THOMAS JEFFERSON

THOMAS JEFFERSON

WRITINGS

Autobiography

A Summary View of the Rights of British America

Notes on the State of Virginia

Public Papers

Addresses, Messages, and Replies

Miscellany

Letters

THE LIBRARY OF AMERICA

Some of the material in this volume is reprinted by
permission of the holders of copyright and publication rights.
Acknowledgements will be found on pages 1535–46.

Distributed to the trade in the United States
and Canada by the Viking Press.

Published outside North America by the Press Syndicate
of the University of Cambridge,
The Pitt Building, Trumpington Street, Cambridge CB2IRP, England
ISBN O 521 26344 I

Library of Congress Catalog Card Number: 83-19917
For Cataloging in Publication Data, see end of *Notes* section.
ISBN 0-940450-16-X

First Printing

Manufactured in the United States of America

MERRILL D. PETERSON
WROTE THE NOTES AND SELECTED
THE TEXTS FOR THIS VOLUME

Grateful acknowledgement is made to the National Endowment for the Humanities and the Ford Foundation for their generous financial support of this series.

The publishers express their appreciation to the Library Company of Philadelphia, the Library of Congress, the American Philosophical Society, the Missouri Historical Society, the Massachusetts Historical Society, the Milbank Memorial Library of Teachers College, Columbia University, and the University of Virginia for the use of manuscript and printed materials.

Contents

Each section has its own table of contents.

AUTOBIOGRAPHY

AUTOBIOGRAPHY

1743–1790

With the Declaration of Independence

January 6, 1821

AT THE AGE of 77, I begin to make some memoranda and state some recollections of dates & facts concerning myself, for my own more ready reference & for the information of my family.

The tradition in my father's family was that their ancestor came to this country from Wales, and from near the mountain of Snowdon, the highest in Gr. Br. I noted once a case from Wales in the law reports where a person of our name was either pl. or def. and one of the same name was Secretary to the Virginia company. These are the only instances in which I have met with the name in that country. I have found it in our early records, but the first particular information I have of any ancestor was my grandfather who lived at the place in Chesterfield called Ozborne's and ownd. the lands afterwards the glebe of the parish. He had three sons, Thomas who died young, Field who settled on the waters of Roanoke and left numerous descendants, and Peter my father, who settled on the lands I still own called Shadwell adjoining my present residence. He was born Feb. 29, 1707/8, and intermarried 1739. with Jane Randolph, of the age of 19. daur of Isham Randolph one of the seven sons of that name & family settled at Dungeoness in Goochld. They trace their pedigree far back in England & Scotland, to which let every one ascribe the faith & merit he chooses.

My father's education had been quite neglected; but being of a strong mind, sound judgment and eager after information, he read much and improved himself insomuch that he was chosen with Joshua Fry professor of Mathem. in W. & M. college to continue the boundary line between Virginia & N. Caroline which had been begun by Colo Byrd, and was afterwards employed with the same Mr. Fry to make the 1st map of Virginia which had ever been made, that of Capt Smith being merely a conjectural sketch. They possessed ex-

3

cellent materials for so much of the country as is below the blue ridge; little being then known beyond that ridge. He was the 3d or 4th settler of the part of the country in which I live, which was about 1737. He died Aug. 17. 1757, leaving my mother a widow who lived till 1776, with 6 daurs & 2. sons, myself the elder. To my younger brother he left his estate on James river called Snowden after the supposed birth-place of the family. To myself the lands on which I was born & live. He placed me at the English school at 5. years of age and at the Latin at 9. where I continued until his death. My teacher Mr. Douglas a clergyman from Scotland was but a superficial Latinist, less instructed in Greek, but with the rudiments of these languages he taught me French, and on the death of my father I went to the revd Mr. Maury a correct classical scholar, with whom I continued two years, and then went to Wm. and Mary college, to wit in the spring of 1760, where I continued 2. years. It was my great good fortune, and what probably fixed the destinies of my life that Dr. Wm. Small of Scotland was then professor of Mathematics, a man profound in most of the useful branches of science, with a happy talent of communication, correct and gentlemanly manners, & an enlarged & liberal mind. He, most happily for me, became soon attached to me & made me his daily companion when not engaged in the school; and from his conversation I got my first views of the expansion of science & of the system of things in which we are placed. Fortunately the Philosophical chair became vacant soon after my arrival at college, and he was appointed to fill it per interim: and he was the first who ever gave in that college regular lectures in Ethics, Rhetoric & Belles lettres. He returned to Europe in 1762, having previously filled up the measure of his goodness to me, by procuring for me, from his most intimate friend G. Wythe, a reception as a student of law, under his direction, and introduced me to the acquaintance and familiar table of Governor Fauquier, the ablest man who had ever filled that office. With him, and at his table, Dr. Small & Mr. Wythe, his amici omnium horarum, & myself, formed a partie quarree, & to the habitual conversations on these occasions I owed much instruction. Mr. Wythe continued to be my faithful and beloved Mentor in youth, and my most affectionate friend through life. In 1767, he led me into the practice of the law at the bar of the General court, at which I continued until the revolution shut up the courts of justice. [For a sketch of the life & character of Mr. Wythe see my letter of Aug. 31. 20. to Mr. John Saunderson]

In 1769, I became a member of the legislature by the choice of the county in which I live, & continued in that until it was closed by the revolution. I made one effort in that body for the permission of the emancipation of slaves, which was rejected: and indeed, during the regal government, nothing liberal could expect success. Our minds were circumscribed within narrow limits by an habitual belief that it was our duty to be subordinate to the mother country in all matters of government, to direct all our labors in subservience to her interests, and even to observe a bigoted intolerance for all religions but hers. The difficulties with our representatives were of habit and despair, not of reflection & conviction. Experience soon proved that they could bring their minds to rights on the first summons of their attention. But the king's council, which acted as another house of legislature, held their places at will & were in most humble obedience to that will: the Governor too, who had a negative on our laws held by the same tenure, & with still greater devotedness to it: and last of all the Royal negative closed the last door to every hope of amelioration.

On the 1st of January, 1772 I was married to Martha Skelton widow of Bathurst Skelton, & daughter of John Wayles, then 23. years old. Mr. Wayles was a lawyer of much practice, to which he was introduced more by his great industry, punctuality & practical readiness, than to eminence in the science of his profession. He was a most agreeable companion, full of pleasantry & good humor, and welcomed in every society. He acquired a handsome fortune, died in May, 1773, leaving three daughters, and the portion which came on that event to Mrs. Jefferson, after the debts should be paid, which were very considerable, was about equal to my own patrimony, and consequently doubled the ease of our circumstances.

When the famous Resolutions of 1765, against the Stamp-act, were proposed, I was yet a student of law in Wmsbg. I attended the debate however at the door of the lobby of the

H. of Burgesses, & heard the splendid display of Mr. Henry's talents as a popular orator. They were great indeed; such as I have never heard from any other man. He appeared to me to speak as Homer wrote. Mr. Johnson, a lawyer & member from the Northern Neck, seconded the resolns, & by him the learning & the logic of the case were chiefly maintained. My recollections of these transactions may be seen pa. 60, Wirt's life of P. H., to whom I furnished them.

In May, 1769, a meeting of the General Assembly was called by the Govr., Ld. Botetourt. I had then become a member; and to that meeting became known the joint resolutions & address of the Lords & Commons of 1768−9, on the proceedings in Massachusetts. Counter-resolutions, & an address to the King, by the H. of Burgesses were agreed to with little opposition, & a spirit manifestly displayed of considering the cause of Massachusetts as a common one. The Governor dissolved us: but we met the next day in the Apollo of the Raleigh tavern, formed ourselves into a voluntary convention, drew up articles of association against the use of any merchandise imported from Gr. Britain, signed and recommended them to the people, repaired to our several counties, & were re elected without any other exception than of the very few who had declined assent to our proceedings.

Nothing of particular excitement occurring for a considerable time our countrymen seemed to fall into a state of insensibility to our situation. The duty on tea not yet repealed & the Declaratory act of a right in the British parl to bind us by their laws in all cases whatsoever, still suspended over us. But a court of inquiry held in R. Island in 1762, with a power to send persons to England to be tried for offences committed here was considered at our session of the spring of 1773. as demanding attention. Not thinking our old & leading members up to the point of forwardness & zeal which the times required, Mr. Henry, R. H. Lee, Francis L. Lee, Mr. Carr & myself agreed to meet in the evening in a private room of the Raleigh to consult on the state of things. There may have been a member or two more whom I do not recollect. We were all sensible that the most urgent of all measures was that of coming to an understanding with all the other colonies to consider the British claims as a common cause to all, & to

produce an unity of action: and for this purpose that a commee of correspondce in each colony would be the best instrument for intercommunication: and that their first measure
would probably be to propose a meeting of deputies from
every colony at some central place, who should be charged
with the direction of the measures which should be taken by
all. We therefore drew up the resolutions which may be seen
in Wirt pa 87. The consulting members proposed to me to
move them, but I urged that it should be done by Mr. Carr,
my friend & brother in law, then a new member to whom I
wished an opportunity should be given of making known to
the house his great worth & talents. It was so agreed; he
moved them, they were agreed to nem. con. and a commee
of correspondence appointed of whom Peyton Randolph, the
Speaker, was chairman. The Govr. (then Ld. Dunmore) dissolved us, but the commee met the next day, prepared a circular letter to the Speakers of the other colonies, inclosing to
each a copy of the resolns and left it in charge with their
chairman to forward them by expresses.

The origination of these commees of correspondence between the colonies has been since claimed for Massachusetts,
and Marshall II. 151, has given into this error, altho' the very
note of his appendix to which he refers, shows that their es-
tablmt was confined to their own towns. This matter will be
seen clearly stated in a letter of Samuel Adams Wells to me of
Apr. 2., 1819, and my answer of May 12. I was corrected by
the letter of Mr. Wells in the information I had given Mr.
Wirt, as stated in his note, pa. 87, that the messengers of Mas-
sach. & Virga crossed each other on the way bearing similar
propositions, for Mr. Wells shows that Mass. did not adopt
the measure but on the receipt of our proposn delivered at
their next session. Their message therefore which passed ours,
must have related to something else, for I well remember P.
Randolph's informing me of the crossing of our messengers.

The next event which excited our sympathies for Massachusets was the Boston port bill, by which that port was to be
shut up on the 1st of June, 1774. This arrived while we were
in session in the spring of that year. The lead in the house on
these subjects being no longer left to the old members, Mr.
Henry, R. H. Lee, Fr. L. Lee, 3. or 4. other members, whom

I do not recollect, and myself, agreeing that we must boldly
take an unequivocal stand in the line with Massachusetts, determined to meet and consult on the proper measures in the
council chamber, for the benefit of the library in that room.
We were under conviction of the necessity of arousing our
people from the lethargy into which they had fallen as to
passing events; and thought that the appointment of a day of
general fasting & prayer would be most likely to call up &
alarm their attention. No example of such a solemnity had
existed since the days of our distresses in the war of 55. since
which a new generation had grown up. With the help therefore of Rushworth, whom we rummaged over for the revolutionary precedents & forms of the Puritans of that day,
preserved by him, we cooked up a resolution, somewhat
modernizing their phrases, for appointing the 1st day of June,
on which the Port bill was to commence, for a day of fasting,
humiliation & prayer, to implore heaven to avert from us the
evils of civil war, to inspire us with firmness in support of our
rights, and to turn the hearts of the King & parliament to
moderation & justice. To give greater emphasis to our proposition, we agreed to wait the next morning on Mr. Nicholas,
whose grave & religious character was more in unison with
the tone of our resolution and to solicit him to move it. We
accordingly went to him in the morning. He moved it the
same day; the 1st of June was proposed and it passed without
opposition. The Governor dissolved us as usual. We retired
to the Apollo as before, agreed to an association, and instructed the commee of correspdce to propose to the corresponding commees of the other colonies to appoint deputies
to meet in Congress at such place, *annually*, as should be convenient to direct, from time to time, the measures required
by the general interest: and we declared that an attack on any
one colony should be considered as an attack on the whole.
This was in May. We further recommended to the several
counties to elect deputies to meet at Wmsbg the 1st of Aug
ensuing, to consider the state of the colony, & particularly to
appoint delegates to a general Congress, should that measure
be acceded to by the commees of correspdce generally. It was
acceded to, Philadelphia was appointed for the place, and the
5th of Sep. for the time of meeting. We returned home, and

in our several counties invited the clergy to meet assemblies of the people on the 1st of June, to perform the ceremonies of the day, & to address to them discourses suited to the occasion. The people met generally, with anxiety & alarm in their countenances, and the effect of the day thro' the whole colony was like a shock of electricity, arousing every man & placing him erect & solidly on his centre. They chose universally delegates for the convention. Being elected one for my own county I prepared a draught of instructions to be given to the delegates whom we should send to the Congress, and which I meant to propose at our meeting. In this I took the ground which, from the beginning I had thought the only one orthodox or tenable, which was that the relation between Gr. Br. and these colonies was exactly the same as that of England & Scotland after the accession of James & until the Union, and the same as her present relations with Hanover, having the same Executive chief but no other necessary political connection; and that our emigration from England to this country gave her no more rights over us, than the emigrations of the Danes and Saxons gave to the present authorities of the mother country over England. In this doctrine however I had never been able to get any one to agree with me but Mr. Wythe. He concurred in it from the first dawn of the question What was the political relation between us & England? Our other patriots Randolph, the Lees, Nicholas, Pendleton stopped at the half-way house of John Dickinson who admitted that England had a right to regulate our commerce, and to lay duties on it for the purposes of regulation, but not of raising revenue. But for this ground there was no foundation in compact, in any acknowledged principles of colonization, nor in reason: expatriation being a natural right, and acted on as such, by all nations, in all ages. I set out for Wmsbg some days before that appointed for our meeting, but was taken ill of a dysentery on the road, & unable to proceed. I sent on therefore to Wmsbg two copies of my draught, the one under cover to Peyton Randolph, who I knew would be in the chair of the convention, the other to Patrick Henry. Whether Mr. Henry disapproved the ground taken, or was too lazy to read it (for he was the laziest man in reading I ever knew) I never learned: but he communicated it to nobody. Peyton Randolph informed the convention he had received such a paper from a member prevented by sickness from offering it in his place, and he laid it on the table for perusal. It was read generally by the members, approved by many, but thought too bold for the present state of things; but they printed it in pamphlet form under the title of "A Summary view of the rights of British America." It found its way to England, was taken up by the opposition, interpolated a little by Mr. Burke so as to make it answer opposition purposes, and in that form ran rapidly thro' several editions. This information I had from Parson Hurt, who happened at the time to be in London, whether he had gone to receive clerical orders. And I was informed afterwards by Peyton Randolph that it had procured me the honor of having my name inserted in a long list of proscriptions enrolled in a bill of attainder commenced in one of the houses of parliament, but suppressed in embryo by the hasty step of events which warned them to be a little cautious. Montague, agent of the H. of Burgesses in England made extracts from the bill, copied the names, and sent them to Peyton Randolph. The names I think were about 20 which he repeated to me, but I recollect those only of Hancock, the two Adamses, Peyton Randolph himself, Patrick Henry, & myself.* The convention met on the 1st of Aug, renewed their association, appointed delegates to the Congress, gave them instructions very temperately & properly expressed, both as to style & matter; and they repaired to Philadelphia at the time appointed. The splendid proceedings of that Congress at their 1st session belong to general history, are known to every one, and need not therefore be noted here. They terminated their session on the 26th of Octob, to meet again on the 10th May ensuing. The convention at their ensuing session of Mar, '75, approved of the proceedings of Congress, thanked their delegates and reappointed the same persons to represent the colony at the meeting to be held in May: and foreseeing the probability that Peyton Randolph their president and Speaker also of the H. of B. might be called off, they added me, in that event to the delegation.

Mr. Randolph was according to expectation obliged to leave the chair of Congress to attend the Gen. Assembly sum-

*See Girardin's *History of Virginia*, Appendix No. 12, note.

moned by Ld. Dunmore to meet on the 1st day of June 1775. Ld. North's conciliatory propositions, as they were called, had been received by the Governor and furnished the subject for which this assembly was convened. Mr. Randolph accordingly attended, and the tenor of these propositions being generally known, as having been addressed to all the governors, he was anxious that the answer of our assembly, likely to be the first, should harmonize with what he knew to be the sentiments and wishes of the body he had recently left. He feared that Mr. Nicholas, whose mind was not yet up to the mark of the times, would undertake the answer, & therefore pressed me to prepare an answer. I did so, and with his aid carried it through the house with long and doubtful scruples from Mr. Nicholas and James Mercer, and a dash of cold water on it here & there, enfeebling it somewhat, but finally with unanimity or a vote approaching it. This being passed, I repaired immediately to Philadelphia, and conveyed to Congress the first notice they had of it. It was entirely approved there. I took my seat with them on the 21st of June. On the 24th, a commee which had been appointed to prepare a declaration of the causes of taking up arms, brought in their report (drawn I believe by J. Rutledge) which not being liked they recommitted it on the 26th, and added Mr. Dickinson and myself to the committee. On the rising of the house, the commee having not yet met, I happened to find myself near Govr W. Livingston, and proposed to him to draw the paper. He excused himself and proposed that I should draw it. On my pressing him with urgency, " we are as yet but new acquaintances, sir, said he, why are you so earnest for my doing it?" "Because, said I, I have been informed that you drew the Address to the people of Gr. Britain, a production certainly of the finest pen in America." "On that, says he, perhaps sir you may not have been correctly informed." I had received the information in Virginia from Colo Harrison on his return from that Congress. Lee, Livingston & Jay had been the commee for that draught. The first, prepared by Lee, had been disapproved & recommitted. The second was drawn by Jay, but being presented by Govr Livingston, had led Colo Harrison into the error. The next morning, walking in the hall of Congress, many members being assembled but the house not yet formed, I observed Mr. Jay, speaking to R. H. Lee, and leading him by the button of his coat, to me. "I understand, sir, said he to me, that this gentleman informed you that Govr Livingston drew the Address to the people of Gr Britain." I assured him at once that I had not received that information from Mr. Lee & that not a word had ever passed on the subject between Mr. Lee & myself; and after some explanations the subject was dropt. These gentlemen had had some sparrings in debate before, and continued ever very hostile to each other.

I prepared a draught of the Declaration committed to us. It was too strong for Mr. Dickinson. He still retained the hope of reconciliation with the mother country, and was unwilling it should be lessened by offensive statements. He was so honest a man, & so able a one that he was greatly indulged even by those who could not feel his scruples. We therefore requested him to take the paper, and put it into a form he could approve. He did so, preparing an entire new statement, and preserving of the former only the last 4. paragraphs & half of the preceding one. We approved & reported it to Congress, who accepted it. Congress gave a signal proof of their indulgence to Mr. Dickinson, and of their great desire not to go too fast for any respectable part of our body, in permitting him to draw their second petition to the King according to his own ideas, and passing it with scarcely any amendment. The disgust against this humility was general; and Mr. Dickinson's delight at its passage was the only circumstance which reconciled them to it. The vote being passed, altho' further observn on it was out of order, he could not refrain from rising and expressing his satisfaction and concluded by saying "there is but one word, Mr. President, in the paper which I disapprove, & that is the word *Congress*," on which Ben Harrison rose and said "there is but on word in the paper, Mr. President, of which I approve, and that is the word *Congress*."

On the 22d of July Dr. Franklin, Mr. Adams, R. H. Lee, & myself, were appointed a commee to consider and report on Ld. North's conciliatory resolution. The answer of the Virginia assembly on that subject having been approved I was requested by the commee to prepare this report, which will account for the similarity of feature in the two instruments.

On the 15th of May, 1776, the convention of Virginia instructed their delegates in Congress to propose to that body
to declare the colonies independent of G. Britain, and appointed a commee to prepare a declaration of rights and plan
of government.

*   *   *

In Congress, Friday June 7. 1776. The delegates from Virginia
moved in obedience to instructions from their constituents that the
Congress should declare that these United colonies are & of right
ought to be free & independent states, that they are absolved from
all allegiance to the British crown, and that all political connection
between them & the state of Great Britain is & ought to be, totally
dissolved; that measures should be immediately taken for procuring
the assistance of foreign powers, and a Confederation be formed to
bind the colonies more closely together.

The house being obliged to attend at that time to some other
business, the proposition was referred to the next day, when the
members were ordered to attend punctually at ten o'clock.

Saturday June 8. They proceeded to take it into consideration and
referred it to a committee of the whole, into which they immediately
resolved themselves, and passed that day & Monday the 10th in debating on the subject.

It was argued by Wilson, Robert R. Livingston, E. Rutledge,
Dickinson and others

That tho' they were friends to the measures themselves, and saw
the impossibility that we should ever again be united with Gr. Britain, yet they were against adopting them at this time:

That the conduct we had formerly observed was wise & proper
now, of deferring to take any capital step till the voice of the people
drove us into it:

That they were our power, & without them our declarations could
not be carried into effect;

That the people of the middle colonies (Maryland, Delaware,
Pennsylva, the Jerseys & N. York) were not yet ripe for bidding
adieu to British connection, but that they were fast ripening & in a
short time would join in the general voice of America:

That the resolution entered into by this house on the 15th of May
for suppressing the exercise of all powers derived from the crown,
had shown, by the ferment into which it had thrown these middle
colonies, that they had not yet accommodated their minds to a separation from the mother country:

That some of them had expressly forbidden their delegates to con-

sent to such a declaration, and others had given no instructions, &
consequently no powers to give such consent:

That if the delegates of any particular colony had no power to
declare such colony independant, certain they were the others could
not declare it for them; the colonies being as yet perfectly independant of each other:

That the assembly of Pennsylvania was now sitting above stairs,
their convention would sit within a few days, the convention of New
York was now sitting, & those of the Jerseys & Delaware counties
would meet on the Monday following, & it was probable these bodies would take up the question of Independance & would declare to
their delegates the voice of their state:

That if such a declaration should now be agreed to, these delegates
must retire & possibly their colonies might secede from the Union:

That such a secession would weaken us more than could be compensated by any foreign alliance:

That in the event of such a division, foreign powers would either
refuse to join themselves to our fortunes, or, having us so much in
their power as that desperate declaration would place us, they would
insist on terms proportionably more hard and prejudicial:

That we had little reason to expect an alliance with those to whom
alone as yet we had cast our eyes:

That France & Spain had reason to be jealous of that rising power
which would one day certainly strip them of all their American possessions:

That it was more likely they should form a connection with the
British court, who, if they should find themselves unable otherwise
to extricate themselves from their difficulties, would agree to a partition of our territories, restoring Canada to France, & the Floridas
to Spain, to accomplish for themselves a recovery of these colonies:

That it would not be long before we should receive certain information of the disposition of the French court, from the agent whom
we had sent to Paris for that purpose:

That if this disposition should be favorable, by waiting the event
of the present campaign, which we all hoped would be successful,
we should have reason to expect an alliance on better terms:

That this would in fact work no delay of any effectual aid from
such ally, as, from the advance of the season & distance of our situation, it was impossible we could receive any assistance during this
campaign:

That it was prudent to fix among ourselves the terms on which
we should form alliance, before we declared we would form one at
all events:

And that if these were agreed on, & our Declaration of Independance ready by the time our Ambassador should be prepared to sail, it would be as well as to go into that Declaration at this day.

On the other side it was urged by J. Adams, Lee, Wythe, and others

That no gentleman had argued against the policy or the right of separation from Britain, nor had supposed it possible we should ever renew our connection; that they had only opposed its being now declared:

That the question was not whether, by a declaration of independance, we should make ourselves what we are not; but whether we should declare a fact which already exists:

That as to the people or parliament of England, we had alwais been independent of them, their restraints on our trade deriving efficacy from our acquiescence only, & not from any rights they possessed of imposing them, & that so far our connection had been federal only & was now dissolved by the commencement of hostilities:

That as to the King, we had been bound to him by allegiance, but that this bond was now dissolved by his assent to the late act of parliament, by which he declares us out of his protection, and by his levying war on us, a fact which had long ago proved us out of his protection; it being a certain position in law that allegiance & protection are reciprocal, the one ceasing when the other is withdrawn:

That James the IId. never declared the people of England out of his protection yet his actions proved it & the parliament declared it:

No delegates then can be denied, or ever want, a power of declaring an existing truth:

That the delegates from the Delaware counties having declared their constituents ready to join, there are only two colonies Pennsylvania & Maryland whose delegates are absolutely tied up, and that these had by their instructions only reserved a right of confirming or rejecting the measure:

That the instructions from Pennsylvania might be accounted for from the times in which they were drawn, near a twelvemonth ago, since which the face of affairs has totally changed:

That within that time it had become apparent that Britain was determined to accept nothing less than a carte-blanche, and that the King's answer to the Lord Mayor Aldermen & common council of London, which had come to hand four days ago, must have satisfied every one of this point:

That the people wait for us to lead the way:

That *they* are in favour of the measure, tho' the instructions given by some of their *representatives* are not:

That the voice of the representatives is not always consonant with the voice of the people, and that this is remarkably the case in these middle colonies:

That the effect of the resolution of the 15th of May has proved this, which, raising the murmurs of some in the colonies of Pennsylvania & Maryland, called forth the opposing voice of the freer part of the people, & proved them to be the majority, even in these colonies:

That the backwardness of these two colonies might be ascribed partly to the influence of proprietary power & connections, & partly to their having not yet been attacked by the enemy:

That these causes were not likely to be soon removed, as there seemed no probability that the enemy would make either of these the seat of this summer's war:

That it would be vain to wait either weeks or months for perfect unanimity, since it was impossible that all men should ever become of one sentiment on any question:

That the conduct of some colonies from the beginning of this contest, had given reason to suspect it was their settled policy to keep in the rear of the confederacy, that their particular prospect might be better, even in the worst event:

That therefore it was necessary for those colonies who had thrown themselves forward & hazarded all from the beginning, to come forward now also, and put all again to their own hazard:

That the history of the Dutch revolution, of whom three states only confederated at first proved that a secession of some colonies would not be so dangerous as some apprehended:

That a declaration of Independence alone could render it consistent with European delicacy for European powers to treat with us, or even to receive an Ambassador from us:

That till this they would not receive our vessels into their ports, nor acknowledge the adjudications of our courts of admiralty to be legitimate, in cases of capture of British vessels:

That though France & Spain may be jealous of our rising power, they must think it will be much more formidable with the addition of Great Britain; and will therefore see it their interest to prevent a coalition; but should they refuse, we shall be but where we are; whereas without trying we shall never know whether they will aid us or not:

That the present campaign may be unsuccessful, & therefore we had better propose an alliance while our affairs wear a hopeful aspect:

That to await the event of this campaign will certainly work delay, because during this summer France may assist us effectually by cutting off those supplies of provisions from England & Ireland on which the enemy's armies here are to depend; or by setting in motion the great power they have collected in the West Indies, & calling our enemy to the defence of the possessions they have there:

That it would be idle to lose time in settling the terms of alliance, till we had first determined we would enter into alliance:

That it is necessary to lose no time in opening a trade for our people, who will want clothes, and will want money too for the paiment of taxes:

And that the only misfortune is that we did not enter into alliance with France six months sooner, as besides opening their ports for the vent of our last year's produce, they might have marched an army into Germany and prevented the petty princes there from selling their unhappy subjects to subdue us.

It appearing in the course of these debates that the colonies of N. York, New Jersey, Pennsylvania, Delaware, Maryland, and South Carolina were not yet matured for falling from the parent stem, but that they were fast advancing to that state, it was thought most prudent to wait a while for them, and to postpone the final decision to July 1. but that this might occasion as little delay as possible a committee was appointed to prepare a declaration of independence. The commee were J. Adams, Dr. Franklin, Roger Sherman, Robert R. Livingston & myself. Committees were also appointed at the same time to prepare a plan of confederation for the colonies, and to state the terms proper to be proposed for foreign alliance. The committee for drawing the declaration of Independence desired me to do it. It was accordingly done, and being approved by them, I reported it to the house on Friday the 28th of June when it was read and ordered to lie on the table. On Monday, the 1st of July the house resolved itself into a commee of the whole & resumed the consideration of the original motion made by the delegates of Virginia, which being again debated through the day, was carried in the affirmative by the votes of N. Hampshire, Connecticut, Massachusetts, Rhode Island, N. Jersey, Maryland, Virginia, N. Carolina, & Georgia. S. Carolina and Pennsylvania voted against it. Delaware having but two members present, they were divided. The delegates for New York declared they were for it themselves & were assured their constituents were for it, but that their instructions having been drawn near a twelvemonth before, when reconciliation was still the general object, they were enjoined by them to do nothing which should impede that object. They therefore thought themselves not justifiable in voting on either side, and asked leave to withdraw from the question, which was given them. The commee rose & reported their resolution to the house. Mr. Edward Rutledge of S. Carolina then requested the determination might be put off to the next day, as he believed his colleagues, tho' they disapproved of the resolution, would then join in it for the sake of unanimity. The ultimate question whether the house would agree to the resolution of the committee was accordingly postponed to the next day, when it was again moved and S. Carolina concurred in voting for it. In the meantime a third member had come post from the Delaware counties and turned the vote of that colony in favour of the resolution. Members of a different sentiment attending that morning from Pennsylvania also, their vote was changed, so that the whole 12 colonies who were authorized to vote at all, gave their voices for it; and within a few days, the convention of N. York approved of it and thus supplied the void occasioned by the withdrawing of her delegates from the vote.

Congress proceeded the same day to consider the declaration of Independance which had been reported & lain on the table the Friday preceding, and on Monday referred to a commee of the whole. The pusillanimous idea that we had friends in England worth keeping terms with, still haunted the minds of many. For this reason those passages which conveyed censures on the people of England were struck out, lest they should give them offence. The clause too, reprobating the enslaving the inhabitants of Africa, was struck out in complaisance to South Carolina and Georgia, who had never attempted to restrain the importation of slaves, and who on the contrary still wished to continue it. Our northern brethren also I believe felt a little tender under those censures; for tho' their people have very few slaves themselves yet they had been pretty considerable carriers of them to others. The debates having taken up the greater parts of the 2d 3d & 4th days of July were, in the evening of the last, closed the declaration was reported by the commee, agreed to by the house and signed by every member present except Mr. Dickinson. As the sentiments of men are known not only by what they receive, but what they reject also, I will state the form of the declaration as originally reported. The parts struck out by Congress shall be distinguished by a black line drawn under them; & those inserted by them shall be placed in the margin or in a concurrent column.

A Declaration by the Representatives of the United States of America, in General Congress Assembled.

When in the course of human events it becomes necessary for one people to dissolve the political bands which have connected them with another, and to assume among the powers of the earth the separate & equal station to which the laws of nature and of nature's God entitle them, a decent respect to the opinions of mankind requires that they should declare the causes which impel them to the separation.

We hold these truths to be self-evident: that all men are created equal; that they are endowed by their creator with <u>inherent and</u> inalienable rights; that among these _{certain} are life, liberty, & the pursuit of happiness: that to secure these rights, governments are instituted among men, deriving their just powers from the consent of the governed; that whenever any form of government becomes destructive of these ends, it is the right of the people to alter or abolish it, & to institute new government, laying it's foundation on such principles, & organizing it's powers in such form, as to them shall seem most likely to effect their safety & happiness. Prudence indeed will dictate that governments long established should not be changed for light & transient causes; and accordingly all experience hath shown that mankind are more disposed to suffer while evils are sufferable, than to right themselves by abolishing the forms to which they are accustomed. But when a long train of abuses & usurpations <u>begun at a distinguished period and</u> pursuing invariably the same object, evinces a design to reduce them under absolute despotism, it is their right, it is their duty to throw off such government, & to provide new guards for their future security. Such has been the patient sufferance of these colonies; & such is now the necessity which constrains them to <u>expunge</u> their former systems of government. The _{alter} history of the present king of Great Britain is a history of <u>unremitting</u> injuries & usurpations, <u>among which</u> _{repeated} <u>appears no solitary fact to contradict the uniform tenor of the rest but all have</u> in direct object the establishment _{all having} of an absolute tyranny over these states. To prove this let facts

19

be submitted to a candid world <u>for the truth of which we pledge a faith yet unsullied by falsehood.</u>

He has refused his assent to laws the most wholesome & necessary for the public good.

He has forbidden his governors to pass laws of immediate & pressing importance, unless suspended in their operation till his assent should be obtained; & when so suspended, he has utterly neglected to attend to them.

He has refused to pass other laws for the accommodation of large districts of people, unless those people would relinquish the right of representation in the legislature, a right inestimable to them, & formidable to tyrants only.

He has called together legislative bodies at places unusual, uncomfortable, and distant from the depository of their public records, for the sole purpose of fatiguing them into compliance with his measures.

He has dissolved representative houses repeatedly <u>& continually</u> for opposing with manly firmness his invasions on the rights of the people.

He has refused for a long time after such dissolutions to cause others to be elected, whereby the legislative powers, incapable of annihilation, have returned to the people at large for their exercise, the state remaining in the meantime exposed to all the dangers of invasion from without & convulsions within.

He has endeavored to prevent the population of these states; for that purpose obstructing the laws for naturalization of foreigners, refusing to pass others to encourage their migrations hither, & raising the conditions of new appropriations of lands.

^{obstructed}   He has <u>suffered</u> the administration of justice ^{by}   <u>totally to cease in some of these states</u> refusing his assent to laws for establishing judiciary powers.

He has made <u>our</u> judges dependant on his will alone, for the tenure of their offices, & the amount & paiment of their salaries.

He has erected a multitude of new offices <u>by a self assumed power</u> and sent hither swarms of new officers to harass our people and eat out their substance.

He has kept among us in times of peace standing armies

<u>and ships of war</u> without the consent of our legislatures.

He has affected to render the military independant of, & superior to the civil power.

He has combined with others to subject us to a jurisdiction foreign to our constitutions & unacknowledged by our laws, giving his assent to their acts of pretended legislation for quartering large bodies of armed troops among us; for protecting them by a mock-trial from punishment for any murders which they should commit on the inhabitants of these states; for cutting off our trade with all parts of the world; for imposing taxes on us without our consent; for depriving us [   ] of the benefits of trial by jury; for trans- _{in many} porting us beyond seas to be tried for pretended _{cases} offences; for abolishing the free system of English laws in a neighboring province, establishing therein an arbitrary government, and enlarging it's boundaries, so as to render it at once an example and fit instrument for introducing the same absolute rule into these <u>states</u>; for taking away our _{colonies} charters, abolishing our most valuable laws, and altering fundamentally the forms of our governments; for suspending our own legislatures, & declaring themselves invested with power to legislate for us in all cases whatsoever.

He has abdicated government here <u>withdrawing</u> by declaring <u>his governors, and declaring us out of his allegiance</u> us out of his <u>& protection.</u> protection, and waging war against us.

He has plundered our seas, ravaged our coasts, burnt our towns, & destroyed the lives of our people.

He is at this time transporting large armies of foreign mercenaries to compleat the works of death, desolation & tyranny already begun with circumstances of cruelty and scarcely paralleled in the perfidy [   ] unworthy the head of a civilized most barbarous ages, & nation. totally

He has constrained our fellow citizens taken captive on the high seas to bear arms against their country, to become the executioners of their friends & brethren, or to fall themselves by their hands.

He has [   ] endeavored to bring on the inhabi- excited tants of our frontiers the merciless Indian savages, domestic insurrection whose known rule of warfare is an undistinguished among us, & has destruction of all ages, sexes, & conditions of existence.

He has incited treasonable insurrections of our fellow-citizens, with the allurements of forfeiture & confiscation of our property.

He has waged cruel war against human nature itself, violating it's most sacred rights of life and liberty in the persons of a distant people who never offended him, captivating & carrying them into slavery in another hemisphere, or to incur miserable death in their transportation thither. This piratical warfare, the opprobium of INFIDEL powers, is the warfare of the CHRISTIAN king of Great Britain. Determined to keep open a market where MEN should be bought & sold, he has prostituted his negative for suppressing every legislative attempt to prohibit or to restrain this execrable commerce. And that this assemblage of horrors might want no fact of distinguished die, he is now exciting those very people to rise in arms among us, and to purchase that liberty of which he has deprived them, by murdering the people on whom he also obtruded them: thus paying off former crimes committed against the LIBERTIES of one people, with crimes which he urges them to commit against the LIVES of another.

In every stage of these oppressions we have petitioned for redress in the most humble terms: our repeated petitions have been answered only by repeated injuries.

A prince whose character is thus marked by every act which may define a tyrant is unfit to be the ruler of a free [ ] people who mean to be free. Future ages will scarcely believe that the hardiness of one man adventured, within the short compass of twelve years only, to lay a foundation so broad & so undisguised for tyranny over a people fostered & fixed in principles of freedom.

Nor have we been wanting in attentions to our British brethren. We have warned them from time to time an unwarrantable of attempts by their legislature to extend a jurisdiction over these our states. We have reminded us them of the circumstances of our emigration & settlement here, no one of which could warrant so strange a pretension: that these were effected at the expense of our own blood & treasure, unassisted by the wealth or the strength of Great

Britain: that in constituting indeed our several forms of government, we had adopted one common king, thereby laying a foundation for perpetual league & amity with them: but that submission to their parliament was no part of our constitution, nor ever in idea, if history may be credited: and, we [ ] appealed to their native justice and magna-   have
nimity as well as to the ties of our common   and we have
kindred to disavow these usurpations which were   conjured
likely to interrupt our connection and correspon-   them by
dence. They too have been deaf to the voice of   inevitably   would
justice & of consanguinity, and when occasions have been given them, by the regular course of their laws, of removing from their councils the disturbers of our harmony, they have, by their free election, re-established them in power. At this very time too they are permitting their chief magistrate to send over not only soldiers of our common blood,   We must
but Scotch & foreign mercenaries to invade & de-   therefore
stroy us. These facts have given the last stab to agonizing affection, and manly spirit bids us to renounce forever these unfeeling brethren. We must endeavor to forget our former love for them, and hold them as we hold the rest of mankind, enemies in war, in peace friends. We might have been a free and a great people together; but a communication of grandeur & of freedom it seems is below their dig-   and hold
nity. Be it so, since they will have it. The road to   them as we
happiness & to glory is open to us too. We will tread   of mankind,
it apart from them, and acquiesce in the necessity   enemies in
which denounces our eternal separation [ ]!   war, in
   peace
   friends.

We therefore the represen- tatives of the United States of America in General Congress assembled do in the name & by authority of the good people of these states reject & renounce all allegiance & subjection to the kings of Great Britain & all others who may hereafter claim by, through or under them: we utterly dissolve all political

We therefore the represen- tatives of the United States of America in General Congress assembled, appealing to the supreme judge of the world for the rectitude of our inten- tions, do in the name, & by the authority of the good people of these colonies, sol- emnly publish & declare that these united colonies are & of right ought to be free &

connection which may heretofore have subsisted be-
tween us & the people or
parliament of Great Britain:
& finally we do assert & declare these colonies to be free
& independent states, & that
as free & independent states,
they have full power to levy
war, conclude peace, contract
alliances, establish commerce,
& to do all other acts &
things which independent
states may of right do.

And for the support of
this declaration we mutually
pledge to each other our
lives, our fortunes, & our sacred honor.

independent states; that they
are absolved from all allegiance to the British crown,
and that all political connection between them & the
state of Great Britain is, &
ought to be, totally dis-
solved; & that as free & independent states they have
full power to levy war, conclude peace, contract alliances, establish commerce &
to do all other acts & things
which independant states
may of right do.

And for the support of this
declaration, with a firm reliance on the protection of divine providence we mutually
pledge to each other our
lives, our fortunes, & our sacred honor.

The Declaration thus signed on the 4th, on paper was engrossed on parchment, & signed again on the 2d. of August.

*   *   *

Some erroneous statements of the proceedings on the declaration
of independence having got before the public in latter times, Mr.
Samuel A. Wells asked explanations of me, which are given in my
letter to him of May 12. 19. before and now again referred to. I took
notes in my place while these things were going on, and at their
close wrote them out in form and with correctness and from 1 to 7
of the two preceding sheets are the originals then written; as the
two following are of the earlier debates on the Confederation, which
I took in like manner.

On Friday July 12. the Committee appointed to draw the articles
of confederation reported them, and on the 22d. the house resolved
themselves into a committee to take them into consideration. On the
30th. & 31st. of that month & 1st. of the ensuing, those articles were
debated which determined the proportion or quota of money which

each state should furnish to the common treasury, and the manner of voting in Congress. The first of these articles was expressed in the original draught in these words. "Art. XI. All charges of war & all other expenses that shall be incurred for the common defence, or general welfare, and allowed by the United States assembled, shall be defrayed out of a common treasury, which shall be supplied by the several colonies in proportion to the number of inhabitants of every age, sex & quality, except Indians not paying taxes, in each colony, a true account of which, distinguishing the white inhabitants, shall be triennially taken & transmitted to the Assembly of the United States."

Mr. [Samuel] Chase moved that the quotas should be fixed, not by the number of inhabitants of every condition, but by that of the "white inhabitants." He admitted that taxation should be alwais in proportion to property, that this was in theory the true rule, but that from a variety of difficulties, it was a rule which could never be adopted in practice. The value of the property in every State could never be estimated justly & equally. Some other measure for the wealth of the State must therefore be devised, some standard referred to which would be more simple. He considered the number of inhabitants as a tolerably good criterion of property, and that this might alwais be obtained. He therefore thought it the best mode which we could adopt, with one exception only. He observed that negroes are property, and as such cannot be distinguished from the lands or personalities held in those States where there are few slaves, that the surplus of profit which a Northern farmer is able to lay by, he invests in cattle, horses, &c. whereas a Southern farmer lays out that same surplus in slaves. There is no more reason therefore for taxing the Southern states on the farmer's head, & on his slave's head, than the Northern ones on their farmer's heads & the heads of their cattle, that the method proposed would therefore tax the Southern states according to their numbers & their wealth conjunctly, while the Northern would be taxed on numbers only: that negroes in fact should not be considered as members of the state more than cattle & that they have no more interest in it.

Mr. John Adams observed that the numbers of people were taken by this article as an index of the wealth of the state, & not as subjects of taxation, that as to this matter it was of no consequence by what name you called your people, whether by that of freemen or of slaves. That in some countries the labouring poor were called freemen, in others they were called slaves; but that the difference as to the state was imaginary only. What matters it whether a landlord employing ten labourers in his farm, gives them annually as much money as will buy them the necessaries of life, or gives them those necessaries at short hand. The ten labourers add as much wealth annually to the state, increase it's exports as much in the one case as the other. Certainly 500 freemen produce no more profits, no greater surplus for the paiment of taxes than 500 slaves. Therefore the state in which are the labourers called freemen should be taxed no more than that in which are those called slaves. Suppose by any extraordinary operation of nature or of law one half the labourers of a state could in the course of one night be transformed into slaves: would the state be made the poorer or the less able to pay taxes? That the condition of the laboring poor in most countries, that of the fishermen particularly of the Northern states, is as abject as that of slaves. It is the number of labourers which produce the surplus for taxation, and numbers therefore indiscriminately, are the fair index of wealth. That it is the use of the word "property" here, & it's application to some of the people of the state, which produces the fallacy. How does the Southern farmer procure slaves? Either by importation or by purchase from his neighbor. If he imports a slave, he adds one to the number of labourers in his country, and proportionably to it's profits & abilities to pay taxes. If he buys from his neighbor it is only a transfer of a labourer from one farm to another, which does not change the annual produce of the state, & therefore should not change it's tax. That if a Northern farmer works ten labourers on his farm, he can, it is true, invest the surplus of ten men's labour in cattle: but so may the Southern farmer working ten slaves. That a state of one hundred thousand freemen can maintain no more cattle than one of one hundred thousand slaves. Therefore they have no more of that kind of property. That a slave may indeed from the custom of speech be more properly called the wealth of his master, than the free labourer might be called the wealth of his employer: but as to the state, both were equally it's wealth, and should therefore equally add to the quota of it's tax.

Mr. [Benjamin] Harrison proposed as a compromise, that two slaves should be counted as one freeman. He affirmed that slaves did not do so much work as freemen, and doubted if two effected more than one. That this was proved by the price of labor. The hire of a labourer in the Southern colonies being from 8 to £12. while in the Northern it was generally £24.

Mr. [James] Wilson said that if this amendment should take place the Southern colonies would have all the benefit of slaves, whilst the Northern ones would bear the burthen. That slaves increase the profits of a state, which the Southern states mean to take to themselves; that they also increase the burthen of defence, which would of course fall so much the heavier on the Northern. That slaves occupy the places of freemen and eat their food. Dismiss your slaves & freemen will take their places. It is our duty to lay every discouragement on the importation of slaves; but this amendment would give the jus trium liberorum to him who would import slaves. That other kinds of property were pretty equally distributed thro' all the colonies: there were as many cattle, horses, & sheep, in the North as the South, & South as the North; but not so as to slaves. That experience has shown that those colonies have been alwais able to pay most which have the most inhabitants, whether they be black or white, and the practice of the Southern colonies has alwais been to make every farmer pay poll taxes upon all his labourers whether they be black or white. He acknowledges indeed that freemen work the most; but they consume the most also. They do not produce a greater surplus for taxation. The slave is neither fed nor clothed so expensively as a freeman. Again white women are exempted from labor generally, but negro women are not. In this then the Southern states have an advantage as the article now stands. It has sometimes been said that slavery is necessary because the commodities they raise would be too dear for market if cultivated by freemen; but now it is said that the labor of the slave is the dearest.

Mr. Payne urged the original resolution of Congress, to proportion the quotas of the states to the number of souls.

Dr. [John] Witherspoon was of opinion that the value of lands & houses was the best estimate of the wealth of a nation, and that it was practicable to obtain such a valuation. This is the true barometer of wealth. The one now proposed is imperfect in itself, and unequal between the States. It has been objected that negroes eat the food of freemen & therefore should be taxed. Horses also eat the food of freemen; therefore they also should be taxed. It has been said too that in carrying slaves into the estimate of the taxes the state is to pay, we do no more than those states themselves do, who alwais take slaves into the estimate of the taxes the individual is to pay. But the cases are not parallel. In the Southern colonies slaves pervade the whole colony; but they do not pervade the whole continent. That as to the original resolution of Congress to proportion the quotas according to the souls, it was temporary only, & related to the monies heretofore emitted: whereas we are now entering into a new compact, and therefore stand on original ground.

Aug 1. The question being put the amendment proposed was rejected by the votes of N. Hampshire, Massachusetts, Rhode island, Connecticut, N. York, N. Jersey, & Pennsylvania, against those of Delaware, Maryland, Virginia, North & South Carolina. Georgia was divided.

The other article was in these words. "Art. XVII. In determining questions each colony shall have one vote."

July 30. 31. Aug 1.   Present 41. members. Mr. Chase observed that this article was the most likely to divide us of any one proposed in the draught then under consideration. That the larger colonies had threatened they would not confederate at all if their weight in congress should not be equal to the numbers of people they added to the confederacy; while the smaller ones declared against a union if they did not retain an equal vote for the protection of their rights. That it was of the utmost consequence to bring the parties together, as should we sever from each other, either no foreign power will ally with us at all, or the different states will form different alliances, and thus increase the horrors of those scenes of civil war and bloodshed which in such a state of separation & independance would render us a miserable people. That our importance, our interests, our peace required that we should confederate, and that mutual sacrifices should be made to effect a compromise of this difficult question. He was of opinion the smaller colonies would lose their rights, if they were not in some instances allowed an equal vote; and therefore that a discrimination should take place among the questions which would come before Congress. That the smaller states should be secured in all questions concerning life or liberty & the greater ones in all respecting property. He therefore proposed that in votes relating to money, the voice of each colony should be proportioned to the number of its inhabitants.

Dr. Franklin thought that the votes should be so proportioned in all cases. He took notice that the Delaware counties had bound up their Delegates to disagree to this article. He thought it a very extraordinary language to be held by any state, that they would not confederate with us unless we would let them dispose of our money. Certainly if we vote equally we ought to pay equally; but the smaller states will hardly purchase the privilege at this price. That had he lived in a state where the representation, originally equal, had become unequal by time & accident he might have submitted rather than disturb government; but that we should be very wrong to set out in this practice when it is in our power to establish what is right. That at the time of the Union between England and Scotland the latter had made the objection which the smaller states now do. But experience had proved that no unfairness had ever been shown them. That their advocates had prognosticated that it would again happen as in times of old, that the whale would swallow Jonas, but he thought the prediction reversed in event and that Jonas had swallowed the whale, for the Scotch had in fact got possession of the government and gave laws to the English. He reprobated the original agreement of Congress to vote by colonies and therefore was for their voting in all cases according to the number of taxables.

Dr. Witherspoon opposed every alteration of the article. All men admit that a confederacy is necessary. Should the idea get abroad that there is likely to be no union among us, it will damp the minds of the people, diminish the glory of our struggle, & lessen it's importance; because it will open to our view future prospects of war & dissension among ourselves. If an equal vote be refused, the smaller states will become vassals to the larger; & all experience has shown that the vassals & subjects of free states are the most enslaved. He instanced the Helots of Sparta & the provinces of Rome. He observed that foreign powers discovering this blemish would make it a handle for disengaging the smaller states from so unequal a confederacy. That the colonies should in fact be considered as individuals; and that as such, in all disputes they should have an equal vote; that they are now collected as individuals making a bargain with each other, & of course had a right to vote as individuals. That in the East India company they voted by persons, & not by their proportion of stock. That the Belgic confederacy voted by provinces. That in questions of war the smaller states were as much interested as the larger, & therefore should vote equally; and indeed that the larger states were more likely to bring war on the confederacy in proportion as their frontier was more extensive. He admitted that equality of representation was an excellent principle, but then it must be of things which are coordinate; that is, of things similar & of the same nature: that nothing relating to individuals could ever come before Congress; nothing but what would respect colonies. He distinguished between an incorporating & a federal union. The union of England was an incorporating one; yet Scotland had suffered by that union: for that it's inhabitants were drawn from it by the hopes of places & employments. Nor was it an instance of equality of representation; because while Scotland was allowed nearly a thirteenth of representation they were to pay only one fortieth of the land tax. He expressed his hopes that in the present enlightened state of men's minds we might expect a lasting confederacy, if it was founded on fair principles.

John Adams advocated the voting in proportion to numbers. He said that we stand here as the representatives of the people. That in some states the people are many, in others they are few; that therefore their vote here should be proportioned to the numbers from whom it comes. Reason, justice, & equity never had weight enough on the face of the earth to govern the councils of men. It is interest alone which does it, and it is interest alone which can be trusted. That therefore the interests within doors should be the mathematical representatives of the interests without doors. That the individuality of the colonies is a mere sound. Does the individuality of a colony increase it's wealth or numbers. If it does, pay equally. If it does not add weight in the scale of the confederacy, it cannot add to their rights, nor weigh in argument. A. has £50. B. £500. C. £1000. in partnership. Is it just they should equally dispose of the monies of the partnership? It has been said we are independent individuals making a bargain together. The question is not what we are now, but what we ought to be when our bargain shall be made. The confederacy is to make us one individual only; it is to form us, like separate parcels of metal, into one common mass. We shall no longer retain our separate individuality, but become a single individual as to all questions submitted to the confederacy. Therefore all those reasons which prove the justice & expediency of equal representation in other assemblies, hold good here. It has been objected that a proportional vote will endanger the smaller states. We answer that an equal vote will endanger the larger. Virginia, Pennsylvania, & Massachusetts are the three greater colonies. Consider their distance, their difference of produce, of interests & of manners, & it is apparent they can never have an interest or inclination to combine for the oppression of the smaller. That the smaller will naturally divide on all questions with the larger. Rhode isld, from it's relation, similarity & intercourse will generally pursue the same objects with Massachusetts; Jersey, Delaware & Maryland, with Pennsylvania.

Dr. [Benjamin] Rush took notice that the decay of the liberties of the Dutch republic proceeded from three causes. 1. The perfect unanimity requisite on all occasions. 2. Their obligation to consult their constituents. 3. Their voting by provinces. This last destroyed the equality of representation, and the liberties of great Britain also are sinking from the same defect. That a part of our rights is deposited in the hands of our legislatures. There it was admitted there should be an equality of representation. Another part of our rights is deposited in the hands of Congress: why is it not equally necessary there should be an equal representation there? Were it possible to collect the whole body of the people together, they would determine the questions submitted to them by their majority. Why should not the same majority decide when voting here by their representatives? The larger colonies are so providentially divided in situation as to render every fear of their combining visionary. Their interests are different, & their circumstances dissimilar. It is more probable they will become rivals & leave it in the power of the smaller states to give preponderance to any scale they please. The voting by the number of free inhabitants will have one excellent effect, that of inducing the colonies to discourage slavery & to encourage the increase of their free inhabitants.

Mr. [Stephen] Hopkins observed there were 4 larger, 4 smaller,

& 4 middle-sized colonies. That the 4 largest would contain more than half the inhabitants of the confederated states, & therefore would govern the others as they should please. That history affords no instance of such a thing as equal representation. The Germanic body votes by states. The Helvetic body does the same; & so does the Belgic confederacy. That too little is known of the ancient confederations to say what was their practice.

Mr. Wilson thought that taxation should be in proportion to wealth, but that representation should accord with the number of freemen. That government is a collection or result of the wills of all. That if any government could speak the will of all, it would be perfect; and that so far as it departs from this it becomes imperfect. It has been said that Congress is a representation of states; not of individuals. I say that the objects of its care are all the individuals of the states. It is strange that annexing the name of "State" to ten thousand men, should give them an equal right with forty thousand. This must be the effect of magic, not of reason. As to those matters which are referred to Congress, we are not so many states, we are one large state. We lay aside our individuality, whenever we come here. The Germanic body is a burlesque on government; and their practice on any point is a sufficient authority & proof that it is wrong. The greatest imperfection in the constitution of the Belgic confederacy is their voting by provinces. The interest of the whole is constantly sacrificed to that of the small states. The history of the war in the reign of Q. Anne sufficiently proves this. It is asked shall nine colonies put it into the power of four to govern them as they please? I invert the question, and ask shall two millions of people put it in the power of one million to govern them as they please? It is pretended too that the smaller colonies will be in danger from the greater. Speak in honest language & say the minority will be in danger from the majority. And is there an assembly on earth where this danger may not be equally pretended? The truth is that our proceedings will then be consentaneous with the interests of the majority, and so they ought to be. The probability is much greater that the larger states will disagree than that they will combine. I defy the wit of man to invent a possible case or to suggest any one thing on earth which shall be for the interests of Virginia, Pennsylvania & Massachusetts, and which will not also be for the interest of the other states.

*   *   *

These articles reported July 12. 76 were debated from day to day, & time to time for two years, were ratified July 9, '78, by 10 states, by N. Jersey on the 26th. of Nov. of the same year, and by Delaware on the 23d. of Feb. following. Maryland alone held off 2 years more, acceding to them Mar 1, 81. and thus closing the obligation.

Our delegation had been renewed for the ensuing year commencing Aug. 11. but the new government was now organized, a meeting of the legislature was to be held in Oct. and I had been elected a member by my county. I knew that our legislation under the regal government had many very vicious points which urgently required reformation, and I thought I could be of more use in forwarding that work. I therefore retired from my seat in Congress on the 2d. of Sep. resigned it, and took my place in the legislature of my state, on the 7th. of October.

On the 11th. I moved for leave to bring in a bill for the establishmt of courts of justice, the organization of which was of importance; I drew the bill it was approved by the commee, reported and passed after going thro' it's due course.

On the 12th. I obtained leave to bring in a bill declaring tenants in tail to hold their lands in fee simple. In the earlier times of the colony when lands were to be obtained for little or nothing, some provident individuals procured large grants, and, desirous of founding great families for themselves, settled them on their descendants in fee-tail. The transmission of this property from generation to generation in the same name raised up a distinct set of families who, being privileged by law in the perpetuation of their wealth were thus formed into a Patrician order, distinguished by the splendor and luxury of their establishments. From this order too the king habitually selected his Counsellors of State, the hope of which distinction devoted the whole corps to the interests & will of the crown. To annul this privilege, and instead of an aristocracy of wealth, of more harm and danger, than benefit, to society, to make an opening for the aristocracy of virtue and talent, which nature has wisely provided for the direction of the interests of society, & scattered with equal hand through all it's conditions, was deemed essential to a well ordered republic. To effect it no violence was necessary, no deprivation of natural right, but rather an enlargement of it by a repeal of the law. For this would authorize the present holder to divide the property among his children equally, as his affections were divided; and would place them, by natural generation on the level of their fellow citizens. But this repeal was strongly opposed by Mr. Pendleton, who was zealously attached to ancient establishments; and who, taken all in all, was the ablest man in debate I have ever met with. He had not indeed the poetical fancy of Mr. Henry, his sublime imagination, his lofty and overwhelming diction; but he was cool, smooth and persuasive; his language flowing, chaste & embellished, his conceptions quick, acute and full of resource; never vanquished; for if he lost the main battle, he returned upon you, and regained so much of it as to make it a drawn one, by dexterous manœuvres, skirmishes in detail, and the recovery of small advantages which, little singly, were important altogether. You never knew when you were clear of him, but were harassed by his perseverance until the patience was worn down of all who had less of it than himself. Add to this that he was one of the most virtuous & benevolent of men, the kindest friend, the most amiable & pleasant of companions, which ensured a favorable reception to whatever came from him. Finding that the general principle of entails could not be maintained, he took his stand on an amendment which he proposed, instead of an absolute abolition, to permit the tenant in tail to convey in fee simple, if he chose it: and he was within a few votes of saving so much of the old law. But the bill passed finally for entire abolition.

In that one of the bills for organizing our judiciary system which proposed a court of chancery, I had provided for a trial by jury of all matters of fact in that as well as in the courts of law. He defeated it by the introduction of 4. words only, *"if either party chuse."* The consequence has been that as no suitor will say to his judge, "Sir, I distrust you, give me a jury" juries are rarely, I might say perhaps never seen in that court, but when called for by the Chancellor of his own accord.

The first establishment in Virginia which became permanent was made in 1607. I have found no mention of negroes in the colony until about 1650. The first brought here as slaves were by a Dutch ship; after which the English commenced the trade and continued it until the revolutionary war. That suspended, ipso facto, their further importation for the present, and the business of the war pressing constantly on the legislature, this subject was not acted on finally until the year 78. when I brought in a bill to prevent their further importation. This passed without opposition, and stopped the increase of the evil by importation, leaving to future efforts its final eradication.

The first settlers of this colony were Englishmen, loyal subjects to their king and church, and the grant to Sr. Walter Raleigh contained an express Proviso that their laws "should not be against the true Christian faith, now professed in the church of England." As soon as the state of the colony admitted, it was divided into parishes, in each of which was established a minister of the Anglican church, endowed with a fixed salary, in tobacco, a glebe house and land with the other necessary appendages. To meet these expenses all the inhabitants of the parishes were assessed, whether they were or not, members of the established church. Towards Quakers who came here they were most cruelly intolerant, driving them from the colony by the severest penalties. In process of time however, other sectarisms were introduced, chiefly of the Presbyterian family; and the established clergy, secure for life in their glebes and salaries, adding to these generally the emoluments of a classical school, found employment enough, in their farms and schoolrooms for the rest of the week, and devoted Sunday only to the edification of their flock, by service, and a sermon at their parish church. Their other pastoral functions were little attended to. Against this inactivity the zeal and industry of sectarian preachers had an open and undisputed field; and by the time of the revolution, a majority of the inhabitants had become dissenters from the established church, but were still obliged to pay contributions to support the Pastors of the minority. This unrighteous compulsion to maintain teachers of what they deemed religious errors was grievously felt during the regal government, and without a hope of relief. But the first republican legislature which met in 76. was crowded with petitions to abolish this spiritual tyranny. These brought on the severest contests in which I have ever been engaged. Our great opponents were Mr. Pendleton & Robert Carter Nicholas, honest men, but zealous churchmen. The petitions were referred to the commee of the whole house on the state of the country; and after desperate contests in that committee, almost daily from the 11th of Octob. to the 5th of December, we prevailed so far only as to repeal the laws which rendered criminal the maintenance of any religious opinions, the forbearance of repairing to church, or the exercise of any mode of worship: and further, to exempt dissenters from contributions to the support of the established church; and to suspend, only until the next session levies on the members of that church for the salaries of their own incumbents. For although the majority of our citizens were dissenters, as has been observed, a majority of the legislature were churchmen. Among these however were some reasonable and liberal men, who enabled us, on some points, to obtain feeble majorities. But our opponents carried in the general resolutions of the commee of Nov. 19. a declaration that religious assemblies ought to be regulated, and that provision ought to be made for continuing the succession of the clergy, and superintending their conduct. And in the bill now passed was inserted an express reservation of the question Whether a general assessment should not be established by law, on every one, to the support of the pastor of his choice; or whether all should be left to voluntary contributions; and on this question, debated at every session from 76 to 79 (some of our dissenting allies, having now secured their particular object, going over to the advocates of a general assessment) we could only obtain a suspension from session to session until 79. when the question against a general assessment was finally carried, and the establishment of the Anglican church entirely put down. In justice to the two honest but zealous opponents, who have been named I must add that altho', from their natural temperaments, they were more disposed generally to acquiesce in things as they are, than to risk innovations, yet whenever the public will had once decided, none were more faithful or exact in their obedience to it.

The seat of our government had been originally fixed in the peninsula of Jamestown, the first settlement of the colonists; and had been afterwards removed a few miles inland to Williamsburg. But this was at a time when our settlements had not extended beyond the tide water. Now they had crossed the Alleghany; and the center of population was very far removed from what it had been. Yet Williamsburg was still the depository of our archives, the habitual residence of the Governor & many other of the public functionaries, the established place for the sessions of the legislature, and the magazine of our military stores: and it's situation was so exposed that it might be taken at any time in war, and, at this time particularly, an enemy might in the night run up either of the rivers between which it lies, land a force above, and take possession of the place, without the possibility of saving either persons or things. I had proposed it's removal so early as Octob. 76. but it did not prevail until the session of May. '79.

Early in the session of May 79. I prepared, and obtained leave to bring in a bill declaring who should be deemed citizens, asserting the natural right of expatriation, and prescribing the mode of exercising it. This, when I withdrew from the house on the 1st of June following, I left in the hands of George Mason and it was passed on the 26th of that month.

In giving this account of the laws of which I was myself the mover & draughtsman, I by no means mean to claim to myself the merit of obtaining their passage. I had many occasional and strenuous coadjutors in debate, and one most steadfast, able, and zealous; who was himself a host. This was George Mason, a man of the first order of wisdom among those who acted on the theatre of the revolution, of expansive mind, profound judgment, cogent in argument, learned in the lore of our former constitution, and earnest for the republican change on democratic principles. His elocution was neither flowing nor smooth, but his language was strong, his manner most impressive, and strengthened by a dash of biting cynicism when provocation made it seasonable.

Mr. Wythe, while speaker in the two sessions of 1777. between his return from Congress and his appointment to the Chancery, was an able and constant associate in whatever was before a committee of the whole. His pure integrity, judgment and reasoning powers gave him great weight. Of him see more in some notes inclosed in my letter of August 31. 1821, to Mr. John Saunderson.

Mr. Madison came into the House in 1776. a new member and young; which circumstances, concurring with his extreme modesty, prevented his venturing himself in debate before his removal to the Council of State in Nov. 77. From thence he went to Congress, then consisting of few members. Trained in these successive schools, he acquired a habit of self-possession which placed at ready command the rich resources of his luminous and discriminating mind, & of his extensive information, and rendered him the first of every assembly afterwards of which he became a member. Never wandering from his subject into vain declamation, but pursuing it closely in language pure, classical, and copious, soothing always the feelings of his adversaries by civilities and softness of expression, he rose to the eminent station which he held in the great National convention of 1787. and in that of Virginia which followed, he sustained the new constitution in all its parts, bearing off the palm against the logic of George Mason, and the fervid declamation of Mr. Henry. With these consummate powers were united a pure and spotless virtue which no calumny has ever attempted to sully. Of the powers and polish of his pen, and of the wisdom of his administration in the highest office of the nation, I need say nothing. They have spoken, and will forever speak for themselves.

So far we were proceeding in the details of reformation only; selecting points of legislation prominent in character & principle, urgent, and indicative of the strength of the general pulse of reformation. When I left Congress, in 76. it was in the persuasion that our whole code must be reviewed, adapted to our republican form of government, and, now that we had no negatives of Councils, Governors & Kings to restrain us from doing right, that it should be corrected, in all it's parts, with a single eye to reason, & the good of those for whose government it was framed. Early therefore in the session of 76. to which I returned, I moved and presented a bill for the revision of the laws; which was passed on the 24th. of October, and on the 5th. of November Mr. Pendleton, Mr. Wythe, George Mason, Thomas L. Lee and myself were appointed a committee to execute the work. We agreed to meet at Fredericksburg to settle the plan of operation and to distribute the work. We met there accordingly, on the 13th. of January 1777. The first question was whether we should propose to abolish the whole existing system of laws, and prepare a new and complete Institute, or preserve the general system, and only modify it to the present state of things. Mr. Pendleton, contrary to his usual disposition in favor of antient things, was for the former proposition, in which he was joined by Mr. Lee. To this it was objected that to abrogate our whole system would be a bold measure, and probably far beyond the views of the legislature; that they had been in the practice of revising from time to time the laws of the colony, omitting the expired, the repealed and the obsolete, amending only those retained, and probably meant we should now do the same, only including the British statutes as well as our own: that to compose a new Institute like those of Justinian and Bracton, or that of Blackstone, which was the model proposed by Mr. Pendleton, would be an arduous undertaking, of vast research, of great consideration & judgment; and when reduced to a text, every word of that text, from the imperfection of human language, and it's incompetence to express distinctly every shade of idea, would become a subject of question & chicanery until settled by repeated adjudications; that this would involve us for ages in litigation, and render property uncertain until, like the statutes of old, every word had been tried, and settled by numerous decisions, and by new volumes of reports & commentaries; and that no one of us probably would undertake such a work, which, to be systematical, must be the work of one hand. This last was the opinion of Mr. Wythe, Mr. Mason & myself. When we proceeded to the distribution of the work, Mr. Mason excused himself as, being no lawyer, he felt himself unqualified for the work, and he resigned soon after. Mr. Lee excused himself on the same ground, and died indeed in a short time. The other two gentlemen therefore and myself divided the work among us. The common law and statutes to the 4. James I. (when our separate legislature was established) were assigned to me; the British statutes from that period to the present day to Mr. Wythe, and the Virginia laws to Mr. Pendleton. As the law of Descents, & the criminal law fell of course within my portion, I wished the commee to settle the leading principles of these, as a guide for me in framing them. And with respect to the first, I proposed to abolish the law of primogeniture, and to make real estate descendible in parcenary to the next of kin, as personal property is by the statute of distribution.

Mr. Pendleton wished to preserve the right of primogeniture, but seeing at once that that could not prevail, he proposed we should adopt the Hebrew principle, and give a double portion to the elder son. I observed that if the eldest son could eat twice as much, or do double work, it might be a natural evidence of his right to a double portion; but being on a par in his powers & wants, with his brothers and sisters, he should be on a par also in the partition of the patrimony, and such was the decision of the other members.

On the subject of the Criminal law, all were agreed that the punishment of death should be abolished, except for treason and murder; and that, for other felonies should be substituted hard labor in the public works, and in some cases, the Lex talionis. How this last revolting principle came to obtain our approbation, I do not remember. There remained indeed in our laws a vestige of it in a single case of a slave. It was the English law in the time of the Anglo-Saxons, copied probably from the Hebrew law of "an eye for an eye, a tooth for a tooth," and it was the law of several antient people. But the modern mind had left it far in the rear of it's advances. These points however being settled, we repaired to our respective homes for the preparation of the work.

Feb. 6. In the execution of my part I thought it material not to vary the diction of the antient statutes by modernizing it, nor to give rise to new questions by new expressions. The text of these statutes had been so fully explained and defined by numerous adjudications, as scarcely ever now to produce a question in our courts. I thought it would be useful also, in all new draughts, to reform the style of the later British statutes, and of our own acts of assembly, which from their verbosity, their endless tautologies, their involutions of case within case, and parenthesis within parenthesis, and their multiplied efforts at certainty by *saids* and *aforesaids*, by *ors* and by *ands*, to make them more plain, do really render them more perplexed and incomprehensible, not only to common readers, but to the lawyers themselves. We were employed in this work from that time to Feb. 1779, when we met at Williamsburg, that is to say, Mr. Pendleton, Mr. Wythe & myself, and meeting day by day, we examined critically our several parts, sentence by sentence, scrutinizing and amending until we had agreed on the whole. We then returned home, had fair copies made of our several parts, which were reported to the General Assembly June 18. 1779. by Mr. Wythe and myself, Mr. Pendleton's residence being distant, and he having authorized us by letter to declare his approbation. We had in this work brought so much of the Common law as it was thought necessary to alter, all the British statutes from Magna Charta to the present day, and all the laws of Virginia, from the establishment of our legislature, in the 4th. Jac. 1. to the present time, which we thought should be retained, within the compass of 126 bills, making a printed folio of 90 pages only. Some bills were taken out occasionally, from time to time, and passed; but the main body of the work was not entered on by the legislature until after the general peace, in 1785. when by the unwearied exertions of Mr. Madison, in opposition to the endless quibbles, chicaneries, perversions, vexations and delays of lawyers and demi-lawyers, most of the bills were passed by the legislature, with little alteration.

The bill for establishing religious freedom, the principles of which had, to a certain degree, been enacted before, I had drawn in all the latitude of reason & right. It still met with opposition; but, with some mutilations in the preamble, it was finally passed; and a singular proposition proved that it's protection of opinion was meant to be universal. Where the preamble declares that coercion is a departure from the plan of the holy author of our religion, an amendment was proposed, by inserting the word "Jesus Christ," so that it should read "a departure from the plan of Jesus Christ, the holy author of our religion." The insertion was rejected by a great majority, in proof that they meant to comprehend, within the mantle of it's protection, the Jew and the Gentile, the Christian and Mahometan, the Hindoo, and infidel of every denomination.

Beccaria and other writers on crimes and punishments had satisfied the reasonable world of the unrightfulness and inefficacy of the punishment of crimes by death; and hard labor on roads, canals and other public works, had been suggested as a proper substitute. The Revisors had adopted these opinions; but the general idea of our country had not yet advanced to that point. The bill therefore for proportioning crimes and punishments was lost in the House of Delegates by a majority of a single vote. I learnt afterwards that the substitute of hard labor in public was tried (I believe it was in Pennsylvania) without success. Exhibited as a public spectacle, with shaved heads and mean clothing, working on the high roads produced in the criminals such a prostration of character, such an abandonment of self-respect, as, instead of reforming, plunged them into the most desperate & hardened depravity of morals and character.—To pursue the subject of this law.—I was written to in 1785 (being then in Paris) by Directors appointed to superintend the building of a Capitol in Richmond, to advise them as to a plan, and to add to it one of a prison. Thinking it a favorable opportunity of introducing into the state an example of architecture in the classic style of antiquity, and the Maison quarrée of Nismes, an antient Roman temple, being considered as the most perfect model existing of what may be called Cubic architecture, I applied to M. Clerissault, who had published drawings of the Antiquities of Nismes, to have me a model of the building made in stucco, only changing the order from Corinthian to Ionic, on account of the difficulty of the Corinthian capitals. I yielded with reluctance to the taste of Clerissault, in his preference of the modern capital of Scamozzi to the more noble capital of antiquity. This was executed by the artist whom Choiseul Gouffier had carried with him to Constantinople, and employed while Ambassador there, in making those beautiful models of the remains of Grecian architecture which are to be seen at Paris. To adapt the exterior to our use, I drew a plan for the interior, with the apartments necessary for legislative, executive & judiciary purposes, and accommodated in their size and distribution to the form and dimensions of the building. These were forwarded to the Directors in 1786. and were carried into execution, with some variations not for the better, the most important to which however admit of future correction. With respect of the plan of a Prison, requested at the same time, I had heard of a benevolent society in England which had been indulged by the government in an experiment of the effect of labor in *solitary confinement* on some of their criminals, which experiment had succeeded beyond expectation. The same idea had

been suggested in France, and an Architect of Lyons had proposed a plan of a well contrived edifice on the principle of
solitary confinement. I procured a copy, and as it was too
large for our purposes, I drew one on a scale, less extensive,
but susceptible of additions as they should be wanting. This
I sent to the Directors instead of a plan of a common prison,
in the hope that it would suggest the idea of labor in solitary
confinement instead of that on the public works, which we
had adopted in our Revised Code. It's principle accordingly,
but not it's exact form, was adopted by Latrobe in carrying
the plan into execution, by the erection of what is now called
the Penitentiary, built under his direction. In the meanwhile
the public opinion was ripening by time, by reflection, and
by the example of Pensylva, where labor on the highways had
been tried without approbation from 1786 to 89. & had been
followed by their Penitentiary system on the principle of confinement and labor, which was proceeding auspiciously. In
1796. our legislature resumed the subject and passed the law
for amending the Penal laws of the commonwealth. They
adopted solitary, instead of public labor, established a gradation in the duration of the confinement, approximated the
style of the law more to the modern usage, and instead of the
settled distinctions of murder & manslaughter, preserved in
my bill, they introduced the new terms of murder in the 1st
& 2d degree. Whether these have produced more or fewer
questions of definition I am not sufficiently informed of our
judiciary transactions to say. I will here however insert the
text of my bill, with the notes I made in the course of my
researches into the subject.

Feb. 7. The acts of assembly concerning the College of
Wm. & Mary, were properly within Mr. Pendleton's portion
of our work. But these related chiefly to it's revenue, while
it's constitution, organization and scope of science were derived from it's charter. We thought, that on this subject a
systematical plan of general education should be proposed,
and I was requested to undertake it. I accordingly prepared
three bills for the Revisal, proposing three distinct grades of
education, reaching all classes. 1. Elementary schools for all
children generally, rich and poor. 2. Colleges for a middle

degree of instruction, calculated for the common purposes of
life, and such as would be desirable for all who were in easy
circumstances. And 3d. an ultimate grade for teaching the sciences generally, & in their highest degree. The first bill proposed to lay off every county into Hundreds or Wards, of a
proper size and population for a school, in which reading,
writing, and common arithmetic should be taught; and that
the whole state should be divided into 24 districts, in each of
which should be a school for classical learning, grammar, geography, and the higher branches of numerical arithmetic.
The second bill proposed to amend the constitution of Wm.
& Mary College, to enlarge it's sphere of science, and to
make it in fact an University. The third was for the establishment of a library. These bills were not acted on until the same
year '96. and then only so much of the first as provided for
elementary schools. The College of Wm. & Mary was an establishment purely of the Church of England, the Visitors
were required to be all of that Church; the Professors to subscribe it's 39 Articles, it's Students to learn it's Catechism,
and one of its fundamental objects was declared to be to raise
up Ministers for that church. The religious jealousies therefore of all the dissenters took alarm lest this might give an
ascendancy to the Anglican sect and refused acting on that
bill. Its local eccentricity too and unhealthy autumnal climate
lessened the general inclination towards it. And in the Elementary bill they inserted a provision which completely defeated it, for they left it to the court of each county to
determine for itself when this act should be carried into execution, within their county. One provision of the bill was that
the expenses of these schools should be borne by the inhabitants of the county, every one in proportion to his general
tax-rate. This would throw on wealth the education of the
poor; and the justices, being generally of the more wealthy
class, were unwilling to incur that burthen, and I believe it
was not suffered to commence in a single county. I shall recur
again to this subject towards the close of my story, if I should
have life and resolution enough to reach that term; for I am
already tired of talking about myself.

The bill on the subject of slaves was a mere digest of the

existing laws respecting them, without any intimation of a plan for a future & general emancipation. It was thought better that this should be kept back, and attempted only by way of amendment whenever the bill should be brought on. The principles of the amendment however were agreed on, that is to say, the freedom of all born after a certain day, and deportation at a proper age. But it was found that the public mind would not yet bear the proposition, nor will it bear it even at this day. Yet the day is not distant when it must bear and adopt it, or worse will follow. Nothing is more certainly written in the book of fate than that these people are to be free. Nor is it less certain that the two races, equally free, cannot live in the same government. Nature, habit, opinion has drawn indelible lines of distinction between them. It is still in our power to direct the process of emancipation and deportation peaceably and in such slow degree as that the evil will wear off insensibly, and their place be pari passu filled up by free white laborers. If on the contrary it is left to force itself on, human nature must shudder at the prospect held up. We should in vain look for an example in the Spanish deportation or deletion of the Moors. This precedent would fall far short of our case.

I considered 4 of these bills, passed or reported, as forming a system by which every fibre would be eradicated of antient or future aristocracy; and a foundation laid for a government truly republican. The repeal of the laws of entail would prevent the accumulation and perpetuation of wealth in select families, and preserve the soil of the country from being daily more & more absorbed in Mortmain. The abolition of primogeniture, and equal partition of inheritances removed the feudal and unnatural distinctions which made one member of every family rich, and all the rest poor, substituting equal partition, the best of all Agrarian laws. The restoration of the rights of conscience relieved the people from taxation for the support of a religion not theirs; for the establishment was truly of the religion of the rich, the dissenting sects being entirely composed of the less wealthy people; and these, by the bill for a general education, would be qualified to understand their rights, to maintain them, and to exercise with intelligence their parts in self-government: and all this would be effected without the violation of a single natural right of any one individual citizen. To these too might be added, as a further security, the introduction of the trial by jury, into the Chancery courts, which have already ingulfed and continue to ingulf, so great a proportion of the jurisdiction over our property.

On the 1st of June 1779. I was appointed Governor of the Commonwealth and retired from the legislature. Being elected also one of the Visitors of Wm. & Mary college, a self-electing body, I effected, during my residence in Williamsburg that year, a change in the organization of that institution by abolishing the Grammar school, and the two professorships of Divinity & Oriental languages, and substituting a professorship of Law & Police, one of Anatomy Medicine and Chemistry, and one of Modern languages; and the charter confining us to six professorships, we added the law of Nature & Nations, & the Fine Arts to the duties of the Moral professor, and Natural history to those of the professor of Mathematics and Natural philosophy.

Being now, as it were, identified with the Commonwealth itself, to write my own history during the two years of my administration, would be to write the public history of that portion of the revolution within this state. This has been done by others, and particularly by Mr. Girardin, who wrote his Continuation of Burke's history of Virginia while at Milton, in this neighborhood, had free access to all my papers while composing it, and has given as faithful an account as I could myself. For this portion therefore of my own life, I refer altogether to his history. From a belief that under the pressure of the invasion under which we were then laboring the public would have more confidence in a Military chief, and that the Military commander, being invested with the Civil power also, both might be wielded with more energy promptitude and effect for the defence of the state, I resigned the administration at the end of my 2d. year, and General Nelson was appointed to succeed me.

Soon after my leaving Congress in Sep. '76, to wit on the last day of that month, I had been appointed, with Dr. Franklin, to go to France, as a Commissioner to negotiate treaties of alliance and commerce with that government. Silas Deane, then in France, acting as agent* for procuring military stores, was joined with us in commission. But such was the state of my family that I could not leave it, nor could I expose it to the dangers of the sea, and of capture by the British ships, then covering the ocean. I saw too that the laboring oar was really at home, where much was to be done of the most permanent interest in new modelling our governments, and much to defend our fanes and fire-sides from the desolations of an invading enemy pressing on our country in every point. I declined therefore and Dr. Lee was appointed in my place. On the 15th. of June 1781. I had been appointed with Mr. Adams, Dr. Franklin, Mr. Jay, and Mr. Laurens a Minister plenipotentiary for negotiating peace, then expected to be effected thro' the mediation of the Empress of Russia. The same reasons obliged me still to decline; and the negotiation was in fact never entered on. But, in the autumn of the next year 1782 Congress receiving assurances that a general peace would be concluded in the winter and spring, they renewed my appointment on the 13th. of Nov. of that year. I had two months before that lost the cherished companion of my life, in whose affections, unabated on both sides, I had lived the last ten years in unchequered happiness. With the public interests, the state of my mind concurred in recommending the change of scene proposed; and I accepted the appointment, and left Monticello on the 19th. of Dec. 1782. for Philadelphia, where I arrived on the 27th. The Minister of France, Luzerne, offered me a passage in the Romulus frigate, which I accepting. But she was then lying a few miles below Baltimore blocked up in the ice. I remained therefore a month in Philadelphia, looking over the papers in the office of State in order to possess myself of the general state of our foreign relations, and then went to Baltimore to await the liberation of the frigate from the ice. After waiting there nearly a month, we received information that a Provisional treaty of peace had been signed by our Commissioners on the 3d. of

*His ostensible character was to be that of a merchant, his real one that of agent for military supplies, and also for sounding the dispositions of the government of France, and seeing how far they would favor us, either secretly or openly. His appointment had been by the Committee of Foreign Correspondence, March, 1776.

Sept. 1782. to become absolute on the conclusion of peace between France and Great Britain. Considering my proceeding to Europe as now of no utility to the public, I returned immediately to Philadelphia to take the orders of Congress, and was excused by them from further proceeding. I therefore returned home, where I arrived on the 15th. of May, 1783.

On the 6th. of the following month I was appointed by the legislature a delegate to Congress, the appointment to take place on the 1st. of Nov. ensuing, when that of the existing delegation would expire. I accordingly left home on the 16th. of Oct. arrived at Trenton, where Congress was sitting, on the 3d. of Nov. and took my seat on the 4th., on which day Congress adjourned to meet at Annapolis on the 26th.

Congress had now become a very small body, and the members very remiss in their attendance on it's duties insomuch that a majority of the states, necessary by the Confederation to constitute a house even for minor business did not assemble until the 13th. of December.

They as early as Jan. 7. 1782. had turned their attention to the monies current in the several states, and had directed the Financier, Robert Morris, to report to them a table of rates at which the foreign coins should be received at the treasury. That officer, or rather his assistant, Gouverneur Morris, answered them on the 15th in an able and elaborate statement of the denominations of money current in the several states, and of the comparative value of the foreign coins chiefly in circulation with us. He went into the consideration of the necessity of establishing a standard of value with us, and of the adoption of a money-Unit. He proposed for the Unit such a fraction of pure silver as would be a common measure of the penny of every state, without leaving a fraction. This common divisor he found to be 1–1440 of a dollar, or 1–1600 of the crown sterling. The value of a dollar was therefore to be expressed by 1440 units, and of a crown by 1600. Each Unit containing a quarter of a grain of fine silver. Congress turning again their attention to this subject the following year, the financier, by a letter of Apr. 30, 1783. further explained and urged the Unit he had proposed; but nothing more was done on it until the ensuing year, when it was again taken up, and referred to a commee of which I was a member. The general

views of the financier were sound, and the principle was ingenious on which he proposed to found his Unit. But it was
too minute for ordinary use, too laborious for computation
either by the head or in figures. The price of a loaf of bread
1–20 of a dollar would be 72. units.

A pound of butter 1–5 of a dollar 288. units.

A horse or bullock of 80. D value would require a notation of
6. figures, to wit 115,200, and the public debt, suppose of 80.
millions, would require 12. figures, to wit 115,200,000,000 units.
Such a system of money-arithmetic would be entirely unmanageable for the common purposes of society. I proposed
therefore, instead of this, to adopt the Dollar as our Unit of
account and payment, and that it's divisions and sub-divisions
should be in the decimal ratio. I wrote some Notes on the
subject, which I submitted to the consideration of the financier. I received his answer and adherence to his general system, only agreeing to take for his Unit 100. of those he first
proposed, so that a Dollar should be 14 40–100 and a crown
16. units. I replied to this and printed my notes and reply on
a flying sheet, which I put into the hands of the members of
Congress for consideration, and the Committee agreed to report on my principle. This was adopted the ensuing year and
is the system which now prevails. I insert here the Notes and
Reply, as shewing the different views on which the adoption
of our money system hung. The division into dimes, cents &
mills is now so well understood, that it would be easy of introduction into the kindred branches of weights & measures.
I use, when I travel, an Odometer of Clarke's invention which
divides the mile into cents, and I find every one comprehend
a distance readily when stated to them in miles & cents; so
they would in feet and cents, pounds & cents, &c.

The remissness of Congress, and their permanent session,
began to be a subject of uneasiness and even some of the
legislatures had recommended to them intermissions, and periodical sessions. As the Confederation had made no provision for a visible head of the government during vacations of
Congress, and such a one was necessary to superintend the
executive business, to receive and communicate with foreign
ministers & nations, and to assemble Congress on sudden and

extraordinary emergencies, I proposed early in April the appointment of a commee to be called the Committee of the states, to consist of a member from each state, who should remain in session during the recess of Congress: that the functions of Congress should be divided into Executive and Legislative, the latter to be reserved, and the former, by a general resolution to be delegated to that Committee. This proposition was afterwards agreed to; a Committee appointed, who entered on duty on the subsequent adjournment of Congress, quarrelled very soon, split into two parties, abandoned their post, and left the government without any visible head until the next meeting in Congress. We have since seen the same thing take place in the Directory of France; and I believe it will forever take place in any Executive consisting of a plurality. Our plan, best I believe, combines wisdom and practicability, by providing a plurality of Counsellors, but a single Arbiter for ultimate decision. I was in France when we heard of this schism, and separation of our Committee, and, speaking with Dr. Franklin of this singular disposition of men to quarrel and divide into parties, he gave his sentiments as usual by way of Apologue. He mentioned the Eddystone lighthouse in the British channel as being built on a rock in the mid-channel, totally inaccessible in winter, from the boisterous character of that sea, in that season. That therefore, for the two keepers employed to keep up the lights, all provisions for the winter were necessarily carried to them in autumn, as they could never be visited again till the return of the milder season. That on the first practicable day in the spring a boat put off to them with fresh supplies. The boatmen met at the door one of the keepers and accosted him with a How goes it friend? Very well. How is your companion? I do not know. Don't know? Is not he here? I can't tell. Have not you seen him to-day? No. When did you see him? Not since last fall. You have killed him? Not I, indeed. They were about to lay hold of him, as having certainly murdered his companion; but he desired them to go up stairs & examine for themselves. They went up, and there found the other keeper. They had quarrelled it seems soon after being left there, had divided into two parties, assigned the cares below to one, and those above to the other, and had never spoken to or seen one another since.

But to return to our Congress at Annapolis, the definitive treaty of peace which had been signed at Paris on the 3d. of Sep. 1783. and received here, could not be ratified without a House of 9. states. On the 23d. of Dec. therefore we addressed letters to the several governors, stating the receipt of the definitive treaty, that 7 states only were in attendance, while 9. were necessary to its ratification, and urging them to press on their delegates the necessity of their immediate attendance. And on the 26th. to save time I moved that the Agent of Marine (Robert Morris) should be instructed to have ready a vessel at this place, at N. York, & at some Eastern port, to carry over the ratification of the treaty when agreed to. It met the general sense of the house, but was opposed by Dr. Lee on the ground of expense which it would authorize the agent to incur for us; and he said it would be better to ratify at once & send on the ratification. Some members had before suggested that 7 states were competent to the ratification. My motion was therefore postponed and another brought forward by Mr. Read of S. C. for an immediate ratification. This was debated the 26th. and 27th. Reed, Lee, [Hugh] Williamson & Jeremiah Chace urged that ratification was a mere matter of form, that the treaty was conclusive from the moment it was signed by the ministers; that although the Confederation requires the assent of 9. *states* to *enter into* a treaty, yet that it's conclusion could not be called *entrance into it*; that supposing 9. states requisite, it would be in the power of 5. states to keep us always at war; that 9. states had virtually authorized the ratifion having ratified the provisional treaty, and instructed their ministers to agree to a definitive one in the same terms, and the present one was in fact substantially and almost verbatim the same; that there now remain but 67. days for the ratification, for it's passage across the Atlantic, and it's exchange; that there was no hope of our soon having 9. states present; in fact that this was the ultimate point of time to which we could venture to wait; that if the ratification was not in Paris by the time stipulated, the treaty would become void; that if ratified by 7 states, it would go under our seal without it's being known to Gr. Britain that only 7. had concurred; that it was a question of which they had no right to take cognizance, and we were only answerable for it to our constituents; that it was like the ratification which Gr. Britain had received from the Dutch by the negotiations of Sr. Wm. Temple.

On the contrary, it was argued by Monroe, Gerry, Howel, Ellery & myself that by the modern usage of Europe the ratification was considered as the act which gave validity to a treaty, until which it was not obligatory.* That the commission to the ministers reserved the ratification to Congress; that the treaty itself stipulated that it should be ratified; that it became a 2d. question who were competent to the ratification? That the Confederation expressly required 9 states to enter into any treaty; that, by this, that instrument must have intended that the assent of 9. states should be necessary as well to the *completion* as to the *commencement* of the treaty, it's object having been to guard the rights of the Union in all those important cases where 9. states are called for; that, by the contrary construction, 7 states, containing less than one third of our whole citizens, might rivet on us a treaty, commenced indeed under commission and instructions from 9. states, but formed by the minister in express contradiction to such instructions, and in direct sacrifice of the interests of so great a majority; that the definitive treaty was admitted not to be a verbal copy of the provisional one, and whether the departures from it were of substance or not, was a question on which 9. states alone were competent to decide; that the circumstances of the ratification of the provisional articles by 9. states, the instructions to our ministers to form a definitive one by them, and their actual agreement in substance, do not render us competent to ratify in the present instance; if these circumstances are in themselves a ratification, nothing further is requisite than to give attested copies of them, in exchange for the British ratification; if they are not, we remain where we were, without a ratification by 9. states, and incompetent ourselves to ratify; that it was but 4. days since the seven states now present unanimously concurred in a resolution to be forwarded to the governors of the absent states, in which

*Vattel, L. 2, § 156. L. 4, § 77. 1. Mably Droit D'Europe, 86.

they stated as a cause for urging on their delegates, that 9.
states were necessary to ratify the treaty; that in the case of
the Dutch ratification, Gr. Britain had courted it, and therefore was glad to accept it as it was; that they knew our constitution, and would object to a ratification by 7. that if that
circumstance was kept back, it would be known hereafter, &
would give them ground to deny the validity of a ratification
into which they should have been surprised and cheated, and
it would be a dishonorable prostitution of our seal; that there
is a hope of 9. states; that if the treaty would become null if
not ratified in time, it would not be saved by an imperfect
ratification; but that in fact it would not be null, and would
be placed on better ground, going in unexceptionable form,
tho' a few days too late, and rested on the small importance
of this circumstance, and the physical impossibilities which
had prevented a punctual compliance in point of time; that
this would be approved by all nations, & by Great Britain
herself, if not determined to renew the war, and if determined, she would never want excuses, were this out of the
way. Mr. Reade gave notice he should call for the yeas &
nays; whereon those in opposition prepared a resolution expressing pointedly the reasons of the dissent from his motion.
It appearing however that his proposition could not be carried, it was thought better to make no entry at all. Massachusetts alone would have been for it; Rhode Island, Pennsylvania and Virginia against it, Delaware, Maryland & N.
Carolina, would have been divided.

Our body was little numerous, but very contentious. Day
after day was wasted on the most unimportant questions. My
colleague Mercer was one of those afflicted with the morbid
rage of debate, of an ardent mind, prompt imagination, and
copious flow of words, he heard with impatience any logic
which was not his own. Sitting near me on some occasion of
a trifling but wordy debate, he asked how I could sit in silence hearing so much false reasoning which a word should
refute? I observed to him that to refute indeed was easy, but
to silence impossible. That in measures brought forward by
myself, I took the laboring oar, as was incumbent on me; but
that in general I was willing to listen. If every sound argument or objection was used by some one or other of the nu-

merous debaters, it was enough: if not, I thought it sufficient
to suggest the omission, without going into a repetition of
what had been already said by others. That this was a waste
and abuse of the time and patience of the house which could
not be justified. And I believe that if the members of deliberative bodies were to observe this course generally, they
would do in a day what takes them a week, and it is really
more questionable, than may at first be thought, whether Bonaparte's dumb legislature which said nothing and did much,
may not be preferable to one which talks much and does
nothing. I served with General Washington in the legislature
of Virginia before the revolution, and, during it, with Dr.
Franklin in Congress. I never heard either of them speak ten
minutes at a time, nor to any but the main point which was
to decide the question. They laid their shoulders to the great
points, knowing that the little ones would follow of themselves. If the present Congress errs in too much talking, how
can it be otherwise in a body to which the people send 150.
lawyers, whose trade it is to question everything, yield nothing, & talk by the hour? That 150. lawyers should do business
together ought not to be expected. But to return again to our
subject.

Those who thought 7. states competent to the ratification
being very restless under the loss of their motion, I proposed,
on the 3d. of January to meet them on middle ground, and
therefore moved a resolution which premising that there were
but 7. states present, who were unanimous for the ratification,
but, that they differed in opinion on the question of compe-
tency. That those however in the negative were unwilling that
any powers which it might be supposed they possessed
should remain unexercised for the restoration of peace, provided it could be done saving their good faith, and without
importing any opinion of Congress that 7. states were competent, and resolving that treaty be ratified so far as they had
power; that it should be transmitted to our ministers with
instructions to keep it uncommunicated; to endeavor to obtain 3. months longer for exchange of ratifications; that they
should be informed that so soon as 9. states shall be present
a ratification by 9. shall be sent them; if this should get to
them before the ultimate point of time for exchange, they

were to use it, and not the other; if not, they were to offer the act of the 7. states in exchange, informing them the treaty had come to hand while Congress was not in session, that but 7. states were as yet assembled, and these had unanimously concurred in the ratification. This was debated on the 3d. and 4th. and on the 5th. a vessel being to sail for England from this port (Annapolis) the House directed the President to write to our ministers accordingly.

Jan. 14. Delegates from Connecticut having attended yesterday, and another from S. Carolina coming in this day, the treaty was ratified without a dissenting voice, and three instruments of ratification were ordered to be made out, one of which was sent by Colo. Harmer, another by Colo. Franks, and the 3d. transmitted to the agent of Marine to be forwarded by any good opportunity.

Congress soon took up the consideration of their foreign relations. They deemed it necessary to get their commerce placed with every nation on a footing as favorable as that of other nations; and for this purpose to propose to each a distinct treaty of commerce. This act too would amount to an acknowledgment by each of our independance and of our reception into the fraternity of nations; which altho', as possessing our station of right and in fact, we would not condescend to ask, we were not unwilling to furnish opportunities for receiving their friendly salutations & welcome. With France the United Netherlands and Sweden we had already treaties of commerce, but commissions were given for those countries also, should any amendments be thought necessary. The other states to which treaties were to be proposed were England, Hamburg, Saxony, Prussia, Denmark, Russia, Austria, Venice, Rome, Naples, Tuscany, Sardinia, Genoa, Spain, Portugal, the Porte, Algiers, Tripoli, Tunis & Morocco.

Mar. 16. On the 7th. of May Congress resolved that a Minister Plenipotentiary should be appointed in addition to Mr. Adams & Dr. Franklin for negotiating treaties of commerce with foreign nations, and I was elected to that duty. I accordingly left Annapolis on the 11th. Took with me my elder daughter then at Philadelphia (the two others being too young for the voyage) & proceeded to Boston in quest of a passage. While passing thro' the different states, I made a point of informing myself of the state of the commerce of each, went on to New Hampshire with the same view and returned to Boston. From thence I sailed on the 5th. of July in the Ceres a merchant ship of Mr. Nathaniel Tracey, bound to Cowes. He was himself a passenger, and, after a pleasant voyage of 19. days from land to land, we arrived at Cowes on the 26th. I was detained there a few days by the indisposition of my daughter. On the 30th. we embarked for Havre, arrived there on the 31st. left it on the 3d. of August, and arrived at Paris on the 6th. I called immediately on Doctr. Franklin at Passy, communicated to him our charge, and we wrote to Mr. Adams, then at the Hague to join us at Paris.

Before I had left America, that is to say in the year 1781. I had received a letter from M. de Marbois, of the French legation in Philadelphia, informing me he had been instructed by his government to obtain such statistical accounts of the different states of our Union, as might be useful for their information; and addressing to me a number of queries relative to the state of Virginia. I had always made it a practice whenever an opportunity occurred of obtaining any information of our country, which might be of use to me in any station public or private, to commit it to writing. These memoranda were on loose papers, bundled up without order, and difficult of recurrence when I had occasion for a particular one. I thought this a good occasion to embody their substance, which I did in the order of Mr. Marbois' queries, so as to answer his wish and to arrange them for my own use. Some friends to whom they were occasionally communicated wished for copies; but their volume rendering this too laborious by hand, I proposed to get a few printed for their gratification. I was asked such a price however as exceeded the importance of the object. On my arrival at Paris I found it could be done for a fourth of what I had been asked here. I therefore corrected and enlarged them, and had 200. copies printed, under the title of Notes on Virginia. I gave a very few copies to some particular persons in Europe, and sent the rest to my friends in America. An European copy, by the death of the owner, got into the hands of a bookseller, who engaged it's translation, & when ready for the press, communicated his intentions & manuscript to me, without any other permission than that of suggesting corrections. I never had seen so wretched an attempt at translation. Interverted, abridged, mutilated, and often reversing the sense of the original, I found it a blotch of errors from beginning to end. I corrected some of the most material, and in that form it was printed in French. A London bookseller, on seeing the translation, requested me to permit him to print the English original. I thought it best to do so to let the world see that it was not really so bad as the French translation had made it appear. And this is the true history of that publication.

Mr. Adams soon joined us at Paris, & our first employment was to prepare a general form to be proposed to such nations as were disposed to treat with us. During the negotiations for peace with the British Commissioner David Hartley, our Commissioners had proposed, on the suggestion of Doctr. Franklin, to insert an article exempting from capture by the public or private armed ships of either belligerent, when at war, all merchant vessels and their cargoes, employed merely in carrying on the commerce between nations. It was refused by England, and unwisely, in my opinion. For in the case of a war with us, their superior commerce places infinitely more at hazard on the ocean than ours; and as hawks abound in proportion to game, so our privateers would swarm in proportion to the wealth exposed to their prize, while theirs would be few for want of subjects of capture. We inserted this article in our form, with a provision against the molestation of fishermen, husbandmen, citizens unarmed and following their occupations in unfortified places, for the humane treatment of prisoners of war, the abolition of contraband of war, which exposes merchant vessels to such vexatious & ruinous detentions and abuses; and for the principle of free bottoms, free goods.

In a conference with the Count de Vergennes, it was thought better to leave to legislative regulation on both sides such modifications of our commercial intercourse as would voluntarily flow from amicable dispositions. Without urging, we sounded the ministers of the several European nations at the court of Versailles, on their dispositions towards mutual commerce, and the expediency of encouraging it by the protection of a treaty. Old Frederic of Prussia met us cordially and without hesitation, and appointing the Baron de Thulemeyer, his minister at the Hague, to negotiate with us, we communicated to him our Project, which with little alteration by the King, was soon concluded. Denmark and Tuscany entered also into negotiations with us. Other powers appearing indifferent we did not think it proper to press them. They seemed in fact to know little about us, but as rebels who had been successful in throwing off the yoke of the mother country. They were ignorant of our commerce, which had been always monopolized by England, and of the exchange of articles it might offer advantageously to both parties. They were inclined therefore to stand aloof until they could see better what relations might be usefully instituted with us. The negotiations therefore begun with Denmark & Tuscany we protracted designedly until our powers had expired; and abstained from making new propositions to others having no colonies; because our commerce being an exchange of raw for wrought materials, is a competent price for admission into the colonies of those possessing them: but were we to give it, without price, to others, all would claim it without price on the ordinary ground of gentis amicissimæ.

Mr. Adams being appointed Min. Pleny. of the U S. to London, left us in June, and in July 1785. Dr. Franklin returned to America, and I was appointed his successor at Paris. In Feb. 1786. Mr. Adams wrote to me pressingly to join him in London immediately, as he thought he discovered there some symptoms of better disposition towards us. Colo. Smith, his Secretary of legation, was the bearer of his urgencies for my immediate attendance. I accordingly left Paris on the 1st. of March, and on my arrival in London we agreed on a very summary form of treaty, proposing an exchange of citizenship for our citizens, our ships, and our productions generally, except as to office. On my presentation as usual to the King and Queen at their levées, it was impossible for anything to be more ungracious than their notice of Mr. Adams & myself. I saw at once that the ulcerations in the narrow mind of that mulish being left nothing to be expected on the subject of my attendance; and on the first conference with the Marquis of Caermarthen, his Minister of foreign affairs, the

distance and disinclination which he betrayed in his conversation, the vagueness & evasions of his answers to us, confirmed me in the belief of their aversion to have anything to
do with us. We delivered him however our Projét, Mr. Adams
not despairing as much as I did of it's effect. We afterwards,
by one or more notes, requested his appointment of an interview and conference, which, without directly declining, he
evaded by pretences of other pressing occupations for the moment. After staying there seven weeks, till within a few days
of the expiration of our commission, I informed the minister
by note that my duties at Paris required my return to that
place, and that I should with pleasure be the bearer of any
commands to his Ambassador there. He answered that he had
none, and wishing me a pleasant journey, I left London the
26th. arrived at Paris on the 30th. of April.

While in London we entered into negotiations with the
Chevalier Pinto, Ambassador of Portugal at that place. The
only article of difficulty between us was a stipulation that our
bread stuff should be received in Portugal in the form of flour
as well as of grain. He approved of it himself, but observed
that several Nobles, of great influence at their court, were the
owners of wind mills in the neighborhood of Lisbon which
depended much for their profits on manufacturing our wheat,
and that this stipulation would endanger the whole treaty. He
signed it however, & it's fate was what he had candidly por-
tended.

My duties at Paris were confined to a few objects; the receipt of our whale-oils, salted fish, and salted meats on favorable terms, the admission of our rice on equal terms with that
of Piedmont, Egypt & the Levant, a mitigation of the monopolies of our tobacco by the Farmers-general, and a free
admission of our productions into their islands; were the
principal commercial objects which required attention; and
on these occasions I was powerfully aided by all the influence
and the energies of the Marquis de La Fayette, who proved
himself equally zealous for the friendship and welfare of both
nations; and in justice I must also say that I found the government entirely disposed to befriend us on all occasions, and
to yield us every indulgence not absolutely injurious to them-

selves. The Count de Vergennes had the reputation with the diplomatic corps of being wary & slippery in his diplomatic intercourse; and so he might be with those whom he knew to be slippery and double-faced themselves. As he saw that I had no indirect views, practised no subtleties, meddled in no intrigues, pursued no concealed object, I found him as frank, as honorable, as easy of access to reason as any man with whom I had ever done business; and I must say the same for his successor Montmorin, one of the most honest and worthy of human beings.

Our commerce in the Mediterranean was placed under early alarm by the capture of two of our vessels and crews by the Barbary cruisers. I was very unwilling that we should acquiesce in the European humiliation of paying a tribute to those lawless pirates, and endeavored to form an association of the powers subject to habitual depredations from them. I accordingly prepared and proposed to their ministers at Paris, for consultation with their governments, articles of a special confederation in the following form.

＊　　　＊　　　＊

"Proposals for concerted operation among the powers at war with the Piratical States of Barbary.

1. It is proposed that the several powers at war with the Piratical States of Barbary, or any two or more of them who shall be willing, shall enter into a convention to carry on their operations against those states, in concert, beginning with the Algerines.

2. This convention shall remain open to any other power who shall at any future time wish to accede to it; the parties reserving a right to prescribe the conditions of such accession, according to the circumstances existing at the time it shall be proposed.

3. The object of the convention shall be to compel the piratical states to perpetual peace, without price, & to guarantee that peace to each other.

4. The operations for obtaining this peace shall be constant cruises on their coast with a naval force now to be agreed on. It is not proposed that this force shall be so considerable as to be inconvenient to any party. It is believed that half a dozen frigates, with as many Tenders or Xebecs, one half of which shall be in cruise, while the other half is at rest, will suffice.

5. The force agreed to be necessary shall be furnished by the par-

ties in certain quotas now to be fixed; it being expected that each will be willing to contribute in such proportion as circumstance may render reasonable.

6. As miscarriages often proceed from the want of harmony among officers of different nations, the parties shall now consider & decide whether it will not be better to contribute their quotas in money to be employed in fitting out, and keeping on duty, a single fleet of the force agreed on.

7. The difficulties and delays too which will attend the management of these operations, if conducted by the parties themselves separately, distant as their courts may be from one another, and incapable of meeting in consultation, suggest a question whether it will not be better for them to give full powers for that purpose to their Ambassadors or other ministers resident at some one court of Europe, who shall form a Committee or Council for carrying this convention into effect; wherein the vote of each member shall be computed in proportion to the quota of his sovereign, and the majority so computed shall prevail in all questions within the view of this convention. The court of Versailles is proposed, on account of it's neighborhood to the Mediterranean, and because all those powers are represented there, who are likely to become parties to this convention.

8. To save to that council the embarrassment of personal solicitations for office, and to assure the parties that their contributions will be applied solely to the object for which they are destined, there shall be no establishment of officers for the said Council, such as Commis, Secretaries, or any other kind, with either salaries or perquisites, nor any other lucrative appointments but such whose functions are to be exercised on board the sd vessels.

9. Should war arise between any two of the parties to this convention it shall not extend to this enterprise, nor interrupt it; but as to this they shall be reputed at peace.

10. When Algiers shall be reduced to peace, the other pyratical states, if they refuse to discontinue their pyracies shall become the objects of this convention, either successively or together as shall seem best.

11. Where this convention would interfere with treaties actually existing between any of the parties and the sd states of Barbary, the treaty shall prevail, and such party shall be allowed to withdraw from the operations against that state."

*   *   *

Spain had just concluded a treaty with Algiers at the expense of 3. millions of dollars, and did not like to relinquish the benefit of that until the other party should fail in their observance of it. Portugal, Naples, the two Sicilies, Venice, Malta, Denmark and Sweden were favorably disposed to such an association; but their representatives at Paris expressed apprehensions that France would interfere, and, either openly or secretly support the Barbary powers; and they required that I should ascertain the dispositions of the Count de Vergennes on the subject. I had before taken occasion to inform him of what we were proposing, and therefore did not think it proper to insinuate any doubt of the fair conduct of his government; but stating our propositions, I mentioned the apprehensions entertained by us that England would interfere in behalf of those piratical governments. "She dares not do it," said he. I pressed it no further. The other agents were satisfied with this indication of his sentiments, and nothing was now wanting to bring it into direct and formal consideration, but the assent of our government, and their authority to make the formal proposition. I communicated to them the favorable prospect of protecting our commerce from the Barbary depredations, and for such a continuance of time as, by an exclusion of them from the sea, to change their habits & characters from a predatory to an agricultural people: towards which however it was expected they would contribute a frigate, and it's expenses to be in constant cruise. But they were in no condition to make any such engagement. Their recommendatory powers for obtaining contributions were so openly neglected by the several states that they declined an engagement which they were conscious they could not fulfill with punctuality; and so it fell through.

May 17. In 1786. while at Paris I became acquainted with John Ledyard of Connecticut, a man of genius, of some science, and of fearless courage, & enterprise. He had accompanied Capt Cook in his voyage to the Pacific, had distinguished himself on several occasions by an unrivalled intrepidity, and published an account of that voyage with details unfavorable to Cook's deportment towards the savages, and lessening our regrets at his fate. Ledyard had come to Paris in the hope of forming a company to engage in the fur trade of the Western coast of America. He was disappointed in this, and being out of business, and of a roaming, restless character, I suggested to him the enterprise of exploring the Western part of our continent, by passing thro St. Petersburg to Kamschatka, and procuring a passage thence in some of the Russian vessels to Nootka Sound, whence he might make his way across the continent to America; and I undertook to have the permission of the Empress of Russia solicited. He eagerly embraced the proposition, and M. de Sémoulin, the Russian Ambassador, and more particularly Baron Grimm the special correspondent of the Empress, solicited her permission for him to pass thro' her dominions to the Western coast of America. And here I must correct a material error which I have committed in another place to the prejudice of the Empress. In writing some Notes of the life of Capt Lewis, prefixed to his expedition to the Pacific, I stated that the Empress gave the permission asked, & afterwards retracted it. This idea, after a lapse of 26 years, had so insinuated itself into my mind, that I committed it to paper without the least suspicion of error. Yet I find, on recurring to my letters of that date that the Empress refused permission at once, considering the enterprise as entirely chimerical. But Ledyard would not relinquish it, persuading himself that by proceeding to St. Petersburg he could satisfy the Empress of it's practicability and obtain her permission. He went accordingly, but she was absent on a visit to some distant part of her dominions,* and he pursued his course to within 200. miles of Kamschatka, where he was overtaken by an arrest from the Empress, brought back to Poland, and there dismissed. I must therefore in justice, acquit the Empress of ever having for a moment countenanced, even by the indulgence of an innocent passage thro' her territories this interesting enterprise.

May 18. The pecuniary distresses of France produced this year a measure of which there had been no example for near two centuries, & the consequences of which, good and evil, are not yet calculable. For it's remote causes we must go a little back.

Celebrated writers of France and England had already sketched good principles on the subject of government. Yet the American Revolution seems first to have awakened the

*The Crimea.

thinking part of the French nation in general from the sleep of despotism in which they were sunk. The officers too who had been to America, were mostly young men, less shackled by habit and prejudice, and more ready to assent to the suggestions of common sense, and feeling of common rights. They came back with new ideas & impressions. The press, notwithstanding it's shackles, began to disseminate them. Conversation assumed new freedoms. Politics became the theme of all societies, male and female, and a very extensive & zealous party was formed which acquired the appellation of the Patriotic party, who, sensible of the abusive government under which they lived, sighed for occasions of reforming it. This party comprehended all the honesty of the kingdom sufficiently at it's leisure to think, the men of letters, the easy Bourgeois, the young nobility partly from reflection, partly from mode, for these sentiments became matter of mode, and as such united most of the young women to the party. Happily for the nation, it happened at the same moment that the dissipations of the Queen and court, the abuses of the pension-list, and dilapidations in the administration of every branch of the finances, had exhausted the treasures and credit of the nation, insomuch that it's most necessary functions were paralyzed. To reform these abuses would have overset the minister; to impose new taxes by the authority of the King was known to be impossible from the determined opposition of the parliament to their enregistry. No resource remained then but to appeal to the nation. He advised therefore the call of an assembly of the most distinguished characters of the nation, in the hope that by promises of various and valuable improvements in the organization and regimen of the government, they would be induced to authorize new taxes, to controul the opposition of the parliament, and to raise the annual revenue to the level of expenditures. An Assembly of Notables therefore, about 150. in number named by the King, convened on the 22d. of Feb. The Minister (Calonne) stated to them that the annual excess of expenses beyond the revenue, when Louis XVI. came to the throne, was 37. millions of livres; that 440. millns. had been borrowed to reestablish the navy; that the American war had cost them 1440. millns. (256. mils. of Dollars) and that the interest of these sums, with other increased expenses had added 40 millns. more to the annual deficit. (But a subseqt. and more candid estimate made it 56. millns.) He proffered them an universal redress of grievances, laid open those grievances fully, pointed out sound remedies, and covering his canvas with objects of this magnitude, the deficit dwindled to a little accessory, scarcely attracting attention. The persons chosen were the most able & independent characters in the kingdom, and their support, if it could be obtained, would be enough for him. They improved the occasion for redressing their grievances, and agreed that the public wants should be relieved; but went into an examination of the causes of them. It was supposed that Calonne was conscious that his accounts could not bear examination; and it was said and believed that he asked of the King to send 4. members to the Bastile, of whom the M. de la Fayette was one, to banish 20. others, & 2. of his Ministers. The King found it shorter to banish him. His successor went on in full concert with the Assembly. The result was an augmentation of the revenue, a promise of economies in it's expenditure, of an annual settlement of the public accounts before a council, which the Comptroller, having been heretofore obliged to settle only with the King in person, of course never settled at all; an acknowledgment that the King could not lay a new tax, a reformation of the criminal laws, abolition of torture, suppression of Corvées, reformation of the gabelles, removal of the interior custom houses, free commerce of grain internal & external, and the establishment of Provincial assemblies; which alltogether constituted a great mass of improvement in the condition of the nation. The establishment of the Provincial assemblies was in itself a fundamental improvement. They would be of the choice of the people, one third renewed every year, in those provinces where there are no States, that is to say over about three fourths of the kingdom. They would be partly an Executive themselves, & partly an Executive council to the Intendant, to whom the Executive power, in his province had been heretofore entirely delegated. Chosen by the people, they would soften the execution of hard laws, & having a right of representation to the King, they would censure bad laws, suggest good ones, expose abuses, and their representations, when united, would command respect. To the other advantages might be added the precedent itself of calling the Assemblée des Notables, which would perhaps grow into habit. The hope was that the improvements thus promised would be carried into effect, that they would be maintained during the present reign, & that that would be long enough for them to take some root in the constitution, so that they might come to be considered as a part of that, and be protected by time, and the attachment of the nation.

The Count de Vergennes had died a few days before the meeting of the Assembly, & the Count de Montmorin had been named Minister of foreign affairs in his place. Villedeuil succeeded Calonnes as Comptroller general, & Lomenie de Bryenne, Archbishop of Thoulouse, afterwards of Sens, & ultimately Cardinal Lomenie, was named Minister principal, with whom the other ministers were to transact the business of their departments, heretofore done with the King in person, and the Duke de Nivernois, and M. de Malesherbes were called to the Council. On the nomination of the Minister principal the Marshals de Segur & de Castries retired from the departments of War & Marine, unwilling to act subordinately, or to share the blame of proceedings taken out of their direction. They were succeeded by the Count de Brienne, brother of the Prime minister, and the Marquis de la Luzerne, brother to him who had been Minister in the United States.

May 24. A dislocated wrist, unsuccessfully set, occasioned advice from my Surgeon to try the mineral waters of Aix in Provence as a corroborant. I left Paris for that place therefore on the 28th. of Feb. and proceeded up the Seine, thro' Champagne & Burgundy, and down the Rhone thro' the Beaujolais by Lyons, Avignon, Nismes to Aix, where finding on trial no benefit from the waters, I concluded to visit the rice country of Piedmont, to see if anything might be learned there to benefit the rivalship of our Carolina rice with that, and thence to make a tour of the seaport towns of France, along it's Southern and Western coast, to inform myself if anything could be done to favor our commerce with them. From Aix therefore I took my route by Marseilles, Toulon, Hieres, Nice, across the Col de Tende, by Coni, Turin, Vercelli, Novara, Milan, Pavia, Novi, Genoa. Thence returning along the

coast by Savona, Noli, Albenga, Oneglia, Monaco, Nice, An-
tibes, Frejus, Aix, Marseilles, Avignon, Nismes, Montpellier,
Frontignan, Cette, Agde, and along the canal of Languedoc,
by Bezieres, Narbonne, Cascassonne, Castelnaudari, thro' the
Souterrain of St. Feriol and back by Castelnaudari, to Toulouse, thence to Montauban & down the Garonne by Langon
to Bordeaux. Thence to Rochefort, la Rochelle, Nantes,
L'Orient, then back by Rennes to Nantes, and up the Loire
by Angers, Tours, Amboise, Blois to New Orleans, thence
direct to Paris where I arrived on the 10th. of June. Soon after
my return from this journey to wit, about the latter part of
July, I received my younger daughter Maria from Virginia by
the way of London, the youngest having died some time before.

The treasonable perfidy of the Prince of Orange, Stadtholder & Captain General of the United Netherlands, in the
war which England waged against them for entering into a
treaty of commerce with the U. S. is known to all. As their
Executive officer, charged with the conduct of the war, he
contrived to baffle all the measures of the States General, to
dislocate all their military plans, & played false into the hands
of England and against his own country on every possible
occasion, confident in her protection, and in that of the King
of Prussia, brother to his Princess. The States General indignant at this patricidal conduct applied to France for aid, according to the stipulations of the treaty concluded with her
in 85. It was assured to them readily, and in cordial terms, in
a letter from the Ct. de Vergennes to the Marquis de Verac,
Ambassador of France at the Hague, of which the following
is an extract.

"Extrait de la depeche de Monsr. le Comte de Vergennes
à Monsr. le Marquis de Verac, Ambassadeur de France à la
Haye, du 1er Mars 1786.

"Le Roi concourrera, autant qu'il sera en son pouvoir, au
succes de la chose, et vous inviterez de sa part les patriotes
de lui communiquer leurs vues, leurs plans, et leurs en-
vieux. Vous les assurerez que le roi prend un interêt veritable à leurs personnes comme à leur cause, et qu' ils peuvent
compter sur sa protection. Ils doivent y compter d' autant

plus, Monsieur, que nous ne dissimulons pas que si Monsr. le Stadhoulder reprend son ancienne influence, le systeme Anglois ne tardera pas de prevaloir, et que notre alliance deviendroit un être de raison. Les Patriotes sentiront facilement que cette position seroit incompatible avec la dignité, comme avec la consideration de sa majesté. Mais dans le cas, Monsieur, ou les chefs des Patriotes auroient à craindre une scission, ils auroient le temps suffisant pour ramener ceux de leurs amis que les Anglomanes ont egarés, et preparer les choses de maniere que la question de nouveau mise en deliberation soit decidé selon leurs desirs. Dans cette hypothese, le roi vous autorise à agir de concert avec eux, de suivre la direction qu' ils jugeront devoir vous donner, et d' employer tous les moyens pour augmenter le nombre des partisans de la bonne cause. Il me reste, Monsieur, il me reste Monsieur, de vous parler de la sureté personelle des patriotes. Vous les assurerez que dans tout etat de cause, le roi les prend sous sa protection immediate, et vous ferez connoitre partout ou vous le jugerez necessaire, que sa Majesté regarderoit comme une offense personnelle tout ce qu' on entreprenderoit contre leur liberte. Il est à presumer que ce langage, tenu avec energie, en imposera à l'audace des Anglomanes et que Monsr. le Prince de Nassau croira courir quelque risque en provoquant le ressentiment de sa Majesté."

This letter was communicated by the Patriots to me when at Amsterdam in 1788. and a copy sent by me to Mr. Jay in my letter to him of Mar. 16. 1788.

The object of the Patriots was to establish a representative and republican government. The majority of the States general were with them, but the majority of the populace of the towns was with the Prince of Orange; and that populace was played off with great effect by the triumvirate of * * * Harris the English Ambassador afterwards Ld. Malmesbury, the Prince of Orange a stupid man, and the Princess as much a man as either of her colleagues, in audaciousness, in enterprise, & in the thirst of domination. By these the mobs of the Hague were excited against the members of the States general, their persons were insulted & endangered in the streets, the sanctuary of their houses was violated, and the Prince whose function & duty it was to repress and punish these violations of order, took no steps for that purpose. The States General, for their own protection were therefore obliged to place their militia under the command of a Committee. The Prince filled the courts of London and Berlin with complaints at this usurpation of his prerogatives, and forgetting that he was but the first servant of a republic, marched his regular troops against the city of Utrecht, where the States were in session. They were repulsed by the militia. His interests now became marshalled with those of the public enemy & against his own country. The States therefore, exercising their rights of sovereignty, deprived him of all his powers. The great Frederic had died in August 86.* He had never intended to break with France in support of the Prince of Orange. During the illness of which he died, he had thro' the Duke of Brunswick, declared to the Marquis de la Fayette, who was then at Berlin, that he meant not to support the English interest in Holland: that he might assure the government of France his only wish was that some honorable place in the Constitution should be reserved for the Stadtholder and his children, and that he would take no part in the quarrel unless an entire abolition of the Stadtholderate should be attempted. But his place was now occupied by Frederic William, his great nephew, a man of little understanding, much caprice, & very inconsiderate; and the Princess his sister, altho' her husband was in arms against the legitimate authorities of the country, attempting to go to Amsterdam for the purpose of exciting the mobs of that place and being refused permission to pass a military post on the way, he put the Duke of Brunswick at the head of 20,000 men, and made demonstrations of marching on Holland. The King of France hereupon declared, by his Chargé des Affaires in Holland that if the Prussian troops continued to menace Holland with an invasion, his Majesty, in quality of Ally, was determined to succor that province.† In answer to this Eden gave official information to Count Montmorin, that England must consider as at an end, it's convention with France relative to giving notice of it's naval

*lre to Jay Aug. 6. 87.
†My lre Sep. 22. 87.

armaments and that she was arming generally.* War being now imminent, Eden questioned me on the effect of our treaty with France in the case of a war, & what might be our dispositions. I told him frankly and without hesitation that our dispositions would be neutral, and that I thought it would be the interest of both these powers that we should be so; because it would relieve both from all anxiety as to feeding their W. India islands. That England too, by suffering us to remain so, would avoid a heavy land-war on our continent, which might very much cripple her proceedings elsewhere; that our treaty indeed obliged us to receive into our ports the armed vessels of France, with their prizes, and to refuse admission to the prizes made on her by her enemies: that there was a clause also by which we guaranteed to France her American possessions, which might perhaps force us into the war, if these were attacked. "Then it will be war, said he, for they will assuredly be attacked."† Liston, at Madrid, about the same time, made the same inquiries of Carmichael. The government of France then declared a determination to form a camp of observation at Givet, commenced arming her marine, and named the Bailli de Suffrein their Generalissimo on the Ocean. She secretly engaged also in negotiations with Russia, Austria, & Spain to form a quadruple alliance. The Duke of Brunswick having advanced to the confines of Holland, sent some of his officers to Givet to reconnoitre the state of things there, and report them to him. He said afterwards that "if there had been only a few tents at that place, he should not have advanced further, for that the King would not merely for the interest of his sister, engage in a war with France." But finding that there was not a single company there, he boldly entered the country, took their towns as fast as he presented himself before them, and advanced on Utrecht. The States had appointed the Rhingrave of Salm their Commander-in-chief, a Prince without talents, without courage, and without principle. He might have held out in Utrecht for a considerable time, but he surrendered the place without firing a gun, literally ran away & hid himself so that for months it was not known what had become of him. Am-

*My lre to J. Jay Sep. 24.
†lre to Carm. Dec. 15.

sterdam was then attacked and capitulated. In the meantime the negotiations for the quadruple alliance were proceeding favorably. But the secrecy with which they were attempted to be conducted, was penetrated by Fraser, Chargé des affaires of England at St. Petersburg, who instantly notified his court, and gave the alarm to Prussia. The King saw at once what would be his situation between the jaws of France, Austria, and Russia. In great dismay he besought the court of London not to abandon him, sent Alvensleben to Paris to explain and soothe, and England thro' the D. of Dorset and Eden, renewed her conferences for accommodation. The Archbishop, who shuddered at the idea of war, and preferred a peaceful surrender of right to an armed vindication of it, received them with open arms, entered into cordial conferences, and a declaration, and counter declaration were cooked up at Versailles and sent to London for approbation. They were approved there, reached Paris at 1 o'clock of the 27th. and were signed that night at Versailles. It was said and believed at Paris that M. de Montmorin, literally "pleuroit comme un enfant," when obliged to sign this counter declaration; so distressed was he by the dishonor of sacrificing the Patriots after assurances so solemn of protection, and absolute encouragement to proceed.* The Prince of Orange was reinstated in all his powers, now become regal. A great emigration of the Patriots took place, all were deprived of office, many exiled, and their property confiscated. They were received in France, and subsisted for some time on her bounty. Thus fell Holland, by the treachery of her chief, from her honorable independence to become a province of England, and so also her Stadtholder from the high station of the first citizen of a free republic, to be the servile Viceroy of a foreign sovereign. And this was effected by a mere scene of bullying & demonstration, not one of the parties, France England or Prussia having ever really meant to encounter actual war for the interest of the Prince of Orange. But it had all the effect of a real and decisive war.

Our first essay in America to establish a federative government had fallen, on trial, very short of it's object. During the

*My lre to Jay Nov. 3. lre to J. Adams, Nov. 13.

war of Independance, while the pressure of an external enemy hooped us together, and their enterprises kept us necessarily on the alert, the spirit of the people, excited by danger, was a supplement to the Confederation, and urged them to zealous exertions, whether claimed by that instrument, or not. But when peace and safety were restored, and every man became engaged in useful and profitable occupation, less attention was paid to the calls of Congress. The fundamental defect of the Confederation was that Congress was not authorized to act immediately on the people, & by it's own officers. Their power was only requisitory, and these requisitions were addressed to the several legislatures, to be by them carried into execution, without other coercion than the moral principle of duty. This allowed in fact a negative to every legislature, on every measure proposed by Congress; a negative so frequently exercised in practice as to benumb the action of the federal government, and to render it inefficient in it's general objects, & more especially in pecuniary and foreign concerns. The want too of a separation of the legislative, executive, & judiciary functions worked disadvantageously in practice. Yet this state of things afforded a happy augury of the future march of our confederacy, when it was seen that the good sense and good dispositions of the people, as soon as they perceived the incompetence of their first compact, instead of leaving it's correction to insurrection and civil war, agreed with one voice to elect deputies to a general convention, who should peaceably meet and agree on such a constitution as " would ensure peace, justice, liberty, the common defence & general welfare."

This Convention met at Philadelphia on the 25th. of May '87. It sate with closed doors and kept all it's proceedings secret, until it's dissolution on the 17th. of September, when the results of their labors were published all together. I received a copy early in November, and read and contemplated it's provisions with great satisfaction. As not a member of the Convention however, nor probably a single citizen of the Union, had approved it in all it's parts, so I too found articles which I thought objectionable. The absence of express declarations ensuring freedom of religion, freedom of the press, freedom of the person under the uninterrupted protection of the Habeas corpus, & trial by jury in civil as well as in criminal cases excited my jealousy; and the re-eligibility of the President for life, I quite disapproved. I expressed freely in letters to my friends, and most particularly to Mr. Madison & General Washington, my approbations and objections. How the good should be secured, and the ill brought to rights was the difficulty. To refer it back to a new Convention might endanger the loss of the whole. My first idea was that the 9. states first acting should accept it unconditionally, and thus secure what in it was good, and that the 4. last should accept on the previous condition that certain amendments should be agreed to, but a better course was devised of accepting the whole and trusting that the good sense & honest intentions of our citizens would make the alterations which should be deemed necessary. Accordingly all accepted, 6. without objection, and 7. with recommendations of specified amendments. Those respecting the press, religion, & juries, with several others, of great value, were accordingly made; but the Habeas corpus was left to the discretion of Congress, and the amendment against the reeligibility of the President was not proposed by that body. My fears of that feature were founded on the importance of the office, on the fierce contentions it might excite among ourselves, if continuable for life, and the dangers of interference either with money or arms, by foreign nations, to whom the choice of an American President might become interesting. Examples of this abounded in history; in the case of the Roman emperors for instance, of the Popes while of any significance, of the German emperors, the Kings of Poland, & the Deys of Barbary. I had observed too in the feudal History, and in the recent instance particularly of the Stadtholder of Holland, how easily offices or tenures for life slide into inheritances. My wish therefore was that the President should be elected for 7. years & be ineligible afterwards. This term I thought sufficient to enable him, with the concurrence of the legislature, to carry thro' & establish any system of improvement he should propose for the general good. But the practice adopted I think is better allowing his continuance for 8. years with a liability to be dropped at half way of the term, making that a period of probation.

That his continuance should be restrained to 7. years was the opinion of the Convention at an early stage of it's session, when it voted that term by a majority of 8. against 2. and by a simple majority that he should be ineligible a second time. This opinion &c. was confirmed by the house so late as July 26. referred to the committee of detail, reported favorably by them, and changed to the present form by final vote on the last day but one only of their session. Of this change three states expressed their disapprobation, N. York by recommending an amendment that the President should not be eligible a third time, and Virginia and N. Carolina that he should not be capable of serving more than 8. in any term of 16. years. And altho' this amendment has not been made in form, yet practice seems to have established it. The example of 4 Presidents voluntarily retiring at the end of their 8th year, & the progress of public opinion that the principle is salutary, have given it in practice the force of precedent & usage; insomuch that should a President consent to be a candidate for a 3d. election, I trust he would be rejected on this demonstration of ambitious views.

But there was another amendment of which none of us thought at the time and in the omission of which lurks the germ that is to destroy this happy combination of National powers in the General government for matters of National concern, and independent powers in the states for what concerns the states severally. In England it was a great point gained at the Revolution, that the commissions of the judges, which had hitherto been during pleasure, should thenceforth be made during good behavior. A Judiciary dependent on the will of the King had proved itself the most oppressive of all tools in the hands of that Magistrate. Nothing then could be more salutary than a change there to the tenure of good behavior; and the question of good behavior left to the vote of a simple majority in the two houses of parliament. Before the revolution we were all good English Whigs, cordial in their free principles, and in their jealousies of their executive Magistrate. These jealousies are very apparent in all our state constitutions; and, in the general government in this instance, we have gone even beyond the English caution, by requiring a vote of two thirds in one of the Houses for removing a judge; a vote so impossible where* any defence is made, before men of ordinary prejudices & passions, that our judges are effectually independent of the nation. But this ought not to be. I would not indeed make them dependant on the Executive authority, as they formerly were in England; but I deem it indispensable to the continuance of this government that they should be submitted to some practical & impartial controul: and that this, to be imparted, must be compounded of a mixture of state and federal authorities. It is not enough that honest men are appointed judges. All know the influence of interest on the mind of man, and how unconsciously his judgment is warped by that influence. To this bias add that of the esprit de corps, of their peculiar maxim and creed that "it is the office of a good judge to enlarge his jurisdiction," and the absence of responsibility, and how can we expect impartial decision between the General government, of which they are themselves so eminent a part, and an individual state from which they have nothing to hope or fear. We have seen too that, contrary to all correct example, they are in the habit of going out of the question before them, to throw an anchor ahead and grapple further hold for future advances of power. They are then in fact the corps of sappers & miners, steadily working to undermine the independant rights of the States, & to consolidate all power in the hands of that government in which they have so important a freehold estate. But it is not by the consolidation, or concentration of powers, but by their distribution, that good government is effected. Were not this great country already divided into states, that division must be made, that each might do for itself what concerns itself directly, and what it can so much better do than a distant authority. Every state again is divided into counties, each to take care of what lies within it's local bounds; each county again into townships or wards, to manage minuter details; and every ward into farms, to be governed each by it's individual proprietor. Were we directed from Washington when to sow, & when to reap, we should soon want bread. It is by

*In the impeachment of judge Pickering of New Hampshire, a habitual & maniac drunkard, no defence was made. Had there been, the party vote of more than one third of the Senate would have acquitted him.

this partition of cares, descending in gradation from general to particular, that the mass of human affairs may be best managed for the good and prosperity of all. I repeat that I do not charge the judges with wilful and ill-intentioned error; but honest error must be arrested where it's toleration leads to public ruin. As, for the safety of society, we commit honest maniacs to Bedlam, so judges should be withdrawn from their bench, whose erroneous biases are leading us to dissolution. It may indeed injure them in fame or in fortune; but it saves the republic, which is the first and supreme law.

Among the debilities of the government of the Confederation, no one was more distinguished or more distressing than the utter impossibility of obtaining, from the states, the monies necessary for the payment of debts, or even for the ordinary expenses of the government. Some contributed a little, some less, & some nothing, and the last furnished at length an excuse for the first to do nothing also. Mr. Adams, while residing at the Hague, had a general authority to borrow what sums might be requisite for ordinary & necessary expenses. Interest on the public debt, and the maintenance of the diplomatic establishment in Europe, had been habitually provided in this way. He was now elected Vice President of the U S. was soon to return to America, and had referred our bankers to me for future councel on our affairs in their hands. But I had no powers, no instructions, no means, and no familiarity with the subject. It had always been exclusively under his management, except as to occasional and partial deposits in the hands of Mr. Grand, banker in Paris, for special and local purposes. These last had been exhausted for some time, and I had fervently pressed the Treasury board to replenish this particular deposit; as Mr. Grand now refused to make further advances. They answered candidly that no funds could be obtained until the new government should get into action, and have time to make it's arrangements. Mr. Adams had received his appointment to the court of London while engaged at Paris, with Dr. Franklin and myself, in the negotiations under our joint commissions. He had repaired thence to London, without returning to the Hague to take leave of that government. He thought it necessary however to do so now, before he should leave Europe, and accordingly

went there. I learned his departure from London by a letter from Mrs. Adams received on the very day on which
he would arrive at the Hague. A consultation with him, &
some provision for the future was indispensable, while we
could yet avail ourselves of his powers. For when they
would be gone, we should be without resource. I was daily
dunned by a company who had formerly made a small loan
to the U S. the principal of which was now become due;
and our bankers in Amsterdam had notified me that the interest on our general debt would be expected in June; that
if we failed to pay it, it would be deemed an act of bankruptcy and would effectually destroy the credit of the U S.
and all future prospect of obtaining money there; that the
loan they had been authorized to open, of which a third
only was filled, and now ceased to get forward, and rendered desperate that hope of resource. I saw that there was
not a moment to lose, and set out for the Hague on the 2d.
morning after receiving the information of Mr. Adams's journey. I went the direct road by Louvres, Senlis, Roye, Pont St.
Maxence, Bois le duc, Gournay, Peronne, Cambray, Bou-
chain, Valenciennes, Mons, Bruxelles, Malines, Antwerp,
Mordick, and Rotterdam, to the Hague, where I happily
found Mr. Adams. He concurred with me at once in opinion
that something must be done, and that we ought to risk ourselves on doing it without instructions, to save the credit of
the U S. We foresaw that before the new government could
be adopted, assembled, establish it's financial system, get the
money into the treasury, and place it in Europe, considerable
time would elapse; that therefore we had better provide at
once for the years 88. 89. & 90. in order to place our government at it's ease, and our credit in security, during that trying
interval. We set out therefore by the way of Leyden for Amsterdam, where we arrived on the 10th. I had prepared an
estimate showing that

		Florins.
there would be necessary for the year	88—	531,937–10
	89—	538,540
	90—	473,540
Total,		1,544,017–10

	Flor.	
to meet this the bankers had in hand	79,268–2–8	
& the unsold bonds would yield	542,800	622,068–2–8
leaving a deficit of		921,949–7–4
we proposed then to borrow a million yielding . . .		920,000
which would leave a small deficiency of		1,949–7–4

Mr. Adams accordingly executed 1000. bonds, for 1000. florins each, and deposited them in the hands of our bankers, with instructions however not to issue them until Congress should ratify the measure. This done, he returned to London, and I set out for Paris; and as nothing urgent forbade it, I determined to return along the banks of the Rhine to Strasburg, and thence strike off to Paris. I accordingly left Amsterdam on the 30th of March, and proceeded by Utrecht, Nimeguen, Cleves, Duysberg, Dusseldorf, Cologne, Bonne, Coblentz, Nassau, Hocheim, Frankfort, & made an excursion to Hanau, thence to Mayence and another excursion to Rudesheim, & Johansberg; then by Oppenheim, Worms, and Manheim, and an excursion to Heidelberg, then by Spire, Carlsruh, Rastadt & Kelh, to Strasburg, where I arrived Apr. 16th, and proceeded again on the 18th, by Phalsbourg, Fenestrange, Dieuze, Moyenvie, Nancy, Toul, Ligny, Barleduc, St. Diziers, Vitry, Chalons sur Marne, Epernay, Chateau Thierri, Meaux, to Paris where I arrived on the 23d. of April; and I had the satisfaction to reflect that by this journey our credit was secured, the new government was placed at ease for two years to come, and that as well as myself were relieved from the torment of incessant duns, whose just complaints could not be silenced by any means within our power.

A Consular Convention had been agreed on in 84. between Dr. Franklin and the French government containing several articles so entirely inconsistent with the laws of the several states, and the general spirit of our citizens, that Congress withheld their ratification, and sent it back to me with instructions to get those articles expunged or modified so as to render them compatible with our laws. The minister retired unwillingly from these concessions, which indeed authorized the exercise of powers very offensive in a free state. After much discussion it was reformed in a considerable degree, and the Convention was signed by the Count Montmorin and myself, on the 14th. of Nov. 88 not indeed such as I would have wished; but such as could be obtained with good humor & friendship.

On my return from Holland, I had found Paris still in high fermentation as I had left it. Had the Archbishop, on the close of the assembly of Notables, immediately carried into operation the measures contemplated, it was believed they would all have been registered by the parliament, but he was slow, presented his edicts, one after another, & at considerable intervals of time, which gave time for the feelings excited by the proceedings of the Notables to cool off, new claims to be advanced, and a pressure to arise for a fixed constitution, not subject to changes at the will of the King. Nor should we wonder at this pressure when we consider the monstrous abuses of power under which this people were ground to powder, when we pass in review the weight of their taxes, and inequality of their distribution; the oppressions of the tythes, of the tailles, the corvées, the gabelles, the farms & barriers; the shackles on Commerce by monopolies; on Industry by gilds & corporations; on the freedom of conscience, of thought, and of speech; on the Press by the Censure; and of person by lettres de Cachet; the cruelty of the criminal code generally, the atrocities of the Rack, the venality of judges, and their partialities to the rich; the Monopoly of Military honors by the Noblesse; the enormous expenses of the Queen, the princes & the Court; the prodigalities of pensions; & the riches, luxury, indolence & immorality of the clergy. Surely under such a mass of misrule and oppression, a people might justly press for a thoro' reformation, and might even dismount their rough-shod riders, & leave them to walk on their own legs. The edicts relative to the corvées & free circulation of grain, were first presented to the parliament and registered. But those for the impôt territorial, & stamp tax, offered some time after, were refused by the parliament, which proposed a call of the States General as alone competent to their authorization. Their refusal produced a Bed of justice, and their exile to Troyes. The advocates however refusing to attend them, a suspension in the administration of justice took place. The Parliament held out for awhile, but the ennui of their exile and absence from Paris begun at length to be felt, and some dispositions for compromise to appear. On their consent therefore to prolong some of the former taxes, they were recalled from exile, the King met them in session Nov. 19. 87. promised to call the States General in the year 92. and a majority expressed their assent to register an edict for successive and annual loans from 1788. to 92. But a protest being entered by the Duke of Orleans and this encouraging others in a disposition to retract, the King ordered peremptorily the registry of the edict, and left the assembly abruptly. The parliament immediately protested that the votes for the enregistry had not been legally taken, and that they gave no sanction to the loans proposed. This was enough to discredit and defeat them. Hereupon issued another edict for the establishment of a cour plenière, and the suspension of all the parliaments in the kingdom. This being opposed as might be expected by reclamations from all the parliaments & provinces, the King gave way and by an edict of July 5. 88 renounced his cour plenière, & promised the States General for the 1st. of May of the ensuing year: and the Archbishop finding the times beyond his faculties, accepted the promise of a Cardinal's hat, was removed [Sep. 88] from the ministry, and Mr. Necker was called to the department of finance. The innocent rejoicings of the people of Paris on this change provoked the interference of an officer of the city guards, whose order for their dispersion not being obeyed, he charged them with fixed bayonets, killed two or three, and wounded many. This dispersed them for the moment; but they collected the next day in great numbers, burnt 10. or 12. guard houses, killed two or three of the guards, & lost 6. or 8. more of their own number. The city was hereupon put under martial law, and after awhile the tumult subsided. The effect of this change of ministers, and the promise of the States General at an early day, tranquillized the nation. But two great questions now occurred. 1. What proportion shall the number of deputies of the tiers etat bear to those of the Nobles and Clergy? And 2. shall they sit in the same, or in distinct apartments? Mr. Necker, desirous of avoiding himself these knotty questions, proposed a second call of the same Notables, and that their advice should be asked on the subject. They met

Nov. 9. 88. and, by five bureaux against one, they recommended the forms of the States General of 1614. wherein the houses were separate, and voted by orders, not by persons. But the whole nation declaring at once against this, and that the tiers etat should be, in numbers, equal to both the other orders, and the Parliament deciding for the same proportion, it was determined so to be, by a declaration of Dec. 27. 88. A Report of Mr. Necker to the King, of about the same date, contained other very important concessions. 1. That the King could neither lay a new tax, nor prolong an old one. 2. It expressed a readiness to agree on the periodical meeting of the States. 3. To consult on the necessary restriction on lettres de Cachet. And 4. how far the Press might be made free. 5. It admits that the States are to appropriate the public money; and 6. that Ministers shall be responsible for public expenditures. And these concessions came from the very heart of the King. He had not a wish but for the good of the nation, and for that object no personal sacrifice would ever have cost him a moment's regret. But his mind was weakness itself, his constitution timid, his judgment null, and without sufficient firmness even to stand by the faith of his word. His Queen too, haughty and bearing no contradiction, had an absolute ascendency over him; and around her were rallied the King's brother d'Artois, the court generally, and the aristocratic part of his ministers, particularly Breteuil, Broglio, Vauguyon, Foulon, Luzerne, men whose principles of government were those of the age of Louis XIV. Against this host the good counsels of Necker, Montmorin, St. Priest, altho' in unison with the wishes of the King himself, were of little avail. The resolutions of the morning formed under their advice, would be reversed in the evening by the influence of the Queen & court. But the hand of heaven weighed heavily indeed on the machinations of this junto; producing collateral incidents, not arising out of the case, yet powerfully co-exciting the nation to force a regeneration of it's government, and overwhelming with accumulated difficulties this liberticide resistance. For, while laboring under the want of money for even ordinary purposes, in a government which required a million of livres a day, and driven to the last ditch by the universal call for liberty, there came on a winter of such severe cold, as was without example in the memory of man, or in the written records of history. The Mercury was at times 50° below the freezing point of Fahrenheit and 22° below that of Reaumur. All out-door labor was suspended, and the poor, without the wages of labor, were of course without either bread or fuel. The government found it's necessities aggravated by that of procuring immense quantities of fire-wood, and of keeping great fires at all the cross-streets, around which the people gathered in crowds to avoid perishing with cold. Bread too was to be bought, and distributed daily gratis, until a relaxation of the season should enable the people to work: and the slender stock of bread-stuff had for some time threatened famine, and had raised that article to an enormous price. So great indeed was the scarcity of bread that from the highest to the lowest citizen, the bakers were permitted to deal but a scanty allowance per head, even to those who paid for it; and in cards of invitation to dine in the richest houses, the guest was notified to bring his own bread. To eke out the existence of the people, every person who had the means, was called on for a weekly subscription, which the Curés collected and employed in providing messes for the nourishment of the poor, and vied with each other in devising such economical compositions of food as would subsist the greatest number with the smallest means. This want of bread had been foreseen for some time past and M. de Montmorin had desired me to notify it in America, and that, in addition to the market price, a premium should be given on what should be brought from the U S. Notice was accordingly given and produced considerable supplies. Subsequent information made the importations from America, during the months of March, April & May, into the Atlantic ports of France, amount to about 21,000 barrels of flour, besides what went to other ports, and in other months, while our supplies to their West-Indian islands relieved them also from that drain. This distress for bread continued till July.

Hitherto no acts of popular violence had been produced by the struggle for political reformation. Little riots, on ordinary incidents, had taken place, as at other times, in different parts of the kingdom, in which some lives, perhaps a dozen or twenty, had been lost, but in the month of April a more serious one occurred in Paris, unconnected indeed with the revolutionary principle, but making part of the history of the day. The Fauxbourg St. Antoine is a quarter of the city inhabited entirely by the class of day-laborers and journeymen in every line. A rumor was spread among them that a great paper manufacturer, of the name of Reveillon, had proposed, on some occasion, that their wages should be lowered to 15 sous a day. Inflamed at once into rage, & without inquiring into it's truth, they flew to his house in vast numbers, destroyed everything in it, and in his magazines & work shops, without secreting however a pin's worth to themselves, and were continuing this work of devastation when the regular troops were called in. Admonitions being disregarded, they were of necessity fired on, and a regular action ensued, in which about 100. of them were killed, before the rest would disperse. There had rarely passed a year without such a riot in some part or other of the Kingdom; and this is distinguished only as cotemporary with the revolution, altho' not produced by it.

The States General were opened on the 5th. of May 89. by speeches from the King, the Garde des Sceaux Lamoignon, and Mr. Necker. The last was thought to trip too lightly over the constitutional reformations which were expected. His notices of them in this speech were not as full as in his previous 'Rapport au Roi.' This was observed to his disadvantage. But much allowance should have been made for the situation in which he was placed between his own counsels, and those of the ministers and party of the court. Overruled in his own opinions, compelled to deliver, and to gloss over those of his opponents, and even to keep their secrets, he could not come forward in his own attitude.

The composition of the assembly, altho' equivalent on the whole to what had been expected, was something different in it's elements. It has been supposed that a superior education would carry into the scale of the Commons a respectable portion of the Noblesse. It did so as to those of Paris, of it's vicinity and of the other considerable cities, whose greater intercourse with enlightened society had liberalized their minds, and prepared them to advance up to the measure of the times. But the Noblesse of the country, which constituted two thirds of that body, were far in their rear. Residing constantly on their patrimonial feuds, and familiarized by daily habit with Seigneurial powers and practices, they had not yet learned to suspect their inconsistence with reason and right. They were willing to submit to equality of taxation, but not to descend from their rank and prerogatives to be incorporated in session with the tiers etat. Among the clergy, on the other hand, it had been apprehended that the higher orders of the hierarchy, by their wealth and connections, would have carried the elections generally. But it proved that in most cases the lower clergy had obtained the popular majorities. These consisted of the Curés, sons of the peasantry who had been employed to do all the drudgery of parochial services for 10. 20. or 30 Louis a year; while their superiors were consuming their princely revenues in palaces of luxury & indolence.

The objects for which this body was convened being of the first order of importance, I felt it very interesting to understand the views of the parties of which it was composed, and especially the ideas prevalent as to the organization contemplated for their government. I went therefore daily from Paris to Versailles, and attended their debates, generally till the hour of adjournment. Those of the Noblesse were impassioned and tempestuous. They had some able men on both sides, and actuated by equal zeal. The debates of the Commons were temperate, rational and inflexibly firm. As preliminary to all other business, the awful questions came on, Shall the States sit in one, or in distinct apartments? And shall they vote by heads or houses? The opposition was soon found to consist of the Episcopal order among the clergy, and two thirds of the Noblesse; while the tiers etat were, to a man, united and determined. After various propositions of compromise had failed, the Commons undertook to cut the Gordian knot. The Abbe Sieyes, the most logical head of the nation, (author of the pamphlet Qu'est ce que le tiers etat? which had electrified that country, as Paine's Common sense did us) after an impressive speech on the 10th of June, moved that a last invitation should be sent to the Nobles and Clergy, to attend in the Hall of the States, collectively or individually for the verification of powers, to which the commons would proceed immediately, either in their presence or absence. This verifi-

cation being finished, a motion was made, on the 15th. that
they should constitute themselves a National assembly; which
was decided on the 17th. by a majority of four fifths. During
the debates on this question, about twenty of the Curés had
joined them, and a proposition was made in the chamber of
the clergy that their whole body should join them. This was
rejected at first by a small majority only; but, being afterwards
somewhat modified, it was decided affirmatively, by a majority of eleven. While this was under debate and unknown to
the court, to wit, on the 19th. a council was held in the afternoon at Marly, wherein it was proposed that the King should
interpose by a declaration of his sentiments, in a *seance royale*.
A form of declaration was proposed by Necker, which, while
it censured in general the proceedings both of the Nobles and
Commons, announced the King's views, such as substantially
to coincide with the Commons. It was agreed to in council,
the *seance* was fixed for the 22d. the meetings of the States
were till then to be suspended, and everything, in the meantime, kept secret. The members the next morning (20th.) repairing to their house as usual, found the doors shut and
guarded, a proclamation posted up for a seance royale on the
22d. and a suspension of their meetings in the meantime.
Concluding that their dissolution was now to take place, they
repaired to a building called the "Jeu de paume" (or Tennis
court) and there bound themselves by oath to each other,
never to separate of their own accord, till they had settled a
constitution for the nation, on a solid basis, and if separated
by force, that they would reassemble in some other place. The
next day they met in the church of St. Louis, and were joined
by a majority of the clergy. The heads of the Aristocracy saw
that all was lost without some bold exertion. The King was
still at Marly. Nobody was permitted to approach him but
their friends. He was assailed by falsehoods in all shapes. He
was made to believe that the Commons were about to absolve
the army from their oath of fidelity to him, and to raise their
pay. The court party were now all rage and desperate. They
procured a committee to be held consisting of the King and
his ministers, to which Monsieur & the Count d'Artois
should be admitted. At this committee the latter attacked Mr.
Necker personally, arraigned his declaration, and proposed

one which some of his prompters had put into his hands. Mr. Necker was brow-beaten and intimidated, and the King shaken. He determined that the two plans should be deliberated on the next day and the seance royale put off a day longer. This encouraged a fiercer attack on Mr. Necker the next day. His draught of a declaration was entirely broken up, & that of the Count d'Artois inserted into it. Himself and Montmorin offered their resignation, which was refused, the Count d'Artois saying to Mr. Necker "No sir, you must be kept as the hostage; we hold you responsible for all the ill which shall happen." This change of plan was immediately whispered without doors. The Noblesse were in triumph; the people in consternation. I was quite alarmed at this state of things. The soldiery had not yet indicated which side they should take, and that which they should support would be sure to prevail. I considered a successful reformation of government in France, as ensuring a general reformation thro Europe, and the resurrection, to a new life, of their people, now ground to dust by the abuses of the governing powers. I was much acquainted with the leading patriots of the assembly. Being from a country which had successfully passed thro' a similar reformation, they were disposed to my acquaintance, and had some confidence in me. I urged most strenuously an immediate compromise; to secure what the government was now ready to yield, and trust to future occasions for what might still be wanting. It was well understood that the King would grant at this time 1. Freedom of the person by Habeas corpus. 2. Freedom of conscience. 3. Freedom of the press. 4. Trial by jury. 5. A representative legislature. 6. Annual meetings. 7. The origination of laws. 8. The exclusive right of taxation and appropriation. And 9. The responsibility of ministers; and with the exercise of these powers they would obtain in future whatever might be further necessary to improve and preserve their constitution. They thought otherwise however, and events have proved their lamentable error. For after 30. years of war, foreign and domestic, the loss of millions of lives, the prostration of private happiness, and foreign subjugation of their own country for a time, they have obtained no more, nor even that securely. They were unconscious of (for who could foresee?) the melancholy sequel of their well-meant perseverance; that their physical force would be usurped by a first tyrant to trample on the independance, and even the existence, of other nations: that this would afford fatal example for the atrocious conspiracy of Kings against their people; would generate their unholy and homicide alliance to make common cause among themselves, and to crush, by the power of the whole, the efforts of any part, to moderate their abuses and oppressions.

When the King passed, the next day, thro' the lane formed from the Chateau to the Hotel des etats, there was a dead silence. He was about an hour in the House delivering his speech & declaration. On his coming out a feeble cry of "Vive le Roy" was raised by some children, but the people remained silent & sullen. In the close of his speech he had ordered that the members should follow him, & resume their deliberations the next day. The Noblesse followed him, and so did the clergy, except about thirty, who, with the tiers, remained in the room, and entered into deliberation. They protested against what the King had done, adhered to all their former proceedings, and resolved the inviolability of their own persons. An officer came to order them out of the room in the King's name. "Tell those who sent you, said Mirabeau, that we shall not move hence but at our own will, or the point of the bayonet." In the afternoon the people, uneasy, began to assemble in great numbers in the courts, and vicinities of the palace. This produced alarm. The Queen sent for Mr. Necker. He was conducted amidst the shouts and acclamations of the multitude who filled all the apartments of the palace. He was a few minutes only with the queen, and what passed between them did not transpire. The King went out to ride. He passed thro' the crowd to his carriage and into it, without being in the least noticed. As Mr. Neckar followed him universal acclamations were raised of "vive Monsr. Neckar, vive le sauveur de la France opprimée." He was conducted back to his house with the same demonstrations of affection and anxiety. About 200. deputies of the Tiers, catching the enthusiasm of the moment, went to his house, and extorted from him a promise that he would not resign. On the 25th. 48. of the Nobles joined the tiers, & among them the D. of Orleans. There were then with them 164 members of the Clergy, altho' the minority of that body still sat apart & called themselves the chamber of the clergy. On the 26th. the Archbp. of Paris joined the tiers, as did some others of the clergy and of the Noblesse.

These proceedings had thrown the people into violent ferment. It gained the souldiery, first of the French guards, extended to those of every other denomination, except the Swiss, and even to the body guards of the King. They began to quit their barracks, to assemble in squads, to declare they would defend the life of the King, but would not be the murderers of their fellow-citizens. They called themselves the souldiers *of the nation*, and left now no doubt on which side they would be, in case of rupture. Similar accounts came in from the troops in other parts of the kingdom, giving good reason to believe they would side with their fathers and brothers rather than with their officers. The operation of this medicine at Versailles was as sudden as it was powerful. The alarm there was so compleat that in the afternoon of the 27th. the King wrote with his own hand letters to the Presidents of the clergy and Nobles, engaging them immediately to join the Tiers. These two bodies were debating & hesitating when notes from the Ct. d'Artois decided their compliance. They went in a body and took their seats with the tiers, and thus rendered the union of the orders in one chamber compleat.

The Assembly now entered on the business of their mission, and first proceeded to arrange the order in which they would take up the heads of their constitution, as follows:

First, and as Preliminary to the whole a general Declaration of the Rights of Man. Then specifically the Principles of the Monarchy; rights of the Nation; rights of the King; rights of the citizens; organization & rights of the National assembly; forms necessary for the enactment of laws; organization & functions of the provincial & municipal assemblies; duties and limits of the Judiciary power; functions & duties of the military power.

A declaration of the rights of man, as the preliminary of their work, was accordingly prepared and proposed by the Marquis de la Fayette.

But the quiet of their march was soon disturbed by information that troops, and particularly the foreign troops, were advancing on Paris from various quarters. The King had been probably advised to this on the pretext of preserving peace in Paris. But his advisers were believed to have other things in contemplation. The Marshal de Broglio was appointed to their command, a high flying aristocrat, cool and capable of everything. Some of the French guards were soon arrested, under other pretexts, but really on account of their dispositions in favor of the National cause. The people of Paris forced their prison, liberated them, and sent a deputation to the Assembly to solicit a pardon. The Assembly recommended peace and order to the people of Paris, the prisoners to the king, and asked from him the removal of the troops. His answer was negative and dry, saying they might remove themselves, if they pleased, to Noyons or Soissons. In the meantime these troops, to the number of twenty or thirty thousand, had arrived and were posted in, and between Paris and Versailles. The bridges and passes were guarded. At three o'clock in the afternoon of the 11th July the Count de la Luzerne was sent to notify Mr. Neckar of his dismission, and to enjoin him to retire instantly without saying a word of it to anybody. He went home, dined, and proposed to his wife a visit to a friend, but went in fact to his country house at St. Ouen, and at midnight set out for Brussels. This was not known until the next day, 12th when the whole ministry was changed, except Villedeuil, of the Domestic department, and Barenton, Garde des sceaux. The changes were as follows.

The Baron de Breteuil, president of the council of finance; de la Galaisiere, Comptroller general in the room of Mr. Neckar; the Marshal de Broglio, minister of War, & Foulon under him in the room of Puy-Segur; the Duke de la Vauguyon, minister of foreign affairs instead of the Ct. de Montmorin; de La Porte, minister of Marine, in place of the Ct. de la Luzerne; St. Priest was also removed from the council. Luzerne and Puy-Segur had been strongly of the Aristocratic party in the Council, but they were not considered as equal to the work now to be done. The King was now compleatly in the hands of men, the principal among whom had been noted thro' their lives for the Turkish despotism of their characters, and who were associated around the King as proper instruments for what was to be executed. The news of this change began to be known at Paris about 1. or 2. o'clock. In the afternoon a body of about 100 German cavalry were advanced and drawn up in the Place Louis XV. and about 200. Swiss posted at a little distance in their rear. This drew people to the spot, who thus accidentally found themselves in front of the troops, merely at first as spectators; but as their numbers increased, their indignation rose. They retired a few steps, and posted themselves on and behind large piles of stones, large and small, collected in that Place for a bridge which was to be built adjacent to it. In this position, happening to be in my carriage on a visit, I passed thro' the lane they had formed, without interruption. But the moment after I had passed, the people attacked the cavalry with stones. They charged, but the advantageous position of the people, and the showers of stones obliged the horse to retire, and quit the field altogether, leaving one of their number on the ground, & the Swiss in their rear not moving to their aid. This was the signal for universal insurrection, and this body of cavalry, to avoid being massacred, retired towards Versailles. The people now armed themselves with such weapons as they could find in armorer's shops and private houses, and with bludgeons, and were roaming all night thro' all parts of the city, without any decided object. The next day (13th.) the assembly pressed on the king to send away the troops, to permit the Bourgeoisie of Paris to arm for the preservation of order in the city, and offer to send a deputation from their body to tranquillize them; but their propositions were refused. A committee of magistrates and electors of the city are appointed by those bodies to take upon them it's government. The people, now openly joined by the French guards, force the prison of St. Lazare, release all the prisoners, and take a great store of corn, which they carry to the Corn-market. Here they get some arms, and the French guards begin to form & train them. The City-committee determined to raise 48.000. Bourgeoise, or rather to restrain their numbers to 48.000. On the 14th. they send one of their members (Mons. de Corny) to the Hotel des Invalides, to ask arms for their Garde-Bourgeoise. He was followed by, and he found there a great collection of people. The Governor of the Invalids came out and represented the impossibility of his delivering arms without the orders of those from whom he received them. De Corny advised the people then to retire, and retired himself; but the people took possession of the arms. It was remarkable that not only the Invalids themselves made no opposition, but that a body of 5000. foreign troops, within 400. yards, never stirred. M. de Corny and five others were then sent to ask arms of M. de Launay, governor of the Bastile. They found a great collection of people already before the place, and they immediately planted a flag of truce, which was answered by a like flag hoisted on the Parapet. The deputation prevailed on the people to fall back a little, advanced themselves to make their demand of the Governor, and in that instant a discharge from the Bastile killed four persons, of those nearest to the deputies. The deputies retired. I happened to be at the house of M. de Corny when he returned to it, and received from him a narrative of these transactions. On the retirement of the deputies, the people rushed forward & almost in an instant were in possession of a fortification defended by 100. men, of infinite strength, which in other times had stood several regular sieges, and had never been taken. How they forced their entrance has never been explained. They took all the arms, discharged the prisoners, and such of the garrison as were not killed in the first moment of fury, carried the Governor and Lt. Governor to the Place de Grève (the place of public execution) cut off their heads, and sent them thro' the city in triumph to the Palais royal. About the same instant a treacherous correspondence having been discovered in M. de Flesselles, prevot des marchands, they seized him in the Hotel de Ville where he was in the execution of his office, and cut off his head. These events carried imperfectly to Versailles were the subject of two successive deputations from the assembly to the king, to both of which he gave dry and hard answers for nobody had as yet been permitted to inform him truly and fully of what had passed at Paris. But at night the Duke de Liancourt forced his way into the king's bed chamber, and obliged him to hear a full and animated detail of the disasters of the day in Paris. He went to bed fearfully impressed. The decapitation of de Launai worked powerfully thro' the night on the whole aristocratic party, insomuch that, in the morning, those of the greatest influence on the Count d'Artois represented to him the absolute necessity that the king should give up everything to the Assembly. This according with the dispositions of the king, he went about 11. o'clock, accompanied only by his brothers, to the Assembly, & there read to them a speech, in which he asked their interposition to re-establish order. Altho' couched in terms of some caution, yet the manner in which it was delivered made it evident that it was meant as a surrender at discretion. He returned to the Chateau afoot, accompanied by the assembly. They sent off a deputation to quiet Paris, at the head of which was the Marquis de la Fayette who had, the same morning, been named Commandant en chef of the Milice Bourgeoise, and Mons Bailly, former President of the States General, was called for as Prevot des marchands. The demolition of the Bastile was now ordered and begun. A body of the Swiss guards of the regiment of Ventimille, and the city horse guards joined the people. The alarm at Versailles increased. The foreign troops were ordered off instantly. Every minister resigned. The king confirmed Bailly as Prevot des Marchands, wrote to Mr. Neckar to recall him, sent his letter open to the assembly, to be forwarded by them, and invited them to go with him to Paris the next day, to satisfy the city of his dispositions; and that night, and the next morning the Count D'Artois and M. de Montesson a deputy connected with him, Madame de Polignac, Madame de Guiche, and the Count de Vaudreuil, favorites of the queen, the Abbe de Vermont her confessor, the Prince of Condé and Duke of Bourbon fled. The king came to Paris, leaving the queen in consternation for his return. Omitting the less important figures of the procession, the king's carriage was in the center, on each side of it the assembly, in two ranks afoot, at their head the M. de la Fayette, as Commander-in-chief, on horseback, and Bourgeois guards before and behind. About 60.000 citizens of all forms and conditions, armed with the muskets of the Bastile and Invalids, as far as they would go, the rest with pistols, swords, pikes, pruning hooks, scythes &c. lined all the streets thro' which the procession passed, and with the crowds of people in the streets, doors & windows, saluted them everywhere with cries of "vive la nation," but not a single "vive le roy" was heard. The King landed at the Hotel de Ville. There M.

Bailly presented and put into his hat the popular cockade, and addressed him. The King being unprepared, and unable to answer, Bailly went to him, gathered from him some scraps of sentences, and made out an answer, which he delivered to the audience as from the king. On their return the popular cries were "vive le roy et la nation." He was conducted by a garde bourgeoise to his palace at Versailles, & thus concluded an amende honorable as no sovereign ever made, and no people ever received.

And here again was lost another precious occasion of sparing to France the crimes and cruelties thro' which she has since passed, and to Europe, & finally America the evils which flowed on them also from this mortal source. The king was now become a passive machine in the hands of the National assembly, and had he been left to himself, he would have willingly acquiesced in whatever they should devise as best for the nation. A wise constitution would have been formed, hereditary in his line, himself placed at it's head, with powers so large as to enable him to do all the good of his station, and so limited as to restrain him from it's abuse. This he would have faithfully administered, and more than this I do not believe he ever wished. But he had a Queen of absolute sway over his weak mind, and timid virtue; and of a character the reverse of his in all points. This angel, as gaudily painted in the rhapsodies of the Rhetor Burke, with some smartness of fancy, but no sound sense was proud, disdainful of restraint, indignant at all obstacles to her will, eager in the pursuit of pleasure, and firm enough to hold to her desires, or perish in their wreck. Her inordinate gambling and dissipations, with those of the Count d'Artois and others of her clique, had been a sensible item in the exhaustion of the treasury, which called into action the reforming hand of the nation; and her opposition to it her inflexible perverseness, and dauntless spirit, led herself to the Guillotine, & drew the king on with her, and plunged the world into crimes & calamities which will forever stain the pages of modern history. I have ever believed that had there been no queen, there would have been no revolution. No force would have been provoked nor exercised. The king would have gone hand in hand with the wisdom of his sounder counsellors, who, guided by the increased lights of the age, wished only, with the same pace, to advance the principles of their social institution. The deed which closed the mortal course of these sovereigns, I shall neither approve nor condemn. I am not prepared to say that the first magistrate of a nation cannot commit treason against his country, or is unamenable to it's punishment: nor yet that where there is no written law, no regulated tribunal, there is not a law in our hearts, and a power in our hands, given for righteous employment in maintaining right, and redressing wrong. Of those who judged the king, many thought him wilfully criminal, many that his existence would keep the nation in perpetual conflict with the horde of kings, who would war against a regeneration which might come home to themselves, and that it were better that one should die than all. I should not have voted with this portion of the legislature. I should have shut up the Queen in a Convent, putting harm out of her power, and placed the king in his station, investing him with limited powers, which I verily believe he would have honestly exercised, according to the measure of his understanding. In this way no void would have been created, courting the usurpation of a military adventurer, nor occasion given for those enormities which demoralized the nations of the world, and destroyed, and is yet to destroy millions and millions of it's inhabitants. There are three epochs in history signalized by the total extinction of national morality. The first was of the successors of Alexander, not omitting himself. The next the successors of the first Cæsar, the third our own age. This was begun by the partition of Poland, followed by that of the treaty of Pilnitz; next the conflagration of Copenhagen; then the enormities of Bonaparte partitioning the earth at his will, and devastating it with fire and sword; now the conspiracy of kings, the successors of Bonaparte, blasphemously calling themselves the Holy Alliance, and treading in the footsteps of their incarcerated leader, not yet indeed usurping the government of other nations avowedly and in detail, but controuling by their armies the forms in which they will permit them to be governed; and reserving in petto the order and extent of the usurpations further meditated. But I will return from a digression, anticipated too in time, into which I have been led by reflection on the criminal passions which refused to the world a favorable occasion of saving it from the afflictions it has since suffered.

M. Necker had reached Basle before he was overtaken by the letter of the king, inviting him back to resume the office he had recently left. He returned immediately, and all the other ministers having resigned, a new administration was named, to wit St. Priest & Montmorin were restored; the Archbishop of Bordeaux was appointed Garde des sceaux; La Tour du Pin Minister of War; La Luzerne Minister of Marine. This last was believed to have been effected by the friendship of Montmorin; for altho' differing in politics, they continued firm in friendship, & Luzerne, altho' not an able man was thought an honest one. And the Prince of Bauvau was taken into the Council.

Seven princes of the blood royal, six ex-ministers, and many of the high Noblesse having fled, and the present ministers, except Luzerne, being all of the popular party, all the functionaries of government moved for the present in perfect harmony.

In the evening of Aug. 4. and on the motion of the Viscount de Noailles brother in law of La Fayette, the assembly abolished all titles of rank, all the abusive privileges of feudalism, the tythes and casuals of the clergy, all provincial privileges, and, in fine, the Feudal regimen generally. To the suppression of tythes the Abbe Sieyes was vehemently opposed; but his learned and logical arguments were unheeded, and his estimation lessened by a contrast of his egoism (for he was beneficed on them) with the generous abandonment of rights by the other members of the assembly. Many days were employed in putting into the form of laws the numerous demolitions of ancient abuses; which done, they proceeded to the preliminary work of a Declaration of rights. There being much concord of sentiment on the elements of this instrument, it was liberally framed, and passed with a very general approbation. They then appointed a Committee for the reduction of a projet of a Constitution, at the head of which was the Archbishop of Bordeaux. I received from him, as Chairman of the Committee a letter of July 20. requesting me to attend and assist at their deliberations; but I excused myself on the obvious considerations that my mission was to the king as Chief Magistrate of the nation, that my duties were limited to the concerns of my own country, and forbade me to intermeddle with the internal transactions of that in which I had been received under a specific character only. Their plan of a constitution was discussed in sections, and so reported from time to time, as agreed to by the Committee. The first respected the general frame of the government; and that this should be formed into three departments, Executive, Legislative and Judiciary was generally agreed. But when they proceeded to subordinate developments, many and various shades of opinion came into conflict, and schism, strongly marked, broke the Patriots into fragments of very discordant principles. The first question Whether there should be a king, met with no open opposition, and it was readily agreed that the government of France should be monarchical & hereditary. Shall the king have a negative on the laws? shall that negative be absolute, or suspensive only? Shall there be two chambers of legislation? or one only? If two, shall one of them be hereditary? or for life? or for a fixed term? and named by the king? or elected by the people? These questions found strong differences of opinion, and produced repulsive combinations among the Patriots. The Aristocracy was cemented by a common principle of preserving the ancient regime, or whatever should be nearest to it. Making this their Polar star, they moved in phalanx, gave preponderance on every question to the minorities of the Patriots, and always to those who advocated the least change. The features of the new constitution were thus assuming a fearful aspect, and great alarm was produced among the honest patriots by these dissensions in their ranks. In this uneasy state of things, I received one day a note from the Marquis de la Fayette, informing me that he should bring a party of six or eight friends to ask a dinner of me the next day. I assured him of their welcome. When they arrived, they were La Fayette himself, Duport, Barnave, Alexander La Meth, Blacon, Mounier, Maubourg, and Dagout. These were leading patriots, of honest but differing opinions sensible of the necessity of effecting a coalition by mutual sacrifices, knowing each other, and not afraid therefore to unbosom themselves mutually. This last was a material principle in the selection. With this view the Marquis had invited the conference and had fixed the time & place inadvertently as to the embarrassment under which it might place me. The cloth being removed and wine set on the table, after the American manner, the Marquis introduced the objects of the conference by summarily reminding them of the state of things in the Assembly, the course which the principles of the constitution were taking, and the inevitable result, unless checked by more concord among the Patriots themselves. He observed that altho' he also had his opinion, he was ready to sacrifice it to that of his brethren of the same cause: but that a common opinion must now be formed, or the Aristocracy would carry everything, and that whatever they should now agree on, he, at the head of the National force, would maintain. The discussions began at the hour of four, and were continued till ten o'clock in the evening; during which time I was a silent witness to a coolness and candor of argument unusual in the conflicts of political opinion; to a logical reasoning, and chaste eloquence, disfigured by no gaudy tinsel of rhetoric or declamation, and truly worthy of being placed in parallel with the finest dialogues of antiquity, as handed to us by Xenophon, by Plato and Cicero. The result was an agreement that the king should have a suspensive veto on the laws, that the legislature should be composed of a single body only, & that to be chosen by the people. This Concordate decided the fate of the constitution. The Patriots all rallied to the principles thus settled, carried every question agreeably to them, and reduced the Aristocracy to insignificance and impotence. But duties of exculpation were now incumbent on me. I waited on Count Montmorin the next morning, and explained to him with truth and candor how it had happened that my house had been made the scene of conferences of such a character. He told me he already knew everything which had passed, that, so far from taking umbrage at the use made of my house on that occasion, he earnestly wished I would habitually assist at such conferences, being sure I should be useful in moderating the warmer spirits, and promoting a wholesome and practicable reformation only. I told him I knew too well the duties I owed to the king, to the nation, and to my own country to take any part in councils concerning their internal government, and that I should persevere with care in the character of a neutral and passive spectator, with wishes only and very sincere ones, that those measures might prevail which would be for the greatest good of the nation. I have no doubt indeed that this conference was previously known and approved by this honest minister, who was in confidence and communication with the patriots, and wished for a reasonable reform of the Constitution.

Here I discontinue my relation of the French revolution. The minuteness with which I have so far given it's details is disproportioned to the general scale of my narrative. But I have thought it justified by the interest which the whole world must take in this revolution. As yet we are but in the first chapter of it's history. The appeal to the rights of man, which had been made in the U S. was taken up by France, first of the European nations. From her the spirit has spread over those of the South. The tyrants of the North have allied indeed against it, but it is irresistible. Their opposition will only multiply it's millions of human victims; their own satellites will catch it, and the condition of man thro' the civilized world will be finally and greatly ameliorated. This is a wonderful instance of great events from small causes. So inscrutable is the arrangement of causes & consequences in this world that a two-penny duty on tea, unjustly imposed in a sequestered part of it, changes the condition of all it's inhabitants. I have been more minute in relating the early transactions of this regeneration because I was in circumstances peculiarly favorable for a knowledge of the truth. Possessing the confidence and intimacy of the leading patriots, & more than all of the Marquis Fayette, their head and Atlas, who had no secrets from me, I learnt with correctness the views & proceedings of that party; while my intercourse with the diplomatic missionaries of Europe at Paris, all of them with the court, and eager in prying into it's councils and proceedings, gave me a knolege of these also. My information was always and immediately committed to writing, in letters to Mr. Jay, and often to my friends, and a recurrence to these letters now insures me against errors of memory.

These opportunities of information ceased at this period, with my retirement from this interesting scene of action. I had been more than a year soliciting leave to go home with a view to place my daughters in the society & care of their friends, and to return for a short time to my station at Paris. But the metamorphosis thro' which our government was then passing from it's Chrysalid to it's Organic form suspended it's action in a great degree; and it was not till the last of August that I received the permission I had asked.—And here I cannot leave this great and good country without expressing my sense of it's preeminence of character among the nations of the earth. A more benevolent people, I have never known, nor greater warmth & devotedness in their select friendships. Their kindness and accommodation to strangers is unparalleled, and the hospitality of Paris is beyond anything I had conceived to be practicable in a large city. Their eminence too in science, the communicative dispositions of their scientific men, the politeness of the general manners, the ease and vivacity of their conversation, give a charm to their society to be found nowhere else. In a comparison of this with other countries we have the proof of primacy, which was given to Themistocles after the battle of Salamis. Every general voted to himself the first reward of valor, and the second to Themistocles. So ask the travelled inhabitant of any nation, In what country on earth would you rather live?—Certainly in my own, where are all my friends, my relations, and the earliest & sweetest affections and recollections of my life. Which would be your second choice? France.

On the 26th. of Sep. I left Paris for Havre, where I was detained by contrary winds until the 8th. of Oct. On that day, and the 9th. I crossed over to Cowes, where I had engaged the Clermont, Capt. Colley, to touch for me. She did so, but here again we were detained by contrary winds until the 22d. when we embarked and landed at Norfolk on the 23d. of November. On my way home I passed some days at Eppington in Chesterfield, the residence of my friend and connection, Mr. Eppes, and, while there, I received a letter from the President, Genl. Washington, by express, covering an appointment to be Secretary of State. I received it with real regret. My wish had been to return to Paris, where I had left my household establishment, as if there myself, and to see the end of the Revolution, which, I then thought would be certainly and happily closed in less than a year. I then meant to return home, to withdraw from Political life, into which I had been impressed by the circumstances of the times, to sink into the bosom of my family and friends, and devote myself to studies more congenial to my mind. In my answer of Dec. 15. I expressed these dispositions candidly to the President, and my preference of a return to Paris; but assured him that if it was believed I could be more useful in the administration of the government, I would sacrifice my own inclinations without hesitation, and repair to that destination; this I left to his decision. I arrived at Monticello on the 23d. of Dec. where I received a second letter from the President, expressing his continued wish that I should take my station there, but leaving me still at liberty to continue in my former office, if I could not reconcile myself to that now proposed. This silenced my reluctance, and I accepted the new appointment.

In the interval of my stay at home my eldest daughter had been happily married to the eldest son of the Tuckahoe branch of Randolphs, a young gentleman of genius, science and honorable mind, who afterwards filled a dignified station in the General Government, & the most dignified in his own State. I left Monticello on the 1st of March 1790. for New York. At Philadelphia I called on the venerable and beloved Franklin. He was then on the bed of sickness from which he never rose. My recent return from a country in which he had left so many friends, and the perilous convulsions to which they had been exposed, revived all his anxieties to know what part they had taken, what had been their course, and what their fate. He went over all in succession, with a rapidity and animation almost too much for his strength. When all his inquiries were satisfied, and a pause took place, I told him I had learnt with much pleasure that, since his return to America, he had been occupied in preparing for the world the history of his own life. I cannot say much of that, said he; but I will give you a sample of what I shall leave: and he directed his little grandson (William Bache) who was standing by the bedside, to hand him a paper from the table to which he pointed. He did so; and the Doctr. putting it into my hands, desired me to take it and read it at my leisure. It was about a quire of folio paper, written in a large and running hand very like his own. I looked into it slightly, then shut it and said I

would accept his permission to read it and would carefully
return it. He said, "no, keep it." Not certain of his meaning,
I again looked into it, folded it for my pocket, and said again,
I would certainly return it. "No," said he, "keep it." I put it
into my pocket, and shortly after took leave of him. He died
on the 17th. of the ensuing month of April; and as I understood that he had bequeathed all his papers to his grandson
William Temple Franklin, I immediately wrote to Mr. Franklin to inform him I possessed this paper, which I should consider as his property, and would deliver to his order. He came
on immediately to New York, called on me for it, and I delivered it to him. As he put it into his pocket, he said carelessly
he had either the original, or another copy of it, I do not
recollect which. This last expression struck my attention forc-
ibly, and for the first time suggested to me the thought that
Dr. Franklin had meant it as a confidential deposit in my
hands, and that I had done wrong in parting from it. I have
not yet seen the collection he published of Dr. Franklin's
works, and therefore know not if this is among them. I have
been told it is not. It contained a narrative of the negotiations
between Dr. Franklin and the British Ministry, when he was
endeavoring to prevent the contest of arms which followed.
The negotiation was brought about by the intervention of
Ld. Howe and his sister, who, I believe, was called Lady
Howe, but I may misremember her title. Ld. Howe seems to
have been friendly to America, and exceedingly anxious to
prevent a rupture. His intimacy with Dr. Franklin, and his
position with the Ministry induced him to undertake a mediation between them; in which his sister seemed to have been
associated. They carried from one to the other, backwards
and forwards, the several propositions and answers which
past, and seconded with their own intercessions the importance of mutual sacrifices to preserve the peace & connection
of the two countries. I remember that Ld. North's answers
were dry, unyielding, in the spirit of unconditional submission, and betrayed an absolute indifference to the occurrence
of a rupture; and he said to the mediators distinctly, at last
that "a rebellion was not to be deprecated on the part of
Great Britain; that the confiscations it would produce would
provide for many of their friends." This expression was re-

ported by the mediators to Dr. Franklin, and indicated so cool and calculated a purpose in the Ministry, as to render compromise hopeless, and the negotiation was discontinued. If this is not among the papers published, we ask what has become of it? I delivered it with my own hands into those of Temple Franklin. It certainly established views so atrocious in the British government that it's suppression would to them be worth a great price. But could the grandson of Dr. Franklin be in such degree an accomplice in the parricide of the memory of his immortal grandfather? The suspension for more than 20. years of the general publication bequeathed and confided to him, produced for awhile hard suspicions against him: and if at last all are not published, a part of these suspicions may remain with some.

I arrived at New York on the 21st. of Mar. where Congress was in session.

So far July 29. 21.

A SUMMARY VIEW OF
THE RIGHTS OF
BRITISH AMERICA

A SUMMARY VIEW OF THE
RIGHTS OF BRITISH AMERICA

RESOLVED, that it be an instruction to the said deputies, when assembled in general congress with the deputies from the other states of British America, to propose to the said congress that an humble and dutiful address be presented to his majesty, begging leave to lay before him, as chief magistrate of the British empire, the united complaints of his majesty's subjects in America; complaints which are excited by many unwarrantable encroachments and usurpations, attempted to be made by the legislature of one part of the empire, upon those rights which God and the laws have given equally and independently to all. To represent to his majesty that these his states have often individually made humble application to his imperial throne to obtain, through its intervention, some redress of their injured rights, to none of which was ever even an answer condescended; humbly to hope that this their joint address, penned in the language of truth, and divested of those expressions of servility which would persuade his majesty that we are asking favours, and not rights, shall obtain from his majesty a more respectful acceptance. And this his majesty will think we have reason to expect when he reflects that he is no more than the chief officer of the people, appointed by the laws, and circumscribed with definite powers, to assist in working the great machine of government, erected for their use, and consequently subject to their superintendance. And in order that these our rights, as well as the invasions of them, may be laid more fully before his majesty, to take a view of them from the origin and first settlement of these countries.

To remind him that our ancestors, before their emigration to America, were the free inhabitants of the British dominions in Europe, and possessed a right which nature has given to all men, of departing from the country in which chance, not choice, has placed them, of going in quest of new habitations, and of there establishing new societies, under such laws and regulations as to them shall seem most likely to promote public happiness. That their Saxon ancestors had, under this universal law, in like manner left their native wilds and woods in the north of Europe, had possessed themselves of the island of Britain, then less charged with inhabitants, and had established there that system of laws which has so long been the glory and protection of that country. Nor was ever any claim of superiority or dependence asserted over them by that mother country from which they had migrated; and were such a claim made, it is believed that his majesty's subjects in Great Britain have too firm a feeling of the rights derived to them from their ancestors, to bow down the sovereignty of their state before such visionary pretensions. And it is thought that no circumstance has occurred to distinguish materially the British from the Saxon emigration. America was conquered, and her settlements made, and firmly established, at the expence of individuals, and not of the British public. Their own blood was spilt in acquiring lands for their settlement, their own fortunes expended in making that settlement effectual; for themselves they fought, for themselves they conquered, and for themselves alone they have right to hold. Not a shilling was ever issued from the public treasures of his majesty, or his ancestors, for their assistance, till of very late times, after the colonies had become established on a firm and permanent footing. That then, indeed, having become valuable to Great Britain for her commercial purposes, his parliament was pleased to lend them assistance against an enemy, who would fain have drawn to herself the benefits of their commerce, to the great aggrandizement of herself, and danger of Great Britain. Such assistance, and in such circumstances, they had often before given to Portugal, and other allied states, with whom they carry on a commercial intercourse; yet these states never supposed, that by calling in her aid, they thereby submitted themselves to her sovereignty. Had such terms been proposed, they would have rejected them with disdain, and trusted for better to the moderation of their enemies, or to a vigorous exertion of their own force. We do not, however, mean to under-rate those aids, which to us were doubtless valuable, on whatever principles granted; but we would shew that they cannot give a title to that authority which the British parliament would arrogate over us, and that they may amply be repaid by our giving to the inhabitants of Great Britain such exclusive privileges in trade as may be advantageous to them, and at the same time not too restrictive to ourselves. That settlements having been thus effected in the wilds of America, the emigrants thought proper to adopt that system of laws under which they had hitherto lived in the mother country, and to continue their union with her by submitting themselves to the same common sovereign, who was thereby made the central link connecting the several parts of the empire thus newly multiplied.

But that not long were they permitted, however far they thought themselves removed from the hand of oppression, to hold undisturbed the rights thus acquired, at the hazard of their lives, and loss of their fortunes. A family of princes was then on the British throne, whose treasonable crimes against their people brought on them afterwards the exertion of those sacred and sovereign rights of punishment reserved in the hands of the people for cases of extreme necessity, and judged by the constitution unsafe to be delegated to any other judicature. While every day brought forth some new and unjustifiable exertion of power over their subjects on that side the water, it was not to be expected that those here, much less able at that time to oppose the designs of despotism, should be exempted from injury.

Accordingly that country, which had been acquired by the lives, the labours, and the fortunes, of individual adventurers, was by these princes, at several times, parted out and distributed among the favourites and *followers of their fortunes, and, by an assumed right of the crown alone, were erected into distinct and independent governments; a measure which

*1632 Maryland was granted to lord Baltimore, 14. c. 2. Pennsylvania to Penn, and the province of Carolina was in the year 1663 granted by letters patent of majesty, king Charles II. in the 15th year of his reign, in propriety, unto the right honourable Edward earl of Clarendon, George duke of Albemarle, William earl of Craven, John lord Berkeley, Anthony lord Ashley, sir George Carteret, sir John Coleton, knight and baronet, and sir William Berkeley, knight; by which letters patent the laws of England were to be in force in Carolina: But the lords proprietors had power, *with the consent of the inhabitants*, to make bye-laws for the better government of the said province; so that no money could be received, or law made, without the consent of the inhabitants, or their representatives.

it is believed his majesty's prudence and understanding would prevent him from imitating at this day, as no exercise of such a power, of dividing and dismembering a country, has ever occurred in his majesty's realm of England, though now of very antient standing; nor could it be justified or acquiesced under there, or in any other part of his majesty's empire.

That the exercise of a free trade with all parts of the world, possessed by the American colonists, as of natural right, and which no law of their own had taken away or abridged, was next the object of unjust encroachment. Some of the colonies having thought proper to continue the administration of their government in the name and under the authority of his majesty king Charles the first, whom, notwithstanding his late deposition by the commonwealth of England, they continued in the sovereignty of their state; the parliament for the commonwealth took the same in high offence, and assumed upon themselves the power of prohibiting their trade with all other parts of the world, except the island of Great Britain. This arbitrary act, however, they soon recalled, and by solemn treaty, entered into on the 12th day of March, 1651, between the said commonwealth by their commissioners, and the colony of Virginia by their house of burgesses, it was expressly stipulated, by the 8th article of the said treaty, that they should have "free trade as the people of England do enjoy to all places and with all nations, according to the laws of that commonwealth." But that, upon the restoration of his majesty king Charles the second, their rights of free commerce fell once more a victim to arbitrary power; and by several acts* of his reign, as well as of some of his successors, the trade of the colonies was laid under such restrictions, as shew what hopes they might form from the justice of a British parliament, were its uncontrouled power admitted over these states. History has informed us that bodies of men, as well as individuals, are susceptible of the spirit of tyranny. A view of these acts of parliament for regulation, as it has been affectedly called, of the American trade, if all other evidence were removed out of the case, would undeniably evince the truth of this observation. Besides the duties they impose on our

*12. c. 2. c. 18. 15. c. 2. c. 11. 25. c. 2. c. 7. 7. 8. W. M. c. 22. 11. W. 3. 4. Anne. 6. G. 2. c. 13.

articles of export and import, they prohibit our going to any markets northward of Cape Finesterre, in the kingdom of Spain, for the sale of commodities which Great Britain will not take from us, and for the purchase of others, with which she cannot supply us, and that for no other than the arbitrary purposes of purchasing for themselves, by a sacrifice of our rights and interests, certain privileges in their commerce with an allied state, who in confidence that their exclusive trade with America will be continued, while the principles and power of the British parliament be the same, have indulged themselves in every exorbitance which their avarice could dictate, or our necessities extort; have raised their commodities, called for in America, to the double and treble of what they sold for before such exclusive privileges were given them, and of what better commodities of the same kind would cost us elsewhere, and at the same time give us much less for what we carry thither than might be had at more convenient ports. That these acts prohibit us from carrying in quest of other purchasers the surplus of our tobaccoes remaining after the consumption of Great Britain is supplied; so that we must leave them with the British merchant for whatever he will please to allow us, to be by him reshipped to foreign markets, where he will reap the benefits of making sale of them for full value. That to heighten still the idea of parliamentary justice, and to shew with what moderation they are like to exercise power, where themselves are to feel no part of its weight, we take leave to mention to his majesty certain other acts of British parliament, by which they would prohibit us from manufacturing for our own use the articles we raise on our own lands with our own labour. By an act* passed in the 5th Year of the reign of his late majesty king George the second, an American subject is forbidden to make a hat for himself of the fur which he has taken perhaps on his own soil; an instance of despotism to which no parallel can be produced in the most arbitrary ages of British history. By one other act,† passed in the 23d year of the same reign, the iron which we make we are forbidden to manufacture, and heavy as that article is, and necessary in every branch of husbandry, besides

*5. G. 2.   †23. G. 2. C. 29.

commission and insurance, we are to pay freight for it to
Great Britain, and freight for it back again, for the purpose
of supporting not men, but machines, in the island of Great
Britain. In the same spirit of equal and impartial legislation is
to be viewed the act of parliament,* passed in the 5th year of
the same reign, by which American lands are made subject to
the demands of British creditors, while their own lands were
still continued unanswerable for their debts; from which one
of these conclusions must necessarily follow, either that justice is not the same in America as in Britain, or else that the
British parliament pay less regard to it here than there. But
that we do not point out to his majesty the injustice of these
acts, with intent to rest on that principle the cause of their
nullity; but to shew that experience confirms the propriety of
those political principles which exempt us from the jurisdiction of the British parliament. The true ground on which we
declare these acts void is, that the British parliament has no
right to exercise authority over us.

That these exercises of usurped power have not been confined to instances alone, in which themselves were interested,
but they have also intermeddled with the regulation of the
internal affairs of the colonies. The act of the 9th of Anne for
establishing a post office in America seems to have had little
connection with British convenience, except that of accommodating his majesty's ministers and favourites with the sale
of a lucrative and easy office.

That thus have we hastened through the reigns which preceded his majesty's, during which the violations of our right
were less alarming, because repeated at more distant intervals
than that rapid and bold succession of injuries which is likely
to distinguish the present from all other periods of American
story. Scarcely have our minds been able to emerge from the
astonishment into which one stroke of parliamentary thunder
has involved us, before another more heavy, and more alarming, is fallen on us. Single acts of tyranny may be ascribed to
the accidental opinion of a day; but a series of oppressions,
begun at a distinguished period, and pursued unalterably
through every change of ministers, too plainly prove a deliberate and systematical plan of reducing us to slavery.

*5. G. 270.

That the act* passed in the 4th year of his majesty's reign, intitled "An act for granting certain duties in the British colonies and plantations in America, &c."

One other act†, passed in the 5th year of his reign, intitled "An act for granting and applying certain stamp duties and other duties in the British colonies and plantations in America, &c."

One other act‡, passed in the 6th year of his reign, intituled "An act for the better securing the dependency of his majesty's dominions in America upon the crown and parliament of Great Britain;" and one other act§, passed in the 7th year of his reign, intituled "An act for granting duties on paper, tea, &c." form that connected chain of parliamentary usurpation, which has already been the subject of frequent applications to his majesty, and the houses of lords and commons of Great Britain; and no answers having yet been condescended to any of these, we shall not trouble his majesty with a repetition of the matters they contained.

But that one other act‖, passed in the same 7th year of the reign, having been a peculiar attempt, must ever require peculiar mention; it is intituled "An act for suspending the legislature of New York." One free and independent legislature hereby takes upon itself to suspend the powers of another, free and independent as itself; thus exhibiting a phœnomenon unknown in nature, the creator and creature of its own power. Not only the principles of common sense, but the common feelings of human nature, must be surrendered up before his majesty's subjects here can be persuaded to believe that they hold their political existence at the will of a British parliament. Shall these governments be dissolved, their property annihilated, and their people reduced to a state of nature, at the imperious breath of a body of men, whom they never saw, in whom they never confided, and over whom they have no powers of punishment or removal, let their crimes against the American public be ever so great? Can any one reason be

*4. G. 3. c. 15.
†5. G. 3. c. 12.
‡6. G. 3. c. 12.
§7. G. 3.
‖ 7. G. 3. c. 59.

assigned why 160,000 electors in the island of Great Britain should give law to four millions in the states of America, every individual of whom is equal to every individual of them, in virtue, in understanding, and in bodily strength? Were this to be admitted, instead of being a free people, as we have hitherto supposed, and mean to continue ourselves, we should suddenly be found the slaves, not of one, but of 160,000 tyrants, distinguished too from all others by this singular circumstance, that they are removed from the reach of fear, the only restraining motive which may hold the hand of a tyrant.

That by "an act* to discontinue in such manner and for such time as are therein mentioned the landing and discharging, lading or shipping, of goods, wares, and merchandize, at the town and within the harbour of Boston, in the province of Massachusetts Bay, in North America," which was passed at the last session of British parliament; a large and populous town, whose trade was their sole subsistence, was deprived of that trade, and involved in utter ruin. Let us for a while suppose the question of right suspended, in order to examine this act on principles of justice: An act of parliament had been passed imposing duties on teas, to be paid in America, against which act the Americans had protested as inauthoritative. The East India company, who till that time had never sent a pound of tea to America on their own account, step forth on that occasion the assertors of parliamentary right, and send hither many ship loads of that obnoxious commodity. The masters of their several vessels, however, on their arrival in America, wisely attended to admonition, and returned with their cargoes. In the province of New England alone the remonstrances of the people were disregarded, and a compliance, after being many days waited for, was flatly refused. Whether in this the master of the vessel was governed by his obstinacy, or his instructions, let those who know, say. There are extraordinary situations which require extraordinary interposition. An exasperated people, who feel that they possess power, are not easily restrained within limits strictly regular. A number of them assembled in the town of Boston, threw the tea into the ocean, and dispersed without doing any

*14. G. 3.

other act of violence. If in this they did wrong, they were known and were amenable to the laws of the land, against which it could not be objected that they had ever, in any instance, been obstructed or diverted from their regular course in favour of popular offenders. They should therefore not have been distrusted on this occasion. But that ill fated colony had formerly been bold in their enmities against the house of Stuart, and were now devoted to ruin by that unseen hand which governs the momentous affairs of this great empire. On the partial representations of a few worthless ministerial dependents, whose constant office it has been to keep that government embroiled, and who, by their treacheries, hope to obtain the dignity of the British knighthood, without calling for a party accused, without asking a proof, without attempting a distinction between the guilty and the innocent, the whole of that antient and wealthy town is in a moment reduced from opulence to beggary. Men who had spent their lives in extending the British commerce, who had invested in that place the wealth their honest endeavours had merited, found themselves and their families thrown at once on the world for subsistence by its charities. Not the hundredth part of the inhabitants of that town had been concerned in the act complained of; many of them were in Great Britain and in other parts beyond sea; yet all were involved in one indiscriminate ruin, by a new executive power, unheard of till then, that of a British parliament. A property, of the value of many millions of money, was sacrificed to revenge, not repay, the loss of a few thousands. This is administering justice with a heavy hand indeed! and when is this tempest to be arrested in its course? Two wharfs are to be opened again when his majesty shall think proper. The residue which lined the extensive shores of the bay of Boston are forever interdicted the exercise of commerce. This little exception seems to have been thrown in for no other purpose than that of setting a precedent for investing his majesty with legislative powers. If the pulse of his people shall beat calmly under this experiment, another and another will be tried, till the measure of despotism be filled up. It would be an insult on common sense to pretend that this exception was made in order to restore its commerce to that great town. The trade which cannot be re-

ceived at two wharfs alone must of necessity be transferred to
some other place; to which it will soon be followed by that
of the two wharfs. Considered in this light, it would be an
insolent and cruel mockery at the annihilation of the town of
Boston.

By the act* for the suppression of riots and tumults in the
town of Boston, passed also in the last session of parliament,
a murder committed there is, if the governor pleases, to be
tried in the court of King's Bench, in the island of Great Britain, by a jury of Middlesex. The witnesses, too, on receipt of
such a sum as the governor shall think it reasonable for them
to expend, are to enter into recognizance to appear at the
trial. This is, in other words, taxing them to the amount of
their recognizance, and that amount may be whatever a governor pleases; for who does his majesty think can be prevailed
on to cross the Atlantic for the sole purpose of bearing evidence to a fact? His expences are to be borne, indeed, as they
shall be estimated by a governor; but who are to feed the wife
and children whom he leaves behind, and who have had no
other subsistence but his daily labour? Those epidemical disorders, too, so terrible in a foreign climate, is the cure of
them to be estimated among the articles of expence, and their
danger to be warded off by the almighty power of parliament? And the wretched criminal, if he happen to have offended on the American side, stripped of his privilege of trial
by peers of his vicinage, removed from the place where alone
full evidence could be obtained, without money, without
counsel, without friends, without exculpatory proof, is tried
before judges predetermined to condemn. The cowards who
would suffer a countryman to be torn from the bowels of
their society, in order to be thus offered a sacrifice to parliamentary tyranny, would merit that everlasting infamy now
fixed on the authors of the act! A clause† for a similar purpose had been introduced into an act, passed in the 12th year
of his majesty's reign, intitled "An act for the better securing
and preserving his majesty's dockyards, magazines, ships, ammunition, and stores;" against which, as meriting the same
censures, the several colonies have already protested.

*14. G. 3.
†12. G. 3. c. 24.

That these are the acts of power, assumed by a body of men, foreign to our constitutions, and unacknowledged by our laws, against which we do, on behalf of the inhabitants of British America, enter this our solemn and determined protest; and we do earnestly entreat his majesty, as yet the only mediatory power between the several states of the British empire, to recommend to his parliament of Great Britain the total revocation of these acts, which, however nugatory they be, may yet prove the cause of further discontents and jealousies among us.

That we next proceed to consider the conduct of his majesty, as holding the executive powers of the laws of these states, and mark out his deviations from the line of duty: By the constitution of Great Britain, as well as of the several American states, his majesty possesses the power of refusing to pass into a law any bill which has already passed the other two branches of legislature. His majesty, however, and his ancestors, conscious of the impropriety of opposing their single opinion to the united wisdom of two houses of parliament, while their proceedings were unbiassed by interested principles, for several ages past have modestly declined the exercise of this power in that part of his empire called Great Britain. But by change of circumstances, other principles than those of justice simply have obtained an influence on their determinations; the addition of new states to the British empire has produced an addition of new, and sometimes opposite interests. It is now, therefore, the great office of his majesty, to resume the exercise of his negative power, and to prevent the passage of laws by any one legislature of the empire, which might bear injuriously on the rights and interests of another. Yet this will not excuse the wanton exercise of this power which we have seen his majesty practise on the laws of the American legislatures. For the most trifling reasons, and sometimes for no conceivable reason at all, his majesty has rejected laws of the most salutary tendency. The abolition of domestic slavery is the great object of desire in those colonies, where it was unhappily introduced in their infant state. But previous to the enfranchisement of the slaves we have, it is necessary to exclude all further importations from Africa; yet our repeated attempts to effect this by prohibitions, and by imposing duties which might amount to a prohibition, have been hitherto defeated by his majesty's negative: Thus preferring the immediate advantages of a few African corsairs to the lasting interests of the American states, and to the rights of human nature, deeply wounded by this infamous practice. Nay, the single interposition of an interested individual against a law was scarcely ever known to fail of success, though in the opposite scale were placed the interests of a whole country. That this is so shameful an abuse of a power trusted with his majesty for other purposes, as if not reformed, would call for some legal restrictions.

With equal inattention to the necessities of his people here has his majesty permitted our laws to lie neglected in England for years, neither confirming them by his assent, nor annulling them by his negative; so that such of them as have no suspending clause we hold on the most precarious of all tenures, his majesty's will, and such of them as suspend themselves till his majesty's assent be obtained, we have feared, might be called into existence at some future and distant period, when time, and change of circumstances, shall have rendered them destructive to his people here. And to render this grievance still more oppressive, his majesty by his instructions has laid his governors under such restrictions that they can pass no law of any moment unless it have such suspending clause; so that, however immediate may be the call for legislative interposition, the law cannot be executed till it has twice crossed the atlantic, by which time the evil may have spent its whole force.

But in what terms, reconcileable to majesty, and at the same time to truth, shall we speak of a late instruction to his majesty's governor of the colony of Virginia, by which he is forbidden to assent to any law for the division of a county, unless the new county will consent to have no representative in assembly? That colony has as yet fixed no boundary to the westward. Their western counties, therefore, are of indefinite extent; some of them are actually seated many hundred miles from their eastern limits. Is it possible, then, that his majesty can have bestowed a single thought on the situation of those people, who, in order to obtain justice for injuries, however great or small, must, by the laws of that colony, attend their county court, at such a distance, with all their witnesses, monthly, till their litigation be determined? Or does his majesty seriously wish, and publish it to the world, that his subjects should give up the glorious right of representation, with all the benefits derived from that, and submit themselves the absolute slaves of his sovereign will? Or is it rather meant to confine the legislative body to their present numbers, that they may be the cheaper bargain whenever they shall become worth a purchase.

One of the articles of impeachment against Tresilian, and the other judges of Westminister Hall, in the reign of Richard the second, for which they suffered death, as traitors to their country, was, that they had advised the king that he might dissolve his parliament at any time; and succeeding kings have adopted the opinion of these unjust judges. Since the establishment, however, of the British constitution, at the glorious revolution, on its free and antient principles, neither his majesty, nor his ancestors, have exercised such a power of dissolution in the island of Great Britain; and when his majesty was petitioned, by the united voice of his people there, to dissolve the present parliament, who had become obnoxious to them, his ministers were heard to declare, in open parliament, that his majesty possessed no such power by the constitution. But how different their language and his practice here! To declare, as their duty required, the known rights of their country, to oppose the usurpations of every foreign judicature, to disregard the imperious mandates of a minister or governor, have been the avowed causes of dissolving houses of representatives in America. But if such powers be really vested in his majesty, can he suppose they are there placed to awe the members from such purposes as these? When the representative body have lost the confidence of their constituents, when they have notoriously made sale of their most valuable rights, when they have assumed to themselves powers which the people never put into their hands, then indeed their continuing in office becomes dangerous to the state, and calls for an exercise of the power of dissolution. Such being the causes for which the representative body should, and should not, be dissolved, will it not appear strange to an unbiassed observer, that that of Great Britain was not dissolved, while those of the colonies have repeatedly incurred that sentence?

But your majesty, or your governors, have carried this power beyond every limit known, or provided for, by the laws: After dissolving one house of representatives, they have refused to call another, so that, for a great length of time, the legislature provided by the laws has been out of existence. From the nature of things, every society must at all times possess within itself the sovereign powers of legislation. The feelings of human nature revolt against the supposition of a state so situated as that it may not in any emergency provide against dangers which perhaps threaten immediate ruin. While those bodies are in existence to whom the people have delegated the powers of legislation, they alone possess and may exercise those powers; but when they are dissolved by the lopping off one or more of their branches, the power reverts to the people, who may exercise it to unlimited extent, either assembling together in person, sending deputies, or in any other way they may think proper. We forbear to trace consequences further; the dangers are conspicuous with which this practice is replete.

That we shall at this time also take notice of an error in the nature of our land holdings, which crept in at a very early period of our settlement. The introduction of the feudal tenures into the kingdom of England, though antient, is well enough understood to set this matter in a proper light. In the earlier ages of the Saxon settlement feudal holdings were certainly altogether unknown; and very few, if any, had been introduced at the time of the Norman conquest. Our Saxon ancestors held their lands, as they did their personal property, in absolute dominion, disencumbered with any superior, answering nearly to the nature of those possessions which the feudalists term allodial. William, the Norman, first introduced that system generally. The lands which had belonged to those who fell in the battle of Hastings, and in the subsequent insurrections of his reign, formed a considerable proportion of the lands of the whole kingdom. These he granted out, subject to feudal duties, as did he also those of a great number of his new subjects, who, by persuasions or threats, were induced to surrender them for that purpose. But still much was left in the hands of his Saxon subjects; held of no superior, and not subject to feudal conditions. These, therefore, by express laws, enacted to render uniform the system of military defence, were made liable to the same military duties as if they had been feuds; and the Norman lawyers soon found means to saddle them also with all the other feudal burthens. But still they had not been surrendered to the king, they were not derived from his grant, and therefore they were not holden of him. A general principle, indeed, was introduced, that "all lands in England were held either mediately or immediately of the crown," but this was borrowed from those holdings, which were truly feudal, and only applied to others for the purposes of illustration. Feudal holdings were therefore but exceptions out of the Saxon laws of possession, under which all lands were held in absolute right. These, therefore, still form the basis, or ground-work, of the common law, to prevail wheresoever the exceptions have not taken place. America was not conquered by William the Norman, nor its lands surrendered to him, or any of his successors. Possessions there are undoubtedly of the allodial nature. Our ancestors, however, who migrated hither, were farmers, not lawyers. The fictitious principle that all lands belong originally to the king, they were early persuaded to believe real; and accordingly took grants of their own lands from the crown. And while the crown continued to grant for small sums, and on reasonable rents; there was no inducement to arrest the error, and lay it open to public view. But his majesty has lately taken on him to advance the terms of purchase, and of holding to the double of what they were; by which means the acquisition of lands being rendered difficult, the population of our country is likely to be checked. It is time, therefore, for us to lay this matter before his majesty, and to declare that he has no right to grant lands of himself. From the nature and purpose of civil institutions, all the lands within the limits which any particular society has circumscribed around itself are assumed by that society, and subject to their allotment only. This may be done by themselves, assembled collectively, or by their legislature, to whom they may have delegated sovereign authority; and if they are alloted in neither of these ways, each individual of the society may appropriate to himself such lands as he finds vacant, and occupancy will give him title.

That in order to enforce the arbitrary measures before complained of, his majesty has from time to time sent among us large bodies of armed forces, not made up of the people here, nor raised by the authority of our laws: Did his majesty possess such a right as this, it might swallow up all our other rights whenever he should think proper. But his majesty has no right to land a single armed man on our shores, and those whom he sends here are liable to our laws made for the suppression and punishment of riots, routs, and unlawful assemblies; or are hostile bodies, invading us in defiance of law. When in the course of the late war it became expedient that a body of Hanoverian troops should be brought over for the defence of Great Britain, his majesty's grandfather, our late sovereign, did not pretend to introduce them under any authority he possessed. Such a measure would have given just alarm to his subjects in Great Britain, whose liberties would not be safe if armed men of another country, and of another spirit, might be brought into the realm at any time without the consent of their legislature. He therefore applied to parliament, who passed an act for that purpose, limiting the number to be brought in and the time they were to continue. In like manner is his majesty restrained in every part of the empire. He possesses, indeed, the executive power of the laws in every state; but they are the laws of the particular state which he is to administer within that state, and not those of any one within the limits of another. Every state must judge for itself the number of armed men which they may safely trust among them, of whom they are to consist, and under what restrictions they shall be laid.

To render these proceedings still more criminal against our laws, instead of subjecting the military to the civil powers, his majesty has expressly made the civil subordinate to the military. But can his majesty thus put down all law under his feet? Can he erect a power superior to that which erected himself? He has done it indeed by force; but let him remember that force cannot give right.

That these are our grievances which we have thus laid before his majesty, with that freedom of language and sentiment which becomes a free people claiming their rights, as derived from the laws of nature, and not as the gift of their chief magistrate: Let those flatter who fear; it is not an American art. To give praise which is not due might be well from the venal, but would ill beseem those who are asserting the rights of human nature. They know, and will therefore say, that kings are the servants, not the proprietors of the people. Open your breast, sire, to liberal and expanded thought. Let not the name of George the third be a blot in the page of history. You are surrounded by British counsellors, but remember that they are parties. You have no ministers for American affairs, because you have none taken from among us, nor amenable to the laws on which they are to give you advice. It behoves you, therefore, to think and to act for yourself and your people. The great principles of right and wrong are legible to every reader; to pursue them requires not the aid of many counsellors. The whole art of government consists in the art of being honest. Only aim to do your duty, and mankind will give you credit where you fail. No longer persevere in sacrificing the rights of one part of the empire to the inordinate desires of another; but deal out to all equal and impartial right. Let no act be passed by any one legislature which may infringe on the rights and liberties of another. This is the important post in which fortune has placed you, holding the balance of a great, if a well poised empire. This, sire, is the advice of your great American council, on the observance of which may perhaps depend your felicity and future fame, and the preservation of that harmony which alone can continue both to Great Britain and America the reciprocal advantages of their connection. It is neither our wish, nor our interest, to separate from her. We are willing, on our part, to sacrifice every thing which reason can ask to the restoration of that tranquillity for which all must wish. On their part, let them be ready to establish union and a generous plan. Let them name their terms, but let them be just. Accept of every commercial preference it is in our power to give for such things as we can raise for their use, or they make for ours. But let them not think to exclude us from going to other markets to dispose of those commodities which they cannot use, or to supply those wants which they cannot supply. Still less let it be proposed that our properties within our own territories shall be taxed or regulated by any power on earth but our own. The God who gave us life gave us liberty at the same time; the hand of force may destroy, but cannot disjoin them. This, sire, is our last, our determined resolution; and that you will be pleased to interpose with that efficacy which your earnest endeavours may ensure to procure redress of these our great grievances, to quiet the minds of your subjects in British America, against any apprehensions of future encroachment, to establish fraternal love and harmony through the whole empire, and that these may continue to the latest ages of time, is the fervent prayer of all British America!

NOTES ON THE
STATE OF VIRGINIA

ADVERTISEMENT

THE following Notes were written in Virginia in the year 1781, and somewhat corrected and enlarged in the winter of 1782, in answer to Queries proposed to the Author, by a Foreigner of Distinction, then residing among us. The subjects are all treated imperfectly; some scarcely touched on. To apologize for this by developing the circumstances of the time and place of their composition, would be to open wounds which have already bled enough. To these circumstances some of their imperfections may with truth be ascribed; the great mass to the want of information and want of talents in the writer. He had a few copies printed, which he gave among his friends: and a translation of them has been lately published in France, but with such alterations as the laws of the press in that country rendered necessary. They are now offered to the public in their original form and language.

Feb. 27, 1787.

Contents

QUERY I

Virginia is bounded on the East by the Atlantic: on the North by a line of latitude, crossing the Eastern Shore through Watkins's Point, being about 37°. 57′. North latitude; from thence by a streight line to Cinquac, near the mouth of Patowmac; thence by the Patowmac, which is common to Virginia and Maryland, to the first fountain of its northern branch; thence by a meridian line, passing through that fountain till it intersects a line running East and West, in latitude 39°. 43′. 42.4″ which divides Maryland from Pennsylvania, and which was marked by Messrs. Mason and Dixon; thence by that line, and a continuation of it westwardly to the completion of five degrees of longitude from the eastern boundary of Pennsylvania, in the same latitude, and thence by a meridian line to the Ohio: On the West by the Ohio and Missisipi, to latitude 36°. 30′. North: and on the South by the line of latitude last-mentioned. By admeasurements through nearly the whole of this last line, and supplying the unmeasured parts from good data, the Atlantic and Missisipi, are found in this latitude to be 758 miles distant, equal to 13°. 38′. of longitude, reckoning 55 miles and 3144 feet to the degree. This being our comprehension of longitude, that of our latitude, taken between this and Mason and Dixon's line, is 3°. 13′. 42.4″. equal to 223.3 miles, supposing a degree of a great circle to be 69 m. 864 f. as computed by Cassini. These boundaries include an area somewhat triangular, of 121525 square miles, whereof 79650 lie westward of the Allegany mountains, and 57034 westward of the meridian of the mouth of the Great Kanhaway. This state is therefore one third larger than the islands of Great Britain and Ireland, which are reckoned at 88357 square miles.

These limits result from, 1. The antient charters from the crown of England. 2. The grant of Maryland to the Lord Baltimore, and the subsequent determinations of the British court as to the extent of that grant. 3. The grant of Pennsylvania to William Penn, and a compact between the general

assemblies of the commonwealths of Virginia and Pennsylvania as to the extent of that grant. 4. The grant of Carolina,
and actual location of its northern boundary, by consent of
both parties. 5. The treaty of Paris of 1763. 6. The confirmation of the charters of the neighbouring states by the
convention of Virginia at the time of constituting their commonwealth. 7. The cession made by Virginia to Congress of
all the lands to which they had title on the North side of the
Ohio.

QUERY II

A notice of its rivers, rivulets, and how far they are navigable?

Rivers and Navigation

An inspection of a map of Virginia, will give a better idea of the geography of its rivers, than any description in writing. Their navigation may be imperfectly noted.

Roanoke, so far as it lies within this state, is no where navigable, but for canoes, or light batteaux; and, even for these, in such detached parcels as to have prevented the inhabitants from availing themselves of it at all.

James River, and its waters, afford navigation as follows.

The whole of *Elizabeth River*, the lowest of those which run into James River, is a harbour, and would contain upwards of 300 ships. The channel is from 150 to 200 fathom wide, and at common flood tide, affords 18 feet water to Norfolk. The Strafford, a 60 gun ship, went there, lightening herself to cross the bar at Sowell's point. The Fier Rodrigue, pierced for 64 guns, and carrying 50, went there without lightening. Craney island, at the mouth of this river, commands its channel tolerably well.

Nansemond River is navigable to Sleepy hole, for vessels of 250 tons; to Suffolk, for those of 100 tons; and to Milner's, for those of 25.

Pagan Creek affords 8 or 10 feet water to Smithfeild, which admits vessels of 20 ton.

Chickahominy has at its mouth a bar, on which is only 12 feet water at common flood tide. Vessels passing that, may go 8 miles up the river; those of 10 feet draught may go four miles further, and those of six tons burthen, 20 miles further.

Appamattox may be navigated as far as Broadways, by any vessel which has crossed Harrison's bar in James river; it keeps 8 or 9 feet water a mile or two higher up to Fisher's bar, and 4 feet on that and upwards to Petersburgh, where all navigation ceases.

James River itself affords harbour for vessels of any size in Hampton Road, but not in safety through the whole winter; and there is navigable water for them as far as Mulberry island. A 40 gun ship goes to James town, and, lightening herself, may pass to Harrison's bar, on which there is only 15 feet water. Vessels of 250 tons may go to Warwick; those of 125 go to Rocket's, a mile below Richmond; from thence is about 7 feet water to Richmond; and about the center of the town, four feet and a half, where the navigation is interrupted by falls, which in a course of six miles, descend about 80 feet perpendicular: above these it is resumed in canoes and batteaux, and is prosecuted safely and advantageously to within 10 miles of the Blue ridge; and even through the Blue ridge a ton weight has been brought; and the expence would not be great, when compared with its object, to open a tolerable navigation up Jackson's river and Carpenter's creek, to within 25 miles of Howard's creek of Green briar, both of which have then water enough to float vessels into the Great Kanhaway. In some future state of population, I think it possible, that its navigation may also be made to interlock with that of the Patowmac, and through that to communicate by a short portage with the Ohio. It is to be noted, that this river is called in the maps *James River*, only to its confluence with the Rivanna; thence to the Blue ridge it is called the Fluvanna; and thence to its source, Jackson's river. But in common speech, it is called James river to its source.

The *Rivanna*, a branch of James river, is navigable for canoes and batteaux to its intersection with the South West mountains, which is about 22 miles; and may easily be opened to navigation through those mountains to its fork above Charlottesville.

York River, at York town, affords the best harbour in the state for vessels of the largest size. The river there narrows to the width of a mile, and is contained within very high banks, close under which the vessels may ride. It holds 4 fathom water at high tide for 25 miles above York to the mouth of Poropotank, where the river is a mile and a half wide, and the channel only 75 fathom, and passing under a high bank. At the confluence of *Pamunkey* and *Mattapony*, it is reduced to 3 fathom depth, which continues up Pamunkey to Cumberland, where the width is 100 yards, and up Mattapony to within two miles of Frazer's ferry, where it becomes 2½ fathom deep, and holds that about five miles. Pamunkey is then capable of navigation for loaded flats to Brockman's bridge, 50 miles above Hanover town, and Mattapony to Downer's bridge, 70 miles above its mouth.

Piankatank, the little rivers making out of *Mobjack bay* and those of the *Eastern shore*, receive only very small vessels, and these can but enter them.

Rappahanock affords 4 fathom water to Hobb's hole, and 2 fathom from thence to Fredericksburg.

Patowmac is 7½ miles wide at the mouth; 4½ at Nomony bay; 3 at Aquia; 1½ at Hallooing point; 1¼ at Alexandria. Its soundings are, 7 fathom at the mouth; 5 at St. George's island; 4½ at Lower Matchodic; 3 at Swan's point, and thence up to Alexandria; thence 10 feet water to the falls, which are 13 miles above Alexandria. These falls are 15 miles in length, and of very great descent, and the navigation above them for batteaux and canoes, is so much interrupted as to be little used. It is, however, used in a small degree up the Cohongoronta branch as far as Fort Cumberland, which was at the mouth of Wills's creek: and is capable, at no great expence, of being rendered very practicable. The Shenandoah branch interlocks with James river about the Blue ridge, and may perhaps in future be opened.

The *Missisipi* will be one of the principal channels of future commerce for the country westward of the Alleghaney. From the mouth of this river to where it receives the Ohio, is 1000 miles by water, but only 500 by land, passing through the Chickasaw country. From the mouth of the Ohio to that of the Missouri, is 230 miles by water, and 140 by land. From thence to the mouth of the Illinois river, is about 25 miles. The Missisipi, below the mouth of the Missouri, is always muddy, and abounding with sand bars, which frequently change their places. However, it carries 15 feet water to the mouth of the Ohio, to which place it is from one and a half to two miles wide, and thence to Kaskaskia from one mile to a mile and a quarter wide. Its current is so rapid, that it never can be stemmed by the force of the wind alone, acting on sails. Any vessel, however, navigated with oars, may come up at any time, and receive much aid from the wind. A batteau passes from the mouth of Ohio to the mouth of Missisipi in three weeks, and is from two to three months getting up again. During its floods, which are periodical as those of the

Nile, the largest vessels may pass down it, if their steerage can be ensured. These floods begin in April, and the river returns into its banks early in August. The inundation extends further on the western than eastern side, covering the lands in some places for 50 miles from its banks. Above the mouth of the Missouri, it becomes much such a river as the Ohio, like it clear, and gentle in its current, not quite so wide, the period of its floods nearly the same, but not rising to so great a height. The streets of the village at Cohoes are not more than 10 feet above the ordinary level of the water, and yet were never overflowed. Its bed deepens every year. Cohoes, in the memory of many people now living, was insulated by every flood of the river. What was the Eastern channel has now become a lake, 9 miles in length and one in width, into which the river at this day never flows. This river yields turtle of a peculiar kind, perch, trout, gar, pike, mullets, herrings, carp, spatula fish of 50 lb. weight, cat fish of an hundred pounds weight, buffalo fish, and sturgeon. Alligators or crocodiles have been seen as high up as the Acansas. It also abounds in herons, cranes, ducks, brant, geese, and swans. Its passage is commanded by a fort established by this state, five miles below the mouth of Ohio, and ten miles above the Carolina boundary.

The Missouri, since the treaty of Paris, the Illinois and Northern branches of the Ohio since the cession to Congress, are no longer within our limits. Yet having been so heretofore, and still opening to us channels of extensive communication with the western and north-western country, they shall be noted in their order.

The *Missouri* is, in fact, the principal river, contributing more to the common stream than does the Missisipi, even after its junction with the Illinois. It is remarkably cold, muddy and rapid. Its overflowings are considerable. They happen during the months of June and July. Their commencement being so much later than those of the Missisipi, would induce a belief that the sources of the Missouri are northward of those of the Missisipi, unless we suppose that the cold increases again with the ascent of the land from the Missisipi westwardly. That this ascent is great, is proved by the rapidity of the river. Six miles above the mouth it is brought within

the compass of a quarter of a mile's width: yet the Spanish
Merchants at Pancore, or St. Louis, say they go two thousand
miles up it. It heads far westward of the Rio Norte, or North
River. There is, in the villages of Kaskaskia, Cohoes and St.
Vincennes, no inconsiderable quantity of plate, said to have
been plundered during the last war by the Indians from the
churches and private houses of Santa Fé, on the North River,
and brought to these villages for sale. From the mouth of
Ohio to Santa Fé are forty days journey, or about 1000 miles.
What is the shortest distance between the navigable waters of
the Missouri, and those of the North River, or how far this
is navigable above Santa Fé, I could never learn. From Santa
Fé to its mouth in the Gulph of Mexico is about 1200 miles.
The road from New Orleans to Mexico crosses this river at
the post of Rio Norte, 800 miles below Santa Fé: and from
this post to New Orleans is about 1200 miles; thus making
2000 miles between Santa Fé and New Orleans, passing
down the North river, Red river and Missisipi; whereas it is
2230 through the Missouri and Missisipi. From the same post
of Rio Norte, passing near the mines of La Sierra and La-
iguana, which are between the North river and the river Sa-
lina to Sartilla, is 375 miles; and from thence, passing the
mines of Charcas, Zaccatecas and Potosi, to the city of Mexico is 375 miles; in all, 1550 miles from Santa Fé to the city of
Mexico. From New Orleans to the city of Mexico is about
1950 miles: the roads, after setting out from the Red river,
near Natchitoches, keeping generally parallel with the coast,
and about two hundred miles from it, till it enters the city of
Mexico.

The *Illinois* is a fine river, clear, gentle, and without rapids;
insomuch that it is navigable for batteaux to its source. From
thence is a portage of two miles only to the Chickago, which
affords a batteau navigation of 16 miles to its entrance into
lake Michigan. The Illinois, about 10 miles above its mouth,
is 300 yards wide.

The *Kaskaskia* is 100 yards wide at its entrance into the
Missisipi, and preserves that breadth to the Buffalo plains, 70
miles above. So far also it is navigable for loaded batteaux,
and perhaps much further. It is not rapid.

The *Ohio* is the most beautiful river on earth. Its current gentle, waters clear, and bosom smooth and unbroken by rocks and rapids, a single instance only excepted.

It is ¼ of a mile wide at Fort Pitt:

500 yards at the mouth of the Great Kanhaway:

1 mile and 25 poles at Louisville:

¼ of a mile on the rapids, three or four miles below Louisville:

½ a mile where the low country begins, which is 20 miles above Green river:

1¼ at the receipt of the Tanissee:

And a mile wide at the mouth.

Its length, as measured according to its meanders by Capt. Hutchings, is as follows:

From Fort Pitt

	Miles.		Miles.
To Log's town	18½	Little Miami	126¼
Big Beaver creek	10¾	Licking creek	8
Little Beaver cr.	13½	Great Miami	26¾
Yellow creek	11¾	Big Bones	32½
Two creeks	21¾	Kentuckey	44¼
Long reach	53¾	Rapids	77¼
End Long reach	16½	Low country	155¾
Muskingum	25½	Buffalo river	64½
Little Kanhaway	12¼	Wabash	97¼
Hockhocking	16	Big cave	42¾
Great Kanhaway	82½	Shawanee river	52½
Guiandot	43¾	Cherokee river	13
Sandy creek	14½	Massac	11
Sioto	48¾	Missisipi	46
			1188

In common winter and spring tides it affords 15 feet water to Louisville, 10 feet to La Tarte's rapids, 40 miles above the mouth of the great Kanhaway, and a sufficiency at all times for light batteaux and canoes to Fort Pitt. The rapids are in latitude 38°. 8′. The inundations of this river begin about the last of March, and subside in July. During these a first rate man of war may be carried from Louisville to New Orleans, if the sudden turns of the river and the strength of its current will admit a safe steerage. The rapids at Louisville descend about 30 feet in a length of a mile and a half. The bed of the river there is a solid rock, and is divided by an island into two branches, the southern of which is about 200 yards wide, and is dry four months in the year. The bed of the northern branch is worn into channels by the constant course of the water, and attrition of the pebble stones carried on with that, so as to be passable for batteaux through the greater part of the year. Yet it is thought that the southern arm may be the most easily opened for constant navigation. The rise of the waters in these rapids does not exceed 10 or 12 feet. A part of this island is so high as to have been never overflowed, and to command the settlement at Louisville, which is opposite to it. The fort, however, is situated at the head of the falls. The ground on the South side rises very gradually.

The *Tanissee*, Cherokee or Hogohege river is 600 yards wide at its mouth, ¼ of a mile at the mouth of Holston, and 200 yards at Chotee, which is 20 miles above Holston, and 300 miles above the mouth of the Tanissee. This river crosses the southern boundary of Virginia, 58 miles from the Missisipi. Its current is moderate. It is navigable for loaded boats of any burthen to the Muscleshoals, where the river passes through the Cumberland mountain. These shoals are 6 or 8 miles long, passable downwards for loaded canoes, but not upwards, unless there be a swell in the river. Above these the navigation for loaded canoes and batteaux continues to the Long island. This river has its inundations also. Above the Chickamogga towns is a whirlpool called the Sucking-pot, which takes in trunks of trees or boats, and throws them out again half a mile below. It is avoided by keeping very close to the bank, on the South side. There are but a few miles portage between a branch of this river and the navigable waters of the river Mobile, which runs into the gulph of Mexico.

Cumberland, or Shawanee river, intersects the boundary between Virginia and North Carolina 67 miles from the Missisipi, and again 198 miles from the same river, a little above the entrance of Obey's river into the Cumberland. Its clear fork crosses the same boundary about 300 miles from the Missisipi. Cumberland is a very gentle stream, navigable for loaded batteaux 800 miles, without interruption; then intervene some rapids of 15 miles in length, after which it is again navigable 70 miles upwards, which brings you within 10 miles of the Cumberland mountains. It is about 120 yards wide through its whole course, from the head of its navigation to its mouth.

The *Wabash* is a very beautiful river, 400 yards wide at the mouth, and 300 at St. Vincennes, which is a post 100 miles above the mouth, in a direct line. Within this space there are two small rapids, which give very little obstruction to the navigation. It is 400 yards wide at the mouth, and navigable 30 leagues upwards for canoes and small boats. From the mouth of Maple river to that of Eel river is about 80 miles in a direct line, the river continuing navigable, and from one to two hundred yards in width. The Eel river is 150 yards wide, and affords at all times navigation for periaguas, to within 18 miles of the Miami of the lake. The Wabash, from the mouth of Eel river to Little river, a distance of 50 miles direct, is interrupted with frequent rapids and shoals, which obstruct the navigation, except in a swell. Little river affords navigation during a swell to within 3 miles of the Miami, which thence affords a similar navigation into lake Erié, 100 miles distant in a direct line. The Wabash overflows periodically in correspondence with the Ohio, and in some places two leagues from its banks.

Green River is navigable for loaded batteaux at all times 50 miles upwards; but it is then interrupted by impassable rapids, above which the navigation again commences, and continues good 30 or 40 miles to the mouth of Barren river.

Kentucky river is 90 yards wide at the mouth, and also at Boonsborough, 80 miles above. It affords a navigation for loaded batteaux 180 miles in a direct line, in the winter tides.

The *Great Miami* of the Ohio, is 200 yards wide at the mouth. At the Piccawee towns, 75 miles above, it is reduced to 30 yards; it is, nevertheless, navigable for loaded canoes 50 miles above these towns. The portage from its western branch into the Miami of Lake Erié, is 5 miles; that from its eastern branch into Sandusky river, is of 9 miles.

Salt river is at all times navigable for loaded batteaux 70 or 80 miles. It is 80 yards wide at its mouth, and keeps that width to its fork, 25 miles above.

The *Little Miami* of the Ohio, is 60 or 70 yards wide at its mouth, 60 miles to its source, and affords no navigation.

The *Sioto* is 250 yards wide at its mouth, which is in latitude

38°. 22′. and at the Saltlick towns, 200 miles above the mouth, it is yet 100 yards wide. To these towns it is navigable for loaded batteaux, and its eastern branch affords navigation almost to its source.

Great Sandy river is about sixty yards wide, and navigable sixty miles for loaded batteaux.

Guiandot is about the width of the river last mentioned, but is more rapid. It may be navigated by canoes sixty miles.

The *Great Kanhaway* is a river of considerable note for the fertility of its lands, and still more, as leading towards the headwaters of James river. Nevertheless, it is doubtful whether its great and numerous rapids will admit a navigation, but at an expence to which it will require ages to render its inhabitants equal. The great obstacles begin at what are called the great falls, 90 miles above the mouth, below which are only five or six rapids, and these passable, with some difficulty, even at low water. From the falls to the mouth of Greenbriar is 100 miles, and thence to the lead mines 120. It is 280 yards wide at its mouth.

Hock-hocking is 80 yards wide at its mouth, and yields navigation for loaded batteaux to the Press-place, 60 miles above its mouth.

The *Little Kanhaway* is 150 yards wide at the mouth. It yields a navigation of 10 miles only. Perhaps its northern branch, called Junius's creek, which interlocks with the western of Monongahela, may one day admit a shorter passage from the latter into the Ohio.

The *Muskingum* is 280 yards wide at its mouth, and 200 yards at the lower Indian towns, 150 miles upwards. It is navigable for small batteaux to within one mile of a navigable part of Cayahoga river, which runs into lake Erié.

At Fort Pitt the river Ohio loses its name, branching into the Monongahela and Alleghaney.

The *Monongahela* is 400 yards wide at its mouth. From thence is 12 or 15 miles to the mouth of Yohoganey, where it is 300 yards wide. Thence to Redstone by water is 50 miles, by land 30. Then to the mouth of Cheat river by water 40 miles, by land 28, the width continuing at 300 yards, and the navigation good for boats. Thence the width is about 200 yards to the western fork, 50 miles higher, and the navigation frequently interrupted by rapids; which however with a swell of two or three feet become very passable for boats. It then admits light boats, except in dry seasons, 65 miles further to the head of Tygarts valley, presenting only some small rapids and falls of one or two feet perpendicular, and lessening in its width to 20 yards. The *Western fork* is navigable in the winter 10 or 15 miles towards the northern of the Little Kanhaway, and will admit a good waggon road to it. The *Yohoganey* is the principal branch of this river. It passes through the Laurel mountain, about 30 miles from its mouth; is so far from 300 to 150 yards wide, and the navigation much obstructed in dry weather by rapids and shoals. In its passage through the mountain it makes very great falls, admitting no navigation for ten miles to the Turkey foot. Thence to the great crossing, about 20 miles, it is again navigable, except in dry seasons, and at this place is 200 yards wide. The sources of this river are divided from those of the Patowmac by the Alleghaney mountain. From the falls, where it intersects the Laurel mountain, to Fort Cumberland, the head of the navigation on the Patowmac, is 40 miles of very mountainous road. Wills's creek, at the mouth of which was Fort Cumberland, is 30 or 40 yards wide, but affords no navigation as yet. *Cheat* river, another considerable branch of the Monongahela, is 200 yards wide at its mouth, and 100 yards at the Dunkard's settlement, 50 miles higher. It is navigable for boats, except in dry seasons. The boundary between Virginia and Pennsylvania crosses it about three or four miles above its mouth.

The *Alleghaney* river, with a slight swell, affords navigation for light batteaux to Venango, at the mouth of French creek, where it is 200 yards wide; and it is practised even to Le Bœuf, from whence there is a portage of 15 miles to Presque Isle on Lake Erié.

The country watered by the Missisipi and its eastern branches, constitutes five-eighths of the United States, two of which five-eighths are occupied by the Ohio and its waters: the residuary streams which run into the Gulph of Mexico, the Atlantic, and the St. Laurence water, the remaining three-eighths.

Before we quit the subject of the western waters, we will take a view of their principal connections with the Atlantic.

These are three; the Hudson's river, the Patowmac, and the Missisipi itself. Down the last will pass all heavy commodities. But the navigation through the Gulph of Mexico is so dangerous, and that up the Missisipi so difficult and tedious, that it is thought probable that European merchandize will not return through that channel. It is most likely that flour, timber, and other heavy articles will be floated on rafts, which will themselves be an article for sale as well as their loading, the navigators returning by land or in light batteaux. There will therefore be a competition between the Hudson and Patowmac rivers for the residue of the commerce of all the country westward of Lake Erié, on the waters of the lakes, of the Ohio, and upper parts of the Missisipi. To go to New-York, that part of the trade which comes from the lakes or their waters must first be brought into Lake Erié. Between Lake Superior and its waters and Huron are the rapids of St. Mary, which will permit boats to pass, but not larger vessels. Lakes Huron and Michigan afford communication with Lake Erié by vessels of 8 feet draught. That part of the trade which comes from the waters of the Missisipi must pass from them through some portage into the waters of the lakes. The portage from the Illinois river into a water of Michigan is of one mile only. From the Wabash, Miami, Muskingum, or Alleghaney, are portages into the waters of Lake Erié, of from one to fifteen miles. When the commodities are brought into, and have passed through Lake Erié, there is between that and Ontario an interruption by the falls of Niagara, where the portage is of 8 miles; and between Ontario and the Hudson's river are portages at the falls of Onondago, a little above Oswego, of a quarter of a mile; from Wood creek to the Mohawks river two miles; at the little falls of the Mohawks river half a mile, and from Schenectady to Albany 16 miles. Besides the increase of expence occasioned by frequent change of carriage, there is an increased risk of pillage produced by committing merchandize to a greater number of hands successively. The Patowmac offers itself under the following circumstances. For the trade of the lakes and their waters westward of Lake Erié, when it shall have entered that lake, it must coast along its southern shore, on account of the number and excellence of its harbours, the northern, though shortest, having few harbours, and these unsafe. Having reached Cayahoga, to proceed on to New-York it will have 825 miles and five portages: whereas it is but 425 miles to Alexandria, its emporium on the Patowmac, if it turns into the Cayahoga, and passes through that, Bigbeaver, Ohio, Yohoganey, (or Monongalia and Cheat) and Patowmac, and there are but two portages; the first of which between Cayahoga and Beaver may be removed by uniting the sources of these waters, which are lakes in the neighbourhood of each other, and in a champaign country; the other from the waters of Ohio to Patowmac will be from 15 to 40 miles, according to the trouble which shall be taken to approach the two navigations. For the trade of the Ohio, or that which shall come into it from its own waters or the Missisipi, it is nearer through the Patowmac to Alexandria than to New-York by 580 miles, and it is interrupted by one portage only. There is another circumstance of difference too. The lakes themselves never freeze, but the communications between them freeze, and the Hudson's river is itself shut up by the ice three months in the year; whereas the channel to the Chesapeak leads directly into a warmer climate. The southern parts of it very rarely freeze at all, and whenever the northern do, it is so near the sources of the rivers, that the frequent floods to which they are there liable break up the ice immediately, so that vessels may pass through the whole winter, subject only to accidental and short delays. Add to all this, that in case of a war with our neighbours the Anglo-Americans or the Indians, the route to New-York becomes a frontier through almost its whole length, and all commerce through it ceases from that moment.—But the channel to New-York is already known to practice; whereas the upper waters of the Ohio and the Patowmac, and the great falls of the latter, are yet to be cleared of their fixed obstructions.

QUERY III

A notice of the best sea-ports of the state, and how big are the vessels they can receive?

Having no ports but our rivers and creeks, this Query has been answered under the preceding one.

QUERY IV

A notice of its Mountains?

Mountains For the particular geography of our mountains I must refer to Fry and Jefferson's map of Virginia; and to Evans's analysis of his map of America for a more philosophical view of them than is to be found in any other work. It is worthy notice, that our mountains are not solitary and scattered confusedly over the face of the country; but that they commence at about 150 miles from the sea-coast, are disposed in ridges one behind another, running nearly parallel with the sea-coast, though rather approaching it as they advance north-eastwardly. To the south-west, as the tract of country between the sea-coast and the Mississipi becomes narrower, the mountains converge into a single ridge, which, as it approaches the Gulph of Mexico, subsides into plain country, and gives rise to some of the waters of that Gulph, and particularly to a river called the Apalachicola, probably from the Apalachies, an Indian nation formerly residing on it. Hence the mountains giving rise to that river, and seen from its various parts, were called the Apalachian mountains, being in fact the end or termination only of the great ridges passing through the continent. European geographers however extended the name northwardly as far as the mountains extended; some giving it, after their separation into different ridges, to the Blue ridge, others to the North mountain, others to the Alleghaney, others to the Laurel ridge, as may be seen in their different maps. But the fact I believe is, that none of these ridges were ever known by that name to the inhabitants, either native or emigrant, but as they saw them so called in European maps. In the same direction generally are the veins of lime-stone, coal and other minerals hitherto discovered: and so range the falls of our great rivers. But the courses of the great rivers are at right angles with these. James and Patowmac penetrate through all the ridges of mountains eastward of the Alleghaney; that is broken by no watercourse. It is in fact the spine of the country between the Atlantic on one side, and the Missisipi and St. Laurence on the other. The passage of the Patowmac through the Blue ridge is per-

142

haps one of the most stupendous scenes in nature. You stand on a very high point of land. On your right comes up the Shenandoah, having ranged along the foot of the mountain an hundred miles to seek a vent. On your left approaches the Patowmac, in quest of a passage also. In the moment of their junction they rush together against the mountain, rend it asunder, and pass off to the sea. The first glance of this scene hurries our senses into the opinion, that this earth has been created in time, that the mountains were formed first, that the rivers began to flow afterwards, that in this place particularly they have been dammed up by the Blue ridge of mountains, and have formed an ocean which filled the whole valley; that continuing to rise they have at length broken over at this spot, and have torn the mountain down from its summit to its base. The piles of rock on each hand, but particularly on the Shenandoah, the evident marks of their disrupture and avulsion from their beds by the most powerful agents of nature, corroborate the impression. But the distant finishing which nature has given to the picture is of a very different character. It is a true contrast to the fore-ground. It is as placid and delightful, as that is wild and tremendous. For the mountain being cloven asunder, she presents to your eye, through the cleft, a small catch of smooth blue horizon, at an infinite distance in the plain country, inviting you, as it were, from the riot and tumult roaring around, to pass through the breach and participate of the calm below. Here the eye ultimately composes itself; and that way too the road happens actually to lead. You cross the Patowmac above the junction, pass along its side through the base of the mountain for three miles, its terrible precipices hanging in fragments over you, and within about 20 miles reach Frederic town and the fine country round that. This scene is worth a voyage across the Atlantic. Yet here, as in the neighbourhood of the natural bridge, are people who have passed their lives within half a dozen miles, and have never been to survey these monuments of a war between rivers and mountains, which must have shaken the earth itself to its center.—The height of our mountains has not yet been estimated with any degree of exactness. The Alleghaney being the great ridge which divides the waters of the Atlantic from those of the Missisipi, its summit is doubtless more elevated above the ocean than that of any other mountain. But its relative height, compared with the base on which it stands, is not so great as that of some others, the country rising behind the successive ridges like the steps of stairs. The mountains of the Blue ridge, and of these the Peaks of Otter, are thought to be of a greater height, measured from their base, than any others in our country, and perhaps in North America. From data, which may found a tolerable conjecture, we suppose the highest peak to be about 4000 feet perpendicular, which is not a fifth part of the height of the mountains of South America, nor one third of the height which would be necessary in our latitude to preserve ice in the open air unmelted through the year. The ridge of mountains next beyond the Blue ridge, called by us the North mountain, is of the greatest extent; for which reason they were named by the Indians the Endless mountains.

A substance supposed to be Pumice, found floating on the Missisipi, has induced a conjecture, that there is a volcano on some of its waters: and as these are mostly known to their sources, except the Missouri, our expectations of verifying the conjecture would of course be led to the mountains which divide the waters of the Mexican Gulph from those of the South Sea; but no volcano having ever yet been known at such a distance from the sea, we must rather suppose that this floating substance has been erroneously deemed Pumice.

QUERY V

Its Cascades and Caverns?

The only remarkable Cascade in this country, is that Falling spring of the Falling Spring in Augusta. It is a water of James river, where it is called Jackson's river, rising in the warm spring mountains about twenty miles South West of the warm spring, and flowing into that valley. About three quarters of a mile from its source, it falls over a rock 200 feet into the valley below. The sheet of water is broken in its breadth by the rock in two or three places, but not at all in its height. Between the sheet and rock, at the bottom, you may walk across dry. This Cataract will bear no comparison with that of Niagara, as to the quantity of water composing it; the sheet being only 12 or 15 feet wide above, and somewhat more spread below; but it is half as high again, the latter being only 156 feet, according to the mensuration made by order of M. Vaudreuil, Governor of Canada, and 130 according to a more recent account.

In the lime-stone country, there are many caverns Madison's cave of very considerable extent. The most noted is called Madison's Cave, and is on the North side of the Blue ridge, near the intersection of the Rockingham and Augusta line with the South fork of the southern river of Shenandoah. It is in a hill of about 200 feet perpendicular height, the ascent of which, on one side, is so steep, that you may pitch a biscuit from its summit into the river which washes its base. The entrance of the cave is, in this side, about two thirds of the way up. It extends into the earth about 300 feet, branching into subordinate caverns, sometimes ascending a little, but more generally descending, and at length terminates, in two different places, at basons of water of unknown extent, and which I should judge to be nearly on a level with the water of the river; however, I do not think they are formed by refluent water from that, because they are never turbid; because they do not rise and fall in correspondence with that in times of flood, or of drought; and because the water is always cool. It is probably one of the many reservoirs with which the interior parts of the earth are supposed to abound,

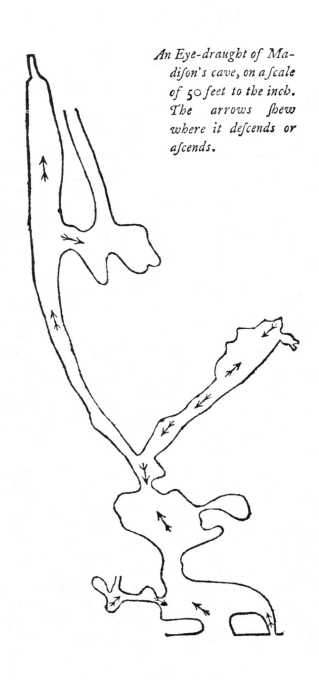

An Eye-draught of Madison's cave, on a scale of 50 feet to the inch. The arrows shew where it descends or ascends.

and which yield supplies to the fountains of water, distinguished from others only by its being accessible. The vault of this cave is of solid lime-stone, from 20 to 40 or 50 feet high, through which water is continually percolating. This, trickling down the sides of the cave, has incrusted them over in the form of elegant drapery; and dripping from the top of the vault generates on that, and on the base below, stalactites of a conical form, some of which have met and formed massive columns.

Another of these caves is near the North mountain, in the county of Frederick, on the lands of Mr. Zane. The entrance into this is on the top of an extensive ridge. You descend 30 or 40 feet, as into a well, from whence the cave then extends, nearly horizontally, 400 feet into the earth, preserving a breadth of from 20 to 50 feet, and a height of from 5 to 12 feet. After entering this cave a few feet, the mercury, which in the open air was at 50°. rose to 57°. of Farenheit's thermometer, answering to 11°. of Reaumur's, and it continued at that to the remotest parts of the cave. The uniform temperature of the cellars of the observatory of Paris, which are 90 feet deep, and of all subterranean cavities of any depth, where no chymical agents may be supposed to produce a factitious heat, has been found to be 10°. of Reamur, equal to 54½°. of Farenheit. The temperature of the cave above-mentioned so nearly corresponds with this, that the difference may be ascribed to a difference of instruments.

At the Panther gap, in the ridge which divides the waters of the Cow and the Calf pasture, is what is called the *Blowing cave*. It is in the side of a hill, is of about 100 feet diameter, and emits constantly a current of air of such force, as to keep the weeds prostrate to the distance of twenty yards before it. This current is strongest in dry frosty weather, and in long spells of rain weakest. Regular inspirations and expirations of air, by caverns and fissures, have been probably enough accounted for, by supposing them combined with intermitting fountains; as they must of course inhale air while their reservoirs are emptying themselves, and again emit it while they are filling. But a constant issue of air, only varying in its force as the weather is drier or damper, will require a new hypothesis. There is another blowing cave in the Cumberland mountain, about a mile from where it crosses the Carolina line. All we know of this is, that it is not constant, and that a fountain of water issues from it.

Natural bridge

The *Natural bridge*, the most sublime of Nature's works, though not comprehended under the present head, must not be pretermitted. It is on the ascent of a hill, which seems to have been cloven through its length by some great convulsion. The fissure, just at the bridge, is, by some admeasurements, 270 feet deep, by others only 205. It is about 45 feet wide at the bottom, and 90 feet at the top; this of course determines the length of the bridge, and its height from the water. Its breadth in the middle, is about 60 feet, but more at the ends, and the thickness of the mass at the summit of the arch, about 40 feet. A part of this thickness is constituted by a coat of earth, which gives growth to many large trees. The residue, with the hill on both sides, is one solid rock of lime-stone. The arch approaches the Semi-elliptical form; but the larger axis of the ellipsis, which would be the cord of the arch, is many times longer than the transverse. Though the sides of this bridge are provided in some parts with a parapet of fixed rocks, yet few men have resolution to walk to them and look over into the abyss. You involuntarily fall on your hands and feet, creep to the parapet and peep over it. Looking down from this height about a minute, gave me a violent head ach. If the view from the top be painful and intolerable, that from below is delightful in an equal extreme. It is impossible for the emotions arising from the sublime, to be felt beyond what they are here: so beautiful an arch, so elevated, so light, and springing as it were up to heaven, the rapture of the spectator is really indescribable! The fissure continuing narrow, deep, and streight for a considerable distance above and below the bridge, opens a short but very pleasing view of the North mountain on one side, and Blue ridge on the other, at the distance each of them of about five miles. This bridge is in the county of Rock bridge, to which it has given name, and affords a public and commodious passage over a valley, which cannot be crossed elsewhere for a considerable distance. The stream passing under it is called Cedar creek. It is a water of James river, and sufficient in the driest seasons to turn a grist-mill, though its fountain is not more than two miles above.*

*Don Ulloa mentions a break, similar to this, in the province of Angaraez, in South America. It is from 16 to 22 feet wide, 111 feet deep, and of 1.3 miles continuance, English measures. Its breadth at top is not sensibly greater than at bottom. But the following fact is remarkable, and will furnish some light for conjecturing the probable origin of our natural bridge. 'Esta caxa, ó cauce está cortada en péna viva con tanta precision, que las desigualdades del un lado entrantes, corresponden á las del otro lado salientes, como si aquella altura se hubiese abierto expresamente, con sus bueltas y tortuosidades, para darle transito á los aguas por entre los dos murallones que la forman; siendo tal su igualdad, que si llegasen á juntarse se endentarían uno con otro sin dexar hueco.' Not. Amer. II. §. 10. Don Ulloa inclines to the opinion, that this channel has been affected by the wearing of the water which runs through it, rather than that the mountain should have been broken open by any convulsion of nature. But if it had been worn by the running of water, would not the rocks which form the sides, have been worn plane? or if, meeting in some parts with veins of harder stone, the water had left prominences on the one side, would not the same cause have sometimes, or perhaps generally, occasioned prominences on the other side also? Yet Don Ulloa tells us, that on the other side there are always corresponding cavities, and that these tally with the prominences so perfectly, that, were the two sides to come together, they would fit in all their indentures, without leaving any void. I think that this does not resemble the effect of running water, but looks rather as if the two sides had parted asunder. The sides of the break, over which is the Natural bridge of Virginia, consisting of a veiny rock which yields to time, the correspondence between the salient and re-entering inequalities, if it existed at all, has now disappeared. This break has the advantage of the one described by Don Ulloa in its finest circumstance; no portion in that instance having held together, during the separation of the other parts, so as to form a bridge over the Abyss.

QUERY VI

1. Minerals   *A notice of the mines and other subterraneous riches; its trees, plants, fruits, &c.*

Gold   I knew a single instance of gold found in this state. It was interspersed in small specks through a lump of ore, of about four pounds weight, which yielded seventeen pennyweight of gold, of extraordinary ductility. This ore was found on the North side of Rappahanoc, about four miles below the falls. I never heard of any other indication of gold in its neighbourhood.

Lead   On the Great Kanhaway, opposite to the mouth of Cripple creek, and about twenty-five miles from our southern boundary, in the county of Montgomery, are mines of lead. The metal is mixed, sometimes with earth, and sometimes with rock, which requires the force of gunpowder to open it; and is accompanied with a portion of silver, too small to be worth separation under any process hitherto attempted there. The proportion yielded is from 50 to 80 lb. of pure metal from 100 lb. of washed ore. The most common is that of 60 to the 100 lb. The veins are at sometimes most flattering; at others they disappear suddenly and totally. They enter the side of the hill, and proceed horizontally. Two of them are wrought at present by the public, the best of which is 100 yards under the hill. These would employ about 50 labourers to advantage. We have not, however, more than 30 generally, and these cultivate their own corn. They have produced 60 tons of lead in the year; but the general quantity is from 20 to 25 tons. The present furnace is a mile from the ore-bank, and on the opposite side of the river. The ore is first waggoned to the river, a quarter of a mile, then laden on board of canoes and carried across the river, which is there about 200 yards wide, and then again taken into waggons and carried to the furnace. This mode was originally adopted, that they might avail themselves of a good situation on a creek, for a pounding mill: but it would be easy to have the furnace and pounding mill on the same side of the river, which would yield water, without any dam, by a canal of about half a mile in length. From the furnace the lead is transported 130 miles along a good road, leading through the peaks of Otter to Lynch's ferry, or Winston's, on James river, from whence it is carried by water about the same distance to Westham. This land carriage may be greatly shortened, by delivering the lead on James river, above the blue ridge, from whence a ton weight has been brought on two canoes. The Great Kanhaway has considerable falls in the neighbourhood of the mines. About seven miles below are three falls, of three or four feet perpendicular each; and three miles above is a rapid of three miles continuance, which has been compared in its descent to the great fall of James river. Yet it is the opinion, that they may be laid open for useful navigation, so as to reduce very much the portage between the Kanhaway and James river.

A valuable lead mine is said to have been lately discovered in Cumberland, below the mouth of Red river. The greatest, however, known in the western country, are on the Missisipi, extending from the mouth of Rock river 150 miles upwards. These are not wrought, the lead used in that country being from the banks on the Spanish side of the Missisipi, opposite to Kaskaskia.

A mine of copper was once opened in the county of Amherst, on the North side of James river, and **Copper** another in the opposite country, on the South side. However, either from bad management or the poverty of the veins, they were discontinued. We are told of a rich mine of native copper on the Ouabache, below the upper Wiaw.

The mines of iron worked at present are Callaway's, Ross's, and Ballendine's, on the South side of **Iron** James river; Old's on the North side, in Albemarle; Miller's in Augusta, and Zane's in Frederic. These two last are in the valley between the Blue ridge and North mountain. Callaway's, Ross's, Millar's, and Zane's, make about 150 tons of bar iron each, in the year. Ross's makes also about 1600 tons of pig iron annually; Ballendine's 1000; Callaway's, Millar's, and Zane's, about 600 each. Besides these, a forge of Mr. Hunter's, at Fredericksburgh, makes about 300 tons a year of bar iron, from pigs imported from Maryland; and Taylor's forge on Neapsco of Patowmac, works in the same way, but to what extent I am not informed. The indications of iron in other places are numerous, and dispersed through all the middle country. The toughness of the cast iron of Ross's and Zane's furnaces is very remarkable. Pots and other utensils, cast thinner than usual, of this iron, may be safely thrown into, or out of the waggons in which they are transported. Salt-pans made of the same, and no longer wanted for that purpose, cannot be broken up, in order to be melted again, unless previously drilled in many parts.

In the western country, we are told of iron mines between the Muskingum and Ohio; of others on Kentucky, between the Cumberland and Barren rivers, between Cumberland and Tannissee, on Reedy creek, near the Long island, and on Chesnut creek, a branch of the Great Kanhaway, near where it crosses the Carolina line. What are called the iron banks, on the Missisipi, are believed, by a good judge, to have no iron in them. In general, from what is hitherto known of that country, it seems to want iron.

Black lead   Considerable quantities of black lead are taken occasionally for use from Winterham, in the county of Amelia. I am not able, however, to give a particular state of the mine. There is no work established at it, those who want, going and procuring it for themselves.

Pit coal   The country on James river, from 15 to 20 miles above Richmond, and for several miles northward and southward, is replete with mineral coal of a very excellent quality. Being in the hands of many proprietors, pits have been opened, and before the interruption of our commerce were worked to an extent equal to the demand.

In the western country coal is known to be in so many places, as to have induced an opinion, that the whole tract between the Laurel mountain, Missisipi, and Ohio, yields coal. It is also known in many places on the North side of the Ohio. The coal at Pittsburg is of very superior quality. A bed of it at that place has been a-fire since the year 1765. Another coal-hill on the Pike-run of Monongahela has been a-fire ten years; yet it has burnt away about twenty yards only.

Precious stones   I have known one instance of an Emerald found in this country. Amethysts have been frequent, and chrystals common; yet not in such numbers any of them as to be worth seeking.

There is very good marble, and in very great abundance, on

James river, at the mouth of Rockfish. The samples
I have seen, were some of them of a white as pure
as one might expect to find on the surface of the earth: but
most of them were variegated with red, blue, and purple.
None of it has been ever worked. It forms a very large preci-
pice, which hangs over a navigable part of the river. It is said
there is marble at Kentucky.

    Marble

But one vein of lime-stone is known below the
Blue ridge. Its first appearance, in our country, is
in Prince William, two miles below the Pignut ridge of mountains; thence it passes on nearly parallel with that, and crosses
the Rivanna about five miles below it, where it is called the
South-west ridge. It then crosses Hardware, above the mouth
of Hudson's creek, James river at the mouth of Rockfish, at the
marble quarry before spoken of, probably runs up that river to
where it appears again at Ross's iron-works, and so passes off
south-westwardly by Flat creek of Otter river. It is never more
than one hundred yards wide. From the Blue ridge westwardly
the whole country seems to be founded on a rock of lime-stone,
besides infinite quantities on the surface, both loose and fixed.
This is cut into beds, which range, as the mountains and sea-
coast do, from south-west to north-east, the lamina of each bed
declining from the horizon towards a parallelism with the axis
of the earth. Being struck with this observation, I made, with a
quadrant, a great number of trials on the angles of their decli-
nation, and found them to vary from 22°. to 60°. but averag-
ing all my trials, the result was within one-third of a degree
of the elevation of the pole or latitude of the place, and much
the greatest part of them taken separately were little different
from that: by which it appears, that these lamina are, in the
main, parallel with the axis of the earth. In some instances,
indeed, I found them perpendicular, and even reclining the
other way: but these were extremely rare, and always attended
with signs of convulsion, or other circumstances of singularity, which admitted a possibility of removal from their original position. These trials were made between Madison's cave
and the Patowmac. We hear of lime-stone on the Missisipi
and Ohio, and in all the mountainous country between the
eastern and western waters, not on the mountains themselves,
but occupying the vallies between them.

    Limestone

Near the eastern foot of the North mountain are immense bodies of *Schist*, containing impressions of shells in a variety of forms. I have received petrified shells of very different kinds from the first sources of the Kentucky, which bear no resemblance to any I have ever seen on the tide-waters. It is said that shells are found in the Andes, in South-America, fifteen thousand feet above the level of the ocean. This is considered by many, both of the learned and unlearned, as a proof of an universal deluge. To the many considerations opposing this opinion, the following may be added. The atmosphere, and all its contents, whether of water, air, or other matters, gravitate to the earth; that is to say, they have weight. Experience tells us, that the weight of all these together never exceeds that of a column of mercury of 31 inches height, which is equal to one of rain-water of 35 feet high. If the whole contents of the atmosphere then were water, instead of what they are, it would cover the globe but 35 feet deep; but as these waters, as they fell, would run into the seas, the superficial measure of which is to that of the dry parts of the globe as two to one, the seas would be raised only 52½ feet above their present level, and of course would overflow the lands to that height only. In Virginia this would be a very small proportion even of the champaign country, the banks of our tide-waters being frequently, if not generally, of a greater height. Deluges beyond this extent then, as for instance, to the North mountain or to Kentucky, seem out of the laws of nature. But within it they may have taken place to a greater or less degree, in proportion to the combination of natural causes which may be supposed to have produced them. History renders probable some instances of a partial deluge in the country lying round the Mediterranean sea. It has been often *supposed, and is not unlikely, that that sea was once a lake. While such, let us admit an extraordinary collection of the waters of the atmosphere from the other parts of the globe to have been discharged over that and the countries whose waters run into it. Or without supposing it

* 2. Buffon Epoques, 96.

a lake, admit such an extraordinary collection of the waters of the atmosphere, and an influx of waters from the Atlantic ocean, forced by long continued Western winds. That lake, or that sea, may thus have been so raised as to overflow the low lands adjacent to it, as those of Egypt and Armenia, which, according to a tradition of the Egyptians and Hebrews, were overflowed about 2300 years before the Christian æra; those of Attica, said to have been overflowed in the time of Ogyges, about 500 years later; and those of Thessaly, in the time of Deucalion, still 300 years posterior. But such deluges as these will not account for the shells found in the higher lands. A second opinion has been entertained, which is, that, in times anterior to the records either of history or tradition, the bed of the ocean, the principal residence of the shelled tribe, has, by some great convulsion of nature, been heaved to the heights at which we now find shells and other remains of marine animals. The favourers of this opinion do well to suppose the great events on which it rests to have taken place beyond all the æras of history; for within these, certainly none such are to be found: and we may venture to say further, that no fact has taken place, either in our own days, or in the thousands of years recorded in history, which proves the existence of any natural agents, within or without the bowels of the earth, of force sufficient to heave, to the height of 15,000 feet, such masses as the Andes. The difference between the power necessary to produce such an effect, and that which shuffled together the different parts of Calabria in our days, is so immense, that, from the existence of the latter we are not authorised to infer that of the former.

M. de Voltaire has suggested a third solution of this difficulty (Quest. encycl. Coquilles). He cites an instance in Touraine, where, in the space of 80 years, a particular spot of earth had been twice metamorphosed into soft stone, which had become hard when employed in building. In this stone shells of various kinds were produced, discoverable at first only with the microscope, but afterwards growing with the stone. From this fact, I suppose, he would have us infer, that, besides the usual process for generating shells by the elaboration of earth and water in animal vessels, nature may have

provided an equivalent operation, by passing the same materials through the pores of calcareous earths and stones: as we
see calcareous dropstones generating every day by the per-
colation of water through lime-stone, and new marble forming in the quarries from which the old has been taken out;
and it might be asked, whether it is more difficult for nature
to shoot the calcareous juice into the form of a shell, than
other juices into the forms of chrystals, plants, animals, according to the construction of the vessels through which they
pass? There is a wonder somewhere. Is it greatest on this
branch of the dilemma; on that which supposes the existence
of a power, of which we have no evidence in any other case;
or on the first, which requires us to believe the creation of a
body of water, and its subsequent annihilation? The establishment of the instance, cited by M. de Voltaire, of the growth
of shells unattached to animal bodies, would have been that
of his theory. But he has not established it. He has not even
left it on ground so respectable as to have rendered it an object of enquiry to the literati of his own country. Abandoning
this fact, therefore, the three hypotheses are equally unsatisfactory; and we must be contented to acknowledge, that this
great phænomenon is as yet unsolved. Ignorance is preferable
to error; and he is less remote from the truth who believes
nothing, then he who believes what is wrong.

Stone   There is great abundance (more especially when
           you approach the mountains) of stone, white, blue,
brown, &c. fit for the chissel, good mill-stone, such also as
stands the fire, and slate-stone. We are told of flint, fit for
gun-flints, on the Meherrin in Brunswic, on the Missisipi between the mouth of Ohio and Kaskaskia, and on others of
the western waters. Isinglass or mica is in several places; loadstone also, and an Asbestos of a ligneous texture, is sometimes to be met with.

Earths   Marle abounds generally. A clay, of which, like
           the Sturbridge in England, bricks are made, which
will resist long the violent action of fire, has been found on
Tuckahoe creek of James river, and no doubt will be found in
other places. Chalk is said to be in Botetourt and Bedford. In
the latter county is some earth, believed to be Gypseous.
Ochres are found in various parts.

In the lime-stone country are many caves, the
earthy floors of which are impregnated with nitre.   Nitre
On Rich creek, a branch of the Great Kanhaway, about 60
miles below the lead mines, is a very large one, about 20 yards
wide, and entering a hill a quarter or half a mile. The vault is
of rock, from 9 to 15 or 20 feet above the floor. A Mr. Lynch,
who gives me this account, undertook to extract the nitre.
Besides a coat of the salt which had formed on the vault and
floor, he found the earth highly impregnated to the depth of
seven feet in some places, and generally of three, every bushel
yielding on an average three pounds of nitre. Mr. Lynch having made about 1000 lb. of the salt from it, consigned it to
some others, who have since made 10,000 lb. They have done
this by pursuing the cave into the hill, never trying a second
time the earth they have once exhausted, to see how far or
soon it receives another impregnation. At least fifty of these
caves are worked on the Greenbriar. There are many of them
known on Cumberland river.

The country westward of the Alleghaney abounds
with springs of common salt. The most remarkable   Salt
we have heard of are at Bullet's lick, the Big bones, the Blue
licks, and on the North fork of Holston. The area of Bullet's
lick is of many acres. Digging the earth to the depth of three
feet, the water begins to boil up, and the deeper you go, and
the drier the weather, the stronger is the brine. A thousand
gallons of water yield from a bushel to a bushel and a half of
salt, which is about 80 lb. of water to one lb. of salt; but of
sea-water 25 lb. yield one lb. of salt. So that sea-water is more
than three times as strong as that of these springs. A salt
spring has been lately discovered at the Turkey foot on Yohogany, by which river it is overflowed, except at very low
water. Its merit is not yet known. Duning's lick is also as yet
untried, but it is supposed to be the best on this side the
Ohio. The salt springs on the margin of the Onondago lake
are said to give a saline taste to the waters of the lake.

There are several Medicinal springs, some of   Medicinal
which are indubitably efficacious, while others   springs
seem to owe their reputation as much to fancy, and change
of air and regimen, as to their real virtues. None of them
having undergone a chemical analysis in skilful hands, nor

been so far the subject of observations as to have produced a reduction into classes of the disorders which they relieve, it is in my power to give little more than an enumeration of them.

The most efficacious of these are two springs in Augusta, near the first sources of James river, where it is called Jackson's river. They rise near the foot of the ridge of mountains, generally called the Warm spring mountain, but in the maps Jackson's mountains. The one is distinguished by the name of the Warm spring, and the other of the Hot spring. The Warm spring issues with a very bold stream, sufficient to work a grist-mill, and to keep the waters of its bason, which is 30 feet in diameter, at the vital warmth, viz. 96°. of Farenheit's thermometer. The matter with which these waters is allied is very volatile; its smell indicates it to be sulphureous, as also does the circumstance of its turning silver black. They relieve rheumatisms. Other complaints also of very different natures have been removed or lessened by them. It rains here four or five days in every week.

The *Hot spring* is about six miles from the Warm, is much smaller, and has been so hot as to have boiled an egg. Some believe its degree of heat to be lessened. It raises the mercury in Farenheit's thermometer to 112 degrees, which is fever heat. It sometimes relieves where the Warm spring fails. A fountain of common water, issuing within a few inches of its margin, gives it a singular appearance. Comparing the temperature of these with that of the Hot springs of Kamschatka, of which Krachininnikow gives an account, the difference is very great, the latter raising the mercury to 200°. which is within 12°. of boiling water. These springs are very much resorted to in spite of a total want of accommodation for the sick. Their waters are strongest in the hottest months, which occasions their being visited in July and August principally.

The Sweet springs are in the county of Botetourt, at the eastern foot of the Alleghaney, about 42 miles from the Warm springs. They are still less known. Having been found to relieve cases in which the others had been ineffectually tried, it is probable their composition is different. They are different also in their temperature, being as cold as common water: which is not mentioned, however, as a proof of a distinct impregnation. This is among the first sources of James river.

On Patowmac river, in Berkeley county, above the North mountain, are Medicinal springs, much more frequented than those of Augusta. Their powers, however, are less, the waters weakly mineralized, and scarcely warm. They are more visited, because situated in a fertile, plentiful, and populous country, better provided with accommodations, always safe from the Indians, and nearest to the more populous states.

In Louisa county, on the head waters of the South Anna branch of York river, are springs of some medicinal virtue. They are not much used however. There is a weak chalybeate at Richmond; and many others in various parts of the country, which are of too little worth, or too little note, to be enumerated after those before-mentioned.

We are told of a Sulphur spring on Howard's creek of Greenbriar, and another at Boonsborough on Kentuckey.

In the low grounds of the Great Kanhaway, 7 miles above the mouth of Elk river, and 67 above that of the Kanhaway itself, is a hole in the earth of the capacity of 30 or 40 gallons, from which issues constantly a bituminous vapour in so strong a current, as to give to the sand about its orifice the motion which it has in a boiling spring. On presenting a lighted candle or torch within 18 inches of the hole, it flames up in a column of 18 inches diameter, and four or five feet height, which sometimes burns out within 20 minutes, and at other times has been known to continue three days, and then has been left still burning. The flame is unsteady, of the density of that of burning spirits, and smells like burning pit coal. Water sometimes collects in the bason, which is remarkably cold, and is kept in ebullition by the vapour issuing through it. If the vapour be fired in that state, the water soon becomes so warm that the hand cannot bear it, and evaporates wholly in a short time. This, with the circumjacent lands, is the property of his Excellency General Washington and of General Lewis. *Burning spring*

There is a similar one on Sandy river, the flame of which is a column of about 12 inches diameter, and 3 feet high. General Clarke, who informs me of it, kindled the vapour, staid about an hour, and left it burning.

The mention of uncommon springs leads me to that of Syphon fountains. There is one of these *Syphon fountains* near the intersection of the Lord Fairfax's boundary with the North mountain, not far from Brock's gap, on the stream of which is a grist-mill, which grinds two bushel of grain at every flood of the spring. Another, near the Cow-pasture river, a mile and a half below its confluence with the Bull-pasture river, and 16 or 17 miles from the Hot springs, which intermits once in every twelve hours. One also near the mouth of the North Holston.

After these may be mentioned the *Natural Well*, on the lands of a Mr. Lewis in Frederick county. It is somewhat larger than a common well: the water rises in it as near the surface of the earth as in the neighbouring artificial wells, and is of a depth as yet unknown. It is said there is a current in it tending sensibly downwards. If this be true, it probably feeds some fountain, of which it is the natural reservoir, distinguished from others, like that of Madison's cave, by being accessible. It is used with a bucket and windlass as an ordinary well.

Vegetables   A complete catalogue of the trees, plants, fruits, &c. is probably not desired. I will sketch out those which would principally attract notice, as being 1. Medicinal, 2. Esculent, 3. Ornamental, or 4. Useful for fabrication; adding the Linnæan to the popular names, as the latter might not convey precise information to a foreigner. I shall confine myself too to native plants.

1. Senna.   Cassia ligustrina.
Arsmart.   Polygonum Sagittatum.
Clivers, or goose-grass.   Galium spurium.
Lobelia of several species.
Palma Christi.   Ricinus.
James-town weed.   Datura Stramonium.
Mallow.   Malva rotundifolia.
Syrian mallow.   Hibiscus moschentos.
                Hibiscus virginicus.
Indian mallow.   Sida rhombifolia.
                Sida abutilon.
Virginia Marshmallow.   Napæa hermaphrodita.
                        Napæa dioica.
Indian physic.   Spiræa trifoliata.

Euphorbia Ipecacuanhæ.
Pleurisy root.   Asclepias decumbens.
Virginia snake-root.   Aristolochia serpentaria.
Black snake-root.   Actæa racemosa.
Seneca rattlesnake-root.   Polygala Senega.
Valerian.   Valeriana locusta radiata.
Gentiana, Saponaria, Villosa & Centaurium.
Ginseng.   Panax quinquefolium.
Angelica.   Angelica sylvestris.
Cassava.   Jatropha urens.

2. Tuckahoe.   Lycoperdon tuber.
Jerusalem artichoke.   Helianthus tuberosus.
Long potatoes.   Convolvulas batatas.
Granadillas. Maycocks. Maracocks. Passiflora
   incarnata.
Panic.   Panicum of many species.
Indian millet.   Holcus laxus.
                            Holcus striosus.
Wild oat.   Zizania aquatica.
Wild pea.   Dolichos of Clayton.
Lupine.   Lupinus perennis.
Wild hop.   Humulus lupulus.
Wild cherry.   Prunus Virginiana.
Cherokee plumb.   Prunus sylvestris fructu majori. ⎫
Wild plumb.   Prunus sylvestris fructu minori. ⎬ Clayton.
Wild crab-apple.   Pyrus coronaria.   ⎭
Red mulberry.   Morus rubra.
Persimmon.   Diospyros Virginiana.
Sugar maple.   Acer saccharinum.
Scaly bark hiccory.   Juglans alba cortice squamoso.
   Clayton.
Common hiccory.   Juglans alba, fructu minore rancido.
   Clayton.
Paccan, or Illinois nut. Not described by Linnæus, Millar,
   or Clayton. Were I to venture to describe this, speaking
   of the fruit from memory, and of the leaf from plants of
   two years growth, I should specify it as the Juglans alba,
   foliolis lanceolatis, acuminatis, serratis, tomentosis, fructu
   minore, ovato, compresso, vix insculpto, dulci, putamine,

tenerrimo. It grows on the Illinois, Wabash, Ohio, and Missisipi. It is spoken of by Don Ulloa under the name of Pacanos, in his Noticias Americanas. Entret. 6.

Black walnut.   Juglans nigra.
White walnut.   Juglans alba.
Chesnut.   Fagus castanea.
Chinquapin.   Fagus pumila.
Hazlenut.   Corylus avellana.
Grapes.   Vitis. Various kinds, though only three described by Clayton.
Scarlet Strawberries.   Fragaria Virginiana of Millar.
Whortleberries.   Vaccinium uliginosum?
Wild gooseberries.   Ribes grossularia.
Cranberries.   Vaccinium oxycoccos.
Black raspberries.   Rubus occidentalis.
Blackberries.   Rubus fruticosus.
Dewberries.   Rubus cæsius.
Cloud-berries.   Rubus chamæmorus.

3. Plane-tree.   Platanus occidentalis.
Poplar.   Liriodendron tulipifera.
                Populus heterophylla.
Black poplar.   Populus nigra.
Aspen.   Populus tremula.
Linden, or lime.   Tilia Americana.
Red flowering maple.   Acer rubrum.
Horse-chesnut, or Buck's-eye.   Æsculus pavia.
Catalpa.   Bignonia catalpa.
Umbrella.   Magnolia tripetala.
Swamp laurel.   Magnolia glauca.
Cucumber-tree.   Magnolia acuminata.
Portugal bay.   Laurus indica.
Red bay.   Laurus borbonia.
Dwarf-rose bay.   Rhododendron maximum.
Laurel of the western country.   Qu. species?
Wild pimento.   Laurus benzoin.
Sassafras.   Laurus sassafras.
Locust.   Robinia pseudo-acacia.
Honey-locust.   Gleditsia. 1. β.
Dogwood.   Cornus florida.

Fringe or snow-drop tree. Chionanthus Virginica.
Barberry. Berberis vulgaris.
Redbud, or Judas-tree. Cercis Canadensis.
Holly. Ilex aquifolium.
Cockspur hawthorn. Cratægus coccinea.
Spindle-tree. Euonymus Europæus.
Evergreen spindle-tree. Euonymus Americanus.
Itea Virginica.
Elder. Sambucus nigra.
Papaw. Annona triloba.
Candleberry myrtle. Myrica cerifera.
Dwarf-laurel. Kalmia angustifolia. ⎤ called ivy
              Kalmia latifolia   ⎦ with us.
Ivy. Hedera quinquefolia.
Trumpet honeysuckle. Lonicera sempervirens.
Upright honeysuckle. Azalea nudiflora.
Yellow jasmine. Bignonia sempervirens.
Calycanthus floridus.
American aloe. Agave Virginica.
Sumach. Rhus. Qu. species?
Poke. Phytolacca decandra.
Long moss. Tillandsia Usneoides.

4. Reed. Arundo phragmitis.
Virginia hemp. Acnida cannabina.
Flax. Linum Virginianum.
Black, or pitch-pine. Pinus tæda.
White pine. Pinus strobus.
Yellow pine. Pinus Virginica.
Spruce pine. Pinus foliis singularibus. Clayton.
Hemlock spruce fir. Pinus Canadensis.
Abor vitæ. Thuya occidentalis.
Juniper. Juniperus virginica (called cedar with us).
Cypress. Cupressus disticha.
White cedar. Cupressus Thyoides.
Black oak. Quercus nigra.
White oak. Quercus alba.
Red oak. Quercus rubra.
Willow oak. Quercus phellos.
Chesnut oak. Quercus prinus.

Black jack oak.   Quercus aquatica.   Clayton.   Query?
Ground oak.   Quercus pumila.   Clayton.
Live oak.   Quercus Virginiana.   Millar.
Black Birch.   Betula nigra.
White birch.   Betula alba.
Beach.   Fagus sylvatica.
Ash.   Fraxinus Americana.
        Fraxinus Novæ Angliæ.   Millar.
Elm.   Ulmus Americana.
Willow.   Salix.   Query species?
Sweet Gum.   Liquidambar styraciflua.

The following were found in Virginia when first visited by
the English; but it is not said whether of spontaneous
growth, or by cultivation only. Most probably they were natives of more southern climates, and handed along the continent from one nation to another of the savages.

Tobacco.   Nicotiana.
Maize.   Zea mays.
Round potatoes.   Solanum tuberosum.
Pumpkins.   Cucurbita pepo.
Cymlings.   Cucurbita verrucosa.
Squashes.   Cucurbita melopepo.

There is an infinitude of other plants and flowers, for an
enumeration and scientific description of which I must refer
to the Flora Virginica of our great botanist Dr. Clayton, published by Gronovius at Leyden, in 1762. This accurate observer was a native and resident of this state, passed a long
life in exploring and describing its plants, and is supposed to
have enlarged the botanical catalogue as much as almost any
man who has lived.

Besides these plants, which are native, our *Farms* produce
wheat, rye, barley, oats, buck wheat, broom corn, and Indian
corn. The climate suits rice well enough wherever the lands
do. Tobacco, hemp, flax, and cotton, are staple commodities.
Indico yields two cuttings. The silk-worm is a native, and the
mulberry, proper for its food, grows kindly.

We cultivate also potatoes, both the long and the round,
turnips, carrots, parsneps, pumpkins, and ground nuts (Ar-
achis.) Our grasses are Lucerne, St. Foin, Burnet, Timothy,

ray and orchard grass; red, white, and yellow clover; green-swerd, blue grass, and crab grass.

The *gardens* yield musk melons, water melons, tomatas, okra, pomegranates, figs, and the esculent plants of Europe.

The *orchards* produce apples, pears, cherries, quinces, peaches, nectarines, apricots, almonds, and plumbs.

Our quadrupeds have been mostly described by Linnæus and Mons. de Buffon. Of these the Mam-moth, or big buffalo, as called by the Indians, must certainly have been the largest. Their tradition is, that he was carnivo-rous, and still exists in the northern parts of America. A delega-tion of warriors from the Delaware tribe having visited the governor of Virginia, during the present revolution, on matters of business, after these had been discussed and settled in coun-cil, the governor asked them some questions relative to their country, and, among others, what they knew or had heard of the animal whose bones were found at the Saltlicks, on the Ohio. Their chief speaker immediately put himself into an atti-tude of oratory, and with a pomp suited to what he conceived the elevation of his subject, informed him that it was a tradition handed down from their fathers, 'That in antient times a herd of these tremendous animals came to the Big-bone licks, and began an universal destruction of the bear, deer, elks, buffa-loes, and other animals, which had been created for the use of the Indians: that the Great Man above, looking down and seeing this, was so enraged that he seized his lightning, de-scended on the earth, seated himself on a neighbouring mountain, on a rock, of which his seat and the print of his feet are still to be seen, and hurled his bolts among them till the whole were slaughtered, except the big bull, who present-ing his forehead to the shafts, shook them off as they fell; but missing one at length, it wounded him in the side; whereon, springing round, he bounded over the Ohio, over the Wa-bash, the Illinois, and finally over the great lakes, where he is living at this day.' It is well known that on the Ohio, and in many parts of America further north, tusks, grinders, and skeletons of unparalleled magnitude, are found in great num-bers, some lying on the surface of the earth, and some a little below it. A Mr. Stanley, taken prisoner by the Indians near the mouth of the Tanissee, relates, that, after being transferred

Animals *(margin note)*

through several tribes, from one to another, he was at length carried over the mountains west of the Missouri to a river which runs westwardly; that these bones abounded there; and that the natives described to him the animal to which they belonged as still existing in the northern parts of their country; from which description he judged it to be an elephant. Bones of the same kind have been lately found, some feet below the surface of the earth, in salines opened on the North Holston, a branch of the Tanissee, about the latitude of 36½°. North. From the accounts published in Europe, I suppose it to be decided, that these are of the same kind with those found in Siberia. Instances are mentioned of like animal remains found in the more southern climates of both hemispheres; but they are either so loosely mentioned as to leave a doubt of the fact, so inaccurately described as not to authorize the classing them with the great northern bones, or so rare as to found a suspicion that they have been carried thither as curiosities from more northern regions. So that on the whole there seem to be no certain vestiges of the existence of this animal further south than the salines last mentioned. It is remarkable that the tusks and skeletons have been ascribed by the naturalists of Europe to the elephant, while the grinders have been given to the hippopotamus, or river-horse. Yet it is acknowledged, that the tusks and skeletons are much larger than those of the elephant, and the grinders many times greater than those of the hippopotamus, and essentially different in form. Wherever these grinders are found, there also we find the tusks and skeleton; but no skeleton of the hippopotamus nor grinders of the elephant. It will not be said that the hippopotamus and elephant came always to the same spot, the former to deposit his grinders, and the latter his tusks and skeleton. For what became of the parts not deposited there? We must agree then that these remains belong to each other, that they are of one and the same animal, that this was not a hippopotamus, because the hippopotamus had no tusks nor such a frame, and because the grinders differ in their size as well as in the number and form of their points. That it was not an elephant, I think ascertained by proofs equally decisive. I will not avail myself of the authority of the celebrated *anatomist, who, from an examination of the form and structure of the tusks, has declared they were essentially different from those of the elephant; because another †anatomist, equally celebrated, has declared, on a like examination, that they are precisely the same. Between two such authorities I will suppose this circumstance equivocal. But, 1. The skeleton of the mammoth (for so the incognitum has been called) bespeaks an animal of five or six times the cubic volume of the elephant, as Mons. de Buffon has admitted. 2. The grinders are five times as large, are square, and the grinding surface studded with four or five rows of blunt points: whereas those of the elephant are broad and thin, and their grinding surface flat. 3. I have never heard an instance, and suppose there has been none, of the grinder of an elephant being found in America. 4. From the known temperature and constitution of the elephant he could never have existed in those regions where the remains of the mammoth have been found. The elephant is a native only of the torrid zone and its vicinities: if, with the assistance of warm apartments and warm clothing, he has been preserved in life in the temperate climates of Europe, it has only been for a small portion of what would have been his natural period, and no instance of his multiplication in them has ever been known. But no bones of the mammoth, as I have before observed, have been ever found further south than the salines of the Holston, and they have been found as far north as the Arctic circle. Those, therefore, who are of opinion that the elephant and mammoth are the same, must believe, 1. That the elephant known to us can exist and multiply in the frozen zone; or, 2. That an internal fire may once have warmed those regions, and since abandoned them, of which, however, the globe exhibits no unequivocal indications; or, 3. That the obliquity of the ecliptic, when these elephants lived, was so great as to include within the tropics all those regions in which the bones are found; the tropics being, as is before observed, the natural limits of habitation for the elephant. But if it be admitted that this obliquity has

*Hunter.
†D'Aubenton.

really decreased, and we adopt the highest rate of decrease yet pretended, that is, of one minute in a century, to transfer the northern tropic to the Arctic circle, would carry the existence of these supposed elephants 250,000 years back; a period far beyond our conception of the duration of animal bones left exposed to the open air, as these are in many instances. Besides, though these regions would then be supposed within the tropics, yet their winters would have been too severe for the sensibility of the elephant. They would have had too but one day and one night in the year, a circumstance to which we have no reason to suppose the nature of the elephant fitted. However, it has been demonstrated, that, if a variation of obliquity in the ecliptic takes place at all, it is vibratory, and never exceeds the limits of 9 degrees, which is not sufficient to bring these bones within the tropics. One of these hypotheses, or some other equally voluntary and inadmissible to cautious philosophy, must be adopted to support the opinion that these are the bones of the elephant. For my own part, I find it easier to believe that an animal may have existed, resembling the elephant in his tusks, and general anatomy, while his nature was in other respects extremely different. From the 30th degree of South latitude to the 30th of North, are nearly the limits which nature has fixed for the existence and multiplication of the elephant known to us. Proceeding thence northwardly to 36½ degrees, we enter those assigned to the mammoth. The further we advance North, the more their vestiges multiply as far as the earth has been explored in that direction; and it is as probable as otherwise, that this progression continues to the pole itself, if land extends so far. The center of the Frozen zone then may be the Achmé of their vigour, as that of the Torrid is of the elephant. Thus nature seems to have drawn a belt of separation between these two tremendous animals, whose breadth indeed is not precisely known, though at present we may suppose it about 6½ degrees of latitude; to have assigned to the elephant the regions South of these confines, and those North to the mammoth, founding the constitution of the one in her extreme of heat, and that of the other in the extreme of cold. When the Creator has therefore separated their nature as far as the extent of the scale of animal life allowed to this planet would

permit, it seems perverse to declare it the same, from a partial resemblance of their tusks and bones. But to whatever animal we ascribe these remains, it is certain such a one has existed in America, and that it has been the largest of all terrestrial beings. It should have sufficed to have rescued the earth it inhabited, and the atmosphere it breathed, from the imputation of impotence in the conception and nourishment of animal life on a large scale: to have stifled, in its birth, the opinion of a writer, the most learned too of all others in the science of animal history, that in the new world, Buffon.
'La nature vivante est beaucoup moins agissante, xviii. 122. ed. beaucoup moins forte:' that nature is less active, Paris. 1764. less energetic on one side of the globe than she is on the other. As if both sides were not warmed by the same genial sun; as if a soil of the same chemical composition, was less capable of elaboration into animal nutriment; as if the fruits and grains from that soil and sun, yielded a less rich chyle, gave less extension to the solids and fluids of the body, or produced sooner in the cartilages, membranes, and fibres, that rigidity which restrains all further extension, and terminates animal growth. The truth is, that a Pigmy and a Patagonian, a Mouse and a Mammoth, derive their dimensions from the same nutritive juices. The difference of increment depends on circumstances unsearchable to beings with our capacities. Every race of animals seems to have received from their Maker certain laws of extension at the time of their formation. Their elaborative organs were formed to produce this, while proper obstacles were opposed to its further progress. Below these limits they cannot fall, nor rise above them. What intermediate station they shall take may depend on soil, on climate, on food, on a careful choice of breeders. But all the manna of heaven would never raise the Mouse to the bulk of the Mammoth.

The opinion advanced by the Count de Buffon, xviii. 100 is 1. That the animals common both to the old and –156. new world, are smaller in the latter. 2. That those peculiar to the new, are on a smaller scale. 3. That those which have been domesticated in both, have degenerated in America: and 4. That on the whole it exhibits fewer species. And the reason he thinks is, that the heats of America are less; that more waters are spread over its surface by nature, and fewer of these drained off by the hand of man. In other words, that *heat* is friendly, and *moisture* adverse to the production and developement of large quadrupeds. I will not meet this hypothesis on its first doubtful ground, whether the climate of America be comparatively more humid? Because we are not furnished with observations sufficient to decide this question. And though, till it be decided, we are as free to deny, as others are to affirm the fact, yet for a moment let it be supposed. The hypothesis, after this supposition, proceeds to another; that *moisture* is unfriendly to animal growth. The truth of this is inscrutable to us by reasonings a priori. Nature has hidden from us her modus agendi. Our only appeal on such questions is to experience; and I think that experience is against the supposition. It is by the assistance of *heat* and *moisture* that vegetables are elaborated from the elements of earth, air, water, and fire. We accordingly see the more humid climates produce the greater quantity of vegetables. Vegetables are mediately or immediately the food of every animal: and in proportion to the quantity of food, we see animals not only multiplied in their numbers, but improved in their bulk, as far as the laws of their nature will admit. Of this opinion is the Count de Buffon himself in another part of his work: 'en general il paroit que les pays un peu *froids* conviennent mieux à nos boeufs que les pays chauds, et qu'ils sont d'autant plus gros et plus grands que le climat est plus *humide* et plus abondans en paturages. Les boeufs de Danemarck, de la Podolie, de l'Ukraine et de la Tartarie qu'habitent les Calmouques sont les plus grands de tous.' Here then a race of animals, and one of the largest too, has been increased in its dimensions by *cold* and *moisture*, in direct opposition to the hypothesis, which supposes that these two circumstances diminish animal bulk, and that it is their contraries *heat* and *dryness* which enlarge it. But when we appeal to experience, we are not to rest satisfied with a single fact. Let us therefore try our question on more general ground. Let us take two portions of the earth, Europe and America for instance, sufficiently extensive to give operation to general causes; let us consider the circumstances peculiar to each, and observe their

viii. 134.

effect on animal nature. America, running through the torrid as well as temperate zone, has more *heat*, collectively taken, than Europe. But Europe, according to our hypothesis, is the *dryest*. They are equally adapted then to animal productions; each being endowed with one of those causes which befriend animal growth, and with one which opposes it. If it be thought unequal to compare Europe with America, which is so much larger, I answer, not more so than to compare America with the whole world. Besides, the purpose of the comparison is to try an hypothesis, which makes the size of animals depend on the *heat* and *moisture* of climate. If therefore we take a region, so extensive as to comprehend a sensible distinction of climate, and so extensive too as that local accidents, or the intercourse of animals on its borders, may not materially affect the size of those in its interior parts, we shall comply with those conditions which the hypothesis may reasonably demand. The objection would be the weaker in the present case, because any intercourse of animals which may take place on the confines of Europe and Asia, is to the advantage of the former, Asia producing certainly larger animals than Europe. Let us then take a comparative view of the Quadrupeds of Europe and America, presenting them to the eye in three different tables, in one of which shall be enumerated those found in both countries; in a second those found in one only; in a third those which have been domesticated in both. To facilitate the comparison, let those of each table be arranged in gradation according to their sizes, from the greatest to the smallest, so far as their sizes can be conjectured. The weights of the large animals shall be expressed in the English avoirdupoise pound and its decimals: those of the smaller in the ounce and its decimals. Those which are marked thus *, are actual weights of particular subjects, deemed among the largest of their species. Those marked thus †, are furnished by judicious persons, well acquainted with the species, and saying, from conjecture only, what the largest individual they had seen would probably have weighed. The other weights are taken from Messrs. Buffon and D'Aubenton, and are of such subjects as came casually to their hands for dissection. This circumstance must be remembered where

A comparative View of the Quadrupeds of Europe
and of America.

I. *Aboriginals of both.*

	Europe.	America.
	lb.	lb.
Mammoth		
Buffalo. Bison		*1800
White bear. Ours blanc		
Caribou. Renne		
Bear. Ours	153.7	*410
Elk. Elan. Orignal, palmated		
Red deer. Cerf	288.8	*273
Fallow deer. Daim	167.8	
Wolf. Loup	69.8	
Roe. Chevreuil	56.7	
Glutton. Glouton. Carcajou		
Wild cat. Chat sauvage		†30
Lynx. Loup cervier	25.	
Beaver. Castor	18.5	*45
Badger. Blaireau	13.6	
Red Fox. Renard	13.5	
Grey Fox. Isatis		
Otter. Loutre	8.9	†12
Monax. Marmotte	6.5	
Vison. Fouine	2.8	
Hedgehog. Herisson	2.2	
Martin. Marte	1.9	†6
	oz.	
Water rat. Rat d'eau	7.5	
Wesel. Belette	2.2	oz.
Flying squirrel. Polatouche	2.2	†4
Shrew mouse. Musaraigne	1.	

their weights and mine stand opposed: the latter being stated, not to produce a conclusion in favour of the American species, but to justify a suspension of opinion until we are better informed, and a suspicion in the mean time that there is no uniform difference in favour of either; which is all I pretend.

II. *Aboriginals of one only.*

Europe.		America.	
	lb.		lb.
Sanglier. Wild boar	280.	Tapir	534.
Mouflon. Wild sheep	56.	Elk, round horned	†450.
Bouquetin. Wild goat		Puma	
Lievre. Hare	7.6	Jaguar	218.
Lapin. Rabbet	3.4	Cabiai	109.
Putois. Polecat	3.3	Tamanoir	109.
Genette	3.1	Tamandua	65.4
Desman. Muskrat	oz.	Cougar of N. Amer.	75.
Ecureuil. Squirrel	12.	Cougar of S. Amer.	59.4
Hermine. Ermin	8.2	Ocelot	
Rat. Rat	7.5	Pecari	46.3
Loirs	3.1	Jaguaret	43.6
Lerot. Dormouse	1.8	Alco	
Taupe. Mole	1.2	Lama	
Hamster	.9	Paco	
Zisel		Paca	32.7
Leming		Serval	
Souris. Mouse	.6	Sloth. Unau	27 ¼
		Saricovienne	
		Kincajou	
		Tatou Kabassou	21.8
		Urson. Urchin	
		Raccoon. Raton	16.5
		Coati	
		Coendou	16.3
		Sloth. Aï	13.
		Sapajou Ouarini	
		Sapajou Coaita	9.8
		Tatou Encubert	
		Tatou Apar	
		Tatou Cachica	7.
		Little Coendou	6.5
		Opossum. Sarigue	
		Tapeti	
		Margay	
		Crabier	
		Agouti	4.2
		Sapajou Saï	3.5
		Tatou Cirquinçon	
		Tatou Tatouate	3.3

II. Table continued.

Europe.	America.	
	Mouffette Squash	
	Mouffette Chinche	
	Mouffette Conepate.	
	Scunk	
	Mouffette. Zorilla	
	Whabus. Hare. Rabbet	
	Aperea	
	Akouchi	
	Ondatra. Muskrat	
	Pilori	
	Great grey squirrel	†2.7
	Fox squirrel of Virginia	†2.625
	Surikate	2.
	Mink	†2.
	Sapajou. Sajou	1.8
	Indian pig. Cochon	
	d'Inde	1.6
	Sapajou. Saïmiri	1.5
	Phalanger	
	Coquallin	
	Lesser grey squirrel	†1.5
	Black squirrel	†1.5
	Red squirrel	10. oz.
	Sagoin Saki	
	Sagoin Pinche	
	Sagoin Tamarin	oz.
	Sagoin Ouistiti	4.4
	Sagoin Marikine	
	Sagoin Mico	
	Cayopollin	
	Fourmillier	
	Marmose	
	Sarigue of Cayenne	
	Tucan	
	Red mole	oz.
	Ground squirrel	4.

III. *Domesticated in both.*

	Europe.	America.
	lb.	lb.
Cow	763.	*2500
Horse		*1366
Ass		
Hog		*1200
Sheep		*125
Goat		*80
Dog	67.6	
Cat	7.	

I have not inserted in the first table the *Phoca nor leather-winged bat, because the one living half the year in the water, and the other being a winged animal, the individuals of each species may visit both continents.

Of the animals in the 1st table Mons. de Buffon himself informs us, [XXVII. 130. XXX. 213.] that the beaver, the otter, and shrew mouse, though of the same species, are larger in America than Europe. This should therefore have corrected the generality of his expressions XVIII. 145. and elsewhere, that the animals common to the two countries, are considerably less in America than in Europe, ' & cela sans aucune exception.' He tells us too, [Quadrup. VIII. 334. edit. Paris, 1777] that on examining a bear from America, he remarked no difference, 'dans *la forme* de cet ours d'Amerique comparé a celui d'Europe.' But adds from Bartram's journal, that an American bear weighed 400 lb. English, equal to 367 lb. French: whereas we find the European bear examined by Mons. D'Aubenton, [XVII. 82.] weighed but 141 lb. French. That the palmated Elk is larger in America than Europe we are informed by Kalm, a Naturalist who visited the former by public appointment for the express I. 233. Lond. 1772.

---

*It is said, that this animal is seldom seen above 30 miles from shore, or beyond the 56th degree of latitude. The interjacent islands between Asia and America admit his passing from one continent to the other without exceeding these bounds. And, in fact, travellers tell us that these islands are places of principal resort for them, and especially in the season of bringing forth their young.

purpose of examining the subjects of Natural history. In this
fact Pennant concurs with him. [Barrington's Mis-
cellanies.] The same Kalm tells us that the Black Moose, or
Renne of America, is as high as a tall horse; and
Catesby, that it is about the bigness of a middle sized ox. The
same account of their size has been given me by many
who have seen them. But Mons. D'Aubenton says
that the Renne of Europe is but about the size of a Red-deer.
The wesel is larger in America than in Europe, as
may be seen by comparing its dimensions as reported
by Mons. D'Aubenton and Kalm. The latter tells us, that the
lynx, badger, red fox, and flying squirrel, are the
same in America as in Europe: by which expression
I understand, they are the same in all material circumstances, in size as well as others: for if they were smaller,
they would differ from the European. Our grey fox
is, by Catesby's account, little different in size and
shape from the European fox. I presume he means the red fox
of Europe, as does Kalm, where he says, that in size
'they do not quite come up to our foxes.' For proceeding next to the red fox of America, he says 'they are entirely the same with the European sort.' Which shews he had in
view one European sort only, which was the red. So that the
result of their testimony is, that the American grey fox is somewhat less than the European red; which is equally true of the
grey fox of Europe, as may be seen by comparing the
measures of the Count de Buffon and Mons. D'Aubenton. The white bear of America is as large as that
of Europe. The bones of the Mammoth which
have been found in America, are as large as those found in the
old world. It may be asked, why I insert the Mammoth, as if it
still existed? I ask in return, why I should omit it, as if it did
not exist? Such is the œconomy of nature, that no instance
can be produced of her having permitted any one race of her
animals to become extinct; of her having formed any link in
her great work so weak as to be broken. To add to this, the
traditionary testimony of the Indians, that this animal still exists in the northern and western parts of America, would be
adding the light of a taper to that of the meridian sun. Those
parts still remain in their aboriginal state, unexplored and un-

Ib. 233.

I. xxvii.

XXIV. 162.

XV. 42.

I. 359. I. 48.
221. 251. II.
52.

II. 78.

I. 220.

XXVII. 63.
XIV. 119.
Harris,
II.387.
Buffon.
Quad. IX. 1.

disturbed by us, or by others for us. He may as well exist there now, as he did formerly where we find his bones. If he be a carnivorous animal, as some Anatomists have conjectured, and the Indians affirm, his early retirement may be accounted for from the general destruction of the wild game by the Indians, which commences in the first instant of their connection with us, for the purpose of purchasing matchcoats, hatchets, and fire locks, with their skins. There remain then the buffalo, red deer, fallow deer, wolf, roe, glutton, wild cat, monax, vison, hedge-hog, martin, and water rat, of the comparative sizes of which we have not sufficient testimony. It does not appear that Messrs. de Buffon and D'Aubenton have measured, weighed, or seen those of America. It is said of some of them, by some travellers, that they are smaller than the European. But who were these travellers? Have they not been men of a very different description from those who have laid open to us the other three quarters of the world? Was natural history the object of their travels? Did they measure or weigh the animals they speak of? or did they not judge of them by sight, or perhaps even from report only? Were they acquainted with the animals of their own country, with which they undertake to compare them? Have they not been so ignorant as often to mistake the species? A true answer to these questions would probably lighten their authority, so as to render it insufficient for the foundation of an hypothesis. How unripe we yet are, for an accurate comparison of the animals of the two countries, will appear from the work of Mons. de Buffon. The ideas we should have formed of the sizes of some animals, from the information he had received at his first publications concerning them, are very different from what his subsequent communications give us. And indeed his candour in this can never be too much praised. One sentence of his book must do him immortal honour. 'J'aime autant une personne qui me releve d'une erreur, qu'une autre qui m'apprend une verité, parce qu'en effet une erreur corrigée est une verité.' He seems to have thought the Cabiai he first examined wanted little of its full growth. 'Il n'etoit pas encore tout-a-fait adulte.' Yet he weighed but 46½ lb. and he found afterwards, that these animals, when full grown,

Quad. IX. 158.

XXV. 184.

Quad. IX. 132.

weigh 100 lb. He had supposed, from the examination of a
jaguar, said to be two years old, which weighed but
16 lb. 12 oz. that, when he should have acquired his
full growth, he would not be larger than a middle sized dog.
But a subsequent account raises his weight to 200
lb. Further information will, doubtless, produce
further corrections. The wonder is, not that there is yet something in this great work to correct, but that there is so little.
The result of this view then is, that of 26 quadrupeds common to both countries, 7 are said to be larger in America, 7
of equal size, and 12 not sufficiently examined. So that the first
table impeaches the first member of the assertion, that of the
animals common to both countries, the American are smallest, 'et cela sans aucune exception.' It shews it not just, in all
the latitude in which its author has advanced it, and probably
not to such a degree as to found a distinction between the
two countries.

Proceeding to the second table, which arranges the animals
found in one of the two countries only, Mons. de Buffon
observes, that the tapir, the elephant of America, is but of the
size of a small cow. To preserve our comparison, I will add
that the wild boar, the elephant of Europe, is little more than
half that size. I have made an elk with round or cylindrical
horns, an animal of America, and peculiar to it; because I
have seen many of them myself, and more of their horns; and
because I can say, from the best information, that, in Virginia,
this kind of elk has abounded much, and still exists in smaller
numbers; and I could never learn that the palmated kind had
been seen here at all. I suppose this confined to the more
Northern latitudes*. I have made our hare or rabbet peculiar,

*The descriptions of Theodat, Denys and La Hontan, cited by Mons. de
Buffon under the article Elan, authorize the supposition, that the flat-horned
elk is found in the northern parts of America. It has not however extended
to our latitudes. On the other hand, I could never learn that the round-
horned elk has been seen further North than the Hudson's river. This agrees
with the former elk in its general character, being, like that, when compared
with a deer, very much larger, its ears longer, broader, and thicker in proportion, its hair much longer, neck and tail shorter, having a dewlap before
the breast (caruncula gutturalis Linnæi) a white spot often, if not always; of
a foot diameter, on the hinder part of the buttocks round the tail; its gait a
trot, and attended with a rattling of the hoofs: but distinguished from that

XIX. 2.

Quad. IX.
41.

believing it to be different from both the European animals of those denominations, and calling it therefore by its Algon-quin name Whabus, to keep it distinct from these. Kalm is of the same opinion. I have enumer-ated the squirrels according to our own knowledge, derived from daily sight of them, because I am not able to reconcile with that the European appellations and descriptions. I have heard of other species, but they have never come within my own notice. These, I think, are the only instances in which I have departed from the authority of Mons. de Buffon in the construction of this table. I take him for my ground work, because I think him the best informed of any Naturalist who has ever written. The result is, that there are 18 quadrupeds peculiar to Europe; more than four times as many, to wit 74,

Kalm II. 340.I. 82.

---

decisively by its horns, which are not palmated, but round and pointed. This is the animal described by Catesby as the Cervus major Americanus, the Stag of America, le Cerf de l'Amerique. But it differs from the Cervus as totally, as does the palmated elk from the dama. And in fact it seems to stand in the same relation to the palmated elk, as the red deer does to the fallow. It has abounded in Virginia, has been seen, within my knowledge, on the Eastern side of the Blue ridge since the year 1765, is now common beyond those mountains, has been often brought to us and tamed, and their horns are in the hands of many. I should designate it as the 'Alces Americanus cornibus teretibus.' It were to be wished, that Naturalists, who are acquainted with the renne and elk of Europe, and who may hereafter visit the northern parts of America, would examine well the animals called there by the names of grey and black moose, caribou, orignal, and elk. Mons. de Buffon has done what could be done from the materials in his hands, towards clearing up the confusion introduced by the loose application of these names among the an-imals they are meant to designate. He reduces the whole to the renne and flat-horned elk. From all the information I have been able to collect, I strongly suspect they will be found to cover three, if not four distinct species of animals. I have seen skins of a moose, and of the caribou: they differ more from each other, and from that of the round-horned elk, than I ever saw two skins differ which belonged to different individuals of any wild species. These differences are in the colour, length, and coarseness of the hair, and in the size, texture, and marks of the skin. Perhaps it will be found that there is, 1. the moose, black and grey, the former being said to be the male, and the latter the female. 2. The caribou or renne. 3. The flat-horned elk, or orignal. 4. The round-horned elk. Should this last, though possessing so nearly the characters of the elk, be found to be the same with the Cerf d'Ardennes or Brandhirtz of Germany, still there will remain the three species first enumerated.

peculiar to America; that the *first of these 74 weighs more than the whole column of Europeans; and consequently this second table disproves the second member of the assertion, that the animals peculiar to the new world are on a smaller scale, so far as that assertion relied on European animals for support: and it is in full opposition to the theory which makes the animal volume to depend on the circumstances of *heat* and *moisture*.

The IIId. table comprehends those quadrupeds only which are domestic in both countries. That some of these, in some parts of America, have become less than their original stock, is doubtless true; and the reason is very obvious. In a thinly peopled country, the spontaneous productions of the forests and waste fields are sufficient to support indifferently the do-mestic animals of the farmer, with a very little aid from him in the severest and scarcest season. He therefore finds it more convenient to receive them from the hand of nature in that indifferent state, than to keep up their size by a care and nourishment which would cost him much labour. If, on this low fare, these animals dwindle, it is no more than they do in those parts of Europe where the poverty of the soil, or pov-erty of the owner, reduces them to the same scanty subsis-tance. It is the uniform effect of one and the same cause, whether acting on this or that side of the globe. It would be erring therefore against that rule of philosophy, which teaches us to ascribe like effects to like causes, should we impute this diminution of size in America to any imbecility or want of uniformity in the operations of nature. It may be affirmed with truth that, in those countries, and with those individuals of America, where necessity or curiosity has produced equal attention as in Europe to the nourishment of animals, the horses, cattle, sheep, and hogs of the one continent are as

*The Tapir is the largest of the animals peculiar to America. I collect his weight thus. Mons. de Buffon says, XXIII. 274. that he is of the size of a Zebu, or a small cow. He gives us the measures of a Zebu, ib. 94. as taken by himself, viz. 5 feet 7 inches from the muzzle to the root of the tail, and 5 feet 1 inch circumference behind the fore legs. A bull, measuring in the same way 6 feet 9 inches and 5 feet 2 inches, weighed 600 lb. VIII. 153. The Zebu then, and of course the Tapir, would weigh about 500 lb. But one individual of every species of European peculiars would probably weigh less than 400 lb. These are French measures and weights.

large as those of the other. There are particular instances, well
attested, where individuals of this country have imported
good breeders from England, and have improved their size by
care in the course of some years. To make a fair comparison
between the two countries, it will not answer to bring together animals of what might be deemed the middle or ordinary size of their species; because an error in judging of that
middle or ordinary size would vary the result of the comparison. Thus Monsieur D'Aubenton considers a
horse of 4 feet 5 inches high and 400 lb. weight   VII. 432.
French, equal to 4 feet 8.6 inches and 436 lb. English, as a middle sized horse. Such a one is deemed a small horse in America.
The extremes must therefore be resorted to. The same anatomist dissected a horse of 5 feet 9 inches height, French measure,
equal to 6 feet 1.7 English. This is near 6 inches
higher than any horse I have seen: and could it be   VII. 474.
supposed that I had seen the largest horses in America, the
conclusion would be, that ours have diminished, or that we
have bred from a smaller stock. In Connecticut and Rhode-
Island, where the climate is favorable to the production of grass,
bullocks have been slaughtered which weighed 2500, 2200, and
2100 lb. nett; and those of 1800 lb. have been frequent. I have
seen a *hog weigh 1050 lb. after the blood, bowels, and hair
had been taken from him. Before he was killed an attempt
was made to weigh him with a pair of steel-yards, graduated
to 1200 lb. but he weighed more. Yet this hog was probably
not within fifty generations of the European stock. I am well
informed of another which weighed 1100 lb. gross. Asses have
been still more neglected than any other domestic animal in
America. They are neither fed nor housed in the most rigorous season of the year. Yet they are larger than those measured by Mons. D'Aubenton, of 3 feet 7¼ inches, 3   VIII. 48. 35.
feet 4 inches, and 3 feet 2½ inches, the latter weigh-   66.
ing only 215.8 lb. These sizes, I suppose, have been produced
by the same negligence in Europe, which has produced a like
diminution here. Where care has been taken of them on that
side of the water, they have been raised to a size bordering
on that of the horse; not by the *heat* and *dryness* of the cli-

---

*In Williamsburg, April, 1769.

mate, but by good food and shelter. Goats have been also much neglected in America. Yet they are very prolific here, bearing twice or three times a year, and from one to five kids at a birth. Mons. de Buffon has been sensible of a difference in this circumstance in favour of America. But what are their greatest weights I cannot say. A large sheep here weighs 100 lb. I observe Mons. D'Aubenton calls a ram of 62 lb. one of the middle size. But to say what are the extremes of growth in these and the other domestic animals of America, would require information of which no one individual is possessed. The weights actually known and stated in the third table preceding will suffice to shew, that we may conclude, on probable grounds, that, with equal food and care, the climate of America will preserve the races of domestic animals as large as the European stock from which they are derived; and consequently that the third member of Mons. de Buffon's assertion, that the domestic animals are subject to degeneration from the climate of America, is as probably wrong as the first and second were certainly so.

XVIII. 96.

IX. 41.

That the last part of it is erroneous, which affirms that the species of American quadrupeds are comparatively few, is evident from the tables taken all together. By these it appears that there are an hundred species aboriginal of America. Mons. de Buffon supposes about double that number existing on the whole earth. Of these Europe, Asia, and Africa, furnish suppose 126; that is, the 26 common to Europe and America, and about 100 which are not in America at all. The American species then are to those of the rest of the earth, as 100 to 126, or 4 to 5. But the residue of the earth being double the extent of America, the exact proportion would have been but as 4 to 8.

XXX. 219.

Hitherto I have considered this hypothesis as applied to brute animals only, and not in its extension to the man of America, whether aboriginal or transplanted. It is the opinion of Mons. de Buffon that the former furnishes no exception to it. 'Quoique le sauvage du nouveau monde soit à-peu-près de même stature que l'homme de notre monde, cela ne suffit pas pour qu'il puisse faire une exception au fait général du rapetissement de la nature vivante dans tout

XVIII. 146.

ce continent: le sauvage est foible & petit par les organes de la
génération; il n'a ni poil, ni barbe, & nulle ardeur pour sa
femelle; quoique plus léger que l'Européen parce qu'il a plus
d'habitude à courir, il est cependant beaucoup moins fort de
corps; il est aussi bien moins sensible, & cependant plus crain-
tif & plus lâche; il n'a nulle vivacité, nulle activité dans l'ame;
celle du corps est moins un exercice, un mouvement volon-
taire qu'une nécessité d'action causée par le besoin; otez lui la
faim & la soif, vous détruirez en meme temps le principe actif
de tous ses mouvemens; il demeurera stupidement en repos
sur ses jambes ou couché pendant des jours entiers. Il ne faut
pas aller chercher plus loin la cause de la vie dispersée des
sauvages & de leur éloignement pour la société: la plus pré-
cieuse étincelle du feu de la nature leur a été refusée; ils man-
quent d'ardeur pour leur femelle, & par consequent d'amour
pour leur semblables: ne connoissant pas l'attachement le plus
vif, le plus tendre de tous, leurs autres sentimens de ce genre
sont froids & languissans; ils aiment foiblement leurs pères &
leurs enfans; la société la plus intime de toutes, celle de la
même famille, n'a donc chez eux que de foibles liens; la société d'une famille à l'autre n'en a point du tout: dès lors nulle
réunion, nulle république, nulle ètat social. La physique de
l'amour fait chez eux le moral des mœurs; leur cœur est glacé,
leur société froide, & leur empire dur. Ils ne regardent leurs
femmes que comme des servantes de peine ou des bêtes de
somme qu'ils chargent, sans ménagement, du fardeau de leur
chasse, & qu'ils forcent sans pitié, sans reconnoissance, à des
ouvrages qui souvent sont audessus de leurs forces: ils n'ont
que peu d'enfans; ils en ont peu de soin; tout se ressent de
leur premier défaut; ils sont indifférents parce qu'ils sont peu
puissans, & cette indifférence pour le sexe est la tâche origi-
nelle qui flétrit la nature, qui l'empêche de s'épanouir, & qui
détruisant les germes de la vie, coupe en même temps la racine de la société. L'homme ne fait donc point d'exception ici.
La nature en lui refusant les puissances de l'amour l'a plus
maltraité & plus rapetissé qu'aucun des animaux.' An afflicting picture indeed, which, for the honor of human nature, I
am glad to believe has no original. Of the Indian of South
America I know nothing; for I would not honor with the
appellation of knowledge, what I derive from the fables pub-

lished of them. These I believe to be just as true as the fables of Æsop. This belief is founded on what I have seen of man, white, red, and black, and what has been written of him by authors, enlightened themselves, and writing amidst an enlightened people. The Indian of North America being more within our reach, I can speak of him somewhat from my own knowledge, but more from the information of others better acquainted with him, and on whose truth and judgment I can rely. From these sources I am able to say, in contradiction to this representation, that he is neither more defective in ardor, nor more impotent with his female, than the white reduced to the same diet and exercise: that he is brave, when an enterprize depends on bravery; education with him making the point of honor consist in the destruction of an enemy by stratagem, and in the preservation of his own person free from injury; or perhaps this is nature; while it is education which teaches us to *honor force more than finesse: that he will defend himself against an host of enemies, always chusing to be killed, rather than to †surrender, though it be to the

*Sol Rodomonte sprezza di venire
  Se non, dove la via meno è sicura.   Ariosto. 14. 117.

†In so judicious an author as Don Ulloa, and one to whom we are indebted for the most precise information we have of South America, I did not expect to find such assertions as the following. 'Los Indios vencidos son los mas cobardes y pusilanimes que se peuden vér:—se hacen inocentes, se humillan hasta el desprecio, disculpan su inconsiderado arrojo, y con las súplicas y los ruegos dán seguras pruebas de su pusilanimidad.—ó lo que resieren las historias de la Conquista, sobre sus grandes acciones, es en un sentido figurado, ó el caracter de estas gentes no es ahora segun era entonces; pero lo que no tiene duda es, que las Naciones de la parte Septentrional subsisten en la misma libertad que siempre han tenido, sin haber sido sojuzgados por algun Principe extrano, y que viven segun su régimen y costumbres de toda la vida, sin que haya habido motivo para que muden de caracter; y en estos se vé lo mismo, que sucede en los del Peru, y de toda la América Meridional, reducidos, y que nunca lo han estado.' Noticias Americanas. Entretenimiento XVIII. §. 1. Don Ulloa here admits, that the authors who have described the Indians of South America, before they were enslaved, had represented them as a brave people, and therefore seems to have suspected that the cowardice which he had observed in those of the present race might be the effect of subjugation. But, supposing the Indians of North America to be cowards also, he concludes the ancestors of those of South America to have been so too, and therefore that those authors have given fictions for truths. He was probably not acquainted himself with the Indians of North America, and had formed his opinion of them from hear-say. Great numbers of French, of En-

whites, who he knows will treat him well: that in other situations also he meets death with more deliberation, and endures tortures with a firmness unknown almost to religious enthusiasm with us: that he is affectionate to his children, careful of them, and indulgent in the extreme: that his affections comprehend his other connections, weakening, as with us, from circle to circle, as they recede from the center: that his friendships are strong and faithful to the uttermost *extremity: that his sensibility is keen, even the warriors weeping most bitterly on the loss of their children, though in general they endeavour to appear superior to human events: that his vivacity and activity of mind is equal to ours in the same situation; hence his eagerness for hunting, and for games of chance. The women are submitted to unjust drudgery. This I believe is the case with every barbarous people. With such, force is law. The stronger sex therefore imposes on the weaker. It is civilization alone which replaces women in the

---

glish, and of Americans, are perfectly acquainted with these people. Had he had an opportunity of enquiring of any of these, they would have told him, that there never was an instance known of an Indian begging his life when in the power of his enemies: on the contrary, that he courts death by every possible insult and provocation. His reasoning then would have been reversed thus. 'Since the present Indian of North America is brave, and authors tell us, that the ancestors of those of South America were brave also; it must follow, that the cowardice of their descendants is the effect of subjugation and ill treatment.' For he observes, ib. §. 27. that 'los obrages los aniquilan por la inhumanidad con que se les trata.'

*A remarkable instance of this appeared in the case of the late Col. Byrd, who was sent to the Cherokee nation to transact some business with them. It happened that some of our disorderly people had just killed one or two of that nation. It was therefore proposed in the council of the Cherokees that Col. Byrd should be put to death, in revenge for the loss of their countrymen. Among them was a chief called Silòuee, who, on some former occasion, had contracted an acquaintance and friendship with Col. Byrd. He came to him every night in his tent, and told him not to be afraid, they should not kill him. After many days deliberation, however, the determination was, contrary to Silòuee's expectation, that Byrd should be put to death, and some warriors were dispatched as executioners. Silòuee attended them, and when they entered the tent, he threw himself between them and Byrd, and said to the warriors, 'this man is my friend: before you get at him, you must kill me.' On which they returned, and the council respected the principle so much as to recede from their determination.

enjoyment of their natural equality. That first teaches us to subdue the selfish passions, and to respect those rights in others which we value in ourselves. Were we in equal barbarism, our females would be equal drudges. The man with them is less strong than with us, but their woman stronger than ours; and both for the same obvious reason; because our man and their woman is habituated to labour, and formed by it. With both races the sex which is indulged with ease is least athletic. An Indian man is small in the hand and wrist for the same reason for which a sailor is large and strong in the arms and shoulders, and a porter in the legs and thighs.—They raise fewer children than we do. The causes of this are to be found, not in a difference of nature, but of circumstance. The women very frequently attending the men in their parties of war and of hunting, child-bearing becomes extremely inconvenient to them. It is said, therefore, that they have learnt the practice of procuring abortion by the use of some vegetable; and that it even extends to prevent conception for a considerable time after. During these parties they are exposed to numerous hazards, to excessive exertions, to the greatest extremities of hunger. Even at their homes the nation depends for food, through a certain part of every year, on the gleanings of the forest: that is, they experience a famine once in every year. With all animals, if the female be badly fed, or not fed at all, her young perish: and if both male and female be reduced to like want, generation becomes less active, less productive. To the obstacles then of want and hazard, which nature has opposed to the multiplication of wild animals, for the purpose of restraining their numbers within certain bounds, those of labour and of voluntary abortion are added with the Indian. No wonder then if they multiply less than we do. Where food is regularly supplied, a single farm will shew more of cattle, than a whole country of forests can of buffaloes. The same Indian women, when married to white traders, who feed them and their children plentifully and regularly, who exempt them from excessive drudgery, who keep them stationary and unexposed to accident, produce and raise as many children as the white women. Instances are known, under these circumstances, of their rearing a dozen children. An inhuman practice once prevailed in this country of making slaves of the

Indians. It is a fact well known with us, that the Indian women so enslaved produced and raised as numerous families as either the whites or blacks among whom they lived.—It has been said, that Indians have less hair than the whites, except on the head. But this is a fact of which fair proof can scarcely be had. With them it is disgraceful to be hairy on the body. They say it likens them to hogs. They therefore pluck the hair as fast as it appears. But the traders who marry their women, and prevail on them to discontinue this practice, say, that nature is the same with them as with the whites. Nor, if the fact be true, is the consequence necessary which has been drawn from it. Negroes have notoriously less hair than the whites; yet they are more ardent. But if cold and moisture be the agents of nature for diminishing the races of animals, how comes she all at once to suspend their operation as to the physical man of the new world, whom the Count acknowledges to be 'à peu près de même stature que l'homme de notre monde,' and to let loose their influence on his moral faculties? How has this 'combination of the elements and other physical causes, so contrary to the enlargement of animal nature in this new world, these obstacles to the developement and formation of great germs,' been arrested and suspended, so as to permit the human body to acquire its just dimensions, and by what inconceivable process has their action been directed on his mind alone? To judge of the truth of this, to form a just estimate of their genius and mental powers, more facts are wanting, and great allowance to be made for those circumstances of their situation which call for a display of particular talents only. This done, we shall probably find that they are formed in mind as well as in body, on the same module with the *'Homo sapiens Europæus.' The principles of their society forbidding all compulsion, they are to be led to duty and to enterprize by personal influence and persuasion. Hence eloquence in council, bravery and address in war, become the foundations of all consequence with them. To these acquirements all their faculties are directed. Of their bravery and address in war we have multiplied proofs, because we have been the subjects on which they were exer-

XVIII. 145.

*Linn. Syst. Definition of a Man.

cised. Of their eminence in oratory we have fewer examples, because it is displayed chiefly in their own councils. Some, however, we have of very superior lustre. I may challenge the whole orations of Demosthenes and Cicero, and of any more eminent orator, if Europe has furnished more eminent, to produce a single passage, superior to the speech of Logan, a Mingo chief, to Lord Dunmore, when governor of this state. And, as a testimony of their talents in this line, I beg leave to introduce it, first stating the incidents necessary for understanding it. In the spring of the year 1774, a robbery and murder were committed on an inhabitant of the frontiers of Virginia, by two Indians of the Shawanee tribe. The neighbouring whites, according to their custom, undertook to punish this outrage in a summary way. Col. Cresap, a man infamous for the many murders he had committed on those much-injured people, collected a party, and proceeded down the Kanhaway in quest of vengeance. Unfortunately a canoe of women and children, with one man only, was seen coming from the opposite shore, unarmed, and unsuspecting an hostile attack from the whites. Cresap and his party concealed themselves on the bank of the river, and the moment the canoe reached the shore, singled out their objects, and, at one fire, killed every person in it. This happened to be the family of Logan, who had long been distinguished as a friend of the whites. This unworthy return provoked his vengeance. He accordingly signalized himself in the war which ensued. In the autumn of the same year, a decisive battle was fought at the mouth of the Great Kanhaway, between the collected forces of the Shawanees, Mingoes, and Delawares, and a detachment of the Virginia militia. The Indians were defeated, and sued for peace. Logan however disdained to be seen among the suppliants. But, lest the sincerity of a treaty should be distrusted, from which so distinguished a chief absented himself, he sent by a messenger the following speech to be delivered to Lord Dunmore.

'I appeal to any white man to say, if ever he entered Logan's cabin hungry, and he gave him not meat; if ever he came cold and naked, and he clothed him not. During the course of the last long and bloody war, Logan remained idle in his cabin, an advocate for peace. Such was my love for the whites, that my countrymen pointed as they passed, and said, 'Logan is the friend of white men.' I had even thought to have lived with you, but for the injuries of one man. Col. Cresap, the last spring, in cold blood, and unprovoked, murdered all the relations of Logan, not sparing even my women and children. There runs not a drop of my blood in the veins of any living creature. This called on me for revenge. I have sought it: I have killed many: I have fully glutted my vengeance. For my country, I rejoice at the beams of peace. But do not harbour a thought that mine is the joy of fear. Logan never felt fear. He will not turn on his heel to save his life. Who is there to mourn for Logan?—Not one.'

Before we condemn the Indians of this continent as wanting genius, we must consider that letters have not yet been introduced among them. Were we to compare them in their present state with the Europeans North of the Alps, when the Roman arms and arts first crossed those mountains, the comparison would be unequal, because, at that time, those parts of Europe were swarming with numbers; because numbers produce emulation, and multiply the chances of improvement, and one improvement begets another. Yet I may safely ask, How many good poets, how many able mathematicians, how many great inventors in arts or sciences, had Europe North of the Alps then produced? And it was sixteen centuries after this before a Newton could be formed. I do not mean to deny, that there are varieties in the race of man, distinguished by their powers both of body and mind. I believe there are, as I see to be the case in the races of other animals. I only mean to suggest a doubt, whether the bulk and faculties of animals depend on the side of the Atlantic on which their food happens to grow, or which furnishes the elements of which they are compounded? Whether nature has enlisted herself as a Cis or Trans-Atlantic partisan? I am induced to suspect, there has been more eloquence than sound reasoning displayed in support of this theory; that it is one of those cases where the judgment has been seduced by a glowing pen: and whilst I render every tribute of honor and esteem to the celebrated Zoologist, who has added, and is still adding, so many precious things to the treasures of science, I must doubt whether in this instance he has not cherished error also, by lending her for a moment his vivid imagination and bewitching language.

So far the Count de Buffon has carried this new theory of the tendency of nature to belittle her productions on this side the Atlantic. Its application to the race of whites, transplanted from Europe, remained for the Abbé Raynal. 'On doit etre étonné (he says) que l'Amerique n'ait pas encore produit un bon poëte, un habile mathematicien, un homme de genie dans un seul art, ou une seule science.' 7. Hist. Philos. p. 92. ed. Maestricht. 1774. 'America has not yet produced one good poet.' When we shall have existed as a people as long as the Greeks did before they produced a Homer, the Romans a Virgil, the French a Racine and Voltaire, the English a Shakespeare and Milton, should this reproach be still true, we will enquire from what unfriendly causes it has proceeded, that the other countries of Europe and quarters of the earth shall not have inscribed any name in the roll of poets*. But neither has America produced 'one able mathematician, one man of genius in a single art or a single science.' In war we have produced a Washington, whose memory will be adored while liberty shall have votaries, whose name will triumph over time, and will in future ages assume its just station among the most celebrated worthies of the world, when that wretched philosophy shall be forgotten which would have arranged him among the degeneracies of nature. In physics we have produced a Franklin, than whom no one of the present age has made more important discoveries, nor has enriched philosophy with more, or more ingenious solutions of the phænomena of nature. We have supposed Mr. Rittenhouse second to no astronomer living: that in genius he must be the first, because he is self-taught. As an artist he has exhibited as great a proof of mechanical genius as the world has ever produced. He has not indeed made a world; but he has by imitation approached nearer its Maker than any man who has

*Has the world as yet produced more than two poets, acknowledged to be such by all nations? An Englishman, only, reads Milton with delight, an Italian Tasso, a Frenchman the Henriade, a Portuguese Camouens: but Homer and Virgil have been the rapture of every age and nation: they are read with enthusiasm in their originals by those who can read the originals, and in translations by those who cannot.

lived from the creation to this day*. As in philosophy and war, so in government, in oratory, in painting, in the plastic art, we might shew that America, though but a child of yesterday, has already given hopeful proofs of genius, as well of the nobler kinds, which arouse the best feelings of man, which call him into action, which substantiate his freedom, and conduct him to happiness, as of the subordinate, which serve to amuse him only. We therefore suppose, that this reproach is as unjust as it is unkind; and that, of the geniuses which adorn the present age, America contributes its full share. For comparing it with those countries, where genius is most cultivated, where are the most excellent models for art, and scaffoldings for the attainment of science, as France and England for instance, we calculate thus. The United States contain three millions of inhabitants; France twenty millions; and the British islands ten. We produce a Washington, a Franklin, a Rittenhouse. France then should have half a dozen in each of these lines, and Great-Britain half that number, equally eminent. It may be true, that France has: we are but just becoming acquainted with her, and our acquaintance so far gives us high ideas of the genius of her inhabitants. It would be injuring too many of them to name particularly a Voltaire, a Buffon, the constellation of Encyclopedists, the Abbé Raynal himself, &c. &c. We therefore have reason to believe she can produce her full quota of genius. The present war having so long cut off all communication with Great-Britain, we are not able to make a fair estimate of the state of science in that country. The spirit in which she wages war is the only sample before our eyes, and that does not seem the legitimate offspring either of science or of civilization. The sun of her glory is fast descending to the horizon. Her philosophy has crossed the Channel, her freedom the Atlantic, and herself seems passing to that awful dissolution, whose issue is not given human foresight to scan†.

*There are various ways of keeping truth out of sight. Mr. Rittenhouse's model of the planetary system has the plagiary appellation of an Orrery; and the quadrant invented by Godfrey, an American also, and with the aid of which the European nations traverse the globe, is called Hadley's quadrant.

†In a later edition of the Abbé Raynal's work, he has withdrawn his censure from that part of the new world inhabited by the Federo-Americans;

Having given a sketch of our minerals, vegetables, and quadrupeds, and being led by a proud theory to make a comparison of the latter with those of Europe, and to extend it to the Man of America, both aboriginal and emigrant, I will proceed to the remaining articles comprehended under the present query.

Between ninety and an hundred of our birds have been described by Catesby. His drawings are better as to form and attitude, than colouring, which is generally too high. They are the following.

---

but has left it still on the other parts. North America has always been more accessible to strangers than South. If he was mistaken then as to the former, he may be so as to the latter. The glimmerings which reach us from South America enable us only to see that its inhabitants are held under the accumulated pressure of slavery, superstition, and ignorance. Whenever they shall be able to rise under this weight, and to shew themselves to the rest of the world, they will probably shew they are like the rest of the world. We have not yet sufficient evidence that there are more *lakes* and *fogs* in South America than in other parts of the earth. As little do we know what would be their operation on the mind of man. That country has been visited by Spaniards and Portugueze chiefly, and almost exclusively. These, going from a country of the old world remarkably dry in its soil and climate, fancied there were more lakes and fogs in South America than in Europe. An inhabitant of Ireland, Sweden, or Finland, would have formed the contrary opinion. Had South America then been discovered and seated by a people from a fenny country, it would probably have been represented as much drier than the old world. A patient pursuit of facts, and cautious combination and comparison of them, is the drudgery to which man is subjected by his Maker, if he wishes to attain sure knowledge.

BIRDS OF VIRGINIA.

Linnean Designation.	Catesby's Designation.		Popular Names.	Buffon oiseaux.
Lanius tyrannus	Muscicapa coronâ rubrâ	1.55	Tyrant. Field martin	8.398
Vultur aura	Buteo specie Gallo-pavonis	1.6	Turkey buzzard	1.246
Falco leucocephalus	Aquila capite albo	1.1	Bald Eagle	1.138
Falco sparverius	Accipiter minor	1.5	Little hawk. Sparrow hawk	
Falco columbarius	Accipiter palumbarius	1.3	Pigeon hawk	1.338
Falco furcatus	Accipiter caudâ furcatâ	1.4	Forked tail hawk	1.286.312
	Accipiter piscatorius	1.2	Fishing hawk	1.199
Strix asio	Noctua aurita minor	1.7	Little owl	1.141
Psittacus Caroliniensis	Psitticus Caroliniensis	1.11	Parrot of Carolina. Perroquet	11.383
Corvus cristatus	Pica glandaria, cærulea, cristata	1.15	Blue jay	5.164
Oriolus Baltimore	Icterus ex aureo nigroque varius	1.48	Baltimore bird	5.318
Oriolus spurius	Icterus minor	1.49	Bastard Baltimore	5.321
Gracula quiscula	Monedula purpurea	1.12	Purple jackdaw. Crow blackbird	5.134
Cuculus Americanus	Cuculus Caroliniensis	1.9	Carolina cuckow	12.62
Picus principalis	Picus maximus rostro albo	1.16	White bill woodpecker	13.69
Picus pileatus	Picus niger maximus, capite rubro	1.17	Larger red-crested woodpecker	13.72
Picus erythrocephalus	Picus capite toto rubro	1.20	Red-headed woodpecker	13.83
Picus auratus	Picus major alis aureis	1.18	Gold winged woodpecker. Yucker	13.59
Picus Carolinus	Picus ventre rubro	1.19	Red bellied woodpecker	13.105
Picus pubescens	Picus varius minimus	1.21	Smallest spotted woodpecker	13.113
Picus villosus	Picus medius quasi-villosus	1.19	Hairy woodpecker. Speck. woodpec.	13.111
Picus varius	Picus varius minor ventre luteo	1.21	Yellow bellied woodpecker	13.115

Linnæan Designation.	Catesby's Designation.		Popular Names.		*Buffon oiseaux.*
Sitta Europaea	Sitta capite nigro	1.22	Nuthatch		10.213
	Sitta capite fusco	1.22	Small Nuthatch		10.214
Alcedo alcyon	Ispida	1.69	Kingfisher		13.310
Certhia pinus	Parus Americanus lutescens	1.61	Pinecreeper		9.433
Trochilus colubris	Mellivora avis Caroliniensis	1.65	Humming bird		11.16
Anas Canadensis	Anser Canadensis	1.92	Wild goose		17.122
Anas bucephala	Anas minor purpureo capite	1.95	Buffel's head duck		17.356
Anas rustica	Anas minor ex albo & fusco vario	1.98	Little brown duck		17.443
Anas discors	Querquedula Americana variegata	1.100	White face teal		17.403
Anas discors. β.	Querquedula Americana fusca	1.99	Blue wing teal		17.405
Anas sponsa	Anas Americanus cristatus elegans	1.97	Summer duck		17.351
	Anas Americanus lato rostro	1.96	Blue wing shoveler		17.275
Mergus cucullatus	Anas cristatus	1.94	Round crested duck		15.437
Colymbus podiceps	Prodicipes minor rostro vario	1.91	Pied bill dopchick		15.383
Ardea Herodias	Ardea cristata maxima Americana	3.10	Largest crested heron		14.113
Ardea violacea	Ardea stellaris cristata Americana	1.79	Crested bittern		14.134
Ardea cerulea	Ardea cerulea	1.76	Blue heron. Crane		14.131
Ardea virescens	Ardea stellaris minima	1.80	Small bittern		14.142
Ardea æquinoctialis	Ardea alba minor Caroliniensis	1.77	Little white heron		14.136
	Ardea stellaris Americana	1.78	Brown bittern. Indian hen		14.175
Tantalus loculator	Pelicanus Americanus	1.81	Wood pelican		13.403
Tantalus alber	Numenius albus	1.82	White curlew		15.62
Tantalus fuscus	Numenius fuscus	1.83	Brown curlew		15.64
Charadrius vociferus	Pluvialis vociferus	1.71	Chattering plover. Kildee		15.151
Hæmatopus ostralegus	Hæmatopus	1.85	Oyster Catcher		15.185

Linnæan Designation.	Catesby's Designation.		Popular Names.	Buffon oiseaux.
Rallus Virginianus	Gallinula Americana	1.70	Soree. Ral-bird	15.256
Meleagris Gallopavo	Gallopavo Sylvestris	xliv.	Wild turkey	3,187.229
Tetrao Virginianus	Perdix Sylvestris Virginiana	3.12	American partridge. American quail	4.237
	Urogallus minor, or a kind of Lagopus	3.1	Pheasant. Mountain partridge	3.409
Columba passerina	Turtur minimus guttatus	1.26	Ground dove	4.404
Columba migratoria	Palumbus migratorius	1.23	Pigeon of passage. Wild pigeon	4.351
Columba Caroliniensis	Turtur Caroliniensis	1.24	Turtle. Turtle dove	4.401
Alauda alpestris	Alauda gutture flavo	1.32	Lark. Sky lark	9.79
Alauda magna	Alauda magna	1.33	Field lark. Large lark	6.59
	Sturnus niger alis superné rubentibus	1.13	Red winged starling. Marsh blackbird	5.293
Turdus migratorius	Turdus pilaris migratorius	1.29	Fieldfare of Carolina. Robin redbreast	5.426 / 9.257
Turdus rufus	Turdus ruffus	1.28	Fox coloured thrush. Thrush	5.449
Turdus polyglottos	Turdus minor cinereo albus non maculatus	1.27	Mocking bird	5.451
	Turdus minimus	1.31	Little thrush	5.400
Ampelis garrulus. β.	Garrulus Caroliniensis	1.46	Chatterer	6.162
Loxia Cardinalis	Coccothraustes rubra	1.38	Red bird. Virginia nightingale	6.185
Loxia Cærulea	Coccothraustes cærulea	1.39	Blue gross beak	8.125
Emberiza hyemalis	Passer nivalis	1.36	Snow bird	8.47
Emberiza Oryzivora	Hortulanus Caroliniensis	1.14	Rice bird	8.49
Emberiza Ciris	Fringilla tricolor	1.44	Painted finch	7.247
Tanagra cyanea	Linaria cærulea	1.45	Blue linnet	7.122
	Passerculus	1.35	Little sparrow	7.120
	Passer fuscus	1.34	Cowpen bird	7.196
Fringilla erythrophthalma	Passer niger oculis rubris	1.34	Towhe bird	7.201

Linnaean Designation.	Catesby's Designation.		Popular Names.	Buffon oiseaux.
Fringilla tristis	Carduelis Americanus	1.43	American goldfinch. Lettuce bird	7.297
	Fringilla purpurea	1.41	Purple finch	8.129
Muscicapa crinita	Muscicapa cristata ventre luteo	1.52	Crested flycatcher	8.379
Muscicapa rubra	Muscicapa rubra	1.56	Summer red bird	8.410
Muscicapa ruticilla	Ruticilla Americana	1.67	Red start	{ 8.349 9.259
Muscicapa Caroliniensis	Muscicapa vertice nigro	1.66	Cat bird	8.372
	Muscicapa nigrescens	1.53	Black-cap flycatcher	8.341
	Muscicapa fusca	1.54	Little brown flycatcher	8.344
	Muscicapa oculis rubris	1.54	Red-eyed flycatcher	8.337
Motacilla Sialis	Rubicula Americana cerulea	1.47	Blue bird	9.308
Motacilla regulus	Regulus cristatus	3.13	Wren	10.58
Motacilla trochilus. β.	Oenanthe Americana pectore luteo	1.50	Yellow-breasted chat	6.96
Parus bicolor	Parus cristatus	1.57	Crested titmouse	10.181
Parus Americanus	Parus fringillaris	1.64	Finch creeper	9.442
Parus Virginianus	Parus uropygeo luteo	1.58	Yellow rump	10.184
	Parus cucullo nigro	1.60	Hooded titmouse	10.183
	Parus Americanus gutture luteo	1.62	Yellow-throated creeper	
	Parus Caroliniensis	1.63	Yellow titmouse	
Hirundo Pelasgia	Hirundo cauda aculeata Americana	3.8	American swallow	9.431
Hirundo purpurea	Hirundo purpurea	1.51	Purple martin. House martin	12.478
Caprimulgus Europaeus α	Caprimulgus	1.8	Goatsucker. Great bat	12.445
Caprimulgus Europaeus β	Caprimulgus minor Americanus	3.16	Whip-poor Will	12.243
				12.246

Besides these, we have

The Royston crow. Corvus
   cornix.
   Crane. Ardea Canadensis.
   House swallow. Hirundo
   rustica.
   Ground swallow. Hirundo
   riparia.
   Greatest grey eagle.
   Smaller turkey buzzard,
   with a feathered head.
   Greatest owl, or night-
   hawk.
   Wethawk, which feeds
   flying.
   Raven.
   Water pelican of the Missi-
   sipi, whose pouch holds
   a peck.
   Swan.
   Loon.

The Cormorant.
   Duck and Mallard.
   Widgeon.
   Sheldrach, or Canvas back.
   Black head.
   Ballcoot.
   Sprigtail.
   Didapper, or Dopchick.
   Spoon billed duck.
   Water-witch.
   Water-pheasant.
   Mow-bird.
   Blue peter.
   Water wagtail.
   Yellow-legged snipe.
   Squatting snipe.
   Small plover.
   Whistling plover.
   Woodcock.
   Red bird, with black head,
   wings and tail.

And doubtless many others which have not yet been described and classed.

To this catalogue of our indigenous animals, I will add a
short account of an anomaly of nature, taking place sometimes in the race of negroes brought from Africa, who,
though black themselves, have in rare instances, white children, called Albinos. I have known four of these myself, and
have faithful accounts of three others. The circumstances in
which all the individuals agree are these. They are of a pallid
cadaverous white, untinged with red, without any coloured
spots or seams; their hair of the same kind of white, short,
coarse, and curled as is that of the negro; all of them well
formed, strong, healthy, perfect in their senses, except that of
sight, and born of parents who had no mixture of white
blood. Three of these Albinos were sisters, having two other
full sisters, who were black. The youngest of the three was
killed by lightning, at twelve years of age. The eldest died at
about 27 years of age, in child-bed, with her second child. The
middle one is now alive in health, and has issue, as the eldest

had, by a black man, which issue was black. They are uncommonly shrewd, quick in their apprehensions and in reply. Their eyes are in a perpetual tremulous vibration, very weak, and much affected by the sun: but they see better in the night than we do. They are of the property of Col. Skipwith, of Cumberland. The fourth is a negro woman, whose parents came from Guinea, and had three other children, who were of their own colour. She is freckled, her eye-sight so weak that she is obliged to wear a bonnet in the summer; but it is better in the night than day. She had an Albino child by a black man. It died at the age of a few weeks. These were the property of Col. Carter, of Albemarle. A sixth instance is a woman of the property of a Mr. Butler, near Petersburgh. She is stout and robust, has issue a daughter, jet black, by a black man. I am not informed as to her eye sight. The seventh instance is of a male belonging to a Mr. Lee, of Cumberland. His eyes are tremulous and weak. He is tall of stature, and now advanced in years. He is the only male of the Albinos which have come within my information. Whatever be the cause of the disease in the skin, or in its colouring matter, which produces this change, it seems more incident to the female than male sex. To these I may add the mention of a negro man within my own knowledge, born black, and of black parents; on whose chin, when a boy, a white spot appeared. This continued to increase till he became a man, by which time it had extended over his chin, lips, one cheek, the under jaw and neck on that side. It is of the Albino white, without any mixture of red, and has for several years been stationary. He is robust and healthy, and the change of colour was not accompanied with any sensible disease, either general or topical.

Of our fish and insects there has been nothing like a full description or collection. More of them are described in Catesby than in any other work. Many also are to be found in Sir Hans Sloane's Jamaica, as being common to that and this country. The honey-bee is not a native of our continent. Marcgrave indeed mentions a species of honey-bee in Brasil. But this has no sting, and is therefore different from the one we have, which resembles perfectly that of Europe. The Indians concur with us in the tradition that it was brought from

Europe; but when, and by whom, we know not. The bees have generally extended themselves into the country, a little in advance of the white settlers. The Indians therefore call them the white man's fly, and consider their approach as indicating the approach of the settlements of the whites. A question here occurs, How far northwardly have these insects been found? That they are unknown in Lapland, I infer from Scheffer's information, that the Laplanders eat the pine bark, prepared in a certain way, instead of those things sweetened with sugar. 'Hoc comedunt pro rebus saccharo conditis.' Scheff. Lapp. c. 18. Certainly, if they had honey, it would be a better substitute for sugar than any preparation of the pine bark. Kalm tells us the honey bee cannot live through the winter in Canada. They furnish then I. 126. an additional proof of the remarkable fact first observed by the Count de Buffon, and which has thrown such a blaze of light on the field of natural history, that no animals are found in both continents, but those which are able to bear the cold of those regions where they probably join.

QUERY VII

Climate *A notice of all what can increase the progress of human knowledge?*

Under the latitude of this query, I will presume it not improper nor unacceptable to furnish some data for estimating the climate of Virginia. Journals of observations on the quantity of rain, and degree of heat, being lengthy, confused, and too minute to produce general and distinct ideas, I have taken five years observations, to wit, from 1772 to 1777, made in Williamsburgh and its neighbourhood, have reduced them to an average for every month in the year, and stated those averages in the following table, adding an analytical view of the winds during the same period.

The rains of every month, (as of January for instance) through the whole period of years, were added separately, and an average drawn from them. The coolest and warmest point of the same day in each year of the period were added separately, and an average of the greatest cold and greatest heat of that day, was formed. From the averages of every day in the month, a general average for the whole month was formed. The point from which the wind blew was observed two or three times in every day. These observations, in the month of January for instance, through the whole period amounted to 337. At 73 of these, the wind was from the North; at 47, from the North-east, &c. So that it will be easy to see in what proportion each wind usually prevails in each month: or, taking the whole year, the total of observations through the whole period having been 3698, it will be observed that 611 of them were from the North, 558 from the North-east, &c.

Though by this table it appears we have on an average 47 inches of rain annually, which is considerably more than usually falls in Europe, yet from the information I have collected, I suppose we have a much greater proportion of sunshine here than there. Perhaps it will be found there are twice as many cloudy days in the middle parts of Europe, as in the United States of America. I mention the middle parts of Europe, because my information does not extend to its northern or southern parts.

	Fall of rain, &c. in inches.	Least & greatest daily heat by Farenheit's thermometer.		W I N D S.								
		8.A.M.	4.P.M.	N.	N. E.	E.	S. E.	S.	S. W.	W.	N. W.	Total.
Jan.	3.192	38½	to 44	73	47	32	10	11	78	40	46	337
Feb.	2.049	41	47½	61	52	24	11	4	63	30	31	276
Mar.	3.95	48	54½	49	44	38	28	14	83	29	33	318
April	3.68	56	62½	35	44	54	19	9	58	18	20	257
May	2.871	63	70½	27	36	62	23	7	74	32	20	281
June	3.751	71½	78¼	22	34	43	24	13	81	25	25	267
July	4.497	77	82½	41	44	75	15	7	95	32	19	328
Aug.	9.153	76¼	81	43	52	40	30	9	103	27	30	334
Sept.	4.761	69½	74¼	70	60	51	18	10	81	18	37	345
Oct.	3.633	61¼	66½	52	77	64	15	6	56	23	34	327
Nov.	2.617	47¾	53½	74	21	20	14	9	63	35	58	294
Dec.	2.877	43	48¾	64	37	18	16	10	91	42	56	334
Total.	47.038	8.A.M.	4.P.M.	611	548	521	223	109	926	351	409	3698

In an extensive country, it will of course be expected that the climate is not the same in all its parts. It is remarkable that, proceeding on the same parallel of latitude westwardly, the climate becomes colder in like manner as when you proceed northwardly. This continues to be the case till you attain the summit of the Alleghaney, which is the highest land between the ocean and the Missisipi. From thence, descending in the same latitude to the Missisipi, the change reverses; and, if we may believe travellers, it becomes warmer there than it is in the same latitude on the sea side. Their testimony is strengthened by the vegetables and animals which subsist and multiply there naturally, and do not on our sea coast. Thus Catalpas grow spontaneously on the Missisipi, as far as the latitude of 37°. and reeds as far as 38°. Perroquets even winter on the Sioto, in the 39th degree of latitude. In the summer of 1779, when the thermometer was at 90°. at Monticello, and 96 at Williamsburgh, it was 110°. at Kaskaskia. Perhaps the mountain, which overhangs this village on the North side, may, by its reflexion, have contributed somewhat to produce this heat. The difference of temperature of the air at the sea coast, or on Chesapeak bay, and at the Alleghaney, has not been ascertained; but cotemporary observations, made at Williamsburgh, or in its neighbourhood, and at Monticello, which is on the most eastern ridge of mountains, called the South West, where they are intersected by the Rivanna, have furnished a ratio by which that difference may in some degree be conjectured. These observations make the difference between Williamsburgh and the nearest mountains, at the position before mentioned, to be on an average 6⅛ degrees of Farenheit's thermometer. Some allowance however is to be made for the difference of latitude between these two places, the latter being 38°. 8′. 17″. which is 52′. 22″. North of the former. By cotemporary observations of between five and six weeks, the averaged and almost unvaried difference of the height of mercury in the barometer, at those two places, was .784 of an inch, the atmosphere at Monticello being so much the lightest, that is to say, about 1/37 of its whole weight. It should be observed, however, that the hill of Monticello is of 500 feet perpendicular height above the river which washes its base. This position being nearly central between our northern and southern boundaries, and between the bay and Allegha-ney, may be considered as furnishing the best average of the temperature of our climate. Williamsburgh is much too near the South-eastern corner to give a fair idea of our general temperature.

But a more remarkable difference is in the winds which prevail in the different parts of the country. The following table exhibits a comparative view of the winds prevailing at Williamsburgh, and at Monticello. It is formed by reducing nine months observations at Monticello to four principal points, to wit, the North-east, South-east, South-west, and North-west; these points being perpendicular to, or parallel with our coast, mountains and rivers: and by reducing, in like manner, an equal number of observations, to wit, 421. from the preceding table of winds at Williamsburgh, taking them proportionably from every point.

	N. E.	S. E.	S. W.	N. W.	Total.
Williamsburgh	127	61	132	101	421
Monticello	32	91	126	172	421

By this it may be seen that the South-west wind prevails equally at both places; that the North-east is, next to this, the principal wind towards the sea coast, and the North-west is the predominant wind at the mountains. The difference be-tween these two winds to sensation, and in fact, is very great. The North-east is loaded with vapour, insomuch, that the salt makers have found that their crystals would not shoot while that blows; it brings a distressing chill, is heavy and oppres-sive to the spirits: the North-west is dry, cooling, elastic and animating. The Eastern and South-eastern breezes come on generally in the afternoon. They have advanced into the coun-try very sensibly within the memory of people now living. They formerly did not penetrate far above Williamsburgh. They are now frequent at Richmond, and every now and then reach the mountains. They deposit most of their moisture however before they get that far. As the lands become more cleared, it is probable they will extend still further westward.

Going out into the open air, in the temperate, and in the

warm months of the year, we often meet with bodies of warm air, which, passing by us in two or three seconds, do not afford time to the most sensible thermometer to seize their temperature. Judging from my feelings only, I think they approach the ordinary heat of the human body. Some of them perhaps go a little beyond it. They are of about 20 or 30 feet diameter horizontally. Of their height we have no experience; but probably they are globular volumes wafted or rolled along with the wind. But whence taken, where found, or how generated? They are not to be ascribed to Volcanos, because we have none. They do not happen in the winter when the farmers kindle large fires in clearing up their grounds. They are not confined to the spring season, when we have fires which traverse whole counties, consuming the leaves which have fallen from the trees. And they are too frequent and general to be ascribed to accidental fires. I am persuaded their cause must be sought for in the atmosphere itself, to aid us in which I know but of these constant circumstances; a dry air; a temperature as warm at least as that of the spring or autumn; and a moderate current of wind. They are most frequent about sun-set; rare in the middle parts of the day; and I do not recollect having ever met with them in the morning.

The variation in the weight of our atmosphere, as indicated by the barometer, is not equal to two inches of mercury. During twelve months observation at Williamsburgh, the extremes were 29, and 30.86 inches, the difference being 1.86 of an inch: and in nine months, during which the height of the mercury was noted at Monticello, the extremes were 28.48 and 29.69 inches, the variation being 1.21 of an inch. A gentleman, who has observed his barometer many years, assures me it has never varied two inches. Cotemporary observations, made at Monticello and Williamsburgh, proved the variations in the weight of air to be simultaneous and corresponding in these two places.

Our changes from heat to cold, and cold to heat, are very sudden and great. The mercury in Farenheit's thermometer has been known to descend from 92°. to 47°. in thirteen hours.

It is taken for granted, that the preceding table of averaged

heat will not give a false idea on this subject, as it proposes
to state only the ordinary heat and cold of each month, and
not those which are extraordinary. At Williamsburgh in August 1766, the mercury in Farenheit's thermometer was at 98°.
corresponding with 29⅓ of Reaumur. At the same place in
January 1780, it was at 6°. corresponding with 11½ below o.
of Reaumur. I believe *these may be considered to be nearly
the extremes of heat and cold in that part of the country. The
latter may most certainly, as, at that time, York river, at York
town, was frozen over, so that people walked across it; a circumstance which proves it to have been colder than the winter of 1740, 1741, usually called the cold winter, when York
river did not freeze over at that place. In the same season of
1780, Chesapeak bay was solid, from its head to the mouth of
Patowmac. At Annapolis, where it is 5¼ miles over between
the nearest points of land, the ice was from 5 to 7 inches thick
quite across, so that loaded carriages went over on it. Those,
our extremes of heat and cold, of 6°. and 98°. were indeed
very distressing to us, and were thought to put the extent of
the human constitution to considerable trial. Yet a Siberian
would have considered them as scarcely a sensible variation.
At Jenniseitz in that country, in latitude 58°. 27′. we are told,
that the cold in 1735 sunk the mercury by Farenheit's scale to
126°. below nothing; and the inhabitants of the same country
use stove rooms two or three times a week, in which they
stay two hours at a time, the atmosphere of which raises the
mercury to 135°. above nothing. Late experiments shew that
the human body will exist in rooms heated to 140°. of Reaumur, equal to 347°. of Farenheit, and 135°. above boiling water. The hottest point of the 24 hours is about four o'clock,
P. M. and the dawn of day the coldest.

The access of frost in autumn, and its recess in the spring,
do not seem to depend merely on the degree of cold; much
less on the air's being at the freezing point. White frosts are
frequent when the thermometer is at 47°. have killed young
plants of Indian corn at 48°. and have been known at 54°.

*At Paris, in 1753, the mercury in Reaumur's thermometer was at 30½
above o, and in 1776, it was at 16 below o. The extremities of heat and cold
therefore at Paris, are greater than at Williamsburgh, which is in the hottest
part of Virginia.

Black frost, and even ice, have been produced at 38½°. which is 6½ degrees above the freezing point. That other circumstances must be combined with the cold to produce frost, is evident from this also, that on the higher parts of mountains, where it is absolutely colder than in the plains on which they stand, frosts do not appear so early by a considerable space of time in autumn, and go off sooner in the spring, than in the plains. I have known frosts so severe as to kill the hiccory trees round about Monticello, and yet not injure the tender fruit blossoms then in bloom on the top and higher parts of the mountain; and in the course of 40 years, during which it has been settled, there have been but two instances of a general loss of fruit on it: while, in the circumjacent country, the fruit has escaped but twice in the last seven years. The plants of tobacco, which grow from the roots of those which have been cut off in the summer, are frequently green here at Christmas. This privilege against the frost is undoubtedly combined with the want of dew on the mountains. That the dew is very rare on their higher parts, I may say with certainty, from 12 years observations, having scarcely ever, during that time, seen an unequivocal proof of its existence on them at all during summer. Severe frosts in the depth of winter prove that the region of dews extends higher in that season than the tops of the mountains: but certainly, in the summer season, the vapours, by the time they attain that height, are become so attenuated as not to subside and form a dew when the sun retires.

The weavil has not yet ascended the high mountains.

A more satisfactory estimate of our climate to some, may perhaps be formed, by noting the plants which grow here, subject however to be killed by our severest colds. These are the fig, pomegranate, artichoke, and European walnut. In mild winters, lettuce and endive require no shelter; but generally they need a slight covering. I do not know that the want of long moss, reed, myrtle, swamp laurel, holly and cypress, in the upper country, proceeds from a greater degree of cold, nor that they were ever killed with any degree of cold in the lower country. The aloe lived in Williamsburgh in the open air through the severe winter of 1779, 1780.

A change in our climate however is taking place very sensibly. Both heats and colds are become much more moderate within the memory even of the middle-aged. Snows are less frequent and less deep. They do not often lie, below the mountains, more than one, two, or three days, and very rarely a week. They are remembered to have been formerly frequent, deep, and of long continuance. The elderly inform me the earth used to be covered with snow about three months in every year. The rivers, which then seldom failed to freeze over in the course of the winter, scarcely ever do so now. This change has produced an unfortunate fluctuation between heat and cold, in the spring of the year, which is very fatal to fruits. From the year 1741 to 1769, an interval of twenty-eight years, there was no instance of fruit killed by the frost in the neighbourhood of Monticello. An intense cold, produced by constant snows, kept the buds locked up till the sun could obtain, in the spring of the year, so fixed an ascendency as to dissolve those snows, and protect the buds, during their de-velopement, from every danger of returning cold. The accu-mulated snows of the winter remaining to be dissolved all together in the spring, produced those overflowings of our rivers, so frequent then, and so rare now.

Having had occasion to mention the particular situation of Monticello for other purposes, I will just take notice that its elevation affords an opportunity of seeing a phænomenon which is rare at land, though frequent at sea. The seamen call it *looming*. Philosophy is as yet in the rear of the seamen, for so far from having accounted for it, she has not given it a name. Its principal effect is to make distant objects appear larger, in opposition to the general law of vision, by which they are diminished. I knew an instance, at York town, from whence the water prospect eastwardly is without termination, wherein a canoe with three men, at a great distance, was taken for a ship with its three masts. I am little acquainted with the phænomenon as it shews itself at sea; but at Monti-cello it is familiar. There is a solitary mountain about 40 miles off, in the South, whose natural shape, as presented to view there, is a regular cone; but, by the effect of looming, it some-times subsides almost totally into the horizon; sometimes it rises more acute and more elevated; sometimes it is hemi-spherical; and sometimes its sides are perpendicular, its top flat, and as broad as its base. In short it assumes at times the most whimsical shapes, and all these perhaps successively in the same morning. The Blue ridge of mountains comes into view, in the North East, at about 100 miles distance, and, approaching in a direct line, passes by within 20 miles, and goes off to the South-west. This phænomenon begins to shew itself on these mountains, at about 50 miles distance, and continues beyond that as far as they are seen. I remark no particular state, either in the weight, moisture, or heat of the atmosphere, necessary to produce this. The only constant circumstances are, its appearance in the morning only, and on objects at least 40 or 50 miles distant. In this latter circumstance, if not in both, it differs from the looming on the water. Refraction will not account for this metamorphosis. That only changes the proportions of length and breadth, base and altitude, preserving the general outlines. Thus it may make a circle appear elliptical, raise or depress a cone, but by none of its laws, as yet developed, will it make a circle appear a square, or a cone a sphere.

QUERY VIII

The number of its inhabitants?
Population
The following table shews the number of persons imported for the establishment of our colony in its infant state, and the census of inhabitants at different periods, extracted from our historians and public records, as particularly as I have had opportunities and leisure to examine them. Successive lines in the same year shew successive periods of time in that year. I have stated the census in two different columns, the whole inhabitants having been sometimes numbered, and sometimes the *tythes* only. This term, with us, includes the free males above 16 years of age, and slaves above that age of both sexes. A further examination of our records would render this history of our population much more satisfactory and perfect, by furnishing a greater number of intermediate terms. Those however which are here stated will enable us to calculate, with a considerable degree of precision, the rate at which we have increased. During the infancy of the colony, while numbers were small, wars, importations, and other accidental circumstances render the progression fluctuating and irregular. By the year 1654, however, it becomes tolerably uniform, importations having in a great measure ceased from the dissolution of the company, and the inhabitants become too numerous to be sensibly affected by Indian wars. Beginning at that period, therefore, we find that from thence to the year 1772, our tythes had increased from 7209 to 153,000. The whole term being of 118 years, yields a duplication once in every 27¼ years. The intermediate enumerations taken in 1700, 1748, and 1759, furnish proofs of the uniformity of this progression. Should this rate of increase continue, we shall have between six and seven millions of inhabitants within 95 years. If we suppose our country to be bounded, at some future day, by the meridian of the mouth of the Great Kanhaway, (within which it has been before conjectured, are 64,491 square miles) there will then be 100 inhabitants for every square mile, which is nearly the state of population in the British islands.

Years	Settlers imported.	Census of Inhabitants.	Census of Tythes.
1607	100		
		40	
	120		
1608		130	
	70		
1609		490	
	16		
		60	
1610	150		
		200	
1611	3 ship loads		
	300		
1612	80		
1617		400	
1618	200		
	40		
		600	
1619	1216		
1621	1300		
1622		3800	
		2500	
1628		3000	
1632			2000
1644			4822
1645			5000
1652			7000
1654			7209
1700			22,000
1748			82,100
1759			105,000
1772			153,000
1782		567,614	

Here I will beg leave to propose a doubt. The present desire of America is to produce rapid population by as great importations of foreigners as possible. But is this founded in good policy? The advantage proposed is the multiplication of numbers. Now let us suppose (for example only) that, in this state, we could double our numbers in one year by the importation of foreigners; and this is a greater accession than the most sanguine advocate for emigration has a right to expect. Then I say, beginning with a double stock, we shall attain any given degree of population only 27 years and 3 months sooner than if we proceed on our single stock. If we propose four millions and a half as a competent population for this state, we should be 54½ years attaining it, could we at once double our numbers; and 81¾ years, if we rely on natural propagation, as may be seen by the following table.

In the first column are stated periods of 27¼ years; in the second are our numbers, at each period, as they will be if we proceed on our actual stock; and in the third are what they

	Proceeding on our present stock.	Proceeding on a double stock.
1781	567,614	1,135,228
1808¼	1,135,228	2,270,456
1835½	2,270,456	4,540,912
1862¾	4,540,912	

would be, at the same periods, were we to set out from the double of our present stock. I have taken the term of four millions and a half of inhabitants for example's sake only. Yet I am persuaded it is a greater number than the country spoken of, considering how much inarrable land it contains, can clothe and feed, without a material change in the quality of their diet. But are there no inconveniences to be thrown into the scale against the advantage expected from a multiplication of numbers by the importation of foreigners? It is for the happiness of those united in society to harmonize as much as possible in matters which they must of necessity transact together. Civil government being the sole object of forming societies, its administration must be conducted by common consent. Every species of government has its specific principles. Ours perhaps are more peculiar than those of any other in the universe. It is a composition of the freest principles of the English constitution, with others derived from natural right and natural reason. To these nothing can be more opposed than the maxims of absolute monarchies. Yet, from such, we are to expect the greatest number of emigrants. They will bring with them the principles of the governments they leave, imbibed in their early youth; or, if able to throw them off, it will be in exchange for an unbounded licentiousness, passing, as is usual, from one extreme to another. It would be a miracle were they to stop precisely at the point of temperate liberty. These principles, with their language, they will transmit to their children. In proportion to their numbers, they will share with us the legislation. They will infuse into it their spirit, warp and bias its direction, and render it a heterogeneous, incoherent, distracted mass. I may appeal to experience, during the present contest, for a verification of these conjectures. But, if they be not certain in event, are they not possible, are they not probable? Is it not safer to wait with patience 27 years and three months longer, for the attainment of any degree of population desired, or expected? May not our government be more homogeneous, more peaceable, more durable? Suppose 20 millions of republican Americans thrown all of a sudden into France, what would be the condition of that kingdom? If it would be more turbulent, less happy, less strong, we may believe that the addition of half a million of foreigners to our present numbers would produce a similar effect here. If they come of themselves, they are entitled to all the rights of citizenship: but I doubt the expediency of inviting them by extraordinary encouragements. I mean not that these doubts should be extended to the importation of useful artificers. The policy of that measure depends on very different considerations. Spare no expence in obtaining them. They will after a while go to the plough and the hoe; but, in the mean time, they will teach us something we do not know. It is not so in agriculture. The indifferent state of that among us does not proceed from a want of knowledge merely; it is from our having such quantities of land to waste as we please. In Europe the object is to make the most of their land, labour being abundant: here it is to make the most of our labour, land being abundant.

It will be proper to explain how the numbers for the year 1782 have been obtained; as it was not from a perfect census of the inhabitants. It will at the same time develope the proportion between the free inhabitants and slaves. The following return of taxable articles for that year was given in.

- 53,289 free males above 21 years of age.
- 211,698 slaves of all ages and sexes.
- 23,766 not distinguished in the returns, but said to be titheable slaves.
- 195,439 horses.
- 609,734 cattle.
- 5,126 wheels of riding-carriages.
- 191 taverns.

There were no returns from the 8 counties of Lincoln, Jefferson, Fayette, Monongalia, Yohogania, Ohio, Northampton, and York. To find the number of slaves which should have been returned instead of the 23,766 titheables, we must mention that some observations on a former census had given reason to believe that the numbers above and below 16 years of age were equal. The double of this number, therefore, to wit, 47,532 must be added to 211,698, which will give us 259,230 slaves of all ages and sexes. To find the number of free inhabitants, we must repeat the observation, that those above and below 16 are nearly equal. But as the number 53,289 omits the males between 16 and 21, we must supply them from conjecture. On a former experiment it had appeared that about one-third of our militia, that is, of the males between 16 and 50, were unmarried. Knowing how early marriage takes place here, we shall not be far wrong in supposing that the unmarried part of our militia are those between 16 and 21. If there be young men who do not marry till after 21, there are as many who marry before that age. But as the men above 50 were not included in the militia, we will suppose the unmarried, or those between 16 and 21, to be one-fourth of the whole number above 16, then we have the following calculation:

53,289	free males above 21 years of age.
17,763	free males between 16 and 21.
71,052	free males under 16.
142,104	free females of all ages.
284,208	free inhabitants of all ages.
259,230	slaves of all ages.
543,438	inhabitants, exclusive of the 8 counties from which

were no returns. In these 8 counties in the years 1779 and 1780 were 3,161 militia. Say then,

3,161	free males above the age of 16.
3,161	ditto under 16.
6,322	free females.
12,644	free inhabitants in these 8 counties. To find the

number of slaves, say, as 284,208 to 259,230, so is 12,644 to 11,532. Adding the third of these numbers to the first, and the fourth to the second, we have,

296,852	free inhabitants.
270,762	slaves.
567,614	inhabitants of every age, sex, and condition. But

296,852, the number of free inhabitants, are to 270,762, the number of slaves, nearly as 11 to 10. Under the mild treatment our slaves experience, and their wholesome, though coarse, food, this blot in our country increases as fast, or faster, than the whites. During the regal government, we had at one time obtained a law, which imposed such a duty on the importation of slaves, as amounted nearly to a prohibition, when one inconsiderate assembly, placed under a peculiarity of circumstance, repealed the law. This repeal met a joyful sanction from the then sovereign, and no devices, no expedients, which could ever after be attempted by subsequent assemblies, and they seldom met without attempting them, could succeed in getting the royal assent to a renewal of the duty. In the very first session held under the republican government, the assembly passed a law for the perpetual prohibition of the importation of slaves. This will in some measure stop the increase of this great political and moral evil, while the minds of our citizens may be ripening for a complete emancipation of human nature.

QUERY IX

The number and condition of the militia and regular troops, and their pay?
Military

The following is a state of the militia, taken from returns of 1780 and 1781, except in those counties marked with an asterisk, the returns from which are somewhat older.

Situation.	Counties.	Militia.	Situation.		Counties.	Militia.
Westward of the Allegany. 4458.	Lincoln	600		**Between James river and Carolina. 6959.**	Greenesville	500
	Jefferson	300			Dinwiddie	*750
	Fayette	156			Chesterfield	655
	Ohio				Prince George	382
	Monongalia	*1000			Surry	380
	Washington	*829			Sussex	*700
	Montgomery	1071			Southampton	874
	Green-briar	502			Isle of Wight	*600
Between the Allegany and Blue ridge. 7673.	Hampshire	930			Nansemond	*644
	Berkeley	*1100			Norfolk	*880
	Frederick	1143	**19,012.**		Princess Anne	*594
	Shenando	*925		**Between James and York rivers. 3009.**	Henrico	619
	Rockingham	875			Hanover	796
	Augusta	1375			New Kent	*418
	Rockbridge	*625			Charles City	286
	Botetourt	*700			James City	235
Between the Blue ridge and Tide waters. 18,828	Loudoun	1746			Williamsburg	129
	Fauquier	1078			York	*244
	Culpeper	1513			Warwick	*100
	Spotsylvania	480			Elizabeth City	182
	Orange	*600	**ON THE TIDE WATERS AND IN THAT PARALLEL.**	**Between York and Rappaha- nock. 3269.**	Caroline	805
	Louisa	603			King William	436
	Goochland	*550			King & Queen	500
	Fluvanna	*296			Essex	468
	Albemarle	873			Middlesex	*210
	Amherst	896			Gloucester	850
	Buckingham	*625		**Between Rappaha- noc & Patowmac. 4137.**	Fairfax	652
	Bedford	1300			Prince William	614
	Henry	1004			Stafford	*500
	Pittsylvania	*725			King George	483
	Halifax	*1139			Richmond	412
	Charlotte	612			Westmoreland	544
	Prince Edward	589			Northumberl.	630
	Cumberland	408			Lancaster	302
	Powhatan	330		**East. Shore. 1638.**	Accomac	*1208
	Amelia	*1125			Northampton	*430
	Lunenburg	677		Whole Militia of the State		49,971
	Mecklenburg	1100				
	Brunswic	559				

Every able-bodied freeman, between the ages of 16 and 50, is enrolled in the militia. Those of every county are formed into companies, and these again into one or more battalions, according to the numbers in the county. They are commanded by colonels, and other subordinate officers, as in the regular service. In every county is a county-lieutenant, who commands the whole militia of his county, but ranks only as a colonel in the field. We have no general officers always existing. These are appointed occasionally, when an invasion or insurrection happens, and their commission determines with the occasion. The governor is head of the military, as well as civil power. The law requires every militia-man to provide himself with the arms usual in the regular service. But this injunction was always indifferently complied with, and the arms they had have been so frequently called for to arm the regulars, that in the lower parts of the country they are entirely disarmed. In the middle country a fourth or fifth part of them may have such firelocks as they had provided to destroy the noxious animals which infest their farms; and on the western side of the Blue ridge they are generally armed with rifles. The pay of our militia, as well as of our regulars, is that of the Continental regulars. The condition of our regulars, of whom we have none but Continentals, and part of a battalion of state troops, is so constantly on the change, that a state of it at this day would not be its state a month hence. It is much the same with the condition of the other Continental troops, which is well enough known.

QUERY X

Marine

The marine?

Before the present invasion of this state by the British under the command of General Phillips, we had three vessels of 16 guns, one of 14, five small gallies, and two or three armed boats. They were generally so badly manned as seldom to be in condition for service. Since the perfect possession of our rivers assumed by the enemy, I believe we are left with a single armed boat only.

QUERY XI

Aborigines *A description of the Indians established in that state?*

When the first effectual settlement of our colony was made, which was in 1607, the country from the sea-coast to the mountains, and from Patowmac to the most southern waters

<table>
<tr><td></td><td colspan="5" align="center">M A N N A H O A C S.</td><td></td></tr>
<tr><td rowspan="2"></td><td rowspan="2">TRIBES.</td><td rowspan="2">COUNTRY.</td><td rowspan="2">CHIEF TOWN.</td><td colspan="2">WARRIORS.</td><td rowspan="2">TRIBES.</td></tr>
<tr><td>1607</td><td>1669</td></tr>
<tr><td rowspan="5">Between
PATOWMAC
and
RAPPAHANOC.</td><td>Whonkenties</td><td>Fauquier</td><td></td><td></td><td></td><td>Tauxenents
Patówomekes</td></tr>
<tr><td>Tegninaties</td><td>Culpeper</td><td></td><td></td><td></td><td>Cuttatawomans
Pissasecs</td></tr>
<tr><td>Ontponies</td><td>Orange</td><td></td><td></td><td></td><td>Onaumanìents
Rappahànocs</td></tr>
<tr><td>Tauxitanians</td><td>Fauquier</td><td></td><td></td><td></td><td>Moràughtacunds
Secacaonies</td></tr>
<tr><td>Hassinungaes</td><td>Culpeper</td><td></td><td></td><td></td><td>Wighcocòmicoes
Cuttatawomans</td></tr>
<tr><td rowspan="3">Between
RAPPAHANOC
and
YORK.</td><td>Stegarakies</td><td>Orange</td><td></td><td></td><td></td><td>Nantaughtacunds
Màttapomènts</td></tr>
<tr><td>Shackakonies</td><td>Spotsylvania</td><td></td><td></td><td></td><td>Pamùnkies</td></tr>
<tr><td>Mannahoacs</td><td>Stafford
Spotsylvania</td><td></td><td></td><td></td><td>Wèrowocòmicos
Payànkatanks</td></tr>
<tr><td rowspan="4"></td><td colspan="5" align="center">M O N A C A N S.</td><td>Youghtanunds
Chickahòminies</td></tr>
<tr><td rowspan="2">Between
YORK
and
JAMES.</td><td>Monacans</td><td>James R. above
the falls</td><td>Fork of
James R.</td><td></td><td>30</td><td>Powhatans
Arrowhàtocs
Wèanocs</td></tr>
<tr><td>Monasiccapanoes</td><td>Louisa. Fluvanna</td><td></td><td></td><td>Paspahèghes
Chìskiacs
Kecoughtáns</td></tr>
<tr><td rowspan="3">Between
JAMES
and
CAROLINA.</td><td>Monahassanoes</td><td>Bedford.
Buckingham</td><td></td><td></td><td></td><td rowspan="2">Appamàttocs
Quiocohànocs
Wàrrasqeaks</td></tr>
<tr><td>Massinacacs</td><td>Cumberland</td><td></td><td></td><td></td></tr>
<tr><td>Mohemenchoes</td><td>Powhatan</td><td></td><td></td><td></td><td>Nansamònds
Chèsapeaks</td></tr>
<tr><td>EASTERN
SHORE.</td><td></td><td></td><td></td><td></td><td></td><td>Accohanocs
Accomàcks</td></tr>
</table>

W E S T:

of James river, was occupied by upwards of forty different tribes of Indians. Of these the *Powhatans*, the *Mannahoacs*, and *Monacans*, were the most powerful. Those between the sea-coast and falls of the rivers, were in amity with one another, and attached to the *Powhatans* as their link of union. Those between the falls of the rivers and the mountains, were divided into two confederacies; the tribes inhabiting the head waters of Patowmac and Rappahanoc being attached to the

NORTH.

P O W H A T A N S.

COUNTRY.	CHIEF TOWN.	WARRIORS.		
		1607	1669	
Fairfax	About General Washington's	40		By the name of Matchotics. U. Matchodic. Nanzaticos. Nanzatico. Appamatox Matox.
Stafford. King George	Patowmac creek	200		
King George	About Lamb creek	20	60	
King Geo. Richmond	Above Leeds town	—		
Westmoreland	Nomony river	100		
Richmond county	Rappahanoc creek	100	30	
Lancaster. Richmond	Moratico river	80	40	
Northumberland	Coan river	30		by the name of Totuskeys.
Northumberland	Wicocomico river	130	70	
Lancaster	Corotoman	30		
Essex. Caroline	Port tobacco creek	150	60	
Mattapony river	— — — —	30	20	
King William	Romuncock	300	50	
Gloucester	About Rosewell	40		
Piankatank river	Turk's Ferry. Grimesby	55		
Pamunkey river	— — — —	60		
Chickahominy river	Orapaks	250	60	
Henrico	Powhatan. Mayo's	40	10	
Henrico	Arrohatocs	30		
Charles city	Weynoke	100	15	
Charles city. James city	Sandy point	40		
York	Chiskiac	45	15	
Elizabeth city	Roscows	20		
Chesterfield	Bermuda hundred	60	50	
Surry	About Upper Chipoak	25	3 Pohics	Nottoways / Meherrics / Tuteloes — 1669 / 90 / 50
Isle of Wight	Warrasqueac			
Nansamond	About the mouth of West. branch	200	45	
Princess Anne	About Lynhaven river	100		
Accom. Northampton	Accohanoc river	40		
Northampton	About Cheriton's	80		

EAST.

SOUTH.

Mannahoacs; and those on the upper parts of James river to the *Monacans*. But the *Monacans* and their friends were in amity with the *Mannahoacs* and their friends, and waged joint and perpetual war against the *Powhatans*. We are told that the *Powhatans*, *Mannahoacs*, and *Monacans*, spoke languages so radically different, that interpreters were necessary when they transacted business. Hence we may conjecture, that this was not the case between all the tribes, and probably that each spoke the language of the nation to which it was attached; which we know to have been the case in many particular instances. Very possibly there may have been antiently three different stocks, each of which multiplying in a long course of time, had separated into so many little societies. This practice results from the circumstance of their having never submitted themselves to any laws, any coercive power, any shadow of government. Their only controuls are their manners, and that moral sense of right and wrong, which, like the sense of tasting and feeling, in every man makes a part of his nature. An offence against these is punished by contempt, by exclusion from society, or, where the case is serious, as that of murder, by the individuals whom it concerns. Imperfect as this species of coercion may seem, crimes are very rare among them: insomuch that were it made a question, whether no law, as among the savage Americans, or too much law, as among the civilized Europeans, submits man to the greatest evil, one who has seen both conditions of existence would pronounce it to be the last: and that the sheep are happier of themselves, than under care of the wolves. It will be said, that great societies cannot exist without government. The Savages therefore break them into small ones.

The territories of the *Powhatan* confederacy, south of the Patowmac, comprehended about 8000 square miles, 30 tribes, and 2400 warriors. Capt. Smith tells us, that within 60 miles of James town were 5000 people, of whom 1500 were warriors. From this we find the proportion of their warriors to their whole inhabitants, was as 3 to 10. The *Powhatan* confederacy then would consist of about 8000 inhabitants, which was one for every square mile; being about the twentieth part of our present population in the same territory, and the hundredth of that of the British islands.

Besides these, were the *Nottoways*, living on Nottoway river, the *Meherrins* and *Tuteloes* on Meherrin river, who were connected with the Indians of Carolina, probably with the Chowanocs.

The preceding table contains a state of these several tribes, according to their confederacies and geographical situation, with their numbers when we first became acquainted with them, where these numbers are known. The numbers of some of them are again stated as they were in the year 1669, when an attempt was made by the assembly to enumerate them. Probably the enumeration is imperfect, and in some measure conjectural, and that a further search into the records would furnish many more particulars. What would be the melancholy sequel of their history, may however be augured from the census of 1669; by which we discover that the tribes therein enumerated were, in the space of 62 years, reduced to about one-third of their former numbers. Spirituous liquors, the small-pox, war, and an abridgment of territory, to a people who lived principally on the spontaneous productions of nature, had committed terrible havock among them, which generation, under the obstacles opposed to it among them, was not likely to make good. That the lands of this country were taken from them by conquest, is not so general a truth as is supposed. I find in our historians and records, repeated proofs of purchase, which cover a considerable part of the lower country; and many more would doubtless be found on further search. The upper country we know has been acquired altogether by purchases made in the most unexceptionable form.

Westward of all these tribes, beyond the mountains, and extending to the great lakes, were the *Massawomecs*, a most powerful confederacy, who harrassed unremittingly the *Powhatans* and *Manahoacs*. These were probably the ancestors of the tribes known at present by the name of the *Six Nations*.

Very little can now be discovered of the subsequent history of these tribes severally. The *Chickahominies* removed, about the year 1661, to Mattapony river. Their chief, with one from each of the tribes of the Pamunkies and Mattaponies, attended the treaty of Albany in 1685. This seems to have been the last chapter in their history. They retained however their separate name so late as 1705, and were at length blended with the Pamunkies and Mattaponies, and exist at present only under their names. There remain of the *Mattaponies* three or four men only, and they have more negro than Indian blood in them. They have lost their language, have reduced themselves, by voluntary sales, to about fifty acres of land, which lie on the river of their own name, and have, from time to time, been joining the Pamunkies, from whom they are distant but 10 miles. The *Pamunkies* are reduced to about 10 or 12 men, tolerably pure from mixture with other colours. The older ones among them preserve their language in a small degree, which are the last vestiges on earth, as far as we know, of the Powhatan language. They have about 300 acres of very fertile land, on Pamunkey river, so encompassed by water that a gate shuts in the whole. Of the *Nottoways*, not a male is left. A few women constitute the remains of that tribe. They are seated on Nottoway river, in Southampton county, on very fertile lands. At a very early period, certain lands were marked out and appropriated to these tribes, and were kept from encroachment by the authority of the laws. They have usually had trustees appointed, whose duty was to watch over their interests, and guard them from insult and injury.

The *Monacans* and their friends, better known latterly by the name of *Tuscaroras*, were probably connected with the Massawomecs, or Five Nations. For though we are *told their languages were so different that the intervention of interpreters was necessary between them, yet do we also †learn that the Erigas, a nation formerly inhabiting on the Ohio, were of the same original stock with the Five Nations, and that they partook also of the Tuscarora language. Their dialects might, by long separation, have become so unlike as to be unintelligible to one another. We know that in 1712, the Five Nations received the Tuscaroras into their confederacy, and made them the Sixth Nation. They received the Meherrins and Tuteloes also into their protection: and it is most probable, that the remains of many other of the tribes, of whom we find no particular account, retired westwardly in

*Smith.
†Evans.

like manner, and were incorporated with one or other of the western tribes.

I know of no such thing existing as an Indian monument: for I would not honour with that name arrow points, stone hatchets, stone pipes, and half-shapen images. Of labour on the large scale, I think there is no remain as respectable as would be a common ditch for the draining of lands: unless indeed it be the Barrows, of which many are to be found all over this country. These are of different sizes, some of them constructed of earth, and some of loose stones. That they were repositories of the dead, has been obvious to all: but on what particular occasion constructed, was matter of doubt. Some have thought they covered the bones of those who have fallen in battles fought on the spot of interment. Some ascribed them to the custom, said to prevail among the Indians, of collecting, at certain periods, the bones of all their dead, wheresoever deposited at the time of death. Others again supposed them the general sepulchres for towns, conjectured to have been on or near these grounds; and this opinion was supported by the quality of the lands in which they are found, (those constructed of earth being generally in the softest and most fertile meadow-grounds on river sides) and by a tradition, said to be handed down from the Aboriginal Indians, that, when they settled in a town, the first person who died was placed erect, and earth put about him, so as to cover and support him; that, when another died, a narrow passage was dug to the first, the second reclined against him, and the cover of earth replaced, and so on. There being one of these in my neighbourhood, I wished to satisfy myself whether any, and which of these opinions were just. For this purpose I determined to open and examine it thoroughly. It was situated on the low grounds of the Rivanna, about two miles above its principal fork, and opposite to some hills, on which had been an Indian town. It was of a spheroidical form, of about 40 feet diameter at the base, and had been of about twelve feet altitude, though now reduced by the plough to seven and a half, having been under cultivation about a dozen years. Before this it was covered with trees of twelve inches diameter, and round the base was an excavation of five feet depth and width, from whence the earth had been taken of which the hillock was formed. I first dug superficially in several parts of it, and came to collections of human bones, at different depths, from six inches to three feet below the surface. These were lying in the utmost confusion, some vertical, some oblique, some horizontal, and directed to every point of the compass, entangled, and held together in clusters by the earth. Bones of the most distant parts were found together, as, for instance, the small bones of the foot in the hollow of a scull, many sculls would sometimes be in contact, lying on the face, on the side, on the back, top or bottom, so as, on the whole, to give the idea of bones emptied promiscuously from a bag or basket, and covered over with earth, without any attention to their order. The bones of which the greatest numbers remained, were sculls, jaw-bones, teeth, the bones of the arms, thighs, legs, feet, and hands. A few ribs remained, some vertebræ of the neck and spine, without their processes, and one instance only of the *bone which serves as a base to the vertebral column. The sculls were so tender, that they generally fell to pieces on being touched. The other bones were stronger. There were some teeth which were judged to be smaller than those of an adult; a scull, which, on a slight view, appeared to be that of an infant, but it fell to pieces on being taken out, so as to prevent satisfactory examination; a rib, and a fragment of the under-jaw of a person about half grown; another rib of an infant; and part of the jaw of a child, which had not yet cut its teeth. This last furnishing the most decisive proof of the burial of children here, I was particular in my attention to it. It was part of the right-half of the under-jaw. The processes, by which it was articulated to the temporal bones, were entire; and the bone itself firm to where it had been broken off, which, as nearly as I could judge, was about the place of the eye-tooth. Its upper edge, wherein would have been the sockets of the teeth, was perfectly smooth. Measuring it with that of an adult, by placing their hinder processes together, its broken end extended to the penultimate grinder of the adult. This bone was white, all the others of a sand colour. The bones of

*The os sacrum.

infants being soft, they probably decay sooner, which might be the cause so few were found here. I proceeded then to make a perpendicular cut through the body of the barrow, that I might examine its internal structure. This passed about three feet from its center, was opened to the former surface of the earth, and was wide enough for a man to walk through and examine its sides. At the bottom, that is, on the level of the circumjacent plain, I found bones; above these a few stones, brought from a cliff a quarter of a mile off, and from the river one-eighth of a mile off; then a large interval of earth, then a stratum of bones, and so on. At one end of the section were four strata of bones plainly distinguishable; at the other, three; the strata in one part not ranging with those in another. The bones nearest the surface were least decayed. No holes were discovered in any of them, as if made with bullets, arrows, or other weapons. I conjectured that in this barrow might have been a thousand skeletons. Every one will readily seize the circumstances above related, which militate against the opinion, that it covered the bones only of persons fallen in battle; and against the tradition also, which would make it the common sepulchre of a town, in which the bodies were placed upright, and touching each other. Appearances certainly indicate that it has derived both origin and growth from the accustomary collection of bones, and deposition of them together; that the first collection had been deposited on the common surface of the earth, a few stones put over it, and then a covering of earth, that the second had been laid on this, had covered more or less of it in proportion to the number of bones, and was then also covered with earth; and so on. The following are the particular circumstances which give it this aspect. 1. The number of bones. 2. Their confused position. 3. Their being in different strata. 4. The strata in one part having no correspondence with those in another. 5. The different states of decay in these strata, which seem to indicate a difference in the time of inhumation. 6. The existence of infant bones among them.

But on whatever occasion they may have been made, they are of considerable notoriety among the Indians: for a party passing, about thirty years ago, through the part of the country where this barrow is, went through the woods directly to it, without any instructions or enquiry, and having staid about it some time, with expressions which were construed to be those of sorrow, they returned to the high road, which they had left about half a dozen miles to pay this visit, and pursued their journey. There is another barrow, much resembling this in the low grounds of the South branch of Shenandoah, where it is crossed by the road leading from the Rock-fish gap to Staunton. Both of these have, within these dozen years, been cleared of their trees and put under cultivation, are much reduced in their height, and spread in width, by the plough, and will probably disappear in time. There is another on a hill in the Blue ridge of mountains, a few miles North of Wood's gap, which is made up of small stones thrown together. This has been opened and found to contain human bones, as the others do. There are also many others in other parts of the country.

Great question has arisen from whence came those aboriginal inhabitants of America? Discoveries, long ago made, were sufficient to shew that a passage from Europe to America was always practicable, even to the imperfect navigation of ancient times. In going from Norway to Iceland, from Iceland to Groenland, from Groenland to Labrador, the first traject is the widest: and this having been practised from the earliest times of which we have any account of that part of the earth, it is not difficult to suppose that the subsequent trajects may have been sometimes passed. Again, the late discoveries of Captain Cook, coasting from Kamschatka to California, have proved that, if the two continents of Asia and America be separated at all, it is only by a narrow streight. So that from this side also, inhabitants may have passed into America: and the resemblance between the Indians of America and the Eastern inhabitants of Asia, would induce us to conjecture, that the former are the descendants of the latter, or the latter of the former: excepting indeed the Eskimaux, who, from the same circumstance of resemblance, and from identity of language, must be derived from the Groenlanders, and these probably from some of the northern parts of the old continent. A knowledge of their several languages would be the most certain evidence of their derivation which could be produced. In fact, it is the best proof of the affinity of nations which ever can be referred to. How many ages have elapsed since the English, the Dutch, the Germans, the Swiss, the Norwegians, Danes and Swedes have separated from their common stock? Yet how many more must elapse before the proofs of their common origin, which exist in their several languages, will disappear? It is to be lamented then, very much to be lamented, that we have suffered so many of the Indian tribes already to extinguish, without our having previously collected and deposited in the records of literature, the general rudiments at least of the languages they spoke. Were vocabularies formed of all the languages spoken in North and South America, preserving their appellations of the most common objects in nature, of those which must be present to every nation barbarous or civilised, with the inflections of their nouns and verbs, their principles of regimen and concord, and these deposited in all the public libraries, it would furnish opportunities to those skilled in the languages of the old world to compare them with these, now, or at any future time, and hence to construct the best evidence of the derivation of this part of the human race.

But imperfect as is our knowledge of the tongues spoken in America, it suffices to discover the following remarkable fact. Arranging them under the radical ones to which they may be palpably traced, and doing the same by those of the red men of Asia, there will be found probably twenty in America, for one in Asia, of those radical languages, so called because, if they were ever the same, they have lost all resemblance to one another. A separation into dialects may be the work of a few ages only, but for two dialects to recede from one another till they have lost all vestiges of their common origin, must require an immense course of time; perhaps not less than many people give to the age of the earth. A greater number of those radical changes of language having taken place among the red men of America, proves them of greater antiquity than those of Asia.

I will now proceed to state the nations and numbers of the Aborigines which still exist in a respectable and independant form. And as their undefined boundaries would render it difficult to specify those only which may be within any certain limits, and it may not be unacceptable to present a more general view of them, I will reduce within the form of a Catalogue all those within, and circumjacent to, the United States, whose names and numbers have come to my notice. These are taken from four different lists, the first of which was given in the year 1759 to General Stanwix by George Croghan, Deputy agent for Indian affairs under Sir William Johnson; the second was drawn up by a French trader of considerable note, resident among the Indians many years, and annexed to Colonel Bouquet's printed account of his expedition in 1764. The third was made out by Captain Hutchins, who visited most of the tribes, by order, for the purpose of learning their numbers in 1768. And the fourth by John Dodge, an Indian trader, in 1779, except the numbers marked *, which are from other information.

TRIBES.	Croghan. 1759.	Bouquet. 1764.	Hutchins. 1768.	Where they reside.
Oswegatchies	— —	— —	100	At Swagatchy, on the river St. Laurence
Connasedagoes	— —	— — ⎫	300	Near Montreal
Cohunnewagoes	— —	200 ⎬		
Orondocs	— —	— — ⎭	100	Near Trois Rivieres
Abenakies	— —	350	150	Near Trois Rivieres
Little Algonkins	— —	— —	100	Near Trois Rivieres
Michmacs	— —	700	— —	River St. Laurence
Amelistes	— —	550	— —	River St. Laurence
Chalas	— —	130	— —	River St. Laurence
Nipissins	— —	400	— —	Towards the heads of the Ottawas river
Algonquins	— —	300	— —	Towards the heads of the Ottawas river
Round heads	— —	2500	— —	Riviere aux Tetes boules on the East side of Lake Superior
Messasagues	— —	2000	— —	Lakes Huron and Superior
Christinaux. Kris	— —	3000	— —	Lake Christinaux
Assinaboes	— —	1500	— —	Lake Assinaboes
Blancs, or Barbus	— —	1500	— —	
Sioux of the Meadows ⎫		2500 ⎫		
Sioux of the Woods ⎬	10,000	1800 ⎬	10,000	On the heads of the Missisipi
Sioux ⎭		— ⎭		and Westward of that river
Ajoues	— —	1100	— —	North of the Padoucas
Panis. White	— —	2000	— —	South of the Missouri
Panis. Freckled	— —	1700	— —	South of the Missouri
Padoucas	— —	500	— —	South of the Missouri
Grandes eaux	— —	1000	— —	
Canses	— —	1600	— —	South of the Missouri
Osages	— —	600	— —	South of the Missouri
Missouris	400	3000	— —	On the river Missouri
Arkanzas	— —	2000	— —	On the river Arkanzas
Caouitas	— —	700	— —	East of the Alibamous

Northward and Westward of the United States.

Within the Limits of the United States.

TRIBES.	Croghan. 1759.	Bouquet. 1764.	Hutchins. 1768.	Dodge. 1779.	Where they reside.
Mohocks	—	——	160	100	Mohocks river. [of Susquehanna.
Onèidas	—	——	300	400	E. side of Oneida L. and head branches
Tuscaròras	—	——	200		Between the Oneidas and Onondàgoes.
Onondàgoes	—	1550	260	230	Near Onondago L. [of Susquehanna.
Cayùgas	—	——	200	220	On the Cayuga L. near the N. branch
Sènecas	—	——	1000	650	On the waters of Susquehanna, of Ontario, and the heads of the Ohio.
Aughquàgahs	—	——	150	—	East branch of Susquehanna, and on Aughquagah.
Nànticocs	—	——	100	—	Utsanango, Chaghtnet, and Owegy, on the East branch of Susquehanna.
Mohìccons	—	——	100	—	In the same parts.
Conòies	—	——	30	—	In the same parts.
Sapòonies	—	——	30	—	At Diahago and other villages up the N. branch of Susquehanna.
Mùnsies	—	——	150	*150	At Diahago and other villages up the N. branch of Susquehanna.
Delawares, or Linnelinopies	—	—	150	*500	At Diahago and other villages up the N. branch of Susquehanna.
Delawares, or Linnelinopies	600	600	600		Between Ohio and L. Erie and the branches of Beaver creek, Cayahoga and Muskingham.
Shàwanees	400	500	300	300	Sioto and the branches of Muskingham.
Mìngoes	—	—	——	60	On a branch of Sioto.
Mohìccons	—	—		*60	
Cohunnewagos	—	—	300	—	Near Sandusky.
Wyandots	300	300	300	180	Near Fort St. Joseph's and Detroit.
Wyandots			250		
Twightwees	300	—	250	—	Miami river near Fort Miami.
Miamis	—	350	——	300	Miami river, about Fort St. Joseph.
Ouiàtonons	200	400	300	*300	On the banks of the Wabash, near Fort Ouiatonon.
Pìankishas	300	250	300	*400	On the banks of the Wabash, near Fort Ouiatonon.
Shàkies	—	—	200	—	On the banks of the Wabash, near Fort Ouiatonon.

TRIBES.	Croghan. 1759.	Bouquet. 1764.	Hutchins. 1768.	Dodge. 1779.	Where they reside.
Kaskaskias	— ⎫	600	300	—	Near Kaskaskia.
Illinois	400 ⎭		300	—	Near Cahokia. Qu. If not the same with the Mitchigamis?
Piorias	—	800	— —	—	On the Illinois R. called Pianrias, but supposed to mean Piorias.
Poutëòtamies ⎫	—	350	300	450	Near St. Joseph's and Fort Detroit.
Ottàwas ⎪	— ⎫	—	550	*300	Near St. Joseph's and Fort Detroit.
Chìppawas ⎪	— ⎪	— ⎫		—	On Saguinam bay of Lake Huron.
Ottawas ⎪	— ⎪	— ⎬	200	—	On Saguinam bay of Lake Huron.
Chippawas ⎬	— ⎪	— ⎭	400 ⎫	—	Near Michillimakinac.
Ottawas ⎪	— ⎪	—	250	5450	Near Michillimakinac.
Chippawas ⎪	2000 ⎬	5900	400		Near Fort St. Mary's on Lake Superior.
Chippawas ⎪	— ⎪	—	— —	—	Several other villages along the banks of Lake Superior. Numbers unknown.
Chippawas ⎪	— ⎪	— ⎫	— — ⎫	—	Near Puans bay, on Lake Michigan.
Shakies ⎭	200 ⎭	400 ⎬	550 ⎭	—	Near Puans bay, on Lake Michigan.
Mynonàmies	—	— ⎭	— —	—	Near Puans bay, on Lake Michigan.
Ouisconsings	—	550	— —	—	Ouisconsing River.
Kìckapous	600	300 ⎫	— —	250 ⎫	
Otogamies. Foxes	—	— ⎪	— —	— ⎪	
Màscoutens	—	500 ⎪		— ⎪	On Lake Michigan, and between that and the Missisipi.
Miscòthins	—	— ⎬	4000	— ⎬	
Outimacs	—	— ⎪	— —	— ⎪	
Musquakies	200	250 ⎭	— —	250 ⎭	
Sioux. Eastern	—	—	— —	500	On the Eastern heads of Missisipi, and the islands of Lake Superior.
			Galphin. 1768.		
Cherokees	1500	2500	3000	—	Western parts of North Carolina.
Chickasaws	—	750	500	—	Western parts of Georgia.
Catawbas	—	150	— —	—	On the Catawba R. in S. Carolina.

Within the Limits of the United States.

TRIBES.	Croghan. 1759.	Bouquet. 1764.	Galphin. 1768.	Dodge. 1779.	Where they reside.
Chacktaws	2000	4500	6000	—	Western parts of Georgia.
Upper Creeks	—	—	3000	—	Western parts of Georgia.
Lower Creeks	—	1180			
Natchez	—	150	——	—	
Alibamous	—	600	——	—	Alibama R. in the Western parts of Georgia.

The following tribes are also mentioned:

Croghan's catal.	Lezar	400	From the mouth of Ohio to the mouth of Wabash.
	Webings	200	On the Missisipi below the Shakies.
	Ousasoys. Grand Tuc.	4000	On White creek, a branch of the Missisipi.
	Linways	1000	On the Missisipi.
Bouquet's.	Les Puans	700	Near Puans bay.
	Folle avoine	350	Near Puans bay.
	Ouanakina	300	
	Chiakanessou	350	Conjectured to be tribes of the creeks.
	Machecous	800	
	Souikilas	200	
Dodge's.	Mineamis	2000	North-west of L. Michigan, to the heads of Missisipi, and up to L. Superior.
	Piankishas Mascoutins Vermillions	800	On and near the Wabash, towards the Illinois.

But, apprehending these might be different appellations for some of the tribes already enumerated, I have not inserted them in the table, but state them separately as worthy of further inquiry. The variations observable in numbering the same tribe may sometimes be ascribed to imperfect information, and sometimes to a greater or less comprehension of settlements under the same name.

QUERY XII

A notice of the counties, cities, townships, and villages?

The counties have been enumerated under Query IX. They are 74 in number, of very unequal size and population. Of these 35 are on the tide waters, or in that parallel; 23 are in the Midlands, between the tide waters and Blue ridge of mountains; 8 between the Blue ridge and Alleghaney; and 8 westward of the Alleghaney.

The state, by another division, is formed into parishes, many of which are commensurate with the counties: but sometimes a county comprehends more than one parish, and sometimes a parish more than one county. This division had relation to the religion of the state, a Parson of the Anglican church, with a fixed salary, having been heretofore established in each parish. The care of the poor was another object of the parochial division.

We have no townships. Our country being much intersected with navigable waters, and trade brought generally to our doors, instead of our being obliged to go in quest of it, has probably been one of the causes why we have no towns of any consequence. Williamsburgh, which, till the year 1780, was the seat of our government, never contained above 1800 inhabitants; and Norfolk, the most populous town we ever had, contained but 6000. Our towns, but more properly our villages or hamlets, are as follows.

On *James river* and its waters, Norfolk, Portsmouth, Hampton, Suffolk, Smithfield, Williamsburgh, Petersburg, Richmond the seat of our government, Manchester, Charlottesville, New London.

On *York river* and its waters, York, Newcastle, Hanover.

On *Rappahannoc*, Urbanna, Portroyal, Fredericksburg, Falmouth.

On *Patowmac* and its waters, Dumfries, Colchester, Alexandria, Winchester, Staunton.

On *Ohio*, Louisville.

There are other places at which, like some of the foregoing, the *laws* have said there shall be towns; but *Nature* has said there shall not, and they remain unworthy of enumeration. *Norfolk* will probably be the emporium for all the trade of the Chesapeak bay and its waters; and a canal of 8 or 10 miles will bring to it all that of Albemarle sound and its waters. Secondary to this place, are the towns at the head of the tidewaters, to wit, Petersburgh on Appamattox, Richmond on James river, Newcastle on York river, Alexandria on Patowmac, and Baltimore on the Patapsco. From these the distribution will be to subordinate situations in the country. Accidental circumstances however may controul the indications of nature, and in no instances do they do it more frequently than in the rise and fall of towns.

QUERY XIII

The constitution of the state, and its several charters?

Consti-
tution

Queen Elizabeth by her letters-patent, bearing date March 25, 1584, licensed Sir Walter Raleigh to search for remote heathen lands, not inhabited by Christian people, and granted to him, in fee simple, all the soil within 200 leagues of the places where his people should, within 6 years, make their dwellings or abidings; reserving only, to herself and her successors, their allegiance and one fifth part of all the gold and silver ore they should obtain. Sir Walter immediately sent out two ships which visited Wococon island in North Carolina, and the next year dispatched seven with 107 men, who settled in Roanoke island, about latitude 35°. 50.′ Here Okisko, king of the Weopomeiocs, in a full council of his people, is said to have acknowledged himself the homager of the Queen of England, and, after her, of Sir Walter Raleigh. A supply of 50 men were sent in 1586, and 150 in 1587. With these last, Sir Walter sent a Governor, appointed him twelve assistants, gave them a charter of incorporation, and instructed them to settle on Chesapeak bay. They landed however at Hatorask. In 1588, when a fleet was ready to sail with a new supply of colonists and necessaries, they were detained by the Queen to assist against the Spanish Armada. Sir Walter having now expended 40,000 l. in these enterprizes, obstructed occasionally by the crown, without a shilling of aid from it, was under a necessity of engaging others to adventure their money. He therefore, by deed bearing date the 7th of March 1589, by the name of Sir Walter Raleigh, Chief Governor of Assamàcomòc, (probably Acomàc), alias Wingadacoia, alias Virginia, granted to Thomas Smith and others, in consideration of their adventuring certain sums of money, liberty of trade to his new country, free from all customs and taxes for seven years, excepting the fifth part of the gold and silver ore to be obtained; and stipulated with them, and the other assistants, then in Virginia, that he would confirm the deed of incorporation which he had given in 1587, with all the prerogatives, jurisdictions, royalties and privileges granted to him by the Queen. Sir

Walter, at different times, sent five other adventures hither, the last of which was in 1602: for in 1603 he was attainted, and put into close imprisonment, which put an end to his cares over his infant colony. What was the particular fate of the colonists he had before sent and seated, has never been known: whether they were murdered, or incorporated with the savages.

Some gentlemen and merchants, supposing that by the attainder of Sir Walter Raleigh the grant to him was forfeited, not enquiring over carefully whether the sentence of an English court could affect lands not within the jurisdiction of that court, petitioned king James for a new grant of Virginia to them. He accordingly executed a grant to Sir Thomas Gates and others, bearing date the 9th of March 1607, under which, in the same year a settlement was effected at Jamestown and ever after maintained. Of this grant however no particular notice need be taken, as it was superseded by letters-patent of the same king, of May 23, 1609, to the Earl of Salisbury and others, incorporating them by the name of 'the Treasurer and Company of adventurers and planters of the City of London for the first colony in Virginia,' granting to them and their successors all the lands in Virginia from Point Comfort along the sea coast to the northward 200 miles, and from the same point along the sea coast to the southward 200 miles, and all the space from this precinct on the sea coast up into the land, West and North-west, from sea to sea, and the islands within one hundred miles of it, with all the commodities, jurisdictions, royalties, privileges, franchises and pre-eminences within the same, and thereto and thereabouts, by sea and land, appertaining, in as ample manner as had before been granted to any adventurer: to be held of the king and his successors, in common soccage, yielding one fifth part of the gold and silver ore to be therein found, for all manner of services; establishing a council in England for the direction of the enterprise, the members of which were to be chosen and displaced by the voice of the majority of the company and adventurers, and were to have the nomination and revocation of governors, officers, and ministers, which by them should be thought needful for the colony, the power of establishing laws and forms of government and magistracy, obligatory not only within the colony, but also on the seas in going and coming to and from it; authorising them to carry thither any persons who should consent to go, freeing them for ever from all taxes and impositions on any goods or merchandize on importation into the colony, or exportation out of it, except the five per cent. due for custom on all goods imported into the British dominions, according to the ancient trade of merchants; which five per cent. only being paid, they might, within 13 months, re-export the same goods into foreign parts, without any custom, tax, or other duty, to the king or any his officers or deputies: with powers of waging war against those who should annoy them: giving to the inhabitants of the colony all the rights of natural subjects, as if born and abiding in England; and declaring that these letters should be construed, in all doubtful parts, in such manner as should be most for the benefit of the grantees.

Afterwards, on the 12th of March 1612, by other letters-patent, the king added to his former grants, all islands in any part of the ocean between the 30th and 41st degrees of latitude, and within 300 leagues of any of the parts before granted to the Treasurer and company, not being possessed or inhabited by any other christian prince or state, nor within the limits of the northern colony.

In pursuance of the authorities given to the company by these charters, and more especially of that part in the charter of 1609, which authorised them to establish a form of government, they on the 24th of July 1621, by charter under their common seal, declared that from thenceforward there should be two supreme councils in Virginia, the one to be called the council of state, to be placed and displaced by the treasurer, council in England, and company, from time to time, whose office was to be that of assisting and advising the governor; the other to be called the general assembly, to be convened by the governor once yearly or oftener, which was to consist of the council of state, and two burgesses out of every town, hundred, or plantation, to be respectively chosen by the inhabitants. In this all matters were to be decided by the greater part of the votes present; reserving to the governor a negative voice; and they were to have power to treat, consult, and conclude all emergent occasions concerning the public weal, and to make laws for the behoof and government of the colony, imitating and following the laws and policy of England as nearly as might be: providing that these laws should have no force till ratified in a general quarter court of the company in England, and returned under their common seal, and declaring that, after the government of the colony should be well framed and settled, no orders of the council in England should bind the colony unless ratified in the said general assembly. The king and company quarrelled, and, by a mixture of law and force, the latter were ousted of all their rights, without retribution, after having expended 100,000 l. in establishing the colony, without the smallest aid from government. King James suspended their powers by proclamation of July 15, 1624, and Charles I. took the government into his own hands. Both sides had their partisans in the colony: but in truth the people of the colony in general thought themselves little concerned in the dispute. There being three parties interested in these several charters, what passed between the first and second it was thought could not affect the third. If the king seized on the powers of the company, they only passed into other hands, without increase or diminution, while the rights of the people remained as they were. But they did not remain so long. The northern parts of their country were granted away to the Lords Baltimore and Fairfax, the first of these obtaining also the rights of separate jurisdiction and government. And in 1650 the parliament, considering itself as standing in the place of their deposed king, and as having succeeded to all his powers, without as well as within the realm, began to assume a right over the colonies, passing an act for inhibiting their trade with foreign nations. This succession to the exercise of the kingly authority gave the first colour for parliamentary interference with the colonies, and produced that fatal precedent which they continued to follow after they had retired, in other respects, within their proper functions. When this colony, therefore, which still maintained its opposition to Cromwell and the parliament, was induced in 1651 to lay down their arms, they previously secured their most essential rights, by a solemn convention, which having never seen in print, I will here insert literally from the records.

'ARTICLES agreed on & concluded at James Cittie in Virginia for the surrendering and settling of that plantation under ẙ obedience & goverment of the common wealth of England by the Commissioners of the Councill of state by authoritie of the parliamt. of England & by the Grand assembly of the Governour, Councill & Burgesses of that countrey.

'First it is agreed and consted that the plantation of Virginia, and all the inhabitants thereof shall be and remaine in due obedience and subjection to the Comon wealth of England, according to ẙ lawes there established, and that this submission and subscription bee acknowledged a voluntary act not forced nor constrained by a conquest upon the countrey, and that they shall have & enjoy such freedomes and priviledges as belong to the free borne people of England, and that the former government by the Comissions and Instructions be void and null.

'2ly, Secondly that the Grand assembly as formerly shall convene & transact the affairs of Virginia wherein nothing is to be acted or done contrarie to the government of the Comon wealth of England & the lawes there established.

'3ly, That there shall be a full & totall remission and indempnitie of all acts, words, or writeings done or spoken against the parliament of England in relation to the same.

'4ly, That Virginia shall have & enjoy ẙ antient bounds and Lymitts granted by the charters of the former kings, and that we shall seek a new charter from the parliament to that purpose against any that have intrencht upon ẙ rights thereof.

'5ly, That all the pattents of land granted under the collony seale by any of the precedent governours shall be & remaine in their full force & strength.

'6ly, That the priviledge of haveing ffiftie acres of land for every person transported in that collonie shall continue as formerly granted.

'7ly, That ẙ people of Virginia have free trade as ẙ people of England do enjoy to all places and with all nations according to ẙ lawes of that common wealth, and that Virginia shall enjoy all priviledges equall with any English plantations in America.

'8ly, That Virginia shall be free from all taxes, customs & impositions whatsoever, & none to be imposed on them without consent of the Grand assembly, And soe that neither ffortes nor castles bee erected or garrisons maintained without their consent.

'9ly, That noe charge shall be required from this country in respect of this present ffleet.

'10ly, That for the future settlement of the countrey in their due obedience, the Engagement shall be tendred to all ỹ inhabitants according to act of parliament made to that purpose, that all persons who shall refuse to subscribe the said engagement, shall have a yeare's time if they please to remove themselves & their estates out of Virginia, and in the mean time during the said yeare to have equall justice as formerly.

'11ly, That ỹ use of the booke of common prayer shall be permitted for one yeare ensueinge with referrence to the consent of ỹ major part of the parishes, provided that those things which relate to kingshipp or that government be not used publiquely, and the continuance of ministers in their places, they not misdemeaning themselves, and the payment of their accustomed dues and agreements made with them respectively shall be left as they now stand dureing this ensueing yeare.

'12ly, That no man's cattell shall be questioned as ỹ companies unles such as have been entrusted with them or have disposed of them without order.

'13ly, That all ammunition, powder & armes, other then for private use, shall be delivered up, securitie being given to make satisfaction for it.

'14ly, That all goods allreadie brought hither by ỹ Dutch or others which are now on shoar shall be free from surprizall.

'15ly, That the quittrents granted unto us by the late kinge for seaven yeares bee confirmed.

'16ly, That ỹ commissioners for the parliament subscribeing these articles engage themselves & the honour of the parliament for the full performance thereof: and that the present governour & ỹ councill & the burgesses do likewise subscribe & engage the whole collony on their parts.

RICH. BENNETT.————Seale.

W^m. CLAIBORNE.————Seale.

EDMOND CURTIS.————Seale.

'Theise articles were signed & sealed by the Commissioners of the Councill of state for the Commonwealth of England the twelveth day of March 1651.'

Then follow the articles stipulated by the governor and council, which relate merely to their own persons and property, and then the ensuing instrument:

'An act of indempnitie made att the surrender of the countrey.

'Whereas by the authoritie of the parliament of England wee the commissioners appointed by the councill of state authorized thereto having brought a fleete & force before James cittie in Virginia to reduce that collonie under the obedience of the commonwealth of England, & findeing force raised by the Governour & countrey to make opposition against the said ffleet whereby assured danger appearinge of the ruine & destruction of ſ plantation, for prevention whereof the Burgesses of all the severall plantations being called to advise & assist therein, uppon long & serious debate, and in sad contemplation of the greate miseries & certaine destruction which were soe neerely hovering over the whole countrey; Wee the said Comissioners have thought fitt & condescended and granted to signe & confirme under our hands, seales, & by our oath, Articles bearinge date with theise presents, and do further declare that by ſ authoritie of the parliament & commonwealth of England derived unto us theire Comissioners, that according to the articles in generall wee have granted an act of indempnitie and oblivion to all the inhabitants of this colloney from all words, actions, or writings that have been spoken acted or writt against the parliament or commonwealth of England or any other person from the beginning of the world to this daye. And this wee have done that all the inhabitants of the collonie may live quietly & securely under the comonwealth of England. And wee do promise that the parliament and commonwealth of England shall confirme & make good all those transactions of ours.

Wittnes our hands & seales this 12th of March 1651. Richard Bennett—Seale. W^m. Claiborne—Seale. Edm. Curtis—Seale.'

The colony supposed, that, by this solemn convention, entered into with arms in their hands, they had secured the *antient limits of their country, †its free trade, its exemption from ‡taxation but by their own assembly, and exclusion of §military force from among them. Yet in every of these points was this convention violated by subsequent kings and parliaments, and other infractions of their constitution, equally dangerous, committed. Their General Assembly, which was composed of the council of state and burgesses, sitting together and deciding by plurality of voices, was split into two houses, by which the council obtained a separate negative on their laws. Appeals from their supreme court, which had been fixed by law in their General Assembly, were arbitrarily revoked to England, to be there heard before the king and council. Instead of four hundred miles on the sea coast, they were reduced, in the space of thirty years, to about one hundred miles. Their trade with foreigners was totally suppressed, and, when carried to Great-Britain, was there loaded with imposts. It is unnecessary, however, to glean up the several instances of injury, as scattered through American and British history, and the more especially as, by passing on to the accession of the present king, we shall find specimens of them all, aggravated, multiplied and crouded within a small compass of time, so as to evince a fixed design of considering our rights natural, conventional and chartered as mere nullities. The following is an epitome of the first fifteen years of his reign. The colonies were taxed internally and externally; their essential interests sacrificed to individuals in Great-Britain; their legislatures suspended; charters annulled; trials by juries taken away; their persons subjected to transportation across the Atlantic, and to trial before foreign judicatories; their supplications for redress thought beneath answer; them-

* Art. 4.
† Art. 7.
‡ Art. 8.
§ Art. 8.

selves published as cowards in the councils of their mother country and courts of Europe; armed troops sent among them to enforce submission to these violences; and actual hostilities commenced against them. No alternative was presented but resistance, or unconditional submission. Between these could be no hesitation. They closed in the appeal to arms. They declared themselves independent States. They confederated together into one great republic; thus securing to every state the benefit of an union of their whole force. In each state separately a new form of government was established. Of ours particularly the following are the outlines. The executive powers are lodged in the hands of a governor, chosen annually, and incapable of acting more than three years in seven. He is assisted by a council of eight members. The judiciary powers are divided among several courts, as will be hereafter explained. Legislation is exercised by two houses of assembly, the one called the house of Delegates, composed of two members from each county, chosen annually by the citizens possessing an estate for life in 100 acres of uninhabited land, or 25 acres with a house on it, or in a house or lot in some town: the other called the Senate, consisting of 24 members, chosen quadrennially by the same electors, who for this purpose are distributed into 24 districts. The concurrence of both houses is necessary to the passage of a law. They have the appointment of the governor and council, the judges of the superior courts, auditors, attorney-general, treasurer, register of the land office, and delegates to congress. As the dismemberment of the state had never had its confirmation, but, on the contrary, had always been the subject of protestation and complaint, that it might never be in our own power to raise scruples on that subject, or to disturb the harmony of our new confederacy, the grants to Maryland, Pennsylvania, and the two Carolinas, were ratified.

This constitution was formed when we were new and unexperienced in the science of government. It was the first too which was formed in the whole United States. No wonder then that time and trial have discovered very capital defects in it.

1. The majority of the men in the state, who pay and fight for its support, are unrepresented in the legislature, the roll

of freeholders intitled to vote, not including generally the half of those on the roll of the militia, or of the tax-gatherers.

2. Among those who share the representation, the shares are very unequal. Thus the county of Warwick, with only one hundred fighting men, has an equal representation with the county of Loudon, which has 1746. So that every man in Warwick has as much influence in the government as 17 men in Loudon. But lest it should be thought that an equal interspersion of small among large counties, through the whole state, may prevent any danger of injury to particular parts of it, we will divide it into districts, and shew the proportions of land, of fighting men, and of representation in each.

	Square miles.	Fighting men.	Delegates	Senators.
Between the sea-coast and falls of the rivers	*11,205	19,012	71	12
Between the falls of the rivers and the Blue ridge of mountains	18,759	18,828	46	8
Between the Blue ridge and the Alleghaney	11,911	7,673	16	2
Between the Alleghaney and the Ohio	†79,650	4,458	16	2
Total	121,525	49,971	149	24

An inspection of this table will supply the place of commentaries on it. It will appear at once that nineteen thousand men, living below the falls of the rivers, possess half the senate, and want four members only of possessing a majority of the house of delegates; a want more than supplied by the vicinity of their situation to the seat of government, and of course the greater degree of convenience and punctuality with which their members may and will attend in the legislature. These nineteen thousand, therefore, living in one part of the country, give law to upwards of thirty thousand, living in another, and appoint all their chief officers executive and judiciary. From the difference of their situation and circumstances, their interests will often be very different.

3. The senate is, by its constitution, too homogeneous with the house of delegates. Being chosen by the same electors, at

* Of these, 542 are on the Eastern shore.
† Of these, 22,616 are Eastward of the meridian of the mouth of the Great Kanhaway.

the same time, and out of the same subjects, the choice falls of course on men of the same description. The purpose of establishing different houses of legislation is to introduce the influence of different interests or different principles. Thus in Great-Britain it is said their constitution relies on the house of commons for honesty, and the lords for wisdom; which would be a rational reliance if honesty were to be bought with money, and if wisdom were hereditary. In some of the American states the delegates and senators are so chosen, as that the first represent the persons, and the second the property of the state. But with us, wealth and wisdom have equal chance for admission into both houses. We do not therefore derive from the separation of our legislature into two houses, those benefits which a proper complication of principles is capable of producing, and those which alone can compensate the evils which may be produced by their dissensions.

4. All the powers of government, legislative, executive, and judiciary, result to the legislative body. The concentrating these in the same hands is precisely the definition of despotic government. It will be no alleviation that these powers will be exercised by a plurality of hands, and not by a single one. 173 despots would surely be as oppressive as one. Let those who doubt it turn their eyes on the republic of Venice. As little will it avail us that they are chosen by ourselves. An *elective despotism* was not the government we fought for; but one which should not only be founded on free principles, but in which the powers of government should be so divided and balanced among several bodies of magistracy, as that no one could transcend their legal limits, without being effectually checked and restrained by the others. For this reason that convention, which passed the ordinance of government, laid its foundation on this basis, that the legislative, executive and judiciary departments should be separate and distinct, so that no person should exercise the powers of more than one of them at the same time. But no barrier was provided between these several powers. The judiciary and executive members were left dependant on the legislative, for their subsistence in office, and some of them for their continuance in it. If therefore the legislature assumes executive and judiciary powers, no opposition is likely to be made; nor, if made, can it be

effectual; because in that case they may put their proceedings
into the form of an act of assembly, which will render them
obligatory on the other branches. They have accordingly, in
many instances, decided rights which should have been left to
judiciary controversy: and the direction of the executive, during the whole time of their session, is becoming habitual and
familiar. And this is done with no ill intention. The views of
the present members are perfectly upright. When they are led
out of their regular province, it is by art in others, and inad-
vertence in themselves. And this will probably be the case for
some time to come. But it will not be a very long time. Mankind soon learn to make interested uses of every right and
power which they possess, or may assume. The public money
and public liberty, intended to have been deposited with three
branches of magistracy, but found inadvertently to be in the
hands of one only, will soon be discovered to be sources of
wealth and dominion to those who hold them; distinguished
too by this tempting circumstance, that they are the instrument, as well as the object of acquisition. With money we will
get men, said Cæsar, and with men we will get money. Nor
should our assembly be deluded by the integrity of their own
purposes, and conclude that these unlimited powers will
never be abused, because themselves are not disposed to
abuse them. They should look forward to a time, and that not
a distant one, when corruption in this, as in the country from
which we derive our origin, will have seized the heads of government, and be spread by them through the body of the
people; when they will purchase the voices of the people, and
make them pay the price. Human nature is the same on every
side of the Atlantic, and will be alike influenced by the same
causes. The time to guard against corruption and tyranny, is
before they shall have gotten hold on us. It is better to keep
the wolf out of the fold, than to trust to drawing his teeth
and talons after he shall have entered. To render these considerations the more cogent, we must observe in addition,

5. That the ordinary legislature may alter the constitution
itself. On the discontinuance of assemblies, it became necessary to substitute in their place some other body, competent
to the ordinary business of government, and to the calling
forth the powers of the state for the maintenance of our op-

position to Great-Britain. Conventions were therefore introduced, consisting of two delegates from each county, meeting
together and forming one house, on the plan of the former
house of Burgesses, to whose places they succeeded. These
were at first chosen anew for every particular session. But in
March 1775, they recommended to the people to chuse a convention, which should continue in office a year. This was
done accordingly in April 1775, and in the July following that
convention passed an ordinance for the election of delegates
in the month of April annually. It is well known, that in July
1775, a separation from Great-Britain and establishment of Republican government had never yet entered into any person's
mind. A convention therefore, chosen under that ordinance,
cannot be said to have been chosen for purposes which certainly did not exist in the minds of those who passed it. Under this ordinance, at the annual election in April 1776, a
convention for the year was chosen. Independance, and the
establishment of a new form of government, were not even
yet the objects of the people at large. One extract from the
pamphlet called Common Sense had appeared in the Virginia
papers in February, and copies of the pamphlet itself had got
into a few hands. But the idea had not been opened to the
mass of the people in April, much less can it be said that they
had made up their minds in its favor. So that the electors of
April 1776, no more than the legislators of July 1775, not thinking of independance and a permanent republic, could not
mean to vest in these delegates powers of establishing them,
or any authorities other than those of the ordinary legislature.
So far as a temporary organization of government was necessary to render our opposition energetic, so far their organization was valid. But they received in their creation no
powers but what were given to every legislature before and
since. They could not therefore pass an act transcendant to
the powers of other legislatures. If the present assembly pass
any act, and declare it shall be irrevocable by subsequent assemblies, the declaration is merely void, and the act repeal-
able, as other acts are. So far, and no farther authorized, they
organized the government by the ordinance entitled a Constitution or Form of government. It pretends to no higher authority than the other ordinances of the same session; it does

not say, that it shall be perpetual; that it shall be unalterable
by other legislatures; that it shall be transcendant above the
powers of those, who they knew would have equal power
with themselves. Not only the silence of the instrument is a
proof they thought it would be alterable, but their own practice also: for this very convention, meeting as a House of Delegates in General Assembly with the new Senate in the
autumn of that year, passed acts of assembly in contradiction
to their ordinance of government; and every assembly from
that time to this has done the same. I am safe therefore in the
position, that the constitution itself is alterable by the ordinary legislature. Though this opinion seems founded on the
first elements of common sense, yet is the contrary maintained
by some persons. 1. Because, say they, the conventions were
vested with every power necessary to make effectual opposition to Great-Britain. But to complete this argument, they
must go on, and say further, that effectual opposition could
not be made to Great-Britain, without establishing a form of
government perpetual and unalterable by the legislature;
which is not true. An opposition which at some time or
other was to come to an end, could not need a perpetual institution to carry it on: and a government, amendable as its
defects should be discovered, was as likely to make effectual
resistance, as one which should be unalterably wrong.
Besides, the assemblies were as much vested with all powers
requisite for resistance as the conventions were. If therefore
these powers included that of modelling the form of government in the one case, they did so in the other. The assemblies
then as well as the conventions may model the government;
that is, they may alter the ordinance of government. 2. They
urge, that if the convention had meant that this instrument
should be alterable, as their other ordinances were, they
would have called it an ordinance: but they have called it a
constitution, which ex vi termini means 'an act above the
power of the ordinary legislature.' I answer that *constitutio*,
constitutum, *statutum*, *lex*, are convertible terms. '*Constitutio*
dicitur jus quod a principe conditur.' '*Constitutum*, quod ab
imperatoribus rescriptum statutumve est.' '*Statutum*, idem
quod lex.' Calvini Lexicon juridicum. *Constitution* and *statute*

were originally terms of the *civil law, and from thence introduced by Ecclesiastics into the English law. Thus in the statute 25 Hen. 8. c. 19. §. 1. '*Constitutions* and *ordinances*' are used
as synonimous. The term *constitution* has many other signifi-
cations in physics and in politics; but in Jurisprudence, whenever it is applied to any act of the legislature, it invariably
means a statute, law, or ordinance, which is the present case.
No inference then of a different meaning can be drawn from
the adoption of this title: on the contrary, we might conclude,
that, by their affixing to it a term synonimous with ordinance,
or statute, they meant it to be an ordinance or statute. But of
what consequence is their meaning, where their power is denied? If they meant to do more than they had power to do,
did this give them power? It is not the name, but the authority which renders an act obligatory. Lord Coke says, 'an article of the statute 11 R. 2. c. 5. that no person should attempt
to revoke any ordinance then made, is repealed, for that such
restraint is against the jurisdiction and power of the parliament.' 4. inst. 42. and again, 'though divers parliaments have
attempted to restrain subsequent parliaments, yet could they
never effect it; for the latter parliament hath ever power to
abrogate, suspend, qualify, explain, or make void the former
in the whole or in any part thereof, notwithstanding any
words of restraint, prohibition, or penalty, in the former: for
it is a maxim in the laws of the parliament, quod leges pos-
teriores priores contrarias abrogant.' 4. inst. 43.—To get rid
of the magic supposed to be in the word *constitution*, let us
translate it into its definition as given by those who think it
above the power of the law; and let us suppose the convention instead of saying, 'We, the ordinary legislature, establish
a *constitution*,' had said, 'We, the ordinary legislature, establish
an act *above the power of the ordinary legislature*.' Does not this
expose the absurdity of the attempt? 3. But, say they, the people have acquiesced, and this has given it an authority superior to the laws. It is true, that the people did not rebel
against it: and was that a time for the people to rise in rebellion? Should a prudent acquiescence, at a critical time, be con-

---

* To *bid*, to *set*, was the antient legislative word of the English. Ll. Hlo-
tharii & Eadrici. Ll. Inae. Ll. Eadwerdi. Ll. Aathelstani.

strued into a confirmation of every illegal thing done during
that period? Besides, why should they rebel? At an annual
election, they had chosen delegates for the year, to exercise the
ordinary powers of legislation, and to manage the great contest in which they were engaged. These delegates thought the
contest would be best managed by an organized government.
They therefore, among others, passed an ordinance of government. They did not presume to call it perpetual and unalterable. They well knew they had no power to make it so; that
our choice of them had been for no such purpose, and at a
time when we could have no such purpose in contemplation.
Had an unalterable form of government been meditated, perhaps we should have chosen a different set of people. There
was no cause then for the people to rise in rebellion. But to
what dangerous lengths will this argument lead? Did the acquiescence of the colonies under the various acts of power
exercised by Great-Britain in our infant state, confirm these
acts, and so far invest them with the authority of the people
as to render them unalterable, and our present resistance
wrong? On every unauthoritative exercise of power by the
legislature, must the people rise in rebellion, or their silence
be construed into a surrender of that power to them? If so,
how many rebellions should we have had already? One certainly for every session of assembly. The other states in the
Union have been of opinion, that to render a form of government unalterable by ordinary acts of assembly, the people
must delegate persons with special powers. They have accordingly chosen special conventions to form and fix their governments. The individuals then who maintain the contrary
opinion in this country, should have the modesty to suppose
it possible that they may be wrong and the rest of America
right. But if there be only a possibility of their being wrong,
if only a plausible doubt remains of the validity of the ordinance of government, is it not better to remove that doubt,
by placing it on a bottom which none will dispute? If they be
right, we shall only have the unnecessary trouble of meeting
once in convention. If they be wrong, they expose us to the
hazard of having no fundamental rights at all. True it is, this
is no time for deliberating on forms of government. While an
enemy is within our bowels, the first object is to expel him.

But when this shall be done, when peace shall be established, and leisure given us for intrenching within good forms, the rights for which we have bled, let no man be found indolent enough to decline a little more trouble for placing them beyond the reach of question. If any thing more be requisite to produce a conviction of the expediency of calling a convention, at a proper season, to fix our form of government, let it be the reflection,

6. That the assembly exercises a power of determining the Quorum of their own body which may legislate for us. After the establishment of the new form they adhered to the *Lex majoris partis*, founded in *common law as well as common right. It is the †natural law of every assembly of men, whose numbers are not fixed by any other law. They continued for some time to require the presence of a majority of their whole number, to pass an act. But the British parliament fixes its own quorum: our former assemblies fixed their own quorum: and one precedent in favour of power is stronger than an hundred against it. The house of delegates therefore have ‡lately voted that, during the present dangerous invasion, forty members shall be a house to proceed to business. They have been moved to this by the fear of not being able to collect a house. But this danger could not authorize them to call that a house which was none: and if they may fix it at one number, they may at another, till it loses its fundamental character of being a representative body. As this vote expires with the present invasion, it is probable the former rule will be permitted to revive: because at present no ill is meant. The power however of fixing their own quorum has been avowed, and a precedent set. From forty it may be reduced to four, and from four to one: from a house to a committee, from a committee to a chairman or speaker, and thus an oligarchy or monarchy be substituted under forms supposed to be regular. 'Omnia mala exempla ex bonis orta sunt: sed ubi imperium ad ignaros aut minus bonos pervenit, novum illud exemplum ab dignis et idoneis ad indignos et non idoneos fertur.' When therefore it is considered, that there is no legal obstacle to the

* Bro. abr. Corporations. 31. 34. Hakewell, 93.
† Puff. Off. hom. l. 2. c. 6. §. 12.
‡ June 4, 1781.

assumption by the assembly of all the powers legislative, executive, and judiciary, and that these may come to the hands of the smallest rag of delegation, surely the people will say, and their representatives, while yet they have honest representatives, will advise them to say, that they will not acknowledge as laws any acts not considered and assented to by the major part of their delegates.

In enumerating the defects of the constitution, it would be wrong to count among them what is only the error of particular persons. In December 1776, our circumstances being much distressed, it was proposed in the house of delegates to create a *dictator*, invested with every power legislative, executive and judiciary, civil and military, of life and of death, over our persons and over our properties: and in June 1781, again under calamity, the same proposition was repeated, and wanted a few votes only of being passed.—One who entered into this contest from a pure love of liberty, and a sense of injured rights, who determined to make every sacrifice, and to meet every danger, for the re-establishment of those rights on a firm basis, who did not mean to expend his blood and substance for the wretched purpose of changing this master for that, but to place the powers of governing him in a plurality of hands of his own choice, so that the corrupt will of no one man might in future oppress him, must stand confounded and dismayed when he is told, that a considerable portion of that plurality had meditated the surrender of them into a single hand, and, in lieu of a limited monarch, to deliver him over to a despotic one! How must we find his efforts and sacrifices abused and baffled, if he may still by a single vote be laid prostrate at the feet of one man! In God's name, from whence have they derived this power? Is it from our ancient laws? None such can be produced. Is it from any principle in our new constitution, expressed or implied? Every lineament of that expressed or implied, is in full opposition to it. Its fundamental principle is, that the state shall be governed as a commonwealth. It provides a republican organization, proscribes under the name of *prerogative* the exercise of all powers undefined by the laws; places on this basis the whole system of our laws; and, by consolidating them together, chuses that they shall be left to stand or fall together, never providing for any circumstances, nor admitting that such could arise, wherein either should be suspended, no, not for a moment. Our antient laws expressly declare, that those who are but delegates themselves shall not delegate to others powers which require judgment and integrity in their exercise.—Or was this proposition moved on a supposed right in the movers of abandoning their posts in a moment of distress? The same laws forbid the abandonment of that post, even on ordinary occasions; and much more a transfer of their powers into other hands and other forms, without consulting the people. They never admit the idea that these, like sheep or cattle, may be given from hand to hand without an appeal to their own will.—Was it from the necessity of the case? Necessities which dissolve a government, do not convey its authority to an oligarchy or a monarchy. They throw back, into the hands of the people, the powers they had delegated, and leave them as individuals to shift for themselves. A leader may offer, but not impose himself, nor be imposed on them. Much less can their necks be submitted to his sword, their breath be held at his will or caprice. The necessity which should operate these tremendous effects should at least be palpable and irresistible. Yet in both instances, where it was feared, or pretended with us, it was belied by the event. It was belied too by the preceding experience of our sister states, several of whom had grappled through greater difficulties without abandoning their forms of government. When the proposition was first made, Massachusets had found even the government of committees sufficient to carry them through an invasion. But we at the time of that proposition were under no invasion. When the second was made, there had been added to this example those of Rhode-Island, New-York, New-Jersey, and Pennsylvania, in all of which the republican form had been found equal to the task of carrying them through the severest trials. In this state alone did there exist so little virtue, that fear was to be fixed in the hearts of the people, and to become the motive of their exertions and the principle of their government? The very thought alone was treason against the people; was treason against mankind in general; as rivetting for ever the chains which bow down their necks, by giving to their oppressors a proof, which they would have trumpeted through the universe, of the imbecility of republican government, in times of pressing danger, to shield them from harm. Those who assume the right of giving away the reins of government in any case, must be sure that the herd, whom they hand on to the rods and hatchet of the dictator, will lay their necks on the block when he shall nod to them. But if our assemblies supposed such a resignation in the people, I hope they mistook their character. I am of opinion, that the government, instead of being braced and invigorated for greater exertions under their difficulties, would have been thrown back upon the bungling machinery of county committees for administration, till a convention could have been called, and its wheels again set into regular motion. What a cruel moment was this for creating such an embarrassment, for putting to the proof the attachment of our countrymen to republican government! Those who meant well, of the advocates for this measure, (and most of them meant well, for I know them personally, had been their fellow-labourers in the common cause, and had often proved the purity of their principles), had been seduced in their judgment by the example of an ancient republic, whose constitution and circumstances were fundamentally different. They had sought this precedent in the history of Rome, where alone it was to be found, and where at length too it had proved fatal. They had taken it from a republic, rent by the most bitter factions and tumults, where the government was of a heavy-handed unfeeling aristocracy, over a people ferocious, and rendered desperate by poverty and wretchedness; tumults which could not be allayed under the most trying circumstances, but by the omnipotent hand of a single despot. Their constitution therefore allowed a temporary tyrant to be erected, under the name of a Dictator; and that temporary tyrant, after a few examples, became perpetual. They misapplied this precedent to a people, mild in their dispositions, patient under their trial, united for the public liberty, and affectionate to their leaders. But if from the constitution of the Roman government there resulted to their Senate a power of submitting all their rights to the will of one man, does it follow, that the assembly of Virginia have the same authority? What clause in our constitution has substituted that of Rome, by way of residuary provision, for all cases not otherwise provided for? Or if they may step ad libitum into any other form of government for precedents to rule us by, for what oppression may not a precedent be found in this world of the bellum omnium in omnia?—Searching for the foundations of this proposition, I can find none which may pretend a colour of right or reason, but the defect before developed, that there being no barrier between the legislative, executive, and judiciary departments, the legislature may seize the whole: that having seized it, and possessing a right to fix their own quorum, they may reduce that quorum to one, whom they may call a chairman, speaker, dictator, or by any other name they please.—Our situation is indeed perilous, and I hope my countrymen will be sensible of it, and will apply, at a proper season, the proper remedy; which is a convention to fix the constitution, to amend its defects, to bind up the several branches of government by certain laws, which when they transgress their acts shall become nullities; to render unnecessary an appeal to the people, or in other words a rebellion, on every infraction of their rights, on the peril that their acquiescence shall be construed into an intention to surrender those rights.

QUERY XIV

The administration of justice and description of the laws? Laws

The state is divided into counties. In every county are appointed magistrates, called justices of the peace, usually from eight to thirty or forty in number, in proportion to the size of the county, of the most discreet and honest inhabitants. They are nominated by their fellows, but commissioned by the governor, and act without reward. These magistrates have jurisdiction both criminal and civil. If the question before them be a question of law only, they decide on it themselves: but if it be of fact, or of fact and law combined, it must be referred to a jury. In the latter case, of a combination of law and fact, it is usual for the jurors to decide the fact, and to refer the law arising on it to the decision of the judges. But this division of the subject lies with their discretion only. And if the question relate to any point of public liberty, or if it be one of those in which the judges may be suspected of bias, the jury undertake to decide both law and fact. If they be mistaken, a decision against right, which is casual only, is less dangerous to the state, and less afflicting to the loser, than one which makes part of a regular and uniform system. In truth, it is better to toss up cross and pile in a cause, than to refer it to a judge whose mind is warped by any motive whatever, in that particular case. But the common sense of twelve honest men gives still a better chance of just decision, than the hazard of cross and pile. These judges execute their process by the sheriff or coroner of the county, or by constables of their own appointment. If any free person commit an offence against the commonwealth, if it be below the degree of felony, he is bound by a justice to appear before their court, to answer it on indictment or information. If it amount to felony, he is committed to jail, a court of these justices is called; if they on examination think him guilty, they send him to the jail of the general court, before which court he is to be tried first by a grand jury of 24, of whom 13 must concur in opinion: if they find him guilty, he is then tried by a jury of 12 men of the county where the offence was committed, and by their verdict, which must be unanimous, he is acquitted or condemned without appeal. If the criminal be a slave the trial by the county court is final. In every case however, except that of high treason, there resides in the governor a power of pardon. In high treason, the pardon can only flow from the general assembly. In civil matters these justices have jurisdiction in all cases of whatever value, not appertaining to the department of the admiralty. This jurisdiction is twofold. If the matter in dispute be of less value than 4⅙ dollars, a single member may try it at any time and place within his county, and may award execution on the goods of the party cast. If it be of that or greater value, it is determinable before the county court, which consists of four at the least of those justices, and assembles at the court-house of the county on a certain day in every month. From their determination, if the matter be of the value of ten pounds sterling, or concern the title or bounds of lands, an appeal lies to one of the superior courts.

There are three superior courts, to wit, the high-court of chancery, the general court, and court of admiralty. The first and second of these receive appeals from the county courts, and also have original jurisdiction where the subject of controversy is of the value of ten pounds sterling, or where it concerns the title or bounds of land. The jurisdiction of the admiralty is original altogether. The high-court of chancery is composed of three judges, the general court of five, and the court of admiralty of three. The two first hold their sessions at Richmond at stated times, the chancery twice in the year, and the general court twice for business civil and criminal, and twice more for criminal only. The court of admiralty sits at Williamsburgh whenever a controversy arises.

There is one supreme court, called the court of appeals, composed of the judges of the three superior courts, assembling twice a year at stated times at Richmond. This court receives appeals in all civil cases from each of the superior courts, and determines them finally. But it has no original jurisdiction.

If a controversy arise between two foreigners of a nation in alliance with the United States, it is decided by the Consul for their State, or, if both parties chuse it, by the ordinary courts of justice. If one of the parties only be such a foreigner, it is triable before the courts of justice of the country. But if it shall have been instituted in a county court, the foreigner may remove it into the general court, or court of chancery, who are to determine it at their first sessions, as they must also do if it be originally commenced before them. In cases of life and death, such foreigners have a right to be tried by a jury, the one half foreigners, the other natives.

All public accounts are settled with a board of auditors, consisting of three members, appointed by the general assembly, any two of whom may act. But an individual, dissatisfied with the determination of that board, may carry his case into the proper superior court.

A description of the laws.

The general assembly was constituted, as has been already shewn, by letters-patent of March the 9th, 1607, in the 4th year of the reign of James the First. The laws of England seem to have been adopted by consent of the settlers, which might easily enough be done whilst they were few and living all together. Of such adoption however we have no other proof than their practice, till the year 1661, when they were expressly adopted by an act of the assembly, except so far as 'a difference of condition' rendered them inapplicable. Under this adoption, the rule, in our courts of judicature was, that the common law of England, and the general statutes previous to the 4th of James, were in force here; but that no subsequent statutes were, *unless we were named in them*, said the judges and other partisans of the crown, but *named or not named*, said those who reflected freely. It will be unnecessary to attempt a description of the laws of England, as that may be found in English publications. To those which were established here, by the adoption of the legislature, have been since added a number of acts of assembly passed during the monarchy, and ordinances of convention and acts of assembly enacted since the establishment of the republic. The following variations from the British model are perhaps worthy of being specified.

Debtors unable to pay their debts, and making faithful delivery of their whole effects, are released from confinement, and their persons for ever discharged from restraint for such previous debts: but any property they may afterwards acquire will be subject to their creditors.

The poor, unable to support themselves, are maintained by an assessment on the titheable persons in their parish. This assessment is levied and administered by twelve persons in each parish, called vestrymen, originally chosen by the house-keepers of the parish, but afterwards filling vacancies in their own body by their own choice. These are usually the most discreet farmers, so distributed through their parish, that every part of it may be under the immediate eye of some one of them. They are well acquainted with the details and œconomy of private life, and they find sufficient inducements to execute their charge well, in their philanthropy, in the approbation of their neighbours, and the distinction which that gives them. The poor who have neither property, friends, nor strength to labour, are boarded in the houses of good farmers, to whom a stipulated sum is annually paid. To those who are able to help themselves a little, or have friends from whom they derive some succours, inadequate however to their full maintenance, supplementory aids are given, which enable them to live comfortably in their own houses, or in the houses of their friends. Vagabonds, without visible property or vocation, are placed in workhouses, where they are well cloathed, fed, lodged, and made to labour. Nearly the same method of providing for the poor prevails through all our states; and from Savannah to Portsmouth you will seldom meet a beggar. In the larger towns indeed they sometimes present themselves. These are usually foreigners, who have never obtained a settlement in any parish. I never yet saw a native American begging in the streets or highways. A subsistence is easily gained here: and if, by misfortunes, they are thrown on the charities of the world, those provided by their own country are so comfortable and so certain, that they never think of relinquishing them to become strolling beggars. Their situation too, when sick, in the family of a good farmer, where every member is emulous to do them kind offices, where they are visited by all the neighbours, who bring them the little rarities which their sickly appetites may crave, and who take by rotation the nightly watch over them, when their condition requires it, is without comparison better than in a general hospital, where the sick, the dying, and the dead are crammed together, in the same rooms, and often in the same beds. The disadvantages, inseparable from general hospitals, are such as can never be counterpoised by all the regularities of medicine and regimen. Nature and kind nursing save a much greater proportion in our plain way, at a smaller expence, and with less abuse. One branch only of hospital institution is wanting with us; that is, a general establishment for those labouring under difficult cases of chirurgery. The aids of this art are not equivocal. But an able chirurgeon cannot be had in every parish. Such a receptacle should therefore be provided for those patients: but no others should be admitted.

Marriages must be solemnized either on special licence, granted by the first magistrate of the county, on proof of the consent of the parent or guardian of either party under age, or after solemn publication, on three several Sundays, at some place of religious worship, in the parishes where the parties reside. The act of solemnization may be by the minister of any society of Christians, who shall have been previously licensed for this purpose by the court of the county. Quakers and Menonists however are exempted from all these conditions, and marriage among them is to be solemnized by the society itself.

A foreigner of any nation, not in open war with us, becomes naturalized by removing to the state to reside, and taking an oath of fidelity: and thereupon acquires every right of a native citizen: and citizens may divest themselves of that character, by declaring, by solemn deed, or in open court, that they mean to expatriate themselves, and no longer to be citizens of this state.

Conveyances of land must be registered in the court of the county wherein they lie, or in the general court, or they are void, as to creditors, and subsequent purchasers.

Slaves pass by descent and dower as lands do. Where the descent is from a parent, the heir is bound to pay an equal share of their value in money to each of his brothers and sisters.

Slaves, as well as lands, were entailable during the mon-

archy: but, by an act of the first republican assembly, all
donees in tail, present and future, were vested with the absolute dominion of the entailed subject.

Bills of exchange, being protested, carry 10 per cent. interest from their date.

No person is allowed, in any other case, to take more than
five per cent. per annum simple interest, for the loan of
monies.

Gaming debts are made void, and monies actually paid to
discharge such debts (if they exceeded 40 shillings) may be
recovered by the payer within three months, or by any other
person afterwards.

Tobacco, flour, beef, pork, tar, pitch, and turpentine, must
be inspected by persons publicly appointed, before they can
be exported.

The erecting iron-works and mills is encouraged by many
privileges; with necessary cautions however to prevent their
dams from obstructing the navigation of the water-courses.
The general assembly have on several occasions shewn a great
desire to encourage the opening the great falls of James and
Patowmac rivers. As yet, however, neither of these have been
effected.

The laws have also descended to the preservation and improvement of the races of useful animals, such as horses, cattle, deer; to the extirpation of those which are noxious, as
wolves, squirrels, crows, blackbirds; and to the guarding our
citizens against infectious disorders, by obliging suspected
vessels coming into the state, to perform quarantine, and by
regulating the conduct of persons having such disorders
within the state.

The mode of acquiring lands, in the earliest times of our
settlement, was by petition to the general assembly. If the
lands prayed for were already cleared of the Indian title, and
the assembly thought the prayer reasonable, they passed the
property by their vote to the petitioner. But if they had not
yet been ceded by the Indians, it was necessary that the petitioner should previously purchase their right. This purchase
the assembly verified, by enquiries of the Indian proprietors;
and being satisfied of its reality and fairness, proceeded further to examine the reasonableness of the petition, and its

consistence with policy; and, according to the result, either granted or rejected the petition. The company also sometimes, though very rarely, granted lands, independantly of the general assembly. As the colony increased, and individual applications for land multiplied, it was found to give too much occupation to the general assembly to enquire into and execute the grant in every special case. They therefore thought it better to establish general rules, according to which all grants should be made, and to leave to the governor the execution of them, under these rules. This they did by what have been usually called the land laws, amending them from time to time, as their defects were developed. According to these laws, when an individual wished a portion of unappropriated land, he was to locate and survey it by a public officer, appointed for that purpose: its breadth was to bear a certain proportion to its length: the grant was to be executed by the governor: and the lands were to be improved in a certain manner, within a given time. From these regulations there resulted to the state a sole and exclusive power of taking conveyances of the Indian right of soil: since, according to them, an Indian conveyance alone could give no right to an individual, which the laws would acknowledge. The state, or the crown, thereafter, made general purchases of the Indians from time to time, and the governor parcelled them out by special grants, conformed to the rules before described, which it was not in his power, or in that of the crown, to dispense with. Grants, unaccompanied by their proper legal circumstances, were set aside regularly by *scire facias*, or by bill in Chancery. Since the establishment of our new government, this order of things is but little changed. An individual, wishing to appropriate to himself lands still unappropriated by any other, pays to the public treasurer a sum of money proportioned to the quantity he wants. He carries the treasurer's receipt to the auditors of public accompts, who thereupon debit the treasurer with the sum, and order the register of the land-office to give the party a warrant for his land. With this warrant from the register, he goes to the surveyor of the county where the land lies on which he has cast his eye. The surveyor lays it off for him, gives him its exact description, in the form of a certificate, which certificate he returns to the land-office, where a grant is made out, and is signed by the governor. This vests in him a perfect dominion in his lands, transmissible to whom he pleases by deed or will, or by descent to his heirs if he die intestate.

Many of the laws which were in force during the monarchy being relative merely to that form of government, or inculcating principles inconsistent with republicanism, the first assembly which met after the establishment of the commonwealth appointed a committee to revise the whole code, to reduce it into proper form and volume, and report it to the assembly. This work has been executed by three gentlemen, and reported; but probably will not be taken up till a restoration of peace shall leave to the legislature leisure to go through such a work.

The plan of the revisal was this. The common law of England, by which is meant, that part of the English law which was anterior to the date of the oldest statutes extant, is made the basis of the work. It was thought dangerous to attempt to reduce it to a text: it was therefore left to be collected from the usual monuments of it. Necessary alterations in that, and so much of the whole body of the British statutes, and of acts of assembly, as were thought proper to be retained, were digested into 126 new acts, in which simplicity of stile was aimed at, as far as was safe. The following are the most remarkable alterations proposed:

To change the rules of descent, so as that the lands of any person dying intestate shall be divisible equally among all his children, or other representatives, in equal degree.

To make slaves distributable among the next of kin, as other moveables.

To have all public expences, whether of the general treasury, or of a parish or county, (as for the maintenance of the poor, building bridges, court-houses, &c.) supplied by assessments on the citizens, in proportion to their property.

To hire undertakers for keeping the public roads in repair, and indemnify individuals through whose lands new roads shall be opened.

To define with precision the rules whereby aliens should become citizens, and citizens make themselves aliens.

To establish religious freedom on the broadest bottom.

To emancipate all slaves born after passing the act. The bill reported by the revisors does not itself contain this proposition; but an amendment containing it was prepared, to be offered to the legislature whenever the bill should be taken up, and further directing, that they should continue with their parents to a certain age, then be brought up, at the public expence, to tillage, arts or sciences, according to their geniusses, till the females should be eighteen, and the males twenty-one years of age, when they should be colonized to such place as the circumstances of the time should render most proper, sending them out with arms, implements of houshold and of the handicraft arts, feeds, pairs of the useful domestic animals, &c. to declare them a free and independant people, and extend to them our alliance and protection, till they shall have acquired strength; and to send vessels at the same time to other parts of the world for an equal number of white inhabitants; to induce whom to migrate hither, proper encouragements were to be proposed. It will probably be asked, Why not retain and incorporate the blacks into the state, and thus save the expence of supplying, by importation of white settlers, the vacancies they will leave? Deep rooted prejudices entertained by the whites; ten thousand recollections, by the blacks, of the injuries they have sustained; new provocations; the real distinctions which nature has made; and many other circumstances, will divide us into parties, and produce convulsions which will probably never end but in the extermination of the one or the other race.—To these objections, which are political, may be added others, which are physical and moral. The first difference which strikes us is that of colour. Whether the black of the negro resides in the reticular membrane between the skin and scarf-skin, or in the scarf-skin itself; whether it proceeds from the colour of the blood, the colour of the bile, or from that of some other secretion, the difference is fixed in nature, and is as real as if its seat and cause were better known to us. And is this difference of no importance? Is it not the foundation of a greater or less share of beauty in the two races? Are not the fine mixtures of red and white, the expressions of every passion by greater or less suffusions of colour in the one, preferable to that eternal monotony, which reigns in the countenances, that immoveable veil of black which covers all the emotions of the other race? Add to these, flowing hair, a more elegant symmetry of form, their own judgment in favour of the whites, declared by their preference of them, as uniformly as is the preference of the Oranootan for the black women over those of his own species. The circumstance of superior beauty, is thought worthy attention in the propagation of our horses, dogs, and other domestic animals; why not in that of man? Besides those of colour, figure, and hair, there are other physical distinctions proving a difference of race. They have less hair on the face and body. They secrete less by the kidnies, and more by the glands of the skin, which gives them a very strong and disagreeable odour. This greater degree of transpiration renders them more tolerant of heat, and less so of cold, than the whites. Perhaps too a difference of structure in the pulmonary apparatus, which a late ingenious *experimentalist has discovered to be the principal regulator of animal heat, may have disabled them from extricating, in the act of inspiration, so much of that fluid from the outer air, or obliged them in expiration, to part with more of it. They seem to require less sleep. A black, after hard labour through the day, will be induced by the slightest amusements to sit up till midnight, or later, though knowing he must be out with the first dawn of the morning. They are at least as brave, and more adventuresome. But this may perhaps proceed from a want of forethought, which prevents their seeing a danger till it be present. When present, they do not go through it with more coolness or steadiness than the whites. They are more ardent after their female: but love seems with them to be more an eager desire, than a tender delicate mixture of sentiment and sensation. Their griefs are transient. Those numberless afflictions, which render it doubtful whether heaven has given life to us in mercy or in wrath, are less felt, and sooner forgotten with them. In general, their existence appears to participate more of sensation than reflection. To this must be ascribed their disposition to sleep when abstracted from their diversions, and unemployed in labour. An animal whose body is at rest, and who does not reflect, must be disposed to sleep

*Crawford.

of course. Comparing them by their faculties of memory, reason, and imagination, it appears to me, that in memory they are equal to the whites; in reason much inferior, as I think one could scarcely be found capable of tracing and comprehending the investigations of Euclid; and that in imagination they are dull, tasteless, and anomalous. It would be unfair to follow them to Africa for this investigation. We will consider them here, on the same stage with the whites, and where the facts are not apocryphal on which a judgment is to be formed. It will be right to make great allowances for the difference of condition, of education, of conversation, of the sphere in which they move. Many millions of them have been brought to, and born in America. Most of them indeed have been confined to tillage, to their own homes, and their own society: yet many have been so situated, that they might have availed themselves of the conversation of their masters; many have been brought up to the handicraft arts, and from that circumstance have always been associated with the whites. Some have been liberally educated, and all have lived in countries where the arts and sciences are cultivated to a considerable degree, and have had before their eyes samples of the best works from abroad. The Indians, with no advantages of this kind, will often carve figures on their pipes not destitute of design and merit. They will crayon out an animal, a plant, or a country, so as to prove the existence of a germ in their minds which only wants cultivation. They astonish you with strokes of the most sublime oratory; such as prove their reason and sentiment strong, their imagination glowing and elevated. But never yet could I find that a black had uttered a thought above the level of plain narration; never see even an elementary trait of painting or sculpture. In music they are more generally gifted than the whites with accurate ears for tune and time, and they have been found capable of imagining a small catch*. Whether they will be equal to the composition of a more extensive run of melody, or of complicated harmony, is yet to be proved. Misery is often the parent of

*The instrument proper to them is the Banjar, which they brought hither from Africa, and which is the original of the guitar, its chords being precisely the four lower chords of the guitar.

Ƀ. Ƀ.

the most affecting touches in poetry.—Among the blacks is
misery enough, God knows, but no poetry. Love is the peculiar œstrum of the poet. Their love is ardent, but it kindles
the senses only, not the imagination. Religion indeed has produced a Phyllis Whately; but it could not produce a poet. The
compositions published under her name are below the dignity
of criticism. The heroes of the Dunciad are to her, as Hercules to the author of that poem. Ignatius Sancho has approached nearer to merit in composition; yet his letters do
more honour to the heart than the head. They breathe the
purest effusions of friendship and general philanthropy, and
shew how great a degree of the latter may be compounded
with strong religious zeal. He is often happy in the turn of
his compliments, and his stile is easy and familiar, except
when he affects a Shandean fabrication of words. But his
imagination is wild and extravagant, escapes incessantly from
every restraint of reason and taste, and, in the course of its
vagaries, leaves a tract of thought as incoherent and eccentric,
as is the course of a meteor through the sky. His subjects
should often have led him to a process of sober reasoning: yet
we find him always substituting sentiment for demonstration.
Upon the whole, though we admit him to the first place
among those of his own colour who have presented themselves to the public judgment, yet when we compare him with
the writers of the race among whom he lived, and particularly
with the epistolary class, in which he has taken his own stand,
we are compelled to enroll him at the bottom of the column.
This criticism supposes the letters published under his name
to be genuine, and to have received amendment from no
other hand; points which would not be of easy investigation.
The improvement of the blacks in body and mind, in the first
instance of their mixture with the whites, has been observed
by every one, and proves that their inferiority is not the effect
merely of their condition of life. We know that among the
Romans, about the Augustan age especially, the condition of
their slaves was much more deplorable than that of the blacks
on the continent of America. The two sexes were confined in
separate apartments, because to raise a child cost the master
more than to buy one. Cato, for a very restricted indulgence

to his slaves in this particular, *took from them a certain price. But in this country the slaves multiply as fast as the free inhabitants. Their situation and manners place the commerce between the two sexes almost without restraint.—The same Cato, on a principle of œconomy, always sold his sick and superannuated slaves. He gives it as a standing precept to a master visiting his farm, to sell his old oxen, old waggons, old tools, old and diseased servants, and every thing else become useless. 'Vendat boves vetulos, plaustrum vetus, ferramenta vetera, servum senem, servum morbosum, & si quid aliud supersit vendat.' Cato de re rusticâ. c. 2. The American slaves cannot enumerate this among the injuries and insults they receive. It was the common practice to expose in the island of Æsculapius, in the Tyber, diseased slaves, whose cure was like to become tedious. The Emperor Claudius, by an edict, gave freedom to such of them as should recover, and first declared, that if any person chose to kill rather than to expose them, it should be deemed homicide. The exposing them is a crime of which no instance has existed with us; and were it to be followed by death, it would be punished capitally. We are told of a certain Vedius Pollio, who, in the presence of Augustus, would have given a slave as food to his fish, for having broken a glass. With the Romans, the regular method of taking the evidence of their slaves was under torture. Here it has been thought better never to resort to their evidence. When a master was murdered, all his slaves, in the same house, or within hearing, were condemned to death. Here punishment falls on the guilty only, and as precise proof is required against him as against a freeman. Yet notwithstanding these and other discouraging circumstances among the Romans, their slaves were often their rarest artists. They excelled too in science, insomuch as to be usually employed as tutors to their master's children. Epictetus, Terence, and Phædrus, were slaves. But they were of the race of whites. It is not their condition then, but nature, which has produced the distinction.—Whether further observation will or will not verify the conjecture, that

Suet. Claud. 25.

*Τὸς δὸλὸς εταξεν ὡρισμενὸ νομισματος ὁμιλειν ταις θεραπαινισιν. —Plutarch.   Cato.

nature has been less bountiful to them in the endowments of the head, I believe that in those of the heart she will be found to have done them justice. That disposition to theft with which they have been branded, must be ascribed to their situation, and not to any depravity of the moral sense. The man, in whose favour no laws of property exist, probably feels himself less bound to respect those made in favour of others. When arguing for ourselves, we lay it down as a fundamental, that laws, to be just, must give a reciprocation of right: that, without this, they are mere arbitrary rules of conduct, founded in force, and not in conscience: and it is a problem which I give to the master to solve, whether the religious precepts against the violation of property were not framed for him as well as his slave? And whether the slave may not as justifiably take a little from one, who has taken all from him, as he may slay one who would slay him? That a change in the relations in which a man is placed should change his ideas of moral right and wrong, is neither new, nor peculiar to the colour of the blacks. Homer tells us it was so 2600 years ago.

Ἥμισυ, γαζ τ᾽ ἀρετῆς ἀποαίνυlαι εὐρύθπα Ζεὺς
Ἀνερος, ευτ᾽ ἄν μιν κατὰ δὔλιον ἦμαζ ἔλησιν.

Od. 17. 323.

> Jove fix'd it certain, that whatever day
> Makes man a slave, takes half his worth away.

But the slaves of which Homer speaks were whites. Notwithstanding these considerations which must weaken their respect for the laws of property, we find among them numerous instances of the most rigid integrity, and as many as among their better instructed masters, of benevolence, gratitude, and unshaken fidelity.—The opinion, that they are inferior in the faculties of reason and imagination, must be hazarded with great diffidence. To justify a general conclusion, requires many observations, even where the subject may be submitted to the Anatomical knife, to Optical glasses, to analysis by fire, or by solvents. How much more then where it is a faculty, not a substance, we are examining; where it eludes the research of all the senses; where the conditions of its existence are various and variously combined; where the effects of those which are present or absent bid defiance to calculation; let me add too, as a circumstance of great tenderness, where our conclusion would degrade a whole race of men from the rank in the scale of beings which their Creator may perhaps have given them. To our reproach it must be said, that though for a century and a half we have had under our eyes the races of black and of red men, they have never yet been viewed by us as subjects of natural history. I advance it therefore as a suspicion only, that the blacks, whether originally a distinct race, or made distinct by time and circumstances, are inferior to the whites in the endowments both of body and mind. It is not against experience to suppose, that different species of the same genus, or varieties of the same species, may possess different qualifications. Will not a lover of natural history then, one who views the gradations in all the races of animals with the eye of philosophy, excuse an effort to keep those in the department of man as distinct as nature has formed them? This unfortunate difference of colour, and perhaps of faculty, is a powerful obstacle to the emancipation of these people. Many of their advocates, while they wish to vindicate the liberty of human nature, are anxious also to preserve its dignity and beauty. Some of these, embarrassed by the question 'What further is to be done with them?' join themselves in opposition with those who are actuated by sordid avarice only. Among the Romans emancipation required but one effort. The slave, when made free, might mix with, without staining the blood of his master. But with us a second is necessary, unknown to history. When freed, he is to be removed beyond the reach of mixture.

The revised code further proposes to proportion crimes and punishments. This is attempted on the following scale.

I. Crimes whose punishment extends to *Life*.
  1. High treason. Death by hanging.
                      Forfeiture of lands and goods to the commonwealth.
  2. Petty treason. Death by hanging. Dissection.
                      Forfeiture of half the lands and goods to the representatives of the party slain.

3. Murder. 1. by poison. Death by poison.
                           Forfeiture of one-half as before.
            2. in Duel.   Death by hanging. Gibbeting, if the
                           challenger.
                           Forfeiture of one-half as before, unless it
                           be the party challenged, then the forfei-
                           ture is to the commonwealth.
            3. in any other way. Death by hanging.
                           Forfeiture of one-half as before.
      4. Manslaughter. The second offence is murder.
   II. Crimes whose punishment goes to *Limb*.
      1. Rape,   ⎫
      2. Sodomy,   ⎬ Dismemberment.
      3. Maiming, ⎫ Retaliation, and the forfeiture of half the lands and
      4. Disfiguring, ⎭ goods to the sufferer.
  III. Crimes punishable by *Labour*.

1.	Manslaughter, 1st offence.	Labour VII. years for the public.	Forfeiture of half as in murder.
2.	Counterfeiting money.	Labour VI. years.	Forfeiture of lands and goods to the commonwealth.
3.	Arson.	Labour V. years.	Reparation three-fold.
4.	Asportation of vessels.		
5.	Robbery.	Labour IV. years.	Reparation double.
6.	Burglary.		
7.	Housebreaking.	Labour III. years.	Reparation.
8.	Horse-stealing.		
9.	Grand Larceny.	Labour II. years.	Reparation. Pillory.
10.	Petty Larceny.	Labour I. year.	Reparation. Pillory.
11.	Pretensions to witch-craft, &c.	Ducking.	Stripes.
12.	Excusable homicide.	to be pitied, not punished.	
13.	Suicide.		
14.	Apostacy. Heresy.		

Pardon and privilege of clergy are proposed to be abolished; but if the verdict be against the defendant, the court in
their discretion, may allow a new trial. No attainder to cause
a corruption of blood, or forfeiture of dower. Slaves guilty of
offences punishable in others by labour, to be transported to
Africa, or elsewhere, as the circumstances of the time admit,
there to be continued in slavery. A rigorous regimen proposed for those condemned to labour.

Another object of the revisal is, to diffuse knowledge more

generally through the mass of the people. This bill proposes
to lay off every county into small districts of five or six miles
square, called hundreds, and in each of them to establish a
school for teaching reading, writing, and arithmetic. The tutor to be supported by the hundred, and every person in it
entitled to send their children three years gratis, and as much
longer as they please, paying for it. These schools to be under
a visitor, who is annually to chuse the boy, of best genius in
the school, of those whose parents are too poor to give them
further education, and to send him forward to one of the
grammar schools, of which twenty are proposed to be erected
in different parts of the country, for teaching Greek, Latin,
geography, and the higher branches of numerical arithmetic.
Of the boys thus sent in any one year, trial is to be made at
the grammar schools one or two years, and the best genius of
the whole selected, and continued six years, and the residue
dismissed. By this means twenty of the best geniusses will be
raked from the rubbish annually, and be instructed, at the
public expence, so far as the grammer schools go. At the end
of six years instruction, one half are to be discontinued (from
among whom the grammar schools will probably be supplied
with future masters); and the other half, who are to be chosen
for the superiority of their parts and disposition, are to be
sent and continued three years in the study of such sciences
as they shall chuse, at William and Mary college, the plan of
which is proposed to be enlarged, as will be hereafter explained, and extended to all the useful sciences. The ultimate
result of the whole scheme of education would be the teaching all the children of the state reading, writing, and common
arithmetic: turning out ten annually of superior genius, well
taught in Greek, Latin, geography, and the higher branches
of arithmetic: turning out ten others annually, of still superior
parts, who, to those branches of learning, shall have added
such of the sciences as their genius shall have led them to: the
furnishing to the wealthier part of the people convenient
schools, at which their children may be educated, at their own
expence.—The general objects of this law are to provide an
education adapted to the years, to the capacity, and the condition of every one, and directed to their freedom and happiness. Specific details were not proper for the law. These

must be the business of the visitors entrusted with its execution. The first stage of this education being the schools of the hundreds, wherein the great mass of the people will receive their instruction, the principal foundations of future order will be laid here. Instead therefore of putting the Bible and Testament into the hands of the children, at an age when their judgments are not sufficiently matured for religious enquiries, their memories may here be stored with the most useful facts from Grecian, Roman, European and American history. The first elements of morality too may be instilled into their minds; such as, when further developed as their judgments advance in strength, may teach them how to work out their own greatest happiness, by shewing them that it does not depend on the condition of life in which chance has placed them, but is always the result of a good conscience, good health, occupation, and freedom in all just pursuits.—Those whom either the wealth of their parents or the adoption of the state shall destine to higher degrees of learning, will go on to the grammar schools, which constitute the next stage, there to be instructed in the languages. The learning Greek and Latin, I am told, is going into disuse in Europe. I know not what their manners and occupations may call for: but it would be very ill-judged in us to follow their example in this instance. There is a certain period of life, say from eight to fifteen or sixteen years of age, when the mind, like the body, is not yet firm enough for laborious and close operations. If applied to such, it falls an early victim to premature exertion; exhibiting indeed at first, in these young and tender subjects, the flattering appearance of their being men while they are yet children, but ending in reducing them to be children when they should be men. The memory is then most susceptible and tenacious of impressions; and the learning of languages being chiefly a work of memory, it seems precisely fitted to the powers of this period, which is long enough too for acquiring the most useful languages antient and modern. I do not pretend that language is science. It is only an instrument for the attainment of science. But that time is not lost which is employed in providing tools for future operation: more especially as in this case the books put into the hands of the youth for this purpose may be such as will at the same

time impress their minds with useful facts and good principles. If this period be suffered to pass in idleness, the mind
becomes lethargic and impotent, as would the body it inhab-
its if unexercised during the same time. The sympathy between body and mind during their rise, progress and decline,
is too strict and obvious to endanger our being misled while
we reason from the one to the other.—As soon as they are of
sufficient age, it is supposed they will be sent on from the
grammar schools to the university, which constitutes our
third and last stage, there to study those sciences which may
be adapted to their views.—By that part of our plan which
prescribes the selection of the youths of genius from among
the classes of the poor, we hope to avail the state of those
talents which nature has sown as liberally among the poor as
the rich, but which perish without use, if not sought for and
cultivated.—But of all the views of this law none is more important, none more legitimate, than that of rendering the
people the safe, as they are the ultimate, guardians of their
own liberty. For this purpose the reading in the first stage,
where *they* will receive their whole education, is proposed, as
has been said, to be chiefly historical. History by apprising
them of the past will enable them to judge of the future; it
will avail them of the experience of other times and other
nations; it will qualify them as judges of the actions and designs of men; it will enable them to know ambition under
every disguise it may assume; and knowing it, to defeat its
views. In every government on earth is some trace of human
weakness, some germ of corruption and degeneracy, which
cunning will discover, and wickedness insensibly open, cultivate, and improve. Every government degenerates when
trusted to the rulers of the people alone. The people themselves therefore are its only safe depositories. And to render
even them safe their minds must be improved to a certain
degree. This indeed is not all that is necessary, though it be
essentially necessary. An amendment of our constitution must
here come in aid of the public education. The influence over
government must be shared among all the people. If every
individual which composes their mass participates of the ultimate authority, the government will be safe; because the corrupting the whole mass will exceed any private resources of

wealth: and public ones cannot be provided but by levies on the people. In this case every man would have to pay his own price. The government of Great-Britain has been corrupted, because but one man in ten has a right to vote for members of parliament. The sellers of the government therefore get nine-tenths of their price clear. It has been thought that corruption is restrained by confining the right of suffrage to a few of the wealthier of the people: but it would be more effectually restrained by an extension of that right to such numbers as would bid defiance to the means of corruption.

Lastly, it is proposed, by a bill in this revisal, to begin a public library and gallery, by laying out a certain sum annually in books, paintings, and statues.

QUERY XV

*The colleges and public establishments, the roads, build-
ings, &c.?*
The college of William and Mary is the only public
seminary of learning in this state. It was founded in the
time of king William and queen Mary, who granted to it
20,000 acres of land, and a penny a pound duty on certain
tobaccoes exported from Virginia and Maryland, which had
been levied by the statute of 25 Car. 2. The assembly also gave
it, by temporary laws, a duty on liquors imported, and skins
and firs exported. From these resources it received upwards
of 3000 l. communibus annis. The buildings are of brick, sufficient for an indifferent accommodation of perhaps an
hundred students. By its charter it was to be under the government of twenty visitors, who were to be its legislators, and
to have a president and six professors, who were incorporated. It was allowed a representative in the general assembly.
Under this charter, a professorship of the Greek and Latin
languages, a professorship of mathematics, one of moral philosophy, and two of divinity, were established. To these were
annexed, for a sixth professorship, a considerable donation by
Mr. Boyle of England, for the instruction of the Indians, and
their conversion to Christianity. This was called the professorship of Brafferton, from an estate of that name in England,
purchased with the monies given. The admission of the learners of Latin and Greek filled the college with children. This
rendering it disagreeable and degrading to young gentlemen
already prepared for entering on the sciences, they were discouraged from resorting to it, and thus the schools for mathematics and moral philosophy, which might have been of
some service, became of very little. The revenues too were
exhausted in accommodating those who came only to acquire
the rudiments of science. After the present revolution, the visitors, having no power to change those circumstances in the
constitution of the college which were fixed by the charter,
and being therefore confined in the number of professorships,
undertook to change the objects of the professorships. They

excluded the two schools for divinity, and that for the Greek
and Latin languages, and substituted others; so that at present they stand thus:

A Professorship for Law and Police:
      Anatomy and Medicine:
      Natural Philosophy and Mathematics:
      Moral Philosophy, the Law of Nature
        and Nations, the Fine Arts:
      Modern Languages:
      For the Brafferton.

And it is proposed, so soon as the legislature shall have
leisure to take up this subject, to desire authority from them
to increase the number of professorships, as well for the purpose of subdividing those already instituted, as of adding others for other branches of science. To the professorships usually
established in the universities of Europe, it would seem
proper to add one for the antient languages and literature of
the North, on account of their connection with our own language, laws, customs, and history. The purposes of the Brafferton institution would be better answered by maintaining a
perpetual mission among the Indian tribes, the object of
which, besides instructing them in the principles of Christianity, as the founder requires, should be to collect their traditions, laws, customs, languages, and other circumstances
which might lead to a discovery of their relation with one
another, or descent from other nations. When these objects
are accomplished with one tribe, the missionary might pass
on to another.

The roads are under the government of the county courts,
subject to be controuled by the general court. They order new
roads to be opened wherever they think them necessary. The
inhabitants of the county are by them laid off into precincts,
to each of which they allot a convenient portion of the public
roads to be kept in repair. Such bridges as may be built without the assistance of artificers, they are to build. If the stream
be such as to require a bridge of regular workmanship, the
court employs workmen to build it, at the expence of the
whole county. If it be too great for the county, application is
made to the general assembly, who authorize individuals to

build it, and to take a fixed toll from all passengers, or give sanction to such other proposition as to them appears reasonable.

Ferries are admitted only at such places as are particularly pointed out by law, and the rates of ferriage are fixed.

Taverns are licensed by the courts, who fix their rates from time to time.

The private buildings are very rarely constructed of stone or brick; much the greatest proportion being of scantling and boards, plaistered with lime. It is impossible to devise things more ugly, uncomfortable, and happily more perishable. There are two or three plans, on one of which, according to its size, most of the houses in the state are built. The poorest people build huts of logs, laid horizontally in pens, stopping the interstices with mud. These are warmer in winter, and cooler in summer, than the more expensive constructions of scantling and plank. The wealthy are attentive to the raising of vegetables, but very little so to fruits. The poorer people attend to neither, living principally on milk and animal diet. This is the more inexcusable, as the climate requires indispensably a free use of vegetable food, for health as well as comfort, and is very friendly to the raising of fruits.—The only public buildings worthy mention are the Capitol, the Palace, the College, and the Hospital for Lunatics, all of them in Williamsburg, heretofore the seat of our government. The Capitol is a light and airy structure, with a portico in front of two orders, the lower of which, being Doric, is tolerably just in its proportions and ornaments, save only that the inter-colonnations are too large. The upper is Ionic, much too small for that on which it is mounted, its ornaments not proper to the order, nor proportioned within themselves. It is crowned with a pediment, which is too high for its span. Yet, on the whole, it is the most pleasing piece of architecture we have. The Palace is not handsome without: but it is spacious and commodious within, is prettily situated, and, with the grounds annexed to it, is capable of being made an elegant seat. The College and Hospital are rude, mis-shapen piles, which, but that they have roofs, would be taken for brick-kilns. There are no other public buildings but churches and court-houses, in which no attempts are made at elegance.

natural constructions not
appealing the — Lunar..

Indeed it would not be easy to execute such an attempt, as a workman could scarcely be found here capable of drawing an order. The genius of architecture seems to have shed its maledictions over this land. Buildings are often erected, by individuals, of considerable expence. To give these symmetry and taste would not increase their cost. It would only change the arrangement of the materials, the form and combination of the members. This would often cost less than the burthen of barbarous ornaments with which these buildings are sometimes charged. But the first principles of the art are unknown, and there exists scarcely a model among us sufficiently chaste to give an idea of them. Architecture being one of the fine arts, and as such within the department of a professor of the college, according to the new arrangement, perhaps a spark may fall on some young subjects of natural taste, kindle up their genius, and produce a reformation in this elegant and useful art. But all we shall do in this way will produce no permanent improvement to our country, while the unhappy prejudice prevails that houses of brick or stone are less wholesome than those of wood. A dew is often observed on the walls of the former in rainy weather, and the most obvious solution is, that the rain has penetrated through these walls. The following facts however are sufficient to prove the error of this solution. 1. This dew on the walls appears when there is no rain, if the state of the atmosphere be moist. 2. It appears on the partition as well as the exterior walls. 3. So also on pavements of brick or stone. 4. It is more copious in proportion as the walls are thicker; the reverse of which ought to be the case, if this hypothesis were just. If cold water be poured into a vessel of stone, or glass, a dew forms instantly on the outside: but if it be poured into a vessel of wood, there is no such appearance. It is not supposed, in the first case, that the water has exuded through the glass, but that it is precipitated from the circumambient air; as the humid particles of vapour, passing from the boiler of an alembic through its refrigerant, are precipitated from the air, in which they were suspended, on the internal surface of the refrigerant. Walls of brick or stone act as the refrigerant in this instance. They are sufficiently cold to condense and precipitate the moisture suspended in the air of the room, when it is heavily charged therewith. But walls of wood are not so. The question then is, whether air in which this moisture is left floating, or that which is deprived of it, be most wholesome? In both cases the remedy is easy. A little fire kindled in the room, whenever the air is damp, prevents the precipitation on the walls: and this practice, found healthy in the warmest as well as coldest seasons, is as necessary in a wooden as in a stone or a brick house. I do not mean to say, that the rain never penetrates through walls of brick. On the contrary I have seen instances of it. But with us it is only through the northern and eastern walls of the house, after a north-easterly storm, these being the only ones which continue long enough to force through the walls. This however happens too rarely to give a just character of unwholesomeness to such houses. In a house, the walls of which are of well-burnt brick and good mortar, I have seen the rain penetrate through but twice in a dozen or fifteen years. The inhabitants of Europe, who dwell chiefly in houses of stone or brick, are surely as healthy as those of Virginia. These houses have the advantage too of being warmer in winter and cooler in summer than those of wood, of being cheaper in their first construction, where lime is convenient, and infinitely more durable. The latter consideration renders it of great importance to eradicate this prejudice from the minds of our countrymen. A country whose buildings are of wood, can never increase in its improvements to any considerable degree. Their duration is highly estimated at 50 years. Every half century then our country becomes a tabula rasa, whereon we have to set out anew, as in the first moment of seating it. Whereas when buildings are of durable materials, every new edifice is an actual and permanent acquisition to the state, adding to its value as well as to its ornament.

QUERY XVI

The measures taken with regard of the estates and pos-
sessions of the rebels, commonly called Tories?

A Tory has been properly defined to be a traitor in thought,
but not in deed. The only description, by which the laws have
endeavoured to come at them, was that of non-jurors, or persons refusing to take the oath of fidelity to the state. Persons
of this description were at one time subjected to double taxation, at another to treble, and lastly were allowed retribution, and placed on a level with good citizens. It may be
mentioned as a proof both of the lenity of our government,
and unanimity of its inhabitants, that though this war has
now raged near seven years, not a single execution for treason
has taken place.

Under this query I will state the measures which have been
adopted as to British property, the owners of which stand on
a much fairer footing than the Tories. By our laws, the same
as the English in this respect, no alien can hold lands, nor
alien enemy maintain an action for money, or other moveable
thing. Lands acquired or held by aliens become forfeited to
the state; and, on an action by an alien enemy to recover
money, or other moveable property, the defendant may plead
that he is an alien enemy. This extinguishes his right in the
hands of the debtor or holder of his moveable property. By
our separation from Great-Britain, British subjects became
aliens, and being at war, they were alien enemies. Their lands
were of course forfeited, and their debts irrecoverable. The
assembly however passed laws, at various times, for saving
their property. They first sequestered their lands, slaves, and
other property on their farms, in the hands of commissioners,
who were mostly the confidential friends or agents of the
owners, and directed their clear profits to be paid into the
treasury: and they gave leave to all persons owing debts to
British subjects to pay them also into the treasury. The monies so to be brought in were declared to remain the property
of the British subject, and, if used by the state, were to be
repaid, unless an improper conduct in Great-Britain should
render a detention of it reasonable. Depreciation had at that

time, though unacknowledged and unperceived by the Whigs, begun in some small degree. Great sums of money were paid in by debtors. At a later period, the assembly, adhering to the political principles which forbid an alien to hold lands in the state, ordered all British property to be sold: and, become sensible of the real progress of depreciation, and of the losses which would thence occur, if not guarded against, they ordered that the proceeds of the sales should be converted into their then worth in tobacco, subject to the future direction of the legislature. This act has left the question of retribution more problematical. In May 1780 another act took away the permission to pay into the public treasury debts due to British subjects.

QUERY XVII

The different religions received into that state?

The first settlers in this country were emigrants from England, of the English church, just at a point of time when it was flushed with complete victory over the religious of all other persuasions. Possessed, as they became, of the powers of making, administering, and executing the laws, they shewed equal intolerance in this country with their Presbyterian brethren, who had emigrated to the northern government. The poor Quakers were flying from persecution in England. They cast their eyes on these new countries as asylums of civil and religious freedom; but they found them free only for the reigning sect. Several acts of the Virginia assembly of 1659, 1662, and 1693, had made it penal in parents to refuse to have their children baptized; had prohibited the unlawful assembling of Quakers; had made it penal for any master of a vessel to bring a Quaker into the state; had ordered those already here, and such as should come thereafter, to be imprisoned till they should abjure the country; provided a milder punishment for their first and second return, but death for their third; had inhibited all persons from suffering their meetings in or near their houses, entertaining them individually, or disposing of books which supported their tenets. If no capital execution took place here, as did in New-England, it was not owing to the moderation of the church, or spirit of the legislature, as may be inferred from the law itself; but to historical circumstances which have not been handed down to us. The Anglicans retained full possession of the country about a century. Other opinions began then to creep in, and the great care of the government to support their own church, having begotten an equal degree of indolence in its clergy, two-thirds of the people had become dissenters at the commencement of the present revolution. The laws indeed were still oppressive on them, but the spirit of the one party had subsided into moderation, and of the other had risen to a degree of determination which commanded respect.

The present state of our laws on the subject of religion is this. The convention of May 1776, in their declaration of

283

rights, declared it to be a truth, and a natural right, that the exercise of religion should be free; but when they proceeded to form on that declaration the ordinance of government, instead of taking up every principle declared in the bill of rights, and guarding it by legislative sanction, they passed over that which asserted our religious rights, leaving them as they found them. The same convention, however, when they met as a member of the general assembly in October 1776, repealed all *acts of parliament* which had rendered criminal the maintaining any opinions in matters of religion, the forbearing to repair to church, and the exercising any mode of worship; and suspended the laws giving salaries to the clergy, which suspension was made perpetual in October 1779. Statutory oppressions in religion being thus wiped away, we remain at present under those only imposed by the common law, or by our own acts of assembly. At the common law, *heresy* was a capital offence, punishable by burning. Its definition was left to the ecclesiastical judges, before whom the conviction was, till the statute of the 1 El. c. 1. circumscribed it, by declaring, that nothing should be deemed heresy, but what had been so determined by authority of the canonical scriptures, or by one of the four first general councils, or by some other council having for the grounds of their declaration the express and plain words of the scriptures. Heresy, thus circumscribed, being an offence at the common law, our act of assembly of October 1777, c. 17. gives cognizance of it to the general court, by declaring, that the jurisdiction of that court shall be general in all matters at the common law. The execution is by the writ *De hæretico comburendo*. By our own act of assembly of 1705, c. 30, if a person brought up in the Christian religion denies the being of a God, or the Trinity, or asserts there are more Gods than one, or denies the Christian religion to be true, or the scriptures to be of divine authority, he is punishable on the first offence by incapacity to hold any office or employment ecclesiastical, civil, or military; on the second by disability to sue, to take any gift or legacy, to be guardian, executor, or administrator, and by three years imprisonment, without bail. A father's right to the custody of his own children being founded in law on his right of guardianship, this being taken away, they may of course be severed from him, and put, by the authority of a court, into more orthodox hands. This is a summary view of that religious slavery, under which a people have been willing to remain, who have lavished their lives and fortunes for the establishment of their civil freedom. *The error seems not sufficiently eradicated, that the operations of the mind, as well as the acts of the body, are subject to the coercion of the laws. But our rulers can have authority over such natural rights only as we have submitted to them. The rights of conscience we never submitted, we could not submit. We are answerable for them to our God. The legitimate powers of government extend to such acts only as are injurious to others. But it does me no injury for my neighbour to say there are twenty gods, or no god. It neither picks my pocket nor breaks my leg. If it be said, his testimony in a court of justice cannot be relied on, reject it then, and be the stigma on him. Constraint may make him worse by making him a hypocrite, but it will never make him a truer man. It may fix him obstinately in his errors, but will not cure them. Reason and free enquiry are the only effectual agents against error. Give a loose to them, they will support the true religion, by bringing every false one to their tribunal, to the test of their investigation. They are the natural enemies of error, and of error only. Had not the Roman government permitted free enquiry, Christianity could never have been introduced. Had not free enquiry been indulged, at the æra of the reformation, the corruptions of Christianity could not have been purged away. If it be restrained now, the present corruptions will be protected, and new ones encouraged. Was the government to prescribe to us our medicine and diet, our bodies would be in such keeping as our souls are now. Thus in France the emetic was once forbidden as a medicine, and the potatoe as an article of food. Government is just as infallible too when it fixes systems in physics. Galileo was sent to the inquisition for affirming that the earth was a sphere: the government had declared it to be as flat as a trencher, and Galileo was obliged to abjure his error. This error however at length prevailed, the earth became a globe, and Descartes declared it was whirled round its

*Furneaux passim.

axis by a vortex. The government in which he lived was wise enough to see that this was no question of civil jurisdiction, or we should all have been involved by authority in vortices. In fact, the vortices have been exploded, and the Newtonian principle of gravitation is now more firmly established, on the basis of reason, than it would be were the government to step in, and to make it an article of necessary faith. Reason and experiment have been indulged, and error has fled before them. It is error alone which needs the support of government: Truth can stand by itself. Subject opinion to coercion: whom will you make your inquisitors? Fallible men; men governed by bad passions, by private as well as public reasons. And why subject it to coercion? To produce uniformity. But is uniformity of opinion desireable? No more than of face and stature. Introduce the bed of Procrustes then, and as there is danger that the large men may beat the small, make us all of a size, by lopping the former and stretching the latter. Difference of opinion is advantageous in religion. The several sects perform the office of a Censor morum over each other. Is uniformity attainable? Millions of innocent men, women, and children, since the introduction of Christianity, have been burnt, tortured, fined, imprisoned; yet we have not advanced one inch towards uniformity. What has been the effect of coercion? To make one half the world fools, and the other half hypocrites. To support roguery and error all over the earth. Let us reflect that it is inhabited by a thousand millions of people. That these profess probably a thousand different systems of religion. That ours is but one of that thousand. That if there be but one right, and ours that one, we should wish to see the 999 wandering sects gathered into the fold of truth. But against such a majority we cannot effect this by force. Reason and persuasion are the only practicable instruments. To make way for these, free enquiry must be indulged; and how can we wish others to indulge it while we refuse it ourselves. But every state, says an inquisitor, has established some religion. No two, say I, have established the same. Is this a proof of the infallibility of establishments? Our sister states of Pennsylvania and New York, however, have long subsisted without any establishment at all. The experiment was new and doubtful when they made it. It has answered beyond conception. They flourish infinitely. Religion is well supported; of various kinds, indeed, but all good enough; all sufficient to preserve peace and order: or if a sect arises, whose tenets would subvert morals, good sense has fair play, and reasons and laughs it out of doors, without suffering the state to be troubled with it. They do not hang more malefactors than we do. They are not more disturbed with religious dissensions. On the contrary, their harmony is unparalleled, and can be ascribed to nothing but their unbounded tolerance, because there is no other circumstance in which they differ from every nation on earth. They have made the happy discovery, that the way to silence religious disputes, is to take no notice of them. Let us too give this experiment fair play, and get rid, while we may, of those tyrannical laws. It is true, we are as yet secured against them by the spirit of the times. I doubt whether the people of this country would suffer an execution for heresy, or a three years imprisonment for not comprehending the mysteries of the Trinity. But is the spirit of the people an infallible, a permanent reliance? Is it government? Is this the kind of protection we receive in return for the rights we give up? Besides, the spirit of the times may alter, will alter. Our rulers will become corrupt, our people careless. A single zealot may commence persecutor, and better men be his victims. It can never be too often repeated, that the time for fixing every essential right on a legal basis is while our rulers are honest, and ourselves united. From the conclusion of this war we shall be going down hill. It will not then be necessary to resort every moment to the people for support. They will be forgotten, therefore, and their rights disregarded. They will forget themselves, but in the sole faculty of making money, and will never think of uniting to effect a due respect for their rights. The shackles, therefore, which shall not be knocked off at the conclusion of this war, will remain on us long, will be made heavier and heavier, till our rights shall revive or expire in a convulsion.

QUERY XVIII

Manners   *The* particular *customs and manners that may happen to be received in that state?*

It is difficult to determine on the standard by which the manners of a nation may be tried, whether *catholic*, or *particular*. It is more difficult for a native to bring to that standard the manners of his own nation, familiarized to him by habit. There must doubtless be an unhappy influence on the manners of our people produced by the existence of slavery among us. The whole commerce between master and slave is a perpetual exercise of the most boisterous passions, the most unremitting despotism on the one part, and degrading submissions on the other. Our children see this, and learn to imitate it; for man is an imitative animal. This quality is the germ of all education in him. From his cradle to his grave he is learning to do what he sees others do. If a parent could find no motive either in his philanthropy or his self-love, for restraining the intemperance of passion towards his slave, it should always be a sufficient one that his child is present. But generally it is not sufficient. The parent storms, the child looks on, catches the lineaments of wrath, puts on the same airs in the circle of smaller slaves, gives a loose to his worst of passions, and thus nursed, educated, and daily exercised in tyranny, cannot but be stamped by it with odious peculiarities. The man must be a prodigy who can retain his manners and morals undepraved by such circumstances. And with what execration should the statesman be loaded, who permitting one half the citizens thus to trample on the rights of the other, transforms those into despots, and these into enemies, destroys the morals of the one part, and the amor patriæ of the other. For if a slave can have a country in this world, it must be any other in preference to that in which he is born to live and labour for another: in which he must lock up the faculties of his nature, contribute as far as depends on his individual endeavours to the evanishment of the human race, or entail his own miserable condition on the endless generations proceeding from him. With the morals of the people, their industry also is destroyed. For in a warm climate, no

288

man will labour for himself who can make another labour for him. This is so true, that of the proprietors of slaves a very small proportion indeed are ever seen to labour. And can the liberties of a nation be thought secure when we have removed their only firm basis, a conviction in the minds of the people that these liberties are of the gift of God? That they are not to be violated but with his wrath? Indeed I tremble for my country when I reflect that God is just: that his justice cannot sleep for ever: that considering numbers, nature and natural means only, a revolution of the wheel of fortune, an exchange of situation, is among possible events; that it may become probable by supernatural interference! The Almighty has no attribute which can take side with us in such a contest.—But it is impossible to be temperate and to pursue this subject through the various considerations of policy, of morals, of history natural and civil. We must be contented to hope they will force their way into every one's mind. I think a change already perceptible, since the origin of the present revolution. The spirit of the master is abating, that of the slave rising from the dust, his condition mollifying, the way I hope preparing, under the auspices of heaven, for a total emancipation, and that this is disposed, in the order of events, to be with the consent of the masters, rather than by their extirpation.

other side

QUERY XIX

*The present state of manufactures, commerce, interior
and exterior trade?*

We never had an interior trade of any importance. Our exterior commerce has suffered very much from the beginning of the present contest. During this time we have manufactured within our families the most necessary articles of cloathing. Those of cotton will bear some comparison with the same kinds of manufacture in Europe; but those of wool, flax and hemp are very coarse, unsightly, and unpleasant: and such is our attachment to agriculture, and such our preference for foreign manufactures, that be it wise or unwise, our people will certainly return as soon as they can, to the raising raw materials, and exchanging them for finer manufactures than they are able to execute themselves.

The political œconomists of Europe have established it as a principle that every state should endeavour to manufacture for itself: and this principle, like many others, we transfer to America, without calculating the difference of circumstance which should often produce a difference of result. In Europe the lands are either cultivated, or locked up against the cultivator. Manufacture must therefore be resorted to of necessity not of choice, to support the surplus of their people. But we have an immensity of land courting the industry of the husbandman. Is it best then that all our citizens should be employed in its improvement, or that one half should be called off from that to exercise manufactures and handicraft arts for the other? Those who labour in the earth are the chosen people of God, if ever he had a chosen people, whose breasts he has made his peculiar deposit for substantial and genuine virtue. It is the focus in which he keeps alive that sacred fire, which otherwise might escape from the face of the earth. Corruption of morals in the mass of cultivators is a phænomenon of which no age nor nation has furnished an example. It is the mark set on those, who not looking up to heaven, to their own soil and industry, as does the husbandman, for their subsistance, depend for it on the casualties and caprice of customers. Dependance begets subservience and venality, suffocates the germ of virtue, and prepares fit tools for the designs of ambition. This, the natural progress and consequence of the arts, has sometimes perhaps been retarded by accidental circumstances: but, generally speaking, the proportion which the aggregate of the other classes of citizens bears in any state to that of its husbandmen, is the proportion of its unsound to its healthy parts, and is a good-enough barometer whereby to measure its degree of corruption. While we have land to labour then, let us never wish to see our citizens occupied at a work-bench, or twirling a distaff. Carpenters, masons, smiths, are wanting in husbandry: but, for the general operations of manufacture, let our work-shops remain in Europe. It is better to carry provisions and materials to workmen there, than bring them to the provisions and materials, and with them their manners and principles. The loss by the transportation of commodities across the Atlantic will be made up in happiness and permanence of government. The mobs of great cities add just so much to the support of pure government, as sores do to the strength of the human body. It is the manners and spirit of a people which preserve a republic in vigour. A degeneracy in these is a canker which soon eats to the heart of its laws and constitution.

QUERY XX

Commercial productions *A notice of the commercial productions particular to the state, and of those objects which the inhabitants are obliged to get from Europe and from other parts of the world?*

Before the present war we exported, communibus annis, according to the best information I can get, nearly as follows:

A R T I C L E S.	Quantity.	Price in dollars.	Am. in dollars.
Tobacco	55,000 hhds. of 1000 lb.	at 30 d. per hhd.	1,650,000
Wheat	800,000 bushels	at 5/6 d. per bush.	666,666⅔
Indian corn	600,000 bushels	at ⅓ d. per bush.	200,000
Shipping	— — —	— —	100,000
Masts, planks, skantling, shingles, staves	— — —	— —	66,666⅔
Tar, pitch, turpentine	30,000 barrels	at 1⅓ d. per bar.	40,000
Peltry, viz. skins of deer, beavers, otters, muskrats, racoons, foxes	180 hhds. of 600 lb.	at 5/12 d. per lb.	42,000
Pork	4,000 barrels	at 10 d. per bar.	40,000
Flax-seed, hemp, cotton	— — —	— —	8,000
Pit-coal, pig-iron	— — —	— —	6,666⅔
Peas	5,000 bushels	at ⅔ d. per bush.	3,333⅓
Beef	1,000 barrels	at 3⅓ d. per bar.	3,333⅓
Sturgeon, white shad, herring	— — —	— —	3,333⅓
Brandy from peaches and apples, and whiskey	— — —	— —	1,666⅔
Horses	— — —	— —	1,666⅔

This sum is equal to 850,000 l. Virginia money, 607,142 guineas. ・ 2,833,333⅓ D.

In the year 1758 we exported seventy thousand hogsheads of tobacco, which was the greatest quantity ever produced in this country in one year. But its culture was fast declining at the commencement of this war and that of wheat taking its place: and it must continue to decline on the return of peace. I suspect that the change in the temperature of our climate has become sensible to that plant, which, to be good, requires an extraordinary degree of heat. But it requires still more indispensably an uncommon fertility of soil: and the price which it commands at market will not enable the planter to produce this by manure. Was the supply still to depend on Virginia and Maryland alone, as its culture becomes more difficult, the price would rise, so as to enable the planter to surmount those difficulties and to live. But the western country on the Missisipi, and the midlands of Georgia, having fresh and fertile lands in abundance, and a hotter sun, will be able to undersell these two states, and will oblige them to abandon the raising tobacco altogether. And a happy obligation for them it will be. It is a culture productive of infinite wretchedness. Those employed in it are in a continued state of exertion beyond the powers of nature to support. Little food of any kind is raised by them; so that the men and animals on these farms are badly fed, and the earth is rapidly impoverished. The cultivation of wheat is the reverse in every circumstance. Besides cloathing the earth with herbage, and preserving its fertility, it feeds the labourers plentifully, requires from them only a moderate toil, except in the season of harvest, raises great numbers of animals for food and service, and diffuses plenty and happiness among the whole. We find it easier to make an hundred bushels of wheat than a thousand weight of tobacco, and they are worth more when made. The weavil indeed is a formidable obstacle to the cultivation of this grain with us. But principles are already known which must lead to a remedy. Thus a certain degree of heat, to wit, that of the common air in summer, is necessary to hatch the egg. If subterranean granaries, or others, therefore, can be contrived below that temperature, the evil will be cured by cold. A degree of heat beyond that which hatches the egg, we know will kill it. But in aiming at this we easily run into that which produces putrefaction. To produce putrefaction, however, three agents are requisite, heat, moisture, and the external air. If the absence of any one of these be secured, the other two may safely be admitted. Heat is the one we want. Moisture then, or external air, must be excluded. The former has been done by exposing the grain in kilns to the action of fire, which produces heat, and extracts moisture at the same time: the latter, by putting the grain into hogsheads, covering it with a coat of lime, and heading it up. In this situation its bulk produces a heat sufficient to kill the egg; the moisture is suffered to remain indeed, but the external air is excluded. A nicer operation yet has been attempted; that is, to produce an intermediate temperature of heat between that which kills the egg, and that which produces putrefaction. The threshing the grain as soon as it is cut, and laying it in its chaff in large heaps, has been found very nearly to hit this temperature, though not perfectly, nor always. The heap generates heat sufficient to kill most of the eggs, whilst the chaff commonly restrains it from rising into putrefaction. But all these methods abridge too much the quantity which the farmer can manage, and enable other countries to undersell him which are not infested with this insect. There is still a desideratum then to give with us decisive triumph to this branch of agriculture over that of tobacco.—The culture of wheat, by enlarging our pasture, will render the Arabian horse an article of very considerable profit. Experience has shewn that ours is the particular climate of America where he may be raised without degeneracy. Southwardly the heat of the sun occasions a deficiency of pasture, and northwardly the winters are too cold for the short and fine hair, the particular sensibility and constitution of that race. Animals transplanted into unfriendly climates, either change their nature and acquire new fences against the new difficulties in which they are placed, or they multiply poorly and become extinct. A good foundation is laid for their propagation here by our possessing already great numbers of horses of that blood, and by a decided taste and preference for them established among the people. Their patience of heat without injury, their superior wind, fit them better in this and the more southern climates even for the drudgeries of the plough and waggon. Northwardly they will become an object only to persons of taste and fortune, for the saddle and light carriages. To these, and for these uses, their fleetness and beauty will recommend them.—Besides these there will be other valuable substitutes when the cultivation of tobacco shall be discontinued, such as cotton in the eastern parts of the state, and hemp and flax in the western.

It is not easy to say what are the articles either of necessity, comfort, or luxury, which we cannot raise, and which we therefore shall be under a necessity of importing from abroad, as every thing hardier than the olive, and as hardy as the fig, may be raised here in the open air. Sugar, coffee and tea, indeed, are not between these limits; and habit having placed them among the necessaries of life with the wealthy part of our citizens, as long as these habits remain, we must go for them to those countries which are able to furnish them.

Weights,
Measures,
Money *The weights, measures, and the currency of the hard money? Some details relating to the exchange with Europe?*

Our weights and measures are the same which are fixed by acts of parliament in England.—How it has happened that in this as well as the other American states the nominal value of coin was made to differ from what it was in the country we had left, and to differ among ourselves too, I am not able to say with certainty. I find that in 1631 our house of burgesses desired of the privy council in England, a coin debased to twenty-five per cent: that in 1645 they forbid dealing by barter for tobacco, and established the Spanish piece of eight at six shillings, as the standard of their currency: that in 1655 they changed it to five shillings sterling. In 1680 they sent an address to the king, in consequence of which, by proclamation in 1683, he fixed the value of French crowns, rixdollars and pieces of eight at six shillings, and the coin of New-England at one shilling. That in 1710, 1714, 1727, and 1762, other regulations were made, which will be better presented to the eye stated in the form of a table as follows:

	1710.	1714.	1727.	1762.
Guineas	— —	26s		
British gold coin not milled, coined gold of Spain and France, chequins, Arabian gold, moidores of Portugal	— —	5s the dwt.		
Coined gold of the empire	— —	5s the dwt.	— —	4s3 the dwt.
English milled silver money, in proportion to the crown, at	— —	5s10	6s3	
Pieces of eight of Mexico, Seville, and Pillar, ducatoons of Flanders, French ecus, or silver Louis, crusados of Portugal	3¾ d. the dwt.	— —	4 d. the dwt.	
Peru pieces, cross dollars, and old rixdollars of the empire	3½ d. the dwt.	— —	3¾ d. the dwt.	
Old British silver coin not milled	— —	3¾ d. the dwt.		

The first symptom of the depreciation of our present paper-money, was that of silver dollars selling at six shillings, which had before been worth but five shillings and ninepence. The assembly thereupon raised them by law to six shillings. As the dollar is now likely to become the money-unit of America, as it passes at this rate in some of our sister-states, and as it facilitates their computation in pounds and shillings, & e converso, this seems to be more convenient than it's former denomination. But as this particular coin now stands higher than any other in the proportion of 133⅓ to 125, or 16 to 15, it will be necessary to raise the others in the same proportion.

QUERY XXII

The public income and expences?

The nominal amount of these varying constantly and rapidly, with the constant and rapid depreciation of our paper-money, it becomes impracticable to say what they are. We find ourselves cheated in every essay by the depreciation intervening between the declaration of the tax and its actual receipt. It will therefore be more satisfactory to consider what our income may be when we shall find means of collecting what the people may spare. I should estimate the whole taxable property of this state at an hundred millions of dollars, or thirty millions of pounds our money. One per cent on this, compared with any thing we ever yet paid, would be deemed a very heavy tax. Yet I think that those who manage well, and use reasonable œconomy, could pay one and a half per cent, and maintain their houshould comfortably in the mean time, without aliening any part of their principal, and that the people would submit to this willingly for the purpose of supporting their present contest. We may say then, that we could raise, and ought to raise, from one million to one million and a half of dollars annually, that is from three hundred to four hundred and fifty thousand pounds, Virginia money.

Of our expences it is equally difficult to give an exact state, and for the same reason. They are mostly stated in paper money, which varying continually, the legislature endeavours at every session, by new corrections, to adapt the nominal sums to the value it is wished they should bear. I will state them therefore in real coin, at the point at which they endeavour to keep them.

	Dollars.
The annual expences of the general assembly are about	20,000
The governor	3,333⅓
The council of state	10,666⅔
Their clerks	1,166⅔
Eleven judges	11000
The clerk of the chancery	666⅔
The attorney general	1,000

Three auditors and a solicitor	5,333⅓
Their clerks	2,000
The treasurer	2,000
His clerks	2,000
The keeper of the public jail	1,000
The public printer	1,666⅔
Clerks of the inferior courts	43,333⅓
Public levy: this is chiefly for the expences of criminal justice	40,000
County levy, for bridges, court houses, prisons, &c.	40,000
Members of congress	7000
Quota of the Federal civil list, supposed ⅙ of about 78,000 dollars	13,000
Expences of collection, 6 per cent. on the above	12,310
The clergy receive only voluntary contributions: suppose them on an average ⅛ of a dollar a tythe on 200,000 tythes	25,000
Contingencies, to make round numbers not far from truth	7,523⅓
	250,000

Dollars, or 53,571 guineas. This estimate is exclusive of the military expence. That varies with the force actually employed, and in time of peace will probably be little or nothing. It is exclusive also of the public debts, which are growing while I am writing, and cannot therefore be now fixed. So it is of the maintenance of the poor, which being merely a matter of charity, cannot be deemed expended in the administration of government. And if we strike out the 25,000 dollars for the services of the clergy, which neither makes part of that administration, more than what is paid to physicians or lawyers, and being voluntary, is either much or nothing as every one pleases, it leaves 225,000 dollars, equal to 48,208 guineas, the real cost of the apparatus of government with us. This, divided among the actual inhabitants of our country, comes to about two-fifths of a dollar, 21d sterling, or 42 sols, the price which each pays annually for the protection of the residue of his property, that of his person, and the other advantages of a free government. The public revenues of Great Britain divided in like manner on its inhabitants would be sixteen times greater. Deducting even the double of the expences of government, as before estimated, from the million and a half of dollars which we before supposed might be annually paid without distress, we may conclude that this state can contribute one million of dollars annually towards supporting the federal army, paying the federal debt, building a federal navy, or opening roads, clearing rivers, forming safe ports, and other useful works.

To this estimate of our abilities, let me add a word as to the application of them, if, when cleared of the present contest, and of the debts with which that will charge us, we come to measure force hereafter with any European power. Such events are devoutly to be deprecated. Young as we are, and with such a country before us to fill with people and with happiness, we should point in that direction the whole generative force of nature, wasting none of it in efforts of mutual destruction. It should be our endeavour to cultivate the peace and friendship of every nation, even of that which has injured us most, when we shall have carried our point against her. Our interest will be to throw open the doors of commerce, and to knock off all its shackles, giving perfect freedom to all persons for the vent of whatever they may chuse to bring into our ports, and asking the same in theirs. Never was so much false arithmetic employed on any subject, as that which has been employed to persuade nations that it is their interest to go to war. Were the money which it has cost to gain, at the close of a long war, a little town, or a little territory, the right to cut wood here, or to catch fish there, expended in improving what they already possess, in making roads, opening rivers, building ports, improving the arts, and finding employment for their idle poor, it would render them much stronger, much wealthier and happier. This I hope will be our wisdom. And, perhaps, to remove as much as possible the occasions of making war, it might be better for us to abandon the ocean altogether, that being the element whereon we shall be principally exposed to jostle with other nations: to leave to others to bring what we shall want, and to carry what we can spare. This would make us invulnerable to Europe, by offering none of our property to their prize, and would turn all

our citizens to the cultivation of the earth; and, I repeat it
again, cultivators of the earth are the most virtuous and independant citizens. It might be time enough to seek employment for them at sea, when the land no longer offers it. But
the actual habits of our countrymen attach them to commerce. They will exercise it for themselves. Wars then must
sometimes be our lot; and all the wise can do, will be to avoid
that half of them which would be produced by our own follies, and our own acts of injustice; and to make for the other
half the best preparations we can. Of what nature should
these be? A land army would be useless for offence, and not
the best nor safest instrument of defence. For either of these
purposes, the sea is the field on which we should meet an
European enemy. On that element it is necessary we should
possess some power. To aim at such a navy as the greater
nations of Europe possess, would be a foolish and wicked
waste of the energies of our countrymen. It would be to pull
on our own heads that load of military expence, which makes
the European labourer go supperless to bed, and moistens his
bread with the sweat of his brows. It will be enough if we
enable ourselves to prevent insults from those nations of Europe which are weak on the sea, because circumstances exist,
which render even the stronger ones weak as to us. Providence has placed their richest and most defenceless possessions at our door; has obliged their most precious commerce
to pass as it were in review before us. To protect this, or to
assail us, a small part only of their naval force will ever be
risqued across the Atlantic. The dangers to which the elements expose them here are too well known, and the greater
dangers to which they would be exposed at home, were any
general calamity to involve their whole fleet. They can attack
us by detachment only; and it will suffice to make ourselves
equal to what they may detach. Even a smaller force than they
may detach will be rendered equal or superior by the quick-
ness with which any check may be repaired with us, while
losses with them will be irreparable till too late. A small naval
force then is sufficient for us, and a small one is necessary.
What this should be, I will not undertake to say. I will only
say, it should by no means be so great as we are able to make
it. Suppose the million of dollars, or 300,000 pounds, which

Virginia could annually spare without distress, to be applied to the creating a navy. A single year's contribution would build, equip, man, and send to sea a force which should carry 300 guns. The rest of the confederacy, exerting themselves in the same proportion, would equip in the same time 1500 guns more. So that one year's contributions would set up a navy of 1800 guns. The British ships of the line average 76 guns; their frigates 38. 1800 guns then would form a fleet of 30 ships, 18 of which might be of the line, and 12 frigates. Allowing 8 men, the British average, for every gun, their annual expence, including subsistence, cloathing, pay, and ordinary repairs, would be about 1280 dollars for every gun, or 2,304,000 dollars for the whole. I state this only as one year's possible exertion, without deciding whether more or less than a year's exertion should be thus applied.

The value of our lands and slaves, taken conjunctly, doubles in about twenty years. This arises from the multiplication of our slaves, from the extension of culture, and increased demand for lands. The amount of what may be raised will of course rise in the same proportion.

QUERY XXIII

The histories of the state, the memorials published   Histories,
in its name in the time of its being a colony, and   &c.
the pamphlets relating to its interior or exterior affairs present or
antient?

Captain Smith, who next to Sir Walter Raleigh may be considered as the founder of our colony, has written its history, from the first adventures to it till the year 1624. He was a member of the council, and afterwards president of the colony; and to his efforts principally may be ascribed its support against the opposition of the natives. He was honest, sensible, and well informed; but his style is barbarous and uncouth. His history, however, is almost the only source from which we derive any knowledge of the infancy of our state.

The reverend William Stith, a native of Virginia, and president of its college, has also written the history of the same period, in a large octavo volume of small print. He was a man of classical learning, and very exact, but of no taste in style. He is inelegant, therefore, and his details often too minute to be tolerable, even to a native of the country, whose history he writes.

Beverley, a native also, has run into the other extreme; he has comprised our history, from the first propositions of Sir Walter Raleigh to the year 1700, in the hundredth part of the space which Stith employs for the fourth part of the period.

Sir William Keith has taken it up at its earliest period, and continued it to the year 1725. He is agreeable enough in style, and passes over events of little importance. Of course he is short, and would be preferred by a foreigner.

During the regal government, some contest arose on the exaction of an illegal fee by governor Dinwiddie, and doubtless there were others on other occasions not at present recollected. It is supposed, that these are not sufficiently interesting to a foreigner to merit a detail.

The petition of the council and burgesses of Virginia to the king, their memorial to the lords, and remonstrance to the commons in the year 1764, began the present contest: and these having proved ineffectual to prevent the passage of the stamp-act, the resolutions of the house of burgesses of 1765 were passed, declaring the independance of the people of Virginia on the parliament of Great-Britain, in matters of taxation. From that time till the declaration of independence by congress in 1776, their journals are filled with assertions of the public rights.

The pamphlets published in this state on the controverted question were,

- 1766, An Enquiry into the Rights of the British Colonies, by Richard Bland.
- 1769, The Monitor's Letters, by Dr. Arthur Lee.
- 1774, *A summary View of the Rights of British America.
- —— Considerations, &c. by Robert Carter Nicholas.

Since the declaration of independance this state has had no controversy with any other, except with that of Pennsylvania, on their common boundary. Some papers on this subject passed between the executive and legislative bodies of the two states, the result of which was a happy accommodation of their rights.

To this account of our historians, memorials, and pamphlets, it may not be unuseful to add a chronological catalogue of American state-papers, as far as I have been able to collect their titles. It is far from being either complete or correct. Where the title alone, and not the paper itself, has come under my observation, I cannot answer for the exactness of the date. Sometimes I have not been able to find any date at all, and sometimes have not been satisfied that such a paper exists. An extensive collection of papers of this description has been for some time in a course of preparation by a †gentleman fully equal to the task, and from whom, therefore, we may hope ere long to receive it. In the mean time accept this as the result of my labours, and as closing the tedious detail which you have so undesignedly drawn upon yourself.

1496, Mar. 5.   II. H. 7.   Pro Johanne Caboto et filiis suis super terra incognita investiganda. 12. Ry. 595. 3. Hakl. 4. 2. Mem. Am. 409.

*By the author of these Notes.
†Mr. Hazard.

Billa signata anno 13. Henrici septimi. 3. Hakluyt's voiages 5.	1498, Feb. 3.	13. H. 7.
De potestatibus ad terras incognitas investigandum. 13. Rymer. 37.	1502, Dec. 19.	18. H. 7.
Commission de François I. à Jacques Cartier pour l'establissement du Canada. L'Escarbot. 397. 2. Mem. Am. 416.	1540, Oct. 17.	
An act against the exaction of money, or any other thing, by any officer for license to traffique into Iseland and Newfoundland, made in An. 2. Edwardi sexti. 3. Hakl. 131.	1548,	2. E. 6.
The letters-patent granted by her Majestie to Sir Humphrey Gilbert, knight, for the inhabiting and planting of our people in America. 3. Hakl. 135.	1578, June 11,	20. El.
Letters-patents of Queen Elizabeth to Adrian Gilbert and others, to discover the Northwest passage to China. 3. Hakl. 96.	1583, Feb. 6.	
The letters-patents granted by the Queen's majestie to M. Walter Raleigh, now knight, for the discovering and planting of new lands and countries, to continue the space of 6 years and no more. 3. Hakl. 243.	1584, Mar. 25,	26 El.
An assignment by Sir Walter Raleigh for continuing the action of inhabiting and planting his people in Virginia. Hakl. 1st. ed. publ. in 1589, p. 815.	Mar. 7.	31. El.
Lettres de Lieutenant General de l'Acadie & pays circonvoisins pour le Sieur de Monts. L'Escarbot. 417.	1603, Nov. 8.	
Letters-patent to Sir Thomas Gates, Sir George Somers and others, for two several colonies to be made in Virginia and other parts of America. Stith. Append. No. 1.	1606, Apr. 10,	4. Jac. 1.
An ordinance and constitution enlarging the council of the two colonies in Vir-	1607, Mar. 9,	4. Jac. 1.

		ginia and America, and augmenting their authority, M. S.
1609, May 23.	7. Jac. 1.	The second charter to the treasurer and company for Virginia, erecting them into a body politick. Stith. Ap. 2.
1610, Apr. 10.	Jac. 1.	Letters-patents to the E. of Northampton, granting part of the island of New-foundland. 1. Harris. 861.
1611, Mar. 12.	9. Jac. 1.	A third charter to the treasurer and company for Virginia.—Stith. App. 3.
1617,	Jac. 1.	A commission to Sir Walter Raleigh. Qu.?
1620, Apr. 7.	18. Jac. 1.	Commissio specialis concernens le garbling herbæ Nicotianæ. 17. Rym. 190.
1620, June 29.	18. Jac. 1.	A proclamation for restraint of the disordered trading of tobacco. 17. Rym. 233.
1620, Nov. 3.	Jac. 1.	A grant of New England to the council of Plymouth.
1621, July 24.	Jac. 1.	An ordinance and constitution of the treasurer, council and company in England, for a council of state and general assembly in Virginia. Stith. App. 4.
1621, Sep. 10–20.	Jac. 1.	A grant of Nova Scotia to Sir William Alexander. 2. Mem. de l'Amerique. 193.
1622, Nov. 6.	20. Jac. 1.	A proclamation prohibiting interloping and disorderly trading to New England in America. 17. Rym. 416.
1623, May 9.	21. Jac. 1.	De Commissione speciali Willielmo Jones militi directa. 17. Rym. 490.
1623.		A grant to Sir Edmund Ployden, of New Albion. Mentioned in Smith's examination. 82.
1624, July 15.	22. Jac. 1.	De Commissione Henrico vice-comiti Mandevill & aliis. 17. Rym. 609.
1624, Aug. 26.	22. Jac. 1.	De Commissione speciali concernenti gubernationem in Virginia. 17. Rym. 618.
1624, Sep. 29.	22. Jac. 1.	A proclamation concerning tobacco. 17. Rym. 621.

De concessione demiss. Edwardo Dich-   1624, Nov. 9.   22. Jac. 1.
field et aliis. 17. Rym. 633.

A proclamation for the utter prohibiting   1625, Mar. 2.   22. Jac. 1.
the importation and use of all tobacco
which is not of the proper growth of
the colony of Virginia and the Somer
islands, or one of them. 17. Rym. 668.

De commissione directa Georgio Yardeley   1625, Mar. 4.   1. Car. 1.
militi et aliis. 18. Rym. 311.

Proclamatio de herba Nicotianâ. 18. Rym.   1625, Apr. 9.   1. Car. 1.
19.

A proclamation for settlinge the planta-   1625, May 13.   1. Car. 1.
tion of Virginia. 18. Rym. 72.

A grant of the soil, barony, and domains   1625, July 12.
of Nova Scotia to Sir Wm. Alexander
of Minstrie. 2. Mem. Am. 226.

Commissio directa Johanni Wolstenholme   1626, Jan. 31.   2. Car. 1.
militi et aliis. 18. Ry. 831.

A proclamation touching tobacco. Ry.   1626, Feb. 17.   2. Car. 1.
848.

A grant of Massachuset's bay by the   1627, Mar. 19. qu.?
council of Plymouth to Sir Henry Ros-   2. Car. 1.
well and others.

De concessione commissionis specialis pro   1627, Mar. 26.   3. Car. 1.
concilio in Virginia. 18. Ry. 980.

De proclamatione de signatione de to-   1627, Mar. 30.   3. Car. 1.
bacco. 18. Ry. 886.

De proclamatione pro ordinatione de to-   1627, Aug. 9.   3. Car. 1.
bacco. 18. Ry. 920.

A confirmation of the grant of Massachu-   1628, Mar. 4.   3. Car. 1.
set's bay by the crown.

The capitulation of Quebec. Champlain   1629, Aug. 19.
part. 2. 216. 2. Mem. Am. 489.

A proclamation concerning tobacco. 19.   1630, Jan. 6.   5. Car. 1.
Ry. 235.

Conveyance of Nova Scotia (Port-royal   1630, April 30.
excepted) by Sir William Alexander to
Sir Claude St. Etienne Lord of la Tour
and of Uarre and to his son Sir Charles

de St. Etienne Lord of St. Denniscourt, on condition that they continue subjects to the king of Scotland under the great seal of Scotland.

1630–31, Nov. 24. 6. Car. 1. A proclamation forbidding the disorderly trading with the salvages in New England in America, especially the furnishing the natives in those and other parts of America by the English with weapons and habiliments of warre. 19. Ry. 210. 3. Rushw. 82.

1630, Dec. 5. 6. Car. 1. A proclamation prohibiting the selling arms, &c. to the savages in America. Mentioned 3. Rushw. 75.

1630, Car. 1. A grant of Connecticut by the council of Plymouth to the E. of Warwick.

1630, Car. 1. A confirmation by the crown of the grant of Connecticut [said to be in the petty bag office in England].

1631, Mar. 19. 6. Car. 1. A conveiance of Connecticut by the E. of Warwick to Lord Say and Seal and others. Smith's examination, App. No. 1.

1631, June 27. 7. Car. 1. A special commission to Edward Earle of Dorsett and others for the better plantation of the colony of Virginia. 19. Ry. 301.

1631, June 29. 7. Car. 1. Litere continentes promissionem regis ad tradendum castrum et habitationem de Kebec in Canada ad regem Francorum. 19. Ry. 303.

1632, Mar. 29. 8. Car. 1. Traité entre le roy Louis XIII. et Charles roi d'Angleterre pour la restitution de la nouvelle France, la Cadie et Canada et des navires et merchandises pris de part et d'autre. Fait a St. Germain. 19. Ry. 361. 2. Mem. Am. 5.

1632, June 20. 8. Car. 1. A grant of Maryland to Cæcilius Calvert, Baron of Baltimore in Ireland.

1633, July 3. 9. Car. 1. A petition of the planters of Virginia against the grant to Lord Baltimore.

Order of council upon the dispute between the Virginia planters and lord Baltimore. Votes of repres. of Pennsylvania. V.	1633, July 3.
A proclamation to prevent abuses growing by the unordered retailing of tobacco. Mentioned 3. Rushw. 191.	1633, Aug. 13. 9. Car. 1.
A special commission to Thomas Young to search, discover and find out what parts are not yet inhabited in Virginia and America and other parts thereunto adjoining. 19. Ry. 472.	1633, Sept. 23. 9. Car. 1.
A proclamation for preventing of the abuses growing by the unordered retailing of tobacco. 19. Ry. 474.	1633, Oct. 13. 9. Car. 1.
A proclamation restraining the abusive venting of tobacco. 19. Rym. 522.	1634, Mar. 13. Car. 1.
A proclamation concerning the landing of tobacco, and also forbidding the planting thereof in the king's dominions. 19. Ry. 553.	1634, May 19. 10. Car. 1.
A commission to the Archbishop of Canterbury and 11 others, for governing the American colonies.	1634, Car. 1.
A commission concerning tobacco. M. S.	1634, June 19. 10. Car. 1.
A commission from Lord Say and Seal, and others, to John Winthrop to be governor of Connecticut. Smith's App.	1635, July 18. 11. Car. 1.
A grant to Duke Hamilton.	1635, Car. 1.
De commissione speciali Johanni Harvey militi pro meliori regimine coloniae in Virginia. 20. Ry. 3.	1636, Apr. 2. 12. Car. 1.
A proclamation concerning tobacco. Title in 3. Rush. 617.	1637, Mar. 14. Car. 1.
De commissione speciali Georgio domino Goring et aliis concessâ concernente venditionem de tobacco absque licentiâ regiâ. 20. Ry. 116.	1636–7, Mar. 16. 12. Car. 1.
A proclamation against the disorderly transporting his Majesty's subjects to	1637, Apr. 30. 13. Car. 1.

the plantations within the parts of America. 20. Ry. 143. 3. Rush. 409.

1637, May 1. 13. Car. 1. An order of the privy council to stay 8 ships now in the Thames from going to New-England. 3. Rush. 409.

1637, Car. 1. A warrant of the Lord Admiral to stop unconformable ministers from going beyond sea. 3. Rush. 410.

1638, Apr. 4. Car. 1. Order of council upon Claiborne's petition against Lord Baltimore. Votes of representatives of Pennsylvania. vi.

1638, Apr. 6. 14. Car. 1. An order of the king and council that the attorney-general draw up a proclamation to prohibit transportation of passengers to New-England without licence. 3. Rush. 718.

1638, May 1. 14. Car. 1. A proclamation to restrain the transporting of passengers and provisions to New-England without licence. 20. Ry. 223.

1639, Mar. 25. Car. 1. A proclamation concerning tobacco. Title 4. Rush. 1060.

1639, Aug. 19. 15. Car. 1. A proclamation declaring his majesty's pleasure to continue his commission and letters patents for licensing retailers of tobacco. 20. Ry. 348.

1639, Dec. 16. 15. Car. 1. De commissione speciali Henrico Ashton armigero et aliis ad amovendum Henricum Hawley gubernatorem de Barbadoes. 20. Ry. 357.

1639, Car. 1. A proclamation concerning retailers of tobacco. 4. Rush. 966.

1641, Aug. 9. 17. Car. 1. De constitutione gubernatoris et concilii pro Virginia. 20. Ry. 484.

1643, Car. 1. Articles of union and confederacy entered into by Massachusets, Plymouth, Connecticut and New-haven. 1. Neale. 223.

1644, Car. 1. Deed from George Fenwick to the old Connecticut jurisdiction.

An ordinance of the lords and commons

assembled in parliament, for exempting from custom and imposition all commodities exported for, or imported from New-England, which has been very prosperous and without any public charge to this state, and is likely to prove very happy for the propagation of the gospel in those parts. Tit. in Amer. library 90. 5. No date. But seems by the neighbouring articles to have been in 1644.

An act for charging of tobacco brought from New-England with custom and excise. Title in American library. 99. 8.   1644, June 20.   Car. 2.

An act for the advancing and regulating the trade of this commonwealth. Tit. Amer. libr. 99. 9.   1644, Aug. 1.   Car. 2.

Grant of the Northern neck of Virginia to Lord Hopton, Lord Jermyn, Lord Culpeper, Sir John Berkely, Sir William Moreton, Sir Dudly Wyatt, and Thomas Culpeper.   Sept. 18. 1. Car. 2.

An act prohibiting trade with the Barbadoes, Virginia, Bermudas and Antego. Scoble's Acts. 1027.   1650, Oct. 3.   2. Car. 2.

A declaration of Lord Willoughby, governor of Barbadoes, and of his council, against an act of parliament of 3d of October 1650. 4. Polit. register. 2. cited from 4. Neale. hist. of the Puritans. App. No. 12. but not there.   1650,   Car. 2.

A final settlement of boundaries between the Dutch New Netherlands and Connecticut.   1650,   Car. 2.

Instructions for Captain Robert Dennis, Mr. Richard Bennet, Mr. Thomas Stagge, and Capt. William Clabourne, appointed commissioners for the reducing of Virginia and the inhabitants thereof to their due obedience to the   1651, Sept. 26. 3. Car. 2.

commonwealth of England. 1. Thurloe's
state papers. 197.

1651, Oct. 9.   3. Car. 2.   An act for increase of shipping and encouragement of the navigation of this
nation. Scobell's acts. 1449.

1651–2, Mar. 12.   Articles agreed on and concluded at James
4.Car. 2.   cittie in Virginia for the surrendering
and settling of that plantation under the
obedience and government of the commonwealth of England, by the commissioners of the council of state, by
authoritie of the parliament of England,
and by the grand assembly of the governor, council, and burgesse of that
state. M. S. [Ante. pa. 201.]

1651–2, Mar. 12.   An act of indempnitie made at the surren-
4. Car. 2.   der of the countrey [of Virginia.]
[Ante. p. 206.]

1654, Aug. 16.   Capitulation de Port-Royal. mem. Am.
507.

1655,   Car. 2.   A proclamation of the protector relating
to Jamaica. 3. Thurl. 75.

1655, Sept. 26. 7. Car. 2.   The protector to the commissioners of
Maryland. A letter. 4. Thurl. 55.

1655, Oct. 8.   7. Car. 2.   An instrument made at the council of Jamaica, Oct. 8, 1655, for the better carry-
ing on of affairs there. 4. Thurl. 71.

1655, Nov. 3.   Treaty of Westminster between France
and England. 6. corps diplom. part 2.
p. 121. 2. Mem. Am. 10.

1656, Mar. 27. 8. Car. 2.   The assembly at Barbadoes to the Protector. 4. Thurl. 651.

1656, Aug. 9.   A grant by Cromwell to Sir Charles de
Saint Etienne, a baron of Scotland,
Crowne and Temple. A French transla-
tion of it. 2. Mem. Am. 511.

1656,   Car. 2.   A paper concerning the advancement of
trade. 5. Thurl. 80.

1656,   Car. 2.   A brief narration of the English rights

to the Northern parts of America. 5. Thurl. 81.

Mr. R. Bennet and Mr. S. Matthew to Secretary Thurloe. 5. Thurl. 482. — 1656, Oct. 10. 8. Car. 2.

Objections against the Lord Baltimore's patent, and reasons why the government of Maryland should not be put into his hands. 5. Thurl. 482. — 1656, Oct. 10. 8. Car. 2.

A paper relating to Maryland. 5. Thurl. 483. — 1656, Oct. 10. 8. Car. 2.

A breviet of the proceedings of the lord Baltimore and his officers and compliers in Maryland against the authority of the parliament of the commonwealth of England and against his highness the lord protector's authority laws and government. 5. Thurl. 486. — 1656, Oct. 10. 8. Car. 2.

The assembly of Virginia to secretary Thurlow. 5. Thurl. 497. — 1656, Oct. 15. 8. Car. 2.

The governor of Barbadoes to the protector. 6. Thurl. 169. — 1657, Apr. 4. 9. Car. 2.

Petition of the general court at Hartford upon Connecticut for a charter. Smith's exam. App. 4. — 1661, Car. 2.

Charter of the colony of Connecticut. Smith's examn. App. 6. — 1662, Ap. 23. 14. Car. 2.

The first charter granted by Charles II. to the proprietaries of Carolina, to wit, to the Earl of Clarendon, Duke of Albemarle, Lord Craven, Lord Berkeley, Lord Ashley, Sir George Carteret, Sir William Berkeley, and Sir John Colleton. 4. mem. Am. 554. — 1662–3, Mar. 24. Apr. 4. 15. Car. 2.

The concessions and agreement of the lords proprietors of the province of New Cæsarea, or New-Jersey, to and with all and every of the adventurers and all such as shall settle or plant there. Smith's New-Jersey. App. 1. — 1664, Feb. 10.

1664, Mar. 12. 20. Car. 2.	A grant of the colony of New-York to the Duke of York.
1664, Apr. 26. 16. Car. 2.	A commission to Colonel Nichols and others to settle disputes in New-England. Hutch. Hist. Mass. Bay. App. 537.
1664, Apr. 26.	The commission to Sir Robert Carre and others to put the Duke of York in possession of New-York, New-Jersey, and all other lands thereunto appertaining.
	Sir Robert Carre and others proclamation to the inhabitants of New-York, New-Jersey, &c. Smith's N. J. 36.
1664, June 23, 24. 16. C. 2.	Deeds of lease and release of New-Jersey by the Duke of York to Lord Berkeley and Sir George Carteret.
	A conveiance of the Delaware counties to William Penn.
1664, Aug. 19–29, 20–30, 24. Aug. 25. Sept. 4.	Letters between Stuyvesant and Colonel Nichols on the English right. Smith's N. J. 37–42.
1664, Aug. 27.	Treaty between the English and Dutch for the surrender of the New-Netherlands. Sm. N. Jers. 42.
Sept. 3.	Nicoll's commission to Sir Robert Carre to reduce the Dutch on Delaware bay. Sm. N. J. 47.
	Instructions to Sir Robert Carre for reducing of Delaware bay and settling the people there under his majesty's obedience. Sm. N. J. 47.
1664, Oct. 1.	Articles of capitulation between Sir Robert Carre and the Dutch and Swedes on Delaware bay and Delaware river. Sm. N. J. 49.
1664, Dec. 1. 16. Car. 2.	The determination of the commissioners of the boundary between the Duke of York and Connecticut. Sm. Ex. Ap. 9.
1664.	The New Haven case. Smith's Ex. Ap. 20.

The second charter granted by Charles II. to the same proprietors of Carolina. 4. Mem. Am. 586.

1665, June 13–24.
17. C. 2.

Declaration de guerre par la France contre l'Angleterre. 3. Mem. Am. 123.

1666, Jan. 26.

Declaration of war by the king of England against the king of France.

1666, Feb. 9. 17. Car. 2.

The treaty of peace between France and England made at Breda. 7. Corps Dipl. part 1. p. 41. 2. Mem. Am. 32.

1667, July 31.

The treaty of peace and alliance between England and the United Provinces made at Breda. 7. Cor. Dip. p. 1. p. 44. 2. Mem. Am. 40.

1667, July 31.

Acte de la cession de l'Acadie au roi de France. 2. Mem. Am. 292.

1667–8, Feb. 17.

Directions from the governor and council of New York for a better settlement of the government on Delaware. Sm. N. J. 51.

1668, April 21.

Lovelace's order for customs at the Hoar-kills. Sm. N. J. 55.

1668.

A confirmation of the grant of the northern neck of Virginia to the Earl of St. Alban's, Lord Berkeley, Sir William Moreton and John Tretheway.

16— May 8. 21. Car. 2.

Incorporation of the town of Newcastle or Amstell.

1672.

A demise of the colony of Virginia to the Earl of Arlington and Lord Culpeper for 31 years. M. S.

1673, Feb. 25. 25. Car. 2.

Treaty at London between king Charles II. and the Dutch. Article VI.

1673–4.

Remonstrances against the two grants of Charles II. of Northern and Southern Virginia. Ment^d. Beverley. 65.

Sir George Carteret's instructions to Governor Carteret.

1674, July 13.

Governor Andros's proclamation on

1674, Nov. 9.

taking possession of Newcastle for the Duke of York. Sm. N. J. 78.

1675, Oct. 1.   27. Car. 2.   A proclamation for prohibiting the importation of commodities of Europe into any of his majesty's plantations in Africa, Asia, or America, which were not laden in England: and for putting all other laws relating to the trade of the plantations in effectual execution.

1676, Mar. 3.   The concessions and agreements of the proprietors, freeholders and inhabitants of the province of West-New-Jersey in America. Sm. N. J. App. 2.

1676, July 1.   A deed quintipartite for the division of New-Jersey.

1676, Aug. 18.   Letter from the proprietors of New-Jersey to Richard Hartshorne. Sm. N. J. 80.

Proprietors instructions to James Wasse and Richard Hartshorne. Sm. N. J. 83.

1676, Oct. 10. 28. Car. 2.   The charter of king Charles II. to his subjects of Virginia. M. S.

1676.   Cautionary epistle from the trustees of Byllinge's part of New-Jersey. Sm. N. J. 84.

1677, Sept. 10.   Indian deed for the lands between Rankokas creek and Timber creek, in New-Jersey.

1677, Sept. 27.   Indian deed for the lands from Oldman's creek to Timber creek, in New-Jersey.

1677, Oct. 10.   Indian deed for the lands from Rankokas creek to Assunpink creek, in New-Jersey.

1678, Dec. 5.   The will of Sir George Carteret, sole proprietor of East-Jersey, ordering the same to be sold.

1680, Feb. 16.   An order of the king in council for the better encouragement of all his majesty's subjects in their trade to his majesty's plantations, and for the better information of all his majesty's loving

subjects in these matters. Lond. Gaz
No. 1596. Title in Amer. library. 134. 6.

Arguments against the customs demanded   1680.
in New-West-Jersey by the governor of
New-York, addressed to the Duke's
commissioners. Sm. N. J. 117.

Extracts of proceedings of the committee
of trade and plantations; copies of let-   June 14. 23. 25.
ters, reports, &c. between the board of   1680,   Oct. 16.
trade, Mr. Penn, Lord Baltimore and   Nov. 4. 8. 11.
Sir John Werden, in the behalf of the   18. 20. 23.
Duke of York and the settlement of the   Dec. 16.
Pennsylvania boundaries by the L. C. J.   1680–1, Jan. 15. 22.
North. Votes of Repr. Pennsyl. vii.–   Feb. 24.
xiii.

A grant of Pennsylvania to William Penn.   1681, Mar. 4.   Car. 2.
Votes of Represen. Pennsylv. xviii.

The king's declaration to the inhabitants   1681, Apr. 2.
and planters of the province of Pennsyl-
vania. Vo. Rep. Penn. xxiv.

Certain conditions or concessions agreed   1681, July 11.
upon by William Penn, proprietary and
governor of Pennsylvania, and those
who are the adventurers and purchasers
in the same province. Votes of Rep.
Pennsylv. xxiv.

Fundamental laws of the province of   1681, Nov. 9.
West-New-Jersey. Sm. N. J. 126.

The methods of the commissioners for   1681–2, Jan. 14.
settling and regulation of lands in New-
Jersey. Sm. N. J. 130.

Indentures of lease and release by the ex-   1681–2, Feb. 1. 2.
ecutors of Sir George Carteret to Wil-
liam Penn and 11 others, conveying
East-Jersey.

The Duke of York's fresh grant of East-   1682, Mar. 14.
New-Jersey to the 24 proprietors.

The Frame of the government of the   1682, Apr. 25.
province of Pennsylvania, in America.
Votes of Repr. Penn. xxvii.

1682, Aug. 21.	The Duke of York's deed for Pennsylvania. Vo. Repr. Penn. xxxv.
1682, Aug. 24.	The Duke of York's deed of feoffment of Newcastle and twelve miles circle to William Penn. Vo. Repr. Penn.
1682, Aug. 24.	The Duke of York's deed of feoffment of a tract of land 12 miles south from Newcastle to the Whorekills, to William Penn. Vo. Repr. Penn. xxxvii.
1682, Nov. 27. 34. Car. 2.	A commission to Thomas Lord Culpeper to be lieutenant and governor-general of Virginia. M. S.
1682, 10th month, 6th day.	An act of union for annexing and uniting of the counties of Newcastle, Jones's and Whorekill's alias Deal, to the province of Pennsylvania, and of naturalization of all foreigners in the province and counties aforesaid.
1682, Dec. 6.	An act of settlement.
1683, Apr. 2.	The frame of the government of the province of Pennsylvania and territories thereunto annexed in America.

1683, Apr. 17, 27.   1684, Feb. 12.   1685, Mar. 17. ⎫ Proceedings of
May 30.   July 2, 16, 23.   Aug. 18. 26. ⎪ the committee
June 12.   Sept. 30.   Sept. 2. ⎬ of trade and
    Dec. 9.   Oct. 8. 17, 31. ⎪ plantations in
        Nov. 7. ⎭ the dispute be-
tween Lord Baltimore and Mr. Penn. Vo. R. P. xiii–xviii.

1683, July 17.	A commission by the proprietors of East-New-Jersey to Robert Barclay to be governor. Sm. N. J. 166.
1683, July 26. 35. Car. 2.	An order of council for issuing a quo warranto against the charter of the colony of the Massachuset's bay in New-England, with his majesty's declaration that in case the said corporation of Masschuset's bay shall before prosecution had upon the same quo warranto make a full submission and entire res-

ignation to his royal pleasure, he will
then regulate their charter in such a
manner as shall be for his service and
the good of that colony. Title in Amer.
library. 139. 6.

A commission to Lord Howard of Ef-   1683, Sept. 28. 35. Car. 2.
fingham to be lieutenant and governor-
general of Virginia. M. S.

The humble address of the chief gover-   1684, May 3.
nor, council and representatives of the
island of Nevis, in the West-Indies, presented to his majesty by Colonel Nethe-
way and Captain Jefferson, at Windsor,
May 3, 1684. Title in Amer. libr. 142. 3.
cites Lond. Gaz. No. 1927.

A treaty with the Indians at Albany.   1684, Aug. 2.

A treaty of neutrality for America be-   1686, Nov. 16.
tween France and England. 7. Corps.
Dipl. part 2. p. 44. 2. Mem. Am. 40.

By the king, a proclamation for the more   1687, Jan. 20.
effectual reducing and suppressing of pi-
rates and privateers in America, as well
on the sea as on the land in great numbers, committing frequent robberies
and piracies, which hath occasioned a
great prejudice and obstruction to trade
and commerce, and given a great scan-
dal and disturbance to our government
in those parts. Title Amer. libr. 147. 2.
cites Lond. Gaz. No. 2315.

Constitution of the council of proprietors   1687, Feb. 12.
of West-Jersey. Smith's N. Jersey. 199.

A confirmation of the grant of the north-   1687, qu. Sept. 27.
ern neck of Virginia to Lord Culpeper.   4. Jac. 2.

Governor Coxe's declaration to the coun-   1687, Sept. 5.
cil of proprietors of West-Jersey. Sm.
N. J. 190.

Provisional treaty of Whitehall concerning   1687, Dec. 16.
America between France and England.
2. Mem. de l'Am. 89.

Governor Coxe's narrative relating to the division line, directed to the council of proprietors of West-Jersey. Sm. App. N. 4.

The representation of the council of proprietors of West-Jersey to Governor Burnet. Smith. App. No. 5.

The remonstrance and petition of the inhabitants of East-New-Jersey to the king. Sm. App. No. 8.

The memorial of the proprietors of East-New-Jersey to the Lords of trade. Sm. App. No. 9.

1688, Sept. 5.   Agreement of the line of partition between East and West-New-Jersey. Sm. N. J. 196.

1691.   Conveiance of the government of West-Jersey and territories by Dr. Coxe, to the West-Jersey society.

1691, Oct. 7.   A charter granted by King William and Queen Mary to the inhabitants of the province of Massachuset's bay in New-England. 2. Mem. de l'Am. 593.

1696, Nov. 7.   The frame of government of the province of Pennsylvania and the territories thereunto belonging, passed by Governor Markham. Nov. 7, 1696.

1697, Sept. 20.   The treaty of peace between France and England, made at Ryswick. 7. Corps Dipl. part. 2. p. 399. 2. Mem. Am. 89.

1699, July 5.   The opinion and answer of the lords of trade to the memorial of the proprietors of East-New-Jersey. Sm. App. No. 10.

1700, Jan. 15.   The memorial of the proprietors of East-New-Jersey to the Lords of trade. Sm. App. No. 11.

The petition of the proprietors of East and West-New-Jersey to the Lords justices of England. Sm. App. No. 12.

A confirmation of the boundary between the colonies of New-York and Connecticut, by the crown.   1700,   W. 3.

The memorial of the proprietors of East and West-Jersey to the king. Sm. App. No. 14.   1701, Aug. 12.

Representation of the lords of trade to the lords justices. Sm. App. No. 13.   1701, Oct. 2.

A treaty with the Indians.   1701.

Report of lords of trade to king William of draughts of a commission and instructions for a governor of New-Jersey. Sm. N. J. 262.   1701–2, Jan. 6.

Surrender from the proprietors of E. and W. N. Jersey of their pretended right of government to her majesty Q. Anne. Sm. N. J. 211.   1702, Apr. 15.

The Queen's acceptance of the surrender of government of East and West-Jersey. Sm. N. J. 219.   1702, Apr. 17.

Instructions to lord Cornbury. Sm. N. J. 230.   1702, Nov. 16.

A commission from Queen Anne to Lord Cornbury, to be captain-general and governor in chief of New-Jersey. Sm. N. J. 220.   1702, Dec. 5.

Recognition by the council of proprietors of the true boundary of the deeds of Sept. 10 and Oct. 10, 1677. (New-Jersey). Sm. N. J. 96.   1703, June 27.

Indian deed for the lands above the falls of the Delaware in West-Jersey.   1703.

Indian deed for the lands at the head of Rankokus river in West-Jersey.

A proclamation by Queen Anne for settling and ascertaining the current rates of foreign coins in America. Sm. N. J. 281.   1704, June 18.

Additional instructions to Lord Cornbury. Sm. N. J. 235.   1705, May 3.

1707, May 3.	Additional instructions to Lord Cornbury. Sm. N. J. 258.
1707, Nov. 20.	Additional instructions to Lord Cornbury. Sm. N. J. 259.
1707.	An answer by the council of proprietors for the western division of New-Jersey, to questions, proposed to them by Lord Cornbury. Sm. N. J. 285.
1708–9, Feb. 28.	Instructions to Colonel Vetch in his negociations with the governors of America. Sm. N. J. 364.
1708–9, Feb. 28.	Instructions to the governor of New-Jersey and New-York. Sm. N. J. 361.
1710, Aug.	Earl of Dartmouth's letter to governor Hunter.
1711, Apr. 22.	Premieres propositions de la France. 6. Lamberty, 669. 2. Mem. Am. 341.
1711, Oct. 8.	Réponses de la France aux demandes préliminaires de la Grande-Bretagne. 6. Lamb. 681. 2. Mem. Amer. 344.
1711, $\frac{\text{Sept. 27.}}{\text{Oct. 8.}}$	Demandes préliminaires plus particulieres de la Grande-Bretagne, avec les réponses. 2. Mem. de l'Am. 346.
1711, $\frac{\text{Sept. 27.}}{\text{Oct. 8.}}$	L'acceptation de la part de la Grande-Bretagne. 2. Mem. Am. 356.
1711, Dec. 23.	The queen's instructions to the Bishop of Bristol and Earl of Strafford, her plenipotentiaries, to treat of a general peace. 6. Lamberty, 744. 2. Mem. Am. 358.
1712, $\frac{\text{May 24.}}{\text{June 10.}}$	A memorial of Mr. St. John to the Marquis de Torci, with regard to North America, to commerce, and to the suspension of arms. 7. Recueil de Lamberty, 161. 2. Mem. de l'Amer. 376.
1712, June 10.	Réponse du roi de France au memoire de Londres. 7. Lamberty, p. 163. 2. Mem. Am. 380.
1712, Aug. 19.	Traité pour une suspension d'armes entre Louis XIV. roi de France, & Anne,

reigne de la Grande-Bretagne, fait à
Paris. 8. Corps Diplom. part. 1. p. 308.
2. Mem. d'Am. 104.

Offers of France to England, demands of   1712, Sept. 10.
England, and the answers of France. 7.
Rec. de Lamb. 491. 2. Mem. Am. 390.

Traité de paix & d'amitié entre Louis XIV.   1713, $\frac{\text{Mar. 31.}}{\text{Apr. 11.}}$
roi de France, & Anne, reine de la
Grande-Bretagne, fait à Utrecht. 15.
Corps Diplomatique de Dumont, 339.
id. Latin. 2. Actes & memoires de la
pais d'Utrecht, 457. id. Lat. Fr. 2. Mem.
Am. 113.

Traité de navigation & de commerce entre   1713, $\frac{\text{Mar. 31.}}{\text{Apr. 11.}}$
Louis XIV. roi de France, & Anne,
reine de la Grande-Bretagne. Fait à
Utrecht. 8. Corps. Dipl. part. 1. p. 345.
2. Mem. de l'Am. 137.

A treaty with the Indians.   1726.

The petition of the representatives of the   1728, Jan.
province of New-Jersey, to have a dis-
tinct governor. Sm. N. J. 421.

Deed of release by the government of   1732,   G. 2.
Connecticut to that of New-York.

The charter granted by George II. for   1732, June 9–20. 5. G. 2.
Georgia. 4. Mem. de l'Am. 617.

Petition of Lord Fairfax, that a commis-   1733.
sion might issue for running and mark-
ing the dividing line between his
district and the province of Virginia.

Order of the king in council for Commis-   1733, Nov. 29.
sioners to survey and settle the said di-
viding line between the proprietary and
royal territory.

Report of the lords of trade relating to   1736, Aug. 5.
the separating the government of the
province of New-Jersey from New-
York. Sm. N. J. 423.

Survey and report of the commissioners   1737, Aug. 10.

appointed on the part of the crown to settle the line between the crown and Lord Fairfax.

1737, Aug. 11.   Survey and report of the commissioners appointed on the part of Lord Fairfax to settle the line between the crown and him.

1738, Dec. 21.   Order of reference of the surveys between the crown and Lord Fairfax to the council for plantation affairs.

1744, June   Treaty with the Indians of the 6 nations at Lancaster.

1745, Apr. 6.   Report of the council for plantation affairs, fixing the head springs of Rappahanoc and Patowmac, and a commission to extend the line.

1745, Apr. 11.   Order of the king in council confirming the said report of the council for plantation affairs.

1748, Apr. 30.   Articles préliminaires pour parvenir à la paix, signés à Aix-la-Chapelle entre les ministres de France, de la Grande-Bretagne, & des Provinces-Unies des Pays-Bas. 2. Mem. de l'Am. 159.

1748, May 21.   Declaration des ministres de France, de la Grande-Bretagne, & des Provinces-Unies des Pays-Bas, pour rectifier les articles I. & II. des préliminaires. 2. Mem. Am. 165.

1748, Oct. 7–18.
22. G. 2.   The general and definitive treaty of peace concluded at Aix-la-Chapelle. Lond. Mag. 1748. 503 French. 2. Mem. Am. 169.

1754.   A treaty with the Indians.

1758, Aug. 7.   A conference between Governor Bernard and Indian nations at Burlington. Sm. N. J. 449.

1758, Oct. 8.   A conference between Governor Denny, Governor Bernard and others, and Indian nations at Easton. Sm. N. J. 455.

The capitulation of Niagara.   1759, July 25.   33. G. 2.

The king's proclamation promising lands   175—
    to souldiers.

The definitive treaty concluded at Paris.   1763, Feb. 10.   3. G. 3.
    Lond. Mag. 1763. 149.

A proclamation for regulating the cessions   1763, Oct. 7.   G. 3.
    made by the last treaty of peace. Guth.
    Geogr. Gram. 623.

The king's proclamation against settling   1763.
    on any lands on the waters, westward
    of the Alleghaney.

Deed from the six nations of Indians to   1768, Nov. 3.
    William Trent and others for lands be-
    twixt the Ohio and Monongahela.
    View of the title to Indiana. Phil. Sty-
    ner and Cist. 1776.

Deed from the six nations of Indians to   1768, Nov. 5.
    the crown for certain lands and settling
    a boundary. M. S.

PUBLIC PAPERS

Contents

Resolutions of Congress on Lord North's Conciliatory Proposal

In Congress

THE SEVERAL Assemblies of NEW JERSEY, PENNSYLVANIA and VIRGINIA, having referred to the Congress a resolution of the House of Commons of GREAT BRITAIN, which resolution is in these words, viz.

Lunae, 20° die Feb. 1775.

The House in a Committee on the American papers. Motion made, and question proposed.

THAT *it is the opinion of this Committee, that when the General Council and Assembly, or General Court of any of his Majesty's provinces, or colonies in America, shall propose to make provision, according to the condition, circumstance, or situation of such province or colony, for contributing their proportion to the common defence (such proportion to be raised under the authority of the General Court, or General Assembly of such province or colony, and disposable by Parliament) and shall engage to make provision also, for the support of the civil government, and the Administration of justice in such province or colony, it will be proper if such proposal shall be approved by his Majesty and the two Houses of Parliament; and for so long as such provision shall be made accordingly, to forbear in respect of such province or colony, to lay any duty, tax, or assessment, or to impose any further duty, tax or assessment, except only such duties as it may be expedient to continue to levy or impose, for the regulation of commerce, the net produce of the duties last mentioned, to be carried to the account of such province or colony respectively.*

The Congress took the said resolution into consideration, and are thereupon of opinion:

That the colonies of America are entitled to the sole and exclusive privilege of giving and granting their own money; that this involves a right of deliberating whether they will make any gift, for what purposes it shall be made, and what shall be it's amount; and that it is a high breach of this privilege for any body of men, extraneous to their constitutions, to prescribe the purposes for which money shall be levied on them, to take to themselves the authority of judging of their conditions, circumstances and situations; and of determining the amount of the contribution to be levied.

That as the colonies possess a right of appropriating their gifts, so are they entitled at all times to enquire into their application, to see that they be not wasted among the venal and corrupt for the purpose of undermining the civil rights of the givers, nor yet be diverted to the support of standing armies, inconsistent with their freedom and subversive of their quiet. To propose therefore, as this resolution does, that the monies given by the colonies shall be subject to the disposal of parliament alone, is to propose that they shall relinquish this right of enquiry, and put it in the power of others to render their gifts, ruinous, in proportion as they are liberal.

That this privilege of giving or of withholding our monies is an important barrier against the undue exertion of prerogative, which if left altogether without controul may be exercised to our great oppression; and all history shews how efficacious is its intercession for redress of grievances and re-establishment of rights, and how improvident it would be to part with so powerful a mediator.

We are of opinion that the proposition contained in this resolution is unreasonable and insidious: unreasonable, because, if we declare we accede to it, we declare without reservation, we will purchase the favour of Parliament, not knowing at the same time at what price they will please to estimate their favor: It is insidious, because, individual colonies, having bid and bidden again, till they find the avidity of the seller too great for all their powers to satisfy; are then to return into opposition, divided from their sister colonies whom the minister will have previously detached by a grant of easier terms, or by an artful procrastination of a definitive answer.

That the suspension of the exercise of their pretended power of taxation being expressly made commensurate with the continuance of our gifts, these must be perpetual to make that so. Whereas no experience has shewn that a gift of perpetual revenue secures a perpetual return of duty or of kind disposition. On the contrary, the Parliament itself, wisely attentive to this observation, are in the established practice of granting their supplies from year to year only.

Desirous and determined as we are to consider in the most dispassionate view every seeming advance towards a reconciliation made by the British Parliament, let our brethren of Britain reflect what would have been the sacrifice to men of free spirits had even fair terms been proffered, as these insidious proposals were with circumstances of insult and defiance. A proposition to give our money, accompanied with large fleets and armies, seems addressed to our fears rather than to our freedom. With what patience would Britons have received articles of treaty from any power on earth when borne on the point of a bayonet by military plenipotentiaries?

We think the attempt unnecessary to raise upon us by force or by threats our proportional contributions to the common defence, when all know, and themselves acknowledge we have fully contributed, whenever called upon to do so in the character of freemen.

We are of opinion it is not just that the colonies should be required to oblige themselves to other contributions, while Great Britain possesses a monopoly of their trade. This of itself lays them under heavy contribution. To demand therefore, additional aids in the form of a tax, is to demand the double of their equal proportion, if we are to contribute equally with the other parts of the empire, let us equally with them enjoy free commerce with the whole world. But while the restrictions on our trade shut to us the resources of wealth, is it just we should bear all other burthens equally with those to whom every resource is open.

We conceive that the British Parliament has no right to intermeddle with our provisions for the support of civil government, or administration of justice. The provisions we have made are such as please ourselves, and are agreeable to our own circumstances; they answer the substantial purposes of government and of justice, and other purposes than these should not be answered. We do not mean that our people shall be burthened with oppressive taxes to provide sinecures for the idle or the wicked, under colour of providing for a civil list. While Parliament pursue their plan of civil government within their own jurisdiction, we also hope to pursue ours without molestation.

We are of opinion the proposition is altogether unsatisfactory because it imports only a suspension of the mode, not a renunciation of the pretended right to tax us: Because too it does not propose to repeal the several Acts of Parliament passed for the purposes of restraining the trade and altering the form of government of one of our Colonies; extending the boundaries and changing the government of Quebec; enlarging the jurisdiction of the Courts of Admiralty and Vice Admiralty; taking from us the rights of trial by a Jury of the vicinage in cases affecting both life and property; transporting us into other countries to be tried for criminal offences; exempting by mock-trial the murderers of Colonists from punishment; and quartering soldiers on us in times of profound peace. Nor do they renounce the power of suspending our own Legislatures, and of legislating for us themselves in all cases whatsoever. On the contrary, to shew they mean no discontinuance of injury, they pass acts, at the very time of holding out this proposition, for restraining the commerce and fisheries of the Provinces of New-England, and for interdicting the trade of other Colonies with all foreign nations and with each other. This proves unequivocally they mean not to relinquish the exercise of indiscriminate legislation over us.

Upon the whole, this proposition seems to have been held up to the world, to deceive it into a belief that there was nothing in dispute between us but the *mode* of levying taxes; and that the Parliament having now been so good as to give up this, the Colonies are unreasonable if not perfectly satisfied: Whereas in truth, our adversaries still claim a right of demanding *ad libitum*, and of taxing us themselves to the full amount of their demand, if we do not comply with it. This leaves us without any thing we can call property. But, what is of more importance, and what in this proposal they keep out of sight, as if no such point was now in contest between us, they claim a right to alter our Charters and established laws, and leave us without any security for our Lives or Liberties. The proposition seems also to have been calculated more particularly to lull into fatal security our well-affected fellow subjects on the other side the water, till time should be given for the operation of those arms, which a British Minister pronounced would instantaneously reduce the "cowardly" sons of America to unreserved submission. But when the world reflects, how inadequate to justice are these vaunted terms; when it attends to the rapid and bold succession of injuries, which, during a course of eleven years, have been aimed at these Colonies; when it reviews the pacific and respectful expostulations, which, during that whole time, were the sole arms we opposed to them; when it observes that our complaints were either not heard at all, or were answered with new and accumulated injury; when it recollects that the Minister himself on an early occasion declared, "that he would never treat with America, till he had brought her to his feet," and that an avowed partisan of Ministry has more lately denounced against us the dreadful sentence *"delenda est Carthago,"* that this was done in presence of a British Senate, and being unreproved by them, must be taken to be their own sentiment, (especially as the purpose has already in part been carried into execution by their treatment of Boston, and burning of Charlestown) when it considers the great armaments with which they have invaded us, and the circumstances of cruelty with which these have commenced and prosecuted hostilities; when these things, we say, are laid together, and attentively considered, can the world be deceived into an opinion that we are unreasonable, or can it hesitate to believe with us, that nothing but our own exertions may defeat the ministerial sentence of death or abject submission.

By Order of the Congress,

JOHN HANCOCK, *President.*

Philadelphia, July 31, 1775.

Draft Constitution for Virginia

[*June, 1776.*]

Fair Copy

[*A Bil*]l for new-modelling the form of Government and for establishing the Fundamental principles thereof in future.

Whereas George
Guelf king of Great Britain and Ireland and Elector of Hanover, heretofore entrusted with the exercise of the kingly office in this government hath endeavored to pervert the same into a detestable and insupportable tyranny;

by putting his negative on laws the most wholesome & necessary for ye public good;

by denying to his governors permission to pass laws of immediate and pressing importance, unless suspended in their operations for his assent, and, when so suspended, neglecting to attend to them for many years;

by refusing to pass certain other laws, unless the person to be benefited by them would relinquish the inestimable right of representation in the legislature

by dissolving legislative assemblies repeatedly and continually for opposing with manly firmness his invasions on the rights of the people;

when dissolved, by refusing to call others for a long space of time, thereby leaving the political system without any legislative head;

by endeavoring to prevent the population of our country, & for that purpose obstructing the laws for the naturalization of foreigners & raising the condition [*lacking appro*]priations of lands;

[*by keeping among u*]s, in times of peace, standing armies and ships of war;

[*lacking*]ing to render the military independent of & superior to the civil power;

by combining with others to subject us to a foreign jurisdiction, giving his assent to their pretended acts of legislation.

for quartering large bodies of troops among us;

for cutting off our trade with all parts of the world;

for imposing taxes on us without our consent;

for depriving us of the benefits of trial by jury;

for transporting us beyond seas to be tried for pretended offences; and

for suspending our own legislatures & declaring themselves invested with power to legislate for us in all cases whatsoever;

by plundering our seas, ravaging our coasts, burning our towns and destroying the lives of our people;

by inciting insurrections of our fellow subjects with the allurements of forfeiture & confiscation;

by prompting our negroes to rise in arms among us; those very negroes whom ~~he hath from time to time~~ by an inhuman use of his negative he hath refused permission to exclude by law;

by endeavoring to bring on the inhabitants of our frontiers the merciless Indian savages, whose known rule of warfare is an undistinguished destruction of all ages, sexes, & conditions of existence;

by transporting at this time a large army of foreign mercenaries [*to complete*] the works of death, desolation & tyranny already begun with circum[*stances*] of cruelty & perfidy so unworthy the head of a civilized nation;

by answering our repeated petitions for redress with a repetition of injuries;

and finally by abandoning the helm of government and declaring us out of his allegiance & protection;

by which several acts of misrule the said George Guelf has forfeited the kingly office and has rendered it necessary for the preservation of the people that he should be immediately deposed from the same, and divested of all its privileges, powers, & prerogatives:

And forasmuch as the public liberty may be more certainly secured by abolishing an office which all experience hath shewn to be inveterately inimical thereto ~~or which~~ and it will thereupon become further necessary to re-establish such ancient principles as are friendly to the rights of the people and to declare certain others which may co-operate with and fortify the same in future.

Be it therefore enacted by the authority of the people that

the said, George   Guelf be, and he hereby is deposed
from the kingly office within this government and absolutely
divested of all it's rights, powers, and prerogatives: and that
he and his descendants and all persons acting by or through
him, and all other persons whatsoever shall be and forever
remain incapable of the same: and that the said office shall
henceforth cease and never more either in name or substance
be re-established within this colony.

And be it further enacted by the authority aforesaid that
the following fundamental laws and principles of government
shall henceforth be established.

The Legislative, Executive and Judiciary offices shall be
kept forever separate; no person exercising the one shall be
capable of appointment to the others, or to either of them.

I. LEGISLATIVE.

Legislation shall be exercised by two separate houses, to wit
a house of Representatives, and a house of Senators, which
shall be called the General Assembly of Virginia.

Ho. of
Represen-
tatives

The sd house of Representatives shall be composed of persons chosen by the people annually on
the [1st day of October] and shall meet in General
assembly on the [1st day of November] following and so from
time to time on their own adjournments, or at any time when
summoned by the Administrator and shall continue sitting so
long as they shall think the publick service requires.

Vacancies in the said house by death or disqualification
shall be filled by the electors under a warrant from the
Speaker of the said house.

Electors

All male persons of full age and sane mind having
a freehold estate in [one fourth of an acre] of land
in any town, or in [25] acres of land in the country, and all

Elected

persons resident in the colony who shall have paid
scot and lot to government the last [two years] shall
have right to give their vote in the election of their respective
representatives. And every person so qualified to elect shall be
capable of being elected, provided he shall have given no
bribe either directly or indirectly to any elector, and shall take
an oath of fidelity to the state and of duty in his office, before

he enters on the exercise thereof. During his continuance in the said office he shall hold no public pension nor post of profit, either himself, or by another for his use.

The number of Representatives for each county or borough shall be so proportioned to the numbers of it's qualified electors that the whole number of representatives shall not exceed [300] nor be less than [125.] for the present there shall be one representative for every [   ] qualified electors in each county or borough: but whenever this or any future proportion shall be likely to exceed or fall short of the limits beforementioned, it shall be again adjusted by the house of representatives.

The house of Representatives when met shall be free to act according to their own judgment and conscience.

The Senate shall consist of not less than [15] nor more than [50] members who shall be appointed by **Senate** the house of Representatives. One third of them shall be removed out of office by lot at the end of the first [three] years and their places be supplied by a new appointment; one other third shall be removed by lot in like manner at the end of the second [three] years and their places be supplied by a new appointment; after which one third shall be removed annually at the end of every [three] years according to seniority. When once removed, they shall be forever incapable of being reappointed to that house. Their qualifications shall be an oath of fidelity to the state, and of duty in their office, the being [31] years of age at the least, and the having given no bribe directly or indirectly to obtain their appointment. While in the senatorial office they shall be incapable of holding any public pension or post of profit either themselves, or by others for their use.

The judges of the General court and of the High court of Chancery shall have session and deliberative voice, but not suffrage in the house of Senators.

The Senate and the house of representatives shall each of them have power to originate and amend bills; save only that bills for levying money ~~bills~~ shall be originated and amended by the representatives only: the assent of both houses shall be requisite to pass a law.

The General assembly shall have no power to pass any law

inflicting death for any crime, excepting murder, & ~~such~~ those offences in the military service for which they shall think punishment by death absolutely necessary: and all capital punishments in other cases are hereby abolished. Nor shall they have power to prescribe torture in any case whatever: nor shall there be power anywhere to pardon crimes or to remit fines or punishments: nor shall any law for levying money be in force longer than [ten years] from the time of its commencement.

[Two thirds] of the members of either house shall be a Quorum to proceed to business.

II. EXECUTIVE.

The executive powers shall be exercised in manner following.

Adminis-trator One person to be called the [Administrator] shall be annually appointed by the house of Representatives on the second day of their first session, who after having acted [one] year shall be incapable of being again appointed to that office until he shall have been out of the same [three] years.

Deputy Admr. Under him shall be appointed by the same house and at the same time, a Deputy-Administrator to assist his principal in the discharge of his office, and to succeed, in case of his death before the year shall have expired, to the whole powers thereof during the residue of the year.

The administrator shall possess the power formerly held by the king: save only that, he shall be bound by acts of legislature tho' not expressly named;

he shall have no negative on the bills of the Legislature;

he shall be liable to action, tho' not to personal restraint for private duties or wrongs;

he shall not possess the prerogatives;

of dissolving, proroguing or adjourning either house of Assembly;

of declaring war or concluding peace;

of issuing letters of marque or reprisal;

of raising or introducing armed forces, building armed vessels, forts or strongholds;

of coining monies or regulating their values;

of regulating weights and measures;

of erecting courts, offices, boroughs, corporations, fairs, markets, ports, beacons, lighthouses, seamarks.

of laying embargoes, or prohibiting the exportation of any commodity for a longer space than [40] days.

of retaining or recalling a member of the state but by legal process pro delicto vel contractu.

of making denizens.

~~of pardoning crimes, or remitting fines or punishments.~~

of creating dignities or granting rights of precedence.

but these powers shall be exercised by the legislature alone, and excepting also those powers which by these fundamentals are given to others, or abolished.

A Privy council shall be annually appointed by the house of representatives whose duties it shall be to give advice to the Administrator when called on by him. With them the Deputy Administrator shall have session and suffrage.

Privy Council

Delegates to represent this colony in the American Congress shall be appointed when necessary by the house of Representatives. After serving [one] year in that office they shall not be capable of being re-appointed to the same during an interval of [one] year.

Delegates

A Treasurer shall be appointed by the house of Representatives who shall issue no money but by authority of both houses.

Treasurer

An Attorney general shall be appointed by the house of Representatives

Attorney Genrl.

High Sheriffs and Coroners of counties shall be annually elected by those qualified to vote for representatives: and no person who shall have served as high sheriff [one] year shall be capable of being re-elected to the said office in the same county till he shall have been out of office [five] years.

High Sheriffs, &c.

All other Officers civil and military shall be appointed by the Administrator; but such appoint-

Other Officers

ment shall be subject to the negative of the Privy council,
saving however to the Legislature a power of transferring to
any other persons the appointment of such officers or any of
them.

III. JUDICIARY.

The Judiciary powers shall be exercised
First, by County courts and other inferior jurisdictions:
Secondly, by a General court & a High court of Chancery:
Thirdly, by a Court of Appeals.

County Courts, &c. The judges of the county courts and other inferior jurisdictions shall be appointed by the Administrator, subject to the negative of the privy council. They
shall not be fewer than [five] in number. Their jurisdictions
shall be defined from time to time by the legislature: and they
shall be removable for misbehavior by the court of Appeals.

Genl. Court and High Ct. of Chancery The Judges of the General court and of the High
court of Chancery shall be appointed by the Admin-
istrator and Privy council. If kept united they shall
be [5] in number, if separate, there shall be [5] for the General
court & [3] for the High court of Chancery. The appointment
shall be made from the faculty of the law, and of such persons
of that faculty as shall have actually exercised the same at the
bar of some court or courts of record within this colony for
[seven] years. They shall hold their commissions during good
behavior, for breach of which they shall be removable by the
court of Appeals. Their jurisdiction shall be defined from time
to time by the Legislature.

Court of Appeals The Court of Appeals shall consist of not less
than [7] nor more than [11] members, to be appointed by the house of Representatives: they shall hold their
offices during good behavior, for breach of which they shall
be removable by an act of the legislature only. Their jurisdiction shall be to determine finally all causes removed before
them from the General Court or High Court of Chancery, or
of the county courts or other inferior jurisdictions for misbehavior: [to try impeachments against high offenders lodged
before them by the house of representatives for such crimes
as shall hereafter be precisely defined by the Legislature, and

for the punishment of which, the said legislature shall have previously prescribed certain and determinate pains.] In this court the judges of the General court and High court of Chancery shall have session and deliberative voice, but no suffrage.

All facts in causes whether of Chancery, Common, Ecclesiastical, or Marine law, shall be tried by a jury upon evidence given vivâ voce, in open court: but where witnesses are out of the colony or unable to attend through sickness or other invincible necessity, their deposition may be submitted to the credit of the jury.

Juries

All Fines or Amercements shall be assessed, & Terms of imprisonment for Contempts & Misdemeanors shall be fixed by the verdict of a Jury.

Fines, &c.

All Process Original & Judicial shall run in the name of the court from which it issues.

Process

Two thirds of the members of the General court, High court of Chancery, or Court of Appeals shall be a Quorum to proceed to business.

Quorum

IV. Rights, Private and Public.

Unappropriated or Forfeited lands shall be appropriated by the Administrator with the consent of the Privy council.

Lands

Every person of full age neither owning nor having owned [50] acres of land, shall be entitled to an appropriation of [50] acres or to so much as shall make up what he owns or has owned [50] acres in full and absolute dominion. And no other person shall be capable of taking an appropriation.

Lands heretofore holden of the crown in fee simple, and those hereafter to be appropriated shall be holden in full and absolute dominion, of no superior whatever.

No lands shall be appropriated until purchased of the Indian native proprietors; nor shall any purchases be made of them but on behalf of the public, by authority of acts of the General assembly to be passed for every purchase specially.

The territories contained within the charters erecting the colonies of Maryland, Pennsylvania, North and South Carolina, are hereby ceeded, released, & forever confirmed to the people of those colonies respectively, with all the rights of property, jurisdiction and government and all other rights whatsoever which might at any time heretofore have been claimed by this colony. The Western and Northern extent of this country shall in all other respects stand as fixed by the charter of

until by act of the Legislature one or more territories shall be laid off Westward of the Alleghaney mountains for new colonies, which colonies shall be established on the same fundamental laws contained in this instrument, and shall be free and independent of this colony and of all the world.

Descents shall go according to the laws Gavelkind, save only that females shall have equal rights with males.

Slaves   No person hereafter coming into this county shall be held within the same in slavery under any pretext whatever.

Naturalization   All persons who by their own oath or affirmation, or by other testimony shall give satisfactory proof to any court of record in this colony that they propose to reside in the same [7] years at the least and who shall subscribe the fundamental laws, shall be considered as residents and entitled to all the rights of persons natural born.

Religion   All persons shall have full and free liberty of religious opinion; nor shall any be compelled to frequent or maintain any religious institution.

Arms   No freeman shall be debarred the use of arms [within his own lands].

Standing Armies   There shall be no standing army but in time of actual war.

Free Press   Printing presses shall be free, except so far as by commission of private injury cause may be given of private action.

Forfeitures   All Forfeitures heretofore going to the king, shall go the state; save only such as the legislature may hereafter abolish.

The royal claim to Wrecks, waifs, strays, treasure-
trove, royal mines, royal fish, royal birds, are declared to have been usurpations on common right.

Wrecks

No Salaries or Perquisites shall be given to any
officer but by some future act of the legislature. No
salaries shall be given to the Administrator, members of the
legislative houses, judges of the court of Appeals, judges of
the County courts, or other inferior jurisdictions, Privy counsellors, or Delegates to the American Congress: but the reasonable expences of the Administrator, members of the house
of representatives, judges of the court of Appeals, Privy counsellors, & Delegates for subsistence while acting in the duties
of their office, may be borne by the public, if the legislature
shall so direct.

Salaries

No person shall be capable of acting in any office
Civil, Military [or Ecclesiastical] ~~The Qualifications~~
~~of all not otherwise directed, shall be an oath of fidelity to~~
~~state and the having given no bribe to obtain their office~~ who
shall have given any bribe to obtain such office, or who shall
not previously take an oath of fidelity to the state.

*Qualifica-
tions*

None of these fundamental laws and principles of government shall be repealed or altered, but by the personal consent
of the people on summons to meet in their respective counties on one and the same day by an act of Legislature to be
passed for every special occasion: and if in such county meetings the people of two thirds of the counties shall give their
suffrage for any particular alteration or repeal referred to
them by the said act, the same shall be accordingly repealed
or altered, and such repeal or alteration shall take it's place
among these fundamentals and stand on the same footing
with them, in lieu of the article repealed or altered.

The laws heretofore in force in this colony shall remain in
force, except so far as they are altered by the foregoing fundamental laws, or so far as they may be hereafter altered by
acts of the Legislature.

A Bill for Establishing Religious Freedom

SECTION I. Well aware that the opinions and belief of men depend not on their own will, but follow involuntarily the evidence proposed to their minds; that Almighty God hath created the mind free, and manifested his supreme will that free it shall remain by making it altogether insusceptible of restraint; that all attempts to influence it by temporal punishments, or burthens, or by civil incapacitations, tend only to beget habits of hypocrisy and meanness, and are a departure from the plan of the holy author of our religion, who being lord both of body and mind, yet chose not to propagate it by coercions on either, as was in his Almighty power to do, but to extend it by its influence on reason alone; that the impious presumption of legislators and rulers, civil as well as ecclesiastical, who, being themselves but fallible and uninspired men, have assumed dominion over the faith of others, setting up their own opinions and modes of thinking as the only true and infallible, and as such endeavoring to impose them on others, hath established and maintained false religions over the greatest part of the world and through all time: That to compel a man to furnish contributions of money for the propagation of opinions which he disbelieves and abhors, is sinful and tyrannical; that even the forcing him to support this or that teacher of his own religious persuasion, is depriving him of the comfortable liberty of giving his contributions to the particular pastor whose morals he would make his pattern, and whose powers he feels most persuasive to righteousness; and is withdrawing from the ministry those temporary rewards, which proceeding from an approbation of their personal conduct, are an additional incitement to earnest and unremitting labours for the instruction of mankind; that our civil rights have no dependance on our religious opinions, any more than our opinions in physics or geometry; that therefore the proscribing any citizen as unworthy the public confidence by laying upon him an incapacity of being called to offices of trust and emolument, unless he profess or re-

nounce this or that religious opinion, is depriving him injuriously of those privileges and advantages to which, in
common with his fellow citizens, he has a natural right; that
it tends also to corrupt the principles of that very religion it
is meant to encourage, by bribing, with a monopoly of
worldly honours and emoluments, those who will externally
profess and conform to it; that though indeed these are criminal who do not withstand such temptation, yet neither are
those innocent who lay the bait in their way; that the opinions of men are not the object of civil government, nor under
its jurisdiction; that to suffer the civil magistrate to intrude
his powers into the field of opinion and to restrain the profession or propagation of principles on supposition of their ill
tendency is a dangerous falacy, which at once destroys all religious liberty, because he being of course judge of that tendency will make his opinions the rule of judgment, and
approve or condemn the sentiments of others only as they
shall square with or differ from his own; that it is time
enough for the rightful purposes of civil government for its
officers to interfere when principles break out into overt acts
against peace and good order; and finally, that truth is great
and will prevail if left to herself; that she is the proper and
sufficient antagonist to error, and has nothing to fear from
the conflict unless by human interposition disarmed of her
natural weapons, free argument and debate; errors ceasing to
be dangerous when it is permitted freely to contradict them.

SECT. II. WE the General Assembly of Virginia do enact
that no man shall be compelled to frequent or support any
religious worship, place, or ministry whatsoever, nor shall be
enforced, restrained, molested, or burthened in his body or
goods, nor shall otherwise suffer, on account of his religious
opinions or belief; but that all men shall be free to profess,
and by argument to maintain, their opinions in matters of
religion, and that the same shall in no wise diminish, enlarge,
or affect their civil capacities.

SECT. III. AND though we well know that this Assembly,
elected by the people for the ordinary purposes of legislation
only, have no power to restrain the acts of succeeding Assem-

blies, constituted with powers equal to our own, and that therefore to declare this act irrevocable would be of no effect in law; yet we are free to declare, and do declare, that the rights hereby asserted are of the natural rights of mankind, and that if any act shall be hereafter passed to repeal the present or to narrow its operation, such act will be an infringement of natural right.

A Bill for Proportioning Crimes and Punishments

SECTION I. Whereas it frequently happens that wicked and dissolute men, resigning themselves to the dominion of inordinate passions, commit violations on the lives, liberties, and property of others, and the secure enjoyment of these having principally induced men to enter into society, government would be defective in its principal purpose, were it not to restrain such criminal acts by inflicting due punishments on those who perpetrate them; but it appears at the same time equally deducible from the purposes of society, that a member thereof, committing an inferior injury, does not wholly forfeit the protection of his fellow citizens, but after suffering a punishment in proportion to his offence, is entitled to their protection from all greater pain, so that it becomes a duty in the Legislature to arrange in a proper scale the crimes which it may be necessary for them to repress, and to adjust thereto a corresponding gradation of punishments. And whereas the reformation of offenders, though an object worthy the attention of the laws, is not effected at all by capital punishments which exterminate instead of reforming, and should be the last melancholy resource against those whose existence is become inconsistent with the safety of their fellow citizens; which also weaken the State by cutting off so many, who, if reformed, might be restored sound members to society, who, even under a course of correction, might be rendered useful in various labours for the public, and would be, living, and long-continued spectacles to deter others from committing the like offences. And forasmuch as the experience of all ages and countries hath shewn, that cruel and sanguinary laws defeat their own purpose, by engaging the benevolence of mankind to withhold prosecutions, to smother testimony, or to listen to it with bias; and by producing in many instances a total dispensation and impunity under the names of pardon and privilege of clergy; when, if the punishment were only proportioned to the injury, men would feel it their inclination, as well as their duty, to see the laws observed; and the power of dispensation, so dangerous and mischievous, which produces crimes by holding up a hope of impunity, might totally be abolished, so that men while contemplating to perpetrate a crime would see their punishment ensuing as necessarily as effects follow their causes; for rendering crimes and punishments, therefore, more proportionate to each other,

SECT. II. Be it enacted by the General Assembly, that no crime shall be henceforth punished by the deprivation of life or limb,* except those herein after ordained to be so punished.

SECT. III.† If a man do levy war‡ against the Commonwealth *in the same*, or be adherent to the enemies of the Commonwealth *within the same*,§ giving to them aid or comfort in the Commonwealth, or elsewhere, and thereof be convicted, of open deed, by the evidence of two sufficient and lawful witnesses, or his own voluntary confession, the said cases, and no‖ others, shall be adjudged treasons which extend

---

*This takes away the punishment of cutting off the hand of a person striking another, or drawing his sword in one of the superior courts of justice. Stamf. P. C. 38. 33. H. 8. c. 12. In an earlier stage of the Common law, it was death. Gif hwa gefeohte on Cyninges huse sy he scyldig ealles his yrfes, and sy on Cyninges dome hwæther he lif age de nage; si quis in regis domo pugnet, perdat omnem suam hæreditatem, et in regis sit arbitrio, possideat vitam an non possideat. Ll. Inae. 6. Gif hwa on Cyninges healle gefeohte, oththe his wæpne gebrede, and hine mon gefo, sy thæt on Cyninges dome swa death, swa lif, swa he him forgyfan wille: si quis in aula regia pugnet, vel arma sua extrahat et capiatur, sit in regis arbitrio tam mors quam vita, sicut ei condonare voluerit. Ll. Alfr. 7, Gif hwa on Cyninges hirede gefeohte tholige thæt lifes, buton se Cyning him gearian wille: si quis in regia dimicat, perdat vitam, nisi rex hoc illi condonare velit. Ll. Cnuti. 56. 4. Bl. 125.

†25. E. 3. st. 5. c. 2. 7. W. 3. c. 3. § 2.

‡Though the crime of an accomplice in treason is not here described, yet, Lord Coke says, the partaking and maintaining a treason herein described, makes him a principal in that treason: it being a rule that in treason all are principals. 3 Inst. 138. 2 Inst. 590. 1 H. 6. 5.

§These words in the English statute narrow its operation. A man adhering to the enemies of the Commonwealth, in a foreign country, would certainly not be guilty of treason with us, if these words be retained. The convictions of treason of that kind in England have been under that branch of the statute which makes the compassing the king's death treason. Foster 196, 197. But as we omit that branch, we must by other means reach this flagrant case.

‖The stat. 25. E. 3. directs all other cases of treasons to await the opinion of Parliament. This has the effect of negative words, excluding all other treasons. As we drop that part of the statute, we must, by negative words, pre-

to the commonwealth, and the person so convicted shall suffer death, by hanging,* and shall forfeit his lands and goods
to the commonwealth.

SECT. IV. If any person commit petty treason, or a husband
murder his wife, a parent† his child, or a child his parent, he
shall suffer death, by hanging, and his body be delivered to
Anatomists to be dissected.

SECT. V. Whosoever committeth murder by poisoning,
shall suffer death by poison.

SECT. VI. Whosoever committeth murder by way of duel,
shall suffer death by hanging; and if he were the challenger,

---

vent an inundation of common law treasons. I strike out the word "it,"
therefore, and insert "the said cases, and no others." Quære, how far those
negative words may effect the case of accomplices above mentioned? Though
if their case was within the statute, so as that it needed not await the opinion
of Parliament, it should seem to be also within our act, so as not be ousted
by the negative words.

*This implies "by the neck." See 2 Hawk. 544 notes n. o.

†By the stat. 21. Jac. 1. c. 27. and Act Ass. 1170. c. 12. concealment by the
mother of the death of a bastard child is made murder. In justification of
this, it is said, that shame is a feeling which operates so strongly on the mind,
as frequently to induce the mother of such a child to murder it, in order to
conceal her disgrace. The act of concealment, therefore, proves she was influenced by shame, and that influence produces a presumption that she murdered the child. The effect of this law then is, to make what, in its nature, is
only presumptive evidence of a murder conclusive of that fact. To this I answer, 1. So many children die before or soon after birth, that to presume all
those murdered who are found dead, is a presumption which will lead us
oftener wrong than right, and consequently would shed more blood than it
would save. 2. If the child were born dead, the mother would naturally
choose rather to conceal it, in hopes of still keeping a good character in the
neighborhood. So that the act of concealment is far from proving the guilt
of murder on the mother. 3. If shame be a powerful affection of the mind, is
not parental love also? Is it not the strongest affection known? Is it not
greater than even that of self-preservation? While we draw presumptions
from shame, one affection of the mind against the life of the prisoner, should
we not give some weight to presumptions from parental love, an affection at
least as strong, in favor of life? If concealment of the fact is a presumptive
evidence of murder, so strong as to overbalance all other evidence that may
possibly be produced to take away the presumption, why not trust the force
of this incontestable presumption to the jury, who are, in a regular course,
to hear presumptive, as well as positive testimony? If the presumption arising
from the act of concealment, may be destroyed by proof positive or circumstantial to the contrary, why should the legislature preclude that contrary
proof? Objection. The crime is difficult to prove, being usually committed in

his body, after death, shall be gibbetted.* He who removeth
it from the gibbet shall be guilty of a misdemeanor, and the
officer shall see that it be replaced.

SECT. VII. Whosoever shall commit murder in any other
way shall suffer death by hanging.

SECT. VIII. And in all cases of Petty treason and murder,
one half of the lands and goods of the offender shall be forfeited to the next of kin to the person killed, and the other
half descend and go to his own representatives. Save only,
where one shall slay the challenger in a duel,† in which case,
no part of his lands or goods shall be forfeited to the kindred
of the party slain, but instead thereof, a moiety shall go to
the commonwealth.

SECT. IX. The same evidence‡ shall suffice, and order and
course§ of trial be observed in cases of Petty treason as in
those of other‖ murders.

---

secret. Answer. But circumstantial proof will do; for example, marks of violence, the behavior, countenance, &c. of the prisoner, &c. And if conclusive
proof be difficult to be obtained, shall we therefore fasten irremovably upon
equivocal proof? Can we change the nature of what is contestable, and make
it incontestable? Can we make that conclusive which God and nature have
made inconclusive? Solon made no law against parricide, supposing it impossible that any one could be guilty of it; and the Persians, from the same
opinion, adjudged all who killed their reputed parents to be bastards; and
although parental be yet stronger than filial affection, we admit saticide
proved on the most equivocal testimony, whilst they rejected all proof of an
act certainly not more repugnant to nature, as of a thing impossible, unprov-
able. See Beccaria, § 31.

*25. G. 2. c. 37.

†Quære, if the estates of both parties in a duel, should not be forfeited?
The deceased is equally guilty with a suicide.

‡Quære, if these words may not be omitted? By the Common law, one
witness in treason was sufficient. Foster 233. Plowd. 8. a. Mirror c. 3. § 34.
Waterhouse on Fortesc. de laud. 252. Carth. 144. per Holt. But Lord Coke,
contra 3 inst. 26. The stat. 1. E. 6. c. 12. & 5. E. 6. c. 11. first required two
witnesses in treason. The clause against high treason supra, does the same as
to high treason; but it seems if 1st and 5th E. 6. are dropped, Petty treason
will be tried and proved, as at Common law, by one witness. But quære,
Lord Coke being contra, whose opinion it is ever dangerous to neglect.

§These words are intended to take away the peremptory challenge of
thirty-five jurors. The same words being used 1. 2. Ph. & M. c. 10. are deemed
to have restored the peremptory challenge in high treason; and consequently
are sufficient to take it away. Foster 237.

‖Petty treason is considered in law only as an aggravated murder. Foster

SECT. X. Whosoever shall be guilty of manslaughter,* shall, for the first offence, be condemned to hard† labour for seven years in the public works; shall forfeit one half of his lands and goods to the next of kin to the person slain; the other half to be sequestered during such term, in the hands, and to the use, of the commonwealth, allowing a reasonable part of the profits for the support of his family. The second offence shall be deemed murder.

SECT. XI. And where persons meaning to commit a trespass‡ only, or larceny, or other unlawful deed, and doing an act from which involuntary homicide hath ensued, have heretofore been adjudged guilty of manslaughter or of murder, by transferring such their unlawful intention to an act, much more penal than they could have in probable contemplation; no such case shall hereafter be deemed manslaughter unless manslaughter was intended, nor murder, unless murder was intended.

SECT. XII. In other cases of homicide the law will not add to the miseries of the party, by punishments or forfeitures.§

---

107. 323. A pardon of all murders, pardons Petty treason. 1 Hale P. C. 378. see 2 H. P. C. 340. 342. It is also included in the word "felony," so that a pardon of all felonies, pardons Petty treason.

*Manslaughter is punishable at law, by burning in the hands, and forfeiture of chattels.

†It is best, in this act, to lay down principles only, in order that it may not forever be undergoing change; and, to carry into effect the minuter parts of it, frame a bill "for the employment and government of felons, or malefactors, condemned to labor for the Commonwealth," which may serve as an Appendix to this, and in which all the particulars requisite may be directed; and as experience will, from time to time, be pointing out amendments, these may be made without touching this fundamental act. See More's Utopia p. 50. for some good hints. Fugitives might, in such a bill, be obliged to work two days for every one they absent themselves.

‡The shooting at a wild fowl, and killing a man, is homicide by misadventure. Shooting at a pullet, without any design to take it away, is manslaughter; and with a design to take it away, is murder. 6 Sta. tr. 222. To shoot at the poultry of another, and thereby set fire to his house, is arson, in the opinion of some. Dalt. c. 116. 1. Hale's P. C. 569. c. contra.

§Beccaria. § 32. Suicide. Homicides are, 1. Justifiable. 2. Excusable. 3. Felonious. For the last, punishments have been already provided. The first are held to be totally without guilt, or rather commendable. The second are in some cases not quite unblamable. These should subject the party to marks of contrition; viz., the killing of a man in defence of property; so also in defence

SECT. XIII. Whenever sentence of death shall have been pronounced against any person for treason or murder, execution thereof shall be done on the next day but one, after

---

of one's person, which is a species of excusable homicide; because, although cases may happen where these also are commendable, yet most frequently they are done on too slight appearance of danger; as in return for a blow, kick, fillip, &c.; or on a person's getting into a house, not animo furandi, but perhaps veneris causa, &c. Bracton says, "si quis furem nocturnum occident, ita demum impune foret, si parcere ei sine periculo suo non potuit, si autem potuit, aliter erit." "Item erit si quis hamsokne quæ dicitur invasio domus contra pacem domini regis in domo sua se defenderit, et invasor occisus fuerit; impersecutus et insultus remanebit, si ille quem invasit aliter se defendere non potuit; dicitur enim quod non est dignus habere pacem qui non vult observare eam." L. 3. c. 23. § 3. "Qui latronem occiderit, non tenetur, nocturnum vel diurum, si aliter periculum evadere non possit; tenetur tamen si possit. Item non tenetur si per infortunium, et non animo et voluntate occidendi, nec dolus, nec culpa ejus inveniatur." L. 3. c. 36. § 1. The stat. 24. H. 8. c. 5. is therefore merely declaratory of the Common law. See on the general subject Puffend. 2. 5. § 10. 11. 12. 16. 17. Excusable homicides are by misadventure, or in self-defence. It is the opinion of some lawyers, that the Common law punished these with death, and that the statute of Marlbridge c. 26. and Gloucester, c. 9. first took away this by giving them title to a pardon, as matter of right, and a writ of restitution of their goods. See 2. Inst. 148. 315. 3. Inst. 55. Bracton L. 3. c. 4. § 2. Fleta L. 1. c. 23. § 14. 15. 21. E. 3. 23. But it is believed never to have been capital. 1. H. P. C. 425. 1 Hawk. 75. Foster, 282. 4. Bl. 188. It seems doubtful also, whether at Common law, the party forfeited all his chattels in this case, or only paid a weregild. Foster, ubi supra, doubts, and thinks it of no consequence, as the statute of Gloucester entitles the party to Royal grace, which goes as well to forfeiture as life. To me there seems no reason for calling these excusable homicides, and the killing a man in defence of property, a justifiable homicide. The latter is less guiltless than misadventure or self-defence.

Suicide is by law punishable by forfeiture of chattels. This bill exempts it from forfeiture. The suicide injures the State less than he who leaves it with his effects. If the latter then be not punished, the former should not. As to the example, we need not fear its influence. Men are too much attached to life, to exhibit frequent instances of depriving themselves of it. At any rate, the quasi-punishment of confiscation will not prevent it. For if one be found who can calmly determine to renounce life, who is so weary of his existence here, as rather to make experiment of what is beyond the grave, can we suppose him, in such a state of mind, susceptible of influence from the losses to his family from confiscation? That men in general, too, disapprove of this severity, is apparent from the constant practice of juries finding the suicide in a state of insanity; because they have no other way of saving the forfeiture. Let it then be done away.

such sentence, unless it be Sunday, and then on the Monday following.*

SECT. XIV. Whosoever shall be guilty of rape,† *polygamy*,‡

*Beccaria. § 19. 25. G. 2. c. 37.

†13. E. 1. c. 34. Forcible abduction of a woman having substance is felony by 3. H. 7. c. 2. 3 Inst. 61. 4 Bl. 208. If goods be taken, it will be felony as to them, without this statute; and as to the abduction of the woman, quære if not better to leave that, and also kidnapping, 4. Bl. 219. to the Common law remedies, viz., fine, imprisonment, and pillory, Raym. 474. 2 Show. 221. Skin. 47. Comb. 10. the writs of Homine replegiando, Capias in Withernam, Habeas corpus, and the action of trespass? Rape was felony at the Common law. 3. Inst. 60. but see 2. Inst. 181. further—for its definition see 2. Inst. 180. Bracton, L. 3. c. 28. § 1. says the punishment of rape is "amissio membrorum, ut sit membrum pro membro, quia virgo, cum corrumpitur, membrum amittit, et ideo corruptor puniatur in eo in quo deliquit; oculus igitur amittat propter aspectum decoris quo virginem concupivit; amittat et testiculos qui calorem stupri induxerunt. Olim quidem corruptores virginitatis et castitatis suspendebantur et eorum fautores, &c. Modernis tamen temporibus aliter observatur," &c. And Fleta, "solet justiciarius pro quolibet mahemio ad amissionem testiculorum vel oculorum convictum condemnare, sed non sine errore, eo quod id judicium nisi in corruptione virginum tantum competebat; nam pro virginitatis corruptione solebant abscidi et merito judiciari, ut sic pro membro quod abstulit, membrum per quod deliquit amitteret, viz., testiculos, qui calorem stupri induxerunt," &c. Fleta, L. 1. c. 40. § 4. "Gif theow man theowne to nydhed genyde, gabte mid his eowende:" "Si servus servam ad stuprum coegerit, compenset hoc virga sua virili. Si quis puellam," &c. Ll. Aelfridi. 25. "Hi purgist femme per forze forfait ad les membres." Ll. Gul. conq. 19. In Dyer, 305, a man was indicted, and found guilty of a rape on a girl of seven years old. The court "doubted of the rape of so tender a girl; but if she had been nine years old, it would have been otherwise." 14. Eliz. Therefore the statute 18. Eliz. c. 6. says, "For plain declaration of law, be it enacted, that if any person shall unlawfully and carnally know and abuse any woman child, under the age of ten years, &c., he shall suffer as a felon, without allowance of clergy." Lord Hale, however, 1. P. C. 630. thinks it rape independent of that statute, to know carnally, a girl under twelve, the age of consent. Yet 4. Bl. 212. seems to neglect this opinion; and as it was founded on the words of 3. E. 1. c. 13. and this is with us omitted, the offence of carnally knowing a girl under twelve, or ten years of age, will not be distinguished from that of any other.

‡1. Jac. 1. c. 11. Polygamy was not penal till the statute 1. Jac. The law contented itself with the nullity of the act. 4. Bl. 163. 3. Inst. 88.

But no one shall be punished for Polygamy, who shall have married after probable information of the death of his or her husband or wife, or after his or her husband or wife, hath absented him or herself, so that no notice of his or her being alive hath reached such person for seven years together, or hath suffered the punishments before prescribed for rape, polygamy, or sodomy.

or sodomy* with man or woman, shall be punished; if a man, by castration,† a woman, by boring through the cartilage of her nose a hole of one half inch in diameter at the least.

SECT. XV. Whosoever on purpose,‡ shall disfigure another, by cutting out or disabling the tongue, slitting or cutting off a nose, lip, or ear, branding, or otherwise, shall be maimed, or disfigured in like§ sort; or if that cannot be, for want of the same part, then as nearly as may be, in some other part of at least equal value and estimation, in the opinion of a jury, and moreover, shall forfeit one half of his lands and goods to the sufferer.

*§ 25. H. 8. c. 6. Buggery is twofold. 1. With mankind, 2. with beasts. Buggery is the Genus, of which Sodomy and Bestiality, are the species. 12. Co. 37. says, "note that Sodomy is with mankind." But Finch's L. B. 3. c. 24. "Sodomiary is a carnal copulation against nature, to wit, of man or woman in the same sex, or of either of them with beasts." 12. Co. 36. says, "it appears by the ancient authorities of the law that this was felony." Yet the 25. H. 8. declares it felony, as if supposed not to be so. Britton, c. 9. says, that Sodomites are to be burnt. F. N. B. 269. b. Fleta, L. 1. c. 37. says, "pecorantes et Sodomitæ in terra vivi confodiantur." The Mirror makes it treason. Bestiality can never make any progress; it cannot therefore be injurious to society in any great degree, which is the true measure of criminality in foro civili, and will ever be properly and severely punished, by universal derision. It may, therefore, be omitted. It was anciently punished with death, as it has been latterly. Ll. Aelfrid. 31. and 25. H. 8. c. 6. see Beccaria. § 31. Montesq.

† Bracton, Fleta, &c.

‡ 22. 23. Car. 2. c. 1. Maiming was felony at the Common law. Britton, c. 25. 'Mahemium autem dici poteri, aubia aliquis in aliqua parte sui corporis læsionem acceperit, per quam affectus sit inutilis ad pugnandum: ut si manus amputetur, vel pes, oculus privetur, vel scerda de osse capitis laveter, vel si quis dentes præcisores amiserit, vel castratus fuerit, et talis pro mahemiato poterit adjudicari.' Fleta L. 1. c. 40. 'Et volons que nul maheme ne soit tenus forsque de membre tollet dount home es plus feble a combatre, sicome del oyl, ou de la mayn, ou del pie, ou de la tete debruse, ou de les dentz devant.' Britton, c. 25. For further definitions, see Bracton, L. 3. c. 24 § 3. 4. Finch L. B. 3. c. 12. Co. L. 126. a. b. 288. a. 3. Bl. 121. 4. Bl. 205. Stamf. P. C. L. 1. c. 41. I do not find any of these definitions confine the offence to wilful and malicious perpetrations of it. 22. 23. Car. 2. c. 1. called the Coventry act, has the words 'on purpose and of malice forethought.' Nor does the Common law prescribe the same punishment for disfiguring, as for maiming.

§ The punishment was by retaliation. "Et come ascun appele serra de tele felonie atteint et attende jugement, si soit le jugement tiel que il perde autriel membre come il avera tollet al pleintyfe. Et sy la pleynte soi faite de femme que avera tollet a home ses membres, en tiel cas perdra la femme la une meyn

SECT. XVI. Whosoever shall counterfeit* any coin current by law within this commonwealth, or any paper bills issued in the nature of money, or of certificates of loan, on the credit of this commonwealth, or of all or any of the United States of America, or any Inspectors' notes for tobacco, or shall pass any such counterfeited coin, paper bills, or notes, knowing them to be counterfeit; or, for the sake of lucre, shall diminish† each, or any such coin, shall be condemned to hard labour six years in the public works, and shall forfeit all his lands and goods to the commonwealth.

SECT. XVII. The making false any such paper bill, or note, shall be deemed counterfeiting.

SECT. XVIII.‡ Whosoever committeth arson, shall be con-

---

par jugement, come le membre dount ele axera trespasse." Britton, c. 25. Fleta, B. 1. c. 40. Ll. Ælfr. 19. 40.

*25. E. 3. st. 5 c. 2. 5. El. c. 11. 18. El. c. 1. 8. 9. W. 3. c. 26. 15. 16. G. 2. c. 28. 7. Ann. c. 25. By the laws of Æthelstan and Canute, this was punished by cutting off the hand. "Gif se mynetere ful wurthe slea man tha hand of, the he that ful mid worthe and sette uppon tha mynet smiththan." In English characters and words "if the minter foul [criminal] wert, slay the hand off, that he the foul [crime] with wrought, and set upon the mint-smithery." Ll. Aethelst. 14. "Et si quis praeter hanc, falsam fecerit, perdat manum quacum falsam confecit." Ll. Cnuti. 8. It had been death by the Ll. Æthelredi sub fine. By those of H. 1. "si quis cum falso denario inventus fuerit—fiat justitia mea, saltem de dextro pugno et de testiculis." Anno 1108. Operæ pretium vero est audire quam severus rex fuerit in pravos. Monetarios enim fere omnes totius Angliæ fecit ementulari, et manus dextras abscindi, quia monetam furtive corruperant. Wilkins ib. et anno 1125. When the Common law became settled, it appears to have been punishable by death. "Est aluid genus criminis quod sub nomine falsi continetur, et tangit coronam domini regis, et ultimum inducit supplicium, sicut de illis qui falsam fabricant monetam, et qui de re non reproba, faciunt reprobam; sicut sunt retonsores denariorum." Bract. L. 3. c § 2. Fleta, L. 1. c. 22. § 4. Lord Hale thinks it was deemed petty treason at common law. 1. H. P. C. 220. 224. The bringing in false money with *intent* to merchandize, and make payment of it, is treason, by 25. E. 3. But the best proof of the intention, is the act of passing it, and why not leave room for repentance here, as in other cases of felonies intended? 1. H. P. C. 229.

†Clipping, filing, rounding, impairing, scaling, lightening, (the words in the statutes) are included in "diminishing;" gilding, in the word "casing;" coloring in the word "washing;" and falsifying, or making, is "counterfeiting."

‡43 L. c. 13. confined to four counties. 22. 23. Car. 2. c. 7. 9. G. 1. c. 22. 9. G. 3. c. 29.

demned to hard labour five years in the public works, and shall make good the loss of the sufferers threefold.*

Sect. XIX. If any person shall, within this Commonwealth, or, being a citizen thereof, shall without the same, wilfully destroy† or run‡ away with any sea-vessel, or goods laden on board thereof, or plunder or pilfer any wreck, he shall be condemned to hard labour five years in the public works, and shall make good the loss of the sufferers threefold.

Sect. XX. Whosoever committeth a robbery,§ shall be condemned to hard labour four years in the public works, and shall make double reparation to the persons injured.

Sect. XXI. Whatsoever act, if committed on any mansion-

---

*Arson was a felony at Common law—3. Inst. 66; punished by a fine, Ll. Aethelst. 6. But Ll. Cnuti, 61. make it a "scelus inexpiable." "Hus brec and bærnet and open thyfth æberemorth and hlaford swice æfter woruld laga is botleds." Word for word, "house break and burnt, and open theft, and manifest murther, and lord-treachery, afterworld's law is bootless." Bracton says it was punished by death. "Si quis turbida seditione incendium fecerit nequiter et in felonia, vel ob inimicitias, vel praedandi causa, capitali puniatur pœna vel sententia." Bract. L. 3. 27. He defines it as commissible by burning "aedes alienas." Ib. Britton, c. 9. "Ausi soit enquis de ceux que felonisement en temps de pees eient autre *blees* ou autre *mesons* ars, et ceux que serrount de ceo atteyntz, soient ars issint que eux soient punys par mesme cele chose dount ilz pecherent." Fleta, L. 1. c. 37. is a copy of Bracton. The Mirror c. 1. § 8. says, "Ardours sont que ardent citie, ville, maison home, maison beast, ou auters chatelx, de lour felonie en temps de pace pour haine ou vengeance." Again, c. 2. § 11. pointing out the words of the appellor "jeo dise que Sebright, &c., entiel meason ou *biens* mist de feu." Coke 3. Inst. 67. says, "the ancient authors extended this felony further than houses, viz., to sacks of corn, waynes or carts of coal, wood or other goods." He denies it as commissible, not only on the inset houses, parcel of the mansion house, but the outset also, as barn, stable, cowhouse, sheep house, dairy house, mill house, and the like, parcel of the mansion house. But "burning of a barn, being no parcel of a mansion house, is no felony," unless there be corn or hay within it. Ib. The 22. 23. Car. 2. and 9. G. 1. are the principal statutes against arson. They extend the offence beyond the Common law.
†1. Ann. st. 2. c. 9. 12. Ann. c. 18. 4. G. 1. c. 12. 26. G. 2. c. 19.
‡11. 12. W. 3. c. 7.
§Robbery was a felony at Common law. 3 Inst. 68. "Scelus inexpiable," by the Ll. Cnuti. 61. [See before in Arson.] It was punished with death. Britt. c. 15, "de robbours et de larouns et de semblables mesfesours, soit ausi ententivement enquis—et tauntost soient ceux robbours juges a la mort." Fleta says, "si quis convictus fuerit de bonis viri robbatis vel asportatis ad sectam regis judicium capitale subibit. L. 1. c. 39. See also Bract. L. 3. c. 32. § 1.

house, would be deemed a burglary,* shall be burglary, if committed on any other house; and he who is guilty of burglary, shall be condemned to hard labour four years in the public works, and shall make double reparation to the persons injured.

Sect. XXII. Whatsoever act, if committed in the night time, shall constitute the crime of burglary, shall, if committed in the day, be deemed house-breaking†; and whoever is

---

*Burglary was felony at the Common law. 3 Inst. 63. It was not distinguished by ancient authors, except the Mirror, from simple House-breaking, ib. 65. Burglary and House-breaking were called "Hamsockne diximus etiam de pacis violatione et de immunitatibus domus, si quis hoc in posterum fecerit ut perdat omne quod habet, et sit in regis arbitrio utrum vitam habeat. Eac we quædon be mundbryce and be ham socnum, sethe hit ofer this do thæt he dolie ealles thæs the age, and sy on Cyninges dome hwæther he life age; and we quoth of mound-breach, and of home-seeking he who it after this do, that he dole all that he owe [owns], and is in king's doom whether he life owes [owns.] Ll. Eadmundi, c. 6. and see Ll. Cnuti. 61. "hus brec," in notes on Arson. ante. A Burglar was also called a Burgessor. "Et soit enquis de Burgessours et sunt tenus Burgessours trestous ceux que *felonisement* en temps de pees debrusont esglises ou auter mesons, ou murs ou portes de nos cytes, ou de nos Burghes." Britt. c. 10. "Burglaria est nocturna diruptio habitaculi alicu jus, vel ecclesiæ, etiam murorum, partarumve civitatis aut burgi, ad feloniam aliquam perpetrandam. *Noctanter* dico, recentiores secutus; veteres enim hoc non adjungunt." Spelm. gloss. verb. Burglaria. It was punished with death. Ib. citn. from the office of a Coroner. It may be committed in the outset houses, as well as inset. 3 Inst. 65. though not under the same roof or contiguous, provided they be within the Curtilage or Homestall. 4 Bl. 225. As by the Common law, all felonies were clergiable, the stat. 23 H. 8. c. 1. 5. E. 6. c. 9. and 18 El. c. 7. first distinguished them, by taking the clerical privilege of impunity from the principals, and 3. 4. W. M. c. 9. from accessories before the fact. No *statute* defines what Burglary is. The 12 Ann. c. 7. decides the doubt whether, where breaking is subsequent to entry, it is Burglary. Bacon's Elements had affirmed, and 1. H. P. C. 554. had denied it. Our bill must distinguish them by different degrees of punishment.

†At the Common law, the offence of Housebreaking was not distinguished from Burglary, and neither of them from any other larceny. The statutes at first took away clergy from Burglary, which made a leading distinction between the two offences. Later statutes, however, have taken clergy from so many cases of Housebreaking, as nearly to bring the offences together again. These are 23 H. 8. c. 1. 1 E. 6. c. 12. 5 and 6 E. 6. c. 9. 3 and 4 W. M. c. 9. 39 El. c. 15. 10 and 11 W. 3 c. 23. 12 Ann. c. 7. See Barr. 428. 4 Bl. 240. The circumstances which in these statutes characterize the offence, seem to have been occasional and unsystematical. The houses on which Burglary may be committed, and the circumstances which constitute that crime being ascertained, it will be better to define Housebreaking by the same subjects and

guilty thereof, shall be condemned to hard labour three years
in the public works, and shall make reparation to the persons
injured.

SECT. XXIII. Whosoever shall be guilty of horse-stealing,*
shall be condemned to hard labour three years in the public
works, and shall make reparation to the person injured.

SECT. XXIV. Grand larceny† shall be where the goods stolen
are of the value of five dollars; and whosoever shall be guilty
thereof, shall be forthwith put in the pillory for one half hour,
shall be condemned to hard labour‡ two years in the public
works, and shall make reparation to the person injured.

---

circumstances, and let the crimes be distinguished only by the hour at which
they are committed, and the degree of punishment.

*The offence of Horse-stealing seems properly distinguishable from other
larcenies, here, where these animals generally run at large, the temptation
being so great and frequent, and the facility of commission so remarkable.
See 1 E. 6. c. 12. 23 E. 6. c. 33. 31 El. c. 12.

†The distinction between grand and petty larceny, is very ancient. At first
8d. was the sum which constituted grand larceny. Ll. Æthelst. c. 1. "Ne parcatur ulli furi, qui furtum manutenens captus sit, supra 12. annos nato, et
supra 8. denarios." Afterwards, in the same king's reign it was raised to 12d.
"non parcatur alicui furi ultra 12 denarios, et ultra 12 annos nato—ut occide-
mus illum et capiamus omne quod possidet, et imprimis sumamus rei furto
ablatæ pretium ab haerede, ac dividatur postea reliquum in duas partes, una
pars uxori, si munda, et facinoris conscia non sit; et residuum in duo, dimidium capiat rex, dimidium societas." Ll. Aethelst. Wilkins, p. 65.

‡Ll. Inae. c. 7. "Si quis furetur ita ut uxor ejus et infans ipsius nesciant,
solvat 60. solidos poenæ loco. Si autem furetur testantibus omnibus
hæredibus suis, *abeant omnes in servitutem.*" Ina was king of the West-Saxons,
and began to reign A. C. 688. After the union of the Heptarchy, i. e. temp.
Æthelst, inter 924 and 940, we find it punishable with death as above. So it
was inter 1017 and 1035, i. e. temp. Cnuti. Ll. Cnuti. 61. cited in notes on
Arson. In the time of William the conqueror, it seems to have been made
punishable by fine only. Ll. Gul. conq. apud Wilk. p. 218, 220. This commu-
tation, however, was taken away by Ll. H. 1. anno 1108. "Si quis in furto vel
latrocinio deprehensus fuisset, suspenderetur; sublata wirgildorum, id est, pe-
cuniaræ redemptionis lege." Larceny is the felonious taking and carrying
away of the personal goods of another. 1. As to the taking, the 3. 4. W. M.
c. 9 § 5. is not additional to the Common law, but declaratory of it; because
where only the care or use, and not the possession, of things is delivered, to
take them was larceny at the Common law. The 33 H. 6. c. 1. and 21, H. 8. c.
7. indeed, have added to the Common law, by making it larceny in a servant
to convert things of his master's. But quære, if they should be imitated more
than as to other breaches of trust in general. 2. As to the subject of larceny,

SECT. XXV. Petty larceny shall be, where the goods stolen are of less value than five dollars; whosoever shall be guilty thereof, shall be forthwith put in the pillory for a quarter of an hour, shall be condemned to hard labour for one year in the public works, and shall make reparation to the persons injured.

SECT. XXVI. Robbery* or larceny of bonds, bills obligatory, bills of exchange, or promissory notes, for the payment of money or tobacco, lottery tickets, paper bills issued in the nature of money, or certificates of loan on the credit of this commonwealth, or of all or any of the United States of America, or inspectors notes for tobacco, shall be punished in the same manner as robbery or larceny of the money or tobacco due on, or represented by such papers.

SECT. XXVII. Buyers† and receivers of goods taken by way of robbery or larceny, knowing them to have been so taken, shall be deemed accessaries to such robbery or larceny after the fact.

SECT. XXVIII. Prison-breakers,‡ also, shall be deemed accessaries after the fact, to traitors or felons whom they enlarge from prison.§

---

4 G. 2. c. 32. 6 G. 3. c. 36. 48. 45. El. c. 7. 15 Car. 2. c. 2. 23 G. 2. c. 26. 31 G. 2. c. 35. 9 G. 3. c. 41. 25 G. 2. c. 10. have extended larceny to things of various sorts either real, or fixed to the reality. But the enumeration is unsystematical, and in this country, where the produce of the earth is so spontaneous, as to have rendered things of this kind scarcely a breach of civility or good manners, in the eyes of the people, quære, if it would not too much enlarge the field of Criminal law? The same may be questioned of 9 G. 1. c. 22. 13 Car. 2. c. 10. 10 G. 2. c. 32. 5 G. 3. c. 14. 22 and 23 Car. 2. c. 25. 37 E. 3. c. 19. making it felony to steal animals feræ naturæ.

*2 G. 2. c. 25 § 3. 7 G. 3. c. 50.

†3. 4. W. M. c. 9. § 4. 5 Ann. c. 31. § 5. 4 G. 1. c. 11. § 1.

‡1 E. 2.

§Breach of prison at the Common law was capital, without regard to the crime for which the party was committed. "Cum pro criminis qualitate in carcerem recepti fuerint, conspiraverint (ut ruptis vinculis aut fracto carcere) evadant, amplius (quam causa pro qua recepti sunt exposeit) puniendi sunt, videlicet ultimo supplicio, quamvis ex eo crimine innocentes inveniantur, propter quod inducti sunt in carcerem et imparcati." Bracton L. 3. c. 9. § 4. Britt. c. 11. Fleta, L. 1. c. 26. § 4. Yet in the Y. B. Hill. 1. H. 7. 2. Hussey says, that by the opinion of Billing and Coke, and all the justices, it was a felony in strangers only, but not in the prisoner himself. S. C. Fitz. Abr.

SECT. XXIX. All attempts to delude the people, or to abuse their understanding by exercise of the pretended arts of witchcraft, conjuration, enchantment, or sorcery, or by pretended prophecies, shall be punished by ducking and whipping, at the discretion of a jury, not exceeding fifteen stripes.*

SECT. XXX. If the principal offenders be fled,† or secreted from justice, in any case not touching life or member, the accessaries may, notwithstanding, be prosecuted as if their principal were convicted.‡

Coron. 48. They are the principal felons, not accessaries. ib. Whether it was felony in the prisoner at Common law, is doubted. Stam. P. C. 30. b. The Mirror c. 5. § 1, says "abusion est a tener escape de prisoner, ou de bruserie del gaole pur peche mortell, car cel usage nest garrant per nul ley, ne in nul part est use forsque in cest realme, et en France, eins [mais] est leu garrantie de ceo faire per la ley de nature." 2 Inst. 589. The stat. 1. E. 2. de fraugentibus prisonam, restrained the judgment of life and limb for prison breaking, to cases where the offence of the prisoner required such judgment.

It is not only vain, but wicked, in a legislator to frame laws in opposition to the laws of nature, and to arm them with the terrors of death. This is truly creating crimes in order to punish them. The law of nature impels every one to escape from confinement; it should not, therefore, be subjected to punishment. Let the legislator restrain his criminal by walls, not by parchment. As to strangers breaking prison to enlarge an offender, they should, and may be fairly considered as accessaries after the fact. This bill says nothing of the prisoner releasing himself by breach of jail, he will have the benefit of the first section of the bill, which repeals the judgment of life and death at the common law.

*Gif wiccan owwe wigleras nansworan, owwe morthwyrhtan owwe fule afylede æbere horcwenan ahwhar on lande wurthan agytene, thonne fyrsie man of earde and clænsie tha theode, owwe on earde forfare hi mid ealle, buton hi geswican and the deoper gebetan: if witches, or weirds, man-swearers, murther-wroughters, or foul, defiled, open whore-queens, anywhere in the land were gotten, then force them off earth, and cleanse the nation, or in earth forth-fare them withal, but on they beseech, and deeply better. Ll. Ed. et Guthr. c. 11. "Sagæ, mulieres barbara, factitantes sacrificia, aut pestiferi, si cui mortem intulerint, neque id inficiari poterint, capitis poena esto." Ll. Æthelst. c. 6. apud Lambard. Ll. Aelfr. 30. Ll. Cnuti. c. 4. "Mesme cel jugement (d'etrears) eyent sorcers, et sorceresses, &c. ut supra. Fleta ut et ubi supra." 3. Inst. 44. Trial of witches before Hale in 1664. The statutes 33 H. 8. c. 8. 5 El. c. 16 and 1 Jac. 1. c. 12. seem to be only in confirmation of the Common law. 9 G. 2. c. 25. punishes them with pillory, and a year's imprisonment. 3 E. 6. c. 15. 5 El. c. 15. punish fond, fantastical and false prophecies, by fine and imprisonment.

†1 Ann. c. 9. § 2.

‡As every treason includes within it a misprision of treason, so every felony

Sect. XXXI. If any offender stand mute of obstinacy,* or challenge peremptorily more of the jurors than by law he may, being first warned of the consequence thereof, the court shall proceed as if he had confessed the charge.†

Sect. XXXII. Pardon and privilege of clergy, shall henceforth be abolished, that none may be induced to injure through hope of impunity. But if the verdict be against the defendant, and the court, before whom the offence is heard and determined, shall doubt that it may be untrue for default of testimony, or other cause, they may direct a new trial to be had.‡

---

includes a misprision, or misdemeanor. 1 Hale P. C. 652. 708. "Licet fuerit felonia, tamen in eo continetur misprisio." 2 R. 3. 10. Both principal and accessary, therefore, may be proceeded against in any case, either for felony or misprision, at the Common law. Capital cases not being mentioned here, accessaries to them will of course be triable for misprisions, if the offender flies.

*E. 1. c. 12.

†Whether the judgment of penance lay at Common law. See 2 Inst. 178. 2 H. P. C. 321. 4 Bl. 322. It was given on standing mute; but on challenging more than the legal number, whether that sentence, or sentence of death is to be given, seems doubtful. 2 H. P. C. 316. Quære, whether it would not be better to consider the supernumerary challenge as merely void, and to proceed in the trial? Quære too, in case of silence?

‡"Cum Clericus sic de crimine convictus degradetur non sequitur alia poena pro uno delicto, vel pluribus ante degradationem perpetratis. Satis enim sufficit ei pro poena degradatio, quæ est magna capitis diminutio, nisi forte convictus fuerit de apostatia, quia hinc primo degradetur, et postea per manum laicalem comburetur, secundum quod accidit in concilio Oxoni celebrato a bonæ memoriæ S. Cantuanen. Archiepiscopo de quodam diacono, qui se apostatavit pro quadam Judaæ; qui cum esset per episcopum degradatus, statim fuit igni traditus per manum laicalem." Bract. L. 3. c. 9. § 2. "Et mesme cel jugement (i. e. qui ils soient ars eyent) sorcers et sorceresses, et sodomites et mescreauntz apertement atteyntz." Britt. c. 9. "Christiani autem Apostatæ, sortilegii, et hujusmodi detractari debent et comburi." Fleta, L. 1. c. 37. § 2 see 3. Inst. 39. 12. Rep. 92. 1 H. P. C. 393. The extent of the clerical privilege at the Common law. 1. As to the crimes, seems very obscure and uncertain. It extended to no case where the judgment was not of life, or limb. Note in 2. H. P. C. 326. This therefore excluded it in trespass, petty larceny, or killing se defendendo. In high treason against the person of the King, it seems not to have been allowed. Note 1. H. P. C. 185. Treasons, therefore, not against the King's person immediately, petty treasons and felonies, seem to have been the cases where it was allowed; and even of those, not for insidiatio varium, depopulatio agrorum, or combustio domorum. The statute

SECT. XXXIII. No attainder shall work corruption of blood in any case.

SECT. XXXIV. In all cases of forfeiture, the widow's dower shall be saved to her, during her title thereto; after which it shall be disposed of as if no such saving had been.

SECT. XXXV. The aid of Counsel,* and examination of their witnesses on oath, shall be allowed to defendants in criminal prosecutions.

SECT. XXXVI. Slaves guilty of any offence† punishable in others by labour in the public works, shall be transported to such parts in the West-Indies, South-America, or Africa, as the Governor shall direct, there to be continued in slavery.

---

de Clero, 25 E. 3. st. 3. c. 4. settled the law on this head. 2. As to the persons, it extended to all clerks, always, and toties quoties. 2 H. P. C. 374. To nuns also. Fitz. Abr. Corone. 461. 22. E. 3. The clerical habit and tonsure were considered as evidence of the person being clerical. 26. Assiz. 19. 20. E. 2. Fitz. Corone. 233. By the 9 E. 4. 28. b. 34. H. 6. 49 a. b. a simple reading became the evidence. This extended impunity to a great number of laymen, and toties quoties. The stat. 4 H. 7. c. 13. directed that real clerks should, upon a second arraignment, produce their orders, and all others to be burnt in the hand with M. or T. on the first allowance of clergy, and not to be admitted to it a second time. A heretic, Jew, or Turk (as being incapable of orders) could not have clergy. 11. Co. Rep. 29 b. But a Greek, or other alien, reading in a book of his own country, might. Bro. Clergie. 20. So a blind man, if he could speak Latin. Ib. 21. qu. 11. Rep. 29. b. The orders entitling the party, were bishops, priests, deacons and subdeacons, the inferior being reckoned Clerici in minoribus. 2. H. P. C. 373. Quære, however, if this distinction is not founded on the stat. 23 H. 8. c. 1. 25 H. 8. c. 32. By merely dropping all the statutes, it should seem that none but clerks would be entitled to this privilege, and that they would, toties quoties.

*1 Ann. c. 9.

†Manslaughter, counterfeiting, arson, asportation of vessels, robbery, burglary, house-breaking, horse-stealing, larceny.

A Bill for the More General Diffusion of Knowledge

SECTION I. WHEREAS it appeareth that however certain forms of government are better calculated than others to protect individuals in the free exercise of their natural rights, and are at the same time themselves better guarded against degeneracy, yet experience hath shewn, that even under the best forms, those entrusted with power have, in time, and by slow operations, perverted it into tyranny; and it is believed that the most effectual means of preventing this would be, to illuminate, as far as practicable, the minds of the people at large, and more especially to give them knowledge of those facts, which history exhibiteth, that, possessed thereby of the experience of other ages and countries, they may be enabled to know ambition under all its shapes, and prompt to exert their natural powers to defeat its purposes; And whereas it is generally true that the people will be happiest whose laws are best, and are best administered, and that laws will be wisely formed, and honestly administered, in proportion as those who form and administer them are wise and honest; whence it becomes expedient for promoting the publick happiness that those persons, whom nature hath endowed with genius and virtue, should be rendered by liberal education worthy to receive, and able to guard the sacred deposit of the rights and liberties of their fellow citizens, and that they should be called to that charge without regard to wealth, birth or other accidental condition or circumstance; but the indigence of the greater number disabling them from so educating, at their own expence, those of their children whom nature hath fitly formed and disposed to become useful instruments for the public, it is better that such should be sought for and educated at the common expence of all, than that the happiness of all should be confided to the weak or wicked:

SECT. II. BE it therefore enacted by the General Assembly, that in every county within this commonwealth, there shall be chosen annually, by the electors qualified to vote for Delegates, three of the most honest and able men of their county, to be called the Aldermen of the county; and that the election of the said Aldermen shall be held at the same time and place, before the same persons, and notified and conducted in the same manner as by law is directed for the annual election of Delegates for the county.

SECT. III. THE person before whom such election is holden shall certify to the court of the said county the names of the Aldermen chosen, in order that the same may be entered of record, and shall give notice of their election to the said Aldermen within a fortnight after such election.

SECT. IV. THE said Aldermen on the first Monday in October, if it be fair, and if not, then on the next fair day, excluding Sunday, shall meet at the court-house of their county, and proceed to divide their said county into hundreds, bounding the same by water courses, mountains, or limits, to be run and marked, if they think necessary, by the county surveyor, and at the county expence, regulating the size of the said hundreds, according to the best of their discretion, so as that they may contain a convenient number of children to make up a school, and be of such convenient size that all the children within each hundred may daily attend the school to be established therein, distinguishing each hundred by a particular name; which division, with the names of the several hundreds, shall be returned to the court of the county and be entered of record, and shall remain unaltered until the increase or decrease of inhabitants shall render an alteration necessary, in the opinion of any succeeding Aldermen, and also in the opinion of the court of the county.

SECT. V. THE electors aforesaid residing within every hundred shall meet on the third Monday in October after the first election of Aldermen, at such place, within their hundred, as the said Aldermen shall direct, notice thereof being previously given to them by such person residing within the hundred as the said Aldermen shall require who is hereby enjoined to obey such requisition, on pain of being punished by amercement and imprisonment. The electors being so assembled shall choose the most convenient place within their hundred for building a school-house. If two or more places, having a greater number of votes than any others, shall yet be equal between themselves, the Aldermen, or such of them as are not of the same hundred, on information thereof, shall decide between them. The said Aldermen shall forthwith proceed to have a school-house built at the said place, and shall see that the same be kept in repair, and, when necessary, that it be rebuilt; but whenever they shall think necessary that it be rebuilt, they shall give notice as before directed, to the electors of the hundred to meet at the said school-house, on such day as they shall appoint, to determine by vote, in the manner before directed, whether it shall be rebuilt at the same, or what other place in the hundred.

SECT. VI. AT every of these schools shall be taught reading, writing, and common arithmetick, and the books which shall be used therein for instructing the children to read shall be such as will at the same time make them acquainted with Græcian, Roman, English, and American history. At these schools all the free children, male and female, resident within the respective hundred, shall be intitled to receive tuition gratis, for the term of three years, and as much longer, at their private expence, as their parents, guardians or friends, shall think proper.

SECT. VII. OVER ten of these schools (or such other number nearest thereto, as the number of hundreds in the county will admit, without fractional divisions) an overseer shall be appointed annually by the Aldermen at their first meeting, eminent for his learning, integrity, and fidelity to the commonwealth, whose business and duty it shall be, from time to time, to appoint a teacher to each school, who shall give assurance of fidelity to the commonwealth, and to remove him as he shall see cause; to visit every school once in every half year at the least, to examine the schollars; see that any general plan of reading and instruction recommended by the visiters of William and Mary College shall be observed; and to superintend the conduct of the teacher in every thing relative to his school.

SECT. VIII. EVERY teacher shall receive a salary of by the year, which, with the expences of building and repairing the school houses, shall be provided in such manner as other county expences are by law directed to be provided and shall also have his diet, lodging, and washing found him, to be levied in like manner, save only that such levy shall be on the inhabitants of each hundred for the board of their own teacher only.

SECT. IX. AND in order that grammer schools may be rendered convenient to the youth in every part of the commonwealth, BE it farther enacted, that on the first Monday in November, after the first appointment of overseers for the hundred schools, if fair, and if not, then on the next fair day, excluding Sunday, after the hour of one in the afternoon, the said overseers appointed for the schools in the counties of Princess Ann, Norfolk, Nansemond and Isle-of-Wight, shall meet at Nansemond court house; those for the counties of Southampton, Sussex, Surry and Prince George, shall meet at Sussex court-house; those for the counties of Brunswick, Mecklenburg and Lunenburg, shall meet at Lunenburg court-house; those for the counties of Dinwiddie, Amelia and Chesterfield, shall meet at Chesterfield court-house; those for the counties of Powhatan, Cumberland, Goochland, Henrico and Hanover, shall meet at Henrico court-house; those for the counties of Prince Edward, Charlotte and Halifax, shall meet at Charlotte court-house; those for the counties of Henry, Pittsylvania and Bedford, shall meet at Pittsylvania court-house; those for the counties of Buckingham, Amherst, Albemarle and Fluvanna, shall meet at Albemarle court-house; those for the counties of Botetourt, Rockbridge, Montgomery, Washington and Kentucky, shall meet at Botetourt court-house; those for the counties of Augusta, Rockingham and Greenbrier, shall meet at Augusta court-house; those for the counties of Accomack and Northampton, shall meet at Accomack court-house; those for the counties of Elizabeth City, Warwick, York, Gloucester, James City, Charles City and New

Kent, shall meet at James City court-house; those for the counties of Middlesex, Essex, King and Queen, King William and Caroline, shall meet at King and Queen court-house; those for the counties of Lancaster, Northumberland, Richmond and Westmoreland, shall meet at Richmond court-house; those for the counties of King George, Stafford, Spotsylvania, Prince William and Fairfax, shall meet at Spotsylvania court-house; those for the counties of Loudoun and Fauquier, shall meet at Loudoun court-house; those for the counties of Culpeper, Orange and Louisa, shall meet at Orange court-house; those for the counties of Shenandoah and Frederick, shall meet at Frederick court-house; those for the counties of Hampshire and Berkeley, shall meet at Berkeley court house; and those for the counties of Yohogania, Monongalia and Ohio, shall meet at Monongalia court-house; and shall fix on such place in some one of the counties in their district as shall be most proper for situating a grammar school-house, endeavouring that the situation be as central as may be to the inhabitants of the said counties, that it be furnished with good water, convenient to plentiful supplies of provision and fuel, and more than all things that it be healthy. And if a majority of the overseers present should not concur in their choice of any one place proposed, the method of determining shall be as follows: If two places only were proposed, and the votes be divided, they shall decide between them by fair and equal lot; if more than two places were proposed, the question shall be put on those two which on the first division had the greater number of votes; or if no two places had a greater number of votes than the others, as where the votes shall have been equal between one or both of them and some other or others, then it shall be decided by fair and equal lot (unless it can be agreed by a majority of votes) which of the places having equal numbers shall be thrown out of the competition, so that the question shall be put on the remaining two, and if on this ultimate question the votes shall be equally divided, it shall then be decided finally by lot.

SECT. X. THE said overseers having determined the place at which the grammer school for their district shall be built, shall forthwith (unless they can otherwise agree with the proprietors of the circumjacent lands as to location and price) make application to the clerk of the county in which the said house is to be situated, who shall thereupon issue a writ, in the nature of a writ of ad quod damnum, directed to the sheriff of the said county commanding him to summon and impannel twelve fit persons to meet at the place, so destined for the grammer school-house, on a certain day, to be named in the said writ, not less than five, nor more than ten, days from the date thereof; and also to give notice of the same to the proprietors and tenants of the lands to be viewed, if they be to be found within the county, and if not, then to their agents therein if any they have. Which freeholders shall be charged by the said sheriff impartially, and to the best of their skill and judgement to view the lands round about the said place, and to locate and circumscribe, by certain metes and bounds, one hundred acres thereof, having regard therein principally to the benefit and convenience of the said school, but respecting in some measure also the convenience of the said proprietors, and to value and appraise the same in so many several respective interests and estates therein. And after such location and appraisement so made, the said sheriff shall forthwith return the same under the hands and seals of the said jurors, together with the writ, to the clerk's office of the said county and the right and property of the said proprietors and tenants in the said lands so circumscribed shall be immediately devested and be transferred to the commonwealth for the use of the said grammar school, in full and absolute dominion, any want of consent or disability to consent in the said owners or tenants notwithstanding. But it shall not be lawful for the said overseers so to situate the said grammar school-house, nor to the said jurors so to locate the said lands, as to include the mansion-house of the proprietor of the lands, nor the offices, curtilage, or garden, thereunto immediately belonging.

SECT. XI. THE said overseers shall forthwith proceed to have a house of brick or stone, for the said grammar school, with necessary offices, built on the said lands, which grammer school-house shall contain a room for the school, a hall to dine in, four rooms for a master and usher, and ten or twelve lodging rooms for the scholars.

SECT. XII. To each of the said grammar schools shall be allowed out of the public treasury, the sum of pounds, out of which shall be paid by the Treasurer, on warrant from the Auditors, to the proprietors or tenants of the lands located, the value of their several interests as fixed by the jury, and the balance thereof shall be delivered to the said overseers to defray the expence of the said buildings.

SECT. XIII. IN these grammar schools shall be taught the Latin and Greek languages, English grammar, geography, and the higher part of numerical arithmetick, to wit, vulgar and decimal fractions, and the extraction of the square and cube roots.

SECT. XIV. A visiter from each county constituting the district shall be appointed, by the overseers, for the county, in the month of October annually, either from their own body or from their county at large, which visiters or the greater part of them, meeting together at the said grammar school on the first Monday in November, if fair, and if not, then on the next fair day, excluding Sunday, shall have power to choose their own Rector, who shall call and preside at future meetings, to employ from time to time a master, and if necessary, an usher, for the said school, to remove them at their will, and to settle the price of tuition to be paid by the scholars. They shall also visit the school twice in every year at the least, either together or separately at their discretion, examine the scholars, and see that any general plan of instruction recommended by the visiters of William and Mary College shall be observed. The said masters and ushers, before they enter on the execution of their office, shall give assurance of fidelity to the commonwealth.

SECT. XV. A steward shall be employed, and removed at will by the master, on such wages as the visiters shall direct; which steward shall see to the procuring provisions, fuel, servants for cooking, waiting, house cleaning, washing, mending, and gardening on the most reasonable terms; the expence of which, together with the steward's wages, shall be divided equally among all the scholars boarding either on the public or private expence. And the part of those who are on private expence, and also the price of their tuitions due to the master or usher, shall be paid quarterly by the respective scholars, their parents, or guardians, and shall be recoverable, if withheld, together with costs, on motion in any Court of Record, ten days notice thereof being previously given to the party, and a jury impannelled to try the issue joined, or enquire of the damages. The said steward shall also, under the direction of the visiters, see that the houses be kept in repair, and necessary enclosures be made and repaired, the accounts for which, shall, from time to time, be submitted to the Auditors, and on their warrant paid by the Treasurer.

SECT. XVI. EVERY overseer of the hundred schools shall, in the month of September annually, after the most diligent and impartial examination and enquiry, appoint from among the boys who shall have been two years at the least at some one of the schools under his superintendance, and whose parents are too poor to give them farther education, some one of the best and most promising genius and disposition, to proceed to the grammar school of his district; which appointment shall be made in the court-house of the county, on the court day for that month, if fair, and if not, then on the next fair day, excluding Sunday, in the presence of the Aldermen, or two of them at the least, assembled on the bench for that purpose, the said overseer being previously sworn by them to make such appointment, without favor or affection, according to the best of his skill and judgment, and being interrogated by the said Aldermen, either on their own motion, or on suggestions from the parents, guardians, friends, or teachers of the children, competitors for such appointment; which teachers shall attend for the information of the Aldermen. On which interrogatories the said Aldermen, if they be not satisfied with the appointment proposed, shall have right to negative it; whereupon the said visiter may proceed to make a new appointment, and the said Aldermen again to interrogate and negative, and so toties quoties until an appointment be approved.

SECT. XVII. EVERY boy so appointed shall be authorised to proceed to the grammar school of his district, there to be educated and boarded during such time as is hereafter limited; and his quota of the expences of the house together with a compensation to the master or usher for his tuition, at the rate of twenty dollars by the year, shall be paid by the Treasurer quarterly on warrant from the Auditors.

SECT. XVIII. A visitation shall be held, for the purpose of probation, annually at the said grammar school on the last Monday in September, if fair, and if not, then on the next fair day, excluding Sunday, at which one third of the boys sent thither by appointment of the said overseers, and who shall have been there one year only, shall be discontinued as public foundationers, being those who, on the most diligent examination and enquiry, shall be thought to be of the least promising genius and disposition; and of those who shall have been there two years, all shall be discontinued, save one only the best in genius and disposition, who shall be at liberty to continue there four years longer on the public foundation, and shall thence forward be deemed a senior.

SECT. XIX. THE visiters for the districts which, or any part of which, be southward and westward of James river, as known by that name, or by the names of Fluvanna and Jackson's river, in every other year, to wit, at the probation meetings held in the years, distinguished in the Christian computation by odd numbers, and the visiters for all the other districts at their said meetings to be held in those years, distinguished by even numbers, after diligent examination and enquiry as before directed, shall chuse one among the said seniors, of the best learning and most hopeful genius and disposition, who shall be authorised by them to proceed to William and Mary College, there to be educated, boarded, and clothed, three years; the expence of which annually shall be paid by the Treasurer on warrant from the Auditors.

A Bill Declaring Who Shall Be Deemed
Citizens of this Commonwealth

SECTION I. BE it enacted by the General Assembly, that all white persons born within the territory of this commonwealth and all who have resided therein two years next before the passing of this act, and all who shall hereafter migrate into the same; and shall before any court of record give satisfactory proof by their own oath or affirmation, that they intend to reside therein, and moreover shall give assurance of fidelity to the commonwealth; and all infants wheresoever born, whose father, if living, or otherwise, whose mother was, a citizen at the time of their birth, or who migrate hither, their father, if living, or otherwise their mother becoming a citizen, or who migrate hither without father or mother, shall be deemed citizens of this commonwealth, until they relinquish that character in manner as herein after expressed: And all others not being citizens of any the United States of America, shall be deemed aliens. The clerk of the court shall enter such oath of record, and give the person taking the same a certificate thereof, for which he shall receive the fee of one dollar. And in order to preserve to the citizens of this commonwealth, that natural right, which all men have of relinquishing the country, in which birth, or other accident may have thrown them, and, seeking subsistance and happiness wheresoever they may be able, or may hope to find them: And to declare unequivocally what circumstances shall be deemed evidence of an intention in any citizen to exercise that right, it is enacted and declared, that whensoever any citizen of this commonwealth, shall by word of mouth in the presence of the court of the county, wherein he resides, or of the General Court, or by deed in writing, under his hand and seal, executed in the presence of three witnesses, and by them proved in either of the said courts, openly declare to the same court, that he relinquishes the character of a citizen, and shall depart the commonwealth; or whensoever he shall without such declaration depart the commonwealth and enter into the service of any other state, not in enmity with this, or any other of the United States of America, or do any act whereby he shall become a subject or citizen of such state, such person shall be considered as having exercised his natural right of expatriating himself, and shall be deemed no citizen of this commonwealth from the time of his departure. The free white inhabitants of every of the states, parties to the American confederation, paupers, vagabonds and fugitives from justice excepted, shall be intitled to all rights, privileges, and immunities of free citizens in this commonwealth, and shall have free egress, and regress, to and from the same, and shall enjoy therein, all the privileges of trade, and commerce, subject to the same duties, impositions and restrictions as the citizens of this commonwealth. And if any person guilty of, or charged with treason, felony, or other high misdemeanor, in any of the said states, shall flee from justice and be found in this commonwealth, he shall, upon demand of the Governor, or Executive power of the state, from which he fled, be delivered up to be removed to the state having jurisdiction of his offence. Where any person holding property, within this commonwealth, shall be attainted within any of the said states, parties to the said confederation, of any of those crimes, which by the laws of this commonwealth shall be punishable by forfeiture of such property, the said property shall be disposed of in the same manner as it would have been if the owner thereof had been attainted of the like crime in this commonwealth.

Report on Government for Western Territory

March 1, 1784

THE COMMITTEE appointed to prepare a plan for the temporary Government of the Western territory have agreed to the following resolutions:

Resolved that the territory ceded or to be ceded by Individual States to the United States whensoever the same shall have been purchased of the Indian Inhabitants & offered for sale by the U. S. shall be formed into distinct States bounded in the following manner as nearly as such cessions will admit, that is to say; Northwardly & Southwardly by parallels of latitude so that each state shall comprehend from South to North two degrees of latitude beginning to count from the completion of thirty-one degrees North of the equator, but any territory Northwardly of the 47th degree shall make part of the state—next below, and Eastwardly & Westwardly they shall be bounded, those on the Mississippi by that river on one side and the meridian of the lowest point of the rapids of Ohio on the other; and those adjoining on the East by the same meridian on their Western side, and on their eastern by the meridian of the Western cape of the mouth of the Great Kanhaway. And the territory eastward of this last meridian between the Ohio, Lake Erie & Pennsylvania shall be one state.

That the settlers within the territory so to be purchased & offered for sale shall, either on their own petition, or on the order of Congress, receive authority from them, with appointments of time and place for their free males of full age to meet together for the purpose of establishing a temporary government, to adopt the constitution & laws of any one of these states, so that such laws nevertheless shall be subject to alteration by their ordinary legislature, and to erect, subject to a like alteration counties or townships for the election of members for their legislature.

That such temporary government shall only continue in force in any state until it shall have acquired 20,000 free inhabitants, when, giving due proof thereof to Congress, they shall receive from them authority with appointments of time and place to call a Convention of representatives to establish a permanent Constitution & Government for themselves.

Provided that both the temporary & permanent Governments be established on these principles as their basis. 1, That they shall forever remain a part of the United States of America. 2, That in their persons, property & territory, they shall be subject to the Government of the United States in Congress assembled and to the articles of confederation in all those cases in which the original states shall be so subject. 3, That they shall be subject to pay a part of the federal debts contracted or to be contracted to be apportioned on them by Congress, according to the same common rule and measure by which apportionments thereof shall be made on the other states. 4, That their respective Governments shall be in republican forms, and shall admit no person to be a citizen, who holds any hereditary title. 5, That after the year 1800 of the Christian æra, there shall be neither slavery nor involuntary servitude in any of the said states, otherwise than in punishment of crimes, whereof the party shall have been duly convicted to have been personally guilty.

That whenever any of the sd states shall have, of free inhabitants as many as shall then be in any one the least numerous of the thirteen original states, such state shall be admitted by it's delegates into the Congress of the United States, on an equal footing with the said original states: After which the assent of two thirds of the United States in Congress assembled shall be requisite in all those cases, wherein by the Confederation the assent of nine States is now required. Provided the consent of nine states to such admission may be obtained according to the eleventh of the Articles of Confederation. Until such admission by their delegates into Congress, any of the said states, after the establishment of their temporary Government, shall have authority to keep a sitting Member in Congress, with a right of debating, but not of voting.

That the territory Northward of the 45th degree, that is to say of the completion of 45° from the Equator & extending to the Lake of the Woods, shall be called SYLVANIA:

That of the territory under the 45th & 44th degrees that which lies Westward of Lake Michigan shall be called MICHIGANIA, and that which is Eastward thereof within the peninsula formed by the lakes & waters of Michigan, Huron, St. Clair and Erie, shall be called CHERRONESUS, and shall include any part of the peninsula which may extend above the 45th degree.

Of the territory under the 43^d & 42^d degrees, that to the Westward thro' which the Assenisipi or Rock river runs shall be called ASSENISIPIA, and that to the Eastward in which are the fountains of the Muskingum, the two Miamis of Ohio, the Wabash, the Illinois, the Miami of the lake and Sandusky rivers, shall be called METROPOTAMIA.

Of the territory which lies under the 41st & 40th degrees the Western, thro which the river Illinois runs, shall be called ILLINOIA; that next adjoining to the Eastward SARATOGA, and that between this last & Pennsylvania & extending from the Ohio to Lake Erie shall be called WASHINGTON.

Of the territory which lies under the 39th & 38th degrees to which shall be added so much of the point of land within the fork of the Ohio & Missisipi as lies under the 37th degree, that to the Westward within & adjacent to which are the confluences of the rivers Wabash, Shawanee, Tanisse, Ohio, Illinois, Missisipi & Missouri, shall be called POLYPOTAMIA, and that to the Eastward farther up the Ohio otherwise called the PELISIPI shall be called PELISIPIA.

That the preceding articles shall be formed into a charter of Compact, shall be duly executed by the President of the U. S. in Congress assembled under his hand and the seal of the United States, shall be promulgated, and shall stand as fundamental constitutions between the thirteen original States, & those now newly described unalterable but by the joint consent of the U. S. in Congress assembled and of the particular state within which such alteration is proposed to be made.

Observations on the Whale-Fishery

WHALE OIL enters, as a raw material, into several branches of manufacture, as of wool, leather, soap: it is used also in painting, architecture and navigation. But its great consumption is in lighting houses and cities. For this last purpose however it has a powerful competitor in the vegetable oils. These do well in warm, still weather, but they fix with cold, they extinguish easily with the wind, their crop is precarious, depending on the seasons, and to yield the same light, a larger wick must be used, and greater quantity of oil consumed. Estimating all these articles of difference together, those employed in lighting cities find their account in giving about 25 per cent. more for whale than for vegetable oils. But higher than this the whale oil, in its present form, cannot rise; because it then becomes more advantageous to the city-lighters to use others. This competition then limits its price, higher than which no encouragement can raise it, and becomes, as it were, a law of its nature, but, at this low price, the whale fishery is the poorest business into which a merchant or sailor can enter. If the sailor, instead of wages, has a part of what is taken, he finds that this, one year with another, yields him less than he could have got as wages in any other business. It is attended too with great risk, singular hardships, and long absences from his family. If the voyage is made solely at the expence of the merchant, he finds that, one year with another, it does not reimburse him his expences. As, for example, an English ship of 300 ton, and 42. hands brings home, communibus annis, after a four months voyage, 25. ton of oil, worth 437l. 10s. sterl. but the wages of the officers and seamen will be 400l. The Outfit then and the merchant's profit must be paid by the government. And it is accordingly on this idea that the British bounty is calculated. From the poverty of this business then it has happened that the nations, who have taken it up, have successively abandoned it. The Basques began it. But, tho' the most economical and enterprising of the inhabitants of France, they could not continue it; and it is said they never employed more than 30. ships a year. The Dutch and Hanse towns succeeded

them. The latter gave it up long ago tho' they have continued
to lend their name to British and Dutch oils. The English
carried it on, in competition with the Dutch, during the last,
and beginning of the present century. But it was too little
profitable for them in comparison with other branches of
commerce open to them. In the mean time too the inhabitants of the barren Island of Nantucket had taken up this fishery, invited to it by the whales presenting themselves on
their own shore. To them therefore the English relinquished
it, continuing to them, as British subjects, the importation of
their oils into England duty free, while foreigners were subject to a duty of 18l. 5s. sterl. a ton. The Dutch were enabled
to continue it long, because, 1. They are so near the northern
fishing grounds, that a vessel begins her fishing very soon after she is out of port. 2. They navigate with more economy
than the other nations of Europe. 3. Their seamen are content
with lower wages: and 4. their merchants with a lower profit
on their capital. Under all these favorable circumstances however, this branch of business, after long languishing, is at
length nearly extinct with them. It is said they did not send
above half a dozen ships in pursuit of the whale this present
year. The Nantuckois then were the only people who exercised this fishery to any extent at the commencement of the
late war. Their country, from its barrenness, yielding no subsistence, they were obliged to seek it in the sea which surrounded them. Their economy was more rigorous than
that of the Dutch. Their seamen, instead of wages, had a
share in what was taken. This induced them to fish with
fewer hands, so that each had a greater dividend in the profit.
It made them more vigilant in seeking game, bolder in pursuing it, and parcimonious in all their expences. London was
their only market. When therefore, by the late revolution,
they became aliens in great Britain, they became subject to
the alien duty of 18l. 5s. the ton of oil, which being more than
equal to the price of the common whale oil, they were
obliged to abandon that fishery. So that this people, who before the war had employed upwards of 300 vessels a year in
the whale fishery, (while great Britain had herself never employed one hundred) have now almost ceased to exercise it.
But they still had the seamen, the most important material for

this fishery; and they still retained the spirit of fishing: so that at the reestablishment of peace they were capable in a very short time of reviving their fishery in all its splendor. The British government saw that the moment was critical. They knew that their own share in that fishery was as nothing. That the great mass of fishermen was left with a nation now separated from them: that these fishermen however had lost their ancient market, had no other resource within their country to which they could turn, and they hoped therefore they might, in the present moment of distress, be decoyed over to their establishments, and be added to the mass of their seamen. To effect this they offered extravagant advantages to all persons who should exercise the whale fishery from British establishments. But not counting with much confidence on a long connection with their remaining possessions on the continent of America, foreseeing that the Nantuckois would settle in them preferably, if put on an equal footing with those of great Britain, and that thus they might have to purchase them a second time, they confined their high offers to settlers in Great Britain. The Nantuckois, left without resource by the loss of their market, began to think of removing to the British dominions: some to Nova Scotia, preferring smaller advantages, in the neighbourhood of their ancient country and friends; others to great Britain postponing country and friends to high premiums. A vessel was already arrived from Halifax to Nantucket to take off some of those who proposed to remove; two families had gone on board and others were going, when a letter was received there, which had been written by Monsieur le Marquis de la Fayette to a gentleman in Boston, and transmitted by him to Nantucket. The purport of the letter was to dissuade their accepting the British proposals, and to assure them that their friends in France would endeavour to do something for them. This instantly suspended their design: not another went on board, and the vessel returned to Halifax with only the two families.

In fact the French Government had not been inattentive to the views of the British, nor insensible of the crisis. They saw the danger of permitting five or six thousand of the best seamen existing to be transferred by a single stroke to the marine strength of their enemy, and to carry over with them an art which they possessed almost exclusively. The counterplan which they set on foot was to tempt the Nantuckois by high offers to come and settle in France. This was in the year 1785. The British however had in their favour a sameness of language, religion, laws, habits and kindred. 9 families only, of 33 persons in the whole came to Dunkirk; so that this project was not likely to prevent their emigration to the English establishments, if nothing else had happened.

France had effectually aided in detaching the U. S. of America from the *force* of Great Britain. But as yet they seemed to have indulged only a silent wish to detach them from her *commerce*. They had done nothing to induce that event. In the same year 1785, while M. de Calonne was in treaty, with the Nantuckois, an estimate of the commerce of the U. S. was submitted to the count de Vergennes, and it was shewn that, of 3. millions of pounds sterling to which their exports amounted, one third might be brought to France and exchanged against her productions and manufactures advantageously for both nations, provided the obstacles of prohibition, monopoly, and duty were either done away or moderated as far as circumstances would admit. A committee, which had been appointed to investigate a particular one of these subjects, was thereupon instructed to extend its researches to the whole, and see what advantages and facilities the Government could offer for the encouragement of a general commerce with the United States. The Committee was composed of persons well skilled in commerce; and, after labouring assiduously for several months, they made their report: the result of which was given in the letter of his Majesty's Comptroller General of the 2d of Octob. 1786. wherein he stated the principles which should be established for the future regulation of the commerce between France and the United States. It was become tolerably evident, at the date of this letter, that the terms offered to the Nantuckois would not produce their emigration to Dunkirk; and that it would be safest in every event to offer some other alternative which might prevent their acceptance of the British offers. The obvious one was to open the ports of France to their oils, so that they might still exercise their fishery, remaining in their native country, and find a new market for its produce instead of that which they had lost. The article of Whale oil was accordingly distinguished, in the letter of M. de Calonne, by an immediate abatement of duty, and promise of further abatement after the year 1790. This letter was instantly sent to America, and bid fair to produce there the effect intended, by determining the fishermen to carry on their trade from their own homes, with the advantage only of a free market in France, rather than remove to Great Britain where a free market and great bounty were offered them. An Arret was still to be prepared to give legal sanction to the letter of M. de Calonne. M. Lambert, with a patience and assiduity almost unexampled, went through all the investigations necessary to assure himself that the conclusions of the Committee had been just. Frequent conferences on this subject were held in his presence; the Deputies of the Chambers of Commerce were heard, and the result was the Arret of Dec. 29. 1787. confirming the abatements of duty present and future, which the letter of Octob. 1786. had promised, and reserving to his Majesty to grant still further favours to that production, if on further information he should find it for the interest of the two Nations.

The English had now begun to deluge the markets of France with their whale oils: and they were enabled by the great premiums given by their Government to undersell the French fisherman, aided by feebler premiums, and the American aided by his poverty alone. Nor is it certain that these speculations were not made at the risk of the British Government, to suppress the French and American fishermen in their only market. Some remedy seemed necessary. Perhaps it would not have been a bad one to subject, by a general law, the merchandize of every nation and of every nature to pay additional duties in the ports of France exactly equal to the premiums and drawbacks given on the same merchandise by their own government. This might not only counteract the effect of premium in the instance of whale oils, but attack the whole British system of bounties and drawbacks by the aid of which they make London the center of commerce for the whole earth. A less general remedy, but an effectual one, was to prohibit the oils of all *European* nations: the treaty with England requiring only that she should be treated as well as

the most favoured *European* nation. But the remedy adopted
was to prohibit all oils without exception.

To know how this remedy will operate we must consider
the quantity of whale oil which France consumes annually,
the quantity she obtains from her own fishery; and if she obtains less than she consumes, we are to consider what will
follow this prohibition.

The annual consumption of France, as stated by a person
who has good opportunities of knowing it, is as follows.

	pesant.	*quintaux.*	*tons.*
Paris according to the registers of 1786.	2,800,000	28,000	1750
27. other cities lighted by M. Sangrain	800,000	8,000	500
Rouen.	500,000	5,000	312½
Bordeaux.	600,000	6,000	375
Lyon	300,000	3,000	187½
Other cities, leather and light	3,000,000	30,000	1875
	8,000,000	80,000	5000

Other calculations, reduce the consumption to about half
this. It is treating these with sufficient respect to place them
on an equal footing with the estimate of the person before
alluded to, and to suppose the truth half way between them.
We will call then the present consumption of France only
60,000 quintals, or 3750 ton a year. This consumption is increasing fast as the practice of lighting cities is becoming
more general, and the superior advantages of lighting them
with whale oil are but now beginning to be known.

What do the fisheries of France furnish? she has employed
this year 15. vessels in the Southern, and 2 in the Northern
fishery, carrying 4500 tons in the whole or 265 each on an
average. The English ships, led by Nantuckois as well as the
French, have as I am told never averaged, in the Southern
fishery, more than one fifth of their burthen, in the best year.
The 15 ships of France, according to this ground of calculation, and supposing the present to have been one of the best
years, should have brought, one with another, one fifth of 265
tons, or 53 tons each. But we are told they have brought near

the double of that, to wit 100 tons each and 1500 tons in the whole. Supposing the 2. Northern vessels to have brought home the cargo which is common from the Northern fishery, to wit, 25 tons each, the whole produce this year will then be 1550 tons. This is 5½ months provision or two fifths of the annual consumption. To furnish for the whole year, would require 40 ships of the same size, in years as fortunate as the present, and 85 communibus annis, 44 tons, or one sixth of the burthen, being as high an average as should be counted on, one year with another: and the number must be increased with the increasing consumption. France then is evidently not yet in a condition to supply her own wants. It is said indeed she has a large stock on hand unsold occasioned by the English competition. 33,000 quintals, including this year's produce, are spoken of. This is between 6. and 7. months provision: and supposing, by the time this is exhausted, that the next year's supply comes in, that will enable her to go on 5. or 6. months longer; say a twelvemonth in the whole. But, at the end of the twelvemonth, what is to be done? The Manufactures depending on this article cannot maintain their competition against those of other countries, if deprived of their equal means. When the alternative then shall be presented of letting them drop, or opening the ports to foreign whale oil, it is presumable the latter will be adopted, as the lesser evil. But it will be too late for America: her fishery, annihilated during the late war, only began to raise its head on the prospect of market held out by this country. Crushed by the Arret of Sept. 28. in its first feeble effort to revive, it will rise no more. Expeditions, which require the expence of the outfit of vessels, and from 9. to 12 months navigation, as the Southern fishery does, most frequented by the Americans, cannot be undertaken in sole reliance on a market which is opened and shut from one day to another, with little or no warning. The English alone then will remain to furnish these supplies, and they must be received even from them. We must accept bread from our enemies, if our friends cannot furnish it. This comes exactly to the point to which that government has been looking. She fears no rival in the whale fishery but America. Or rather, it is the whale fishery of America of which she is endeavouring to possess herself. It is for this

object she is making the present extraordinary efforts by
bounties and other encouragements: and her success so far is
very flattering. Before the war she had not 100 vessels in the
whale trade, while America employed 309. In 1786. Great Britain employed 151 vessels, in 1787. 286. in 1788. 314. nearly the
ancient American number; while the latter is fallen to about
80. They have just changed places then, England having
gained exactly what America has lost. France by her ports and
markets holds the balance between the two contending parties, and gives the victory, by opening and shutting them, to
which she pleases. We have still precious remains of seamen
educated in this fishery, and capable by their poverty, their
boldness and address, of recovering it from the English, in
spite of their bounties. But this Arret endangers the transferring to Great Britain every man of them who is not invincibly
attached to his native soil. There is no other nation in present
condition to maintain a competition with Great Britain in the
whale fishery. The expence at which it is supported on her
part seems enormous. 255 vessels, of 75,436 tons, employed by
her this year in the Northern fishery, at 42 men each; and 59.
in the Southern at 18 men each makes 11,772 men. These are
known to have cost the government 15l. each, or 176,580l. in
the whole, and that to employ the principal part of them from
3. to 4. months only. The Northern ships have brought home
20. and the Southern 60. tons of oil on an average, making
8,640 tons, every ton of oil then has cost the government 20l.
in bounty. Still, if they can beat us out of the field and have
it to themselves, they will think their money well employed.
If France undertakes solely the competition against them, she
must do it at equal expence. The trade is too poor to support
itself. The 85 ships necessary to supply even her present consumption, bountied as the English are, will require a sacrifice
of 1,285,200 livres a year, to maintain 3,570 seamen, and that a
part of the year only. And if she will push it to 12,000 men
in competition with England, she must sacrifice, as they do,
4. or 5. millions a year. The same number of men might, with
the same bounty, be kept in as constant employ carrying
stone from Bayonne to Cherburg, or coal from Newcastle to
Havre, in which navigations they would be always at hand,
and become as good seamen. The English consider among

their best sailors those employed in carrying coal from New-castle to London. France cannot expect to raise her fishery, even to the supply of her own consumption, in one year or in several years. Is it not better then, by keeping her ports open to the U. S. to enable them to aid in maintaining the field against the common adversary, till she shall be in condi-tion to take it herself, and to supply her own wants? Other-wise her supplies must aliment that very force which is keeping her under. On our part, we can never be dangerous competitors to France. The extent to which we can exercise this fishery is limited to that of the barren island of Nan-tucket, and a few similar barren spots; its duration to the pleasure of this government, as we have no other market.

A material observation must be added here. Sudden vicis-situdes of opening and shutting ports, do little injury to mer-chants settled on the opposite coast, watching for the opening, like the return of a tide, and ready to enter with it. But they ruin the adventurer whose distance requires 6 months notice. Those who are now arriving from America, in consequence of the Arret of Dec. 29. will consider it as the false light which has led them to their ruin. They will be apt to say that they come to the ports of France by invitation of that Arret, that the subsequent one of Sept. 28. which drives them from those ports, founds itself on a single principle, viz. 'that the prohibition of foreign oils is the most useful encour-agement which can be given to that branch of industry.' They will say that, if this be a true principle, it was as true on the 29th. of Dec. 1787. as on the 28th. of Sept. 1788. It was then weighed against other motives, judged weaker, and over-ruled, and it is hard it should be now revived to ruin them.

The Refinery for whale oil lately established at Rouen, seems to be an object worthy of national attention. In order to judge of its importance, the different qualities of whale oil must be noted. Three qualities are known in the American and English markets. 1. That of the Spermaceti whale. 2. Of the Groenland whale. 3. Of the Brazil whale. 1. The Sperma-ceti whale found by the Nantucketmen in the neighbourhood of the western Islands, to which they had gone in pursuit of other whales, retired thence to the coast of Guinea, afterwards to that of Brazil, and begins now to be best found in the latitude of the cape of good hope, and even of cape Horn. He is an active, fierce animal and requires vast address and boldness in the fisherman. The inhabitants of Brazil make little expeditions from their coast, and take some of these fish. But the Americans are the only distant people who have been in the habit of seeking and attacking them in numbers. The British however, led by the Nantuckois whom they have decoyed into their service, have begun this fishery. In 1785 they had 18 ships in it; in 1787, 38: in 1788, 54. or as some say 64. I have calculated on the middle number 59. Still they take but a very small proportion of their own demand. We furnish the rest. Theirs is the only market to which we carry that oil, because it is the only one where its properties are known. It is luminous, resists coagulation by cold to the 41st. degree of Farenheit's thermometer, and 4th. of Reaumur's, and yields no smell at all. It is used therefore within doors to lighten shops, and even in the richest houses for antichambers, stairs, galleries, &c. it sells at the London market for treble the price of common whale oil. This enables the adventurer to pay the duty of 18l. 5s. sterl. the ton, and still to have a living profit. Besides the mass of oil produced from the whole body of the whale, his head yields 3. or 4. barrels of what is called head-matter, from which is made the solid Spermaceti used for medicine and candles. This sells by the pound at double the price of the oil. The disadvantage of this fishery is that the sailors are from 9. to 12. months absent on the voyage, of course they are not at hand on any sudden emergency, and are even liable to be taken before they know that a war is begun. It must be added on the subject of this whale, that he is rare, and shy, soon abandoning the grounds where he is hunted. This fishery being less losing than the other, and often profitable, will occasion it to be so thronged soon, as to bring it on a level with the other. It will then require the same expensive support, or to be abandoned.

2. The Groenland whale oil is next in quality. It resists coagulation by cold to 36°. of Farenheit and 2°. of Reaumur; but it has a smell insupportable within doors, and is not luminous. It sells therefore in London at about 16l. the ton. This whale is clumsy and timid, he dives when struck, and comes up to breathe by the first cake of ice, where the fisher-

men need little address or courage to find and take him. This is the fishery mostly frequented by European nations; it is this fish which yields the fin in quantity, and the voyages last about 3. or 4. months.

3. The third quality is that of the small Brazil whale. He was originally found on the coast of Nantucket, and first led that people to this pursuit. He retired first to the banks of Newfoundland, then to the western islands; and is now found within soundings on the coast of Brazil, during the months of December, January, February and March. This oil chills at 50°. of Farenheit and 8°. of Reaumur, is black and offensive, worth therefore but 13l. the ton in London. In warm summer nights however it burns better than the Groenland oil.

The qualities of the oils thus described, it is to be added that an individual has discovered methods 1. of converting a great part of the oil of the spermaceti whale into the solid substance called spermaceti, heretofore produced from his head alone. 2. Of refining the Groenland whale oil, so as to take from it all smell and render it limpid and luminous, as that of the spermaceti whale. 3. of curdling the oil of the Brazil whale into tallow, resembling that of the beef, and answering all its purposes. This person is engaged by the company which has established the Refinery at Rouen: their works will cost them half a million of livres, will be able to refine all the oil which can be used in the kingdom, and even to supply foreign markets.—The effect of this refinery then would be 1. to supplant the solid spermaceti of all other nations by theirs of equal quality and lower price. 2. to substitute, instead of spermaceti oil, their black whale oil, refined, of equal quality and lower price. 3. to render the worthless oil of the Brazil whale equal in value to tallow: and 4. by accomodating these oils to uses, to which they could never otherwise have been applied, they will extend the demand beyond its present narrow limits to any supply which can be furnished, and thus give the most effectual encouragement and extension to the whale fishery. But these works were calculated on the Arret of Dec. 29. which admitted here freely and fully the produce of the American fishery. If confined to that of the French fishery alone, the enterprise may fail for want of matter to work on.

After this review of the whale fishery as a Political institution, a few considerations shall be added on its produce as a basis of Commercial exchange between France and the United-States. The discussions it has undergone on former occasions, in this point of view, leaves little new to be now urged.

The United-States not possessing mines of the precious metals, they can purchase necessaries from other nations so far only as their produce is received in exchange. Without enumerating our smaller articles, we have three of principal importance, proper for the French market, to wit, Tobacco, whale oil, and rice. The first and most important is Tobacco. This might furnish an exchange for 8. millions of the productions of this country: but it is under a monopoly, and that not of a mercantile, but a financiering company, whose interest is to pay in money, and not in merchandise; and who are so much governed by the spirit of simplifying their purchases and proceedings, that they find means to elude every endeavour on the part of government to make them diffuse their purchases among the merchants in general. Little profit is derived from this then as an article of exchange for the produce and manufactures of France. Whale oil might be next in importance; but that is now prohibited. American Rice is not yet of great, but it is of growing consumption in France, and being the only article of the three which is free, it may become a principal basis of exchange. Time and trial may add a fourth, that is, timber. But some essays, rendered unsuccessful by unfortunate circumstances, place that at present under a discredit, which it will be found hereafter not to have merited. The English know its value, and were supplied with it before the war. A spirit of hostility, since that event, led them to seek Russian rather than American supplies. A new spirit of hostility has driven them back from Russia, and they are now making contracts for American timber. But of the three articles before mentioned, proved by experience to be suitable for the French market, one is prohibited, one under monopoly, and one alone free, and that the smallest and of very limited consumption. The way to encourage purchasers is to multiply their means of payment. Whale oil might be an important one. In one scale is the interest of the millions who are lighted, shod or clothed with the help of it, and the thousands of labourers and manufacturers who would be employed in producing the articles which might be given in exchange for it, if received from America. In the other scale are the interests of the adventurers in the whale fishery; each of whom indeed, politically considered may be of more importance to the state than a simple labourer or manufacturer: but to make the estimate with the accuracy it merits, we should multiply the numbers in each scale into their individual importance, and see which preponderates.

Both governments have seen with concern that their commercial intercourse does not grow as rapidly as they would wish. The system of the United States is to use neither prohibitions nor premiums. Commerce there regulates itself freely, and asks nothing better. Where a government finds itself under the necessity of undertaking that regulation, it would seem that it should conduct it as an intelligent merchant would: that is to say, invite customers to purchase, by facilitating their means of payment, and by adapting goods to their taste. If this idea be just, government here has two operations to attend to, with respect to the commerce of the United States. 1. To do away, or to moderate, as much as possible, the prohibitions and monopolies of their materials for payment. 2. To encourage the institution of the principal manufactures which the necessities, or the habits of their new customers call for. Under this latter head a hint shall be suggested which must find its apology in the motive from which it flows, that is, a desire of promoting mutual interests and close friendship. 600,000 of the labouring poor of America, comprehending slaves under that denomination, are clothed in three of the simplest manufactures possible, to wit, Oznabrigs, Plains, and Duffel blankets. The first is a linen, the two last woollens. It happens too that they are used exactly by those who cultivate the tobacco and rice and in a good degree by those employed in the whale fishery. To these manufactures they are so habituated, that no substitute will be received. If the vessels which bring tobacco, rice and whale oil, do not find them in the ports of delivery, they must be sought where they can be found. That is in England at present. If they were made in France they would be gladly taken in ex-

change there. The quantities annually used by this description
of people, and their value are as follows.

Oznabrigs 2,700,000 aunes a 16. sous the aune worth	2,160,000l.
Plains 1,350,000 aunes a 2. livres the aune . .	2,700,000
Duffel blankets 300,000 a 7livres. 4sous. each .	2,160,000
	7,020,000

It would be difficult to say how much should be added for
the consumption of inhabitants of other descriptions. A great
deal surely. But the present view shall be confined to the one
description named. 7 millions of livres, are 9 millions of days
work of those who raise card, spin and weave the wool and
flax; and at 300 working days to the year, would maintain
30,000 people. To introduce these simple manufactures suppose government to give 5 per cent. on the value of what
should be exported of them, for 10. years to come. If none
should be exported, nothing would be to be paid; but on the
other hand, if the manufactures, with this encouragement
should rise to the full demand, it will be a sacrifice of
351,000livres. a year for 10. years only, to produce a perpetual
subsistence for more than 30,000 people, (for the demand
will grow with our population) while she must expend perpetually 1,285,000livres. a year to maintain the 3,570 seamen,
who would supply her with whale oil: that is to say, for each
seaman as much as for 30. labourers and manufacturers.

But to return to our subject, and to conclude.

Whether then we consider the Arret of Sept. 28. in a political or a commercial light, it would seem that the U. S.
should be excepted from its operation. Still more so when
they invoke against it the amity subsisting between the two
nations, the desire of binding them together by every possible
interest and connection, the several acts in favour of this exception, the dignity of legislation which admits not of
changes backwards and forwards, the interests of commerce
which require steady regulations, the assurances of the
friendly motives which have led the king to pass these acts,
and the hope that no cause will arise to change either his
motives or his measures towards us.

Plan for Establishing Uniformity in the Coinage, Weights, and Measures of the United States

COMMUNICATED TO THE HOUSE OF REPRESENTATIVES, JULY 13, 1790

New York, July 4, 1790

S IR:—In obedience to the order of the House of Representatives of January 15th, I have now the honor to enclose
you a report on the subject of measures, weights, and coins.
The length of time which intervened between the date of the
order and my arrival in this city, prevented my receiving it till
the 15th of April; and an illness which followed soon after
added, unavoidably, some weeks to the delay; so that it was
not till about the 20th May that I was able to finish the report. A desire to lessen the number of its imperfections induced me still to withhold it awhile, till, on the 15th of June,
came to my hands, from Paris, a printed copy of a proposition
made by the Bishop of Autun, to the National Assembly of
France, on the subject of weights and measures; and three
days afterwards I received, through the channel of the public
papers, the speech of Sir John Riggs Miller, of April 13th, in
the British House of Commons, on the same subject. In the
report which I had prepared, and was then about to give in,
I had proposed the latitude of 38°, as that which should fix
our standard, because it was the medium latitude of the
United States; but the proposition before the National Assembly of France, to take that of 45° as being a middle term
between the equator and both poles, and a term which consequently might unite the nations of both hemispheres, appeared to me so well chosen, and so just, that I did not
hesitate a moment to prefer it to that of 38°. It became necessary, of course, to conform all my calculations to that standard—an operation which has been retarded by my other occupations.

These circumstances will, I hope, apologize for the delay
which has attended the execution of the order of the House;
and, perhaps, a disposition on their part to have due regard
for the proceedings of other nations, engaged on the same

subject, may induce them still to defer deciding ultimately on it till their next session. Should this be the case, and should any new matter occur in the meantime, I shall think it my duty to communicate it to the House, as supplemental to the present report.

I have the honor to be, with sentiments of the most profound respect,

Sir, your most obedient and most humble servant.

The Secretary of State, to whom was referred, by the House of Representatives, to prepare and report a proper plan or plans for establishing uniformity in the currency, weights, and measures of the United States, in obedience thereto, makes the following report:—

To obtain uniformity in measures, weights, and coins, it is necessary to find some measure of invariable length, with which, as a standard, they may be compared.

There exists not in nature, as far as has been hitherto observed, a single subject or species of subject, accessible to man, which presents one constant and uniform dimension.

The globe of the earth itself, indeed, might be considered as invariable in all its dimensions, and that its circumference would furnish an invariable measure; but no one of its circles, great or small, is accessible to admeasurement through all its parts, and the various trials to measure definite portions of them, have been of such various result as to show there is no dependence on that operation for certainty.

Matter, then, by its mere extension, furnishing nothing invariable, its motion is the only remaining resource.

The motion of the earth round its axis, though not absolutely uniform and invariable, may be considered as such for every human purpose. It is measured obviously, but unequally, by the departure of a given meridian from the sun, and its return to it, constituting a solar day. Throwing together the inequalities of solar days, a mean interval, or day, has been found, and divided, by very general consent, into 86,400 equal parts.

A pendulum, vibrating freely, in small and equal arcs, may be so adjusted in its length, as, by its vibrations, to make this division of the earth's motion into 86,400 equal parts, called seconds of mean time.

Such a pendulum, then, becomes itself a measure of determinate length, to which all others may be referred to as to a standard.

But even a pendulum is not without its uncertainties.

1. The difficulty of ascertaining, in practice, its centre of oscillation, as depending on the form of the bob, and its distance from the point of suspension; the effect of the weight of the suspending wire towards displacing the centre of oscillation; that centre being seated within the body of the bob, and therefore inaccessible to the measure, are sources of considerable uncertainty.

2. Both theory and experience prove that, to preserve its isochronism, it must be shorter towards the equator, and longer towards the poles.

3. The height of the situation above the common level, as being an increment to the radius of the earth, diminishes the length of the pendulum.

4. The pendulum being made of metal, as is best, it varies its length with the variations in the temperature of the atmosphere.

5. To continue small and equal vibrations, through a sufficient length of time, and to count these vibrations, machinery and a power are necessary, which may exert a small but constant effort to renew the waste of motion; and the difficulty is so to apply these, as that they shall neither retard or accelerate the vibrations.

1. In order to avoid the uncertainties which respect the centre of oscillation, it has been proposed by Mr. Leslie, an ingenious artist of Philadelphia, to substitute, for the pendulum, a uniform cylindrical rod, without a bob.

Could the diameter of such a rod be infinitely small, the centre of oscillation would be exactly at two-thirds of the whole length, measured from the point of suspension. Giving it a diameter which shall render it sufficiently inflexible, the centre will be displaced, indeed; but, in a second rod not the (1) six hundred thousandth part of its length, and not the hundredth part as much as in a second pendulum with a

spherical bob of proper diameter. This displacement is so infinitely minute, then, that we may consider the centre of oscillation, for all practical purposes, as residing at two-thirds
of the length from the centre of suspension. The distance between these two centres might be easily and accurately ascertained in practice. But the whole rod is better for a standard
than any portion of it, because sensibly defined at both its
extremities.

2. The uncertainty arising from the difference of length requisite for the second pendulum, or the second rod, in different latitudes, may be avoided by fixing on some one latitude,
to which our standard shall refer. That of 38°, as being the
middle latitude of the United States, might seem the most
convenient, were we to consider ourselves alone; but connected with other nations by commerce and science, it is better to fix on that parallel which bids fairest to be adopted by
them also. The 45th, as being the middle term between the
equator and pole, has been heretofore proposed in Europe,
and the proposition has been lately renewed there under circumstances which may very possibly give it some effect. This
parallel is distinguished with us also as forming our principal
northern boundary. Let the completion of the 45th degree,
then, give the standard for our union, with the hope that it
may become a line of union with the rest of the world.

The difference between the second rod for 45° of latitude,
and that for 31°, our other extreme, is to be examined.

The second *pendulum* for 45° of latitude, according to Sir
Isaac Newton's computation, must be of (2) 39.14912 inches
English measure; and a *rod*, to vibrate in the same time, must
be of the same length between the centres of suspension and
oscillation; and, consequently, its whole length 58.7 (or, more
exactly, 58.72368) inches. This is longer than the rod which
shall vibrate seconds in the 31° of latitude, by about $\frac{1}{679}$ part
of its whole length; a difference so minute, that it might be
neglected, as insensible, for the common purposes of life, but,
in cases requiring perfect exactness, the second rod, found by
trial of its vibrations in any part of the United States, may be
corrected by computation for the (3) latitude of the place, and
so brought exactly to the standard of 45°.

3. By making the experiment in the level of the ocean, the

difference will be avoided, which a higher position might occasion.

4. The expansion and contraction of the rod with the change of temperature, is the fourth source of uncertainty before mentioned. According to the high authority so often quoted, an iron rod, of given length, may vary, between summer and winter, in temperate latitudes, and in the common exposure of house clocks, from $\frac{1}{1728}$ to $\frac{1}{2592}$ of its whole length, which, in a rod of 58.7 inches, will be from about two to three hundredths of an inch. This may be avoided by adjusting and preserving the standard in a cellar, or other place, the temperature of which never varies. Iron is named for this purpose, because the least expansible of the metals.

5. The practical difficulty resulting from the effect of the machinery and moving power is very inconsiderable in the present state of the arts; and, in their progress towards perfection, will become less and less. To estimate and obviate this, will be the artist's province. It is as nothing when compared with the sources of inaccuracy hitherto attending measures.

Before quitting the subject of the inconveniences, some of which attend the pendulum alone, others both the pendulum and rod, it must be added that the rod would have an accidental but very precious advantage over the pendulum in this country, in the event of our fixing the foot at the nearest aliquot part of either; for the difference between the common foot, and those so to be deduced, would be three times greater in the case of the pendulum than in that of the rod.

Let the standard of measure, then, be a uniform cylindrical rod of iron, of such length as, in latitude 45°, in the level of the ocean, and in a cellar, or other place, the temperature of which does not vary through the year, shall perform its vibrations in small and equal arcs, in one second of mean time.

A standard of invariable length being thus obtained, we may proceed to identify, by that, the measures, weights and coins of the United States; but here a doubt presents itself as to the extent of the reformation meditated by the House of Representatives. The experiment made by Congress in the year one thousand seven hundred and eighty-six, by declaring that there should be one money of account and payment through the United States, and that its parts and multiples should be in a decimal ratio, has obtained such general approbation, both at home and abroad, that nothing seems wanting but the actual coinage, to banish the discordant pounds, shillings, pence, and farthings of the different States, and to establish in their stead the new denominations. Is it in contemplation with the House of Representatives to extend a like improvement to our measures and weights, and to arrange them also in a decimal ratio? The facility which this would introduce into the vulgar arithmetic would, unquestionably, be soon and sensibly felt by the whole mass of the people, who would thereby be enabled to compute for themselves whatever they should have occasion to buy, to sell, or to measure, which the present complicated and difficult ratios place beyond their computation for the most part. Or, is it the opinion of the Representatives that the difficulty of changing the established habits of a whole nation opposes an insuperable bar to this improvement? Under this uncertainty, the Secretary of State thinks it his duty to submit alternative plans, that the House may, at their will, adopt either the one or the other, exclusively, or the one for the present and the other for a future time, when the public mind may be supposed to have become familiarized to it.

I. And first, on the supposition that the present measures and weights are to be retained but to be rendered uniform and invariable, by bringing them to the same invariable standard.

The first settlers of these States, having come chiefly from England, brought with them the measures and weights of that country. These alone are generally established among us, either by law or usage; and these, therefore, are alone to be retained and fixed. We must resort to that country for information of what they are, or ought to be.

This rests, principally, on the evidence of certain standard measures and weights, which have been preserved, of long time, in different deposits. But differences among these having been known to exist, the House of Commons, in the years 1757 and 1758, appointed committees to inquire into the original standards of their weights and measures. These committees, assisted by able mathematicians and artists, examined and compared with each other the several standard measures and weights, and made reports on them in the years 1758 and 1759. The circumstances under which these reports were made entitle them to be considered, as far as they go, as the best written testimony existing of the standard measures and weights of England; and as such, they will be relied on in the progress of this report.

MEASURES OF LENGTH.

The measures of length in use among us are:

The league of 3 miles,
The mile of 8 furlongs,
The furlong of 40 poles or perches,
The pole or perch of 5½ yards,
The fathom of 2 yards,
The ell of a yard and quarter,
The yard of 3 feet,
The foot of 12 inches, and
The inch of 10 lines.

On this branch of their subject, the committee of 1757–1758, says that the standard measures of length at the receipt of the exchequer, are a yard, supposed to be of the time of Henry VII., and a yard and ell supposed to have been made about the year 1601; that they are brass rods, very coarsely made, their divisions not exact, and the rods bent; and that in the year 1742, some members of the Royal Society had been at great pains in taking an exact measure of these standards, by very curious instruments, prepared by the ingenious Mr. Graham; that the Royal Society had had a brass rod made pursuant to their experiments, which was made so accurately, and by persons so skilful and exact, that it was thought not easy to obtain a more exact one; and the committee, in fact, found it to agree with the standards at the exchequer, as near as it was possible. They furnish no means, to persons at a distance, of knowing what this standard is. This, however, is supplied by the evidence of the second pendulum, which, according to the authority before quoted, is, at London, 39.1682 English inches, and, consequently, the second rod there is of 58.7523 of the same inches. When we shall have found, then, by actual trial, the second rod for 45° by adding the difference of their computed length, to wit: 287/10000 of an inch, or rather 3/10 of a line (which in practice will endanger less error than an attempt at so minute a fraction as the ten thousandth parts of an inch) we shall have the second rod of London, or a true measure of 58¾ English inches. Or, to shorten the operation, without varying the result,

Let the standard rod of 45° be divided into 587⅕ equal parts, and let each of these parts be declared a line.

10 lines an inch,	5½ yards a perch or pole,
12 inches a foot,	40 poles or perches a
3 feet a yard,	furlong,
3 feet 9 inches an ell,	8 furlongs a mile,
6 feet a fathom,	3 miles a league.

SUPERFICIAL MEASURES.

Our measures of surface are, the acre of 4 roods and the rood of 40 square poles; so established by a statute of 33 Edw. I. Let them remain the same.

MEASURES OF CAPACITY.

The measures of capacity in use among us are the following names and proportions:

The gill, four of which make a pint.

Two pints make a quart.

Two quarts a pottle.

Two pottles a gallon.

Two gallons a peck, dry measure.

Eight gallons make a measure called a firkin, in liquid substances, and a bushel, dry.

Two firkins, or bushels, make a measure called a rundlet or kilderkin, liquid, and a strike, dry.

Two kilderkins, or strikes, make a measure called a barrel, liquid, and a coomb, dry; this last term being ancient and little used.

Two barrels, or coombs, make a measure called a hogshead, liquid, or a quarter, dry; each being the quarter of a ton.

A hogshead and a third make a tierce, or third of a ton.

Two hogsheads make a pipe, butt, or puncheon; and

Two pipes make a ton.

But no one of these measures is of a determinate capacity. The report of the committee of 1757–8, shows that the gallon is of very various content; and that being the unit, all the others must vary with it.

The gallon and bushel contain—

224 and 1792 cubic inches, according to the standard wine gallon preserved at Guildhall.

231 and 1848, according to the statute of 5th of Anne.

264.8 and 2118.4, according to the ancient Rumford quart, of 1228, examined by the committee.

265.5 and 2124, according to three standard bushels preserved in the Exchequer, to wit: one of Henry VII., without a rim; one dated 1091, supposed for 1591, or 1601, and one dated 1601.

266.25 and 2130, according to the ancient Rumford gallon of 1228, examined by the committee.

268.75 and 2150, according to the Winchester bushel, as declared by statute 13, 14, William III., which has been the model for some of the grain States.

271, less 2 spoonfuls, and 2168, less 16 spoonfuls, according to a standard gallon of Henry VII., and another dated 1601, marked E. E., both in the Exchequer.

271 and 2168, according to a standard gallon in the Exchequer, dated 1601, marked E., and called the corn gallon.

272 and 2176, according to the three standard corn gallons last mentioned, as measured in 1688, by an artist for the Commissioners of the Excise, generally used in the seaport towns, and by mercantile people, and thence introduced into some of the grain States.

277.18 and 2217.44, as established for the measure of coal by the statute 12 Anne.

278 and 2224, according to the standard bushel of Henry VII., with a copper rim, in the Exchequer.

278.4 and 2227.2 according to two standard pints of 1601 and 1602, in the Exchequer.

280 and 2240, according to the standard quart of 1601, in the Exchequer.

282 and 2256, according to the standard gallon for beer and ale in the Treasury.

There are, moreover, varieties on these varieties, from the barrel to the ton, inclusive; for, if the barrel be of herrings, it must contain 28 gallons by the statute 13 Eliz. c. 11. If of wine, it must contain 31½ gallons by the statute 2 Henry VI. c. 11, and 1 Rich. III. c. 15. If of beer or ale, it must contain 34 gallons by the statute 1 William and Mary, c. 24, and the higher measures in proportion.

In those of the United States which have not adopted the statutes of William and Mary, and of Anne before cited, nor their substance, the wine gallon of 231 cubic inches rests on the authority of very long usage, before the 5th of Anne, the origin and foundation of which are unknown; the bushel is the Winchester bushel, by the 11 Henry VII. undefined; and the barrel of ale 32 gallons, and of beer 36 gallons, by the statute 23 Henry VIII. c. 4.

The Secretary of State is not informed whether there have been any, and what, alterations of these measures by the laws of the particular States.

It is proposed to retain this series of measures, but to fix the gallon to one determinate capacity, as the unit of measure, both wet and dry; for convenience is in favor of abolishing the distinction between wet and dry measures.

The wine gallon, whether of 224 or 231 cubic inches, may be altogether disregarded, as concerning, principally, the mercantile and the wealthy, the least numerous part of the society, and the most capable of reducing one measure to another by calculation. This gallon is little used among the mass of farmers, whose chief habits and interests are in the size of the corn bushel.

Of the standard measures before stated, two are principally distinguished in authority and practice. The statute bushel of 2150 cubic inches, which gives a gallon of 268.75 cubic inches, and the standard gallon of 1601, called the corn gallon of 271 or 272 cubic inches, which has introduced the mercantile bushel of 2276 inches. The former of these is most used in some of the grain States, the latter in others. The middle term of 270 cubic inches may be taken as a mutual compromise of convenience, and as offering this general advantage: that the bushel being of 2160 cubic inches, is exactly a cubic foot and a quarter, and so facilitates the conversion of wet and dry measures into solid contents and tonnage, and simplifies the

connection of measures and weights, as will be shown hereafter. It may be added, in favor of this, as a medium measure,
that eight of the standard, or statute measures before enumerated, are below this term, and nine above it.

The measures to be made for use, being four sided, with
    rectangular sides and bottom.
The pint will be 3 inches square, and 3¾ inches deep;
The quart 3 inches square, and 7½ inches deep;
The pottle 3 inches square, and 15 inches deep, or 4½, 5,
    and 6 inches.
The gallon 6 inches square, and 7½ inches deep, or 5, 6,
    and 9 inches;
The peck 6, 9, and 10 inches;
The half bushel 12 inches square, and 7½ inches deep; and
The bushel 12 inches square, and 15 inches deep, or 9, 15,
    and 16 inches.
Cylindrical measures have the advantage of superior
strength, but square ones have the greater advantage of en-
abling every one who has a rule in his pocket, to verify their
contents by measuring them. Moreover, till the circle can be
squared, the cylinder cannot be cubed, nor its contents exactly
expressed in figures.

Let the measures of capacity, then, for the United States
    be—
A gallon of 270 cubic inches;
The gallon to contain 2 pottles;
The pottle 2 quarts;
The quart 2 pints;
The pint 4 gills;
Two gallons to make a peck;
Eight gallons a bushel or firkin;
Two bushels, or firkin, a strike or kilderkin;
Two strikes, or kilderkins, a coomb or barrel;
Two coombs, or barrels, a quarter or hogshead;
A hogshead and a third one tierce;
Two hogsheads a pipe, butt, or puncheon; and
Two pipes a ton.
And let all measures of capacity of dry subjects be stricken
    with a straight strike.

WEIGHTS.

There are two series of weights in use among us; the one called avoirdupois, the other troy.

In the Avoirdupois series:

The pound is divided into 16 ounces;
The ounce into 16 drachms;
The drachm into 4 quarters.

In the Troy series:

The pound is divided into 12 ounces;
The ounce (according to the subdivision of the apothecaries) into 8 drachms;
The drachm into 3 scruples;
The scruple into 20 grains.

According to the subdivision for gold and silver, the ounce is divided into twenty pennyweights, and the pennyweight into twenty-four grains.

So that the pound troy contains 5760 grains, of which 7000 are requisite to make the pound avoirdupois; of course the weight of the pound troy is to that of the pound avoirdupois as 5760 to 7000, or as 144 to 175.

It is remarkable that this is exactly the proportion of the ancient liquid gallon of Guildhall of 224 cubic inches, to the corn gallon of 272; for 224 are to 272 as 144 to 175. (4.)

It is further remarkable still, that this is also the exact proportion between the specific weight of any measure of wheat, and of the same measure of water: for the statute bushel is of 64 pounds of wheat. Now as 144 to 175, so are 64 pounds to 77.7 pounds; but 77.7 pounds is known to be the weight of (5.) 2150.4 cubic inches of pure water, which is exactly the content of the Winchester bushel, as declared by the statute 13, 14, Will. 3. That statute determined the bushel to be a cylinder of 18½ inches diameter, and 8 inches depth. Such a cylinder, as nearly as it can be cubed, and expressed in figures, contains 2150.425 cubic inches; a result which reflects authority on the declaration of Parliament, and induces a favorable opinion of the care with which they investigated the contents of the ancient bushel, and also a belief that there might exist evidence of it at that day, unknown to the committees of 1758 and 1759.

We find, then, in a continued proportion 64 to 77.7 as 224 to 272, and as 144 to 175, that is to say, the specific weight of a measure of wheat, to that of the same measure of water, as the cubic contents of the wet gallon, to those of the dry; and as the weight of a pound troy to that of a pound avoirdupois.

This seems to have been so combined as to render it indifferent whether a thing were dealt out by weight or measure; for the dry gallon of wheat, and the liquid one of wine, were of the same weight; and the avoirdupois pound of wheat, and the troy pound of wine, were of the same measure. Water and the vinous liquors, which enter most into commerce, are so nearly of a weight, that the difference, in moderate quantities, would be neglected by both buyer and seller; some of the wines being a little heavier, and some a little lighter, than water.

Another remarkable correspondence is that between weights and measures. For 1000 ounces avoirdupois of pure water fill a cubic foot, with mathematical exactness.

What circumstances of the times, or purposes of barter or commerce, called for this combination of weights and measures, with the subjects to be exchanged or purchased, are not now to be ascertained. But a triple set of exact proportionals representing weights, measures, and the things to be weighed and measured, and a relation so integral between weights and solid measures, must have been the result of design and scientific calculation, and not a mere coincidence of hazard. It proves that the dry and wet measures, the heavy and light weights, must have been original parts of the system they compose—contrary to the opinion of the committee of 1757, 1758, who thought that the avoirdupois weight was not an ancient weight of the kingdom, nor ever even a legal weight, but during a single year of the reign of Henry VIII.; and, therefore, concluded, otherwise than will be here proposed, to suppress it altogether. Their opinion was founded chiefly on the silence of the laws as to this weight. But the harmony here developed in the system of weights and measures, of which the avoirdupois makes an essential member, corrobo-

rated by a general use, from very high antiquity, of that, or
of a nearly similar weight under another (6.) name, seem
stronger proofs that this is legal weight, than the mere silence
of the written laws is of the contrary.

Be this as it may, it is in such general use with us, that, on
the principle of popular convenience, its higher denominations, at least, must be preserved. It is by the avoirdupois
pound and ounce that our citizens have been used to buy and
sell. But the smaller subdivisions of drachms and quarters are
not in use with them. On the other hand, they have been used
to weigh their money and medicine with the pennyweights
and grains troy weight, and are not in the habit of using the
pounds and ounces of that series. It would be for their convenience, then, to suppress the pound and ounce troy, and
the drachm and quarter avoirdupois; and to form into one
series the avoirdupois pound and ounce, and the troy pennyweight and grain. The avoirdupois ounce contains 18 pennyweights 5½ grains troy weight. Divide it, then, into 18
pennyweights, and the pennyweight, as heretofore, into 24
grains, and the new pennyweight will contain between a third
and a quarter of a grain more than the present troy pennyweight; or, more accurately, it will be to that as 875 to 864—
a difference not to be noticed, either in money or medicine,
below the denomination of an ounce.

But it will be necessary to refer these weights to a determinate mass of some substance, the specific gravity of which
is invariable. Rain water is such a substance, and may be referred to everywhere, and through all time. It has been found
by accurate experiments that a cubic foot of rain water weighs
1000 ounces avoirdupois, standard weights of the exchequer.
It is true that among these standard weights the committee
report small variations; but this experiment must decide in
favor of those particular weights, between which, and an integral mass of water, so remarkable a coincidence has been
found. To render this standard more exact, the water should
be weighed always in the same temperature of air; as heat, by
increasing its volume, lessens its specific gravity. The cellar of
uniform temperature is best for this also.

Let it, then, be established that an ounce is of the weight
of a cube of rain water, of one-tenth of a foot; or, rather, that

it is the thousandth part of the weight of a cubic foot of rain water, weighed in the standard temperature; that the series of weights of the United States shall consist of pounds, ounces, pennyweights, and grains; whereof

24 grains shall be one pennyweight;

18 pennyweights one ounce;

16 ounces one pound.

COINS.

Congress, in 1786, established the money unit at 375.64 troy grains of pure silver. It is proposed to enlarge this by about the third of a grain in weight, or a mill in value; that is to say, to establish it at 376 (or, more exactly, 375.989343) instead of 375.64 grains; because it will be shown that this, as the unit of coin, will link in system with the units of length, surface, capacity, and weight, whenever it shall be thought proper to extend the decimal ratio through all these branches. It is to preserve the possibility of doing this, that this very minute alteration is proposed.

We have this proportion, then, 875 to 864, as 375.989343 grains troy to 371.2626277; the expression of the unit in the new grains.

Let it be declared, therefore, that the money unit, or dollar of the United States, shall contain 371.262 American grains of pure silver.

If nothing more, then, is proposed, than to render uniform and stable the system we already possess, this may be effected on the plan herein detailed; the sum of which is: 1st. That the present measures of length be retained, and fixed by an invariable standard. 2d. That the measures of surface remain as they are, and be invariable also as the measures of length to which they are to refer. 3d. That the unit of capacity, now so equivocal, be settled at a medium and convenient term, and defined by the same invariable measures of length. 4th. That the more known terms in the two kinds of weights be retained, and reduced to one series, and that they be referred to a definite mass of some substance, the specific gravity of which never changes. And 5th. That the quantity of pure silver in the money unit be expressed in parts of the weights so defined.

In the whole of this no change is proposed, except an insensible one in the troy grain and pennyweight, and the very minute one in the money unit.

II. But if it be thought that, either now, or at any future time, the citizens of the United States may be induced to undertake a thorough reformation of their whole system of measures, weights and coins, reducing every branch to the same decimal ratio already established in their coins, and thus bringing the calculation of the principal affairs of life within the arithmetic of every man who can multiply and divide plain numbers, greater changes will be necessary.

The unit of measure is still that which must give law through the whole system; and from whatever unit we set out, the coincidences between the old and new ratios will be rare. All that can be done, will be to choose such a unit as will produce the most of these. In this respect the second rod has been found, on trial, to be far preferable to the second pendulum.

MEASURES OF LENGTH.

Let the second rod, then, as before described, be the standard of measure; and let it be divided into five equal parts, each of which shall be called a foot; for, perhaps, it may be better generally to retain the name of the nearest present measure, where there is one tolerably near. It will be about one quarter of an inch shorter than the present foot.

Let the foot be divided into 10 inches;
The inch into 10 lines;
The line into 10 points;

Let 10 feet make a decad;
10 decads one rood;
10 roods a furlong;
10 furlongs a mile.

SUPERFICIAL MEASURES.

Superficial measures have been estimated, and so may continue to be, in squares of the measures of length, except in the case of lands, which have been estimated by squares, called roods and acres. Let the rood be equal to a square, every side of which is 100 feet. This will be 6.483 English feet less than the English (7.) rood every way, and 1311 square feet less in its whole contents; that is to say, about one-eighth; in which proportion, also, 4 roods will be less than the present acre.

Measures of Capacity.

Let the unit of capacity be the cubic foot, to be called a bushel. It will contain 1620.05506862 cubic inches, English; be about one-fourth less than that before proposed to be adopted as a medium; one-tenth less than the bushel made from 8 of the Guildhall gallons; and one-fourteenth less than the bushel made from 8 Irish gallons of 217.6 cubic inches.

Let the bushel be divided into 10 pottles;

Each pottle into 10 demi-pints;

Each demi-pint into 10 metres, which will be of a cubic inch each.

Let 10 bushels be a quarter, and

10 quarters a last, or double ton.

The measures for use being four-sided, and the sides and bottoms rectangular, the bushel will be a foot cube.

The pottle 5 inches square and four inches deep;

The demi-pint 2 inches square, and 2½ inches deep;

The metre, an inch cube.

Weights.

Let the weight of a cubic inch of rain water, or the thousandth part of a cubic foot, be called an ounce; and let the ounce be divided into 10 double scruples:

The double scruple into 10 carats;

The carat into 10 minims or demi-grains;

The minim into 10 mites.

Let 10 ounces make a pound;

10 pounds a stone;

16 stones a kental;

10 kentals a hogshead.

Coins.

Let the money unit, or dollar, contain eleventh-twelfths of an ounce of pure silver. This will be 376 troy grains, (or more exactly, 375.989343 troy grains,) which will be about a third of a grain, (or more exactly, .349343 of a grain,) more than the present unit. This, with the twelfth of alloy already established, will make the dollar or unit, of the weight of an ounce, or of a cubic inch of rain water, exactly. The series of mills, cents, dimes, dollars, and eagles, to remain as already established. (8.)

The second rod, or the second pendulum, expressed in the measures of other countries, will give the proportion between their measures and those of the United States.

Measures, weights and coins, thus referred to standards unchangeable in their nature, (as is the length of a rod vibrating seconds, and the weight of a definite mass of rain water,) will themselves be unchangeable. These standards, too, are such as to be accessible to all persons, in all times and places. The measures and weights derived from them fall in so nearly with some of those now in use, as to facilitate their introduction; and being arranged in decimal ratio, they are within the calculation of every one who possesses the first elements of arithmetic, and of easy comparison, both for foreigners and citizens, with the measures, weights, and coins of other countries.

A gradual introduction would lessen the inconveniences which might attend too sudden a substitution, even of an easier for a more difficult system. After a given term, for instance, it might begin in the custom-houses, where the merchants would become familiarized to it. After a further term, it might be introduced into all legal proceedings, and merchants and traders in foreign commodities might be required to use it in their dealings with one another. After a still further term, all other descriptions of people might receive it into common use. Too long a postponement, on the other hand, would increase the difficulties of its reception with the increase of our population.

Appendix, containing illustrations and developments of some passages of the preceding report.

(1.) In the second pendulum with a spherical bob, call the distance between the centres of suspension and of the bob, 2×19.575, or 2d, and the radius of the bob $= r$; then 2d : $r :: r : {}^{rr}\!/2d$ and $\frac{2}{5}$ of this last proportional expresses the displacement of the centre of oscillation, to wit: ${}^{2rr}\!/5 \times 2d = {}^{rr}\!/5d$.

Two inches have been proposed as a proper diameter for such a bob. In that case r will be $= 1$. inch, and $r/5d = 1/9787$ inches.

In the cylindrical second rod, call the length of the rod, 3×19.575. or 3d, and its radius $= r$ and $r/2 \times 3d = r/6d$ will express the displacement of the centre of oscillation. It is thought the rod will be sufficiently inflexible if it be $1/5$ of an inch in diameter. Then r will be $= .1$ inch, and $r/6d = 1/11745$ inches, which is but the 120th part of the displacement in the case of the pendulum with a spherical bob, and but the 689,710th part of the whole length of the rod. If the rod be even of half an inch diameter, the displacement will be but $1/1879$ of an inch, or $1/110356$ of the length of the rod.

(2.) Sir Isaac Newton computes the pendulum for 45° to be 36 pouces 8.428 lignes. Picard made the English foot 11 pouces 2.6 lignes, and Dr. Maskelyne 11 pouces 3.11 lignes. D'Alembert states it at 11 pouces 3 lignes, which has been used in these calculations as a middle term, and gives us 36 pouces 8.428 lignes $= 39.1491$ inches. This length for the pendulum of 45° had been adopted in this report before the Bishop of Autun's proposition was known here. He relies on Mairan's ratio for the length of the pendulum in the latitude of Paris, to wit: $504 : 257 :: 72$ pouces to a 4th proportional, which will be 36.71428 pouces $= 39.1619$ inches, the length of the pendulum for latitude 48° 50′. The difference between this and the pendulum for 45° is .0113 of an inch; so that the pendulum for 45° would be estimated, according to Mairan, at $39.1619 - .0113 = 39.1506$ inches, almost precisely the same with Newton's computation herein adopted.

(3.) Sir Isaac Newton's computations for the different degrees of latitude, from 30° to 45°, are as follows:

	Pieds.	Lignes.		Pieds.	Lignes.
30°	3	7.948	42°	3	8.327
35	3	8.099	43	3	8.361
40	3	8.261	44	3	8.394
41	3	8.294	45	3	8.428

(4.) Or, more exactly, $144 : 175 :: 224 : 272.2$.

(5.) Or, more exactly, $62.5 : 1728 :: 77.7 : 2150.39$.

(6.) The merchant's weight.

(7.) The Eng. rood contains 10,890 sq. feet $= 104.355$ feet sq.

(8.) *The Measures, Weights, and Coins of the Decimal System,
estimated in those of England, now used in the United States.*

1. MEASURES OF LENGTH.

	Feet.	Equivalent in English measure.
The point, .	.001	. .011 inch.
The line, .	.01	. .117
The inch, .	.1	. 1.174, about $\frac{1}{7}$ more than the Eng. inch.
The foot, . 1.	}. 11.744736 }. .978728 feet,	about $\frac{1}{48}$ less than the English foot.
The decad, .	10.	. 9.787, about $\frac{1}{48}$ less than the 10 feet rod of the carpenters.
The rood, .	100.	. 97.872, about $\frac{1}{16}$ less than the side of an English square rood.
The furlong,	1000.	. 978.728, about $\frac{1}{3}$ more than the Eng. fur.
The mile, .	10000.	. 9787.28, about $1\frac{6}{7}$ English mile, nearly the Scotch and Irish mile, and $\frac{1}{2}$ the German mile.

2. SUPERFICIAL MEASURE.

	Roods.	
The hundredth,	. .01	. 95.69 square feet English.
The tenth,	. .1	. 957.9
The rood,	. 1.	. 9579.085
The double acre,	. 10.	. 2.199, or say 2.2 acres English.
The square furlong, .	100.	. 22.

3. MEASURE OF CAPACITY.

	Bushels.	Cub. Inches.
The metre,	. .001	. 1.62
The demi-pint,	. .01	. 16.2, about $\frac{1}{24}$ less than the English half-pint.
The pottle,	. .1	. 162.005, about $\frac{1}{6}$ more than the English pottle.
The bushel,	. 1.	{ 1620.05506862 { .937531868414884352 cub feet. }

about $\frac{1}{4}$ less than the middle sized English bushel.

The quarter,	. 10.	.	9.375, about ⅕ less than the Eng. qr.
The last,	. 100.	.	93.753, about ⅐ more than the Eng. last.

4. WEIGHTS.

	Pounds.	Avoirdupois.	Troy.
Mite,	.00001	. . . . . .	.041 grains, about ⅕ less than the English mite.
Minim, or demi-grain, }	.0001	. . . . .	.4101, about ⅕ less than half-grain troy.
Carat,	.001	. . . . .	4.101, about 1/40 more than the carat troy.
Double scruple, }	.01	. . . . .	41.017, about 1/40 more than 2 scruples troy.
Ounce,	.1	{ .937531868414884352 oz. } about 1/16 less than the ounce avoirdupois.	{ 410.170192431 .85452 oz.
Pound,	1.	{ 9.375 .585957417759 lb. }	.712101 lb., about ¼ less than the pound troy.
Stone,	10.	{ 93.753 oz. 5.8595 lb. }	7.121 about ¼ less than the English stone of 8 lbs. avoirdupois.
Kental,	100.	{ 937.531 oz. 58.5957 lb. }	71.21 about 4/10 less than the English kental of 100 lbs. avoirdupois.
Hogshead,	1000.	{ 9375.318 oz. 585.9574 lb. }	712.101

5. COINS.

	Dollars.		Troy grains
The mill,	.001	Dollar, . 1.	{ 375.98934306 pure silver. 34.18084937 alloy.
The cent,	.01		
The dime,	.1	Eagle, . 10.	410.17019243

Postscript.

January 10, 1791

It is scarcely necessary to observe that the measures, weights, and coins, proposed in the preceding report, will be derived altogether from mechanical operations, viz.: A rod, vibrating seconds, divided into five equal parts, one of these subdivided, and multiplied decimally, for every measure of length, surface, and capacity, and these last filled with water, to determine the weights and coins. The arithmetical estimates in the report were intended only to give an idea of what the new measures, weights, and coins, would be nearly, when compared with the old. The length of the standard or second rod, therefore, was assumed from that of the pendulum; and as there has been small differences in the estimates of the pendulum by different persons, that of Sir Isaac Newton was taken, the highest authority the world has yet known. But, if even he has erred, the measures, weights, and coins proposed, will not be an atom the more or less. In cubing the new foot, which was estimated at .978728 of an English foot, or 11.744736 English inches, an arithmetical error of an unit happened in the fourth column of decimals, and was repeated in another line in the sixth column, so as to make the result one ten thousandth and one millionth of a foot too much. The thousandth part of this error (about one ten millionth of a foot) consequently fell on the metre of measure, the ounce weight, and the unit of money. In the last it made a difference of about the twenty-fifth part of a grain Troy, in weight, or the ninety-third of a cent in value. As it happened, this error was on the favorable side, so that the detection of it approximates our estimate of the new unit exactly that much nearer to the old, and reduces the difference between them to 34, instead of 38 hundredths of a grain Troy; that is to say, the money unit instead of 375.64 Troy grains of pure silver, as established heretofore, will now be 375.98934306 grains, as far as our knowledge of the length of the second pendulum enables us to judge; and the current of authorities since Sir Isaac Newton's time, gives reason to believe that his estimate is more probably above than below the truth, consequently future corrections of it will bring the estimate of the new unit still nearer to the old.

The numbers in which the arithmetical error before mentioned showed itself in the table, at the end of the report, have been rectified, and the table re-printed.

The head of superficial measures in the last part of the report, is thought to be not sufficiently developed. It is proposed that the rood of land, being 100 feet square, (and nearly a quarter of the present acre,) shall be the unit of land measure. This will naturally be divided into tenths and hundredths, the latter of which will be a square decad. Its multiples will also, of course, be tens, which may be called double acres, and hundreds, which will be equal to a square furlong each. The surveyor's chain should be composed of 100 links of one foot each.

Opinion on the Constitutionality of a National Bank

February 15, 1791

THE BILL for establishing a National Bank undertakes among other things:—

1. To form the subscribers into a corporation.

2. To enable them in their corporate capacities to receive grants of land; and so far is against the laws of *Mortmain*.[1]

3. To make alien subscribers capable of holding lands; and so far is against the laws of *Alienage*.

4. To transmit these lands, on the death of a proprietor, to a certain line of successors; and so far changes the course of *Descents*.

5. To put the lands out of the reach of forfeiture or escheat; and so far is against the laws of *Forfeiture and Escheat*.

6. To transmit personal chattels to successors in a certain line; and so far is against the laws of *Distribution*.

7. To give them the sole and exclusive right of banking under the national authority; and so far is against the laws of Monopoly.

8. To communicate to them a power to make laws paramount to the laws of the States: for so they must be construed, to protect the institution from the control of the State legislatures; and so, probably, they will be construed.

I consider the foundation of the Constitution as laid on this ground: That "all powers not delegated to the United States, by the Constitution, nor prohibited by it to the States, are reserved to the States or to the people." [XIIth amendment.] To take a single step beyond the boundaries thus specially drawn around the powers of Congress, is to take possession of a boundless field of power, no longer susceptible of any definition.

The incorporation of a bank, and the powers assumed by this bill, have not, in my opinion, been delegated to the United States, by the Constitution.

---

[1] Though the Constitution controls the laws of Mortmain so far as to permit Congress itself to hold land for certain purposes, yet not so far as to permit them to communicate a similar right to other corporate bodies.

I. They are not among the powers specially enumerated: for these are: 1st. A power to lay taxes for the purpose of paying the debts of the United States; but no debt is paid by this bill, nor any tax laid. Were it a bill to raise money, its origination in the Senate would condemn it by the Constitution.

2d. "To borrow money." But this bill neither borrows money nor ensures the borrowing it. The proprietors of the bank will be just as free as any other money holders, to lend or not to lend their money to the public. The operation proposed in the bill, first, to lend them two millions, and then to borrow them back again, cannot change the nature of the latter act, which will still be a payment, and not a loan, call it by what name you please.

3. To "regulate commerce with foreign nations, and among the States, and with the Indian tribes." To erect a bank, and to regulate commerce, are very different acts. He who erects a bank, creates a subject of commerce in its bills; so does he who makes a bushel of wheat, or digs a dollar out of the mines; yet neither of these persons regulates commerce thereby. To make a thing which may be bought and sold, is not to prescribe regulations for buying and selling. Besides, if this was an exercise of the power of regulating commerce, it would be void, as extending as much to the internal commerce of every State, as to its external. For the power given to Congress by the Constitution does not extend to the internal regulation of the commerce of a State, (that is to say of the commerce between citizen and citizen,) which remain exclusively with its own legislature; but to its external commerce only, that is to say, its commerce with another State, or with foreign nations, or with the Indian tribes. Accordingly the bill does not propose the measure as a regulation of trade, but as "productive of considerable advantages to trade." Still less are these powers covered by any other of the special enumerations.

II. Nor are they within either of the general phrases, which are the two following:—

1. To lay taxes to provide for the general welfare of the United States, that is to say, "to lay taxes for *the purpose* of providing for the general welfare." For the laying of taxes is

the *power*, and the general welfare the *purpose* for which the power is to be exercised. They are not to lay taxes *ad libitum for any purpose they please*; but only *to pay the debts or provide for the welfare of the Union*. In like manner, they are not *to do anything they please* to provide for the general welfare, but only to *lay taxes* for that purpose. To consider the latter phrase, not as describing the purpose of the first, but as giving a distinct and independent power to do any act they please, which might be for the good of the Union, would render all the preceding and subsequent enumerations of power completely useless.

It would reduce the whole instrument to a single phrase, that of instituting a Congress with power to do whatever would be for the good of the United States; and, as they would be the sole judges of the good or evil, it would be also a power to do whatever evil they please.

It is an established rule of construction where a phrase will bear either of two meanings, to give it that which will allow some meaning to the other parts of the instrument, and not that which would render all the others useless. Certainly no such universal power was meant to be given them. It was intended to lace them up straitly within the enumerated powers, and those without which, as means, these powers could not be carried into effect. It is known that the very power now proposed *as a means* was rejected as *an end* by the Convention which formed the Constitution. A proposition was made to them to authorize Congress to open canals, and an amendatory one to empower them to incorporate. But the whole was rejected, and one of the reasons for rejection urged in debate was, that then they would have a power to erect a bank, which would render the great cities, where there were prejudices and jealousies on the subject, adverse to the reception of the Constitution.

2. The second general phrase is, "to make all laws *necessary* and proper for carrying into execution the enumerated powers." But they can all be carried into execution without a bank. A bank therefore is not *necessary*, and consequently not authorized by this phrase.

It has been urged that a bank will give great facility or convenience in the collection of taxes. Suppose this were true:

yet the Constitution allows only the means which are "*necessary*," not those which are merely "convenient" for effecting the enumerated powers. If such a latitude of construction be allowed to this phrase as to give any non-enumerated power, it will go to every one, for there is not one which ingenuity may not torture into a *convenience* in some instance *or other*, to *some one* of so long a list of enumerated powers. It would swallow up all the delegated powers, and reduce the whole to one power, as before observed. Therefore it was that the Constitution restrained them to the *necessary* means, that is to say, to those means without which the grant of power would be nugatory.

But let us examine this convenience and see what it is. The report on this subject, page 3, states the only *general* convenience to be, the preventing the transportation and re-transportation of money between the States and the treasury, (for I pass over the increase of circulating medium, ascribed to it as a want, and which, according to my ideas of paper money, is clearly a demerit.) Every State will have to pay a sum of tax money into the treasury; and the treasury will have to pay, in every State, a part of the interest on the public debt, and salaries to the officers of government resident in that State. In most of the States there will still be a surplus of tax money to come up to the seat of government for the officers residing there. The payments of interest and salary in each State may be made by treasury orders on the State collector. This will take up the greater part of the money he has collected in his State, and consequently prevent the great mass of it from being drawn out of the State. If there be a balance of commerce in favor of that State against the one in which the government resides, the surplus of taxes will be remitted by the bills of exchange drawn for that commercial balance. And so it must be if there was a bank. But if there be no balance of commerce, either direct or circuitous, all the banks in the world could not bring up the surplus of taxes but in the form of money. Treasury orders then, and bills of exchange may prevent the displacement of the main mass of the money collected, without the aid of any bank; and where these fail, it cannot be prevented even with that aid.

Perhaps, indeed, bank bills may be a more *convenient* vehicle than treasury orders. But a little *difference* in the degree of *convenience*, cannot constitute the necessity which the constitution makes the ground for assuming any non-enumerated power.

Besides; the existing banks will, without a doubt, enter into arrangements for lending their agency, and the more favorable, as there will be a competition among them for it; whereas the bill delivers us up bound to the national bank, who are free to refuse all arrangement, but on their own terms, and the public not free, on such refusal, to employ any other bank. That of Philadelphia, I believe, now does this business, by their post-notes, which, by an arrangement with the treasury, are paid by any State collector to whom they are presented. This expedient alone suffices to prevent the existence of that *necessity* which may justify the assumption of a non-enumerated power as a means for carrying into effect an enumerated one. The thing may be done, and has been done, and well done, without this assumption; therefore, it does not stand on that degree of *necessity* which can honestly justify it.

It may be said that a bank whose bills would have a currency all over the States, would be more convenient than one whose currency is limited to a single State. So it would be still more convenient that there should be a bank, whose bills should have a currency all over the world. But it does not follow from this superior conveniency, that there exists anywhere a power to establish such a bank; or that the world may not go on very well without it.

Can it be thought that the Constitution intended that for a shade or two of *convenience*, more or less, Congress should be authorised to break down the most ancient and fundamental laws of the several States; such as those against Mortmain, the laws of Alienage, the rules of descent, the acts of distribution, the laws of escheat and forfeiture, the laws of monopoly? Nothing but a necessity invincible by any other means, can justify such a prostitution of laws, which constitute the pillars of our whole system of jurisprudence. Will Congress be too straight-laced to carry the constitution into honest effect, unless they may pass over the foundation-laws of the State government for the slightest convenience of theirs?

The negative of the President is the shield provided by the

constitution to protect against the invasions of the legislature: 1. The right of the Executive. 2. Of the Judiciary. 3. Of the States and State legislatures. The present is the case of a right remaining exclusively with the States, and consequently one of those intended by the Constitution to be placed under its protection.

It must be added, however, that unless the President's mind on a view of everything which is urged for and against this bill, is tolerably clear that it is unauthorised by the Constitution; if the pro and the con hang so even as to balance his judgment, a just respect for the wisdom of the legislature would naturally decide the balance in favor of their opinion. It is chiefly for cases where they are clearly misled by error, ambition, or interest, that the Constitution has placed a check in the negative of the President.

Opinion on the French Treaties

April 28, 1793

I PROCEED, in compliance with the requisition of the President, to give an opinion in writing on the general Question, Whether the U S. have a right to renounce their treaties with France, or to hold them suspended till the government of that country shall be established?

In the Consultation at the President's on the 19th inst. the Secretary of the Treasury took the following positions & consequences. 'France was a monarchy when we entered into treaties with it: but it has now declared itself a Republic, & is preparing a Republican form of government. As it may issue in a Republic, or a Military despotism, or in something else which may possibly render our alliance with it dangerous to ourselves, we have a right of election to renounce the treaty altogether, or to declare it suspended till their government shall be settled in the form it is ultimately to take; and then we may judge whether we will call the treaties into operation again, or declare them forever null. Having that right of election now, if we receive their minister without any qualifications, it will amount to an act of election to continue the treaties; & if the change they are undergoing should issue in a form which should bring danger on us, we shall not be then free to renounce them. To elect to continue them is equivalent to the making a new treaty at this time in the same form, that is to say, with a clause of guarantee; but to make a treaty with a clause of guarantee, during a war, is a departure from neutrality, and would make us associates in the war. To renounce or suspend the treaties therefore is a necessary act of neutrality.'

If I do not subscribe to the soundness of this reasoning, I do most fully to its ingenuity.—I shall now lay down the principles which according to my understanding govern the case.

I consider the people who constitute a society or nation as the source of all authority in that nation, as free to transact their common concerns by any agents they think proper, to change these agents individually, or the organisation of them in form or function whenever they please: that all the acts done by those agents under the authority of the nation, are the acts of the nation, are obligatory on them, & enure to their use, & can in no wise be annulled or affected by any change in the form of the government, or of the persons administering it. Consequently the Treaties between the U S. and France, were not treaties between the U S. & Louis Capet, but between the two nations of America & France, and the nations remaining in existance, tho' both of them have since changed their forms of government, the treaties are not annulled by these changes.

The Law of nations, by which this question is to be determined, is composed of three branches. 1. The Moral law of our nature. 2. The Usages of nations. 3. Their special Conventions. The first of these only, concerns this question, that is to say the Moral law to which Man has been subjected by his creator, & of which his feelings, or Conscience as it is sometimes called, are the evidence with which his creator has furnished him. The Moral duties which exist between individual and individual in a state of nature, accompany them into a state of society & the aggregate of the duties of all the individuals composing the society constitutes the duties of that society towards any other; so that between society & society the same moral duties exist as did between the individuals composing them while in an unassociated state, their maker not having released them from those duties on their forming themselves into a nation. Compacts then between nation & nation are obligatory on them by the same moral law which obliges individuals to observe their compacts. There are circumstances however which sometimes excuse the non-performance of contracts between man & man: so are there also between nation & nation. When performance, for instance, becomes *impossible*, non-performance is not immoral. So if performance becomes *self-destructive* to the party, the law of self-preservation overrules the laws of obligation to others. For the reality of these principles I appeal to the true fountains of evidence, the head & heart of every rational & honest man. It is there Nature has written her moral laws, & where every man may read them for himself. He will never read there the permission to annul his obligations for a time, or

for ever, whenever they become 'dangerous, useless, or disagreeable.' Certainly not when merely *useless* or *disagreeable*,
as seems to be said in an authority which has been quoted,
Vattel. 2. 197, and tho he may under certain degrees of *danger*,
yet the danger must be imminent, & the degree great. Of
these, it is true, that nations are to be judges for themselves,
since no one nation has a right to sit in judgment over another. But the tribunal of our consciences remains, & that
also of the opinion of the world. These will revise the sentence we pass in our own case, & as we respect these, we
must see that in judging ourselves we have honestly done the
part of impartial & vigorous judges.

But Reason, which gives this right of self-liberation from a
contract in certain cases, has subjected it to certain just limitations.

I. The danger which absolves us must be great, inevitable
& imminent. Is such the character of that now apprehended
from our treaties with France? What is that danger. 1. Is it
that if their government issues in a military despotism, an alliance with them may taint us with despotic principles? But
their government, when we allied ourselves to it, was a perfect despotism, civil & military, yet the treaties were made in
that very state of things, & therefore that danger can furnish
no just cause. 2. Is it that their government may issue in a
republic, and too much strengthen our republican principles?
But this is the hope of the great mass of our constituents, &
not their dread. They do not look with longing to the happy
mean of a limited monarchy. 3. But says the doctrine I am
combating, the change the French are undergoing may possibly end in something we know not what, and bring on us
danger we know not whence. In short it may end in a Raw-
head & bloody-bones in the dark. Very well. Let Rawhead &
bloody bones come, & then we shall be justified in making
our peace with him, by renouncing our antient friends & his
enemies. For observe, it is not the *possibility of danger*, which
absolves a party from his contract: for that possibility always
exists, & in every case. It existed in the present one at the
moment of making the contract. If *possibilities* would avoid
contracts, there never could be a valid contract. For possibilities hang over everything. Obligation is not suspended, till

the danger is become real, & the moment of it so imminent, that we can no longer avoid decision without forever losing the opportunity to do it. But can a danger which has not yet taken it's shape, which does not yet exist, & never may exist, which cannot therefore be defined, can such a danger I ask, be so imminent that if we fail to pronounce on it in this moment we can never have another opportunity of doing it?

4. The danger apprehended, is it that, the treaties remaining valid, the clause guarantying their West India islands will engage us in the war? But does the Guarantee engage us to enter into the war in any event?

Are we to enter into it before we are called on by our allies? Have we been called on by them?—shall we ever be called on? Is it their interest to call on us?

Can they call on us before their islands are invaded, or imminently threatened?

If they can save them themselves, have they a right to call on us?

Are we obliged to go to war at once, without trying peaceable negociations with their enemy?

If all these questions be against us, there are still others behind.

Are we in a condition to go to war?

Can we be expected to begin before we are in condition?

Will the islands be lost if we do not save them? Have we the means of saving them?

If we cannot save them are we bound to go to war for a desperate object?

Will not a 10. years forbearance in us to call them into the guarantee of our posts, entitle us to some indulgence?

Many, if not most of these questions offer grounds of doubt whether the clause of guarantee will draw us into the war. Consequently if this be the danger apprehended, it is not yet certain enough to authorize us in sound morality to declare, at this moment, the treaties null.

5. Is the danger apprehended from the 17th article of the treaty of Commerce, which admits French ships of war & privateers to come and go freely, with prizes made on their enemies, while their enemies are not to have the same privilege with prizes made on the French? But Holland & Prussia

have approved of this article in our treaty with France, by
subscribing to an express Salvo of it in our treaties with them.
[Dutch treaty 22. Convention 6. Prussian treaty 19.] And England in her last treaty with France [art. 40] has entered into
the same stipulation verbatim, & placed us in her ports on
the same footing on which she is in ours, in case of a war of
either of us with France. If we are engaged in such a war,
England must receive prizes made on us by the French, &
exclude those made on the French by us. Nay further, in this
very article of her treaty with France, is a salvo of any similar
article in any anterior treaty of either party, and ours with
France being anterior, this salvo confirms it expressly. Neither
of these three powers then have a right to complain of this
article in our treaty.

6. Is the danger apprehended from the 22.^{d} Art. of our
treaty of commerce, which prohibits the enemies of France
from fitting out privateers in our ports, or selling their prizes
here. But we are free to refuse the same thing to France, there
being no stipulation to the contrary, and we ought to refuse
it on principles of fair neutrality.

7. But the reception of a Minister from the Republic of
France, without qualifications, it is thought will bring us into
danger: because this, it is said, will determine the continuance
of the treaty, and take from us the right of self-liberation
when at any time hereafter our safety would require us to use
it. The reception of the Minister at all (in favor of which Col.^{o}
Hamilton has given his opinion, tho reluctantly as he confessed) is an acknolegement of the legitimacy of their government: and if the qualifications meditated are to deny that
legitimacy, it will be a curious compound which is to admit
& deny the same thing. But I deny that the reception of a
Minister has any thing to do with the treaties. There is not a
word, in either of them, about sending ministers. This has
been done between us under the common usage of nations,
& can have no effect either to continue or annul the treaties.

But how can any act of election have the effect to continue
a treaty which is acknoleged to be going on still? For it was
not pretended the treaty was void, but only voidable if we
chuse to declare it so. To make it void would require an act
of election, but to let it go on requires only that we should

do nothing, and doing nothing can hardly be an infraction of peace or neutrality.

But I go further & deny that the most explicit declaration made at this moment that we acknolege the obligation of the treatys could take from us the right of non-compliance at any future time when compliance would involve us in great & inevitable danger.

I conclude then that few of these sources threaten any danger at all; and from none of them is it inevitable: & consequently none of them give us the right at this moment of releasing ourselves from our treaties.

II. A second limitation on our right of releasing ourselves is that we are to do it from so much of the treaties only as is bringing great & inevitable danger on us, & not from the residue, allowing to the other party a right at the same time to determine whether on our non-compliance with that part they will declare the whole void. This right they would have, but we should not. Vattel. 2. 202. The only part of the treaties which can really lead us into danger is the clause of guarantee. That clause is all then we could suspend in any case, and the residue will remain or not at the will of the other party.

III. A third limitation is that where a party from necessity or danger withholds compliance with part of a treaty, it is bound to make compensation where the nature of the case admits & does not dispense with it. 2. Vattel 324. Wolf. 270. 443. If actual circumstances excuse us from entering into the war under the clause of guarantee, it will be a question whether they excuse us from compensation. Our weight in the war admits of an estimate; & that estimate would form the measure of compensation.

If in withholding a compliance with any part of the treaties, we do it without just cause or compensation, we give to France a cause of war, and so become associated in it on the other side. An injured friend is the bitterest of foes, & France had not discovered either timidity, or over-much forbearance on the late occasions. Is this the position we wish to take for our constituents? It is certainly not the one they would take for themselves.

I will proceed now to examine the principal authority which has been relied on for establishing the right of self liberation; because tho' just in part, it would lead us far beyond justice, if taken in all the latitude of which his expressions would admit. Questions of natural right are triable by their conformity with the moral sense & reason of man. Those who write treatises of natural law, can only declare what their own moral sense & reason dictate in the several cases they state. Such of them as happen to have feelings & a reason coincident with those of the wise & honest part of mankind, are respected & quoted as witnesses of what is morally right or wrong in particular cases. Grotius, Puffendorf, Wolf, & Vattel are of this number. Where they agree their authority is strong. But where they differ, & they often differ, we must appeal to our own feelings and reason to decide between them.

The passages in question shall be traced through all these writers, that we may see wherein they concur, & where that concurrence is wanting. It shall be quoted from them in the order in which they wrote, that is to say, from Grotius first, as being the earliest writer, Puffendorf next, then Wolf, & lastly Vattel as latest in time.

The doctrine then of Grotius, Puffendorf & Wolf is that 'treaties remain obligatory notwithstanding any change in the form of government, except in the single case where the preservation of that form was the object of the treaty.' There the treaty extinguishes, not by the election or declaration of the party remaining in statu quo; but independantly of that, by the evanishment of the object. Vattel lays down, in fact, the same doctrine, that treaties continue obligatory, notwithstanding a change of government by the will of the other party, that to oppose that will would be a wrong, & that the ally remains an ally notwithstanding the change. So far he concurs with all the previous writers. But he then adds what they had not said, nor would say 'but if this change renders the alliance *useless*, dangerous, or *disagreeable* to it, it is free to renounce it.' It was unnecessary for him to have specified the exception of *danger* in this particular case, because that exception exists in all cases & it's extent has been considered. But when he adds that, because a contract is become merely *useless* or *disagreeable*, we are free to renounce it, he is in opposition to Grotius, Puffendorf, & Wolf, who admit no such licence against the obligation of treaties, & he is in opposition to the morality of every honest man, to whom we may safely appeal to decide whether he feels himself free to renounce a contract the moment it becomes merely *useless* or *disagreeable*, to him? We may appeal too to Vattel himself, in those parts of his book where he cannot be misunderstood, & to his known character, as one of the most zealous & constant advocates for the preservation of good faith in all our dealings. Let us hear him on other occasions; & first where he shews what degree of danger or injury will authorize self-liberation from a treaty. 'If simple lezion' (lezion means the loss sustained by selling a thing for less than half value, which degree of loss rendered the sale void by the Roman law), 'if simple lezion, says he, or some degree of disadvantage in a treaty does not suffice to render it invalid, it is not so as to inconveniences which would go to the *ruin* of the nation. As every treaty ought to be made by a sufficient power, a treaty pernicious to the state is null, & not at all obligatory; no governor of a nation having power to engage things capable of *destroying* the state, for the safety of which the empire is trusted to him. The nation itself, bound necessarily to whatever it's preservation & safety require, cannot enter into engagements contrary to it's indispensable obligations.' Here then we find that the degree of injury or danger which he deems sufficient to liberate us from a treaty, is that which would go to the absolute *ruin* or *destruction* of the state; not simply the lezion of the Roman law, not merely the being disadvantageous, or dangerous. For as he says himself § 158. 'lezion cannot render a treaty invalid. It is his duty, who enters into engagements, to weigh well all things before be concludes. He may do with his property what he pleases, he may relinquish his rights, renounce his advantages, as he judges proper: the acceptant is not obliged to inform himself of his motives, nor to weigh their just value. If we could free ourselves from a compact because we find ourselves injured by it, there would be nothing firm in the contracts of nations. Civil laws may set limits to lezion, & determine the degree capable of producing a nullity of the contract. But sovereigns acknolege no judge. How establish lezion among them? Who will determine the degree sufficient to invalidate a treaty? The happiness & peace

Grotius. 2. 16. 16.

'Hither must be referred the common question, concerning personal & real treaties. If indeed it be with a free people, there can be no doubt but that the engagement is in it's nature real, because the subject is a permanent thing, and even tho' the government of the state be changed into a Kingdom, the treaty remains, because the same body remains, tho' the head is changed, and, as we have before said, the government which is exercised by a King, does not cease to be the government of the people. There is an *exception*, when the object seems peculiar to the government as if free cities contract a league for the defence of their freedom.'

Puffendorf. 8. 9. 6.

'It is certain that every alliance made with a republic, is real, & continues consequently to the term agreed on by the treaty, altho' the magistrates who concluded it be dead before, or that the form of government is changed, even from a democracy to a monarchy: for in this case the people does not cease to be the same, and the King, in the case supposed, being established by the consent of the people, who abolished the republican government, is understood to accept the engagements which the people contracting it had contracted, as being free & governing themselves. There must nevertheless be an *Exception* of the alliances contracted with a

Wolf. 1146.

'The alliance which is made with a free people, or with a popular government, is a real alliance; and as when the form of government changes, the people remains the same, (for it is the association which forms the people, & not the manner of administering the government) this alliance subsists, tho' the form of government changes, as is evident, the reason of the alliance was particular to the popular state.'

Vattel. 2. 197.

'The same question presents itself in real alliances, & in general on every alliance made with a state, & not in particular with a King for the defense of his person. We ought without doubt to defend our ally against all invasion, against all foreign violence, & even against rebel subjects. We ought in like manner to defend a republic against the enterprises of an oppressor of the public liberty. But we ought to recollect that we are the ally of the state, or of the nation, & not it's judge. If the nation has deposed it's King in form, if the people of a republic has driven away it's magistrates, & have established themselves free, or if they have acknoleged the authority of an view to preserve the present government. As if two Republics league for neutral defence against those who would undertake to invade their liberty: for if one of these two people consent afterwards voluntarily to change the form of their government, the alliance ends of itself, because the reason on which it was founded no longer subsists.'

usurper, whether expressly or tacitly, to oppose these domestic arrangements, to contest their justice or validity, would be to meddle with the government of the nation, & to do it an injury. The ally remains the ally of the state, notwithstanding the change which has taken place. *But if this change renders the alliance useless, dangerous or disagreeable to it, it is free to renounce it. For it may say with truth, that it would not have allied itself with this nation, if it had been under the present form of it's government.'*

of nations require manifestly that their treaties should not depend on a means of nullity so vague & so dangerous.'

Let us hear him again on the general subject of the observance of treaties § 163. 'It is demonstrated in natural law that he who promises another confers on him a perfect right to require the thing promised, & that, consequently, not to observe a perfect promise, is to violate the right of another; it is as manifest injustice as to plunder any one of their right. All the tranquillity, the happiness & security of mankind rest on justice, on the obligation to respect the rights of others. The respect of others for our rights of domain & property is the security of our actual possessions; the faith of promises is our security for the things which cannot be delivered or executed on the spot. No more security, no more commerce among men, if they think themselves not obliged to preserve faith, to keep their word. This obligation then is as necessary as it is natural & indubitable, among nations who live together in a state of nature, & who acknolege no superior on earth, to maintain order & peace in their society. Nations & their governors then ought to observe inviolably their promises & their treaties. This great truth, altho' too often neglected in practice, is generally acknoleged by all nations: the reproach of perfidy is a bitter affront among sovereigns: now he who does not observe a treaty is assuredly perfidious, since he violates his faith. On the contrary nothing is so glorious to a prince & his nation, as the reputation of inviolable fidelity to his word.' Again § 219. 'Who will doubt that treaties are of the things sacred among nations? They decide matters the most important. They impose rules on the pretensions of sovereigns: they cause the rights of nations to be acknoleged, they assure their most precious interests. Among political bodies, sovereigns, who acknolege no superior on earth, treaties are the only means of adjusting their different pretensions, of establishing a rule, to know on what to count, on what to depend. But treaties are but vain words if nations do not consider them as respectable engagements, as rules, inviolable for sovereigns, & sacred through the whole earth. § 220. The faith of treaties, that firm & sincere will, that invariable constancy in fulfilling engagements, of which a declaration is made in a treaty, is there holy & sacred, among nations, whose safety & repose it ensures; & if nations will not be wanting to themselves, they will load with infamy whoever violates his faith.'

After evidence so copious & explicit of the respect of this author for the sanctity of treaties, we should hardly have expected that his authority would have been resorted to for a wanton invalidation of them whenever they should become merely *useless* or *disagreeable*. We should hardly have expected that, rejecting all the rest of his book, this scrap would have been culled, & made the hook whereon to hang such a chain of immoral consequences. Had the passage accidentally met our eye, we should have imagined it had fallen from the author's pen under some momentary view, not sufficiently developed to found a conjecture what he meant: and we may certainly affirm that a fragment like this cannot weigh against the authority of all other writers, against the uniform & systematic doctrine of every work from which it is torn, against the moral feelings & the reason of all honest men. If the terms of the fragment are not misunderstood, they are in full contradiction to all the written & unwritten evidences of morality: if they are misunderstood, they are no longer a foundation for the doctrines which have been built on them.

But even had this doctrine been as true as it is manifestly false, it would have been asked, to whom is it that the treaties with France have become *disagreeable*? How will it be proved that they are *useless*?

The conclusion of the sentence suggests a reflection too strong to be suppressed 'for the party may say with truth that it would not have allied itself with this nation, if it had been under the present form of it's government.' The Republic of the U.S. allied itself with France when under a despotic government. She changes her government, declares it shall be a Republic, prepares a form of Republic extremely free, and in the mean time is governing herself as such, and it is proposed that America shall declare the treaties void because 'it may say with truth that it would not have allied itself with that nation, if it had been under the present form of it's government!' Who is the American who can say with truth that he would not have allied himself to France if she had been a republic? or that a Republic of any form would be as *disagreeable* as her antient despotism?

Upon the whole I conclude

That the treaties are still binding, notwithstanding the change of government in France: that no part of them, but the clause of guarantee, holds up *danger*, even at a distance.

And consequently that a liberation from no other part could be proposed in any case: that if that clause may ever bring *danger*, it is neither extreme, nor imminent, nor even probable: that the authority for renouncing a treaty, when *useless* or *disagreeable*, is either misunderstood, or in opposition to itself, to all their writers, & to every moral feeling: that were it not so, these treaties are in fact neither useless nor disagreeable.

That the receiving a Minister from France at this time is an act of no significance with respect to the treaties, amounting neither to an admission nor a denial of them, forasmuch as he comes not under any stipulation in them:

That were it an explicit admission, or were an express declaration of this obligation now to be made, it would not take from us that right which exists at all times of liberating ourselves when an adherence to the treaties would be *ruinous* or *destructive* to the society: and that the not renouncing the treaties now is so far from being a breach of neutrality, that the doing it would be the breach, by giving just cause of war to France.

Report on the Privileges and Restrictions on the Commerce of the United States in Foreign Countries

December 16, 1793

The Secretary of State, to whom was referred by the House of Representatives, the report of a committee on the written message of the President of the United States, of the 14th of February, 1791, with instructions to report to Congress the nature and extent of the privileges and restrictions of the commercial intercourse of the United States with foreign nations, and the measures which he should think proper to be adopted for the improvement of the commerce and navigation of the same, has had the same under consideration, and thereupon makes the following Report:

THE COUNTRIES with which the United States have their chief commercial intercourse are Spain, Portugal, France, Great Britain, the United Netherlands, Denmark, and Sweden, and their American possessions; and the articles of export, which constitute the basis of that commerce, with their respective amounts, are,

Breadstuff, that is to say, bread grains, meals, and bread, to the annual amount of.	$7,649,887
Tobacco	4,349,567
Rice	1,753,796
Wood	1,263,534
Salted fish	941,696
Pot and pearl ash	839,093
Salted meats	599,130
Indigo	537,379
Horses and mules	339,753
Whale oil	252,591
Flax seed	236,072
Tar, pitch and turpentine	217,177
Live provisions	137,743
Ships	
Foreign goods	620,274

To descend to articles of smaller value than these, would lead into a minuteness of detail neither necessary nor useful to the present object.

The proportions of our exports, which go to the nations

before mentioned, and to their dominions, respectively, are as follows:

To Spain and its dominions	$2,005,907
Portugal and its dominions.	1,283,462
France and its dominions	4,698,735
Great Britain and its dominions	9,363,416
The United Netherlands and their dominions	1,963,880
Denmark and its dominions	224,415
Sweden and its dominions	47,240

Our imports from the same countries, are

Spain and its dominions	335,110
Portugal and its dominions.	595,763
France and its dominions	2,068,348
Great Britain and its dominions	15,285,428
United Netherlands and their dominions	1,172,692
Denmark and its dominions	351,364
Sweden and its dominions	14,325

These imports consist mostly of articles on which industry has been exhausted.

Our *navigation*, depending on the same commerce, will appear by the following statement of the tonnage of our own vessels, entering in our ports, from those several nations and their possessions, in one year: that is to say, from October, 1789, to September, 1790, inclusive, as follows:

	Tons.
Spain	19,695
Portugal	23,576
France	116,410
Great Britain	43,580
United Netherlands	58,858
Denmark	14,655
Sweden	750

Of our commercial objects, Spain receives favorably our breadstuff, salted fish, wood, ships, tar, pitch, and turpentine. On our meals, however, as well as on those of other foreign countries, when re-exported to their colonies, they have lately imposed duties of from half-a-dollar to two dollars the barrel, the duties being so proportioned to the current price of their own flour, as that both together are to make the constant sum of nine dollars per barrel.

They do not discourage our rice, pot and pearl ash, salted provisions, or whale oil; but these articles, being in small demand at their markets, are carried thither but in a small degree. Their demand for rice, however, is increasing. Neither tobacco nor indigo are received there. Our commerce is permitted with their Canary islands under the same conditions.

Themselves, and their colonies, are the actual consumers of what they receive from us.

Our navigation is free with the kingdom of Spain; foreign goods being received there in our ships on the same conditions as if carried in their own, or in the vessels of the country of which such goods are the manufacture or produce.

Portugal receives favorably our grain and bread, salted fish, and other salted provisions, wood, tar, pitch and turpentine.

For flax-seed, pot and pearl ash, though not discouraged, there is little demand.

Our ships pay 20 per cent. on being sold to their subjects, and are then free-bottoms.

Foreign goods (except those of the East Indies) are received on the same footing in our vessels as in their own, or any others; that is to say, on general duties of from 20 to 28 per cent., and, consequently, our navigation is unobstructed by them. Tobacco, rice, and meals, are prohibited.

Themselves and their colonies consume what they receive from us.

These regulations extend to the Azores, Madeira, and the Cape de Verd islands, except that in these, meals and rice are received freely.

France receives favorably our bread-stuffs, rice, wood, pot and pearl ashes.

A duty of 5 sous the quintal, or nearly 4½ cents, is paid on our tar, pitch, and turpentine. Our whale oils pay 6 livres the quintal, and are the only foreign whale oils admitted. Our indigo pays 5 livres the quintal, their own 2½; but a difference of quality, still more than a difference of duty, prevents its seeking that market.

Salted beef is received freely for re-exportation; but if for home consumption, it pays five livres the quintal. Other salted provisions pay that duty in all cases, and salted fish is made lately to pay the prohibitory one of twenty livres the quintal.

Our ships are free to carry thither all foreign goods which may be carried in their own or any other vessels, except tobaccoes not of our own growth; and they participate with theirs, the exclusive carriage of our whale oils and tobaccoes.

During their former government, our tobacco was under a monopoly, but paid no duties; and our ships were freely sold in their ports and converted into national bottoms. The first national assembly took from our ships this privilege. They emancipated tobacco from its monopoly, but subjected it to duties of eighteen livres, fifteen sous the quintal, carried in their own vessels, and five livres carried in ours—a difference more than equal to the freight of the article.

They and their colonies consume what they receive from us.

Great Britain receives our pot and pearl ashes free, whilst those of other nations pay a duty of two shillings and three pence the quintal. There is an equal distinction in favor of our bar iron; of which article, however, we do not produce enough for our own use. Woods are free from us, whilst they pay some small duty from other countries. Indigo and flaxseed are free from all countries. Our tar and pitch pay eleven pence, sterling, the barrel. From other alien countries they pay about a penny and a third more.

Our tobacco, for their own consumption, pays one shilling and three pence, sterling, the pound, custom and excise, besides heavy expenses of collection; and rice, in the same case, pays seven shillings and four pence, sterling, the hundred weight; which rendering it too dear, as an article of common food, it is consequently used in very small quantity.

Our salted fish and other salted provisions, except bacon, are prohibited. Bacon and whale oils are under prohibitory duties, so are our grains, meals, and bread, as to internal consumption, unless in times of such scarcity as may raise the price of wheat to fifty shillings, sterling, the quarter, and other grains and meals in proportion.

Our ships, though purchased and navigated by their own

subjects, are not permitted to be used, even in their trade with us.

While the vessels of other nations are secured by standing laws, which cannot be altered but by the concurrent will of the three branches of the British legislature, in carrying thither any produce or manufacture of the country to which they belong, which may be lawfully carried in any vessels, ours, with the same prohibition of what is foreign, are further prohibited by a standing law (12 Car. 2, 18, sect. 3), from carrying thither all and any of our own domestic productions and manufactures. A subsequent act, indeed, has authorized their executive to permit the carriage of our own productions in our own bottoms, at its sole discretion; and the permission has been given from year to year by proclamation, but subject every moment to be withdrawn on that single will; in which event, our vessels having anything on board, stand interdicted from the entry of all British ports. The disadvantage of a tenure which may be so suddenly discontinued, was experienced by our merchants on a late occasion,* when an official notification that this law would be stricly enforced, gave them just apprehensions for the fate of their vessels and cargoes despatched or destined for the ports of Great Britain. The minister of that court, indeed, frankly expressed his personal convictions that the words of the order went farther than was intended, and so he afterwards officially informed us: but the embarrassments of the moment were real and great, and the possibility of their renewal lays our commerce to that country under the same species of discouragement as to other countries, where it is regulated by a single legislator; and the distinction is too remarkable not to be noticed, that our navigation is excluded from the security of fixed laws, while that security is given to the navigation of others.

Our vessels pay in their ports one shilling and nine pence, sterling, per ton, light and trinity dues, more than is paid by British ships, except in the port of London, where they pay the same as British.

The greater part of what they receive from us, is reexported to other countries, under the useless charges of an

*April 12, 1792.

intermediate deposit, and double voyage. From tables published in England, and composed, as is said, from the books
of their customhouses, it appears, that of the indigo imported
there in the years 1773, '4, '5, one-third was re-exported; and
from a document of authority, we learn, that of the rice and
tobacco imported there before the war, four-fifths were re-
exported. We are assured, indeed, that the quantities sent
thither for re-exportation since the war, are considerably diminished, yet less so than reason and national interest would
dictate. The whole of our grain is re-exported when wheat
is below fifty shillings the quarter, and other grains in proportion.

The *United Netherlands* prohibit our pickled beef and pork,
meals and bread of all sorts, and lay a prohibitory duty on
spirits distilled from grain.

All other of our productions are received on varied duties,
which may be reckoned, on a medium, at about three per
cent.

They consume but a small proportion of what they receive.
The residue is partly forwarded for consumption in the inland
parts of Europe, and partly re-shipped to other maritime
countries. On the latter portion they intercept between us and
the consumer, so much of the value as is absorbed in the
charges attending and intermediate deposit.

Foreign goods, except some East India articles, are received
in vessels of any nation.

Our ships may be sold and neutralized there, with exceptions of one or two privileges, which somewhat lessen their
value.

Denmark lays considerable duties on our tobacco and rice,
carried in their own vessels, and half as much more, if carried
in ours; but the exact amount of these duties is not perfectly
known here. They lay such duties as amount to prohibitions
on our indigo and corn.

Sweden receives favorably our grains and meals, salted provisions, indigo, and whale oil.

They subject our rice to duties of sixteen mills the pound
weight, carried in their own vessels, and of forty per cent.
additional on that, or twenty-two and four-tenths mills, carried in ours or any others. Being thus rendered too dear as an

article of common food, little of it is consumed with them. They consume some of our tobaccoes, which they take circuitously through Great Britain, levying heavy duties on them also; their duties of entry, town duties, and excise, being 4 34 dollars the hundred weight, if carried in their own vessels, and of forty per cent. on that additional, if carried in our own or any other vessels.

They prohibit altogether our bread, fish, pot and pearl ashes, flax-seed, tar, pitch, and turpentine, wood (except oak timber and masts), and all foreign manufactures.

Under so many restrictions and prohibitions, our navigation with them is reduced to almost nothing.

With our neighbors, an order of things much harder presents itself.

Spain and *Portugal* refuse, to all those parts of America which they govern, all direct intercourse with any people but themselves. The commodities in mutual demand between them and their neighbors, must be carried to be exchanged in some port of the dominant country, and the transportation between that and the subject state, must be in a domestic bottom.

France, by a standing law, permits her West India possessions to receive directly our vegetables, live provisions, horses, wood, tar, pitch, turpentine, rice, and maize, and prohibits our other bread stuff; but a suspension of this prohibition having been left to the colonial legislatures, in times of scarcity, it was formerly suspended occasionally, but latterly without interruption.

Our fish and salted provisions (except pork) are received in their islands under a duty of three colonial livres the quintal, and our vessels are as free as their own to carry our commodities thither, and to bring away rum and molasses.

Great Britain admits in her islands our vegetables, live provisions, horses, wood, tar, pitch, and turpentine, rice and bread stuff, by a proclamation of her executive, limited always to the term of a year, but hitherto renewed from year to year. She prohibits our salted fish and other salted provisions. She does not permit our vessels to carry thither our own produce. Her vessels alone may take it from us, and bring in exchange rum, molasses, sugar, coffee, cocoa-nuts, ginger, and pimento. There are, indeed, some freedoms in the island of Dominica, but, under such circumstances, as to be little used by us. In the British continental colonies, and in Newfoundland, all our productions are prohibited, and our vessels forbidden to enter their ports. Their governors, however, in times of distress, have power to permit a temporary importation of certain articles in their own bottoms, but not in ours.

Our citizens cannot reside as merchants or factors within any of the British plantations, this being expressly prohibited by the same statute of 12 Car. 2, c. 18, commonly called the navigation act.

In the *Danish American* possessions a duty of 5 per cent. is levied on our corn, corn meal, rice, tobacco, wood, salted fish, indigo, horses, mules and live stock, and of 10 per cent. on our flour, salted pork and beef, tar, pitch and turpentine.

In the American islands of the *United Netherlands* and Sweden, our vessels and produce are received, subject to duties, not so heavy as to have been complained of; but they are heavier in the Dutch possessions on the continent.

To sum up these restrictions, so far as they are important:

FIRST. In Europe—

Our bread stuff is at most times under prohibitory duties in England, and considerably dutied on re-exportation from Spain to her colonies.

Our tobaccoes are heavily dutied in England, Sweden and France, and prohibited in Spain and Portugal.

Our rice is heavily dutied in England and Sweden, and prohibited in Portugal.

Our fish and salted provisions are prohibited in England, and under prohibitory duties in France.

Our whale oils are prohibited in England and Portugal.

And our vessels are denied naturalization in England, and of late in France.

SECOND. In the West Indies—

All intercourse is prohibited with the possessions of Spain and Portugal.

Our salted provisions and fish are prohibited by England.

Our salted pork and bread stuff (except maize) are received under temporary laws only, in the dominions of France, and our salted fish pays there a weighty duty.

THIRD. In the article of navigation—

Our own carriage of our own tobacco is heavily dutied in Sweden, and lately in France.

We can carry no article, not of our own production, to the British ports in Europe. Nor even our own produce to her American possessions.

Such being the restrictions on the commerce and navigation of the United States; the question is, in what way they may best be removed, modified or counteracted?

As to commerce, two methods occur. 1. By friendly arrangements with the several nations with whom these restrictions exist; Or, 2. By the separate act of our own legislatures for countervailing their effects.

There can be no doubt but that of these two, friendly arrangements is the most eligible. Instead of embarrassing commerce under piles of regulating laws, duties, and prohibitions, could it be relieved from all its shackles in all parts of the world, could every country be employed in producing that which nature has best fitted it to produce, and each be free to exchange with others mutual surplusses for mutual wants, the greatest mass possible would then be produced of those things which contribute to human life and human happiness; the numbers of mankind would be increased, and their condition bettered.

Would even a single nation begin with the United States this system of free commerce, it would be advisable to begin it with that nation; since it is one by one only that it can be extended to all. Where the circumstances of either party render it expedient to levy a revenue, by way of impost, on commerce, its freedom might be modified, in that particular, by mutual and equivalent measures, preserving it entire in all others.

Some nations, not yet ripe for free commerce in all its extent, might still be willing to mollify its restrictions and regulations for us, in proportion to the advantages which an intercourse with us might offer. Particularly they may concur with us in reciprocating the duties to be levied on each side, or in compensating any excess of duty by equivalent advantages of another nature. Our commerce is certainly of a character to entitle it to favor in most countries. The commodities we offer are either necessaries of life, or materials for manufacture, or convenient subjects of revenue; and we take in exchange, either manufactures, when they have received the last finish of art and industry, or mere luxuries. Such customers may reasonably expect welcome and friendly treatment at every market. Customers, too, whose demands, increasing with their wealth and population, must very shortly give full employment to the whole industry of any nation whatever, in any line of supply they may get into the habit of calling for from it.

But should any nation, contrary to our wishes, suppose it may better find its advantage by continuing its system of prohibitions, duties and regulations, it behooves us to protect our citizens, their commerce and navigation, by counter prohibitions, duties and regulations, also. Free commerce and navigation are not to be given in exchange for restrictions and vexations; nor are they likely to produce a relaxation of them.

Our navigation involves still higher considerations. As a branch of industry, it is valuable, but as a resource of defence, essential.

Its value, as a branch of industry, is enhanced by the dependence of so many other branches on it. In times of general peace it multiplies competitors for employment in transportation, and so keeps that at its proper level; and in times of war, that is to say, when those nations who may be our principal carriers, shall be at war with each other, if we have not within ourselves the means of transportation, our produce must be exported in belligerent vessels, at the increased expense of war-freight and insurance, and the articles which will not bear that, must perish on our hands.

But it is as a resource of defence that our navigation will admit neither negligence nor forbearance. The position and circumstances of the United States leave them nothing to fear on their land-board, and nothing to desire beyond their present rights. But on their seaboard, they are open to injury, and they have there, too, a commerce which must be protected. This can only be done by possessing a respectable body of citizen-seamen, and of artists and establishments in readiness for ship-building.

Were the ocean, which is the common property of all, open

to the industry of all, so that every person and vessel should be free to take employment wherever it could be found, the United States would certainly not set the example of appropriating to themselves, exclusively, any portion of the common stock of occupation. They would rely on the enterprise and activity of their citizens for a due participation of the benefits of the seafaring business, and for keeping the marine class of citizens equal to their object. But if particular nations grasp at undue shares, and, more especially, if they seize on the means of the United States, to convert them into aliment for their own strength, and withdraw them entirely from the support of those to whom they belong, defensive and protecting measures become necessary on the part of the nation whose marine resources are thus invaded; or it will be disarmed of its defence; its productions will lie at the mercy of the nation which has possessed itself exclusively of the means of carrying them, and its politics may be influenced by those who command its commerce. The carriage of our own commodities, if once established in another channel, cannot be resumed in the moment we may desire. If we lose the seamen and artists whom it now occupies, we lose the present means of marine defence, and time will be requisite to raise up others, when disgrace or losses shall bring home to our feelings the error of having abandoned them. The materials for maintaining our due share of navigation, are ours in abundance. And, as to the mode of using them, we have only to adopt the principles of those who put us on the defensive, or others equivalent and better fitted to our circumstances.

The following principles, being founded in reciprocity, appear perfectly just, and to offer no cause of complaint to any nation:

1. Where a nation imposes high duties on our productions, or prohibits them altogether, it may be proper for us to do the same by theirs; first burdening or excluding those productions which they bring here, in competition with our own of the same kind; selecting next, such manufactures as we take from them in greatest quantity, and which, at the same time, we could the soonest furnish to ourselves, or obtain from other countries; imposing on them duties lighter at first, but heavier and heavier afterwards, as other channels of supply

open. Such duties having the effect of indirect encouragement to domestic manufactures of the same kind, may induce the manufacturer to come himself into these States, where cheaper subsistence, equal laws, and a vent of his wares, free of duty, may ensure him the highest profits from his skill and industry. And here, it would be in the power of the State governments to co-operate essentially, by opening the resources of encouragement which are under their control, extending them liberally to artists in those particular branches of manufacture for which their soil, climate, population and other circumstances have matured them, and fostering the precious efforts and progress of *household* manufacture, by some patronage suited to the nature of its objects, guided by the local informations they possess, and guarded against abuse by their presence and attentions. The oppressions on our agriculture, in foreign ports, would thus be made the occasion of relieving it from a dependence on the councils and conduct of others, and of promoting arts, manufactures and population at home.

2. Where a nation refuses permission to our merchants and factors to reside within certain parts of their dominions, we may, if it should be thought expedient, refuse residence to theirs in any and every part of ours, or modify their transactions.

3. Where a nation refuses to receive in our vessels any productions but our own, we may refuse to receive, in theirs, any but their own productions. The first and second clauses of the bill reported by the committee, are well formed to effect this object.

4. Where a nation refuses to consider any vessel as ours which has not been built within our territories, we should refuse to consider as theirs, any vessel not built within their territories.

5. Where a nation refuses to our vessels the carriage even of our own productions, to certain countries under their domination, we might refuse to theirs of every description, the carriage of the same productions to the same countries. But as justice and good neighborhood would dictate that those who have no part in imposing the restriction on us, should not be the victims of measures adopted to defeat its effect, it

may be proper to confine the restrictions to vessels owned or navigated by any subjects of the same dominant power, other than the inhabitants of the country to which the said productions are to be carried. And to prevent all inconvenience to the said inhabitants, and to our own, by too sudden a check on the means of transportation, we may continue to admit the vessels marked for future exclusion, on an advanced tonnage, and for such length of time only, as may be supposed necessary to provide against that inconvenience.

The establishment of some of these principles by Great Britain, alone, has already lost to us in our commerce with that country and its possessions, between eight and nine hundred vessels of near 40,000 tons burden, according to statements from official materials, in which they have confidence. This involves a proportional loss of seamen, shipwrights, and ship-building, and is too serious a loss to admit forbearance of some effectual remedy.

It is true we must expect some inconvenience in practice from the establishment of discriminating duties. But in this, as in so many other cases, we are left to choose between two evils. These inconveniences are nothing when weighed against the loss of wealth and loss of force, which will follow our perseverance in the plan of indiscrimination. When once it shall be perceived that we are either in the system or in the habit of giving equal advantages to those who extinguish our commerce and navigation by duties and prohibitions, as to those who treat both with liberality and justice, liberality and justice will be converted by all into duties and prohibitions. It is not to the moderation and justice of others we are to trust for fair and equal access to market with our productions, or for our due share in the transportation of them; but to our own means of independence, and the firm will to use them. Nor do the inconveniences of discrimination merit consideration. Not one of the nations before mentioned, perhaps not a commercial nation on earth, is without them. In our case one distinction alone will suffice: that is to say, between nations who favor our productions and navigation, and those who do not favor them. One set of moderate duties, say the present duties, for the first, and a fixed advance on these as to some articles, and prohibitions as to others, for the last.

Still, it must be repeated that friendly arrangements are preferable with all who will come into them; and that we should carry into such arrangements all the liberality and spirit of accommodation which the nature of the case will admit.

France has, of her own accord, proposed negotiations for improving, by a new treaty on fair and equal principles, the commercial relations of the two countries. But her internal disturbances have hitherto prevented the prosecution of them to effect, though we have had repeated assurances of a continuance of the disposition.

Proposals of friendly arrangement have been made on our part, by the present government, to that of Great Britain, as the message states; but, being already on as good a footing in law, and a better in fact, than the most favored nation, they have not, as yet, discovered any disposition to have it meddled with.

We have no reason to conclude that friendly arrangements would be declined by the other nations, with whom we have such commercial intercourse as may render them important. In the meanwhile, it would rest with the wisdom of Congress to determine whether, as to those nations, they will not surcease *ex parte* regulations, on the reasonable presumption that they will concur in doing whatever justice and moderation dictate should be done.

Draft of the Kentucky Resolutions

1. *Resolved*, That the several States composing the United States of America, are not united on the principle of unlimited submission to their General Government; but that, by a compact under the style and title of a Constitution for the United States, and of amendments thereto, they constituted a General Government for special purposes,—delegated to that government certain definite powers, reserving, each State to itself, the residuary mass of right to their own self-government; and that whensoever the General Government assumes undelegated powers, its acts are unauthoritative, void, and of no force; that to this compact each State acceded as a State, and is an integral party, its co-States forming, as to itself, the other party: that the government created by this compact was not made the exclusive or final judge of the extent of the powers delegated to itself; since that would have made its discretion, and not the Constitution, the measure of its powers; but that, as in all other cases of compact among powers having no common judge, each party has an equal right to judge for itself, as well of infractions as of the mode and measure of redress.

2. *Resolved*, That the Constitution of the United States, having delegated to Congress a power to punish treason, counterfeiting the securities and current coin of the United States, piracies, and felonies committed on the high seas, and offences against the law of nations, and no other crimes whatsoever; and it being true as a general principle, and one of the amendments to the Constitution having also declared, that "the powers not delegated to the United States by the Constitution, nor prohibited by it to the States, are reserved to the States respectively, or to the people," therefore the act of Congress, passed on the 14th day of July, 1798, and intituled "An Act in addition to the act intituled An Act for the punishment of certain crimes against the United States," as also the act passed by them on the — day of June, 1798, intituled "An Act to punish frauds committed on the bank of the United States," (and all their other acts which assume to

create, define, or punish crimes, other than those so enumerated in the Constitution,) are altogether void, and of no force; and that the power to create, define, and punish such other crimes is reserved, and, of right, appertains solely and exclusively to the respective States, each within its own territory.

3. *Resolved*, That it is true as a general principle, and is also expressly declared by one of the amendments to the Constitution, that "the powers not delegated to the United States by the Constitution, nor prohibited by it to the States, are reserved to the States respectively, or to the people;" and that no power over the freedom of religion, freedom of speech, or freedom of the press being delegated to the United States by the Constitution, nor prohibited by it to the States, all lawful powers respecting the same did of right remain, and were reserved to the States or the people: that thus was manifested their determination to retain to themselves the right of judging how far the licentiousness of speech and of the press may be abridged without lessening their useful freedom, and how far those abuses which cannot be separated from their use should be tolerated, rather than the use be destroyed. And thus also they guarded against all abridgment by the United States of the freedom of religious opinions and exercises, and retained to themselves the right of protecting the same, as this State, by a law passed on the general demand of its citizens, had already protected them from all human restraint or interference. And that in addition to this general principle and express declaration, another and more special provision has been made by one of the amendments to the Constitution, which expressly declares, that "Congress shall make no law respecting an establishment of religion, or prohibiting the free exercise thereof, or abridging the freedom of speech or of the press:" thereby guarding in the same sentence, and under the same words, the freedom of religion, of speech, and of the press: insomuch, that whatever violated either, throws down the sanctuary which covers the others, and that libels, falsehood, and defamation, equally with heresy and false religion, are withheld from the cognizance of federal tribunals. That, therefore, the act of Congress of the United States, passed on the 14th day of July, 1798, intituled "An Act in addition to the act intituled An Act for the punishment of cer-

tain crimes against the United States," which does abridge the freedom of the press, is not law, but is altogether void, and of no force.

4. *Resolved*, That alien friends are under the jurisdiction and protection of the laws of the State wherein they are: that no power over them has been delegated to the United States, nor prohibited to the individual States, distinct from their power over citizens. And it being true as a general principle, and one of the amendments to the Constitution having also declared, that "the powers not delegated to the United States by the Constitution, nor prohibited by it to the States, are reserved to the States respectively, or to the people," the act of the Congress of the United States, passed on the — day of July, 1798, intituled "An Act concerning aliens," which assumes powers over alien friends, not delegated by the Constitution, is not law, but is altogether void, and of no force.

5. *Resolved*, That in addition to the general principle, as well as the express declaration, that powers not delegated are re-served, another and more special provision, inserted in the Constitution from abundant caution, has declared that "the migration or importation of such persons as any of the States now existing shall think proper to admit, shall not be prohib-ited by the Congress prior to the year 1808;" that this commonwealth does admit the migration of alien friends, described as the subject of the said act concerning aliens: that a provision against prohibiting their migration, is a provision against all acts equivalent thereto, or it would be nugatory: that to remove them when migrated, is equivalent to a pro-hibition of their migration, and is, therefore, contrary to the said provision of the Constitution, and void.

6. *Resolved*, That the imprisonment of a person under the protection of the laws of this commonwealth, on his failure to obey the simple *order* of the President to depart out of the United States, as is undertaken by said act intituled "An Act concerning aliens," is contrary to the Constitution, one amendment to which has provided that "no person shall be deprived of liberty without due process of law;" and that an-other having provided that "in all criminal prosecutions the accused shall enjoy the right to public trial by an impartial jury, to be informed of the nature and cause of the accusation,

to be confronted with the witnesses against him, to have compulsory process for obtaining witnesses in his favor, and to have the assistance of counsel for his defence," the same act, undertaking to authorize the President to remove a person out of the United States, who is under the protection of the law, on his own suspicion, without accusation, without jury, without public trial, without confrontation of the witnesses against him, without hearing witnesses in his favor, without defence, without counsel, is contrary to the provision also of the Constitution, is therefore not law, but utterly void, and of no force: that transferring the power of judging any person, who is under the protection of the laws, from the courts to the President of the United States, as is undertaken by the same act concerning aliens, is against the article of the Constitution which provides that "the judicial power of the United States shall be vested in courts, the judges of which shall hold their offices during good behavior;" and that the said act is void for that reason also. And it is further to be noted, that this transfer of judiciary power is to that magistrate of the General Government who already possesses all the Executive, and a negative on all legislative powers.

7. *Resolved*, That the construction applied by the General Government (as is evidenced by sundry of their proceedings) to those parts of the Constitution of the United States which delegate to Congress a power "to lay and collect taxes, duties, imports, and excises, to pay the debts, and provide for the common defence and general welfare of the United States," and "to make all laws which shall be necessary and proper for carrying into execution the powers vested by the Constitution in the government of the United States, or in any department or officer thereof," goes to the destruction of all limits prescribed to their power by the Constitution: that words meant by the instrument to be subsidiary only to the execution of limited powers, ought not to be so construed as themselves to give unlimited powers, nor a part to be so taken as to destroy the whole residue of that instrument: that the proceedings of the General Government under color of these articles, will be a fit and necessary subject of revisal and correction, at a time of greater tranquillity, while those specified in the preceding resolutions call for immediate redress.

8th. *Resolved*, That a committee of conference and correspondence be appointed, who shall have in charge to communicate the preceding resolutions to the legislatures of the several States; to assure them that this commonwealth continues in the same esteem of their friendship and union which it has manifested from that moment at which a common danger first suggested a common union: that it considers union, for specified national purposes, and particularly to those specified in their late federal compact, to be friendly to the peace, happiness and prosperity of all the States: that faithful to that compact, according to the plain intent and meaning in which it was understood and acceded to by the several parties, it is sincerely anxious for its preservation: that it does also believe, that to take from the States all the powers of self-government and transfer them to a general and consolidated government, without regard to the special delegations and reservations solemnly agreed to in that compact, is not for the peace, happiness or prosperity of these States; and that therefore this commonwealth is determined, as it doubts not its co-States are, to submit to undelegated, and consequently unlimited powers in no man, or body of men on earth: that in cases of an abuse of the delegated powers, the members of the General Government, being chosen by the people, a change by the people would be the constitutional remedy; but, where powers are assumed which have not been delegated, a nullification of the act is the rightful remedy: that every State has a natural right in cases not within the compact, (casus non fœderis,) to nullify of their own authority all assumptions of power by others within their limits: that without this right, they would be under the dominion, absolute and unlimited, of whosoever might exercise this right of judgment for them: that nevertheless, this commonwealth, from motives of regard and respect for its co-States, has wished to communicate with them on the subject: that with them alone it is proper to communicate, they alone being parties to the compact, and solely authorized to judge in the last resort of the powers exercised under it, Congress being not a party, but merely the creature of the compact, and subject as to its assumptions of power to the final judgment of those by whom, and for whose use itself and its powers were all created and modified: that if the acts before specified should stand, these conclusions would flow from them; that the General Government may place any act they think proper on the list of crimes, and punish it themselves whether enumerated or not enumerated by the Constitution as cognizable by them: that they may transfer its cognizance to the President, or any other person, who may himself be the accuser, counsel, judge and jury, whose *suspicions* may be the evidence, his *order* the sentence, his *officer* the executioner, and his breast the sole record of the transaction: that a very numerous and valuable description of the inhabitants of these States being, by this precedent, reduced, as outlaws, to the absolute dominion of one man, and the barrier of the Constitution thus swept away from us all, no rampart now remains against the passions and the powers of a majority in Congress to protect from a like exportation, or other more grievous punishment, the minority of the same body, the legislatures, judges, governors, and counsellors of the States, nor their other peaceable inhabitants, who may venture to reclaim the constitutional rights and liberties of the States and people, or who for other causes, good or bad, may be obnoxious to the views, or marked by the suspicions of the President, or be thought dangerous to his or their election, or other interests, public or personal: that the friendless alien has indeed been selected as the safest subject of a first experiment; but the citizen will soon follow, or rather, has already followed, for already has a sedition act marked him as its prey: that these and successive acts of the same character, unless arrested at the threshold, necessarily drive these States into revolution and blood, and will furnish new calumnies against republican government, and new pretexts for those who wish it to be believed that man cannot be governed but by a rod of iron: that it would be a dangerous delusion were a confidence in the men of our choice to silence our fears for the safety of our rights: that confidence is everywhere the parent of despotism—free government is founded in jealousy, and not in confidence; it is jealousy and not confidence which prescribes limited constitutions, to bind down those whom we are obliged to trust with power: that our Constitution has accordingly fixed the limits to which, and no further, our confidence may go; and let the honest advocate of confidence read the alien and sedition acts, and say if the Constitution has not been wise in fixing limits to the government it created, and whether we should be wise in destroying those limits. Let him say what the government is, if it be not a tyranny, which the men of our choice have conferred on our President, and the President of our choice has assented to, and accepted over the friendly strangers to whom the mild spirit of our country and its laws have pledged hospitality and protection: that the men of our choice have more respected the bare *suspicions* of the President, than the solid right of innocence, the claims of justification, the sacred force of truth, and the forms and substance of law and justice. In questions of power, then, let no more be heard of confidence in man, but bind him down from mischief by the chains of the Constitution. That this commonwealth does therefore call on its co-States for an expression of their sentiments on the acts concerning aliens, and for the punishment of certain crimes herein before specified, plainly declaring whether these acts are or are not authorized by the federal compact. And it doubts not that their sense will be so announced as to prove their attachment unaltered to limited government, whether general or particular. And that the rights and liberties of their co-States will be exposed to no dangers by remaining embarked in a common bottom with their own. That they will concur with this commonwealth in considering the said acts as so palpably against the Constitution as to amount to an undisguised declaration that that compact is not meant to be the measure of the powers of the General Government, but that it will proceed in the exercise over these States, of all powers whatsoever: that they will view this as seizing the rights of the States, and consolidating them in the hands of the General Government, with a power assumed to bind the States, not merely as the cases made federal, (casus fœderis,) but in all cases whatsoever, by laws made, not with their consent, but by others against their consent: that this would be to surrender the form of government we have chosen, and live under one deriving its powers from its own will, and not from our authority; and that the co-States, recurring to their natural right in cases not made federal, will concur in declaring these acts void, and of no force, and will each take measures of its own for providing that neither these acts, nor any others of the General Government not plainly and intentionally authorized by the Constitution, shall be exercised within their respective territories.

9th. *Resolved*, That the said committee be authorized to communicate by writing or personal conferences, at any times or places whatever, with any person or person who may be appointed by any one or more co-States to correspond or confer with them; and that they lay their proceedings before the next session of Assembly.

Report of the Commissioners for the University of Virginia

August 4, 1818

THE COMMISSIONERS for the University of Virginia, having met, as by law required, at the tavern, in Rockfish Gap, on the Blue Ridge, on the first day of August, of this present year, 1818; and having formed a board, proceeded on that day to the discharge of the duties assigned to them by the act of the Legislature, entitled "An act, appropriating part of the revenue of the literary fund, and for other purposes;" and having continued their proceedings by adjournment, from day to day, to Tuesday, the 4th day of August, have agreed to a report on the several matters with which they were charged, which report they now respectfully address and submit to the Legislature of the State.

The first duty enjoined on them, was to enquire and report a site, in some convenient and proper part of the State, for an university, to be called the "University of Virginia." In this enquiry, they supposed that the governing considerations should be the healthiness of the site, the fertility of the neighboring country, and its centrality to the white population of the whole State. For, although the act authorized and required them to receive any voluntary contributions, whether conditional or absolute, which might be offered through them to the President and Directors of the Literary Fund, for the benefit of the University, yet they did not consider this as establishing an auction, or as pledging the location to the highest bidder.

Three places were proposed, to wit: Lexington, in the county of Rockbridge, Staunton, in the county of Augusta, and the Central College, in the county of Albemarle. Each of these was unexceptionable as to healthiness and fertility. It was the degree of centrality to the white population of the State which alone then constituted the important point of comparison between these places; and the Board, after full enquiry, and impartial and mature consideration, are of opinion, that the central point of the white population of the State is nearer to the Central College than to either Lexington or

Staunton, by great and important differences; and all other circumstances of the place in general being favorable to it, as a position for an university, they do report the Central College, in Albemarle, to be a convenient and proper part of the State for the University of Virginia.

2. The Board having thus agreed on a proper site for the University, to be reported to the Legislature, proceed to the second of the duties assigned to them—that of proposing a plan for its buildings—and they are of opinion that it should consist of distinct houses or pavilions, arranged at proper distances on each side of a lawn of a proper breadth, and of indefinite extent, in one direction, at least; in each of which should be a lecturing room, with from two to four apartments, for the accommodation of a professor and his family; that these pavilions should be united by a range of dormitories, sufficient each for the accommodation of two students only, this provision being deemed advantageous to morals, to order, and to uninterrupted study; and that a passage of some kind, under cover from the weather, should give a communication along the whole range. It is supposed that such pavilions, on an average of the larger and smaller, will cost each about $5,000; each dormitory about $350, and hotels of a single room, for a refectory, and two rooms for the tenant, necessary for dieting the students, will cost about $3500 each. The number of these pavilions will depend on the number of professors, and that of the dormitories and hotels on the number of students to be lodged and dieted. The advantages of this plan are: greater security against fire and infection; tranquillity and comfort to the professors and their families thus insulated; retirement to the students; and the admission of enlargement to any degree to which the institution may extend in future times. It is supposed probable, that a building of somewhat more size in the middle of the grounds may be called for in time, in which may be rooms for religious worship, under such impartial regulations as the Visitors shall prescribe, for public examinations, for a library, for the schools of music, drawing, and other associated purposes.

3, 4. In proceeding to the third and fourth duties prescribed by the Legislature, of reporting "the branches of learning, which should be taught in the University, and the number and description of the professorships they will require," the Commissioners were first to consider at what point it was understood that university education should commence? Certainly not with the alphabet, for reasons of expediency and impracticability, as well from the obvious sense of the Legislature, who, in the same act, make other provision for the primary instruction of the poor children, expecting, doubtless, that in other cases it would be provided by the parent, or become, perhaps, subject of future and further attention of the Legislature. The objects of this primary education determine its character and limits. These objects would be,

To give to every citizen the information he needs for the transaction of his own business;

To enable him to calculate for himself, and to express and preserve his ideas, his contracts and accounts, in writing;

To improve, by reading, his morals and faculties;

To understand his duties to his neighbors and country, and to discharge with competence the functions confided to him by either;

To know his rights; to exercise with order and justice those he retains; to choose with discretion the fiduciary of those he delegates; and to notice their conduct with diligence, with candor, and judgment;

And, in general, to observe with intelligence and faithfulness all the social relations under which he shall be placed.

To instruct the mass of our citizens in these, their rights, interests and duties, as men and citizens, being then the objects of education in the primary schools, whether private or public, in them should be taught reading, writing and numerical arithmetic, the elements of mensuration, (useful in so many callings,) and the outlines of geography and history. And this brings us to the point at which are to commence the higher branches of education, of which the Legislature require the development; those, for example, which are,

To form the statesmen, legislators and judges, on whom public prosperity and individual happiness are so much to depend;

To expound the principles and structure of government, the

laws which regulate the intercourse of nations, those formed municipally for our own government, and a sound spirit of legislation, which, banishing all arbitrary and unnecessary restraint on individual action, shall leave us free to do whatever does not violate the equal rights of another;

To harmonize and promote the interests of agriculture, manufactures and commerce, and by well informed views of political economy to give a free scope to the public industry;

To develop the reasoning faculties of our youth, enlarge their minds, cultivate their morals, and instill into them the precepts of virtue and order;

To enlighten them with mathematical and physical sciences, which advance the arts, and administer to the health, the subsistence, and comforts of human life;

And, generally, to form them to habits of reflection and correct action, rendering them examples of virtue to others, and of happiness within themselves.

These are the objects of that higher grade of education, the benefits and blessings of which the Legislature now propose to provide for the good and ornament of their country, the gratification and happiness of their fellow-citizens, of the parent especially, and his progeny, on which all his affections are concentrated.

In entering on this field, the Commissioners are aware that they have to encounter much difference of opinion as to the extent which it is expedient that this institution should occupy. Some good men, and even of respectable information, consider the learned sciences as useless acquirements; some think that they do not better the condition of man; and others that education, like private and individual concerns, should be left to private individual effort; not reflecting that an establishment embracing all the sciences which may be useful and even necessary in the various vocations of life, with the buildings and apparatus belonging to each, are far beyond the reach of individual means, and must either derive existence from public patronage, or not exist at all. This would leave us, then, without those callings which depend on education, or send us to other countries to seek the instruction they require. But the Commissioners are happy in considering the statute under which they are assembled as proof that the

Legislature is far from the abandonment of objects so interesting. They are sensible that the advantages of well-directed education, moral, political and economical, are truly above all estimate. Education generates habits of application, of order, and the love of virtue; and controls, by the force of habit, any innate obliquities in our moral organization. We should be far, too, from the discouraging persuasion that man is fixed, by the law of his nature, at a given point; that his improvement is a chimera, and the hope delusive of rendering ourselves wiser, happier or better than our forefathers were. As well might it be urged that the wild and uncultivated tree, hitherto yielding sour and bitter fruit only, can never be made to yield better; yet we know that the grafting art implants a new tree on the savage stock, producing what is most estimable both in kind and degree. Education, in like manner, engrafts a new man on the native stock, and improves what in his nature was vicious and perverse into qualities of virtue and social worth. And it cannot be but that each generation succeeding to the knowledge acquired by all those who preceded it, adding to it their own acquisitions and discoveries, and handing the mass down for successive and constant accumulation, must advance the knowledge and well-being of mankind, not *infinitely*, as some have said, but *indefinitely*, and to a term which no one can fix and foresee. Indeed, we need look back half a century, to times which many now living remember well, and see the wonderful advances in the sciences and arts which have been made within that period. Some of these have rendered the elements themselves subservient to the purposes of man, have harnessed them to the yoke of his labors, and effected the great blessings of moderating his own, of accomplishing what was beyond his feeble force, and extending the comforts of life to a much enlarged circle, to those who had before known its necessaries only. That these are not the vain dreams of sanguine hope, we have before our eyes real and living examples. What, but education, has advanced us beyond the condition of our indigenous neighbors? And what chains them to their present state of barbarism and wretchedness, but a bigotted veneration for the supposed superlative wisdom of their fathers, and the preposterous idea that they are to look backward for better things, and not forward, longing, as it should seem, to return to the days of eating acorns and roots, rather than indulge in the degeneracies of civilization? And how much more encouraging to the achievements of science and improvement is this, than the desponding view that the condition of man cannot be ameliorated, that what has been must ever be, and that to secure ourselves where we are, we must tread with awful reverence in the footsteps of our fathers. This doctrine is the genuine fruit of the alliance between Church and State; the tenants of which, finding themselves but too well in their present condition, oppose all advances which might unmask their usurpations, and monopolies of honors, wealth, and power, and fear every change, as endangering the comforts they now hold. Nor must we omit to mention, among the benefits of education, the incalculable advantage of training up able counsellors to administer the affairs of our country in all its departments, legislative, executive and judiciary, and to bear their proper share in the councils of our national government; nothing more than education advancing the prosperity, the power, and the happiness of a nation.

Encouraged, therefore, by the sentiments of the Legislature, manifested in this statute, we present the following tabular statement of the branches of learning which we think should be taught in the University, forming them into groups, each of which are within the powers of a single professor:

I. Languages, ancient:
    Latin,
    Greek,
    Hebrew.

II. Languages, modern:
    French,
    Spanish,
    Italian,
    German,
    Anglo-Saxon.

III. Mathematics, pure:
    Algebra,
    Fluxions,
    Geometry, Elementary, Transcendental.
    Architecture, Military, Naval.

IV. Physico-Mathematics:
    Mechanics,
    Statics,
    Dynamics,
    Pneumatics,
    Acoustics,
    Optics,
    Astronomy,
    Geography.

V. Physics, or Natural
    Philosophy:
    Chemistry,
    Mineralogy.

VI. Botany, Zoology.

VII. Anatomy, Medicine.

VIII. Government,
    Political Economy,
    Law of Nature and
      Nations,
    History, being inter-
      woven with Politics
      and Law.

IX. Law, municipal.

X. Ideology,
    General Grammar,
    Ethics, Rhetoric,
    Belles Lettres,
      and the fine arts.

Some of the terms used in this table being subject to a difference of acceptation, it is proper to define the meaning and comprehension intended to be given them here:

Geometry, Elementary, is that of straight lines and of the circle.

    Transcendental, is that of all other curves; it includes, of course, *Projectiles*, a leading branch of the military art.

Military Architecture includes Fortification, another branch of that art.

Statics respect matter generally, in a state of rest, and include Hydrostatics, or the laws of fluids particularly, at rest or in equilibrio.

Dynamics, used as a general term, include
    Dynamics proper, or the laws of *solids* in motion; and
    Hydrodynamics, or Hydraulics, those of *fluids* in motion.

Pneumatics teach the theory of air, its weight, motion, condensation, rarefaction, &c.

Acoustics, or Phonics, the theory of sound.

Optics, the laws of light and vision.

Physics, or Physiology, in a general sense, mean the doctrine of the physical objects of our senses.

Chemistry is meant, with its other usual branches, to comprehend the theory of agriculture.

Mineralogy, in addition to its peculiar subjects, is here understood to embrace what is real in geology.

Ideology is the doctrine of thought.

General Grammar explains the construction of language.

Some articles in this distribution of sciences will need observation. A professor is proposed for ancient languages, the Latin, Greek, and Hebrew, particularly; but these languages being the foundation common to all the sciences, it is difficult to foresee what may be the extent of this school. At the same time, no greater obstruction to industrious study could be proposed than the presence, the intrusions and the noisy turbulence of a multitude of small boys; and if they are to be placed here for the rudiments of the languages, they may be so numerous that its character and value as an University will be merged in those of a Grammar school. It is, therefore, greatly to be wished, that preliminary schools, either on private or public establishment, could be distributed in districts through the State, as preparatory to the entrance of students into the University. The tender age at which this part of education commences, generally about the tenth year, would weigh heavily with parents in sending their sons to a school so distant as the central establishment would be from most of them. Districts of such extent as that every parent should be within a day's journey of his son at school, would be desirable in cases of sickness, and convenient for supplying their ordinary wants, and might be made to lessen sensibly the expense of this part of their education. And where a sparse population would not, within such a compass, furnish subjects sufficient to maintain a school, a competent enlargement of district must, of necessity, there be submitted to. At these district schools or colleges, boys should be rendered able to read the easier authors, Latin and Greek. This would be useful and sufficient for many not intended for an University education. At these, too, might be taught English grammar, the higher branches of numerical arithmetic, the geometry of straight lines and of the circle, the elements of navigation, and geography to a sufficient degree, and thus afford to greater numbers the means of being qualified for the various vocations of life, needing more instruction than merely menial or prædial labor, and the same advantages to youths whose education may have been neglected until too late to lay a foundation in the learned languages. These institutions, intermediate between the primary schools and University, might then be the passage of entrance for youths into the University, where their classical learning might be critically completed, by a study of the authors of highest degree; and it is at this stage only that they should be received at the University. Giving then a portion of their time to a finished knowledge of the Latin and Greek, the rest might be appropriated to the modern languages, or to the commencement of the course of science for which they should be destined. This would generally be about the fifteenth year of their age, when they might go with more safety and contentment to that distance from their parents. Until this preparatory provision shall be made, either the University will be overwhelmed with the grammar school, or a separate establishment, under one or more ushers, for its lower classes, will be advisable, at a mile or two distant from the general one; where, too, may be exercised the stricter government necessary for young boys, but unsuitable for youths arrived at years of discretion.

The considerations which have governed the specification of languages to be taught by the professor of modern languages were, that the French is the language of general intercourse among nations, and as a depository of human science, is unsurpassed by any other language, living or dead; that the Spanish is highly interesting to us, as the language spoken by so great a portion of the inhabitants of our continents, with whom we shall probably have great intercourse ere long, and is that also in which is written the greater part of the earlier history of America. The Italian abounds with works of very superior order, valuable for their matter, and still more distinguished as models of the finest taste in style and composition. And the German now stands in a line with that of the most learned nations in richness of erudition and advance in the sciences. It is too of common descent with the language of our own country, a branch of the same original Gothic stock, and furnishes valuable illustrations for us. But in this point of view, the Anglo-Saxon is of peculiar value. We have placed it among the modern languages, because it is in fact that which we speak, in the earliest form in which we have knowledge of it. It has been undergoing, with time, those gradual changes which all languages, ancient and modern, have experienced; and even now needs only to be printed in the modern character and orthography to be intelligible, in a considerable degree, to an English reader. It has this value, too, above the Greek and Latin, that while it gives the radix of the mass of our language, they explain its innovations only. Obvious proofs of this have been presented to the modern reader in the disquisitions of Horn Tooke; and Fortescue Aland has well explained the great instruction which may be derived from it to a full understanding of our ancient common law, on which, as a stock, our whole system of law is engrafted. It will form the first link in the chain of an historical review of our language through all its successive changes to the present day, will constitute the foundation of that critical instruction in it which ought to be found in a seminary of general learning, and thus reward amply the few weeks of attention which would alone be requisite for its attainment; a language already fraught with all the eminent science of our parent country, the future vehicle of whatever we may ourselves achieve, and destined to occupy so much space on the globe, claims distinguished attention in American education.

Medicine, where fully taught, is usually subdivided into several professorships, but this cannot well be without the accessory of an hospital, where the student can have the benefit of attending clinical lectures, and of assisting at operations of surgery. With this accessory, the seat of our University is not yet prepared, either by its population or by the numbers of poor who would leave their own houses, and accept of the charities of an hospital. For the present, therefore, we propose but a single professor for both medicine and anatomy. By him the medical science may be taught, with a history and explanations of all its successive theories from Hippocrates to the present day; and anatomy may be fully treated. Vegetable pharmacy will make a part of the botanical course, and mineral and chemical pharmacy of those of mineralogy and chemistry. This degree of medical information is such as the mass of scientific students would wish to possess, as enabling them in their course through life, to estimate with satisfaction the extent and limits of the aid to human life and health, which they may understandingly expect from that art; and it constitutes such a foundation for those intended for the profession, that the finishing course of practice at the bed-sides of the sick, and at the operations of surgery in a hospital, can neither be long nor expensive. To seek this finishing elsewhere, must therefore be submitted to for a while.

In conformity with the principles of our Constitution, which places all sects of religion on an equal footing, with the jealousies of the different sects in guarding that equality from encroachment and surprise, and with the sentiments of the Legislature in favor of freedom of religion, manifested on former occasions, we have proposed no professor of divinity; and the rather as the proofs of the being of a God, the creator, preserver, and supreme ruler of the universe, the author of all the relations of morality, and of the laws and obligations these infer, will be within the province of the professor of ethics; to which adding the developments of these moral obligations, of those in which all sects agree, with a knowledge of the languages, Hebrew, Greek, and Latin, a basis will be formed common to all sects. Proceeding thus far without offence to the Constitution, we have thought it proper at this point to leave every sect to provide, as they think fittest, the means of further instruction in their own peculiar tenets.

We are further of opinion, that after declaring by law that certain sciences shall be taught in the University, fixing the number of professors they require, which we think should, at present, be ten, limiting (except as to the professors who shall be first engaged in each branch,) a maximum for their salaries, (which should be a certain but moderate subsistence, to be made up by liberal tuition fees, as an excitement to assiduity,) it will be best to leave to the discretion of the visitors, the grouping of these sciences together, according to the accidental qualifications of the professors; and the introduction also of other branches of science, when enabled by private donations, or by public provision, and called for by the increase of population, or other change of circumstances; to establish beginnings, in short, to be developed by time, as those who come after us shall find expedient. They will be more advanced than we are in science and in useful arts, and will know best what will suit the circumstances of their day.

We have proposed no formal provision for the gymnastics of the school, although a proper object of attention for every institution of youth. These exercises with ancient nations, constituted the principal part of the education of their youth. Their arms and mode of warfare rendered them severe in the extreme; ours, on the same correct principle, should be adapted to our arms and warfare; and the manual exercise, military manœuvres, and tactics generally, should be the frequent exercises of the students, in their hours of recreation. It is at that age of aptness, docility, and emulation of the practices of manhood, that such things are soonest learnt and longest remembered. The use of tools too in the manual arts is worthy of encouragement, by facilitating to such as choose it, an admission into the neighboring workshops. To these should be added the arts which embellish life, dancing, music, and drawing; the last more especially, as an important part of military education. These innocent arts furnish amusement and happiness to those who, having time on their hands, might less inoffensively employ it. Needing, at the same time, no regular incorporation with the institution, they may be left to accessory teachers, who will be paid by the individuals employing them, the University only providing proper apartments for their exercise.

The fifth duty prescribed to the Commissioners, is to propose such general provisions as may be properly enacted by the Legislature, for the better organizing and governing the University.

In the education of youth, provision is to be made for, 1, tuition; 2, diet; 3, lodging; 4, government; and 5, honorary excitements. The first of these constitutes the proper functions of the professors; 2, the dieting of the students should be left to private boarding houses of their own choice, and at their own expense; to be regulated by the Visitors from time to time, the house only being provided by the University within its own precincts, and thereby of course subjected to the general regimen, moral or sumptuary, which they shall prescribe. 3. They should be lodged in dormitories, making a part of the general system of buildings. 4. The best mode of

government for youth, in large collections, is certainly a desideratum not yet attained with us. It may be well questioned whether *fear* after a certain age, is a motive to which we should have ordinary recourse. The human character is susceptible of other incitements to correct conduct, more worthy of employ, and of better effect. Pride of character, laudable ambition, and moral dispositions are innate correctives of the indiscretions of that lively age; and when strengthened by habitual appeal and exercise, have a happier effect on future character than the degrading motive of fear. Hardening them to disgrace, to corporal punishments, and servile humiliations cannot be the best process for producing erect character. The affectionate deportment between father and son, offers in truth the best example for that of tutor and pupil; and the experience and practice of other* countries, in this respect, may be worthy of enquiry and consideration with us. It will then be for the wisdom and discretion of the Visitors to devise and perfect a proper system of government, which, if it be founded in reason and comity, will be more likely to nourish in the minds of our youth the combined spirit of order and self-respect, so congenial with our political institutions, and so important to be woven into the American character.
5. What qualifications shall be required to entitle to entrance into the University, the arrangement of the days and hours of lecturing for the different schools, so as to facilitate to the students the circle of attendance on them; the establishment of periodical and public examinations, the premiums to be given for distinguished merit; whether honorary degrees shall be conferred, and by what appellations; whether the title to these shall depend on the time the candidate has been at the University, or, where nature has given a greater share of understanding, attention, and application; whether he shall not be allowed the advantages resulting from these endowments, with other minor items of government, we are of opinion should be entrusted to the Visitors; and the statute under which we act having provided for the appointment of these, we think they should moreover be charged with

---

*A police exercised by the students themselves, under proper discretion, has been tried with success in some countries, and the rather as forming them for initiation into the duties and practices of civil life.

The erection, preservation, and repair of the buildings, the care of the grounds and appurtenances, and of the interest of the University generally.

That they should have power to appoint a bursar, employ a proctor, and all other necessary agents.

To appoint and remove professors, two-thirds of the whole number of Visitors voting for the removal.

To prescribe their duties and the course of education, in conformity with the law.

To establish rules for the government and discipline of the students, not contrary to the laws of the land.

To regulate the tuition fees, and the rent of the dormitories they occupy.

To prescribe and control the duties and proceedings of all officers, servants, and others, with respect to the buildings, lands, appurtenances, and other property and interests of the University.

To draw from the literary fund such moneys as are by law charged on it for this institution; and in general

To direct and do all matters and things which, not being inconsistent with the laws of the land, to them shall seem most expedient for promoting the purposes of the said institution; which several functions they should be free to exercise in the form of by-laws, rules, resolutions, orders, instructions, or otherwise, as they should deem proper.

That they should have two stated meetings in the year, and occasional meetings at such times as they should appoint, or on a special call with such notice as themselves shall prescribe by a general rule; which meetings should be at the University, a majority of them constituting a quorum for business; and that on the death or resignation of a member, or on his removal by the President and Directors of the Literary Fund, or the Executive, or such other authority as the Legislature shall think best, such President and Directors, or the Executive, or other authority, shall appoint a successor.

That the said Visitors should appoint one of their own body to be Rector, and with him be a body corporate, under the style and title of the Rector and Visitors of the University of Virginia, with the right, as such, to use a common seal; that they should have capacity to plead and be impleaded in all courts of justice, and in all cases interesting to the University, which may be the subjects of legal cognizance and jurisdiction; which pleas should not abate by the determination of their office, but should stand revived in the name of their successors, and they should be capable in law and in trust for the University, of receiving subscriptions and donations, real and personal, as well from bodies corporate, or persons associated, as from private individuals.

And that the said Rector and Visitors should, at all times, conform to such laws as the Legislature may, from time to time, think proper to enact for their government; and the said University should, in all things, and at all times, be subject to the control of the Legislature.

And lastly, the Commissioners report to the Legislature the following conditional offers to the President and Directors of the Literary Fund, for the benefit of the University:

On the condition that Lexington, or its vicinity, shall be selected as the site of the University, and that the same be permanently established there within two years from the date, John Robinson, of Rockbridge county, has executed a deed to the President and Directors of the Literary Fund, to take effect at his death, for the following tracts of land, to wit:

400 acres on the North fork of James river, known by the name of Hart's bottom, purchased of the late Gen. Bowyer.

171 acres adjoining the same, purchased of James Griggsby.

203 acres joining the last mentioned tract, purchased of William Paxton.

112 acres lying on the North river, above the lands of Arthur Glasgow, conveyed to him by William Paxton's heirs.

500 acres adjoining the lands of Arthur Glasgow, Benjamin Camden and David Edmonson.

545 acres lying in Pryor's gap, conveyed to him by the heirs of William Paxton, deceased.

260 acres lying in Childer's gap, purchased of Wm. Mitchell.

300 acres lying, also, in Childer's gap, purchased of Nicholas Jones.

500 acres lying on Buffalo, joining the lands of Jas. Johnston.

340 acres on the Cowpasture river, conveyed to him by

General James Breckenridge—reserving the right of selling the two last mentioned tracts, and converting them into other lands contiguous to Hart's bottom, for the benefit of the University; also the whole of his slaves, amounting to 57 in number; one lot of 22 acres, joining the town of Lexington, to pass immediately on the establishment of the University, together with all the personal estate of every kind, subject only to the payment of his debts and fulfillment of his contracts.

It has not escaped the attention of the Commissioners, that the deed referred to is insufficient to pass the estate in the lands intended to be conveyed, and may be otherwise defective; but if necessary, this defect may be remedied before the meeting of the Legislature, which the Commissioners are advised will be done.

The Board of Trustees of Washington College have also proposed to transfer the whole of their funds, viz: 100 shares in the funds of the James River Company, 31 acres of land upon which their buildings stand, their philosophical apparatus, their expected interest in the funds of the Cincinnati Society, the libraries of the Graham and Washington Societies, and $3,000 in cash, on condition that a reasonable provision be made for the present professors. A subscription has also been offered by the people of Lexington and its vicinity, amounting to $17,878, all which will appear from the deed and other documents, reference thereto being had.

In this case, also, it has not escaped the attention of the Commissioners, that questions may arise as to the power of the trustees to make the above transfers.

On the condition that the Central College shall be made the site of the University, its whole property, real and personal, in possession or in action, is offered. This consists of a parcel of land of 47 acres, whereon the buildings of the college are begun, one pavilion and its appendix of dormitories being already far advanced, and with one other pavilion, and equal annexation of dormitories, being expected to be completed during the present season—of another parcel of 153 acres, near the former, and including a considerable eminence very favorable for the erection of a future observatory; of the proceeds of the sales of two glebes, amounting to $3,280 86 cents; and of a subscription of $41,248, on papers in hand, besides what is on outstanding papers of unknown amount, not yet returned—out of these sums are to be taken, however, the cost of the lands, of the buildings, and other works done, and for existing contracts. For the conditional transfer to these to the President and Directors of the Literary Fund, a regular power, signed by the subscribers and founders of the Central College generally, has been given to its Visitors and Proctor, and a deed conveying the said property accordingly to the President and Directors of the Literary Fund, has been duly executed by the said Proctor, and acknowledged for record in the office of the clerk of the county court of Albemarle.

Signed and certified by the members present, each in his proper hand-writing, this 4th day of August, 1818.

TH: JEFFERSON,
CREED TAYLOR,
PETER RANDOLPH,
WM. BROCKENBROUGH,
ARCH'D RUTHERFORD,
ARDH'D STUART,
JAMES BRECKENRIDGE,
HENRY E. WATKINS,
JAMES MADISON,
A. T. MASON,
HUGH HOLMES,

PHIL. C. PENDLETON,
SPENCER ROANE,
JOHN M. C. TAYLOR,
J. G. JACKSON,
PHIL. SLAUGHTER,
WM. H. CABELL,
NAT. H. CLAIBORNE,
WM. A. C. DADE,
WILLIAM JONES,
THOMAS WILSON.

Memorial on the Book Duty

November 30, 1821

To the Senate and House of Representatives of the United States of America in Congress assembled:

THE PETITION of the rector and visiters of the University of Virginia, on behalf of those for whom they are in the office of preparing the means of instruction, as well as of others seeking it elsewhere, respectfully representeth:

That the Commonwealth of Virginia has thought proper lately to establish a university for instruction, generally, in all the useful branches of science, of which your petitioners are appointed rector and visiters, and, as such, are charged with attention to the interests of those who shall be committed to their care.

That they observe, by the tariff of duties imposed by the laws of Congress on importations into the United States, an article peculiarly inauspicious to the objects of their own, and of all other literary institutions throughout the United States.

That at an early period of the present Government, when our country was burdened with a heavy debt, contracted in the war of Independence, and its resources for revenue were untried and uncertain, the National Legislature thought it as yet inexpedient to indulge in scruples as to the subjects of taxation, and, among others, imposed a duty on books imported from abroad, which has been continued, and now is, of fifteen per cent., on their prime cost, raised by ordinary custom-house charges to eighteen per cent., and by the importer's profits to perhaps twenty-five per cent., and more.

That, after many years' experience, it is certainly found that the reprinting of books in the United States is confined chiefly to those in our native language, and of popular characters, and to cheap editions of a few of the classics for the use of schools; while the valuable editions of the classical authors, even learned works in the English language, and books in all foreign living languages, (vehicles of the important discoveries and improvements in science and the arts, which are daily advancing the interest and happiness of other nations,) are unprinted here, and unobtainable from abroad but under the burden of a heavy duty.

That of many important books, in different branches of science, it is believed that there is not a single copy in the United States; of others, but a few; and these too distant and difficult of access for students and writers generally.

That the difficulty resulting from this mode of procuring books of the first order in the sciences, and in foreign languages, ancient and modern, is an unfair impediment to the American student, who, for want of these aids, already possessed or easily procurable in all countries except our own, enters on his course with very unequal means, with wants unknown to his foreign competitors, and often with that imperfect result which subjects us to reproaches not unfelt by minds alive to the honor and mortified sensibilities of their country.

That, to obstruct the acquisition of books from abroad, as an encouragement of the progress of literature at home, is burying the fountain to increase the flow of its waters.

That books, and especially those of the rare and valuable character, thus burdened, are not articles of consumption, but of permanent preservation and value, lasting often as many centuries as the houses we live in, of which examples are to be found in every library of note.

That books, therefore, are capital, often the only capital of professional men on their outset in life, and of students destined for professions, (as most of our scholars are,) and barely able, too, for the most part, to meet the expenses of tuition, and less to pay as extra tax on the books necessary for their instruction, that they are consequently less instructed than they would be; and that our citizens at large do not derive from their employment all the benefits which higher qualifications would procure them.

That this is the only form of capital on which a tax of from 18 to 25 per cent. is first levied on the gross, and the proprietor then subject to all other taxes in detail, as those holding capitals in other forms, on which no such extra tax has been previously levied.

That it is true that no duty is required on books imported for seminaries of learning; but these, locked up in libraries, can be of no avail to the practical man, when he wishes a recurrence to them for the uses of life.

That more than thirty years' experience of the resources of our country prove them equal to all its debts and wants, and permit its Legislature now to favor such objects as the public interests recommend to favor.

That the value of science to a republican people; the security it gives to liberty, by enlightening the minds of its citizens; the protection it affords against foreign power; the virtues it inculcates; the just emulation of the distinction it confers on nations foremost in it; in short, its identification with power, morals, order, and happiness, (which merits to it premiums of encouragement rather than repressive taxes,) are topics, which your petitioners do not permit themselves to urge on the wisdom of Congress, before whose minds these considerations are always present, and bearing with their just weight.

And they conclude, therefore, with praying that Congress will be pleased to bestow on this important subject the attention it merits, and give the proper relief to the candidates of science among ourselves, devoting themselves to the laudable object of qualifying themselves to become the instructors and benefactors of their fellow-citizens.

And your petitioners, as in duty bound, shall ever pray, &c.

From the Minutes of the Board of Visitors, University of Virginia, 1822–1825

Report to the President and Directors of the Literary Fund (extract)

October 7, 1822

IN THE SAME REPORT of the commissioners of 1818 it was stated by them that "in conformity with the principles of our constitution, which places all sects of religion on an equal footing, with the jealousies of the different sects in guarding that equality from encroachment or surprise, and with the sentiments of the legislature in freedom of religion, manifested on former occasions, they had not proposed that any professorship of divinity should be established in the University; that provision, however, was made for giving instruction in the Hebrew, Greek and Latin languages, the depositories of the originals, and of the earliest and most respected authorities of the faith of every sect, and for courses of ethical lectures, developing those moral obligations in which all sects agree. That, proceeding thus far, without offence to the constitution, they had left, at this point, to every sect to take into their own hands the office of further instruction in the peculiar tenet of each."

It was not, however, to be understood that instruction in religious opinion and duties was meant to be precluded by the public authorities, as indifferent to the interests of society. On the contrary, the relations which exist between man and his Maker, and the duties resulting from those relations, are the most interesting and important to every human being, and the most incumbent on his study and investigation. The want of instruction in the various creeds of religious faith existing among our citizens presents, therefore, a chasm in a general institution of the useful sciences. But it was thought that this want, and the entrustment to each society of instruction in its own doctrine, were evils of less danger than a permission to the public authorities to dictate modes or principles of religious instruction, or than opportunities furnished them by giving countenance or ascendancy to any one sect over another. A remedy, however, has been suggested of promising aspect, which, while it excludes the public authorities from the domain of religious freedom, will give to the sectarian schools of divinity the full benefit the public provisions made for instruction in the other branches of science. These branches are equally necessary to the divine as to the other professional or civil characters, to enable them to fulfill the duties of their calling with understanding and usefulness. It has, therefore, been in contemplation, and suggested by some pious individuals, who perceive the advantages of associating other studies with those of religion, to establish their religious schools on the confines of the University, so as to give to their students ready and convenient access and attendance on the scientific lectures of the University; and to maintain, by that means, those destined for the religious professions on as high a standing of science, and of personal weight and respectability, as may be obtained by others from the benefits of the University. Such establishments would offer the further and greater advantage of enabling the students of the University to attend religious exercises with the professor of their particular sect, either in the rooms of the building still to be erected, and destined to that purpose under impartial regulations, as proposed in the same report of the commissioners, or in the lecturing room of such professor. To such propositions the Visitors are disposed to lend a willing ear, and would think it their duty to give every encouragement, by assuring to those who might choose such a location for their schools, that the regulations of the University should be so modified and accommodated as to give every facility of access and attendance to their students, with such regulated use also as may be permitted to the other students, of the library which may hereafter be acquired, either by public or private munificence. But always understanding that these schools shall be independent of the University and of each other. Such an arrangement would complete the circle of the useful sciences embraced by this institution, and would fill the chasm now existing, on principles which would leave inviolate the constitutional freedom of religion, the most inalienable and sacred of all human rights, over which the people and authorities of this state, individually and publicly, have ever manifested the most watchful jealousy: and could this jealousy be now alarmed, in the opinion of the legislature, by what is here suggested, the idea will be relinquished on any surmise of disapprobation which they might think proper to express.

March 4, 1825

A resolution was moved and agreed to in the following words:

Whereas, it is the duty of this Board to the government under which it lives, and especially to that of which this University is the immediate creation, to pay especial attention to the principles of government which shall be inculcated therein, and to provide that none shall be inculcated which are incompatible with those on which the Constitutions of this State, and of the United States were genuinely based, in the common opinion; and for this purpose it may be necessary to point out specially where these principles are to be found legitimately developed:

Resolved, that it is the opinion of this Board that as to the general principles of liberty and the rights of man, in nature and in society, the doctrines of Locke, in his "Essay concerning the true original extent and end of civil government," and of Sidney in his "Discourses on government," may be considered as those generally approved by our fellow citizens of this, and the United States, and that on the distinctive principles of the government of our State, and of that of the United States, the best guides are to be found in, 1. The Declaration of Independence, as the fundamental act of union of these States. 2. The book known by the title of "The Federalist," being an authority to which appeal is habitually made by all, and rarely declined or denied by any as evidence of the general opinion of those who framed, and of those who accepted the Constitution of the United States, on questions as to its genuine meaning. 3. The Resolutions of the General Assembly of Virginia in 1799 on the subject of the alien and sedition laws, which appeared to accord with the predominant sense of the people of the United States. 4. The valedictory address of President Washington, as conveying political lessons of peculiar value. And that in the branch of the school of law, which is to treat on the subject of civil polity, these shall be used as the text and documents of the school.

Resolved, that it be communicated to the Faculty of the professors of the University, as the earnest request and recommendation of the rector and Visitors, that so far as can be effected by their exertions, they cause the statutes and rules enacted for the government of the University, to be exactly and strictly observed; that the roll of each school particularly be punctually called at the hour at which its students should attend; that the absent and the tardy, without reasonable cause, be noted, and a copy of these notations be communicated by mail or otherwise to the parent or guardian of each student respectively, on the first days of every month during the term (instead of the days prescribed in a former statute for such communications).

That it is requested of them to make known to the students that it is with great regret that some breaches of order, committed by the unworthy few who lurk among them unknown, render necessary the extension to all of processes afflicting to the feelings of those who are conscious of their own correctness, and who are above all participation in these vicious irregularities. While the offenders continue unknown the tarnish of their faults spreads itself over the worthy also, and confounds all in a common censure. But that it is in their power to relieve themselves from the imputations and painful proceedings to which they are thereby subjected, by lending their aid to the faculty, on all occasions towards detecting the real guilty. The Visitors are aware that a prejudice prevails too extensively among the young that it is dishonorable to bear witness one against another. While this prevails, and under the form of a matter of conscience, they have been unwilling to authorize constraint, and have therefore, in their regulations on this subject, indulged the error, however unfounded in reason or morality. But this loose principle in the ethics of school-boy combinations, is unworthy of mature and regulated minds, and is accordingly condemned by the laws of their country, which, in offences within their cognisance, compel those who have knowledge of a fact, to declare it for the purposes of justice, and of the general good and safety of society. And certainly, where wrong has been done, he who knows and conceals the doer of it, makes himself an accomplice, and justly censurable as such. It becomes then but an act of justice to themselves, that the innocent and the worthy should throw off with disdain all communion of character with such offenders, should determine no longer to screen the irregular and the vicious under the respect of their cloak, and to notify them, even by a solemn association for the purpose, that they will co-operate with the faculty in future, for preservation of order, the vindication of their own character, and the reputation and usefulness of an institution which their country has so liberally established for their improvement, and to place within their reach those acquirements in knowledge on which their future happiness and fortunes depend. Let the good and the virtuous of the alumni of the University do this, and the disorderly will then be singled out for observation, and deterred by punishment, or disabled by expulsion, from infecting with their inconsideration the institution itself, and the sound mass of those which it is preparing for virtue and usefulness.

Draft Declaration and Protest of the Commonwealth of Virginia, on the Principles of the Constitution of the United States of America, and on the Violations of them

December 1825

W E, the General Assembly of Virginia, on behalf, and in the name of the people thereof, do declare as follows:

The States in North America which confederated to establish their independence of the government of Great Britain, of which Virginia was one, became, on that acquisition, free and independent States, and as such, authorized to constitute governments, each for itself, in such form as it thought best.

They entered into a compact, (which is called the Constitution of the United States of America,) by which they agreed to unite in a single government as to their relations with each other, and with foreign nations, and as to certain other articles particularly specified. They retained at the same time, each to itself, the other rights of independent government, comprehending mainly their domestic interests.

For the administration of their federal branch, they agreed to appoint, in conjunction, a distinct set of functionaries, legislative, executive, and judiciary, in the manner settled in that compact: while to each, severally, and of course, remained its original right of appointing, each for itself, a separate set of functionaries, legislative, executive, and judiciary, also, for administering the domestic branch of their respective governments.

These two sets of officers, each independent of the other, constitute thus a *whole* of government, for each State separately; the powers ascribed to the one, as specifically made federal, exercised over the whole, the residuary powers, retained to the other, exercisable exclusively over its particular State, foreign herein, each to the others, as they were before the original compact.

To this construction of government and distribution of its powers, the Commonwealth of Virginia does religiously and affectionately adhere, opposing, with equal fidelity and firmness, the usurpation of either set of functionaries on the rightful powers of the other.

But the federal branch has assumed in some cases, and claimed in others, a right of enlarging its own powers by constructions, inferences, and indefinite deductions from those directly given, which this assembly does declare to be usurpations of the powers retained to the independent branches, mere interpolations into the compact, and direct infractions of it.

They claim, for example, and have commenced the exercise of a right to construct roads, open canals, and effect other internal improvements within the territories and jurisdictions exclusively belonging to the several States, which this assembly does declare has not been given to that branch by the constitutional compact, but remains to each State among its domestic and unalienated powers, exercisable within itself and by its domestic authorities alone.

This assembly does further disavow and declare to be most false and unfounded, the doctrine that the compact, in authorizing its federal branch to lay and collect taxes, duties, imposts and excises to pay the debts and provide for the common defence and general welfare of the United States, has given them thereby a power to do whatever *they* may think, or pretend, would promote the general welfare, which construction would make that, of itself, a complete government, without limitation of powers; but that the plain sense and obvious meaning were, that they might levy the taxes necessary to provide for the general welfare, by the various acts of power therein specified and delegated to them, and by no others.

Nor is it admitted, as has been said, that the people of these States, by not investing their federal branch with all the means of bettering their condition, have denied to themselves any which may effect that purpose; since, in the distribution of these means they have given to that branch those which belong to its department, and to the States have reserved separately the residue which belong to them separately. And thus by the organization of the two branches taken together, have completely secured the first object of human association, the full improvement of their condition, and reserved to themselves all the faculties of multiplying their own blessings.

Whilst the General Assembly thus declares the rights retained by the States, rights which they have never yielded, and which this State will never voluntarily yield, they do not mean to raise the banner of disaffection, or of separation from their sister States, co-parties with themselves to this compact. They know and value too highly the blessings of their Union as to foreign nations and questions arising among themselves, to consider every infraction as to be met by actual resistance. They respect too affectionately the opinions of those possessing the same rights under the same instrument, to make every difference of construction a ground of immediate rupture. They would, indeed, consider such a rupture as among the greatest calamities which could befall them; but not the greatest. There is yet one greater, submission to a government of unlimited powers. It is only when the hope of avoiding this shall become absolutely desperate, that further forebearance could not be indulged. Should a majority of the co-parties, therefore, contrary to the expectation and hope of this assembly, prefer, at this time, acquiescence in these assumptions of power by the federal member of the government, we will be patient and suffer much, under the confidence that time, ere it be too late, will prove to them also the bitter consequences in which that usurpation will involve us all. In the meanwhile, we will breast with them, rather than separate from them, every misfortune, save that only of living under a government of unlimited powers. We owe every other sacrifice to ourselves, to our federal brethren, and to the world at large, to pursue with temper and perseverance the great experiment which shall prove that man is capable of living in society, governing itself by laws self-imposed, and securing to its members the enjoyment of life, liberty, property, and peace; and further to show, that even when the government of its choice shall manifest a tendency to degeneracy, we are not at once to despair but that the will and the watchfulness of its sounder parts will reform its aberrations, recall it to original and legitimate principles, and restrain it within the rightful limits of self-government. And these are the objects of this Declaration and Protest.

Supposing then, that it might be for the good of the whole, as some of its co-States seem to think, that the power of making roads and canals should be added to those directly given to the federal branch, as more likely to be systematically and beneficially directed, than by the independent action of the several States, this commonwealth, from respect to these opinions, and a desire of conciliation with its co-States, will consent, in concurrence with them, to make this addition, provided it be done regularly by an amendment of the compact, in the way established by that instrument, and provided also, it be sufficiently guarded against abuses, compromises, and corrupt practices, not only of possible, but of probable occurrence.

And as a further pledge of the sincere and cordial attachment of this commonwealth to the union of the whole, so far as has been consented to by the compact called "The Constitution of the United States of America," (constructed according to the plain and ordinary meaning of its language, to the common intendment of the time, and of those who framed it;) to give also to all parties and authorities, time for reflection and for consideration, whether, under a temperate view of the possible consequences, and especially of the constant obstructions which an equivocal majority must ever expect to meet, they will still prefer the assumption of this power rather than its acceptance from the free will of their constituents; and to preserve peace in the meanwhile, we proceed to make it the duty of our citizens, until the legislature shall otherwise and ultimately decide, to acquiesce under those acts of the federal branch of our government which we have declared to be usurpations, and against which, in point of right, we do protest as null and void, and never to be quoted as precedents of right.

We therefore do enact, and be it enacted by the General Assembly of Virginia, that all citizens of this commonwealth, and persons and authorities within the same, shall pay full obedience at all times to the acts which may be passed by the Congress of the United States, the object of which shall be the construction of post roads, making canals of navigation, and maintaining the same in any part of the United States, in like manner as if said acts were, *totidem verbis*, passed by the legislature of this commonwealth.

ADDRESSES, MESSAGES, AND REPLIES

Contents

INDIAN ADDRESSES

Response to the Citizens of Albemarle

February 12, 1790

GENTLEMEN,

The testimony of esteem with which you are pleased to honour my return to my native country fills me with gratitude and pleasure. While it shews that my absence has not lost me your friendly recollection, it holds out the comfortable hope that when the hour of retirement shall come, I shall again find myself amidst those with whom I have long lived, with whom I wish to live, and whose affection is the source of my purest happiness. Their favor was the door thro' which I was ushered on the stage of public life; and while I have been led on thro' it's varying scenes, I could not be unmindful of those who assigned me my first part.

My feeble and obscure exertions in their service, and in the holy cause of freedom, have had no other merit than that they were my best. We have all the same. We have been fellow-labourers and fellow-sufferers, and heaven has rewarded us with a happy issue from our struggles. It rests now with ourselves alone to enjoy in peace and concord the blessings of self-government, so long denied to mankind: to shew by example the sufficiency of human reason for the care of human affairs and that the will of the majority, the Natural law of every society, is the only sure guardian of the rights of man. Perhaps even this may sometimes err. But it's errors are honest, solitary and short-lived.—Let us then, my dear friends, for ever bow down to the general reason of the society. We are safe with that, even in it's deviations, for it soon returns again to the right way. These are lessons we have learnt together. We have prospered in their practice, and the liberality with which you are pleased to approve my attachment to the general rights of mankind assures me we are still together in these it's kindred sentiments.

Wherever I may be stationed, by the will of my country, it will be my delight to see, in the general tide of happiness, that yours too flows on in just place and measure. That it may flow thro' all times, gathering strength as it goes, and spreading the happy influence of reason and liberty over the face of the earth, is my fervent prayer to heaven.

First Inaugural Address

March 4, 1801

FRIENDS AND FELLOW-CITIZENS,

Called upon to undertake the duties of the first executive office of our country, I avail myself of the presence of that portion of my fellow-citizens which is here assembled to express my grateful thanks for the favor with which they have been pleased to look toward me, to declare a sincere consciousness that the task is above my talents, and that I approach it with those anxious and awful presentiments which the greatness of the charge and the weakness of my powers so justly inspire. A rising nation, spread over a wide and fruitful land, traversing all the seas with the rich productions of their industry, engaged in commerce with nations who feel power and forget right, advancing rapidly to destinies beyond the reach of mortal eye—when I contemplate these transcendent objects, and see the honor, the happiness, and the hopes of this beloved country committed to the issue and the auspices of this day, I shrink from the contemplation, and humble myself before the magnitude of the undertaking. Utterly, indeed, should I despair did not the presence of many whom I here see remind me that in the other high authorities provided by our Constitution I shall find resources of wisdom, of virtue, and of zeal on which to rely under all difficulties. To you, then, gentlemen, who are charged with the sovereign functions of legislation, and to those associated with you, I look with encouragement for that guidance and support which may enable us to steer with safety the vessel in which we are all embarked amidst the conflicting elements of a troubled world.

During the contest of opinion through which we have passed the animation of discussions and of exertions has sometimes worn an aspect which might impose on strangers unused to think freely and to speak and to write what they think; but this being now decided by the voice of the nation, announced according to the rules of the Constitution, all will, of course, arrange themselves under the will of the law, and unite in common efforts for the common good. All, too, will bear in mind this sacred principle, that though the will of the majority is in all cases to prevail, that will to be rightful must be reasonable; that the minority possess their equal rights, which equal law must protect, and to violate would be oppression. Let us, then, fellow-citizens, unite with one heart and one mind. Let us restore to social intercourse that harmony and affection without which liberty and even life itself are but dreary things. And let us reflect that, having banished from our land that religious intolerance under which mankind so long bled and suffered, we have yet gained little if we countenance a political intolerance as despotic, as wicked, and capable of as bitter and bloody persecutions. During the throes and convulsions of the ancient world, during the agonizing spasms of infuriated man, seeking through blood and slaughter his long-lost liberty, it was not wonderful that the agitation of the billows should reach even this distant and peaceful shore; that this should be more felt and feared by some and less by others, and should divide opinions as to measures of safety. But every difference of opinion is not a difference of principle. We have called by different names brethren of the same principle. We are all Republicans, we are all Federalists. If there be any among us who would wish to dissolve this Union or to change its republican form, let them stand undisturbed as monuments of the safety with which error of opinion may be tolerated where reason is left free to combat it. I know, indeed, that some honest men fear that a republican government can not be strong, that this Government is not strong enough; but would the honest patriot, in the full tide of successful experiment, abandon a government which has so far kept us free and firm on the theoretic and visionary fear that this Government, the world's best hope, may by possibility want energy to preserve itself? I trust not. I believe this, on the contrary, the strongest Government on earth. I believe it the only one where every man, at the call of the law, would fly to the standard of the law, and would meet invasions of the public order as his own personal concern. Sometimes it is said that man can not be trusted with the government of himself. Can he, then, be trusted with the government of others? Or have we found angels in the forms of kings to govern him? Let history answer this question.

Let us, then, with courage and confidence pursue our own

Federal and Republican principles, our attachment to union and representative government. Kindly separated by nature and a wide ocean from the exterminating havoc of one quarter of the globe; too high-minded to endure the degradations of the others; possessing a chosen country, with room enough for our descendants to the thousandth and thousandth generation; entertaining a due sense of our equal right to the use of our own faculties, to the acquisitions of our own industry, to honor and confidence from our fellow-citizens, resulting not from birth, but from our actions and their sense of them; enlightened by a benign religion, professed, indeed, and practiced in various forms, yet all of them inculcating honesty, truth, temperance, gratitude, and the love of man; acknowledging and adoring an overruling Providence, which by all its dispensations proves that it delights in the happiness of man here and his greater happiness hereafter—with all these blessings, what more is necessary to make us a happy and a prosperous people? Still one thing more, fellow-citizens—a wise and frugal Government, which shall restrain men from injuring one another, shall leave them otherwise free to regulate their own pursuits of industry and improvement, and shall not take from the mouth of labor the bread it has earned. This is the sum of good government, and this is necessary to close the circle of our felicities.

About to enter, fellow-citizens, on the exercise of duties which comprehend everything dear and valuable to you, it is proper you should understand what I deem the essential principles of our Government, and consequently those which ought to shape its Administration. I will compress them within the narrowest compass they will bear, stating the general principle, but not all its limitations. Equal and exact justice to all men, of whatever state or persuasion, religious or political; peace, commerce, and honest friendship with all nations, entangling alliances with none; the support of the State governments in all their rights, as the most competent administrations for our domestic concerns and the surest bulwarks against antirepublican tendencies; the preservation of the General Government in its whole constitutional vigor, as the sheet anchor of our peace at home and safety abroad; a jealous care of the right of election by the people—a mild and

safe corrective of abuses which are lopped by the sword of
revolution where peaceable remedies are unprovided; absolute acquiescence in the decisions of the majority, the vital
principle of republics, from which is no appeal but to force,
the vital principle and immediate parent of despotism; a well-
disciplined militia, our best reliance in peace and for the first
moments of war till regulars may relieve them; the supremacy
of the civil over the military authority; economy in the public
expense, that labor may be lightly burthened; the honest payment of our debts and sacred preservation of the public faith;
encouragement of agriculture, and of commerce as its hand-
maid; the diffusion of information and arraignment of all
abuses at the bar of the public reason; freedom of religion;
freedom of the press, and freedom of person under the protection of the habeas corpus, and trial by juries impartially
selected. These principles form the bright constellation which
has gone before us and guided our steps through an age of
revolution and reformation. The wisdom of our sages and
blood of our heroes have been devoted to their attainment.
They should be the creed of our political faith, the text of
civic instruction, the touchstone by which to try the services
of those we trust; and should we wander from them in moments of error or of alarm, let us hasten to retrace our steps
and to regain the road which alone leads to peace, liberty, and
safety.

I repair, then, fellow-citizens, to the post you have assigned
me. With experience enough in subordinate offices to have
seen the difficulties of this the greatest of all, I have learnt to
expect that it will rarely fall to the lot of imperfect man to
retire from this station with the reputation and the favor
which bring him into it. Without pretensions to that high
confidence you reposed in our first and greatest revolutionary
character, whose preeminent services had entitled him to the
first place in his country's love and destined for him the fairest page in the volume of faithful history, I ask so much confidence only as may give firmness and effect to the legal
administration of your affairs. I shall often go wrong through
defect of judgment. When right, I shall often be thought
wrong by those whose positions will not command a view of
the whole ground. I ask your indulgence for my own errors,

which will never be intentional, and your support against the errors of others, who may condemn what they would not if seen in all its parts. The approbation implied by your suffrage is a great consolation to me for the past, and my future solicitude will be to retain the good opinion of those who have bestowed it in advance, to conciliate that of others by doing them all the good in my power, and to be instrumental to the happiness and freedom of all.

Relying, then, on the patronage of your good will, I advance with obedience to the work, ready to retire from it whenever you become sensible how much better choice it is in your power to make. And may that Infinite Power which rules the destinies of the universe lead our councils to what is best, and give them a favorable issue for your peace and prosperity.

To Elias Shipman and Others, a Committee of the Merchants of New Haven

Washington, July 12, 1801

GENTLEMEN,

I have received the remonstrance you were pleased to address to me, on the appointment of Samuel Bishop to the office of collector of New Haven, lately vacated by the death of David Austin. The right of our fellow citizens to represent to the public functionaries their opinion on proceedings interesting to them, is unquestionably a constitutional right, often useful, sometimes necessary, and will always be respectfully acknoleged by me.

Of the various executive duties, no one excites more anxious concern than that of placing the interests of our fellow citizens in the hands of honest men, with understandings sufficient for their station. No duty, at the same time, is more difficult to fulfil. The knolege of characters possessed by a single individual is, of necessity, limited. To seek out the best through the whole Union, we must resort to other information, which, from the best of men, acting disinterestedly and with the purest motives, is sometimes incorrect. In the case of Samuel Bishop, however, the subject of your remonstrance, time was taken, information was sought, & such obtained as could leave no room for doubt of his fitness. From private sources it was learnt that his understanding was sound, his integrity pure, his character unstained. And the offices confided to him within his own State, are public evidences of the estimation in which he is held by the State in general, and the city & township particularly in which he lives. He is said to be the town clerk, a justice of the peace, mayor of the city of New Haven, an office held at the will of the legislature, chief judge of the court of common pleas for New Haven county, a court of high criminal and civil jurisdiction wherein most causes are decided without the right of appeal or review, and sole judge of the court of probates, wherein he singly decides all questions of wills, settlement of estates, testate and intestate, appoints guardians, settles their accounts, and in fact has under his jurisdiction and care all the property real and personal of persons dying. The two last offices, in the annual gift of the legislature, were given to him in May last. Is it possible that the man to whom the legislature of Connecticut has so recently committed trusts of such difficulty & magnitude, is 'unfit to be the collector of the district of New Haven,' tho' ackноleged in the same writing, to have obtained all this confidence 'by a long life of usefulness?' It is objected, indeed, in the remonstrance, that he is 77. years of age; but at a much more advanced age, our Franklin was the ornament of human nature. He may not be able to perform in person, all the details of his office; but if he gives us the benefit of his understanding, his integrity, his watchfulness, and takes care that all the details are well performed by himself or his necessary assistants, all public purposes will be answered. The remonstrance, indeed, does not allege that the office *has been* illy conducted, but only apprehends that it *will be* so. Should this happen in event, be assured I will do in it what shall be just and necessary for the public service. In the meantime, he should be tried without being prejudged.

The removal, as it is called, of Mr. Goodrich, forms another subject of complaint. Declarations by myself in favor of *political tolerance*, exhortations to *harmony* and affection in social intercourse, and to respect for the *equal rights* of the minority, have, on certain occasions, been quoted & misconstrued into assurances that the tenure of offices was to be undisturbed. But could candor apply such a construction? It is not indeed in the remonstrance that we find it; but it leads to the explanations which that calls for. When it is considered, that during the late administration, those who were not of a particular sect of politics were excluded from all office; when, by a steady pursuit of this measure, nearly the whole offices of the U S were monopolized by that sect; when the public sentiment at length declared itself, and burst open the doors of honor and confidence to those whose opinions they more approved, was it to be imagined that this monopoly of office was still to be continued in the hands of the minority? Does it violate their *equal rights*, to assert some rights in the majority also? Is it *political intolerance* to claim a proportionate share in the direction of the public affairs? Can they not *harmonize* in society unless they have everything in their own hands? If the will of the nation, manifested by their various elections, calls for an administration of government according with the opinions of those elected; if, for the fulfilment of that will, displacements are necessary, with whom can they so justly begin as with persons appointed in the last moments of an administration, not for its own aid, but to begin a career at the same time with their successors, by whom they had never been approved, and who could scarcely expect from them a cordial cooperation? Mr. Goodrich was one of these. Was it proper for him to place himself in office, without knowing whether those whose agent he was to be would have confidence in his agency? Can the preference of another, as the successor to Mr. Austin, be candidly called a removal of Mr. Goodrich? If a due participation of office is a matter of right, how are vacancies to be obtained? Those by death are few; by resignation, none. Can any other mode than that of removal be proposed? This is a painful office; but it is made my duty, and I meet it as such. I proceed in the operation with deliberation & inquiry, that it may injure the best men least, and effect the purposes of justice & public utility with the least private distress; that it may be thrown, as much as possible, on delinquency, on oppression, on intolerance, on incompetence, on ante-revolutionary adherence to our enemies.

The remonstrance laments "that a change in the administration must produce a change in the subordinate officers;" in other words, that it should be deemed necessary for all officers to think with their principal. But on whom does this imputation bear? On those who have excluded from office every shade of opinion which was not theirs? Or on those who have been so excluded? I lament sincerely that unessential differences of political opinion should ever have been deemed sufficient to interdict half the society from the rights and the blessings of self-government, to proscribe them as characters unworthy of every trust. It would have been to me a circumstance of great relief, had I found a moderate participation of office in the hands of the majority. I would gladly have left to time and accident to raise them to their just share. But their total exclusion calls for prompter correctives. I shall correct the procedure; but that done, disdain to follow it, shall return with joy to that state of things, when the only questions concerning a candidate shall be, is he honest? Is he capable? Is he faithful to the Constitution?

I tender you the homage of my high respect.

First Annual Message

December 8, 1801

FELLOW CITIZENS OF THE SENATE AND HOUSE OF REPRESENTATIVES:

It is a circumstance of sincere gratification to me that on meeting the great council of our nation, I am able to announce to them, on the grounds of reasonable certainty, that the wars and troubles which have for so many years afflicted our sister nations have at length come to an end, and that the communications of peace and commerce are once more opening among them. While we devoutly return thanks to the beneficent Being who has been pleased to breathe into them the spirit of conciliation and forgiveness, we are bound with peculiar gratitude to be thankful to him that our own peace has been preserved through so perilous a season, and ourselves permitted quietly to cultivate the earth and to practice and improve those arts which tend to increase our comforts. The assurances, indeed, of friendly disposition, received from all the powers with whom we have principal relations, had inspired a confidence that our peace with them would not have been disturbed. But a cessation of the irregularities which had effected the commerce of neutral nations, and of the irritations and injuries produced by them, cannot but add to this confidence; and strengthens, at the same time, the hope, that wrongs committed on offending friends, under a pressure of circumstances, will now be reviewed with candor, and will be considered as founding just claims of retribution for the past and new assurances for the future.

Among our Indian neighbors, also, a spirit of peace and friendship generally prevailing and I am happy to inform you that the continued efforts to introduce among them the implements and the practice of husbandry, and of the household arts, have not been without success; that they are becoming more and more sensible of the superiority of this dependence for clothing and subsistence over the precarious resources of hunting and fishing; and already we are able to announce, that instead of that constant diminution of their numbers, produced by their wars and their wants, some of them begin to experience an increase of population.

To this state of general peace with which we have been blessed, one only exception exists. Tripoli, the least considerable of the Barbary States, had come forward with demands unfounded either in right or in compact, and had permitted itself to denounce war, on our failure to comply before a given day. The style of the demand admitted but one answer. I sent a small squadron of frigates into the Mediterranean, with assurances to that power of our sincere desire to remain in peace, but with orders to protect our commerce against the threatened attack. The measure was seasonable and salutary. The bey had already declared war in form. His cruisers were out. Two had arrived at Gibraltar. Our commerce in the Mediterranean was blockaded, and that of the Atlantic in peril. The arrival of our squadron dispelled the danger. One of the Tripolitan cruisers having fallen in with, and engaged the small schooner Enterprise, commanded by Lieutenant Sterret, which had gone as a tender to our larger vessels, was captured, after a heavy slaughter of her men, without the loss of a single one on our part. The bravery exhibited by our citizens on that element, will, I trust, be a testimony to the world that it is not the want of that virtue which makes us seek their peace, but a conscientious desire to direct the energies of our nation to the multiplication of the human race, and not to its destruction. Unauthorized by the constitution, without the sanction of Congress, to go out beyond the line of defence, the vessel being disabled from committing further hostilities, was liberated with its crew. The legislature will doubtless consider whether, by authorizing measures of offence, also, they will place our force on an equal footing with that of its adversaries. I communicate all material information on this subject, that in the exercise of the important function considered by the constitution to the legislature exclusively, their judgment may form itself on a knowledge and consideration of every circumstance of weight.

I wish I could say that our situation with all the other Barbary states was entirely satisfactory. Discovering that some delays had taken place in the performance of certain articles stipulated by us, I thought it my duty, by immediate measures for fulfilling them, to vindicate to ourselves the right of considering the effect of departure from stipulation on their side. From the papers which will be laid before you, you will be enabled to judge whether our treaties are regarded by them as fixing at all the measure of their demands, or as guarding from the exercise of force our vessels within their power; and to consider how far it will be safe and expedient to leave our affairs with them in their present posture.

I lay before you the result of the census lately taken of our inhabitants, to a conformity with which we are to reduce the ensuing rates of representation and taxation. You will perceive that the increase of numbers during the last ten years, proceeding in geometrical ratio, promises a duplication in little more than twenty-two years. We contemplate this rapid growth, and the prospect it holds up to us, not with a view to the injuries it may enable us to do to others in some future day, but to the settlement of the extensive country still remaining vacant within our limits, to the multiplications of men susceptible of happiness, educated in the love of order, habituated to self-government, and value its blessings above all price.

Other circumstances, combined with the increase of numbers, have produced an augmentation of revenue arising from consumption, in a ratio far beyond that of population alone, and though the changes of foreign relations now taking place so desirably for the world, may for a season affect this branch of revenue, yet, weighing all probabilities of expense, as well as of income, there is reasonable ground of confidence that we may now safely dispense with all the internal taxes, comprehending excises, stamps, auctions, licenses, carriages, and refined sugars, to which the postage on newspapers may be added, to facilitate the progress of information, and that the remaining sources of revenue will be sufficient to provide for the support of government to pay the interest on the public debts, and to discharge the principals in shorter periods than the laws or the general expectations had contemplated. War, indeed, and untoward events, may change this prospect of things, and call for expenses which the imposts could not meet; but sound principles will not justify our taxing the industry of our fellow citizens to accumulate treasure for wars to happen we know not when, and which might not perhaps happen but from the temptations offered by that treasure.

These views, however, of reducing our burdens, are formed

on the expectation that a sensible, and at the same time a salutary reduction, may take place in our habitual expenditures. For this purpose, those of the civil government, the army, and navy, will need revisal.

When we consider that this government is charged with the external and mutual relations only of these states; that the states themselves have principal care of our persons, our property, and our reputation, constituting the great field of human concerns, we may well doubt whether our organization is not too complicated, too expensive; whether offices or officers have not been multiplied unnecessarily, and sometimes injuriously to the service they were meant to promote. I will cause to be laid before you an essay toward a statement of those who, under public employment of various kinds, draw money from the treasury or from our citizens. Time has not permitted a perfect enumeration, the ramifications of office being too multipled and remote to be completely traced in a first trial. Among those who are dependent on executive discretion, I have begun the reduction of what was deemed necessary. The expenses of diplomatic agency have been considerably diminished. The inspectors of internal revenue who were found to obstruct the accountability of the institution, have been discontinued. Several agencies created by executive authority, on salaries fixed by that also, have been suppressed, and should suggest the expediency of regulating that power by law, so as to subject its exercises to legislative inspection and sanction. Other reformations of the same kind will be pursued with that caution which is requisite in removing useless things, not to injure what is retained. But the great mass of public offices is established by law, and, therefore, by law alone can be abolished. Should the legislature think it expedient to pass this roll in review, and try all its parts by the test of public utility, they may be assured of every aid and light which executive information can yield. Considering the general tendency to multiply offices and dependencies, and to increase expense to the ultimate term of burden which the citizen can bear, it behooves us to avail ourselves of every occasion which presents itself for taking off the surcharge; that it may never be seen here that, after leaving to labor the smallest portion of its earnings on which it can subsist, government shall itself consume the residue of what it was instituted to guard.

In our care, too, of the public contributions intrusted to our direction, it would be prudent to multiply barriers against their dissipation, by appropriating specific sums to every specific purpose susceptible of definition; by disallowing applications of money varying from the appropriation in object, or transcending it in amount; by reducing the undefined field of contingencies, and thereby circumscribing discretionary powers over money; and by bringing back to a single department all accountabilities for money where the examination may be prompt, efficacious, and uniform.

An account of the receipts and expenditures of the last year, as prepared by the secretary of the treasury, will as usual be laid before you. The success which has attended the late sales of the public lands, shows that with attention they may be made an important source of receipt. Among the payments, those made in discharge of the principal and interest of the national debt, will show that the public faith has been exactly maintained. To these will be added an estimate of appropriations necessary for the ensuing year. This last will of course be effected by such modifications of the systems of expense, as you shall think proper to adopt.

A statement has been formed by the secretary of war, on mature consideration, of all the posts and stations where garrisons will be expedient, and of the number of men requisite for each garrison. The whole amount is considerably short of the present military establishment. For the surplus no particular use can be pointed out. For defence against invasion, their number is as nothing; nor is it conceived needful or safe that a standing army should be kept up in time of peace for that purpose. Uncertain as we must ever be of the particular point in our circumference where an enemy may choose to invade us, the only force which can be ready at every point and competent to oppose them, is the body of neighboring citizens as formed into a militia. On these, collected from the parts most convenient, in numbers proportioned to the invading foe, it is best to rely, not only to meet the first attack, but if it threatens to be permanent, to maintain the defence until regulars may be engaged to relieve them. These considerations render it important that we should at every session continue to amend the defects which from time to time show themselves in the laws for regulating the militia, until they are sufficiently perfect. Nor should we now or at any time separate, until we can say we have done everything for the militia which we could do were an enemy at our door.

The provisions of military stores on hand will be laid before you, that you may judge of the additions still requisite.

With respect to the extent to which our naval preparations should be carried, some difference of opinion may be expected to appear; but just attention to the circumstances of every part of the Union will doubtless reconcile all. A small force will probably continue to be wanted for actual service in the Mediterranean. Whatever annual sum beyond that you may think proper to appropriate to naval preparations, would perhaps be better employed in providing those articles which may be kept without waste or consumption, and be in readiness when any exigence calls them into use. Progress has been made, as will appear by papers now communicated, in providing materials for seventy-four gun ships as directed by law.

How far the authority given by the legislature for procuring and establishing sites for naval purposes has been perfectly understood and pursued in the execution, admits of some doubt. A statement of the expenses already incurred on that subject, shall be laid before you. I have in certain cases suspended or slackened these expenditures, that the legislature might determine whether so many yards are necessary as have been contemplated. The works at this place are among those permitted to go on; and five of the seven frigates directed to be laid up, have been brought and laid up here, where, besides the safety of their position, they are under the eye of the executive administration, as well as of its agents and where yourselves also will be guided by your own view in the legislative provisions respecting them which may from time to time be necessary. They are preserved in such condition, as well the vessels as whatever belongs to them, as to be at all times ready for sea on a short warning. Two others are yet to be laid up so soon as they shall have reserved the repairs requisite to put them also into sound condition. As a superintending officer will be necessary at each yard, his duties and emoluments, hitherto fixed by the executive, will be a more proper subject for legislation. A communication will also be made of our progress in the execution of the law respecting the vessels directed to be sold.

The fortifications of our harbors, more or less advanced, present considerations of great difficulty. While some of them are on a scale sufficiently proportioned to the advantages of their position, to the efficacy of their protection, and the importance of the points within it, others are so extensive, will cost so much in their first erection, so much in their maintenance, and require such a force to garrison them, as to make it questionable what is best now to be done. A statement of those commenced or projected, of the expenses already incurred, and estimates of their future cost, so far as can be foreseen, shall be laid before you, that you may be enabled to judge whether any attention is necessary in the laws respecting this subject.

Agriculture, manufactures, commerce, and navigation, the four pillars of our prosperity, are the most thriving when left most free to individual enterprise. Protection from casual embarrassments, however, may sometimes be seasonably interposed. If in the course of your observations or inquiries they should appear to need any aid within the limits of our constitutional powers, your sense of their importance is a sufficient assurance they will occupy your attention. We cannot, indeed, but all feel an anxious solicitude for the difficulties under which our carrying trade will soon be placed. How far it can be relieved, otherwise than by time, is a subject of important consideration.

The judiciary system of the United States, and especially that portion of it recently erected, will of course present itself to the contemplation of Congress: and that they may be able to judge of the proportion which the institution bears to the business it has to perform, I have caused to be procured from the several States, and now lay before Congress, an exact statement of all the causes decided since the first establishment of the courts, and of those which were depending when additional courts and judges were brought in to their aid.

And while on the judiciary organization, it will be worthy your consideration, whether the protection of the inestimable

institution of juries has been extended to all the cases involving the security of our persons and property. Their impartial
selection also being essential to their value, we ought further
to consider whether that is sufficiently secured in those States
where they are named by a marshal depending on executive
will, or designated by the court or by officers dependent on
them.

I cannot omit recommending a revisal of the laws on the
subject of naturalization. Considering the ordinary chances of
human life, a denial of citizenship under a residence of fourteen years is a denial to a great proportion of those who ask
it, and controls a policy pursued from their first settlement by
many of these States, and still believed of consequence to
their prosperity. And shall we refuse the unhappy fugitives
from distress that hospitality which the savages of the wilder-
ness extended to our fathers arriving in this land? Shall
oppressed humanity find no asylum on this globe? The
constitution, indeed, has wisely provided that, for admission
to certain offices of important trust, a residence shall be required sufficient to develop character and design. But might
not the general character and capabilities of a citizen be safely
communicated to every one manifesting a *bona fide* purpose
of embarking his life and fortunes permanently with us? with
restrictions, perhaps, to guard against the fraudulent usurpation of our flag; an abuse which brings so much embarrassment and loss on the genuine citizen, and so much danger to
the nation of being involved in war, that no endeavor should
be spared to detect and suppress it.

These, fellow citizens, are the matters respecting the state
of the nation, which I have thought of importance to be submitted to your consideration at this time. Some others of less
moment, or not yet ready for communication, will be the subject of separate messages. I am happy in this opportunity of
committing the arduous affairs of our government to the collected wisdom of the Union. Nothing shall be wanting on my
part to inform, as far as in my power, the legislative judgment, nor to carry that judgment into faithful execution. The
prudence and temperance of your discussions will promote,
within your own walls, that conciliation which so much befriends national conclusion; and by its example will encourage

among our constituents that progress of opinion which is tending to unite them in object and in will. That all should be satisfied with any one order of things is not to be expected, but I indulge the pleasing persuasion that the great body of our citizens will cordially concur in honest and disinterested efforts, which have for their object to preserve the general and State governments in their constitutional form and equilibrium; to maintain peace abroad, and order and obedience to the laws at home; to establish principles and practices of administration favorable to the security of liberty and prosperity, and to reduce expenses to what is necessary for the useful purposes of government.

To Messrs. Nehemiah Dodge and Others, a Committee of the Danbury Baptist Association, in the State of Connecticut

GENTLEMEN,

The affectionate sentiments of esteem and approbation which you are so good as to express towards me, on behalf of the Danbury Baptist Association, give me the highest satisfaction. My duties dictate a faithful and zealous pursuit of the interests of my constituents, and in proportion as they are persuaded of my fidelity to those duties, the discharge of them becomes more and more pleasing.

Believing with you that religion is a matter which lies solely between man and his God, that he owes account to none other for his faith or his worship, that the legislative powers of government reach actions only, and not opinions, I contemplate with sovereign reverence that act of the whole American people which declared that their legislature should "make no law respecting an establishment of religion, or prohibiting the free exercise thereof," thus building a wall of separation between church and State. Adhering to this expression of the supreme will of the nation in behalf of the rights of conscience, I shall see with sincere satisfaction the progress of those sentiments which tend to restore to man all his natural rights, convinced he has no natural right in opposition to his social duties.

I reciprocate your kind prayers for the protection and blessing of the common Father and Creator of man, and tender you for yourselves and your religious association, assurances of my high respect and esteem.

Third Annual Message

October 17, 1803

TO THE SENATE AND HOUSE OF REPRESENTATIVES OF THE UNITED STATES:

In calling you together, fellow citizens, at an earlier day than was contemplated by the act of the last session of Congress, I have not been insensible to the personal inconveniences necessarily resulting from an unexpected change in your arrangements. But matters of great public concernment have rendered this call necessary, and the interest you feel in these will supersede in your minds all private considerations.

Congress witnessed, at their last session, the extraordinary agitation produced in the public mind by the suspension of our right of deposit at the port of New Orleans, no assignment of another place having been made according to treaty. They were sensible that the continuance of that privation would be more injurious to our nation than any consequences which could flow from any mode of redress, but reposing just confidence in the good faith of the government whose officer had committed the wrong, friendly and reasonable representations were resorted to, and the right of deposit was restored.

Previous, however, to this period, we had not been unaware of the danger to which our peace would be perpetually exposed while so important a key to the commerce of the western country remained under foreign power. Difficulties, too, were presenting themselves as to the navigation of other streams, which, arising within our territories, pass through those adjacent. Propositions had, therefore, been authorized for obtaining, on fair conditions, the sovereignty of New Orleans, and of other possessions in that quarter interesting to our quiet, to such extent as was deemed practicable; and the provisional appropriation of two millions of dollars, to be applied and accounted for by the president of the United States, intended as part of the price, was considered as conveying the sanction of Congress to the acquisition proposed. The enlightened government of France saw, with just discernment, the importance to both nations of such liberal arrangements as might best and permanently promote the peace, friendship, and interests of both; and the property and sovereignty of all

Louisiana, which had been restored to them, have on certain conditions been transferred to the United States by instruments bearing date the 30th of April last. When these shall have received the constitutional sanction of the senate, they will without delay be communicated to the representatives also, for the exercise of their functions, as to those conditions which are within the powers vested by the constitution in Congress. While the property and sovereignty of the Mississippi and its waters secure an independent outlet for the produce of the western States, and an uncontrolled navigation through their whole course, free from collision with other powers and the dangers to our peace from that source, the fertility of the country, its climate and extent, promise in due season important aids to our treasury, an ample provision for our posterity, and a wide-spread field for the blessings of freedom and equal laws.

With the wisdom of Congress it will rest to take those ulterior measures which may be necessary for the immediate occupation and temporary government of the country; for its incorporation into our Union; for rendering the change of government a blessing to our newly-adopted brethren; for securing to them the rights of conscience and of property: for confirming to the Indian inhabitants their occupancy and self-government, establishing friendly and commercial relations with them, and for ascertaining the geography of the country acquired. Such materials for your information, relative to its affairs in general, as the short space of time has permitted me to collect, will be laid before you when the subject shall be in a state for your consideration.

Another important acquisition of territory has also been made since the last session of Congress. The friendly tribe of Kaskaskia Indians with which we have never had a difference, reduced by the wars and wants of savage life to a few individuals unable to defend themselves against the neighboring tribes, has transferred its country to the United States, reserving only for its members what is sufficient to maintain them in an agricultural way. The considerations stipulated are, that we shall extend to them our patronage and protection, and give them certain annual aids in money, in implements of agriculture, and other articles of their choice. This country, among the most fertile within our limits, extending along the Mississippi from the mouth of the Illinois to and up the Ohio, though not so necessary as a barrier since the acquisition of the other bank, may yet be well worthy of being laid open to immediate settlement, as its inhabitants may descend with rapidity in support of the lower country should future circumstances expose that to foreign enterprise. As the stipulations in this treaty also involve matters within the competence of both houses only, it will be laid before Congress as soon as the senate shall have advised its ratification.

With many other Indian tribes, improvements in agriculture and household manufacture are advancing, and with all our peace and friendship are established on grounds much firmer than heretofore. The measure adopted of establishing trading houses among them, and of furnishing them necessaries in exchange for their commodities, at such moderated prices as leave no gain, but cover us from loss, has the most conciliatory and useful effect upon them, and is that which will best secure their peace and good will.

The small vessels authorized by Congress with a view to the Mediterranean service, have been sent into that sea, and will be able more effectually to confine the Tripoline cruisers within their harbors, and supersede the necessity of convoy to our commerce in that quarter. They will sensibly lessen the expenses of that service the ensuing year.

A further knowledge of the ground in the north-eastern and north-western angles of the United States has evinced that the boundaries established by the treaty of Paris, between the British territories and ours in those parts, were too imperfectly described to be susceptible of execution. It has therefore been thought worthy of attention, for preserving and cherishing the harmony and useful intercourse subsisting between the two nations, to remove by timely arrangements what unfavorable incidents might otherwise render a ground of future misunderstanding. A convention has therefore been entered into, which provides for a practicable demarkation of those limits to the satisfaction of both parties.

An account of the receipts and expenditures of the year ending 30th September last, with the estimates for the service of the ensuing year, will be laid before you by the secretary of the treasury so soon as the receipts of the last quarter shall be returned from the more distant States. It is already ascertained that the amount paid into the treasury for that year has been between eleven and twelve millions of dollars, and that the revenue accrued during the same term exceeds the sum counted on as sufficient for our current expenses, and to extinguish the public debt within the period heretofore proposed.

The amount of debt paid for the same year is about three millions one hundred thousand dollars, exclusive of interest, and making, with the payment of the preceding year, a discharge of more than eight millions and a half of dollars of the principal of that debt, besides the accruing interest; and there remain in the treasury nearly six millions of dollars. Of these, eight hundred and eighty thousand have been reserved for payment of the first instalment due under the British convention of January 8th, 1802, and two millions are what have been before mentioned as placed by Congress under the power and accountability of the president, toward the price of New Orleans and other territories acquired, which, remaining untouched, are still applicable to that object, and go in diminution of the sum to be funded for it.

Should the acquisition of Louisiana be constitutionally confirmed and carried into effect, a sum of nearly thirteen millions of dollars will then be added to our public debt, most of which is payable after fifteen years; before which term the present existing debts will all be discharged by the established operation of the sinking fund. When we contemplate the ordinary annual augmentation of imposts from increasing population and wealth, the augmentation of the same revenue by its extension to the new acquisition, and the economies which may still be introduced into our public expenditures, I cannot but hope that Congress in reviewing their resources will find means to meet the intermediate interests of this additional debt without recurring to new taxes, and applying to this object only the ordinary progression of our revenue. Its extraordinary increase in times of foreign war will be the proper and sufficient fund for any measures of safety or precaution which that state of things may render necessary in our neutral position.

Remittances for the instalments of our foreign debt having been found impracticable without loss, it has not been thought expedient to use the power given by a former act of Congress of continuing them by reloans, and of redeeming instead thereof equal sums of domestic debt, although no difficulty was found in obtaining that accommodation.

The sum of fifty thousand dollars appropriated by Congress for providing gun-boats, remains unexpended. The favorable and peaceful turn of affairs on the Mississippi rendered an immediate execution of that law unnecessary, and time was desirable in order that the institution of that branch of our force might begin on models the most approved by experience. The same issue of events dispensed with a resort to the appropriation of a million and a half of dollars contemplated for purposes which were effected by happier means.

We have seen with sincere concern the flames of war lighted up again in Europe, and nations with which we have the most friendly and useful relations engaged in mutual destruction. While we regret the miseries in which we see others involved let us bow with gratitude to that kind Providence which, inspiring with wisdom and moderation our late legislative councils while placed under the urgency of the greatest wrongs, guarded us from hastily entering into the sanguinary contest, and left us only to look on and to pity its ravages. These will be heaviest on those immediately engaged. Yet the nations pursuing peace will not be exempt from all evil. In the course of this conflict, let it be our endeavor, as it is our interest and desire, to cultivate the friendship of the belligerent nations by every act of justice and of incessant kindness; to receive their armed vessels with hospitality from the distresses of the sea, but to administer the means of annoyance to none; to establish in our harbors such a police as may maintain law and order; to restrain our citizens from embarking individually in a war in which their country takes no part; to punish severely those persons, citizen or alien, who shall usurp the cover of our flag for vessels not entitled to it, infecting thereby with suspicion those of real Americans, and committing us into controversies for the redress of wrongs not our own; to exact from every nation the observance, toward our vessels and citizens, of those principles and practices which all civilized people acknowledge; to merit the character of a just nation, and maintain that of an independent one, preferring every consequence to insult and habitual wrong. Congress will consider whether the existing laws enable us efficaciously to maintain this course with our citizens in all places, and with others while within the limits of our jurisdiction, and will give them the new modifications necessary for these objects. Some contraventions of right have already taken place, both within our jurisdictional limits and on the high seas. The friendly disposition of the governments from whose agents they have proceeded, as well as their wisdom and regard for justice, leave us in reasonable expectation that they will be rectified and prevented in future; and that no act will be countenanced by them which threatens to disturb our friendly intercourse. Separated by a wide ocean from the nations of Europe, and from the political interests which entangle them together, with productions and wants which render our commerce and friendship useful to them and theirs to us, it cannot be the interest of any to assail us, nor ours to disturb them. We should be most unwise, indeed, were we to cast away the singular blessings of the position in which nature has placed us, the opportunity she has endowed us with of pursuing, at a distance from foreign contentions, the paths of industry, peace, and happiness; of cultivating general friendship, and of bringing collisions of interest to the umpirage of reason rather than of force. How desirable then must it be, in a government like ours, to see its citizens adopt individually the views, the interests, and the conduct which their country should pursue, divesting themselves of those passions and partialities which tend to lessen useful friendships, and to embarrass and embroil us in the calamitous scenes of Europe. Confident, fellow citizens, that you will duly estimate the importance of neutral dispositions toward the observance of neutral conduct, that you will be sensible how much it is our duty to look on the bloody arena spread before us with commiseration indeed, but with no other wish than to see it closed, I am persuaded you will cordially cherish these dispositions in all discussions among yourselves, and in all communications with your constituents; and I anticipate with satisfaction the measures of wisdom which the great interests now committed to *you* will give you an opportunity of providing, and *myself* that of approving and carrying into execution with the fidelity I owe to my country.

Second Inaugural Address

March 4, 1805

Proceeding, fellow citizens, to that qualification which the constitution requires, before my entrance on the charge again conferred upon me, it is my duty to express the deep sense I entertain of this new proof of confidence from my fellow citizens at large, and the zeal with which it inspires me, so to conduct myself as may best satisfy their just expectations.

On taking this station on a former occasion, I declared the principles on which I believed it my duty to administer the affairs of our commonwealth. My conscience tells me that I have, on every occasion, acted up to that declaration, according to its obvious import, and to the understanding of every candid mind.

In the transaction of your foreign affairs, we have endeavored to cultivate the friendship of all nations, and especially of those with which we have the most important relations. We have done them justice on all occasions, favored where favor was lawful, and cherished mutual interests and intercourse on fair and equal terms. We are firmly convinced, and we act on that conviction, that with nations, as with individuals, our interests soundly calculated, will ever be found inseparable from our moral duties; and history bears witness to the fact, that a just nation is taken on its word, when recourse is had to armaments and wars to bridle others.

At home, fellow citizens, you best know whether we have done well or ill. The suppression of unnecessary offices, of useless establishments and expenses, enabled us to discontinue our internal taxes. These covering our land with officers, and opening our doors to their intrusions, had already begun that process of domiciliary vexation which, once entered, is scarcely to be restrained from reaching successively every article of produce and property. If among these taxes some minor ones fell which had not been inconvenient, it was because their amount would not have paid the officers who collected them, and because, if they had any merit, the state authorities might adopt them, instead of others less approved.

The remaining revenue on the consumption of foreign articles, is paid cheerfully by those who can afford to add foreign luxuries to domestic comforts, being collected on our seaboards and frontiers only, and incorporated with the transactions of our mercantile citizens, it may be the pleasure and pride of an American to ask, what farmer, what mechanic, what laborer, ever sees a tax-gatherer of the United States? These contributions enable us to support the current expenses of the government, to fulfil contracts with foreign nations, to extinguish the native right of soil within our limits, to extend those limits, and to apply such a surplus to our public debts, as places at a short day their final redemption, and that redemption once effected, the revenue thereby liberated may, by a just repartition among the states, and a corresponding amendment of the constitution, be applied, *in time of peace*, to rivers, canals, roads, arts, manufactures, education, and other great objects within each state. *In time of war*, if injustice, by ourselves or others, must sometimes produce war, increased as the same revenue will be increased by population and consumption, and aided by other resources reserved for that crisis, it may meet within the year all the expenses of the year, without encroaching on the rights of future generations, by burdening them with the debts of the past. War will then be but a suspension of useful works, and a return to a state of peace, a return to the progress of improvement.

I have said, fellow citizens, that the income reserved had enabled us to extend our limits; but that extension may possibly pay for itself before we are called on, and in the meantime, may keep down the accruing interest; in all events, it will repay the advances we have made. I know that the acquisition of Louisiana has been disapproved by some, from a candid apprehension that the enlargement of our territory would endanger its union. But who can limit the extent to which the federative principle may operate effectively? The larger our association, the less will it be shaken by local passions; and in any view, is it not better that the opposite bank of the Mississippi should be settled by our own brethren and children, than by strangers of another family? With which shall we be most likely to live in harmony and friendly intercourse?

In matters of religion, I have considered that its free exercise is placed by the constitution independent of the powers of the general government. I have therefore undertaken, on no occasion, to prescribe the religious exercises suited to it; but have left them, as the constitution found them, under the direction and discipline of state or church authorities acknowledged by the several religious societies.

The aboriginal inhabitants of these countries I have regarded with the commiseration their history inspires. Endowed with the faculties and the rights of men, breathing an ardent love of liberty and independence, and occupying a country which left them no desire but to be undisturbed, the stream of overflowing population from other regions directed itself on these shores; without power to divert, or habits to contend against, they have been overwhelmed by the current, or driven before it; now reduced within limits too narrow for the hunter's state, humanity enjoins us to teach them agriculture and the domestic arts; to encourage them to that industry which alone can enable them to maintain their place in existence, and to prepare them in time for that state of society, which to bodily comforts adds the improvement of the mind and morals. We have therefore liberally furnished them with the implements of husbandry and household use; we have placed among them instructors in the arts of first necessity; and they are covered with the ægis of the law against aggressors from among ourselves.

But the endeavors to enlighten them on the fate which awaits their present course of life, to induce them to exercise their reason, follow its dictates, and change their pursuits with the change of circumstances, have powerful obstacles to encounter; they are combated by the habits of their bodies, prejudice of their minds, ignorance, pride, and the influence of interested and crafty individuals among them, who feel themselves something in the present order of things, and fear to become nothing in any other. These persons inculcate a sanctimonious reverence for the customs of their ancestors; that whatsoever they did, must be done through all time; that reason is a false guide, and to advance under its counsel, in their physical, moral, or political condition, is perilous innovation; that their duty is to remain as their Creator made them, ignorance being safety, and knowledge full of danger; in short, my friends, among them is seen the action and counteraction of good sense and bigotry; they, too, have their anti-philosophers, who find an interest in keeping things in their present state, who dread reformation, and exert all their faculties to maintain the ascendency of habit over the duty of improving our reason, and obeying its mandates.

In giving these outlines, I do not mean, fellow citizens, to arrogate to myself the merit of the measures; that is due, in the first place, to the reflecting character of our citizens at large, who, by the weight of public opinion, influence and strengthen the public measures; it is due to the sound discretion with which they select from among themselves those to whom they confide the legislative duties; it is due to the zeal and wisdom of the characters thus selected, who lay the foundations of public happiness in wholesome laws, the execution of which alone remains for others; and it is due to the able and faithful auxiliaries, whose patriotism has associated with me in the executive functions.

During this course of administration, and in order to disturb it, the artillery of the press has been levelled against us, charged with whatsoever its licentiousness could devise or dare. These abuses of an institution so important to freedom and science, are deeply to be regretted, inasmuch as they tend to lessen its usefulness, and to sap its safety; they might, indeed, have been corrected by the wholesome punishments reserved and provided by the laws of the several States against falsehood and defamation; but public duties more urgent press on the time of public servants, and the offenders have therefore been left to find their punishment in the public indignation.

Nor was it uninteresting to the world, that an experiment should be fairly and fully made, whether freedom of discussion, unaided by power, is not sufficient for the propagation and protection of truth—whether a government, conducting itself in the true spirit of its constitution, with zeal and purity, and doing no act which it would be unwilling the whole world should witness, can be written down by falsehood and defamation. The experiment has been tried; you have witnessed the scene; our fellow citizens have looked on, cool and collected; they saw the latent source from which these outrages proceeded; they gathered around their public functionaries, and when the constitution called them to the decision by suffrage, they pronounced their verdict, honorable to those who had served them, and consolatory to the friend of man, who believes he may be intrusted with his own affairs.

No inference is here intended, that the laws, provided by the State against false and defamatory publications, should not be enforced; he who has time, renders a service to public morals and public tranquillity, in reforming these abuses by the salutary coercions of the law; but the experiment is noted, to prove that, since truth and reason have maintained their ground against false opinions in league with false facts, the press, confined to truth, needs no other legal restraint; the public judgment will correct false reasonings and opinions, on a full hearing of all parties; and no other definite line can be drawn between the inestimable liberty of the press and its demoralizing licentiousness. If there be still improprieties which this rule would not restrain, its supplement must be sought in the censorship of public opinion.

Contemplating the union of sentiment now manifested so generally, as auguring harmony and happiness to our future course, I offer to our country sincere congratulations. With those, too, not yet rallied to the same point, the disposition to do so is gaining strength; facts are piercing through the veil drawn over them; and our doubting brethren will at length see, that the mass of their fellow citizens, with whom they cannot yet resolve to act, as to principles and measures, think as they think, and desire what they desire; that our wish, as well as theirs, is, that the public efforts may be directed honestly to the public good, that peace be cultivated, civil and religious liberty unassailed, law and order preserved; equality of rights maintained, and that state of property, equal or unequal, which results to every man from his own industry, or that of his fathers. When satisfied of these views, it is not in human nature that they should not approve and support them; in the meantime, let us cherish them with patient affection; let us do them justice, and more than justice, in all competitions of interest; and we need not doubt that truth, reason, and their own interests, will at length prevail, will gather them into the fold of their country, and will complete their entire union of opinion, which gives to a nation the blessing of harmony, and the benefit of all its strength.

I shall now enter on the duties to which my fellow citizens have again called me, and shall proceed in the spirit of those principles which they have approved. I fear not that any motives of interest may lead me astray; I am sensible of no passion which could seduce me knowingly from the path of justice; but the weakness of human nature, and the limits of my own understanding, will produce errors of judgment sometimes injurious to your interests. I shall need, therefore, all the indulgence I have heretofore experienced—the want of it will certainly not lessen with increasing years. I shall need, too, the favor of that Being in whose hands we are, who led our forefathers, as Israel of old, from their native land, and planted them in a country flowing with all the necessaries and comforts of life; who has covered our infancy with his providence, and our riper years with his wisdom and power; and to whose goodness I ask you to join with me in supplications, that he will so enlighten the minds of your servants, guide their councils, and prosper their measures, that whatsoever they do, shall result in your good, and shall secure to you the peace, friendship, and approbation of all nations.

Sixth Annual Message

December 2, 1806

To the Senate and House of Representatives of the United States in Congress assembled:

It would have given me, fellow citizens, great satisfaction to announce in the moment of your meeting that the difficulties in our foreign relations, existing at the time of your last separation, had been amicably and justly terminated. I lost no time in taking those measures which were most likely to bring them to such a termination, by special missions charged with such powers and instructions as in the event of failure could leave no imputation on either our moderation or forbearance. The delays which have since taken place in our negotiations with the British government appears to have proceeded from causes which do not forbid the expectation that during the course of the session I may be enabled to lay before you their final issue. What will be that of the negotiations for settling our differences with Spain, nothing which had taken place at the date of the last despatches enables us to pronounce. On the western side of the Mississippi she advanced in considerable force, and took post at the settlement of Bayou Pierre, on the Red river. This village was originally settled by France, was held by her as long as she held Louisiana, and was delivered to Spain only as a part of Louisiana. Being small, insulated, and distant, it was not observed, at the moment of redelivery to France and the United States, that she continued a guard of half a dozen men which had been stationed there. A proposition, however, having been lately made by our commander-in-chief, to assume the Sabine river as a temporary line of separation between the troops of the two nations until the issue of our negotiations shall be known; this has been referred by the Spanish commandant to his superior, and in the meantime, he has withdrawn his force to the western side of the Sabine river. The correspondence on this subject, now communicated, will exhibit more particularly the present state of things in that quarter.

The nature of that country requires indispensably that an unusual proportion of the force employed there should be cavalry or mounted infantry. In order, therefore, that the commanding officer might be enabled to act with effect, I had authorized him to call on the governors of Orleans and Mississippi for a corps of five hundred volunteer cavalry. The temporary arrangement he has proposed may perhaps render this unnecessary. But I inform you with great pleasure of the promptitude with which the inhabitants of those territories have tendered their services in defence of their country. It has done honor to themselves, entitled them to the confidence of their fellow-citizens in every part of the Union, and must strengthen the general determination to protect them efficaciously under all circumstances which may occur.

Having received information that in another part of the United States a great number of private individuals were combining together, arming and organizing themselves contrary to law, to carry on military expeditions against the territories of Spain, I thought it necessary, by proclamations as well as by special orders, to take measures for preventing and suppressing this enterprise, for seizing the vessels, arms, and other means provided for it, and for arresting and bringing to justice its authors and abettors. It was due to that good faith which ought ever to be the rule of action in public as well as in private transactions; it was due to good order and regular government, that while the public force was acting strictly on the defensive and merely to protect our citizens from aggression, the criminal attempts of private individuals to decide for their country the question of peace or war, by commencing active and unauthorized hostilities, should be promptly and efficaciously suppressed.

Whether it will be necessary to enlarge our regular force will depend on the result of our negotiation with Spain; but as it is uncertain when that result will be known, the provisional measures requisite for that, and to meet any pressure intervening in that quarter, will be a subject for your early consideration.

The possession of both banks of the Mississippi reducing to a single point the defence of that river, its waters, and the country adjacent, it becomes highly necessary to provide for that point a more adequate security. Some position above its mouth, commanding the passage of the river, should be rendered sufficiently strong to cover the armed vessels which may be stationed there for defence, and in conjunction with them to present an insuperable obstacle to any force attempting to pass. The approaches to the city of New Orleans, from the eastern quarter also, will require to be examined, and more effectually guarded. For the internal support of the country, the encouragement of a strong settlement on the western side of the Mississippi, within reach of New Orleans, will be worthy the consideration of the legislature.

The gun-boats authorized by an act of the last session are so advanced that they will be ready for service in the ensuing spring. Circumstances permitted us to allow the time necessary for their more solid construction. As a much larger number will still be wanting to place our seaport towns and waters in that state of defence to which we are competent and they entitled, a similar appropriation for a further provision for them is recommended for the ensuing year.

A further appropriation will also be necessary for repairing fortifications already established, and the erection of such works as may have real effect in obstructing the approach of an enemy to our seaport towns, or their remaining before them.

In a country whose constitution is derived from the will of the people, directly expressed by their free suffrages; where the principal executive functionaries, and those of the legislature, are renewed by them at short periods; where under the characters of jurors, they exercise in person the greatest portion of the judiciary powers; where the laws are consequently so formed and administered as to bear with equal weight and favor on all, restraining no man in the pursuits of honest industry, and securing to every one the property which that acquires, it would not be supposed that any safeguards could be needed against insurrection or enterprise on the public peace or authority. The laws, however, aware that these should not be trusted to moral restraints only, have wisely provided punishments for these crimes when committed. But would it not be salutary to give also the means of preventing their commission? Where an enterprise is meditated by private individuals against a foreign nation in amity with the United States, powers of prevention to a certain extent are given by the laws; would they not be as reasonable and useful were the enterprise preparing against the United States? While adverting to this branch of the law, it is proper to observe, that in enterprises meditated against foreign nations, the ordinary process of binding to the observance of the peace and good behavior, could it be extended to acts to be done out of the jurisdiction of the United States, would be effectual in some cases where the offender is able to keep out of sight every indication of his purpose which could draw on him the exercise of the powers now given by law.

The states on the coast of Barbary seem generally disposed at present to respect our peace and friendship; with Tunis alone some uncertainty remains. Persuaded that it is our interest to maintain our peace with them on equal terms, or not at all, I propose to send in due time a reinforcement into the Mediterranean, unless previous information shall show it to be unnecessary.

We continue to receive proofs of the growing attachment of our Indian neighbors, and of their disposition to place all their interests under the patronage of the United States. These dispositions are inspired by their confidence in our justice, and in the sincere concern we feel for their welfare; and as long as we discharge these high and honorable functions with the integrity and good faith which alone can entitle us to their continuance, we may expect to reap the just reward in their peace and friendship.

The expedition of Messrs. Lewis and Clarke, for exploring the river Missouri, and the best communication from that to the Pacific ocean, has had all the success which could have been expected. They have traced the Missouri nearly to its source, descended the Columbia to the Pacific ocean, ascertained with accuracy the geography of that interesting communication across our continent, learned the character of the country, of its commerce, and inhabitants; and it is but justice to say that Messrs. Lewis and Clarke, and their brave companions, have by this arduous service deserved well of their country.

The attempt to explore the Red river, under the direction of Mr. Freeman, though conducted with a zeal and prudence meriting entire approbation, has not been equally successful. After proceeding up it about six hundred miles, nearly as far as the French settlements had extended while the country was in their possession, our geographers were obliged to return without completing their work.

Very useful additions have also been made to our knowledge of the Mississippi by Lieutenant Pike, who has ascended to its source, and whose journal and map, giving the details of the journey, will shortly be ready for communication to both houses of Congress. Those of Messrs. Lewis and Clarke, and Freeman, will require further time to be digested and prepared. These important surveys, in addition to those before possessed, furnish materials for commencing an accurate map of the Mississippi, and its western waters. Some principal rivers, however, remain still to be explored, toward which the authorization of Congress, by moderate appropriations, will be requisite.

I congratulate you, fellow-citizens, on the approach of the period at which you may interpose your authority constitutionally, to withdraw the citizens of the United States from all further participation in those violations of human rights which have been so long continued on the unoffending inhabitants of Africa, and which the morality, the reputation, and the best interests of our country, have long been eager to proscribe. Although no law you may pass can take prohibitory effect till the first day of the year one thousand eight hundred and eight, yet the intervening period is not too long to prevent, by timely notice, expeditions which cannot be completed before that day.

The receipts at the treasury during the year ending on the 30th of September last, have amounted to near fifteen millions of dollars, which have enabled us, after meeting the current demands, to pay two millions seven hundred thousand dollars of the American claims, in part of the price of Louisiana; to pay of the funded debt upward of three millions of principal, and nearly four of interest; and in addition, to reimburse, in the course of the present month, near two millions of five and a half per cent. stock. These payments and reimbursements of the funded debt, with those which have been made in the four years and a half preceding, will, at the close of the present year, have extinguished upwards of twenty-three millions of principal.

The duties composing the Mediterranean fund will cease by law at the end of the present season. Considering, however, that they are levied chiefly on luxuries, and that we have an impost on salt, a necessary of life, the free use of which otherwise is so important, I recommend to your consideration the suppression of the duties on salt, and the continuation of the Mediterranean fund, instead thereof, for a short time, after which that also will become unnecessary for any purpose now within contemplation.

When both of these branches of revenue shall in this way be relinquished, there will still ere long be an accumulation of moneys in the treasury beyond the instalments of public debt which we are permitted by contract to pay. They cannot, then, without a modification assented to by the public creditors, be applied to the extinguishment of this debt, and the complete liberation of our revenues—the most desirable of all objects; nor, if our peace continues, will they be wanting for any other existing purpose. The question, therefore, now comes forward,—to what other objects shall these surpluses be appropriated, and the whole surplus of impost, after the entire discharge of the public debt, and during those intervals when the purposes of war shall not call for them? Shall we suppress the impost and give that advantage to foreign over domestic manufactures? On a few articles of more general and necessary use, the suppression in due season will doubtless be right, but the great mass of the articles on which impost is paid is foreign luxuries, purchased by those only who are rich enough to afford themselves the use of them. Their patriotism would certainly prefer its continuance and application to the great purposes of the public education, roads, rivers, canals, and such other objects of public improvement as it may be thought proper to add to the constitutional enumeration of federal powers. By these operations new channels of communication will be opened between the States; the lines of separation will disappear, their interests will be identified, and their union cemented by new and indissoluble ties. Education is here placed among the articles of public care, not that it would be proposed to take its ordinary branches out of the hands of private enterprise, which manages so much better all the concerns to which it is equal; but a public institution can alone supply those sciences which, though rarely called for, are yet necessary to complete the circle, all the parts of which contribute to the improvement of the country, and some of them to its preservation. The subject is now proposed for the consideration of Congress, because, if approved by the time the State legislatures shall have deliberated on this extension of the federal trusts, and the laws shall be passed, and other arrangements made for their execution, the necessary funds will be on hand and without employment. I suppose an amendment to the constitution, by consent of the States, necessary, because the objects now recommended are not among those enumerated in the constitution, and to which it permits the public moneys to be applied.

The present consideration of a national establishment for education, particularly, is rendered proper by this circumstance also, that if Congress, approving the proposition, shall yet think it more eligible to found it on a donation of lands, they have it now in their power to endow it with those which will be among the earliest to produce the necessary income. This foundation would have the advantage of being independent on war, which may suspend other improvements by requiring for its own purposes the resources destined for them.

This, fellow citizens, is the state of the public interest at the present moment, and according to the information now possessed. But such is the situation of the nations of Europe, and such too the predicament in which we stand with some of them, that we cannot rely with certainty on the present aspect of our affairs that may change from moment to moment, during the course of your session or after you shall have separated. Our duty is, therefore, to act upon things as they are, and to make a reasonable provision for whatever they may be. Were armies to be raised whenever a speck of war is visible in our horizon, we never should have been without them. Our resources would have been exhausted on dangers which have never happened, instead of being reserved for what is really to take place. A steady, perhaps a quickened pace in preparations for the defence of our seaport towns and waters; an early settlement of the most exposed and vulnerable parts of our country; a militia so organized that its effective portions can be called to any point in the Union, or volunteers instead of them to serve a sufficient time, are means which may always be ready yet never preying on our resources until actually called into use. They will maintain the public interests while a more permanent force shall be in course of preparation. But much will depend on the promptitude with which these means can be brought into activity. If war be forced upon us in spite of our long and vain appeals to the justice of nations, rapid and vigorous movements in its outset will go far toward securing us in its course and issue, and toward throwing its burdens on those who render necessary the resort from reason to force.

The result of our negotiations, or such incidents in their course as may enable us to infer their probable issue; such further movements also on our western frontiers as may show whether war is to be pressed there while negotiation is protracted elsewhere, shall be communicated to you from time to time as they become known to me, with whatever other information I possess or may receive, which may aid your deliberations on the great national interests committed to your charge.

Special Message on the Burr Conspiracy

January 22, 1807

TO THE SENATE AND HOUSE OF REPRESENTATIVES OF THE UNITED STATES:

Agreeably to the request of the House of Representatives, communicated in their resolution of the sixteenth instant, I proceed to state under the reserve therein expressed, information received touching an illegal combination of private individuals against the peace and safety of the Union, and a military expedition planned by them against the territories of a power in amity with the United States, with the measures I have pursued for suppressing the same.

I had for some time been in the constant expectation of receiving such further information as would have enabled me to lay before the legislature the termination as well as the beginning and progress of this scene of depravity, so far it has been acted on the Ohio and its waters. From this the state and safety of the lower country might have been estimated on probable grounds, and the delay was indulged the rather, because no circumstance had yet made it necessary to call in the aid of the legislative functions. Information now recently communicated has brought us nearly to the period contemplated. The mass of what I have received, in the course of these transactions, is voluminous, but little has been given under the sanction of an oath, so as to constitute formal and legal evidence. It is chiefly in the form of letters, often containing such a mixture of rumors, conjectures, and suspicions, as render it difficult to sift out the real facts, and unadvisable to hazard more than general outlines, strengthened by concurrent information, or the particular credibility of the relater. In this state of the evidence, delivered sometimes too under the restriction of private confidence, neither safety nor justice will permit the exposing names, except that of the principal actor, whose guilt is placed beyond question.

Some time in the latter part of September, I received intimations that designs were in agitation in the western country, unlawful and unfriendly to the peace of the Union; and that the prime mover in these was Aaron Burr, heretofore distinguished by the favor of his country. The grounds of these intimations being inconclusive, the objects uncertain, and the fidelity of that country known to be firm, the only measure taken was to urge the informants to use their best endeavors to get further insight into the designs and proceedings of the suspected persons, and to communicate them to me.

It was not until the latter part of October, that the objects of the conspiracy began to be perceived, but still so blended and involved in mystery that nothing distinct could be singled out for pursuit. In this state of uncertainty as to the crime contemplated, the acts done, and the legal course to be pursued, I thought it best to send to the scene where these things were principally in transaction, a person, in whose integrity, understanding, and discretion, entire confidence could be reposed, with instructions to investigate the plots going on, to enter into conference (for which he had sufficient credentials) with the governors and all other officers, civil and military, and with their aid to do on the spot whatever should be necessary to discover the designs of the conspirators, arrest their means, bring their persons to punishment, and to call out the force of the country to suppress any unlawful enterprise in which it should be found they were engaged. By this time it was known that many boats were under preparation, stores of provisions collecting, and an unusual number of suspicious characters in motion on the Ohio and its waters. Besides despatching the confidential agent to that quarter, orders were at the same time sent to the governors of the Orleans and Mississippi territories, and to the commanders of the land and naval forces there, to be on their guard against surprise, and in constant readiness to resist any enterprise which might be attempted on the vessels, posts, or other objects under their care; and on the 8th of November, instructions were forwarded to General Wilkinson to hasten an accommodation with the Spanish commander on the Sabine, and as soon as that was effected, to fall back with his principal force to the hither bank of the Mississippi, for the defence of the intersecting points on that river. By a letter received from that officer on the 25th of November, but dated October 21st, we learn that a confidential agent of Aaron Burr had been deputed to him, with communications partly written in cipher and partly oral, explaining his designs, exaggerating his resources, and making such offers of emolument and command, to engage him and the army in his unlawful enterprise, as he had flattered himself would be successful. The general, with the honor of a soldier and fidelity of a good citizen, immediately despatched a trusty officer to me with information of what had passed, proceeding to establish such an understanding with the Spanish commandant on the Sabine as permitted him to withdraw his force across the Mississippi, and to enter on measures for opposing the projected enterprise.

The general's letter, which came to hand on the 25th of November, as has been mentioned, and some other information received a few days earlier, when brought together, developed Burr's general designs, different parts of which only had been revealed to different informants. It appeared that he contemplated two distinct objects, which might be carried on either jointly or separately, and either the one or the other first, as circumstances should direct. One of these was the severance of the Union of these States by the Alleghany mountains; the other, an attack on Mexico. A third object was provided, merely ostensible, to wit: the settlement of a pretended purchase of a tract of country on the Washita, claimed by a Baron Bastrop. This was to serve as the pretext for all his preparations, an allurement for such followers as really wished to acquire settlements in that country, and a cover under which to retreat in the event of final discomfiture of both branches of his real design.

He found at once that the attachment of the western country to the present Union was not to be shaken; that its dissolution could not be effected with the consent of its inhabitants, and that his resources were inadequate, as yet, to effect it by force. He took his course then at once, determined to seize on New Orleans, plunder the bank there, possess himself of the military and naval stores, and proceed on his expedition to Mexico; and to this object all his means and preparations were now directed. He collected from all the quarters where himself or his agents possessed influence, all the ardent, restless, desperate, and disaffected persons who were ready for any enterprise analogous to their characters. He seduced good and well-meaning citizens, some by assurances that he possessed the confidence of the government and was acting under its secret patronage, a pretence which obtained some credit from the state of our differences with Spain; and others by offers of land in Bastrop's claim on the Washita.

This was the state of my information of his proceedings about the last of November, at which time, therefore, it was first possible to take specific measures to meet them. The proclamation of November 27th, two days after the receipt of General Wilkinson's information, was now issued. Orders were despatched to every intersecting point on the Ohio and Mississippi, from Pittsburg to New Orleans, for the employment of such force either of the regulars or of the militia, and of such proceedings also of the civil authorities, as might enable them to seize on all the boats and stores provided for the enterprise, to arrest the persons concerned, and to suppress effectually the further progress of the enterprise. A little before the receipt of these orders in the State of Ohio, our confidential agent, who had been diligently employed in investigating the conspiracy, had acquired sufficient information to open himself to the governor of that State, and apply for the immediate exertion of the authority and power of the State to crush the combination. Governor Tiffin and the legislature, with a promptitude, an energy, and patriotic zeal, which entitle them to a distinguished place in the affection of their sister States, effected the seizure of all the boats, provisions, and other preparations within their reach, and thus gave a first blow, materially disabling the enterprise in its outset.

In Kentucky, a premature attempt to bring Burr to justice, without sufficient evidence for his conviction, had produced a popular impression in his favor, and a general disbelief of his guilt. This gave him an unfortunate opportunity of hastening his equipments. The arrival of the proclamation and orders, and the application and information of our confidential agent, at length awakened the authorities of that State to the truth, and then produced the same promptitude and energy of which the neighboring State had set the example. Under an act of their legislature of December 23d, militia was instantly ordered to different important points, and measures taken for doing whatever could yet be done. Some boats (accounts vary from five to double or treble that number) and persons (differently estimated from one to three hundred) had in the meantime passed the falls of the Ohio, to rendezvous at the mouth of the Cumberland, with others expected down that river.

Not apprized, till very late, that any boats were building on Cumberland, the effect of the proclamation had been trusted to for some time in the State of Tennessee; but on the 19th of December, similar communications and instructions with those of the neighboring States were despatched by express to the governor, and a general officer of the western division of the State, and on the 23d of December our confidential agent left Frankfort for Nashville, to put into activity the means of that State also. But by information received yesterday I learn that on the 22d of December, Mr. Burr descended the Cumberland with two boats merely of accommodation, carrying with him from that State no quota toward his unlawful enterprise. Whether after the arrival of the proclamation, of the orders, or of our agent, any exertion which could be made by that State, or the orders of the governor of Kentucky for calling out the militia at the mouth of Cumberland, would be in time to arrest these boats, and those from the falls of the Ohio, is still doubtful.

On the whole, the fugitives from Ohio, with their associates from Cumberland, or any other place in that quarter, cannot threaten serious danger to the city of New Orleans.

By the same express of December nineteenth, orders were sent to the governors of New Orleans and Mississippi, supplementary to those which had been given on the twenty-fifth of November, to hold the militia of their territories in readiness to co-operate for their defence, with the regular troops and armed vessels then under command of General Wilkinson. Great alarm, indeed, was excited at New Orleans by the exaggerated accounts of Mr. Burr, disseminated through his emissaries, of the armies and navies he was to assemble there. General Wilkinson had arrived there himself on the 24th of November and had immediately put into activity the resources of the place for the purpose of its defence; and on the tenth of December he was joined by his troops from the Sabine. Great zeal was shown by the inhabitants generally, the merchants of the place readily agreeing to the most laudable exertions and sacrifices for manning the armed vessels with their seamen, and the other citizens manifesting unequivocal fidelity to the Union, and a spirit of determined resistance to their expected assailants.

Surmises have been hazarded that this enterprise is to receive aid from certain foreign powers. But these surmises are without proof or probability. The wisdom of the measures sanctioned by Congress at its last session had placed us in the paths of peace and justice with the only powers with whom we had any differences, and nothing has happened since which makes it either their interest or ours to pursue another course. No change of measures has taken place on our part; none ought to take place at this time. With the one, friendly arrangement was then proposed, and the law deemed necessary on the failure of that was suspended to give time for a fair trial of the issue. With the same power, negotiation is still preferred and provisional measures only are necessary to meet the event of rupture. While, therefore, we do not deflect in the slightest degree from the course we then assumed, and are still pursuing, with mutual consent, to restore a good understanding, we are not to impute to them practices as irreconcilable to interest as to good faith, and changing necessarily the relations of peace and justice between us to those of war. These surmises are, therefore, to be imputed to the vauntings of the author of this enterprise, to multiply his partisans by magnifying the belief of his prospects and support.

By letters from General Wilkinson, of the 14th and 18th of September, which came to hand two days after date of the resolution of the House of Representatives, that is to say, on the morning of the 18th instant, I received the important affidavit, a copy of which I now communicate, with extracts of so much of the letters as come within the scope of the resolution. By these it will be seen that of three of the principal emissaries of Mr. Burr, whom the general had caused to be apprehended, one had been liberated by *habeas corpus*, and the two others, being those particularly employed in the endeavor to corrupt the general and army of the United States, have been embarked by him for our ports in the Atlantic States, probably on the consideration that an impartial trial could not be expected during the present agitations of New Orleans, and that that city was not as yet a safe place of confinement. As soon as these persons shall arrive, they will be delivered to the custody of the law, and left to such course of trial, both as to place and process, as its functionaries may direct. The presence of the highest judicial authorities, to be assembled at this place within a few days, the means of pursuing a sounder course of proceedings here than elsewhere, and the aid of the executive means, should the judges have occasion to use them, render it equally desirable for the criminals as for the public, that being already removed from the place where they were first apprehended, the first regular arrest should take place here, and the course of proceedings receive here its proper direction.

Special Message on Gun-Boats

February 10, 1807

To the Senate and House of Representatives of the
United States:

In compliance with the request of the House of Representatives, expressed in their resolution of the 5th instant, I proceed to give such information as is possessed, of the effect of
gun-boats in the protection and defense of harbors, of the
numbers thought necessary, and of the proposed distribution
of them among the ports and harbors of the United States.

Under the present circumstances, and governed by the intentions of the legislature, as manifested by their annual appropriations of money for the purposes of defence, it has
been concluded to combine—1st, land batteries, furnished
with heavy cannon and mortars, and established on all the
points around the place favorable for preventing vessels from
lying before it; 2d, movable artillery which may be carried, as
an occasion may require, to points unprovided with fixed batteries; 3d, floating batteries; and 4th, gun-boats, which may
oppose an enemy at its entrance and co-operate with the batteries for his expulsion.

On this subject professional men were consulted as far as
we had opportunity. General Wilkinson, and the late General
Gates, gave their opinions in writing, in favor of the system,
as will be seen by their letters now communicated. The higher
officers of the navy gave the same opinions in separate conferences, as their presence at the seat of government offered
occasions of consulting them, and no difference of judgment
appeared on the subjects. Those of Commodore Barron and
Captain Tingey, now here, are recently furnished in writing,
and transmitted herewith to the legislature.

The efficacy of gun-boats for the defence of harbors, and of
other smooth and enclosed waters, may be estimated in part
from that of galleys, formerly much used, but less powerful,
more costly in their construction and maintenance, and requiring more men. But the gun-boat itself is believed to be in
use with every modern maritime nation for the purpose of
defence. In the Mediterranean, on which are several small
powers, whose system like ours is peace and defence, few har-

bors are without this article of protection. Our own experience there of the effect of gun-boats for harbor service, is recent. Algiers is particularly known to have owed to a great provision of these vessels the safety of its city, since the epoch of their construction. Before that it had been repeatedly insulted and injured. The effect of gun-boats at present in the neighborhood of Gibraltar, is well known, and how much they were used both in the attack and defence of that place during a former war. The extensive resort to them by the two greatest naval powers in the world, on an enterprise of invasion not long since in prospect, shows their confidence in their efficacy for the purposes for which they are suited. By the northern powers of Europe, whose seas are particularly adapted to them, they are still more used. The remarkable action between the Russian flotilla of gun-boats and galleys, and a Turkish fleet of ships-of-the-line and frigates, in the Liman sea, 1788, will be readily recollected. The latter, commanded by their most celebrated admiral, were completely defeated, and several of their ships-of-the-line destroyed.

From the opinions given as to the number of gun-boats necessary for some of the principal seaports, and from a view of all the towns and ports from Orleans to Maine inclusive, entitled to protection, in proportion to their situation and circumstances, it is concluded, that to give them a due measure of protection in time of war, about two hundred gun-boats will be requisite. According to first ideas, the following would be their general distribution, liable to be varied on more mature examination, and as circumstances shall vary, that is to say:—

To the Mississippi and its neighboring waters, forty gun-boats.

To Savannah and Charleston, and the harbors on each side, from St. Mary's to Currituck, twenty-five.

To the Chesapeake and its waters, twenty.

To Delaware bay and river, fifteen.

To New York, the Sound, and waters as far as Cape Cod, fifty.

To Boston and the harbors north of Cape Cod, fifty.

The flotilla assigned to these several stations, might each be under the care of a particular commandant, and the vessels composing them would, in ordinary, be distributed among the harbors within the station in proportion to their importance.

Of these boats a proper proportion would be of the larger size, such as those heretofore built, capable of navigating any seas, and of reinforcing occasionally the strength of even the most distant port when menaced with danger. The residue would be confined to their own or the neighboring harbors, would be smaller, less furnished for accommodation, and consequently less costly. Of the number supposed necessary, seventy-three are built or building, and the hundred and twenty-seven still to be provided, would cost from five to six hundred thousand dollars. Having regard to the convenience of the treasury, as well as to the resources of building, it has been thought that one half of these might be built in the present year, and the other half the next. With the legislature, however, it will rest to stop where we are, or at any further point, when they shall be of opinion that the number provided shall be sufficient for the object.

At times when Europe as well as the United States shall be at peace, it would not be proposed that more than six or eight of these vessels should be kept afloat. When Europe is in war, treble that number might be necessary to be distributed among those particular harbors which foreign vessels of war are in the habit of frequenting, for the purpose of preserving order therein.

But they would be manned, in ordinary, with only their complement for navigation, relying on the seamen and militia of the port if called into action on sudden emergency. It would be only when the United States should themselves be at war, that the whole number would be brought into actual service, and would be ready in the first moments of the war to co-operate with other means for covering at once the line of our seaports. At all times, those unemployed would be withdrawn into places not exposed to sudden enterprise, hauled up under sheds from the sun and weather, and kept in preservation with little expense for repairs or maintenance.

It must be superfluous to observe, that this species of naval armament is proposed merely for defensive operation; that it can have but little effect toward protecting our commerce in the open seas even on our coast; and still less can it become an excitement to engage in offensive maritime war, toward which it would furnish no means.

Eighth Annual Message

November 8, 1808

To the Senate and House of Representatives of the United States:

It would have been a source, fellow citizens, of much gratification, if our last communications from Europe had enabled me to inform you that the belligerent nations, whose disregard of neutral rights has been so destructive to our commerce, had become awakened to the duty and true policy of revoking their unrighteous edicts. That no means might be omitted to produce this salutary effect, I lost no time in availing myself of the act authorizing a suspension, in whole or in part, of the several embargo laws. Our ministers at London and Paris were instructed to explain to the respective governments there, our disposition to exercise the authority in such manner as would withdraw the pretext on which the aggressions were originally founded, and open a way for a renewal of that commercial intercourse which it was alleged on all sides had been reluctantly obstructed. As each of those governments had pledged its readiness to concur in renouncing a measure which reached its adversary through the incontestable rights of neutrals only, and as the measure had been assumed by each as a retaliation for an asserted acquiescence in the aggressions of the other, it was reasonably expected that the occasion would have been seized by both for evincing the sincerity of their profession, and for restoring to the commerce of the United States its legitimate freedom. The instructions to our ministers with respect to the different belligerents were necessarily modified with reference to their different circumstances, and to the condition annexed by law to the executive power of suspension, requiring a degree of security to our commerce which would not result from a repeal of the decrees of France. Instead of a pledge, therefore, of a suspension of the embargo as to her in case of such a repeal, it was presumed that a sufficient inducement might be found in other considerations, and particularly in the change produced by a compliance with our just demands by one belligerent, and a refusal by the other, in the relations between the other and the United States. To Great Britain, whose power on the ocean is so ascendant, it was deemed not inconsistent with that condition to state explicitly, that on her rescinding her orders in relation to the United States their trade would be opened with her, and remain shut to her enemy, in case of his failure to rescind his decrees also. From France no answer has been received, nor any indication that the requisite change in her decrees is contemplated. The favorable reception of the proposition to Great Britain was the less to be doubted, as her orders of council had not only been referred for their vindication to an acquiescence on the part of the United States no longer to be pretended, but as the arrangement proposed, while it resisted the illegal decrees of France, involved, moreover, substantially, the precise advantages professedly aimed at by the British orders. The arrangement has nevertheless been rejected.

This candid and liberal experiment having thus failed, and no other event having occurred on which a suspension of the embargo by the executive was authorized, it necessarily remains in the extent originally given to it. We have the satisfaction, however, to reflect, that in return for the privations by the measure, and which our fellow citizens in general have borne with patriotism, it has had the important effects of saving our mariners and our vast mercantile property, as well as of affording time for prosecuting the defensive and provisional measures called for by the occasion. It has demonstrated to foreign nations the moderation and firmness which govern our councils, and to our citizens the necessity of uniting in support of the laws and the rights of their country, and has thus long frustrated those usurpations and spoliations which, if resisted, involve war; if submitted to, sacrificed a vital principle of our national independence.

Under a continuance of the belligerent measures which, in defiance of laws which consecrate the rights of neutrals, overspread the ocean with danger, it will rest with the wisdom of Congress to decide on the course best adapted to such a state of things; and bringing with them, as they do, from every part of the Union, the sentiments of our constituents, my confidence is strengthened, that in forming this decision they will, with an unerring regard to the essential rights and interests of the nation, weigh and compare the painful alternatives out of which a choice is to be made. Nor should I do justice to the virtues which on other occasions have marked the character of our fellow citizens, if I did not cherish an equal confidence that the alternative chosen, whatever it may be, will be maintained with all the fortitude and patriotism which the crisis ought to inspire.

The documents containing the correspondences on the subject of the foreign edicts against our commerce, with the instructions given to our ministers at London and Paris, are now laid before you.

The communications made to Congress at their last session explained the posture in which the close of the discussion relating to the attack by a British ship of war on the frigate Chesapeake left a subject on which the nation had manifested so honorable a sensibility. Every view of what had passed authorized a belief that immediate steps would be taken by the British government for redressing a wrong, which, the more it was investigated, appeared the more clearly to require what had not been provided for in the special mission. It is found that no steps have been taken for the purpose. On the contrary, it will be seen, in the documents laid before you, that the inadmissible preliminary which obstructed the adjustment is still adhered to; and, moreover, that it is now brought into connection with the distinct and irrelative case of the orders in council. The instructions which had been given to our ministers at London with a view to facilitate, if necessary, the reparation claimed by the United States, are included in the documents communicated.

Our relations with the other powers of Europe have undergone no material changes since your last session. The important negotiations with Spain, which had been alternately suspended and resumed, necessarily experience a pause under the extraordinary and interesting crisis which distinguished her internal situation.

With the Barbary powers we continue in harmony, with the exception of an unjustifiable proceeding of the dey of Algiers toward our consul to that regency. Its character and circumstances are now laid before you, and will enable you to decide how far it may, either now or hereafter, call for any measures not within the limits of the executive authority.

With our Indian neighbors the public peace has been steadily maintained. Some instances of individual wrong have, as at other times, taken place, but in nowise implicating the will of the nation. Beyond the Mississippi, the Iowas, the Sacs, and the Alabamas, have delivered up for trial and punishment individuals from among themselves accused of murdering citizens of the United States. On this side of the Mississippi, the Creeks are exerting themselves to arrest offenders of the same kind; and the Choctaws have manifested their readiness and desire for amicable and just arrangements respecting depredations committed by disorderly persons of their tribe. And, generally, from a conviction that we consider them as part of ourselves, and cherish with sincerity their rights and interests, the attachment of the Indian tribes is gaining strength daily—is extending from the nearer to the more remote, and will amply requite us for the justice and friendship practised towards them. Husbandry and household manufacture are advancing among them, more rapidly with the southern than the northern tribes, from circumstances of soil and climate; and one of the two great divisions of the Cherokee nation have now under consideration to solicit the citizenship of the United States, and to be identified with us in laws and government, in such progressive manner as we shall think best.

In consequence of the appropriations of the last session of Congress for the security of our seaport towns and harbors, such works of defence have been erected as seemed to be called for by the situation of the several places, their relative importance, and the scale of expense indicated by the amount of the appropriation. These works will chiefly be finished in the course of the present season, except at New York and New Orleans, where most was to be done; and although a great proportion of the last appropriation has been expended on the former place, yet some further views will be submitted by Congress for rendering its security entirely adequate against naval enterprise. A view of what has been done at the several places, and of what is proposed to be done, shall be communicated as soon as the several reports are received.

Of the gun-boats authorized by the act of December last, it has been thought necessary to build only one hundred and three in the present year. These, with those before possessed, are sufficient for the harbors and waters exposed, and the residue will require little time for their construction when it is deemed necessary.

Under the act of the last session for raising an additional military force, so many officers were immediately appointed as were necessary for carrying on the business of recruiting, and in proportion as it advanced, others have been added. We have reason to believe their success has been satisfactory, although such returns have not yet been received as enable me to present to you a statement of the numbers engaged.

I have not thought it necessary in the course of the last season to call for any general detachments of militia or volunteers under the law passed for that purpose. For the ensuing season, however, they will require to be in readiness should their services be wanted. Some small and special detachments have been necessary to maintain the laws of embargo on that portion of our northern frontier which offered peculiar facilities for evasion, but these were replaced as soon as it could be done by bodies of new recruits. By the aid of these, and of the armed vessels called into actual service in other quarters, the spirit of disobedience and abuse which manifested itself early, and with sensible effect while we were unprepared to meet it, has been considerably repressed.

Considering the extraordinary character of the times in which we live, our attention should unremittingly be fixed on the safety of our country. For a people who are free, and who mean to remain so, a well-organized and armed militia is their best security. It is, therefore, incumbent on us, at every meeting, to revise the condition of the militia, and to ask ourselves if it is prepared to repel a powerful enemy at every point of our territories exposed to invasion. Some of the States have paid a laudable attention to this object; but every degree of neglect is to be found among others. Congress alone have power to produce a uniform state of preparation in this great organ of defence; the interests which they so deeply feel in their own and their country's security will present this as among the most important objects of their deliberation.

Under the acts of March 11th and April 23d, respecting arms, the difficulty of procuring them from abroad, during the present situation and dispositions of Europe, induced us to direct our whole efforts to the means of internal supply. The public factories have, therefore, been enlarged, additional machineries erected, and in proportion as artificers can be found or formed, their effect, already more than doubled, may be increased so as to keep pace with the yearly increase of the militia. The annual sums appropriated by the latter act, have been directed to the encouragement of private factories of arms, and contracts have been entered into with individual undertakers to nearly the amount of the first year's appropriation.

The suspension of our foreign commerce, produced by the injustice of the belligerent powers, and the consequent losses and sacrifices of our citizens, are subjects of just concern. The situation into which we have thus been forced, has impelled us to apply a portion of our industry and capital to internal manufactures and improvements. The extent of this conversion is daily increasing, and little doubt remains that the establishments formed and forming will—under the auspices of cheaper materials and subsistence, the freedom of labor from taxation with us, and of protecting duties and prohibitions—become permanent. The commerce with the Indians, too, within our own boundaries, is likely to receive abundant aliment from the same internal source, and will secure to them peace and the progress of civilization, undisturbed by practices hostile to both.

The accounts of the receipts and expenditures during the year ending on the 30th day of September last, being not yet made up, a correct statement will hereafter be transmitted from the Treasury. In the meantime, it is ascertained that the receipts have amounted to near eighteen millions of dollars, which, with the eight millions and a half in the treasury at the beginning of the year, have enabled us, after meeting the current demands and interest incurred, to pay two millions three hundred thousand dollars of the principal of our funded debt, and left us in the treasury, on that day, near fourteen millions of dollars. Of these, five millions three hundred and fifty thousand dollars will be necessary to pay what will be due on the first day of January next, which will complete the reimbursement of the eight per cent. stock. These payments, with those made in the six years and a half preceding, will have extinguished thirty-three millions five hundred and eighty thousand dollars of the principal of the funded debt, being the whole which could be paid or purchased within the limits of the law and our contracts; and the amount of principal thus discharged will have liberated the revenue from about two millions of dollars of interest, and added that sum annually to the disposable surplus. The probable accumulation of the surpluses of revenue beyond what can be applied to the payment of the public debt, whenever the freedom and safety of our commerce shall be restored, merits the consideration of Congress. Shall it lie unproductive in the public vaults? Shall the revenue be reduced? Or shall it rather be appropriated to the improvements of roads, canals, rivers, education, and other great foundations of prosperity and union, under the powers which Congress may already possess, or such amendment of the constitution as may be approved by the States? While uncertain of the course of things, the time may be advantageously employed in obtaining the powers necessary for a system of improvement, should that be thought best.

Availing myself of this the last occasion which will occur of addressing the two houses of the legislature at their meeting, I cannot omit the expression of my sincere gratitude for the repeated proofs of confidence manifested to me by themselves and their predecessors since my call to the administration, and the many indulgences experienced at their hands. The same grateful acknowledgments are due to my fellow citizens generally, whose support has been my great encouragement under all embarrassments. In the transaction of their business I cannot have escaped error. It is incident to our imperfect nature. But I may say with truth, my errors have been of the understanding, not of intention; and that the advancement of their rights and interests has been the constant motive for every measure. On these considerations I solicit their indulgence. Looking forward with anxiety to their future destinies, I trust that, in their steady character unshaken by difficulties, in their love of liberty, obedience to law, and support of the public authorities, I see a sure guaranty of the permanence of our republic; and retiring from the charge of their affairs, I carry with me the consolation of a firm persuasion that Heaven has in store for our beloved country long ages to come of prosperity and happiness.

To the Inhabitants of Albemarle County, in Virginia

April 3, 1809

Returning to the scenes of my birth and early life, to the society of those with whom I was raised, and who have been ever dear to me, I receive, fellow citizens and neighbors, with inexpressible pleasure, the cordial welcome you are so good as to give me. Long absent on duties which the history of a wonderful era made incumbent on those called to them, the pomp, the turmoil, the bustle and splendor of office, have drawn but deeper sighs for the tranquil and irresponsible occupations of private life, for the enjoyment of an affectionate intercourse with you, my neighbors and friends, and the endearments of family love, which nature has given us all, as the sweetener of every hour. For these I gladly lay down the distressing burthen of power, and seek, with my fellow citizens, repose and safety under the watchful cares, the labors, and perplexities of younger and abler minds. The anxieties you express to administer to my happiness, do, of themselves, confer that happiness, and the measure will be complete, if my endeavors to fulfil my duties in the several public stations to which I have been called, have obtained for me the approbation of my country. The part which I have acted on the theatre of public life, has been before them; and to their sentence I submit it; but the testimony of my native country, of the individuals who have known me in private life, to my conduct in its various duties and relations, is the more grateful, as proceeding from eye witnesses and observers, from triers of the vicinage. Of you, then, my neighbors, I may ask, in the face of the world, " whose ox have I taken, or whom have I defrauded? Whom have I oppressed, or of whose hand have I received a bribe to blind mine eyes therewith?" On your verdict I rest with conscious security. Your wishes for my happiness are received with just sensibility, and I offer sincere prayers for your own welfare and prosperity.

To Brother John Baptist de Coigne

Charlottesville, June 1781

BROTHER JOHN BAPTIST DE COIGNE,—I am very much pleased with the visit you have made us, and particularly that it has happened when the wise men from all parts of our country were assembled together in council, and had an opportunity of hearing the friendly discourse you held to me. We are all sensible of your friendship, and of the services you have rendered, and I now, for my countrymen, return you thanks, and, most particularly, for your assistance to the garrison which was besieged by the hostile Indians. I hope it will please the great being above to continue you long in life, in health and in friendship to us; and that your son will afterwards succeed you in wisdom, in good disposition, and in power over your people. I consider the name you have given as particularly honorable to me, but I value it the more as it proves your attachment to my country. We, like you, are Americans, born in the same land, and having the same interests. I have carefully attended to the figures represented on the skins, and to their explanation, and shall always keep them hanging on the walls in remembrance of you and your nation. I have joined with you sincerely in smoking the pipe of peace; it is a good old custom handed down by your ancestors, and as such I respect and join in it with reverence. I hope we shall long continue to smoke in friendship together. You find us, brother, engaged in war with a powerful nation. Our forefathers were Englishmen, inhabitants of a little island beyond the great water, and, being distressed for land, they came and settled here. As long as we were young and weak, the English whom we had left behind, made us carry all our wealth to their country, to enrich them; and, not satisfied with this, they at length began to say we were their slaves, and should do whatever they ordered us. We were now grown up and felt ourselves strong, we knew we were free as they were, that we came here of our own accord and not at their biddance, and were determined to be free as long as we should exist. For this reason they made war on us. They have now waged that war six years, and have not yet won more land from us than will serve to bury the warriors they have lost. Your old father, the king of France, has joined us in the war, and done many good things for us. We are bound forever to love him, and wish you to love him, brother, because he is a good and true friend to us. The Spaniards have also joined us, and other powerful nations are now entering into the war to punish the robberies and violences the English have committed on them. The English stand alone, without a friend to support them, hated by all mankind because they are proud and unjust. This quarrel, when it first began, was a family quarrel between us and the English, who were then our brothers. We, therefore, did not wish you to engage in it at all. We are strong enough of ourselves without wasting your blood in fighting our battles. The English, knowing this, have been always suing to the Indians to help them fight. We do not wish you to take up the hatchet. We love and esteem you. We wish you to multiply and be strong. The English, on the other hand, wish to set you and us to cutting one another's throats, that when we are dead they may take all our land. It is better for you not to join in this quarrel, unless the English have killed any of your warriors or done you any other injury. If they have, you have a right to go to war with them, and revenge the injury, and we have none to restrain you. Any free nation has a right to punish those who have done them an injury. I say the same, brother, as to the Indians who treat you ill. While I advise you, like an affectionate friend, to avoid unnecessary war, I do not assume the right of restraining you from punishing your enemies. If the English have injured you, as they have injured the French and Spaniards, do like them and join us in the war. General Clarke will receive you and show you the way to their towns. But if they have not injured you, it is better for you to lie still and be quiet. This is the advice which has been always given by the great council of the Americans. We must give the same, because we are but one of thirteen nations, who have agreed to act and speak together. These nations keep a council of wise men always sitting together, and each of us separately follow their advice. They have the care of all the people and the lands between the Ohio and Mississippi, and will see that no wrong be committed on them. The French settled at Kaskaskias, St. Vincennes, and the Cohos, are subject to that council, and they will punish them if they do you any injury. If you will make known to me any just cause of complaint against them, I will represent it to the great council at Philadelphia, and have justice done you.

Our good friend, your father, the King of France, does not lay any claim to them. Their misconduct should not be imputed to him. He gave them up to the English the last war, and we have taken them from the English. The Americans alone have a right to maintain justice in all the lands on this side the Mississippi,—on the other side the Spaniards rule. You complain, brother, of the want of goods for the use of your people. We know that your wants are great, notwithstanding we have done everything in our power to supply them, and have often grieved for you. The path from hence to Kaskaskias is long and dangerous; goods cannot be carried to you in that way. New Orleans has been the only place from which we could get goods for you. We have bought a great deal there; but I am afraid not so much of them have come to you as we intended. Some of them have been sold of necessity to buy provisions for our posts. Some have been embezzled by our own drunken and roguish people. Some have been taken by the Indians and many by the English.

The Spaniards, having now taken all the English posts on the Mississippi, have opened that channel free for our commerce, and we are in hopes of getting goods for you from them. I will not boast to you, brother, as the English do, nor promise more than we shall be able to fulfil. I will tell you honestly, what indeed your own good sense will tell you, that a nation at war cannot buy so many goods as when in peace. We do not make so many things to send over the great waters to buy goods, as we made and shall make again in time of peace. When we buy those goods, the English take many of them, as they are coming to us over the great water. What we get in safe, are to be divided among many, because we have a great many soldiers, whom we must clothe. The remainder we send to our brothers the Indians, and in going, a great deal of it is stolen or lost. These are the plain reasons why you cannot get so much from us in war as in peace. But peace is not far off. The English cannot hold out long, because all the world is against them. When that takes place, brother, there will not be an Englishman left on this side the great water. What will those foolish nations then do, who have made us their enemies, sided with the English, and laughed at you for not being as wicked as themselves? They are clothed for a day, and will be naked forever after; while you, who have submitted to short inconvenience, will be well supplied through the rest of your lives. Their friends will be gone and their enemies left behind; but your friends will be here, and will make you strong against all your enemies. For the present you shall have a share of what little goods we can get. We will order some immediately up the Mississippi for you and for us. If they be little, you will submit to suffer a little as your brothers do for a short time. And when we shall have beaten our enemies and forced them to make peace, we will share more plentifully. General Clarke will furnish you with ammunition to serve till we can get some from New Orleans. I must recommend to you particular attention to him. He is our great, good, and trusty warrior; and we have put everything under his care beyond the Alleghanies. He will advise you in all difficulties, and redress your wrongs. Do what he tells you, and you will be sure to do right. You ask us to send schoolmasters to educate your son and the sons of your people. We desire above all things, brother, to instruct you in whatever we know ourselves. We wish to learn you all our arts and to make you wise and wealthy. As soon as there is peace we shall be able to send you the best of schoolmasters; but while the war is raging, I am afraid it will not be practicable. It shall be done, however, before your son is of an age to receive instruction.

This, brother, is what I had to say to you. Repeat it from me to all your people, and to our friends, the Kickapous, Piorias, Piankeshaws and Wyattanons. I will give you a commission to show them how much we esteem you. Hold fast the chain of friendship which binds us together, keep it bright as the sun, and let them, you and us, live together in perpetual love.

To Brother Handsome Lake

Washington, November 3, 1802

TO BROTHER HANDSOME LAKE:—

I have received the message in writing which you sent me through Captain Irvine, our confidential agent, placed near you for the purpose of communicating and transacting between us, whatever may be useful for both nations. I am happy to learn you have been so far favored by the Divine spirit as to be made sensible of those things which are for your good and that of your people, and of those which are hurtful to you; and particularly that you and they see the ruinous effects which the abuse of spirituous liquors have produced upon them. It has weakened their bodies, enervated their minds, exposed them to hunger, cold, nakedness, and poverty, kept them in perpetual broils, and reduced their population. I do not wonder then, brother, at your censures, not only on your own people, who have voluntarily gone into these fatal habits, but on all the nations of white people who have supplied their calls for this article. But these nations have done to you only what they do among themselves. They have sold what individuals wish to buy, leaving to every one to be the guardian of his own health and happiness. Spirituous liquors are not in themselves bad, they are often found to be an excellent medicine for the sick; it is the improper and intemperate use of them, by those in health, which makes them injurious. But as you find that your people cannot refrain from an ill use of them, I greatly applaud your resolution not to use them at all. We have too affectionate a concern for your happiness to place the paltry gain on the sale of these articles in competition with the injury they do you. And as it is the desire of your nation, that no spirits should be sent among them, I am authorized by the great council of the United States to prohibit them. I will sincerely cöoperate with your wise men in any proper measures for this purpose, which shall be agreeable to them.

You remind me, brother, of what I said to you, when you visited me the last winter, that the lands you then held would remain yours, and shall never go from you but when you should be disposed to sell. This I now repeat, and will ever abide by. We, indeed, are always ready to buy land; but we will never ask but when you wish to sell; and our laws, in order to protect you against imposition, have forbidden individuals to purchase lands from you; and have rendered it necessary, when you desire to sell, even to a State, that an agent from the United States should attend the sale, see that your consent is freely given, a satisfactory price paid, and report to us what has been done, for our approbation. This was done in the late case of which you complain. The deputies of your nation came forward, in all the forms which we have been used to consider as evidence of the will of your nation. They proposed to sell to the State of New York certain parcels of land, of small extent, and detached from the body of your other lands; the State of New York was desirous to buy. I sent an agent, in whom we could trust, to see that your consent was free, and the sale fair. All was reported to be free and fair. The lands were your property. The right to sell is one of the rights of property. To forbid you the exercise of that right would be a wrong to your nation. Nor do I think, brother, that the sale of lands is, under all circumstances, injurious to your people. While they depended on hunting, the more extensive the forest around them, the more game they would yield. But going into a state of agriculture, it may be as advantageous to a society, as it is to an individual, who has more land than he can improve, to sell a part, and lay out the money in stocks and implements of agriculture, for the better improvement of the residue. A little land well stocked and improved, will yield more than a great deal without stock or improvement. I hope, therefore, that on further reflection, you will see this transaction in a more favorable light, both as it concerns the interest of your nation, and the exercise of that superintending care which I am sincerely anxious to employ for their subsistence and happiness. Go on then, brother, in the great reformation you have undertaken. Persuade our red brethren then to be sober, and to cultivate their lands; and their women to spin and weave for their families. You will soon see your women and children well fed and clothed, your men living happily in peace and plenty, and your numbers increasing from year to year. It will be a great glory to you to have been the instrument of so happy a change, and your children's children, from generation to generation, will repeat your name with love and gratitude forever. In all your enterprises for the good of your people, you may count with confidence on the aid and protection of the United States, and on the sincerity and zeal with which I am myself animated in the furthering of this humane work. You are our brethren of the same land; we wish your prosperity as brethren should do. Farewell.

To the Brothers of the Choctaw Nation

December 17, 1803

BROTHERS OF THE CHOCTAW NATION:—

We have long heard of your nation as a numerous, peaceable, and friendly people; but this is the first visit we have had from its great men at the seat of our government. I welcome you here; am glad to take you by the hand, and to assure you, for your nation, that we are their friends. Born in the same land, we ought to live as brothers, doing to each other all the good we can, and not listening to wicked men, who may endeavor to make us enemies. By living in peace, we can help and prosper one another; by waging war, we can kill and destroy many on both sides; but those who survive will not be the happier for that. Then, brothers, let it forever be peace and good neighborhood between us. Our seventeen States compose a great and growing nation. Their children are as the leaves of the trees, which the winds are spreading over the forest. But we are just also. We take from no nation what belongs to it. Our growing numbers make us always willing to buy lands from our red brethren, when they are willing to sell. But be assured we never mean to disturb them in their possessions. On the contrary, the lines established between us by mutual consent, shall be sacredly preserved, and will protect your lands from all encroachments by our own people or any others. We will give you a copy of the law, made by our great Council, for punishing our people, who may encroach on your lands, or injure you otherwise. Carry it with you to your homes, and preserve it, as the shield which we spread over you, to protect your land, your property and persons.

It is at the request which you sent me in September, signed by Puckshanublee and other chiefs, and which you now repeat, that I listen to your proposition to sell us lands. You say you owe a great debt to your merchants, that you have nothing to pay it with but lands, and you pray us to take lands, and pay your debt. The sum you have occasion for, brothers, is a very great one. We have never yet paid as much to any of our red brethren for the purchase of lands. You propose to us some on the Tombigbee, and some on the Mississippi. Those on the Mississippi suit us well. We wish to have establishments on that river, as resting places for our boats, to furnish them provisions, and to receive our people who fall sick on the way to or from New Orleans, which is now ours. In that quarter, therefore, we are willing to purchase as much as you will spare. But as to the manner in which the line shall be run, we are not judges of it here, nor qualified to make any bargain. But we will appoint persons hereafter to treat with you on the spot, who, knowing the country and quality of the lands, will be better able to agree with you on a line which will give us a just equivalent for the sum of money you want paid.

You have spoken, brothers, of the lands which your fathers formerly sold and marked off to the English, and which they ceded to us with the rest of the country they held here; and you say that, though you do not know whether your fathers were paid for them, you have marked the line over again for us, and do not ask repayment. It has always been the custom, brothers, when lands were bought of the red men, to pay for them immediately, and none of us have ever seen an example of such a debt remaining unpaid. It is to satisfy their immediate wants that the red men have usually sold lands; and in such a case, they would not let the debt be unpaid. The presumption from custom then is strong; so it is also from the great length of time since your fathers sold these lands. But we have, moreover, been informed by persons now living, and who assisted the English in making the purchase, that the price was paid at the time. Were it otherwise, as it was their contract, it would be their debt, not ours.

I rejoice, brothers, to hear you propose to become cultivators of the earth for the maintenance of your families. Be assured you will support them better and with less labor, by raising stock and bread, and by spinning and weaving clothes, than by hunting. A little land cultivated, and a little labor, will procure more provisions than the most successful hunt; and a woman will clothe more by spinning and weaving, than a man by hunting. Compared with you, we are but as of yesterday in this land. Yet see how much more we have multiplied by industry, and the exercise of that reason which you possess in common with us. Follow then our example, brethren, and we will aid you with great pleasure.

The clothes and other necessaries which we sent you the last year, were, as you supposed, a present from us. We never meant to ask land or any other payment for them; and the store which we sent on, was at your request also; and to accommodate you with necessaries at a reasonable price, you wished of course to have it on your land; but the land would continue yours, not ours.

As to the removal of the store, the interpreter, and the agent, and any other matters you may wish to speak about, the Secretary at War will enter into explanations with you, and whatever he says, you may consider as said by myself, and what he promises you will be faithfully performed.

I am glad, brothers, you are willing to go and visit some other parts of our country. Carriages shall be ready to convey you, and you shall be taken care of on your journey; and when you shall have returned here and rested yourselves to your own mind, you shall be sent home by land. We had provided for your coming by land, and were sorry for the mistake which carried you to Savannah instead of Augusta, and exposed you to the risks of a voyage by sea. Had any accident happened to you, though we could not help it, it would have been a cause of great mourning to us. But we thank the Great Spirit who took care of you on the ocean, and brought you safe and in good health to the seat of our great Council; and we hope His care will accompany and protect you, on your journey and return home; and that He will preserve and prosper your nation in all its just pursuits.

To the Chiefs of the Cherokee Nation

Washington, January 10, 1806

MY FRIENDS AND CHILDREN, CHIEFLY OF THE CHERO-
KEE NATION,—Having now finished our business and finished it I hope to mutual satisfaction, I cannot take leave of
you without expressing the satisfaction I have received from
your visit. I see with my own eyes that the endeavors we have
been making to encourage and lead you in the way of improving your situation have not been unsuccessful; it has been
like grain sown in good ground, producing abundantly. You
are becoming farmers, learning the use of the plough and
the hoe, enclosing your grounds and employing that labor
in their cultivation which you formerly employed in hunting
and in war; and I see handsome specimens of cotton cloth
raised, spun and wove by yourselves. You are also raising
cattle and hogs for your food, and horses to assist your labors.
Go on, my children, in the same way and be assured the further you advance in it the happier and more respectable you
will be.

Our brethren, whom you have happened to meet here from
the West and Northwest, have enabled you to compare your
situation now with what it was formerly. They also make the
comparison, and they see how far you are ahead of them, and
seeing what you are they are encouraged to do as you have
done. You will find your next want to be mills to grind your
corn, which by relieving your women from the loss of time
in beating it into meal, will enable them to spin and weave
more. When a man has enclosed and improved his farm,
builds a good house on it and raised plentiful stocks of animals, he will wish when he dies that these things shall go to
his wife and children, whom he loves more than he does his
other relations, and for whom he will work with pleasure during his life. You will, therefore, find it necessary to establish
laws for this. When a man has property, earned by his own
labor, he will not like to see another come and take it from
him because he happens to be stronger, or else to defend it
by spilling blood. You will find it necessary then to appoint
good men, as judges, to decide contests between man and
man, according to reason and to the rules you shall establish.

561

If you wish to be aided by our counsel and experience in these things we shall always be ready to assist you with our advice.

My children, it is unnecessary for me to advise you against spending all your time and labor in warring with and destroying your fellow-men, and wasting your own members. You already see the folly and iniquity of it. Your young men, however, are not yet sufficiently sensible of it. Some of them cross the Mississippi to go and destroy people who have never done them an injury. My children, this is wrong and must not be; if we permit them to cross the Mississippi to war with the Indians on the other side of that river, we must let those Indians cross the river to take revenge on you. I say again, this must not be. The Mississippi now belongs to us. It must not be a river of blood. It is now the water-path along which all our people of Natchez, St. Louis, Indiana, Ohio, Tennessee, Kentucky and the western parts of Pennsylvania and Virginia are constantly passing with their property, to and from New Orleans. Young men going to war are not easily restrained. Finding our people on the river they will rob them, perhaps kill them. This would bring on a war between us and you. It is better to stop this in time by forbidding your young men to go across the river to make war. If they go to visit or to live with the Cherokees on the other side of the river we shall not object to that. That country is ours. We will permit them to live in it.

My children, this is what I wished to say to you. To go on in learning to cultivate the earth and to avoid war. If any of your neighbors injure you, our beloved men whom we place with you will endeavor to obtain justice for you and we will support them in it. If any of your bad people injure your neighbors, be ready to acknowledge it and to do them justice. It is more honorable to repair a wrong than to persist in it. Tell all your chiefs, your men, women and children, that I take them by the hand and hold it fast. That I am their father, wish their happiness and well-being, and am always ready to promote their good.

My children, I thank you for your visit and pray to the Great Spirit who made us all and planted us all in this land to live together like brothers that He will conduct you safely to your homes, and grant you to find your families and your friends in good health.

To the Wolf and People of the Mandan Nation

Washington, December 30, 1806

MY CHILDREN, THE WOLF AND PEOPLE OF THE MANDAN NATION:—I take you by the hand of friendship and give you a hearty welcome to the seat of the government of the United States. The journey which you have taken to visit your fathers on this side of our island is a long one, and your having undertaken it is a proof that you desired to become acquainted with us. I thank the Great Spirit that he has protected you through the journey and brought you safely to the residence of your friends, and I hope He will have you constantly in his safe keeping, and restore you in good health to your nations and families.

My friends and children, we are descended from the old nations which live beyond the great water, but we and our forefathers have been so long here that we seem like you to have grown out of this land. We consider ourselves no longer of the old nations beyond the great water, but as united in one family with our red brethren here. The French, the English, the Spaniards, have now agreed with us to retire from all the country which you and we hold between Canada and Mexico, and never more to return to it. And remember the words I now speak to you, my children, they are never to return again. We are now your fathers; and you shall not lose by the change. As soon as Spain had agreed to withdraw from all the waters of the Missouri and Mississippi, I felt the desire of becoming acquainted with all my red children beyond the Mississippi, and of uniting them with us as we have those on this side of that river, in the bonds of peace and friendship. I wished to learn what we could do to benefit them by furnishing them the necessaries they want in exchange for their furs and peltries. I therefore sent our beloved man, Captain Lewis, one of my own family, to go up the Missouri river to get acquainted with all the Indian nations in its neighborhood, to take them by the hand, deliver my talks to them, and to inform us in what way we could be useful to them. Your nation received him kindly, you have taken him by the hand and been friendly to him. My children, I thank you for the services you rendered him, and for your attention to his words.

He will now tell us where we should establish trading houses to be convenient to you all, and what we must send to them.

My friends and children, I have now an important advice to give you. I have already told you that you and all the red men are my children, and I wish you to live in peace and friendship with one another as brethren of the same family ought to do. How much better is it for neighbors to help than to hurt one another; how much happier must it make them. If you will cease to make war on one another, if you will live in friendship with all mankind, you can employ all your time in providing food and clothing for yourselves and your families. Your men will not be destroyed in war, and your women and children will lie down to sleep in their cabins without fear of being surprised by their enemies and killed or carried away. Your numbers will be increased instead of diminishing, and you will live in plenty and in quiet. My children, I have given this advice to all your red brethren on this side of the Mississippi; they are following it, they are increasing in their numbers, are learning to clothe and provide for their families as we do. Remember then my advice, my children, carry it home to your people, and tell them that from the day that they have become all of the same family, from the day that we became father to them all, we wish, as a true father should do, that we may all live together as one household, and that before they strike one another, they should go to their father and let him endeavor to make up the quarrel.

My children, you are come from the other side of our great island, from where the sun sets, to see your new friends at the sun rising. You have now arrived where the waters are constantly rising and falling every day, but you are still distant from the sea. I very much desire that you should not stop here, but go and see your brethren as far as the edge of the great water. I am persuaded you have so far seen that every man by the way has received you as his brothers, and has been ready to do you all the kindness in his power. You will see the same thing quite to the sea shore; and I wish you, therefore, to go and visit our great cities in that quarter, and see how many friends and brothers you have here. You will then have travelled a long line from west to east, and if you had time to go from north to south, from Canada to Florida, you would find it as long in that direction, and all the people as sincerely your friends. I wish you, my children, to see all you can, and to tell your people all you see; because I am sure the more they know of us, the more they will be our hearty friends. I invite you, therefore, to pay a visit to Baltimore, Philadelphia, New York, and the cities still beyond that, if you are willing to go further. We will provide carriages to convey you and a person to go with you to see that you want for nothing. By the time you come back the snows will be melted on the mountains, the ice in the rivers broken up, and you will be wishing to set out on your return home.

My children, I have long desired to see you; I have now opened my heart to you, let my words sink into your hearts and never be forgotten. If ever lying people or bad spirits should raise up clouds between us, call to mind what I have said, and what you have seen yourselves. Be sure there are some lying spirits between us; let us come together as friends and explain to each other what is misrepresented or misunderstood, the clouds will fly away like morning fog, and the sun of friendship appear and shine forever bright and clear between us.

My children, it may happen that while you are here occasion may arise to talk about many things which I do not now particularly mention. The Secretary at War will always be ready to talk with you, and you are to consider whatever he says as said by myself. He will also take care of you and see that you are furnished with all comforts here.

MISCELLANY

Contents

Reply to the Representations of Affairs in America by British Newspapers

[before November 20, 1784]

I AM an officer lately returned from service & residence in the U.S. of America. I have fought & bled for that country because I thought it's cause just. From the moment of peace to that in which I left it, I have seen it enjoying all the happiness which easy government, order & industry are capable of giving to a people. On my return to my native country what has been my astonishment to find all the public papers of Europe filled with accounts of the anarchy & destractions supposed to exist in that country. I have received serious condolances from all my friends on the bitter fruits of so prosperous a war. These friends I know to be so well disposed towards America that they wished the reverse of what they repeated from the public papers. I have enquired into the source of all this misinformation & have found it not difficult to be traced. The printers on the Continent have not yet got into the habit of taking the American newspapers. Whatever they retail therefore on the subject of America, they take from the English. If your readers will reflect a moment they will recollect that every unfavourable account they have seen of the transactions in America has been taken from the English papers only. Nothing is known in Europe of the situation of the U.S. since the acknowlegement of their independance but thro' the channel of these papers.

But these papers have been under the influence of two ruling motives 1. deep-rooted hatred springing from an unsuccesful attempt to injure 2. a fear that their island will be depopulated by the emigration of it's inhabitants to America. Hence no paper comes out without a due charge of paragraphs manufactured by persons employed for that purpose. According to these America is a scene of continued riot & anarchy. Wearied out with contention, it is on the verge of falling again into the lap of Gr. Br. for repose. It's citizens are groaning under the oppression of heavy taxes. They are flying for refuge to the frozen regions which still remain subject to Gr. Br. Their assemblies and congresses are become odious, in one paragraph represented as tyrranising over their constituents, & in another as possessing no power or influence at all, &c. &c. The truth is as follows without aggravation or diminution. There was a mutiny of 300 souldiers in Philadelphia soon after the peace; & Congress thinking the executive of that state did not act with proper energy to suppress & punish it they left that city in disgust. Yet in this mutiny there neither was blood shed nor a blow struck. There has lately been a riot in Charlestown, occasioned by the feuds between the whigs who had been driven from their country by the British while they possessed it, and the tories who were permitted to remain by the Americans when they recovered it. There were a few instances in other states where individuals disgusted with some articles in the peace undertook to call town meetings, published the resolves of the few citizens whom they could prevail upon to meet as if they had been the resolves of the whole town, and endeavored unsuccesfully to engage the people in the execution of their private views. It is beleived that these attempts have not been more than ten or a dozen thro' the whole 13 states & not one of them has been succesful: on the contrary where any illegal act has been committed by the demagogues they have been put under a due course of legal prosecution. The British when they evacuated New York having carried off, contrary to the express articles of the treaty of peace, a great deal of property belonging to the citizens of the U.S. & particularly to those of the state of Virginia, amounting as has been said to half a million of pounds sterling, the assembly of that state lately resolved that till satisfaction was made for this, the article respecting British debts ought not to be carried into full execution, submitting nevertheless this their opinion to Congress and declaring that if they thought otherwise, all laws obstructing the recovery of debts should be immediately repealed. Yet even this was opposed by a respectable minority in their senate who entered a protest against it in strong terms. The protest as it stands in the records follows immediately the resolutions protested against & therefore does not recite them. The English papers publish the protest without the resolutions and thus lead Europe to beleive that the resolutions had definitively decided against the paiment of British debts. Yet nothing is less true. This is a faithful history of the high sounded disturbances of America. Those who have visited that country since the peace will vouch that it is impossible for any governments to be more tranquil & orderly than they are. What were the mutiny of 300 souldiers in Philada, the riot of whigs & tories in Charlestown to the riots of London under L.ᵈ G. Gordon, and of London & the country in general in the late elections? Where is there any country of equal extent with the U.S. in which fewer disturbances have happened in the same space of time? Where has there been an instance of an army disbanded as was that of America without receiving a shilling of the long arrearages due them or even having their accounts settled & yet disbanded peaceably? Instead of resorting as is too often the case with disbanded armies to beggary or robbery for a livelihood they returned every man to his home & resumed his axe & spade; & it is a fact as true as it is singular that on the disbanding of an army of 30,000 men in America there have been but two or three instances of any of those who composed it being brought to the bar of justice as criminals: and that you may travel from one end to the other of the continent without seeing a beggar. With respect to the people their confidence in their rulers in general is what common sense will tell us it must be, where they are of their own choice annually, unbribed by money, undebauched by feasting, & drunkenness. It would be difficult to find one man among them who would not consider a return under the dominion of Gr. Br. as the greatest of all possible miseries. Their taxes are light, as they should be with a people so lately wasted in the most cruel manner by war. They pay in proportion to their property from one half to one & a half per cent annually on it's whole value as estimated by their neighbors, the different states requiring more or less as they have been less or more ravaged by their enemies. Where any taxes are imposed they are very trifling & are calculated cheifly to bring merchants into contribution with the farmers. Against their emigration to the remaining British dominions the superior rigor of their climate, the inferiority of their soil, the nature of their governments and their being actually inhabited by their most mortal enemies the tory refugees, will be an eternal security. During the course of the war the English papers were constantly filled with accounts of their great victories, their armies were daily gaining. Yet Europe saw that they were daily losing ground in America, & formed it's idea of the truth not from what it heard but from what it saw. They wisely considered an enlargement of territory on the one side & contraction of it on the other as the best indication on which side victory really was. It is hoped that Europe will be as wise & as just now: that they will not consider the fabricated papers of England as any evidence of truth; but that they will continue to judge of causes from effects. If the distractions of America were what these papers pretend, some great facts would burst out & lay their miseries open to the eyes of all the world: no such effects appear, therefore no such causes exist. If any such existed they would appear in the American newspapers which are as free as any on earth. But none such can be found in them. These are the testimonials to which I appeal for beleif. To bring more home to every reader the reliance which may be put on the English papers let him examine, if a Frenchman, what account they give of the affairs of France, if a Dutchman, what of the United Netherl[ds], if an Irishman, what of Ireland &c. If he finds that those of his own country with which he happens to be acquainted are wickedly misrepresented, let him consider how much more likely to be so are those of a nation so hated as America. America was the great pillar on which British glory was raised: America has been the instrument for levelling that glory with the dust. A little ill humour therefore might have found excuse in our commiseration: but an apostasy from truth, under whatever misfortunes, calls up feelings of a very different order.

Answers and Observations for Démeunier's Article on the United States in the *Encyclopédie Methodique, 1786*

1. From *Answers to Démeunier's First Queries*

January 24, 1786

11. The Confederation is a wonderfully perfect instrument, considering the circumstances under which it was formed. There are however some alterations which experience proves to be wanting. These are principally three. 1. To establish a general rule for the admission of new states into the Union. By the Confederation no new state, except Canada, can be permitted to have a vote in Congress without first obtaining the consent of all the thirteen legislatures. It becomes necessary to agree what districts may be established into separate states, and at what period of their population they may come into Congress. The act of Congress of April 23, 1784, has pointed out what ought to be agreed on, to say also what number of votes must concur when the number of voters shall be thus enlarged. 2. The Confederation in it's eighth article, decides that the quota of money to be contributed by the several states shall be proportioned to the value of landed property in the state. Experience has shown it impracticable to come at this value. Congress have therefore recommended to the states to agree that their quotas shall be in proportion to the number of their inhabitants, counting 5 slaves however but as equal to 3 free inhabitants. I believe all the states have agreed to this alteration except Rhode island. 3. The Confederation forbids the states individually to enter into treaties of commerce, or of any other nature, with foreign nations: and it authorizes Congress to establish such treaties, with two reservations however, viz., that they shall agree to no treaty which would 1. restrain the legislatures from imposing such duties on foreigners, as natives are subjected to; or 2. from prohibiting the exportation or importation of any species of commodities. Congress may therefore be said to have a power to regulate commerce, so far as it can be effected by conventions with other nations, & by conventions which do not infringe the two fundamental reservations before mentioned.

But this is too imperfect. Because till a convention be made with any particular nation, the commerce of any one of our states with that nation may be regulated by the State itself, and even when a convention is made, the regulation of the commerce is taken out of the hands of the several states only so far as it is covered or provided for by that convention or treaty. But treaties are made in such general terms, that the greater part of the regulations would still result to the legislatures. Let us illustrate these observations by observing how far the commerce of France & of England can be affected by the state legislatures. As to England, any one of the legislatures may impose on her goods double the duties which are paid other nations; may prohibit their goods altogether; may refuse them the usual facilities for recovering their debts or withdrawing their property, may refuse to receive their Consuls or to give those Consuls any jurisdiction. But with France, whose commerce is protected by a treaty, no state can give any molestation to that commerce which is defended by the treaty. Thus, tho' a state may exclude the importation of all wines (because one of the reservations aforesaid is that they may prohibit the importation of any species of commodities) yet they cannot prohibit the importation of *French* wines particularly while they allow wines to be brought in from other countries. They cannot impose heavier duties on French commodities than on those of other nations. They cannot throw peculiar obstacles in the way of their recovery of debts due to them &c. &c. because those things are provided for by treaty. Treaties however are very imperfect machines for regulating commerce in the detail. The principal objects in the regulation of our commerce would be: 1. to lay such duties, restrictions, or prohibitions on the goods of any particular nation as might oblige that nation to concur in just & equal arrangements of commerce. 2. To lay such uniform duties on the articles of commerce throughout all the states, as may avail them of that fund for assisting to bear the burthen of public expenses. Now this cannot be done by the states separately; because they will not separately pursue the same plan. New Hampshire cannot lay a given duty on a particular article, unless Massachusetts will do the same; because it will turn the importation of that article from her ports into those of Massachusetts, from whence they will be smuggled into New Hampshire by land. But tho Massachusetts were willing to concur with N Hampshire in laying the same duty, yet she cannot do it, for the same reason, unless Rhode island will also, nor can Rhode island without Connecticut, nor Connecticut without N York, nor N York without N Jersey, & so on quite to Georgia. It is visible therefore that the commerce of the states cannot be regulated to the best advantage but by a single body, and no body so proper as Congress. Many of the states have agreed to add an article to the Confederation for allowing to Congress the regulation of their commerce, only providing that the revenues to be raised on it, shall belong to the state in which they are levied. Yet it is believed that Rhode island will prevent this also. An everlasting recurrence to this same obstacle will occasion a question to be asked. How happens it that Rhode island is opposed to every useful proposition? Her geography accounts for it, with the aid of one or two observations. The cultivators of the earth are the most virtuous citizens, and possess most of the amor patriæ. Merchants are the least virtuous, and possess the least of the amor patriæ. The latter reside principally in the seaport towns, the former in the interior country. Now it happened that of the territory constituting Rhode island & Connecticut, the part containing the seaports was erected into a state by itself & called Rhode island, & that containing the interior country was erected into another state called Connecticut. For tho it has a little seacoast, there are no good ports in it. Hence it happens that there is scarcely one merchant in the whole state of Connecticut, while there is not a single man in Rhode island who is not a merchant of some sort. Their whole territory is but a thousand square miles, and what of that is in use is laid out in grass farms almost entirely. Hence they have scarcely any body employed in agriculture. All exercise some species of commerce. This circumstance has decided the characters of these two states. The remedies to this evil are hazardous. One would be to consolidate the two states into one. Another would be to banish Rhode island from the union. A third to compel her submission to the will of the other twelve. A fourth for the other twelve to govern themselves according to the new propositions and to let

Rhode island go on by herself according to the antient articles. But the dangers & difficulties attending all these remedies are obvious.

These are the only alterations proposed to the confederation, and the last of them is the only additional power which
Congress is thought to need.

21. Broils among the states may happen in the following
ways: 1. A state may be embroiled with the other twelve by
not complying with the lawful requisitions of Congress. 2.
Two states may differ about their boundaries. But the
method of settling these is fixed by the Confederation, and
most of the states which have any differences of this kind
are submitting them to this mode of determination; and
there is no danger of opposition to the decree by any state.
The individuals interested may complain, but this can produce no difficulty. 3. Other contestations may arise between
two states, such as pecuniary demands, affrays among their
citizens, & whatever else may arise between any two nations. With respect to these, there are two opinions. One
that they are to be decided according to the 9th article of
the Confederation, which says that "Congress shall be the
last resort in all differences between two or more states,
concerning boundary jurisdiction, *or any other cause whatever*"; and prescribes the mode of decision, and the weight
of reason is undoubtedly in favor of this opinion, yet there
are some who question it.

It has been often said that the decisions of Congress are
impotent because the Confederation provides no compulsory
power. But when two or more nations enter into compact, it
is not usual for them to say what shall be done to the party
who infringes it. Decency forbids this, and it is unnecessary
as indecent, because the right of compulsion naturally results
to the party injured by the breach. When any one state in the
American Union refuses obedience to the Confederation by
which they have bound themselves, the rest have a natural
right to compel them to obedience. Congress would probably
exercise long patience before they would recur to force; but
if the case ultimately required it, they would use that recurrence. Should this case ever arise, they will probably coerce

by a naval force, as being more easy, less dangerous to liberty, & less likely to produce much bloodshed.

It has been said too that our governments both federal and particular want energy; that it is difficult to restrain both individuals & states from committing wrong. This is true, & it is an inconvenience. On the other hand that energy which absolute governments derive from an armed force, which is the effect of the bayonet constantly held at the breast of every citizen, and which resembles very much the stillness of the grave, must be admitted also to have it's inconveniences. We weigh the two together, and like best to submit to the former. Compare the number of wrongs committed with impunity by citizens among us, with those committed by the sovereign in other countries, and the last will be found most numerous, most oppressive on the mind, and most degrading of the dignity of man.

2. From *Observations on Démeunier's Manuscript*

OBSERVATIONS ON THE ARTICLE ETATS-UNIS
PREPARED FOR THE ENCYCLOPEDIE.

June 22, 1786

1. II. 17. 29. Pa 8. The Malefactors sent to America were not sufficient in number to merit enumeration as one class out of three which peopled America. It was at a late period of their history that this practice began. I have no book by me which enables me to point out the date of it's commencement. But I do not think the whole number sent would amount to 2000 & being principally men, eaten up with disease, they married seldom & propagated little. I do not suppose that themselves & their descendants are at present 4000, which is little more than one thousandth part of the whole inhabitants.

Indented servants formed a considerable supply. These were poor Europeans who went to America to settle themselves. If they could pay their passage it was well. If not, they must find means of paying it. They were at liberty therefore to make an agreement with any person they chose, to serve him such a length of time as they agreed on, on condition that he would repay to the master of the vessel the expenses of their passage. If being foreigners unable to speak the lan-

guage, they did not know how to make a bargain for themselves the captain of the vessel contracted for them with such
persons as he could. This contract was by deed indented,
which occasioned them to be called indented servants. Sometimes they were called Redemptioners, because by their agreement with the master of the vessel they could *redeem*
themselves from his power by paying their passage, which
they frequently effected by hiring themselves on their arrival
as is before mentioned. In some states I know that these people had a right of marrying themselves without their master's
leave, & I did suppose they had that right everywhere. I did
not know that in any of the states they demanded so much as
a week for every day's absence without leave. I suspect this
must have been at a very early period while the governments
were in the hands of the first emigrants, who being mostly
labourers, were narrow-minded and severe. I know that in
Virginia the laws allowed their servitude to be protracted
only two days for every one they were absent without leave.
So mild was this kind of servitude, that it was very frequent
for foreigners who carried to America money enough, not
only to pay their passage, but to buy themselves a farm, it
was common I say for them to indent themselves to a master
for three years, for a certain sum of money, with a view to
learn the husbandry of the country. I will here make a general
observation. So desirous are the poor of Europe to get to
America, where they may better their condition, that, being
unable to pay their passage, they will agree to serve two or
three years on their arrival there, rather than not go. During
the time of that service they are better fed, better clothed, and
have lighter labour than while in Europe. Continuing to work
for hire a few years longer, they buy a farm, marry, and enjoy
all the sweets of a domestic society of their own. The American governments are censured for permitting this species of
servitude which lays the foundation of the happiness of these
people. But what should these governments do? Pay the passage of all those who chuse to go into their country? They
are not able; nor, were they able, do they think the purchase
worth the price? Should they exclude these people from their
shores? Those who know their situations in Europe & America, would not say that this is the alternative which humanity

dictates. It is said that these people are deceived by those who carry them over. But this is done in Europe. How can the American governments prevent it? Should they punish the deceiver? It seems more incumbent on the European government, where the act is done, and where a public injury is sustained from it. However it is only in Europe that this deception is heard of. The individuals are generally satisfied in America with their adventure, and very few of them wish not to have made it. I must add that the Congress have nothing to do with this matter. It belongs to the legislatures of the several states.

Ib. l. 12. "Mal-aisé d' indiquer la nuance precise &c." In forming a scale of crimes & punishments, two considerations have principal weight. 1. The atrocity of the crime. 2. The peculiar circumstances of a country which furnish greater temptations to commit it, or greater facilities for escaping detection. The punishment must be heavier to counterbalance this. Was the first the only consideration, all nations would form the same scale. But as the circumstances of a country have influence on the punishment, and no two countries exist precisely under the same circumstances, no two countries will form the same scale of crimes & punishments. For example in America, the inhabitants let their horses go at large in the uninclosed lands which are so extensive as to maintain them altogether. It is easy therefore to steal them & easy to escape. Therefore the laws are obliged to oppose these temptations with a heavier degree of punishment. For this reason the stealing of a horse in America is punished more severely than stealing the same value in any other form. In Europe where horses are confined so securely that it is impossible to steal them, that species of theft need not be punished more severely than any other. In some countries of Europe, stealing fruit from trees is punished capitally. The reason is that it being impossible to lock fruit trees up in coffers, as we do our money, it is impossible to oppose physical bars to this species of theft. Moral ones are therefore opposed by the laws. This to an unreflecting American, appears the most enormous of all the abuses of power; because he has been used to see fruits hanging in such quantities that if not taken

by men they would rot: he has been used to consider it therefore as of no value, as not furnishing materials for the commission of a crime. This must serve as an apology for the
arrangements of crimes & punishments in the scale under our
consideration. A different one would be formed here; & still
different ones in Italy, Turkey, China, &c.

Pa. 240. "Les officiers Americains &c." to pa 264. "qui le
meritoient." I would propose to new-model this Section in
the following manner. 1. Give a succinct history of the origin
& establishment of the Cincinnati. 2. Examine whether in its
present form it threatens any dangers to the state. 3. Propose
the most practicable method of preventing them.

Having been in America during the period in which this
institution was formed, and being then in a situation which
gave me opportunities of seeing it in all it's stages, I may
venture to give M. de Meusnier materials for the 1st branch
of the preceding distribution of the subject. The 2d and 3d he
will best execute himself. I should write it's history in the
following form.

When, on the close of that war which established the independance of America, it's army was about to be disbanded,
the officers, who during the course of it had gone thro the
most trying scenes together, who by mutual aids & good offices had become dear to one another, felt with great oppression of mind the approach of that moment which was to
separate them never perhaps to meet again. They were from
different states & from distant parts of the same state. Hazard
alone could therefore give them but rare & partial occasions
of seeing each other. They were of course to abandon altogether the hope of ever meeting again, or to devise some occasion which might bring them together. And why not come
together on purpose at stated times? Would not the trouble
of such a journey be greatly overpaid by the pleasure of seeing
each other again, by the sweetest of all consolations, the talking over the scenes of difficulty & of endearment they had
gone through? This too would enable them to know who of
them should succeed in the world, who should be unsuccessful, and to open the purses of all to every labouring brother.
This idea was too soothing not to be cherished in conversa-

tion. It was improved into that of a regular association with an organized administration, with periodical meetings general & particular, fixed contributions for those who should be in distress, & a badge by which not only those who had not had occasion to become personally known should be able to recognize one another, but which should be worn by their descendants to perpetuate among them the friendships which had bound their ancestors together. Genl. Washington was at that moment oppressed with the operation of disbanding an army which was not paid, and the difficulty of this operation was increased by some two or three of the states having expressed sentiments which did not indicate a sufficient attention to their paiment. He was sometimes present when his officers were fashioning in their conversations their newly proposed society. He saw the innocence of it's origin, & foresaw no effects less innocent. He was at that time writing his valedictory letter to the states, which has been so deservedly applauded by the world. Far from thinking it a moment to multiply the causes of irritation, by thwarting a proposition which had absolutely no other basis but of benevolence & friendship, he was rather satisfied to find himself aided in his difficulties by this new incident, which occupied, &, at the same time soothed the minds of the officers. He thought too that this institution would be one instrument the more for strengthening the federal bond, & for promoting federal ideas. The institution was formed. They incorporated into it the officers of the French army & navy by whose sides they had fought, and with whose aid they had finally prevailed, extending it to such grades as they were told might be permitted to enter into it. They sent an officer to France to make the proposition to them & to procure the badges which they had devised for their order. The moment of disbanding the army having come on before they could have a full meeting to appoint their president, the General was prayed to act in that office till their first general meeting which was to be held at Philadelphia in the month of May following. The laws of the society were published. Men who read them in their closets, unwarmed by those sentiments of friendship which had produced them, inattentive to those pains which an approaching separation had excited in the minds of the institutors, Pol-

iticians, who see in everything only the dangers with which it
threatens civil society, in fine the labouring people, who,
shielded by equal laws, had never seen any difference between
man and man, but had read of terrible oppressions which
people of their description experience in other countries from
those who are distinguished by titles & badges, began to be
alarmed at this new institution. A remarkable silence however
was observed. Their sollicitudes were long confined within
the circles of private conversation. At length however a Mr.
Burke, chief justice of South Carolina, broke that silence. He
wrote against the new institution; foreboding it's dangers
very imperfectly indeed, because he had nothing but his imagination to aid him. An American could do no more: for to
detail the real evils of aristocracy they must be seen in Europe. Burke's fears were thought exaggerations in America;
while in Europe it is known that even Mirabeau has but
faintly sketched the curses of hereditary aristocracy as they are
experienced here, and as they would have followed in America had this institution remained. The epigraph of Burke's
pamphlet was "Blow ye the trumpet in Zion." It's effect corresponded with it's epigraph. This institution became first the
subject of general conversation. Next it was made the subject
of deliberation in the legislative assemblies of some of the
States. The governor of South Carolina censured it in an address to his Assembly. The assemblies of Massachusetts,
Rhode island and Pennsylvania condemned it's principles.
No circumstance indeed brought the consideration of it expressly before Congress, yet it had sunk deep into their
minds. An offer having been made to them on the part of the
Polish order of divine providence to receive some of their distinguished citizens into that order, they made that an occasion to declare that these distinctions were contrary to the
principles of their confederation. The uneasiness excited by
this institution had very early caught the notice of General
Washington. Still recollecting all the purity of the motives
which gave it birth, he became sensible that it might produce
political evils which the warmth of these motives had masked.
Add to this that it was disapproved by the mass of citizens of
the Union. This alone was reason strong enough in a country
where the will of the majority is the law, & ought to be the

law. He saw that the objects of the institution were too light
to be opposed to considerations as serious as these; and that
it was become necessary to annihilate it absolutely. On this
therefore he was decided. The first annual meeting at Philadelphia was now at hand. He went to that, determined to
exert all his influence for it's suppression. He proposed it to
his fellow officers, and urged it with all his powers. It met an
opposition which was observed to cloud his face with an anxiety that the most distressful scenes of the war had scarcely
ever produced. It was canvassed for several days, & at length
it was no more a doubt what would be it's ultimate fate. The
order was on the point of receiving it's annihilation by the
vote of a very great majority of it's members. In this moment
their envoy arrived from France, charged with letters from the
French officers accepting with cordiality the proposed badges
of union, with sollicitations from others to be received into
the order, & with notice that their respectable sovereign had
been pleased to recognize it, & permit his officers to wear it's
badges. The prospect now changed. The question assumed a
new form. After the offer made by them, & accepted by their
friends, in what words could they clothe a proposition to retract it which would not cover themselves with the reproaches
of levity & ingratitude? which would not appear an insult to
those whom they loved? Federal principles, popular discontent, were considerations whose weight was known & felt by
themselves. But would foreigners know & feel them equally?
Would they so far acknowledge their cogency as to permit
without any indignation the eagle & ribbon to be torn from
their breasts by the very hands which had placed them there?
The idea revolted the whole society. They found it necessary
then to preserve so much of their institution as might continue to support this foreign branch, while they should prune
off every other which would give offence to their fellow citizens; thus sacrificing on each hand to their friends & to their
country. The society was to retain it's existence, it's name,
it's meetings, & it's charitable funds: but these last were to
be deposited with their respective legislatures; the order was
to be no longer hereditary; a reformation which had been
pressed even from this side of the Atlantic; it was to be communicated to no new members; the general meetings instead

of annual were to be triennial only. The eagle & ribbon indeed were retained; because they were worn, & they wished
them to be worn, by their friends who were in a country
where they would not be objects of offence; but themselves
never wore them. They laid them up in their bureaus with the
medals of American Independance, with those of the trophies
they had taken & the battles they had won. But through all
the United States no officer is seen to offend the public eye
with the display of this badge. These changes have tranquillized the American states. Their citizens do justice to the circumstances which prevented a total annihilation of the order.
They feel too much interest in the reputation of their officers,
and value too much whatever may serve to recall to the memory of their allies the moments wherein they formed but one
people. Tho they are obliged by a prudent foresight to keep
out everything from among themselves which might pretend
to divide them into orders, and to degrade one description of
men below another, yet they hear with pleasure that their allies whom circumstances have already placed under these distinctions, are willing to consider it as one to have aided them
in the establishment of their liberties & to wear a badge
which may recall to their remembrance; and it would be an
extreme affliction to them if the domestic reformation which
has been found necessary, if the censures of individual writers,
or if any other circumstance should discourage the wearing
their badge, or lessen it's reputation.

This short but true history of the order of the Cincinnati,
taken from the mouths of persons on the spot who were privy
to it's origin & progress, & who knew it's present state, is
the best apology which can be made for an institution which
appeared to be, & was really, so heterogeneous to the governments in which it was erected.

It should be further considered that, in America, no other
distinction between man & man had ever been known, but
that of persons in office exercising powers by authority of the
laws, and private individuals. Among these last the poorest
labourer stood on equal ground with the wealthiest million-
naire, & generally on a more favoured one whenever their
rights seem to jar. It has been seen that a shoemaker, or other
artisan, removed by the voice of his country from his work

bench into a chair of office, has instantly commanded all the respect and obedience which the laws ascribe to his office. But of distinction by birth or badge they had no more idea than they had of the mode of existence in the moon or planets. They had heard only that there were such, & knew that they must be wrong. A due horror of the evils which flow from these distinctions could be excited in Europe only, where the dignity of man is lost in arbitrary distinctions, where the human species is classed into several stages of degradation, where the many are crushed under the weight of the few, & where the order established can present to the contemplation of a thinking being no other picture than that of God almighty & his angels trampling under foot the hosts of the damned. No wonder then that the institution of the Cincinnati should be innocently conceived by one order of American citizens, could raise in the other orders only a slow, temperate, & rational opposition, and could be viewed in Europe as a detestable parricide.

The 2d & 3d branches of this subject, no body can better execute than M. de. Meusnier. Perhaps it may be curious to him to see how they strike an American mind at present. He shall therefore have the ideas of one who was an enemy to the institution from the first moment of it's conception, but who was always sensible that the officers neither foresaw, nor intended the injury they were doing to their country.

As to the question then, whether any evil can proceed from the institution as it stands at present, I am of opinion there may. 1. From the meetings. These will keep the officers formed into a body; will continue a distinction between the civil & military which it would be for the good of the whole to obliterate as soon as possible; & the military assemblies will not only keep alive the jealousies & the fears of the civil government, but give ground for these fears & jealousies. For when men meet together, they will make business if they have none; they will collate their grievances, some real, some imaginary, all highly painted; they will communicate to each other the sparks of discontent; & this may engender a flame which will consume their particular, as well as the general, happiness. 2. The charitable part of the institution is still more likely to do mischief, as it perpetuates the dangers apprehended in the preceding clause. For here is a fund provided of permanent existence. To whom will it belong? To the descendants of American officers of a certain description. These descendants then will form a body, having sufficient interest to keep up an attention to their description, to continue meetings, & perhaps, in some moment, when the political eye shall be slumbering, or the firmness of their fellow-citizens realized, to replace the insignia of the order & revive all its pretensions. What good can the officers propose which may weigh against these possible evils? The securing their descendants against want? Why afraid to trust them to the same fertile soil, & the same genial climate which will secure from want the descendants of their other fellow citizens? Are they afraid they will be reduced to labour the earth for their sustenance? They will be rendered thereby both honester and happier. An industrious farmer occupies a more dignified place in the scale of beings, whether moral or political, than a lazy lounger, valuing himself on his family, too proud to work, & drawing out a miserable existence by eating on that surplus of other men's labour which is the sacred fund of the helpless poor. A pitiful annuity will only prevent them from exerting that industry & those talents which would soon lead them to better fortune.

How are these evils to be prevented? 1. At their first general meeting let them distribute the funds on hand to the existing objects of their destination, & discontinue all further contributions. 2. Let them declare at the same time that their meetings general & particular shall henceforth cease. 3. Let them melt up their eagles & add the mass to the distributable fund that their descendants may have no temptation to hang them in their button holes.

These reflections are not proposed as worthy the notice of M. de Meusnier. He will be so good as to treat the subject in his own way, & no body has a better. I will only pray him to avail us of his forcible manner to evince that there is evil to be apprehended even from the ashes of this institution, & to exhort the society in America to make their reformation complete; bearing in mind that we must keep the passions of men on our side even when we are persuading them to do what they ought to do.

Pa. 272. "Comportera peut etre une population de thirty millions."

The territories of the United States contain about a million of square miles, English. There is in them a greater proportion of fertile lands than in the British dominions in Europe. Suppose the territory of the U.S. then to attain an equal degree of population with the British European dominions, they will have an hundred millions of inhabitants. Let us extend our views to what may be the population of the two continents of North & South America supposing them divided at the narrowest part of the isthmus of Panama. Between this line and that of 50° of north latitude the northern continent contains about 5 millions of square miles, and South of this line of division the Southern continent contains about 7 millions of square miles. I do not pass the 50th degree of northern latitude in my reckoning, because we must draw a line somewhere, & considering the soil & climate beyond that, I would only avail my calculation of it, as a make weight, to make good what the colder regions within that line may be supposed to fall short in their future population. Here are 12 millions of square miles then, which at the rate of population before assumed, will nourish 1200 millions of inhabitants, a number greater than the present population of the whole globe is supposed to amount to. If those who propose medals for the resolution of questions, about which nobody makes any question, those who have invited discussions on the pretended problem Whether the discovery of America was for the good of mankind? if they, I say, would have viewed it only as doubling the numbers of mankind, & of course the quantum of existence & happiness, they might have saved the money & the reputation which their proposition has cost them. The present population of the inhabited parts of the U.S. is of about 10. to the square mile; & experience has shown us, that wherever we reach that the inhabitants become uneasy, as too much compressed, and go off in great numbers to search for vacant country. Within 40 years the whole territory will be peopled at that rate. We may fix that then as the term beyond which the people of those states will not be restrained within their present limits; we may fix it too as the term of population, which they will not exceed till the whole of those two continents are filled up to that mark, that is to say, till they shall contain 120 millions of inhabitants. The soil of the country on the western side of the Mississippi, it's climate, & it's vicinity to the U.S. point it out as the first which will receive population from that nest. The present occupiers will just have force enough to repress & restrain the emigrations to a certain degree of consistence. We have seen lately a single person go & decide on a settlement in Kentucky, many hundred miles from any white inhabitant, remove thither with his family and a few neighbors, & though perpetually harassed by the Indians, that settlement in the course of 10 years has acquired 30.000 inhabitants, it's numbers are increasing while we are writing, and the state of which it formerly made a part has offered it independance.

3. *To Jean Nicolas Démeunier*

June 26, 1786

Mr. Jefferson presents his compliments to M. de Meusnier & sends him copies of the 13th, 23d, & 24th articles of the treaty between the K. of Prussia & the United States.

In the negociation with the Minister of Portugal at London, the latter objected to the 13th article. The observations which were made in answer to his objections Mr. Jefferson incloses. They are a commentary on the 13th article. Mr. de Meusnier will be so good as to return the sheet on which these observations are as Mr. Jefferson does not retain a copy of it.

If M. de Meusnier proposes to mention the facts of cruelty of which he & Mr. Jefferson spoke yesterday, the 24th article will introduce them properly, because they produced a sense of the necessity of that article. These facts are 1. The death of upwards of 11,000 Americans in one prison ship (the Jersey) and in the space of 3. years. 2. General Howe's permitting our prisoners taken at the battle of Germantown and placed under a guard in the yard of the Statehouse of Philadelphia to be so long without any food furnished them that many perished with hunger. Where the bodies laid, it was seen that they had eaten all the grass round them within their reach, after they had lost the power of rising, or moving from their place. 3. The 2d fact was the act of a commandg officer; the 1st of several commanding officers, & for so long a time as must suppose the approbation of government. But the following was the act of government itself. During the periods that our affairs seemed unfavourable & theirs successful, that is to say, after the evacuation of New York, and again after the taking of Charlestown in South Carolina, they regularly sent our prisoners taken on the seas & carried to England to the E. Indies. This is so certain, that in the month of Novemb. or Decemb. 1785, Mr. Adams having officially demanded a delivery of the American prisoners sent to the East Indies, Ld. Cærmarthen answered officially "that orders were issued immediately for their discharge." M. de Meusnier is at liberty to quote this fact. 4. A fact not only of the government, but of the parliament, who passed an act for that purpose in the beginning of the war, was the obliging our prisoners taken at sea to join them and fight against their countrymen. This they effected by starving & whipping them. The insult on Capt. Stanhope, which happened at Boston last year, was a consequence of this. Two persons, Dunbar & Lorthrope, whom Stanhope had treated in this manner (having particularly inflicted 24 lashes on Dunbar), meeting him at Boston, attempted to beat him. But the people interposed & saved him. The fact is referred to in that paragraph of the declaration of independance which sais "he has constrained our fellow citizens taken captive on the high seas, to bear arms against their country, to become the executioners of their friends & brethren, or to fall themselves by their hands." This was the most afflicting to our prisoners of all the cruelties exercised on them. The others affected the body only, but this the mind— they were haunted by the horror of having perhaps themselves shot the ball by which a father or a brother fell. Some of them had constancy enough to hold out against half allowance of food & repeated whippings. These were generally sent to England & from thence to the East Indies. One of these escaped from the East Indies and got back to Paris, where he gave an account of his sufferings to Mr. Adams, who happened to be then at Paris.

M. de Meusnier, where he mentions that the slave-law has been passed in Virginia, without the clause of emancipation, is pleased to mention that neither Mr. Wythe nor Mr. Jeffer-

son were present to make the proposition they had meditated; from which people, who do not give themselves the
trouble to reflect or enquire, might conclude hastily that their
absence was the cause why the proposition was not made; &
of course that there were not in the assembly persons of virtue & firmness enough to propose the clause for emancipation. This supposition would not be true. There were persons
there who wanted neither the virtue to propose, nor talents
to enforce the proposition had they seen that the disposition
of the legislature was ripe for it. These worthy characters
would feel themselves wounded, degraded, & discouraged by
this idea. Mr. Jefferson would therefore be obliged to M. de
Meusnier to mention it in some such manner as this. "Of the
two commissioners who had concerted the amendatory clause
for the gradual emancipation of slaves Mr. Wythe could not
be present as being a member of the judiciary department,
and Mr. Jefferson was absent on the legation to France. But
there wanted not in that assembly men of virtue enough to
propose, & talents to vindicate this clause. But they saw that
the moment of doing it with success was not yet arrived, and
that an unsuccessful effort, as too often happens, would only
rivet still closer the chains of bondage, and retard the moment
of delivery to this oppressed description of men. What a stupendous, what an incomprehensible machine is man! who can
endure toil, famine, stripes, imprisonment & death itself in
vindication of his own liberty, and the next moment be deaf
to all those motives whose power supported him thro' his
trial, and inflict on his fellow men a bondage, one hour of
which is fraught with more misery than ages of that which he
rose in rebellion to oppose. But we must await with patience
the workings of an overruling providence, & hope that that
is preparing the deliverance of these, our suffering brethren.
When the measure of their tears shall be full, when their
groans shall have involved heaven itself in darkness, doubtless
a god of justice will awaken to their distress, and by diffusing
light & liberality among their oppressors, or at length by his
exterminating thunder, manifest his attention to the things of
this world, and that they are not left to the guidance of a
blind fatality."

Thoughts on English Prosody

TO CHASTELLUX

October 1786

Among the topics of conversation which stole off like so many minutes the few hours I had the happiness of possessing you at Monticello, the measures of English verse was one. I thought it depended like Greek and Latin verse, on long and short syllables arranged into regular feet. You were of a different opinion. I did not pursue this subject after your departure, because it always presented itself with the painful recollection of a pleasure which in all human probability I was never to enjoy again. This probability like other human calculations has been set aside by events; and we have again discussed on this side the Atlantic a subject which had occupied us during some pleasing moments on the other. A daily habit of walking in the Bois de Boulogne gave me an opportunity of turning this subject in my mind and I determined to present you my thoughts on it in the form of a letter. I for some time parried the difficulties which assailed me, but at length I found they were not to be opposed, and their triumph was complete. Error is the stuff of which the web of life is woven and he who lives longest and wisest is only able to weave out the more of it. I began with the design of converting you to my opinion that the arrangement of long and short syllables into regular feet constituted the harmony of English verse. I ended by discovering that you were right in denying that proposition. The next object was to find out the real circumstance which gives harmony to English poetry and laws to those who make it. I present you with the result. It is a tribute due to your friendship. It is due you also as having recalled me from an error in my native tongue and that, too, in a point the most difficult of all others to a foreigner, the law of its poetical numbers.

Thoughts on English Prosody

Every one knows the difference between verse and prose in his native language; nor does he need the aid of prosody to enable him to read or to repeat verse according to its just rhythm. It is the business of the poet so to arrange his words as that, repeated in their accustomed measures they shall strike the ear with that regular rhythm which constitutes verse.

It is for foreigners principally that Prosody is necessary; not knowing the accustomed measures of words, they require the aid of rules to teach them those measures and to enable them to read verse so as to make themselves or others sensible of its music. I suppose that the system of rules or exceptions which constitutes Greek and Latin prosody, as shown with us, was unknown to those nations, and that it has been invented by the moderns to whom those languages were foreign. I do not mean to affirm this, however, because you have not searched into the history of this art, nor am I at present in a situation which admits of that search. By industrious examination of the Greek and Latin verse it has been found that pronouncing certain combinations of vowels and consonants long, and certain others short, the actual arrangement of those long and short syllables, as found in their verse, constitutes a rhythm which is regular and pleasing to the ear, and that pronouncing them with any other measures, the run is unpleasing, and ceases to produce the effect of the verse. Hence it is concluded and rationally enough that the Greeks and Romans pronounced those syllables long or short in reading their verse; and as we observe in modern languages that the syllables of words have the same measures both in verse and prose, we ought to conclude that they had the same also in those ancient languages, and that we must lengthen or shorten in their prose the same syllables which we lengthen or shorten in their verse. Thus, if I meet with the word *præteritos* in Latin prose and want to know how the Romans pronounced it, I search for it in some poet and find it in the line of Virgil, *"O mihi præteritos referat si Jupiter annos!"* where it is evident that *præ* is long and *te* short in direct opposition to the pronunciation which we often hear. The length allowed to a syllable is called its quantity, and hence we say that the Greek and Latin languages are to be pronounced according to quantity.

Those who have undertaken to frame a prosody for the English language have taken quantity for their basis and have mounted the English poetry on Greek and Latin feet. If this foundation admits of no question, the prosody of Doctor Johnson, built upon it, is perhaps the best. He comprehends under three different feet every combination of long and short syllables which he supposes can be found in English verse, to wit: 1. a long and a short, which is the trochee of the Greeks and Romans; 2. a short and a long, which is their iambus; and 3. two short and a long, which is their anapest. And he thinks that all English verse may be resolved into these feet.

It is true that in the English language some one syllable of a word is always sensibly distinguished from the others by an emphasis of pronunciation or by an accent as we call it. But I am not satisfied whether this accented syllable be pronounced longer, louder, or harder, and the others shorter, lower, or softer. I have found the nicest ears divided on the question. Thus in the word *calenture*, nobody will deny that the first syllable is pronounced more emphatically than the others; but many will deny that it is longer in pronunciation. In the second of the following verses of Pope, I think there are but two short syllables.

Oh! be thou bless'd with all that Heav'n can send
Long health, long youth, long pleasure, and a friend.

Innumerable instances like this might be produced. It seems, therefore, too much to take for the basis of a system a postulatum which one-half of mankind will deny. But the superstructure of Doctor Johnson's prosody may still be supported by substituting for its basis accent instead of quantity; and nobody will deny us the existence of accent.

In every word of more than one syllable there is some one syllable strongly distinguishable in pronunciation by its emphasis or accent.

If a word has more than two syllables it generally admits of a subordinate emphasis or accent on the alternate syllables counting backwards and forwards from the principal one, as in this verse of Milton:

> Well if thrown out as supernumerary,

where the principal accent is on *nu*, but there is a lighter one on *su* and *ra* also. There are some few instances indeed wherein the subordinate accent is differently arranged, as *parisyllabic, Constantinople*. It is difficult, therefore, to introduce words of this kind into verse.

That the accent shall never be displaced from the syllable whereon usage hath established it is the fundamental law of English verse.

There are but three arrangements into which these accents can be thrown in the English language which entitled the composition to be distinguished by the name of verse. That is, 1. Where the accent falls on all the odd syllables; 2. Where it falls on all the even syllables; 3. When it falls on every third syllable. If the reason of this be asked, no other can be assigned but that it results from the nature of the sounds which compose the English language and from the construction of the human ear. So, in the infinite gradations of sounds from the lowest to the highest in the musical scale, those only give pleasure to the ear which are at the intervals we call whole tones and semitones. The reason is that it has pleased God to make us so. The English poet then must so arrange his words that their established accents shall fall regularly in one of these three orders. To aid him in this he has at his command the whole army of monosyllables which in the English language is a very numerous one. These he may accent or not, as he pleases. Thus is this verse:

> 'Tis júst resentment añd becómes the brave.
>
> —Pope

the monosyllable *and* standing between two unaccented syllables catches the accent and supports the measure. The same monosyllable serves to fill the interval between two accents in the following instance:

From úse obscúre and súbtle, bút to knów.
—MILTON

The monosyllables *with* and *in* receive the accent in one of the following instances and suffer it to pass over them in the other.

The témpted *wíth* dishónor fóul, suppósed.
—MILTON
Attémpt *with* cónfidénce, the wórk is dóne.
—HOPKINS
Which múst be mútual *iń* propórtion dúe.
—MILTON
Too múch of órnamént *in* oútward shéw.
—MILTON

The following lines afford other proofs of this license.

Yet, yét, I lóve—from Abelard it came.
—POPE

Flow, flow, my stream this devious way.
—SHENSTONE

The Greeks and Romans in like manner had a number of syllables which might in any situation be pronounced long or short without offending the ear. They had others which they could make long or short by changing their position. These were of great avail to the poets. The following is an example:

Πολλάκις ὦ πολυφάμε, τὰ | μη καλὰ | καλὰ πε | φανλαι.
—THEOCRITUS
’Αγες, ’Αγες βροτολοιγὲ, μιαι φόνε τει χεσιπλητα.
—HOM. IL.
Μετσα δε τεμ’ χε θεοισι, το | νδ μετρον | εστιν ἀγίσον.
—PHOCYL.

where the word Ages, being used twice, the first syllable is long in the first and short in the second instance, and the second is short in the first and long in the second instance.

But though the poets have great authority over the monosyllables, yet it is not altogether absolute. The following is a proof of this:

> Through the dark póstern óf time lóng eláps'd.
> —YOUNG

It is impossible to read this without throwing the accent on the monosyllable *of* and yet the ear is shocked and revolts at this.

That species of our verse wherein the accent falls on all the odd syllables, I shall call, from that circumstance, odd or imparisyllabic verse. It is what has been heretofore called trochaic verse. To the foot which composes it, it will still be convenient and most intelligible to retain the ancient name of Trochee, only remembering that by that term we do not mean a long and a short syllable, but an accented and unaccented one.

That verse wherein the accent is on the even syllables may be called even or parisyllabic verse, and corresponds with what has been called iambic verse; retaining the term iambus for the name of the foot we shall thereby mean an unaccented and an accented syllable.

That verse wherein the accent falls on every third syllable, may be called trisyllabic verse; it is equivalent to what has been called anapestic; and we will still use the term anapest to express two unaccented and one accented syllable.

Accent then is, I think, the basis of English verse; and it leads us to the same threefold distribution of it to which the hypothesis of *quantity* had led Dr. Johnson. While it preserves to us the simplicity of his classification it relieves us from the doubtfulness, if not the error, on which it was founded.

OBSERVATIONS ON THE THREE MEASURES.

Wherever a verse should regularly begin or end with an accented syllable, that unaccented syllable may be suppressed.

Bréd on pláins, or bórn in válleys,
    Whó would bíd those scénes adiéu?
Stránger tó the árts of málice,
    Whó would éver coúrts pursúe?
                    —Shenstone

Rúin séize thée, rúthléss kíng!
    Confúsioń on thy bánners wáit;
Though, fanńed by Cónquest's crímson wíng,
    They móck the aír with ídle sťate.
Helḿ, nor haúlberk's twísted máil,
Nor ev́'n thy vírtues, Týrant, sháll aváil
To sáve thy sécret soúl from ńightly féars.
From Cámbria's cúrse, from Cámbria's téars!
                    —Gray

Y̆e Shép | herds! give eár | to my láv,
    And táke no more heéd of my shéep;
They have nóthing to dó but to sťray;
    I have ńothing to dó but to wéep.
                    —Shenstone

In the first example the unaccented syllable with which the imparisyllabic (odd) verse should end is omitted in the second and fourth lines. In the second example the unaccented syllable with which the parisyllabic (even) verse should begin is omitted in the first and fifth lines. In the third instance one of the unaccented syllables with which the trisyllabic (triple) verse should begin, is omitted in the first and second lines and in the first of the following line both are omitted:

Uńder this márble, or uńder this síll
Or uńder this túrf, or é'en what you will
Lies one who ne'er car'd, and still cares not a pin
What they said, or may say, of the mortal within;
But who, living or dying, serene still and free,
Trusts in God that as well as he was he shall be.
                    —Pope

An accented syllable may be prefixed to a verse which should regularly begin with an accent and added to one which should end with an accent, thus:

> 1. Daúntless ón his nátive sánds
> The drágon-són of Mona stánds;
> In glittering árms and glóry drést,
> Hígh he réars his rúby crést.
> Thére the thúndering strókes begín,
> Thére the préss, and thére the dín;
> Talymalfra's rocky shore
> —Gray

Again:

> Thére Confúsion, Térror's chíld,
> Cónflict fiérce, and Rúin wild,
> Ágoný, that pánts for bréath,
> Despair, and hónoráble death.
> —Gray

> 2. Whát is this world? thy schóol Oh! mísery!
> Our ónly lésson is to léarn to súffer;
> And hé who knóws not thát, was bórn for nóthing.
> My cómfort is each móment tákes awáy
> A gráin at léast from the dead lóad that's ón me
> And gíves a néarer próspect óf the gráve.
> —Young

> 3. Says Ríchard to Thómas (and seém'd half afráid),
> "I'm thinking to márry thy místress's máid;
> Now, becaúse Mrs. Lúcy to theé is well knówn,
> I will dó't if thou bídst me, or lét it alóne."
> Said Thomás to Ríchard, "To spéak my opínion,
> There is nót such a bítch in King Géorge's domínion;
> And I fírmly beliéve, if thou knéw'st her as Í do,
> Thou wouldst choóse out a whipping-post fírst to be
>   tied to.
> She's peévish, she's thiévish, she's úgly, shé's old,
> And a liár, and a fóol, and a slút, and a scóld."

Next dáy Richard hásten'd to chúrch and was wéd,
And ere níght had infórm'd her what Thómas had sáid.
                                          —SHENSTONE

An accented syllable can never be either omitted or added without changing the character of the verse. In fact it is the number of accented syllables which determines the length of the verse. That is to say, the number of feet of which it consists.

Imparisyllabic verse being made up of Trochees should regularly end with an unaccented syllable; and in that case if it be in rhyme both syllables of the foot must be rhymed. But most frequently the unaccented syllable is omitted according to the license before mentioned and then it suffices to rhyme the accented one. The following is given as a specimen of this kind of verse.

> Shépherd, woúldst thou hére obtaín
> Pléasure unalloý'd with páin?
> Joý that súits the rúral sphére?
> Géntle shépherd, lénd an eár.
>
> Leárn to rélish cálm delíght
> Vérdant váles and foúntains bríght;
> Treés that nód o'er slóping hílls,
> Cavés that écho tínkling rílls.
>
> Íf thou cánst no chárm disclóse
> Ín the símplest búd that blóws;
> Gó, forsake thy pláin and fóld;
> Joín the crówd, and toil for góld.
>
> Tránquil pleásures néver clóy;
> Bánish eách tumúltuous jóy;
> All but lóve—for love inspíres
> Fónder wíshes, wármer fíres
>
> Sée, to sweeten thy repose,
> The blóssom buds, the fountain flows;

> Ló! to crown thy healthful board,
> Áll that milk and fruits afford.
>
> Séek no more—the rest is vain;
> Pléasure ending soon in pain:
> Ańguish lightly gilded o'er;
> Close thy wish, and seek no more.
>   —SHENSTONE

Parisyllabic verse should regularly be composed of all iambuses; that is to say, all its even syllables should be accented. Yet it is very common for the first foot of the line to be a trochee as in this verse:

> Yé who e'er lóst an ańgel, píty me!

Sometimes a trochee is found in the midst of this verse. But this is extremely rare indeed. The following, however, are instances of it taken from Milton.

> To dó ought góod *néver* will bé our tásk
> Behésts obéy, *wórthiest* to bé obéyed.
>
> Than sélf-esteém, *groúnded* on júst and ríght
> Leans the huge elephant the *wisest* of brutes!

In these instances it has not a good effect, but in the following it has:

> This hánd is mine—*óh! what* a hánd is hére!
> So soft, souls sink into it and are lost.

When this trochee is placed at the beginning of a verse, if it be not too often repeated it produces a variety in the measure which is pleasing. The following is a specimen of the parisyllabic verse, wherein the instances of this trochee beginning the verse are noted:

> *Píty* the sórrows óf a poór old mán,
>   Whose trembling limbs have bórne him tó your doór.

Whose days are dwindled tó the shórtest span;
  Oh! give relief, and Heáven will bless your stóre.

These táttered clóthes my póverty bespeák,
  These hoáry locks proclaim my léngthen'd yéars
And mány a fúrrow in my grief-worn chéek
  Has been the chánnel to a flóod of teárs.

Yon hoúse, erécted on the rísing gróund,
  With témpting aspect, dréw me fróm my róad;
For plénty there a résidénce has fóund,
  And grándeur á magníficent abóde.

Hard is the fáte of thé infírm and póor!
  Here, as I craved a mórsel of their bréad,
A pámper'd ménial drove me from the dóor,
  To seék a shélter in an húmbler shed.

Oh! take me tó your hóspitáble dóme;
  Keén blows the wind, and piércing is the cóld;
Short is my pássage tó the friéndly tómb,
  For I am poór, and miserábly óld.

<u>Heáven sends</u> misfórtunes; why should we repíne!
  Tis Heáven has broúght me tó the státe you seé;
And yoúr condition máy be soón like míne,
  The child of sórrow and of mísery.

                                                —Moss

Trisyllabic verse consists altogether of anapests, that is, of
feet made up of two unaccented and one accented syllable;
and it does not admit a mixture of any other feet. The following is a specimen of this kind of verse:

  I have foúnd out a gift for my fair;
    I have foúnd where the woód-pigeons bréed;
  But lét me that plúnder forbeár,
    She will sáy 'twas a bárbarous déed:

  For he ne'er could be trúe, she averr'd,
    Who could rób a poor bird of its yoúng;

And I lovéd her the móre when I héard
Such ténderness fall from her tóngue.
                                        —SHENSTONE

The following are instances of an iambus in an anapestic verse:

Or únder this túrf, or ev'ń what they wíll.
                                        —POPE
It néver was knówn that círcular létters.
                                        —SWIFT

They are extremely rare and are deformities, which cannot be admitted to belong to the verse, notwithstanding the authority of the writers from whom they are quoted. Indeed, the pieces from which they are taken are merely pieces of sport on which they did not mean to rest their poetical merit.

But to what class shall we give the following species of verse? "God save great Washington." It is triple verse, but the accent is on the first syllable of the foot instead of the third. Is this an attempt at dactylian verse? or shall we consider it still as anapestic, wherein either the two unaccented syllables which should begin the verse are omitted; or else the two which should end it are, in reciting, transposed to the next verse to complete the first anapest of that, as in Virgil in the following instance, the last syllable of the line belongs to the next, being amalgamated with that into one.

I am not able to recollect another instance of this kind of verse and a single example cannot form a class. It is not worth while, therefore, to provide a foreigner with a critical investigation of its character.

OF ELISION.

The vowels only suffer elision except that "v" is also omitted in the word over and "w" in will, "h" in have. This is actually made in most cases, as it was with the Greeks. Sometimes, however, it is neglected to be done, and in those cases the reader must make it for himself, as in the following examples:

Thou yet *mightest* act the friendly part
And lass *unnoticed* from malignant right
And *fallen* to save his injur'd land
Impatient for *it is* past the promis'd hour.

He *also against* the house of God was bold
Anguish and doubt and fear and sor*row and* pain
Of Phlegma with *the he*roic race was joined
Damasco, or Maroc*co, or* Trebisond
All her *original* brightness, nor appear'd
Open or understood must be resolv'd.

OF SYNECPHONESIS.

Diphthongs are considered as forming one syllable. But vowels belonging to different syllables are sometimes forced to coalesce into a diphthong if the measure requires it. Nor is this coalescence prevented by the intervention of an "h," a "w" or a liquid. In this case the two syllables are run into one another with such rapidity as to take but the time of one. The following are examples:

And wish th*e a*venging fight
B*e it* so, for I submit, his doom is fair.
When wint'ry winds deform the plent*eo*us year
Droop'd their fair leaves, nor knew th*e u*nfriendly soil
The rad*ia*nt morn resumed her orient pride
While born to bring the Muse's happ*ie*r days
A patr*io*t's hand protects a poet's lays
Ye midnight lamps, ye cur*iou*s homes
That eagle gen*ius*! had he let fall—

Fair fancy wept; and ech*oi*ng sighs confest
The sounding forest fluct*ua*tes in the storm
Thy greatest infl*ue*nce own
Iss*uei*ng from out the portals of the morn
What groves nor streams bestow a virt*uou*s mind
With man*y a* proof of recollected love.
With kind concern our pit*yi*ng eyes o'erflow
Lies yet a little embr*yo* unperceiv'd—

Now Marg*are*t's curse is fall'n upon our heads
And ev*en a* Shakespeare to her fame be born
When min*era*l fountains vainly bear
O how self-fettered was my grov*eli*ng soul!
To ev*ery* sod which wraps the dead
And beam protection on a wand*eri*ng maid
Him or his children, ev*il he* may be sure
Love unlibid*inou*s resigned, nor jealousy
And left t*o he*rself, if evil thence ensue.
Big swell'd my heart and own'd the p*owe*rful maid
Proceeding, runs low bell*owi*ng round the hills
Thy cherishing, thy hon*ouri*ng, and thy love
With all its shad*owy* shapes is shown
The shepherd's so civil y*ou ha*ve nothing to fear.

The elision of a vowel is often actually made where the coalescence before noted be more musical. Perhaps a vowel should never suffer elision when it is followed by a vowel or where only an "h," a " w" or a liquid intervenes between that and a next vowel, or in other words there should never be an elision where synecphonesis may take place. Consider the following instances:

Full of the dear ecstatic pow'r, and sick
Dare not th' infectious sigh; thy pleading look
While ev'ning draws her crimson curtains round
And fright the tim'rous game
Fills ev'ry nerve, and pants in ev'ry vein.

Full of the dear ecstatic power, and sick
Dare not the infectious sigh; thy pleading look
While evening draws her crimson curtains round
And fright the timorous game
Fills every nerve, and pants in every vein.

The pronunciation in these instances with the actual elision is less agreeable to my ear than by synecphonesis.

OF RULES FOR THE ACCENT.

Accent deciding the measure of English verse as quantity does that of the Latin, and rules having been formed for teaching the quantity of the Latins it would be expected that rules should also be offered for indicating to foreigners the accented syllable of every word in English. Such rules have been attempted. Were they to be so completely formed as that the rules and their necessary exceptions would reach every word in the language, they would be too great a charge on the memory and too complicated for use either in reading or conversation. In the imperfect manner in which they have been hitherto proposed they would lead into infinite errors. It is usage which has established the accent of every word, or rather I might say it has been caprice or chance, for nothing can be more arbitrary or less consistent. I am of opinion it is easier for a foreigner to learn the accent of every word individually, than the rules which would teach it. This his dictionary will teach him, if, when he recurs to it for the meaning of a word, he will recollect that he should notice also on which syllable is its accent. Or he may learn the accent by reading poetry, which differs our language from Greek and Latin, wherein you must learn their prosody in order to read their poetry. Knowing that with us the accent is on every odd syllable or on every even one or on every third, he has only to examine of which of these measures the verse is to be able to read it correctly. But how shall he distinguish the measure to which the verse belongs?

If he can find in the piece any one word the accent of which he already knows, that word will enable him to distinguish if it be parisyllabic or imparisyllabic. Let us suppose, for example, he would read the following piece:

> How sleep the brave, who sink to rest,
> By all their country's wishes blest!
> When Spring, with dewy fingers cold,
> Returns to deck their hallowed mould,
> She there shall dress a *sweeter* sod
> Than Fancy's feet have ever trod.
>
> By fairy hands their knell is rung;
> By forms unseen their dirge is sung;
> There Honor comes, a pilgrim gray,
> To bless the turf that wraps their clay;

And Freedom shall a while repair,
To dwell a weeping hermit there!
—COLLINS

He finds the word *sweeter*, the accent of which he has already
learned to be on the first syllable, sweet. He observes that that
is an even syllable, being the sixth of the line. He knows then
that it is parisyllabic verse and from that he can accent the
whole piece. If he does not already know the accent of a single word he must look in his dictionary for some one, and
that will be a key to the whole piece. He should take care not
to rely on the first foot of any line, because, as has been before observed, that is often a trochee even in the parisyllabic
verse. Without consulting his dictionary at all, or knowing a
single accent, the following observation will enable him to
distinguish between these two species of verse when they are
in rhyme. An odd number of syllables with a single rhyme, or
an even number with a double rhyme, prove the verse to be
imparisyllabic. An even number of syllables with a single
rhyme, or an odd number with a double one, prove it to be
parisyllabic, *e. g.*:

Learn by this unguarded lover
    When your secret sighs prevail
Not to let your tongue discover
    Raptures that you should conceal.
                    —CUNNINGHAM

He sung and hell consented
    To hear the poet's prayer
Stern Proserpine relented
    And gave him back the fair.
                    —POPE

If in thus examining the seat of the accent he finds it is
alternately on an odd and an even syllable, that is to say, on
the third, sixth, ninth, twelfth syllables, the verse is trisyllabic.

With her how I stray'd amid fóuntains and bowers!
Or loíter'd behínd, and collected the flowérś!

Then breathless with ardor my fair one pursued,
And to think with what kindness my garland she view'd!
But be still, my fond heart! this emotion give o'er;
Fain wouldst thou forget thou must love her no more.
—SHENSTONE

It must be stated that in this kind of verse we should count backward from the last syllable, if it be a single rhyme, or the last but one if it be double; because one of the unaccented syllables which should begin the verse is so often omitted. This last syllable in the preceding example should be the twelfth. When the line is full it is accented of course. Consulting the dictionary, therefore, we find in the first line the ninth syllable accented; in the second, the sixth; in the third line the accented syllables there being alternately odd and even, to wit, the third, sixth, ninth and twelfth, we know the verse must be trisyllabic.

The foreigner then first determining the measure of the verse, may read it boldly. He will commit a few errors, indeed; let us see what they are likely to be. In imparisyllabic verse none, because that consists of trochees invariably; if an unaccented syllable happens to be prefixed to the verse, he will discover it by the number of syllables. In parisyllabic verse, when a trochee begins the verse, he will pronounce that foot wrong. This will perhaps happen once in ten lines; in some authors more, in others less. In like manner he will pronounce wrong the trochee in the middle of the line. But this he will encounter once in some hundreds of times. In the trisyllabic verse he can never commit an error if he counts from the end of the line. These imperfections are as few as a foreigner can possibly expect in the beginning; and he will reduce their number in proportion as he acquires by practice a knowledge of the accents.

The subject of accent cannot be quitted till we apprise him of another imperfection which will show itself in his reading, and which will be longer removing. Though there be accents on the first, the second or the third syllables of the foot, as has been before explained, yet is there subordination among these accents, a modulation in their tone of which it is impossible to give a precise idea in writing. This is intimately connected with the sense; and though a foreigner will readily find to what words that would give distinguished emphasis, yet nothing but habit can enable him to give actually the different shades of emphasis which his judgment would dictate to him. Even natives have very different powers as to this article. This difference exists both in the organ and the judgment. Foote is known to have read Milton so exquisitely that he received great sums of money for reading him to audiences who attended him regularly for that purpose. This difference, too, enters deeply into the merit of theatrical actors. The foreigner, therefore, must acquiesce under a want of perfection which is the lot of natives in common with himself.

We will proceed to give examples which may explain what is here meant, distinguishing the accents into four shades by these marks ""'' ''' '' ' the greater number of marks denoting the strongest accents.

> Oh when the growling winds contend and all
> The sounding forest fluctuates in the storm
> To sink in warm repose, and hear the din
> Howl o'er the steady battlements, delights
> Above the luxury of vulgar sleep.
>
> —ARMSTRONG

> Life's cares are comforts; such by heav'n design'd
> He that has none, must make them or be wretched
> Cares are employments; and without employ
> The soul is on a rack, the rack of rest.
>
> —YOUNG

> O! lost to virtue, lost to manly thought,
> Lost to the noble sallies of the soul!
> Who think it solitude, to be alone.
> Communion sweet! communion large and high!
> Our reason, guardian angel, and our God!
> Then nearest these, when others most remote;
> And all, ere long, shall be remote, but these.
>
> —YOUNG

By nature's law, what may be, may be now;
There's no prerogative in human hours.
In human hearts what bolder thought can rise,
Than man's presumption on to-morrow's dawn?
Where is to-morrow? In another world.
For numbers this is certain; the reverse
Is sure to none; and yet on this perhaps,
This peradventure, infamous for lies,
As on a rock of adamant, we build
Our mountain hopes; spin out eternal schemes.
As we the fatal sisters could outspin,
And, big with life's futurities, expire.

— YOUNG

Cowards die many times before their deaths:
The valiant never taste of death but once.
Of all the wonders that I yet have heard,
It seems to me most strange that men should fear,
Seeing that death, a necessary end,
Will come when it will come.

I cannot tell what you and other men
Think of this life, but for my single self,
I had as lief not be as live to be
In awe of such a thing as I myself.
I was born free as Cæsar, so were you;
We both have fed as well, and we can both
Endure the winter's cold as well as he.

The cloud-capp'd towers, the gorgeous palaces,
The solemn temples, the great globe itself,
Yea, all which it inherit, shall dissolve,
And, like this insubstantial pageant faded,
Leave not a rack behind.

I am far from presuming to give this accentuation as perfect. No two persons will accent the same passage alike. No
person but a real adept would accent it twice alike. Perhaps
two real adepts who should utter the same passage with infinite perfection yet by throwing the energy into different

words might produce very different effects. I suppose that in
those passages of Shakespeare, for example, no man but Gar-
rick ever drew their full tone out of them, if I may borrow an
expression from music. Let those who are disposed to criti-
cise, therefore, try a few experiments themselves. I have essayed these short passages to let the foreigner see that the
accent is not equal; that they are not to be read monoto-
nously. I chose, too, the most pregnant passages, those
wherein every word teems with latent meaning, that he might
form an idea of the degrees of excellence of which this art is
capable. He must not apprehend that all poets present the
same difficulty. It is only the most brilliant passages. The
great mass, even of good poetry, is easily enough read. Take
the following examples, wherein little differences in the enunciation will not change the meaning sensibly.

Here, in cool grot and mossy cell,
We rural fays and faeries dwell;
Though rarely seen by mortal eye,
When the pale Moon, ascending high,
Darts through yon lines her quivering beams,
We frisk it near these crystal streams.

Her beams, reflected from the wave,
Afford the light our revels crave;
The turf, with daisies broider'd o'er,
Exceeds, we wot, the Parian floor;
Nor yet for artful strains we call,
But listen to the water's fall.

Would you then taste our tranquil scene,
Be sure your bosoms be serene:
Devoid of hate, devoid of strife,
Devoid of all that poisons life:
And much it 'vails you, in their place
To graft the love of human race.

And tread with awe these favor'd bowers,
Nor wound the shrubs, nor bruise the flowers;
So may your path with sweets abound;

So may your couch with rest be crown'd!
But harm betide the wayward swain,
Who dares our hallow'd haunts profane!
—SHENSTONE

To fair Fidele's grassy tomb
  Soft maids and village hinds shall bring
Each opening sweet, of earliest bloom,
  And rifle all the breathing Spring.

No wailing ghost shall dare appear
  To vex with shrieks this quiet grove,
But shepherd lads assemble here,
  And melting virgins own their love.

No wither'd witch shall here be seen,
  No goblins lead their nightly crew;
The female fays shall haunt the green,
  And dress thy grave with pearly dew;

The red-breast oft at evening hours
  Shall kindly lend his little aid,
With hoary moss, and gather'd flowers,
  To deck the ground where thou art laid.

When howling winds, and beating rain,
  In tempests shake thy sylvan cell;
Or 'midst the chase on every plain,
  The tender thought on thee shall dwell.

Each lonely scene shall thee restore,
  For thee the tear be duly shed;
Belov'd, till life can charm no more
  And mourn'd, till Pity's self be dead.
—COLLINS

OF THE LENGTH OF VERSE.

Having spoken of feet which are only the constituent part
of verse, it becomes necessary to say something of its larger
divisions, and even of the verse itself. For what is a verse?
This question naturally occurs, and it is not sufficiently an-

MISCELLANY

swered by saying it is a whole line. Should the printer think
proper to print the following passage in this manner:

Ὣς εἰπὼν οὗ παιδὸς ὀρέξατο φαίδιμος Ἕκτωρ. ἂψ δ' ὁ
παῖς πρὸς κόλπον ἐϋζώνοιο τιθήνης ἐκλίνθη ἰάχων, πατρὸς
φίλου ὄψιν ἀτυχθείς, ταρβήσας χαλκόν τε ἰδὲ λόφον
ἱππιοχαίτην, δεινὸν ἀπ' ἀκροτάτης κόρυθος νεύοντα νοήσας
ἐκ δ' ἐγέλασσε πατήρ τε φίλος καὶ πότνια μήτηρ. αὐτίκ' ἀπὸ
κρατὸς κόρυθ' εἵλετο φαίδιμος Ἕκτωρ, καὶ τὴν μὲν
κατέθηκεν ἐπὶ χθονὶ παμφανόωσαν· αὐτὰρ ὅ γ' ὃν φίλον
υἱὸν ἐπεὶ κύσε πῆλέ τε χερσίν, εἶπεν ἐπευξάμενος Διΐ τ'
ἄλλοισίν τε θεοῖσι· Ζεῦ ἄλλοι τε θεοί, δότε δὴ καὶ τόνδε
γενέσθαι παῖδ' ἐμόν, ὡς καὶ ἐγώ περ, ἀριπρεπέα Τρώεσσιν,
ὧδε βίην τ' ἀγαθὸν καὶ Ἰλίου ἶφι ἀνάσσειν· καὶ ποτέ τις
εἴποι, 'πατρός γ' ὅδε πολλὸν ἀμείνων' ἐκ πολέμου ἀνιόντα·
φέροι δ' ἔναρα βροτόεντα κτείνας δήϊον ἄνδρα, χαρείη δὲ
φρένα μήτηρ. Ὣς εἰπὼν ἀλόχοιο φίλης ἐν χερσὶν ἔθηκε
παῖδ' ἑόν· ἡ δ' ἄρα μιν κηώδεϊ δέξατο κόλπῳ δακρυόεν
γελάσασα· πόσις δ' ἐλέησε νοήσας, χειρί τέ μιν κατέρεξεν
ἔπος τ' ἔφατ' ἔκ τ' ὀνόμαζε·

it would still be verse; it would still immortalize its author
were every other syllable of his compositions lost. The poet
then does not depend on the printer to give a character to his
work. He has studied the human ear. He has discovered that
in any rhythmical composition the ear is pleased to find at
certain regular intervals a pause where it may rest, by which
it may divide the composition into parts, as a piece of music
is divided into bars. He contrives to mark this division by a
pause in the sense or at least by an emphatical word which
may force the pause so that the ear may feel the regular return
of the pause. The interval then between these regular pauses
constitutes a verse. In the morsel before cited this interval
comprehends six feet, and though it is written in the manner
of prose, yet he who can read it without pausing at every
sixth foot, like him who is insensible to the charm of music,
who is insensible of love or of gratitude, is an unfavored son
of nature to whom she has given a faculty fewer than to others of her children, one source of pleasure the less in a world
where there are none to spare. A well-organized ear makes
the pause regularly whether it be printed as verse or as prose.

But not only the organization of the ear but the character of the language have influence in determining the length of the verse. Otherwise the constitution of the ear being the same with all nations the verse would be of the same length in all languages, which is not the case. But the difference in language occasions the ear to be pleased with a difference of interval in the pause. The language of Homer enabled him to compose in verse of six feet; the English language cannot bear this. They may be of one, two, three, four, or five feet, as in the following examples:

One foot.

> Turning
> Burning
> Changing
> Ranging
> I mourn
> I sigh
> I burn
> I die
> Let us part—
> Let us part
> Will you break
> My poor heart?

Two feet.

> Flow'ry mountains
> Mossy fountains
> Shady woods
> Crystal floods
> To me the rose
> No longer glows
> Ev'ry plant
> Has lost its scent.

> Prithee Cupid no more
> Hurl thy darts at threescore
> To thy girls and thy boys
> Give thy pains and thy joys.

Three feet.

> Farewell fear and sorrow
> Pleasure till to-morrow.

> Yes, ev'ry flow'r that blows
>   I passed unheeded by
> Till this enchanting rose
>   Had fix'd my wand'ring eye.
>   —CUNNINGHAM

> The rose though a beautiful red
>   Looks faded to Phyllis's bloom;
> And the breeze from the bean-flower bed
>   To her breath's but a feeble perfume;
> A lily I plucked in full pride
>   Its freshness with hers to compare,
> And foolishly thought till I try'd
>   The flow'ret was equally fair.
>   —CUNNINGHAM

Four feet.

> From the dark tremendous cell
> Where the fiends of magic dwell
> Now the sun hath left the skies
> Daughters of Enchantment, rise!
>   —CUNNINGHAM

> Come Hope, and to my pensive eye
> Thy far foreseeing tube apply
> Whose kind deception steals us o'er
> The gloomy waste that lies before.
>   —LANGHORNE

> 'Mongst lords and fine ladies we shepherds are told
> The dearest affections are barter'd for gold
> That discord in wedlock is often their lot
> While Cupid and Hymen shake hands in a cot.
>   —CUNNINGHAM

Here the parisyllabic alone bears one foot more.

Oh liberty! thou goddess heav'nly bright
Profuse of bliss, and pregnant with delight,
Eternal pleasures in thy presence reign,
And smiling Plenty leads thy wanton train;
Eas'd of her load subjection grows more light,
And Poverty looks cheerful in thy sight;
Thou mak'st the gloomy face of nature gay
Giv'st beauty to the sun, and pleasure to the day.
—ADDISON

The last line furnishes an instance of six feet, usually called an Alexandrian; but no piece is ever wholly in that measure. A single line only is tolerated now and then, and is never a beauty. Formerly it was thought that the language bore lines of seven feet in length, as in the following:

'Tis he whose ev'ry thought and deed by rules of virtue
    moves;
Whose gen'rous tongue disdains to speak the thing his heart
    disproves
Who never did a slander forge his neighbor's fame to
    wound;
Nor listen to a false report by malice whisper'd round.
—PSALM 15

But a little attention shows that there is as regular a pause at the fourth foot as at the seventh, and as verse takes its denomination from the shortest regular intervals, this is no more than an alternate verse of four and of three feet. It is, therefore, usually written as in the following stanzas of the same piece:

Who to his plighted vows and trust
    Has ever firmly stood
And, though he promise to his loss,
    He makes his promise good.

The man who by this steady course
    Has happiness ensur'd
When earth's foundations shake, will stand
    By Providence secur'd.

We may justly consider, therefore, verses of five feet as the longest the language sustains, and it is remarkable that not only this length, though the extreme, is generally the most esteemed, but that it is the only one which has dignity enough to support blank verse, that is, verse without rhyme. This is attempted in no other measure. It constitutes, therefore, the most precious part of our poetry. The poet, unfettered by rhyme, is at liberty to prune his diction of those tautologies, those feeble nothings necessary to introtrude the rhyming word. With no other trammel than that of measure he is able to condense his thoughts and images and to leave nothing but what is truly poetical. When enveloped in all the pomp and majesty of his subject he sometimes even throws off the restraint of the regular pause:

> Of Man's first disobedience, and the fruit
> Of that forbidden tree, whose mortal taste
> Brought death into the world, and all our woe,
> With loss of Eden, till one greater Man
> Restore us, and regain the blissful seat,
> Sing, heavenly Muse! that on the sacred top
> Of Oreb, or of Sinai, didst inspire
> That shepherd, who first taught the chosen seed,
> In the beginning, how the Heavens and Earth
> Rose out of Chaos.

> Then stay'd the fervid wheels, and in his hand
> He took the golden compasses, prepared
> In God's eternal store, to circumscribe
> This universe, and all created things
> One foot he centred, and the other turn'd
> Round, through the vast profundity obscure
> And said, "Thus far extend."

There are but two regular pauses in this whole passage of seven verses. They are constantly drowned by the majesty of the rhythm and sense. But nothing less than this can authorize such a license. Take the following proof from the same author:

> Again, God said, "Let there be firmament
> Amid the waters, and let it divide
> The waters from the waters;" and God made
> The firmament. —MILTON 7: 261

And God said, Let there be a firmament in the midst of the waters, and let it divide the waters from the waters.

And God made the firmament. —GENESIS 1: 6

I have here placed Moses and Milton side by side, that he who can may distinguish which verse belongs to the poet. To do this he will not have the aid either of the sentiment, diction or measure of poetry. The original is so servilely copied that though it be cut into pieces of ten syllables, no pause is marked between these portions.

What proves the excellence of blank verse is that the taste lasts longer than that for rhyme. The fondness for the jingle leaves us with that for the rattles and baubles of childhood, and if we continue to read rhymed verse at a later period of life it is such only where the poet has had force enough to bring great beauties of thought and diction into this form. When young any composition pleases which unites a little sense, some imagination, and some rhythm, in doses however small. But as we advance in life these things fall off one by one, and I suspect we are left at last with only Homer and Virgil, perhaps with Homer alone. He like

> Hope travels on nor quits us when we die.

Having noted the different lengths of line which the English poet may give to his verse it must be further observed that he may intermingle these in the same verse according to his fancy.

The following are selected as examples:

> A tear bedews my Delia's eye,
> To think yon playful kid must die;
> From crystal spring, and flowery mead,
> Must, in his prime of life, recede!

She tells with what delight he stood,
To trace his features in the flood;
Then skipp'd aloof with quaint amaze,
And then drew near again to gaze.
                              —SHENSTONE

Full many a gem of purest ray serene
  The dark unfathomed caves of ocean bear;
Full many a flower is born to blush unseen,
  And waste its sweetness on the desert air.

Some village Hampden, that, with dauntless breast,
  The little tyrant of his fields withstood,
Some mute inglorious Milton here may rest,
  Some Cromwell, guiltless of his country's blood.
                              —GRAY

There shall my plaintive song recount
    Dark themes of hopeless woe,
And faster than the drooping fount
    I'll teach mine eyes to flow.

There leaves, in spite of Autumn green
    Shall shade the hallow'd ground,
And Spring will there again be seen
    To call forth flowers around.
                              —SHENSTONE

O Health! capricious maid!
    Why dost thou shun my peaceful bower,
    Where I had hope to share thy power,
And bless thy lasting aid?
                              —SHENSTONE

The man whose mind, on virtue bent
Pursues some greatly good intent
        With undivided aim
Serene beholds the angry crowd
Nor can their clamors fierce and loud
        His stubborn purpose tame.

Ye gentle Bards! give ear,
　Who talk of amorous rage,
Who spoil the lily, rob the rose,
Come learn of me to weep your woes:
　"O sweet! O sweet Anne Page!"
　　　　　—SHENSTONE

Too long a stranger to repose,
At length from Pain's abhorred couch I rose
　And wander'd forth alone,
To court once more the balmy breeze,
And catch the verdure of the trees,
　Ere yet their charms were flown.
　　　　　—SHENSTONE

O thou, by Nature taught
To breathe her genuine thought,
In numbers warmly pure, and sweetly strong;
Who first, on mountains wild,
In Fancy, loveliest child,
Thy babe, and Pleasure's, nursed the powers of song!
　　　　　—COLLINS

　　'Twas in a land of learning,
　　The Muse's favorite city,
　　Such pranks of late
　　Were play'd by a rat,
　　As—tempt one to be witty.
　　　　　—SHENSTONE

Yet stay, O stay! celestial Pow'rs!
　And with a hand of kind regard
Dispel the boisterous storm that low'rs
　Destruction on the fav'rite bard;
O watch with me his last expiring breath
And snatch him from the arms of dark oblivious death.
　　　　　—GRAY

　　What is grandeur, what is power?
　　Heavier toil, superior pain.

What the bright reward we gain?
The grateful memory of the good.
Sweet is the breath of vernal shower,
The bee's collected treasures sweet,
Sweet music's melting fall, but sweeter yet
The still small voice of gratitude.

Methinks I hear, in accents low,
The sportive, kind reply:
Poor moralist! and what art thou?
A solitary fly!
Thy joys no glittering female meets,
No hive hast thou of hoarded sweets,
No painted plumage to display;
On hasty wings thy youth is flown;
Thy sun is set, thy spring is gone—
We frolic while 'tis May.

—GRAY

Then let me rove some wild and heathy scene;
Or find some ruin, 'midst its dreary dells,
    Whose walls more awful nod
    By thy religious gleams.

Or, if chill blustering winds, or driving rain,
Prevent my willing feet, be mine the hut,
    That, from the mountain's side,
    Views wilds, and swelling floods.

—COLLINS

Though the license to intermingle the different measures admits an infinitude of combinations, yet this becomes less and less pleasing in proportion as they depart from that simplicity and regularity of which the ear is most sensible. When these are wholly or nearly neglected, as in the lyric pieces, the poet renounces one of the most fascinating charms of his art. He must then look well to his matter and supply in sublimity or other beauties the loss of regular measure. In effect these pieces are seldom read twice.

A Tour to some of the Gardens of England

[*Memorandums made on a tour to some of the gardens in England, described by Whateley in his book on gardening.*] While his descriptions, in point of style, are models of perfect elegance and classical correctness, they are as remarkable for their exactness. I always walked over the gardens with his book in my hand, examined with attention the particular spots he described, found them so justly characterized by him as to be easily recognized, and saw with wonder, that his fine imagination had never been able to seduce him from the truth. My inquiries were directed chiefly to such practical things as might enable me to estimate the expense of making and maintaining a garden in that style. My journey was in the months of March and April, 1786.

Chiswick.—Belongs to Duke of Devonshire. A garden about six acres;—the octagonal dome has an ill effect, both within and without: the garden shows still too much of art. An obelisk of very ill effect; another in the middle of a pond useless.

Hampton-Court.—Old fashioned. Clipt yews grown wild.

Twickenham.—Pope's original garden, three and a half acres. Sir Wm. Stanhope added one and a half acre. This is a long narrow slip, grass and trees in the middle, walk all round. Now Sir Wellbore Ellis's. Obelisk at bottom of Pope's garden, as monument to his mother. Inscription, "Ah! Editha, matrum optima, mulierum amantissima, Vale." The house about thirty yards from the Thames: the ground shelves gently to the water side; on the back of the house passes the street, and beyond that the garden. The grotto is under the street, and goes out level to the water. In the centre of the garden a mound with a spiral walk round it. A rookery.

Esher-Place.—The house in a bottom near the river; on the other side the ground rises pretty much. The road by which we come to the house forms a dividing line in the middle of the front; on the right are heights, rising one beyond and above another, with clumps of trees; on the farthest a temple.

A hollow filled up with a clump of trees, the tallest in the bottom, so that the top is quite flat. On the left the ground descends. Clumps of trees, the clumps on each hand balance finely—a most lovely mixture of concave and convex. The garden is of about forty-five acres, besides the park which joins. Belongs to Lady Frances Pelham.

Claremont.—Lord Clive's. Nothing remarkable.

Paynshill.—Mr. Hopkins. Three hundred and twenty-three acres, garden and park all in one. Well described by Whateley. Grotto said to have cost £7,000. Whateley says one of the bridges is of stone, but both now are of wood, the lower sixty feet high: there is too much evergreen. The dwelling-house built by Hopkins, ill-situated: he has not been there in five years. He lived there four years while building the present house. It is not finished; its architecture is incorrect. A Doric temple, beautiful.

Woburn.—Belongs to Lord Peters. Lord Loughborough is the present tenant for two lives. Four people to the farm, four to the pleasure garden, four to the kitchen garden. All are intermixed, the pleasure garden being merely a highly-ornamented walk through and round the divisions of the farm and kitchen garden.

Caversham.—Sold by Lord Cadogan to Major Marsac. Twenty-five acres of garden, four hundred acres of park, six acres of kitchen garden. A large lawn, separated by a sunk fence from the garden, appears to be part of it. A straight, broad gravel walk passes before the front and parallel to it, terminated on the right by a Doric temple, and opening at the other end on a fine prospect. This straight walk has an ill effect. The lawn in front, which is pasture, well disposed with clumps of trees.

Wotton.—Now belongs to the Marquis of Buckingham, son of George Grenville. The lake covers fifty acres, the river five acres, the basin fifteen acres, the little river two acres—equal to seventy-two acres of water. The lake and great river are on a level, they fall into the basin five feet below, and that again into the little river five feet lower. These waters lie in form of an L: the house is in middle of open side, fronting the angle. A walk goes round the whole, three miles in circumference, and containing within it about three hundred acres: sometimes it passes close to the water, sometimes so far off as to leave large pasture grounds between it and the water. But two hands to keep the pleasure grounds in order; much neglected. The water affords two thousand brace of carp a year. There is a Palladian bridge, of which, I think, Whateley does not speak.

Stowe.—Belongs to the Marquis of Buckingham, son of George Grenville, and who takes it from Lord Temple. Fifteen men and eighteen boys employed in keeping pleasure grounds. Within the walk are considerable portions separated by inclosures and used for pasture. The Egyptian pyramid is almost entirely taken down by the late Lord Temple, to erect a building there, in commemoration of Mr. Pitt, but he died before beginning it, and nothing is done to it yet. The grotto and two rotundas are taken away. There are four levels of water, receiving it one from the other. The basin contains seven acres, the lake below that ten acres. Kent's building is called the temple of Venus. The inclosure is entirely by ha-ha. At each end of the front line there is a recess like the bastion of a fort. In one of these is the temple of Friendship, in the other the temple of Venus. They are seen the one from the other, the line of sight passing, not through the garden, but through the country parallel to the line of the garden. This has a good effect. In the approach to Stowe, you are brought a mile through a straight avenue, pointing to the Corinthian arch and to the house, till you get to the arch, then you turn short to the right. The straight approach is very ill. The Corinthian arch has a very useless appearance, inasmuch as it has no pretension to any destination. Instead of being an object from the house, it is an obstacle to a very pleasing distant prospect. The Grecian valley being clear of trees, while the hill on each side is covered with them, is much deepened to appearance.

Leasowes, in Shropshire.—Now the property of Mr. Horne by purchase. One hundred and fifty acres within the walk. The waters small. This is not even an ornamented farm—it is only a grazing farm with a path round it, here and there a seat of board, rarely anything better. Architecture has contributed nothing. The obelisk is of brick. Shenstone had but three hundred pounds a year, and ruined himself by what he did to this farm. It is said that he died of the heart-aches which his debts occasioned him. The part next the road is of red earth, that on the further part gray. The first and second cascades are beautiful. The landscape at number eighteen, and prospect at thirty-two, are fine. The walk through the wood is umbrageous and pleasing. The whole arch of prospect may be of ninety degrees. Many of the inscriptions are lost.

Hagley, now Lord Wescot's.—One thousand acres: no distinction between park and garden—both blended, but more of the character of garden. Eight or nine laborers keep it in order. Between two and three hundred deer in it, some few of them red deer. They breed sometimes with the fallow. This garden occupying a descending hollow between the Clent and Witchbury hills, with the spurs from those hills, there is no level in it for a spacious water. There are, therefore, only some small ponds. From one of these there is a fine cascade; but it can only be occasionally, by opening the sluice. This is in a small, dark, deep hollow, with recesses of stone in the banks on every side. In one of these is a Venus predique, turned half round as if inviting you with her into the recess. There is another cascade seen from the portico on the bridge. The castle is triangular, with a round tower at each angle, one only entire; it seems to be between forty and fifty feet high. The ponds yield a great deal of trout. The walks are scarcely gravelled.

Blenheim.—Twenty-five hundred acres, of which two hundred is garden, one hundred and fifty water, twelve kitchen garden, and the rest park. Two hundred people employed to keep it in order, and to make alterations and additions. About fifty of these employed in pleasure grounds. The turf is mowed once in ten days. In summer, about two thousand fallow deer in the park, and two or three thousand sheep. The palace of Henry II. was remaining till taken down by Sarah, widow of the first Duke of Marlborough. It was on a round spot levelled by art, near what is now water, and but a little above it. The island was a part of the high road leading to the palace. Rosamond's bower was near where is now a little grove, about two hundred yards from the palace. The well is near where the bower was. The water here is very beautiful, and very grand. The cascade from the lake, a fine one; except this the garden has no great beauties. It is not laid out in fine lawns and woods, but the trees are scattered thinly over the ground, and every here and there small thickets of shrubs, in oval raised beds, cultivated, and flowers among the shrubs. The gravelled walks are broad—art appears too much. There are but a few seats in it, and nothing of architecture more dignified. There is no one striking position in it. There has been a great addition to the length of the river since Whateley wrote.

Enfield Chase.—One of the four lodges. Garden about sixty acres. Originally by Lord Chatham, now in the tenure of Dr. Beaver, who married the daughter of Mr. Sharpe. The lease lately renewed—not in good repair. The water very fine; would admit of great improvement by extending walks, &c., to the principal water at the bottom of the lawn.

Moor Park.—The lawn about thirty acres. A piece of ground up the hill of six acres. A small lake. Clumps of spruce firs. Surrounded by walk—separately inclosed—destroys unity. The property of Mr. Rous, who bought of Sir Thomas Dundas. The building superb; the principal front a Corinthian portico of four columns; in front of the wings a colonnade, Ionic, subordinate. Back front a terrace, four Corinthian pilasters. Pulling down wings of building; removing deer; wants water.

Kew.—Archimedes' screw for raising water. A horizontal shaft made to turn the oblique one of the screw by a patent machinery of this form:

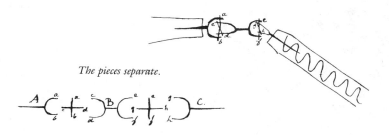

The pieces separate.

A is driven by its shank into the horizontal axis of the wheel which turns the machine.

B is an intermediate iron to connect the motion of A and C.

C is driven by its shank into the axis of the screw.

D is a cross axis, the ends, a and b, going into the corresponding holes a and b of the iron A, and the ends, c and d, going into the corresponding holes c and d of the iron B.

E is another cross axis, the ends, e and f, going into the corresponding holes e and f of the iron B, and the ends, g and h, going into the corresponding holes g and h of the iron C.

Memorandums on a Tour from Paris to Amsterdam, Strasburg, and back to Paris

Amsterdam.—Joists of houses placed, not with their sides horizontally and perpendicularly, but diamond wise, thus: ◇ first, for greater strength; second, to arch between with brick, thus: Windows opening so that they admit air and not rain. The upper sash opens on a horizontal axis, or pins in the centre of the sides, the lower sash slides up.

Manner of fixing a flag staff on the mast of a vessel: *a* is the bolt on which it turns; *b* a bolt which is taken in and out to fasten it or to let it down. When taken out, the lower end of the staff is shoved out of its case, and the upper end being heaviest brings itself down: a rope must have been previously fastened to the butt end, to pull it down again when you want to raise the flag end. Dining tables letting down with single or double leaves, so as to take the room of their thickness only with a single leaf when open, thus: or thus: double-leaves open: shut, thus: or thus: shut:

Peat costs about one doit each, or twelve and a half stivers the hundred. One hundred make seven cubic feet, and to keep a tolerably comfortable fire for a study or chamber, takes about six every hour and a half.

A machine for drawing light *empty* boats over a dam at Amsterdam. It is an axis in peritrochio fixed on the dam. From the dam each way is a sloping stage, the boat is presented to this, the rope of the axis made fast to it, and it is drawn up. The water on one side of the dam is about four feet higher than on the other.

The camels used for lightening ships over the Pampus will raise the ships eight feet. There are beams passing through the ship's sides, projecting to the off side of the camel and resting on it; of course that alone would keep the camel close to the ship. Besides this, there are a great number of wind-lasses on the camels, the ropes of which are made fast to the gunwale of the ship. The camel is shaped to the ship on the near side, and straight on the off one. When placed along side, water is let into it so as nearly to sink it; in this state it receives the beams, &c., of the ship, and then the water is pumped out.

Wind saw mills. See the plans detailed in the moolen book which I bought. A circular foundation of brick is raised about three or four feet high, and covered with a curb or sill of wood, and has little rollers under its sill which make it turn easily on the curb. A hanging bridge projects at each end about fifteen or twenty feet beyond the circular area, thus:

horizontally, and thus: in the profile

to increase the play of the timbers on the frame. The wings are at one side, as at *a*; there is a shelter over the hanging bridges, but of plank with scarce any frame, very light.

A bridge across a canal formed by two scows, which open each to the opposite shore and let boats pass.

A lanthern over the street door, which gives light equally into the antechamber and the street. It is a hexagon, and oc-cupies the place of the middle pane of glass in the circular top of the street door.

A bridge on a canal, turning on a swivel, by which means it is arranged along the side of the canal so as not to be in the way of boats when not in use. When used, it is turned across the canal. It is, of course, a little more than double the width of the canal.

Hedges of beach, which, not losing the old leaf till the new bud pushes it off, has the effect of an evergreen as to cover.

Mr. Ameshoff, merchant at Amsterdam. The distribution of his aviary is worthy of notice. Each kind of the large birds has its coop eight feet wide and four feet deep; the middle of the front is occupied by a broad glass window, on one side of which is a door for the keeper to enter at, and on the other a little trap-door for the birds to pass in and out. The floor strewed with clean hay. Before each coop is a court of eight by sixteen feet, with wire in front and netting above, if the fowls be able to fly. For such as require it, there are bushes of evergreen growing in their court for them to lay their eggs under. The coops are frequently divided into two stories: the upper for those birds which perch, such as pigeons, &c., the lower for those which feed on the ground, as pheasants, partridges, &c. The court is in common for both stories, because the birds do no injury to each other. For the water-fowl there is a pond of water passing through the courts, with a movable separation. While they are breeding they must be separate, afterwards they may come together. The small birds are some of them in a common aviary, and some in cages.

The Dutch wheel-barrow is in this form: which is very convenient for loading and unloading.

Mr. Hermen Hend Damen, merchant-broker of Amsterdam, tells me that the emigrants to America come from the Palatinate down the Rhine, and take shipping from Amsterdam. Their passage is ten guineas if paid here, and eleven if paid in America. He says they might be had in any number to go to America, and settle lands as tenants on half stocks or metairies. Perhaps they would serve their employer one year as an indemnification for the passage, and then be bound to remain on his lands seven years. They would come to Amsterdam at their own expense. He thinks they would employ more than fifty acres each; but *quære*, especially if they have fifty acres for their wife also?

Hodson.—The best house. Stadhonderian, his son, in the government. Friendly, but old and very infirm.

Hope.—The first house in Amsterdam. His first object England; but it is supposed he would like to have the American business also, yet he would probably make our affairs subordinate to those of England.

Vollenhoven.—An excellent old house; connected with no party.

Sapportus.—A broker, very honest and ingenuous, well-disposed; acts for Hope, but will say with truth what he can do for us. The best person to consult with as to the best house to undertake a piece of business. He has brothers in London in business. Jacob Van Staphorst tells me there are about fourteen millions of florins, new money, placed in loans in Holland every year, being the savings of individuals out of their annual revenue, &c. Besides this, there are every year reimbursements of old loans from some quarter or other to be replaced at interest in some new loan.

1788. March 16th. Baron Steuben has been generally suspected of having suggested the first idea of the self-styled Order of Cincinnati. But Mr. Adams tells me, that in the year 1776 he had called at a tavern in the State of New York to dine, just at the moment when the British army was landing at Frog's Neck. Generals Washington, Lee, Knox and Parsons, came to the same tavern. He got into conversation with Knox. They talked of ancient history—of Fabius, who used to raise the Romans from the dust; of the present contest, &c.; and General Knox, in the course of the conversation, said he should wish for some ribbon to wear in his hat, or in his button hole, to be transmitted to his descendants as a badge and a proof that he had fought in defence of their liberties. He spoke of it in such precise terms, as showed he had revolved it in his mind before. Mr. Adams says he and Knox were standing together in the door of the tavern, and does not recollect whether General Washington and the others were near enough to hear the conversation, or were even in the room at that moment. Baron Steuben did not arrive in America till above a year after that. Mr. Adams is now fifty-three years old, *i.e.* nine years more than I am.

It is said this house will cost four tons of silver, or forty

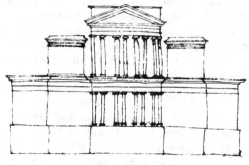

HOPE'S HOUSE, NEAR HARLAEM.

thousand pounds sterling. The separation between the middle building and wings in the upper story has a capricious appearance, yet a pleasing one. The right wing of the house (which is the left in the plan) extends back to a great length, so as to make the ground plan in the form of an L. The parapet has a pannel of wall, and a pannel of ballusters alternately, which lighten it. There is no portico, the columns being backed against the wall of the front.

March 30th, 31st. *Amsterdam. Utrecht. Nimeguen.* The lower parts of the low countries seem partly to have been gained from the sea, and partly to be made up of the plains of the Yssel, the Rhine, the Maese and the Schelde united. To Utrecht nothing but plains are seen, a rich black mould, wet, lower than the level of the waters which intersect it; almost entirely in grass; few or no farm-houses, as the business of grazing requires few laborers. The canal is lined with country houses, which bespeak the wealth and cleanliness of the country; but generally in an uncouth state, and exhibiting no regular architecture. After passing Utrecht, the hills north-east of the Rhine come into view, and gather in towards the river, till at Wyck Dursted they are within three or four miles, and at Amelengen they join the river. The plains, after passing Utrecht, become more sandy; the hills are very poor and sandy, generally waste in broom, sometimes a little corn. The plains are in corn, grass, and willow. The plantations of the latter are immense, and give it the air of an uncultivated country. There are now few châteaux; farm-houses abound, built generally of brick, and covered with tile or thatch. There are some apple-trees, but no forest; a few inclosures of willow wattling. In the gardens are hedges of beach, one foot apart, which, not losing its old leaves till they are pushed off in the spring by the young ones, gives the shelter of evergreens. The Rhine is here about three hundred yards wide, and the road to Nimeguen passing it a little below Wattelingen, leaves Hetern in sight on the left. On this side, the plains of the Rhine, the Ling, and the Waal unite. The Rhine and Waal are crossed on vibrating boats, the rope supported by a line of seven little barks. The platform by which you go on to the ferry-boat is supported by boats. The view from the hill at Cress is sublime. It commands the Waal, and extends far up the Rhine. That also up and down the Waal from the Bellevue of Nimeguen, is very fine. The château here is pretended to have lodged Julius Cæsar. This is giving it an antiquity of at least eighteen centuries, which must be apocryphal. Some few sheep to-day, which were feeding in turnip patches.

April 1st. *Cranenburg. Cleves. Santen. Reynberg. Hoogstraat.* The transition from ease and opulence to extreme poverty is remarkable on crossing the line between the Dutch and Prussian territories. The soil and climate are the same; the governments alone differ. With the poverty, the fear also of slaves is visible in the faces of the Prussian subjects. There is an improvement, however, in the physiognomy, especially could it be a little brightened up. The road leads generally over the hills, but sometimes through skirts of the plains of the Rhine. These are always extensive and good. They want manure, being visibly worn down. The hills are almost always sandy, barren, uncultivated, and insusceptible of culture, covered with broom and moss; here and there a little indifferent forest, which is sometimes of beach. The plains are principally in corn; some grass and willow. There are no châteaux, nor houses that bespeak the existence even of a middle class. Universal and equal poverty overspreads the whole. In the villages, too, which seem to be falling down, the over-proportion of women is evident. The cultivators seem to live on their farms. The farm-houses are of mud, the better sort of brick; all covered over with thatch. Cleves is little more than a village. If there are shops or magazines of merchandise in it, they show little. Here and there at a window some small articles are hung up within the glass. The goose-berry beginning to leaf.

April 2d. Passed the Rhine at *Essenberg.* It is there about a quarter of a mile wide, or five hundred yards. It is crossed in a scow with sails. The wind being on the quarter, we were eight or ten minutes only in the passage. Duysberg is but a village in fact, walled in; the buildings mostly of brick. No new ones, which indicate a thriving state. I had understood that near that were remains of the encampment of Varus, in which he and his legions fell by the arms of Arminius (in the time of Tiberius I think it was), but there was not a person to be found in Duysberg who could understand either English, French, Italian, or Latin. So I could make no inquiry.

From *Duysberg* to *Dusseldorf* the road leads sometimes over the hills, sometimes through the plains of the Rhine, the quality of which are as before described. On the hills, how-ever, are considerable groves of oak, of spontaneous growth, which seem to be of more than a century; but the soil being barren, the trees, though high, are crooked and knotty. The undergrowth is broom and moss. In the plains is corn en-tirely. As they are become rather sandy for grass, there are no inclosures on the Rhine at all. The houses are poor and ruin-ous, mostly of brick, and scantling mixed. A good deal of grape cultivated.

Dusseldorf. The gallery of paintings is sublime, particularly the room of Vanderwerff. The plains from Dusseldorf to Co-logne are much more extensive, and go off in barren downs at some distance from the river. These downs extend far, ac-cording to appearance. They are manuring the plains with lime. A gate at the Elector's château on this road in this form. We cross at Cologne on a pendulum boat. I observe the hog of this country (Westphalia), of which the celebrated ham is made, is tall, gaunt, and with heavy lop ears. Fatted at a year old, would weigh one hundred or one hundred and twenty pounds. At two years old, two hundred pounds. Their principal food is acorns. The pork, fresh, sells at two and a half pence sterling the pound. The hams, ready made, at eight and a half pence sterling the pound. One hundred and six pounds of this coun-try is equal to one hundred pounds of Holland. About four pounds of fine Holland salt is put on one hundred pounds of pork. It is smoked in a room which has no chimney. Well-informed people here tell me there is no other part of the world where the bacon is smoked. They do not know that we do it. Cologne is the principal market of exportation. They find that the small hog makes the sweetest meat.

Cologne is a sovereign city, having no territory out of its walls. It contains about sixty thousand inhabitants; appears to have much commerce, and to abound with poor. Its com-merce is principally in the hands of Protestants, of whom there are about sixty houses in the city. They are extremely restricted in their operations, and otherwise oppressed in every form by the government, which is Catholic, and exces-sively intolerant. Their Senate, some time ago, by a majority of twenty-two to eighteen, allowed them to have a church;

but it is believed this privilege will be revoked. There are about two hundred and fifty Catholic churches in the city. The Rhine is here about four hundred yards wide. This city is in 51° latitude, wanting about 6′. Here the vines begin, and it is the most northern spot on the earth on which wine is made. Their first grapes came from Orleans, since that from Alsace, Champagne, &c. It is thirty-two years only since the first vines were sent from Cassel, near Mayence, to the Cape of Good Hope, of which the Cape wine is now made. Afterwards new supplies were sent from the same quarter. That I suppose is the most southern spot on the globe where wine is made, and it is singular that the same vine should have furnished two wines as much opposed to each other in quality as in situation. I was addressed here by Mr. Damen, of Amsterdam, to Mr. Jean Jaques Peuchen, of this place, Merchant.

April 4th. *Cologne. Bonne. Andernach. Coblentz.* I saw many walnut trees to-day in the open fields. It would seem as if this tree and wine required the same climate. The soil begins now to be reddish, both on the hills and in the plains. Those from Cologne to Bonne extend about three miles from the river on each side; but a little above Bonne they become contracted, and continue from thence to be from one mile to nothing, comprehending both sides of the river. They are in corn, some clover and rape, and many vines. These are planted in rows three feet apart both ways. The vine is left about six or eight feet high, and stuck with poles ten or twelve feet high. To these poles they are tied in two places, at the height of about two and four feet. They are now performing this operation. The hills are generally excessively steep, a great proportion of them barren; the rest in vines principally, sometimes small patches of corn. In the plains, though rich, I observed they dung their vines plentifully; and it is observed here, as elsewhere, that the plains yield much wine, but bad. The good is furnished from the hills. The walnut, willow, and apple tree beginning to leaf.

Andernach is the port on the Rhine to which the famous millstones of Cologne are brought; the quarry, as some say, being at Mendich, three or four leagues from thence. I suppose they have been called Cologne millstones, because the merchants of that place having the most extensive correspondence, have usually sent them to all parts of the world. I observed great collections of them at Cologne. This is one account.

April 5. *Coblentz. Nassau.* Another account is, that these stones are cut at Triers and brought down the Moselle. I could not learn the price of them at the quarry; but I was shown a grindstone of the same stone, five feet diameter, which cost at Triers six florins. It was of but half the thickness of a millstone. I supposed, therefore, that two millstones would cost about as much as three of these grindstones, *i. e.* about a guinea and a half. This country abounds with slate.

The best Moselle wines are made about fifteen leagues from hence, in an excessively mountainous country. The first quality (without any comparison) is that made on the mountain of Brownberg, adjoining to the village of Dusmond; and the best crops is that of the Baron Breidbach Burrhesheim, grand chambellan et grand Baillif de Coblentz. His Receveur, of the name of Mayer, lives at Dusmond. The last fine year was 1783, which sells now at fifty louis the foudre, which contains six aumes of one hundred and seventy bottles each, equal about one thousand one hundred and ten bottles. This is about twenty-two sous Tournois the bottle. In general, the Baron Burresheim's crops will sell as soon as made, say at the vintage, for one hundred and thirty, one hundred and forty, and one hundred and fifty ecus the foudre (the ecu is one and a half florin of Holland), say two hundred. 2. Vialen is the second quality, and sells new at one hundred and twenty ecus the foudre. 3. Crach-Bispost is the third, and sells for about one hundred and five ecus. I compared Crach of 1783 with Baron Burrhesheim's of the same year. The latter is quite clear of acid, stronger, and very sensibly the best. 4. Selting, which sells at one hundred ecus. 5. Kous-Berncastle, the fifth quality, sells at eighty or ninety. After this there is a gradation of qualities down to thirty ecus. These wines must be five or six years old before they are quite ripe for drinking. One thousand plants yield a foudre of wine a year in the most plentiful vineyards. In other vineyards, it will take two thousand or two thousand and five hundred plants to yield a foudre. The culture of one thousand plants costs about one louis a year. A day's labor of a man is paid in winter twenty kreitzers (*i. e.* one-third of a florin), in summer twenty-six; a woman's is half that. The red wines of this country are very indifferent, and will not keep. The Moselle is here from one hundred to two hundred yards wide; the Rhine three hundred to four hundred. A jessamine in the Count de Moustier's garden in leaf.

In the Elector of Treves' palace at *Coblentz*, are large rooms very well warmed by warm air conveyed from an oven below, through tubes which open into the rooms. An oil and vinegar cruet in this form: At Coblentz we pass the river on a pendulum boat, and the road to Nassau is over tremendous hills, on which is here and there a little corn, more vines, but mostly barren. In some of these barrens are forests of beach and oak, tolerably large, but crooked and knotty; the undergrowth beach brush, broom, and moss. The soil of the plains, and of the hills where they are cultivable, is reddish. Nassau is a village the whole rents of which should not amount to more than a hundred or two guineas. Yet it gives the title of Prince to the house of Orange to which it belongs.

April 6th. *Nassau. Schwelbach. Wisbaden. Hocheim. Frankfort.* The road from Nassau to Schwelbach is over hills, or rather mountains, both high and steep; always poor, and above half of them barren in beach and oak. At Schwelbach there is some chesnut. The other parts are either in winter grain, or preparing for that of the spring. Between Schwelbach and Wisbaden we come in sight of the plains of the Rhine, which are very extensive. From hence the lands, both high and low, are very fine, in corn, vines, and fruit trees. The country has the appearance of wealth, especially in the approach to Frankfort.

April 7th. *Frankfort.* Among the poultry, I have seen no turkies in Germany till I arrive at this place. The Stork, or Crane, is very commonly tame here. It is a miserable, dirty, ill-looking bird. The Lutheran is the reigning religion here, and is equally intolerant to the Catholic and Calvinist, excluding them from the free corps.

April 8th. *Frankfort. Hanau.* The road goes through the plains of the Maine, which are mulatto, and very fine. They are well cultivated till you pass the line between the republic and the landgraviate of Hesse, when you immediately see the effect of the difference of government, notwithstanding the tendency which the neighborhood of such a commercial town as Frankfort has to counteract the effects of tyranny in its vicinities, and to animate them in spite of oppression. In Frankfort all is life, bustle, and motion; in Hanau the silence and quiet of the mansions of the dead. Nobody is seen moving in the streets; every door is shut; no sound of the saw, the hammer, or other utensil of industry. The drum and fife is all that is heard. The streets are cleaner than a German floor, because nobody passes them. At Williamsbath, near Hanau, is a country seat of the Landgrave. There is a ruin which is clever. It presents the remains of an old castle.

The ground plan is in this form: ⊏⊐ The upper story in this: ◯ A circular room of thirty-one and a half feet diameter within. The four little square towers at the corners finish at the floor of the upper story, so as to be only platforms to walk out on. Over the circular room is a platform also, which is covered by the broken parapet which once crowned the top, but is now fallen off some parts, whilst the other parts remain. I like better, however, the form of the ruin at Hagley, in England, which was thus. There is a centry box here, covered over with bark, so as to look exactly like the trunk of an old tree. This is a good idea; and may be of much avail in a garden. There is a hermitage in which is a good figure of a hermit in plaster, colored to the life, with a table and book before him, in the attitude of reading and contemplation. In a little cell is his bed; in another his books, some tools, &c.; in another his little provision of firewood, &c. There is a monument erected to the son of the present landgrave, in the form of a pyramid, the base of which is eighteen and a half feet. The side declines from the perpendicular about twenty-two and a half degrees. An arch is carried through it both ways so as to present a door in each side. In the middle of this, at the crossing of the two arches, is a marble monument with this inscription: "ante tempus." He died at twelve years of age. Between Hanau and Frankfort, in sight of the road, is the village of

Bergen, where was fought the battle of Bergen in the war before last. Things worth noting here are: 1. A folding ladder. 2. Manner of packing china cups and saucers, the former in a circle within the latter. 3. The marks of different manufactures of china, to wit: Dresden with two swords. Hecks with a wheel with ⚹ , Frankendaal with 🜍 (for Charles Theodore), and a ♔ over it. Berlin with   4. The top rail of a wagon supported by the washers on the ends of the axle-trees.

April 10th. *Frankfort. Hocheim. Mayence.* The little tyrants round about having disarmed their people, and made it very criminal to kill game, one knows when they quit the territory of Frankfort by the quantity of game which is seen. In the Republic, everybody being allowed to be armed, and to hunt on their own lands, there is very little game left in its territory. The hog hereabouts resembles extremely the little hog of Virginia. Round like that, a small head, and short upright ears. This makes the ham of Mayence so much esteemed at Paris.

We cross the Rhine at Mayence on a bridge one thousand eight hundred and forty feet long, supported by forty-seven boats. It is not in a direct line, but curved up against the stream; which may strengthen it if the difference between the upper and lower curve be sensible, if the planks of the floor be thick, well jointed together, and forming sectors of circles, so as to act on the whole as the stones of an arch. But it has by no means this appearance. Near one end, one of the boats has an axis in peritrochio, and a chain, by which it may be let drop down stream some distance, with the portion of the floor belonging to it, so as to let a vessel through. Then it is wound up again into place, and to consolidate it the more with the adjoining parts, the loose section is a little higher, and has at each end a folding stage, which folds back on it when it moves down, and when brought up again into place, these stages are folded over on the bridge. This whole operation takes but four or five minutes. In the winter the bridge is taken away entirely, on account of the ice. And then everything passes on the ice, through the whole winter.

April 11th. *Mayence. Rudesheim. Johansberg. Markebrom.* The women do everything here. They dig the earth, plough, saw, cut and split wood, row, tow the batteaux, &c. In a small but dull kind of batteau, with two hands rowing with a kind of large paddle, and a square sail, but scarcely a breath of wind, we went down the river at the rate of five miles an hour, making it three and a half hours to Rudesheim. The floats of wood which go with the current only, go one mile and a half an hour. They go night and day. There are five boat-mills abreast here. Their floats seem to be about eight feet broad. The Rhine yields salmon, carp, pike, and perch, and the little rivers running into it yield speckled trout. The plains from Maintz to Rudesheim are good and in corn; the hills mostly in vines. The banks of the river are so low that, standing up in the batteau, I could generally see what was in the plains. Yet they are seldom overflowed.

Though they begin to make wine, as has been said, at Cologne, and continue it up the river indefinitely, yet it is only from Rudesheim to Hocheim that wines of the very first qual-

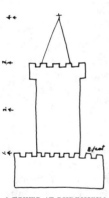

A TOWER AT RUDESHEIM.

ity are made. The river happens there to run due east and west, so as to give its hills on that side a southern aspect. And even in this canton, it is only Hocheim, Johansberg, and Rudesheim, that are considered as of the very first quality. Johansberg is a little mountain (berg signifies mountain), whereon is a religious house, about fifteen miles below Mayence, and near the village of Vingel. It has a southern aspect, the soil a barren mulatto clay, mixed with a good deal of stone, and some slate. This wine used to be but on a par with Hocheim and Rudesheim; but the place having come to the Bishop of Fulda, he improved its culture so as to render it stronger; and since the year 1775, it sells at double the price of the other two. It has none of the acid of the Hocheim and other Rhenish wines. There are about sixty tons made in a good year, which sell, as soon as of a drinkable age, at one thousand franks each. The tun here contains seven and a-half aumes of one hundred and seventy bottles each. Rudesheim is a village of about eighteen or twenty miles below Mayence. Its fine wines are made on the hills about a mile below the village, which look to the south, and on the middle and lower parts of them. They are terraced. The soil is gray, about one-half of slate and rotten stone, the other half of barren clay, excessively steep. Just behind the village also is a little spot, called Hinder House, belonging to the Counts of Sicken and Oschstein, whereon each makes about a ton of wine of the very first quality. This spot extends from the bottom to the top of the hill. The vignerons of Rudesheim dung their wines about once in five or six years, putting a one-horse tumbrel load of dung on every twelve feet square. One thousand plants yield about four aumes in a good year. The best crops are,

The Chanoines of Mayence, who make . . . 15	pieces of 7½ aumes.	
Le Comte de Sicken 6	"	"
Le Comte d'Oschstein 9	"	"
L'Electeur de Mayence 6	"	"
Le Comte de Meternisch 6	"	"
Monsieur de Boze 5	"	"
M. Ackerman, baliff et aubergiste des 3 couronnes 8	"	"
M. Ackerman le fils, aubergiste à la couronne . 5	"	"
M. Lynn, aubergiste de l'ange 5	"	"
Baron de Wetzel 7	"	"
Convent de Mariahousen, des religieuses Benedictines 7	"	"
M. Johan Yung 8	"	"
M. de Rieden 5	"	"
92		

These wines begin to be drinkable at about five years old. The proprietors sell them old or young, according to the prices offered, and according to their own want of money. There is always a little difference between different casks, and therefore when you choose and buy a single cask, you pay three, four, five or six hundred florins for it. They are not at all acid, and to my taste much preferable to Hocheim, though but of the same price. Hocheim is a village about three miles above Mayence, on the Maine, where it empties into the Rhine. The spot whereon the good wine is made is the hill side from the church down to the plain, a gentle slope of about a quarter of a mile wide, and extending half a mile towards Mayence. It is of south-western aspect, very poor, sometimes gray, sometimes mulatto, with a moderate mixture of small broken stone. The wines are planted three feet apart, and stuck with sticks about six feet high. The wine, too, is cut at that height. They are dunged once in three or four years. One thousand plants yield from one to two aumes a year: they begin to yield a little at three years old, and continue to one hundred years, unless sooner killed by a cold winter. Dick, keeper of the Rothen-house tavern at Frankfort, a great wine merchant, who has between three and four hundred tons of wine in his cellars, tells me that Hocheim of the year 1783, sold, as soon as it was made, at ninety florins the aume, Rudesheim of the same year, as soon as made, at one hundred and fifteen florins, and Markebronn seventy florins. But a peasant of Hocheim tells me that the best crops of Hocheim in the good years, when sold new, sell but for about thirty-two or thirty-three florins the aume; but that it is only the poorer proprietors who sell new. The fine crops are,

Count Ingleheim about . . 10 tuns.		
Baron d'Alberg . . . . 8 "		All of these keep till about fif-
Count Schimbon . . . 14 "		teen years old, before they sell,
The Chanoines of Mayence . 18 "		unless they are offered a very
Counsellor Schik de Vetsler . 15 "		good price sooner.
Convent of Jacobsberg . . 8 "		
The Chanoine of Fechbach . 10 "		
The Carmelites of Frankfort. 8 "		Who only sell by the bottle in their own tavern in Frankfort.
The Bailiff of Hocheim . . 11 "		Who sells at three or four years old.
Zimmerman, a bourgeois. . 4 "		These being poor, sell new.
Feldman, a carpenter. . . 2 "		

Markebronn (bronn signifies a spring, and is probably of affinity with the Scotch word, burn) is a little canton in the same range of hills, adjoining to the village of Hagenheim, about three miles above Johansberg, subject to the elector of Mayence. It is a sloping hill side of southern aspect, mulatto, poor, and mixed with some stone. This yields wine of the second quality.

April 12th. *Mayence. Oppenheim. Dorms. Manheim.* On the road between Mayence and Oppenheim are three cantons, which are also esteemed as yielding wines of the second qual-

ity. These are Laudenheim, Bodenheim, and Nierstein. Laudenheim is a village about four or five miles from Mayence.
Its wines are made on a steep hill side, the soil of which is
gray, poor and mixed with some stone. The river there happens to make a short turn to the south-west, so as to present
its hills to the south-east. Bodenheim is a village nine miles,
and Nierstein another about ten or eleven miles from Mayence. Here, too, the river is north-east and south-west, so as
to give the hills between these villages a south-east aspect;
and at Thierstein, a valley making off, brings the face of the
hill round to the south. The hills between these villages are
almost perpendicular, of a vermilion red, very poor, and having as much rotten stone as earth. It is to be observed that
these are the only cantons on the south side of the river which
yield good wine, the hills on this side being generally exposed
to the cold winds, and turned from the sun. The annexed bill
of prices current, will give an idea of the estimation of these
wines respectively.

With respect to the grapes in this country, there are three
kinds in use for making white wine, (for I take no notice of
the red wines, as being absolutely worthless.) 1. The Klempe-
rien, of which the inferior qualities of Rhenish wines are
made, and is cultivated because of its hardness. The wines of
this grape descend as low as one hundred florins the tun of
eight aumes. 2. The Rhysslin grape, which grows only from
Hocheim down to Rudesheim. This is small and delicate, and
therefore succeeds only in this chosen spot. Even at Rudesheim it yields a fine wine only in the little spot called Hinder
House, before mentioned; the mass of good wines made at
Rudesheim, below the village, being of the third kind of
grape, which is called the Orleans grape.

To Oppenheim the plains of the Rhine and Maine are
united. From that place we see the commencement of the
Berg-strasse, or mountains which separate at first the plains
of the Rhine and Maine, then cross the Neckar at Heidelberg,
and from thence forms the separation between the plains of
the Neckar and Rhine, leaving those of the Rhine about ten
or twelve miles wide. These plains are sometimes black, sometimes mulatto, always rich. They are in corn, potatoes, and

some willow. On the other side again, that is, on the west side, the hills keep at first close to the river. They are about one hundred and fifty, or two hundred feet high, sloping, red, good, and mostly in vines. Above Oppenheim, they begin to go off till they join the mountains of Lorraine and Alsace, which separate the waters of the Moselle and Rhine, leaving to the whole valley of the Rhine about twenty or twenty-five miles breadth. About Worms these plains are sandy, poor, and often covered only with small pine.

April 13th. *Manheim*. There is a bridge over the Rhine here, supported on thirty-nine boats, and one over the Neckar on eleven boats. The bridge over the Rhine is twenty-one and a half feet wide from rail to rail. The boats are four feet deep, fifty-two feet long, and nine feet eight inches broad. The space between boat and boat is eighteen feet ten inches. From these data the length of the bridge should be 9ft. 8in. + 18ft. 10in. × 40 = 1140 feet. In order to let vessels pass through, two boats well framed together, with their flooring, are made to fall down stream together. Here, too, they make good ham. It is fattened on round potatoes and Indian corn. The farmers smoke what is for their own use in their chimneys. When it is made for sale, and in greater quantities than the chimney will hold, they make the smoke of the chimney pass into an adjoining loft, or apartment, from which it has no issue; and here they hang their hams.

An economical curtain bedstead. The bedstead is seven feet by four feet two inches. From each leg there goes up an iron rod three-eighths of an inch in diameter. Those from the legs at the foot of the bed meeting at top as in the margin, and

those from the head meeting in like manner, so that the two at the foot form one point, and the two at the head another. On these points lays an oval iron rod, whose long diameter is five feet, and short one three feet one inch. There is a hole through this rod at each end, by which it goes on firm on the point of the upright rods. Then a nut screws it down firmly. Ten breadths of stuff two feet ten inches wide, and eight feet six inches long, form the curtains. There is no top nor vallons. The rings are fastened within two and a half or three inches of the top on the inside, which two and a half or three inches stand up, and are an ornament somewhat like a ruffle.

I have observed all along the Rhine that they make the oxen draw by the horns. A pair of very handsome chariot horses, large, bay, and seven years old, sell for fifty louis. One pound of beef sells for eight kreitzers, (*i. e.* eight sixtieths of a florin;) one pound of mutton or veal, six kreitzers; one pound of pork, seven and a half kreitzers; one pound of ham, twelve kreitzers; one pound of fine wheat bread, two kreitzers; one pound of butter, twenty kreitzers; one hundred and sixty pounds of wheat, six francs; one hundred and sixty pounds of maize, five francs; one hundred and sixty pounds of potatoes, one franc; one hundred pounds of hay, one franc; a cord of wood (which is 4 4 and 6 feet), seven francs; a laborer by the day receives twenty-four kreitzers, and feeds himself. A journee or arpent of land (which is eight by two hundred steps), such as the middling plains of the Rhine, will sell for two hundred francs. There are more soldiers here than other inhabitants, to wit: six thousand soldiers and four thousand males of full age of the citizens, the whole number of whom is reckoned at twenty thousand.

April 14th. *Manheim. Dossenheim. Heidelberg. Schwetzingen. Manheim.* The elector placed, in 1768, two males and five females of the Angora goat at Dossenheim, which is at the foot of the Bergstrasse mountains. He sold twenty-five last year, and has now seventy. They are removed into the mountains four leagues beyond Dossenheim. Heidelberg is on the Neckar just where it issues from the Bergstrasse mountains, occupying the first skirt of plain which it forms. The château is up the hill a considerable height. The gardens lie above the château, climbing up the mountain in terraces. This château is the most noble ruin I have ever seen, having been reduced to that state by the French in the time of Louis XIV., 1693. Nothing remains under cover but the chapel. The situation is romantic and pleasing beyond expression. It is on a great scale much like the situation of Petrarch's château, at Vaucluse, on a small one. The climate, too, is like that of Italy. The apple, the pear, cherry, peach, apricot, and almond, are all in bloom. There is a station in the garden to which the château re-echoes distinctly four syllables. The famous ton of Heidelberg was new built in 1751, and made to contain thirty foudres more than the ancient one. It is said to contain two hundred and thirty-six foudres of one thousand two hundred bottles each. I measured it, and found its length external to be twenty-eight feet ten inches; its diameter at the end twenty feet three inches; the thickness of the staves seven and a half inches; thickness of the hoops seven and a half inches; besides a great deal of external framing. There is no wine in it now. The gardens at Schwetzingen show how much money may be laid out to make an ugly thing. What is called the English quarter, however, relieves the eye from the straight rows of trees, round and square basins, which constitute the great mass of the garden. There are some tolerable morsels of Grecian architecture, and a good ruin. The Aviary, too, is clever. It consists of cells of about eight feet wide, arranged round, and looking into a circular area of about forty or fifty feet diameter. The cells have doors both of wire and glass, and have small shrubs in them. The plains of the Rhine on this side are twelve miles wide, bounded by the Bergstrasse mountains. These appear to be eight hundred or a thousand feet high; the lower part in vines, from which is made what is called the vin de Nichar; the upper in chesnut. There are some cultivated spots however, quite to the top. The plains are generally mulatto, in corn principally; they are planting potatoes in some parts, and leaving others open for maize

and tobacco. Many peach and other fruit trees on the lower part of the mountain. The paths on some parts of these mountains are somewhat in the style represented in the margin.

Manheim. Kaeferthal. Manheim. Just beyond Kaeferthal is an extensive, sandy waste, planted in pine, in which the elector has about two hundred sangliers, tamed. I saw about fifty; the heavies I am told, would weigh about three hundred pounds. They are fed on round potatoes, and range in the forest of pines. At the village of Kaeferthal is a plantation of rhubarb, begun in 1769 by a private company. It contains twenty arpens or jourries, and its culture costs about four or five hundred francs a year; it sometimes employs forty or fifty laborers at a time. The best age to sell the rhubarb at is the fifth or sixth year, but the sale being dull, they keep it sometimes to the tenth year; they find it best to let it remain in the ground. They sell about two hundred kentals a year at two or three francs a pound, and could sell double that quantity from the ground if they could find a market. The apothecaries of Francfort and of England are the principal buyers. It is in beds, resembling lettice-beds; the plants four, five or six feet apart. When dug, a thread is passed through every piece of root, and it is hung separate in a kind of rack; when dry it is rasped; what comes off is given to the cattle.

April 15. *Manheim. Spire. Carlsruhe.* The valley preserves its width, extending on each side of the river about ten or twelve miles, but the soil loses much in its quality, becoming sandy and lean, often barren and overgrown with pine thicket. At Spire is nothing remarkable. Between that and Carlsruhe we pass the Rhine in a common skow with oars, where it is between three and four hundred yards wide. Carlsruhe is the residence of the Margrave of Baden, a sovereign prince. His château is built in the midst of a natural forest of several leagues diameter, and of the best trees I have seen in these countries: they are mostly oak, and would be deemed but indifferent in America. A great deal of money has been spent to do more harm than good to the ground—cutting a number of straight allies through the forest. He has a pheasantry of the gold and silver kind, the latter very tame, but the former excessively shy. A little inclosure of stone, two and a half feet high and thirty feet diameter, in which are two tamed beavers. There is a pond of fifteen feet diameter in the centre, and at each end a little cell for them to retire into, which is stowed with boughs and twigs with leaves on them, which is their principal food. They eat bread also;—twice a week the water is changed. They cannot get over this wall. Some cerfs of a peculiar kind, spotted like fawns, the horns remarkably long, small and sharp, with few points. I am not sure there were more than two to each main beam, and if I saw distinctly, there came out a separate and subordinate beam from the root of each. Eight angora goats—beautiful animals—all white. This town is only an appendage of the château, and but a moderate one. It is a league from Durlach, half way between that and the river. I observe they twist the flues of their stoves in any form for ornament merely, without smoking, as thus, *e. g.*

April 16. *Carlsruhe. Rastadt. Scholhoven. Bischofheim. Kehl. Strasburg.* The valley of the Rhine still preserves its breadth, but varies in quality; sometimes a rich mulatto loom, sometimes a poor sand, covered with small pine. The culture is generally corn. It is to be noted, that through the whole of my route through the Netherlands and the valley of the Rhine, there is a little red clover every here and there, and a great deal of grape cultivated. The seed of this is sold to be made into oil. The grape is now in blossom. No inclosures. The fruit trees are generally blossoming through the whole valley. The high mountains of the Bergstrasse, as also of Alsace, are covered with snow. Within this day or two, the every-day dress of the country women here is black. Rastadt is a seat also of the Margrave of Baden. Scholhoven and Kehl are in his territory, but not Bischofheim. I see no beggars since I entered his government, nor is the traveller obliged to ransom himself every moment by a chausiee gold. The roads are excellent, and made so, I presume, out of the coffers of the prince. From Cleves till I enter the Margravate of Baden, the roads have been strung with beggars—in Hesse the most, and the road tax very heavy. We pay it cheerfully, however, through the territory of Francfort and thence up the Rhine, because fine gravelled roads are kept up; but through the Prussian, and other parts of the road below Francfort, the roads are only as made by the carriages, there not appearing to have been ever a day's work employed on them. At Strasburgh we pass the Rhine on a wooden bridge.

At *Brussels and Antwerp*, the fuel is pit-coal, dug in Brabant. Through all Holland it is turf. From Cleves to Cologne it is pit-coal brought from England. They burn it in open stoves. From thence it is wood, burnt in close stoves, till you get to Strasburg, where the open chimney comes again into use.

April 16th, 17th, 18th. *Strasburg*. The vin de paille is made in the neighborhood of Colmar, in Alsace, about ———— from this place. It takes its name from the circumstance of spreading the grapes on straw, where they are preserved till spring, and then made into wine. The little juice then remaining in them makes a rich sweet wine, but the dearest in the world, without being the best by any means. They charge nine florins the bottle for it in the taverns of Strasburg. It is the caprice of wealth alone which continues so losing an operation. This wine is sought because dear; while the better wine of Frontignan is rarely seen at a good table because it is cheap.

Strasburg. Saverne. Phalsbourg. As far as Saverne the country is in waiving hills and hollows; red, rich enough; mostly in small grain, but some vines; a little stone. From Saverne to Phalsbourg we cross a considerable mountain, which takes an hour to rise it.

April 19th. *Phalsbourg. Fenestrange. Moyenvic. Nancy.* Asparagus to-day at Moyenvic. The country is always either mountainous or hilly; red, tolerably good, and in small grain. On the hills about Fenestrange, Moyenvic, and Nancy, are some small vineyards where a bad wine is made. No inclosures. Some good sheep, indifferent cattle, and small horses. The most forest I have seen in France, principally of beech, pretty large. The houses, as in Germany, are of scantling, filled in with wicker and mortar, and covered either with thatch or tiles. The people, too, here as there, are gathered in villages. Oxen plough here with collars and hames. The awkward figure of their mould-board leads one to consider what should be its form. The offices of the mould-board are to receive the sod after the share has cut under it, to raise it gradually, and to reverse it. The fore-end of it then, should be horizontal to enter under the sod, and the hind end perpendicular to throw it over; the intermediate surface changing gradually from the horizontal to the perpendicular. It should be as wide as the furrow, and of a length suited to the construction of the plough. The following would seem a good method of making it: Take a block, whose length, breadth and thickness, is that of your intended mould-board, suppose two and a half feet long and eight inches broad and thick. Draw the lines *a d* and *c d*, figure 1, with a saw, the toothed edge of which is straight, enter at *a* and cut on, guiding the hind part of the saw on the line *a b*, and the fore part on the line *a d*, till the saw reaches the points *c* and *d*, then enter it at *c* and cut on, guiding it by the lines *c b* and *c d* till it reaches the points *b* and *d*. The quarter, *a b c d*, will then be completely cut out, and the diagonal from *d* to *b* laid bare. The piece may now be represented as in figure 2. Then saw in transversely at every two inches till the saw reaches the line *c e*, and the diagonal *b d*, and cut out the pieces with an adze. The upper surface will thus be formed. With a gauge opened to eight inches, and guided by the lines *c e*, scribe the upper edge of the board from *d b*, cut that edge perpendicular to the face of the board, and scribe it of the proper thickness. Then form the underside by the upper, by cutting transversely with the saw and taking out the piece with an adze. As the upper edge of the wing of the share rises a little, the fore end of the board, *b c*, will rise as much from a strict horizontal position, and will throw the hind end, *e d*, exactly as much beyond the perpendicular, so as to promote the reversing of the sod. The women here, as in Germany, do all sorts of work. While one considers them as useful and rational companions, one cannot forget that they are also objects of our pleasures; nor can they ever forget it. While employed in dirt and drudgery, some tag of a ribbon, some ring, or bit of bracelet, earbob or necklace, or something of that kind, will show that the desire of pleasing is never suspended in them. It is an honorable circumstance for man, that the first moment he is at his ease, he allots the internal employments to his female partner, and takes the external on himself. And this circumstance, or its reverse, is a pretty good indication that a people are, or are not at their ease. Among the Indians, this indication fails from a particular cause: every Indian man is a soldier or warrior, and the whole body of warriors constitute a standing army, always employed in war or hunting. To support that army, there remain no laborers but the women. Here, then, is so heavy a military establishment, that the civil part of the nation is reduced to women only. But this is a barbarous perversion of the natural destination of the two sexes. Women are formed by nature for attentions, not for hard labor. A woman never forgets one of the numerous train of little offices which belong to her. A man forgets often.

April 20th. *Nancy. Toule. Void. Ligny en Barrois. Bar le Duc. St. Dizier.* Nancy itself is a neat little town, and its environs very agreeable. The valley of the little branch of the Moselle, on which it is, is about a mile wide: the road then crossing the head-waters of the Moselle, the Maes, and the Marne, the country is very hilly, and perhaps a third of it poor and in forests of beech: the other two-thirds from poor up to middling, red, and stony. Almost entirely in corn, now and then only some vines on the hills. The Moselle at Toule is thirty or forty yards wide: the Maese near Void about half that: the Marne at St. Dizier about forty yards. They all make good plains of from a quarter of a mile to a mile wide. The hills of the Maese abound with chalk. The rocks coming down from the tops of the hills, on all the road of this day, at regular intervals like the ribs of an animal, have a very irregular appearance. Considerable flocks of sheep and asses, and, in the approach to St. Dizier, great plantations of apple and cherry trees; here and there peach tree, all in general bloom. The roads through Lorraine are strung with beggars.

April 21st. *St. Dizier. Vitry le Français. Chalons sur Marne. Epernay.* The plains of the Marne and Sault uniting, appear boundless to the eye till we approach their confluence at Vitry, where the hills come in on the right; after that the plains are generally about a mile, mulatto, of middling quality, sometimes stony. Sometimes the ground goes off from the river so sloping, that one does not know whether to call it high or low land. The hills are mulatto also, but whitish, occasioned by the quantity of chalk which seems to constitute their universal base. They are poor, and principally in vines. The streams of water are of the color of milk, occasioned by the chalk also. No inclosures, some flocks of sheep; children gathering dung in the roads. Here and there a château; but none considerable.

April 22d. *Epernay.* The hills abound with chalk. Of this they make lime, not so strong as stone lime, and therefore to be used in greater proportion. They cut the blocks into regular forms also, like stone, and build houses of it. The common earth too, well impregnated with this, is made into mortar, moulded in the form of brick, dried in the sun, and houses built of them which last one hundred or two hundred years. The plains here are a mile wide, red, good, in corn, clover, Luzerne, St. Foin. The hills are in vines, and this being precisely the canton where the most celebrated wines of Champagne are made, details must be entered into. Remember, however, that they will always relate to the white wines, unless where the red are expressly mentioned. The reason is that their red wines, though much esteemed on the spot, are by no means esteemed elsewhere equally with their white; nor do they merit equal esteem.

A Topographical sketch of the position of the wine villages, the course of the hills, and consequently the aspect of the vine-yards.

Soil, meagre, mulatto clay, mixed with small broken stone, and a little hue of chalk. Very dry.

Aspect, may be better seen by the annexed diagram. The

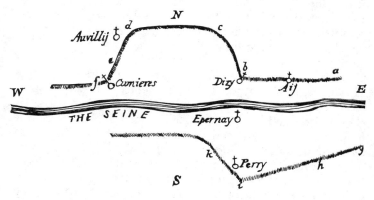

wine of Aij is made from *a* to *b*, those of Dizy from *b* to *c*, Auvillij *d* to *e*, Cumieres *e* to *f*, Epernay *g* to *h*, Perij *i* to *k*. The hills are generally about two hundred and fifty feet high. The good wine is made only in the middle region. The lower region, however, is better than the upper; because this last is exposed to cold winds, and a colder atmosphere.

Culture. The vines are planted two feet apart. Afterwards they are multiplied (provignés). When a stock puts out two shoots they lay them down, spread them open and cover them with earth, so as to have in the end about a plant for every square foot. For performing this operation they have a hook, of this shape, ⌒ and nine inches long, which, being stuck in the ground, holds down the main stock, while the laborer separates and covers the new shoot. They leave two buds above the ground. When the vine has shot up high enough, they stick it with split sticks of oak, from an inch to an inch and a half square, and four feet long, and tie the vine to its stick with straw. These sticks cost two florins the hundred, and will last forty years. An arpent, one year with another, in the fine vineyards, gives twelve pieces, and in the inferior vineyards twenty-five pieces, of two hundred bottles each. An arpent of the first quality sells for three thousand florins, and there have been instances of seven thousand two hundred florins. The arpent contains one hundred verges, of twenty-two pieds square. The arpent of inferior quality sells at one thousand florins. They plant the vines in a hole about a foot deep, and fill that hole with good mould, to make the plant take. Otherwise it would perish. Afterwards, if ever they put dung, it is very little. During wheat harvest there is a month or six weeks that nothing is done in the vineyard, that is to say, from the 1st of August to the beginning of vintage. The vintage commences early in September, and lasts a month. A day's work of a laborer in the busiest season is twenty sous, and he feeds himself: in the least busy season it is fifteen sous. Corn lands are rented from four florins to twenty-four; but vine lands are never rented. The three façons (or workings) of an arpent cost fifteen florins. The whole year's expense of an arpent is worth one hundred florins.

Grapes.—The bulk of their grapes are purple, which they prefer for making even white wine. They press them very lightly, without treading or permitting them to ferment at all, for about an hour; so that it is the beginning of the running only which makes the bright wine. What follows the beginning is of a straw color, and therefore not placed on a level with the first. The last part of the juice, produced by strong pressure, is red and ordinary. They choose the bunches with as much care, to make wine of the very first quality, as if to eat. Not above one-eighth of the whole grapes will do for this purpose. The white grape, though not so fine for wine as the red, when the red can be produced, and more liable to rot in a moist season, yet grows better if the soil be excessively poor, and therefore in such a soil is preferred, or rather, is used of necessity, because there the red would not grow at all.

Wine.—The white wines are either mousseux, sparkling, or non-mousseux, still. The sparkling are little drunk in France, but are almost alone known and drunk in foreign countries. This makes so great a demand, and so certain a one, that it is the dearest by about an eighth, and therefore they endeavor to make all sparkling if they can. This is done by bottling in the spring, from the beginning of March till June. If it succeeds, they lose abundance of bottles, from one-tenth to one-third. This is another cause increasing the price. To make the still wine, they bottle in September. This is only done when they know from some circumstance that the wine will not be sparkling. So if the spring bottling fails to make a sparkling wine, they decant it into other bottles in the fall, and it then makes the very best still wine. In this operation, it loses from one-tenth to one-twentieth by sediment. They let it stand in the bottles in this case forty-eight hours, with only a napkin spread over their mouths, but no cork. The best sparkling wine, decanted in this manner, makes the best still wine, and which will keep much longer than that originally made still by being bottled in September. The sparkling wines lose their briskness the older they are, but they gain in quality with age to a certain length. These wines are in perfection from two to ten years old, and will even be very good to fifteen. 1766 was the best year ever known. 1775 and 1776 next to that. 1783 is the last good year, and that not to be compared with those. These wines stand icing very well.

Aij. M. Dorsay makes one thousand and one hundred pieces, which sell, as soon as made, at three hundred florins, and in good years four hundred florins, in the cask. I paid in his cellar, to M. Louis, his homme d'affaires, for the remains of the year 1783, three florins ten sous the bottle. Sparkling Champagne, of the same degree of excellence, would have cost four florins, (the piece and demiqueue are the same; the feuillette is one hundred bottles.) M. le Duc makes four hundred to five hundred pieces. M. de Villermont, three hundred pieces. M. Janson, two hundred and fifty pieces. All of the first quality, red and white in equal quantities.

Auvillaij. The Benedictine monks make one thousand pieces, red and white, but three-fourths red, both of the first quality. The king's table is supplied by them. This enables them to sell at five hundred and fifty florins the piece. Though their white is hardly as good as Dorsay's, their red is the best. L'Abbatiale, belonging to the bishop of the place, makes one thousand to twelve hundred pieces, red and white, three-fourths red, at four hundred to five hundred and fifty florins, because neighbors to the monks.

Cumieres is all of the second quality, both red and white, at one hundred and fifty to two hundred florins the piece.

Epernay. Madame Jermont makes two hundred pieces at three hundred florins. M. Patelaine, one hundred and fifty pieces. M. Mare, two hundred pieces. M. Chertems, sixty pieces. M. Lauchay, fifty pieces. M. Cousin (Aubergiste de l'hôtel de Róhan à Epernay), one hundred pieces. M. Pierrot, one hundred pieces. Les Chanoines regulieres d'Epernay, two hundred pieces. Mesdames les Ursulines religieuses, one hundred pieces. M. Gilette, two hundred pieces. All of the first quality; red and white in equal quantities.

Pierrij. M. Casotte makes five hundred pieces. M. de la Motte, three hundred pieces. M. de Failli, three hundred pieces. I tasted his wine of 1779, one of the good years. It was fine, though not equal to that of M. Dorsay, of 1783. He sells it at two florins ten sous to merchants, and three florins to individuals. Les Seminaristes, one hundred and fifty pieces. M. Hoquart, two hundred pieces. All of the first quality; white and red in equal quantities.

At Cramont, also, there are some wines of the first quality made. At Avisi also, and Aucy, Le Meni, Mareuil, Verzis-Verzenni. This last place belongs to the Marquis de Sillery. The wines are carried to Sillery, and there stored, whence they are called Vins de Sillery, though not made at Sillery.

All these wines of Epernay and Pierrij sell almost as dear as

M. Dorsay's, their quality being nearly the same. There are many small proprietors who might make wine of the first quality, if they would cull their grapes, but they are too poor for this. Therefore, the proprietors before named, whose names are established, buy of the poorer ones the right to cull their vineyards, by which means they increase their quantity, as they find about one-third of the grapes will make wines of the first quality.

The lowest-priced wines of all are thirty florins the piece, red or white. They make brandy of the pumice. In very bad years, when their wines become vinegar, they are sold for six florins the piece, and made into brandy. They yield one-tenth brandy.

White Champagne is deemed good in proportion as it is silky and still. Many circumstances derange the scale of wines. The proprietor of the best vineyard, in the best year, having bad weather come upon him while he is gathering his grapes, makes a bad wine, while his neighbor, holding a more indifferent vineyard, which happens to be ingathering while the weather is good, makes a better. The M. de Casotte at Pierrij formerly was the first house. His successors, by some imperceptible change of culture, have degraded the quality of their wines. Their cellars are admirably made, being about six, eight or ten feet wide, vaulted, and extending into the ground, in a kind of labyrinth, to a prodigious distance, with an air-hole of two feet diameter every fifty feet. From the top of the vault to the surface of the earth, is from fifteen to thirty feet. I have nowhere seen cellars comparable to these. In packing their bottles, they lay on their side; then cross them at each end, they lay laths, and on these another row of bottles, heads and points; and so on. By this means, they can take out a bottle from the top, or where they will.

April 23d. *Epernay. Château Thieray. St. Jean. Meaux. Vergalant. Paris.* From Epernay to St. Jean the road leads over hills, which in the beginning are indifferent, but get better towards the last. The plains, wherever seen, are inconsiderable. After passing St. Jean, the hills become good, and the plains increase. The country about Vergalant is pretty. A skirt of a low ridge which runs in on the extensive plains of the

Marne and Seine, is very picturesque. The general bloom of fruit trees proves there are more of them than I had imagined from travelling in other seasons, when they are less distinguishable at a distance from the forest trees.

Travelling notes for Mr. Rutledge and Mr. Shippen

June 3, 1788

General Observations.—On arriving at a town, the first thing is to buy the plan of the town, and the book noting its curiosities. Walk round the ramparts when there are any, go to the top of a steeple to have a view of the town and its environs.

When you are doubting whether a thing is worth the trouble of going to see, recollect that you will never again be so near it, that you may repent the not having seen it, but can never repent having seen it. But there is an opposite extreme too, that is, the seeing too much. A judicious selection is to be aimed at, taking care that the indolence of the moment have no influence in the decision. Take care particularly not to let the porters of churches, cabinets, &c., lead you through all the little details of their profession, which will load the memory with trifles, fatigue the attention, and waste that and your time. It is difficult to confine these people to the few objects worth seeing and remembering. They wish for your money, and suppose you give it the more willingly the more they detail to you.

When one calls in the taverns for the *vin du pays*, they give what is natural and unadulterated and cheap: when *vin etrangere* is called for, it only gives a pretext for charging an extravagant price for an unwholsome stuff, very often of their own brewery. The people you will naturally see the most of will be tavern keepers, *valets de place*, and postilions. These are the hackneyed rascals of every country. Of course they must never be considered when we calculate the national character.

Objects of attention for an American.—1. Agriculture. Everything belonging to this art, and whatever has a near relation to it. Useful or agreeable animals which might be transported to America. Species of plants for the farmer's garden, according to the climate of the different States.

2. Mechanical arts, so far as they respect things necessary in America, and inconvenient to be transported thither ready-made, such as forges, stone quarries, boats, bridges, (very especially,) &c., &c.

3. Lighter mechanical arts, and manufactures. Some of these will be worth a superficial view; but circumstances rendering it impossible that America should become a manufacturing country during the time of any man now living, it would be a waste of attention to examine these minutely.

4. Gardens, peculiarly worth the attention of an American, because it is the country of all others where the noblest gardens may be made without expense. We have only to cut out the superabundant plants.

5. Architecture worth great attention. As we double our numbers every twenty years, we must double our houses. Besides, we build of such perishable materials, that one half of our houses must be rebuilt in every space of twenty years, so that in that time, houses are to be built for three-fourths of our inhabitants. It is, then, among the most important arts; and it is desirable to introduce taste into an art which shows so much.

6. Painting. Statuary. Too expensive for the state of wealth among us. It would be useless, therefore, and preposterous, for us to make ourselves connoisseurs in those arts. They are worth seeing, but not studying.

7. Politics of each country, well worth studying so far as respects internal affairs. Examine their influence on the happiness of the people. Take every possible occasion for entering into the houses of the laborers, and especially at the moments of their repast; see what they eat, how they are clothed, whether they are obliged to work too hard; whether the government or their landlord takes from them an unjust proportion of their labor; on what footing stands the property they call their own, their personal liberty, &c., &c.

8. Courts. To be seen as you would see the tower of London or menagerie of Versailles, with their lions, tigers, hyenas, and other beast of prey, standing in the same relation to their fellows. A slight acquaintance with them will suffice to show you that, under the most imposing exterior, they are the weakest and worst part of mankind. Their manners, could you ape them, would not make you beloved in your own country, nor would they improve it could you introduce them there to the exclusion of that honest simplicity now prevailing in America, and worthy of being cherished.

In these 3 vols will be found copies of the official opinions given in writing by me to Genl. Washington, while I was Secretary of State, with sometimes the documents belonging to the case. Some of these are the rough draughts, some press-copies, some fair ones. In the earlier part of my acting in that office I took no other note of the passing transactions: but, after awhile, I saw the importance of doing it, in aid of my memory. Very often therefore I made memorandums on loose scraps of paper, taken out of my pocket in the moment, and laid by to be copied fair at leisure, which however they hardly ever were. These scraps therefore, ragged, rubbed, & scribbled as they were, I had bound with the others by a binder who came into my cabinet, did it under my own eye, and without the opportunity of reading a single paper. At this day, after the lapse of 25 years, or more, from their dates, I have given to the whole a calm revisal, when the passions of the time are past away, and the reasons of the transactions act alone on the judgment. Some of the informations I had recorded are now cut out from the rest, because I have seen that they were incorrect, or doubtful, or merely personal or private, with which we have nothing to do. I should perhaps have thought the rest not worth preserving, but for their testimony against the only history of that period which pretends to have been compiled from authentic and unpublished documents. Could these documents, all, be laid open to the public eye, they might be compared, contrasted, weighed, & the truth fairly sifted out of them, for we are not to suppose that every thing found among Genl. Washington's papers is to be taken as gospel truth. Facts indeed of his own writing & inditing, must be believed by all who knew him; and opinions, which were his own, merit veneration and respect; for few men have lived whose opinions were more unbiassed and correct. Not that it is pretended he never felt bias. His passions were naturally strong; but his reason, generally, stronger. But the materials from his own pen make probably an almost insensible part of the mass of papers which fill his presses. He possessed the love, the veneration, and confidence of all. With him were deposited suspicions & certainties, rumors & realities, facts & falsehoods, by all those who were, or who wished to be thought, in correspondence with him, and by the many Anonymi who were ashamed to put their names to their slanders. From such a Congeries history may be made to wear any hue, with which the passions of the compiler, royalist or republican, may chuse to tinge it. Had Genl. Washington himself written from these materials a history of the period they embrace, it would have been a conspicuous monument of the integrity of his mind, the soundness of his judgment, and its powers of discernment between truth & falsehood; principles & pretensions. But the party feelings of his biographer, to whom after his death the collection was confided, has culled from it a composition as different from what Genl. Washington would have offered, as was the candor of the two characters during the period of the war. The partiality of this pen is displayed in lavishments of praise on certain military characters, who had done nothing military, but who afterwards, & before he wrote, had become heroes in party, altho' not in war; and in his reserve on the merits of others, who rendered signal services indeed, but did not earn his praise by apostatising in peace from the republican principles for which they had fought in war. It shews itself too in the cold indifference with which a struggle for the most animating of human objects is narrated. No act of heroism ever kindles in the mind of this writer a single aspiration in favor of the holy cause which inspired the bosom, & nerved the arm of the patriot warrior. No gloom of events, no lowering of prospects ever excites a fear for the issue of a contest which was to change the condition of man over the civilized globe. The sufferings inflicted on endeavors to vindicate the rights of humanity are related with all the frigid insensibility with which a monk would have contemplated the victims of an auto da fé. Let no man believe that Genl. Washington ever intended that his papers should be used for the suicide of the cause, for which he had lived, and for which there never was a moment in which he would not have died. The abuse of these materials is chiefly however manifested in the history of the period immediately following the establishment of the present constitution; and nearly with that my memorandums begin. Were a reader of this period to form his idea of it from this history alone, he would suppose the republican party (who were in truth endeavoring to keep the government within the line of the Constitution, and prevent it's being monarchised in practice) were a mere set of grumblers, and disorganisers, satisfied with no government, without fixed principles of any, and, like a British parliamentary opposition, gaping after loaves and fishes, and ready to change principles, as well as position, at any time, with their adversaries.

But a short review of facts omitted, or uncandidly stated in this history will shew that the contests of that day were contests of principle, between the advocates of republican, and those of kingly government, and that, had not the former made the efforts they did, our government would have been, even at this early day, a very different thing from what the successful issue of those efforts have made it.

The alliance between the states under the old articles of confederation, for the purpose of joint defence against the aggression of Great Britan, was found insufficient, as treaties of alliance generally are, to enforce compliance with their mutual stipulations: and these, once fulfilled, that bond was to expire of itself, & each state to become sovereign and independant in all things. Yet it could not but occur to every one that these separate independencies, like the petty States of Greece, would be eternally at war with each other, & would become at length the mere partisans & satellites of the leading powers of Europe. All then must have looked forward to some further bond of union, which would ensure internal peace, and a political system of our own, independant of that of Europe. Whether all should be consolidated into a single government, or each remain independant as to internal matters, and the whole form a single nation as to what was foreign only, and whether that national government should be a monarchy or republic, would of course divide opinions according to the constitutions, the habits, and the circumstances of each individual. Some officers of the army, as it has always been said and believed (and Steuben and Knox have even been named as the leading agents) trained to monarchy by military habits, are understood to have proposed to Genl. Washington to decide this great question by the army before it's disbandment, and to assume himself the crown, on the assurance of their support. The indignation with which he is said to have scouted this parricid proposition, was equally worthy of his virtue and his wisdom. The next effort was (on suggestion of the same individuals, in the moment of their separation) the establishment of an hereditary order, under the name of the Cincinnati, ready prepared, by that distinction, to be engrafted into the future frame of government, & placing Genl. Washington still at their head. The General* wrote to me on this subject, while I was in Congress at Annapolis, and an extract from my answer is inserted in 5. Marshall's hist. pa. 28. He afterwards called on me at that place, on his way to a meeting of the society, and after a whole evening of consultation he left that place fully determined to use all his endeavors for it's total suppression. But he found it so firmly riveted in the affections of the members that, strengthened as they happened to be by an adventitious occurrence of the moment, he could effect no more than the abolition of it's hereditary principle. He called again on his return, & explained to me fully the opposition which had been made, the effect of the occurrence from France, and the difficulty with which it's duration had been limited to the lives of the present members. Further details will be found among my papers, in his and my letters, and some in the *Encyclop. Method. Dictionnaire d'Econ. politique*, communicated by myself to M. Meusnier, it's author, who had made the establishment of this society the ground, in that work, of a libel on our country. The want of some authority, which should procure justice to the public creditors, and an observance of treaties with foreign nations, produced, some time after, the call of a convention of the States at Annapolis. Altho' at this meeting a difference of opinion was evident on the question of a republican or kingly government, yet, so general thro' the states, was the sentiment in favor of the former, that the friends of the latter confined themselves to a course of obstruction only, and delay, to every thing pro-

*See his lre., Apr. 8, 84.

posed. They hoped that, nothing being done, and all things going from bad to worse, a kingly government might be usurped, and submitted to by the people, as better than anarchy, & wars internal and external the certain consequences of the present want of a general government. The effect of their manœuvres, with the defective attendance of deputies from the states, resulted in the measure of calling a more general convention, to be held at Philadelphia. At this the same party exhibited the same practices, and with the same views of preventing a government of concord, which they foresaw would be republican, and of forcing, thro' anarchy, their way to monarchy. But the mass of that convention was too honest, too wise, and too steady to be baffled or misled by their manœuvres. One of these was, a form of government proposed by Colo. Hamilton, which would have been in fact a compromise between the two parties of royalism & republicanism. According to this, the Executive & one branch of the legislature were to be during good behavior, i. e. for life, and the Governors of the states were to be named by these two permanent organs. This however was rejected, on which Hamilton left the Convention, as desperate, & never returned again until near it's final conclusion. These opinions & efforts, secret or avowed, of the advocates for monarchy, had begotten great jealously thro' the states generally: and this jealousy it was which excited the strong oppositon to the conventional constitution; a jealousy which yielded at last only to a general determination to establish certain amendments as barriers against a government either monarchical or consolidated. In what passed thro' the whole period of these conventions, I have gone on the information of those who were members of them, being absent myself on my mission to France.

I returned from that mission in the 1st. year of the new government, having landed in Virginia in Dec. 89. & proceeded to N. York in March 90. to enter on the office of Secretary of State. Here certainly I found a state of things which, of all I had ever contemplated, I the least expected. I had left France in the first year of its revolution, in the fervor of natural rights, and zeal for reformation. My conscientious devotion to these rights could not be heightened, but it had

been aroused and excited by daily exercise. The President received me cordially, and my Colleagues & the circle of principal citizens, apparently, with welcome. The courtesies of
dinner parties given me as a stranger newly arrived among
them, placed me at once in their familiar society. But I cannot
describe the wonder and mortification with which the table
conversations filled me. Politics were the chief topic, and a
preference of kingly, over republican, government, was evidently the favorite sentiment. An apostate I could not be;
nor yet a hypocrite: and I found myself, for the most part,
the only advocate on the republican side of the question, unless, among the guests, there chanced to be some member of
that party from the legislative Houses. Hamilton's financial
system had then past. It had two objects. 1st as a puzzle, to
exclude popular understanding & inquiry. 2dly, as a machine
for the corruption of the legislature; for he avowed the opinion that man could be governed by one of two motives only,
force or interest: force he observed, in this country, was out
of the question; and the interests therefore of the members
must be laid hold of, to keep the legislature in unison with
the Executive. And with grief and shame it must be acknoleged that his machine was not without effect. That even in
this, the birth of our government, some members were found
sordid enough to bend their duty to their interests, and to
look after personal, rather than public good. It is well known
that, during the war, the greatest difficulty we encountered
was the want of money or means, to pay our souldiers who
fought, or our farmers, manufacturers & merchants who furnished the necessary supplies of food & clothing for them.
After the expedient of paper money had exhausted itself, certificates of debt were given to the individual creditors, with
assurance of payment, so soon as the U. S. should be able.
But the distresses of these people often obliged them to part
with these for the half, the fifth, and even a tenth of their
value; and Speculators had made a trade of cozening them
from the holders, by the most fraudulent practices and persuasions that they would never be paid. In the bill for funding
& paying these, Hamilton made no difference between the
original holders, & the fraudulent purchasers of this paper.
Great & just repugnance arose at putting these two classes of

creditors on the same footing, and great exertions were used to pay to the former the full value, and to the latter the price only which he had paid, with interest. But this would have prevented the game which was to be played, & for which the minds of greedy members were already tutored and prepared. When the trial of strength on these several efforts had indicated the form in which the bill would finally pass, this being known within doors sooner than without, and especially than to those who were in distant parts of the Union, the base scramble began. Couriers & relay horses by land, and swift sailing pilot boats by sea, were flying in all directions. Active part[n]ers & agents were associated & employed in every state, town and country neighborhood, and this paper was bought up at 5/ and even as low as 2/ in the pound, before the holder knew that Congress had already provided for it's redemption at par. Immense sums were thus filched from the poor & ignorant, and fortunes accumulated by those who had themselves been poor enough before. Men thus enriched by the dexterity of a leader, would follow of course the chief who was leading them to fortune, and become the zealous instruments of all his enterprises. This game was over, and another was on the carpet at the moment of my arrival; and to this I was most ignorantly & innocently made to hold the candle. This fiscal maneuvre is well known by the name of the Assumption. Independantly of the debts of Congress, the states had, during the war, contracted separate and heavy debts; and Massachusetts particularly in an absurd attempt, absurdly conducted, on the British post of Penobscot: and the more debt Hamilton could rake up, the more plunder for his mercenaries. This money, whether wisely or foolishly spent, was pretended to have been spent for general purposes, and ought therefore to be paid from the general purse. But it was objected that nobody knew what these debts were, what their amount, or what their proofs. No matter; we will guess them to be 20. millions. But of these 20. millions we do not know how much should be reimbursed to one state, nor how much to another. No matter; we will guess. And so another scramble was set on foot among the several states, and some got much, some little, some nothing. But the main object was obtained, the phalanx of the treasury was rein-

forced by additional recruits. This measure produced the most
bitter & angry contests ever known in Congress, before or
since the union of the states. I arrived in the midst of it. But
a stranger to the ground, a stranger to the actors on it, so
long absent as to have lost all familiarity with the subject, and
as yet unaware of it's object, I took no concern in it. The
great and trying question however was lost in the H. of Representatives. So high were the feuds excited by this subject,
that on it's rejection, business was suspended. Congress met
and adjourned from day to day without doing any thing, the
parties being too much out of temper to do business together. The Eastern members particularly, who, with Smith
from South Carolina, were the principal gamblers in these
scenes, threatened a secession and dissolution. Hamilton was
in despair. As I was going to the President's one day, I met
him in the street. He walked me backwards & forwards before the President's door for half an hour. He painted pathet-
ically the temper into which the legislature had been wrought,
the disgust of those who were called the Creditor states, the
danger of the secession of their members, and the separation
of the states. He observed that the members of the administration ought to act in concert, that tho' this question was
not of my department, yet a common duty should make it a
common concern; that the President was the center on which
all administrative questions ultimately rested, and that all of
us should rally around him, and support with joint efforts
measures approved by him; and that the question having
been lost by a small majority only, it was probable that an
appeal from me to the judgment and discretion of some of
my friends might effect a change in the vote, and the machine
of government, now suspended, might be again set into motion. I told him that I was really a stranger to the whole subject; not having yet informed myself of the system of finances
adopted, I knew not how far this was a necessary sequence;
that undoubtedly if it's rejection endangered a dissolution of
our union at this incipient stage, I should deem that the most
unfortunate of all consequences, to avert which all partial and
temporary evils should be yielded. I proposed to him however
to dine with me the next day, and I would invite another
friend or two, bring them into conference together, and I

thought it impossible that reasonable men, consulting together coolly, could fail, by some mutual sacrifices of opinion, to form a compromise which was to save the union. The discussion took place. I could take no part in it, but an exhortatory one, because I was a stranger to the circumstances which should govern it. But it was finally agreed that, whatever importance had been attached to the rejection of this proposition, the preservation of the union, & and of concord among the states was more important, and that therefore it would be better that the vote of rejection should be rescinded, to effect which some members should change their votes. But it was observed that this pill would be peculiarly bitter to the Southern States, and that some concomitant measure should be adopted to sweeten it a little to them. There had before been propositions to fix the seat of government either at Philadelphia, or at Georgetown on the Potomac; and it was thought that by giving it to Philadelphia for ten years, and to Georgetown permanently afterwards, this might, as an anodyne, calm in some degree the ferment which might be excited by the other measure alone. So two of the Potomac members (White & Lee, but White with a revulsion of stomach almost convulsive) agreed to change their votes, & Hamilton undertook to carry the other point. In doing this the influence he had established over the Eastern members, with the agency of Robert Morris with those of the middle states, effected his side of the engagement, and so the assumption was passed, and 20. millions of stock divided among favored states, and thrown in as pabulum to the stock-jobbing herd. This added to the number of votaries to the treasury and made its Chief the master of every vote in the legislature which might give to the government the direction suited to his political views. I know well, and so must be understood, that nothing like a majority in Congress had yielded to this corruption. Far from it. But a division, not very unequal, had already taken place in the honest part of that body, between the parties styled republican and federal. The latter being monarchists in principle, adhered to Hamilton of course, as their leader in that principle, and this mercenary phalanx added to them ensured him always a majority in both houses: so that the whole action of the legislature was now under the direction of the treasury. Still the machine was not compleat. The effect of the funding system, & of the assumption, would be temporary. It would be lost with the loss of the individual members whom it had enriched, and some engine of influence more permanent must be contrived, while these myrmidons were yet in place to carry it thro' all opposition. This engine was the Bank of the U.S. All that history is known; so I shall say nothing about it. While the government remained at Philadelphia, a selection of members of both houses were constantly kept as Directors, who, on every question interesting to that institution, or to the views of the federal head, voted at the will of that head; and, together with the stockholding members, could always make the federal vote that of the majority. By this combination, legislative expositions were given to the constitution, and all the administrative laws were shaped on the model of England, & so passed. And from this influence we were not relieved until the removal from the precincts of the bank, to Washington. Here then was the real ground of the opposition which was made to the course of administration. It's object was to preserve the legislature pure and independant of the Executive, to restrain the administration to republican forms and principles, and not permit the constitution to be construed into a monarchy, and to be warped in practice into all the principles and pollutions of their favorite English model. Nor was this an opposition to Genl. Washington. He was true to the republican charge confided to him; & has solemnly and repeatedly protested to me, in our private conversations, that he would lose the last drop of his blood in support of it, and he did this the oftener, and with the more earnestness, because he knew my suspicions of Hamilton's designs against it; & wished to quiet them. For he was not aware of the drift, or of the effect of Hamilton's schemes. Unversed in financial projects & calculations, & budgets, his approbation of them was bottomed on his confidence in the man. But Hamilton was not only a monarchist, but for a monarchy bottomed on corruption. In proof of this I will relate an anecdote, for the truth of which I attest the God who made me. Before the President set out on his Southern tour in April 1791. he addressed a letter of the 4th. of that month, from Mt. Vernon to the Secretaries of State,

Treasury & War, desiring that, if any serious and important cases should arise during his absence, they would consult & act on them, and he requested that the Vice-president should also be consulted. This was the only occasion on which that officer was ever requested to take part in a Cabinet question. Some occasion for consultation arising, I invited those gentlemen (and the Attorney genl. as well as I remember) to dine with me in order to confer on the subject. After the cloth was removed, and our question agreed & dismissed, conversation began on other matters and, by some circumstance, was led to the British constitution, on which Mr. Adams observed "purge that constitution of it's corruption, and give to it's popular branch equality of representation, and it would be the most perfect constitution ever devised by the wit of man." Hamilton paused and said, "purge it of it's corruption, and give to it's popular branch equality of representation, & it would become an *impracticable* government: as it stands at present, with all it's supposed defects, it is the most perfect government which ever existed." And this was assuredly the exact line which separated the political creeds of these two gentlemen. The one was for two hereditary branches and an honest elective one: the other for a hereditary king with a house of lords & commons, corrupted to his will, and standing between him and the people. Hamilton was indeed a singular character. Of acute understanding, disinterested, honest, and honorable in all private transactions, amiable in society, and duly valuing virtue in private life, yet so bewitched & perverted by the British example, as to be under thoro' conviction that corruption was essential to the government of a nation. Mr. Adams had originally been a republican. The glare of royalty and nobility, during his mission to England, had made him believe their fascination a necessary ingredient in government, and Shay's rebellion, not sufficiently understood where he then was, seemed to prove that the absence of want and oppression was not a sufficient guarantee of order. His book on the American constitutions having made known his political bias, he was taken up by the monarchical federalists, in his absence, and on his return to the U.S. he was by them made to believe that the general disposition of our citizens was favorable to monarchy. He here wrote his

Davila, as a supplement to the former work, and his election to the Presidency confirmed his errors. Innumerable addresses too, artfully and industriously poured in upon him, deceived him into a confidence that he was on the pinnacle of popularity, when the gulph was yawning at his feet which was to swallow up him and his deceivers. For, when Genl. Washington was withdrawn, these energumeni of royalism, kept in check hitherto by the dread of his honesty, his firmness, his patriotism, and the authority of his name now, mounted on the Car of State & free from controul, like Phäeton on that of the sun, drove headlong & wild, looking neither to right nor left, nor regarding anything but the objects they were driving at; until, displaying these fully, the eyes of the nation were opened, and a general disbandment of them from the public councils took place. Mr. Adams, I am sure, has been long since convinced of the treacheries with which he was surrounded during his administration. He has since thoroughly seen that his constituents were devoted to republican government, and whether his judgment is re-settled on it's ancient basis, or not, he is conformed as a good citizen to the will of the majority, and would now, I am persuaded, maintain it's republican structure with the zeal and fidelity belonging to his character. For even an enemy has said "he is always an honest man, & often a great one." But in the fervor of the fury and follies of those who made him their stalking horse, no man who did not witness it, can form an idea of their unbridled madness, and the terrorism with which they surrounded themselves. The horrors of the French revolution, then raging, aided them mainly, and using that as a raw head and bloody bones they were enabled by their stratagems of X. Y. Z. in which this historian was a leading mountebank, their tales of tub-plots, Ocean massacres, bloody buoys, and pulpit lyings, and slanderings, and maniacal ravings of their Gardiners, their Osgoods and Parishes, to spread alarm into all but the firmest breasts. Their Attorney General had the impudence to say to a republican member that deportation must be resorted to, of which, said he, "you republicans have set the example," thus daring to identify us with the murderous Jacobins of France. These transactions, now recollected but as dreams of the night, were then sad realities; and nothing rescued us from their liberticide effect but the unyielding opposition of those firm spirits who sternly maintained their post, in defiance of terror, until their fellow citizens could be aroused to their own danger, and rally, and rescue the standard of the constitution. This has been happily done. Federalism & monarchism have languished from that moment, until their treasonable combinations with the enemies of their country during the late war, their plots of dismembering the Union & their Hartford convention, has consigned them to the tomb of the dead: and I fondly hope we may now truly say " we are all republicans, all federalists," and that the motto of the standard to which our country will forever rally, will be "federal union, and republican government;" and sure I am we may say that we are indebted, for the preservation of this point of ralliance, to that opposition of which so injurious an idea is so artfully insinuated & excited in this history.

Much of this relation is notorious to the world, & many intimate proofs of it will be found in these notes. From the moment, where they end, of my retiring from the administration, the federalists got unchecked hold of Genl. Washington. His memory was already sensibly impaired by age, the firm tone of mind for which he had been remarkable, was beginning to relax, it's energy was abated; a listlessness of labor, a desire for tranquillity had crept on him, and a willingness to let others act and even think for him. Like the rest of mankind, he was disgusted with atrocities of the French revolution, and was not sufficiently aware of the difference between the rabble who were used as instruments of their perpetration, and the steady & rational character of the American people, in which he had not sufficient confidence. The opposition too of the republicans to the British treaty, and zealous support of the federalists in that unpopular, but favorite measure of theirs, had made him all their own. Understanding moreover that I disapproved of that treaty, & copiously nourished with falsehoods by a malignant neighbor of mine, who ambitioned to be his correspondent, he had become alienated from myself personally, as from the republican body generally of his fellow citizens; & he wrote the letters to Mr. Adams, and Mr. Carroll, over which, in devotion to his imperishable fame, we must forever weep as monuments of mortal decay.

Conversations with the President

1792. Feb. 28. I was to have been with him long enough before 3. o clock (which was the hour & day he received visits) to have opened to him a proposition for doubling the velocity of the post riders, who now travel about 50. miles a day, & might without difficulty go 100. and for taking measures (by way-bills) to know where the delay is, when there is any. I was delayed by business, so as to have scarcely time to give him the outlines. I ran over them rapidly, & observed afterwards that I had hitherto never spoke to him on the subject of the post office, not knowing whether it was considered as a revenue law, or a law for the general accommodation of the citizens; that the law just passed seemed to have removed the doubt, by declaring that the whole profits of the office should be applied to extending the posts & that even the past profits should be refunded by the treasury for the same purpose: that I therefore conceived it was now in the department of the Secretary of State: that I thought it would be advantageous so to declare it for another reason, to wit, that the department of treasury possessed already such an influence as to swallow up the whole Executive powers, and that even the future Presidents (not supported by the weight of character which himself possessed) would not be able to make head against this department. That in urging this measure I had certainly no personal interest, since, if I was supposed to have any appetite for power, yet as my career would certainly be exactly as short as his own, the intervening time was too short to be an object. My real wish was to avail the public of every occasion during the residue of the President's period, to place things on a safe footing.—He was now called on to attend his company, & he desired me to come and breakfast with him the next morning.

Feb. 29. I did so, & after breakfast we retired to his room, & I unfolded my plan for the post-office, and after such an approbation of it as he usually permitted himself on the first presentment of any idea, and desiring me to commit it to writing, he, during that pause of conversation which follows a business closed, said in an affectionate tone, that he had felt much concern at an expression which dropt from me yesterday, & which marked my intention of retiring when he should. That as to himself, many motives obliged him to it. He had through the whole course of the war, and most particularly at the close of it uniformly declared his resolution to retire from public affairs, & never to act in any public office; that he had retired under that firm resolution, that the government however which had been formed being found evidently too inefficacious, and it being supposed that his aid was of some consequence towards bringing the people to consent to one of sufficient efficacy for their own good, he consented to come into the convention, & on the same motive, after much pressing, to take a part in the new government and get it under way. That were he to continue longer, it might give room to say, that having tasted the sweets of office he could not do without them: that he really felt himself growing old, his bodily health less firm, his memory, always bad, becoming worse, and perhaps the other faculties of his mind showing a decay to others of which he was insensible himself, that this apprehension particularly oppressed him, that he found moreover his activity lessened, business therefore more irksome, and tranquility & retirement become an irresistible passion. That however he felt himself obliged for these reasons to retire from the government, yet he should consider it as unfortunate if that should bring on the retirement of the great officers of the government, and that this might produce a shock on the public mind of dangerous consequence. I told him that no man had ever had less desire of entering into public offices than myself; that the circumstance of a perilous war, which brought every thing into danger, & called for all the services which every citizen could render, had induced me to undertake the administration of the government of Virginia, that I had both before & after refused repeated appointments of Congress to go abroad in that sort of office, which if I had consulted my own gratification, would always have been the most agreeable to me, that at the end of two years, I resigned the government of Virginia, & retired with a firm resolution never more to appear in public life, that a domestic loss however happened, and made me fancy that absence, & a change of scene for a time might be expedient for me, that I therefore accepted a foreign appointment limited to two years, that at the close of that, Dr. Franklin having left France, I was appointed to supply his place, which I had accepted, & tho' I continued in it three or four years, it was under the constant idea of remaining only a year or two longer; that the revolution in France coming on, I had so interested myself in the event of that, that when obliged to bring my family home, I had still an idea of returning & awaiting the close of that, to fix the æra of my final retirement; that on my arrival here I found he had appointed me to my present office, that he knew I had not come into it without some reluctance, that it was on my part a sacrifice of inclination to the opinion that I might be more serviceable here than in France, & with a firm resolution in my mind to indulge my constant wish for retirement at no very distant day: that when therefore I received his letter written from Mount Vernon, on his way to Carolina & Georgia, (Apr. 1. 1791) and discovered from an expression in that that he meant to retire from the government ere long, & as to the precise epoch there could be no doubt, my mind was immediately made up to make that the epoch of my own retirement from those labors, of which I was heartily tired. That however I did not believe there was any idea in either of my brethren in the administration of retiring, that on the contrary I had perceived at a late meeting of the trustees of the sinking fund that the Secretary of the Treasury had developed the plan he intended to pursue, & that it embraced years in it's view.— He said that he considered the Treasury department as a much more limited one going only to the single object of revenue, while that of the Secretary of State embracing nearly all the objects of administration, was much more important, & the retirement of the officer therefore would be more noticed: that tho' the government had set out with a pretty general good will of the public, yet that symptoms of dissatisfaction had lately shewn themselves far beyond what he could have expected, and to what height these might arise in case of too great a change in the administration, could not be foreseen.—

I told him that in my opinion there was only a single source of these discontents. Tho' they had indeed appeared to spread themselves over the war department also, yet I considered that as an overflowing only from their real channel which would never have taken place if they had not first been generated in another department, to wit that of the treasury. That a system had there been contrived, for deluging the states with paper money instead of gold & silver, for withdrawing our citizens from the pursuits of commerce, manufactures, buildings, & other branches of useful industry, to occupy themselves & their capitals in a species of gambling, destructive of morality, & which had introduced it's poison into the government itself. That it was a fact, as certainly known as that he & I were then conversing, that particular members of the legislature, while those laws were on the carpet, had feathered their nests with paper, had then voted for the laws, and constantly since lent all the energy of their talents, & instrumentality of their offices to the establishment & enlargement of this system: that they had chained it about our necks for a great length of time, & in order to keep the game in their hands had from time to time aided in making such legislative constructions of the constitution as made it a very different thing from what the people thought they had submitted to; that they had now brought forward a proposition, far beyond every one ever yet advanced, & to which the eyes of many were turned as the decision which was to let us know whether we live under a limited or an unlimited government.—He asked me to what proposition I alluded? I answered to that in the Report on manufactures which, under colour of giving *bounties* for the encouragement of particular manufactures, meant to establish the doctrine that the power given by the Constitution to collect taxes to provide for the *general welfare* of the U.S., permitted Congress to take everything under their management which *they* should deem for the *public welfare*, & which is susceptible of the application of money: consequently that the subsequent enumeration of their powers was not the description to which resort must be had, & did not at all constitute the limits of their authority: that this was a very different question from that of the bank, which was thought an incident to an enumerated power: that therefore this decision was expected with great anxiety: that indeed I hoped the proposition would be rejected, believing there was a majority in both houses against it, and that if it should be, it would be considered as a proof that things were returning into their true channel; & that at any rate I looked forward to the broad representation which would shortly take place for keeping the general constitution on it's true ground, & that this would remove a great deal of the discontent which had shewn itself. The conversation ended with this last topic. It is here stated nearly as much at length as it really was, the expressions preserved where I could recollect them, and their substance always faithfully stated.

July 10. 1792. My lre of —— to the President, directed to him at Mt Vernon, had not found him there, but came to him here. He told me of this & that he would take an occasion of speaking with me on the subject. He did so this day. He began by observing that he had put it off from day to day because the subject was painful, to wit his remaining in office which that letter sollicited. He said that the decln he had made when he quitted his military command of never again acting in public was sincere. That however when he was called on to come forward to set the present govmt in motion, it appeared to him that circumstances were so changed as to justify a change in his resoln: he was made to believe that in 2 years all would be well in motion & he might retire. At the end of two years he found some things still to be done. At the end of the 3d year he thought it was not worth while to disturb the course of things as in one year more his office would expire & he was decided then to retire. Now he was told there would still be danger in it. Certainly if he thought so, he would conquer his longing for retirement. But he feared it would be said his former professions of retirement had been mere affectation, & that he was like other men, when once in office he could not quit it. He was sensible too of a decay of his hearing perhaps his other faculties might fall off & he not be sensible of it. That with respect to the existing causes of uneasiness, he thought there were suspicions against a particular party which had been carried a great deal too far, there might be *desires*, but he did not believe there were *designs* to change the form of govmt into a monarchy. That there might be a few who wished it in the higher walks of life, particularly in the great cities but that the main body of the people in the Eastern states were as steadily for republicanism as in the Southern. That the pieces lately published, & particularly in Freneau's paper seemed to have in view the exciting opposition to the govmt. That this had taken place in Pennsylve as to the excise law, accdg to informn he had recd from Genl Hand that they tended to produce a separation of the Union, the most dreadful of all calamities, and that whatever tended to produce anarchy, tended of course to produce a resort to monarchical government. He considered those papers as attacking him directly, for he must be a fool indeed to swallow the little sugar plumbs here & there thrown out to him. That in condemning the admn of the govmt they condemned him, for if they thought there were measures pursued contrary to his sentiment, they must conceive him too careless to attend to them or too stupid to understand them. That tho indeed he had signed many acts which he did not approve in all their parts, yet he had never put his name to one which he did not think on the whole was eligible. That as to the bank which had been an act of so much complaint, until there was some infallible criterion of reason, a difference of opinion must be tolerated. He did not believe the discontents extended far from the seat of govmt. He had seen & spoken with many people in Maryld & Virginia in his late journey. He found the people contented & happy. He wished however to be better informed on this head. If the discontent were more extensive than he supposed, it might be that the desire that he should remain in the government was not general.

My observns to him tended principally to enforce the topics of my lre. I will not therefore repeat them except where they produced observns from him. I said that the two great complaints were that the national debt was unnecessarily increased, & that it had furnished the means of corrupting both branches of the legislature. That he must know & everybody knew there was a considerable squadron in both whose votes were devoted to the paper & stock-jobbing interest, that the names of a weighty number were known & several others suspected on good grounds. That on examining the votes of these men they would be found uniformly for every treasury measure, & that as most of these measures had been carried by small majorities they were carried by these very votes. That therefore it was a cause of just uneasiness when we saw a legislature legislating for their own interests in opposition to those of the people. He said not a word on the corruption of the legislature, but took up the other point, defended the assumption, & argued that it had not increased the debt, for that all of it was honest debt. He justified the excise law, as one of the best laws which could be past, as nobody would pay the tax who did not chuse to do it. With respect to the increase of the debt by the assumption I observed to him that what was meant & objected to was that it increased the debt of the general govmt and carried it beyond the possibility of paiment. That if the balances had been settled & the debtor states directed to pay their deficiencies to the creditor states, they would have done it easily, and by resources of taxation in their power, and acceptable to the people, by a direct tax in the South, & an excise in the North. Still he said it would be paid by the people. Finding him really approving the treasury system I avoided entering into argument with him on those points.

Bladensbg. Oct. 1. This morning at Mt Vernon I had the following conversation with the President. He opened it by expressing his regret at the resolution in which I appeared so fixed in the lre I had written him of retiring from public affairs. He said that he should be extremely sorry that I should do it as long as he was in office, and that he could not see where he should find another character to fill my office. That as yet he was quite undecided whether to retire in March or not. His inclinations led him strongly to do it. Nobody disliked more the ceremonies of his office, and he had not the least taste or gratification in the execution of it's functions. That he was happy at home alone, and that his presence there was now peculiarly called for by the situation of Majr Washington whom he thought irrecoverable & should he get well he would remove into another part of the country which might better agree with him. That he did not believe his presence necessary: that there were other characters who would do the business as well or better. Still however if his aid was thought necessary to save the cause to which he had devoted his life principally he would make the sacrifice of a longer continuance. That he therefore reserved himself for future decision, as his declaration would be in time if made a month before the day of election. He had desired Mr. Lear to find out from conversation, without appearing to make the inquiry, whether any other person would be desired by any body. He had informed him he judged from conversations that it was the universal desire he should continue, & the expectation that those who expressed a doubt of his continuance did it in the language of apprehension, and not of desire. But this, says he, is only from the north, it may be very different in the South. I thought this meant as an opening to me to say what was the sentiment in the South from which quarter I came. I told him that as far as I knew there was but one voice there which was for his continuance. That as to myself I had ever preferred the pursuits of private life to those of public, which had nothing in them agreeable to me. I explained to him the circumstances of the war which had first called me into public life, and those following the war which had called me from a retirement on which I had determd. That I had constantly kept my eye on my own home, and could no longer refrain from returning to it. As to himself his presence was important, that he was the only man in the U.S. who possessed the confidce of the whole, that govmt was founded in opinion & confidence, and that the longer he remained, the stronger would become the habits of the people in submitting to the govmt. & in thinking it a thing to be maintained. That there was no other person who would be thought anything more than the head of a party. He then expressed his concern at the difference which he found to subsist between the Sec. of the Treasury & myself, of which he said he had not been aware. He knew indeed that there was a marked difference in our political sentiments, but he had never suspected it had gone so far in producing a personal difference, and he wished he could be the mediator to put an end to it. That he thought it important to preserve the check of my opinions in the administration in order to keep things in their proper channel & prevent them from going too far. That as to the idea of transforming this govt into a monarchy he did not believe there were ten men in the U.S. whose opinions were worth attention who entertained such a thought. I told him there were many more than he imagined.

I recalled to his memory a dispute at his own table a little before we left Philada, between Genl. Schuyler on one side & Pinkney & myself on the other, wherein the former maintained the position that hereditary descent was as likely to produce good magistrates as election. I told him that tho' the people were sound, there were a numerous sect who had monarchy in contempln. That the Secy of the Treasury was one of these. That I had heard him say that this constitution was a shilly shally thing of mere milk & water, which could not last, & was only good as a step to something better. That when we reflected that he had endeavored in the convention to make an English constn of it, and when failing in that we saw all his measures tending to bring it to the same thing it was natural for us to be jealous: and particular when we saw that these measures had established corruption in the legislature, where there was a squadron devoted to the nod of the treasury, doing whatever he had directed & ready to do what he should direct. That if the equilibrium of the three great bodies Legislative, Executive, & judiciary could be preserved, if the Legislature could be kept independant, I should never fear the result of such a government but that I could not but be uneasy when I saw that the Executive had swallowed up the legislative branch. He said that as to that interested spirit in the legislature, it was what could not be avoided in any government, unless we were to exclude particular descriptions of men, such as the holders of the funds from all office. I told him there was great difference between the little accidental schemes of self interest which would take place in every body of men & influence their votes, and a regular system for forming a corps of interested persons who should be steadily at the orders of the Treasury. He touched on the merits of the funding system, observed that there was a difference of opinion about it some thinking it very bad, others very good. That experience was the only criterion of right which he knew & this alone would decide which opn was right. That for himself he had seen our affairs desperate & our credit lost, and that this was in a sudden & extraordinary degree raised to the highest pitch. I told him all that was ever necessary to establish our credit, was an efficient govmt & an honest one declaring it would sacredly pay our debts, laying taxes for this purpose & applying them to it. I avoided going further into the subject. He finished by another exhortation to me not to decide too positively on retirement, & here we were called to breakfast.

Feb. 7. 1793. I waited on the President with letters & papers from Lisbon. After going through these I told him that I had for some time suspended speaking with him on the subject of my going out of office because I had understood that the bill for intercourse with foreign nations was likely to be rejected by the Senate in which case the remaining business of the department would be too inconsiderable to make it worth while to keep it up. But that the bill being now passed I was freed from the considerations of propriety which had embarrassed me. That &c. (nearly in the words of a letter to Mr. T. M. Randolph of a few days ago) and that I should be willing, if he had taken no arrangemts. to the contrary to continue somewhat longer, how long I could not say, perhaps till summer, perhaps autumn. He said so far from taking arrangements on the subject, he had never mentioned to any mortal the design of retiring which I had expressed to him, till yesterday having heard that I had given up my house & that it was rented by another, thereupon he mentd. it to Mr. E. Randolph & asked him, as he knew my retirement had been talked of, whether he had heard any persons suggested in conversations to succeed me. He expressed his satisfn at my change of purpose, & his apprehensions that my retirement would be a new source of uneasiness to the public. He said Govr. Lee had that day informed of the genl. discontent prevailing in Virga of which he never had had any conception, much less sound informn: That it appeared to him very alarming. He proceeded to express his earnest wish that Hamilton & myself could coalesce in the measures of the govmt, and urged here the general reasons for it which he had done to me on two former conversns. He said he had proposed the same thing to Ham. who expresd his readiness, and he thought our coalition would secure the general acquiescence of the public. I told him my concurrence was of much less importce than he seemed to imagine; that I kept myself aloof from all cabal & correspondence on the subject of the govmt & saw & spoke with as few as I could. That as to a coalition with Mr. Hamilton, if by that was meant that either was to sacrifice his general system to the other, it was impossible. We had both no doubt formed our conclusions after the most mature consideration and principles conscientiously adopted could not be given up on either side. My wish was to see both houses of Congr. cleansed of all persons interested in the bank or public stocks; & that a pure legislature being given us, I should always be ready to acquiesce under their determns even if contrary to my own opns, for that I subscribe to the principle that the will of the majority honestly expressed should give law. I confirmed him in the fact of the great discontents to the South, that they were grounded on seeing that their judgmts & interests were sacrificed to those of the Eastern states on every occn. & their belief that it was the effect of a corrupt squadron of voters in Congress at the command of the Treasury, & they see that if the votes of those members who had an interest distinct from & contrary to the general interest of their constts had been withdrawn, as in decency & honesty they should have been, the laws would have been the reverse of what they are in all the great questions. I instanced the new assumption carried in the H. of Repr. by the Speaker's votes. On this subject he made no reply. He explained his remaing. in office to have been the effect of strong solicitations after he returned here declaring that he had never mentd. his purpose of going out but to the heads of depnts & Mr. Madison; he expressed the extreme wretchedness of his existence while in office, and went lengthily into the late attacks on him for levees &c—and explained to me how he had been led into them by the persons he consulted at New York, and that if he could but know what the sense of the public was, he would most cheerfully conform to it.

Aug 6. 1793. The President calls on me at my house in the country, and introduces my letter of July 31. announcing that I should resign at the close of the next month. He again expressed his repentance at not having resigned himself, and how much it was increased by seeing that he was to be deserted by those on whose aid he had counted: that he did not know where he should look to find characters to fill up the offices, that mere talents did not suffice for the departmt of state, but it required a person conversant in foreign affairs, perhaps acquainted with foreign courts, that without this the best talents would be awkward & at a loss. He told me that Colo. Hamilton had 3. or 4. weeks ago written to him, informg him that private as well as public reasons had brought him to the determination to retire, & that he should do it towards the close of the next session. He said he had often before intimated dispositions to resign, but never as decisively before: that he supposed he had fixed on the latter part of next session to give an opportunity to Congress to examine into his conduct; that our going out at times so different increased his difficulty, for if he had both places to fill at one he might consult both the particular talents & geographical situation of our successors. He expressed great apprehensions at the fermentation which seemed to be working in the mind of the public, that many descriptions of persons, actuated by different causes appeared to be uniting, what it would end in he knew not, a new Congress was to assemble, more numerous, perhaps of a different spirit; the first expressions of their sentiments would be important: if I would only stay to the end of that it would relieve him considerably.

I expressed to him my excessive repugnance to public life, the particular uneasiness of my situation in this place where the laws of society oblige me always to move exactly in the circle which I know to bear me peculiar hatred, that is to say the wealthy aristocrats, the merchants connected closely with England, the new created paper fortunes; that thus surrounded, my words were caught, multiplied, misconstrued, & even fabricated & spread abroad to my injury, that he saw also that there was such an opposition of views between myself & another part of the admn as to render it peculiarly unpleasing, and to destroy the necessary harmony. Without knowg the views of what is called the Republican party here, or havg any communication with them, I could undertake to assure him from my intimacy with that party in the late Congress, that there was not a view in the Republican party as spread over the U S. which went to the frame of the government, that I believed the next Congress would attempt nothing material but to render their own body independant, that that party were firm in their dispositions to support the government: that the manœuvres of Mr. Genet might produce some little embarrassment, but that he would be abandoned by the Republicans the moment they knew the nature of his conduct, and on the whole no crisis existed which threatened anything.

He said he believed the views of the Republican party were perfectly pure, but when men put a machine into motion it is impossible for them to stop it exactly where they would chuse or to say where it will stop. That the constn we have is an excellent one if we can keep it where it is, that it was indeed supposed there was a party disposed to change it into a monarchical form, but that he could conscientiously declare there was not a man in the U S. who would set his face more decidedly against it than himself. Here I interrupted him by saying "no rational man in the U S. suspects you of any other disposn, but there does not pass a week in which we cannot prove declns dropping from the monarchical party that our governmt is good for nothing, it is a milk & water thing which cannot support itself, we must knock it down & set up something of more energy."—He said if that was the case he thought it a proof of their insanity, for that the republican spirit of the Union was so manifest and so solid that it was astonishg how any one could expect to move them.

He returned to the difficulty of naming my successor, he said Mr. Madison would be his first choice, but that he had always expressed to him such a decision against public office that he could not expect he would undertake it. Mr. Jay would prefer his present office. He sd that Mr. Jay had a great opinion of the talents of Mr. King, that there was also Mr. Smith of S. Carola: E. Rutledge &c. but he observed that name whom he would some objections would be made, some would be called speculators, some one thing, some another, and he asked me to mention any characters occurrg to me. I asked him if Govr. Johnson of Maryld. had occurred to him? He said he had, that he was a man of great good sense, an honest man, & he believed clear of speculations, but this says he is an instance of what I was observing, with all these qualifications Govr. Johnson, from a want of familiarity with foreign affairs, would be in them like a fish out of water, everything would be new to him, & he awkward in everything. I confessed to him that I had considered Johnson rather as fit for the Treasury department. Yes, says he, for that he would be the fittest appointment that could be made; he is a man acquainted with figures, & having as good a knowledge of the resources of this country as any man. I asked him if Chancr. Livingston had occurred to him? He said yes, but he was from N. York, & to appoint him while Hamilton was in & before it should be known he was going out, would excite a newspaper conflagration, as the ultimate arrangement would not be known. He said McLurg had occurred to him as a man of first rate abilities, but it is said that he is a speculator. He asked me what sort of a man Wolcott was. I told him I knew nothing of him myself; I had heard him characterized as a cunning man. I asked him whether some person could not take my office par interim, till he should make an apptment? as Mr. Randolph for instance. Yes, says he, but there you would raise the expectation of keeping it, and I do not know that he is fit for it nor what is thought of Mr. Randolph. I avoided noticing the last observation, & he put the question to me directly. I then told him that I went into society so little as to be unable to answer it: I knew that the embarrassments in his private affairs had obliged him to use expedts which had injured him with the merchts & shopkeepers & affected his character of independance; that these embarrassments were serious, & not likely to cease soon. He said if I would only stay in till the end of another quarter (the last of Dec.) it would get us through the difficulties of this year, and he was satisfied that the affairs of Europe would be settled with this campaign; for that either France would be overwhelmed by it, or the confederacy would give up the contest. By that time too Congress will have manifested it's character & view. I told him that I had set my private affairs in motion in a line which had powerfully called for my presence the last spring, & that they had suffered immensely from my not going home; that I had now calculated them to my return in the fall, and to fail in going then would be the loss of another year, & prejudicial beyond measure. I asked him whether he could not name Govr. Johnson to my office, under an express arrangement that at the close of the session he should take that of the treasury. He said that men never chose to descend: that being once in a higher department he would not like to go into a lower one.* And he concluded by desiring that I would take 2. or 3. days to consider whether I could not stay in till the end of another quarter, for that like a man going to the gallows, he was willing to put it off as long as he could: but if I persisted, he must then look about him & make up his mind to do the best he could: & so he took leave.

"Liberty warring on herself"

Aug. 20. 1793. We met at the President's to examine by paragraphs the draught of a letter I had prepared to Gouverneur Morris on the conduct of Mr. Genet. There was no difference of opinion on any part of it, except on this expression. "An attempt to embroil both, to add still another nation to the enemies of his country, & to draw on both a reproach, which it is hoped will never stain the history of either, that of *liberty warring on herself.*" H. moved to strike out these words "that of liberty warring on herself." He urged generally that it would give offence to the combined powers, that it amounted to a declaration that they were warring on liberty, that we were not called on to declare that the cause of France was that of liberty, that he had at first been with them with all his heart, but that he had long since left them, and was not for encouraging the idea here that the cause of France was the cause of liberty in general, or could have either connection or influence in our affairs. Knox accordg to custom jumped plump into all his opinions. The Pr. with a good deal of positiveness declared in favor of the expression, that he considered the pursuit of France to be that of liberty, however they might sometimes fail of the best means of obtaining it, that he had never at any time entertained a doubt of their ultimate success, if they hung well together, & that as to their dissensions there were such contradictory accts. given that no one could tell what to believe. I observed that it had been supposed among us all along that the present letter might

*He asked me whether I could not arrange my affairs by going home. I told him I did not think the public business would admit of it; that there was never a day now in which the absence of the Secretary of state would not be inconvenient to the public.

become public; that we had therefore 3. parties to attend to,—1. France, 2. her enemies, 3. the people of the U S. That as to the enemies of France it ought not to offend them, because the passage objected to only spoke of an attempt to make the U S. a *free nation*, war on France, a *free nation*, which would be liberty warring on herself, and therefore a true fact. That as to France, we were taking so harsh a measure (desiring her to recall her minister) that a precedent for it could scarcely be found, that we knew that minister would represent to his government that our Executive was hostile to liberty, leaning to monarchy & would endeavor to parry the charges on himself, by rendering suspicious the source from which they flowed. That therefore it was essential to satisfy France not only of our friendship to her, but our attachment to the general cause of liberty, & to hers in particular. That as to the people of the U S. we knew there were suspicions abroad that the Executive in some of it's parts was tainted with a hankering after monarchy, an indisposition towards liberty & towards the French cause; & that it was important by an explicit declaration to remove these suspicions & restore the confidence of the people in their govmt. R. opposed the passage on nearly the same ground with H. He added that he thought it had been agreed that this correspondence should contain no expressions which could give offence to either party. I replied that it had been my opinion in the beginng of the correspondence that while we were censuring the conduct of the French minister, we should make the most cordial declarations of friendship to them: that in the first letter or two of the correspondence I had inserted expressions of that kind, but that himself & the other two gentlemen had struck them out; that I thereupon conformed to their opinions in my subseqt. letters, and had carefully avoided the insertion of a single term of friendship to the French nation, and the letters were as dry & husky as if written between the generals of two enemy nations. That on the present occasion how ever it had been agreed that such expressions ought to be inserted in the letter now under considn, & I had accordly charged it pretty well with them. That I had further thought it essential to satisfy the French & our own citizens of the light in which we viewed their cause, and of our fellow feeling for the general cause of liberty, and had ventured only four words on the subject, that there was not from beginning to end of the letter one other expression or word in favor of liberty, & I should think it singular at least if the single passage of that character should be struck out.—The President again spoke. He came into the idea that attention was due to the two parties who had been mentd. France & the U S. That as to the former, thinking it certain their affairs would issue in a government of some sort, of considerable freedom, it was the only nation with whom our relations could be counted on: that as to the U S. there could be no doubt of their universal attachmt to the cause of France, and of the solidity of their republicanism. He declared his strong attachment to the expression, but finally left it to us to accommodate. It was struck out, of course, and the expressions of affection in the context were a good deal taken down.

Conversations with Aaron Burr

Jan. 26. 1804. Col. Burr the V. P. calls on me in the evening, having previously asked an opportunity of conversing with me. He began by recapitulating summarily that he had come to N. Y. a stranger some years ago, that he found the country in possn of two rich families, (the Livingstons & Clintons) that his pursuits were not political & he meddled not. When the crisis, however of 1800 came on they found their influence worn out, & solicited his aid with the people. He lent it without any views of promotion. That his being named as a candidate for V. P. was unexpected by him. He acceded to it with a view to promote my fame & advancement and from a desire to be with me, whose company and conversation had always been fascinating to him. That since those great families had become hostile to him, and had excited the calumnies which I had seen published. That in this Hamilton had joined and had even written some of the pieces against him. That his attachment to me had been sincere and was still unchanged, altho many little stories had been carried to him, & he supposed to me also, which he despised, but that attachments must be reciprocal or cease to exist, and therefore he asked if any change had taken place in mine towards him; that he had chosen to have this conversn with myself directly & not through any intermediate agent. He reminded me of a letter written to him about the time of counting the votes (say Feb. 1801) mentioning that his election had left a chasm in my arrangements, that I had lost him from my list in the admn. &c. He observed he believed it would be for the interest of the republican cause for him to retire; that a disadvantageous schism would otherwise take place; but that were he to retire, it would be said he shrunk from the public sentence, which he never would do; that his enemies were using my name to destroy him, and something was necessary from me to prevent and deprive them of that weapon, some mark of favor from me, which would declare to the world that he retired with my confidence. I answered by recapitulating to him what had been my conduct previous to the election of 1800. That I never had interfered directly or indirectly with my friends or any others, to influence the election either for him or myself; that I considered it as my duty to be merely passive, except that, in Virginia I had taken some measures to procure for him the unanimous vote of that state, because I thought any failure there might be imputed to me. That in the election now coming on, I was observing the same conduct, held no councils with anybody respecting it, nor suffered any one to speak to me on the subject, believing it my duty to leave myself to the free discussion of the public; that I do not at this moment know, nor have ever heard who were to be proposed as candidates for the public choice, except so far as could be gathered from the newspapers. That as to the attack excited against him in the newspapers, I had noticed it but as the passing wind; that I had seen complaints that Cheetham, employed in publishing the laws, should be permitted to eat the public bread & abuse its second officer: that as to this, the publishers of the laws were appd by the Secy. of the state witht. any reference to me; that to make the notice general, it was often given to one republican & one federal printer of the same place, that these federal printers did not in the least intermit their abuse of me, tho' receiving emoluments from the govmts and that I have never thot it proper to interfere for myself, & consequently not in the case *of* the Vice president. That as to the letter he referred to, I remembered it, and believed he had only mistaken the date at which it was written; that I thought it must have been on the first notice of the event of the election of S. Carolina; and that I had taken that occasion to mention to him that I had intended to have proposed to him one of the great offices, if he had not been elected, but that his election in giving him a higher station had deprived me of his aid in the administration. The letter alluded to was in fact mine to him of Dec. 15. 1800. I now went on to explain to him verbally what I meant by saying I had lost him from my list. That in Genl. Washington's time it had been signified to him that Mr. Adams, the V. President, would be glad of a foreign embassy; that Genl. Washington mentd. it to me, expressed his doubts whether Mr. Adams was a fit character for such an office, & his still greater doubts, indeed his conviction that it would not be justifiable to send away the person who, in case of his death, was provided by the constn to take his place; that it would moreover appear indecent for him to be disposing of the public trusts in apparently buying off a competitor for the public favor. I concurred with him in the opinion, and, if I recollect rightly, Hamilton, Knox, & Randolph were consulted & gave the same opinions. That when Mr. Adams came to the admn, in his first interview with me he mentioned the necessity of a mission to France, and how desirable it would have been to him if he could have got me to undertake it; but that he conceived it would be wrong in him to send me away, and assigned the same reasons Genl Washington had done; and therefore he should appoint Mr. Madison &c. That I had myself contemplated his (Colo. Burr's) appointment to one of the great offices; in case he was not elected V. P. but that as soon as that election was known, I saw it could not be done for the good reasons which had led Genl W. & Mr. A. to the same conclusion, and therefore in my first letter to Colo. Burr after the issue was known, I had mentioned to him that a chasm in my arrangements had been produced by this event. I was thus particular in rectifying the date of this letter, because it gave me an opportunity of explaining the grounds on which it was written which were indirectly an answer to his present hints. He left the matter with me for consideration & the conversation was turned to indifferent subjects. I should here notice that Colo. Burr must have thot that I could swal-

THE ANAS — SELECTIONS 693

low strong things in my own favor, when he founded his acquiescence in the nominn as V. P. to his desire of promoting my honor, the being with me whose company & conversn had always been fascinating to him &c. I had never seen Colo. Burr till he came as a member of Senate. His conduct very soon inspired me with distrust. I habitually cautioned Mr. Madison against trusting him too much. I saw afterwards that under Genl W.'s and Mr. A.'s admns, whenever a great military appmt or a diplomatic one was to be made, he came post to Philada to shew himself & in fact that he was always at market, if they had wanted him. He was indeed told by Dayton in 1800 he might be Secy. at war; but this bid was too late. His election as V. P. was then foreseen. With these impressions of Colo. Burr there never had been an intimacy between us, and but little association. When I destined him for a high appmt, it was out of respect for the favor he had obtained with the republican party by his extraordinary exertions and successes in the N. Y. election in 1800.

1806. April 15. About a month ago, Colo. Burr called on me & entered into a conversation in which he [mentioned] that a little before my coming into office I had written to him a letter intimating that I had destined him for a high employ, had he not been placed by the people in a different one; that he had signified his willingness to resign as V. President to give aid to the admn in any other place; that he had never asked an office however; he asked aid of nobody, but could walk on his own legs, & take care of himself; that I had always used him with politeness, but nothing more: that he aided in bringing on the present order of things, that he had supported the admn, & that he could do me much harm: he wished however to be on differt. ground: he was now disengaged from all particular business, willing to engage in something, should be in town some days, if I should have anything to propose to him. I observed to him that I had always been sensible that he possessed talents which might be employed greatly to the advantage of the public, & that as to myself I had a confidence that if he were employed he would use his talents for the public good: but that he must be sensible the public had withdrawn their confidence from him & that in a government like ours it was necessary to embrace in its admn as great a mass of public confidce as possible, by employing those who had a character with the public, of their own, & not merely a secondary one through the Exve. He observed that if we believed a few newspapers it might be supposed he had lost the public confidence, but that I knew how easy it was to engage newspapers in anything. I observed that I did not refer to that kind of evidence of his having lost the public confidence, but to the late presidential election, when, tho' in possn of the office of V. P. there was not a single voice heard for his retaining it. That as to any harm he could do me, I knew no cause why he should desire it, but at the same time I feared no injury which any man could do me: that I never had done a single act, or been concerned in any transaction, which I feared to have fully laid open, or which could do me any hurt if truly stated: that I had never done a single thing with a view to my personal interest, or that of any friend, or with any other view than that of the greatest public good: that therefore no threat or fear on that head would ever be a motive of action with me. He has continued in town to this time; dined with me this day week & called on me to take leave 2. or 3. days ago. I did not commit these things to writing at the time but I do it now, because in a suit between him & Cheetham, he has had a deposn of Mr. Bayard taken, which seems to have no relation to the suit nor to any other object but to calumniate me. Bayard pretends to have addressed to me, during the pending of the Presidl election in Feb. 1801, through Genl. Saml. Smith, certain condns on which my election might be obtained, & that Genl. Smith after conversing with me gave answers from me. This is absolutely false. No proposn of any kind was ever made to me on that occasion by Genl. Smith, nor any answer authorized by me. And this fact Genl. Smith affirms at this moment. For some matters connected with this see my notes of Feb. 12. & 14. 1801 made at the moment. But the following transactions took place about the same time, that is to say while the Presidential election was in suspense in Congress, which tho' I did not enter at the time they made such an impression on my mind that they are now as fresh as to their principal circumstances as if they had happened yesterday. Coming out of the Senate chamber one day I found Gouverneur Morris on the steps. He stopped me & began a conversn on the strange & portentous state of things then existing, and went on to observe that the reasons why the minority of states were so opposed to my being elected were that they apprehended that 1. I should turn all federalists out of office. 2. put down the navy. 3. wipe off the public debt & 4.

That I need only to declare, or authorize my friends to declare, that I would not take these steps, and instantly the event of the election would be fixed. I told him that I should leave the world to judge of the course I meant to pursue by that which I had pursued hitherto; believing it to be my duty to be passive & silent during the present scene; that I should certainly make no terms, should never go into the office of President by capitulation, nor with my hands tied by any conditions which should hinder me from pursuing the measures which I should deem for the public good. It was understood that Gouverneur Morris had entirely the direction of the vote of Lewis Morris of Vermont, who by coming over to M. Lyon would have added another vote & decided the election. About the same time, I met with Mr. Adams walking in the Pensylve avenue. We conversed on the state of things. I observed to him, that a very dangerous experiment was then in contemplation, to defeat the Presidential election by an act of Congress declaring the right of the Senate to naming a President of the Senate, to devolve on him the govmt during any interregnum: that such a measure would probably produce resistance by force & incalculable consequences which it would be in his power to prevent by negativing such an act. He seemed to think such an act justifiable & observed it was in my power to fix the election by a word in an instant, by declaring I would not turn out the federal officers, not put down the navy, nor sponge the National debt. Finding his mind made up as to the usurpation of the government by the President of the Senate I urged it no further, observed the world must judge as to myself of the future by the past, and turned the conversation to something else. About the same time Dwight Foster of Massachusetts called on me in my room one night & went into a very long conversation on the state of affairs the drift of which was to let me understand that the fears above-mentioned were the only obstacles to my election, to all of which I avoided giving any answer the one way or the other. From this moment he became most bitterly & personally opposed to me, & so has ever continued. I do not recollect that I ever had any particular conversn with Genl. Saml. Smith on this subject. Very possibly I had however, as the general subject & all its parts were the constant themes of conversation in the private *tête à têtes* with our friends. But certain I am that neither he, nor any other republican ever uttered the most distant hint to me about submitting to any conditions or giving any assurances to anybody; and still more certainly was neither he nor any other person ever authorized by me to say what I would or would not do. See a very exact statement of Bayard's conduct on that occasion in a piece among my notes of 1801. which was published by G. Granger with some alterations in the papers of the day under the signature of

Notes on Professor Ebeling's Letter of July 30, 1795

Professor Ebeling mentioning the persons in America from whom he derives information for his work, it may be useful for him to know how far he may rely on their authority.

President Stiles, an excellent man, of very great learning, but remarkable for his credulity.

Dr. Willard.
Dr. Barton
Dr. Ramsay
Mr. Barlow

All these are men of respectable characters worthy of confidence as to any facts they may state, and rendered, by their good sense, good judges of them.

Mr. Morse.
Mr. Webster.

Good authorities for whatever relates to the Eastern states, & perhaps as far South as the Delaware.

But South of that their information is worse than none at all, except as far as they quote good authorities. They both I believe took a single journey through the Southern parts, merely to acquire the right of being considered as eye-witnesses. But to pass once along a public road thro' a country, & in one direction only, to put up at it's taverns, and get into conversation with the idle, drunken individuals who pass their time lounging in these taverns, is not the way to know a country, it's inhabitants, or manners. To generalize a whole nation from these specimens is not the sort of information which Professor Ebeling would wish to compose *his work* from.

Fenno's Gazette of the U.S.
Webster's Minerva.
Columbian centinel.

To form a just judgment of a country from it's newspapers the character of these papers should be known, in order that proper allowances & corrections may be used. This will require a long explanation, without which, these particular papers would give a foreigner a very false view of American affairs.

The people of America, before the revolution-war, being attached to England, had taken up, without examination, the English ideas of the superiority of their constitution over every thing of the kind which ever had been or ever would be tried. The revolution forced them to consider the subject for themselves, and the result was an universal conversion to republicanism. Those who did not come over to this opinion, either left us, & were called Refugees, or staid with us under the name of tories; & some, preferring profit to principle took side with us and floated with the general tide. Our first federal constitution, or confederation as it was called, was framed in the first moments of our separation from England, in the highest point of our jealousies of independance as to her & as to each other. It formed therefore too weak a bond to produce an union of action as to foreign nations. This appeared at once on the establishment of peace, when the pressure of a common enemy which had hooped us together during the war, was taken away. Congress was found to be quite unable to point the action of the several states to a common object. A general desire therefore took place of amending the federal constitution. This was opposed by some of those who wished for monarchy to wit, the Refugees now returned, the old tories, & the timid whigs who prefer tranquility to freedom, hoping monarchy might be the remedy if a state of complete anarchy could be brought on. A Convention however being decided on, some of the monocrats got elected, with a hope of introducing an English constitution, when they found that the great body of the delegates were strongly for adhering to republicanism, & for giving due strength to their government under that form, they then directed their efforts to the assimilation of all the parts of the new government to the English constitution as nearly as was attainable. In this they were not altogether without success; insomuch that the monarchical features of the new constitution produced a violent opposition to it from the most zealous republicans in the several states. For this reason, & because they also thought it carried the principle of a consolidation of the states farther than was requisite for the purpose of producing an union of action as to foreign powers, it is still doubted by some whether a majority of the people of the U.S. were not against adopting it. However it was carried through all the assemblies of the states, tho' by very small majorities in the largest states. The inconveniences of an inefficient government, driving the people as is usual, into the opposite extreme, the elections to the first Congress run very much in favor of those who were known to favor a very strong government. Hence the anti-republicans appeared a considerable majority in both houses of Congress. They pressed forward the plan therefore of strengthening all the features of the government which gave it resemblance to an English constitution, of adopting the English forms & principles of administration, and of forming like them a monied interest, by means of a funding system, not calculated to pay the public debt, but to render it perpetual, and to make it an engine in the hands of the executive branch of government which, added to the great patronage it possessed in the disposal of public offices, might enable it to assume by degrees a kingly authority. The biennial period of Congress being too short to betray to the people, spread over this great continent, this train of things during the first Congress, little change was made in the members to the second. But in the mean time two very distinct parties had formed in Congress; and before the third election, the people in general became apprised of the game which was playing for drawing over them a kind of government which they never had in contemplation. At the 3d. election therefore a decided majority of Republicans were sent to the lower house of Congress; and as information spread still farther among the people after the 4th. election the anti-republicans have become a weak minority. But the members of the Senate being changed but once in 6. years, the completion of that body will be much slower in it's assimilation to that of the people. This will account for the differences which may appear in the proceedings & spirit of the two houses. Still however it is inevitable that the Senate will at length be formed to the republican model of the people, & the two houses of the legislature, once brought to act on the true principles of the Constitution, backed by the people, will be able to defeat the plan of sliding us into monarchy, & to keep the Executive within Republican bounds, notwithstanding the immense patronage it possesses in the disposal of public offices, notwithstanding it has been able to draw into this vortex the judiciary branch of the government & by their expectancy of sharing the other offices in the Executive gift to make them auxiliary to the Executive in all it's views instead of forming a balance between that & the legislature as it was originally intended and notwithstanding the funding phalanx which a respect for public faith must protect, tho it was engaged by false brethren. Two parties then do exist within the U.S. They embrace respectively the following descriptions of persons.

The Anti-republicans consist of
1. The old refugees & tories.
2. British merchants residing among us, & composing the main body of our merchants.
3. American merchants trading on British capital. Another great portion.
4. Speculators & Holders in the banks & public funds.
5. Officers of the federal government with some exceptions.
6. Office-hunters, willing to give up principles for places. A numerous & noisy tribe.
7. Nervous persons, whose languid fibres have more analogy with a passive than active state of things.

The Republican part of our Union comprehends
1. The entire body of landholders throughout the United States.
2. The body of labourers, not being landholders, whether in husbanding or the arts.

The latter is to the aggregate of the former party probably as 500 to one; but their wealth is not as disproportionate, tho' it is also greatly superior, and is in truth the foundation of that of their antagonists. Trifling as are the numbers of the Anti-republican party, there are circumstances which give them an appearance of strength & numbers. They all live in cities, together, & can act in a body readily & at all times; they give chief employment to the newspapers, & therefore have most of them under their command. The Agricultural interest is dispersed over a great extent of country, have little means of inter-communication with each other, and feeling their own strength & will, are conscious that a single exertion of these will at any time crush the machinations against their government. As in the commerce of human life, there are commodities adapted to every demand, so there are newspapers adapted to the Antirepublican palate, and others to the Republican. Of the former class are the Columbian Centinel, the Hartford newspaper, Webster's Minerva, Fenno's Gazette of the U.S., Davies's Richmond paper &c. Of the latter are Adams's Boston paper, Greenleaf's of New York, Freneau's of New Jersey, Bache's of Philadelphia, Pleasant's of Virginia &c. Pleasant's paper comes out twice a week, Greenleaf's & Freneau's once a week, Bache's daily. I do not know how often Adams's. I shall according to your desire endeavor to get Pleasant's for you for 1794, & 95. and will have it forwarded through 96 from time to time to your correspondent at Baltimore.

While on the subject of authorities and information, the following works are recommended to Professor Ebeling.

Minot's history of the insurrection in Massachusetts in 1786. 8vo.

Mazzei. Recherches historiques et politiques sur les E. U. de l'Amerique. 4 vol. 8vo. This is to be had from Paris. The author is an exact man.

The article 'Etats Unis de l'Amerique' in the Dictionnaire d'Economie politique et diplomatique, de l'Encyclopedie methodique. This article occupies about 90. pages, is by De Meusnier, and his materials were worthy of confidence, except so far as they were taken from the Abbé Raynal. Against these effusions of an imagination in delirio it is presumed Professor Ebeling needs not be put on his guard. The earlier editions of the Abbé Raynal's work were equally bad as to both South & North America. A gentleman however of perfect information as to South America, undertook to reform that part of the work, and his changes & additions were for the most part adopted by the Abbé in his latter editions. But the North-American part remains in it's original state of worthlessness.

A Memorandum (Services to My Country)

[c. 1800]

I have sometimes asked myself whether my country is the better for my having lived at all? I do not know that it is. I have been the instrument of doing the following things; but they would have been done by others; some of them, perhaps, a little better.

The Rivanna had never been used for navigation; scarcely an empty canoe had ever passed down it. Soon after I came of age, I examined its obstructions, set on foot a subscription for removing them, got an Act of Assembly passed, and the thing effected, so as to be used completely and fully for carrying down all our produce.

The Declaration of Independence.

I proposed the demolition of the church establishment, and the freedom of religion. It could only be done by degrees; to wit, the Act of 1776, c. 2, exempted dissenters from contributions to the church, and left the church clergy to be supported by voluntary contributions of their own sect; was continued from year to year, and made perpetual 1779, c. 36. I prepared the act for religious freedom in 1777, as part of the revisal, which was not reported to the Assembly till 1779, and that particular law not passed till 1785, and then by the efforts of Mr. Madison.

The act putting an end to entails.

The act prohibiting the importation of slaves.

The act concerning citizens, and establishing the natural right of man to expatriate himself, at will.

The act changing the course of descents, and giving the inheritance to all the children, &c., equally, I drew as part of the revisal.

The act for apportioning crimes and punishments, part of the same work, I drew. When proposed to the legislature, by Mr. Madison, in 1785, it failed by a single vote. G. K. Taylor afterwards, in 1796, proposed the same subject; avoiding the adoption of any part of the diction of mine, the text of which had been studiously drawn in the technical terms of the law, so as to give no occasion for new questions by new expressions. When I drew mine, public labor was thought the best punishment to be substituted for death. But, while I was in France, I heard of a society in England, who had successfully introduced solitary confinement, and saw the drawing of a prison at Lyons, in France, formed on the idea of solitary confinement. And, being applied to by the Governor of Virginia for the plan of a Capitol and Prison, I sent him the Lyons plan, accompanying it with a drawing on a smaller scale, better adapted to our use. This was in June, 1786. Mr. Taylor very judiciously adopted this idea, (which had now been acted on in Philadelphia, probably from the English model) and substituted labor in confinement, to the public labor proposed by the Committee of revisal; which themselves would have done, had they been to act on the subject again. The public mind was ripe for this in 1796, when Mr. Taylor proposed it, and ripened chiefly by the experiment in Philadelphia; whereas, in 1785, when it had been proposed to our assembly, they were not quite ripe for it.

In 1789 and 1790, I had a great number of olive plants, of the best kind, sent from Marseilles to Charleston, for South Carolina and Georgia. They were planted, and are flourishing; and, though not yet multiplied, they will be the germ of that cultivation in those States.

In 1790, I got a cask of heavy upland rice, from the river Denbigh, in Africa, about lat. 9° 30′ North, which I sent to Charleston, in hopes it might supersede the culture of the wet rice, which renders South Carolina and Georgia so pestilential through the summer. It was divided, and a part sent to Georgia. I know not whether it has been attended to in South Carolina; but it has spread in the upper parts of Georgia, so as to have become almost general, and is highly prized. Perhaps it may answer in Tennessee and Kentucky. The greatest service which can be rendered any country is, to add an useful plant to its culture; especially, a bread grain; next in value to bread is oil.

Whether the act for the more general diffusion of knowledge will ever be carried into complete effect, I know not. It was received by the legislature with great enthusiasm at first; and a small effort was made in 1796, by the act to establish public schools, to carry a part of it into effect, viz., that for the establishment of free English schools; but the option given to the courts has defeated the intention of the act.

A Memorandum (Rules of Etiquette)

[*c*. November, 1803]

1. In order to bring the members of society together in the first instance, the custom of the country has established that residents shall pay the first visit to strangers, and, among strangers, first comers to later comers, foreign and domestic; the character of stranger ceasing after the first visits. To this rule there is a single exception. Foreign ministers, from the necessity of making themselves known, pay the first visit to the ministers of the nation, which is returned.

11. When brought together in society, all are perfectly equal, whether foreign or domestic, titled or untitled, in or out of office.

All other observances are but exemplifications of these two principles.

I. 1st. The families of foreign ministers, arriving at the seat of government, receive the first visit from those of the national ministers, as from all other residents.

2d. Members of the Legislature and of the Judiciary, independent of their offices, have a right as strangers to receive the first visit.

II. 1st. No title being admitted here, those of foreigners give no precedence.

2d. Differences of grade among diplomatic members, gives no precedence.

3d. At public ceremonies, to which the government invites the presence of foreign ministers and their families, a convenient seat or station will be provided for them, with any other strangers invited and the families of the national ministers, each taking place as they arrive, and without any precedence.

4th. To maintain the principle of equality, or of pêle mêle, and prevent the growth of precedence out of courtesy, the members of the Executive will practice at their own houses, and recommend an adherence to the ancient usage of the country, of gentlemen in mass giving precedence to the ladies in mass, in passing from one apartment where they are assembled into another.

Epitaph [*1826*]

could the dead feel any interest in Monuments or other remembrances of them, when, as
Anacreon says   Ολιγη δε κεισομεϛθα
           Κονιϛ, οϛτεων λυθεντων
the following would be to my Manes the most
gratifying.
On the grave
    a plain die or cube of 3.f without any
mouldings, surmounted by an Obelisk
of 6.f height, each of a single stone:
on the faces of the Obelisk the following
inscription, & not a word more
               'Here was buried
               Thomas Jefferson

    Author of the Declaration of American Independance
        of the Statute of Virginia for religious freedom
      & Father of the University of Virginia.'
because by these, as testimonials that I have lived, I wish most to
be remembered. to be of the coarse stone of which
my columns are made, that no one might be tempted
hereafter to destroy it for the value of the materials.
my bust by Ciracchi, with the pedestal and truncated
column on which it stands, might be given to the University
if they would place it in the Dome room of the Rotunda.
on the Die of the Obelisk might be engraved

   'Born Apr. 2. 1743. o.s.
   Died ____   '

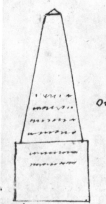

could the dead feel any interest in Monu-
-ments or other remembrances of them, when, as
Anacreon says: Ολιγη δε κεισομεσθα
                    Κονις, οσεων λυθεντων
the following would be to my Manes the most
gratifying.
On the grave
        a plain die or cube of 3.f without any
        mouldings, surmounted by an Obelisk
        of 6.f. height, each of a single stone:
        on the faces of the Obelisk the following
        inscription, & not a word more.
                Here was buried
                Thomas Jefferson
        Author of the Declaration of American Independance
                of the Statute of Virginia for religious freedom
        & Father of the University of Virginia.'
because by these, as testimonials that I have lived, I wish most to
be remembered. ██████ to be of the coarse stone of which
my columns are made, that no one might be tempted
hereafter to destroy it for the value of the materials.
my bust by Ciracchi, with the pedestal and truncated
column on which it stands, might be given to the University
if they would place it in the Dome room of the Rotunda.
on the Die of the Obelisk might be engraved
                Born apr. 2. 1743. O.S.
                Died ____

Jefferson's Design and Inscription for His Tombstone.
Courtesy of the Library of Congress

LETTERS

Contents

CONTENTS

To John Harvie

Shadwell, Jan. 14, 1760

SIR,—I was at Colo. Peter Randolph's about a Fortnight ago, & my Schooling falling into Discourse, he said he thought it would be to my Advantage to go to the College, & was desirous I should go, as indeed I am myself for several Reasons. In the first place as long as I stay at the Mountains the Loss of one fourth of my Time is inevitable, by Company's coming here & detaining me from School. And likewise my Absence will in a great Measure put a Stop to so much Company, & by that Means lessen the Expences of the Estate in House-Keeping. And on the other Hand by going to the College I shall get a more universal Acquaintance, which may hereafter be serviceable to me; & I suppose I can pursue my Studies in the Greek & Latin as well there as here, & likewise learn something of the Mathematics. I shall be glad of your opinion.

OLD COKE AND YOUNG LADIES
To John Page

Fairfield, December 25, 1762

DEAR PAGE,—This very day, to others the day of greatest mirth and jollity, sees me overwhelmed with more and greater misfortunes than have befallen a descendant of Adam for these thousand years past, I am sure; and perhaps, after excepting Job, since the creation of the world. I think his misfortunes were somewhat greater than mine: for although we may be pretty nearly on a level in other respects, yet, I thank my God, I have the advantage of brother Job in this, that Satan has not as yet put forth his hand to load me with bodily afflictions. You must know, dear Page, that I am now in a house surrounded with enemies, who take counsel together against my soul; and when I lay me down to rest, they say among themselves, come let us destroy him. I am sure if there is such a thing as a Devil in this world, he must have been here last night and have had some hand in contriving what happened to me. Do you think the cursed rats (at his instigation, I suppose) did not eat up my pocket-book, which was in my pocket, within a foot of my head? And not contented with plenty for the present, they carried away my jemmy-worked silk garters, and half a dozen new minuets I had just got, to serve, I suppose, as provision for the winter. But of this I should not have accused the Devil, (because, you know rats will be rats, and hunger, without the addition of his instigations, might have urged them to do this,) if something worse, and from a different quarter, had not happened. You know it rained last night, or if you do not know it, I am sure I do. When I went to bed, I laid my watch in the usual place, and going to take her up after I arose this morning, I found her in the same place, it's true! but *Quantum mutatus ab illo!* all afloat in water, let in at a leak in the roof of the house, and as silent and still as the rats that had eat my pocket-book. Now, you know, if chance had had anything to do in this matter, there were a thousand other spots where it might have chanced to leak as well as at this one, which was perpendicularly over my watch. But I'll tell you; it's my opinion that the Devil came and bored the hole over it on purpose. Well, as I was saying, my poor watch had lost her speech. I should not have cared much for this, but something worse attended it; the subtle particles of the water with which the case was filled, had, by their penetration, so overcome the cohesion of the particles of the paper, of which my dear picture and watch-paper were composed, that, in attempting to take them out to dry them, good God! *Mens horret referre!* My cursed fingers gave them such a rent, as I fear I never shall get over. This, cried I, was the last stroke Satan had in reserve for me: he knew I cared not for anything else he could do to me, and was determined to try this last most fatal expedient. *"Multis fortunæ vulneribus percussus, huic uni me imparem sensi, et penitus succubui!"* I would have cried bitterly, but I thought it beneath the dignity of a man, and a man too who had read των οντων, τα μεν εφ'ημιν, τα δ'ȣκ εφ'ημιν. However, whatever misfortunes may attend the picture or lover, my hearty prayers shall be, that all the health and happiness which Heaven can send may be the portion of the original, and that so much goodness may ever meet with what may be most agreeable in this world, as I am sure it must be in the next. And now, although the picture be defaced, there is so lively an image of her imprinted in my mind, that I shall think of her too often, I fear, for my peace of mind; and too often, I am sure, to get through old Coke this winter; for God knows I have not seen him since I packed him up in my trunk in Williamsburg. Well, Page, I do wish the Devil had old Coke, for I am sure I never was so tired of an old dull scoundrel in my life. What! are there so few inquietudes tacked to this momentary life of our's, that we must need be loading ourselves with a thousand more? Or, as brother Job says, (who, by the bye, I think began to whine a little under his afflictions,) "Are not my days few? Cease then, that I may take comfort a little before I go whence I shall not return, even to the land of darkness, and the shadow of death." But the old fellows say we must read to gain knowledge, and gain knowledge to make us happy and admired. *Mere jargon!* Is there any such thing as happiness in this world? No. And as for admiration, I am sure the man who powders most, perfumes most, embroiders most, and talks most nonsense, is most admired. Though to be candid, there are some who have too much good sense to esteem such monkey-like animals as these, in whose formation, as the saying is, the tailors and barbers go halves with God Almighty; and since these are the only persons whose esteem is worth a wish, I do not know but that, upon the whole, the advice of these old fellows may be worth following.

You cannot conceive the satisfaction it would give me to have a letter from you. Write me very circumstantially everything which happened at the wedding. Was she there? because, if she was, I ought to have been at the Devil for not being there too. If there is any news stirring in town or country, such as deaths, courtships, or marriages, in the circle of my acquaintance, let me know it. Remember me affectionately to all the young ladies of my acquaintance, particularly

the Miss Burwells, and Miss Potters, and tell them that
though that heavy earthly part of me, my body, be absent,
the better half of me, my soul, is ever with them; and that my
best wishes shall ever attend them. Tell Miss Alice Corbin that
I verily believe the rats knew I was to win a pair of garters
from her, or they never would have been so cruel as to carry
mine away. This very consideration makes me so sure of the
bet, that I shall ask everybody I see from that part of the
world what pretty gentleman is making his addresses to her.
I would fain ask the favour of Miss Becca Burwell to give me
another watch-paper of her own cutting, which I should esteem much more, though it were a plain round one, than the
nicest in the world cut by other hands—however, I am afraid
she would think this presumption, after my suffering the
other to get spoiled. If you think you can excuse me to her
for this, I should be glad if you would ask her. Tell Miss
Sukey Potter that I heard, just before I came out of town,
that she was offended with me about something, what it is I
do not know; but this I know, that I never was guilty of the
least disrespect to her in my life, either in word or deed; as
far from it as it has been possible for one to be. I suppose
when we meet next, she will be *endeavouring* to repay an
imaginary affront with a real one: but she may save herself
the trouble, for nothing that she can say or do to me shall
ever lessen her in my esteem, and I am determined always to
look upon her as the same honest-hearted, good-humored,
agreeable lady I ever did. Tell—tell—in short, tell them all ten
thousand things more than either you or I can now or ever
shall think of as long as we live.

My mind has been so taken up with thinking of my acquaintances, that, till this moment, I almost imagined myself
in Williamsburg, talking to you in our old unreserved way;
and never observed, till I turned over the leaf, to what an
immoderate size I had swelled my letter—however, that I may
not tire your patience by further additions, I will make but
this one more, that I am sincerely and affectionately, Dear
Page, your friend and servant.

P. S. I am now within an easy day's ride of Shadwell,
whither I shall proceed in two or three days.

A VISIT TO ANNAPOLIS
To John Page

Annapolis, May 25, 1766

DEAR PAGE—I received your last by T. Nelson whom I luckily met on my road hither. surely never did small hero experience greater misadventures than I did on the first two or three days of my travelling. twice did my horse run away with me and greatly endanger the breaking my neck on the first day. on the second I drove two hours through as copious a rain as ever I have seen, without meeting with a single house to which I could repair for shelter. on the third in going through Pamunkey, being unacquainted with the ford, I passed through water so deep as to run over the cushion as I sat on it, and to add to the danger, at that instant one wheel mounted a rock which I am confident was as high as the axle, and rendered it necessary for me to exercise all my skill in the doctrine of gravity, in order to prevent the center of gravity from being left unsupported the consequence of which would according to Bob. Carter's opinion have been the corruition of myself, chair and all into the water. whether that would have been the case or not, let the learned determine: it was not convenient for me to try the experiment at that time, and I therefore threw my whole weight on the mounted wheel and escaped the danger. I confess that on this occasion I was seised with a violent hydrophobia. I had the pleasure of passing two or three days on my way hither at the two Will. Fitzhugh's and Col°. Harrison's where were S. Potter, P. Stith, and Ben Harrison, since which time I have seen no face known to me before, except Cap.ᵗ Mitchell's who is here.—but I will now give you some account of what I have seen in this metropolis. the assembly happens to be sitting at this time. their upper and lower house, as they call them, sit in different houses. I went into the lower, sitting in an old courthouse, which, judging from it's form and appearance, was built in the year one. I was surprised on approaching it to hear as great a noise and hubbub as you will usually observe at a publick meeting of the planters in Virginia. the first object which struck me after my entrance was the figure of a little old man dressed but indifferently, with a yellow queüe wig on, and mounted in the judge's chair. this the gentleman who walked with me informed me was the speaker, a man of a very fair character, but who by the bye, has very little the air of a speaker. at one end of the justices' bench stood a man whom in another place I should from his dress and phis have taken for Goodall the lawyer in Williamsburgh, reading a bill then before the house with a schoolboy tone and an abrupt pause at every half dozen words. this I found to be the clerk of the assembly. the mob (for such was their appearance) sat covered on the justices' and lawyers' benches, and were divided into little clubs amusing themselves in the common chit chat way. I was surprised to see them address the speaker without rising from their seats, and three, four, and five at a time without being checked. when a motion was made, the speaker instead of putting the question in the usual form, only asked the gentlemen whether they chose that such or such a thing should be done, and was answered by a yes sir, or no sir: and tho' the voices appeared frequently to be divided, they never would go to the trouble of dividing the house, but the clerk entered the resolutions, I supposed, as he thought proper. in short everything seems to be carried without the house in general's knowing what was proposed. the situation of this place is extremely beautiful, and very commodious for trade having a most secure port capable of receiving the largest vessels, those of 400 hh'ds being able to brush against the sides of the dock. the houses are in general better than those in Williamsburgh, but the gardens more indifferent. the two towns seem much of a size. they have no publick buildings worth mentioning except a governor's house, the hull of which after being nearly finished, they have suffered to go to ruin. I would give you an account of the rejoicings here on the repeal of the stamp act, but this you will probably see in print before my letter can reach you. I shall proceed tomorrow to Philadelphia where I shall make the stay necessary for inoculation, thence going on to New-York I shall return by water to Williamsburgh, about the middle of July, till which time you have the prayers of

Dear Page

Your affectionate friend

P. S. I should be glad if you could in some indirect manner, without discovering that it was my desire, let J. Randolph know when I propose to be in the city of Williamsburgh.

THE STUDY OF LAW
To Thomas Turpin

Shadwell, Feb. 5, 1769

DEAR SIR,—I am truly concerned that it is not in my power to undertake the superintendance of your son in his studies; but my situation both present and future renders it utterly impossible. I do not expect to be here more than two months in the whole between this and November next, at which time I propose to remove to another habitation which I am about to erect, and on a plan so contracted as that I shall have but one spare bedchamber for whatever visitants I may have. nor have I reason to expect at any future day to pass a greater proportion of my time at home. thus situated it would even have been injustice to Phill to have undertaken to give him an assistance which will not be within my power; a task which I otherwise should with the greatest pleasure have taken on me, and would have desired no higher satisfaction than to see him hold that rank in the profession to which his genius and application must surely advance him. these how-ever encourage me to hope that the presence of an assistant will be little necessary. I always was of opinion that the plac-ing a youth to study with an attorney was rather a prejudice than a help. we are all too apt by shifting on them our busi-ness, to incroach on that time which should be devoted to their studies. the only help a youth wants is to be directed what books to read, and in what order to read them. I have accordingly recommended strongly to Phill to put himself into apprenticeship with no one, but to employ his time for himself alone. to enable him to do this to advantage I have laid down a plan of study which will afford him all the assis-tance a tutor could, without subjecting him to the inconven-ience of expending his own time for the emolument of another. one difficulty only occurs, that is, the want of books.

but this I am in hopes you will think less of remedying when it is considered that had he been placed under the care of another, a proper collection of books must have been provided for him before he engaged in the practice of his profession; for a lawyer without books would be like a workman without tools. the only difference then is that they must now be procured something earlier. should you think it necessary, it would be better to consider the money laid out in books as a part of the provision made for him and to deduct it from what you intended to give him, than that he should be without them. I have given him a catalogue of such as will be necessary, amounting in the whole to about £ 100 sterling, but divided into four invoices. Should Phill enter on the plan of study recommended, I shall endeavor as often as possible to take your house in on my way to and from Williamsburgh as it will afford me the double satisfaction of observing his progress in science and of seeing yourself, my aunt, and the family. I am Dear Sir with great respect

Your most humble servant

A GENTLEMAN'S LIBRARY

*To Robert Skipwith with
a List of Books*

Monticello, Aug. 3, 1771

I sat down with a design of executing your request to form a catalogue of books to the amount of about 50 lib. sterl. But could by no means satisfy myself with any partial choice I could make. Thinking therefore it might be as agreeable to you I have framed such a general collection as I think you would wish and might in time find convenient to procure. Out of this you will chuse for yourself to the amount you mentioned for the present year and may hereafter as shall be convenient proceed in completing the whole. A view of the second column in this catalogue would I suppose extort a smile from the face of gravity. Peace to its wisdom! Let me not awaken it. A little attention however to the nature of the human mind evinces that the entertainments of fiction are useful as well as pleasant. That they are pleasant when well written every person feels who reads. But wherein is its utility asks the reverend sage, big with the notion that nothing can be useful but the learned lumber of Greek and Roman reading with which his head is stored?

I answer, everything is useful which contributes to fix in the principles and practices of virtue. When any original act of charity or of gratitude, for instance, is presented either to our sight or imagination, we are deeply impressed with its beauty and feel a strong desire in ourselves of doing charitable and grateful acts also. On the contrary when we see or read of any atrocious deed, we are disgusted with it's deformity, and conceive an abhorence of vice. Now every emotion of this kind is an exercise of our virtuous dispositions, and dispositions of the mind, like limbs of the body acquire strength by exercise. But exercise produces habit, and in the instance of which we speak the exercise being of the moral feelings produces a habit of thinking and acting virtuously. We never reflect whether the story we read be truth or fiction. If the painting be lively, and a tolerable picture of nature, we are thrown into a reverie, from which if we awaken it is the fault of the writer. I appeal to every reader of feeling and sentiment whether the fictitious murther of Duncan by Macbeth in Shakespeare does not excite in him as great a horror of villany, as the real one of Henry IV. by Ravaillac as related by Davila? And whether the fidelity of Nelson and generosity of Blandford in Marmontel do not dilate his breast and elevate his sentiments as much as any similar incident which real history can furnish? Does he not in fact feel himself a better man while reading them, and privately covenant to copy the fair example? We neither know nor care whether Lawrence Sterne really went to France, whether he was there accosted by the Franciscan, at first rebuked him unkindly, and then gave him a peace offering: or whether the whole be not fiction. In either case we equally are sorrowful at the rebuke, and secretly resolve *we* will never do so: we are pleased with the subsequent atonement, and view with emulation a soul candidly acknowleging it's fault and making a just reparation. Considering history as a moral exercise, her lessons would be too infrequent if confined to real life. Of those recorded by historians few incidents have been attended with such circumstances as to excite in any high degree this sympathetic emotion of virtue. We are therefore wisely framed to be as warmly interested for a fictitious as for a real personage. The field of imagination is thus laid open to our use and lessons may be formed to illustrate and carry home to the heart every moral rule of life. Thus a lively and lasting sense of filial duty is more effectually impressed on the mind of a son or daughter by reading King Lear, than by all the dry volumes of ethics, and divinity that ever were written. This is my idea of well written Romance, of Tragedy, Comedy and Epic poetry.—If you are fond of speculation the books under the head of Criticism will afford you much pleasure. Of Politics and Trade I have given you a few only of the best books, as you would probably chuse to be not unacquainted with those commercial principles which bring wealth into our country, and the constitutional security we have for the enjoiment of that wealth. In Law I mention a few systematical books, as a knowledge of the minutiae of that science is not necessary for a private gentleman. In Religion, History, Natural philosophy, I have followed the same plan in general,—But whence the necessity of this collection? Come to the new Rowanty, from which you may reach your hand to a library formed on a more extensive plan. Separated from each other but a few paces the possessions of each would be open to the other. A spring centrically situated might be the scene of every evening's joy. There we should talk over the lessons of the day, or lose them in music, chess or the merriments of our family companions. The heart thus lightened our pillows would be soft, and health and long life would attend the happy scene. Come then and bring our dear Tibby with you, the first in your affections, and second in mine. Offer prayers for me too at that shrine to which tho' absent I pray continual devotions. In every scheme of happiness she is placed in the foreground of the picture, as the principal figure. Take that away, and it is no picture for me. Bear my affections to Wintipock clothed in the warmest expressions of sincerity; and to yourself be every human felicity. Adieu.

ENCLOSURE

FINE ARTS.

Observations on gardening. Payne. 5/
Webb's essay on painting. 12mo 3/
Pope's Iliad. 18/
——— Odyssey. 15/
Dryden's Virgil. 12mo. 12/
Milton's works. 2 v. 8vo. Donaldson. Edinburgh 1762. 10/
Hoole's Tasso. 12mo. 5/
Ossian with Blair's criticisms. 2 v. 8vo. 10/
Telemachus by Dodsley. 6/
Capell's Shakespear. 12mo. 30/
Dryden's plays. 6v. 12mo. 18/
Addison's plays. 12mo. 3/
Otway's plays. 3 v. 12mo. 9/
Rowe's works. 2 v. 12mo. 6/
Thompson's works. 4 v. 12mo. 12/
Young's works. 4 v. 12mo. 12/
Home's plays. 12mo. 3/
Mallet's works. 3 v. 12mo. 9/
Mason's poetical works. 5/
Terence. Eng. 3/
Moliere. Eng. 15/
Farquhar's plays. 2 v. 12mo. 6/
Vanbrugh's plays. 2 v. 12mo. 6/
Steele's plays. 3/
Congreve's works. 3 v. 12mo. 9/
Garric's dramatic works. 2 v. 8vo. 10/
Foote's dramatic works. 2 v. 8vo. 10/
Rousseau's Eloisa. Eng. 4 v. 12mo. 12/
——— Emilius and Sophia. Eng. 4 v. 12mo. 12/
Marmontel's moral tales. Eng. 2 v. 12mo. 12/
Gil Blas. by Smollett. 6/
Don Quixot. by Smollett 4 v. 12mo. 12/
David Simple. 2 v. 12mo. 6/

Roderic Random. 2 v. 12mo. 6/
Peregrine Pickle. 4 v. 12mo. 12/
Launcelot Graves. 6/
Adventures of a guinea. 2 v. 12mo. 6/
} *these are written by Smollett.*

Pamela. 4 v. 12mo. 12/
Clarissa. 8 v. 12mo. 24/
Grandison. 7 v. 12mo. 9/
Fool of quality. 3 v. 12mo. 9/
} *these are by Richardson.*

Feilding's works. 12 v. 12mo. £1.16
Constantia. 2 v. 12mo. 6/
Solyman and Almena. 12mo. 3/
} *by Langhorne.*

Belle assemblee. 4 v. 12mo. 12/
Vicar of Wakefeild. 2 v. 12mo. 6/. by Dr. Goldsmith
Sidney Bidulph. 5 v. 12mo. 15/
Lady Julia Mandeville. 2 v. 12mo. 6/
Almoran and Hamet. 2 v. 12mo. 6/
Tristam Shandy. 9 v. 12mo. £1.7
Sentimental journey. 2 v. 12mo. 6/
Fragments of antient poetry. Edinburgh. 2/
Percy's Runic poems. 3/
Percy's reliques of antient English poetry. 3 v. 12mo. 9/
Percy's Han Kiou Chouan. 4 v. 12mo. 12/
Percy's Miscellaneous Chinese peices. 2 v. 12mo. 6/
Chaucer. 10/
Spencer. 6 v. 12mo. 15/

Waller's poems. 12mo. 3/

Dodsley's collection of poems. 6 v. 12mo. 18/

Pearch's collection of poems. 4 v. 12mo. 12/

Gray's works. 5/

Ogilvie's poems. 5/

Prior's poems. 2 v. 12mo. Foulis. 6/

Gay's works. 12mo. Foulis. 3/

Shenstone's works. 2 v. 12mo. 6/

Dryden's works. 4 v. 12mo. Foulis. 12/

Pope's works. by Warburton. 12mo. £1.4

Churchill's poems. 4 v. 12mo. 12/

Hudibrass. 3/

Swift's works. 21 v. small 8vo. £ 3.3

Swift's literary correspondence. 3 v. 9/

Spectator. 9 v. 12mo. £ 1.7

Tatler. 5 v. 12mo. 15/

Guardian 2 v. 12mo. 6/

Freeholder. 12mo. 3/

Ld. Lyttleton's Persian letters. 12mo. 3/

CRITICISM ON THE FINE ARTS.

Ld. Kaim's elements of criticism. 2 v. 8vo. 10/

Burke on the sublime and beautiful. 8vo. 5/

Hogarth's analysis of beauty. 4to. £ 1.1

Reid on the human mind. 8vo. 5/

Smith's theory of moral sentiments. 8vo. 5/

Johnson's dictionary. 2 v. fol. £ 3

Capell's prolusions. 12mo. 3/

POLITICKS, TRADE.

Montesquieu's spirit of the laws. 2 v. 12mo. 6/

Locke on government. 8vo. 5/

Sidney on government. 4to. 15/

Marmontel's Belisarius. 12mo. Eng. 3/

Ld. Bolingbroke's political works. 5 v. 8vo. £ 1.5

Montesquieu's rise & fall of the Roman governmt. 12mo. 3/

Steuart's Political oeconomy. 2 v. 4to. £ 1.10

Petty's Political arithmetic. 8vo. 5/

RELIGION.

Locke's conduct of the mind in search of truth. 12mo. 3/

Xenophon's memoirs of Socrates. by Feilding. 8vo. 5/

Epictetus. by Mrs. Carter. 2 v. 12mo. 6/

Antoninus by Collins. 3/

Seneca. by L'Estrange. 8vo. 5/

Cicero's Offices. by Guthrie. 8vo. 5/

Cicero's Tusculan questions. Eng. 3/

Ld. Bolingbroke's Philosophical works. 5 v. 8vo. £ 1.5

Hume's essays. 4 v. 12mo. 12/

Ld. Kaim's Natural religion. 8vo. 6/

Philosophical survey of Nature. 3/

Oeconomy of human life. 2/

Sterne's sermons. 7 v. 12mo. £ 1.1

Sherlock on death. 8vo. 5/

Sherlock on a future state. 5/

LAW.

Ld. Kaim's Principles of equity. fol. £ 1.1

Blackstone's Commentaries. 4 v. 4to. £ 4.4

Cuningham's Law dictionary. 2 v. fol. £ 3

HISTORY. ANTIENT.

Bible. 6/

Rollin's Antient history. Eng. 13 v.
12mo. £ 1.19

Stanyan's Graecian history. 2 v. 8vo.
10/

Livy. (the late translation). 12/

Sallust by Gordon. 12mo. 12/

Tacitus by Gordon. 12mo. 15/

Caesar by Bladen. 8vo. 5/

Josephus. Eng. 1.0

Vertot's Revolutions of Rome. Eng.
9/

Plutarch's lives. by Langhorne. 6 v.
8vo. £ 1.10

Bayle's Dictionary. 5 v. fol. £ 7.10.

Jeffery's Historical & Chronological
chart. 15/

HISTORY. MODERN.

Robertson's History of Charles the
Vth. 3 v. 4to. £ 3.3

Bossuet's history of France. 4 v.
12mo. 12/

Davila. by Farneworth. 2 v. 4to.
£ 1.10.

Hume's history of England. 8 v.
8vo. £ 2.8.

Clarendon's history of the rebellion.
6 v. 8vo. £ 1.10.

Robertson's history of Scotland.
2 v. 8vo. 12/

Keith's history of Virginia. 4to. 12/

Stith's history of Virginia. 6/

NATURAL PHILOSOPHY.
NATURAL HISTORY &c.

Nature displayed. Eng. 7 v. 12mo.

Franklin on Electricity. 4to. 10/

Macqueer's elements of Chemistry.
2 v. 8vo. 10/

Home's principles of agriculture.
8vo. 5/

Tull's horse-hoeing husbandry. 8vo.
5/

Duhamel's husbandry. 4to. 15/

Millar's Gardener's diet. fol. £ 2.10.

Buffon's natural history. Eng.
£ 2.10.

A compendium of Physic & Surgery. Nourse. 12mo. 1765. 3/

Addison's travels. 12mo. 3/

Anson's voiage. 8vo. 6/

Thompson's travels. 2 v. 12mo. 6/

Lady M. W. Montague's letters. 3 v.
12mo. 9/

MISCELLANEOUS.

Ld. Lyttleton's dialogues of the
dead. 8vo. 5/

Fenelon's dialogues of the dead.
Eng. 12mo. 3/

Voltaire's works. Eng. £ 4.

Locke on Education. 12mo. 3/

Owen's Dict. of arts & sciences 4 v.
8vo. £ 2.

THE SUBLIME OSSIAN
To Charles McPherson

Albemarle, in Virga, Feb. 25, 1773

DEAR SIR,—Encouraged by the small acquaintance which I
had the pleasure of having contracted with you during your
residence in this country, I take the liberty of making the

present application to you. I understood you were related to
the gentleman of your name (Mr. James McPherson), to
whom the world is so much indebted for the elegant collection, arrangement, and translation of Ossian's poems. These
pieces have been and will, I think, during my life, continue to
be to me the sources of daily pleasures. The tender and the
sublime emotions of the mind were never before so wrought
up by the human hand. I am not ashamed to own that I think
this rude bard of the North the greatest poet that has ever
existed. Merely for the pleasure of reading his works, I am
become desirous of learning the language in which he sung,
and of possessing his songs in their original form. Mr. Mc-
Pherson, I think, informs us he is possessed of the originals.
Indeed, a gentleman has lately told me he had seen them in
print; but I am afraid he has mistaken a specimen from Te-
mora, annexed to some of the editions of the translation, for
the whole works. If they are printed, it will abridge my request and your trouble, to the sending me a printed copy;
but if there be more such, my petition is, that you would be
so good as to use your interest with Mr. McPherson to obtain
leave to take a manuscript copy of them, and procure it to be
done. I would choose it in a fair, round hand, on fine paper,
with a good margin, bound in parchments as elegantly as possible, lettered on the back, and marbled or gilt on the edges
of the leaves. I would not regard expense in doing this. I
would further beg the favor of you to give me a catalogue of
the books written in that language, and to send me such of
them as may be necessary for learning it. These will, of
course, include a grammar and dictionary. The cost of these,
as well as the copy of Ossian, will be (for me), on demand,
answered by Mr. Alexander McCaul, sometime of Virginia,
merchant, but now of Glasgow, or by your friend Mr. Ninian
Minzees, of Richmond, in Virginia, to whose care the books
may be sent. You can, perhaps, tell me whether we may ever
hope to see any more of those Celtic pieces published. Manuscript copies of any which are in print, it would at any time
give me the greatest happiness to receive. The glow of one
warm thought is to me worth more than money. I hear with
pleasure from your friend that your path through life is likely
to be smoothed by success. I wish the business and the plea-

sures of your situation would admit leisure now and then to scribble a line to one who wishes you every felicity, and would willingly merit the appellation of, dear sir, Your friend and humble servant.

NEWS FROM BOSTON
To William Small

May 7, 1775

DEAR SIR,—I had the pleasure by a gentleman who saw you at Birmingham to hear of your welfare. By Capt. Aselby of the True-patriot belonging to Messrs. Farrell & Jones of Bristol I send you 3 doz. bottles of Madeira, being the half of a present which I had laid by for you. The capt was afraid to take more on board lest it should draw upon him the officers of the customs. The remaining three doz. therefore I propose to send by Capt Drew belonging to the same mercantile house, who is just arrived here. That which goes by Aselby will be delivered by him to your order, the residue by Drew, or by Farrell & Jones, I know not which as yet. I hope you will find it fine as it came to me genuine from the island & has been kept in my own cellar eight years. Within this week we have received the unhappy news of an action of considerable magnitude, between the King's troops and our brethren of Boston, in which it is said five hundred of the former, with the Earl of Percy, are slain. That such an action has occurred, is undoubted, though perhaps the circumstances may not have reached us with truth. This accident has cut off our last hope of reconciliation, and a phrensy of revenge seems to have seized all ranks of people. It is a lamentable circumstance, that the only mediatory power, acknowledged by both parties, instead of leading to a reconciliation of his divided people, should pursue the incendiary purpose of still blowing up the flames, as we find him constantly doing, in every speech and public declaration. This may, perhaps, be intended to intimidate into acquiescence, but the effect has been most unfortunately otherwise. A little knowledge of human nature, and attention to its ordinary workings, might have foreseen that the spirits of the people here were in a state, in which

they were more likely to be provoked, than frightened, by
haughty deportment. And to fill up the measure of irritation,
a proscription of individuals has been substituted in the room
of just trial. Can it be believed, that a grateful people will
suffer those to be consigned to execution, whose sole crime
has been the developing and asserting their rights? Had the
Parliament possessed the power of reflection, they would have
avoided a measure as impotent, as it was inflammatory. When
I saw Lord Chatham's bill, I entertained high hope that a
reconciliation could have been brought about. The difference
between his terms, and those offered by our Congress, might
have been accommodated, if entered on, by both parties, with
a dispostion to accommodate. But the dignity of Parliament,
it seems, can brook no opposition to its power. Strange, that
a set of men, who have made sale of their virtue to the Minister, should yet talk of retaining dignity! But I am getting
into politics, though I sat down only to ask your acceptance
of the wine, and express my constant wishes for your happiness. This however seems to be ensured by your philosophy
& peaceful vocation. I shall still hope that amidst public dis-
sention private friendship may be preserved inviolate and
among the warmest you can ever possess is that of your humble serv.ᵗ

RECONCILIATION OR INDEPENDENCE
To John Randolph

Monticello, August 25, 1775

DEAR SIR,—I received your message by Mr. Braxton & immediately gave him an order on the Treasurer for the money
which the Treasurer assured me should be answered on his
return. I now send the bearer for the violin & such music
appurtaining to her as may be of no use to the young ladies.
I beleive you had no case to her. If so, be so good as to direct
Watt Lenox to get from Prentis's some bays or other coarse
woollen to wrap her in & then to pack her securely in a
wooden box. I am sorry the situation of our country should
render it not eligible to you to remain longer in it. I hope the

returning wisdom of Great Britain will, ere long, put an end to this unnatural contest. There may be people to whose tempers and dispositions contention is pleasing, and who, therefore, wish a continuance of confusion, but to me it is of all states but one, the most horrid. My first wish is a restoration of our just rights; my second, a return of the happy period, when, consistently with duty, I may withdraw myself totally from the public stage, and pass the rest of my days in domestic ease and tranquillity, banishing every desire of ever hearing what passes in the world. Perhaps (for the latter adds considerably to the warmth of the former wish), looking with fondness towards a reconciliation with Great Britain, I cannot help hoping you may be able to contribute towards expediting this good work. I think it must be evident to yourself, that the Ministry have been deceived by their officers on this side of the water, who (for what purpose I cannot tell) have constantly represented the American opposition as that of a small faction, in which the body of the people took little part. This, you can inform them, of your own knowledge, is untrue. They have taken it into their heads, too, that we are cowards, and shall surrender at discretion to an armed force. The past and future operations of the war must confirm or undeceive them on that head. I wish they were thoroughly and minutely acquainted with every circumstance relative to America, as it exists in truth. I am persuaded, this would go far towards disposing them to reconciliation. Even those in Parliament who are called friends to America, seem to know nothing of our real determinations. I observe, they pronounced in the last Parliament, that the Congress of 1774 did not mean to insist rigorously on the terms they held out, but kept something in reserve, to give up; and, in fact, that they would give up everything but the article of taxation. Now, the truth is far from this, as I can affirm, and put my honor to the assertion. Their continuance in this error may, perhaps, produce very ill consequences. The Congress stated the lowest terms they thought possible to be accepted, in order to convince the world they were not unreasonable. They gave up the monopoly and regulation of trade, and all acts of Parliament prior to 1764, leaving to British generosity to render these, at some future time, as easy to America as the interest

of Britain would admit. But this was before blood was spilt.
I cannot affirm, but have reason to think, these terms would
not now be accepted. I wish no false sense of honor, no ignorance of our real intentions, no vain hope thatpartial
concessions of right will be accepted, may induce the Ministry
to trifle with accommodation, till it shall be out of their
power ever to accommodate. If, indeed, Great Britain, dis-
jointed from her colonies, be a match for the most potent
nations of Europe, with the colonies thrown into their scale,
they may go on securely. But if they are not assured of
this, it would be certainly unwise, by trying the event of another campaign, to risk our accepting a foreign aid, which,
perhaps, may not be attainable, but on condition of everlasting avulsion from Great Britain. This would be thought a
hard condition, to those who still wish for re-union with
their parent country. I am sincerely one of those, and would
rather be in dependence on Great Britain, properly limited,
than on anyother nation on earth, or than on no nation.
But I am one of those, too, who, rather than submit to the
rights of legislating for us, assumed by the British Parliament,
and which late experience has shown they will so cruelly
exercise, would lend my hand to sink the whole Island in the
ocean.

If undeceiving the Minister, as to matters of fact, may
change his disposition, it will, perhaps, be in your power, by
assisting to do this, to render service to the whole empire, at
the most critical time, certainly, that it has ever seen. Whether
Britain shall continue the head of the greatest empire on
earth, or shall return to her original station in the political
scale of Europe, depends, perhaps, on the resolutions of the
succeeding winter. God send they may be wise and salutary
for us all. I shall be glad to hear from you as often as you
may be disposed to think of things here. You may be at liberty, I expect, to communicate some things, consistently with
your honor, and the duties you will owe to a protecting nation. Such a communication among individuals, may be mutually beneficial to the contending parties. On this or any
future occasion, if I affirm to you any facts, your knowledge
of me will enable you to decide on their credibility; if I haz-

ard opinions on the dispositions of men or other speculative points, you can only know they are my opinions. My best wishes for your felicity, attend you, wherever you go, and believe me to be assuredly, Your friend and servant.

P. S. My collection of classics, & of books of parliamentary learning particularly is not so complete as I could wish. As you are going to the land of literature & of books you may be willing to dispose of some of yours here & replace them there in better editions. I should be willing to treat on this head with any body you may think proper to empower for that purpose.

SAXONS, NORMANS, AND LAND TENURE

To Edmund Pendleton

Philadelphia, Aug. 13, 1776

DEAR SIR,—Your's of Aug. 3. came to hand yesterday; having had no moment to spare since, I am obliged to set down to answer it at a Committee table while the Committee is collecting. My thoughts therefore on the subject you propose will be merely extempore. The opinion that our lands were allodial possessions is one which I have very long held, and had in my eye during a pretty considerable part of my law reading which I found always strengthened it. It was mentioned in a very hasty production, intended to have been put under a course of severe correction, but produced afterwards to the world in a way with which you are acquainted. This opinion I have thought & still think to prove if ever I should have time to look into books again. But this is only meant with respect to the English law as transplanted here. How far our acts of assembly or acceptance of grants may have converted lands which were allodial into feuds I have never considered. This matter is now become a mere speculative point; & we have it in our power to make it what it ought to be for the public good.

It may be considered in the two points of view 1st. as bringing a revenue into the public treasury. 2d. as a tenure. I have only time to suggest hints on each of these heads. 1. Is it consistent with good policy or free government to establish a perpetual revenue? is it not against the practice of our wise British ancestors? have not the instances in which we have departed from this in Virginia been constantly condemned by the universal voice of our country? is it safe to make the governing power when once seated in office, independent of it's revenue? should we not have in contemplation & prepare for an event (however deprecated) which may happen in the possibility of things; I mean a reacknowledgment of the British tyrant as our king, & previously strip him of every prejudicial possession? Remember how universally the people run into the idea of recalling Charles the 2d after living many years under a republican government.—As to the second was not the separation of the property from the perpetual use of lands a mere fiction? Is not it's history well known, & the purposes for which it was introduced, to wit, the establishment of a military system of defence?

Was it not afterwards made an engine of immense oppression? Is it wanting with us for the purpose of military defence? May not it's other legal effects (such as them at least as are valuable) be performed in other more simple ways? Has it not been the practice of all other nations to hold their lands as their personal estate in absolute dominion? Are we not the better for what we have hitherto abolished of the feudal system? Has not every restitution of the antient Saxon laws had happy effects? Is it not better now that we return at once into that happy system of our ancestors, the wisest & most perfect ever yet devised by the wit of man, as it stood before the 8th century.

The idea of Congress selling out unlocated lands has been sometimes dropped, but we have alwais met the hint with such determined opposition that I believe it will never be proposed.—I am against selling the lands at all. The people who will migrate to the Westward whether they form part of the old, or of a new colony will be subject to their proportion of the Continental debt then unpaid. They ought not to be subject to more. They will be a people little able to pay taxes. There is no equity in fixing upon them the whole burthen of this war, or any other proportion than we bear ourselves. By selling the lands to them, you will disgust them, and cause an avulsion of them from the common union. They will settle the lands in spite of everybody.—I am at the same time clear that they should be appropriated in small quantities. It is said that wealthy foreigners will come in great numbers, & they ought to pay for the liberty we shall have provided for them. True, but make them pay in settlers. A foreigner who brings a settler for every 100, or 200 acres of land to be granted him pays a better price than if he had put into the public treasury 5/ or 5£. That settler will be worth to the public 20 times as much every year, as on our old plan he would have paid in one paiment. I have thrown these loose thoughts together only in obedience to your letter, there is not an atom of them which would not have occurred to you on a moment's contemplation of the subject. Charge yourself therefore with the trouble of reading two pages of such undigested stuff.

By Saturday's post the General wrote us that Ld. Howe had got (I think 100) flat bottomed boats alongside, & 30 of them were then loaded with men; by which it was concluded he was preparing to attack, yet this is Tuesday & we hear nothing further. The General has by his last return, 17000 some odd men, of whom near 4000 are sick & near 3000 at out posts in Long Island &c. So you may say he has but 10000 effective men to defend the works of New York. His works however are good & his men in spirits, which I hope will be equal to an addition of many thousands. He had called for 2000 men from the flying camp which were then embarking to him & would certainly be with him in time even if the attack was immediate. The enemy have (since Clinton & his army joined them) 15.000 men of whom not many are sick. Every influence of Congress has been exerted in vain to double the General's force. It was impossible to prevail on the people to leave their harvest. That is now in, & great numbers are in motion, but they have no chance to be there in time. Should however any disaster befall us at New York they will form a great army on the spot to stop the progress of the enemy. I think there cannot be less than 6 or 8000 men in this city & between it & the flying camp. Our council complain of our calling away two of the Virginia battalions. But is this reasonable. They have no British enemy, & if human reason is of any use to conjecture future events, they will not have one. Their Indian enemy is not to be opposed by their regular battalions. Other colonies of not more than half their military strength have 20 battalions in the field. Think of these things & endeavor to reconcile them not only to this, but to yield greater assistance to the common cause if wanted. I wish every battalion we have was now in New York.—We yesterday received dispatches from the Commissioners at Fort Pitt. I have not read them, but a gentleman who has, tells me they are favorable. The Shawanese & Delewares are disposed to peace. I believe it, for this reason. We had by different advices information from the Shawanese that they should strike us, that this was against their will, but that they must do what the Senecas bid them. At that time we knew the Senecas meditated war. We directed a declaration to be made to the six nations in general that if they did not take the most decisive measures for the preservation of neutrality we would never cease waging war with them while one was to be found on the face of the earth. They immediately changed their conduct and I doubt not have given corresponding information to the Shawanese and Delewares.

I hope the Cherokees will now be driven beyond the Missisipi & that this in future will be declared to the Indians the invariable consequence of their beginning a war. Our contest with Britain is too serious and too great to permit any possibility of avocation from the Indians. This then is the season for driving them off, & our Southern colonies are happily rid of every other enemy & may exert their whole force in that quarter.

I hope to leave this place some time this month.

I am Dear Sir, Your affectionate friend

P. S. Mr. Madison of the college & Mr. Johnson of Fredsb'gh are arrived in New York. They say nothing material had happened in England. The French ministry was changed.

THE VIRGINIA CONSTITUTION
To Edmund Pendleton

Philadelpha, Aug. 26, 1776

DEAR SIR—Your's of the 10th inst. came to hand about three days ago, the post having brought no mail with him the last week. You seem to have misapprehended my proposition for the choice of a Senate. I had two things in view: to get the wisest men chosen, & to make them perfectly independent when chosen. I have ever observed that a choice by the people themselves is not generally distinguished for it's wisdom. This first secretion from them is usually crude & heterogeneous. But give to those so chosen by the people a second choice themselves, & they generally will chuse wise men. For this reason it was that I proposed the representatives (& not the people) should chuse the Senate, & thought I had notwithstanding that made the Senators (when chosen) perfectly independant of their electors. However I should have no objection to the mode of election proposed in the printed plan of your committee, to wit, that the people of each county should chuse twelve electors, who should meet those of the other counties in the same district & chuse a senator. I should prefer this too for another reason, that the upper as well as lower house should have an opportunity of superintending & judging of the situation of the whole state & be not all of one neighborhood as our upper house used to be. So much for the wisdom of the Senate. To make them independent, I had proposed that they should hold their places for nine years, & then go out (one third every three years) & be incapable for ever of being re-elected to that house. My idea was that if they might be re-elected, they would be casting their eye forward to the period of election (however distant) & be currying favor with the electors, & consequently dependant on them. My reason for fixing them in office for a term of years rather than for life, was that they might have in idea that they were at a certain period to return into the mass of the people & become the governed instead of the governor which might still keep alive that regard to the public good that otherwise they might perhaps be induced by their independance to forget. Yet I could submit, tho' not so willingly to an appointment for life, or to any thing rather than a mere creation by & dependance on the people. I think the present mode of election objectionable because the larger county will be able to send & will always send a man (less fit perhaps) of their own county to the exclusion of a fitter who may chance to live in a smaller county.—I wish experience may contradict my fears.—That the Senate as well as lower [or shall I speak truth & call it upper] house should hold no office of profit I am clear; but not that they should of necessity possess distinguished property. You have lived longer than I have and perhaps may have formed a different judgment on better grounds; but my observations do not enable me to say I think integrity the characteristic of wealth. In general I beleive the decisions of the people, in a body, will be more honest & more disinterested than those of wealthy men: & I can never doubt an attachment to his country in any man who has his family & peculium in it:—Now as to the representative house which ought to be so constructed as to answer that character truly. I was for extending the right of suffrage (or in other words the rights of a citizen) to all who had a permanent intention of living in the country. Take what circumstances you please as evidence of this, either the having resided a certain time, or having a family, or having property, any or all of them. Whoever intends to live in a country must wish that country well, & has a natural right of assisting in the preservation of it. I think you cannot distinguish between such a person residing in the country & having no fixed property, & one residing in a township whom you say you would admit to a vote.—The other point of equal representation I think capital & fundamental. I am glad you think an alteration may be attempted in that matter.—The fantastical idea of virtue & the public good being a sufficient security to the state against the commission of crimes, which you say you have heard insisted on by some, I assure you was never mine. It is only the sanguinary hue of our penal laws which I meant to object to. Punishments I know are necessary, & I would provide them, strict & inflexible, but proportioned to the crime. Death might be inflicted for murther & perhaps for treason if you would take out of the description of treason all crimes which are not such in their nature. Rape, buggery &c—punish by castration. All other crimes by working on high roads, rivers, gallies &c. a certain time proportioned to the offence. But as this would be no punishment or change of condition to slaves (me miserum!) let them be sent to other countries. By these means we should be freed from the wickedness of the latter, & the former would be living monuments of public vengeance. Laws thus proportionate & mild should never be dispensed with. Let mercy be the character of the lawgiver, but let the judge be a mere machine. The mercies of the law will be dispensed equally & impartially to every description of men; those of the judge, or of the executive power, will be the eccentric impulses of whimsical, capricious designing man.—I am indebted to you for a topic to deny to the Pensylvania claim to a line 39 complete degrees from the equator. As an advocate I shall certainly insist on it; but I wish they would compromise by an extension of Mason & Dixon's line.—They do not agree to the temporary line proposed by our assembly.

We have assurance (not newspaper, but Official) that the French governors of the West Indies have received orders not only to furnish us with what we want but to protect our ships. They will convoy our vessels, they say, thro' the line of British cruisers. What you will see in the papers of capt Weeks is indubitably true. The inhabitants of S.t Pierre's went out in boats to see the promised battle, but the British captain chose not to shew.—By our last letters from N. York the enemy had landed 8000 men on Long island. On Friday a small party, about 40, of them were out maroding & had got some cattle in a barn. Some riflemen (with whom was our Jamieson) attacked them, took away the cattle, they retired as far as the house of Judge Lifford where were their officer's quarters, they were beaten thence also, & the house burnt by the riflemen. It is alwais supposed you know that good execution was done. One officer was killed & left with 9 guineas in his pocket, which shews they were in a hurry; the swords & fusees of three other officers were found, the owners supposed to be killed or wounded & carried away. On Saturday about 2000 of them attempted to march to Bedford. Colō Hans's battalion of 300 Pennsylvania riflemen having posted themselves in a cornfeild & a wood to advantage attacked them.

The enemy had some of their Jagers with them, who it seems are German riflemen used to the woods. General Sullivan (who commands during the illness of Gen! Green) sent some musquetry to support the riflemen. The enemy gave way & were driven half a mile beyond their former station. Among the dead left on the way, were three Jagers. Gen! Washington had sent over 6 battal! to join Sullivan who had before three thousand, some say & rightly I beleive 6000; & had posted 5 battalions more on the water side ready to join Sullivan if the enemy should make that the field of trial, or to return to N. York if wanted there. A general embarkation was certainly begun. 13. transports crouded with men had fallen down to the narrows & others loading. So that we expect every hour to hear of this great affair. Washington by his last return had 23,000 men of whom however 5000 were sick. Since this, Colō Aylett just returned from there, tells us he has received 16 new England battalions, so that we may certainly hope he has 25,000 effective, which is about the strength of the enemy probably, tho' we have never heard certainly that their last 5000, are come, in which case I should think they have but 20,000. Washington discovers a confidence, which he usually does only on very good grounds. He sais his men are high in spirits. Those ordered to Long island went with the eagerness of young men going to a dance. A few more skirmishes would be an excellent preparative for our people. Provisions on Staten island were become so scarce that a cow sold for ten pounds, a sheep for ten dollars. They were barreling up all the horse flesh they could get.—Colō Lee being not yet come I am still here, & suppose I shall not get away till about this day se'nnight. I shall see you in Williamsburgh the morning of the Assembly. Adieu.

FIRST LETTER TO ADAMS
To John Adams

Williamsburgh, May 16, 1777

DEAR SIR—Matters in our part of the continent are too much in quiet to send you news from hence. Our battalions for the

Continental service were some time ago so far filled as rendered the recommendation of a draught from the militia hardly requisite, and the more so as in this country it ever was the most unpopular and impracticable thing that could be attempted. Our people even under the monarchical government had learnt to consider it as the last of all oppressions. I learn from our delegates that the Confederation is again on the carpet. A great and a necessary work, but I fear almost desperate. The point of representation is what most alarms me, as I fear the great and small colonies are bitterly determined not to cede. Will you be so good as to recollect the proposition I formerly made you in private and try if you can work it into some good to save our union? It was that any proposition might be negatived by the representatives of a majority of the people of America, or of a majority of the colonies of America. The former secures the larger the latter the smaller colonies. I have mentioned it to many here. The good whigs I think will so far cede their opinions for the sake of the Union, and others we care little for. The journals of congress not being printed earlier gives more uneasiness than I would ever wish to see produced by any act of that body, from whom alone I know our salvation can proceed. In our assembly even the best affected think it an indignity to freemen to be voted away life and fortune in the dark. Our house have lately written for a M.S. copy of your journals, not meaning to desire a communication of any thing ordered to be kept secret. I wish the regulation of the post office adopted by Congress last September could be put in practice. It was for the riders to travel night and day, and to go their several stages three times a week. The speedy and frequent communication of intelligence is really of great consequence. So many falshoods have been propagated that nothing now is beleived unless coming from Congress or camp. Our people merely for want of intelligence which they may rely on are become lethargick and insensible of the state they are in. Had you ever a leisure moment I should ask a letter from you sometime directed to the care of Mr. Dick, Fredericksburgh: but having nothing to give in return it would be a tax on your charity as well as your time. The esteem I have for you privately, as well as for your public importance will always render assurances of your health and happiness agreeable. I am Dear Sir Your friend and servt:

"THE FAVORITE PASSION OF MY SOUL"
To Giovanni Fabbroni

Williamsburg in Virginia, June 8, 1778

SIR,—Your letter of Sep. 15. 1777 from Paris comes safe to hand. We have not however had the pleasure of seeing Mr. De Cenis, the bearer of it in this country, as he joined the army in Pennsylvania as soon as he arrived. I should have taken particular pleasure in serving him on your recommendation. From the kind anxiety expressed in your letter as well as from other sources of information we discover that our enemies have filled Europe with Thrasonic accounts of victories they had never won and conquests they were fated never to make. While these accounts alarmed our friends in Europe they afforded us diversion. We have long been out of all fear for the event of the war. I enclose you a list of the killed, wounded, and captives of the enemy from the commencement of hostilities at Lexington in April, 1775, until November, 1777, since which there has been no event of any consequence. This is the best history of the war which can be brought within the compass of a letter. I believe the account to be near the truth, tho' it is difficult to get at the numbers lost by an enemy with absolute precision. Many of the articles have been communicated to us from England as taken from the official returns made by their General. I wish it were in my power to send you as just an account of our loss. But this cannot be done without an application to the war office which being in another county is at this time out of my reach. I think that upon the whole it has been about one half the number lost by them, in some instances more, but in others less. This difference is ascribed to our superiority in taking aim when we fire; every soldier in our army having been intimate with his gun from his infancy. If there could have been a doubt before as to the event of the war it is now totally removed by the interposition of France, & the generous alliance she has entered into with us. Tho' much of my time is employed in the councils of America I have yet a little leisure to indulge my fondness for philosophical studies. I could wish to correspond with you on subjects of that kind. It might not be unacceptable to you to be informed for instance of the true power of our climate as discoverable from the thermometer, from the force & direction of the winds, the quantity of rain, the plants which grow without shelter in winter &c. On the other hand we should be much pleased with contemporary observations on the same particulars in your country, which will give us a comparative view of the two climates. Farenheit's thermometer is the only one in use with us, I make my daily observations as early as possible in the morning & again about 4 o'clock in the afternoon, these generally showing the maxima of cold & heat in the course of 24 hours. I wish I could gratify your Botanical taste; but I am acquainted with nothing more than the first principles of that science; yet myself & my friends may furnish you with any Botanical subjects which this country affords, and are not to be had with you; and I shall take pleasure in procuring them when pointed out by you. The greatest difficulty will be the means of conveyance during the continuance of the war.

If there is a gratification which I envy any people in this world, it is to your country its music. This is the favorite passion of my soul, & fortune has cast my lot in a country where it is in a state of deplorable barbarism. From the line of life in which we conjecture you to be, I have for some time lost the hope of seeing you here. Should the event prove so, I shall ask your assistance in procuring a substitute, who may be a proficient in singing, & on the Harpsichord. I should be contented to receive such an one two or three years hence, when it is hoped he may come more safely and find here a greater plenty of those useful things which commerce alone can furnish. The bounds of an American fortune will not admit the indulgence of a domestic band of musicians, yet I have thought that a passion for music might be reconciled with that economy which we are obliged to observe. I retain for instance among my domestic servants a gardener (Ortolans), a weaver (Tessitore di lino e lin), a cabinet maker (Stipeltaio) and a stone cutter (Scalpellino laborante in piano) to which I would add a vigneron. In a country where like yours music is cultivated and practised by every class of men I suppose there might be found persons of those trades who could perform on the French horn, clarinet or hautboy & bassoon, so that one might have a band of two French horns, two clarinets, & hautboys & a bassoon, without enlarging their domestic expenses. A certainty of employment for a half dozen years, and at the end of that time to find them if they choose a conveyance to their own country might induce them to come here on reasonable wages. Without meaning to give you trouble, perhaps it might be practicable for you in [your] ordinary intercourse with your people, to find out such men disposed to come to America. Sobriety and good nature would be desirable parts of their characters. If you think such a plan practicable, and will be so kind as to inform me what will be necessary to be done on my part I will take care that it shall be done. The necessary expenses, when informed of them, I can remit before they are wanting, to any port in France, with which country alone we have safe correspondence. I am Sir with much esteem your humble servant.

"A TRUE WHIG IN SCIENCE"

To David Rittenhouse

Monticello in Albemarle, Virginia, July 19, 1778

DEAR SIR,—I sincerely congratulate you on the recovery of Philadelphia, and wish it may be found uninjured by the enemy—how far the interests of literature may have suffered by the injury or removal of the Orrery (as it is miscalled) the publick libraries, your papers & implements, are doubts which still excite anxiety. We were much disappointed in Virginia generally on the day of the great eclipse, which proved to be cloudy. In Williamsburgh, where it was total, I understand only the beginning was seen. At this place which is in Lat. 38°–8′ and Longitude West from Williamsburgh about 1°–45′ as is conjectured, eleven digits only were supposed to be covered, as it was not seen at all till the moon had advanced nearly one third over the sun's disc. Afterwards it was seen at intervals through the whole. The egress particularly was visible. It proved however of little use to me for want of a time piece that could be depended on; which circumstance, together with the subsequent restoration of Philadelphia to you, has induced me to trouble you with this letter to remind you of your kind promise of making me an accurate clock; which being intended for astronomical purposes only, I would have divested of all apparatus for striking or for any other purpose, which by increasing it's complication might disturb it's accuracy. A companion to it, for keeping seconds, and which might be moved easily, would greatly add to it's value. The theodolite, for which I spoke to you also, I can now dispense with, having since purchased a most excellent one.

Writing to a philosopher, I may hope to be pardoned for intruding some thoughts of my own tho' they relate to him personally. Your time for two years past has, I believe, been principally employed in the civil government of your country. Tho' I have been aware of the authority our cause would acquire with the world from it's being known that yourself & Doct. Franklin were zealous friends to it and am myself duly impressed with a sense of the arduousness of government, and the obligation those are under who are able to conduct it, yet I am also satisfied there is an order of geniusses above that obligation, & therefore exempted from it, nobody can conceive that nature ever intended to throw away a Newton upon the occupations of a crown. It would have been a prodigality for which even the conduct of providence might have been arraigned, had he been by birth annexed to what was so far below him. Cooperating with nature in her ordinary economy we should dispose of and employ the geniusses of men according to their several orders and degrees. I doubt not there are in your country many persons equal to the task of conducting government: but you should consider that the world has but one Ryttenhouse, & that it never had one before. The amazing mechanical representation of the solar system which you conceived & executed, has never been surpassed by any but the work of which it is a copy. Are those powers then, which being intended for the erudition of the world are, like air and light, the world's common property, to be taken from their proper pursuit to do the commonplace drudgery of governing a single state, a work which may be executed by men of an ordinary stature, such as are always & everywhere to be found? Without having ascended mount Sinai for inspiration, I can pronounce that the precept, in the decalogue of the vulgar, that they shall not make to themselves "the likeness of anything that is in the heavens above" is reversed for you, and that you will fulfill the highest purposes of your creation by employing yourself in the perpetual breach of that inhibition. For my own country in particular you must remember something like a promise that it should be adorned with one of them. The taking of your city by the enemy has hitherto prevented the proposition from being made & approved by our legislature. The zeal of a true whig in science must excuse the hazarding these free thoughts, which flow from a desire of promoting the diffusion of knowledge & of your fame, and from one who can assure you truly that he is with much sincerity & esteem Your most obed.^t & most humble serv.^t

P. S. If you can spare as much time as to give me notice of the receipt of this, & what hope I may form of my clocks, it will oblige me. If sent to Fredericksburgh it will come safe to hand.

WAR AND HUMANITY
To Patrick Henry

Albemarle, March 27, 1779

SIR,—A report prevailing here, that in consequence of some powers from Congress, the Governor and Council have it in contemplation to remove the Convention troops, either wholly or in part, from their present situation, I take the liberty of troubling you with some observations on that subject. The reputation and interest of our country, in general, may be affected by such a measure: it would, therefore, hardly be deemed an indecent liberty in the most private citizen, to offer his thoughts to the consideration of the Executive. The locality of my situation, particularly in the neighborhood of the present barracks, and the public relation in which I stand to the people among whom they are situated, together with a confidence which a personal knowledge of the members of the Executive gives me, that they will be glad of information from any quarter, on a subject interesting to the public, induce me to hope that they will acquit me of impropriety in the present representation.

By an article in the Convention of Saratoga, it is stipulated, on the part of the United States, that the officers shall not be separated from their men. I suppose the term officers, includes *general* as well as *regimental* officers. As there are general officers who command all the troops, no part of them can be separated from these officers without a violation of the article: they cannot, of course, be separated from one another, unless the same general officer could be in different places at the same time. It is true, the article adds the words, "as far as circumstances will admit." This was a necessary qualification; because, in no place in America, I suppose, could there have been found quarters for both officers and men together; those for the officers to be according to their rank. So far, then, as the circumstances of the place where they should be quartered, should render a separation necessary, in order to procure quarters for the officers, according to their rank, the article admits that separation. And these are the circumstances which must have been under the contemplation of the parties; both of whom, and all the world beside (who are ultimate judges in the case), would still understand that they were to be as near in the environs of the camp, as convenient quarters could be procured; and not that the qualification of the article destroyed the article itself, and laid it wholly at our discretion. Congress, indeed, have admitted of this separation; but are they so far lords of right and wrong as that our consciences may be quiet with their dispensation? Or is the case amended by saying they leave it optional in the Governor and Council to separate the troops or not? At the same time that it exculpates not them, it is drawing the Governor and Council into a participation in the breach of faith. If indeed it is only proposed, that a separation of the troops shall be referred to the consent of their officers; that is a very different matter. Hav-

ing carefully avoided conversation with them on public subjects, I cannot say, of my own knowledge, how they would
relish such a proposition. I have heard from others, that they
will choose to undergo anything together, rather than to be
separated, and that they will remonstrate against it in the
strongest terms. The Executive, therefore, if voluntary agents
in this measure, must be drawn into a paper war with them,
the more disagreeable, as it seems that faith and reason will
be on the other side. As an American, I cannot help feeling a
thorough mortification, that our Congress should have permitted an infraction of our public honor; as a citizen of Virginia, I cannot help hoping and confiding, that our Supreme
Executive, whose acts will be considered as the acts of the
Commonwealth, estimate that honor too highly to make its
infraction their own act. I may be permitted to hope, then,
that if any removal takes place, it will be a general one; and,
as it is said to be left to the Governor and Council to determine on this, I am satisfied that, suppressing every other consideration, and weighing the matter dispassionately, they will
determine upon this sole question, Is it for the benefit of
those for whom they act, that the Convention troops should
be removed from among them? Under the head of interest,
these circumstances, viz., the expense of building barracks,
said to have been £25,000, and of removing the troops backwards and forwards, amounting to, I know not how much,
are not to be permitted, merely because they are Continental
expenses; for we are a part of the Continent; we must pay a
shilling of every dollar wasted. But the sums of money
which, by these troops, or on their account, are brought into,
and expended in this State, are a great and local advantage.
This can require no proof. If, at the conclusion of the war,
for instance, our share of the Continental debt should be
twenty millions of dollars, or say that we are called on to
furnish an annual quota of two millions four hundred thousand dollars, to Congress, to be raised by tax, it is obvious
that we should raise these given sums with greater or less
ease, in proportion to the greater or less quantity of money
found in circulation among us. I expect that our circulating
money is [increased?], by the presence of these troops, at the
rate of $30,000 a week, at the least. I have heard, indeed, that

an objection arises to their being kept within this State, from the information of the commissary that they cannot be subsisted here. In attending to the information of that officer, it should be borne in mind that the county of King William and its vicinities are one thing, the territory of Virginia another. If the troops could be fed upon long letters, I believe the gentleman at the head of that department in this country, would be the best commissary upon earth. But till I see him determined to act, not to write; to sacrifice his domestic ease to the duties of his appointment, and apply to the resources of this country, wheresoever they are to be had, I must entertain a different opinion of him. I am mistaken if, for the animal subsistence of the troops hitherto, we are not principally indebted to the genius and exertions of Hawkins, during the very short time he lived after his appointment to that department, by your board. His eye immediately pervaded the whole State, it was reduced at once to a regular machine, to a system, and the whole put into movement and animation by the fiat of a comprehensive mind. If the Commonwealth of Virginia cannot furnish these troops with bread, I would ask of the commissariat, which of the thirteen is now become the grain colony? If we are in danger of famine from the addition of four thousand mouths, what is become of that surplus of bread, the exportation of which used to feed the West Indies and Eastern States, and fill the colony with hard money? When I urge the sufficiency of this State, however, to subsist these troops, I beg to be understood, as having in contemplation the quantity of provisions necessary for their real use, and not as calculating what is to be lost by the wanton waste, mismanagement, and carelessness of those employed about it. If magazines of beef and pork are suffered to rot by slovenly butchering, or for want of timely provision and sale; if quantities of flour are exposed, by the commissaries entrusted with the keeping it, to pillage and destruction; and if, when laid up in the Continental stores, it is still to be embezzled and sold, the land of Egypt itself would be insufficient for their supply, and their removal would be necessary, not to a more plentiful country, but to more able and honest commissaries. Perhaps the magnitude of this question, and its relation to the whole State, may render it worth while to

await the opinion of the National Council, which is now to
meet within a few weeks. There is no danger of distress in
the meantime, as the commissaries affirm they have a great
sufficiency of provisions for some time to come. Should the
measure of removing them into another State be adopted,
and carried into execution, before the meeting of Assembly,
no disapprobation of theirs will bring them back, because
they will then be in the power of others, who will hardly give
them up.

Want of information as to what may be the precise measure
proposed by the Governor and Council, obliges me to shift
my ground, and take up the subject in every possible form.
Perhaps, they have not thought to remove the troops out of
this State altogether, but to some other part of it. Here, the
objections arising from the expenses of removal, and of building new barracks, recur. As to animal food, it may be driven
to one part of the country as easily as to another: that circumstance, therefore, may be thrown out of the question. As to
bread, I suppose they will require about forty or forty-five
thousand bushels of grain a year. The place to which it is to
be brought to them, is about the centre of the State. Besides,
that the country round about is fertile, all the grain made in
the counties adjacent to any kind of navigation, may be
brought by water to within twelve miles of the spot. For
these twelve miles, wagons must be employed; I suppose half
a dozen will be a plenty. Perhaps, this part of the expense
might have been saved, had the barracks been built on the
water; but it is not sufficient to justify their being abandoned
now they are built. Wagonage, indeed, seems to the commissariat an article not worth economising. The most wanton
and studied circuity of transportation has been practised: to
mention only one act, they have bought quantities of flour
for these troops in Cumberland, have ordered it to be wagoned down to Manchester, and wagoned thence up to the
barracks. This fact happened to fall within my own knowledge. I doubt not there are many more such, in order either
to produce their total removal, or to run up the expenses of
the present situation, and satisfy Congress that the nearer
they are brought to the commissary's own bed, the cheaper
they will be subsisted. The grain made in the western counties

may be brought partly in wagons, as conveniently to this as to any other place; perhaps more so, on account of its vicinity to one of the best passes through the Blue Ridge; and partly by water, as it is near to James river, to the navigation of which, ten counties are adjacent above the falls. When I said that the grain might be brought hither from all the counties of the State adjacent to navigation, I did not mean to say it would be proper to bring it from all. On the contrary, I think the commissary should be instructed, after the next harvest, not to send one bushel of grain to the barracks from below the falls of the rivers, or from the northern counties. The counties on tide water are accessible to the calls for our own army. Their supplies ought, therefore, to be husbanded for them. The counties in the northwestern parts of the State are not only within reach for our own grand army, but peculiarly necessary for the support of Macintosh's army; or for the support of any other northwestern expedition, which the uncertain conduct of the Indians should render necessary; insomuch, that if the supplies of that quarter should be misapplied to any other purpose, it would destroy, in embryo, every exertion, either for particular or general safety there. The counties above tide water, in the middle and southern and western parts of the country, are not accessible to calls for either of those purposes, but at such an expense of transportation as the article would not bear. Here, then, is a great field, whose supplies of bread cannot be carried to our army, or rather, which will raise no supplies of bread, because there is nobody to eat them. Was it not, then, wise in Congress to remove to that field four thousand idle mouths, who must otherwise have interfered with the pasture of our own troops? And, if they are removed to any other part of the country, will it not defeat this wise purpose? The mills on the waters of James river, above the falls, open to canoe navigation, are very many. Some of them are of great note, as manufacturers. The barracks are surrounded by mills. There are five or six round about Charlottesville. Any two or three of the whole might, in the course of the winter, manufacture flour sufficient for the year. To say the worst, then, of this situation, it is but twelve miles wrong. The safe custody of these troops is another circumstance worthy consideration. Equally removed from the access of an eastern or western enemy; central to the whole State, so that should they attempt an irruption in any direction, they must pass through a great extent of hostile country; in a neighborhood thickly inhabited by a robust and hardy people zealous in the American cause, acquainted with the use of arms, and the defiles and passes by which they must issue: it would seem, that in this point of view, no place could have been better chosen.

Their health is also of importance. I would not endeavor to show that their lives are valuable to us, because it would suppose a possibility, that humanity was kicked out of doors in America, and interest only attended to. The barracks occupy the top and brow of a very high hill, (you have been untruly told they were in a bottom.) They are free from bog, have four springs which seem to be plentiful, one within twenty yards of the piquet, two within fifty yards, and another within two hundred and fifty, and they propose to sink wells within the piquet. Of four thousand people, it should be expected, according to the ordinary calculations, that one should die every day. Yet, in the space of near three months, there have been but four deaths among them; two infants under three weeks old, and two others by apoplexy. The officers tell me, the troops were never before so healthy since they were embodied.

But is an enemy so execrable, that, though in captivity, his wishes and comforts are to be disregarded and even crossed? I think not. It is for the benefit of mankind to mitigate the horrors of war as much as possible. The practice, therefore, of modern nations, of treating captive enemies with politeness and generosity, is not only delightful in contemplation, but really interesting to all the world, friends, foes, and neutrals. Let us apply this: the officers, after considerable hardships, have all procured quarters, comfortable and satisfactory to them. In order to do this, they were obliged, in many instances, to hire houses for a year certain, and at such exorbitant rents, as were sufficient to tempt independent owners to go out of them, and shift as they could. These houses, in most cases, were much out of repair. They have repaired them at a considerable expense. One of the general officers has taken a place for two years, advanced the rent for the whole time, and been obliged, moreover, to erect additional buildings for the accommodation of part of his family, for which there was not room in the house rented. Independent of the brick work, for the carpentry of these additional buildings, I know he is to pay fifteen hundred dollars. The same gentleman, to my knowledge, has paid to one person three thousand six hundred and seventy dollars for different articles to fix himself commodiously. They have generally laid in their stocks of grain and other provisions, for it is well known that officers do not live on their rations. They have purchased cows, sheep, &c., set in to farming, prepared their gardens, and have a prospect of comfort and quiet before them. To turn to the soldiers: the environs of the barracks are delightful, the ground cleared, laid off in hundreds of gardens, each enclosed in its separate paling; these well prepared, and exhibiting a fine appearance. General Riedezel alone laid out upwards of two hundred pounds in garden seeds for the German troops only. Judge what an extent of ground these seeds would cover. There is little doubt that their own gardens will furnish them a great abundance of vegetables through the year. Their poultry, pigeons and other preparations of that kind, present to the mind the idea of a company of farmers, rather than a camp of soldiers. In addition to the barracks built for them by the public, and now very comfortable, they have built great numbers for themselves, in such messes as fancied each other; and the whole corps, both officers and men, seem now happy and satisfied with their situation. Having thus found the art of rendering captivity itself comfortable, and carried it into execution, at their own great expense and labor, their spirits sustained by the prospect of gratifications rising before their eyes, does not every sentiment of humanity revolt against the proposition of stripping them of all this, and removing them into new situations, where, from the advanced season of the year, no preparations can be made for carrying themselves comfortably through the heats of summer; and when it is known that the necessary advances for the conveniences already provided, have exhausted their funds and left them unable to make the like exertions anew. Again, review this matter, as it may regard appearances. A body of troops, after staying a twelvemonth at Boston, are ordered to take a march of seven hundred miles to Virginia, where, it is said, they may be plentifully subsisted. As soon as they are there, they are ordered on some other march, because, in Virginia, it is said, they cannot be subsisted. Indifferent nations will charge this either to ignorance, or to whim and caprice; the parties interested, to cruelty. They now view the proposition in that light, and it is said, there is a general and firm persuasion among them, that they were marched from Boston with no other purpose than to harass and destroy them with eternal marches. Perseverance in object, though not by the most direct way, is often more laudable than perpetual changes, as often as the object shifts light. A character of steadiness in our councils, is worth more than the subsistence of four thousand people.

There could not have been a more unlucky concurrence of circumstances than when these troops first came. The barracks were unfinished for want of laborers, the spell of weather the worst ever known within the memory of man, no stores of bread laid in, the roads, by the weather and number of wagons, soon rendered impassable: not only the troops themselves were greatly disappointed, but the people in the neighborhood were alarmed at the consequences which a total failure of provisions might produce. In this worst state of things, their situation was seen by many and disseminated through the country, so as to occasion a general dissatisfaction, which even seized the minds of reasonable men, who, if not affected by the contagion, must have foreseen that the prospect must brighten, and that great advantages to the people must necessarily arise. It has, accordingly, so happened. The planters, being more generally sellers than buyers, have felt the benefit of their presence in the most vital part about them, their purses, and are now sensible of its source. I have too good an opinion of their love of order to believe that a removal of these troops would produce any irregular proofs of their disapprobation, but I am well assured it would be extremely odious to them.

To conclude. The separation of these troops would be a breach of public faith, therefore I suppose it is impossible; if they are removed to another State, it is the fault of the commissaries; if they are removed to any other part of the State, it is the fault of the commissaries; and in both cases, the public interest and public security suffer, the comfortable and plentiful subsistence of our own army is lessened, the health of the troops neglected, their wishes crossed, and their comforts torn from them, the character of whim and caprice, or, what is worse, of cruelty, fixed on us as a nation, and, to crown the whole, our own people disgusted with such a proceeding.

I have thus taken the liberty of representing to you the facts and the reasons, which seem to militate against the separation or removal of these troops. I am sensible, however, that the same subject may appear to different persons, in very different lights. What I have urged as reasons, may, to sounder minds, be apparent fallacies. I hope they will appear, at least, so plausible, as to excuse the interposition of

Your Excellency's most obedient and most humble servant.

THE TRAITOR ARNOLD
To J. P. G. Muhlenberg

Richmond, Jan. 31, 1781

SIR,—Acquainted as you are with the treasons of Arnold, I need say nothing for your information, or to give you a proper sentiment of them. You will readily suppose that it is above all things desirable to drag him from those under whose wing he is now sheltered. On his march to and from this place I am certain it might have been done with facility by men of enterprise & firmness. I think it may still be done though perhaps not quite so easily. Having peculiar confidence in the men from the Western side of the Mountains, I meant as soon as they should come down to get the enterprise proposed to a chosen number of them, such whose courage & whose fidelity would be above all doubt. Your perfect knowlege of those men personally, and my confidence in your discretion, induce me to ask you to pick from among them proper characters, in such number as you think best, to reveal to them our desire, & engage them to undertake to seize and bring off this greatest of all traitors. Whether this may be best

effected by their going in as friends & awaiting their opportunity, or otherwise is left to themselves. The smaller the
number the better; so that they be sufficient to manage him.
Every necessary caution must be used on their part, to prevent a discovery of their design by the enemy, as should they
be taken, the laws of war will justify against them the most
rigorous sentence. I will undertake if they are successful in
bringing him off alive, that they shall receive five thousand
guineas reward among them. And to men formed for such an
enterprise it must be a great incitement to know that their
names will be recorded with glory in history with those of
Vanwert, Paulding & Williams. The enclosed order from
Baron Steuben will authorize you to call for & dispose of any
force you may think necessary, to place in readiness for covering the enterprise & securing the retreat of the party. Mr.
Newton the bearer of this, & to whom its contents are communicated in confidence, will provide men of trust to go as
guides. These may be associated in the enterprise or not, as
you please; but let that point be previously settled that no
difficulties may arise as to the parties entitled to participate of
the reward. You know how necessary profound secrecy is in
this business, even if it be not undertaken.

WELCOME TO THE MARQUIS
To Lafayette

Richmond, March 10th, 1781

SIR,—Intending that this shall await your arrival in this State
I with great joy welcome you on that event. I am induced to
from the very great esteem your personal character and the
Hopes I entertain of your relieving us from our enemy within
this State. Could any circumstances have rendered your presence more desirable or more necessary it is the unfortunate
one which obliges me to enclose you the enclosed papers.

I trust that your future Acquaintance with the Executive of
the State will evince to you that among their faults is not to
be counted a want of dispostion to second the views of the
Commander against our common Enemy. We are too much

interested in the present scene & have too much at stake to leave a doubt on that Head. Mild Laws, a People not used to prompt obedience, a want of provisions of War & means of procuring them render our orders often ineffectual, oblige us to temporise & when we cannot accomplish an object in one way to attempt it in another. Your knowledge of these circumstances with a temper to accommodate them ensure me your coöperation in the best way we can, when we shall be able to pursue the way we would wish.

I still hope you will find our preparations not far short of the Information I took the Liberty of giving you in my letter of the 8th instant. I shall be very happy to receive your first Applications for whatever may be necessary for the public service and to convince you of our disposition to promote it as far as the Abilities of the State and Powers of the Executive will enable us.

APPEAL TO THE COMMANDER IN CHIEF
To George Washington

Charlottesville, May 28th, 1781

SIR,—I make no doubt you will have heard, before this shall have the honour of being presented to your Excellency, of the junction of Ld Cornwallis with the force at Petersburg under Arnold, who had succeeded to the command on the death of Majr. Genl Phillips. I am now advised that they have evacuated Petersburg, joined at Westover a reinforcement of 2000 men just arrived from New york, crossed James River, and on the 26th instant, were three miles advanced on their way towards Richmond; at which place Majr Genl the Marquis Fayette, lay with three thousand men Regulars and militia: these being the whole number we could arm, until the arrival of the 1100 arms from Rhode Island, which are about this time at the place where our Public stores are deposited. The whole force of the Enemy within this State, from the best intelligence I have been able to get, is I think about 7000 men, infantry and cavalry, including, also, the small garrison left at Portsmouth: a number of privateers, which are constantly ravaging the Shores of our rivers, prevent us from receiving any aid from the Counties lying on navigable waters; and powerful operations meditated against our Western frontier, by a joint force of British, and Indian Savages, have as your Excellency before knew, obliged us to embody, between two and three thousand men in that quarter. Your Excellency will judge from this State of things, and from what you know of our country, what it may probably suffer during the present campaign. Should the Enemy be able to produce no opportunity of annihilating the Marquis's army a small proportion of their force may yet restrain his movements effectually while the greater part employed in detachment to waste an unarmed country and lead the minds of the people to acquiesce under those events which they see no human power prepared to ward off. We are too far removed from the other scenes of war to say whether the main force of the Enemy be within this State. But I suppose they cannot anywhere spare so great an army for the operations of the field. Were it possible for this circumstance to justify in your Excellency a determination to lend us your personal aid, it is evident from the universal voice, that the presence of their beloved Countryman, whose talents have so long been successfully employed, in establishing the freedom of kindred States, to whose person they have still flattered themselves they retained some right and have ever looked up as their dernier resort in distress. That your appearance among them I say would restore full confidence of salvation, and would render them equal to whatever is not impossible. I cannot undertake to foresee and obviate the difficulties which lie in the way of such a resolution: The whole subject is before you of which I see only detached parts; and your judgment will be formed on a view of the whole. Should the danger of this State and its consequence to the Union be such as to render it best for the whole that you should repair to its assistance the difficulty would be how to keep men out of the field. I have undertaken to hint this matter to your Excellency not only on my own sense of its importance to us but at the solicitations of many members of weight in our Legislature which has not yet Assembled to speak their own desires.

A few days will bring to me that relief which the constitution has prepared for those oppressed with the labours of my office and a long declared resolution of relinquishing it to abler hands has prepared my way for retirement to a private station: still as an individual I should feel the comfortable effects of your presence, and have (what I thought could not have been) an additional motive for that gratitude, esteem, & respect with which I have the honour to be, your Excellency's most obedient humble servant.

LIMITS OF PUBLIC DUTY

To James Monroe

Monticello, May 20, 1782

DEAR SIR,—I have been gratified with the receipt of your two favours of the 6th & 11th inst. It gives me pleasure that your county has been wise enough to enlist your talents into their service. I am much obliged by the kind wishes you express of seeing me also in Richmond, and am always mortified when anything is expected from me which I cannot fulfill, & more especially if it relate to the public service. Before I ventured to declare to my countrymen my determination to retire from public employment, I examined well my heart to know whether it were thoroughly cured of every principle of political ambition, whether no lurking particle remained which might leave me uneasy when reduced within the limits of mere private life. I became satisfied that every fibre of that passion was thoroughly eradicated. I examined also in other views my right to withdraw. I considered that I had been thirteen years engaged in public service, that during that time I had so totally abandoned all attention to my private affairs as to permit them to run into great disorder and ruin, that I had now a family advanced to years which require my attention & instruction, that to these were added the hopeful offspring of a deceased friend whose memory must be forever dear to me who have no other reliance for being rendered useful to themselves & their country, that by a constant sacrifice of time, labour, loss, parental & family duties, I had been so far from gaining the affection of my countrymen,

which was the only reward I ever asked or could have felt,
that I had even lost the small estimation I before possessed.
That however I might have comforted myself under the disapprobation of the well-meaning but uninformed people yet
that of their representatives was a shock on which I had not
calculated: that this indeed had been followed by an exculpatory declaration. But in the meantime I had been suspected
& suspended in the eyes of the world without the least hint
then or afterwards made public which might restrain them
from supposing that I stood arraigned for treason of the heart
and not merely weakness of the head; and I felt that these
injuries, for such they have been since acknowledged had inflicted a wound on my spirit which will only be cured by the
all-healing grave. If reason & inclination unite in justifying
my retirement, the laws of my country are equally in favor of
it. Whether the state may command the political services of
all it's members to an indefinite extent, or if these be among
the rights never wholly ceded to the public power, is a question which I do not find expressly decided in England. Obiter
dictums on the subject I have indeed met with, but the complexion of the times in which these have dropped would generally answer them, besides that this species of authority is
not acknowledged in our profession. In this country however
since the present government has been established the point
has been settled by uniform, pointed & multiplied precedents.
Offices of every kind, and given by every power, have been
daily & hourly declined & resigned from the declaration of
independance to this moment. The genl assembly has accepted these without discrimination of office, and without
ever questioning them in point of right. If a difference between the office of a delegate & any other could ever have
been supposed, yet in the case of Mr. Thompson Mason who
declined the office of delegate & was permitted so to do by
the house that supposition has been proved to be groundless.
But indeed no such distinction of offices can be admitted.
Reason and the opinions of the lawyers putting all on a footing as to this question and so giving to the delegate the aid
of all the precedents of the refusal of other offices. The law
then does not warrant the assumption of such a power by the
state over it's members. For if it does where is that law? nor

yet does reason, for tho' I will admit that this does subject every individual if called on to an equal tour of political duty yet it can never go so far as to submit to it his whole existence. If we are made in some degree for others, yet in a greater are we made for ourselves. It were contrary to feeling & indeed ridiculous to suppose that a man had less right in himself than one of his neighbors or indeed all of them put together. This would be slavery & not that liberty which the bill of rights has made inviolable and for the preservation of which our government has been charged. Nothing could so completely divest us of that liberty as the establishment of the opinion that the state has a *perpetual* right to the services of all it's members. This to men of certain ways of thinking would be to annihilate the blessing of existence; to contradict the giver of life who gave it for happiness & not for wretchedness; and certainly to such it were better that they had never been born. However with these I may think public service & private misery inseparably linked together, I have not the vanity to count myself among those whom the state would think worth oppressing with perpetual service. I have received a sufficient memento to the contrary. I am persuaded that having hitherto dedicated to them the whole of the active & useful part of my life I shall be permitted to pass the rest in mental quiet. I hope too that I did not mistake the modes any more than the matter of right when I preferred a simple act of renunciation to the taking sanctuary under those disqualifications provided by the law for other purposes indeed, but which afford asylum also for rest to the wearied. I dare say you did not expect by the few words you dropped on the right of renunciation to expose yourself to the fatigue of so long a letter, but I wished you to see that if I had done wrong I had been betrayed by a semblance of right at least.

I take the liberty of inclosing to you a letter for Genl Chastellux for which you will readily find means of conveyance. But I meant to give you more trouble with the one to Pelham who lives in the neighborhood of Manchester & to ask the favor of you to send it by your servant express which I am in hopes may be done without absenting him from your person but during those hours in which you will be engaged in the house. I am anxious that it should be received immediately.

Mrs Jefferson has added another daughter to our family. She has been ever since & still continues very dangerously ill. It will give me great pleasure to see you here whenever you can favor us with your company. You will find me still busy but in lighter occupations. But in these & all others you will find me to retain a due sense of your friendship & to be with sincere esteem, Dr Sir

Your mo ob & mo hble servt.

P. S. did you ever receive a copy of the Parl. debates & Histor. Register with a letter left for you with Mr Jas. Buchanan?

"A SINGLE EVENT . . ."

To Chastellux

Ampthill, Nov. 26, 1782

DEAR SIR,—I received your friendly letters of —— and June 30 but the latter not till the 17th of Oct. It found me a little emerging from the stupor of mind which had rendered me as dead to the world as she was whose loss occasioned it. Your letter recalled to my memory that there were persons still living of much value to me. If you should have thought me remiss in not testifying to you sooner how deeply I had been impressed with your worth in the little time I had the happiness of being with you you will I am sure ascribe it to it's true cause the state of dreadful suspense in which I had been kept all the summer & the catastrophe which closed it. Before that event my scheme of life had been determined. I had folded myself in the arms of retirement, and rested all prospects of future happiness on domestic & literary objects. A single event wiped away all my plans and left me a blank which I had not the spirits to fill up. In this state of mind an appointment from Congress found me, requiring me to cross the Atlantic. And that temptation might be added to duty I was informed at the same time from his Excy the Chevalier de Luzerne that a vessel of force would be sailing about the middle of Dec. in which you would be passing to France. I accepted the appointment and my only object now is so to hasten over those obstacles which would retard my departure as to be ready to join you in your voyage, fondly measuring your affections by my own & presuming your consent. It is not certain that by any exertion I can be in Philadelphia by the middle of December. The contrary is most probable. But hoping it will not be much later and counting on those procrastinations which usually attend the departure of vessels of size I have hopes of being with you in time. This will give me full leisure to learn the result of your observations on the natural bridge, to communicate to you my answers to the queries of Monsr de Marbois, to receive edification from you on these and on other subjects of science, considering chess too as a matter of science. Should I be able to get out in tolerable time and any extraordinary delays attend the sailing of the vessel I shall certainly do myself the honor of waiting on his Excy Count Rochambeau at his Head quarters and assuring him in person of my high respect and esteem for him—an object of which I have never lost sight. To yourself I am unable to express the warmth of those sentiments of friendship & attachment with which I have the honour to be, Dr Sir,

> Your most obedt & mo hble servt.

ADVICE TO A YOUNG DAUGHTER
To Martha Jefferson

Annapolis, Nov. 28, 1783

MY DEAR PATSY—After four days journey I arrived here without any accident and in as good health as when I left Philadelphia. The conviction that you would be more improved in the situation I have placed you than if still with me, has solaced me on my parting with you, which my love for you has rendered a difficult thing. The acquirements which I hope you will make under the tutors I have provided for you will render you more worthy of my love, and if they cannot increase it they will prevent it's diminution. Consider the good lady who has taken you under her roof, who has undertaken to see that you perform all your exercises, and to admonish you in all those wanderings from what is right or what is clever to which your inexperience would expose you, consider her I say as your mother, as the only person to whom, since the loss with which heaven has been pleased to afflict you, you can now look up; and that her displeasure or disapprobation on any occasion will be an immense misfortune which should you be so unhappy as to incur by any unguarded act, think no concession too much to regain her good will. With respect to the distribution of your time the following is what I should approve.

from 8. to 10 o'clock practise music.

from 10. to 1. dance one day and draw another

from 1. to 2. draw on the day you dance, and write a letter the next day.

from 3. to 4. read French.

from 4. to 5. exercise yourself in music.

from 5. till bedtime read English, write &c.

Communicate this plan to Mrs. Hopkinson and if she approves of it pursue it. As long as Mrs. Trist remains in Philadelphia cultivate her affections. She has been a valuable friend to you and her good sense and good heart make her valued by all who know her and by nobody on earth more than by me. I expect you will write to me by every post. Inform me what books you read, what tunes you learn, and inclose me your best copy of every lesson in drawing. Write also one letter every week either to your aunt Eppes, your aunt Skipwith, your aunt Carr, or the little lady from whom I now inclose a letter, and always put the letter you so write under cover to me. Take care that you never spell a word wrong. Always before you write a word consider how it is spelt, and if you do not remember it, turn to a dictionary. It produces great praise to a lady to spell well. I have placed my happiness on seeing you good and accomplished, and no distress which this world can now bring on me could equal that of your disappointing my hopes. If you love me then, strive to be good under every situation and to all living creatures, and to acquire those accomplishments which I have put in your power, and which will go far towards ensuring you the warmest love of your affectionate father,

P. S. Keep my letters and read them at times that you may always have present in your mind those things which will endear you to me.

THE MAMMOTH AND WESTERN EXPLORATION
To George Rogers Clark

Annapolis, Dec. 4, 1783

DEAR SIR—I received here about a week ago your obliging letter of Oct. 12. 1783. with the shells and seeds for which I return you many thanks. You are also so kind as to keep alive the hope of getting for me as many of the different species of bones, teeth and tusks of the *Mammoth* as can now be found. This will be most acceptable. Pittsburg and Philadelphia or Winchester will be the surest channel of conveyance. I find they have subscribed a very large sum of money in England for exploring the country from the Missisipi to California. They pretend it is only to promote knolege. I am afraid they have thoughts of colonising into that quarter. Some of us have been talking here in a feeble way of making the attempt to search that country. But I doubt whether we have enough of that kind of spirit to raise the money. How would you like to lead such a party? Tho I am afraid our prospect is not worth asking the question. The definitive treaty of peace is at length arrived. It is not altered from the preliminaries. The cession of the territory West of Ohio to the United states has been at length accepted by Congress with some small alterations of the conditions. We are in daily expectation of receiving it with the final approbation of Virginia. Congress have been lately agitated by questions where they should fix their residence. They first resolved on Trentown. The Southern states however contrived to get a vote that they would give half their time to Georgetown at the Falls of Patowmac. Still we consider the matter as undecided between the Delaware and Patowmac. We urge the latter as the only point of union which can cement us to our Western friends when they shall be formed into separate states. I shall always be happy to hear from you and am with very particular esteem Dr. Sir Your friend & humble servt.,

MORE ADVICE

To Martha Jefferson

Annapolis, Dec. 11, 1783

MY DEAR PATSY—I wrote you by the post this day fortnight, since which I have received two letters from you. I am afraid that you may not have sent to the post office and therefore that my letter may be still lying there. Tho' my business here may not let me write to you every week yet it will not be amiss for you to enquire at the office every week. I wrote to Mr. House by the last post. Perhaps his letter may still be in the office. I hope you will have good sense enough to disregard those foolish predictions that the world is to be at an end soon. The almighty has never made known to any body at what time he created it, nor will he tell any body when he means to put an end to it, if ever he means to do it. As to preparations for that event, the best way is for you to be always prepared for it. The only way to be so is never to do nor say a bad thing. If ever you are about to say any thing amiss or to do any thing wrong, consider before hand. You will feel something within you which will tell you it is wrong and ought not to be said or done: this is your conscience, and be sure to obey it. Our maker has given us all, this faithful internal Monitor, and if you always obey it, you will always be prepared for the end of the world: or for a much more certain event which is death. This must happen to all: it puts an end to the world as to us, and the way to be ready for it is never to do a wrong act. I am glad you are proceeding regularly under your tutors. You must not let the sickness of your French master interrupt your reading French, because you are able to do that with the help of your dictionary. Remember I desired you to send me the best copy you should make of every lesson Mr. Cimitiere should set you. In this I hope you will be punctual because it will let me see how you are going on. Always let me know too what tunes you play.

Present my compliments to Mrs. Hopkinson, Mrs. House and Mrs. Trist. I had a letter from your uncle Eppes last week informing me that Polly is very well, and Lucy recovered from an indispostion. I am my dear Patsy your affectionate father,

AMERICAN "POLITICS & POVERTY"
To Chastellux

Annapolis, Jan. 16, 1784

DEAR SIR—L! Colo Franks being appointed to carry to Paris one of the copies of our ratifñ of the Def. treaty, & being to depart in the instant of his appointm! furnishes me a hasty oppȳ of obtruding myself on your recollection. Should this prove troublesome you must take the blame as having exposed yourself to my esteem by letting me become acquainted with your merit. Our transactions on this side the water must now have become uninteresting to the rest of the world. We are busy however among ourselves endeavoring to get our new governments into regular and concerted motion. For this purpose I beleive we shall find some additions requisite to our Confederation. As yet every thing has gone smoothly since the war. We are diverted with the European acc^{ts} of the anarchy & opposition to govm̃t in America. Nothing can be more untrue than these relations. There was indeed some disatisfaction in the army at not being paid off before they were disbanded, and a very trifling mutiny of 200 souldiers in Philadelphia, on the latter occasion Congress left that place disgusted with the pusillanimity of the govm̃t and not from any want of security to their own persons. The indignation which the other states felt at this insult to their delegates has enlisted them more warmly in support of Congress & the people, the legislature, & the Exec. themselves of Pennsvā have made the most satisfactory atonements. Some people also of warm blood undertook to resolve as commeēs for proscribing the refugees. But they were few, scattered here & there through the several states, were absolutely unnoticed by those both in & out of power, and never expressed an idea of not acquiescing ultimately under the decisions of their governments. The greatest difficulty we find is to get money from them. The reason is not founded in their unwillingness, but in their real inability. You were a witness to the total destruction of our commerce, devastation of our country, and absence of the precious metals. It cannot be expected that these should flow in but through the channels of commerce, or that these channels can be opened in the first instant of peace. Time is requisite to avail ourselves of the productions of the earth, and the first of these will be applied to renew our stock of those necessaries of which we had been totally exhausted. But enough of America it's politics & poverty.—Science I suppose is going on with you rapidly as usual. I am in daily hopes of seeing something from your pen which may portray us to ourselves. Aware of the bias of self love & prejudice in myself and that your pictures will be faithful I am determined to annihilate my own opinions and give full credit to yours. I must caution you to distrust information from my answers to Mons.[r] de Marbois' queries. I have lately had a little leisure to revise them. I found some things should be omitted, many corrected, and more supplied & enlarged. They are swelled to treble bulk. Being now too much for M.S. copies I think the ensuing spring to print a dozen or 20 copies to be given to my friends, not suffering another to go out. As I have presumed to place you in that number I shall take the liberty of sending you a copy as a testimony of the sincere esteem and affection with which I have the honor to be D[r] Sir Your mo. ob. & mo. hbl serv[t]

WESTERN COMMERCE

To George Washington

Annapolis, Mar. 15, 1784

D.[r] SIR,—Since my last nothing new has occurred, I suppose the crippled state of Congress is not new to you. We have only 9 states present, 8. of whom are represented by two members each, and of course, on all great questions not only an unanimity of States but of members is necessary. An unanimity which never can be obtained on a matter of any importance. The consequence is that we are wasting our time & labour in vain efforts to do business.—Nothing less than the presence of 13. States, represented by an odd number of delegates will enable us to get forward a single capital point. The deed for the cession of Western territory by Virginia was executed & accepted on the 1st instant. I hope our country will of herself determine to cede still further to the meridian of the mouth of the great Kanhaway. Further she cannot govern; so far is necessary for her own well being. The reasons which call for this boundary (which will retain all the waters of the Kanhaway) are 1. That within that are our lead mines. 2. This river rising in N. Carola traverses our whole latitude and offers to every part of it a channel for navigation & commerce to the Western Country, but 3. It is a channel which can not be opened but at immense expense and with every facility which an absolute power over both shores will give. 4. This river & it's waters forms a band of good land passing along our whole frontier, and forming on it a barrier which will be strongly seated. 5. For 180 miles beyond these waters is a mountainous barren which can never be inhabited & will of course form a safe separation between us & any other State. 6. This tract of country lies more convenient to receive it's government from Virginia than from any other State. 7. It will preserve to us all the upper parts of Yohogany & Cheat rivers within which much will be done to open these which are the true doors to the Western commerce. The union of this navigation with that of the Patowmac is a subject on which I mentioned that I would take the liberty of writing to you. I am sure it's value and practicability are both well known to you. This is the moment however for seizing it if ever we mean to have it. All the world is becoming commercial. Was it practicable to keep our new empire separated from them we might indulge ourselves in speculating whether commerce contributes to the happiness of mankind. But we cannot separate ourselves from them. Our citizens have had too full a taste of the comforts furnished by the arts & manufactures to be debarred the use of them. We must then in our defence endeavour to share as large a portion as we can of this modern source of wealth & power. That offered to us from the Western Country is under a competition between the Hudson, the Patowmac & the Missisipi itself. Down the last will pass all heavy commodities. But the navigation through the gulf of Mexico is so dangerous, & that up the Missisipi so difficult & tedious, that it is not probable that European merchandize will return through that channel. It is most likely that flour, lumber & other heavy articles will be floated on rafts which will be themselves an article of sale as well as their loading, the navigators returning by land or in light batteaux. There will therefore be a rivalship between the Hudson & Patowmac for the residue of the commerce of all the country Westward of L. Erie, on the waters of the lakes, of the Ohio & upper parts of the Missisipi. To go to N. York, that part of the trade which comes from the lakes or their waters must first be brought into L. Erie. So also must that which comes from the waters of the Missisipi, and of course must cross at some portage into the waters of the lakes. When it shall have entered L. Erie it must coast along it's Southern Shore on account of the number & excellence of it's harbours, the Northern, tho' shortest, having few harbours & these unsafe. Having reached Cuyahoga, to proceed on to N. York will be 970 miles from thence & five portages, whereas it is but 430 miles to Alexandria, if it turns into the Cuyahoga & passes through that, Big beaver, Ohio, Yohogany (or Monongahela & Cheat) & Patowmac, & there are but two portages. For the trade of the Ohio or that which shall come into it from it's own waters or the Missisipi, it is nearer to Alexandria than to New York by 730 miles, and is interrupted by one portage only. Nature then has declared in favour of the Patowmac, and through that channel offers to pour into our lap the whole commerce of the Western world. But unfortunately the channel by the Hudson is already open & known in practice; ours is still to be opened. This is the moment in which the trade of the West will begin to get into motion and to take it's direction. It behoves us then to open our doors to it. I have lately pressed this subject on my friends in the General assembly, proposing to them to endeavor to have a tax laid which shall bring into a separate

chest from five to ten thousand pounds a year, to be employed first in opening the upper waters of the Ohio &
Patowmac, where a little money & time will do a great
deal, leaving the great falls for the last part of the work.
To remove the idea of partiality I have suggested the propriety & justice of continuing this fund till all the rivers
shall be cleared successively. But a most powerful objection always arises to propositions of this kind. It is that
public undertakings are carelessly managed and much
money spent to little purpose. To obviate this objection is
the purpose of my giving you the trouble of this discussion. You have retired from public life. You have weighed this
determination & it would be impertinence in me to touch it.
But would the superintendence of this work break in too
much on the sweets of retirement & repose? If they would I
stop here. Your future time & wishes are sacred in my eye. If
it would be only a dignified amusement to you, what a monument of your retirement would it be! It is one which would
follow that of your public life and bespeak it the work of the
same great hand. I am confident that would you either alone
or jointly with any persons you think proper be willing to
direct this business, it would remove the only objection the
weight of which I apprehend. Tho' the tax should not come
in till the fall, it's proceeds should be anticipated by borrowing from some other fund to enable the work to be begun
this summer. When you view me as not owning, nor ever
having a prospect of owning one inch of land on any water
either of the Patowmac or Ohio, it will tend to apologize for
the trouble I have given you of this long letter, by showing
that my zeal in this business is public & pure. The best atonement for the time I have occupied you will be not to add to
it longer than while I assure you of the sincerity & esteem
with which I have the honour to be D.ʳ Sir Your most obedient & most humble servt.

P. S. The hurry of time in my former letter prevented my
thanking you for your polite & friendly invitation to Mount
Vernon. I shall certainly pay my respects there to Mrs Washington & yourself with great pleasure whenever it shall be in
my power.

THE SOCIETY OF THE CINCINNATI
To George Washington

Annapolis, Apr. 16, 1784

DEAR SIR,—I received your favor of Apr. 8. by Colo. Harrison. The subject of it is interesting, and, so far as you have stood connected with it, has been matter of anxiety to me; because whatever may be the ultimate fate of the institution of the Cincinnati, as in it's course it draws to it some degree of disapprobation, I have wished to see you standing on ground separated from it, and that the character which will be handed to future ages at the head of our revolution may in no instance be compromitted in subordinate altercations. The subject has been at the point of my pen in every letter I have written to you, but has been still restrained by the reflection that you had among your friends more able counsellors, and, in yourself, one abler than them all. Your letter has now rendered a duty what was before a desire, and I cannot better merit your confidence than by a full and free communication of facts & sentiments, as far as they have come within my observation. When the army was about to be disbanded, & the officers to take final leave, perhaps never again to meet, it was natural for men who had accompanied each other thro' so many scenes of hardship, of difficulty and danger, who in a variety of instances must have been rendered mutually dear by those aids & good offices to which their situations had given occasion; it was natural I say for these to seize with fondness any proposition which promised to bring them together again at certain & regular periods. And this I take for granted was the origin & object of this institution; & I have no suspicion that they foresaw, much less intended, those mischiefs, which exist perhaps in the forebodings of politicians only. I doubt however whether, in it's execution, it would be found to answer the wishes of those who framed it, and to foster those friendships it was intended to preserve. The members would be brought together at their annual assemblies no longer to encounter a common enemy, but to encounter one another in debate & sentiment. For something I suppose is to be done at these meetings, & however unimportant, it will suffice to produce difference of opinion, contradiction & irritation. The way to make friends quarrel is to put them in disputation under the public eye. An experience of near twenty years has taught me that few friendships stand this test, & that public assemblies, where every one is free to act & speak, are the most powerful looseners of the bands of private friendship. I think therefore that this institution would fail in it's principal object, the perpetuation of the personal friendships contracted thro' the war.

The objections of those who are opposed to the institution shall be briefly sketched. You will readily fill them up. They urge that it is against the confederation—against the letter of some of our constitutions;—against the spirit of all of them—that the foundation on which all these are built is the natural equality of man, the denial of every preeminence but that annexed to legal office, & particularly the denial of a preeminence by birth; that however, in their present dispositions, citizens might decline accepting honorary instalments into the order, a time may come when a change of dispositions would render these flattering, when a well directed distribution of them might draw into the order all the men of talents, of office & wealth, and in this case would probably procure an ingraftment into the government; that in this they will be supported by their foreign members, & the wishes & influence of foreign courts; that experience has shewn that the hereditary branches of modern governments are the patrons of privilege & prerogative, & not of the natural rights of the people whose oppressors they generally are: that besides these evils, which are remote, others may take place more immediately; that a distinction is kept up between the civil & military, which it is for the happiness of both to obliterate; that when the members assemble they will be proposing to do something, & what that something may be will depend on actual circumstances; that being an organized body under habits of subordination, the first obstructions to enterprize will be already surmounted; that the moderation & virtue of a single character has probably prevented this revolution from being closed as most others have been, by a subversion of that liberty it was intended to establish; that he is not immortal, & his successor, or some of his successors, may be led by false calculation into a less certain road to glory:

What are the sentiments of Congress on this subject, & what line they will pursue, can only be stated conjecturally. Congress, as a body, if left to themselves, will in my opinion say nothing on the subject. They may however be forced into a declaration by instructions from some of the states, or by other incidents. Their sentiments, if forced from them, will be unfriendly to the institution. If permitted to pursue their own path, they will check it by side blows whenever it comes in their way, &, in competitions for office, on equal or nearly equal ground, will give silent preferences to those who are not of the fraternity. My reasons for thinking this are 1. The grounds on which they lately declined the foreign order proposed to be conferred on some of our citizens. 2. The fourth of the fundamental articles of constitution for the new states. I inclose you the report. It has been considered by Congress, recommitted & reformed by a committee according to sentiments expressed on other parts of it, but the principle referred to, having not been controverted at all, stands in this as in the original report. It is not yet confirmed by Congress. 3. Private conversations on this subject with the members. Since the receipt of your letter I have taken occasion to extend these; not indeed to the military members, because, being of the order, delicacy forbade it; but to the others pretty generally; and among these I have as yet found but one who is not opposed to the institution, & that with an anguish of mind, tho' covered under a guarded silence, which I have not seen produced by any circumstance before. I arrived at Philadelphia before the separation of the last Congress, & saw there & at Princetown some of its members not now in delegation. Burke's piece happened to come out at that time, which occasioned this institution to be the subject of conversation. I found the same impressions made on them which their successors have received. I hear from other quarters that it is disagreeable generally to such citizens as have attended to it, & therefore will probably be so to all when any circumstance shall present it to the notice of all.

This, Sir, is as faithful an account of sentiments & facts as I am able to give you. You know the extent of the circle within which my observations are at present circumscribed, & can estimate how far, as forming a part of the general opinion, it may merit notice, or ought to influence your particular conduct.

It remains now to pay obedience to that part of your letter which requests sentiments on the most eligible measures to be pursued by the society at their next meeting. I must be far from pretending to be a judge of what would in fact be the most eligible measures for the society. I can only give you the opinions of those with whom I have conversed, & who, as I have before observed, are unfriendly to it. They lead to these conclusions. 1. If the society proceeds according to it's institution, it will be better to make no applications to Congress on that subject or any other in their associated character. 2. If they should propose to modify it, so as to render it unobjectionable, I think this would not be effected without such a modification as would amount almost to annihilation; for such would it be to part with it's inheritability, it's organization, & it's assemblies. 3. If they shall be disposed to discontinue the whole, it would remain with them to determine whether they would chuse it to be done by their own act only, or by a reference of the matter to Congress which would infallibly produce a recommendation of total discontinuance.

You will be sensible, Sir, that these communications are without all reserve. I supposed such to be your wish, & mean them but as materials with such others as you may collect, for your better judgment to work on. I consider the whole matter as between ourselves alone, having determined to take no active part in this or anything else, which may lead to altercation, or disturb that quiet & tranquillity of mind to which I consign the remaining portion of my life. I have been thrown back by events on a stage where I had never more thought to appear. It is but for a time however, & as a day labourer, free to withdraw, or be withdrawn at will. While I remain I shall pursue in silence the path of right, but in every situation, public or private, I shall be gratified by all occasions of rendering you service, & of convincing you there is no one to whom your reputation & happiness are dearer.

HOT-AIR BALLOONS

To Dr. Philip Turpin

Annapolis, Apr. 28, 1784

DEAR SIR—Supposing you may not have received intelligence to be relied on as to the reality & extent of the late discovery of traversing the air in ballons, & having lately perused a book in which everything is brought together on that subject as low down as Decemb. last, I will give you a detail of it. I will state the several experiments, with the most interesting circumstances attending them, by way of table, which will give you a clearer view & in less compass.

They suppose the minimum of these ballons to be of 6 inches diameter: these are constructed of gold-beaters' skin & filled with inflammeable air. this air produced from iron-filings, the vitriolic acid & distilled water is, in weight, to Atmospheric air as 7. to 43. on an average of the trials: & when produced from the filings of Zinc, the Marine acid & distilled water, is to the Atmospheric air as 5. to 53. or 1. to 10½. but Montgolfier's air is half the weight of Atmospheric. this is produced by burning straw & wool. the straw must be dry & open, & the wool shred very fine, so that they may make a clear flame, with as little smoke as possible. 50 lb. of straw & 5 lb. of wool filled the ballons of Oct. 19. & Nov. 21. in five minutes. these ballons contained 60,000 cubic feet. no analysis of this air is given us. Mons'r de Saintford the author of the book, gives us a very great & useless display of Mathematical learning, which certainly has as yet had very little to do with this discovery: & when he comes to the chemical investigations, which are interesting, he sais little. the ballons sometimes were torn by the pressure of the internal air being insufficiently counteracted in the higher regions of the Atmosphere. these rents were of 6. or 7. f. length, yet the machine descended with a gentle equable motion & not with an accelerated one. by the trials at Versailles & Champ de Mars it appears that they will go with a moderate wind 150. leagues in 24 hours. there are yet two principal desiderata. 1. the cheapest & easiest process of making the lightest inflammable air. 2. an envelopment which will be light, strong, impervious to the air & proof against rain. supplies of gas are desireable

Date of experiment 1783	Place of experiment	Height of Ballon in feet	Diameter of Ballon in feet	Materials of which the Envelop was made	Materials from which the internal air was produced	Weight comp'd with common air	Weight the Ballon could raise	Horizontal distance to which it went the air	Ascent in the air	Miscellaneous circumstances
June 5	Annonay	....	36	paper	straw & wool burnt	½	lbs. 490	1200 toises	1000 toises	
Aug. 27	Champ de Mars	....	12	taffety gum elastic	iron filings unindicated	⅙	35	5 leagues	un-known	
Sept. 12	Academie Koiale	70	....	canvas and paper	straw & wool	½	1250		....	
Sept. 19	Versailles	57	41	cloth	straw & wool	½	696	1700 toises	300 toises	a sheep, duck & cock aboard
Oct. 19	Paris	70	46	....	straw & wool	½	....	50 toises	54 toises	2 men aboard
Nov. 21	Chateau de	70	46	....	....		1700	5000 toises in 20'	1600 toises	2 men aboard
Dec.	....	....	....	....	....	....	....	twenty odd miles	1600 toises	2 men ab'd barom. fell from 28 to 18—Farenhi; thermom. fell 36 deg.

too, without being obliged to carry fire with the machine: for in those in which men ascended there was a store of straw & wool laid in the gallery which surrounded the bottom of the ballon & in which the men stood, & a chaffing dish of 3. feet cube in which they burnt the materials to supply air. it is conjectured that these machines may be guided by oars & raised & depressed by having vessels wherein, by the aid of pumps, they can produce a vacuum or condensation of atmospheric air at will. they are, from some new circumstances, strengthened in the opinion that there are generally opposite or different currents in the atmosphere: & that if the current next the earth is not in the direction which suits you, by ascending higher you may find one that does. between these there is probably a region of eddy where you may be stationary if philosophical experiments be your object. the uses of this discovery are suggested to be 1. transportation of commodities under some circumstances. 2. traversing deserts, countries possessed by an enemy, or ravaged by infectious disorders, pathless & inaccessible mountains. 3. conveying intelligence into a beseiged place, or perhaps enterprising on it, reconnoitring an army &c. 4. throwing new lights on the thermometer, barometer, hygrometer, rain, snow, hail, wind & other phenomena of which the Atmosphere is the theatre. 5. the discovery of the pole which is but one day's journey in a baloon. from where the ice has hitherto stopped adventurers. 6. raising weights; lightening ships over bars. 7. housebreaking, smuggling &c. some of these objects are ludicrous, others serious, important & probable. I will give you the figures of the baloons on the last page.

Congress has determined to adjourn on the 3d of June to meet in November at Trenton. a vessel arrived here yesterday which left London the 25th of March. she brings papers to the 20th of that month. mr. Pitt was still in place, supported by the city of London, the nation in general, & the House of Lords. still however the majority in the H. of commons was against him, tho reduced to 12. it was thought the parliament would be dissolved.

Be so good as to present my dutiful respects to my uncle &
aunt & to be assured of the esteem with which I am Dr.
Sir

your friend & serv't

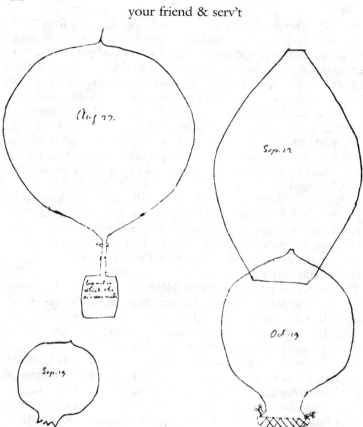

"NIL DESPERANDUM"
To Richard Price

Paris, Feb. 1, 1785

SIR,—The copy of your Observations on the American Revolution which you were so kind as to direct to me came duly to hand, and I should sooner have acknowledged the receipt of it but that I awaited a private conveiance for my letter, having experienced much delay and uncertainty in the posts between this place and London. I have read it with very great pleasure, as have done many others to whom I have communicated it. The spirit which it breathes is as affectionate as the observations themselves are wise and just. I have no doubt it will be reprinted in America and produce much good there. The want of power in the federal head was early perceived, and foreseen to be the flaw in our constitution which might endanger its destruction. I have the pleasure to inform you that when I left America in July the people were becoming universally sensible of this, and a spirit to enlarge the powers of Congress was becoming general. Letters and other information recently received shew that this has continued to increase, and that they are likely to remedy this evil effectually. The happiness of governments like ours, wherein the people are truly the mainspring, is that they are never to be despaired of. When an evil becomes so glaring as to strike them generally, they arrouse themselves, and it is redressed. He only is then the popular man and can get into office who shews the best dispositions to reform the evil. This truth was obvious on several occasions during the late war, and this character in our governments saved us. Calamity was our best physician. Since the peace it was observed that some nations of Europe, counting on the weakness of Congress and the little probability of a union in measure among the States, were proposing to grasp at unequal advantages in our commerce. The people are become sensible of this, and you may be assured that this evil will be immediately redressed, and redressed radically. I doubt still whether in this moment they will enlarge those powers in Congress which are necessary to keep the peace among the States. I think it possible that this may be suffered to lie till some two States commit hostilities on each other, but in that moment the hand of the union will be lifted up and interposed, and the people will themselves demand a general concession to Congress of means to prevent similar mischeifs. Our motto is truly "nil desperandum." The apprehensions you express of danger from the want of powers in Congress, led me to note to you this character in our governments, which, since the retreat behind the Delaware, and the capture of Charlestown, has kept my mind in perfect quiet as to the ultimate fate of our union; and I am sure, from the spirit which breathes thro your book, that whatever promises permanence to that will be a comfort to your mind. I have the honour to be, with very sincere esteem and respect, Sir,

Your most obedient and most humble serv.ᵗ

ON AMERICAN DEGENERACY
To Chastellux

Paris, June 7, 1785

DEAR SIR,—I have been honored with the receipt of your letter of the 2nd instant, and am to thank you, as I do sincerely, for the partiality with which you receive the copy of the Notes on my country. As I can answer for the facts therein reported on my own observation, and have admitted none on the report of others, which were not supported by evidence sufficient to command my own assent, I am not afraid that you should make any extracts you please for the Journal de Physique, which come within their plan of publication. The strictures on slavery and on the constitution of Virginia, are not of that kind, and they are the parts which I do not wish to have made public, at least, till I know whether their publication would do most harm or good. It is possible, that in my own country, these strictures might produce an irritation, which would indispose the people towards the two great objects I have in view; that is, the emancipation of their slaves, and the settlement of their constitution on a firmer and more permanent basis. If I learn from thence, that they will not produce that effect, I have printed and reserved just copies enough to be able to give one to every young man at the

College. It is to them I look, to the rising generation, and not to the one now in power, for these great reformations. The other copy, delivered at your hotel, was for Monsieur de Buffon. I meant to ask the favor of you to have it sent to him, as I was ignorant how to do it. I have one also for Monsieur Daubenton, but being utterly unknown to him, I cannot take the liberty of presenting it, till I can do it through some common acquaintance.

I will beg leave to say here a few words on the general question of the degeneracy of animals in America. 1. As to the degeneracy of the man of Europe transplanted to America, it is no part of Monsieur de Buffon's system. He goes, indeed, within one step of it, but he stops there. The Abbé Raynal alone has taken that step. Your knowledge of America enables you to judge this question, to say, whether the lower class of people in America, are less informed and less susceptible of information, than the lower class in Europe: and whether those in America, who have received such an education as that country can give, are less improved by it than Europeans of the same degree of education. 2. As to the aboriginal man of America, I know of no respectable evidence on which the opinion of his inferiority of genius has been founded, but that of Don Ulloa. As to Robertson, he never was in America, he relates nothing on his own knowledge, he is a compiler only of the relations of others, and a mere translator of the opinions of Monsieur de Buffon. I should as soon, therefore, add the translators of Robertson to the witnesses of this fact, as himself. Paw, the beginner of this charge, was a compiler from the works of others; and of the most unlucky description; for he seems to have read the writings of travellers, only to collect and republish their lies. It is really remarkable, that in three volumes 12mo, of small print, it is scarcely possible to find one truth, and yet, that the author should be able to produce authority for every fact he states, as he says he can. Don Ulloa's testimony is of the most respectable. He wrote of what he saw, but he saw the Indian of South America only, and that, after he had passed through ten generations of slavery. It is very unfair, from this sample, to judge of the natural genius of this race of men; and after supposing that Don Ulloa had not sufficiently calculated the allowance which should be made for this circumstance, we do him no injury in considering the picture he draws of the present Indians of South America, as no picture of what their ancestors were, three hundred years ago. It is in North America we are to seek their original character. And I am safe in affirming, that the proofs of genius given by the Indians of North America, place them on a level with whites in the same uncultivated state. The North of Europe furnishes subjects enough for comparison with them, and for a proof of their equality. I have seen some thousands myself, and conversed much with them, and have found in them a masculine, sound understanding. I have had much information from men who had lived among them, and whose veracity and good sense were so far known to me, as to establish a reliance on their information. They have all agreed in bearing witness in favor of the genius of this people. As to their bodily strength, their manners rendering it disgraceful to labor, those muscles employed in labor will be weaker with them, than with the European laborer; but those which are exerted in the chase, and those faculties which are employed in the tracing an enemy or a wild beast, in contriving ambuscades for him, and in carrying them through their execution, are much stronger than with us, because they are more exercised. I believe the Indian, then, to be, in body and mind, equal to the white man. I have supposed the black man, in his present state, might not be so; but it would be hazardous to affirm, that, equally cultivated for a few generations, he would not become so. 3. As to the inferiority of the other animals of America, without more facts, I can add nothing to what I have said in my Notes.

As to the theory of Monsieur de Buffon, that heat is friendly, and moisture adverse to the production of large animals, I am lately furnished with a fact by Dr. Franklin, which proves the air of London and of Paris to be more humid than that of Philadelphia, and so creates a suspicion that the opinion of the superior humidity of America may, perhaps, have been too hastily adopted. And supposing that fact admitted, I think the physical reasonings urged to show, that in a moist country animals must be small, and that in a hot one they must be large, are not built on the basis of experiment. These questions, however, cannot be decided, ultimately, at this day.

More facts must be collected, and more time flow off, before the world will be ripe for decision. In the mean time, doubt is wisdom.

I have been fully sensible of the anxieties of your situation, and that your attentions were wholly consecrated, where alone they were wholly due, to the succour of friendship and worth. However much I prize your society, I wait with patience the moment when I can have it without taking what is due to another. In the mean time, I am solaced with the hope of possessing your friendship, and that it is not ungrateful to you to receive assurances of that with which I have the honor to be, Dear Sir,

your most obedient,
and most humble servant,

SOME THOUGHTS ON TREATIES
To James Monroe

Paris, June 17, 1785

DEAR SIR,—I received three days ago your favor of Apr. 12. You therein speak of a former letter to me, but it has not come to hand, nor any other of later date than the 14th of December. My last letter to you was of the 11th of May by Mr. Adams who went in the packet of that month. These conveiances are now becoming deranged. We have had expectations of their coming to Havre which would infinitely facilitate the communication between Paris & Congress: but their deliberations on the subject seem to be taking another turn. They complain of the expence, and that their commerce with us is too small to justify it. They therefore talk of sending a packet every six weeks only. The present one therefore, which should have sailed about this time, will not sail until the 1st of July. However the whole matter is as yet undecided. I have hoped that when Mr. St. John arrives from N. York he will get them replaced on their monthly system. By the bye what is the meaning of a very angry resolution of Congress on this subject? I have it not by me and therefore cannot cite it by date, but you will remember it, and will oblige me by explaining it's foundation. This will be handed you by Mr. Otto who comes to America as Chargé des Affaires in the room of Mr. Marbois promoted to the Intendancy of Hispaniola, which office is next to that of Governor. He becomes the head of the civil as the Governor is of the military department. I am much pleased with Otto's appointment. He is good humored, affectionate to America, will see things in a friendly light when they admit of it, in a rational one always, and will not pique himself on writing every trifling circumstance of irritation to his court. I wish you to be acquainted with him, as a friendly intercourse between individuals who do business together produces a mutual spirit of accommodation useful to both parties. It is very much our interest to keep up the affection of this country for us, which is considerable. A court has no affections, but those of the people whom they govern influence their decisions even in the most arbitrary governments.—The negociations between the Emperor & Dutch are spun out to an amazing length. At present there is no apprehension but that they will terminate in peace. This court seems to press it with ardour and the Dutch are averse considering the terms cruel & unjust as they evidently are. The present delays therefore are imputed to their coldness & to their forms. In the mean time the Turk is delaying the demarcation of limits between him and the emperor, is making the most vigorous preparations for war, and has composed his ministry of war-like characters deemed personally hostile to the emperor. Thus time seems to be spinning out both by the Dutch & Turks, & time is wanting for France. Every year's delay is a great thing to her. It is not impossible therefore but that she may secretly encourage the delays of the Dutch & hasten the preparations of the Porte while she is recovering vigour herself and, in order to be able to present such a combination to the emperor as may dictate to him to be quiet. But the designs of these courts are inscrutable. It is our interest to pray that this country may have no continental war till our peace with England is perfectly settled. The merchants of this country continue as loud & furious as ever against the Arret of August 1784, permitting our commerce with their islands to a certain degree. Many of them have actually abandoned their trade. The Ministry are disposed to be firm, but there is a point at which they will give way, that is if the clamours should become such as to endanger their places. It is evident that nothing can be done by us, at this time, if we may hope it hereafter. I like your removal to N. York, and hope Congress will continue there and never execute the idea of building their federal town. Before it could be finished a change of Members in Congress or the admission of new states would remove them somewhere else. It is evident that when a sufficient number of the Western states come in they will remove it to George town. In the mean time it is our interest that it should remain where it is, and give no new pretensions to any other place. I am also much pleased with the proposition to the states to invest Congress with the regulation of their trade, reserving it's revenue to the states. I think it a happy idea, removing the only objection which could have been justly made to the proposition. The time too is the present, before the admission of the Western states. I am very differently affected towards the new plan of opening our land office by dividing the lands among the states and selling them at vendue. It separates still more the interests of the states which ought to be made joint in every possible instance in order to cultivate the idea of our being one nation, and to multiply the instances in which the people shall look up to Congress as their head. And when the states get their portions they will either fool them away, or make a job of it to serve individuals. Proofs of both these practices have been furnished, and by either of them that invaluable fund is lost which ought to pay our public debt. To sell them at vendue, is to give them to the bidders of the day be they many or few. It is ripping up the hen which lays golden eggs. If sold in lots at a fixed price as first proposed, the best lots will be sold first. As these become occupied it gives a value to the interjacent ones, and raises them, tho' of inferior quality, to the price of the first. I send you by Mr. Otto a copy of my book. Be so good as to apologize to Mr. Thomson for my not sending him one by this conveiance. I could not burthen Mr. Otto with more on so long a road as that from here to l'Orient. I will send him one by a Mr. Williams who will go ere long. I have taken measures to prevent it's publication. My reason is that I fear the terms in which I speak of slavery and of our constitution may produce an irritation which will revolt the minds of our countrymen against reformation in these two articles, and thus do more harm than good. I have asked of Mr. Madison to sound this matter as far as he can, and if he thinks it will not produce that effect, I have then copies enough printed to give one to each of the young men at the college, and to my friends in the country.

I am sorry to see a possibility of *A. L.'s being put into* the *Treasury. He* has no *talents* for the *office,* and what *he has* will be *employed* in *rummaging old accounts* to *involve* you in *eternal war with R. M.* and *he* will in a short time *introduce* such *dissensions* into the *Commission* as to *break it up. If he goes* on the *other appointment to Kaskaskia he will produce a revolt* of that *settlement from* the *U. S. I thank you* for *your attention* to *my outfit. For* the *articles* of *household furniture, clothes,* and a *carriage, I have already paid 28,000 livres* and *have* still *more to pay.* For the *greatest part* of *this* I have *been obliged* to *anticipate my salary* from which *however I* shall never be able to *repay* it. *I find* that by a *rigid economy, bordering* however on *meanness I* can *save* perhaps *$500* a *month,* at *least* in *the summer.* The *residue* goes for *expences* so much of *course* & of *necessity that I* cannot *avoid* them *without abandoning all respect* to *my public character. Yet I* will *pray you to touch* this *string,* which *I know to be a tender one* with *Congress* with the utmost delicacy. I had *rather be ruined* in *my fortune,* than in their esteem. If they *allow me half* a *year's salary* as an *outfit I* can *get through my debts in time. If they raise* the *salary* to what *it was, or even pay our house rent* & *taxes, I* can *live with more decency. I trust* that *Mr. A.'s house* at *the Hague* & *Dr. F.'s* at *Passy* the *rent* of which had been always *allowed him* will *give just expectations* of the *same allowance* to *me. Mr. Jay* however did not *charge it. But he lived œconomically* and *laid up money.* I will take the liberty of hazarding to you some thoughts on the policy of entering into treaties with the European nations, and the nature of them. I am not wedded to these ideas, and therefore shall relinquish them chearfully when Congress shall adopt others, and zealously endeavor to carry theirs into effect. First as to the policy of making treaties. Congress, by the Confederation have no original and inherent power over the commerce of the states. But by the 9th article they are authorized to enter into treaties of commerce. The moment these treaties are concluded the jurisdiction of Congress over the commerce of the states springs into existence, and that of the particular states is superseded so far as the articles of the treaty may have taken up the subject. There are two restrictions only on the exercise of the power of treaty by Congress. 1.st that they shall not by such treaty restrain the legislatures of the states from imposing such duties on foreigners as their own people are subject to. 2.dly nor from prohibiting the exportation or importation of any particular species of goods. Leaving these two points free, Congress may by treaty establish any system of commerce they please. But, as I before observed, it is by treaty alone they can do it. Though they may exercise their other powers by resolution or ordinance, those over commerce can only be exercised by forming a treaty, and this probably by an accidental wording of our Confederation. If therefore it is better for the states that Congress should regulate their commerce, it is proper that they should form treaties with all nations with whom we may possibly trade. You see that my primary object in the formation of treaties is to take the commerce of the states out of the hands of the states, and to place it under the superintendence of Congress, so far as the imperfect provisions of our constitution will admit, and until the states shall by new compact make them more perfect. I would say then to every nation on earth, *by treaty*, your people shall trade freely with us, & ours with you, paying no more than the most favoured nation, in order to put an end to the right of individual states acting by fits and starts to interrupt our commerce or to embroil us with any nation. As to the terms of these treaties, the question becomes more difficult. I will mention three different plans. 1. that no duties shall be laid by either party on the productions of the other. 2. that each may be permitted to equalize their duties to those laid by the other. 3. that each shall pay in the ports of the other such duties only as the most favoured nations pay. 1. Were the nations of Europe as free and unembarrassed of established system as we are, I do verily believe they would concur with us in the first plan. But it is impossible. These establishments are fixed upon them, they are interwoven with the body of their laws & the organization of their government & they make a great part of their revenue; they cannot then get rid of them. 2. The plan of equal imposts presents difficulties insurmountable. For how are the equal imposts to be effected? Is it by laying in the ports of A. an equal percent on the goods of B. with that which B. has laid in his ports on the goods of A.? But how are we to find what is that percent? For this is not the usual form of imposts. They generally pay by the ton, by the measure, by the weight, & not by the value. Besides if A. sends a million's worth of goods to B. & takes back but the half of that, and each pays the same percent, it is evident that A. pays the double of what he recovers in the same way with B. This would be our case with Spain. Shall we endeavour to effect equality then by saying A. may levy so much on the sum of B.'s importations into his ports, as B. does on the sum of A's importations into the ports of B.? But how find out that sum? Will either party lay open their custom house books candidly to evince this sum? Does either keep their books so exactly as to be able to do it? This proposition was started in Congress when our institutions were formed, as you may remember, and the impossibility of executing it occasioned it to be disapproved. Besides who should have a right of deciding when the imposts were equal. A. would say to B. my imposts do not raise so much as yours; I raise them therefore. B. would then say you have made them greater than mine, I will raise mine, and thus a kind of auction would be carried on between them, and a mutual imitation, which would end in anything sooner than equality, and right. 3. I confess then to you that I see no alternative left but that which Congress adopted, of each party placing the other on the footing of the most favoured nation. If the nations of Europe from their actual establishments are not at liberty to say to America that she shall trade in their ports duty free they may say she may trade there paying no higher duties than the most favoured nation. And this is valuable in many of these countries where a very great difference is made between different nations. There is no difficulty in the execution of this contract, because there is not a merchant who does not know, or may not know, the duty paid by every nation on every article. This stipulation leaves each party at liberty to regulate their own commerce by general rules; while it secures the other from partial and oppressive discriminations. The difficulty which arises in our case is, with the nations having American territory. Access to the West Indies is indispensably necessary to us. Yet how to gain it, when it is the established system of these nations to exclude all foreigners from their colonies. The only chance seems to be this, our commerce to the mother countries is valuable to them. We must endeavor then to make this the price of an admission into their West Indies, and to those who refuse the admission we must refuse our commerce or load theirs by odious discriminations in our ports. We have this circumstance in our favour too, that what one grants us in their islands, the others will not find it worth their while to refuse. The misfortune is that with this country we gave this price for their aid in the war, and we have now nothing more to offer. She being withdrawn from the competition leaves Gr. Britain much more at liberty to hold out against us. This is the difficult part of the business of treaty, and I own it does not hold out the most flattering prospect.—I wish you would consider this subject and write me your thoughts on it. Mr. Gherry wrote me on the same subject. Will you give me leave to impose on you the trouble of communicating this to him? It is long, and will save me much labour in copying. I hope he will be so indulgent as to consider it as an answer to that part of his letter, and will give me his further thoughts on it.

Shall I send you so much of the Encyclopedia as is already published or reserve it here till you come? It is about 40 vols. which probably is about half the work. Give yourself no uneasiness about the money. Perhaps I may find it convenient to ask you to pay trifles occasionally for me in America. I sincerely wish you may find it convenient to come here. The pleasure of the trip will be less than you expect but the utility greater. It will make you adore your own country, it's soil, it's climate, it's equality, liberty, laws, people & manners. My God! how little do my country men know what precious blessings they are in possession of, and which no other people on earth enjoy. I confess I had no idea of it myself. While we shall see multiplied instances of Europeans going to live in America, I will venture to say no man now living will ever

see an instance of an American removing to settle in Europe
& continuing there. Come then & see the proofs of this, and
on your return add your testimony to that of every thinking
American, in order to satisfy our countrymen how much it is
their interest to preserve uninfected by contagion those peculiarities in their government & manners to which they are
indebted for these blessings. Adieu, my dear friend. Present
me affectionately to your collegues. If any of them think me
worth writing to, they may be assured that in the epistolary
account I will keep the debit side against them. Once more
adieu.

June 19. Since writing the above we receive the following
account. Mons. Pilatre de Rosiere, who has been waiting
some months at Boulogne for a fair wind to cross the channel, at length took his ascent with a companion. The wind
changed after a while and brought him back on the French
coast. Being at a height of about 6000 f. some accident happened to his baloon of inflammable air. It burst, they fell
from that height & were crushed to atoms. There was a
Montgolfier combined with the baloon of inflammable air. It
is suspected the heat of the Montgolfier rarified too much the
inflammable air of the other & occasioned it to burst. The
Montgolfier came down in good order.

ROYAL SCANDAL AND THIRD-RANK BIRDS
To Abigail Adams

Paris, June 21, 1785

DEAR MADAM—I have received duly the honor of your letter,
and am now to return you thanks for your condescension in
having taken the first step for settling a correspondence which
I so much desired; for I now consider it as *settled* and proceed
accordingly. I have always found it best to remove obstacles
first. I will do so therefore in the present case by telling you
that I consider your boasts of the splendour of your city and
of it's superb hackney coaches as a flout, and declaring that I
would not give the polite, self-denying, feeling, hospitable,
goodhumoured people of this country and their amability in

every point of view, (tho' it must be confessed our streets are somewhat dirty, and our fiacres rather indifferent) for ten such races of rich, proud, hectoring, swearing, squibbing, carnivorous animals as those among whom you are; and that I do love this *people* with all my heart, and think that with a better religion and a better form of government and their present governors their condition and country would be most enviable. I pray you to observe that I have used the term *people* and that this is a noun of the masculine as well as feminine gender. I must add too that we are about reforming our fiacres, and that I expect soon an Ordonance that all their drivers shall wear breeches unless any difficulty should arise whether this is a subject for the police or for the general legislation of the country, to take care of. We have lately had an incident of some consequence, as it shews a spirit of treason, and audaciousness which was hardly thought to exist in this country. Some eight or ten years ago a Chevalier —— was sent on a message of state to the princess of —— of —— of (before I proceed an inch further I must confess my profound stupidity; for tho' I have heard this story told fifty times in all it's circumstances, I declare I am unable to recollect the name of the ambassador, the name of the princess, and the nation he was sent to; I must therefore proceed to tell you the naked story, shorn of all those precious circumstances) some chevalier or other was sent on some business or other to some princess or other. Not succeeding in his negociation, he wrote on his return the following song.

Ennivré du brillant poste
Que j'occupe récemment,
Dans une chaise de poste
Je me campe fierement:
Et je vais en ambassade
Au nom de mon souverain
Dire que je suis malade,
Et que lui se porte bien.

Avec une joue enflée
Je debarque tout honteux:
La princesse boursoufflée,
Au lieu d'une, en avoit deux;
Et son altesse sauvage

Sans doute a trouvé mauvais
Que j'eusse sur mon visage
La moitié de ses attraits.

Princesse, le roi mon maitre
M'a pris pour Ambassadeur;
Je viens vous faire connoitre
Quelle est pour vous son ardeur.
Quand vous seriez sous le chaume,
Il donneroit, m'a-t-il dit,
La moitié de son royaume
Pour celle de votre lit.

La princesse à son pupitre
Compose un remerciment:
Elle me donne une epitre
Que j'emporte lestement,

Et je m'en vais dans la rue
Fort satisfait d'ajouter
A l'honneur de l'avoir vue
Le plaisir de la quitter.

This song run through all companies and was known to every body. A book was afterwards printed, with a regular license, called 'Les quatres saisons litteraires' which being a collection of little things, contained this also, and all the world bought it or might buy it if they would, the government taking no notice of it. It being the office of the Journal de Paris to give an account and criticism of new publications, this book came in turn to be criticised by the redacteur, and he happened to select and print in his journal this song as a specimen of what the collection contained. He was seised in his bed that night and has been never since heard of. Our excellent journal de Paris then is suppressed and this bold traitor has been in jail now three weeks, and for ought any body knows will end his days there. Thus you see, madam, the value of energy in government; our feeble republic would in such a case have probably been wrapt in the flames of war and desolation for want of a power lodged in a single hand to punish summarily those who write songs. The fate of poor Pilatre de Rosiere will have reached you before this does, and with more certainty than we yet know it. This will damp for a while the ardor of the Phaetons of our race who are endeavoring to learn us the way to heaven on wings of our own. I took a trip yesterday to Sannois and commenced an acquaintance with the old Countess d'Hocquetout. I received much pleasure from it and hope it has opened a door of admission for me to the circle of literati with which she is environed. I heard there the Nightingale in all it's perfection: and I do not hesitate to pronounce that in America it would be deemed a bird of the third rank only, our mockingbird, and fox-coloured thrush being unquestionably superior to it. The squibs against Mr. Adams are such as I expected from the polished, mild tempered, truth speaking people he is sent to. It would be ill policy to attempt to answer or refute them. But countersquibs I think would be good policy. Be pleased to tell him that as I had before ordered his Madeira and Frontignac to be forwarded, and had asked his orders to Mr. Garvey as to

the residue, which I doubt not he has given, I was afraid to
send another order about the Bourdeaux lest it should produce confusion. In stating my accounts with the United
states, I am at a loss whether to charge house rent or not. It
has always been allowed to Dr. Franklin. Does Mr. Adams
mean to charge this for Auteuil and London? Because if he
does, I certainly will, being convinced by experience that my
expences here will otherwise exceed my allowance. I ask this
information of you, Madam, because I think you know better
than Mr. Adams what may be necessary and right for him to
do in occasions of this class. I will beg the favor of you to
present my respects to Miss Adams. I have no secrets to communicate to her in cypher at this moment, what I write to
Mr. Adams being mere commonplace stuff, not meriting a
communication to the Secretary. I have the honour to be with
the most perfect esteem Dr. Madam Your most obedient and
most humble servt.,

A STATUE OF WASHINGTON

To the Virginia Delegates in Congress

Paris, July 12, 1785

GENTLEMEN,—In consequence of the orders of the Legislative & Executive bodies of Virginia, I have engaged Monsr.
Houdon to make the Statue of Genl. Washington. For this
purpose it is necessary for him to see the General. He therefore goes with Doctr. Franklin, & will have the honor of delivering you this himself. As his journey is at the expence of
the State according to our contract, I will pray you to favor
him with your patronage & counsels, and to protect him as
much as possible from those impositions to which strangers
are but too much exposed. I have advised him to proceed in
the stages to the General's. I have also agreed, if he can see
General Greene & Gates, whose busts he has a desire to
make, that he may make a moderate deviation for this purpose, after he is done with General Washington.

But the most important object with him is to be employed
to make General Washington's equestrian statue for Congress.

Nothing but the expectation of this could have engaged him to have undertaken this voyage. The pedestrian statue for Virginia will not make it worth the business he loses by absenting himself. I was therefore obliged to assure him of my recommendations for this greater work. Having acted in this for the state, you will I hope think yourselves in some measure bound to patronize & urge his being employed by Congress. I would not have done this myself, nor asked you to do it, did I not see that it would be better for Congress to put this business into his hands, than those of any other person living, for these reasons: 1. he is without rivalship the first statuary of this age; as a proof of which he receives orders from every other country for things intended to be capital: 2. he will have seen General Washington, have taken his measures in every part, and of course whatever he does of him will have the merit of being original, from which other workmen can only furnish copies. 3. He is in possession of the house, the furnaces, & all the apparatus provided for making the statue of Louis XV. If any other workman is employed, this will all be to be provided anew and of course to be added to the price of the statue, for no man can ever expect to make two equestrian statues. The addition which this would be to the price will much exceed the expectation of any person who has not seen that apparatus. In truth it is immense. As to the price of the work it will be much greater than Congress is aware of, probably. I have enquired somewhat into this circumstance, and find the prices of those made for two centuries past have been from 120.000 guineas down to 16.000 guineas, according to the size. And as far as I have seen, the smaller they are, the more agreeable. The smallest yet made is infinitely above the size of the life, and they all appear outrée and monstrous. That of Louis XV. is probably the best in the world, and it is the smallest here. Yet it is impossible to find a point of view from which it does not appear a monster, unless you go so far as to lose sight of the features and finer lineaments of the face and body. A statue is not made, like a mountain, to be seen at a great distance. To perceive those minuter circumstances which constitute its beauty you must be near it, and, in that case, it should be so little above the size of the life, as to appear actually of that size from your point of view. I should not therefore fear to propose that the one intended by Congress should be considerably smaller than any of those to be seen here; as I think it will be more beautiful, and also cheaper. I have troubled you with these observations as they have been suggested to me from an actual sight of works in this kind, & supposed they might assist you in making up your minds on this subject. In making a contract with Monsr. Houdon it would not be proper to advance money, but as his disbursements and labour advance. As it is a work of many years, this will render the expence insensible. The pedestrian statue of marble is to take three years. The equestrian of course much more. Therefore the sooner it is begun the better.

"AN HONEST HEART . . . A KNOWING HEAD"

To Peter Carr

Paris, August 19, 1785

DEAR PETER,—I received, by Mr. Mazzei, your letter of April the 20th. I am much mortified to hear that you have lost so much time; and that when you arrived in Williamsburg, you were not at all advanced from what you were when you left Monticello. Time now begins to be precious to you. Every day you lose, will retard a day your entrance on that public stage whereon you may begin to be useful to yourself. However, the way to repair the loss is to improve the future time. I trust, that with your dispositions, even the acquisition of science is a pleasing employment. I can assure you, that the possession of it is, what (next to an honest heart) will above all things render you dear to your friends, and give you fame and promotion in your own country. When your mind shall be well improved with science, nothing will be necessary to place you in the highest points of view, but to pursue the interests of your country, the interests of your friends, and your own interests also, with the purest integrity, the most chaste honor. The defect of these virtues can never be made up by all the other acquirements of body and mind. Make these then your first object. Give up money, give up fame, give up science, give the earth itself and all it contains, rather than do an immoral act. And never suppose, that in any possible situation, or under any circumstances, it is best for you to do a dishonorable thing, however slightly so it may appear to you. Whenever you are to do a thing, though it can never be known but to yourself, ask yourself how you would act were all the world looking at you, and act accordingly. Encourage all your virtuous dispositions, and exercise them whenever an opportunity arises; being assured that they will gain strength by exercise, as a limb of the body does, and that exercise will make them habitual. From the practice of the purest virtue, you may be assured you will derive the most sublime comforts in every moment of life, and in the moment of death. If ever you find yourself environed with difficulties and perplexing circumstances, out of which you are at a loss how to extricate yourself, do what is right, and be assured that that will extricate you the best out of the worst situations. Though you cannot see, when you take one step, what will be the next, yet follow truth, justice, and plain dealing, and never fear their leading you out of the labyrinth, in the easiest manner possible. The knot which you thought a Gordian one, will untie itself before you. Nothing is so mistaken as the supposition, that a person is to extricate himself from a difficulty, by intrigue, by chicanery, by dissimulation, by trimming, by an untruth, by an injustice. This increases the difficulties ten fold; and those who pursue these methods, get themselves so involved at length, that they can turn no way but their infamy becomes more exposed. It is of great importance to set a resolution, not to be shaken, never to tell an untruth. There is no vice so mean, so pitiful, so contemptible; and he who permits himself to tell a lie once, finds it much easier to do it a second and third time, till at length it becomes habitual; he tells lies without attending to it, and truths without the world's believing him. This falsehood of the tongue leads to that of the heart, and in time depraves all its good dispositions.

An honest heart being the first blessing, a knowing head is the second. It is time for you now to begin to be choice in your reading; to begin to pursue a regular course in it; and not to suffer yourself to be turned to the right or left by read-

ing any thing out of that course. I have long ago digested a
plan for you, suited to the circumstances in which you will be
placed. This I will detail to you, from time to time, as you
advance. For the present, I advise you to begin a course of
antient history, reading every thing in the original and not in
translations. First read Goldsmith's history of Greece. This
will give you a digested view of that field. Then take up antient history in the detail, reading the following books, in the
following order: Herodotus, Thucydides, Xenophontis Hel-
lenica, Xenophontis Anabasis, Arrian, Quintus Curtius, Diodorus Siculus, Justin. This shall form the first stage of your
historical reading, and is all I need mention to you now. The
next, will be of Roman history.* From that, we will come
down to modern history. In Greek and Latin poetry, you
have read or will read at school, Virgil, Terence, Horace,
Anacreon, Theocritus, Homer, Euripides, Sophocles. Read
also Milton's Paradise Lost, Shakspeare, Ossian, Pope's and
Swift's works, in order to form your style in your own language. In morality, read Epictetus, Xenophontis Memorabilia, Plato's Socratic dialogues, Cicero's philosophies,
Antoninus, and Seneca. In order to assure a certain progress
in this reading, consider what hours you have free from the
school and the exercises of the school. Give about two of
them, every day, to exercise; for health must not be sacrificed
to learning. A strong body makes the mind strong. As to the
species of exercise, I advise the gun. While this gives a moderate exercise to the body, it gives boldness, enterprise, and
independence to the mind. Games played with the ball, and
others of that nature, are too violent for the body, and stamp
no character on the mind. Let your gun therefore be the constant companion of your walks. Never think of taking a book
with you. The object of walking is to relax the mind. You
should therefore not permit yourself even to think while you
walk; but divert your attention by the objects surrounding
you. Walking is the best possible exercise. Habituate yourself
to walk very far. The Europeans value themselves on having
subdued the horse to the uses of man; but I doubt whether
we have not lost more than we have gained, by the use of this

---

*Livy, Sullust, Cæsar, Cicero's epistles, Suetonius, Tacitus, Gibbon.

animal. No one has occasioned so much, the degeneracy of the human body. An Indian goes on foot nearly as far in a day, for a long journey, as an enfeebled white does on his horse; and he will tire the best horses. There is no habit you will value so much as that of walking far without fatigue. I would advise you to take your exercise in the afternoon: not because it is the best time for exercise, for certainly it is not; but because it is the best time to spare from your studies; and habit will soon reconcile it to health, and render it nearly as useful as if you gave to that the more precious hours of the day. A little walk of half an hour, in the morning, when you first rise, is advisable also. It shakes off sleep, and produces other good effects in the animal economy. Rise at a fixed and an early hour, and go to bed at a fixed and early hour also. Sitting up late at night is injurious to the health, and not useful to the mind. Having ascribed proper hours to exercise, divide what remain, (I mean of your vacant hours) into three portions. Give the principal to History, the other two, which should be shorter, to Philosophy and Poetry. Write to me once every month or two, and let me know the progress you make. Tell me in what manner you employ every hour in the day. The plan I have proposed for you is adapted to your present situation only. When that is changed, I shall propose a corresponding change of plan. I have ordered the following books to be sent to you from London, to the care of Mr. Madison. Herodotus, Thucydides, Xenophon's Hellenics, Anabasis and Memorabilia, Cicero's works, Baretti's Spanish and English Dictionary, Martin's Philosophical Grammar, and Martin's Philosophia Britannica. I will send you the following from hence. Bezout's Mathematics, De la Lande's Astronomy, Muschenbrock's Physics, Quintus Curtius, Justin, a Spanish Grammar, and some Spanish books. You will observe that Martin, Bezout, De la Lande, and Muschenbrock are not in the preceding plan. They are not to be opened till you go to the University. You are now, I expect, learning French. You must push this; because the books which will be put into your hands when you advance into Mathematics, Natural philosophy, Natural history, &c. will be mostly French, these sciences being better treated by the French than the English writers. Our future connection with Spain renders that the most necessary of the modern languages, after the French. When you become a public man, you may have occasion for it, and the circumstance of your possessing that language, may give you a preference over other candidates. I have nothing further to add for the present, but husband well your time, cherish your instructors, strive to make every body your friend; and be assured that nothing will be so pleasing, as your success, to, Dear Peter,

Your's affectionately,

COMMERCE AND SEA POWER
To John Jay

Paris, Aug. 23, 1785

DEAR SIR,—I shall sometimes ask your permission to write you letters, not official but private. The present is of this kind, and is occasioned by the question proposed in yours of June 14. "whether it would be useful to us to carry all our own productions, or none?" Were we perfectly free to decide this question, I should reason as follows. We have now lands enough to employ an infinite number of people in their cultivation. Cultivators of the earth are the most valuable citizens. They are the most vigorous, the most independant, the most virtuous, & they are tied to their country & wedded to it's liberty & interests by the most lasting bonds. As long therefore as they can find employment in this line, I would not convert them into mariners, artisans or anything else. But our citizens will find employment in this line till their numbers, & of course their productions, become too great for the demand both internal & foreign. This is not the case as yet, & probably will not be for a considerable time. As soon as it is, the surplus of hands must be turned to something else. I should then perhaps wish to turn them to the sea in preference to manufactures, because comparing the characters of the two classes I find the former the most valuable citizens. I consider the class of artificers as the panders of vice & the instruments by which the liberties of a country are generally overturned. However we are not free to decide this question on principles of theory only. Our people are decided in the opinion that it is necessary for us to take a share in the occupation of the ocean, & their established habits induce them to require that the sea be kept open to them, and that that line of policy be pursued which will render the use of that element as great as possible to them. I think it a duty in those entrusted with the administration of their affairs to conform themselves to the decided choice of their constituents: and that therefore we should in every instance preserve an equality of right to them in the transportation of commodities, in the right of fishing, & in the other uses of the sea. But what will be the consequence? Frequent wars without a doubt. Their property will be violated on the sea, & in foreign ports, their persons will be insulted, imprisoned &c. for pretended debts, contracts, crimes, contraband, &c., &c. These insults must be resented, even if we had no feelings, yet to prevent their eternal repetition, or in other words, our commerce on the ocean & in other countries must be paid for by frequent war. The justest dispositions possible in ourselves will not secure us against it. It would be necessary that all other nations were just also. Justice indeed on our part will save us from those wars which would have been produced by a contrary disposition. But to prevent those produced by the wrongs of other nations? By putting ourselves in a condition to punish them. Weakness provokes insult & injury, while a condition to punish it often prevents it. This reasoning leads to the necessity of some naval force, that being the only weapon with which we can reach an enemy. I think it to our interest to punish the first insult; because an insult unpunished is the parent of many others. We are not at this moment in a condition to do it, but we should put ourselves into it as soon as possible. If a war with England should take place, it seems to me that the first thing necessary would be a resolution to abandon the carrying trade because we cannot protect it. Foreign nations must in that case be invited to bring us what we want & to take our productions in their own bottoms. This alone could prevent the loss of those productions to us & the acquisition of them to our enemy. Our seamen might be employed in depredations on their trade. But how dreadfully we shall suffer on our coasts, if we have no force on the water, former experience has taught us. Indeed I look forward with horror to the very possible case of war with an European power, & think there is no protection against them but from the possession of some force on the sea. Our vicinity to their West India possessions & to the fisheries is a bridle which a small naval force on our part would hold in the mouths of the most powerful of these countries. I hope our land office will rid us of our debts, & that our first attention then will be to the beginning a naval force of some sort. This alone can countenance our people as carriers on the water, & I suppose them to be determined to continue such.

I wrote you two public letters on the 14th inst., since which I have received yours of July 13. I shall always be pleased to receive from you in a private way such communications as you might not chuse to put into a public letter.

BOOKS FOR A STATESMAN

To James Madison

Paris, September 1, 1785

DEAR SIR,—My last to you by Monsieur de Doradour, was dated May the 11th. Since that, I have received yours of January the 22nd, with six copies of the revisal, and that of April the 27th, by Mr. Mazzei.

All is quiet here. The Emperor and Dutch have certainly agreed, though they have not published their agreement. Most of his schemes in Germany must be postponed, if they are not prevented, by the confederacy of many of the Germanic body, at the head of which is the King of Prussia, and to which the Elector of Hanover is supposed to have acceded. The object of the league is to preserve the members of the empire in their present state. I doubt whether the jealousy entertained of this prince, and which is so fully evidenced by this league, may not defeat the election of his nephew to be King of the Romans, and thus produce an instance of breaking the lineal succession. Nothing is as yet done between him and the Turks. If any thing is produced in that quarter, it will not be for this year. The court of Madrid has obtained the delivery of the crew of the brig Betsey, taken by the Emperor of Morocco. The Emperor had treated them kindly, new clothed them, and delivered them to the Spanish minister, who sent them to Cadiz. This is the only American vessel ever taken by the Barbary States. The Emperor continues to give proofs of his desire to be in friendship with us, or, in other words, of receiving us into the number of his tributaries. Nothing further need be feared from him. I wish the Algerines may be as easily dealt with. I fancy the peace expected between them and Spain, is not likely to take place. I am well informed that the late proceedings in America, have produced a wonderful sensation in England in our favor. I mean the disposition which seems to be becoming general, to invest Congress with the regulation of our commerce, and, in the mean time, the measures taken to defeat the avidity of the British government, grasping at our carrying business. I can add with truth, that it was not till these symptoms appeared in America, that I have been able to discover the smallest token of respect towards the United States, in any part of Europe. There was an enthusiasm towards us, all over Europe, at the moment of the peace. The torrent of lies published unremittingly, in every day's London paper, first made an impression, and produced a coolness. The republication of these lies in most of the papers of Europe, (done probably by authority of the governments, to discourage emigrations) carried them home to the belief of every mind. They supposed every thing in America was anarchy, tumult, and civil war. The reception of the Marquis Fayette gave a check to these ideas. The late proceedings seem to be producing a decisive vibration in our favor. I think it possible that England may ply before them. It is a nation which nothing but views of interest can govern. If they produce us good there, they will here also. The defeat of the Irish propositions is also in our favor.

I have at length made up the purchase of books for you, as far as it can be done at present. The objects which I have not yet been able to get, I shall continue to seek for. Those purchased, are packed this morning in two trunks, and you have the catalogue and prices herein enclosed. The future charges of transportation shall be carried into the next bill. The

amount of the present is 1154 livres 13 sous, which, reckoning
the French crown of six livres at six shillings and eight pence,
Virginia money, is £64, 3s. which sum you will be so good as
to keep in your hands, to be used occasionally in the education of my nephews, when the regular resources disappoint
you. To the same use I would pray you to apply twenty-five
guineas, which I have lent the two Mr. Fitzhughs of Mar-
mion, and which I have desired them to repay into your
hands. You will of course deduct the price of the revisals, and
of any other articles you may have been so kind as to pay for
me. Greek and Roman authors are dearer here, than, I believe, any where in the world. Nobody here reads them;
wherefore they are not reprinted. Don Ulloa, in the original,
is not to be found. The collection of tracts on the economies
of different nations, we cannot find; nor Amelot's travels into
China. I shall send these two trunks of books to Havre, there
to wait a conveyance to America; for as to the fixing the packets there, it is as uncertain as ever. The other articles you mention, shall be procured as far as they can be. Knowing that
some of them would be better got in London, I commissioned Mr. Short, who was going there, to get them. He has
not yet returned. They will be of such a nature, as that I can
get some gentleman who may be going to America, to take
them in his portmanteau. Le Maire being now able to stand
on his own legs, there will be no necessity for your advancing
him the money I desired, if it is not already done. I am anxious to hear from you on the subject of my Notes on Virginia. I have been obliged to give so many of them here, that
I fear their getting published. I have received an application
from the Directors of the public buildings, to procure them a
plan for their capitol. I shall send them one taken from the
best morsel of antient architecture now remaining. It has obtained the approbation of fifteen or sixteen centuries, and is,
therefore, preferable to any design which might be newly
contrived. It will give more room, be more convenient, and
cost less, than the plan they sent me. Pray encourage them to
wait for it, and to execute it. It will be superior in beauty to
any thing in America, and not inferior to any thing in the
world. It is very simple. Have you a copying press? If you

have not, you should get one. Mine (exclusive of paper which costs a guinea a ream) has cost me about fourteen guineas. I would give ten times that sum, to have had it from the date of the stamp act. I hope you will be so good as to continue your communications, both of the great and small kind, which are equally useful to me. Be assured of the sincerity with which I am, Dear Sir,

your friend and servant,

ENCLOSURE

	livres	sous	den
Dictionnaire de Trevoux. 5. vol. fol. @ 5f12 . . .	28	— 0	— 0
La Conquista di Mexico. De Solis. fol. 7f10. relieure 7f	14	— 10	
Traité de morale et de bonheur. 12mo. 2. v. in 1 .	2	— 8	
Wicquefort de l'Ambassadeur. 2. v. 4to. . . .	7	— 4	
Burlamaqui. Principes du droit Politique 4to. 3f12 relieure 2f5	5	— 17	
Conquista de la China por el Tartaro por Palafox. 12mo.	3	—	
Code de l'humanité de Felice. 13. v. 4to. . . .	104	— 0	
13. first livraisons of the Encyclopedie 47. vols. 4to. (being 48f less than subscription) . . .	348	— 0	
14th. livraison of do. 4. v. 4to.	24	— 0	
Peyssonel	2	— 0	
Bibliotheque physico-œconomique. 4. v. 12mo. 10f4. rel. 3f	13	— 4	
Cultivateur Americain. 2. v. 8vo. 7f17. rel. 2f10 .	10	— 7	
Mirabeau sur l'ordre des Cincinnati. 10f10. rel. 1f5 (prohibited)	11	— 15	
Coutumes Amglo-Normands de Houard. 4. v. 4to. 40f rel. 10f.	50	— 0	
Memoires sur l'Amerique 4 v. 4to.	24	— 0	
Tott sur les Turcs. 4. v. in 2. 8vo. 10f. rel. 2f10 .	12	— 10	
Neckar sur l'Administration des Finances de France. 3. v. 12mo. 7f10 rel. 2f5	9	— 15	
le bon-sens. 12mo. 6f rel. 15s (prohibited) . . .	6	— 15	

livres   sous   den

Mably. Principes de morale.

1. v. 12mo. 3	12		
etude de l'histoire 1. . 2	10		
maniere d'ecrire			
l'histoire 1. . . . 2	8		
constitution			
d'Amerique 1.. . . 1	16	relieure de	
sur l'histoire de		11 vols. @	
France. 2. v. . . . 6		15s. 8f5 41 — 1	
droit de l'Europe			
3. v. 7	10		
ordres des societies . . 2			
principes des			
negotiations . . . 2	10		
entretiens de Phocion . 2			
des Romains 2	10		

              32 16

Wanting to complete Mably's works which I have
    not been able to procure
        les principes de legislation
        sur les Grecs
        sur la Pologne.

	livres	sous	den
Chronologie des empires anciennes			
de la Combe.	5 — 0 — 0		
de l'histoire universelle			
de Hornot. . 1. v. 8vo. 4f	4 — 0 — 0		
de l'histoire universelle			
de Berlié . . 1. v. 8vo. 2f10 rel. 1f5	3 — 15		
des empereurs Romains			
par Richer . . 2. v. 8vo. 8f rel. 2f10	10 — 10		
des Juifs . . . 1. v. 8vo. 3f10 rel. 1f5	4 — 15		
de l'histoire universelle			
par Du Fresnoy. 2. v. 8vo. 13f rel. 2f10	15 — 10		
de l'histoire du Nord.			
par La Combe . 2. v. 8vo. 10f. rel. 2f10	12 — 10		
de France. par			
Henault. . 3. v. 8vo. 12f. rel. 5f	15 — 15		

	livres	*sous*	*den*
Memoires de Voltaire. 2. v. in 1. 2f10 rel. 15s. . .	3 — 5 — 0		
Linnaei Philosophia Botanica. 1. v. 8vo. 7f rel. 1f5	8 — 5		
Genera plantarum 1. v. 8vo. 8f rel. 1f5 . . .	9 — 5		
Species plantarum. 4. v. 8vo. 32f rel. 5f . . .	37 — 0		
Systema naturae 4. v. 8vo. 26f rel. 5f . . .	31 — 0		
Clayton. Flora Virginica. 4to. 12f. rel. 2f10. . .	14 — 10		
D'Albon sur l'interet de plusieurs nations. 4. v.			
12mo. 12f. rel. 3f.	15 — 0		
Systeme de la nature de Diderot. 3. v. 8vo. 21f			
(prohibited)	21 — 0		

Coussin histoire Romaine.

     2. v. in 1. 12mo.

     de Constantinople 8. v. in 10.   }   16. vols.

     de l'empire de l'Occident 2. v. }   12mo.   36 — 0 — 0

     de l'eglise. 5. v. in 3.

Droit de la Nature. por Wolff. 6. v. 12mo. 15f rel.			
4f10	19 — 10		
Voyage de Pagét 8vo. 3. v. in 1.	9		

Mirabeau. Ami des hommes 5. v. 12mo. }

   Theorie de l'impot 2. v. in 1. 12mo. }   12

BUFFON. SUPPLEMENT 11. 12. Oiseaux 17. 18.

   Mineraux 1. 2. 3. 4. . . . . 24.

Lettres de Pascal. 12mo. 2f. rel. 15s.	2 — 15		
Le sage à la cour et le roi voiageur (prohibited) .	10 — 15		
Principes de legislation universelle 2. v. 8vo. . .	12 — 0		
Ordonnances de la Marine par Valin. 2. v. 4to. .	22		

Diderot sur les sourds and muets ⌉

     12mo. 3f12. sur les

     aveugles 3f. sur la nature 3f. } 4. v. 12mo.   13 — 7

     sur la morale 3f15 ⌋

Mariana's history of Spain 11. v. 12mo.	21		
2 trunks & packing paper	43 — 0		

                                  1154 — 13

CLIMATE AND AMERICAN CHARACTER
To Chastellux

Paris, Sep. 2, 1785

DEAR SIR,—You were so kind as to allow me a fortnight to read your journey through Virginia. but you should have thought of this indulgence while you were writing it, and have rendered it less interesting if you meant that your readers should have been longer engaged with it. in fact I devoured it at a single meal, and a second reading scarce allowed me sang-froid enough to mark a few errors in the names of persons and places which I note on a paper herein inclosed, with an inconsiderable error or two in facts which I have also noted because I supposed you wished to state them correctly. from this general approbation however you must allow me to except about a dozen pages in the earlier part of the book which I read with a continued blush from beginning to end, as it presented me a lively picture of what I wish to be, but am not. no, my dear Sir, the thousand millionth part of what you there say, is more than I deserve. it might perhaps have passed in Europe at the time you wrote it, and the exaggeration might not have been detected. but consider that the animal is now brought there, and that every one will take his dimensions for himself. the friendly complexion of your mind has betrayed you into a partiality of which the European spectator will be divested. respect to yourself therefore will require indispensably that you expunge the whole of those pages except your own judicious observations interspersed among them on animal and physical subjects. with respect to my countrymen there is surely nothing which can render them uneasy, in the observations made on them. they know that they are not perfect, and will be sensible that you have viewed them with a philanthropic eye. you say much good of them, and less ill than they are conscious may be said with truth. I have studied their character with attention. I have thought them, as you found them, aristocratical, pompous, clannish, indolent, hospitable, and I should have added, disinterested, but you say attached to their interest. this is the only trait in their character wherein our observations differ. I have always thought them so careless of their interests, so thoughtless in their expences and in all their transactions of business that I had placed it among the vices of their character, as indeed most virtues when carried beyond certain bounds degenerate into vices. I had even ascribed this to it's cause, to that warmth of their climate which unnerves and unmans both body and mind. while on this subject I will give you my idea of the characters of the several states.

In the North they are	In the South they are
cool	fiery
sober	voluptuary
laborious	indolent
persevering	unsteady
independant	independant
jealous of their own liberties, and just to those of others	zealous for their own liberties, but trampling on those of others.
interested	generous
chicaning	candid
superstitious and hypocritical in their religion	without attachment or pretensions to any religion but that of the heart.

these characteristics grow weaker and weaker by gradation from North to South and South to North, insomuch that an observing traveller, without the aid of the quadrant may always know his latitude by the character of the people among whom he finds himself. it is in Pennsylvania that the two characters seem to meet and blend, and form a people free from the extremes both of vice and virtue. peculiar circumstances have given to New York the character which climate would have given had she been placed on the South instead of the north side of Pennsylvania. perhaps too other circumstances may have occasioned in Virginia a transplantation of a particular vice foreign to it's climate. you could judge of this with more impartiality than I could, and the probability is that your estimate of them is the most just. I think it for their good that the vices of their character should be pointed out to them that they may amend them; for a malady of either body or mind once known is half cured. I wish you would add to this piece your letter to mr. Madison on the expediency of introducing the arts into America. I found in that a great deal of matter, very many observations, which would be useful to the legislators of America, and to the general mass of citizens. I read it with great pleasure and analysed it's contents that I might fix them in my own mind.

I have the honor to be with very sincere esteem, dear Sir, your most obedient and most humble servt.

"THIS BEAUTIFUL ART"

To James Madison

Paris, September 20, 1785

DEAR SIR,—By Mr. Fitzhugh, you will receive my letter of the first instant. He is still here, and gives me an opportunity of again addressing you much sooner than I should have done, but for the discovery of a great piece of inattention. In that letter I send you a detail of the cost of your books, and desire you to keep the amount in your hands, as if I had forgot that a part of it was in fact your own, as being a balance of what I had remained in your debt. I really did not attend to it in the moment of writing, and when it occurred to me, I revised my memorandum book from the time of our being in Philadelphia together, and stated our account from the beginning, lest I should forget or mistake any part of it. I enclose you this statement. You will always be so good as to let me know, from time to time, your advances for me. Correct with freedom all my proceedings for you, as, in what I do, I have no other desire than that of doing exactly what will be most pleasing to you.

I received this summer a letter from Messrs. Buchanan and Hay, as Directors of the public buildings, desiring I would have drawn for them, plans of sundry buildings, and, in the first place, of a capitol. They fixed, for their receiving this plan, a day which was within about six weeks of that on which their letter came to my hand. I engaged an architect of capital abilities in this business. Much time was requsite, after the external form was agreed on, to make the internal distribution convenient for the three branches of government. This time was much lengthened by my avocations to other objects,

which I had no right to neglect. The plan however was settled. The gentlemen had sent me one which they had thought
of. The one agreed on here, is more convenient, more beautiful, gives more room, and will not cost more than two
thirds of what that would. We took for our model what is
called the Maison quarrée of Nismes, one of the most beautiful, if not the most beautiful and precious morsel of architecture left us by antiquity. It was built by Caius and Lucius
Cæsar, and repaired by Louis XIV., and has the suffrage of all
the judges of architecture, who have seen it, as yielding to no
one of the beautiful monuments of Greece, Rome, Palmyra,
and Balbec, which late travellers have communicated to us. It
is very simple, but it is noble beyond expression, and would
have done honor to our country, as presenting to travellers a
specimen of taste in our infancy, promising much for our ma-
turer age. I have been much mortified with information,
which I received two days ago from Virginia, that the first
brick of the capitol would be laid within a few days. But
surely, the delay of this piece of a summer would have been
repaired by the savings in the plan preparing here, were we
to value its other superiorities as nothing. But how is a taste
in this beautiful art to be formed in our countrymen, unless
we avail ourselves of every occasion when public buildings are
to be erected, of presenting to them models for their study
and imitation? Pray try if you can effect the stopping of this
work. I have written also to E. R. on the subject. The loss
will be only of the laying the bricks already laid, or a part of
them. The bricks themselves will do again for the interior
walls, and one side wall and one end wall may remain, as they
will answer equally well for our plan. This loss is not to be
weighed against the saving of money which will arise, against
the comfort of laying out the public money for something
honorable, the satisfaction of seeing an object and proof of
national good taste, and the regret and mortification of erecting a monument of our barbarism, which will be loaded with
execrations as long as it shall endure. The plans are in good
forwardness, and I hope will be ready within three or four
weeks. They could not be stopped now, but on paying their
whole price, which will be considerable. If the undertakers are
afraid to undo what they have done, encourage them to it by

a recommendation from the Assembly. You see I am an enthusiast on the subject of the arts. But it is an enthusiasm of which I am not ashamed, as its object is to improve the taste of my countrymen, to increase their reputation, to reconcile to them the respect of the world, and procure them its praise.

I shall send off your books, in two trunks, to Havre, within two or three days, to the care of Mr. Limozin, American agent there. I will advise you, as soon as I know by what vessel he forwards them. Adieu.

Your's affectionately,

MARS AND MINERVA
To Abigail Adams

Paris, Sep. 25, 1785

DEAR MADAM—Mr. Short's return the night before last availed me of your favour of Aug. 12. I immediately ordered the shoes you desired which will be ready tomorrow. I am not certain whether this will be in time for the departure of Mr. Barclay or of Colo. Franks, for it is not yet decided which of them goes to London. I have also procured for you three plateaux de dessert with a silvered ballustrade round them, and four figures of Biscuit. The former cost 192^{tt}, the latter 12^{tt} each, making together 240 livres or 10. Louis. The merchant undertakes to send them by the way of Rouen through the hands of Mr. Garvey and to have them delivered in London. There will be some additional expences of packing, transportation and duties here. Those in England I imagine you can save. When I know the amount I will inform you of it, but there will be no occasion to remit it here. With respect to the figures I could only find three of those you named, matched in size. These were Minerva, Diana, and Apollo. I was obliged to add a fourth, unguided by your choice. They offered me a fine Venus; but I thought it out of taste to have two at table at the same time. Paris and Helen were presented. I conceived it would be cruel to remove them from their peculiar shrine. When they shall pass the Atlantic, it will be to sing a requiem over our freedom and happiness. At length a fine Mars was offered, calm, bold, his faulchion not drawn, but ready to be drawn. This will do, thinks I, for the table of the American Minister in London, where those whom it may concern may look and learn that though Wisdom is our guide, and the Song and Chase our supreme delight, yet we offer adoration to that tutelar god also who rocked the cradle of our birth, who has accepted our infant offerings, and has shewn himself the patron of our rights and avenger of our wrongs. The groupe then was closed, and your party formed. Envy and malice will never be quiet. I hear it already whispered to you that in admitting Minerva to your table I have departed from the principle which made me reject Venus: in plain English that I have paid a just respect to the daughter but failed to the mother. No Madam, my respect to both is sincere. Wisdom, I know, is social. She seeks her fellows. But Beauty is jealous, and illy bears the presence of a rival—but, Allons, let us turn over another leaf, and begin the next chapter. I receive by Mr. Short a budget of London papers. They teem with every horror of which human nature is capable. Assassinations, suicides, thefts, robberies, and, what is worse than assassination, theft, suicide or robbery, the blackest slanders! Indeed the man must be of rock, who can stand all this; to Mr. Adams it will be but one victory the more. It would have illy suited me. I do not love difficulties. I am fond of quiet, willing to do my duty, but irritable by slander and apt to be forced by it to abandon my post. These are weaknesses from which reason and your counsels will preserve Mr. Adams. I fancy it must be the quantity of animal food eaten by the English which renders their character insusceptible of civilisation. I suspect it is in their kitchens and not in their churches that their reformation must be worked, and that Missionaries of that description from hence would avail more than those who should endeavor to tame them by precepts of religion or philosophy. But what do the foolish printers of America mean by retailing all this stuff in our papers? As if it was not enough to be slandered by one's enemies without circulating the slanders among his friends also.

To shew you how willingly I shall ever receive and execute your commissions, I venture to impose one on you. From what I recollect of the diaper and damask we used to import from England I think they were better and cheaper than here. You are well acquainted with those of both countries. If you are of the same opinion I would trouble you to send me two sets of table cloths and napkins for 20 covers each, by Colo. Franks or Mr. Barclay who will bring them to me. But if you think they can be better got here I would rather avoid the trouble this commission will give. I inclose you a specimen of what is offered me at 100. livres for the table cloth and 12 napkins. I suppose that, of the same quality, a table cloth 2. aunes wide and 4. aunes long, and 20 napkins of 1. aune each, would cost 7. guineas.—I shall certainly charge the publick my house rent and court taxes. I shall do more. I shall charge my outfit. Without this I can never get out of debt. I think it will be allowed. Congress is too reasonable to expect, where no imprudent expences are incurred, none but those which are required by a decent respect to the mantle with which they cover the public servants, that such expences should be left as a burthen on our private fortunes. But when writing to you, I fancy myself at Auteuil, and chatter on till the last page of my paper awakes me from my reverie, and tells me it is time to assure you of the sincere respect and esteem with which I have the honour to be Dear Madam your most obedient and most humble servt.,

P.S. The cask of wine at Auteuil, I take chearfully. I suppose the seller will apply to me for the price. Otherwise, as I do not know who he is, I shall not be able to find him out.

THE VAUNTED SCENE

To Charles Bellini

Paris, September 30, 1785

DEAR SIR,—Your estimable favor, covering a letter to Mr. Mazzei, came to hand on the 26th instant. The letter to Mr. Mazzei was put into his hands in the same moment, as he happened to be present. I leave to him to convey to you all his complaints, as it will be more agreeable to me to express to you the satisfaction I received, on being informed of your perfect health. Though I could not receive the same pleasing news of Mrs. Bellini, yet the philosophy with which I am told she bears the loss of health, is a testimony the more, how much she deserved the esteem I bear her. Behold me at length on the vaunted scene of Europe! It is not necessary for your information, that I should enter into details concerning it. But you are, perhaps, curious to know how this new scene has struck a savage of the mountains of America. Not advantageously, I assure you. I find the general fate of humanity here, most deplorable. The truth of Voltaire's observation, offers itself perpetually, that every man here must be either the hammer or the anvil. It is a true picture of that country to which they say we shall pass hereafter, and where we are to see God and his angels in splendor, and crowds of the damned trampled under their feet. While the great mass of the people are thus suffering under physical and moral oppression, I have endeavored to examine more nearly the condition of the great, to appreciate the true value of the circumstances in their situation, which dazzle the bulk of spectators, and, especially, to compare it with that degree of happiness which is enjoyed in America, by every class of people. Intrigues of love occupy the younger, and those of ambition, the elder part of the great. Conjugal love having no existence among them, domestic happiness, of which that is the basis, is utterly unknown. In lieu of this, are substituted pursuits which nourish and invigorate all our bad passions, and which offer only moments of ecstacy, amidst days and months of restlessness and torment. Much, very much inferior, this, to the tranquil, permanent felicity with which domestic society in America, blesses most of its inhabitants; leaving them to follow steadily those pursuits which health and reason approve, and rendering truly delicious the intervals of those pursuits.

In science, the mass of the people is two centuries behind ours; their literati, half a dozen years before us. Books, really good, acquire just reputation in that time, and so become known to us, and communicate to us all their advances in knowledge. Is not this delay compensated, by our being placed out of the reach of that swarm of nonsensical publications, which issues daily from a thousand presses, and per-ishes almost in issuing? With respect to what are termed polite manners, without sacrificing too much the sincerity of language, I would wish my countrymen to adopt just so much of European politeness, as to be ready to make all those little sacrifices of self, which really render European manners amiable, and relieve society from the disagreeable scenes to which rudeness often subjects it. Here, it seems that a man might pass a life without encountering a single rudeness. In the pleasures of the table they are far before us, because, with good taste they unite temperance. They do not terminate the most sociable meals by transforming themselves into brutes. I have never yet seen a man drunk in France, even among the lowest of the people. Were I to proceed to tell you how much I enjoy their architecture, sculpture, painting, music, I should want words. It is in these arts they shine. The last of them, particularly, is an enjoyment, the deprivation of which with us, cannot be calculated. I am almost ready to say, it is the only thing which from my heart I envy them, and which, in spite of all the authority of the Decalogue, I do covet. But I am running on in an estimate of things infinitely better known to you than to me, and which will only serve to convince you, that I have brought with me all the prejudices of country, habit and age. But whatever I may allow to be charged to me as prejudice, in every other instance, I have one sentiment at least, founded in reality: it is that of the perfect esteem which your merit and that of Mrs. Bellini have produced, and which will for ever enable me to assure you of the sincere regard, with which I am, Dear Sir,

your friend and servant,

BRITISH HOSTILITY, AMERICAN COMMERCE

To G. K. van Hogendorp

Paris, Oct. 13, 1785

DEAR SIR,—Having been much engaged lately, I have been unable sooner to acknolege the receipt of your favor of Sep. 8. What you are pleased to say on the subject of my Notes is more than they deserve. The condition in which you first saw

them would prove to you how hastily they had been originally written; as you may remember the numerous insertions
I had made in them from time to time, when I could find a
moment for turning to them from other occupations. I have
never yet seen Monsr. de Buffon. He has been in the country
all the summer. I sent him a copy of the book, & have only
heard his sentiments on one particular of it, that of the identity of the Mammoth & Elephant. As to this he retains his
opinion that they are the same. If you had formed any considerable expectations from our Revised code of laws you will
be much disappointed. It contains not more than three or
four laws which could strike the attention of the foreigner.
Had it been a digest of all our laws, it would not have been
comprehensible or instructive but to a native. But it is still
less so, as it digests only the British statutes & our own acts
of assembly, which are but a supplementary part of our law.
The great basis of it is anterior to the date of the Magna
charta, which is the oldest statute extant. The only merit of
this work is that it may remove from our book shelves about
twenty folio volumes of our statutes, retaining all the parts of
them which either their own merit or the established system
of laws required.

You ask me what are those operations of the British nation
which are likely to befriend us, and how they will produce
this effect? The British government as you may naturally suppose have it much at heart to reconcile their nation to the loss
of America. This is essential to the repose, perhaps even to
the safety of the King & his ministers. The most effectual
engines for this purpose are the public papers. You know well
that that government always kept a kind of standing army of
news writers who without any regard to truth, or to what
should be like truth, invented & put into the papers whatever
might serve the minister. This suffices with the mass of the
people who have no means of distinguishing the false from
the true paragraphs of a newspaper. When forced to acknolege our independance they were forced to redouble their efforts to keep the nation quiet. Instead of a few of the papers
formerly engaged, they now engaged every one. No paper
therefore comes out without a dose of paragraphs against
America. These are calculated for a secondary purpose also,

that of preventing the emigrations of their people to America. They dwell very much on American bankruptcies. To explain these would require a long detail, but would shew you that nine tenths of these bankruptcies are truly English bankruptcies in no wise chargeable on America. However they have produced effects the most desirable of all others for us. They have destroyed our credit & thus checked our disposition to luxury; & forcing our merchants to buy no more than they have ready money to pay for, they force them to go to those markets where that ready money will buy most. Thus you see they check our luxury, they force us to connect ourselves with all the world, & they prevent foreign emigrations to our country all of which I consider as advantageous to us. They are doing us another good turn. They attempt without disguise to possess themselves of the carriage of our produce, & to prohibit our own vessels from participating of it. This has raised a general indignation in America. The states see however that their constitutions have provided no means of counteracting it. They are therefore beginning to invest Congress with the absolute power of regulating their commerce, only reserving all revenue arising from it to the state in which it is levied. This will consolidate our federal building very much, and for this we shall be indebted to the British.

You ask what I think on the expediency of encouraging our states to be commercial? Were I to indulge my own theory, I should wish them to practise neither commerce nor navigation, but to stand with respect to Europe precisely on the footing of China. We should thus avoid wars, and all our citizens would be husbandmen. Whenever indeed our numbers should so increase as that our produce would overstock the markets of those nations who should come to seek it, the farmers must either employ the surplus of their time in manufactures, or the surplus of our hands must be employed in manufactures, or in navigation. But that day would, I think be distant, and we should long keep our workmen in Europe, while Europe should be drawing rough materials & even subsistence from America. But this is theory only, & a theory which the servants of America are not at liberty to follow. Our people have a decided taste for navigation & commerce. They take this from their mother country: & their servants are in duty bound to calculate all their measures on this datum: we wish to do it by throwing open all the doors of commerce & knocking off its shackles. But as this cannot be done for others, unless they will do it for us, & there is no great probability that Europe will do this, I suppose we shall be obliged to adopt a system which may shackle them in our ports as they do us in theirs.

With respect to the sale of our lands, that cannot begin till a considerable portion shall have been surveyed. They cannot begin to survey till the fall of the leaf of this year, nor to sell probably till the ensuing spring. So that it will be yet a twelve-month before we shall be able to judge of the efficacy of our land office to sink our national debt. It is made a fundamental that the proceeds shall be solely & sacredly applied as a sinking fund to discharge the capital only of the debt. It is true that the tobaccos of Virginia go almost entirely to England. The reason is that they owe a great debt there which they are paying as fast as they can.—I think I have now answered your several queries, & shall be happy to receive your reflections on the same subjects, & at all times to hear of your welfare & to give you assurances of the esteem with which I have the honor to be Dear Sir your most obedient & most humble servant.

ON EUROPEAN EDUCATION
To John Banister, Jr.

Paris, October 15, 1785

DEAR SIR,—I should sooner have answered the paragraph in your letter, of September the 19th, respecting the best seminary for the education of youth, in Europe, but that it was necessary for me to make inquiries on the subject. The result of these has been, to consider the competition as resting between Geneva and Rome. They are equally cheap, and probably are equal in the course of education pursued. The advantage of Geneva, is, that students acquire there the habit of speaking French. The advantages of Rome, are, the acquiring a local knowledge of a spot so classical and so celebrated;

the acquiring the true pronunciation of the Latin language; a just taste in the fine arts, more particularly those of painting, sculpture, architecture, and music; a familiarity with those objects and processes of agriculture, which experience has shewn best adapted to a climate like ours; and lastly, the advantage of a fine climate for health. It is probable, too, that by being boarded in a French family, the habit of speaking that language may be obtained. I do not count on any advantage to be derived in Geneva, from a familiar acquaintance with the principles of that government. The late revolution has rendered it a tyrannical aristocracy, more likely to give ill, than good ideas to an American. I think the balance in favor of Rome. Pisa is sometimes spoken of, as a place of education. But it does not offer the first and third of the advantages of Rome. But why send an American youth to Europe for education? What are the objects of an useful American education? Classical knowledge, modern languages, chiefly French, Spanish and Italian; Mathematics, Natural philosophy, Natural history, Civil history, and Ethics. In Natural philosophy, I mean to include Chemistry and Agriculture, and in Natural history, to include Botany, as well as the other branches of those departments. It is true that the habit of speaking the modern languages, cannot be so well acquired in America; but every other article can be as well acquired at William and Mary college, as at any place in Europe. When college education is done with, and a young man is to prepare himself for public life, he must cast his eyes (for America) either on Law or Physic. For the former, where can he apply so advantageously as to Mr. Wythe? For the latter, he must come to Europe: the medical class of students, therefore, is the only one which need come to Europe. Let us view the disadvantages of sending a youth to Europe. To enumerate them all, would require a volume. I will select a few. If he goes to England, he learns drinking, horse racing and boxing. These are the peculiarities of English education. The following circumstances are common to education in that, and the other countries of Europe. He acquires a fondness for European luxury and dissipation, and a contempt for the simplicity of his own country; he is fascinated with the privileges of the European aristocrats, and sees, with abhorrence, the lovely equality which the poor enjoy with the rich, in his own country; he contracts a partiality for aristocracy or monarchy; he forms foreign friendships which will never be useful to him, and loses the season of life for forming in his own country, those friendships, which, of all others, are the most faithful and permanent; he is led by the strongest of all the human passions, into a spirit for female intrigue, destructive of his own and others' happiness, or a passion for whores, destructive of his health, and, in both cases, learns to consider fidelity to the marriage bed as an ungentlemanly practice, and inconsistent with happiness; he recollects the voluptuary dress and arts of the European women, and pities and despises the chaste affections and simplicity of those of his own country; he retains, through life, a fond recollection, and a hankering after those places, which were the scenes of his first pleasures and of his first connections; he returns to his own country, a foreigner, unacquainted with the practices of domestic economy, necessary to preserve him from ruin, speaking and writing his native tongue as a foreigner, and therefore unqualified to obtain those distinctions, which eloquence of the pen and tongue ensures in a free country; for I would observe to you, that what is called style in writing or speaking, is formed very early in life, while the imagination is warm, and impressions are permament. I am of opinion, that there never was an instance of a man's writing or speaking his native tongue with elegance, who passed from fifteen to twenty years of age, out of the country where it was spoken. Thus, no instance exists of a person's writing two languages perfectly. That will always appear to be his native language, which was most familiar to him in his youth. It appears to me then, that an American coming to Europe for education, loses in his knowledge, in his morals, in his health, in his habits, and in his happiness. I had entertained only doubts on this head, before I came to Europe: what I see and hear, since I came here, proves more than I had even suspected. Cast your eye over America: who are the men of most learning, of most eloquence, most beloved by their countrymen, and most trusted and promoted by them? They are those who have been educated among them, and whose manners, morals and habits, are perfectly homogeneous with those of the country.

Did you expect by so short a question, to draw such a sermon on yourself? I dare say you did not. But the consequences of foreign education are alarming to me, as an American. I sin, therefore, through zeal, whenever I enter on the subject. You are sufficiently American to pardon me for it. Let me hear of your health, and be assured of the esteem with which I am, Dear Sir,

your friend and servant,

PROPERTY AND NATURAL RIGHT

To James Madison

Fontainebleau, Oct. 28, 1785

DEAR SIR,—Seven o'clock, and retired to my fireside, I have determined to enter into conversation with you. This is a village of about 15,000 inhabitants when the court is not here, and 20,000 when they are, occupying a valley through which runs a brook and on each side of it a ridge of small mountains, most of which are naked rock. The King comes here, in the fall always, to hunt. His court attend him, as do also the foreign diplomatic corps; but as this is not indispensably required and my finances do not admit the expense of a continued residence here, I propose to come occasionally to attend the King's levees, returning again to Paris, distant forty miles. This being the first trip, I set out yesterday morning to take a view of the place. For this purpose I shaped my course towards the highest of the mountains in sight, to the top of which was about a league.

As soon as I had got clear of the town I fell in with a poor woman walking at the same rate with myself and going the same course. Wishing to know the condition of the laboring poor I entered into conversation with her, which I began by enquiries for the path which would lead me into the mountain: and thence proceeded to enquiries into her vocation, condition and circumstances. She told me she was a day laborer at 8 sous or 4d. sterling the day: that she had two children to maintain, and to pay a rent of 30 livres for her house (which would consume the hire of 75 days), that often she

could get no employment and of course was without bread.
As we had walked together near a mile and she had so far
served me as a guide, I gave her, on parting, 24 sous. She
burst into tears of a gratitude which I could perceive was un-
feigned because she was unable to utter a word. She had
probably never before received so great an aid. This little *at-
tendrissement*, with the solitude of my walk, led me into a
train of reflections on that unequal division of property which
occasions the numberless instances of wretchedness which I
had observed in this country and is to be observed all over
Europe.

The property of this country is absolutely concentred in a
very few hands, having revenues of from half a million of
guineas a year downwards. These employ the flower of the
country as servants, some of them having as many as 200 do-
mestics, not laboring. They employ also a great number of
manufacturers and tradesmen, and lastly the class of laboring
husbandmen. But after all there comes the most numerous of
all classes, that is, the poor who cannot find work. I asked
myself what could be the reason so many should be permitted
to beg who are willing to work, in a country where there is a
very considerable proportion of uncultivated lands? These
lands are undisturbed only for the sake of game. It should
seem then that it must be because of the enormous wealth of
the proprietors which places them above attention to the increase of their revenues by permitting these lands to be labored. I am conscious that an equal division of property is
impracticable, but the consequences of this enormous inequality producing so much misery to the bulk of mankind,
legislators cannot invent too many devices for subdividing
property, only taking care to let their subdivisions go hand in
hand with the natural affections of the human mind. The descent of property of every kind therefore to all the children,
or to all the brothers and sisters, or other relations in equal
degree, is a politic measure and a practicable one. Another
means of silently lessening the inequality of property is to
exempt all from taxation below a certain point, and to tax the
higher portions or property in geometrical progression as
they rise. Whenever there are in any country uncultivated
lands and unemployed poor, it is clear that the laws of prop-

erty have been so far extended as to violate natural right. The earth is given as a common stock for man to labor and live on. If for the encouragement of industry we allow it to be appropriated, we must take care that other employment be provided to those excluded from the appropriation. If we do not, the fundamental right to labor the earth returns to the unemployed. It is too soon yet in our country to say that every man who cannot find employment, but who can find uncultivated land, shall be at liberty to cultivate it, paying a moderate rent. But it is not too soon to provide by every possible means that as few as possible shall be without a little portion of land. The small landholders are the most precious part of a state.

The next object which struck my attention in my walk was the deer with which the wood abounded. They were of the kind called "Cerfs," and not exactly of the same species with ours. They are blackish indeed under the belly, and not white as ours, and they are more of the chestnut red; but these are such small differences as would be sure to happen in two races from the same stock breeding separately a number of ages. Their hares are totally different from the animals we call by that name; but their rabbit is almost exactly like him. The only difference is in their manners; the land on which I walked for some time being absolutely reduced to a honey-comb by their burrowing. I think there is no instance of ours burrowing. After descending the hill again I saw a man cutting fern. I went to him under pretence of asking the shortest road to town, and afterwards asked for what use he was cutting fern. He told me that this part of the country furnished a great deal of fruit to Paris. That when packed in straw it acquired an ill taste, but that dry fern preserved it perfectly without communicating any taste at all.

I treasured this observation for the preservation of my apples on my return to my own country. They have no apples here to compare with our Redtown pippin. They have nothing which deserves the name of a peach; there being not sun enough to ripen the plum-peach and the best of their soft peaches being like our autumn peaches. Their cherries and strawberries are fair, but I think lack flavor. Their plums I think are better; so also their gooseberries, and the pears in-

finitely beyond anything we possess. They have nothing better than our sweet-water; but they have a succession of as
good from early in the summer till frost. I am to-morrow to
get [to] M. Malsherbes (an uncle of the Chevalier Luzerne's)
about seven leagues from hence, who is the most curious man
in France as to his trees. He is making for me a collection of
the vines from which the Burgundy, Champagne, Bordeaux,
Frontignac, and other of the most valuable wines of this
country are made. Another gentleman is collecting for me the
best eating grapes, including what we call the raisin. I propose also to endeavor to colonize their hare, rabbit, red and
grey partridge, pheasants of different kinds, and some other
birds. But I find that I am wandering beyond the limits of
my walk and will therefore bid you adieu. Yours affectionately.

"OUR CONFEDERACY . . . THE NEST"

To Archibald Stuart

Paris, Jan. 25, 1786

DEAR SIR,—I have received your favor of the 17th of October, which though you mention as the third you have written
me, is the first which has come to hand. I sincerely thank you
for the communications it contains. Nothing is so grateful to
me at this distance as details both great & small of what is
passing in my own country. Of the latter we receive little
here, because they either escape my correspondents or are
thought unworthy notice. This however is a very mistaken
opinion, as every one may observe by recollecting that when
he has been long absent from his neighborhood the small
news of that is the most pleasing and occupies his first attention either when he meets with a person from thence, or returns thither himself. I shall hope therefore that the letter in
which you have been so good as to give me the minute occurrences in the neighborhood of Monticello may yet come
to hand. And I venture to rely on the many proofs of friendship I have received from you, for a continuance of your favors. This will be the most meritorious as I have nothing to

give you in exchange. The quiet of Europe at this moment furnishes little which can attract your notice. Nor will that quiet be soon disturbed, at least for the current year. Perhaps it hangs on the life of the K. of Prussia, and that hangs by a very slender thread. American reputation in Europe is not such as to be flattering to its citizens. Two circumstances are particularly objected to us, the nonpaiment of our debts, and the want of energy in our government. These discourage a connection with us. I own it to be my opinion that good will arise from the destruction of our credit. I see nothing else which can restrain our disposition to luxury, and the loss of those manners which alone can preserve republican government. As it is impossible to prevent credit, the best way would be to cure it's ill effects by giving an instantaneous recovery to the creditor; this would be reducing purchases on credit to purchases for ready money. A man would then see a poison painted on everything he wished but had not ready money to pay for. I fear from an expression in your letter that the people of Kentucké think of separating not only from Virginia (in which they are right) but also from the confederacy. I own I should think this a most calametous event, and such an one as every good citizen on both sides should set himself against. Our present federal limits are not too large for good government, nor will the increase of votes in Congress produce any ill effect. On the contrary it will drown the little divisions at present existing there. Our confederacy must be viewed as the nest from which all America, North & South is to be peopled. We should take care too, not to think it for the interest of that great continent to press too soon on the Spaniards. Those countries cannot be in better hands. My fear is that they are too feeble to hold them till our population can be sufficiently advanced to gain it from them piece by piece. The navigation of the Mississippi we must have. This is all we are as yet ready to receive. I have made acquaintance with a very sensible candid gentleman here who was in South America during the revolt which took place there while our revolution was working. He says that those disturbances (of which we scarcely heard anything) cost on both sides an hundred thousand lives.—I have made a particular acquaintance here with Monsieur de Buffon, and have a great desire to give him the best idea I can of our elk. Perhaps your situation may enable you to aid me in this. Were it possible, you could not oblige me more than by sending me the horns, skeleton, & skin of an elk. The most desireable form of receiving them would be to have the skin slit from the under paw along the belly to the tail, & down the thighs to the knee, to take the animal out, leaving the legs and hoofs, the bones of the head, & the horns attached to the skin by sewing up the belly & shipping the skin it would present the form of the animal. However as an opportunity of doing this is scarcely expected I shall be glad to receive them detached, packed in a box, & sent to Richmond to the care of Doctor Currie. Every thing of this kind is precious here, and to prevent my adding to your trouble I must close my letter with assurances of the esteem & attachment with which I am Dr Sir Your friend & servt.

P. S. I must add a prayer for some Peccan nuts, 100, if possible, to be packed in a box of sand and sent me. They might come either directly or via N. York.

A ROMAN TEMPLE FOR VIRGINIA

To William Buchanan and James Hay

Paris, January 26, 1786

GENTLEMEN,—I had the honor of writing to you, on the receipt of your orders to procure draughts for the public buildings, and again, on the 13th of August. In the execution of these orders, two methods of proceeding presented themselves to my mind. The one was, to leave to some architect to draw an external according to his fancy, in which way, experience shews, that, about once in a thousand times, a pleasing form is hit upon; the other was, to take some model already devised, and approved by the general suffrage of the world. I had no hesitation in deciding that the latter was best, nor after the decision, was there any doubt what model to take. There is at Nismes, in the south of France, a building called the Maison quarrée, erected in the time of the Cæsars, and which is allowed, without contradiction, to be the most perfect and precious remain of antiquity in existence. Its superiority over any thing at Rome, in Greece, at Balbec or Palmyra, is allowed on all hands; and this single object has placed Nismes in the general tour of travellers. Having not yet had leisure to visit it, I could only judge of it from drawings, and from the relation of numbers who had been to see it. I determined, therefore, to adopt this model, and to have all its proportions justly observed. As it was impossible for a foreign artist to know, what number and sizes of apartments would suit the different corps of our government, nor how they should be connected with one another, I undertook to form that arrangement, and this being done, I committed them to an architect (Monsieur Clerissault) who had studied this art twenty years in Rome, who had particularly studied and measured the Maison quarrée of Nismes, and had published a book containing most excellent plans, descriptions, and observations on it. He was too well acquainted with the merit of that building, to find himself restrained by my injunctions not to depart from his model. In one instance, only, he persuaded me to admit of this. That was, to make the portico two columns deep only, instead of three, as the original is. His reason was, that this latter depth would too much darken the apartments. Economy might be added, as a second reason. I consented to it, to satisfy him, and the plans are so drawn. I knew that it would still be easy to execute the building with a depth of three columns, and it is what I would certainly recommend. We know that the Maison quarrée has pleased, universally, for near two thousand years. By leaving out a column, the proportions will be changed, and perhaps the effect may be injured more than is expected. What is good, is often spoiled by trying to making it better.

The present is the first opportunity which has occurred of sending the plans. You will, accordingly, receive herewith the ground plan, the elevation of the front, and the elevation of the side. The architect having been much busied, and knowing that this was all which would be necessary in the beginning, has not yet finished the sections of the building. They must go by some future occasion, as well as the models of the front and side, which are making in plaister of Paris. These were absolutely necessary for the guide of workmen, not very expert in their art. It will add considerably to the expense, and I would not have incurred it, but that I was sensible of its necessity. The price of the model will be fifteen guineas. I shall know in a few days, the cost of the drawings, which probably will be the triple of the model: however, this is but conjecture. I will make it as small as possible, pay it, and render you an account in my next letter. You will find, on examination, that the body of this building covers an area, but two fifths of that which is proposed and begun; of course, it will take but about one half the bricks; and, of course, this circumstance will enlist all the workmen, and people of the art against the plan. Again, the building begun, is to have four porticoes; this but one. It is true that this will be deeper than those were probably proposed, but even if it be made three columns deep, it will not take half the number of columns. The beauty of this is insured by experience, and by the suffrage of the whole world: the beauty of that is problematical, as is every drawing, however well it looks on paper, till it be actually executed: and though I suppose there is more room in the plan begun, than in that now sent, yet there is enough in this for all the three branches of government, and more than enough is not wanted. This contains sixteen rooms; to wit, four on the first floor, for the General Court, Delegates, lobby, and conference. Eight on the second floor, for the Executive, the Senate, and six rooms for committees and juries: and over four of these smaller rooms of the second floor, are four mezzininos or entresols, serving as offices for the clerks of the Executive, the Senate, the Delegates, and the Court in actual session. It will be an objection, that the work is begun on the other plan. But the whole of this need not be taken to pieces, and of what shall be taken to pieces, the bricks will do for inner work. Mortar never becomes so hard and adhesive to the bricks, in a few months, but that it may be easily chipped off. And upon the whole, the plan now sent will save a great proportion of the expense.

Hitherto, I have spoken of the capitol only. The plans for the prison, also, accompany this. They will explain themselves. I send, also, the plan of the prison proposed at Lyons, which was sent me by the architect, and to which we are indebted for the fundamental idea of ours. You will see, that of a great thing a very small one is made. Perhaps you may find it convenient to build, at first, only two sides, forming an L; but of this, you are the best judges. It has been suggested to me, that fine gravel, mixed in the mortar, prevents the prisoners from cutting themselves out, as that will destroy their tools. In my letter of August the 13th, I mentioned that I could send workmen from hence. As I am in hopes of receiving your orders precisely, in answer to that letter, I shall defer actually engaging any, till I receive them. In like manner, I shall defer having plans drawn for a Governor's house, &c., till further orders; only assuring you, that the receiving and executing these orders, will always give me a very great pleasure, and the more, should I find that what I have done meets your approbation.

I have the honor to be, with sentiments of the most perfect esteem, gentlemen,

your most obedient and
most humble servant,

THE NOTES, HOUDON, AND THE ENCYCLOPÉDIE
To James Madison

Paris, Feb. 8, 1786

DEAR SIR,—My last letters have been of the 1st & 20th of Sep. and the 28th of Oct. Yours unacknowledged are of Aug. 20, Oct. 3, & Nov. 15. I take this the first safe opportunity of enclosing to you the bills of lading for your books, & two others for your namesake of Williamsburgh & for the attorney which I will pray you to forward. I thank you for the communication of the remonstrance against the assessment. Mazzei who is now in Holland promised me to have it published in the Leyden gazette. It will do us great honour. I wish it may be as much approved by our assembly as by the wisest part of Europe. I have heard with great pleasure that our assembly have come to the resolution of giving the regulation of their commerce to the federal head. I will venture to assert that there is not one of it's opposers who, placed on this ground, would not see the wisdom of this measure. The politics of Europe render it indispensably necessary that with respect to everything external we be one nation only, firmly hooped together. Interior government is what each state should keep to itself. If it could be seen in Europe that all our states could be brought to concur in what the Virginia assembly has done, it would produce a total revolution in their opinion of us, and respect for us. And it should ever be held in mind that insult & war are the consequences of a want of respectability in the national character. As long as the states exercise separately those acts of power which respect foreign nations, so long will there continue to be irregularities committing by some one or other of them which will constantly keep us on an ill footing with foreign nations.

I thank you for your information as to my Notes. The copies I have remaining shall be sent over to be given to some of my friends and to select subjects in the college. I have been unfortunate here with this trifle. I gave out a few copies only, & to confidential persons, writing in every copy a restraint against it's publication. Among others I gave a copy to a Mr. Williamos. He died. I immediately took every precaution I could to recover this copy. But by some means or other a bookseller had got hold of it. He employed a hireling translator and was about publishing it in the most injurious form possible. An Abbé Morellet, a man of letters here to whom I had given a copy, got notice of this. He had translated some passages for a particular purpose: and he compounded with the bookseller to translate & give him the whole, on his declining the first publication. I found it necessary to confirm this, and it will be published in French, still mutilated however in it's freest parts. I am now at a loss what to do as to England. Everything, good or bad, is thought worth publishing there; and I apprehend a translation back from the French, and a publication there. I rather believe it will be most eligible to let the original come out in that country; but am not yet decided.

I have purchased little for you in the book way, since I sent the catalogue of my former purchases. I wish first to have your answer to that, and your information what parts of those purchases went out of your plan. You can easily say buy more of this kind, less of that &c. My wish is to conform myself to yours. I can get for you the original Paris edition in folio of the Encyclopedie for 620 livres, 35. vols.; a good edn in 39 vols, 4to, for 380#; and a good one in 39 vols 8vo, for 280#. The new one will be superior in far the greater number of articles: but not in all. And the possession of the ancient one has moreover the advantage of supplying present use. I have bought one for myself, but wait your orders as to you. I remember your purchase of a watch in Philadelphia. If it should not have proved good, you can probably sell her. In that case I can get for you here, one made as perfect as human art can make it for about 24 louis. I have had such a one made by the best & most faithful hand in Paris. It has a second hand, but no repeating, no day of the month, nor other useless thing to impede and injure the movements which are necessary. For 12 louis more you can have in the same cover, but on the back side & absolutely unconnected with the movements of the watch, a pedometer which shall render you an exact account of the distances you walk. Your pleasure hereon shall be awaited.

Houdon is returned. He called on me the other day to remonstrate against the inscription proposed for Genl W.'s statue. He says it is too long to be put on the pedestal. I told him I was not at liberty to permit any alteration, but I would represent his objection to a friend who could judge of it's validity, and whether a change could be authorized. This has been the subject of conversations here, and various devices & inscriptions have been suggested. The one which has appeared best to me may be translated as follows: "Behold, Reader, the form of George Washington. For his worth, ask History: that will tell it, when this stone shall have yielded to the decays of time. His country erects this monument: Houdon makes it." This for one side. On the 2d represent the evacuation of Boston with the motto "Hostibus primum fugatis." On the 3d the capture of the Hessians with "Hostibus iterum devictis." On the 4th the surrender of York, with "Hostibus ultimum debellatis." This is seizing the three most brilliant actions of his military life. By giving out here a wish of receiving mottos for this statue, we might have thousands offered, of which still better might be chosen. The artist made the same objection of length to the inscription for the bust of the M. de la Fayette. An alteration of that might come in time still, if an alteration was wished. However I am not certain that it is desirable in either case. The state of Georgia has given 20.000 acres of land to the Count d' Estaing. This gift is considered here as very honourable to him, and it has gratified him much. I am persuaded that a gift of lands by the state of Virginia to the Marquis de la Fayette would give a good opinion here of our character, and would reflect honour on the Marquis. Nor am I sure that the day will not come when it might be an useful asylum to him. The time of life at which he visited America was too well adapted to receive good & lasting impressions to permit him ever to accommodate himself to the principles of monarchical government; and it will need all his own prudence & that of his friends to make this country a safe residence for him. How glorious, how comfortable in reflection will it be to have prepared a refuge for him in case of a reverse. In the meantime he could settle it with tenants from the freest part of this country, Bretagny. I have never suggested the smallest idea of this kind to him: because the execution of it should convey the first notice. If the state has not a right to give him lands with their own officers, they could buy up at cheap prices the shares of others. I am not certain however whether in the public or private opinion, a similar gift to Count Rochambeau could be dispensed with. If the state could give to both, it would be better: but in any event, I think they should to the Marquis. C. Rochambeau too has really deserved more attention than he has received. Why not set up his bust, that of Gates, Greene, Franklin in your new capitol? A propos of the Capitol. Do my dear friend exert yourself to get the plan begun on set aside, & that adopted which was drawn here. It was taken from a model which has been the admiration of 16. centuries, which has been the object of as many pilgrimages as the tomb of Mahomet: which will give unrivalled honour to our state, and furnish a model whereon to form the taste of our young men. It will cost much less too than the one begun, because it does not cover one half the Area. Ask, if you please, a sight of my letter of Jan. 26 to Messrs. Buchanan & Hay, which will spare me the repeating its substance here.

Everything is quiet in Europe. I recollect but one new invention in the arts which is worth mentioning. It is a mixture of the arts of engraving & printing, rendering both cheaper. Write or draw anything on a plate of brass with the ink of the inventor, and in half an hour he gives you engraved copies of it so perfectly like the original that they could not be suspected to be copies. His types for printing a whole page are all in one solid piece. An author therefore only prints a few copies of his work from time to time as they are called for. This saves the loss of printing more copies than may possibly be sold, and prevents an edition from being ever exhausted.

I am with a lively esteem Dear Sir, your sincere friend & servant.

P. S. Could you procure & send me an hundred or two nuts of the peccan? they would enable me to oblige some characters here whom I should be much gratified to oblige. They should come packed in sand. The seeds of the sugar maple too would be a great present.

BRITISH ARTS AND BRITISH HATRED

To John Page

Paris, May 4, 1786

DEAR SIR,—Your two favours of Mar 15 and Aug 23, 1785, by Monsieur de la Croix came to hand on the 15th of November. His return gives me an opportunity of sending you a copy of the nautical almanacs for 1786, 7, 8, 9. There is no late and interesting publication here, or I would send it by the same conveiance. With these almanacs I pack a copy of some Notes I wrote for Monsr de Marbois in the year 1781, of which I had a few printed here. They were written in haste & for his private inspection. A few friends having asked copies I found it cheaper to print than to write them. One of these got into the hands of a bookseller who getting a bad translation of them made, obliged me to consent that they should appear on condition of their being translated by a better hand. I apprehend therefore they will get further than I intended: tho' as yet they are in few hands. They will offer nothing new to you, not even as an oblation of my friendship for you which is as old almost as we are ourselves. Mazzei brought me your favor of Apr 28. I thank you much for your communications. Nothing can be more grateful at such a distance. It is unfortunate that most people think the occurrences passing daily under their eyes, are either known to all the world, or not worth being known. They therefore do not give them place in their letters. I hope you will be so good as to continue your friendly information. The proceedings of our public bodies, the progress of the public mind on interesting questions, the casualties which happen among our private friends, and whatever is interesting to yourself and family will always be anxiously received by me. There is one circumstance in the work you were concerned in which has not yet come to my knowledge, to wit how far Westward from Fort Pitt does the Western boundary of Pennsylvania pass, and where does it strike the Ohio? The proposition you mention from Mr. Anderson on the purchase of tobacco, I would have made use of, but that I have engaged the abuses of the tobacco trade on a more general scale. I confess their redress does not appear with any certainty: but till I see all hope of removing the evil by the roots, I cannot propose to prune it's branches.

I returned but three or four days ago from a two months trip to England. I traversed that country much, and own both town & country fell short of my expectations. Comparing it with this, I found a much greater proportion of barrens, a soil in other parts not naturally so good as this, not better cultivated, but better manured, & therefore more productive. This proceeds from the practice of long leases there, and short ones here. The labouring people here are poorer than in England. They pay about one half their produce in rent, the English in general about a third. The gardening in that country is the article in which it surpasses all the earth. I mean their pleasure gardening. This indeed went far beyond my ideas. The city of London, tho' handsomer than Paris, is not so handsome as Philadelphia. Their architecture is in the most wretched stile I ever saw, not meaning to except America where it is bad, nor even Virginia where it is worse than in any other part of America, which I have seen. The mechanical arts in London are carried to a wonderful perfection. But of these I need not speak, because of them my countrymen have unfortunately too many samples before their eyes. I consider the extravagance which has seized them as a more baneful evil than toryism was during the war. It is the more so as the example is set by the best and most amiable characters among us. Would that a missionary appear who would make frugality the basis of his religious system, and go thro the land preaching it up as the only road to salvation, I would join his school tho' not generally disposed to seek my religion out of the dictates of my own reason & feelings of my own heart. These things have been more deeply impressed on my mind by what I have heard & seen in England. That nation hates us, their ministers hate us, and their King more than all other men. They have the impudence to avow this, tho' they acknolege our trade important to them. But they say we cannot prevent our countrymen from bringing that into their laps. A conviction of this determines them to make no terms of commerce with us. They say they will pocket our carrying trade as well as their own. Our overtures of commercial arrangement have been treated with a derision which shows their firm persuasion that we shall never unite to suppress their commerce or even to impede it. I think their hostility towards us is much more deeply rooted at present than during the war. In the arts the most striking thing I saw there, new, was the application of the principle of the steam-engine to grist mills. I saw 8 pr. of stones which are worked by steam, and they are to set up 30 pair in the same house. A hundred bushels of coal a day are consumed at present. I do not know in what proportion the consumption will be increased by the additional geer.

Be so good as to present my respects to Mrs. Page & your family, to W. Lewis, F. Willis & their families and to accept yourself assurances of the sincere regard with which I am Dr Sir your affectionate friend & servt.

P. S. Mazzei is still here and will publish soon a book on the subject of America.

WAR ON BARBARY
To John Adams

Paris, July 11, 1786

DEAR SIR—Our instructions relative to the Barbary states having required us to proceed by way of negotiation to obtain their peace, it became our duty to do this to the best of our power. Whatever might be our private opinions, they were to be suppressed, and the line marked out to us, was to be followed. It has been so honestly, and zealously. It was therefore never material for us to consult together on the best plan of conduct towards these states. I acknolege I very early thought it would be best to effect a peace thro' the medium of war. Tho' it is a question with which we have nothing to do, yet as you propose some discussion of it I shall trouble you with my reasons. Of the 4. positions laid down in your letter of the 3d. instant, I agree to the three first, which are in substance that the good offices of our friends cannot procure us a peace without paying it's price, that they cannot materially lessen that price, and that paying it, we can have the peace in spight of the intrigues of our enemies. As to the 4th. that the longer the negotiation is delayed the larger will be the demand, this will depend on the intermediate captures: if they are many and rich the price may be raised; if few and poor it will be lessened. However if it is decided that we shall buy a peace, I know no reason for delaying the operation, but should rather think it ought to be hastened. But I should prefer the obtaining it by war. 1. Justice is in favor of this opinion. 2. Honor favors it. 3. It will procure us respect in Europe, and respect is a safe-guard to interest. 4. It will arm the federal head with the safest of all the instruments of coercion over their delinquent members and prevent them from using what would be less safe. I think that so far you go with me. But in the next steps we shall differ. 5. I think it least expensive. 6. Equally effectual. I ask a fleet of 150. guns, the one half of which shall be in constant cruise. This fleet built, manned and victualled for 6. months will cost 450,000 £ sterling. It's annual expence is 300 £ sterl. a gun, including every thing: this will be 45,000 £ sterl. a year. I take British experience for the basis of my calculations, tho' we know, from our own experience, that we can do, in this way, for pounds lawful, what costs them pounds sterling. Were we to charge all this to the Algerine war it would amount to little more than we must pay if we buy peace. But as it is proper and necessary that we should establish a small marine force (even were we to buy a peace from the Algerines,) and as that force laid up in our dockyards would cost us half as much annually as if kept in order for service, we have a right to say that only 22,500 £ sterl. per ann. should be charged to the Algerine war. 6. It will be as effectual. To all the mismanagements of Spain and Portugal urged to shew that war against those people is ineffectual, I urge a single fact to prove the contrary where there is any management. About 40. year ago, the Algerines having broke their treaty with France, this court sent Monsr. de Massac with one large and two small frigates, he blockaded the harbour of Algiers three months, and they subscribed to the terms he dictated. If it be admitted however that war, on the fairest prospects, is still exposed to incertainties, I weigh against this the greater incertainty of the duration of a peace bought with money, from such a people, from a Dey 80. years old, and by a nation who, on the hypothesis of buying peace, is to have no power on the sea to enforce an observance of it.

So far I have gone on the supposition that the whole weight of this war would rest on us. But 1. Naples will join us. The character of their naval minister (Acton), his known sentiments with respect to the peace Spain is officiously trying to make for them, and his dispositions against the Algerines give the greatest reason to believe it. 2. Every principle of reason tells us Portugal will join us. I state this as taking for granted, what all seem to believe, that they will not be at peace with Algiers. I suppose then that a Convention might be formed between Portugal, Naples and the U.S. by which the burthen of the war might be quotaed on them according to their respective wealth, and the term of it should be when Algiers should subscribe to a peace with all three on equal terms. This might be left open for other nations to accede to, and many, if not most of the powers of Europe (except France, England, Holland and Spain if her peace be made) would sooner or later enter into the confederacy, for the sake of having their peace with the Pyratical states guarantied by the whole. I suppose that in this case our proportion of force would not be the half of what I first calculated on.

These are the reasons which have influenced my judgment on this question. I give them to you to shew you that I am imposed on by a semblance of reason at least, and not with an expectation of their changing your opinion. You have viewed the subject, I am sure in all it's bearings. You have weighed both questions with all their circumstances. You make the result different from what I do. The same facts impress us differently. This is enough to make me suspect an error in my process of reasoning tho' I am not able to detect it. It is of no consequence; as I have nothing to say in the decision, and am ready to proceed heartily on any other plan which may be adopted, if my agency should be thought useful. With respect to the dispositions of the states I am utterly uninformed. I cannot help thinking however that on a view of all circumstances, they might be united in either of the plans.

Having written this on the receipt of your letter, without knowing of any opportunity of sending it, I know not when it will go: I add nothing therefore on any other subject but assurances of the sincere esteem and respect with which I am Dear Sir your friend and servant,

"A CRUSADE AGAINST IGNORANCE"

To George Wythe

Paris, August 13, 1786

DEAR SIR,—Your favors of Jan. 10 & Feb. 10, came to hand on the 20th & 2d of May. I availed myself of the first opportunity which occurred, by a gentleman going to England, of sending to Mr. Joddrel a copy of the Notes on our country, with a line informing him that it was you who had emboldened me to take that liberty. Madison, no doubt, informed you of the reason why I had sent only a single copy to Virginia. Being assured by him that they will not do the harm I had apprehended, but on the contrary may do some good, I propose to send thither the copies remaining on hand, which are fewer than I had intended. But of the numerous corrections they need, there are one or two so essential that I must have them made, by printing a few new leaves & substituting them for the old. This will be done while they are engraving a map which I have constructed of the country from Albemarle sound to Lake Erie, & which will be inserted in the book. A bad French translation which is getting out here, will probably oblige me to publish the original more freely, which it neither deserved nor was ever intended. Your wishes, which are laws to me, will justify my destining a copy for you, otherwise I should as soon have thought of sending you a hornbook; for there is no truth there that which is not familiar to you, and it's errors I should hardly have proposed to treat you with.

Immediately on the receipt of your letter, I wrote to a correspondent at Florence to inquire after the family of Tagliaferro as you desired. I received his answer two days ago, a copy of which I now inclose. The original shall be sent by some other occasion. I will have the copper-plate immediately engraved. This may be ready within a few days, but the probability is that I shall be long getting an opportunity of sending it to you, as these rarely occur. You do not mention the size of the plate but, presuming it is intended for labels for the inside of books, I shall have it made of a proper size for that. I shall omit the word *agisos*, according to the license you allow me, because I think the beauty of a motto is to condense much matter in as few words as possible. The word omitted will be supplied by every reader. The European papers have announced that the assembly of Virginia were occupied on the revisal of their code of laws. This, with some other similar intelligence, has contributed much to convince the people of Europe, that what the English papers are constantly publishing of our anarchy, is false; as they are sensible that such a work is that of a people only who are in perfect tranquillity. Our act for freedom of religion is extremely applauded. The ambassadors & ministers of the several nations of Europe resident at this court have asked of me copies of it to send to their sovereigns, and it is inserted at full length in

several books now in the press; among others, in the new
Encyclopedie. I think it will produce considerable good even
in these countries where ignorance, superstition, poverty, &
oppression of body & mind in every form, are so firmly settled on the mass of the people, that their redemption from
them can never be hoped. If the Almighty had begotten a
thousand sons, instead of one, they would not have sufficed
for this task. If all the sovereigns of Europe were to set themselves to work to emancipate the minds of their subjects from
their present ignorance & prejudices, & that as zealously as
they now endeavor the contrary, a thousand years would not
place them on that high ground on which our common people are now setting out. Ours could not have been so fairly
put into the hands of their own common sense had they not
been separated from their parent stock & kept from contamination, either from them, or the other people of the old
world, by the intervention of so wide an ocean. To know the
worth of this, one must see the want of it here. I think by far
the most important bill in our whole code is that for the diffusion of knowlege among the people. No other sure foundation can be devised, for the preservation of freedom and
happiness. If anybody thinks that kings, nobles, or priests are
good conservators of the public happiness send them here. It
is the best school in the universe to cure them of that folly.
They will see here with their own eyes that these descriptions
of men are an abandoned confederacy against the happiness
of the mass of the people. The omnipotence of their effect
cannot be better proved than in this country particularly,
where notwithstanding the finest soil upon earth, the finest
climate under heaven, and a people of the most benevolent,
the most gay and amiable character of which the human form
is susceptible, where such a people I say, surrounded by so
many blessings from nature, are yet loaded with misery by
kings, nobles and priests, and by them alone. Preach, my dear
Sir, a crusade against ignorance; establish & improve the law
for educating the common people. Let our countrymen know
that the people alone can protect us against these evils, and
that the tax which will be paid for this purpose is not more
than the thousandth part of what will be paid to kings, priests
& nobles who will rise up among us if we leave the people in

ignorance. The people of England, I think, are less oppressed than here. But it needs but half an eye to see, when among them, that the foundation is laid in their dispositions for the establishment of a despotism. Nobility, wealth & pomp are the objects of their adoration. They are by no means the free-minded people we suppose them in America. Their learned men too are few in number, and are less learned and infinitely less emancipated from prejudice than those of this country. An event too seems to be preparing, in the order of things, which will probably decide the fate of that country. It is no longer doubtful that the harbour of Cherburg will be complete, that it will be a most excellent one, & capacious enough to hold the whole navy of France. Nothing has ever been wanting to enable this country to invade that, but a naval force conveniently stationed to protect the transports. This change of situation must oblige the English to keep up a great standing army, and there is no King, who, with sufficient force, is not always ready to make himself absolute. My paper warns me it is time to recommend myself to the friendly recollection of Mrs. Wythe, of Colo. Tagliaferro & his family & particularly of Mr. R. T.; and to assure you of the affectionate esteem with which I am Dear Sir your friend and servt.

EDUCATION OF A FUTURE SON-IN-LAW
To Thomas Mann Randolph, Jr.

Paris, Aug. 27, 1786

DEAR SIR,—I am honoured with your favour of the 16th instant, and desirous, without delay, of manifesting my wishes to be useful to you I shall venture to you some thoughts on the course of your studies, which must be submitted to the better choice with which you are surrounded. A longer race through life may have entitled me to seize some truths which have not yet been presented to your observation & more intimate knowledge of the country in which you are to live & of the circumstances in which you will be placed, may enable me to point your attention to the branches of science which will administer the most to your happiness there. The foundations which you have laid in languages and mathematics are proper for every superstructure. The former exercises our memory while that and no other faculty is yet matured & prevents our acquiring habits of idleness. The latter gives exercise to our reason, as soon as that has acquired a certain degree of strength, and stores the mind with truths which are useful in other branches of science. At this moment then a second order of preparation is to commence. I shall propose to you that it be extensive, comprehending Astronomy, Natural Philosophy (or Physics), Natural History, Anatomy, Botany & Chemistry. No inquisitive mind will be content to be ignorant of any of these branches. But I would advise you to be contented with a course of lectures in most of them, without attempting to make yourself master of the whole. This is more than any genius joined to any length of life is equal to. You will find among them some one study to which your mind will more particularly attach itself. This then I would pursue & propose to attain eminence in. Your own country furnishes the most aliment for Natural History, Botany & Physics & as you express a fondness for the former you might make it your principal object, endeavoring however to make yourself more acquainted with the two latter than with other branches likely to be less useful. In fact you will find botany offering it's charms to you at every step—during summer & Physics in every season. All these branches of science will be better attained by attending courses of lectures in them. You are now in a place where the best courses upon earth are within your reach and being delivered in your native language—you lose no part of their benefit. Such an opportunity you will never again have. I would therefore strongly press on you to fix no other limit to your stay in Edinborough than your having got thro this whole course. The omission of any one part of it will be an affliction & loss to you as long as you live. Beside the comfort of knowledge, every science is auxiliary to every other. While you are attending these courses you can proceed by yourself in a regular series of historical reading. It would be a waste of time to attend a professor of this. It is to be acquired from books and if you pursue it by yourself you can accommodate it to your other reading so as to fill up those chasms of time not otherwise appropriated.

There are portions of the day too when the mind should be eased, particularly after dinner it should be applied to lighter occupation: history is of this kind. It exercises principally the memory. Reflection also indeed is necessary but not generally in a laborious degree. To conduct yourself in this branch of science you have only to consider what æras of it merit a grasp & what a particular attention, & in each æra also to distinguish between the countries the knowledge of whose history will be useful & those where it suffices only to be not altogether ignorant. Having laid down your plan as to the branches of history you would pursue, the order of time will be your sufficient guide. After what you have read in antient history I should suppose Millot's digest would be useful & sufficient. The histories of Greece and Rome are worthy a good degree of attention, they should be read in the original authors. The transition from antient to modern history will be best effected by reading Gibbon's. Then a general history of the principal states of Europe, but particular ones of England. Here too the original writers are to be preferred. Kennet published a considerable collection of these in 3 vols. folio, but there are some others not in his collection well worth being read. After the history of England that of America will claim your attention. Here too original authors & not compilers are best. An author who writes of his own times or of times near his own presents in his own ideas & manner the best picture of the moment of which he writes. History need not be hurried but may give way to the other sciences because history can be pursued after you shall have left your present situation as well as while you remain in it. When you shall have got thro this second order of preparation the study of the law is to be begun. This like history is to be acquired from books. All the aid you will want will be a catalogue of the books to be read & the order in which they are to be read. It being absolutely indifferent in what place you carry on this reading I should propose your doing it in France. The advantages of this will be that you will at the same time acquire the habit of speaking French which is the object of a year or two. You may be giving attention to such of the fine arts as your turn may lead you to & you will be forming an acquaintance with the individuals & characters of a nation with whom we must long remain in the closest intimacy & to whom we are bound by the strong ties of gratitude and policy. A nation in short of the most amiable dispositions on earth, the whole mass of which is penetrated with an affection for us. You might before you return to your own country make a visit to Italy also.

I should have performed the office of but half a friend were I to confine myself to the improvement of the mind only. Knowledge indeed is a desirable, a lovely possession, but I do not scruple to say that health is more so. It is of little consequence to store the mind with science if the body be permitted to become debilitated. If the body be feeble, the mind will not be strong—the sovereign invigorator of the body is exercise, and of all exercises walking is best. A horse gives but a kind of half exercise, and a carriage is no better than a cradle. No one knows, till he tries, how easily a habit of walking is acquired. A person who never walked three miles will in the course of a month become able to walk 15 or 20 without fatigue. I have known some great walkers & had particular accounts of many more: and I never knew or heard of one who was not healthy & long lived. This species of exercise therefore is much to be advised. Should you be disposed to try it, as your health has been feeble, it will be necessary for you to begin with a little, & to increase it by degrees. For the same reason you must probably at first ascribe to it the hours most precious for study, I mean those about the middle of the day. But when you shall find yourself strong you may venture to take your walks in the evening after the digestion of the dinner is pretty well over. This is making a compromise between health & study. The latter would be too much interrupted were you to take from it the early hours of the day and habit will soon render the evening's exercise as salutary as that of the morning. I speak this from my own experience having, from an attachment to study, very early in life, made this arrangement of my time, having ever observed it, & still observing it, & always with perfect success. Not less than two hours a day should be devoted to exercise, and the weather should be little regarded. A person not sick will not be injured by getting wet. It is but taking a cold bath which never gives a cold to any one. Brute animals are the most healthy,

& they are exposed to all weather and, of men, those are healthiest who are the most exposed. The recipe of those two descriptions of beings is simple diet, exercise and the open air, be it's state what it will; and we may venture to say that this recipe will give health & vigor to every other description.—By this time I am sure you will think I have sermonized enough. I have given you indeed a lengthy lecture. I have been led through it by my zeal to serve you; if in the whole you find one useful counsel, that will be my reward, & a sufficient one. Few persons in your own country have started from as advantageous ground as that whereon you will be placed. Nature and fortune have been liberal to you. Every thing honourable or profitable there is placed within your own reach, and will depend on your own efforts. If these are exerted with assiduity, and guided by unswerving honesty, your success is infallible: and that it may be as great as you wish is the sincere desire of Dear Sir, your most affectionate humble servant.

P.S. Be so good as to present me affectionately to your brother & cousin.

ARCHAEOLOGY, LEDYARD, A NEW INVENTION
To Ezra Stiles

Paris, Sep. 1, 1786

SIR,—I am honoured with your letter of May 8. That which you mention to have written in the winter preceding never came to hand. I return you my thanks for the communications relative to the Western country. When we reflect how long we have inhabited those parts of America which lie between the Alleghaney & the ocean, that no monument has ever been found in them which indicated the use of iron among its' aboriginal inhabitants, that they were as far advanced in arts, at least, as the inhabitants on the other side the Alleghaney, a good degree of infidelity may be excused as to the new discoveries which suppose regular fortifications of brickwork to have been in use among the Indians on the waters of the Ohio. Intrenchments of earth they might indeed make: but brick is more difficult. The art of making it may have preceded the use of iron, but it would suppose a greater degree of industry than men in the hunter state usually possess. I should like to know whether General Parsons himself saw actual bricks among the remains of fortification. I suppose the settlement of our continent is of the most remote antiquity. The similitude between its' inhabitants & those of Eastern parts of Asia renders it probable that ours are descended from them or they from ours. The latter is my opinion, founded on this single fact. Among the red inhabitants of Asia there are but a few languages radically different, but among our Indians the number of languages is infinite which are so radically different as to exhibit at present no appearance of their having been derived from a common source. The time necessary for the generation of so many languages must be immense. A countryman of yours, a Mr. Lediard, who was with Capt. Cook on his last voiage, proposes either to go to Kamschatka, cross from thence to the Western side of America, and penetrate through the Continent to our side of it, or to go to Kentucke, & thence penetrate Westwardly to the South sea, the vent from hence lately to London, where if he finds a passage to Kamschatka or the Western coast of America he would avail himself of it: otherwise he proposes to return to our side of America to attempt that route. I think him well calculated for such an enterprise, & wish he may undertake it. Another countryman of yours Mr. Trumbul has paid us a visit here & brought with him two pictures which are the admiration of the Connoisseurs. His natural talents for this art seem almost unparalleled. I send you the 5th & 6th vols. of the *Bibliotheque physico ecconomie* erroneously lettered as the 7th & 8th, which are not yet come out. I inclose with them the article "Etats Unis" of the new Encyclopedie. This article is recently published, & a few copies have been printed separate. For this twelvemonth past little new & excellent has appeared either in literature or the arts. An Abbé Rochon has applied the metal called platina to the telescope instead of the mixed metal of which the specula were formerly composed. It is insusceptible of rust, as gold is, and he thinks it's reflective power equal to that of the mixed metal. He has observed a very curious effect of the natural chrystals, & especially of those of Iceland; which is that lenses made of them have two distinct focuses, and present you the object distinctly at two different distances. This I have seen myself. A new method of copying has been invented here. I called on the inventor, & he presented me a plate of copper, a pen & ink. I wrote a note on the plate, and in about three quarters of an hour he brought me an hundred copies, as perfect as the imagination can conceive. Had I written my name, he could have put it to so many bonds, so that I should have acknoleged the Signature to be my own. The copying of paintings in England is very conceivable. Any number may be taken, which shall give you the true lineaments & colouring of the original without injuring that. This is so like creation, that had I not seen it, I should have doubted it.—The death of the K. of Prussia, which happened on the 17th inst. will probably employ the pens, if not the swords of politicians. We had exchanged the ratifications of our treaty with him. The articles of this which were intended to prevent or miticate wars, by lessening their aliment are so much applauded in Europe that I think the example will be followed. I have the honour to be with very sincere esteem, Dear Sir, your most obedt. humble servant.

"DIALOGUE BETWEEN MY HEAD & MY HEART"
To Maria Cosway

Paris, October 12, 1786

MY DEAR MADAM,—Having performed the last sad office of handing you into your carriage at the pavillon de St. Denis, and seen the wheels get actually into motion, I turned on my heel & walked, more dead than alive, to the opposite door, where my own was awaiting me. Mr. Danquerville was missing. He was sought for, found, & dragged down stairs. We were crammed into the carriage, like recruits for the Bastille, & not having soul enough to give orders to the coachman, he presumed Paris our destination, & drove off. After a considerable interval, silence was broke with a *"Je suis vraiment afflige du depart de ces bons gens."* This was a signal for a mutual confession of distress. We began immediately to talk of Mr. & Mrs. Cosway, of their goodness, their talents, their amiability; & tho we spoke of nothing else, we seemed hardly to have entered into matter when the coachman announced the rue St. Denis, & that we were opposite Mr. Danquerville's. He insisted on descending there & traversing a short passage to his lodgings. I was carried home. Seated by my fireside, solitary & sad, the following dialogue took place between my Head & my Heart:

Head.   Well, friend, you seem to be in a pretty trim.

Heart.   I am indeed the most wretched of all earthly beings. Overwhelmed with grief, every fibre of my frame distended beyond its natural powers to bear, I would willingly meet whatever catastrophe should leave me no more to feel or to fear.

Head.   These are the eternal consequences of your warmth & precipitation. This is one of the scrapes into which you are ever leading us. You confess your follies indeed; but still you hug & cherish them; & no reformation can be hoped, where there is no repentance.

Heart.   Oh, my friend! this is no moment to upbraid my foibles. I am rent into fragments by the force of my grief! If you have any balm, pour it into my wounds; if none, do not harrow them by new torments. Spare me in this awful moment! At any other I will attend with patience to your admonitions.

Head.   On the contrary I never found that the moment of triumph with you was the moment of attention to my admonitions. While suffering under your follies, you may perhaps be made sensible of them, but, the paroxysm over, you fancy it can never return. Harsh therefore as the medicine may be, it is my office to administer it. You will be pleased to remember that when our friend Trumbull used to be telling us of the merits & talents of these good people, I never ceased whispering to you that we had no occasion for new acquaintance; that the greater their merits & talents, the more dangerous their friendship to our tranquillity, because the regret at parting would be greater.

Heart.   Accordingly, Sir, this acquaintance was not the

consequence of my doings. It was one of your projects which threw us in the way of it. It was you, remember, & not I, who desired the meeting at Legrand & Molinos. I never trouble myself with domes nor arches. The Halle aux bleds might have rotted down before I should have gone to see it. But you, forsooth, who are eternally getting us to sleep with your diagrams & crotchets, must go & examine this wonderful piece of architecture. And when you had seen it, oh! it was the most superb thing on earth! What you had seen there was worth all you had yet seen in Paris! I thought so too. But I meant it of the lady & gentleman to whom we had been presented; & not of a parcel of sticks & chips put together in pens. You then, Sir, & not I, have been the cause of the present distress.

Head. It would have been happy for you if my diagrams & crotchets had gotten you to sleep on that day, as you are pleased to say they eternally do. My visit to Legrand & Molinos had public utility for it's object. A market is to be built in Richmond. What a commodious plan is that of Legrand & Molinos; especially if we put on it the noble dome of the Halle aux bleds. If such a bridge as they shewed us can be thrown across the Schuylkill at Philadelphia, the floating bridges taken up & the navigation of that river opened, what a copious resource will be added, of wood & provisions, to warm & feed the poor of that city? While I was occupied with these objects, you were dilating with your new acquaintances, & contriving how to prevent a separation from them. Every soul of you had an engagement for the day. Yet all these were to be sacrificed, that you might dine together. Lying messengers were to be despatched into every quarter of the city, with apologies for your breach of engagement. You particularly had the effrontery to send word to the Dutchess Danville that, on the moment we were setting out to dine with her, despatches came to hand which required immediate attention. You wanted me to invent a more ingenious excuse; but I knew you were getting into a scrape, & I would have nothing to do with it. Well, after dinner to St. Cloud, from St. Cloud to Ruggieri's, from Ruggieri to Krumfoltz, & if the day had been as long as a Lapland summer day, you would still have contrived means among you to have filled it.

Heart. Oh! my dear friend, how you have revived me by recalling to my mind the transactions of that day! How well I remember them all, & that when I came home at night & looked back to the morning, it seemed to have been a month agone. Go on then, like a kind comforter & paint to me the day we went to St. Germains. How beautiful was every object! the Port de Reuilly, the hills along the Seine, the rainbows of the machine of Marly, the terrace of St. Germains, the chateaux, the gardens, the statues of Marly, the pavillon of Lucienne. Recollect too Madrid, Bagatelle, the King's garden, the Dessert. How grand the idea excited by the remains of such a column! The spiral staircase too was beautiful. Every moment was filled with something agreeable. The wheels of time moved on with a rapidity of which those of our carriage gave but a faint idea. And yet in the evening when one took a retrospect of the day, what a mass of happiness had we travelled over! Retrace all those scenes to me, my good companion, & I will forgive the unkindness with which you were chiding me. The day we went to St. Germains was a little too warm, I think; was it not?

Head. Thou art the most incorrigible of all the beings that ever sinned! I reminded you of the follies of the first day, intending to deduce from thence some useful lessons for you, but instead of listening to these, you kindle at the recollection, you retrace the whole series with a fondness which shews you want nothing but the opportunity to act it over again. I often told you during its course that you were imprudently engaging your affections under circumstances that must have cost you a great deal of pain: that the persons indeed were of the greatest merit, possessing good sense, good humour, honest hearts, honest manners, & eminence in a lovely art; that the lady had moreover qualities & accomplishments, belonging to her sex, which might form a chapter apart for her: such as music, modesty, beauty, & that softness of disposition which is the ornament of her sex & charm of ours, but that all these considerations would increase the pang of separation: that their stay here was to be short: that you rack our whole system when you are parted from those you love, complaining that such a separation is worse than death, inasmuch as this ends our sufferings, whereas that only begins them: & that the separation would in this instance be the more severe as you would probably never see them again.

Heart. But they told me they would come back again the next year.

Head. But in the meantime see what you suffer: & their return too depends on so many circumstances that if you had a grain of prudence you would not count upon it. Upon the whole it is improbable & therefore you should abandon the idea of ever seeing them again.

Heart. May heaven abandon me if I do!

Head. Very well. Suppose then they come back. They are to stay two months, & when these are expired, what is to follow? Perhaps you flatter yourself they may come to America?

Heart. God only knows what is to happen. I see nothing impossible in that supposition. And I see things wonderfully contrived sometimes to make us happy. Where could they find such objects as in America for the exercise of their enchanting art? especially the lady, who paints landscapes so inimitably. She wants only subjects worthy of immortality to render her pencil immortal. The Falling Spring, the Cascade of Niagara, the Passage of the Potowmac through the Blue Mountains, the Natural bridge. It is worth a voyage across the Atlantic to see these objects; much more to paint, and make them, & thereby ourselves, known to all ages. And our own dear Monticello, where has nature spread so rich a mantle under the eye? mountains, forests, rocks, rivers. With what majesty do we there ride above the storms! How sublime to look down into the workhouse of nature, to see her clouds, hail, snow, rain, thunder, all fabricated at our feet! and the glorious sun when rising as if out of a distant water, just gilding the tops of the mountains, & giving life to all nature! I hope in God no circumstance may ever make either seek an asylum from grief! With what sincere sympathy I would open every cell of my composition to receive the effusion of their woes! I would pour my tears into their wounds: & if a drop of balm could be found on the top of the Cordilleras, or at the remotest sources of the Missouri, I would go thither myself to seek & to bring it. Deeply practised in the school of affliction, the human heart knows no joy which I have not lost, no sorrow of which I have not drunk! Fortune can present no grief of unknown form to me! Who then can so softly bind up the wound of another as he who has felt the same wound himself? But Heaven forbid they should ever know a sorrow! Let us turn over another leaf, for this has distracted me.

Head.   Well. Let us put this possibility to trial then on another point. When you consider the character which is given of our country by the lying newspapers of London, & their credulous copyers in other countries; when you reflect that all Europe is made to believe we are a lawless banditti, in a state of absolute anarchy, cutting one another's throats, & plundering without distinction, how can you expect that any reasonable creature would venture among us?

Heart.   But you & I know that all this is false: that there is not a country on earth where there is greater tranquillity, where the laws are milder, or better obeyed: where every one is more attentive to his own business, or meddles less with that of others: where strangers are better received, more hospitably treated, & with a more sacred respect.

Head.   True, you & I know this, but your friends do not know it.

Heart.   But they are sensible people who think for themselves. They will ask of impartial foreigners who have been among us, whether they saw or heard on the spot any instances of anarchy. They will judge too that a people occupied as we are in opening rivers, digging navigable canals, making roads, building public schools, establishing academies, erecting busts & statues to our great men, protecting religious freedom, abolishing sanguinary punishments, reforming & improving our laws in general, they will judge I say for themselves whether these are not the occupations of a people at their ease, whether this is not better evidence of our true state than a London newspaper, hired to lie, & from which no truth can ever be extracted but by reversing everything it says.

Head.   I did not begin this lecture my friend with a view to learn from you what America is doing. Let us return then to our point. I wished to make you sensible how imprudent it is to place your affections, without reserve, on objects you must so soon lose, & whose loss when it comes must cost

you such severe pangs. Remember the last night. You knew
your friends were to leave Paris to-day. This was enough to
throw you into agonies. All night you tossed us from one side
of the bed to the other. No sleep, no rest. The poor crippled
wrist too, never left one moment in the same position, now
up, now down, now here, now there; was it to be wondered
at if it's pains returned? The Surgeon then was to be called,
& to be rated as an ignoramus because he could not divine
the cause of this extraordinary change. In fine, my friend, you
must mend your manners. This is not a world to live at random in as you do. To avoid those eternal distresses, to which
you are forever exposing us, you must learn to look forward
before you take a step which may interest our peace. Everything in this world is a matter of calculation. Advance then
with caution, the balance in your hand. Put into one scale the
pleasures which any object may offer; but put fairly into the
other the pains which are to follow, & see which preponderates. The making an acquaintance is not a matter of indifference. When a new one is proposed to you, view it all round.
Consider what advantages it presents, & to what inconveniences it may expose you. Do not bite at the bait of pleasure
till you know there is no hook beneath it. The art of life is
the art of avoiding pain: & he is the best pilot who steers
clearest of the rocks & shoals with which he is beset. Pleasure
is always before us; but misfortune is at our side: while running after that, this arrests us. The most effectual means of
being secure against pain is to retire within ourselves, & to
suffice for our own happiness. Those, which depend on ourselves, are the only pleasures a wise man will count on: for
nothing is ours which another may deprive us of. Hence the
inestimable value of intellectual pleasures. Even in our power,
always leading us to something new, never cloying, we ride
serene & sublime above the concerns of this mortal world,
contemplating truth & nature, matter & motion, the laws
which bind up their existence, & that eternal being who made
& bound them up by those laws. Let this be our employ.
Leave the bustle & tumult of society to those who have not
talents to occupy themselves without them. Friendship is but
another name for an alliance with the follies & the misfortunes of others. Our own share of miseries is sufficient: why

enter then as volunteers into those of another? Is there so little gall poured into our cup that we must needs help to drink that of our neighbor? A friend dies or leaves us: we feel as if a limb was cut off. He is sick: we must watch over him, & participate of his pains. His fortune is shipwrecked; ours must be laid under contribution. He loses a child, a parent, or a partner: we must mourn the loss as if it were our own.

Heart. And what more sublime delight than to mingle tears with one whom the hand of heaven hath smitten! to watch over the bed of sickness, & to beguile it's tedious & it's painful moments! to share our bread with one to whom misfortune has left none! This world abounds indeed with misery: to lighten it's burthen we must divide it with one another. But let us now try the virtues of your mathematical balance, & as you have put into one scale the burthen of friendship, let me put it's comforts into the other. When languishing then under disease, how grateful is the solace of our friends! how are we penetrated with their assiduities & attentions! how much are we supported by their encouragements & kind offices! When heaven has taken from us some object of our love, how sweet is it to have a bosom whereon to recline our heads, & into which we may pour the torrent of our tears! Grief, with such a comfort, is almost a luxury! In a life where we are perpetually exposed to want & accident, yours is a wonderful proposition, to insulate ourselves, to retire from all aid, & to wrap ourselves in the mantle of self-sufficiency! For assuredly nobody will care for him who cares for nobody. But friendship is precious, not only in the shade but in the sunshine of life; & thanks to a benevolent arrangement of things, the greater part of life is sunshine. I will recur for proof to the days we have lately passed. On these indeed the sun shone brightly. How gay did the face of nature appear! Hills, valleys, chateaux, gardens, rivers, every object wore it's liveliest hue! Whence did they borrow it? From the presence of our charming companion. They were pleasing, because she seemed pleased. Alone, the scene would have been dull & insipid: the participation of it with her gave it relish. Let the gloomy monk, sequestered from the world, seek unsocial pleasures in the bottom of his cell! Let the sublimated philosopher grasp visionary happiness while pursuing phantoms dressed in the garb of truth! Their supreme wisdom is supreme folly; & they mistake for happiness the mere absence of pain. Had they ever felt the solid pleasure of one generous spasm of the heart, they would exchange for it all the frigid speculations of their lives, which you have been vaunting in such elevated terms. Believe me then my friend, that that is a miserable arithmetic which could estimate friendship at nothing, or at less than nothing. Respect for you has induced me to enter into this discussion, & to hear principles uttered which I detest & abjure. Respect for myself now obliges me to recall you into the proper limits of your office. When nature assigned us the same habitation, she gave us over it a divided empire. To you she allotted the field of science; to me that of morals. When the circle is to be squared, or the orbit of a comet to be traced; when the arch of greatest strength, or the solid of least resistance is to be investigated, take up the problem; it is yours; nature has given me no cognizance of it. In like manner, in denying to you the feelings of sympathy, of benevolence, of gratitude, of justice, of love, of friendship, she has excluded you from their controul. To these she has adapted the mechanism of the heart. Morals were too essential to the happiness of man to be risked on the incertain combinations of the head. She laid their foundation therefore in sentiment, not in science. That she gave to all, as necessary to all: this to a few only, as sufficing with a few. I know indeed that you pretend authority to the sovereign controul of our conduct in all its parts: & a respect for your grave saws & maxims, a desire to do what is right, has sometimes induced me to conform to your counsels. A few facts however which I can readily recall to your memory, will suffice to prove to you that nature has not organized you for our moral direction. When the poor wearied souldier whom we overtook at Chickahomony with his pack on his back, begged us to let him get up behind our chariot, you began to calculate that the road was full of souldiers, & that if all should be taken up our horses would fail in their journey. We drove on therefore. But soon becoming sensible you had made me do wrong, that tho we cannot relieve all the distressed we should relieve as many as we can, I turned about to take up the souldier; but he had entered a bye path, & was no more to be found; & from that moment to this I could never find him out to ask his forgiveness. Again, when the poor woman came to ask a charity in Philadelphia, you whispered that she looked like a drunkard, & that half a dollar was enough to give her for the ale-house. Those who want the dispositions to give, easily find reasons why they ought not to give. When I sought her out afterwards, & did what I should have done at first, you know that she employed the money immediately towards placing her child at school. If our country, when pressed with wrongs at the point of the bayonet, had been governed by it's heads instead of it's hearts, where should we have been now? Hanging on a gallows as high as Haman's. You began to calculate & to compare wealth and numbers: we threw up a few pulsations of our warmest blood; we supplied enthusiasm against wealth and numbers; we put our existence to the hazard when the hazard seemed against us, and we saved our country: justifying at the same time the ways of Providence, whose precept is to do always what is right, and leave the issue to him. In short, my friend, as far as my recollection serves me, I do not know that I ever did a good thing on your suggestion, or a dirty one without it. I do forever then disclaim your interference in my province. Fill papers as you please with triangles & squares: try how many ways you can hang & combine them together. I shall never envy nor controul your sublime delights. But leave me to decide when & where friendships are to be contracted. You say I contract them at random. So you said the woman at Philadelphia was a drunkard. I receive no one into my esteem till I know they are worthy of it. Wealth, title, office, are no recommendations to my friendship. On the contrary great good qualities are requisite to make amends for their having wealth, title, & office. You confess that in the present case I could not have made a worthier choice. You only object that I was so soon to lose them. We are not immortal ourselves, my friend; how can we expect our enjoyments to be so? We have no rose without it's thorn; no pleasure without alloy. It is the law of our existence; & we must acquiesce. It is the condition annexed to all our pleasures, not by us who receive, but by him who gives them. True, this condition is pressing cruelly on me at this moment.

I feel more fit for death than life. But when I look back on
the pleasures of which it is the consequence, I am conscious
they were worth the price I am paying. Notwithstanding your
endeavours too to damp my hopes, I comfort myself with
expectations of their promised return. Hope is sweeter than
despair, & they were too good to mean to deceive me. In the
summer, said the gentleman; but in the spring, said the lady:
& I should love her forever, were it only for that! Know then,
my friend, that I have taken these good people into my bosom; that I have lodged them in the warmest cell I could find:
that I love them, & will continue to love them through life:
that if fortune should dispose them on one side the globe, &
me on the other, my affections shall pervade it's whole mass
to reach them. Knowing then my determination, attempt not
to disturb it. If you can at any time furnish matter for their
amusement, it will be the office of a good neighbor to do it.
I will in like manner seize any occasion which may offer to
do the like good turn for you with Condorcet, Rittenhouse,
Madison, La Cretelle, or any other of those worthy sons of
science whom you so justly prize.

I thought this a favorable proposition whereon to rest the
issue of the dialogue. So I put an end to it by calling for my
night-cap. Methinks I hear you wish to heaven I had called a
little sooner, & so spared you the ennui of such a sermon. I
did not interrupt them sooner because I was in a mood for
hearing sermons. You too were the subject; & on such a the-
sis I never think the theme long; not even if I am to write it,
and that slowly & awkwardly, as now, with the left hand. But
that you may not be discouraged from a correspondence
which begins so formidably, I will promise you on my honour that my future letters shall be of a reasonable length. I
will even agree to express but half my esteem for you, for fear
of cloying you with too full a dose. But, on your part, no
curtailing. If your letters are as long as the bible, they will
appear short to me. Only let them be brimful of affection. I
shall read them with the dispositions with which Arlequin, in
Les deux billets spelt the words "*je t'aime*," and wished that
the whole alphabet had entered into their composition.

We have had incessant rains since your departure. These

make me fear for your health, as well as that you had an uncomfortable journey. The same cause has prevented me from
being able to give you any account of your friends here. This
voyage to Fontainebleau will probably send the Count de
Moustier & the Marquise de Brehan to America. Danquerville promised to visit me, but has not done it as yet. De la
Tude comes sometimes to take family soup with me, & enter-
tains me with anecdotes of his five & thirty years imprisonment. How fertile is the mind of man which can make the
Bastile & Dungeon of Vincennes yield interesting anecdotes!
You know this was for making four verses on Mme de Pompadour. But I think you told me you did not know the verses.
They were these: *"Sans esprit, sans sentiment, Sans etre belle, ni
neuve, En France on peut avoir le premier amant: Pompadour en
est l' epreuve."* I have read the memoir of his three escapes. As
to myself my health is good, except my wrist which mends
slowly, & my mind which mends not at all, but broods constantly over your departure. The lateness of the season obliges
me to decline my journey into the south of France. Present
me in the most friendly terms to Mr. Cosway, & receive me
into your own recollection with a partiality & a warmth, proportioned, not to my own poor merit, but to the sentiments of sincere affection & esteem with which I have the
honour to be, my dear Madam, your most obedient humble
servant.

HOMER, NEW JERSEY FARMERS, AND THE WHEEL

To St. John de Crèvecoeur

Paris, January 15, 1787

DEAR SIR,—I see by the Journal of this morning, that they
are robbing us of another of our inventions to give it to the
English. The writer, indeed, only admits them to have revived
what he thinks was known to the Greeks, that is, the making
the circumference of a wheel of one single piece. The farmers
in New Jersey were the first who practised it, and they practised it commonly. Dr. Franklin, in one of his trips to London, mentioned this practice to the man now in London,
who has the patent for making those wheels. The idea struck

him. The Doctor promised to go to his shop, and assist him in trying to make the wheel of one piece. The Jersey farmers do it by cutting a young sapling, and bending it, while green and juicy, into a circle; and leaving it so until it becomes perfectly seasoned. But in London there are no saplings. The difficulty was, then, to give to old wood the pliancy of young. The Doctor and the workman labored together some weeks, and succeeded; and the man obtained a patent for it, which has made his fortune. I was in his shop in London, he told me the whole story himself, and acknowledged, not only the origin of the idea, but how much the assistance of Dr. Franklin had contributed to perform the operation on dry wood. He spoke of him with love and gratitude. I think I have had a similar account from Dr. Franklin, but cannot be quite certain. I know, that being in Philadelphia when the first set of patent wheels arrived from London, and were spoken of by the gentleman (an Englishman) who brought them, as a wonderful discovery, the idea of its being a new discovery was laughed at by the Philadelphians, who, in their Sunday parties across the Delaware, had seen every farmer's cart mounted on such wheels. The writer in the paper, supposes the English workman got his idea from Homer. But it is more likely the Jersey farmer got his idea from thence, because ours are the only farmers who can read Homer; because, too, the Jersey practice is precisely that stated by Homer: the English practice very different. Homer's words are (comparing a young hero killed by Ajax to a poplar felled by a workman) literally thus: 'He fell on the ground, like a poplar, which has grown smooth, in the west part of a great meadow; with its branches shooting from its summit. But the chariot maker, with his sharp axe, has felled it, that he may bend a wheel for a beautiful chariot. It lies drying on the banks of the river.' Observe the circumstances which coincide with the Jersey practice. 1. It is a tree growing in a moist place, full of juices and easily bent. 2. It is cut while green. 3. It is bent into the circumference of a wheel. 4. It is left to dry in that form. You, who write French well and readily, should write a line for the Journal, to reclaim the honor of our farmers. Adieu. Yours affectionately,

"THE PEOPLE ARE THE ONLY CENSORS . . ."

To Edward Carrington

Paris, Jan. 16, 1787

DEAR SIR,—Uncertain whether you might be at New York at
the moment of Colo. Franks's arrival, I have inclosed my private letters for Virginia under cover to our delegation in general, which otherwise I would have taken the liberty to inclose
particularly to you, as best acquainted with the situation of
the persons to whom they are addressed. Should this find you
at New York, I will still ask your attention to them. The two
large packages addressed to Colo. N. Lewis contain seeds, not
valuable enough to pay passage, but which I would wish to
be sent by the stage, or any similar quick conveyance. The
letters to Colo. Lewis & Mr. Eppes (who take care of my
affairs) are particularly interesting to me. The package for
Colo. Richd. Cary our judge of Admiralty near Hampton,
contains seeds & roots, not to be sent by Post. Whether they
had better go by the stage, or by water, you will be the best
judge. I beg your pardon for giving you this trouble. But my
situation & your goodness will I hope excuse it. In my letter
to Mr. Jay, I have mentioned the meeting of the Notables
appointed for the 29th inst. It is now put off to the 7th or
8th of next month. This event, which will hardly excite any
attention in America, is deemed here the most important one
which has taken place in their civil line during the present
century. Some promise their country great things from it,
some nothing. Our friend de La Fayette was placed on the
list originally. Afterwards his name disappeared; but finally
was reinstated. This shews that his character here is not considered as an indifferent one; and that it excites agitation. His
education in our school has drawn on him a very jealous eye
from a court whose principles are the most absolute despotism. But I hope he has nearly passed his crisis. The King,
who is a good man, is favorably disposed towards him: & he
is supported by powerful family connections, & by the public
good will. He is the youngest man of the Notables except one
whose office placed him on the list.

The Count de Vergennes has within these ten days had a

very severe attack of what is deemed an unfixed gout. He has
been well enough however to do business to-day. But anxieties for him are not yet quieted. He is a great & good minister, and an accident to him might endanger the peace of
Europe.

The tumults in America, I expected would have produced
in Europe an unfavorable opinion of our political state. But
it has not. On the contrary, the small effect of these tumults
seems to have given more confidence in the firmness of our
governments. The interposition of the people themselves on
the side of government has had a great effect on the opinion
here. I am persuaded myself that the good sense of the people
will always be found to be the best army. They may be led
astray for a moment, but will soon correct themselves. The
people are the only censors of their governors: and even their
errors will tend to keep these to the true principles of their
institution. To punish these errors too severely would be to
suppress the only safeguard of the public liberty. The way to
prevent these irregular interpositions of the people is to give
them full information of their affairs thro' the channel of the
public papers, & to contrive that those papers should penetrate the whole mass of the people. The basis of our governments being the opinion of the people, the very first object
should be to keep that right; and were it left to me to decide
whether we should have a government without newspapers
or newspapers without a government, I should not hesitate a
moment to prefer the latter. But I should mean that every
man should receive those papers & be capable of reading
them. I am convinced that those societies (as the Indians)
which live without government enjoy in their general mass an
infinitely greater degree of happiness than those who live under the European governments. Among the former, public
opinion is in the place of law, & restrains morals as powerfully as laws ever did anywhere. Among the latter, under pretence of governing they have divided their nations into two
classes, wolves & sheep. I do not exaggerate. This is a true
picture of Europe. Cherish therefore the spirit of our people,
and keep alive their attention. Do not be too severe upon
their errors, but reclaim them by enlightening them. If once
they become inattentive to the public affairs, you & I, & Con-

gress & Assemblies, judges & governors shall all become
wolves. It seems to be the law of our general nature, in spite
of individual exceptions; and experience declares that man is
the only animal which devours his own kind, for I can apply
no milder term to the governments of Europe, and to the
general prey of the rich on the poor. The want of news has
led me into disquisition instead of narration, forgetting you
have every day enough of that. I shall be happy to hear from
you sometimes, only observing that whatever passes thro' the
post is read, & that when you write what should be read by
myself only, you must be so good as to confide your letter to
some passenger or officer of the packet. I will ask your permission to write to you sometimes, and to assure you of the
esteem & respect with which I have honour to be Dear Sir
your most obedient & most humble servt.

REBELLION, SECESSION, AND DIPLOMACY
To James Madison

Paris, Jan. 30, 1787

DEAR SIR,—My last to you was of the 16th of Dec, since
which I have received yours of Nov 25, & Dec 4, which afforded me, as your letters always do, a treat on matters public, individual & œconomical. I am impatient to learn your
sentiments on the late troubles in the Eastern states. So far as
I have yet seen, they do not appear to threaten serious consequences. Those states have suffered by the stoppage of the
channels of their commerce, which have not yet found other
issues. This must render money scarce, and make the people
uneasy. This uneasiness has produced acts absolutely unjustifiable; but I hope they will provoke no severities from their
governments. A consciousness of those in power that their
administration of the public affairs has been honest, may perhaps produce too great a degree of indignation: and those
characters wherein fear predominates over hope may apprehend too much from these instances of irregularity. They may
conclude too hastily that nature has formed man insusceptible
of any other government but that of force, a conclusion not

founded in truth, nor experience. Societies exist under three
forms sufficiently distinguishable. 1. Without government, as
among our Indians. 2. Under governments wherein the will
of every one has a just influence, as is the case in England in
a slight degree, and in our states, in a great one. 3. Under
governments of force: as is the case in all other monarchies
and in most of the other republics. To have an idea of the
curse of existence under these last, they must be seen. It is a
government of wolves over sheep. It is a problem, not clear
in my mind, that the 1st condition is not the best. But I believe it to be inconsistent with any great degree of population.
The second state has a great deal of good in it. The mass of
mankind under that enjoys a precious degree of liberty &
happiness. It has it's evils too: the principal of which is the
turbulence to which it is subject. But weigh this against the
oppressions of monarchy, and it becomes nothing. *Malo peri-
culosam libertatem quam quietam servitutem*. Even this evil is
productive of good. It prevents the degeneracy of government, and nourishes a general attention to the public affairs.
I hold it that a little rebellion now and then is a good thing,
& as necessary in the political world as storms in the physical.
Unsuccessful rebellions indeed generally establish the encroachments on the rights of the people which have produced
them. An observation of this truth should render honest republican governors so mild in their punishment of rebellions,
as not to discourage them too much. It is a medicine necessary for the sound health of government. If these transactions
give me no uneasiness, I feel very differently at another piece
of intelligence, to wit, the possibility that the navigation of
the Mississippi may be abandoned to Spain. I never had any
interest Westward of the Alleghaney; & I never will have any.
But I have had great opportunities of knowing the character
of the people who inhabit that country. And I will venture to
say that the act which abandons the navigation of the Mississippi is an act of separation between the Eastern & Western
country. It is a relinquishment of five parts out of eight of the
territory of the United States, an abandonment of the fairest
subject for the paiment of our public debts, & the chaining
those debts on our own necks *in perpetuum*. I have the utmost
confidence in the honest intentions of those who concur in

this measure; but I lament their want of acquaintance with the character & physical advantages of the people who, right or wrong, will suppose their interests sacrificed on this occasion to the contrary interests of that part of the confederacy in possession of present power. If they declare themselves a separate people, we are incapable of a single effort to retain them. Our citizens can never be induced, either as militia or as souldiers, to go there to cut the throats of their own brothers & sons, or rather to be themselves the subjects instead of the perpetrators of the parricide. Nor would that country requite the cost of being retained against the will of it's inhabitants, could it be done. But it cannot be done. They are able already to rescue the navigation of the Mississippi out of the hands of Spain, & to add New Orleans to their own territory. They will be joined by the inhabitants of Louisiana. This will bring on a war between them & Spain; and that will produce the question with us whether it will not be worth our while to become parties with them in the war, in order to reunite them with us, & thus correct our error? & were I to permit my forebodings to go one step further, I should predict that the inhabitants of the U S would force their rulers to take the affirmative of that question. I wish I may be mistaken in all these opinions.

We have for some time expected that the Chevalier de la Luzerne would obtain a promotion in the diplomatic line, by being appointed to some of the courts where this country keeps an ambassador. But none of the vacancies taking place which had been counted on, I think the present disposition is to require his return to his station in America. He told me himself lately, that he should return in the spring. I have never pressed this matter on the court, tho' I knew it to be desirable and desired on our part; because if the compulsion on him to return had been the work of Congress, he would have returned in such ill temper with them, as to disappoint them in the good they expected from it. He would forever have laid at their door his failure of promotion. I did not press it for another reason, which is that I have great reason to believe that the character of the Count de Moustier, who would go were the Chevalier to be otherwise provided for, would give the most perfect satisfaction in America.

As you are now returned into Congress it will become of importance that you should form a just estimate of certain public characters: on which therefore I will give you such notes as my knolege of them has furnished me with. You will compare them with the materials you are otherwise possessed of, and decide on a view of the whole. You know the opinion I *formerly* entertained of *my friend Mr. Adams*. Yourself & the governor were the first who *shook* that opinion. I afterwards saw proofs which *convicted him* of a degree of *vanity*, and of a *blindness* to it, of which no germ *had appeared* in Congress. A *7-month's* intimacy with him *here* and *as* many *weeks* in *London* have given me opportunities of studying him closely. *He is vain, irritable and a bad calculator of* the force & probable effect of the motives which govern men. This is *all* the *ill* which can possibly be *said of him*. He is as disinterested as the being which made him: he is profound in his views: and accurate in his judgment *except where knowledge of the world* is necessary to form a judgment. He is so amiable, that I pronounce you will love him, if ever you become acquainted with him. He would be, as he was, a great man in *Congress*. *Mr. Carmichael*, is, I think, very little *known* in *America*. I never *saw him*, & while I was *in Congress I* formed rather a *disadvantageous idea* of him. His letters, received then, showed him *vain*, & more attentive to *ceremony & etiquette* than we suppose men *of sense* should be. *I* have now a constant correspondence with him, and find *him* a little *hypochondriac* and *discontented*. He possesses very *good understanding*, tho' not of the *first order*. *I have* had great opportunities of *searching into* his *character*, and have availed myself *of them*. Many persons of different nations, *coming* from *Madrid* to *Paris*, all speak of *him as* in *high esteem*, & *I think* it certain that he has more of the *Count de Florida Blanca's friendship*, than any *diplomatic* character at *that court*. As long as this *minister* is in *office*, *Carmichael* can do *more than* any other *person who* could be *sent there*. You will see *Franks, and* doubtless he will be *asking some appointment*. I wish there may be any one for *which* he is *fit*. He is *light, indiscreet, active, honest, affectionate*. Tho' *Bingham* is not in *diplomatic office*, yet as he wishes to be so, I will mention such circumstances of *him, as you might* otherwise be *deceived in*. *He will* make *you believe he* was on the most intimate foot-

ing with the first *characters in Europe*, & versed in the *secrets*
of every *cabinet*. Not a word of this *is true*. *He* had a rage for
being *presented* to *great men*, & had no *modesty* in the methods
by which he could if *he attained acquaintance*. Afterwards it
was with such 90 who were susceptible of impression from
the *beauty of his wife*. I must *except* the Marquis de Bonclearren
who had been an *old acquaintance*.

The *Marquis de La Fayette* is a most valuable *auxiliary to
me*. His *zeal* is unbounded, & his *weight* with those in *power,
great*. His *education* having been merely *military, commerce*
was an unknown field to him. But his good sense enabling
him to *comprehend* perfectly whatever is *explained to him, his
agency* has been very *efficacious*. *He* has a great deal of *sound
genius*, is well *remarked* by the *King*, & rising in *popularity*.
He has nothing against *him, but* the *suspicion* of *republican
principles*. I think he will one day *be of* the *ministry*. His foible
is, a *canine appetite for popularity and fame*; but he will get
above this. *The Count de Vergennes* is *ill*. The possibility of his
recovery, renders it dangerous for *us to express a doubt of it: but*
he is *in danger*. He is *a great minister* in *European affairs*, but
has very *imperfect ideas* of *our institutions, and no confidence in*
them. His *devotion* to the principles of *pure despotism*, renders
him *unaffectionate to our governments*. But *his fear* of *England
makes him value us* as a *make weight*. He is *cool, reserved in
political conversations, but free and familiar* on other *subjects*,
and a very *attentive, agreeable person* to *do business with*. It is
impossible to have a clearer, better *organized head*; but *age* has
chilled his heart. Nothing should be spared, on our part, to
attach this country to us. It is the only one on which we can
rely for support, under every event. Its inhabitants love us
more, I think, than they do any other nation on earth. This
is very much the effect of the good dispositions with which
the French officers returned. In a former letter, I mentioned
to you the dislocation of my wrist. I can make not the least
use of it, except for the single article of writing, though it is
going on five months since the accident happened. I have
great anxieties, lest I should never recover any considerable
use of it. I shall, by the advice of my surgeons, set out in a
fortnight for the waters of Aix, in Provence. I chose these out
of several they proposed to me, because if they fail to be ef-

fectual, my journey will not be useless altogether. It will give me an opportunity of examining the canal of Languedoc, and of acquiring knowledge of that species of navigation, which may be useful hereafter; but more immediately, it will enable me to make the tour of the ports concerned in commerce with us, to examine, on the spot, the defects of the late regulations respecting our commerce, to learn the further improvements which may be made in it, and on my return, to get this business finished. I shall be absent between two and three months, unless anything happens to recall me here sooner, which may always be effected in ten days, in whatever part of my route I may be. In speaking *of characters*, I omitted *those of Reyneval and Hennin*, the *two eyes* of *Count de Vergennes*. The *former* is the most important *character, because possessing* the most of the *confidence* of the *Count. He* is rather *cunning* than *wise*, his views of things being neither *great* nor *liberal. He governs* himself by *principles* which he has *learned* by *rote*, and is *fit only* for the *details* of *execution. His heart* is susceptible of little *passions* but not of *good ones. He* is *brother-in-law* to *M. Gerard*, from whom he received *disadvantageous impressions* of *us, which* cannot be *effaced. He* has much *duplicity. Hennin* is a *philosopher, sincere, friendly, liberal, learned, beloved* by everybody; the *other* by *nobody.* I *think* it a great *misfortune* that the *United States* are in the *department* of the *former.* As particulars of this kind may be useful to you, in your present situation, I may hereafter continue the chapter. I know it will be safely lodged in your discretion.

Feb. 5. Since writing thus far, *Franks* is *returned* from *England. I learn* that *Mr. Adams* desires to be *recalled*, & that *Smith* should be *appointed chargé des affaires* there. It is not for me to decide whether any *diplomatic character* should be *kept* at a *court*, which *keeps* none with *us*. You can judge of *Smith's* abilities by *his letters.* They are not of the *first order*, but they are *good.* For his *honesty*, he is like our friend *Monroe*; turn his *soul* wrong side outwards, and there is not a speck on it. *He* has one *foible*, an *excessive inflammability* of *temper*, but he feels it when it comes on, and has *resolution enough* to *suppress* it, and to *remain silent* till it *passes* over.

I send you by Colo. Franks, your pocket telescope, walking

stick & chemical box. The two former could not be combined together. The latter could not be had in the form you referred to. Having a great desire to have a portable copying machine, & being satisfied from some experiments that the principle of the large machine might be applied in a small one, I planned one when in England & had it made. It answers perfectly. I have since set a workman to making them here, & they are in such demand that he has his hands full. Being assured that you will be pleased to have one, when you shall have tried it's convenience, I send you one by Colo. Franks. The machine costs 96 livres, the appendages 24 livres, and I send you paper & ink for 12 livres; in all 132 livres. There is a printed paper of directions; but you must expect to make many essays before you succeed perfectly. A soft brush, like a shaving brush, is more convenient than the sponge. You can get as much ink & paper as you please from London. The paper costs a guinea a ream.

"THE EMPTY BUSTLE OF PARIS"

To Anne Willing Bingham

Paris, February 7, 1787

I know, Madam, that the twelve month is not yet expired; but it will be, nearly, before this will have the honor of being put into your hands. You are then engaged to tell me, truly and honestly, whether you do not find the tranquil pleasures of America, preferable to the empty bustle of Paris. For to what does that bustle tend? At eleven o'clock, it is day, *chez madame*. The curtains are drawn. Propped on bolsters and pillows, and her head scratched into a little order, the bulletins of the sick are read, and the billets of the well. She writes to some of her acquaintance, and receives the visits of others. If the morning is not very thronged, she is able to get out and hobble round the cage of the Palais royal; but she must hobble quickly, for the *coeffeur's* turn is come; and a tremendous turn it is! Happy, if he does not make her arrive when dinner is half over! The torpitude of digestion a little passed, she flutters half an hour through the streets, by way of paying visits, and then to the spectacles. These finished, another half hour is devoted to dodging in and out of the doors of her very sincere friends, and away to supper. After supper, cards; and after cards, bed; to rise at noon the next day, and to tread, like a mill horse, the same trodden circle over again. Thus the days of life are consumed, one by one, without an object beyond the present moment; ever flying from the ennui of that, yet carrying it with us; eternally in pursuit of happiness, which keeps eternally before us. If death or bankruptcy happen to trip us out of the circle, it is matter for the buz of the evening, and is completely forgotten by the next morning. In America, on the other hand, the society of your husband, the fond cares for the children, the arrangements of the house, the improvements of the grounds, fill every moment with a healthy and an useful activity. Every exertion is encouraging, because to present amusement, it joins the promise of some future good. The intervals of leisure are filled by the society of real friends, whose affections are not thinned to cob-web, by being spread over a thousand objects. This is the picture, in the light it is presented to my mind; now let me have it in yours. If we do not concur this year, we shall the next; or if not then, in a year or two more. You see I am determined not to suppose myself mistaken.

To let you see that Paris is not changed in its pursuits, since it was honored with your presence, I send you its monthly history. But this relating only to the embellishments of their persons, I must add, that those of the city go on well also. A new bridge, for example, is begun at the Place Louis Quinze; the old ones are clearing of the rubbish which encumbered them in the form of houses; new hospitals erecting; magnificent walls of inclosure, and Custom houses at their entrances, &c. &c. &c. I know of no interesting change among those whom you honored with your acquaintance, unless Monsieur de Saint James was of that number. His bankruptcy, and taking asylum in the Bastile, have furnished matter of astonishment. His garden, at the Pont de Neuilly, where, on seventeen acres of ground he had laid out fifty thousand louis, will probably sell for somewhat less money. The workmen of

Paris are making rapid strides towards English perfection. Would you believe, that in the course of the last two years, they have learned even to surpass their London rivals in some articles? Commission me to have you a phaeton made, and if it is not as much handsomer than a London one, as that is than a Fiacre, send it back to me. Shall I fill the box with caps, bonnets, &c.? Not of my own choosing, but—I was going to say, of Mademoiselle Bertin's, forgetting for the moment, that she too is bankrupt. They shall be chosen then by whom you please; or, if you are altogether nonplused by her eclipse, we will call an Assembleé des Notables, to help you out of the difficulty, as is now the fashion. In short, honor me with your commands of any kind, and they shall be faithfully executed. The packets now established from Havre to New York, furnish good opportunities of sending whatever you wish.

I shall end where I began, like a Paris day, reminding you of your engagement to write me a letter of respectable length, an engagement the more precious to me, as it has furnished me the occasion, after presenting my respects to Mr. Bingham, of assuring you of the sincerity of those sentiments of esteem and respect, with which I have the honor to be, Dear Madam, your most obedient and most humble servant,

"A LITTLE REBELLION NOW AND THEN"
To Abigail Adams

Paris, Feb. 22, 1787

DEAR MADAM—I am to acknolege the honor of your letter of Jan. 29. and of the papers you were so good as to send me. They were the latest I had seen or have yet seen. They left off too in a critical moment; just at the point where the Malcontents make their submission on condition of pardon, and before the answer of government was known. I hope they pardoned them. The spirit of resistance to government is so valuable on certain occasions, that I wish it to be always kept alive. It will often be exercised when wrong, but better so than not to be exercised at all. I like a little rebellion now and then. It is like a storm in the Atmosphere. It is wonderful that no letter or paper tells us who is president of Congress, tho' there are letters in Paris to the beginning of January. I suppose I shall hear when I come back from my journey, which will be eight months after he will have been chosen. And yet they complain of us for not giving them intelligence. Our Notables assembled to-day, and I hope before the departure of Mr. Cairnes I shall have heard something of their proceedings worth communicating to Mr. Adams. The most remarkable effect of this convention as yet is the number of puns and bon mots it has generated. I think were they all collected it would make a more voluminous work than the Encyclopedie. This occasion, more than any thing I have seen, convinces me that this nation is incapable of any serious effort but under the word of command. The people at large view every object only as it may furnish puns and bon mots; and I pronounce that a good punster would disarm the whole nation were they ever so seriously disposed to revolt. Indeed, Madam, they are gone. When a measure so capable of doing good as the calling the Notables is treated with so much ridicule, we may conclude the nation desperate, and in charity pray that heaven may send them good kings.—The bridge at the place Louis XV. is begun. The hotel dieu is to be abandoned and new ones to be built. The old houses on the old bridges are in a course of demolition. This is all I know of Paris. We are about to lose the Count d'Aranda, who has desired and obtained his recall. Fernand Nunnez, before destined for London is to come here. The Abbés Arnoux and Chalut are well. The Dutchess Danville somewhat recovered from the loss of her daughter. Mrs. Barrett very homesick, and fancying herself otherwise sick. They will probably remove to Honfleur. This is all our news. I have only to add then that Mr. Cairnes has taken charge of 15. aunes of black lace for you at 9 livres the aune, purchased by Petit and therefore I hope better purchased than some things have been for you; and that I am with sincere esteem Dear Madam your affectionate humble servt.,

THE MAISON CARRÉE
To Madame de Tessé

Nismes, March 20, 1787

Here I am, Madam, gazing whole hours at the Maison quarrée, like a lover at his mistress. The stocking weavers and silk spinners around it, consider me as a hypochondriac Englishman, about to write with a pistol, the last chapter of his history. This is the second time I have been in love since I left Paris. The first was with a Diana at the Chateau de Laye-Epinaye in Beaujolois, a delicious morsel of sculpture, by M. A. Slodtz. This, you will say, was a rule, to fall in love with a female beauty: but with a house! It is out of all precedent. No, Madam, it is not without a precedent, in my own history. While in Paris, I was violently smitten with the Hotel de Salm, and used to go to the Thuileries almost daily, to look at it. The *loueuse des chaises*, inattentive to my passion, never had the complaisance to place a chair there, so that sitting on the parapet, and twisting my neck round to see the object of my admiration, I generally left it with a *torti-colli*.

From Lyons to Nismes I have been nourished with the remains of Roman grandeur. They have always brought you to my mind, because I know your affection for whatever is Roman and noble. At Vienne I thought of you. But I am glad you were not there; for you would have seen me more angry than, I hope, you will ever see me. The Prætorian palace, as it is called, comparable, for its fine proportions, to the Maison quarrée, defaced by the barbarians who have converted it to its present purpose, its beautiful fluted Corinthian columns cut out, in part, to make space for Gothic windows, and hewed down, in the residue, to the plane of the building, was enough, you must admit, to disturb my composure. At Orange too, I thought of you. I was sure you had seen with pleasure, the sublime triumphal arch of Marius at the entrance of the city. I went then to the Arenæ. Would you believe, Madam, that in this eighteenth century, in France, under the reign of Louis XVI. they are at this momont pulling down the circular wall of this superb remain, to pave a road? And that too from a hill which is itself an entire mass of stone, just as fit, and more accessible? A former intendant, a M. de Bas-ville has rendered his memory dear to the traveller and ama-teur, by the pains he took to preserve and restore these monuments of antiquity. The present one (I do not know who he is) is demolishing the object, to make a good road to it. I thought of you again, and I was then in great good hu-mor, at the Pont du Gard, a sublime antiquity, and well pre-served. But most of all here, where Roman taste, genius and magnificence, excite ideas analogous to yours at every step. I could no longer oppose the inclination to avail myself of your permission to write to you, a permission given with too much complaisance by you, and used by me, with too much indis-cretion. Madame de Tott did me the same honor. But she, being only the descendant of some of those puny heroes who boiled their own kettles before the walls of Troy, I shall write to her from a Grecian, rather than a Roman canton: when I shall find myself, for example among her Phocæan relations at Marseilles.

Loving, as you do madam, the precious remains of antiq-uity, loving architecture, gardening, a warm sun and a clear sky, I wonder you have never thought of moving Chaville to Nismes. This, as you know, has not always been deemed im-practicable; and therefore, the next time a *Sur-intendant des batimens du roi*, after the example of M. Colbert, sends per-sons to Nismes to move the Maison quarrée to Paris, that they may not come empty handed, desire them to bring Cha-ville with them, to replace it. A propos of Paris. I have now been three weeks from there, without knowing any thing of what has passed. I suppose I shall meet it all at Aix, where I have directed my letters to be lodged, *poste restante*. My jour-ney has given me leisure to reflect on this Assemblée des No-tables. Under a good and a young King, as the present, I think good may be made of it. I would have the deputies then, by all means, so conduct themselves as to encourage him to repeat the calls of this Assembly. Their first step should be, to get themselves divided into two chambers in-stead of seven; the Noblesse and the Commons separately. The second, to persuade the King, instead of choosing the deputies of the Commons himself, to summon those chosen by the people for the Provincial administrations. The third, as the Noblesse is too numerous to be all of the Assemblée, to obtain permission for that body to choose its own deputies. Two Houses, so elected, would contain a mass of wisdom which would make the people happy, and the King great; would place him in history where no other act can possibly place him. They would thus put themselves in the track of the best guide they can follow, they would soon overtake it, become its guide in turn, and lead to the wholesome modifications wanting in that model, and necessary to constitute a rational government. Should they attempt more than the established habits of the people are ripe for, they may lose all, and retard indefinitely the ultimate object of their aim. These, Madam, are my opinions; but I wish to know yours, which, I am sure, will be better.

From a correspondent at Nismes, you will not expect news. Were I to attempt to give you news, I should tell you stories one thousand years old. I should detail to you the intrigues of the courts of the Cæsars, how they affect us here, the oppressions of their prætors, prefects, &c. I am immersed in antiquities from morning to night. For me, the city of Rome is actually existing in all the splendor of its empire. I am filled with alarms for the event of the irruptions daily making on us, by the Goths, the Visigoths, Ostrogoths, and Vandals, lest they should re-conquer us to our original barbarism. If I am sometimes induced to look forward to the eighteenth century, it is only when recalled to it by the recollection of your goodness and friendship, and by those sentiments of sincere esteem and respect, with which I have the honor to be, Madam, your most obedient and most humble servant,

THE REWARDS OF TRAVEL
To Lafayette

Nice, April 11, 1787

Your head, my dear friend, is full of Notable things; and being better employed, therefore, I do not expect letters from you. I am constantly roving about, to see what I have never seen before, and shall never see again. In the great cities, I go to see what travellers think alone worthy of being seen; but I make a job of it, and generally gulp it all down in a day. On the other hand, I am never satiated with rambling through the fields and farms, examining the culture and cultivators, with a degree of curiosity which makes some take me to be a fool, and others to be much wiser than I am. I have been pleased to find among the people a less degree of physical misery than I had expected. They are generally well clothed, and have a plenty of food, not animal indeed, but vegetable, which is as wholesome. Perhaps they are over worked, the excess of the rent required by the landlord, obliging them to too many hours of labor in order to produce that, and wherewith to feed and clothe themselves. The soil of Champagne and Burgundy I have found more universally good than I had expected, and as I could not help making a comparison with England, I found that comparison more unfavorable to the latter than is generally admitted. The soil, the climate, and the productions are superior to those of England, and the husbandry as good, except in one point; that of manure. In England, long leases for twenty-one years, or three lives, to wit, that of the farmer, his wife, and son, renewed by the son as soon as he comes to the possession, for his own life, his wife's and eldest child's, and so on, render the farms there almost hereditary, make it worth the farmer's while to manure the lands highly, and give the landlord an opportunity of occasionally making his rent keep pace with the improved state of the lands. Here the leases are either during pleasure, or for three, six, or nine years, which does not give the farmer time to repay himself for the expensive operation of well manuring, and therefore, he manures ill, or not at all. I suppose, that could the practice of leasing for three lives be introduced in the whole kingdom, it would, within the term of your life, increase agricultural productions fifty per cent; or were any one proprietor to do it with his own lands, it would increase his rents fifty per cent, in the course of twenty-five years. But I am told the laws do not permit it. The laws then, in this particular, are unwise and unjust, and ought to give that permission. In the southern provinces, where the soil is poor, the climate hot and dry, and there are few animals, they would learn the art, found so precious in England, of making vegetable manure, and thus improving these provinces in the article in which nature has been least kind to them. Indeed, these provinces afford a singular spectacle. Calculating on the poverty of their soil, and their climate by its latitude only, they should have been the poorest in France. On the contrary, they are the richest, from one fortuitous circumstance. Spurs or ramifications of high mountains, making down from the Alps, and as it were, reticulating these provinces, give to the vallies the protection of a particular inclosure to each, and the benefit of a general stagnation of the northern winds produced by the whole of them, and thus countervail the advantage of several degrees of latitude. From the first olive fields of Pierrelatte, to the orangeries of Hieres, has been continued rapture to me. I have often wished for you. I think you have not made this journey. It is a pleasure you have to come, and an improvement to be added to the many you have already made. It will be a great comfort to you, to know, from your own inspection, the condition of all the provinces of your own country, and it will be interesting to them at some future day, to be known to you. This is, perhaps, the only moment of your life in which you can acquire that knowledge. And to do it most effectually, you must be absolutely incognito, you must ferret the people out of their hovels as I have done, look into their kettles, eat their bread, loll on their beds under pretence of resting yourself, but in fact to find if they are soft. You will feel a sublime pleasure in the course of this investigation, and a sublimer one hereafter, when you shall be able to apply your knowledge to the softening of their beds, or the throwing a morsel of meat into their kettle of vegetables.

You will not wonder at the subjects of my letter: they are the only ones which have been presented to my mind for some time past; and the waters must always be what are the fountains from which they flow. According to this, indeed, I should have intermixed, from beginning to end, warm expressions of friendship to you. But, according to the ideas of our country, we do not permit ourselves to speak even truths, when they may have the air of flattery. I content myself, therefore, with saying once for all, that I love you, your wife and children. Tell them so, and adieu.

Yours affectionately,

"THE GRAND RECIPE FOR FELICITY"

To Martha Jefferson

May 21, 1787

I write to you, my dear Patsy, from the Canal of Langue-doc, on which I am at present sailing, as I have been for a week past, cloudless skies above, limpid waters below, and find on each hand a row of nightingales in full chorus. This delightful bird had given me a rich treat before at the fountain of Vaucluse. After visiting the tomb of Laura at Avignon, I went to see this fountain, a noble one of itself, and rendered for ever famous by the songs of Petrarch who lived near it. I arrived there somewhat fatigued, and sat down by the fountain to repose myself. It gushes, of the size of a river, from a secluded valley of the mountain, the ruins of Petrarch's chateau being perched on a rock 200 feet perpendicular above. To add to the enchantment of the scene, every tree and bush was filled with nightingales in full song. I think you told me you had not yet noticed this bird. As you have trees in the garden of the convent, there must be nightingales in them, and this is the season of their song. Endeavor my dear, to make yourself acquainted with the music of this bird, that when you return to your own country you may be able to estimate it's merit in comparison with that of the mocking bird. The latter has the advantage of singing thro' a great part of the year, whereas the nightingale sings but about 5. or 6 weeks in the spring, and a still shorter term and with a more feeble voice in the fall. I expect to be at Paris about the middle of next month. By that time we may begin to expect our dear Polly. It will be a circumstance of inexpressible comfort to me to have you both with me once more. The object most interesting to me for the residue of my life, will be to see you both developing daily those principles of virtue and goodness which will make you valuable to others and happy in your-selves, and acquiring those talents and that degree of science which will guard you at all times against ennui, the most dangerous poison of life. A mind always employed is always happy. This is the true secret, the grand recipe for felicity. The idle are the only wretched. In a world which furnishes so many emploiments which are useful, and so many which are amusing, it is our own fault if we ever know what ennui is, or if we are ever driven to the miserable resource of gaming, which corrupts our dispositions, and teaches us a habit of hostility against all mankind. We are now entering the port of Toulouse, where I quit my bark; and of course must conclude my letter. Be good and be industrious, and you will be what I shall most love in the world. Adieu my dear child. Yours affectionately,

AFFAIRS OF DIPLOMACY
To John Adams

Paris, July 1, 1787

DEAR SIR—I returned about three weeks ago from a very useless voiage. Useless, I mean, as to the object which first suggested it, that of trying the effect of the mineral waters of Aix en Provence on my hand. I tried these because recommended among six or eight others as equally beneficial, and because they would place me at the beginning of a tour to the seaports of Marseilles, Bourdeaux, Nantes and Lorient which I had long meditated, in hopes that a knowlege of the places and persons concerned in our commerce and the information to be got from them might enable me sometimes to be useful. I had expected to satisfy myself at Marseilles of the causes of the difference of quality between the rice of Carolina and that of Piedmont which is brought in quantities to Marseilles. Not being able to do it, I made an excursion of three weeks into the rice country beyond the Alps, going through it from Vercelli to Pavia about 60 miles. I found the difference to be, not in the management as had been supposed both here and in Carolina, but in the species of rice, and I hope to enable them in Carolina to begin the Cultivation of the Piedmont rice and carry it on hand in hand with their own that they may supply both qualities, which is absolutely necessary at this market. I had before endeavored to lead the depot of rice from Cowes to Honfleur and hope to get it received there on such terms as may draw that branch of commerce from England to this country. It is an object of

250,000 guineas a year. While passing thro' the towns of Turin, Milan and Genoa, I satisfied myself of the practicability of introducing our whale oil for their consumption and I suppose it would be equally so in the other great cities of that country. I was sorry that I was not authorized to set the matter on foot. The merchants with whom I chose to ask conferences, met me freely, and communicated fully, knowing I was in a public character. I could however only prepare a disposition to meet our oil merchants. On the article of tobacco I was more in possession of my ground, and put matters into a train for inducing their government to draw their tobaccos directly from the U.S. and not as heretofore from G.B. I am now occupied with the new ministry here to put the concluding hand to the new regulations for our commerce with this country, announced in the letter of M. de Calonnes which I sent you last fall. I am in hopes in addition to those, to obtain a suppression of the duties on Tar, pitch, and turpentine, and an extension of the privileges of American *whale* oil, to their *fish* oils in general. I find that the quantity of Codfish oil brought to Lorient is considerable. This being got off hand (which will be in a few days) the chicaneries and vexations of the farmers on the article of tobacco, and their elusions of the order of Bernis, call for the next attention. I have reason to hope good dispositions in the new ministry towards our commerce with this country. Besides endeavoring on all occasions to multiply the points of contact and connection with this country, which I consider as our surest main-stay under every event, I have had it much at heart to remove from between us every subject of misunderstanding or irritation. Our debts to the king, to the officers, and the farmers are of this description. The having complied with no part of our engagements in these draws on us a great deal of censure, and occasioned a language in the Assemblées des notables very likely to produce dissatisfaction between us. Dumas being on the spot in Holland, I had asked of him some time ago, in confidence, his opinion on the practicability of transferring these debts from France to Holland, and communicated his answer to Congress, pressing them to get you to go over to Holland and try to effect this business. Your knowlege of the ground and former successes occasioned me to take this liberty without consulting you, because I was sure you would not weigh your personal trouble against public good. I have had no answer from Congress, but hearing of your journey to Holland have hoped that some money operation had led you there. If it related to the debts of this country I would ask a communication of what you think yourself at liberty to communicate, as it might change the form of my answers to the eternal applications I receive. The debt to the officers of France carries an interest of about 2000 guineas, so we may suppose it's principal is between 30. and 40,000. This makes more noise against [us] than all our other debts put together.

I send you the arrets which begin the reformation here, and some other publications respecting America: together with copies of letters received from Obryon and Lambe. It is believed that a naval armament has been ordered at Brest in correspondence with that of England. We know certainly that orders are given to form a camp in the neighborhood of Brabant, and that Count Rochambeau has the command of it. It's amount I cannot assert. Report says 15,000 men. This will derange the plans of oeconomy. I take the liberty of putting under your cover a letter for Mrs. Kinloch of South Carolina, with a packet, and will trouble you to enquire for her and have them delivered. The packet is of great consequence, and therefore referred to her care, as she will know the safe opportunities of conveying it. Should you not be able to find her, and can forward the packet to it's address by any very safe conveiance I will beg you to do it. I have the honour to be with sentiments of the most perfect friendship and esteem Dear Sir your most obedient and most humble servant,

"A PEEP . . . INTO ELYSIUM"
To Maria Cosway

Paris, July 1, 1787

You conclude, Madam, from my long silence that I am gone to the other world. Nothing else would have prevented my writing to you so long. I have not thought of you the less, but I took a peep only into Elysium. I entered it at one

door, & came out at another, having seen, as I past, only
Turin, Milan, & Genoa. I calculated the hours it would have
taken to carry me on to Rome, but they were exactly so many
more than I had to spare. Was not this provoking? In thirty
hours from Milan I could have been at the espousals of the
Doge and the Adriatic, but I am born to lose every thing I
love. Why were you not with me? So many enchanting scenes
which only wanted your pencil to consecrate them to fame.
Whenever you go to Italy you must pass at the Col de Tende.
You may go in your chariot in full trot from Nice to Turin,
as if there were no mountain. But have your pallet & pencil
ready: for you will be sure to stop in the passage, at the chateau de Saorgio. Imagine to yourself, madam, a castle & village hanging to a cloud in front, on one hand a mountain
cloven through to let pass a gurgling stream; on the other a
river, over which is thrown a magnificent bridge; the whole
formed into a bason, it's sides shagged with rocks, olive trees,
vines, herds, &c. I insist on your painting it. How do you
do? How have you done? and when are you coming here? If
not at all, what did you ever come for? Only to make people
miserable at losing you. Consider that you are but a day from
Paris. If you come by the way of St. Omers, which is but two
posts further, you will see a new & beautiful country. Come
then, my dear Madam, and we will breakfast every day *á Angloise*, hie away to the Desert, dine under the bowers of
Marly, and forget that we are ever to part again. I received,
in the moment of my departure your favor of Feb. 15. and
long to receive another: but lengthy, warm, & flowing from
the heart, as do the sentiments of friendship & esteem with
which I have the honor to be, dear Madam, your affectionate
friend and servant.

"THE HOMAGE OF REASON"

To Peter Carr

Paris, Aug. 10, 1787

DEAR PETER,—I have received your two letters of Decemb.
30 and April 18, and am very happy to find by them, as well
as by letters from Mr. Wythe, that you have been so fortunate

as to attract his notice & good will; I am sure you will find this to have been one of the most fortunate events of your life, as I have ever been sensible it was of mine. I inclose you a sketch of the sciences to which I would wish you to apply in such order as Mr. Wythe shall advise; I mention also the books in them worth your reading, which submit to his correction. Many of these are among your father's books, which you should have brought to you. As I do not recollect those of them not in his library, you must write to me for them, making out a catalogue of such as you think you shall have occasion for in 18 months from the date of your letter, & consulting Mr. Wythe on the subject. To this sketch I will add a few particular observations.

1. Italian. I fear the learning this language will confound your French and Spanish. Being all of them degenerated dialects of the Latin, they are apt to mix in conversation. I have never seen a person speaking the three languages who did not mix them. It is a delightful language, but late events having rendered the Spanish more useful, lay it aside to prosecute that.

2. Spanish. Bestow great attention on this, & endeavor to acquire an accurate knowlege of it. Our future connections with Spain & Spanish America will render that language a valuable acquisition. The antient history of a great part of America, too, is written in that language. I send you a dictionary.

3. Moral philosophy. I think it lost time to attend lectures in this branch. He who made us would have been a pitiful bungler if he had made the rules of our moral conduct a matter of science. For one man of science, there are thousands who are not. What would have become of them? Man was destined for society. His morality therefore was to be formed to this object. He was endowed with a sense of right & wrong merely relative to this. This sense is as much a part of his nature as the sense of hearing, seeing, feeling; it is the true foundation of morality, & not the το καλον, truth, &c. as fanciful writers have imagined. The moral sense, or conscience, is as much a part of man as his leg or arm. It is given to all human beings in a stronger or weaker degree, as force of members is given them in a greater or less degree. It may

be strengthened by exercise, as may any particular limb of the body. This sense is submitted indeed in some degree to the guidance of reason; but it is a small stock which is required for this: even a less one than what we call common sense. State a moral case to a ploughman & a professor. The former will decide it as well, & often better than the latter, because he has not been led astray by artificial rules. In this branch therefore read good books because they will encourage as well as direct your feelings. The writings of Sterne particularly form the best course of morality that ever was written. Besides these read the books mentioned in the enclosed paper; and above all things lose no occasion of exercising your dispositions to be grateful, to be generous, to be charitable, to be humane, to be true, just, firm, orderly, courageous &c. Consider every act of this kind as an exercise which will strengthen your moral faculties, & increase your worth.

4. Religion. Your reason is now mature enough to examine this object. In the first place divest yourself of all bias in favour of novelty & singularity of opinion. Indulge them in any other subject rather than that of religion. It is too important, & the consequences of error may be too serious. On the other hand shake off all the fears & servile prejudices under which weak minds are servilely crouched. Fix reason firmly in her seat, and call to her tribunal every fact, every opinion. Question with boldness even the existence of a god; because, if there be one, he must more approve of the homage of reason, than that of blindfolded fear. You will naturally examine first the religion of your own country. Read the bible then, as you would read Livy or Tacitus. The facts which are within the ordinary course of nature you will believe on the authority of the writer, as you do those of the same kind in Livy & Tacitus. The testimony of the writer weighs in their favor in one scale, and their not being against the laws of nature does not weigh against them. But those facts in the bible which contradict the laws of nature, must be examined with more care, and under a variety of faces. Here you must recur to the pretensions of the writer to inspiration from god. Examine upon what evidence his pretensions are founded, and whether that evidence is so strong as that its falsehood would be more improbable than a change in the laws of nature in the case he

relates. For example in the book of Joshua we are told the sun stood still several hours. Were we to read that fact in Livy or Tacitus we should class it with their showers of blood, speaking of statues, beasts, &c. But it is said that the writer of that book was inspired. Examine therefore candidly what evidence there is of his having been inspired. The pretension is entitled to your inquiry, because millions believe it. On the other hand you are astronomer enough to know how contrary it is to the law of nature that a body revolving on its axis as the earth does, should have stopped, should not by that sudden stoppage have prostrated animals, trees, buildings, and should after a certain time have resumed its revolution, & that without a second general prostration. Is this arrest of the earth's motion, or the evidence which affirms it, most within the law of probabilities? You will next read the new testament. It is the history of a personage called Jesus. Keep in your eye the opposite pretensions 1. of those who say he was begotten by god, born of a virgin, suspended & reversed the laws of nature at will, & ascended bodily into heaven: and 2. of those who say he was a man of illegitimate birth, of a benevolent heart, enthusiastic mind, who set out without pretensions to divinity, ended in believing them, & was punished capitally for sedition by being gibbeted according to the Roman law which punished the first commission of that offence by whipping, & the second by exile or death *in furcâ*. See this law in the Digest Lib. 48. tit. 19. §. 28. 3. & Lipsius Lib. 2. de cruce. cap. 2. These questions are examined in the books I have mentioned under the head of religion, & several others. They will assist you in your inquiries, but keep your reason firmly on the watch in reading them all. Do not be frightened from this inquiry by any fear of it's consequences. If it ends in a belief that there is no god, you will find incitements to virtue in the comfort & pleasantness you feel in it's exercise, and the love of others which it will procure you. If you find reason to believe there is a god, a consciousness that you are acting under his eye, & that he approves you, will be a vast additional incitement; if that there be a future state, the hope of a happy existence in that increases the appetite to deserve it; if that Jesus was also a god, you will be comforted by a belief of his aid and love. In fine, I repeat that you must lay aside

all prejudice on both sides, & neither believe nor reject anything because any other persons, or description of persons
have rejected or believed it. Your own reason is the only oracle given you by heaven, and you are answerable not for the
rightness but uprightness of the decision. I forgot to observe
when speaking of the new testament that you should read all
the histories of Christ, as well of those whom a council of
ecclesiastics have decided for us to be Pseudo-evangelists, as
those they named Evangelists. Because these Pseudo-evangelists pretended to inspiration as much as the others, and you
are to judge their pretensions by your own reason, & not by
the reason of those ecclesiastics. Most of these are lost. There
are some however still extant, collected by Fabricius which I
will endeavor to get & send you.

    5. Travelling. This makes men wiser, but less happy. When
men of sober age travel, they gather knolege which they may
apply usefully for their country, but they are subject ever after
to recollections mixed with regret, their affections are weakened by being extended over more objects, & they learn new
habits which cannot be gratified when they return home.
Young men who travel are exposed to all these inconveniences
in a higher degree, to others still more serious, and do not
acquire that wisdom for which a previous foundation is requisite by repeated & just observations at home. The glare of
pomp & pleasure is analogous to the motion of their blood,
it absorbs all their affection & attention, they are torn from it
as from the only good in this world, and return to their home
as to a place of exile & condemnation. Their eyes are for ever
turned back to the object they have lost, & it's recollection
poisons the residue of their lives. Their first & most delicate
passions are hackneyed on unworthy objects here, & they
carry home only the dregs, insufficient to make themselves or
anybody else happy. Add to this that a habit of idleness, an
inability to apply themselves to business is acquired & renders
them useless to themselves & their country. These observations are founded in experience. There is no place where your
pursuit of knolege will be so little obstructed by foreign objects as in your own country, nor any wherein the virtues of
the heart will be less exposed to be weakened. Be good, be
learned, & be industrious, & you will not want the aid of

travelling to render you precious to your country, dear to your friends, happy within yourself. I repeat my advice to take a great deal of exercise, & on foot. Health is the first requisite after morality. Write to me often & be assured of the interest I take in your success, as well as of the warmth of those sentiments of attachment with which I am, dear Peter, your affectionate friend.

P.S. Let me know your age in your next letter. Your cousins here are well & desire to be remembered to you.

ENCLOSURE

Antient history. Herodot. Thucyd. Xenoph. hellen. Xenoph. Anab. Q. Curt. Just.
  Livy. Polybius. Sallust. Caesar. Suetonius. Tacitus. Aurel. Victor. Herodian.
  Gibbons' decline of the Roman empire. Milot histoire ancienne.
Mod. hist. English. Tacit. Germ. & Agricole—Hume to the end of H.VI. then Habington's E.IV.—St Thomas Moor's E.5. & R.3.—Ld Bacon's H.7.—Ld Herbert of Cherbury's H.8.—K. Edward's journal (in Burnet) B.^{p.} of Hereford's E.6. & Mary.—Cambden's Eliz.—Wilson's Jac.I.—Ludlow (omit Clarendon as too seducing for a young republican. By and by read him) Burnet's Charles 2. Jac.2. W.^{m.} & Mary & Anne—Ld Orrery down to George 1. & 2.—Burke's G.3.—Robertson's hist. of Scotland.
American. Robertson's America.—Douglass's N. America—Hutcheson's Massachusets. Smith's N. York.—Smith's N. Jersey—Franklin's review of Pennsylvania.—Smith's, Stith's, Keith's, & Beverley's hist. of Virginia
Foreign. Mallet's North.ⁿ Antiquities by Percy—Puffendorf's hist.^y of Europe & Martiniere's of Asia, Africa & America—Milot histoire Moderne. Voltaire histoire universelle—Milot hist. de France—Mariana's hist. of Spain in Span.—Robertson's Charles V.—Watson's Phil. II. & III.—Grotii Belgica. Mosheim's Ecclesiastical history.
Poetry Homer—Milton—Ossian—Sophocles—Aeschylus—Eurip. —Metastasio—Shakesp.—Theocritus—Anacreon [. . .]
Mathematics Bezout & whatever else Mr. Madison recommends.
Astronomy Delalande &.^c as Mr. Madison shall recommend.
Natural Philosophy. Musschenbroeck.

Botany.   Linnaei Philosophia Botanica—Genera plantarum—Spe-
cies plantarum—Gronorii flora [. . .]
Chemistry.   Fourcroy.
Agriculture.   Home's principles of Agriculture—Tull &c.
Anatomy.   Cheselden.
Morality.   The Socratic dialogues—Cicero's Philosophies—Kaim's
principles of Nat! religion—Helvetius de l'esprit et de l'homme.
Locke's Essay.—Lucretius—Traite dé Morale & du bonheur
Religion.   Locke's Conduct of the mind.—Middleton's works—
Bolingbroke's philosoph. works—Hume's essays—Voltaire's
works—Beattie
Politics & Law.   Whatever Mr. Wythe pleases, who will be so good
as to correct also all the preceding articles which are only in-
tended as a groundwork to be finished by his pencil.

REVOLT OF THE NOBLES

To John Adams

Paris, Aug. 30, 1787

DEAR SIR—Since your favor of July 10. mine have been of
July 17. 23 and 28. The last inclosed a bill of exchange from
Mr. Grand on Tessier for £46–17–10 sterl. to answer Genl.
Sullivan's bill for that sum. I hope it got safe to hand, tho' I
have been anxious about it as it went by post and my letters
thro' that channel sometimes miscarry.

From the separation of the Notables to the present moment has been perhaps the most interesting interval ever
known in this country. The propositions of the Government,
approved by the Notables, were precious to the nation and
have been in an honest course of execution, some of them
being carried into effect, and others preparing. Above all the
establishment of the Provincial assemblies, some of which
have begun their sessions, bid fair to be the instrument for
circumscribing the power of the crown and raising the people
into consideration. The election given to them is what will do
this. Tho' the minister who proposed these improvements
seems to have meant them as the price of the new supplies,
the game has been so played as to secure the improvements
to the nation without securing the price. The Notables spoke

softly on the subject of the additional supplies, but the parliament took them up roundly, refused to register the edicts for the new taxes, till compelled in a bed of justice and prefered themselves to be transferred to Troyes rather than withdraw their opposition. It is urged principally against the king, that his revenue is 130. millions more than that of his predecessor was, and yet he demands 120. millions further. You will see this well explained in the 'Conference entre un ministre d'etat et un Conseiller au parlement' which I send you with some other small pamphlets. In the mean time all tongues in Paris (and in France as it is said) have been let loose, and never was a license of speaking against the government exercised in London more freely or more universally. Caracatures, placards, bon mots, have been indulged in by all ranks of people, and I know of no well attested instance of a single punishment. For some time mobs of 10; 20; 30,000 people collected daily, surrounded the parliament house, huzzaed the members, even entered the doors and examined into their conduct, took the horses out of the carriages of those who did well, and drew them home. The government thought it prudent to prevent these, drew some regiments into the neighborhood, multiplied the guards, had the streets constantly patrolled by strong parties, suspended privileged places, forbad all clubs, etc. The mobs have ceased: perhaps this may be partly owing to the absence of parliament. The Count d'Artois, sent to hold a bed of justice in the Cour des Aides, was hissed and hooted without reserve by the populace; the carriage of Madame de (I forget the name) in the queen's livery was stopped by the populace under a belief that it was Madame de Polignac's whom they would have insulted, the queen going to the theater at Versailles with Madame de Polignac was received with a general hiss. The king, long in the habit of drowning his cares in wine, plunges deeper and deeper; the queen cries but sins on. The Count d'Artois is detested, and Monsieur [Louis, Comte de Provence] the general favorite. The Archbishop of Thoulouse is made Ministre principale, a virtuous, patriotic and able character. The Marechal de Castries retired yesterday notwithstanding strong sollicitations to remain in office. The Marechal de Segur retired at the same time, prompted to it by the court. Their successors are not

yet known. M. de St. Prist goes Ambassador to Holland in
the room of Verac transferred to Switzerland, and the Count
de Moustier goes to America in the room of the Chevalier de
la Luzerne who has a promise of the first vacancy. These
nominations are not yet made formally, but they are decided
on and the parties are ordered to prepare for their destination. As it has been long since I have had a confidential conveiance to you, I have brought together the principal facts
from the adjournment of the Notables to the present moment
which, as you will perceive from their nature, required a confidential conveyance. I have done it the rather because, tho'
you will have heard many of them and seen them in the public papers, yet floating in the mass of lies which constitute the
atmospheres of London and Paris, you may not have been
sure of their truth: and I have mentioned every truth of any
consequence to enable you to stamp as false the facts pretermitted. I think that in the course of three months the royal
authority has lost, and the rights of the nation gained, as
much ground, by a revolution of public opinion only, as England gained in all her civil wars under the Stuarts. I rather
believe too they will retain the ground gained, because it is
defended by the young and the middle aged, in opposition to
the old only. The first party increases, and the latter diminishes daily from the course of nature. You may suppose that
under this situation, war would be unwelcome to France. She
will surely avoid it if not forced by the courts of London and
Berlin. If forced, it is probable she will change the system of
Europe totally by an alliance with the two empires, to whom
nothing would be more desireable. In the event of such a
coalition, not only Prussia but the whole European world
must receive from them their laws. But France will probably
endeavor to preserve the present system if it can be done by
sacrifising to a certain degree the pretensions of the patriotic
party in Holland. But of all these matters you can judge, in
your position, where less secrecy is observed, better than I
can. I have news from America as late as July 19. Nothing had
then transpired from the Federal convention. I am sorry they
began their deliberations by so abominable a precedent as
that of tying up the tongues of their members. Nothing can
justify this example but the innocence of their intentions, and

ignorance of the value of public discussions. I have no doubt that all their other measures will be good and wise. It is really an assembly of demigods. Genl. Washington was of opinion they should not separate till October. I have the honour to be with every sentiment of friendship and respect Dear Sir Your most obedient and most humble servant,

A MOOSE FROM NEW HAMPSHIRE
To Buffon

Paris, Octob. 1, 1787

SIR,—I had the honour of informing you some time ago that I had written to some of my friends in America, desiring they would send me such of the spoils of the Moose, Caribou, Elk & deer as might throw light on that class of animals; but more particularly to send me the complete skeleton, skin, & horns of the Moose, in such condition as that the skin might be sewed up & stuffed on it's arrival here. I am happy to be able to present to you at this moment the bones & skin of a Moose, the horns of the Caribou, the elk, the deer, the spiked horned buck, & the Roebuck of America. They all come from New Hampshire & Massachusetts. I give you their popular names, as it rests with yourself to decide their real names. The skin of the Moose was drest with the hair on, but a great deal of it has come off, and the rest is ready to drop off. The horns of the elk are remarkably small. I have certainly seen of them which would have weighed five or six times as much. This is the animal which we call elk in the Southern parts of America, and of which I have given some description in the Notes on Virginia, of which I had the honour of presenting you a copy. I really doubt whether the flat-horned elk exists in America; and I think this may be properly classed with the elk, the principal difference being in the horns. I have seen the Daim, the Cerf, the Chevreuil of Europe. But the animal we call Elk, and which may be distinguished as the Round-horned elk, is very different from them. I have never seen the Brand-hirtz or Cerf d'Ardennes, nor the European elk. Could I get a sight of them I think I should be able to say to which

of them the American elk resembles most, as I am tolerably
well acquainted with that animal. I must observe also that the
horns of the Deer, which accompany these spoils, are not of
the fifth or sixth part of the weight of some that I have seen.
This individual has been of age, according to our method of
judging. I have taken measures particularly to be furnished
with large horns of our elk & our deer, & therefore beg of
you not to consider those now sent as furnishing a specimen
of their ordinary size. I really suspect you will find that the
Moose, the Round horned elk, & the American deer are species not existing in Europe. The Moose is perhaps of a new
class. I wish these spoils, Sir, may have the merit of adding
anything new to the treasures of nature which have so fortunately come under your observation, & of which she seems
to have given you the key: they will in that case be some
gratification to you, which it will always be pleasing to me to
have procured, having the honor to be with sentiments of the
most perfect esteem & respect, Sir, your most obedient, &
most humble servant.

THE NEW CONSTITUTION
To William S. Smith

Paris, Nov. 13, 1787

DEAR SIR,—I am now to acknoledge the receipt of your favors of October the 4th, 8th, & 26th. In the last you apologise
for your letters of introduction to Americans coming here. It
is so far from needing apology on your part, that it calls for
thanks on mine. I endeavor to shew civilities to all the Americans who come here, & will give me opportunities of doing
it: and it is a matter of comfort to know from a good quarter
what they are, & how far I may go in my attentions to them.
Can you send me Woodmason's bills for the two copying
presses for the M. de la Fayette, & the M. de Chastellux? The
latter makes one article in a considerable account, of old
standing, and which I cannot present for want of this article.—I do not know whether it is to yourself or Mr. Adams I
am to give my thanks for the copy of the new constitution. I

beg leave through you to place them where due. It will be yet three weeks before I shall receive them from America. There are very good articles in it: & very bad. I do not know which preponderate. What we have lately read in the history of Holland, in the chapter on the Stadtholder, would have sufficed to set me against a chief magistrate eligible for a long duration, if I had ever been disposed towards one: & what we have always read of the elections of Polish kings should have forever excluded the idea of one continuable for life. Wonderful is the effect of impudent & persevering lying. The British ministry have so long hired their gazetteers to repeat and model into every form lies about our being in anarchy, that the world has at length believed them, the English nation has believed them, the ministers themselves have come to believe them, & what is more wonderful, we have believed them ourselves. Yet where does this anarchy exist? Where did it ever exist, except in the single instance of Massachusetts? And can history produce an instance of rebellion so honourably conducted? I say nothing of it's motives. They were founded in ignorance, not wickedness. God forbid we should ever be 20 years without such a rebellion. The people cannot be all, & always, well informed. The part which is wrong will be discontented in proportion to the importance of the facts they misconceive. If they remain quiet under such misconceptions it is a lethargy, the forerunner of death to the public liberty. We have had 13. states independent 11. years. There has been one rebellion. That comes to one rebellion in a century & a half for each state. What country before ever existed a century & half without a rebellion? & what country can preserve it's liberties if their rulers are not warned from time to time that their people preserve the spirit of resistance? Let them take arms. The remedy is to set them right as to facts, pardon & pacify them. What signify a few lives lost in a century or two? The tree of liberty must be refreshed from time to time with the blood of patriots & tyrants. It is it's natural manure. Our Convention has been too much impressed by the insurrection of Massachusetts: and in the spur of the moment they are setting up a kite to keep the hen-yard in order. I hope in God this article will be rectified before the new constitution is accepted.—You ask me if any thing transpires here on the subject of S. America? Not a word. I know that there are combustible materials there, and that they wait the torch only. But this country probably will join the extinguishers.— The want of facts worth communicating to you has occasioned me to give a little loose to dissertation. We must be contented to amuse, when we cannot inform.

MORE ON THE CONSTITUTION
To John Adams

Paris, Nov. 13, 1787

DEAR SIR—This will be delivered you by young Mr. Rutledge. Your knowledge of his father will introduce him to your notice. He merits it moreover on his own account.

I am now to acknolege your favors of Oct. 8 and 26. That of August 25. was duly received, nor can I recollect by what accident I was prevented from acknoleging it in mine of Sep. 28. It has been the source of my subsistence hitherto, and must continue to be so till I receive letters on the affairs of money from America. Van Staphorsts & Willinks have answered my draughts.—Your books for M. de la Fayette are received here. I will notify it to him, who is at present with his provincial assembly in Auvergne.

Little is said lately of the progress of the negociations between the courts of Petersburg, Vienna, and Versailles. The distance of the former and the cautious, unassuming character of it's minister here is one cause of delays: a greater one is the greediness and instable character of the emperor. Nor do I think that the Principal here [Brienne] will be easily induced to lend himself to any connection which shall threaten a war within a considerable number of years. His own reign will be that of peace only, in all probability; and were any accident to tumble him down, this country would immediately gird on it's sword and buckler, and trust to occurrences for supplies of money. The wound their honour has sustained festers in their hearts, and it may be said with truth that the Archbishop and a few priests, determined to support his measures because proud to see their order come again into power, are the only advocates for the line of conduct which has been pursued. It is said and believed thro' Paris literally that the Count de Monmorin 'pleuroit comme un enfant ["wept like a child"]' when obliged to sign the counter declaration. Considering the phrase as figurative, I believe it expresses the distress of his heart. Indeed he has made no secret of his individual opinion. In the mean time the Principal goes on with a firm and patriotic spirit, in reforming the cruel abuses of the government and preparing a new constitution which will give to this people as much liberty as they are capable of managing. This I think will be the glory of his administration, because, tho' a good theorist in finance, he is thought to execute badly. They are about to open a loan of 100. millions to supply present wants, and it is said the preface of the Arret will contain a promise of the Convocation of the States general during the ensuing year. 12. or 15. provincial assemblies are already in action, and are going on well; and I think that tho' the nation suffers in reputation, it will gain infinitely in happiness under the present administration. I inclose to Mr. Jay a pamphlet which I will beg of you to forward. I leave it open for your perusal. When you shall have read it, be so good as to stick a wafer in it. It is not yet published, nor will be for some days. This copy has been ceded to me as a favor.

How do you like our new constitution? I confess there are things in it which stagger all my dispositions to subscribe to what such an assembly has proposed. The house of federal representatives will not be adequate to the management of affairs either foreign or federal. Their President seems a bad edition of a Polish king. He may be reelected from 4. years to 4. years for life. Reason and experience prove to us that a chief magistrate, so continuable, is an officer for life. When one or two generations shall have proved that this is an office for life, it becomes on every succession worthy of intrigue, of bribery, of force, and even of foreign interference. It will be of great consequence to France and England to have America governed by a Galloman or Angloman. Once in office, and possessing the military force of the union, without either the aid or check of a council, he would not be easily dethroned, even if the people could be induced to withdraw their votes from him. I wish that at the end of the 4. years they had made him for ever ineligible a second time. Indeed I think all the good of this new constitution might have been couched in three or four new articles to be added to the good, old, and venerable fabrick, which should have been preserved even as a religious relique.—Present me and my daughters affectionately to Mrs. Adams. The younger one continues to speak of her warmly. Accept yourself assurances of the sincere esteem and respect with which I have the honour to be, Dear Sir, your friend and servant,

P. S. I am in negociation with de la Blancherie. You shall hear from me when arranged.

OBJECTIONS TO THE CONSTITUTION
To James Madison

Paris, Dec. 20, 1787

DEAR SIR,—My last to you was of Oct. 8 by the Count de Moustier. Yours of July 18. Sep. 6. & Oct. 24. have been successively received, yesterday, the day before & three or four days before that. I have only had time to read the letters, the printed papers communicated with them, however interesting, being obliged to lie over till I finish my dispatches for the packet, which dispatches must go from hence the day after tomorrow. I have much to thank you for. First and most for the cyphered paragraph respecting myself. These little informations are very material towards forming my own decisions. I would be glad even to know when any individual member thinks I have gone wrong in any instance. If I know myself it would not excite ill blood in me, while it would assist to guide my conduct, perhaps to justify it, and to keep me to my duty, alert. I must thank you too for the information in Tho.⁵ Burke's case, tho' you will have found by a subsequent letter that I have asked of you a further investigation of that matter. It is to gratify the lady who is at the head of the Convent wherein my daughters are, & who, by her attachment & attention to them, lays me under great obligations. I shall hope therefore still to receive from you the result of the further enquiries my second letter had asked.—The parcel of rice which you informed me had miscarried accompanied my letter to the Delegates of S. Carolina. Mr. Bourgoin was to be the bearer of both & both were delivered together into the hands of his relation here who introduced him to me, and who at a subsequent moment undertook to convey them to Mr. Bourgoin. This person was an engraver particularly recommended to D! Franklin & Mr. Hopkinson. Perhaps he may have mislaid the little parcel of rice among his baggage.—I am much pleased that the sale of Western lands is so successful. I hope they will absorb all the Certificates of our Domestic debt speedily, in the first place, and that then offered for cash they will do the same by our foreign one.

The season admitting only of operations in the Cabinet, and these being in a great measure secret, I have little to fill a letter. I will therefore make up the deficiency by adding a few words on the Constitution proposed by our Convention. I like much the general idea of framing a government which should go on of itself peaceably, without needing continual recurrence to the state legislatures. I like the organization of the government into Legislative, Judiciary & Executive. I like the power given the Legislature to levy taxes, and for that reason solely approve of the greater house being chosen by the people directly. For tho' I think a house chosen by them will be very illy qualified to legislate for the Union, for foreign nations &c. yet this evil does not weigh against the good of preserving inviolate the fundamental principle that the people are not to be taxed but by representatives chosen immediately by themselves. I am captivated by the compromise of the opposite claims of the great & little states, of the latter to equal, and the former to proportional influence. I am much pleased too with the substitution of the method of voting by persons, instead of that of voting by states: and I like the negative given to the Executive with a third of either house, though I should have liked it better had the Judiciary been associated for that purpose, or invested with a similar and separate power. There are other good things of less moment. I will now add what I do not like. First the omission of a bill of rights providing clearly & without the aid of sophisms for freedom of religion, freedom of the press, protection against standing armies, restriction against monopolies, the eternal & unremitting force of the habeas corpus laws, and trials by jury in all matters of fact triable by the laws of the land & not by the law of nations. To say, as Mr. Wilson does that a bill of rights was not necessary because all is reserved in the case of the general government which is not given, while in the particular ones all is given which is not reserved, might do for the audience to whom it was addressed, but is surely a gratis dictum, opposed by strong inferences from the body of the instrument, as well as from the omission of the clause of our present confederation which had declared that in express terms. It was a hard conclusion to say because there has been no uniformity among the states as to the cases triable by jury, because some have been so incautious as to abandon this mode of trial, therefore the more prudent states shall be reduced to the same level of calamity. It would have been much more just & wise to have concluded the other way that as most of the states had judiciously preserved this palladium, those who had wandered should be brought back to it, and to have established general right instead of general wrong. Let me add that a bill of rights is what the people are entitled to against every government on earth, general or particular, & what no just government should refuse, or rest on inferences. The second feature I dislike, and greatly dislike, is the abandonment in every instance of the necessity of rotation in office, and most particularly in the case of the President. Experience concurs with reason in concluding that the first magistrate will always be re-elected if the Constitution permits it. He is then an officer for life. This once observed, it becomes of so much consequence to certain nations to have a friend or a foe at the head of our affairs that they will interfere with money & with arms. A Galloman or an Angloman will be supported by the nation he befriends. If once elected, and at a second or third election out voted by one or two votes, he will pretend false votes, foul play, hold possession of the reins of government, be supported by the States voting for him, especially if they are the central ones lying in a compact body themselves & separating their opponents: and they will be aided by one nation of Europe, while the majority are aided by another. The election of a President of America some years hence will be much more interesting to certain nations of Europe than ever the election of a king of Poland was. Reflect on all the instances in history antient & modern, of elective monarchies, and say if they do not give foundation for my fears. The Roman emperors, the popes, while they were of any importance, the German emperors till they became hereditary in practice, the kings of Poland, the Deys of the Ottoman dependances. It may be said that if elections are to be attended with these disorders, the seldomer they are renewed the better. But experience shews that the only way to prevent disorder is to render them uninteresting by frequent changes. An incapacity to be elected a second time would have been the only effectual preventative. The power of removing him every fourth year by the vote of the people is a power which will not be exercised. The king of Poland is removeable every day by the Diet, yet he is never removed.—Smaller objections are the Appeal in fact as well as law, and the binding all persons Legislative Executive & Judiciary by oath to maintain that constitution. I do not pretend to decide what would be the best method of procuring the establishment of the manifold good things in this constitution, and of getting rid of the bad. Whether by adopting it in hopes of future amendment, or, after it has been duly weighed & canvassed by the people, after seeing the parts they generally dislike, & those they generally approve, to say to them 'We see now what you wish. Send together your deputies again, let them frame a constitution for you omitting what you have condemned, & establishing the powers you approve. Even these will be a great addition to the energy of your government.'—At all events I hope you will not be discouraged from other trials, if the present one should fail of its full effect.—I have thus told you freely what I like & dislike: merely as a matter of curiosity, for I know your own judgment has been formed on all these points after having heard everything which could be urged on them. I own I am not a friend to a very energetic government. It is always oppressive. The late rebellion in Massachusetts has given more alarm than I think it should have done.

Calculate that one rebellion in 13 states in the course of 11 years, is but one for each state in a century & a half. No country should be so long without one. Nor will any degree of power in the hands of government prevent insurrections. France, with all it's despotism, and two or three hundred thousand men always in arms has had three insurrections in the three years I have been here in every one of which greater numbers were engaged than in Massachusetts & a great deal more blood was spilt. In Turkey, which Montesquieu supposes more despotic, insurrections are the events of every day. In England, where the hand of power is lighter than here, but heavier than with us they happen every half dozen years. Compare again the ferocious depredations of their insurgents with the order, the moderation & the almost self extinguishment of ours.—After all, it is my principle that the will of the majority should always prevail. If they approve the proposed Convention in all it's parts, I shall concur in it chearfully, in hopes that they will amend it whenever they shall find it work wrong. I think our governments will remain virtuous for many centuries; as long as they are chiefly agricultural; and this will be as long as there shall be vacant lands in any part of America. When they get piled upon one another in large cities, as in Europe, they will become corrupt as in Europe. Above all things I hope the education of the common people will be attended to; convinced that on their good sense we may rely with the most security for the preservation of a due degree of liberty. I have tired you by this time with my disquisitions & will therefore only add assurances of the sincerity of those sentiments of esteem & attachment with which I am Dear Sir your affectionate friend & servant

P. S. The instability of our laws is really an immense evil. I think it would be well to provide in our constitutions that there shall always be a twelve-month between the ingrossing a bill & passing it: that it should then be offered to it's passage without changing a word: and that if circumstances should be thought to require a speedier passage, it should take two thirds of both houses instead of a bare majority.

A STRATEGY ON RATIFICATION
To Alexander Donald

Paris, February 7, 1788

DEAR SIR,—I received duly your friendly letter of November the 12th. By this time, you will have seen published by Congress, the new regulations obtained from this court, in favor of our commerce. You will observe, that the arrangement relative to tobacco is a continuation of the order of Berni for five years, only leaving the price to be settled between the buyer and seller. You will see too, that all contracts for tobacco are forbidden, till it arrives in France. Of course, your proposition for a contract is precluded. I fear the prices here will be low, especially if the market be crowded. You should be particularly attentive to the article, which requires that the tobacco should come in French or American bottoms, as this article will, in no instance, be departed from.

I wish with all my soul, that the nine first conventions may accept the new constitution, because this will secure to us the good it contains, which I think great and important. But I equally wish, that the four latest conventions, which ever they be, may refuse to accede to it, till a declaration of rights be annexed. This would probably command the offer of such a declaration, and thus give to the whole fabric, perhaps as much perfection as any one of that kind ever had. By a declaration of rights, I mean one which shall stipulate freedom of religion, freedom of the press, freedom of commerce against monopolies, trial by juries in all cases, no suspensions of the habeas corpus, no standing armies. These are fetters against doing evil, which no honest government should decline. There is another strong feature in the new constitution, which I as strongly dislike. That is, the perpetual reeligibility of the President. Of this I expect no amendment at present, because I do not see that any body has objected to it on your side the water. But it will be productive of cruel distress to our country, even in your day and mine. The importance to France and England, to have our government in the hands of a friend or a foe, will occasion their interference by money, and even by arms. Our President will be of much more consequence to them than a King of Poland. We must take care, however, that neither this, nor any other objection to the new form, produces a schism in our Union. That would be an incurable evil, because near friends falling out, never re-unite cordially; whereas, all of us going together, we shall be sure to cure the evils of our new constitution, before they do great harm. The box of books I had taken the liberty to address to you, is but just gone from Havre for New York. I do not see, at present, any symptoms strongly indicating war. It is true, that the distrust existing between the two courts of Versailles and London, is so great, that they can scarcely do business together. However, the difficulty and doubt of obtaining money make both afraid to enter into war. The little preparations for war, which we see, are the effect of distrust, rather then of a design to commence hostilities. And in such a state of mind, you know, small things may produce a rupture: so that though peace is rather probable, war is very possible.

Your letter has kindled all the fond recollections of antient times; recollections much dearer to me than any thing I have known since. There are minds which can be pleased by honors and preferments; but I see nothing in them but envy and enmity. It is only necessary to possess them, to know how little they contribute to happiness, or rather how hostile they are to it. No attachments soothe the mind so much as those contracted in early life; nor do I recollect any societies which have given me more pleasure, than those of which you have partaken with me. I had rather be shut up in a very modest cottage, with my books, my family and a few old friends, dining on simple bacon, and letting the world roll on as it liked, than to occupy the most splendid post, which any human power can give. I shall be glad to hear from you often. Give me the small news as well as the great. Tell Dr. Currie, that I believe I am indebted to him a letter, but that like the mass of our countrymen, I am not, at this moment, able to pay all my debts; the post being to depart in an hour, and the last stroke of a pen I am able to send by it, being that which assures you of the sentiments of esteem and attachment, with which I am, Dear Sir, your affectionate friend and servant,

"A SON OF NATURE"

To Maria Cosway

Paris, April 24, 1788

I arrived here, my dear friend, the last night, and in a bushel of letters presented me by way of reception, I saw that one was of your handwriting. It is the only one I have yet opened, and I answer it before I open another. I do not think I was in arrears in our epistolary account when I left Paris. In affection I am sure you were greatly my debtor. I often determined during my journey to write to you: but sometimes the fatigue of exercise, and sometimes fatigued attention hindered me.

At Dusseldorff I wished for you much. I surely never saw so precious a collection of paintings. Above all things those of Van der Werff affected me the most. His picture of Sarah delivering Agar to Abraham is delicious. I would have agreed to have been Abraham though the consequence could have been that I should have been dead five or six thousand years. Carlo Dolce became also a violent favorite. I am so little of a connoisseur that I preferred the works of these two authors to the old faded red things of Rubens. I am but a son of nature, loving what I see & feel, without being able to give a reason, nor caring much whether there be one. At Heidelberg I wished for you too. In fact I led you by the hand thro' the whole garden.

I was struck with the resemblance of this scene to that of Vaucluse as seen from what is called the chateau of Petrarch. Nature has formed both on the same sketch, but she has filled up that of Heidelberg with a bolder hand, the river is larger, the mountains more majestic and better clothed. Art too has seconded her views. The chateau of Petrarch is the ruin of a modest country house, that of Heidelberg would stand well along side the pyramids of Egypt. It is certainly the most magnificent ruin after those left us by the antients.

At Strasbourg I sat down to write to you, but for my soul I could think of nothing at Strasbourg but the promontory of noses, of Diego, of Slawkenburgius his historiaga, & the procession of the Strasburgers to meet the man with the nose.

Had I written to you from thence it would have been a continuation of Sterne upon noses, & I knew that nature had not formed me for a Continuator of Sterne: so let it alone till I came here and received your angry letter. It is a proof of your esteem, but I love better to have soft testimonials of it.

You must therefore now write me a letter teeming with affection; such as I feel for you. So much I have no right to ask. Being but just arrived I am not *au fait* of the small news affecting your acquaintances here. I know only that the princess Lubomirski is still here & that she has taken the house that was M. de Simoulin's. When you come again therefore you will be somewhat nearer to me, but not near enough: and still surrounded by a numerous cortege, so that I shall see you only by scraps as I did when you were here last. The time before we were half days & whole days together, & I found this too little. Adieu! God bless you!

Your's affectionately

"AMAZONS AND ANGELS"

To Anne Willing Bingham

Paris, May 11, 1788

DEAR MADAM,—A gentleman going to Philadelphia furnishes me the occasion of sending you some numbers of the Cabinet des Modes & some new theatrical pieces. These last have had great success on the stage, where they have excited perpetual applause. We have now need of something to make us laugh, for the topics of the times are sad and eventful. The gay and thoughtless Paris is now become a furnace of Politics. All the world is now politically mad. Men, women, children talk nothing else, & you know that naturally they talk much, loud & warm. Society is spoilt by it, at least for those who, like myself, are but lookers on.—You too have had your political fever. But our good ladies, I trust, have been too wise to wrinkle their foreheads with politics. They are contented to soothe & calm the minds of their husbands returning ruffled from political debate. They have the good sense to value domestic happiness above all other, and the art to cultivate it beyond all others. There is no part of the earth where so much of this is enjoyed as in America. You agree with me in this; but you think that the pleasures of Paris more than supply its wants; in other words that a Parisian is happier than an American. You will change your opinion, my dear Madam, and come over to mine in the end. Recollect the women of this capital, some on foot, some on horses, & some in carriages hunting pleasure in the streets, in routs & assemblies, and forgetting that they have left it behind them in their nurseries; compare them with our own countrywomen occupied in the tender and tranquil amusements of domestic life, and confess that it is a comparison of Amazons and Angels.— You will have known from the public papers that Monsieur de Buffon, the father, is dead & you have known long ago that the son and his wife are separated. They are pursuing pleasure in opposite directions. Madame de Rochambeau is well: so is Madame de la Fayette. I recollect no other Nouvelles de societé interesting to you. And as for political news of battles & sieges, Turks & Russians, I will not detail them to you, because you would be less handsome after reading them. I have only to add then, what I take a pleasure in repeating, tho' it will be the thousandth time that I have the honour to be with sentiments of very sincere respect & attachment, dear Madam, your most obedient & most humble servant.

"THE CRUMBS OF SCIENCE"
To the Rev. James Madison

Paris, July 19, 1788

DEAR SIR,—My last letter to you was of the 13th of August last. As you seem willing to accept of the crumbs of science on which we are subsisting here, it is with pleasure I continue to hand them on to you, in proportion as they are dealt out. Herschel's volcano in the moon you have doubtless heard of, and placed among the other vagaries of a head, which seems not organised for sound induction. The wildness of the theories hitherto proposed by him, on his own discoveries, seems to authorise us to consider his merit as that of a good optician only. You know also, that Doctor Ingenhouse had discovered, as he supposed, from experiment, that vegetation might be promoted by occasioning streams of the electrical fluid to pass through a plant, and that other physicians had received and confirmed this theory. He now, however, retracts it, and finds by more decisive experiments, that the electrical fluid can neither forward nor retard vegetation. Uncorrected still of the rage of drawing general conclusions from partial and equivocal observations, he hazards the opinion that *light* promotes vegetation. I have heretofore supposed from observation, that light affects the color of living bodies, whether vegetable or animal; but that either the one or the other receives *nutriment* from that fluid, must be permitted to be doubted of, till better confirmed by observation. It is always better to have no ideas, than false ones; to believe nothing, than to believe what is wrong. In my mind, theories are more easily demolished than rebuilt.

An Abbé here, has shaken, if not destroyed, the theory of de Dominis, Descartes and Newton, for explaining the phenomenon of the rainbow. According to that theory, you know, a cone of rays issuing from the sun, and falling on a cloud in the opposite part of the heavens, is reflected back in the form of a smaller cone, the apex of which is the eye of the observer: so that the eye of the observer must be in the axis of both cones, and equally distant from every part of the bow. But he observes, that he has repeatedly seen bows, the one end of which has been very near to him, and the other at a very great distance. I have often seen the same thing myself. I recollect well to have seen the end of a rainbow between myself and a house, or between myself and a bank, not twenty yards distant; and this repeatedly. But I never saw, what he says he has seen, different rainbows at the same time, intersecting each other. I never saw coexistent bows, which were not concentric also. Again, according to the theory, if the sun is in the horizon, the horizon intercepts the lower half of the bow, if above the horizon, that intercepts more than the half, in proportion. So that generally, the bow is less than a semicircle, and never more. He says he has seen it more than a semicircle. I have often seen the leg of the bow below my level. My situation at Monticello admits this, because there is a mountain there in the opposite direction of the afternoon's sun, the valley between which and Monticello, is five hundred feet deep. I have seen a leg of a rainbow plunge down on the river running through the valley. But I do not recollect to have remarked at any time, that the bow was more than half a circle. It appears to me, that these facts demolish the Newtonian hypothesis, but they do not support that erected in its stead by the Abbé. He supposes a cloud between the sun and observer, and that through some opening in that cloud, the rays pass, and form an iris on the opposite part of the heavens, just as a ray passing through a hole in the shutter of a darkened room, and falling on a prism there, forms the prismatic colors on the opposite wall. According to this, we might see bows of more than the half circle, as often as of less. A thousand other objections occur to this hypothesis, which need not be suggested to you. The result is, that we are wiser than we were, by having an error the less in our catalogue; but the blank occasioned by it, must remain for some happier hypothesist to fill up.

The dispute about the conversion and reconversion of water and air, is still stoutly kept up. The contradictory experiments of chemists, leave us at liberty to conclude what we please. My conclusion is, that art has not yet invented sufficient aids, to enable such subtle bodies to make a well defined impression on organs as blunt as ours: that it is laudable to encourage investigation, but to hold back conclusion. Speaking one day with Monsieur de Buffon, on the present ardor of chemical inquiry, he affected to consider chemistry but as cookery, and to place the toils of the laboratory on a footing with those of the kitchen. I think it, on the contrary, among the most useful of sciences, and big with future discoveries for the utility and safety of the human race. It is yet, indeed, a mere embryo. Its principles are contested; experiments seem contradictory; their subjects are so minute as to escape our senses; and their result too fallacious to satisfy the mind. It is probably an age too soon, to propose the establishment of a system. The attempt, therefore, of Lavoisier to reform the chemical nomenclature, is premature. One single experiment may destroy the whole filiation of his terms, and his string of sulphates, sulfites and sulfures, may have served no other end, than to have retarded the progress of the science, by a jargon, from the confusion of which, time will be requisite to extricate us. Accordingly, it is not likely to be admitted generally.

You are acquainted with the properties of the composition of nitre, salt of tartar and sulphur, called pulvis fulminans. Of this, the explosion is produced by heat alone. Monsieur Bertholet, by dissolving silver in the nitrous acid, precipitating it with lime water, and drying the precipitate on ammoniac, has discovered a powder which fulminates most powerfully, on coming into contact with any substance whatever. Once made, it cannot be touched. It cannot be put into a bottle, but must remain in the capsula, where dried. The property of the spathic acid, to corrode flinty substances, has been lately applied by a Mr. Puymaurin, to engrave on glass, as artists engrave on copper, with aquafortis. M. de la Place has discovered, that the secular acceleration and retardation of the moon's motion, is occasioned by the action of the sun, in proportion as his excentricity changes, or, in other words, as the orbit of the earth increases or diminishes. So that this irregularity is now perfectly calculable.

Having seen announced in a gazette, that some person had found in a library of Sicily, an Arabic translation of Livy, which was thought to be complete, I got the chargé des affaires of Naples here, to write to Naples to inquire into the fact. He obtained in answer, that an Arabic translation was found, and that it would restore to us seventeen of the books lost, to wit, from the sixtieth to the seventy-seventh, inclusive: that it was in possession of an Abbé Vella, who, as soon as he shall have finished a work he has on hand, will give us an Italian, and perhaps a Latin translation of this Livy. There are persons, however, who doubt the truth of this discovery, founding their doubts on some personal cricumstances relating to the person who says he has this translation. I find, nevertheless, that the chargé des affaires believes in the discovery, which makes me hope it may be true.

A countryman of ours, a Mr. Ledyard of Connecticut, set out from hence some time ago for St. Petersburg, to go thence to Kamtschatka, thence to cross over to the western coast of America, and penetrate through the continent, to the other side of it. He had got within a few days' journey of Kamtschatka, when he was arrested by order of the Empress of Russia, sent back, and turned adrift in Poland. He went to London; engaged under the auspices of a private society, formed there for pushing discoveries into Africa; passed by this place, which he left a few days ago for Marseilles, where he will embark for Alexandria and Grand Cairo; thence explore the Nile to its source; cross the head of the Niger, and descend that to its mouth. He promises me, if he escapes through his journey, he will go to Kentucky, and endeavor to penetrate westwardly to the South Sea.

The death of M. de Buffon you have heard long ago. I do not know whether we shall have any thing posthumous of his. As to political news, this country is making its way to a good constitution. The only danger is, they may press so fast as to produce an appeal to arms, which might have an unfavorable issue for them. As yet, the appeal is not made. Perhaps the war which seems to be spreading from nation to nation, may reach them: this would insure the calling of the States General, and this, as is supposed, the establishment of a constitution.

I have the honor to be, with sentiments of sincere esteem and respect, Dear Sir, your friend and servant,

"A MONOPOLY OF DESPOTISM"
To St. John de Crèvecoeur

Paris, August 9, 1788

DEAR SIR,—While our second revolution is just brought to a happy end with you, yours here, is but cleverly under way. For some days, I was really melancholy with the apprehension, that arms would be appealed to, and the opposition crushed in its first efforts. But things seem now to wear a better aspect. While the opposition keeps at its highest wholesome point, government, unwilling to draw the sword, is not forced to do it. The contest here is exactly what it was in Holland: a contest between the monarchical and aristocratical parts of the government, for a monopoly of despotism over the people. The aristocracy in Holland, seeing that their common prey was likely to escape out of their clutches, chose rather to retain its former portion, and therefore coalesced with the single head. The people remained victims. Here, I think, it will take a happier turn. The parliamentary part of the aristocracy is alone firmly united. The Noblesse and Clergy, but especially the former, are divided partly between the parliamentary and the despotic party, and partly united with the real patriots, who are endeavoring to gain for the nation what they can, both from the parliamentary and the single despotism. I think I am not mistaken in believing, that the King and some of his ministers are well affected to this band; and surely, that they will make great cessions to the people, rather than small ones to the parliament. They are, accordingly, yielding daily to the national reclamations, and will probably end, in according a well tempered constitution. They promise the States General for the next year, and I have good information that an *Arret* will appear the day after to-morrow, announcing them for May, 1789. How they will be composed, and what they will do, cannot be foreseen. Their convocation, however, will tranquillise the public mind, in a great degree, till their meeting. There are, however, two intervening difficulties. 1. Justice cannot till then continue completely suspended, as it now is. The parliament will not resume their functions, but in their entire body. The baillages are afraid to accept of them. What will be done? 2. There are well founded fears of a bankruptcy before the month of May. In the mean time, the war is spreading from nation to nation. Sweden has commenced hostilities against Russia; Denmark is shewing its teeth against Sweden; Prussia against Denmark; and England too deeply engaged in playing the back game, to avoid coming forward, and dragging this country and Spain in with her. But even war will not prevent the assembly of the States General, because it cannot be carried on without them. War, however, is not the most favorable moment for divesting the monarchy of power. On the contrary, it is the moment when the energy of a single hand, shews itself in the most seducing form.

Your friend the Countess d'Houdetot has had a long illness

at Sanois. She was well enough the other day to come to Paris & was so good as to call on me, as I did also on her, without finding each other. The Dutchess Danville is in the country altogether. Your sons are well. Their master speaks very highly of the genius & application of Aly, and more favorably of the genius than application of the younger. They are both fine lads, and will make you very happy. I am not certain whether more exercise than the rules of the school admit would not be good for Aly. I conferred the other day on this subject with M. le Moine, who seems to be of that opinion, & disposed to give him every possible indulgence.

A very considerable portion of this country, has been desolated by a hail. I considered the newspaper accounts, of hailstones of ten pounds weight, as exaggerations. But in a conversation with the Duke de la Rochefoucaut, the other day, he assured me, that though he could not say he had seen such himself, yet he considered the fact as perfectly established. Great contributions, public and private, are making for the sufferers. But they will be like the drop of water from the finger of Lazarus. There is no remedy for the present evil, nor way to prevent future ones, but to bring the people to such a state of ease, as not to be ruined by the loss of a single crop. This hail may be considered as the *coup de grace* to an expiring victim. In the arts, there is nothing new discovered since you left us, which is worth communicating. Mr. Payne's iron bridge was exhibited here, with great approbation. An idea has been encouraged, of executing it in three arches, at the King's garden. But it will probably not be done.

I am, with sentiments of perfect esteem and attachment, Dear Sir, your most obedient and most humble servant,

COMMERCE, WAR, AND REVOLUTION
To George Washington

Paris, Dec. 4, 1788

SIR,—Your favor of Aug. 31. came to hand yesterday; and a confidential conveiance offering, by the way of London, I avail myself of it to acknolege the receipt.

I have seen, with infinite pleasure, our new constitution accepted by 11. states, not rejected by the 12th. and that the 13th. happens to be a state of the least importance. It is true, that the minorities in most of the accepting states have been very respectable, so much so as to render it prudent, were it not otherwise reasonable, to make some sacrifice to them. I am in hopes that the annexation of the bill of rights to the constitution will alone draw over so great a proportion of the minorities, as to leave little danger in the opposition of the residue; and that this annexation may be made by Congress and the assemblies, without calling a convention which might endanger the most valuable parts of the system. Calculation has convinced me that circumstances may arise, and probably will arise, wherein all the resources of taxation will be necessary for the safety of the state. For tho' I am decidedly of opinion we should take no part in European quarrels, but cultivate peace and commerce with all, yet who can avoid seeing the source of war, in the tyranny of those nations who deprive us of the natural right of trading with our neighbors? The products of the U.S. will soon exceed the European demand: what is to be done with the surplus, when there shall be one? It will be employed, without question, to open by force a market for itself with those placed on the same continent with us, and who wish nothing better. Other causes too are obvious, which may involve us in war; and war requires every resource of taxation & credit. The power of making war often prevents it, and in our case would give efficacy to our desire of peace. If the new government wears the front which I hope it will, I see no impossibility in the availing ourselves of the wars of others to open the other parts of America to our commerce, as the price of our neutrality.

The campaign between the Turks & two empires has been clearly in favor of the former. The emperor is secretly trying to bring about a peace. The alliance between England, Prussia and Holland, (and some suspect Sweden also) renders their mediation decisive whenever it is proposed. They seemed to interpose it so magisterially between Denmark & Sweden, that the former submitted to it's dictates, and there was all reason to believe that the war in the North-Western parts of Europe would be quieted. All of a sudden a new flame bursts out in Poland. The king and his party are devoted to Russia. The opposition rely on the protection of Prussia. They have lately become the majority in the confederated diet, and have passed a vote for subjecting their army to a commission independent of the king, and propose a perpetual diet in which case he will be a perpetual cypher. Russia declares against such a change in their constitution, and Prussia has put an army into readiness for marching at a moment's warning on the frontiers of Poland. These events are too recent to see as yet what turn they will take, or what effect they will have on the peace of Europe. So is that also of the lunacy of the king of England, which is a decided fact, notwithstanding all the stuff the English papers publish about his fevers, his deliriums &c. The truth is that the lunacy declared itself almost at once; and with as few concomitant complaints as usually attend the first development of that disorder. I suppose a regency will be established, and if it consist of a plurality of members it will probably be peaceable. In this event it will much favor the present wishes of this country, which are so decidedly for peace, that they refused to enter into the mediation between Sweden and Russia, lest it should commit them. As soon as the convocation of the States-general was announced, a tranquillity took place thro' the whole kingdom. Happily no open rupture had taken place in any part of it. The parliaments were re-instated in their functions at the same time. This was all they desired, and they had called for the States general only through fear that the crown could not otherwise be forced to re-instate them. Their end obtained, they began to foresee danger to themselves in the States general. They began to lay the foundations for cavilling at the legality of that body, if it's measures should be hostile to them. The court, to clear itself of the dispute, convened the Notables who had acted with general approbation on the former occasion, and referred to them the forms of calling and organising the States-general. These Notables consist principally of nobility & clergy, the few of the tiers etat among them being either parliament-men, or other privileged persons. The court wished that in the future States general the members of the Tiers-etat should equal those of both the other orders, and that they should form but one house, all together, & vote by persons, not by orders. But the Notables, in the true spirit of priests and nobles, combining together against the people, have voted by 5 bureaux out of 6. that the people or tiers etat shall have no greater number of deputies than each of the other orders separately, and that they shall vote by orders: so that two orders concurring in a vote, the third will be over-ruled, for it is not here as in England where each of the three branches has a negative on the other two. If this project of theirs succeeds, a combination between the two houses of clergy & nobles, will render the representation of the Tiers etat merely nugatory. The bureaux are to assemble together to consolidate their separate votes; but I see no reasonable hope of their changing this. Perhaps the king, knowing that he may count on the support of the nation and attach it more closely to him, may take on himself to disregard the opinion of the Notables in this instance, and may call an equal repre-sentation of the people, in which precedents will support him. In every event, I think the present disquiet will end well. The nation has been awaked by our revolution, they feel their strength, they are enlightened, their lights are spreading, and they will not retrograde. The first states general may establish 3. important points without opposition from the court. 1. their own periodical convocation. 2. their exclusive right of taxation (which has been confessed by the king.) 3. the right of registering laws and of previously proposing amendments to them, as the parliaments have by usurpation been in the habit of doing. The court will consent to this from it's hatred to the parliaments, and from the desire of having to do with one rather than many legislatures. If the states are prudent they will not aim at more than this at first, lest they should shock the dispositions of the court, and even alarm the public mind, which must be left to open itself by degrees to succes-sive improvements. These will follow from the nature of things. How far they can proceed, in the end, towards a thor-ough reformation of abuse, cannot be foreseen. In my opin-ion a kind of influence, which none of their plans of reform take into account, will elude them all; I mean the influence of women in the government. The manners of the nation allow them to visit, alone, all persons in office, to sollicit the affairs of the husband, family, or friends, and their sollicitations bid defiance to laws and regulations. This obstacle may seem less to those who, like our countrymen, are in the habit of considering Right, as a barrier against all sollicitation. Nor can such an one, without the evidence of his own eyes, believe the desperate state to which things are reduced in this country from the omnipotence of an influence which, fortunately for the happiness of the sex itself, does not endeavor to extend itself in our country beyond the domestic line.

Your communications to the Count de Moustier, whatever they may have been, cannot have done injury to my endeavors here to open the W. Indies to us. On this head the ministers are invincibly mute, tho' I have often tried to draw them into the subject. I have therefore found it necessary to let it lie till war or other circumstance may force it on. Whenever they are in war with England, they must open the islands to us, and perhaps during that war they may see some price which might make them agree to keep them always open. In the meantime I have laid my shoulder to the opening the markets of this country to our produce, and rendering it's transportation a nursery for our seamen. A maritime force is the only one by which we can act on Europe. Our navigation law (if it be wise to have any) should be the reverse of that of England. Instead of confining *importations* to home-bottoms or those of the *producing* nations, I think we should confine *exportations* to home bottoms or to those of nations *having treaties with us*. Our exportations are heavy, and would nourish a great force of our own, or be a tempting price to the nation to whom we should offer a participation of it in exchange for free access to all their possessions. This is an object to which our government alone is adequate in the gross, but I have ventured to pursue it, here, so far as the consumption of productions by this country extends. Thus in our arrangements relative to tobacco, none can be received here but in French or American bottoms. This is emploiment for nearly 2000 seamen, and puts nearly that number of British out of employ. By the *Arret* of Dec, 1787, it was provided that our whale oils should not be received here but in French or American bottoms, and by later regulations all oils but those of France and America are excluded. This will put 100 English whale vessels immediately out of employ, and 150. ere long;

and call so many of French & American into service. We have
had 6000 seamen formerly in this business, the whole of
whom we have been likely to lose. The consumption of rice
is growing fast in this country, and that of Carolina gaining
ground on every other kind. I am of opinion the whole of
the Carolina rice can be consumed here. It's transportation
employs 2500 sailors, almost all of them English at present;
the rice being deposited at Cowes & brought from thence
here. It would be dangerous to confine this transportation to
French & American bottoms the ensuing year, because they
will be much engrossed by the transportation of wheat &
flour hither, and the crop of rice might lie on hand for want
of vessels; but I see no objections to the extensions of our
principle to this article also, beginning with the year 1790.
However, before there is a necessity of deciding on this I
hope to be able to consult our new government in person, as
I have asked of Congress a leave of absence for 6. months,
that is to say from April to November next. It is necessary for
me to pay a short visit to my native country, first to reconduct
my family thither, and place them in the hands of their
friends, & secondly to place my private affairs under certain
arrangements. When I left my own house, I expected to be
absent but 5 months, & I have been led by events to an absence of 5 years. I shall hope therefore for the pleasure of
personal conferences with your Excellency on the subject of
this letter and others interesting to our country, of getting
my own ideas set to rights by a communication of yours, and
of taking again the tone of sentiment of my own country
which we lose in some degree after a certain absence. You
know doubtless of the death of the Marquise de Chastellux.
The Marquis de La Fayette is out of favor with the court, but
high in favor with the nation. I once feared for his personal
liberty, but I hope he is on safe ground at present. On the
subject of the whale fishery I inclose you some observations I
drew up for the ministry here, in order to obtain a correction
of their *Arret* of Sepr last, whereby they had involved our oils
with the English in a general exclusion from their ports. They
will accordingly correct this, so that our oils will participate
with theirs in the monopoly of their markets. There are several things incidentally introduced which do not seem perti-

nent to the general question. They were rendered necessary by particular circumstances the explanation of which would add to a letter already too long. I will trespass no further then than to assure you of the sentiments of sincere attachment and respect with which I have the honor to be your Excellency's most obedt. humble servant.

P.S. The observations inclosed, tho' printed, have been put into confidential hands only.

CONVENING THE ESTATES GENERAL

To Richard Price

Paris, January 8, 1789

DEAR SIR,—I was favored with your letter of October 26th, and far from finding any of its subjects uninteresting as you apprehend, they were to me, as everything which comes from you, pleasing and instructive. I concur with you strictly in your opinion of the comparative merits of atheism and demonism, and really see nothing but the latter in the being worshipped by many who think themselves Christians. Your opinions and writings will have effect in bringing others to reason on this subject. Our new Constitution, of which you speak also, has succeeded beyond what I apprehended it would have done. I did not at first believe that eleven States out of thirteen would have consented to a plan consolidating them as much into one. A change in their dispositions, which had taken place since I left them, had rendered this consolidation necessary, that is to say, had called for a federal government which could walk upon its own legs, without leaning for support on the State legislatures. A sense of necessity, and a submission to it, is to me a new and consolatory proof that, whenever the people are well-informed, they can be trusted with their own government; that, whenever things get so far wrong as to attract their notice, they may be relied on to set them to rights. You say you are not sufficiently informed about the nature and circumstances of the present struggle here. Having been on the spot from its first origin, and

watched its movements as an uninterested spectator, with no
other bias than a love of mankind, I will give you my ideas
of it. Though celebrated writers of this and other countries
had already sketched good principles on the subject of government, yet the American war seems first to have awakened
the thinking part of this nation in general from the sleep of
despotism in which they were sunk. The officers too who had
been to America, were mostly young men, less shackled by
habit and prejudice, and more ready to assent to the dictates
of common sense and common right. They came back impressed with these. The press, notwithstanding its shackles,
began to disseminate them; conversation, too, assumed new
freedom; politics became the theme of all societies, male and
female, and a very extensive and zealous party was formed,
which may be called the Patriotic party, who, sensible of the
abusive government under which they lived, longed for occasions of reforming it. This party comprehended all the honesty of the kingdom, sufficiently at its leisure to think; the
men of letters, the easy bourgeois, the young nobility, partly
from reflection, partly from mode; for those sentiments became a matter of mode, and as such united most of the young
women to the party. Happily for the nation, it happened that,
at the same moment, the dissipations of the court had exhausted the money and credit of the State, and M. de Calonnes found himself obliged to appeal to the nation, and to
develop to it the ruin of their finances. He had no idea of
supplying the deficit by economies, he saw no means but new
taxes. To tempt the nation to consent to these some douceurs
were necessary. The Notables were called in 1787. The leading
vices of the constitution and administration were ably
sketched out, good remedies proposed, and under the splendor of the propositions, a demand for more money was
couched. The Notables concurred with the minister in the
necessity of reformation, adroitly avoided the demand of
money, got him displaced, and one of their leading men
placed in his room. The archbishop of Thoulouse, by the aid
of the hopes formed of him, was able to borrow some money,
and he reformed considerably the expenses of the court. Notwithstanding the prejudices since formed against him, he appeared to me to pursue the reformation of the laws and

constitution as steadily as a man could do who had to drag
the court after him, and even to conceal from them the consequences of the measures he was leading them into. In his
time the criminal laws were reformed, provincial assemblies
and States established in most of the provinces, the States
General promised, and a solemn acknowledgment made by
the King that he could not impose a new tax without the
consent of the nation. It is true he was continually goaded
forward by the public clamors, excited by the writings and
workings of the Patriots, who were able to keep up the public
fermentation at the exact point which borders on resistance,
without entering on it. They had taken into their alliance the
Parliaments also, who were led, by very singular circumstances, to espouse, for the first time, the rights of the nation.
They had from old causes had personal hostility against M.
de Calonnes. They refused to register his laws or his taxes,
and went so far as to acknowledge they had no power to do
it. They persisted in this with his successor, who therefore
exiled them. Seeing that the nation did not interest themselves much for their recall, they began to fear that the new
judicatures proposed in their place would be established and
that their own suppression would be perpetual. In short, they
found their own strength insufficient to oppose that of the
King. They therefore insisted that the States General should
be called. Here they became united with and supported by
the Patriots, and their joint influence was sufficient to produce the promise of that assembly. I always suspected that the
archbishops had no objections to this force under which they
laid him. But the Patriots and Parliament insisted it was their
efforts which extorted the promise against his will. The re-
establishment of the Parliament was the effect of the same
coalition between the Patriots and Parliament; but, once re-
established, the latter began to see danger in that very power,
the States General, which they had called for in a moment of
despair, but which they now foresaw might very possibly
abridge their powers. They began to prepare grounds for
questioning their legality, as a rod over the head of the States,
and as a refuge if they should really extend their reformations
to them. Mr. Neckar came in at this period and very dexter-
ously disembarrassed the administration of these disputes by

calling the notables to advise the form of calling and constituting the States. The court was well disposed towards the
people, not from principles of justice or love to them; but
they want money. No more can be had from the people. They
are squeezed to the last drop. The clergy and nobles, by their
privileges and influence, have kept their property in a great
measure untaxed hitherto. They then remain to be squeezed,
and no agent is powerful enough for this but the people. The
court therefore must ally itself with the people. But the Notables, consisting mostly of privileged characters, had proposed a method of composing the States, which would have
rendered the voice of the people, or Tiers Etats, in the States
General, inefficient for the purpose of the court. It concurred
then with the Patriots in intriguing with the Parliament to get
them to pass a vote in favor of the rights of the people. This
vote, balancing that of the Notables, has placed the court at
liberty to follow its own views, and they have determined that
the Tiers Etat shall have in the States General as many votes
as the clergy and nobles put together. Still a great question
remains to be decided, that is, shall the States General vote
by orders, or by persons? precedents are both ways. The
clergy will move heaven and earth to obtain the suffrage by
orders, because that parries the effect of all hitherto done for
the people. The people will probably send their deputies expressly instructed to consent to no tax, to no adoption of the
public debts, unless the unprivileged part of the nation has a
voice equal to that of the privileged; that is to say, unless the
voice of the Tiers Etat be equalled to that of the clergy and
nobles. They will have the young noblesse in general on their
side, and the King and court. Against them will be the ancient nobles and the clergy. So that I hope, upon the whole,
that by the time they meet, there will be a majority of the
nobles themselves in favor of the Tiers Etat. So far history.
We are now to come to prophecy; for you will ask, to what
will all this lead? I answer, if the States General do not stum-
ble at the threshold on the question before stated, and which
must be decided before they can proceed to business, then
they will in their first session easily obtain, 1. Their future
periodical convocation of the States. 2. Their exclusive right
to raise and appropriate money which includes that of estab-

lishing a civil list. 3. A participation in legislation; probably at first, it will only be a transfer to them of the portion of it now exercised by parliament, that is to say, a right to propose amendments and a negative. But it must infallibly end in a right of origination. 4. Perhaps they may make a declaration of rights. It will be attempted at least. Two other objects will be attempted, viz., a habeas corpus law and a free press. But probably they may not obtain these in the first session, or with modifications only, and the nation must be left to ripen itself more for their unlimited adoption. Upon the whole, it has appeared to me that the basis of the present struggle is an illumination of the public mind as to the rights of the nation, aided by fortunate incidents; that they can never retrograde, but from the natural progress of things, must press forward to the establishment of a constitution which shall assure to them a good degree of liberty. They flatter themselves they shall form a better constitution than the English. I think it will be better in some points—worse in others. It will be better in the article of representation, which will be more equal. It will be worse, as their situation obliges them to keep up the dangerous machine of a standing army. I doubt, too, whether they will obtain the trial by jury, because they are not sensible of its value.

I am sure I have by this time heartily tired you with this long epistle, and that you will be glad to see it brought to an end, with assurances of the sentiments of esteem and respect with which I have the honor to be, dear Sir, your most obedient, and most humble servant.

BACON, LOCKE, AND NEWTON
To John Trumbull

Paris, Feb. 15, 1789

DEAR SIR,—I have duly received your favor of the 5th. inst. With respect to the busts & pictures I will put off till my return from America all of them except Bacon, Locke and Newton, whose pictures I will trouble you to have copied for me: and as I consider them as the three greatest men that have ever lived, without any exception, and as having laid the foundation of those superstructures which have been raised in the Physical & Moral sciences, I would wish to form them into a knot on the same canvas, that they may not be confounded at all with the herd of other great men. To do this I suppose we need only desire the copyist to draw the three busts in three ovals all contained in a larger oval in some such form as this each bust to be the size of life.

 The large oval would I suppose be about between four & five feet. Perhaps you can suggest a better way of accomplishing my idea. In your hands be it, as well as the subaltern expences you mention. I trouble you with a letter to Mrs. Church. We have no important news here but of the revolution of Geneva which is not yet sufficiently explained. But they have certainly reformed their government. I am with great respect D.ʳ Sir Your affectionate friend & humble serv.ᵗ

"NEITHER FEDERALIST NOR ANTIFEDERALIST"

To Francis Hopkinson

Paris, Mar. 13, 1789

DEAR SIR,—Since my last, which was of Dec. 21. yours of Dec. 9. & 21. are received. Accept my thanks for the papers and pamphlets which accompanied them, and mine & my daughter's for the book of songs. I will not tell you how much they have pleased us, nor how well the last of them merits praise for it's pathos, but relate a fact only, which is that while my elder daughter was playing it on the harpsichord, I happened to look towards the fire & saw the younger one all in tears. I asked her if she was sick? She said 'no; but the tune was so mournful.'—The Editor of the Encyclopedie has published something as to an advanced price on his future volumes, which I understand alarms the subscribers. It was in a paper which I do not take & therefore I have not yet seen it, nor can say what it is.—I hope that by this time you have ceased to make wry faces about your vinegar, and that you have received it safe & good. You say that I have been dished up to you as an antifederalist, and ask me if it be just. My opinion was never worthy enough of notice to merit citing; but since you ask it I will tell it you. I am not a Federalist, because I never submitted the whole system of my opinions to the creed of any party of men whatever in religion, in philosophy, in politics, or in anything else where I was capable of thinking for myself. Such an addiction is the last degradation of a free and moral agent. If I could not go to heaven but with a party, I would not go there at all. Therefore I protest to you I am not of the party of federalists. But I am much farther from that of the Antifederalists. I approved, from the first moment, of the great mass of what is in the new constitution, the consolidation of the government, the organization into Executive legislative & judiciary, the subdivision of the legislative, the happy compromise of interests between the great & little states by the different manner of voting in the different houses, the voting by persons instead of states, the qualified negative on laws given to the Executive which however I should have liked better if associated with the judiciary also as in New York, and the power of taxation. I thought at first that the latter might have been limited. A little reflection soon convinced me it ought not to be. What I disapproved from the first moment also was the want of a bill of rights to guard liberty against the legislative as well as executive branches of the government, that is to say to secure freedom in religion, freedom of the press, freedom from monopolies, freedom from unlawful imprisonment, freedom from a permanent military, and a trial by jury in all cases determinable by the laws of the land. I disapproved also the perpetual reeligibility of the President. To these points of disapprobation I adhere. My first wish was that the 9. first conventions might accept the constitution, as the means of securing to us the great mass of good it contained, and that the 4. last might reject it, as the means of obtaining amendments. But I was corrected in this wish the moment I saw the much better plan of Massachusetts and which had never occurred to me. With respect to the declaration of rights I suppose the majority of the United states are of my opinion: for I apprehend all the antifederalists, and a very respectable proportion of the federalists think that such a declaration should now be annexed. The enlightened part of Europe have given us the greatest credit for inventing this instrument of security for the rights of the people, and have been not a little sur-

prised to see us so soon give it up. With respect to the reeligibility of the president, I find myself differing from the
majority of my countrymen, for I think there are but three
states out of the 11. which have desired an alteration of this.
And indeed, since the thing is established, I would wish it
not to be altered during the life of our great leader, whose
executive talents are superior to those I believe of any man in
the world, and who alone by the authority of his name and
the confidence reposed in his perfect integrity, is fully qualified to put the new government so under way as to secure it
against the efforts of opposition. But having derived from our
error all the good there was in it I hope we shall correct it
the moment we can no longer have the same name at the
helm. These, my dear friend, are my sentiments, by which
you will see I was right in saying I am neither federalist nor
antifederalist; that I am of neither party, nor yet a trimmer
between parties. These my opinions I wrote within a few
hours after I had read the constitution, to one or two friends
in America. I had not then read one single word printed on
the subject. I never had an opinion in politics or religion
which I was afraid to own. A costive reserve on these subjects
might have procured me more esteem from some people, but
less from myself. My great wish is to go on in a strict but
silent performance of my duty; to avoid attracting notice &
to keep my name out of newspapers, because I find the pain
of a little censure, even when it is unfounded, is more acute
than the pleasure of much praise. The attaching circumstance
of my present office is that I can do it's duties unseen by
those for whom they are done.—You did not think, by so
short a phrase in your letter, to have drawn on yourself such
an egotistical dissertation.

A BILL OF RIGHTS
To James Madison

Paris, Mar 15, 1789

DEAR SIR,—I wrote you last on the 12th of Jan. since which
I have received yours of Octob 17, Dec 8 & 12. That of Oct.

17. came to hand only Feb 23. How it happened to be four months on the way, I cannot tell, as I never knew by what hand it came. Looking over my letter of Jan 12th, I remark an error of the word "probable" instead of "improbable," which doubtless however you had been able to correct. Your thoughts on the subject of the Declaration of rights in the letter of Oct 17. I have weighed with great satisfaction. Some of them had not occurred to me before, but were acknoleged just in the moment they were presented to my mind. In the arguments in favor of a declaration of rights, you omit one which has great weight with me, the legal check which it puts into the hands of the judiciary. This is a body, which if rendered independent & kept strictly to their own department merits great confidence for their learning & integrity. In fact what degree of confidence would be too much for a body composed of such men as Wythe, Blair & Pendleton? On characters like these the *"civium ardor prava jubentium"* would make no impression. I am happy to find that on the whole you are a friend to this amendment. The Declaration of rights is like all other human blessings alloyed with some inconveniences, and not accomplishing fully it's object. But the good in this instance vastly overweighs the evil. I cannot refrain from making short answers to the objections which your letter states to have been raised. 1. That the rights in question are reserved by the manner in which the federal powers are granted. Answer. A constitutive act may certainly be so formed as to need no declaration of rights. The act itself has the force of a declaration as far as it goes; and if it goes to all material points nothing more is wanting. In the draught of a constitution which I had once a thought of proposing in Virginia, & printed afterwards, I endeavored to reach all the great objects of public liberty, and did not mean to add a declaration of rights. Probably the object was imperfectly executed; but the deficiencies would have been supplied by others, in the course of discussion. But in a constitutive act which leaves some precious articles unnoticed, and raises implications against others, a declaration of rights becomes necessary by way of supplement. This is the case of our new federal constitution. This instrument forms us into one state

as to certain objects, and gives us a legislative & executive body for these objects. It should therefore guard us against their abuses of power within the field submitted to them. 2. A positive declaration of some essential rights could not be obtained in the requisite latitude. Answer. Half a loaf is better than no bread. If we cannot secure all our rights, let us secure what we can. 3. The limited powers of the federal government & jealousy of the subordinate governments afford a security which exists in no other instance. Answer. The first member of this seems resolvable into the first objection before stated. The jealousy of the subordinate governments is a precious reliance. But observe that those governments are only agents. They must have principles furnished them whereon to found their opposition. The declaration of rights will be the text whereby they will try all the acts of the federal government, In this view it is necessary to the federal government also; as by the same text they may try the opposition of the subordinate governments. 4. Experience proves the inefficacy of a bill of rights. True. But tho it is not absolutely efficacious under all circumstances, it is of great potency always, and rarely inefficacious. A brace the more will often keep up the building which would have fallen with that brace the less. There is a remarkable difference between the characters of the Inconveniences which attend a Declaration of rights, & those which attend the want of it. The inconveniences of the Declaration are that it may cramp government in it's useful exertions. But the evil of this is short-lived, trivial & reparable. The inconveniences of the want of a Declaration are permanent, afflicting & irreparable. They are in constant progression from bad to worse. The executive in our governments is not the sole, it is scarcely the principal object of my jealousy. The tyranny of the legislatures is the most formidable dread at present, and will be for long years. That of the executive will come in it's turn, but it will be at a remote period. I know there are some among us who would now establish a monarchy. But they are inconsiderable in number and weight of character. The rising race are all republicans. We were educated in royalism; no wonder if some of us retain that idolatry still. Our young people are educated in republicanism, an apostasy from that to royalism is unprecedented & impossible. I am much pleased with the prospect that a declaration of rights will be added; and hope it will be done in that way which will not endanger the whole frame of the government, or any essential part of it.

I have hitherto avoided public news in my letters to you, because your situation insured you a communication of my letters to Mr. Jay. This circumstance being changed, I shall in future indulge myself in these details to you. There had been some slight hopes that an accommodation might be affected between the Turks & two empires but these hopes do not strengthen, and the season is approaching which will put an end to them for another campaign at least. The accident to the King of England has had great influence on the affairs of Europe. His mediation joined with that of Prussia, would certainly have kept Denmark quiet, and so have left the two empires in the hands of the Turks & Swedes. But the inactivity to which England is reduced, leaves Denmark more free, and she will probably go on in opposition to Sweden. The K. of Prussia too had advanced so far that he can scarcely retire. This is rendered the more difficult by the troubles he has excited in Poland. He cannot well abandon the party he had brought forward there so that it is very possible he may be engaged in the ensuing campaign. France will be quiet this year, because this year at least is necessary for settling her future constitution. The States will meet the 27th of April: and the public mind will I think by that time be ripe for a just decision of the Question whether they shall vote by orders or persons. I think there is a majority of the nobles already for the latter. If so, their affairs cannot but go on well. Besides settling for themselves a tolerably free constitution, perhaps as free a one as the nation is yet prepared to bear, they will fund their public debts. This will give them such a credit as will enable them to borrow any money they may want, & of course to take the field again when they think proper. And I believe they mean to take the field as soon as they can. The pride of every individual in the nation suffers under the ignominies they have lately been exposed to and I think the states general will give money for a war to wipe off the reproach. There have arisen new bickerings between this court & the Hague, and the papers which have passed shew the most bitter acrimony rankling at the heart of this ministry. They have recalled their ambassador from the Hague without appointing a successor. They have given a note to the Diet of Poland which shews a disapprobation of their measures. The insanity of the King of England has been fortunate for them as it gives them time to put their house in order. The English papers tell you the King is well: and even the English ministry say so. They will naturally set the best foot foremost: and they guard his person so well that it is difficult for the public to contradict them. The King is probably better, but not well by a great deal. 1. He has been bled, and judicious physicians say that in his exhausted state nothing could have induced a recurrence to bleeding but symptoms of relapse. 2. The Prince of Wales tells the Irish deputation he will give them a definitive answer in some days; but if the king had been well he could have given it at once. 3. They talk of passing a standing law for providing a regency in similar cases. They apprehend then they are not yet clear of the danger of wanting a regency. 4. They have carried the king to church; but it was his private chapel. If he be well why do not they shew him publicly to the nation, & raise them from that consternation into which they have been thrown by the prospect of being delivered over to the profligate hands of the prince of Wales. In short, judging from little facts which are known in spite of their teeth the King is better, but not well. Possibly he is getting well, but still, time will be wanting to satisfy even the ministry that it is not merely a lucid interval. Consequently they cannot interrupt France this year in the settlement of her affairs, & after this year it will be too late.

As you will be in a situation to know when the leave of absence will be granted me which I have asked, will you be so good as to communicate it by a line to Mr. Lewis & Mr. Eppes? I hope to see you in the summer, and that if you are not otherwise engaged, you will encamp with me at Monticello for awhile.

SCIENCE AND LIBERTY
To Joseph Willard

Paris, March 24, 1789

SIR,—I have been lately honored with your letter of September the 24th, 1788, accompanied by a diploma for a Doctorate of Laws, which the University of Harvard has been pleased to confer on me. Conscious how little I merit it, I am the more sensible of their goodness and indulgence to a stranger, who has had no means of serving or making himself known to them. I beg you to return them my grateful thanks, and to assure them that this notice from so eminent a seat of science, is very precious to me.

The most remarkable publications we have had in France, for a year or two past, are the following. 'Les voyages d'Anacharsis par l'Abbé Barthelemi,' seven volumes, octavo. This is a very elegant digest of whatever is known of the Greeks; useless, indeed, to him who has read the original authors, but very proper for one who reads modern languages only. The works of the King of Prussia. The Berlin edition is in sixteen volumes, octavo. It is said to have been gutted at Berlin; and here it has been still more mangled. There are one or two other editions published abroad, which pretend to have rectified the maltreatment both of Berlin and Paris. Some time will be necessary to settle the public mind, as to the best edition.

Montignot has given us the original Greek, and a French translation of the seventh book of Potolemy's great work, under the title of 'Etat des etoiles fixes au second siecle,' in quarto. He has given the designation of the same stars by Flamstead and Beyer, and their position in the year 1786. A very remarkable work is the 'Mechanique Analytique,' of Le Grange, in quarto. He is allowed to be the greatest mathematician now living, and his personal worth is equal to his science. The object of his work is to reduce all the principles of mechanics to the single one of the equilibrium, and to give a simple formula applicable to them all. The subject is treated in the algebraic method, without diagrams to assist the conception. My present occupations not permitting me to read any thing which requires a long and undisturbed attention, I

am not able to give you the character of this work from my
own examination. It has been received with great approbation
in Europe. In Italy, the works of Spallanzani on digestion and
generation, are valuable. Though, perhaps, too minute, and
therefore tedious, he has developed some useful truths, and his
book is well worth attention; it is in four volumes, octavo. Clavi-
garo, an Italian also, who has resided thirty-six years in Mexico, has given us a history of that country, which certainly
merits more respect than any other work on the same subject.
He corrects many errors of Dr. Robertson; and though sound
philosophy will disapprove many of his ideas, we must still
consider it as an useful work, and assuredly the best we possess on the same subject. It is in four thin volumes, small
quarto. De la Land has not yet published a fifth volume.

The chemical dispute about the conversion and reconversion of air and water, continues still undecided. Arguments
and authorities are so balanced, that we may still safely believe, as our fathers did before us, that these principles are
distinct. A schism of another kind, has taken place among the
chemists. A particular set of them here, have undertaken to
remodel all the terms of the science, and to give to every substance a new name, the composition, and especially the termination of which, shall define the relation in which it stands
to other substances of the same family. But the science seems
too much in its infancy as yet, for this reformation; because,
in fact, the reformation of this year must be reformed again
the next year, and so on, changing the names of substances as
often as new experiments develope properties in them undiscovered before. The new nomenclature has, accordingly, been
already proved to need numerous and important reformations. Probably it will not prevail. It is espoused by the minority only here, and by very few, indeed, of the foreign
chemists. It is particularly rejected in England.

In the arts, I think two of our countrymen have presented
the most important inventions. Mr. Paine, the author of
Common Sense, has invented an iron bridge, which promises
to be cheaper by a great deal than stone, and to admit of a
much greater arch. He supposes it may be ventured for an
arch of five hundred feet. He has obtained a patent for it in
England, and is now executing the first experiment with an

arch of between ninety and one hundred feet. Mr. Rumsey has also obtained a patent for his navigation by the force of steam, in England, and is soliciting a similar one here. His principal merit is in the improvement of the boiler, and, instead of the complicated machinery of oars and paddles, proposed by others, the substitution of so simple a thing as the reaction of a stream of water on his vessel. He is building a sea vessel at this time in England, and she will be ready for an experiment in May. He has suggested a great number of mechanical improvements in a variety of branches; and upon the whole, is the most original and the greatest mechanical genius I have ever seen. The return of la Peyrouse (whenever that shall happen) will probably add to our knowledge in Geography, Botany and Natural History. What a field have we at our doors to signalise ourselves in! The Botany of America is far from being exhausted, its Mineralogy is untouched, and its Natural History or Zoology, totally mistaken and misrepresented. As far as I have seen, there is not one single species of terrestrial birds common to Europe and America, and I question if there be a single species of quadrupeds. (Domestic animals are to be excepted.) It is for such institutions as that over which you preside so worthily, Sir, to do justice to our country, its productions and its genius. It is the work to which the young men, whom you are forming, should lay their hands. We have spent the prime of our lives in procuring them the precious blessing of liberty. Let them spend theirs in shewing that it is the great parent of *science* and of virtue; and that a nation will be great in both, always in proportion as it is free. Nobody wishes more warmly for the success of your good exhortations on this subject, than he who has the honor to be, with sentiments of great esteem and respect, Sir, your most obedient humble servant,

A REPORT FROM VERSAILLES
To John Jay

Paris, May 9, 1789

SIR,—Since my letter of March the 1st, by the way of Havre, and those of March the 12th and 15th, by the way of London, no opportunity of writing has occurred, till the present to London.

There are no symptoms of accommodation between the Turks and two empires, nor between Russia and Sweden. The Emperor was, on the 16th of the last month, expected to die, certainly; he was, however, a little better when the last news came away, so that hopes were entertained of him; but it is agreed that he cannot get the better of his complaints ultimately, so that his life is not at all counted on. The Danes profess, as yet, to do no more against Sweden than furnish their stipulated aid. The agitation of Poland is still violent, though somewhat moderated by the late change in the demeanor of the King of Prussia. He is much less thrasonic than he was. This is imputed to the turn which the English politics may be rationally expected to take. It is very difficult to get at the true state of the British King; but from the best information we can get, his madness has gone off, but he is left in a state of imbecility and melancholy. They are going to carry him to Hanover, to see whether such a journey may relieve him. The Queen accompanies him. If England should, by this accident, be reduced to inactivity, the southern countries of Europe may escape the present war. Upon the whole, the prospect for the present year, if no unforeseen accident happens, is, certain peace for the powers not already engaged, a probability that Denmark will not become a principal, and a mere possibility that Sweden and Russia may be accommodated. The interior disputes of Sweden are so exactly detailed in the Leyden gazette, that I have nothing to add on that subject.

The revolution of this country has advanced thus far, without encountering any thing which deserves to be called a difficulty. There have been riots in a few instances, in three or four different places, in which there may have been a dozen or twenty lives lost. The exact truth is not to be got at. A few days ago, a much more serious riot took place in this city, in which it became necessary for the troops to engage in regular action with the mob, and probably about one hundred of the latter were killed. Accounts vary from twenty to two hundred. They were the most abandoned banditti of Paris, and never was a riot more unprovoked and unpitied. They began, under a pretence that a paper manufacturer had proposed in an assembly, to reduce their wages to fifteen sous a day. They rifled his house, destroyed every thing in his magazines and shops, and were only stopped in their career of mischief, by the carnage above mentioned. Neither this nor any other of the riots, have had a professed connection with the great national reformation going on. They are such as have happened every year since I have been here, and as will continue to be produced by common incidents. The States General were opened on the 4th instant, by a speech from the throne, one by the Garde des Sceaux, and one from Mr. Neckar. I hope they will be printed in time to send you herewith: lest they should not, I will observe, that that of Mr. Neckar stated the real and ordinary deficit to be fifty-six millions, and that he shewed that this could be made up without a new tax, by economies and bonifications which he specified. Several articles of the latter are liable to the objection, that they are proposed on branches of the revenue, of which the nation has demanded a suppression. He tripped too lightly over the great articles of constitutional reformation, these being not as clearly enounced in this discourse as they were in his 'Rapport au roy,' which I sent you some time ago. On the whole, his discourse has not satisfied the patriotic party. It is now, for the first time, that their revolution is likely to receive a serious check, and begins to wear a fearful appearance. The progress of light and liberality in the order of the Noblesse, has equalled expectation in Paris only, and its vicinities. The great mass of deputies of that order, which come from the country, shew that the habits of tyranny over the people, are deeply rooted in them. They will consent, indeed, to equal taxation; but five-sixths of that chamber are thought to be, decidedly, for voting by orders; so that, had this great preliminary question rested on this body, which formed heretofore the sole hope, that hope would have been completely disappointed. Some aid, however, comes in from a quarter whence none was expected. It was imagined the ecclesiastical elections would have been generally in favor of the higher clergy; on the contrary, the lower clergy have obtained five-sixths of these deputations. These are the sons of peasants, who have done all the drudgery of the service, for ten, twenty and thirty guineas a year, and whose oppressions and penury, contrasted with the pride and luxury of the higher clergy, have rendered them perfectly disposed to humble the latter. They have done it, in many instances, with a boldness they were thought insusceptible of. Great hopes have been formed, that these would concur with the Tiers Etat, in voting by persons. In fact, about half of them seem as yet so disposed; but the bishops are intriguing, and drawing them over with the address which has ever marked ecclesiastical intrigue. The deputies of the Tiers Etat seem, almost to a man, inflexibly determined against the vote by orders. This is the state of parties, as well as can be judged from conversation only, during the fortnight they have been now together. But as no business has been yet begun, no votes as yet taken, this calculation cannot be considered as sure. A middle proposition is talked of, to form the two privileged orders into one chamber. It is thought more possible to bring them into it, than the Tiers Etat. Another proposition is, to distinguish questions, referring those of certain descriptions to a vote by persons, others to a vote by orders. This seems to admit of endless altercation, and the Tiers Etat manifest no respect for that, or any other modification whatever. Were this single question accommodated, I am of opinion, there would not occur the least difficulty in the great and essential points of constitutional reformation. But on this preliminary question the parties are so irreconcilable, that it is impossible to foresee what issue it will have. The Tiers Etat, as constituting the nation, may propose to do the business of the nation, either with or without the minorities in the Houses of Clergy and Nobles, which side with them. In that case, if the King should agree to it, the majorities in those two Houses would secede, and might resist the tax gatherers. This would bring on a civil war. On the other hand, the privileged orders, offering to submit to equal taxation, may propose to the King to continue the government in its former train, resuming to himself the power of taxation. Here, the tax gatherers might be resisted by the people. In fine, it is but too possible, that between parties so animated, the King may incline the balance as he pleases. Happy that he is an honest, unambitious man, who desires neither money nor power for himself; and that his most operative minister, though he has appeared to trim a little, is still, in the main, a friend to public liberty.

I mentioned to you in a former letter, the construction which our bankers at Amsterdam had put on the resolution of Congress, appropriating the last Dutch loan, by which the money for our captives would not be furnished till the end of the year 1790. Orders from the board of treasury, have now settled this question. The interest of the next month is to be first paid, and after that, the money for the captives and foreign officers is to be furnished, before any other payment of interest. This insures it when the next February interest becomes payable. My representations to them, on account of the contracts I had entered into for making the medals, have produced from them the money for that object, which is lodged in the hands of Mr. Grand.

Mr. Neckar, in his discourse, proposes among his bonifications of revenue, the suppression of our two free ports of Bayonne and L'Orient, which he says, occasion a loss of six hundred thousand livres annually, to the crown, by contraband. (The speech being not yet printed, I state this only as it struck my ear when he delivered it. If I have mistaken it, I beg you to receive this as my apology, and to consider what follows, as written on that idea only.) I have never been able to see that these free ports were worth one copper to us. To Bayonne our trade never went, and it is leaving L'Orient. Besides, the right of entrepôt is a perfect substitute for the right of free port. The latter is a little less troublesome only, to the merchants and captains. I should think, therefore, that a thing so useless to us and prejudicial to them might be relinquished by us, on the common principles of friendship. I know the merchants of these ports will make a clamour, because the franchise covers their contraband with all the world. Has Monsieur de Moustier said any thing to you on this subject? It has never been mentioned to me. If not mentioned in either way, it is rather an indecent proceeding, considering that this right of free port is founded in treaty. I shall ask of M. de Montmorin, on the first occasion, whether he has communicated this to you through his minister; and if he has not,

I will endeavor to notice the infraction to him in such manner, as neither to reclaim nor abandon the right of free port, but leave our government free to do either.

The gazettes of France and Leyden, as usual, will accompany this. I am in hourly expectation of receiving from you my leave of absence, and keep my affairs so arranged, that I can leave Paris within eight days after receiving the permission. I have the honor to be, with sentiments of the most perfect esteem and respect, Sir, your most obedient and most humble servant,

A CHARTER FOR FRANCE

To Rabout de St. Etienne, with Draft of a Charter of Rights

Paris, June 3, 1789

SIR,—After you quitted us yesterday evening, we continued our conversation (Mons.ʳ de la Fayette, Mr. Short & myself) on the subject of the difficulties which environ you. The desirable object being to secure the good which the King has offered & to avoid the ill which seems to threaten, an idea was suggested, which appearing to make an impression on Mons.ʳ de la Fayette, I was encouraged to pursue it on my return to Paris, to put it into form, & now to send it to you & him. It is this, that the King, in a *seance royale* should come forward with a Charter of Rights in his hand, to be signed by himself & by every member of the three orders. This charter to contain the five great points which the Resultat of December offered on the part of the King, the abolition of pecuniary privileges offered by the privileged orders, & the adoption of the National debt and a grant of the sum of money asked from the nation. This last will be a cheap price for the preceding articles, and let the same act declare your immediate separation till the next anniversary meeting. You will carry back to your constituents more good than ever was effected before without violence, and you will stop exactly at the point where violence would otherwise begin. Time will be gained, the public mind will continue to ripen & to be informed, a basis of support may be prepared with the people themselves, and expedients occur for gaining still something further at your next meeting, & for stopping again at the point of force. I have ventured to send to yourself & Monsieur de la Fayette a sketch of my ideas of what this act might contain without endangering any dispute. But it is offered merely as a canvas for you to work on, if it be fit to work on at all. I know too little of the subject, & you know too much of it to justify me in offering anything but a hint. I have done it too in a hurry: insomuch that since committing it to writing it occurs to me that the 5th. article may give alarm, that it is in a good degree included in the 4th., and is therefore useless. But after all what excuse can I make, Sir, for this presumption. I have none but an unmeasureable love for your nation and a painful anxiety lest Despotism, after an unaccepted offer to bind it's own hands, should seize you again with tenfold fury. Permit me to add to these very sincere assurances of the sentiments of esteem & respect with which I have the honor to be, Sir, Your most obed.t & most humble serv.t

A Charter of Rights, solemnly established by the King and Nation.

1. The States General shall assemble, uncalled, on the first day of November, annually, and shall remain together so long as they shall see cause. They shall regulate their own elections and proceedings, and until they shall ordain otherwise, their elections shall be in the forms observed in the present year, and shall be triennial.

2. The States General alone shall levy money on the nation, and shall appropriate it.

3. Laws shall be made by the States General only, with the consent of the King.

4. No person shall be restrained of his liberty, but by regular process from a court of justice, authorized by a general law. (Except that a Noble may be imprisoned by order of a court of justice, on the prayer of twelve of his nearest relations.) On complaint of an unlawful imprisonment, to any judge whatever, he shall have the prisoner immediately

brought before him, and shall discharge him, if his imprisonment be unlawful. The officer in whose custody the prisoner
is, shall obey the orders of the judge; and both judge and
officer shall be responsible, civilly and criminally, for a failure
of duty herein.

5. The military shall be subordinate to the civil authority.

6. Printers shall be liable to legal prosecution for printing
and publishing false facts, injurious to the party prosecuting;
but they shall be under no other restraint.

7. All pecuniary privileges and exemptions, enjoyed by any
description of persons, are abolished.

8. All debts already contracted by the King, are hereby
made the debts of the nation; and the faith thereof is pledged
for their payment in due time.

9. Eighty millions of livres are now granted to the King,
to be raised by loan, and reimbursed by the nation; and the
taxes heretofore paid, shall continue to be paid to the end of
the present year, and no longer.

10. The States General shall now separate, and meet again
on the 1st day of November next.

Done, on behalf of the whole nation, by the King and their
representatives in the States General, at Versailles, this ——
day of June, 1789.

Signed by the King, and by every member individually, and
in his presence.

To Diodati

à Paris, ce 3.me Aout 1789

Je viens de recevoir, mon chere Monsieur, l'honneur de
votre lettre du 24. Juillet. La peine avec laquelle je m'exprime
en François feroit que ma reponse seroit bien courte s'il ne
m'etoit pas permis de repondre que dans cette langue. Mais
je sçais qu'avec quelque connoissance de la langue Angloise
vous meme, vous aurez une aide tres suffisante dans Madame
la comtesse que j'ose prier d'ajouter a ses amitiés multipliées
devers moi celle de devenir l'interprete de ce que vais ecrire

en ma propre langue, et qu'elle embellira en la rendant en François.

I presume that your correspondents here have given you a history of all the events which have happened. The Leyden gazette, tho' it contains several inconsiderable errors, gives on the whole a just enough idea. It is impossible to conceive a greater fermentation than has worked in Paris, nor do I believe that so great a fermentation ever produced so little injury in any other place. I have been thro' it daily, have observed the mobs with my own eyes in order to be satisfied of their objects, and declare to you that I saw so plainly the legitimacy of them, that I have slept in my house as quietly thro' the whole as I ever did in the most peaceable moments. So strongly fortified was the despotism of this government by long possession, by the respect & the fears of the people, by possessing the public force, by the imposing authority of forms and of faste, that had it held itself on the defensive only, the national assembly with all their good sense, would probably have only obtained a considerable improvement of the government, not a total revision of it. But, ill informed of the spirit of their nation, the despots around the throne had recourse to violent measures, the forerunners of force. In this they have been completely overthrown, & the nation has made a total resumption of rights, which they had certainly never before ventured even to think of. The National assembly have now as clean a canvas to work on here as we had in America. Such has been the firmness and wisdom of their proceedings in moments of adversity as well as prosperity, that I have the highest confidence that they will use their power justly. As far as I can collect from conversation with their members, the constitution they will propose will resemble that of England in it's outlines, but not in it's defects. They will certainly leave the king possessed completely of the Executive powers, & particularly of the public force. Their legislature will consist of one order only, & not of two as in England: the representation will be equal & not abominably partial as that of England: it will be guarded against corruption, instead of having a majority sold to the king, & rendering his will absolute: whether it will be in one chamber, or broke into two cannot be foreseen. They will meet at certain epochs & sit as long as they please, instead of meeting only when, & sitting only as long as the king pleases as in England. There is a difference of opinion whether the king shall have an absolute, or only a qualified Negative on their acts. The parliaments will probably be suppressed; & juries provided in criminal cases perhaps even in civil ones. This is what appears probable at present. The Assembly is this day discussing the question whether they will have a declaration of rights. Paris has been led by events to assume the government of itself. It has hitherto worn too much the appearance of conformity to continue thus independently of the will of the nation. Reflection will probably make them sensible that the security of all depends on the dependance of all on the national legislature. I have so much confidence on the good sense of man, and his qualifications for self-government, that I am never afraid of the issue where reason is left free to exert her force; and I will agree to be stoned as a false prophet if all does not end well in this country. Nor will it end with this country. Hers is but the first chapter of the history of European liberty.

The capture of the Baron Besenval is very embarrassing for the States general. They are principled against retrospective laws, & will make it one of the corner stones of their new building. But it is very doubtful whether the antient laws will condemn him, and whether the people will permit him to be acquitted. The Duke de la Vauguyon also & his son are taken at Havre.—In drawing the parallel between what England is, & what France is to be I forgot to observe that the latter will have a real constitution, which cannot be changed by the ordinary legislature; whereas England has no constitution at all: that is to say there is not one principle of their government which the parliament does not alter at pleasure. The omnipotence of parliament is an established principle with them.— Postponing my departure to America till the end of September I shall hope to have the pleasure of seeing you at Paris before I go, & of renewing in person to yourself & Madame la Comtesse assurances of those sentiments of respect & attachment with which I have the honor to be Dear Sir your most obedient humble serv.ᵗ

P. S. It is rumored & beleived in Paris that the English have fomented with money the tumults of this place, & that they are arming to attack France. I have never seen any reason to believe either of these rumors.

"THE EARTH BELONGS TO THE LIVING"
To James Madison

Paris, September 6, 1789

DEAR SIR,—I sit down to write to you without knowing by what occasion I shall send my letter. I do it because a subject comes into my head which I would wish to develope a little more than is practicable in the hurry of the moment of making up general despatches.

The question Whether one generation of men has a right to bind another, seems never to have been started either on this or our side of the water. Yet it is a question of such consequences as not only to merit decision, but place also, among the fundamental principles of every government. The course of reflection in which we are immersed here on the elementary principles of society has presented this question to my mind; and that no such obligation can be transmitted I think very capable of proof. I set out on this ground which I suppose to be self evident, *"that the earth belongs in usufruct to the living;"* that the dead have neither powers nor rights over it. The portion occupied by an individual ceases to be his when himself ceases to be, and reverts to the society. If the society has formed no rules for the appropriation of its lands in severalty, it will be taken by the first occupants. These will generally be the wife and children of the decedent. If they have formed rules of appropriation, those rules may give it to the wife and children, or to some one of them, or to the legatee of the deceased. So they may give it to his creditor. But the child, the legatee or creditor takes it, not by any natural right, but by a law of the society of which they are members, and to which they are subject. Then no man can by *natural right* oblige the lands he occupied, or the persons who succeed him in that occupation, to the paiment of debts contracted by him. For if he could, he might during his own life, eat up the usufruct of the lands for several generations to come, and then the lands would belong to the dead, and not to the living, which would be reverse of our principle. What is true of every member of the society individually, is true of them all collectively, since the rights of the whole can be no more than the sum of the rights of individuals. To keep our ideas clear when applying them to a multitude, let us suppose a whole generation of men to be born on the same day, to attain mature age on the same day, and to die on the same day, leaving a succeeding generation in the moment of attaining their mature age all together. Let the ripe age be supposed of 21. years, and their period of life 34. years more, that being the average term given by the bills of mortality to persons who have already attained 21. years of age. Each successive generation would, in this way, come on and go off the stage at a fixed moment, as individuals do now. Then I say the earth belongs to each of these generations during it's course, fully, and in their own right. The 2d. generation receives it clear of the debts and incumbrances of the 1st., the 3d. of the 2d. and so on. For if the 1st. could charge it with a debt, then the earth would belong to the dead and not the living generation. Then no generation can contract debts greater than may be paid during the course of it's own existence. At 21. years of age they may bind themselves and their lands for 34. years to come: at 22. for 33: at 23 for 32. and at 54 for one year only; because these are the terms of life which remain to them at those respective epochs. But a material difference must be noted between the succession of an individual and that of a whole generation. Individuals are parts only of a society, subject to the laws of a whole. These laws may appropriate the portion of land occupied by a decedent to his creditor rather than to any other, or to his child, on condition he satisfies his creditor. But when a whole generation, that is, the whole society dies, as in the case we have supposed, and another generation or society succeeds, this forms a whole, and there is no superior who can give their territory to a third society, who may have lent money to their predecessors beyond their faculty of paying.

What is true of a generation all arriving to self-government on the same day, and dying all on the same day, is true of those on a constant course of decay and renewal, with this only difference. A generation coming in and going out entire, as in the first case, would have a right in the 1st year of their self dominion to contract a debt for 33. years, in the 10th. for 24. in the 20th. for 14. in the 30th. for 4. whereas generations changing daily, by daily deaths and births, have one constant term beginning at the date of their contract, and ending when a majority of those of full age at that date shall be dead. The length of that term may be estimated from the tables of mortality, corrected by the circumstances of climate, occupation &c. peculiar to the country of the contractors. Take, for instance, the table of M. de Buffon wherein he states that 23,994 deaths, and the ages at which they happened. Suppose a society in which 23,994 persons are born every year and live to the ages stated in this table. The conditions of that society will be as follows. 1st. it will consist constantly of 617,703 persons of all ages. 2dly. of those living at any one instant of time, one half will be dead in 24. years 8. months. 3dly. 10,675 will arrive every year at the age of 21. years complete. 4thly. it will constantly have 348,417 persons of all ages above 21. years. 5ly. and the half of those of 21. years and upwards living at any one instant of time will be dead in 18. years 8. months, or say 19. years as the nearest integral number. Then 19. years is the term beyond which neither the representatives of a nation, nor even the whole nation itself assembled, can validly extend a debt.

To render this conclusion palpable by example, suppose that Louis XIV. and XV. had contracted debts in the name of the French nation to the amount of 10.000 milliards of livres and that the whole had been contracted in Genoa. The interest of this sum would be 500 milliards, which is said to be the whole rent-roll, or nett proceeds of the territory of France. Must the present generation of men have retired from the territory in which nature produced them, and ceded it to the Genoese creditors? No. They have the same rights over the soil on which they were produced, as the preceding generations had. They derive these rights not from their predecessors, but from nature. They then and their soil are by nature clear of the debts of their predecessors. Again suppose

Louis XV. and his contemporary generation had said to the money lenders of Genoa, give us money that we may eat, drink, and be merry in our day; and on condition you will demand no interest till the end of 19. years, you shall then forever after receive an annual interest of* 12.^{5} per cent. The money is lent on these conditions, is divided among the living, eaten, drank, and squandered. Would the present generation be obliged to apply the produce of the earth and of their labour to replace their dissipations? Not at all.

I suppose that the received opinion, that the public debts of one generation devolve on the next, has been suggested by our seeing habitually in private life that he who succeeds to lands is required to pay the debts of his ancestor or testator, without considering that this requisition is municipal only, not moral, flowing from the will of the society which has found it convenient to appropriate the lands become vacant by the death of their occupant on the condition of a paiment of his debts; but that between society and society, or generation and generation there is no municipal obligation, no umpire but the law of nature. We seem not to have perceived that, by the law of nature, one generation is to another as one independant nation to another.

The interest of the national debt of France being in fact but a two thousandth part of it's rent-roll, the paiment of it is practicable enough; and so becomes a question merely of honor or expediency. But with respect to future debts; would it not be wise and just for that nation to declare in the constitution they are forming that neither the legislature, nor the nation itself can validly contract more debt, than they may pay within their own age, or within the term of 19. years? And that all future contracts shall be deemed void as to what shall remain unpaid at the end of 19. years from their date? This would put the lenders, and the borrowers also, on their guard. By reducing too the faculty of borrowing within its natural limits, it would bridle the spirit of war, to which too free a course has been procured by the inattention of money

---

*100£ at a compound interest of 6 per cent makes at the end of 19 years an aggregate of principal and interest of £252.14 the interest of which is a £12.^{00} 12.$''$ 7^d which is nearly 12.$''$ p^r cent on the first capital of £100.

lenders to this law of nature, that succeeding generations are not responsible for the preceding.

On similar ground it may be proved that no society can make a perpetual constitution, or even a perpetual law. The earth belongs always to the living generation. They may manage it then, and what proceeds from it, as they please, during their usufruct. They are masters too of their own persons, and consequently may govern them as they please. But persons and property make the sum of the objects of government. The constitution and the laws of their predecessors extinguished them, in their natural course, with those whose will gave them being. This could preserve that being till it ceased to be itself, and no longer. Every constitution, then, and every law, naturally expires at the end of 19. years. If it be enforced longer, it is an act of force and not of right.

It may be said that the succeeding generation exercising in fact the power of repeal, this leaves them as free as if the constitution or law had been expressly limited to 19. years only. In the first place, this objection admits the right, in proposing an equivalent. But the power of repeal is not an equivalent. It might be indeed if every form of government were so perfectly contrived that the will of the majority could always be obtained fairly and without impediment. But this is true of no form. The people cannot assemble themselves; their representation is unequal and vicious. Various checks are opposed to every legislative proposition. Factions get possession of the public councils. Bribery corrupts them. Personal interests lead them astray from the general interests of their constituents; and other impediments arise so as to prove to every practical man that a law of limited duration is much more manageable than one which needs a repeal.

This principle that the earth belongs to the living and not to the dead is of very extensive application and consequences in every country, and most especially in France. It enters into the resolution of the questions Whether the nation may change the descent of lands holden in tail? Whether they may change the appropriation of lands given antiently to the church, to hospitals, colleges, orders of chivalry, and otherwise in perpetuity? whether they may abolish the charges and privileges attached on lands, including the whole catalogue

ecclesiastical and feudal? it goes to hereditary offices, authorities and jurisdictions; to hereditary orders, distinctions and
appellations; to perpetual monopolies in commerce, the arts
or sciences; with a long train of *et ceteras*: and it renders the
question of reimbursement a question of generosity and not
of right. In all these cases the legislature of the day could
authorize such appropriations and establishments for their
own time, but no longer; and the present holders, even where
they or their ancestors have purchased, are in the case of *bona
fide* purchasers of what the seller had no right to convey.

Turn this subject in your mind, my Dear Sir, and particularly as to the power of contracting debts, and develope it
with that perspicuity and cogent logic which is so peculiarly
yours. Your station in the councils of our country gives you
an opportunity of producing it to public consideration, of
forcing it into discussion. At first blush it may be rallied as a
theoretical speculation; but examination will prove it to be
solid and salutary. It would furnish matter for a fine preamble
to our first law for appropriating the public revenue; and it
will exclude, at the threshold of our new government the contagious and ruinous errors of this quarter of the globe, which
have armed despots with means not sanctioned by nature for
binding in chains their fellow-men. We have already given, in
example one effectual check to the Dog of war, by transferring the power of letting him loose from the executive to the
Legislative body, from those who are to spend to those who
are to pay. I should be pleased to see this second obstacle held
out by us also in the first instance. No nation can make a
declaration against the validity of long-contracted debts so
disinterestedly as we, since we do not owe a shilling which
may not be paid with ease principal and interest, within the
time of our own lives. Establish the principle also in the new
law to be passed for protecting copy rights and new inventions, by securing the exclusive right for 19. instead of 14.
years [*a line entirely faded*] an instance the more of our taking
reason for our guide instead of English precedents, the habit
of which fetters us, with all the political herecies of a nation,
equally remarkable for it's encitement from some errors, as
long slumbering under others. I write you no news, because
when an occasion occurs I shall write a separate letter for that.

ADIEU TO FRANCE
To Madame d'Enville

New York, April 2, 1790

I had hoped, Madame la Duchesse, to have again had the honor of paying my respects to you in Paris, but the wish of our government that I should take a share in its administration, has become a law to me. Could I have persuaded myself that public offices were made for private convenience, I should undoubtedly have preferred a continuance in that which placed me nearer to you; but believing on the contrary that a good citizen should take his stand where the public authority marshals him, I have acquiesced. Among the circumstances which reconcile me to my new position the most powerful is the opportunities it will give me of cementing the friendship between our two nations. Be assured that to do this is the first wish of my heart. I have but one system of ethics for men & for nations—to be grateful, to be faithful to all engagements and under all circumstances, to be open & generous, promotes in the long run even the interests of both; and I am sure it promotes their happiness. The change in your government will approximate us to one another. You have had some checks, some horrors since I left you; but the way to heaven, you know, has always been said to be strewed with thorns. Why your nation have had fewer than any other on earth, I do not know, unless it be that it is the best on earth. If I assure you, Madam, moreover, that I consider yourself personally as with the foremost of your nation in every virtue, it is not flattery, my heart knows not that, it is a homage to sacred truth, it is a tribute I pay with cordiality to a character in which I saw but one error; it was that of treating me with a degree of favor I did not merit. Be assured I shall ever retain a lively sense of all your goodness to me, which was a circumstance of principal happiness to me during my stay in Paris. I hope that by this time you have seen that my prognostications of a successful issue to your revolution have been verified. I feared for you during a short interval; but after the declaration of the army, tho' there might be episodes of distress, the denoument was out of doubt. Heaven send that the glorious example of your country may be but the beginning of the history of European liberty, and that you may live many years in health & happiness to see at length that heaven did not make man in it's wrath. Accept the homage of those sentiments of sincere and respectfull esteem with which I have the honor to be, Madame la Duchesse, your most affectionate & obedient humble servant.

READING THE LAW

To John Garland Jefferson

New York, June 11, 1790

DEAR SIR,—Your uncle mr Garland informs me, that, your education being finished, you are desirous of obtaining some clerkship or something else under government whereby you may turn your talents to some account for yourself and he had supposed it might be in my power to provide you with some such office. His commendations of you are such as to induce me to wish sincerely to be of service to you. But there is not, and has not been, a single vacant office at my disposal. Nor would I, as your friend, ever think of putting you into the petty clerkships in the several offices, where you would have to drudge through life for a miserable pittance, without a hope of bettering your situation. But he tells me you are also disposed to the study of the law. This therefore brings it more within my power to serve you. It will be necessary for you in that case to go and live somewhere in my neighborhood in Albemarle. The inclosed letter to Colo. Lewis near Charlottesville will show you what I have supposed could be best done for you there. It is a general practice to study the law in the office of some lawyer. This indeed gives to the student the advantage of his instruction. But I have ever seen that the services expected in return have been more than the instructions have been worth. All that is necessary for a student is access to a library, and directions in what order the books are to be read. This I will take the liberty of suggesting to you, observing previously that as other branches of science, and especially history, are necessary to form a lawyer, these must be carried on together. I will arrange the books to be read into three columns, and propose that you should read those in the first column till 12. oclock every day: those in the 2d. from 12. to 2. those in the 3d. after candlelight, leaving all the afternoon for exercise and recreation, which are as necessary as reading: I will rather say more necessary, because health is worth more than learning.

1st.	2d.	3d.
Coke on Littleton	Dalrymple's feudal system.	Mallet's North antiquit'.
Coke's 2d. 3d. & 4th. institutes.	Hale's history of the Com. law.	
Coke's reports.	Gilbert on Devises	History of England in 3. vols folio compiled by Kennet.
Vaughan's do	Uses.	
Salkeld's	Tenures.	
	Rents	Ludlow's memoirs
Ld. Raymond's	Distresses.	
	Ejectments.	Burnet's history.
Strange's.	Executions.	
	Evidence.	Ld. Orrery's history.
Burrows's	Sayer's law of costs.	Burke's George III.
Kaim's Principles of equity.	Lambard's circonantia.	Robertson's hist. of Scotl'd
Vernon's reports.	Bacon. voce Pleas & Pleadings.	Robertson's hist. of America.
Peere Williams.	Cunningham's law of bills.	
Precedents in Chancery.		Other American histories.
	Molloy de jure maritimo.	
Tracy Atheyns.	Locke on government.	Voltaire's historical works.
Verey.	Montesquieu's Spirit of law.	
	Smith's wealth of nations.	
Hawkin's Pleas of the crown.	Beccaria.	
Blackstone.	Kaim's moral essays.	
Virginia laws.	Vattel's law of nations.	

Should there be any little intervals in the day not otherwise occupied fill them up by reading Lowthe's grammar, Blair's lectures on rhetoric, Mason on poetic & prosaic numbers, Bolingbroke's works for the sake of the stile, which is declamatory & elegant, the English poets for the sake of the style also.

As mr Peter Carr in Goochland is engaged in a course of law reading, and has my books for that purpose, it will be necessary for you to go to mrs Carr's, and to receive such as he shall be then done with, and settle with him a plan of receiving from him regular the before mentioned books as fast as he shall get through them. The losses I have sustained by lending my books will be my apology to you for asking your particular attention to the replacing them in the presses as fast as you finish them, and not to lend them to any body else, nor suffer anybody to have a book out of the Study under cover of your name. You will find, when you get there, that I have had reason to ask this exactness.

I would have you determine beforehand to make yourself a thorough lawyer, & not be contented with a mere smattering. It is superiority of knowledge which can alone lift you above the heads of your competitors, and ensure you success. I think therefore you must calculate on devoting between two & three years to this course of reading, before you think of commencing practice. Whenever that begins, there is an end of reading.

I shall be glad to hear from you from time to time, and shall hope to see you in the fall in Albemarle, to which place I propose a visit in that season. In the mean time wishing you all the industry of patient perseverance which this course of reading will require I am with great esteem Dear Sir Your most obedient friend & servant.

WHIPPOORWILLS AND STRAWBERRIES

To Mary Jefferson

New York, June 13, 1790

MY DEAR MARIA—I have recieved your letter of May 23. which was in answer to mine of May 2. but I wrote you also on the 23d. of May, so that you still owe me an answer to that, which I hope is now on the road. In matters of correspondence as well as of money you must never be in debt. I am much pleased with the account you give me of your occupations, and the making the pudding is as good an article of them as any. When I come to Virginia I shall insist on eating a pudding of your own making, as well as on trying other specimens of your skill. You must make the most of your time while you are with so good an aunt who can learn you every thing. We had not peas nor strawberries here till the 8th. day of this month. On the same day I heard the first Whip-poor-will whistle. Swallows and martins appeared here on the 21st. of April. When did they appear with you? And when had you peas, strawberries, and whip-poor-wills in Virginia? Take notice hereafter whether the whip-poor-wills always come with the strawberries and peas. Send me a copy of the maxims I gave you, also a list of the books I promised you. I have had a long touch of my periodical headach, but a very moderate one. It has not quite left me yet. Adieu, my dear, love your uncle, aunt and cousins, and me more than all. Your's affectionately,

RICE FROM TIMOR AND AFRICA
To Samuel Vaughan, Jr.

Philadelphia, Nov. 27, 1790

DEAR SIR—I feel myself much indebted to Mr. Vaughan your father for the opportunity he has furnished me of a direct correspondence with you, and also to yourself for the seeds of the Mountain rice you have been so good as to send me. I had before received from your brother in London some of the same parcel brought by Capt. Bligh; but it was so late in the spring of the present year that tho the plants came up and grew luxuriantly, they did not produce seed. Your present will enable me to enlarge the experiment I propose for the next year, and for which I had still reserved a few seeds of the former parcel. About two months ago I was fortunate enough to recieve a cask of mountain rice from the coast of Africa. This has enabled me to engage so many persons in the experiment as to be tolerably sure it will be fairly made by some of them. It will furnish also a comparison with that from Timor.

I have the success of this species of rice at heart, because it will not only enable other states to cultivate rice which have not lands susceptible of inundation but because also if the rice be as good as is said, it may take place of the wet rice in the Southern states, & by superseding the necessity of overflowing their lands, save them from the pestilential & mortal fevers brought on by that operation.

We have lately had introduced a plant of the Melon species which, from it's external resemblance to the pumpkin, we have called a pumpkin, distinguishing it specifically as the *potatoe-pumpkin*, on account of the extreme resemblance of it's taste to that of the sweet-potatoe. It is as yet but little known, is well esteemed at our table, and particularly valued by our negroe's. Coming much earlier than the real potatoe, we are so much the sooner furnished with a substitute for that root. I know not from whence it came; so that perhaps it may be originally from your islands. In that case you will only have the trouble of throwing away the few seeds I enclose you herewith. On the other hand, if unknown with you, I think it will probably succeed in the islands, and may add to the catalogue of plants which will do as substitutes for bread. I have always thought that if in the experiments to introduce or to communicate new plants, one species in an hundred is found useful & succeeds, the ninety nine found otherwise are more than paid for. My present situation & occupations are not friendly to agricultural experiments, however strongly I am led to them by inclination. I will ask permission to address myself to you for such seeds as might be worth trying from your quarter, freely offering you reciprocal services in the same or any other line in which you will be so good as to command them. I have the honor to be with great respect & esteem, Sir Your most obedt. & most humble servt,

"A SCOLDING LETTER"

To Martha Jefferson Randolph

Philadelphia, Dec. 23, 1790

MY DEAR DAUGHTER—This is a scolding letter for you all. I have not recieved a scrip of a pen from home since I left it which is now eleven weeks. I think it so easy for you to write me one letter every week, which will be but once in three weeks for each of you, when I write one every week who have not one moment's repose from business from the first to the last moment of the week. Perhaps you think you have nothing to say to me. It is a great deal to say you are all well, or that one has a cold, another a fever &c., besides that there is not a sprig of grass that shoots uninteresting to me, nor any thing that moves, from yourself down to Bergere or Grizzle. Write then my dear daughter punctually on your day, and Mr. Randolph and Polly on theirs. I suspect you may have news to tell me of yourself of the most tender interest to me. Why silent then?

I am still without a house, and consequently without a place to open my furniture. This has prevented my sending you what I was to send for Monticello. In the mean time the river is frozen up so as that no vessel can get out, nor probably will these two months: so that you will be much longer without them than I had hoped. I know how inconvenient this will be and am distressed at it; but there is no help. I send a pamphlet for Mr. Randolph. My best affections to him, Polly and yourself. Adieu my dear,

A HERETICAL SECT
To George Mason

Philadelphia, Feb. 4, 1791

DEAR SIR,—I am to make you my acknowledgments for your favor of Jan. 10, & the information from France which it contained. It confirmed what I had heard more loosely before, and accounts still more recent are to the same effect. I look with great anxiety for the firm establishment of the new government in France, being perfectly convinced that if it takes place there, it will spread sooner or later all over Europe. On the contrary a check there would retard the revival of liberty in other countries. I consider the establishment and success of their government as necessary to stay up our own, and to prevent it from falling back to that kind of Half-way

house, the English constitution. It cannot be denied that we
have among us a sect who believe that to contain whatever is
perfect in human institutions; that the members of this sect
have, many of them, names & offices which stand high in the
estimation of our countrymen. I still rely that the great mass
of our community is untainted with these heresies, as is it's
head. On this I build my hope that we have not laboured in
vain, and that our experiment will still prove that men can be
governed by reason. You have excited my curiosity in saying
"there is a particular circumstance, little attended to, which is
continually sapping the republicanism of the United States."
What is it? What is said in our country of the fiscal arrangements now going on? I really fear their effect when I consider
the present temper of the Southern states. Whether these
measures be right or wrong abstractedly, more attention
should be paid to the general opinion. However, all will
pass—the excise will pass—the bank will pass. The only corrective of what is corrupt in our present form of government
will be the augmentation of the numbers in the lower house,
so as to get a more agricultural representation, which may put
that interest above that of the stock-jobbers.

I had no occasion to sound Mr. Madison on your fears
expressed in your letter. I knew before, as possessing his sentiments fully on that subject, that his value for you was undiminished. I have always heard him say that though you and
he appeared to differ in your systems, yet you were in truth
nearer together than most persons who were classed under
the same appellation. You may quiet yourself in the assurance
of possessing his complete esteem. I have been endeavoring
to obtain some little distinction for our useful customers, the
French. But there is a particular interest opposed to it, which
I fear will prove too strong. We shall soon see. I will send you
a copy of a report I have given in, as soon as it is printed. I
know there is one part of it contrary to your sentiments; yet
I am not sure you will not become sensible that a change
should be slowly preparing. Certainly, whenever I pass your
road, I shall do myself the pleasure of turning into it. Our last
year's experiment, however, is much in favor of that by
Newgate.

MONUMENTS OF THE PAST
To Ebenezer Hazard

Philadelphia, February 18, 1791

SIR,—I return you the two volumes of records, with thanks for the opportunity of looking into them. They are curious monuments of the infancy of our country. I learn with great satisfaction that you are about committing to the press the valuable historical and State papers you have been so long collecting. Time and accident are committing daily havoc on the originals deposited in our public offices. The late war has done the work of centuries in this business. The last cannot be recovered, but let us save what remains; not by vaults and locks which fence them from the public eye and use in consigning them to the waste of time, but by such a multiplication of copies, as shall place them beyond the reach of accident. This being the tendency of your undertaking, be assured there is no one who wishes it more success than, Sir, your most obedient and most humble servant.

MEMORIES OF FRANKLIN
To the Rev. William Smith

Philadelphia, Feb. 19, 1791

DEAR SIR,—I feel both the wish & the duty to communicate, in compliance with your request, whatever, within my knowledge, might render justice to the memory of our great countryman, Dr Franklin, in whom Philosophy has to deplore one of it's principal luminaries extinguished. But my opportunities of knowing the interesting facts of his life have not been equal to my desire of making them known. I could indeed relate a number of those bon mots, with which he used to charm every society, as having heard many of them. But these are not your object. Particulars of greater dignity happened not to occur during his stay of nine months, after my arrival in France.

A little before that, Argand had invented his celebrated lamp, in which the flame is spread into a hollow cylinder, &

thus brought into contact with the air within as well as without. Doct^r Franklin had been on the point of the same discovery. The idea had occurred to him; but he had tried a bull-rush as a wick, which did not succeed. His occupations did not permit him to repeat & extend his trials to the introduction of a larger column of air than could pass through the stem of a bull-rush.

The animal magnetism too of the maniac Mesmer, had just received its death wound from his hand in conjunction with his brethren of the learned committee appointed to unveil that compound of fraud & folly. But, after this, nothing very interesting was before the public, either in philosophy or politics, during his stay; & he was principally occupied in winding up his affairs there.

I can only therefore testify in general that there appeared to me more respect & veneration attached to the character of Doctor Franklin in France, than to that of any other person in the same country, foreign or native. I had opportunities of knowing particularly how far these sentiments were felt by the foreign ambassadors & ministers at the court of Versailles. The fable of his capture by the Algerines, propagated by the English newspapers, excited no uneasiness; as it was seen at once to be a dish cooked up to the palate of their readers. But nothing could exceed the anxiety of his diplomatic brethren, on a subsequent report of his death, which, tho' premature, bore some marks of authenticity.

I found the ministers of France equally impressed with the talents & integrity of Doct^r Franklin. The C^t de Vergennes particularly gave me repeated and unequivocal demonstrations of his entire confidence in him.

When he left Passy, it seemed as if the village had lost its patriarch. On taking leave of the court, which he did by letter, the King ordered him to be handsomely complimented, & furnished him with a litter & mules of his own, the only kind of conveyance the state of his health could bear.

No greater proof of his estimation in France can be given than the late letters of condolence on his death, from the National Assembly of that country, & the Community of Paris, to the President of the United States, & to Congress, and their public mourning on that event. It is, I believe, the first instance of that homage having been paid by a public body of one nation to a private citizen of another.

His death was an affliction which was to happen to us at some time or other. We have reason to be thankful he was so long spared; that the most useful life should be the longest also; that it was protracted so far beyond the ordinary span allotted to man, as to avail us of his wisdom in the establishment of our own freedom, & to bless him with a view of its dawn in the east, where they seemed, till now, to have learned everything, but how to be free.

The succession to Dr Franklin, at the court of France, was an excellent school of humility. On being presented to any one as the minister of America, the commonplace question used in such cases was *"c'est vous, Monsieur, qui remplace le Docteur Franklin?"* "it is you, Sir, who replace Doctor Franklin?" I generally answered, "no one can replace him, Sir: I am only his successor."

These small offerings to the memory of our great & dear friend, whom time will be making greater while it is spunging us from it's records, must be accepted by you, Sir, in that spirit of love & veneration for him, in which they are made; and not according to their insignificance in the eyes of a world, who did not want this mite to fill up the measure of his worth.

CAPITOL ON THE POTOMAC
To Major L'Enfant

Philadelphia, April 10, 1791

SIR,—I am favored with your letter of the 4th instant, and in compliance with your request, I have examined my papers, and found the plans of Frankfort-on-the-Mayne, Carlsruhe, Amsterdam, Strasburg, Paris, Orleans, Bordeaux, Lyons, Montpelier, Marseilles, Turin, and Milan, which I send in a roll by the post. They are on large and accurate scales, having been procured by me while in those respective cities myself. As they are connected with the notes I made in my travels, and often necessary to explain them to myself, I will beg your care of them, and to return them when no longer useful to you, leaving you absolutely free to keep them as long as useful. I am happy that the President has left the planning of the town in such good hands, and have no doubt it will be done to general satisfaction. Considering that the grounds to be reserved for the public are to be paid for by the acre, I think very liberal reservations should be made for them; and if this be about the Tyber and on the back of the town, it will be of no injury to the commerce of the place, which will undoubtedly establish itself on the deep waters towards the eastern branch and mouth of Rock Creek; the water about the mouth of the Tyber not being of any depth. Those connected with the government will prefer fixing themselves near the public grounds in the centre, which will also be convenient to be resorted to as walks from the lower and upper town. Having communicated to the President, before he went away, such general ideas on the subject of the town as occurred to me, I make no doubt that, in explaining himself to you on the subject, he has interwoven with his own ideas, such of mine as he approved. For fear of repeating therefore what he did not approve, and having more confidence in the unbiassed state of his mind, than in my own, I avoided interfering with what he may have expressed to you. Whenever it is proposed to prepare plans for the Capitol, I should prefer the adoption of some one of the models of antiquity, which have had the approbation of thousands of years; and for the President's house, I should prefer the celebrated fronts of modern buildings, which have already received the approbation of all good judges. Such are the Galerie du Louire, the Gardes meubles, and two fronts of the Hotel de Salm. But of this it is yet time enough to consider. In the meantime I am, with great esteem, Sir, your most obedient humble servant.

A NOTE ON INDIAN POLICY
To Charles Carroll

Philadelphia, April 15, 1791

DEAR SIR,—I received last night your favor of the 10th, with Mr. Brown's receipt, and thank you for the trouble you have been so kind as to take in this business.

Our news from the westward is disagreeable. Constant murders committing by the Indians, and their combination threatens to be more and more extensive. I hope we shall give them a thorough drubbing this summer, and then change our tomahawk into a golden chain of friendship. The most economical as well as most humane conduct towards them is to bribe them into peace, and to retain them in peace by eternal bribes. The expedition this year would have served for presents on the most liberal scale for one hundred years; nor shall we otherwise ever get rid of any army, or of our debt. The least rag of Indian depredation will be an excuse to raise troops for those who love to have troops, and for those who think that a public debt is a good thing. Adieu, my dear Sir. Yours affectionately.

BURKE, PAINE, AND MR. ADAMS

To the President of the United States
(GEORGE WASHINGTON)

Philadelphia, May 8, 1791

SIR,—The last week does not furnish one single public event worthy communicating to you: so that I have only to say "all is well." Paine's answer to Burke's pamphlet begins to produce some squibs in our public papers. In Fenno's paper they are Burkites, in the others, Painites. One of Fenno's was evidently from the author of the discourses on Davila. I am afraid the indiscretion of a printer has committed me with my friend Mr. Adams, for whom, as one of the most honest & disinterested men alive, I have a cordial esteem, increased by long habits of concurrence in opinion in the days of his republicanism; and even since his apostacy to hereditary monarchy & nobility, tho' we differ, we differ as friends should do. Beckley had the only copy of Paine's pamphlet, & lent it to me, desiring when I should have read it, that I would send it to a Mr. J. B. Smith, who had asked it for his brother to reprint it. Being an utter stranger to J. B. Smith, both by sight & character I wrote a note to explain to him why I (a stranger to him) sent him a pamphlet, to wit, that Mr. Beckley had desired it; & to take off a little of the dryness of the note, I added that I was glad to find it was to be reprinted, that something would at length be publicly said against the political heresies which had lately sprung up among us, & that I did not doubt our citizens would rally again round the standard of common sense. That I had in my view the Discourses on Davila, which have filled Fenno's papers, for a twelvemonth, without contradiction, is certain, but nothing was ever further from my thoughts than to become myself the contradictor before the public. To my great astonishment however, when the pamphlet came out, the printer had prefixed my note to it, without having given me the most distant hint of it. Mr. Adams will unquestionably take to himself the charge of political heresy, as conscious of his own views of drawing the present government to the form of the English constitution, and, I fear will consider me as meaning to injure him in the public eye. I learn that some Anglo men have censured it in another point of view, as a sanction of Paine's principles tends to give offence to the British government. Their real fear however is that this popular & republican pamphlet, taking wonderfully, is likely at a single stroke to wipe out all the unconstitutional doctrines which their bell-weather Davila has been preaching for a twelvemonth. I certainly never made a secret of my being anti-monarchical, & anti-aristocratical; but I am sincerely mortified to be thus brought forward on the public stage, where to remain, to advance or to retire, will be equally against my love of silence & quiet, & my abhorrence of dispute.—I do not know whether you recollect that the records of Virginia were destroyed by the British in the year 1781. Particularly the transactions of the revolution before that time. I am collecting here all the letters I wrote to Congress while I was in the administration there, and this being done I shall then extend my views to the transactions of my predecessors, in order to replace the whole in the public offices in Virginia. I think that during my administration, say between June 1. 1779. & June 1. 1781. I had the honor of writing frequent letters to you on public affairs, which perhaps may be among your papers at Mount Vernon. Would it be consistent with any general resolution you have formed as to your papers, to let my letters of the above period come here to be copied, in order to make them a part of the records I am endeavoring to restore for the state? or would their selection be too troublesome? if not, I would beg the loan of them, under an assurance that they shall be taken the utmost care of, & safely returned to their present deposit.

The quiet & regular movements of our political affairs leaves nothing to add but constant prayers for your health & welfare and assurances of the sincere respect & attachment of Sir Your most obedient, & most humble servt.

A NORTHERN TOUR

To Thomas Mann Randolph

Bennington, in Vermont, June 5, 1791

DEAR SIR,—Mr. Madison & myself are so far on the tour we had projected. We have visited in the course of it the principal scenes of Genl. Burgoyne's misfortunes to wit the grounds at Stillwater where the action of that name was fought, & particularly the breastworks which cost so much blood to both parties, the encampments at Saratoga & ground where the British piled their arms, the field of the battle of Bennington about 9 miles from this place. We have also visited Forts Wm. Henry & George, Ticonderoga, Crown point, &c. which have been scenes of blood from a very early part of our history. We were more pleased however with the botanical objects which continually presented themselves. Those either unknown or rare in Virgna were the Sugar maple in vast abundance, the Silver fir, White pine, Pitch pine, Spruce pine, a shrub with decumbent stems which they call Juniper, an azalea very different from the nudiflora, with very large clusters of flowers, more thickly set on the branches, of a deeper red, & high pink-fragrance. It is the richest shrub I have seen. The honeysuckle of the gardens growing wild on the banks' of L. George, the paper-birch, an Aspen with a velvet leaf, a shrub-willow with downy catkins, a wild gooseberry, the wild cherry with single fruit (not the bunch cherry) strawberries in abundance. From the Highlands to the lakes it is a limestone country. It is in vast quantities on the Eastern sides of the lakes, but none on the Western sides. The Sandy hill falls & Wing's falls, two very remarkable cataracts of the Hudson of about 35 f. or 40 f. each between F. Edward & F. George are of limestone, in horizontal strata. Those of the Cohoes, on the W. side of the Hudson, & of 70 f. height, we thought not of limestone. We have met with a small red squirrel of the color of our fox-squirrel, with a black stripe on each side, weighing about 6 oz. generally, and in such abundance on L. Champlain particularly as that twenty odd were killed at the house we lodged in opposite Crown point the morning we arrived there, without going 10 yards from the door. We killed 3 crossing the lakes, one of them just as he was getting ashore where it was 3 miles wide, & where with the high wind then blowing he must have made it 5 or 6 miles.

I think I asked the favr. of you to send for Anthony in the season for inoculn, as well as to do what is necessary in the orchard, as to pursue the object of inoculating all the Spontaneous cherry trees in the fields with good fruit.

We have now got over about 400 miles of our tour and have still about 450 more to go over. Arriving here on the Saturday evening, and the laws of the state not permitting us to travel on the Sunday, has given me time to write to you from hence. I expect to be at Philadelphia by the 20th or 21st. I am, with great & sincere esteem Dear Sir yours affectionately.

BREACH OF A FRIENDSHIP

To John Adams

Philadelphia, July 17, 1791

DEAR SIR—I have a dozen times taken up my pen to write to you and as often laid it down again, suspended between opposing considerations. I determine however to write from a conviction that truth, between candid minds, can never do harm.

The first of Paine's pamphlets on the Rights of man, which came to hand here, belonged to Mr. Beckley. He lent it to

Mr. Madison who lent it to me; and while I was reading it Mr. Beckley called on me for it, and, as I had not finished it, he desired me, as soon as I should have done so, to send it to Mr. Jonathan B. Smith, whose brother meant to reprint it. I finished reading it, and, as I had no acquaintance with Mr. Jonathan B. Smith, propriety required that I should explain to him why I, a stranger to him, sent him the pamphlet. I accordingly wrote a note of compliment informing him that I did it at the desire of Mr. Beckley, and, to take off a little of the dryness of the note, I added that I was glad it was to be reprinted here, and that something was to be publicly said against the political heresies which had sprung up among us etc. I thought so little of this note that I did not even keep a copy of it: nor ever heard a tittle more of it till, the week following, I was thunderstruck with seeing it come out at the head of the pamphlet. I hoped however it would not attract notice. But I found on my return from a journey of a month that a writer came forward under the signature of Publicola, attacking not only the author and principles of the pamphlet, but myself as it's sponsor, by name. Soon after came hosts of other writers defending the pamphlet and attacking you by name as the writer of Publicola. Thus were our names thrown on the public stage as public antagonists. That you and I differ in our ideas of the best form of government is well known to us both: but we have differed as friends should do, respecting the purity of each other's motives, and confining our difference of opinion to private conversation. And I can declare with truth in the presence of the almighty that nothing was further from my intention or expectation than to have had either my own or your name brought before the public on this occasion. The friendship and confidence which has so long existed between us required this explanation from me, and I know you too well to fear any misconstruction of the motives of it. Some people here who would wish me to be, or to be thought, guilty of improprieties, have suggested that I was Agricola, that I was Brutus etc. etc. I never did in my life, either by myself or by any other, have a sentence of mine inserted in a newspaper without putting my name to it; and I believe I never shall.

While the empress is refusing peace under a mediation unless Oczakow and it's territory be ceded to her, she is offering
peace on the perfect statu quo to the Porte, if they will conclude it without a mediation. France has struck a severe blow
at our navigation by a difference of duty on tob[acc]o carried
in our and their ships, and by taking from foreign built ships
the capability of naturalization. She has placed our whale oil
on rather a better footing than ever by consolidating the duties into a single one of 6. livres. They amounted before to
some sous over that sum. I am told (I know not how truly)
that England has prohibited our spermaceti oil altogether,
and will prohibit our wheat till the price there is 52/ the
quarter, which it almost never is. We expect hourly to hear
the true event of Genl. Scott's expedition. Reports give favorable hopes of it. Be so good as to present my respectful
compliments to Mrs. Adams and to accept assurances of the
sentiments of sincere esteem and respect with which I am
Dear Sir Your friend and servant.

HOPE FOR "OUR BLACK BRETHREN"

To Benjamin Banneker

Philadelphia, Aug. 30, 1791

SIR,—I thank you sincerely for your letter of the 19th instant
and for the Almanac it contained. No body wishes more than
I do to see such proofs as you exhibit, that nature has given
to our black brethren, talents equal to those of the other colors of men, and that the appearance of a want of them is
owing merely to the degraded condition of their existence,
both in Africa & America. I can add with truth, that no body
wishes more ardently to see a good system commenced for
raising the condition both of their body & mind to what it
ought to be, as fast as the imbecility of their present existence,
and other circumstances which cannot be neglected, will admit. I have taken the liberty of sending your Almanac to
Monsieur de Condorcet, Secretary of the Academy of Sciences at Paris, and member of the Philanthropic society, because I considered it as a document to which your whole

colour had a right for their justification against the doubts which have been entertained of them. I am with great esteem, Sir Your most obed^r humble serv^t.

STRENGTHENING THE STATE GOVERNMENTS
To Archibald Stuart

Philadelphia, Dec. 23, 1791

DEAR SIR,—I received duly your favor of Octob 22. and should have answered it by the gentleman who delivered it, but that he left town before I knew of it.

That it is really important to provide a constitution for our state cannot be doubted: as little can it be doubted that the ordinance called by that name has important defects. But before we attempt it, we should endeavor to be as certain as is practicable that in the attempt we should not make bad worse. I have understood that Mr. Henry has always been opposed to this undertaking: and I confess that I consider his talents and influence such as that, were it decided that we should call a Convention for the purpose of amending, I should fear he might induce that convention either to fix the thing as at present, or change it for the worse. Would it not therefore be well that means should be adopted for coming at his ideas of the changes he would agree to, & for communicating to him those which we should propose? Perhaps he might find ours not so distant from his but that some mutual sacrifices might bring them together.

I shall hazard my own ideas to you as hastily as my business obliges me. I wish to preserve the line drawn by the federal constitution between the general & particular governments as it stands at present, and to take every prudent means of preventing either from stepping over it. Tho' the experiment has not yet had a long enough course to shew us from which quarter encroachments are most to be feared, yet it is easy to foresee from the nature of things that the encroachments of the state governments will tend to an excess of liberty which will correct itself (as in the late instance) while those of the general government will tend to monarchy, which will fortify itself from day to day, instead of working its own cure, as all experience shews. I would rather be exposed to the inconveniencies attending too much liberty than those attending too small a degree of it. Then it is important to strengthen the state governments: and as this cannot be done by any change in the federal constitution, (for the preservation of that is all we need contend for,) it must be done by the states themselves, erecting such barriers at the constitutional line as cannot be surmounted either by themselves or by the general government. The only barrier in their power is a wise government. A weak one will lose ground in every contest. To obtain a wise & an able government, I consider the following changes as important. Render the legislature a desirable station by lessening the number of representatives (say to 100) and lengthening somewhat their term, and proportion them equally among the electors: adopt also a better mode of appointing Senators. Render the Executive a more desirable post to men of abilities by making it more independant of the legislature. To wit, let him be chosen by other electors, for a longer time, and ineligible for ever after. Responsibility is a tremendous engine in a free government. Let him feel the whole weight of it then by taking away the shelter of his executive council. Experience both ways has already established the superiority of this measure. Render the Judiciary respectable by every possible means, to wit, firm tenure in office, competent salaries, and reduction of their numbers. Men of high learning and abilities are few in every country; & by taking in those who are not so, the able part of the body have their hands tied by the unable. This branch of the government will have the weight of the conflict on their hands, because they will be the last appeal of reason.—These are my general ideas of amendments; but, preserving the ends, I should be flexible & conciliatory as to the means. You ask whether Mr. Madison and myself could attend on a convention which should be called? Mr. Madison's engagements as a member of Congress will probably be from October to March or April in every year. Mine are constant while I hold my office, and my attendance would be very unimportant. Were it otherwise, my office should not stand in the way of it. I am with great & sincere esteem, Dr Sir, your friend & servt.

"A STEPPING STONE TO MONARCHY"

To the President of the United States
(GEORGE WASHINGTON)

Philadelphia, May 23, 1792

DEAR SIR,—I have determined to make the subject of a letter, what for some time past, has been a subject of inquietude to my mind without having found a good occasion of disburthening itself to you in conversation, during the busy scenes which occupied you here. Perhaps too you may be able, in your present situation, or on the road, to give it more time & reflection than you could do here at any moment.

When you first mentioned to me your purpose of retiring from the government, tho' I felt all the magnitude of the event, I was in a considerable degree silent. I knew that, to such a mind as yours, persuasion was idle & impertinent: that before forming your decision, you had weighed all the reasons for & against the measure, had made up your mind on full view of them, & that there could be little hope of changing the result. Pursuing my reflections too I knew we were some day to try to walk alone; and if the essay should be made while you should be alive & looking on, we should derive confidence from that circumstance, & resource if it failed. The public mind too was calm & confident, and therefore in a favorable state for making the experiment. Had no change of circumstances intervened, I should not, with any hope of success, have now ventured to propose to you a change of purpose. But the public mind is no longer confident and serene; and that from causes in which you are in no ways personally mixed. Tho these causes have been hackneyed in the public papers in detail, it may not be amiss, in order to calculate the effect they are capable of producing, to take a view of them in the mass, giving to each the form, real or imaginary, under which they have been presented.

It has been urged then that a public debt, greater than we can possibly pay before other causes of adding new debt to it will occur, has been artificially created, by adding together the whole amount of the debtor & creditor sides of accounts, instead of taking only their balances, which could have been paid off in a short time: That this accumulation of debt has

taken for ever out of our power those easy sources of revenue,
which, applied to the ordinary necessities and exigencies of
government, would have answered them habitually, and covered us from habitual murmurings against taxes & tax-gatherers, reserving extraordinary calls, for those extraordinary
occasions which would animate the people to meet them:
That though the calls for money have been no greater than
we must generally expect, for the same or equivalent exigencies, yet we are already obliged to strain the impost till it
produces clamour, and will produce evasion, & war on our
own citizens to collect it: and even to resort to an *Excise* law,
of odious character with the people, partial in it's operation,
unproductive unless enforced by arbitrary & vexatious means,
and committing the authority of the government in parts
where resistance is most probable, & coercion least practicable. They cite propositions in Congress and suspect other
projects on foot still to increase the mass of debt. They say
that by borrowing at ⅔ of the interest, we might have paid
off the principal in ⅔ of the time: but that from this we are
precluded by it's being made irredeemable but in small portions & long terms: That this irredeemable quality was given
it for the avowed purpose of inviting it's transfer to foreign
countries. They predict that this transfer of the principal,
when compleated, will occasion an exportation of 3. millions
of dollars annually for the interest, a drain of coin, of which
as there has been no example, no calculation can be made of
it's consequences: That the banishment of our coin will be
compleated by the creation of 10. millions of paper money, in
the form of bank bills, now issuing into circulation. They
think the 10. or 12. percent annual profit paid to the lenders
of this paper medium taken out of the pockets of the people,
who would have had without interest the coin it is banishing:
That all the capital employed in paper speculation is barren &
useless, producing, like that on a gaming table, no accession
to itself, and is withdrawn from commerce & agriculture
where it would have produced addition to the common mass:
That it nourishes in our citizens habits of vice and idleness
instead of industry & morality: That it has furnished effectual
means of corrupting such a portion of the legislature, as turns
the balance between the honest voters which ever way it is

directed: That this corrupt squadron, deciding the voice of the legislature, have manifested their dispositions to get rid of the limitations imposed by the constitution on the general legislature, limitations, on the faith of which, the states acceded to that instrument: That the ultimate object of all this is to prepare the way for a change, from the present republican form of government, to that of a monarchy, of which the English constitution is to be the model. That this was contemplated in the Convention is no secret, because it's partisans have made none of it. To effect it then was impracticable, but they are still eager after their object, and are predisposing every thing for it's ultimate attainment. So many of them have got into the legislature, that, aided by the corrupt squadron of paper dealers, who are at their devotion, they make a majority in both houses. The republican party, who wish to preserve the government in it's present form, are fewer in number. They are fewer even when joined by the two, three, or half dozen anti-federalists, who, tho they dare not avow it, are still opposed to any general government: but being less so to a republican than a monarchical one, they naturally join those whom they think pursuing the lesser evil.

Of all the mischiefs objected to the system of measures before mentioned, none is so afflicting, and fatal to every honest hope, as the corruption of the legislature. As it was the earliest of these measures, it became the instrument for producing the rest, & will be the instrument for producing in future a king, lords & commons, or whatever else those who direct it may chuse. Withdrawn such a distance from the eye of their constituents, and these so dispersed as to be inaccessible to public information, & particularly to that of the conduct of their own representatives, they will form the most corrupt government on earth, if the means of their corruption be not prevented. The only hope of safety hangs now on the numerous representation which is to come forward the ensuing year. Some of the new members will probably be either in principle or interest, with the present majority, but it is expected that the great mass will form an accession to the republican party. They will not be able to undo all which the two preceding legislatures, & especially the first, have done. Public faith & right will oppose this. But some parts of the system may be rightfully reformed; a liberation from the rest unremittingly pursued as fast as right will permit, & the door shut in future against similar commitments of the nation. Should the next legislature take this course, it will draw upon them the whole monarchical & paper interest. But the latter I think will not go all lengths with the former, because creditors will never, of their own accord, fly off entirely from their debtors. Therefore this is the alternative least likely to produce convulsion. But should the majority of the new members be still in the same principles with the present, & shew that we have nothing to expect but a continuance of the same practices, it is not easy to conjecture what would be the result, nor what means would be resorted to for correction of the evil. True wisdom would direct that they should be temperate & peaceable, but the division of sentiment & interest happens unfortunately to be so geographical, that no mortal can say that what is most wise & temperate would prevail against what is most easy & obvious. I can scarcely contemplate a more incalculable evil than the breaking of the union into two or more parts. Yet when we review the mass which opposed the original coalescence, when we consider that it lay chiefly in the Southern quarter, that the legislature have availed themselves of no occasion of allaying it, but on the contrary whenever Northern & Southern prejudices have come into conflict, the latter have been sacrificed & the former soothed; that the owners of the debt are in the Southern & the holders of it in the Northern division; that the Antifederal champions are now strengthened in argument by the fulfilment of their predictions; that this has been brought about by the Monarchical federalists themselves, who, having been for the new government merely as a stepping stone to monarchy, have themselves adopted the very constructions of the constitution, of which, when advocating it's acceptance before the tribunal of the people, they declared it insusceptible; that the republican federalists, who espoused the same government for it's intrinsic merits, are disarmed of their weapons, that which they denied as prophecy being now become true history: who can be sure that these things may not proselyte the small number which was wanting to place the majority on the other side? And this is the event at which I

tremble, & to prevent which I consider your continuance at
the head of affairs as of the last importance. The confidence
of the whole union is centred in you. Your being at the helm,
will be more than an answer to every argument which can be
used to alarm & lead the people in any quarter into violence
or secession. North & South will hang together, if they have
you to hang on; and, if the first correction of a numerous
representation should fail in it's effect, your presence will give
time for trying others not inconsistent with the union &
peace of the states.

I am perfectly aware of the oppression under which your
present office lays your mind, & of the ardor with which you
pant for retirement to domestic life. But there is sometimes
an eminence of character on which society have such peculiar
claims as to controul the predelection of the individual for a
particular walk of happiness, & restrain him to that alone arising from the present & future benedictions of mankind. This
seems to be your condition, & the law imposed on you by
providence in forming your character, & fashioning the
events on which it was to operate; and it is to motives like
these, & not to personal anxieties of mine or others who have
no right to call on you for sacrifices, that I appeal from your
former determination & urge a revisal of it, on the ground of
change in the aspect of things. Should an honest majority result from the new & enlarged representation; should those
acquiesce whose principles or interest they may controul,
your wishes for retirement would be gratified with less danger, as soon as that shall be manifest, without awaiting the
completion of the second period of four years. One or two
sessions will determine the crisis; and I cannot but hope that
you can resolve to add one or two more to the many years
you have already sacrificed to the good of mankind.

The fear of suspicion that any selfish motive of continuance
in office may enter into this sollicitation on my part obliges
me to declare that no such motive exists. It is a thing of mere
indifference to the public whether I retain or relinquish my
purpose of closing my tour with the first periodical renovation of the government. I know my own measure too well to
suppose that my services contribute any thing to the public
confidence, or the public utility. Multitudes can fill the office

in which you have been pleased to place me, as much to their advantage & satisfaction. I therefore have no motive to consult but my own inclination, which is bent irresistibly on the tranquil enjoyment of my family, my farm, & my books. I should repose among them it is true, in far greater security, if I were to know that you remained at the watch, and I hope it will be so. To the inducements urged from a view of our domestic affairs, I will add a bare mention, of what indeed need only be mentioned, that weighty motives for your continuance are to be found in our foreign affairs. I think it probable that both the Spanish & English negotiations, if not completed before your purpose is known, will be suspended from the moment it is known; & that the latter nation will then use double diligence in fomenting the Indian war.— With my wishes for the future, I shall at the same time express my gratitude for the past, at least my portion in it; & beg permission to follow you whether in public or private life with those sentiments of sincere attachment & respect, with which I am unalterably, Dear Sir, Your affectionate friend & humble servant.

"THE MONSTER ARISTOCRACY"

To Lafayette

Philadelphia, June 16, 1792

Behold you, then, my dear friend, at the head of a great army, establishing the liberties of your country against a foreign enemy. May heaven favor your cause, and make you the channel thro' which it may pour it's favors. While you are exterminating the monster aristocracy, & pulling out the teeth & fangs of it's associate monarchy, a contrary tendency is discovered in some here. A sect has shewn itself among us, who declare they espoused our new constitution, not as a good & sufficient thing itself, but only as a step to an English constitution, the only thing good & sufficient in itself, in their eye. It is happy for us that these are preachers without followers, and that our people are firm & constant in their republican purity. You will wonder to be told that it is from the Eastward chiefly that these champions for a king, lords & commons come. They get some important associates from New York, and are puffed off by a tribe of Agioteurs which have been hatched in a bed of corruption made up after the model of their beloved England. Too many of these stock jobbers & king-jobbers have come into our legislature, or rather too many of our legislature have become stock jobbers & king-jobbers. However the voice of the people is beginning to make itself heard, and will probably cleanse their seats at the ensuing election.—The machinations of our old enemies are such as to keep us still at bay with our Indian neighbors.— What are you doing for your colonies? They will be lost if not more effectually succoured. Indeed no future efforts you can make will ever be able to reduce the blacks. All that can be done in my opinion will be to compound with them as has been done formerly in Jamaica. We have been less zealous in aiding them, lest your government should feel any jealousy on our account. But in truth we as sincerely wish their restoration, and their connection with you, as you do yourselves. We are satisfied that neither your justice nor their distresses will ever again permit their being forced to seek at dear & distant markets those first necessaries of life which they may have at cheaper markets placed by nature at their door, & formed by her for their support.—What is become of Mde de Tessy and Mde de Tott? I have not heard of them since they went to Switzerland. I think they would have done better to have come & reposed under the Poplars of Virginia. Pour into their bosoms the warmest effusions of my friendship & tell them they will be warm and constant unto death. Accept of them also for Mde de la Fayette & your dear children— but I am forgetting that you are in the field of war, & they I hope in those of peace. Adieu my dear friend! God bless you all. Yours affectionately.

THE RIGHTS OF MAN

To Thomas Paine

Philadelphia, June 19, 1792

DEAR SIR,—I received with great pleasure the present of your pamphlets, as well for the thing itself as that it was a testimony of your recollection. Would you believe it possible that in this country there should be high & important characters who need your lessons in republicanism, & who do not heed them? It is but too true that we have a sect preaching up & pouting after an English constitution of king, lords, & commons, & whose heads are itching for crowns, coronets & mitres. But our people, my good friend, are firm and unanimous in their principles of republicanism & there is no better proof of it than that they love what you write and read it with delight. The printers season every newspaper with extracts from your last, as they did before from your first part of the Rights of Man. They have both served here to separate the wheat from the chaff, and to prove that tho' the latter appears on the surface, it is on the surface only. The bulk below is sound & pure. Go on then in doing with your pen what in other times was done with the sword: shew that reformation is more practicable by operating on the mind than on the body of man, and be assured that it has not a more sincere votary nor you a more ardent well-wisher than Yrs. &c.

THE CONFLICT WITH HAMILTON

To the President of the United States

(GEORGE WASHINGTON)

Monticello, Sep. 9, 1792

DEAR SIR,—I received on the 2d inst the letter of Aug 23, which you did me the honor to write me; but the immediate return of our post, contrary to his custom, prevented my answer by that occasion. The proceedings of Spain mentioned in your letter are really of a complexion to excite uneasiness, & a suspicion that their friendly overtures about the Missisipi have been merely to lull us while they should be strengthening their holds on that river. Mr. Carmichael's silence has been long my astonishment: and however it might have justified something very different from a new appointment, yet the public interest certainly called for his junction with Mr. Short as it is impossible but that his knolege of the ground of negotiation of persons & characters, must be useful & even

necessary to the success of the mission. That Spain & Gr Britain may understand one another on our frontiers is very possible; for however opposite their interests or disposition may
be in the affairs of Europe, yet while these do not call them
into opposite action, they may concur as against us. I consider their keeping an agent in the Indian country as a circumstance which requires serious interference on our part; and I
submit to your decision whether it does not furnish a proper
occasion to us to send an additional instruction to Messrs.
Carmichael & Short to insist on a mutual & formal stipulation to forbear employing agents or pensioning any persons
within each other's limits: and if this be refused, to propose
the contrary stipulation, to wit, that each party may freely
keep agents within the Indian territories of the other, in
which case we might soon sicken them of the license.

I now take the liberty of proceeding to that part of your
letter wherein you notice the internal dissentions which have
taken place within our government, & their disagreeable effect on it's movements. That such dissentions have taken
place is certain, & even among those who are nearest to you
in the administration. To no one have they given deeper concern than myself: to no one equal mortification at being myself a part of them. Tho' I take to myself no more than my
share of the general observations of your letter, yet I am so
desirous ever that you should know the whole truth, & believe no more than the truth, that I am glad to seize every
occasion of developing to you whatever I do or think relative
to the government; & shall therefore ask permission to be
more lengthy now than the occasion particularly calls for, or
could otherwise perhaps justify.

When I embarked in the government, it was with a determination to intermeddle not at all with the legislature, & as
little as possible with my co-departments. The first and only
instance of variance from the former part of my resolution, I
was duped into by the Secretary of the Treasury and made a
tool for forwarding his schemes, not then sufficiently understood by me; and of all the errors of my political life, this has
occasioned me the deepest regret. It has ever been my purpose to explain this to you, when, from being actors on the
scene, we shall have become uninterested spectators only. The

second part of my resolution has been religiously observed with the war department; & as to that of the Treasury, has never been farther swerved from than by the mere enuncia-tion of my sentiments in conversation, and chiefly among those who, expressing the same sentiments, drew mine from me. If it has been supposed that I have ever intrigued among the members of the legislatures to defeat the plans of the Sec-retary of the Treasury, it is contrary to all truth. As I never had the desire to influence the members, so neither had I any other means than my friendships, which I valued too highly to risk by usurpations on their freedom of judgment, & the conscientious pursuit of their own sense of duty. That I have utterly, in my private conversations, disapproved of the system of the Secretary of the treasury, I acknolege & avow: and this was not merely a speculative difference. His system flowed from principles adverse to liberty, & was calculated to undermine and demolish the republic, by creating an influ-ence of his department over the members of the legislature. I saw this influence actually produced, & it's first fruits to be the establishment of the great outlines of his project by the votes of the very persons who, having swallowed his bait were laying themselves out to profit by his plans: & that had these persons withdrawn, as those interested in a question ever should, the vote of the disinterested majority was clearly the reverse of what they made it. These were no longer the votes then of the representatives of the people, but of desert-ers from the rights & interests of the people: & it was impos-sible to consider their decisions, which had nothing in view but to enrich themselves, as the measures of the fair majority, which ought always to be respected.—If what was actually doing begat uneasiness in those who wished for virtuous gov-ernment, what was further proposed was not less threatening to the friends of the Constitution. For, in a Report on the subject of manufactures (still to be acted on) it was expressly assumed that the general government has a right to exercise all powers which may be for the *general welfare*, that is to say, all the legitimate powers of government: since no government has a legitimate right to do what is not for the welfare of the governed. There was indeed a sham-limitation of the univer-sality of this power *to cases where money is to be employed*. But about what is it that money cannot be employed? Thus the object of these plans taken together is to draw all the powers of government into the hands of the general legislature, to establish means for corrupting a sufficient corps in that legislature to divide the honest votes & preponderate, by their own, the scale which suited, & to have that corps under the command of the Secretary of the Treasury for the purpose of subverting step by step the principles of the constitution, which he has so often declared to be a thing of nothing which must be changed. Such views might have justified something more than mere expressions of dissent, beyond which, nevertheless, I never went.—Has abstinence from the department committed to me been equally observed by him? To say nothing of other interferences equally known, in the case of the two nations with which we have the most intimate connections, France & England, my system was to give some satisfactory distinctions to the former, of little cost to us, in return for the solid advantages yielded us by them; & to have met the English with some restrictions which might induce them to abate their severities against our commerce. I have always supposed this coincided with your sentiments. Yet the Secretary of the treasury, by his cabals with members of the legislature, & by high-toned declamation on other occasions, has forced down his own system, which was exactly the reverse. He undertook, of his own authority, the conferences with the ministers of those two nations, & was, on every consultation, provided with some report of a conversation with the one or the other of them, adapted to his views. These views, thus made to prevail, their execution fell of course to me; & I can safely appeal to you, who have seen all my letters & proceedings, whether I have not carried them into execution as sincerely as if they had been my own, tho' I ever considered them as inconsistent with the honor & interest of our country. That they have been inconsistent with our interest is but too fatally proved by the stab to our navigation given by the French.—So that if the question be By whose fault is it that Colo Hamilton & myself have not drawn together? the answer will depend on that to two other questions; whose principles of administration best justify, by their purity, conscientious adherence? and which of us has, notwithstanding, stepped farthest into the controul of the department of the other?

To this justification of opinions, expressed in the way of conversation, against the views of Colo Hamilton, I beg leave to add some notice of his late charges against me in Fenno's gazette; for neither the stile, matter, nor venom of the pieces alluded to can leave a doubt of their author. Spelling my name & character at full length to the public, while he conceals his own under the signature of "an American" he charges me 1. With having written letters from Europe to my friends to oppose the present constitution while depending. 2. With a desire of not paying the public debt. 3. With setting up a paper to decry & slander the government. 1. The first charge is most false. No man in the U.S. I suppose, approved of every title in the constitution: no one, I believe approved more of it than I did: and more of it was certainly disproved by my accuser than by me, and of it's parts most vitally republican. Of this the few letters I wrote on the subject (not half a dozen I believe) will be a proof: & for my own satisfaction & justification, I must tax you with the reading of them when I return to where they are. You will there see that my objection to the constitution was that it wanted a bill of rights securing freedom of religion, freedom of the press, freedom from standing armies, trial by jury, & a constant Habeas corpus act. Colo Hamilton's was that it wanted a king and house of lords. The sense of America has approved my objection & added the bill of rights, not the king and lords. I also thought a longer term of service, insusceptible of renewal, would have made a President more independant. My country has thought otherwise, & I have acquiesced implicitly. He wishes the general government should have power to make laws binding the states in all cases whatsoever. Our country has thought otherwise: has he acquiesced? Notwithstanding my wish for a bill of rights, my letters strongly urged the adoption of the constitution, by nine states at least, to secure the good it contained. I at first thought that the best method of securing the bill of rights would be for four states to hold off till such a bill should be agreed to. But the moment I saw Mr. Hancock's proposition to pass the constitution as it stood, and give perpetual instructions to the representatives of every state to insist on a bill of rights, I acknoleged the superiority of his plan, & advocated universal adoption. 2. The second charge is equally untrue. My whole correspondence while in France, & every word, letter, & act on the subject since my return, prove that no man is more ardently intent to see the public debt soon & sacredly paid off than I am. This exactly marks the difference between Colo Hamilton's views & mine, that I would wish the debt paid to morrow; he wishes it never to be paid, but always to be a thing where with to corrupt & manage the legislature. 3. I have never enquired what number of sons, relations & friends of Senators, representatives, printers or other useful partisans Colo Hamilton has provided for among the hundred clerks of his department, the thousand excisemen, custom-house officers, loan officers &c. &c. &c. appointed by him, or at his nod, and spread over the Union; nor could ever have imagined that the man who has the shuffling of millions backwards & forwards from paper into money & money into paper, from Europe to America, & America to Europe, the dealing out of Treasury-secrets among his friends in what time & measure he pleases, and who never slips an occasion of making friends with his means, that such an one I say would have brought forward a charge against me for having appointed the poet Freneau translating clerk to my office, with a salary of 250. dollars a year. That fact stands thus. While the government was at New York I was applied to on behalf of Freneau to know if there was any place within my department to which he could be appointed. I answered there were but four clerkships, all of which I found full, and continued without any change. When we removed to Philadelphia, Mr. Pintard the translating clerk, did not chuse to remove with us. His office then became vacant. I was again applied to there for Freneau, & had no hesitation to promise the clerkship for him. I cannot recollect whether it was at the same time, or afterwards, that I was told he had a thought of setting up a newspaper there. But whether then, or afterwards, I considered it as a circumstance of some value, as it might enable me to do, what I had long wished to have done, that is, to have the material parts of the Leyden gazette brought under your eye & that of the public, in order to possess yourself & them of a juster view of the affairs of Europe than could be obtained from any other public source. This I had ineffectually attempted through the press of Mr. Fenno while in New York, selecting & translating passages myself at first then having it done by Mr. Pintard the translating clerk, but they found their way too slowly into Mr. Fenno's papers. Mr. Bache essayed it for me in Philadelphia, but his being a daily paper, did not circulate sufficiently in the other states. He even tried, at my request, the plan of a weekly paper of recapitulation from his daily paper, in hopes that that might go into the other states, but in this too we failed. Freneau, as translating clerk, & the printer of a periodical paper likely to circulate thro' the states (uniting in one person the parts of Pintard & Fenno) revived my hopes that the thing could at length be effected. On the establishment of his paper therefore, I furnished him with the Leyden gazettes, with an expression of my wish that he could always translate & publish the material intelligence they contained; & have continued to furnish them from time to time, as regularly as I received them. But as to any other direction or indication of my wish how his press should be conducted, what sort of intelligence he should give, what essays encourage, I can protest in the presence of heaven, that I never did by myself or any other, directly or indirectly, say a syllable, nor attempt any kind of influence. I can further protest, in the same awful presence, that I never did by myself or any other, directly or indirectly, write, dictate or procure any one sentence or sentiment to be inserted *in his, or any other gazette*, to which my name was not affixed or that of my office.—I surely need not except here a thing so foreign to the present subject as a little paragraph about our Algerine captives, which I put once into Fenno's paper.—Freneau's proposition to publish a paper, having been about the time that the writings of Publicola, & the discourses on Davila had a good deal excited the public attention, I took for granted from Freneau's character, which had been marked as that of a good whig, that he would give free place to pieces written against the aristocratical & monarchical principles these papers had inculcated. This having been in my mind, it is likely enough I may have expressed it in conversation with others; tho' I do not recollect that I did.

To Freneau I think I could not, because I had still seen him but once, & that was at a public table, at breakfast, at Mrs. Elsworth's, as I passed thro' New York the last year. And I can safely declare that my expectations looked only to the chastisement of the aristocratical & monarchical writers, & not to any criticisms on the proceedings of government: Colo Hamilton can see no motive for any appointment but that of making a convenient partizan. But you Sir, who have received from me recommendations of a Rittenhouse, Barlow, Paine, will believe that talents & science are sufficient motives with me in appointments to which they are fitted: & that Freneau, as a man of genius, might find a preference in my eye to be a translating clerk, & make good title to the little aids I could give him as the editor of a gazette, by procuring subscriptions to his paper, as I did some, before it appeared, & as I have with pleasure done for the labours of other men of genius. I hold it to be one of the distinguishing excellencies of elective over hereditary succesions, that the talents, which nature has provided in sufficient proportion, should be selected by the society for the government of their affairs, rather than that this should be transmitted through the loins of knaves & fools passing from the debauches of the table to those of the bed. Colo Hamilton, alias "Plain facts," says that Freneau's salary began before he resided in Philadelphia. I do not know what quibble he may have in reserve on the word "residence." He may mean to include under that idea the removal of his family; for I believe he removed, himself, before his family did, to Philadelphia. But no act of mine gave commencement to his salary before he so far took up his abode in Philadelphia as to be sufficiently in readiness for the duties of the office. As to the merits or demerits of his paper, they certainly concern me not. He & Fenno are rivals for the public favor. The one courts them by flattery, the other by censure, & I believe it will be admitted that the one has been as servile, as the other severe. But is not the dignity, & even decency of government committed, when one of it's principal ministers enlists himself as an anonymous writer or paragraphist for either the one or the other of them?—No government ought to be without censors: & where the press is free, no one ever will. If virtuous, it need not fear the fair operation of attack &

defence. Nature has given to man no other means of sifting out the truth either in religion, law, or politics. I think it as honorable to the government neither to know, nor notice, it's sycophants or censors, as it would be undignified & criminal to pamper the former & persecute the latter.—So much for the past. A word now of the future.

When I came into this office, it was with a resolution to retire from it as soon as I could with decency. It pretty early appeared to me that the proper moment would be the first of those epochs at which the constitution seems to have contemplated a periodical change or renewal of the public servants. In this I was confirmed by your resolution respecting the same period; from which however I am happy in hoping you have departed. I look to that period with the longing of a wave-worn mariner, who has at length the land in view, & shall count the days & hours which still lie between me & it. In the meanwhile my main object will be to wind up the business of my office avoiding as much as possible all new enterprize. With the affairs of the legislature, as I never did intermeddle, so I certainly shall not now begin. I am more desirous to predispose everything for the repose to which I am withdrawing, than expose it to be disturbed by newspaper contests. If these however cannot be avoided altogether, yet a regard for your quiet will be a sufficient motive for my deferring it till I become merely a private citizen, when the propriety or impropriety of what I may say or do may fall on myself alone. I may then too avoid the charge of misapplying that time which now belonging to those who employ me, should be wholly devoted to their service. If my own justification, or the interests of the republic shall require it, I reserve to myself the right of then appealing to my country, subscribing my name to whatever I write, & using with freedom & truth the facts & names necessary to place the cause in it's just form before that tribunal. To a thorough disregard of the honors & emoluments of office I join as great a value for the esteem of my countrymen, & conscious of having merited it by an integrity which cannot be reproached, & by an enthusiastic devotion to their rights & liberty, I will not suffer my retirement to be clouded by the slanders of a man whose history, from the moment at which history can stoop to notice him, is a tissue of machinations against the liberty of the country which has not only received and given him bread, but heaped it's honors on his head.—Still however I repeat the hope that it will not be necessary to make such an appeal. Though little known to the people of America, I believe that, as far as I am known, it is not as an enemy to the republic, nor an intriguer against it, nor a waster of it's revenue, nor prostitutor of it to the purposes of corruption, as the American represents me; and I confide that yourself are satisfied that, as to dissensions in the newspapers, not a syllable of them has ever proceeded from me; & that no cabals or intrigues of mine have produced those in the legislature, & I hope I may promise, both to you & myself, that none will receive aliment from me during the short space I have to remain in office, which will find ample employment in closing the present business of the department.—Observing that letters written at Mount Vernon on the Monday, & arriving at Richmond on the Wednesday, reach me on Saturday, I have now the honor to mention that the 22d instant will be the last of our post-days that I shall be here, & consequently that no letter from you after the 17th, will find me here. Soon after that I shall have the honor of receiving at Mount Vernon your orders for Philadelphia, & of there also delivering you the little matter which occurs to me as proper for the opening of Congress, exclusive of what has been recommended in former speeches, & not yet acted on. In the meantime & ever I am with great and sincere affection & respect, dear Sir, your most obedient and most humble servant.

"THE WILL OF THE NATION"

To the U.S. Minister to France
(GOUVERNEUR MORRIS)

Philadelphia, Dec. 30, 1792

DEAR SIR—My last to you was of Mar. 7. since which I have received your Nos. 8. and 9. I am apprehensive that your situation must have been difficult during the transition from the late form of government to the re-establishment of some

other legitimate authority, and that you may have been at a
loss to determine with whom business might be done. Nevertheless when principles are well understood their application is less embarrassing. We surely cannot deny to any nation
that right whereon our own government is founded, that
every one may govern itself under whatever forms it pleases,
and change these forms at it's own will, and that it may transact it's business with foreign nations through whatever organ
it thinks proper, whether King, convention, assembly, committee, President, or whatever else it may chuse. The will of
the nation is the only thing essential to be regarded. On the
dissolution of the late constitution in France, by removing so
integral a part of it as the King, the National Assembly, to
whom a part only of the public authority had been delegated,
sensible of the incompetence of their powers to transact the
affairs of the nation legitimately, incited their fellow citizens
to appoint a national convention during this defective state of
the national authority. Duty to our constituents required that
we should suspend paiment of the monies yet unpaid of our
debt to that country, because there was no person or persons
substantially authorized by the nation of France to receive the
monies and give us a good acquittal. On this ground my last
letter desired you to suspend paiments till further orders, with
an assurance, if necessary, that the suspension should not be
continued a moment longer than should be necessary for us
to see the re-establishment of some person or body of persons
with authority to receive and give us a good acquittal. Since
that we learn that a Convention is assembled, invested with
full powers by the nation to transact it's affairs. Tho' we
know that from the public papers only, instead of waiting for
a formal annunciation of it, we hasten to act upon it by authorizing you, if the fact be true, to consider the suspension
of paiment, directed in my last letter, as now taken off, and
to proceed as if it had never been imposed; considering the
Convention, or the government they shall have established as
the lawful representatives of the Nation and authorized to act
for them. Neither the honor nor inclination of our country
would justify our withholding our paiment under a scrupulous attention to forms. On the contrary they lent us that
money when we were under their circumstances, and it seems

providential that we can not only repay them the same sum, but under the same circumstances. Indeed, we wish to omit no opportunity of convincing them how cordially we desire the closest union with them: Mutual good offices, mutual affection and similar principles of government seem to have destined the two people for the most intimate communion, and even for a complete exchange of citizenship among the individuals composing them.

During the fluctuating state of the Assignats of France, I must ask the favor of you to inform me in every letter of the rate of exchange between them & coin, this being necessary for the regulation of our custom houses. We are continuing our supplies to the island of St. Domingo at the request of the Minister of France here. We would wish however to receive a more formal sanction from the government of France than has yet been given. Indeed, we know of none but a vote of the late National Assembly for 4 millions of livres of our debt, sent to the government of St. Domingo, communicated by them to the Minister here, & by him to us. And this was in terms not properly applicable to the form of our advances. We wish therefore for a full sanction of the past & a complete expression of the desires of their government as to future supplies to their colonies. Besides what we have furnished publicly, individual merchants of the U.S. have carried considerable supplies to the island of St. Domingo, which have been sometimes purchased, sometimes taken by force, and bills given by the administration of the colony on the minister here, which have been protested for want of funds. We have no doubt that justice will be done to these

PAEAN TO THE FRENCH REVOLUTION
To William Short

Philadelphia, Jan. 3, 1793

DEAR SIR,—My last private letter to you was of Oct. 16. since which I have received your No. 103, 107, 108, 109, 110, 112, 113 & 114 and yesterday your private one of Sep 15, came to hand. The tone of your letters had for some time given me pain, on account of the extreme warmth with which they censured the proceedings of the Jacobins of France. I considered that sect as the same with the Republican patriots, & the Feuillants as the Monarchical patriots, well known in the early part of the revolution, & but little distant in their views, both having in object the establishment of a free constitution, & differing only on the question whether their chief Executive should be hereditary or not. The Jacobins (as since called) yielded to the Feuillants & tried the experiment of retaining their hereditary Executive. The experiment failed completely, and would have brought on the reestablishment of despotism had it been pursued. The Jacobins saw this, and that the expunging that officer was of absolute necessity. And the Nation was with them in opinion, for however they might have been formerly for the constitution framed by the first assembly, they were come over from their hope in it, and were now generally Jacobins. In the struggle which was necessary, many guilty persons fell without the forms of trial, and with them some innocent. These I deplore as much as any body, & shall deplore some of them to the day of my death. But I deplore them as I should have done had they fallen in battle. It was necessary to use the arm of the people, a machine not quite so blind as balls and bombs, but blind to a certain degree. A few of their cordial friends met at their hands the fate of enemies. But time and truth will rescue & embalm their memories, while their posterity will be enjoying that very liberty for which they would never have hesitated to offer up their lives. The liberty of the whole earth was depending on the issue of the contest, and was ever such a prize won with so little innocent blood? My own affections have been deeply wounded by some of the martyrs to this cause, but rather than it should have failed, I would have seen half the earth desolated. Were there but an Adam & an Eve left in every country, & left free, it would be better than as it now is. I have expressed to you my sentiments, because they are really those of 99. in an hundred of our citizens. The universal feasts, and rejoicings which have lately been had on account of the successes of the French shewed the genuine effusions of their hearts. You have been wounded by the sufferings of your friends, and have by this circumstance been hurried into a temper of mind which would be extremely disrelished if known to your countrymen. The *reserve of the President of the United States* had never permitted me to discover the light in which he viewed it, and as I was more anxious that you should satisfy him than me, I had still avoided explanations with you on the subject. But your 113. induced him to break silence and to notice the extreme acrimony of your expressions. He added that he had been informed the sentiments you expressed *in your conversations* were equally offensive to our allies, & that you should consider yourself as the representative of your country and that what you say might be imputed to your constituents. He desired me therefore to write to you on this subject. He added that he considered *France as the sheet anchor of this country and its friendship as a first object.* There are in the U.S. some characters of opposite principles; some of them are high in office, others possessing great wealth, and all of them hostile to France and fondly looking to England as the staff of their hope. These I named to you on a former occasion. Their prospects have certainly not brightened. Excepting them, this country is entirely republican, friends to the constitution, anxious to preserve it and to have it administered according to it's own republican principles. The little party above mentioned have espoused it only as a stepping stone to monarchy, and have endeavored to approximate it to that in it's administration in order to render it's final transition more easy. The successes of republicanism in France have given the coup de grace to their prospects, and I hope to their projects.—I have developed to you faithfully the sentiments of your country, that you may govern yourself accordingly. I know your republicanism to be pure, and that it is no decay of that which has embittered you against it's votaries in France, but too great a sensibility at the partial evil which it's object has been accomplished there. I have written to you in the stile to which I have been always accustomed with you, and which perhaps it is time I should lay aside. But while old men are sensible enough of their own advance in years, they do not sufficiently recollect it in those whom they have seen young. In writing too the last private letter which will probably be written under present circumstances, in contemplating that your correspondence will shortly be turned over to I know not whom, but certainly to some one not in the habit of considering your interests with the same fostering anxieties I do, I have presented things without reserve, satisfied you will ascribe what I have said to it's true motive, use it for your own best interest, and in that fulfil completely what I had in view.

With respect to the subject of your letter of Sep. 15. you will be sensible that many considerations would prevent my undertaking the reformation of a system with which I am so soon to take leave. It is but common decency to leave to my successor the moulding of his own business.—Not knowing how otherwise to convey this letter to you with certainty, I shall appeal to the friendship and honour of the Spanish commissioners here, to give it the protection of their cover, as a letter of private nature altogether. We have no remarkable event here lately, but the death of Dr. Lee; nor have I anything new to communicate to you of your friends or affairs. I am with unalterable affection & wishes for your prosperity, my dear Sir, your sincere friend and servant.

PEACEABLE COERCION
To James Madison

March 24, 1793

The idea seems to gain credit that the naval powers combined against France will prohibit supplies even of provisions to that country. Should this be formally notified I should suppose Congress would be called, because it is a justifiable cause of war, & as the Executive cannot decide the question of war on the affirmative side, neither ought it to do so on the negative side, by preventing the competent body from deliberating on the question. But I should hope that war would not be their choice. I think it will furnish us a happy opportunity of setting another example to the world, by shewing that nations may be brought to do justice by appeals to their interests as well as by appeals to arms. I should hope that Congress instead of a denunciation of war, would instantly exclude from our ports all the manufactures, produce, vessels & subjects of the nations committing this aggression, during the continuance of the aggression & till full satisfaction made for it. This would work well in many ways, safely in all, & introduce between nations another umpire than arms. It would relieve us too from the risks & the horrors of cutting throats. The death of the king of France has not produced as open condemnations from the Monocrats as I expected. I dined the other day in a company where the subject was discussed. I will name the company in the order in which they manifested their partialities; beginning with the warmest Jacobinism & proceeding by shades to the most heart felt aristocracy. Smith (N.Y.) Coxe. Stewart. T. Shippen. Bingham. Peters. Breck. Meredith. Wolcott. It is certain that the ladies of this city, of the first circle are all open-mouthed against the murderers of a sovereign, and they generally speak those sentiments which the more cautious husband smothers. I believe it is pretty certain that Smith (S.C.) and Miss A. are not to come together. Ternant has at length openly hoisted the flag of monarchy by going into deep mourning for his prince. I suspect he thinks a cessation of his visits to me a necessary accompaniment to this pious duty. A connection between him & Hamilton seems to be springing up. On observing that Duer was secretary to the old board of treasury, I suspect him to have been the person who suggested to Hamilton the letter of mine to that board which he so tortured in his Catullus. Dunlap has refused to print the piece which we had heard of before your departure, and it has been several days in Bache's hands, without any notice of it. The President will leave this about the 27th inst., & return about the 20th of April. Adieu.

THE GALLANT GENET

To James Madison

Phila, May 19, 1793

I wrote you last on the 13th. Since that I have received yours of the 8th. I have scribbled on a separate paper some general notes on the plan of a house you enclosed. I have done more. I have endeavored to throw the same area, the same extent of walls, the same number of rooms, & of the same size, into another form so as to offer a choice to the builder. Indeed I varied my plan by shewing that it would be with alcove bed rooms, to which I am much attached.

I dare say you will have judged from the pusillanimity of the proclamation, from whose pen it came. A fear lest any affection should be discovered is distinguishable enough. This base fear will produce the very evil they wish to avoid. For our constituents seeing that the government does not express their mind, perhaps rather leans the other way, are coming forward to express it themselves. It was suspected that there was not a clear mind in the P.'s counsellors to receive Genet. The citizens however determined to receive him. Arrangements were taken for meeting him at Gray's ferry in a great body. He escaped that by arriving in town with the letters which brought information that he was on the road. The merchants *i.e.* Fitzsimmons & co. were to present an address to *the P.* on the neutrality proclaimed. It contained much wisdom but no affection. You will see it in the papers inclosed. The citizens determined to address *Genet*. Rittenhouse, Hutcheson, Dallas, Sargeant &c. were at the head of it. Tho a select body of only 30. was appointed to present it, yet a vast concourse of people attended them. I have not seen it; but it is understood to be the counter address.—Ternant's hopes of employment in the French army turn out to be without grounds. He is told by the minister of war expressly that the places of Marechal de camp are all full. He thinks it more prudent therefore to remain in America. He delivered yesterday his letters of recall, & Mr. Genet presented his of credence. It is impossible for anything to be more affectionate, more magnanimous than the purport of his mission. 'We know that under present circumstances we have a right to call upon you for the guarantee of our islands. But we do not desire it. We wish you to do nothing but what is for your own good, and we will do all in our power to promote it. Cherish your own peace & prosperity. You have expressed a willingness to enter into a more liberal treaty of commerce with us; I bring full powers (& he produced them) to form such a treaty, and a preliminary decree of the National convention to lay open our country & it's colonies to you for every purpose of utility, without your participating the burthens of maintaining & defending them. We see in you the only person on earth who can love us sincerely & merit to be so loved.' In short he offers everything & asks nothing. Yet I know the offers will be opposed, & suspect they will not be accepted. In short, my dear Sir, it is impossible for you to conceive what is passing in our conclave: and it is evident that one or two at least, under pretence of avoiding war on the one side have no great antipathy to run foul of it on the other, and to make a part in the confederacy of princes against human liberty.—The people in the Western parts of this state have been to the excise officer & threatened to burn his house &c. They were blacked & otherwise disguised so as to be unknown. He has resigned, and H. says there is no possibility of getting the law executed there, & that probably the evil will spread. A proclamation is to be issued, and another instance of my being forced to appear to approve what I have condemned uniformly from it's first conception.

I expect every day to receive from Mr. Pinckney the model of the Scotch threshing machine. It was to have come in a ship which arrived 3. weeks ago, but the workman had not quite finished it. Mr. P. writes me word that the machine from which my model is taken threshes 8. quarters (64. bushels) of oats *an hour*, with 4. horses & 4. men. I hope to get it in time to have one erected at Monticello to clean out the present crop.—I inclose you the pamphlet you desired. Adieu.

THE DEBT OF SERVICE
To James Madison

June 9, 1793

I have to acknolege the receipt of your two favors of May 27 & 29, since the date of my last which was of the 2 inst. In that of the 27th you say 'you must not make your final exit from public life till it will be marked with justifying circumstances which all good citizens will respect, & to which your friends can appeal.'—To my fellow-citizens the debt of service has been fully & faithfully paid. I acknolege that such a debt exists, that a tour of duty, in whatever line he can be most useful to his country, is due from every individual. It is not easy perhaps to say of what length exactly this tour should be, but we may safely say of what length it should not be. Not of our whole life, for instance, for that would be to be born a slave—not even of a very large portion of it. I have now been in the public service four & twenty years; one half of which has been spent in total occupation with their affairs, & absence from my own. I have served my tour then. No positive engagement, by word or deed, binds me to their further service. No commitment of their interests in any enterprise by me requires that I should see them through it.—I am pledged by no act which gives any tribunal a call upon me before I withdraw. Even my enemies do not pretend this. I stand clear then of public right on all points.—My friends I have not committed. No circumstances have attended my passage from office to office, which could lead them, & others through them, into deception as to the time I might remain; & particularly they & all have known with what reluctance I engaged & have continued in the present one, & of my uniform determination to retire from it at an early day.—If the public then has no claim on me, & my friends nothing to justify; the decision will rest on my own feelings alone. There has been a time when these were very different from what they are now: when perhaps the esteem of the world was of higher value in my eye than everything in it. But age, experience & reflection, preserving to that only it's due value, have set a higher on tranquility. The motion of my blood no longer keeps time with the tumult of the world. It leads me to seek for happiness in the lap and love of my family, in the society of my neighbors & my books, in the wholesome occupations of my farm & my affairs, in an interest or affection in every bud that opens, in every breath that blows around me, in an entire freedom of rest or motion, of thought or incogitancy, owing account to myself alone of my hours & actions. What must be the principle of that calculation which should balance against these the circumstances of my present existence! worn down with labours from morning to night, & day to day; knowing them as fruitless to others as they are vexatious to myself, committed singly in desperate & eternal contest against a host who are systematically undermining the public liberty & prosperity, even the rare hours of relaxation sacrificed to the society of persons in the same intentions, of whose hatred I am conscious even in those moments of conviviality when the heart wishes most to open itself to the effusions of friendship & confidence, cut off from my family & friends, my affairs abandoned to chaos & derangement, in short giving everything I love, in exchange for everything I hate, and all this without a single gratification in possession or prospect, in present enjoyment or future wish.—Indeed my dear friend, duty being out of the question, inclination cuts off all argument, & so never let there be more between you & me, on this subject.

I inclose you some papers which have passed on the subject of a new loan. You will see by them that the paper-Coryphæus is either undaunted, or desperate. I believe that the statement inclosed has secured a decision against his proposition.—I dined yesterday in a company where Morris & Bingham were, & happened to sit between them. In the course of a conversation after dinner Morris made one of his warm declarations that after the expiration of his present Senatorial term nothing on earth should ever engage him to serve again in any public capacity. He did this with such solemnity as renders it impossible he should not be in earnest.—The President is not well. Little lingering fevers have been hanging about him for a week or ten days, and have affected his looks most remarkably. He is also extremely affected by the attacks made & kept up on him in the public papers. I think he feels those things more than any person I ever yet met with. I am sincerely sorry to see them. I remember an observation of yours, made when I first went to New York, that the satellites & sycophants which surrounded him had wound up the ceremonials of the government to a pitch of stateliness which nothing but his personal character could have supported, & which no character after him could ever maintain. It appears now that even his will be insufficient to justify them in the appeal of the times to common sense as the arbiter of everything. Naked he would have been sanctimoniously reverenced, but inveloped in the rags of royalty, they

can hardly be torn off without laceration. It is the more unfortunate that this attack is planted on popular ground, on
the love of the people to France & it's cause, which is universal.—Genet mentions freely enough in conversation that
France does not wish to involve us in the war by our guarantee. The information from St. Domingo & Martinique is
that those two islands are disposed & able to resist any attack
which Great Britain can make on them by land. A blockade
would be dangerous, could it be maintained in that climate
for any length of time. I delivered to Genet your letter to
Roland. As the latter is out of office, he will direct it to the
Minister of the Interior. I found every syllable of it strictly
proper. Your ploughs shall be duly attended to. Have you
ever taken notice of Tull's horse-houghing plough? I am persuaded that that, where you wish your work to be very exact,
& our great plough where a less degree will suffice, leave us
nothing to wish for from other countries as to ploughs, under
our circumstances.—I have not yet received my threshing machine. I fear the late long & heavy rains must have extended
to us, & affected our wheat. Adieu. Yours affectionately.

"MY FAMILY, MY FARM, AND MY BOOKS"

To Mrs. Church

Germantown, Nov. 27th, 1793

I have received, my good friend, your kind letter of August
19th, with the extract from that of Lafayette, for whom my
heart has been constantly bleeding. The influence of the
United States has been put into action, as far as it could be
either with decency or effect. But I fear that distance and difference of principle give little hold to General Washington on
the jailers of Lafayette. However, his friends may be assured
that our zeal has not been inactive. Your letter gives me the
first information that our dear friend Madame de Corny has
been, as to her fortune among the victims of the times. Sad
times, indeed! and much lamented victim! I know no country
where the remains of a fortune could place her so much at
her ease as this, and where public esteem is so attached to

worth, regardless of wealth; but our manners, and the state of our society here, are so different from those to which her habits have been formed, that she would lose more perhaps in that scale. And Madame Cosway in a convent! I knew that to much goodness of heart she joined enthusiasm and religion; but I thought that very enthusiasm would have prevented her from shutting up her adoration of the God of the universe within the walls of a cloister; that she would rather have sought the *mountain-top*. How happy should I be that it were *mine* that you, she, and Madame de Corny would seek. You say, indeed, that you are coming to America, but I know that means New York. In the meantime I am going to Virginia. I have at length become able to fix that to the beginning of the new year. I am then to be liberated from the hated occupations of politics, and to remain in the bosom of my family, my farm, and my books. I have my house to build, my fields to farm, and to watch for the happiness of those who labor for mine. I have one daughter married to a man of science, sense, virtue, and competence; in whom indeed I have nothing more to wish. They live with me. If the other shall be as fortunate, in due process of time I shall imagine myself as blessed as the most blessed of the patriarchs. Nothing could then withdraw my thoughts a moment from home but the recollection of my friends abroad. I often put the question, whether yourself and Kitty will ever come to see your friends at Monticello? but it is my affection and not my experience of things which has leave to answer, and I am determined to believe the answer, because in that belief I find I sleep sounder, and wake more cheerful. *En attendant*, God bless you.

Accept the homage of my sincere and constant affection.

"LUCERNE AND POTATOES"
To Tench Coxe

Monticello, May 1, 1794

DEAR SIR,—Your several favors of Feb. 22, 27, & March 16. which had been accumulating in Richmond during the prevalence of the small pox in that place, were lately brought to

me, on the permission given the post to resume his communication. I am particularly to thank you for your favor in forwarding the Bee. Your letters give a comfortable view of
French affairs, and later events seem to confirm it. Over the
foreign powers I am convinced they will triumph completely,
& I cannot but hope that that triumph, & the consequent
disgrace of the invading tyrants, is destined, in the order of
events, to kindle the wrath of the people of Europe against
those who have dared to embroil them in such wickedness,
and to bring at length, kings, nobles, & priests to the scaf-
folds which they have been so long deluging with human
blood. I am still warm whenever I think of these scoundrels,
tho I do it as seldom as I can, preferring infinitely to contemplate the tranquil growth of my lucerne & potatoes. I have so
completely withdrawn myself from these spectacles of usurpation & misrule, that I do not take a single newspaper, nor
read one a month; & I feel myself infinitely the happier for
it. We are alarmed here with the apprehensions of war; and
sincerely anxious that it may be avoided; but not at the expense either of our faith or honor. It seems much the general
opinion here, that the latter has been too much wounded not
to require reparation, & to seek it even in war, if that be
necessary. As to myself, I love peace, and I am anxious that
we should give the world still another useful lesson, by showing to them other modes of punishing injuries than by war,
which is as much a punishment to the punisher as to the sufferer. I love, therefore, mr. Clarke's proposition of cutting off
all communication with the nation which has conducted itself
so atrociously. This, you will say, may bring on war. If it
does, we will meet it like men; but it may not bring on war,
& then the experiment will have been a happy one. I believe
this war would be vastly more unanimously approved than
any one we ever were engaged in; because the aggressions
have been so wanton & bare-faced, and so unquestionably
against our desire.—I am sorry mr. Cooper & Priestly did not
take a more general survey of our country before they fixed
themselves. I think they might have promoted their own advantage by it, and have aided the introduction of our improvement where it is more wanting. The prospect of wheat
for the ensuing year is a bad one. This is all the sort of news

you can expect from me. From you I shall be glad to hear all sort of news, & particularly any improvements in the arts applicable to husbandry or household manufacture.

WHISKEY REBELS AND DEMOCRATIC SOCIETIES

To James Madison

Monticello, Dec. 28, 1794

DEAR SIR,—I have kept mr. Jay's letter a post or two, with an intention of considering attentively the observation it contains; but I have really now so little stomach for anything of that kind, that I have not resolution enough even to endeavor to understand the observations. I therefore return the letter, not to delay your answer to it, and beg you in answering for yourself to assure him of my respects and thankful acceptance of Chalmers' Treaties, which I do not possess, and if you possess yourself of the scope of his reasoning, make any answer to it you please for me. If it had been on the rotation of my crops, I would have answered myself, lengthily perhaps, but certainly *con gusto.*

The denunciation of the democratic societies is one of the extraordinary acts of boldness of which we have seen so many from the fraction of monocrats. It is wonderful indeed, that the President should have permitted himself to be the organ of such an attack on the freedom of discussion, the freedom of writing, printing & publishing. It must be a matter of rare curiosity to get at the modifications of these rights proposed by them, and to see what line their ingenuity would draw between democratical societies, whose avowed object is the nourishment of the republican principles of our constitution, and the society of the Cincinnati, *a self-created* one, carving out for itself hereditary distinctions, lowering over our Constitution eternally, meeting together in all parts of the Union, periodically, with closed doors, accumulating a capital in their separate treasury, corresponding secretly & regularly, & of which society the very persons denouncing the democrats are themselves the fathers, founders, & high officers. Their sight must be perfectly dazzled by the glittering of crowns & coronets, not to see the extravagance of the proposition to suppress the friends of general freedom, while those who wish to confine that freedom to the few, are permitted to go on in their principles & practices. I here put out of sight the persons whose misbehavior has been taken advantage of to slander the friends of popular rights; and I am happy to observe, that as far as the circle of my observation & information extends, everybody has lost sight of them, and views the abstract attempt on their natural & constitutional rights in all it's nakedness. I have never heard, or heard of, a single expression or opinion which did not condemn it as an inexcusable aggression. And with respect to the transactions against the excise law, it appears to me that you are all swept away in the torrent of governmental opinions, or that we do not know what these transactions have been. We know of none which, according to the definitions of the law, have been anything more than riotous. There was indeed a meeting to consult about a separation. But to consult on a question does not amount to a determination of that question in the affirmative, still less to the acting on such a determination; but we shall see, I suppose, what the court lawyers, & courtly judges, & would-be ambassadors will make of it. The excise law is an infernal one. The first error was to admit it by the Constitution; the 2d., to act on that admission; the 3d & last will be, to make it the instrument of dismembering the Union, & setting us all afloat to chuse which part of it we will adhere to. The information of our militia, returned from the Westward, is uniform, that tho the people there let them pass quietly, they were objects of their laughter, not of their fear; that 1000 men could have cut off their whole force in a thousand places of the Alleganey; that their detestation of the excise law is universal, and has now associated to it a detestation of the government; & that separation which perhaps was a very distant & problematical event, is now near, & certain, & determined in the mind of every man. I expected to have seen some justification of arming one part of the society against another; of declaring a civil war the moment before the meeting of that body which has the sole right of declaring war; of being so patient of the kicks & scoffs of our enemies, & rising at a feather against our friends; of adding a million to the public debt & deriding us with recommendations to pay it if we can &c., &c. But the part of the speech which was to be taken as a justification of the armament, reminded me of parson Saunders' demonstration why minus into minus make plus. After a parcel of shreds of stuff from Æsop's fables, and Tom Thumb, he jumps all at once into his Ergo, minus multiplied into minus make plus. Just so the 15,000 men enter after the fables, in the speech.—However, the time is coming when we shall fetch up the leeway of our vessel. The changes in your house, I see, are going on for the better, and even the Augean herd over your heads are slowly purging off their impurities. Hold on then, my dear friend, that we may not shipwreck in the meanwhile. I do not see, in the minds of those with whom I converse, a greater affliction than the fear of your retirement; but this must not be, unless to a more splendid & a more efficacious post. There I should rejoice to see you; I hope I may say, I shall rejoice to see you. I have long had much in my mind to say to you on that subject. But double delicacies have kept me silent. I ought perhaps to say, while I would not give up my own retirement for the empire of the universe, how I can justify wishing one whose happinesss I have so much at heart as yours, to take the front of the battle which is fighting for my security. This would be easy enough to be done, but not at the heel of a lengthy epistle.

Let us quit this, and turn to the fine weather we are basking in. We have had one of our tropical winters. Once only a snow of 3. inches deep, which went off the next day, and never as much ice as would have cooled a bottle of wine. And we have now but a month to go through of winter weather. For February always gives us a good sample of the spring of which it is the harbinger. I recollect no small news interesting to you. You will have heard, I suppose, that Wilson Nicholas has bought Carr's Carrsgrove and Harvey's barracks. I rejoice in the prosperity of a virtuous man, and hope his prosperity will not taint his virtue. Present me respectfully to Mrs. Madison, and pray her to keep you where you are for her own satisfaction and the public good; and accept the cordial affections of all. Adieu.

FARMING

To John Taylor

Monticello, Dec. 29, 1794

DEAR SIR,—I have long owed you a letter, for which my conscience would not have let me rest in quiet but on the consideration that the paiment would not be worth your acceptance. The debt is not merely for a letter the common traffic of every day, but for valuable ideas, which instructed me, which I have adopted, & am acting on them. I am sensible of the truth of your observations that the atmosphere is the great storehouse of matter for recruiting our lands, that tho' efficacious, it is slow in it's operation, and we must therefore give them time instead of the loads of quicker manure given in other countries, that for this purpose we must avail ourselves of the great quantities of land we possess in proportion to our labour, and that while putting them to nurse with the atmosphere, we must protect them from the bite & tread of animals, which are nearly a counterpoise for the benefits of the atmosphere. As good things, as well as evil, go in a train, this relieves us from the labor & expence of crossfences, now very sensibly felt on account of the scarcity & distance of timber. I am accordingly now engaged in applying my cross fences to the repair of the outer ones and substituting rows of peach trees to preserve the boundaries of the fields. And though I observe your strictures on rotations of crops, yet it appears that in this I differ from you only in words. You keep half your lands in culture, the other half at nurse; so I propose to do. Your scheme indeed requires only four years & mine six; but the proportion of labour & rest is the same. My years of rest, however, are employed, two of them in producing clover, yours in volunteer herbage. But I still understand it to be your opinion that clover is best where lands will produce them. Indeed I think that the important improvement for which the world is indebted to Young is the substitution of clover crops instead of unproductive fallows; & the demonstration that lands are more enriched by clover than by volunteer herbage or fallows; and the clover crops are highly valuable. That our red lands which are still in tolerable heart will produce fine clover I know from the experience of the last year; and indeed that of my neighbors had established the fact. And from observations on accidental plants in the feilds which have been considerably harrassed with corn, I believe that even these will produce clover fit for soiling of animals green. I think, therefore, I can count on the success of that improver. My third year of rest will be devoted to cowpenning, & to a trial of the buckwheat dressing. A further progress in surveying my open arable lands has shewn me that I can have 7 fields in each of my farms where I expected only six; consequently that I can add more to the portion of rest & ameliorating crops. I have doubted on a question on which I am sure you can advise me well, whether I had better give this newly acquired year as an addition to the continuance of my clover, or throw it with some improving crop between two of my crops of grain, as for instance between my corn & rye. I strongly incline to the latter, because I am not satisfied that one cleansing crop in seven years will be sufficient; and indeed I think it important to separate my exhausting crops by alternations of amelioraters. With this view I think to try an experiment of what Judge Parker informs me he practises. That is, to turn in my wheat stubble the instant the grain is off, and sow turneps to be fed out by the sheep. But whether this will answer in our fields which are harrassed, I do not know. We have been in the habit of sowing only our freshest lands in turneps, hence a presumption that wearied lands will not bring them. But Young's making turneps to be fed on by sheep the basis of his improvement of poor lands, affords evidence that tho they may not bring great crops, they will bring them in a sufficient degree to improve the lands. I will try that experiment, however, this year, as well as the one of buckwheat. I have also attended to another improver mentioned by you, the winter-vetch, & have taken measures to get the seed of it from England, as also of the Siberian vetch which Millar greatly commends, & being a biennial might perhaps take the place of clover in lands which do not suit that. The winter vetch I suspect may be advantageously thrown in between crops, as it gives a choice to use it as green feed in the spring if fodder be run short, or to turn it in as a green-dressing. My rotation, with these amendments, is as follows:–

1. Wheat, followed the same year by turneps, to be fed on by the sheep.

2. Corn & potatoes mixed, & in autumn the vetch to be used as fodder in the spring if wanted, or to be turned in as a dressing.

3. Peas or potatoes, or both according to the quality of the field.

4. Rye and clover sown on it in the spring. Wheat may be substituted here for rye, when it shall be found that the 2^d, 3^d, 5th, & 6th fields will subsist the farm.

5. Clover.

6. Clover, & in autumn turn it in & sow the vetch.

7. Turn in the vetch in the spring, then sow buckwheat & turn that in, having hurdled off the poorest spots for cow-penning. In autumn sow wheat to begin the circle again.

I am for throwing the whole force of my husbandry on the wheat-field, because it is the only one which is to go to market to produce money. Perhaps the clover may bring in something in the form of stock. The other feilds are merely for the consumption of the farm. Melilot, mentioned by you, I never heard of. The horse bean I tried this last year. It turned out nothing. The President has tried it without success. An old English farmer of the name of Spuryear, settled in Delaware, has tried it there with good success; but he told me it would not do without being well shaded, and I think he planted it among his corn for that reason. But he acknoleged our pea was as good an ameliorater & a more valuable pulse, as being food for man as well as horse. The succory is what Young calls Chicoria Intubus. He sent some seed to the President, who gave me some, & I gave it to my neighbors to keep up till I should come home. One of them has cultivated it with great success, is very fond of it, and gave me some seed which I sowed last spring. Tho' the summer was favorable it came on slowly at first, but by autumn became large & strong. It did not seed that year, but will the next, & you shall be furnished with seed. I suspect it requires rich ground, & then produces a heavy crop for green feed for horses & cattle. I had poor success with my potatoes last year, not having made more than 60 or 70 bushels to the acre. But my neighbors having made good crops, I am not disheartened. The first step towards the recovery of our lands is to find substitutes for corn & bacon. I count on potatoes, clover, & sheep. The two former to feed every animal on the farm except my negroes, & the latter to feed them, diversified with rations of salted fish & molasses, both of them wholesome, agreeable, & cheap articles of food.

For pasture I rely on the forests by day, & soiling in the evening. Why could we not have a moveable airy cow house, to be set up in the middle of the feild which is to be dunged, & soil our cattle in that thro' the summer as well as winter, keeping them constantly up & well littered? This, with me, would be in the clover feild of the 1.st year, because during the 2.^{d} year it would be rotting, and would be spread on it in fallow the beginning of the 3.^{d}, but such an effort would be far above the present tyro state of my farming. The grosser barbarisms in culture which I have to encounter, are more than enough for all my attentions at present. The dung-yard must be my last effort but one. The last would be irrigation. It might be thought at first view, that the interposition of these ameliorations or dressings between my crops will be too laborious, but observe that the turneps & two dressings of vetch do not cost a single ploughing. The turning in the wheat-stubble for the turneps is the fallow for the corn of the succeeding year. The 1.st sowing of vetches is on the corn (as is now practised for wheat), and the turning it in is the flush-ploughing for the crop of potatoes & peas. The 2.^{d} sowing of the vetch is on the wheat fallow, & the turning it in is the ploughing necessary for sowing the buckwheat. These three ameliorations, then, will cost but a harrowing each. On the subject of the drilled husbandry, I think experience has established it's preference for some plants, as the turnep, pea, bean, cabbage, corn, &c., and that of the broadcast for other plants as all the bread grains & grasses, except perhaps lucerne & S.^{t} foin in soils & climates very productive of weeds. In dry soils & climates the broadcast is better for lucerne & S.^{t} foin, as all the south of France can testify.

I have imagined and executed a mould-board which may be mathematically demonstrated to be perfect, as far as perfection depends on mathematical principles, and one great circumstance in it's favor is that it may be made by the most bungling carpenter, & cannot possibly vary a hair's breadth in it's form, but by gross negligence. You have seen the musical instrument called a sticcado. Suppose all it's sticks of equal length, hold the fore-end horizontally on the floor to receive the turf which presents itself horizontally, and with the right hand twist the hind-end to the perpendicular, or rather as much beyond the perpendicular as will be necessary to cast over the turf completely. This gives an idea (tho not absolutely exact) of my mould-board. It is on the principle of two wedges combined at right angles, the first in the direct line of the furrow to raise the turf gradually, the other across the furrow to turn it over gradually. For both these purposes the wedge is the instrument of the least resistance. I will make a model of the mould-board & lodge it with Col? Harvie in Richmond for you. This brings me to my thanks for the drill plough lodged with him for me, which I now expect every hour to receive, and the price of which I have deposited in his hands to be called for when you please. A good instrument of this kind is almost the greatest desideratum in husbandry. I am anxious to conjecture beforehand what may be expected from the sowing turneps in jaded ground, how much from the acre, & how large they will be? Will your experience enable you to give me a probable conjecture? Also what is the produce of potatoes, & what of peas in the same kind of ground? It must now have been several pages since you began to cry out 'mercy.' In mercy then I will here finish with my affectionate remembrance to my old friend. Mr. Pendleton, & respects to your fireside, & to yourself assurances of the sincere esteem of, dear Sir,

Your friend & serv[r],

THE GENEVA ACADEMY

To François D'Ivernois

Monticello, in Virginia, Feb. 6, 1795

DEAR SIR,—Your several favors on the affairs of Geneva found me here, in the month of December last. It is now more than a year that I have withdrawn myself from public affairs, which I never liked in my life, but was drawn into by emergencies which threatened our country with slavery, but ended in establishing it free. I have returned, with infinite appetite, to the enjoyment of my farm, my family & my books, and had determined to meddle in nothing beyond their limits. Your proposition, however, for transplanting the college of Geneva to my own country, was too analogous to all my attachments to science, & freedom, the first-born daughter of science, not to excite a lively interest in my mind, and the essays which were necessary to try it's practicability. This depended altogether on the opinions & dispositions of our State legislature, which was then in session. I immediately communicated your papers to a member of the legislature, whose abilities & zeal pointed him out as proper for it, urging him to sound as many of the leading members of the legislature as he could, & if he found their opinions favorable, to bring forward the proposition; but if he should find it desperate, not to hazard it; because I thought it best not to commit the honor either of our State or of your college, by an useless act of eclat. It was not till within these three days that I have had an interview with him, and an account of his proceedings. He communicated the papers to a great number of the members, and discussed them maturely, but privately, with them. They were generally well-disposed to the proposition, and some of them warmly; however, there was no difference of opinion in the conclusion, that it could not be effected. The reasons which they thought would with certainty prevail against it, were 1. that our youth, not familiarized but with their mother tongue, were not prepared to receive instructions in any other; 2d. that the expence of the institution would excite uneasiness in their constituents, & endanger it's permanence; & 3. that it's extent was disproportioned to the narrow state of the population with us. Whatever might be urged on these several subjects, yet as the decision rested with others, there remained to us only to regret that circumstances were such, or were thought to be such, as to disappoint your & our wishes. I should have seen with peculiar satisfaction the establishment of such a mass of science in my country, and should probably have been tempted to approach myself to it, by procuring a residence in it's neighborhood, at those seasons of the year at least when the operations of agriculture are less active and interesting. I sincerely lament the circumstances which have suggested this emigration. I had hoped that Geneva was familiarized to such a degree of liberty, that they might without difficulty or danger fill up the measure to its maximum; a term, which, though in the insulated man, bounded only by his natural powers, must, in society, be so far restricted as to protect himself against the evil passions of his associates, & consequently, them against him. I suspect that the doctrine, that small States alone are fitted to be republics, will be exploded by experience, with some other brilliant fallacies accredited by Montesquieu & other political writers. Perhaps it will be found, that to obtain a just republic (and it is to secure our just rights that we resort to government at all) it must be so extensive as that local egoisms may never reach it's greater part; that on every particular question, a majority may be found in it's councils free from particular interests, and giving, therefore, an uniform prevalence to the principles of justice. The smaller the societies, the more violent & more convulsive their schisms. We have chanced to live in an age which will probably be distinguished in history, for it's experiments in government on a larger scale than has yet taken place. But we shall not live to see the result. The grosser absurdities, such as hereditary magistracies, we shall see exploded in our day, long experience having already pronounced condemnation against them. But what is to be the substitute? This our children or grand children will answer. We may be satisfied with the certain knowledge that none can ever be tried, so stupid, so unrighteous, so oppressive, so destructive of every end for which honest men enter into government, as that which their forefathers had established, & their fathers alone venture to tumble headlong from the stations they have so long abused. It is unfortunate, that the efforts of mankind to recover the freedom of which they have been so long deprived, will be accompanied with violence, with errors, & even with crimes. But while we weep over the means, we must pray for the end.—But I have been insensibly led by the general complexion of the times, from the particular case of Geneva, to those to which it bears no similitude. Of that we hope good things. Its inhabitants must be too much enlightened, too well experienced in the blessings of freedom and undisturbed industry, to tolerate long a contrary state of things. I shall be happy to hear that their government perfects itself, and leaves room for the honest, the industrious & wise; in which case, your own talents, & those of the persons for whom you have interested yourself, will, I am sure, find welcome & distinction. My good wishes will always attend you, as a consequence of the esteem & regard with which I am, Dear Sir, your most obedient & most humble servant.

ABJURING THE PRESIDENCY

To James Madison

Monticello, Apr. 27, 1795

DEAR SIR,—Your letter of Mar 23. came to hand the 7th of April, and notwithstanding the urgent reasons for answering a part of it immediately, yet as it mentioned that you would leave Philadelphia within a few days, I feared that the answer might pass you on the road. A letter from Philadelphia by the last post having announced to me your leaving that place the day preceding it's date, I am in hopes this will find you in Orange. In mine, to which yours of Mar 23. was an answer, I expressed my hope of the only change of position I ever wished to see you make, and I expressed it with entire sincerity, because there is not another person in the U S. who being placed at the helm of our affairs, my mind would be so completely at rest for the fortune of our political bark. The wish too was pure, & unmixed with anything respecting myself personally. For as to myself, the subject had been thoroughly weighed & decided on, & my retirement from office had been meant from all office high or low, without exception. I can say, too, with truth, that the subject had not been presented to my mind by any vanity of my own. I know myself & my fellow citizens too well to have ever thought of it. But the idea was forced upon me by continual insinuations in the public papers, while I was in office. As all these came from a hostile quarter, I knew that their object was to poison the public mind as to my motives, when they were not able to charge me with facts. But the idea being once presented to me, my own quiet required that I should face it & examine it. I did so thoroughly, & had no difficulty to see that every reason which had determined me to retire from the office I then held, operated more strongly against that which was insinuated to be my object. I decided then on those general grounds which could alone be present to my mind at the time, that is to say, reputation, tranquillity, labor; for as to public duty, it could not be a topic of consideration in my case. If these general considerations were sufficient to ground a firm resolution never to permit myself to think of the office, or to be thought of for it, the special ones which have supervened on my retirement, still more insuperably bar the door to it. My health is entirely broken down within the last eight months; my age requires that I should place my affairs in a clear state; these are sound if taken care of, but capable of considerable dangers if longer neglected; and above all things, the delights I feel in the society of my family, and the agricultural pursuits in which I am so eagerly engaged. The little spice of ambition which I had in my younger days has long since evaporated, and I set still less store by a posthumous than present name. In stating to you the heads of reasons which have produced my determination, I do not mean an opening for future discussion, or that I may be reasoned out of it. The question is forever closed with me; my sole object is to avail myself of the first opening ever given me from a friendly quarter (and I could not with decency do it before), of preventing any division or loss of votes, which might be fatal to the Republican interest. If that has any chance of prevailing, it must be by avoiding the loss of a single vote, and by concentrating all its strength on one object. Who this should be, is a question I can more freely discuss with anybody than yourself. In this I painfully feel the loss of Monroe. Had he been here, I should have been at no loss for a channel through which to make myself understood; if I have been misunderstood by anybody through the instrumentality of mr. Fenno & his abettors.—I long to see you. I am proceeding in my agricultural plans with a slow but sure step. To get under full way will require 4. or 5. years. But patience & perseverance will accomplish it. My little essay in red clover, the last year, has had the most encouraging success. I sowed then about 40. acres. I have sowed this year about 120. which the rain now falling comes very opportunely on. From 160. to 200. acres, will be my yearly sowing. The seed-box described in the agricultural transactions of New York, reduces the expense of seeding from 6/ to ⅔ the acre, and does the business better than is possible to be done by the human hand. May we hope a visit from you? If we may, let it be after the middle of May, by which time I hope to be returned from Bedford. I had had a proposition to meet mr. Henry there this month, to confer on the subject of a convention, to the calling of which he is now become a convert. The session of our district court furnished me a just excuse for the time; but the impropriety of my entering into consultation on a measure in which I would take no part, is a permanent one.

Present my most respectful compliments to mrs. Madison, & be assured of the warm attachment of, Dear Sir, yours affectionately.

A NAIL-MAKER
To Jean Nicolas Démeunier

Monticello, Virginia, Apr. 29, 1795

DEAR SIR,—Your favor of Mar. 30. from Philadelphia came to my hands a few days ago. That which you mention to have written from London has never been received; nor had I been able to discover what has been your fortune during the troubles of France after the death of the King. Being thoroughly persuaded that under all circumstances your conduct had been entirely innocent & friendly to the freedom of your country, I had hopes that you had not been obliged to quit your own country. Being myself a warm zealot for the attainment & enjoiment by all mankind of as much liberty, as each may exercise without injury to the equal liberty of his fellow citizens, I have lamented that in France the endeavours to obtain this should have been attended with the effusion of so much blood. I was intimate with the leading characters of the year 1789. So I was with those of the Brissotine party who succeeded them: & have always been persuaded that their views were upright. Those who have followed have been less known to me: but I have been willing to hope that they also meant the establishment of a free government in their country, excepting perhaps the party which has lately been suppressed. The government of those now at the head of affairs appears to hold out many indications of good sense, moderation & virtue; & I cannot but presume from their character as well as your own that you would find a perfect safety in the bosom of your own country. I think it fortunate for the United States to have become the asylum for so many virtuous patriots of different denominations: but their circumstances, with which you were so well acquainted before, enabled them to be but a bare asylum, & to offer nothing for them but an entire freedom to use their own means & faculties as they please. There is no such thing in this country as what would be called wealth in Europe. The richest are but a little at ease, & obliged to pay the most rigorous attention to their affairs to keep them together. I do not mean to speak here of the Beaujons of America. For we have some of these tho' happily they are but ephemeral. Our public œconomy also is such as to offer drudgery and subsistence only to those entrusted with its administration, a wise & necessary precaution against the degeneracy of the public servants. In our private pursuits it is a great advantage that every honest employment is deemed honorable. I am myself a nail-maker. On returning home after an absence of ten years, I found my farms so much deranged that I saw evidently they would be a burden to me instead of a support till I could regenerate them; & consequently that it was necessary for me to find some other resource in the meantime. I thought for awhile of taking up the manufacture of pot-ash, which requires but small advances of money. I concluded at length however to begin a manufacture of nails, which needs little or no capital, & I now employ a dozen little boys from 10. to 16. years of age, overlooking all the details of their business myself & drawing from it a profit on which I can get along till I can put my farms into a course of yielding profit. My new trade of nail-making is to me in this country what an additional title of nobility or the ensigns of a new order are in Europe. In the commercial line, the grocers business is that which requires the least capital in this country. The grocer generally obtains a credit of three months, & sells for ready money so as to be able to make his paiments & obtain a new supply. But I think I have observed that your countrymen who have been obliged to work out their own fortunes here, have succeeded best with a small farm. Labour indeed is dear here, but rents are low & on the whole a reasonable profit & comfortable subsistence results. It is at the same time the most tranquil, healthy, & independent. And since you have been pleased to ask my opinion as to the best way of employing yourself till you can draw funds from France or return there yourself, I do presume that this is the business which would yield the most happiness & contentment to one of your philosophic turn. But at the distance I am from New York, where you seem disposed to fix yourself, & little acquainted with the circumstances of that place I am much less qualified than disposed to suggest to you emploiments analogous to your turn of mind & at the same time to the circumstances of your present situation. Be assured that it will always give me lively pleasure to learn that your pursuits, whatever they may be may lead you to contentment & success, being with very sincere esteem & respect, dear sir, your most obedient servant.

ROGUES AND A TREATY

To Mann Page

Monticello, Aug. 30, 1795

It was not in my power to attend at Fredericksburg according to the kind invitation in your letter, and in that of mr. Ogilvie. The heat of the weather, the business of the farm, to which I have made myself necessary, forbade it; and to give one round reason for all, *mature sanus*, I have laid up my

Rosinante in his stall, before his unfitness for the road shall
expose him faultering to the world. But why did not I answer
you in time? Because, in truth, I am encouraging myself to
grow lazy, and I was sure you would ascribe the delay to
anything sooner than a want of affection or respect to you,
for this was not among the possible causes. In truth, if anything could ever induce me to sleep another night out of my
own house, it would have been your friendly invitation and
my sollicitude for the subject of it, the education of our
youth. I do most anxiously wish to see the highest degrees of
education given to the higher degrees of genius, and to all
degrees of it, so much as may enable them to read & understand what is going on in the world, and to keep their part
of it going on right: for nothing can keep it right but their
own vigilant & distrustful superintendence. I do not believe
with the Rochefoucaults & Montaignes, that fourteen out of
fifteen men are rogues: I believe a great abatement from that
proportion may be made in favor of general honesty. But I
have always found that rogues would be uppermost, and I do
not know that the proportion is too strong for the higher
orders, and for those who, rising above the swinish multitude, always contrive to nestle themselves into the places of
power & profit. These rogues set out with stealing the people's good opinion, and then steal from them the right of
withdrawing it, by contriving laws and associations against
the power of the people themselves. Our part of the country
is in considerable fermentation, on what they suspect to be a
recent roguery of this kind. They say that while all hands were
below deck mending sails, splicing ropes, and every one at his
own business, & the captain in his cabbin attending to his log
book & chart, a rogue of a pilot has run them into an enemy's port. But metaphor apart, there is much dissatisfaction
with mr. Jay & his treaty. For my part, I consider myself now
but as a passenger, leaving the world, & it's government to
those who are likely to live longer in it. That you may be
among the longest of these, is my sincere prayer. After begging you to be the bearer of my compliments & apologies to
mr. Ogilvie, I bid you an affectionate farewell, always wishing
to hear from you.

THE LAWS OF VIRGINIA
To George Wythe

Monticello, January 16, 1796

In my letter which accompanied the box containing my collection of Printed laws, I promised to send you by post a statement of the contents of the box. On taking up the subject I found it better to take a more general view of the whole of the laws I possess, as well Manuscript as printed, as also of those which I do not possess, and suppose to be no longer extant. This general view you will have in the enclosed paper, whereof the articles stated to be printed constitute the contents of the box I sent you. Those in MS. were not sent, because not supposed to have been within your view, and because some of them will not bear removal, being so rotten, that in turning over a leaf it sometimes falls into powder. These I preserve by wrapping & sewing them up in oiled cloth, so that neither air nor moisture can have access to them. Very early in the course of my researches into the laws of Virginia, I observed that many of them were already lost, and many more on the point of being lost, as existing only in single copies in the hands of careful or curious individuals, on whose death they would probably be used for waste paper. I set myself therefore to work, to collect all which were then existing, in order that when the day should come in which the public should advert to the magnitude of their loss in these precious monuments of our property, and our history, a part of their regret might be spared by information that a portion has been saved from the wreck, which is worthy of their attention & preservation. In searching after these remains, I spared neither time, trouble, nor expense; and am of opinion that scarcely any law escaped me, which was in being as late as the year 1778 in the middle or Southern parts of the State. In the Northern parts, perhaps something might still be found. In the clerk's office in the antient counties, some of these MS. copies of the laws may possibly still exist, which used to be furnished at the public expense to every county, before the use of the press was introduced; and in the same places, and in the hands of antient magistrates or of their fam-

ilies, some of the fugitive sheets of the laws of separate sessions, which have been usually distributed since the practice
commenced of printing them. But recurring to what we actually possess, the question is, what means will be the most
effectual for preserving these remains from future loss? All the
care I can take of them, will not preserve them from the
worm, from the natural decay of the paper, from the accidents
of fire, or those of removal when it is necessary for any public
purposes, as in the case of those now sent you. Our experience has proved to us that a single copy, or a few, deposited
in MS. in the public offices, cannot be relied on for any great
length of time. The ravages of fire and of ferocious enemies
have had but too much part in producing the very loss we are
now deploring. How many of the precious works of antiquity
were lost while they were preserved only in manuscript?
Has there ever been one lost since the art of printing has
rendered it practicable to multiply & disperse copies? This
leads us then to the only means of preserving those remains
of our laws now under consideration, that is, a multiplication
of printed copies. I think therefore that there should be
printed at public expense, an edition of all the laws ever
passed by our legislatures which can now be found; that a
copy should be deposited in every public library in America,
in the principal public offices within the State, and some perhaps in the most distinguished public libraries of Europe, and
that the rest should be sold to individuals, towards reimburs-
ing the expences of the edition. Nor do I think that this
would be a voluminous work. The MSS. would probably furnish matter for one printed volume in folio, would comprehend all the laws from 1624 to 1701, which period includes
Purvis. My collection of Fugitive sheets forms, as we know,
two volumes, and comprehends all the extant laws from 1734
to 1783; and the laws which can be gleaned up from the Revisals to supply the chasm between 1701 & 1734, with those
from 1783 to the close of the present century, (by which term
the work might be compleated,) would not be more than the
matter of another volume. So that four volumes in folio,
would give every law ever passed which is now extant;
whereas those who wish to possess as many of them as can
be procured, must now buy the six folio volumes of Revisals,

to wit, Purvis & those of 1732, 1748, 1768, 1783, & 1794, and in all of them possess not one half of what they wish. What would be the expence of the edition I cannot say, nor how much would be reimbursed by the sales; but I am sure it would be moderate, compared with the rates which the public have hitherto paid for printing their laws, provided a sufficient latitude be given as to printers & places. The first step would be to make out a single copy for the MSS., which would employ a clerk about a year or something more, to which expence about a fourth should be added for the collation of the MSS., which would employ 3. persons at a time about half a day, or a day in every week. As I have already spent more time in making myself acquainted with the contents & arrangement of these MSS. than any other person probably ever will, & their condition does not admit their removal to a distance, I will chearfully undertake the direction & superintendence of this work, if it can be done in the neighboring towns of Charlottesville or Milton, farther than which I could not undertake to go from home. For the residue of the work, my printed volumes might be delivered to the Printer.

I have troubled you with these details, because you are in the place where they may be used for the public service, if they admit of such use, & because the order of assembly, which you mention, shews they are sensible of the necessity of preserving such of these laws as relate to our landed property; and a little further consideration will perhaps convince them that it is better to do the whole work once for all, than to be recurring to it by piece-meal, as particular parts of it shall be required, & that too perhaps when the materials shall be lost. You are the best judge of the weight of these observations, & of the mode of giving them any effect they may merit. Adieu affectionately.

"AN AGE OF EXPERIMENTS"

To John Adams

Monticello, Feb. 28, 1796

I am to thank you, my dear Sir, for forwarding Mr. D'Ivernois' book on the French revolution. I recieve every thing

with respect which comes from him. But it is on politics, a
subject I never loved, and now hate. I will not promise therefore to read it thoroughly. I fear the oligarchical executive of
the French will not do. We have always seen a small council
get into cabals and quarrels, the more bitter and relentless the
fewer they are. We saw this in our committee of the states;
and that they were, from their bad passions, incapable of
doing the business of their country. I think that for the
prompt, clear and consistent action so necessary in an Executive, unity of person is necessary as with us. I am aware of
the objection to this, that the office becoming more important may bring on serious discord in elections. In our country
I think it will be long first; not within our day; and we may
safely trust to the wisdom of our successors the remedies of
the evil to arise in theirs. Both experiments however are now
fairly committed, and the result will be seen. Never was a
finer canvas presented to work on than our countrymen. All
of them engaged in agriculture or the pursuits of honest industry, independant in their circumstances, enlightened as to
their rights, and firm in their habits of order and obedience
to the laws. This I hope will be the age of experiments in
government, and that their basis will be founded on principles of honesty, not of mere force. We have seen no instance
of this since the days of the Roman republic, nor do we read
of any before that. Either force or corruption has been the
principle of every modern government, unless the Dutch perhaps be excepted, and I am not well enough informed to except them absolutely. If ever the morals of a people could be
made the basis of their own government, it is our case; and
he who could propose to govern such a people by the corruption of their legislature, before he could have one night of
quiet sleep, must convince himself that the human soul as well
as body is mortal. I am glad to see that whatever grounds of
apprehension may have appeared of a wish to govern us
otherwise than on principles of reason and honesty, we are
getting the better of them. I am sure, from the honesty of
your heart, you join me in detestation of the corruption of
the English government, and that no man on earth is more
incapable than yourself of seeing that copied among us, willingly. I have been among those who have feared the design

to introduce it here, and it has been a strong reason with me for wishing there was an ocean of fire between that island and us. But away politics.

I owe a letter to the Auditor [Richard Harrison] on the subject of my accounts while a foreign minister, and he informs me yours hang on the same difficulties with mine. Before the present government there was a usage either practised on or understood which regulated our charges. This government has directed the future by a law. But this is not retrospective, and I cannot conceive why the treasury cannot settle accounts under the old Congress on the principles that body acted on. I shall very shortly write to Mr. Harrison on this subject, and if we cannot have it settled otherwise I suppose we must apply to the legislature. In this I will act in concert with you if you approve of it. Present my very affectionate respects to Mrs. Adams, and be assured that no one more cordially esteems your virtues than Dear Sir Your sincere friend and servt.

"THE BOISTEROUS SEA OF LIBERTY"

To Philip Mazzei

Monticello, Apr. 24, 1796

MY DEAR FRIEND,—Your letter of Oct. 26. 1795. is just received and gives me the first information that the bills forwarded for you to V. S. & H. of Amsterdam on V. Anderson for £39-17-10½ & on George Barclay for £70-8-6 both of London have been protested. I immediately write to the drawers to secure the money if still unpaid. I wonder I have never had a letter from our friends of Amsterdam on that subject as well as acknoleging the subsequent remittances. Of these I have apprised you by triplicates, but for fear of miscarriage will just mention that on Sep. 8. I forwarded them Hodgden's bill on Robinson Saunderson & Rumney of Whitehaven for £300. and Jan. 31. that of the same on the same for £137-16-6 both received from mr. Blair for your stock sold out. I have now the pleasure to inform you that Dohrman has settled his account with you, has allowed the New York damage of 20. per cent for the protest, & the New York interest of 7. per cent. and after deducting the partial payments for which he held receipts the balance was three thousand & eighty-seven dollars which sum he has paid into mr. Madison's hands & as he (mr. Madison) is now in Philadelphia, I have desired him to invest the money in good bills on Amsterdam & remit them to the V. Staphorsts & H. whom I consider as possessing your confidence as they do mine beyond any house in London. The pyracies of that nation lately extended from the sea to the debts due from them to other nations renders theirs an unsafe medium to do business through. I hope these remittances will place you at your ease & I will endeavor to execute your wishes as to the settlement of the other small matters you mention: tho' from them I expect little. E. R. is bankrupt, or tantamount to it. Our friend M. P. is embarrassed, having lately sold the fine lands he lives on, & being superlatively just & honorable I expect we may get whatever may be in his hands. Lomax is under greater difficulties with less means, so that I apprehend you have little more to expect from this country except the balance which will remain for Colle after deducting the little matter due to me, & what will be recovered by Anthony. This will be decided this summer.

I have written to you by triplicates with every remittance I sent to the V. S. & H. & always recapitulated in each letter the objects of the preceding ones. I enclosed in two of them some seeds of the squash as you desired. Send me in return some seeds of the winter vetch, I mean that kind which is sewn in autumn & stands thro the cold of winter, furnishing a crop of green fodder in March. Put a few seeds in every letter you may write to me. In England only the spring vetch can be had. Pray fail not in this. I have it greatly at heart.

The aspect of our politics has wonderfully changed since you left us. In place of that noble love of liberty, & republican government which carried us triumphantly thro' the war, an Anglican monarchical, & aristocratical party has sprung up, whose avowed object is to draw over us the substance, as they have already done the forms, of the British government. The main body of our citizens, however, remain true to their republican principles; the whole landed interest is republican, and so is a great mass of talents. Against us are the Executive, the Judiciary, two out of three branches of the legislature, all the officers of the government, all who want to be officers, all timid men who prefer the calm of despotism to the boisterous sea of liberty, British merchants & Americans trading on British capitals, speculators & holders in the banks & public funds, a contrivance invented for the purposes of corruption, & for assimilating us in all things to the rotten as well as the sound parts of the British model. It would give you a fever were I to name to you the apostates who have gone over to these heresies, men who were Samsons in the field & Solomons in the council, but who have had their heads shorn by the harlot England. In short, we are likely to preserve the liberty we have obtained only by unremitting labors & perils. But we shall preserve them; and our mass of weight & wealth on the good side is so great, as to leave no danger that force will ever be attempted against us. We have only to awake and snap the Lilliputian cords with which they have been entangling us during the first sleep which succeeded our labors. I will forward the testimonial of the death of mrs. Mazzei, which I can do the more incontrovertibly as she is buried in my grave yard, and I pass her grave daily. The formalities of the proof you require, will occasion delay. John Page & his son Mann are well. The father remarried to a lady from N. York. Beverley Randolph e la sua consorte living & well. Their only child married to the 2d of T. M. Randolph. The eldest son you know married my eldest daughter, is an able learned & worthy character, but kept down by ill health. They have two children & still live with me. My younger daughter well. Colo. Innis is well, & a true republican still as are all those before named. Colo. Monroe is our M. P. at Paris a most worthy patriot & honest man. These are the persons you inquire after. I begin to feel the effects of age. My health has suddenly broke down, with symptoms which give me to believe I shall not have much to encounter of the *tedium vitæ*. While it remains, however, my heart will be warm in it's friendships, and among these, will always foster the affection with which I am, dear Sir, your friend and servant.

AN ENTENTE WITH ADAMS

To James Madison, with Enclosure

Jan. 1, 1797

Yours of Dec. 19. has come safely. The event of the election has never been a matter of doubt in my mind. I knew that the Eastern states were disciplined in the schools of their town meetings to sacrifice differences of opinion to the great object of operating in phalanx, & that the more free & moral agency practiced in the other states would always make up the supplement of their weight. Indeed the vote comes much nearer an equality than I had expected. I know the difficulty of obtaining belief to one's declarations of a disinclination to honors, & that it is greatest with those who still remain in the world. But no arguments were wanting to reconcile me to a relinquishment of the first office or acquiescence under the second. As to the first it was impossible that a more solid unwillingness settled on full calculation, could have existed in any man's mind, short of the degree of absolute refusal. The only view on which I would have gone into it for awhile was to put our vessel on her republican tack before she should be thrown too much to leeward of her true principles. As to the second, it is the only office in the world about which I am unable to decide in my own mind whether I had rather have it or not have it. Pride does not enter into the estimate; for I think with the Romans that the general of today should be a soldier tomorrow if necessary. I can particularly have no feelings which would revolt at a secondary position to mr. Adams. I am his junior in life, was his junior in Congress, his junior in the diplomatic line, his junior lately in the civil government. Before the receipt of your letter I had written the enclosed one to him. I had intended it some time, but had deferred it from time to time under the discouragement of a despair of making him believe I could be sincere in it. The papers by the last post not rendering it necessary to change anything in the letter I enclose it open for your perusal, not only that you may possess the actual state of dispositions between us, but that if anything should render the delivery of it ineligible in your opinion, you may return it to me. If mr. Adams can be induced to administer the government on it's true principles, & to relinquish his bias to an English constitution, it is to be considered whether it would not be on the whole for the public good to come to a good understanding with him as to his future elections. He is perhaps the only sure barrier against Hamilton's getting in.

Since my last I have received a packet of books & pamphlets, the choiceness of which testifies that they come from you. The incidents of Hamilton's insurrection is a curious work indeed. The hero of it exhibits himself in all the attitudes of a dexterous balance master.

The Political progress is a work of value & of a singular complexion. The eye of the author seems to be a natural achromatic, which divests every object of the glare of colour. The preceding work under the same title had the same merit. One is disgusted indeed with the ulcerated state which it presents of the human mind: but to cure an ulcer we must go to its bottom: & no writer has ever done this more radically than this one. The reflections into which he leads one are not flattering to our species. In truth I do not recollect in all the animal kingdom a single species but man which is eternally & systematically engaged in the destruction of its own species. What is called civilization seems to have no other effect on him than to teach him to pursue the principle of bellum omnium in omnia on a larger scale, & in place of the little contests of tribe against tribe, to engage all the quarters of the earth in the same work of destruction. When we add to this that as to the other species of animals, the lions & tigers are mere lambs compared with man as a destroyer, we must conclude that it is in man alone that nature has been able to find a sufficient barrier against the too great multiplication of other animals & of man himself, an equilibriating power against the fecundity of generation. My situation points my views chiefly to his wars in the physical world: yours perhaps exhibit him as equally warring in the moral one. We both, I believe, join in wishing to see him softened. Adieu.

ENCLOSURE TO JOHN ADAMS

Monticello, Dec. 28, 1796

DEAR SIR—The public and the public papers have been much
occupied lately in placing us in a point of opposition to each
other. I trust with confidence that less of it has been felt by
ourselves personally. In the retired canton where I am, I learn
little of what is passing: pamphlets I see never; papers but a
few; and the fewer the happier. Our latest intelligence from
Philadelphia at present is of the 16th. inst. but tho' at that
date your election to the first magistracy seems not to have
been known as a fact, yet with me it has never been doubted.
I knew it impossible you should lose a vote North of the
Delaware, and even if that of Pensylvania should be against
you in the mass, yet that you would get enough South of that
to place your succession out of danger. I have never one single moment expected a different issue: and tho' I know I shall
not be believed, yet it is not the less true that I have never
wished it. My neighbors, as my compurgators, could aver that
fact, because they see my occupations and my attachment to
them. Indeed it is possible that you may be cheated of your
succession by a trick worthy the subtlety of your arch-friend
[Alexander Hamilton] of New York, who has been able to
make of your real friends tools to defeat their and your just
wishes. Most probably he will be disappointed as to you; and
my inclinations place me out of his reach. I leave to others
the sublime delights of riding in the storm, better pleased
with sound sleep and a warm birth below, with the society of
neighbors, friends and fellow laborers of the earth, than of
spies and sycophants. No one then will congratulate you with
purer disinterestedness than myself. The share indeed which I
may have had in the late vote, I shall still value highly, as an
evidence of the share I have in the esteem of my fellow citizens. But while, in this point of view, a few votes less would
be little sensible, the difference in the effect of a few more
would be very sensible and oppressive to me. I have no ambition to govern men. It is a painful and thankless office.
Since the day too on which you signed the treaty of Paris our
horizon was never so overcast. I devoutly wish you may be
able to shun for us this war by which our agriculture, com-

merce and credit will be destroyed. If you are, the glory will be all your own; and that your administration may be filled with glory and happiness to yourself and advantage to us is the sincere wish of one who tho', in the course of our voyage thro' life, various little incidents have happened or been contrived to separate us, retains still for you the solid esteem of the moments when we were working for our independance, and sentiments of respect and affectionate attachment.

"PERFECTLY NEUTRAL AND INDEPENDENT"

To Elbridge Gerry

Philadelphia, May 13, 1797

MY DEAR FRIEND,—Your favor of the 4th instt came to hand yesterday. That of the 4th of Apr, with the one for Monroe, has never been received. The first, of Mar 27, did not reach me till Apr 21, when I was within a few days of setting out for this place, & I put off acknoleging it till I should come here. I entirely commend your dispositions towards mr. Adams; knowing his worth as intimately and esteeming it as much as any one, and acknoleging the preference of his claims, if any I could have had, to the high office conferred on him. But in truth, I had neither claims nor wishes on the subject, tho I know it will be difficult to obtain belief of this. When I retired from this place & the office of Secy of state, it was in the firmest contemplation of never more returning here. There had indeed been suggestions in the public papers, that I was looking towards a succession to the President's chair, but feeling a consciousness of their falsehood, and observing that the suggestions came from hostile quarters, I considered them as intended merely to excite public odium against me. I never in my life exchanged a word with any person, on the subject, till I found my name brought forward generally, in competition with that of mr. Adams. Those with whom I then communicated, could say, if it were necessary, whether I met the call with desire, or even with a ready acquiescence, and whether from the moment of my first acquiescence, I did not devoutly pray that the very thing might happen which has happened. The second office of this government is honorable & easy, the first is but a splendid misery.

You express apprehensions that stratagems will be used, to produce a misunderstanding between the President and myself. Tho not a word having this tendency has ever been hazarded to me by any one, yet I consider as a certainty that nothing will be left untried to alienate him from me. These machinations will proceed from the Hamiltons by whom he is surrounded, and who are only a little less hostile to him than to me. It cannot but damp the pleasure of cordiality, when we suspect that it is suspected. I cannot help fearing, that it is impossible for mr. Adams to believe that the state of my mind is what it really is; that he may think I view him as an obstacle in my way. I have no supernatural power to impress truth on the mind of another, nor he any to discover that the estimate which he may form, on a just view of the human mind as generally constituted, may not be just in its application to a special constitution. This may be a source of private uneasiness to us; I honestly confess that it is so to me at this time. But neither of us are capable of letting it have effect on our public duties. Those who may endeavor to separate us, are probably excited by the fear that I might have influence on the executive councils; but when they shall know that I consider my office as constitutionally confined to legislative functions, and that I could not take any part whatever in executive consultations, even were it proposed, their fears may perhaps subside, & their object be found not worth a machination.

I do sincerely wish with you, that we could take our stand on a ground perfectly neutral & independent towards all nations. It has been my constant object thro public life; and with respect to the English & French, particularly, I have too often expressed to the former my wishes, & made to them propositions verbally & in writing, officially & privately, to official & private characters, for them to doubt of my views, if they would be content with equality. Of this they are in possession of several written & formal proofs, in my own hand writing. But they have wished a monopoly of commerce & influence with us; and they have in fact obtained it. When we take notice that theirs is the workshop to which we go for all we want; that with them centre either immediately or ultimately all the labors of our hands and lands; that to them belongs either openly or secretly the great mass of our navigation; that even the factorage of their affairs here, is kept to themselves by factitious citizenships; that these foreign & false citizens now constitute the great body of what are called our merchants, fill our sea ports, are planted in every little town & district of the interior country, sway everything in the former places by their own votes, & those of their dependants, in the latter, by their insinuations & the influence of their ledgers; that they are advancing fast to a monopoly of our banks & public funds, and thereby placing our public finances under their control; that they have in their alliance the most influential characters in & out of office; when they have shewn that by all these bearings on the different branches of the government, they can force it to proceed in whatever direction they dictate, and bend the interests of this country entirely to the will of another; when all this, I say, is attended to, it is impossible for us to say we stand on independent ground, impossible for a free mind not to see & to groan under the bondage in which it is bound. If anything after this could excite surprise, it would be that they have been able so far to throw dust in the eyes of our own citizens, as to fix on those who wish merely to recover self-government the charge of subserving one foreign influence, because they resist submission to another. But they possess our printing presses, a powerful engine in their government of us. At this very moment, they would have drawn us into a war on the side of England, had it not been for the failure of her bank. Such was their open & loud cry, & that of their gazettes till this event. After plunging us in all the broils of the European nations, there would remain but one act to close our tragedy, that is, to break up our Union; and even this they have ventured seriously & solemnly to propose & maintain by arguments in a Connecticut paper. I have been happy, however, in believing, from the stifling of this effort, that that dose was found too strong, & excited as much repugnance there as it did horror in other parts of our country, & that whatever follies we may be led into as to foreign nations, we shall never give up our Union, the last anchor of our hope, & that alone which is to prevent this heavenly country from becoming an arena of gladiators. Much as I abhor war, and view it as the greatest scourge of mankind, and anxiously as I wish to keep out of the broils of Europe, I would yet go with my brethren into these, rather than separate from them. But I hope we may still keep clear of them, notwithstanding our present thraldom, & that time may be given us to reflect on the awful crisis we have passed through, and to find some means of shielding ourselves in future from foreign influence, political, commercial, or in whatever other form it may be attempted. I can scarcely withhold myself from joining in the wish of Silas Deane, that there were an ocean of fire between us & the old world.

A perfect confidence that you are as much attached to peace & union as myself, that you equally prize independence of all nations, and the blessings of self-government, has induced me freely to unbosom myself to you, and let you see the light in which I have viewed what has been passing among us from the beginning of the war. And I shall be happy, at all times, in an intercommunication of sentiments with you, believing that the dispositions of the different parts of our country have been considerably misrepresented & misunderstood in each part, as to the other, and that nothing but good can result from an exchange of information & opinions between those whose circumstances & morals admit no doubt of the integrity of their views.

I remain, with constant and sincere esteem, Dear Sir, your affectionate friend and servant.

PEACE AND COMMERCE
To Thomas Pinckney

Philadelphia, May 29, 1797

DEAR SIR,—I received from you, before you left England, a letter enclosing one from the Prince of Parma. As I learnt soon after that you were shortly to return to America, I concluded to join my acknolegments of it to my congratulations on your arrival; & both have been delayed by a blameable spirit of procrastination, forever suggesting to our indolence that we need not do to-day what may be done to-morrow. Accept these now in all the sincerity of my heart. It is but lately I have answered the Prince's letter. It required some time to establish arrangements which might effect his purpose, & I wished also to forward a particular article or two of curiosity. You have found on your return a higher style of political difference than you had left here. I fear this is inseparable from the different constitutions of the human mind, & that degree of freedom which permits unrestrained expression. Political dissension is doubtless a less evil than the lethargy of despotism, but still it is a great evil, and it would be as worthy the efforts of the patriot as of the philosopher, to exclude it's influence, if possible, from social life. The good are rare enough at best. There is no reason to subdivide them by artificial lines. But whether we shall ever be able so far to perfect the principles of society, as that political opinions shall, in it's intercourse, be as inoffensive as those of philosophy, mechanics, or any other, may well be doubted. Foreign influence is the present & just object of public hue and cry, &, as often happens, the most guilty are foremost & loudest in the cry. If those who are truly independent, can so trim our vessels as to beat through the waves now agitating us, they will merit a glory the greater as it seems less possible. When I contemplate the spirit which is driving us on here, & that beyond the water which will view us as but a mouthful the more, I have little hope of peace. I anticipate the burning of our sea ports, havoc of our frontiers, household insurgency, with a long train of et ceteras, which is enough for a man to have met once in his life. The exchange, which is to give us new neighbors in Louisiana (probably the present French armies when disbanded) has opened us to combinations of enemies on that side where we are most vulnerable. War is not the best engine for us to resort to, nature has given us one *in our commerce*, which, if properly managed, will be a better instrument for obliging the interested nations of Europe to treat us with justice. If the commercial regulations had been adopted which our legislature were at one time proposing, we should at this moment have been standing on such an eminence of safety & respect as ages can never recover. But having wandered from that, our object should now be to get back, with as little loss as possible, & when peace shall be restored to the world, endeavor so to form our *commercial* regulations as that justice from other nations shall be their mechanical result. I am happy to assure you that the conduct of Gen! Pinckney has met universal approbation. It was marked with that coolness, dignity, & good sense which we expected from him. I am told that the French government had taken up an unhappy idea, that Monroe was recalled for the candor of his conduct in what related to the British treaty, & Gen! Pinckney was sent as having other dispositions towards them. I learn further, that some of their well-informed citizens here are setting them right as to Gen! Pinckney's dispositions, so well known to have been just towards them; & I sincerely hope, not only that he may be employed as envoy extraordinary to them, but that their minds will be better prepared to receive him. I candidly acknolege, however, that I do not think the speech & addresses of Congress as conciliatory as the preceding irritations on both sides would have rendered wise. I shall be happy to hear from you at all times, to make myself useful to you whenever opportunity offers, and to give every proof of the sincerity of the sentiments of esteem & respect with which I am, Dear Sir, your most obedient and most humble servant.

DOMESTIC AFFECTIONS

To Martha Jefferson Randolph

Philadelphia, June 8, 1797

MY DEAR MARTHA—Yours of May 20 came to hand the 1st. inst. I imagine you recieved mine of May 18. about six days after the date of yours. It was written the first post day after my arrival here. The commission you inclosed for Maria is executed, and the things are in the care of Mr. Boyce of Richmond, who is returning from hence with some goods of his own, and will deliver them to Mr. Johnston. I recieve with inexpressible pleasure the information your letter contained. After your own happy establishment, which has given me an inestimable friend to whom I can leave the care of every thing I love, the only anxiety I had remaining was to see Maria also so asociated as to ensure her happiness. She could not have been more so to my wishes, if I had had the whole earth free to have chosen a partner for her. I now see our fireside formed into a groupe, no one member of which has a fibre in their composition which can ever produce any jarring or jealousies among us. No irregular passions, no dangerous bias, which may render problematical the future fortunes and happiness of our descendants. We are quieted as to their condition for at least one generation more. In order to keep us all together, instead of a present provision in Bedford, as in your case, I think to open and resettle the plantation of Pantops for them. When I look to the ineffable pleasures of my family society, I become more and more disgusted with the jealousies, the hatred, and the rancorous and malignant passions of this scene, and lament my having ever again been drawn into public view. Tranquility is now my object. I have seen enough of political honors to know that they are but splendid torments: and however one might be disposed to render services on which any of their fellow citizens should set a value; yet when as many would deprecate them as a public calamity, one may well entertain a modest doubt of their real importance, and feel the impulse of duty to be very weak. The real difficulty is that being once delivered into the hands of others, whose feelings are friendly to the individual and warm to the public cause, how to withdraw from them without leaving a dissatisfaction in their mind, and an impression of pusillanimity with the public.

Congress, in all probability will rise on Saturday the 17th. inst. the day after you will recieve this. I shall leave Philadelphia Monday the 19th. pass a day at Georgetown and a day at Fredericksburg, at which place I wish my *chair* and horses to be Sunday evening the 25th. Of course they must set out Saturday morning the 24th. This gives me the chance of another post, as you will, the evening before that, recieve by the post a letter of a week later date than this, so that if any thing should happen within a week to delay the rising of Congress, I may still notify it and change the time of the departure of my horses. Jupiter must pursue the rout by Noel's to which

he will come the first day, and by Chew's to Fredericksburg
the next. I fix his rout because were any accident to get me
along earlier, or him later, we might meet on the road. Not
yet informed that Mr. Randolph is returned I have thought it
safest to commit this article to my letter to you. The news of
the day I shall write to him. My warmest love to yourself and
Maria. Adieu affectionately.

PATIENCE AND THE REIGN OF WITCHES

To John Taylor

Philadelphia, June 4, 1798

I now inclose you Mr. Martin's patent. A patent had actually been made out on the first description, and how to get
this suppressed and another made for a second invention,
without a second fee, was the difficulty. I practised a little art
in a case where honesty was really on our side, & nothing
against us but the rigorous letter of the law, and having obtained the 1st specification and got the 2^{d} put in its place, a
second patent has been formed, which I now inclose with the
first specification.

I promised you, long ago, a description of a mould board.
I now send it; it is a press copy & therefore dim. It will be
less so by putting a sheet of white paper behind the one you
are reading. I would recommend to you first to have a model
made of about 3 i. to the foot, or ¼ the real dimensions, and
to have two blocks, the 1st of which, after taking out the py-
ramidal piece & sawing it crosswise above & below, should
be preserved in that form to instruct workmen in making the
large & real one. The 2^{d} block may be carried through all the
operations, so as to present the form of the mould board
complete. If I had an opportunity of sending you a model I
would do it. It has been greatly approved here, as it has been
before by some very good judges at my house, where I have
used it for 5 years with entire approbation.

Mr. New shewed me your letter on the subject of the patent, which gave me an opportunity of observing what you
said as to the effect with you of public proceedings, and that

it was not unusual now to estimate the separate mass of Virginia and N. Carolina with a view to their separate existence. It is true that we are compleatly under the saddle of Massachusets & Connecticut, and that they ride us very hard, cruelly insulting our feelings as well as exhausting our strength and substance. Their natural friends, the three other eastern States, join them from a sort of family pride, and they have the art to divide certain other parts of the Union so as to make use of them to govern the whole. This is not new. It is the old practice of despots to use a part of the people to keep the rest in order, and those who have once got an ascendency and possessed themselves of all the resources of the nation, their revenues and offices, have immense means for retaining their advantages. But our present situation is not a natural one. The body of our countrymen is substantially republican through every part of the Union. It was the irresistable influence & popularity of Gen[l] Washington, played off by the cunning of Hamilton, which turned the government over to anti-republican hands, or turned the republican members, chosen by the people, into anti-republicans. He delivered it over to his successor in this state, and very untoward events, since improved with great artifice, have produced on the public mind the impression we see; but still, I repeat it, this is not the natural state. Time alone would bring round an order of things more correspondent to the sentiments of our constituents; but are there not events impending which will do it within a few months? The invasion of England, the public and authentic avowal of sentiments hostile to the leading principles of our Constitution, the prospect of a war in which we shall stand alone, land-tax, stamp-tax, increase of public debt, &c. Be this as it may, in every free & deliberating society there must, from the nature of man, be opposite parties & violent dissensions & discords; and one of these, for the most part, must prevail over the other for a longer or shorter time. Perhaps this party division is necessary to induce each to watch & delate to the people the proceedings of the other. But if on a temporary superiority of the one party, the other is to resort to a scission of the Union, no federal government can ever exist. If to rid ourselves of the present rule of Massachusets & Connecticut we break the Union, will the evil stop there? Suppose the N. England States alone cut off, will our natures be changed? are we not men still to the south of that, & with all the passions of men? Immediately we shall see a Pennsylvania & a Virginia party arise in the residuary confederacy, and the public mind will be distracted with the same party spirit. What a game, too, will the one party have in their hands by eternally threatening the other that unless they do so & so, they will join their Northern neighbors. If we reduce our Union to Virginia & N. Carolina, immediately the conflict will be established between the representatives of these two States, and they will end by breaking into their simple units. Seeing, therefore, that an association of men who will not quarrel with one another is a thing which never yet existed, from the greatest confederacy of nations down to a town meeting or a vestry, seeing that we must have somebody to quarrel with, I had rather keep our New England associates for that purpose than to see our bickerings transferred to others. They are circumscribed within such narrow limits, & their population so full, that their numbers will ever be the minority, and they are marked, like the Jews, with such a peculiarity of character as to constitute from that circumstance the natural division of our parties. A little patience, and we shall see the reign of witches pass over, their spells dissolve, and the people, recovering their true sight, restore their government to it's true principles. It is true that in the mean time we are suffering deeply in spirit, and incurring the horrors of a war & long oppressions of enormous public debt. But who can say what would be the evils of a scission, and when & where they would end? Better keep together as we are, hawl off from Europe as soon as we can, & from all attachments to any portions of it. And if we feel their power just sufficiently to hoop us together, it will be the happiest situation in which we can exist. If the game runs sometimes against us at home we must have patience till luck turns, & then we shall have an opportunity of winning back the *principles* we have lost, for this is a game where principles are the stake. Better luck, therefore, to us all; and health, happiness, & friendly salutations to yourself. Adieu.

P. S. It is hardly necessary to caution you to let nothing of mine get before the public. A single sentence, got hold of by the Porcupines, will suffice to abuse & persecute me in their papers for months.

To Philip Nolan

Philadelphia, June 24, 1798

SIR,—It is sometime since I have understood that there are large herds of horses in a wild state, in the country west of the Mississippi, and have been desirous of obtaining details of their history in that State. Mr. Brown, Senator from Kentucky, informs me it would be in your power to give interesting information on this subject, and encourages me to ask it. The circumstances of the old world have, beyond the records of history, been such as admitted not that animal to exist in a state of nature. The condition of America is rapidly advancing to the same. The present then is probably the only moment in the age of the world, and the herds above mentioned the only subjects, of which we can avail ourselves to obtain what has never yet been recorded, and never can be again in all probability. I will add that your information is the sole reliance, as far as I can at present see, for obtaining this desideratum. You will render to natural history a very acceptable service, therefore, if you will enable our Philosophical society to add so interesting a chapter to the history of this animal. I need not specify to you the particular facts asked for; as your knowledge of the animal in his domesticated, as well as his wild state, will naturally have led your attention to those particulars in the manners, habits, and laws of his existence, which are peculiar to his wild state. I wish you not to be anxious about the form of your information, the exactness of the substance alone is material; and if, after giving in a first letter all the facts you at present possess, you would be so good, on subsequent occasions, as to furnish such others in addition, as you may acquire from time to time, your communications will always be thankfully received, if addressed to me at Monticello; and put into any post office in Kentucky or Tennessee, they will reach me speedily and safely, and will be considered as obligations on, sir, your most obedient, humble servant.

SUFFERANCE OF CALUMNY
To Samuel Smith

Monticello, Aug. 22, 1798

DEAR SIR,—Your favor of Aug 4 came to hand by our last post, together with the "extract of a letter from a gentleman of Philadelphia, dated July 10," cut from a newspaper stating some facts which respect me. I shall notice these facts. The writer says that "the day after the last despatches were communicated to Congress, Bache, Leib, &c., and a Dr. Reynolds were *closeted* with me." If the receipt of visits in my public room, the door continuing free to every one who should call at the same time, may be called *closeting*, then it is true that I was *closeted* with every person who visited me; in no other sense is it true as to any person. I sometimes received visits from Mr. Bache & Dr. Leib. I received them always with pleasure, because they are men of abilities, and of principles the most friendly to liberty & our present form of government. Mr. Bache has another claim on my respect, as being the grandson of Dr. Franklin, the greatest man & ornament of the age and country in which he lived. Whether I was visited by Mr. Bache or Dr. Leib the day after the communication referred to, I do not remember. I know that all my motions at Philadelphia, here, and everywhere, are watched & recorded. Some of these spies, therefore, may remember better than I do, the dates of these visits. If they say these two gentlemen visited me on the day after the communications, as their trade proves their accuracy, I shall not contradict them, tho' I affirm that I do not recollect it. However, as to Dr. Reynolds I can be more particular, because I never saw him but once, which was on an introductory visit he was so kind as to pay me. This, I well remember, was before the communication alluded to, & that during the short conversation I had with him, not one word was said on the subject of any of the communications. Not that I should not have spoken freely on their subject to Dr. Reynolds, as I should also have done to the letter writer, or to any other person who should have introduced the subject. I know my own principles to be pure, & therefore am not ashamed of them. On the contrary, I wish them known, & therefore willingly express them to every one. They are the same I have acted on from the year 1775 to this day, and are the same, I am sure, with those of the great body of the American people. I only wish the real principles of those who censure mine were also known. But warring against those of the people, the delusion of the people is necessary to the dominant party. I see the extent to which that delusion has been already carried, and I see there is no length to which it may not be pushed by a party in possession of the revenues & the legal authorities of the U S, for a short time indeed, but yet long enough to admit much particular mischief. There is no event, therefore, however atrocious, which may not be expected. I have contemplated every event which the Maratists of the day can perpetrate, and am prepared to meet every one in such a way, as shall not be derogatory either to the public liberty or my own personal honor. The letter writer says, I am "for peace; but it is only with France." He has told half the truth. He would have told the whole, if he had added England. I am for peace with both countries. I know that both of them have given, & are daily giving, sufficient cause of war; that in defiance of the laws of nations, they are every day trampling on the rights of all the neutral powers, whenever they can thereby do the least injury, either to the other. But, as I view a peace between France & England the ensuing winter to be certain, I have thought it would have been better for us to continue to bear from France through the present summer, what we have been bearing both from her & England these four years, and still continue to bear from England, and to have required indemnification in the hour of peace, when I verily believe it would have been yielded by both. This seems to be the plan of the other neutral nations; and whether this, or the commencing war on one of them, as we have done, would have been wisest, time & events must decide. But I am quite at a loss on what ground the letter writer can question the opinion, that

France had no intention of making war on us, & was willing to treat with Mr. Gerry, when we have this from Taleyrand's letter, and from the written and verbal information of our envoys. It is true then, that, as with England, we might of right have chosen either peace or war, & have chosen peace, and prudently in my opinion, so with France, we might also of right have chosen either peace or war, & we have chosen war. Whether the choice may be a popular one in the other States, I know not. Here it certainly is not; & I have no doubt the whole American people will rally ere long to the same sentiment, & rejudge those who, at present, think they have all judgment in their own hands.

These observations will show you, how far the imputations in the paragraph sent me approach the truth. Yet they are not intended for a newspaper. At a very early period of my life, I determined never to put a sentence into any newspaper. I have religiously adhered to the resolution through my life, and have great reason to be contented with it. Were I to undertake to answer the calumnies of the newspapers, it would be more than all my own time, & that of 20. aids could effect. For while I should be answering one, twenty new ones would be invented. I have thought it better to trust to the justice of my countrymen, that they would judge me by what they *see* of my conduct on the stage where they have placed me, & what they knew of me *before* the epoch since which a particular party has supposed it might answer some view of theirs to vilify me in the public eye. Some, I know, will not reflect how apocryphal is the testimony of enemies so palpably betraying the views with which they give it. But this is an injury to which duty requires every one to submit whom the public think proper to call into it's councils. I thank you, my dear Sir, for the interest you have taken for me on this occasion. Though I have made up my mind not to suffer calumny to disturb my tranquillity, yet I retain all my sensibilities for the approbation of the good & just. That is, indeed, the chief consolation for the hatred of so many, who, without the least personal knowledge, & on the sacred evidence of Porcupine & Fenno alone, cover me with their implacable hatred. The only return I will ever make them, will be to do them all the good I can, in spite of their teeth.

I have the pleasure to inform you that all your friends in this quarter are well, and to assure you of the sentiments of sincere esteem & respect with which I am, dear Sir, your friend and servant.

A PROFESSION OF POLITICAL FAITH
To Elbridge Gerry

Philadelphia, Jan. 26, 1799

MY DEAR SIR,—Your favor of Nov. 12 was safely delivered to me by mr. Binney, but not till Dec. 28, as I arrived here only three days before that date. It was received with great satisfaction. Our very long intimacy as fellow-laborers in the same cause, the recent expressions of mutual confidence which had preceded your mission, the interesting course which that had taken, & particularly & personally as it regarded yourself, made me anxious to hear from you on your return. I was the more so too, as I had myself during the whole of your absence, as well as since your return, been a constant butt for every shaft of calumny which malice & falsehood could form, & the presses, public speakers, or private letters disseminate. One of these, too, was of a nature to touch yourself; as if, wanting confidence in your efforts, I had been capable of usurping powers committed to you, & authorizing negociations private & collateral to yours. The real truth is, that though Dr Logan, the pretended missionary, about 4. or 5. days before he sailed for Hamburgh, told me he was going there, & thence to Paris, & asked & received from me a certificate of his citizenship, character, & circumstances of life, merely as a protection, should he be molested on his journey, in the present turbulent & suspicious state of Europe, yet I had been led to consider his object as relative to his private affairs; and tho', from an intimacy of some standing, he knew well my wishes for peace and my political sentiments in general, he nevertheless received then no particular declaration of them, no authority to communicate them to any mortal, nor to speak to any one in my name, or in anybody's name, on that, or on any other subject whatever; nor did I write by him a scrip of a pen to any person whatever. This he has himself honestly & publicly declared since his return; & from his well-known character & every other circumstance, every candid man must perceive that his enterprise was dictated by his own enthusiasm, without consultation or communication with any one; that he acted in Paris on his own ground, & made his own way. Yet to give some color to his proceedings, which might implicate the republicans in general, & myself particularly, they have not been ashamed to bring forward a suppositious paper, drawn by one of their own party in the name of Logan, and falsely pretended to have been presented by him to the government of France; counting that the bare mention of my name therein, would connect that in the eye of the public with this transaction. In confutation of these and all future calumnies, by way of anticipation, I shall make to you a profession of my political faith; in confidence that you will consider every future imputation on me of a contrary complexion, as bearing on its front the mark of falsehood & calumny.

I do then, with sincere zeal, wish an inviolable preservation of our present federal constitution, according to the true sense in which it was adopted by the States, that in which it was advocated by it's friends, & not that which it's enemies apprehended, who therefore became it's enemies; and I am opposed to the monarchising it's features by the forms of it's administration, with a view to conciliate a first transition to a President & Senate for life, & from that to a hereditary tenure of these offices, & thus to worm out the elective principle. I am for preserving to the States the powers not yielded by them to the Union, & to the legislature of the Union it's constitutional share in the division of powers; and I am not for transferring all the powers of the States to the general government, & all those of that government to the Executive branch. I am for a government rigorously frugal & simple, applying all the possible savings of the public revenue to the discharge of the national debt; and not for a multiplication of officers & salaries merely to make partisans, & for increasing, by every device, the public debt, on the principle of it's being a public blessing. I am for relying, for internal defence, on our militia solely, till actual invasion, and for such a naval force only as may protect our coasts and harbors from such depredations as we have experienced; and not for a standing army in time of peace, which may overawe the public sentiment; nor for a navy, which, by it's own expenses and the eternal wars in which it will implicate us, will grind us with public burthens, & sink us under them. I am for free commerce with all nations; political connection with none; & little or no diplomatic establishment. And I am not for linking ourselves by new treaties with the quarrels of Europe; entering that field of slaughter to preserve their balance, or joining in the confederacy of kings to war against the principles of liberty. I am for freedom of religion, & against all maneuvres to bring about a legal ascendancy of one sect over another: for freedom of the press, & against all violations of the constitution to silence by force & not by reason the complaints or criticisms, just or unjust, of our citizens against the conduct of their agents. And I am for encouraging the progress of science in all it's branches; and not for raising a hue and cry against the sacred name of philosophy; for awing the human mind by stories of raw-head & bloody bones to a distrust of its own vision, & to repose implicitly on that of others; to go backwards instead of forwards to look for improvement; to believe that government, religion, morality, & every other science were in the highest perfection in ages of the darkest ignorance, and that nothing can ever be devised more perfect than what was established by our forefathers. To these I will add, that I was a sincere well-wisher to the success of the French revolution, and still wish it may end in the establishment of a free & well-ordered republic; but I have not been insensible under the atrocious depredations they have committed on our commerce. The first object of my heart is my own country. In that is embarked my family, my fortune, & my own existence. I have not one farthing of interest, nor one fibre of attachment out of it, nor a single motive of preference of any one nation to another, but in proportion as they are more or less friendly to us. But though deeply feeling the injuries of France, I did not think war the surest means of redressing them. I did believe, that a mission sincerely disposed to preserve peace, would obtain for us a peaceable & honorable settlement & retribution; and I appeal to you to say, whether this might not have been obtained, if either of your colleagues had been of the same sentiment with yourself.

These, my friend, are my principles; they are unquestionably the principles of the great body of our fellow citizens, and I know there is not one of them which is not yours also. In truth, we never differed but on one ground, the funding system; and as, from the moment of it's being adopted by the constituted authorities, I became religiously principled in the sacred discharge of it to the uttermost farthing, we are united now even on that single ground of difference.

I turn now to your inquiries. The enclosed paper will answer one of them. But you also ask for such political information as may be possessed by me, & interesting to yourself in regard to your embassy. As a proof of my entire confidence in you, I shall give it fully & candidly. When Pinckney, Marshall, and Dana, were nominated to settle our differences with France, it was suspected by many, from what was understood of their dispositions, that their mission would not result in a settlement of differences, but would produce circumstances tending to widen the breach, and to provoke our citizens to consent to a war with that nation, & union with England. Dana's resignation & your appointment gave the first gleam of hope of a peaceable issue to the mission. For it was believed that you were sincerely disposed to accommodation; & it was not long after your arrival there, before symptoms were observed of that difference of views which had been suspected to exist. In the meantime, however, the aspect of our government towards the French republic had become so ardent, that the people of America generally took the alarm. To the southward, their apprehensions were early excited. In the Eastern States also, they at length began to break out. Meetings were held in many of your towns, & addresses to the government agreed on in opposition to war. The example was spreading like a wildfire. Other meetings were called in other places, & a general concurrence of sentiment against the apparent inclinations of the government was imminent; when, most critically for the government, the despatches of Octr 22, prepared by your colleague Marshall, with a view to their being made public, dropped into their laps. It was truly a God-send to them, & they made the most of it. Many thousands of copies were printed & dispersed gratis, at the public expence; & the zealots for war co-operated so heartily, that there were instances of single individuals who printed & dispersed 10. or 12,000 copies at their own expence. The odiousness of the corruption supposed in those papers excited a general & high indignation among the people. Unexperienced in such maneuvres, they did not permit themselves even to suspect that the turpitude of private swindlers might mingle itself unobserved, & give it's own hue to the communications of the French government, of whose participation there was neither proof nor probability. It served, however, for a time, the purpose intended. The people, in many places, gave a loose to the expressions of their warm indignation, & of their honest preference of war to dishonor. The fever was long & successfully kept up, and in the meantime, war measures as ardently crowded. Still, however, as it was known that your colleagues were coming away, and yourself to stay, though disclaiming a separate power to conclude a treaty, it was hoped by the lovers of peace, that a project of treaty would have been prepared, ad referendum, on principles which would have satisfied our citizens, & overawed any bias of the government towards a different policy. But the expedition of the Sophia, and, as was supposed, the suggestions of the person charged with your despatches, & his probable misrepresentations of the real wishes of the American people, prevented these hopes. They had then only to look forward to your return for such information, either through the Executive, or from yourself, as might present to our view the other side of the medal. The despatches of Oct 22, 97, had presented one face. That information, to a certain degree, is now received, & the public will see from your correspondence with Taleyrand, that France, as you testify, " was sincere and anxious to obtain a reconciliation, not wishing us to break the British treaty, but only to give her equivalent stipulations; and in general was disposed to a liberal treaty." And they will judge whether mr. Pickering's report shews an inflexible determination to believe no declarations the French government can make, nor any opinion which you, judging on the spot & from actual view, can give of their sincerity, and to meet their designs of peace with operations of war. The alien & sedition acts have already operated in the South as powerful sedatives of the X. Y. Z. inflammation. In your quarter, where violations of principle are either less regarded or more concealed, the direct tax is likely to have the same effect, & to excite inquiries into the object of the enormous expences & taxes we are bringing on. And your information supervening, that we might have a liberal accommodation if we would, there can be little doubt of the reproduction of that general movement, by the despatches of Oct. 22. And tho' small checks & stops, like Logan's pretended embassy, may be thrown in the way from time to time, & may a little retard it's motion, yet the tide is already turned, and will sweep before it all the feeble obstacles of art. The unquestionable republicanism of the American mind will break through the mist under which it has been clouded, and will oblige it's agents to reform the principles & practices of their administration.

You suppose that you have been abused by both parties. As far as has come to my knowledge, you are misinformed. I have never seen or heard a sentence of blame uttered against you by the republicans; unless we were so to construe their wishes that you had more boldly co-operated in a project of a treaty, and would more explicitly state, whether there was in your colleages that flexibility, which persons earnest after peace would have practised? Whether, on the contrary, their demeanor was not cold, reserved, and distant, at least, if not backward? And whether, if they had yielded to those informal conferences which Taleyrand seems to have courted, the liberal accommodation you suppose might not have been effected, even with their agency? Your fellow-citizens think they have a right to full information, in a case of such great concern to them. It is their sweat which is to earn all the expences of the war, and their blood which is to flow in expiation of the causes of it. It may be in your power to save them from these miseries by full communications and unrestrained details, postponing motives of delicacy to those of duty. It rests for you to come forward independently; to take your stand on the high ground of your own character; to disregard calumny, and to be borne above it on the shoulders of your grateful fellow citizens; or to sink into the humble oblivion, to which the Federalists (self-called) have secretly condemned you; and even to be happy if they will indulge you with oblivion, while they have beamed on your colleagues meridian splendor. Pardon me, my dear Sir, if my expressions are strong. My feelings are so much more so, that it is with difficulty I reduce them even to the tone I use. If you doubt the dispositions towards you, look into the papers, on both sides, for the toasts which were given throughout the States on the 4th of July. You will there see whose hearts were with you, and whose were ulcerated against you. Indeed, as soon as it was known that you had consented to stay in Paris, there was no measure observed in the execrations of the war party. They openly wished you might be guillotined, or sent to Cayenne, or anything else. And these expressions were finally stifled from a principle of policy only, & to prevent you from being urged to a justification of yourself. From this principle alone proceed the silence and cold respect they observe towards you. Still, they cannot prevent at times the flames bursting from under the embers, as mr. Pickering's letters, report, & conversations testify, as well as the indecent expressions respecting you, indulged by some of them in the debate on these despatches. These sufficiently show that you are never more to be honored or trusted by them, and that they await to crush you for ever, only till they can do it without danger to themselves.

When I sat down to answer your letter, but two courses presented themselves, either to say nothing or everything; for half confidences are not in my character. I could not hesitate which was due to you. I have unbosomed myself fully; & it will certainly be highly gratifying if I receive like confidence from you. For even if we differ in principle more than I believe we do, you & I know too well the texture of the human mind, & the slipperiness of human reason, to consider differences of opinion otherwise than differences of form or feature. Integrity of views more than their soundness, is the basis of esteem. I shall follow your direction in conveying this by a private hand; tho' I know not as yet when one worthy of confidence will occur. And my trust in you leaves me without a fear that this letter, meant as a confidential communication of my impressions, will ever go out of your hand, or be suffered in anywise to commit my name. Indeed, besides the accidents which might happen to it even under your care, considering the accident of death to which you are liable, I think it safest to pray you, after reading it as often as you please, to destroy at least the 2d & 3d leaves. The 1st contains principles only, which I fear not to avow; but the 2d & 3d contain facts stated for your information, and which, though sacredly conformable to my firm belief, yet would be galling to some, & expose me to illiberal attacks. I therefore repeat my prayer to burn the 2d & 3d leaves. And did we ever expect to see the day, when, breathing nothing but sentiments of love to our country & it's freedom & happiness, our correspondence must be as secret as if we were hatching it's destruction! Adieu, my friend, and accept my sincere & affectionate salutations. I need not add my signature.

"THE SPIRIT OF 1776"
To Thomas Lomax

Monticello, Mar. 12, 1799

DEAR SIR,—Your welcome favor of last month came to my hands in Philadelphia. So long a time has elapsed since we have been separated by events, that it was like a letter from the dead, and recalled to my memory very dear recollections. My subsequent journey through life has offered nothing which, in comparison with those, is not cheerless & dreary. It is a rich comfort sometimes to look back on them.

I take the liberty of enclosing a letter to mr. Baylor, open, because I solicit your perusal of it. It will, at the same time, furnish the apology for my not answering you from Philadelphia. You ask for any communication I may be able to make, which may administer comfort to you. I can give that which is solid. The spirit of 1776 is not dead. It has only been slumbering. The body of the American people is substantially republican. But their virtuous feelings have been played on by some fact with more fiction; they have been the dupes of artful manœuvres, & made for a moment to be willing instruments in forging chains for themselves. But time & truth have dissipated the delusion, & opened their eyes. They see now that France has sincerely wished peace, & their seducers have wished war, as well for the loaves & fishes which arise out of war expences, as for the chance of changing the constitution, while the people should have time to contemplate nothing but the levies of men and money. Pennsylvania, Jersey & N York are coming majestically round to the true principles. In Pensylva, 13. out of 22. counties had already petitioned on the alien & sedition laws. Jersey & N Y had begun the same movement, and tho' the rising of Congress stops that channel for the expression of their sentiment, the sentiment is going on rapidly, & before their next meeting those three States will be solidly embodied in sentiment with the six Southern & Western ones. The atrocious proceedings of France towards this country, had well nigh destroyed its liberties. The Anglomen and monocrats had so artfully confounded the cause of France with that of freedom, that both went down in the same scale. I sincerely join you in abjuring all political connection with every foreign power; and tho I cordially wish well to the progress of liberty in all nations, and would forever give it the weight of our countenance, yet they are not to be touched without contamination from their other bad principles. Commerce with all nations, alliance with none, should be our motto.

Accept assurances of the constant & unaltered affection of, dear Sir, your sincere friend and servant.

FREEDOM OF MIND
To William Green Munford

Monticello, June 18, 1799

DEAR SIR—I have to acknolege the reciept of your favor of May 14 in which you mention that you have finished the 6. first books of Euclid, plane trigonometry, surveying & algebra and ask whether I think a further pursuit of that branch of science would be useful to you. There are some propositions in the latter books of Euclid, & some of Archimedes, which are useful, & I have no doubt you have been made

acquainted with them. Trigonometry, so far as this, is most
valuable to every man. There is scarcely a day in which he will
not resort to it for some of the purposes of common life. The
science of calculation also is indispensible as far as the extraction of the square & cube roots; algebra as far as the qua-
dratic equation & the use of logarithms are often of value in
ordinary cases: but all beyond these is but a luxury; a delicious luxury indeed; but not to be indulged in by one who is
to have a profession to follow for his subsistence. In this light
I view the conic sections, curves of the higher orders, perhaps
even spherical trigonometry, algebraical operations beyond
the 2^d dimension, and fluxions. There are other branches of
science however worth the attention of every man. Astronomy, botany, chemistry, natural philosophy, natural history,
anatomy. Not indeed to be a proficient in them; but to possess their general principles & outlines, so as that we may be
able to amuse and inform ourselves further in any of them as
we proceed through life & have occasion for them. Some
knowledge of them is necessary for our character as well as
comfort. The general elements of astronomy & of natural philosophy are best acquired at an academy where we can have
the benefit of the instruments & apparatus usually provided
there: but the others may well be acquired from books alone
as far as our purposes require. I have indulged myself in these
observations to you, because the evidence cannot be unuseful
to you of a person who has often had occasion to consider
which of his acquisitions in science have been really useful to
him in life, and which of them have been merely a matter of
luxury.

I am among those who think well of the human character
generally. I consider man as formed for society, and endowed
by nature with those dispositions which fit him for society. I
believe also, with Condorcet, as mentioned in your letter, that
his mind is perfectible to a degree of which we cannot as yet
form any conception. It is impossible for a man who takes a
survey of what is already known, not to see what an immensity in every branch of science yet remains to be discovered,
& that too of articles to which our faculties seem adequate.
In geometry & calculation we know a great deal. Yet there are
some desiderata. In anatomy great progress has been made;

but much is still to be acquired. In natural history we possess knowlege; but we want a great deal. In chemistry we are not yet sure of the first elements. Our natural philosophy is in a very infantine state; perhaps for great advances in it, a further progress in chemistry is necessary. Surgery is well advanced; but prodigiously short of what may be. The state of medecine is worse than that of total ignorance. Could we divest ourselves of every thing we suppose we know in it, we should start from a higher ground & with fairer prospects. From Hippocrates to Brown we have had nothing but a succession of hypothetical systems each having it's day of vogue, like the fashions & fancies of caps & gowns, & yielding in turn to the next caprice. Yet the human frame, which is to be the subject of suffering & torture under these learned modes, does not change. We have a few medecines, as the bark, opium, mercury, which in a few well defined diseases are of unquestionable virtue: but the residuary list of the materia medica, long as it is, contains but the charlataneries of the art; and of the diseases of doubtful form, physicians have ever had a false knowlege, worse than ignorance. Yet surely the list of unequivocal diseases & remedies is capable of enlargement; and it is still more certain that in the other branches of science, great fields are yet to be explored to which our faculties are equal, & that to an extent of which we cannot fix the limits. I join you therefore in branding as cowardly the idea that the human mind is incapable of further advances. This is precisely the doctrine which the present despots of the earth are inculcating, & their friends here re-echoing; & applying especially to religion & politics; 'that it is not probable that any thing better will be discovered than what was known to our fathers.' We are to look backwards then & not forwards for the improvement of science, & to find it amidst feudal barbarisms and the fires of Spital-fields. But thank heaven the American mind is already too much opened, to listen to these impostures; and while the art of printing is left to us, science can never be retrograde; what is once acquired of real knowlege can never be lost. To preserve the freedom of the human mind then & freedom of the press, every spirit should be ready to devote itself to martyrdom; for as long as we may think as we will, & speak as we think, the condition of man will proceed in improvement. The generation which is going off the stage has deserved well of mankind for the struggles it has made, & for having arrested that course of despotism which had overwhelmed the world for thousands & thousands of years. If there seems to be danger that the ground they have gained will be lost again, that danger comes from the generation your cotemporary. But that the enthusiasm which character- ises youth should lift its parricide hands against freedom & science, would be such a monstrous phænomenon as I cannot place among possible things in this age & this country. Your college at least has shewn itself incapable of it; and if the youth of any other place have seemed to rally under other banners it has been from delusions which they will soon dis- sipate. I shall be happy to hear from you from time to time, & of your progress in study, and to be useful to you in what- ever is in my power; being with sincere esteem Dear Sir your friend & servt

COMMON LAW AND THE WILL OF THE NATION
To Edmund Randolph

Monticello, Aug. 18, 1799

DEAR SIR,—I received only two days ago your favor of the 12th, and as it was on the eve of the return of our post, it was not possible to make so prompt a despatch of the answer. Of all the doctrines which have ever been broached by the federal government, the novel one, of the common law being in force & cognizable as an existing law in their courts, is to me the most formidable. All their other assumptions of un-given powers have been in the detail. The bank law, the treaty doc- trine, the sedition act, alien act, the undertaking to change the state laws of evidence in the state courts by certain parts of the stamp act, &c., &c., have been solitary, unconsequen- tial, timid things, in comparison with the audacious, bare- faced and sweeping pretension to a system of law for the U S, without the adoption of their legislature, and so infini- tively beyond their power to adopt. If this assumption be yielded to, the state courts may be shut up, as there will then be nothing to hinder citizens of the same state suing each other in the federal courts in every case, as on a bond for instance, because the common law obliges payment of it, & the common law they say is their law. I am happy you have taken up the subject; & I have carefully perused & considered the notes you enclosed, and find but a single paragraph which I do not approve. It is that wherein (page 2.) you say, that laws being emanations from the legislative department, &, when once enacted, continuing in force from a presumption that their will so continues, that that presumption fails & the laws of course fall, on the destruction of that legislative department. I do not think this is the true bottom on which laws & the administering them rest. The whole body of the nation is the sovereign legislative, judiciary and executive power for itself. The inconvenience of meeting to exercise these powers in person, and their inaptitude to exercise them, induce them to appoint special organs to declare their legislative will, to judge & to execute it. It is the will of the nation which makes the law obligatory; it is their will which creates or annihilates the organ which is to declare & announce it. They may do it by a single person, as an Emperor of Russia, (constituting his declarations evidence of their will,) or by a few persons, as the Aristocracy of Venice, or by a complication of councils, as in our former regal government, or our present republican one. The law being law because it is the will of the nation, is not changed by their changing the organ through which they chuse to announce their future will; no more than the acts I have done by one attorney lose their obligation by my changing or discontinuing that attorney. This doctrine has been, in a certain degree sanctioned by the federal executive. For it is precisely that on which the continuance of obligation from our treaty with France was established, and the doctrine was particularly developed in a letter to Gouverneur Morris, written with the approbation of President Washington and his cabinet. Mercer once prevailed on the Virginia Assembly to declare a different doctrine in some resolutions. These met universal disapprobation in this, as well as the other States, and if I mistake not, a subsequent Assembly did something to do away the authority of their former unguarded resolutions. In this case, as in all others, the true principle will be quite as effectual to establish the just deductions, for before the revolution, the nation of Virginia had, by the organs they then thought proper to constitute, established a system of laws, which they divided into three denominations of 1, common law; 2, statute law; 3, Chancery: or if you please, into two only, of 1, common law; 2, Chancery. When, by the declaration of Independence, they chose to abolish their former organs of declaring their will, the acts of will already formally & constitutionally declared, remained untouched. For the nation was not dissolved, was not annihilated; it's will, therefore, remained in full vigor; and on the establishing the new organs, first of a convention, & afterwards a more complicated legislature, the old acts of national will continued in force, until the nation should, by its new organs, declare it's will changed. The common law, therefore, which was not in force when we landed here, nor till we had formed ourselves into a nation, and had manifested by the organs we constituted that the common law was to be our law, continued to be our law, because the nation continued in being, & because though it changed the organs for the future declarations of its will, yet it did not change its former declarations that the common law was it's law. Apply these principles to the present case. Before the revolution there existed no such nation as the U S; they then first associated as a nation, but for special purposes only. They had all their laws to make, as Virginia had on her first establishment as a nation. But they did not, as Virginia had done, proceed to adopt a whole system of laws ready made to their hand. As their association as a nation was only for special purposes, to wit, for the management of their concerns with one another & with foreign nations, and the states composing the association chose to give it powers for those purposes & no others, they could not adopt any general system, because it would have embraced objects on which this association had no right to form or declare a will. It was not the organ for declaring a national will in these cases. In the cases confided to them, they were free to declare the will of the nation, the law; but till it was declared there could be no law. So that the common law did not become, ipso facto, law on the new association;

it could only become so by a positive adoption, & so far only as they were authorized to adopt.

I think it will be of great importance, when you come to the proper part, to portray at full length the consequences of this new doctrine, that the common law is the law of the U S, & that their courts have, of course, jurisdiction co-extensive with that law, that is to say, general over all cases & persons. But, great heavens! Who could have conceived in 1789 that within ten years we should have to combat such windmills. Adieu. Yours affectionately.

IDEAS FOR A UNIVERSITY

To Dr. Joseph Priestley

Philadelphia, Jan. 18, 1800

DEAR SIR,—I have to thank you for the pamphlets you were so kind as to send me. You will know what I thought of them by my having before sent a dozen sets to Virginia to distribute among my friends. Yet I thank you not the less for these, which I value the more as they came from yourself. The stock of them which Campbell had was, I believe, exhausted the first or second day of advertising them. The Papers of political arithmetic, both in your & Mr. Cooper's pamphlets, are the most precious gifts that can be made to us; for we are running navigation mad, & commerce mad, & navy mad, which is worst of all. How desirable is it that you could pursue that subject for us. From the Porcupines of our country you will receive no thanks; but the great mass of our nation will edify & thank you. How deeply have I been chagrined & mortified at the persecutions which fanaticism & monarchy have excited against you, even here! At first I believed it was merely a continuance of the English persecution. But I observe that on the demise of Porcupine & division of his inheritance between Fenno & Brown, the latter (tho' succeeding only to the *federal* portion of Porcupinism, not the *Anglican,* which is Fenno's part) serves up for the palate of his sect, dishes of abuse against you as high seasoned as Porcupine's were. You have sinned against church & king, & can therefore never be forgiven. How sincerely have I regretted that your friend, before he fixed his choice of a position, did not visit the vallies on each side of the blue ridge in Virginia, as Mr. Madison & myself so much wished. You would have found there equal soil, the finest climate & most healthy one on the earth, the homage of universal reverence & love, & the power of the country spread over you as a shield. But since you would not make it your country by adoption, you must now do it by your good offices. I have one to propose to you which will produce their good, & gratitude to you for ages, and in the way to which you have devoted a long life, that of spreading light among men.

We have in that state a college (Wm. & Mary) just well enough endowed to draw out the miserable existence to which a miserable constitution has doomed it. It is moreover eccentric in it's position, exposed to bilious diseases as all the lower country is, & therefore abandoned by the public care, as that part of the country itself is in a considerable degree by it's inhabitants. We wish to establish in the upper & healthier country, & more centrally for the state, an University on a plan so broad & liberal & *modern*, as to be worth patronizing with the public support, and be a temptation to the youth of other states to come and drink of the cup of knowledge & fraternize with us. The first step is to obtain a good plan; that is, a judicious selection of the sciences, & a practicable grouping of some of them together, & ramifying of others, so as to adapt the professorships to our uses & our means. In an institution meant chiefly for use, some branches of science, formerly esteemed, may be now omitted; so may others now valued in Europe, but useless to us for ages to come. As an example of the former, the oriental learning, and of the latter, almost the whole of the institution proposed to Congress by the Secretary of war's report of the 5th inst. Now there is no one to whom this subject is so familiar as yourself. There is no one in the world who, equally with yourself, unites this full possession of the subject with such a knowledge of the state of our existence, as enables you to fit the garment to him who is to *pay* for it & to *wear* it. To you therefore we

Jan. 5, 1800

address our solicitations, and to lessen to you as much as possible the ambiguities of our object, I will venture even to sketch the sciences which seem useful & practicable for us, as they occur to me while holding my pen. Botany, Chemistry, Zoology, Anatomy, Surgery, Medicine, Natl Philosophy, Agriculture, Mathematics, Astronomy, Geology, Geography, Politics, Commerce, History, Ethics, Law, Arts, Finearts. This list is imperfect because I make it hastily, and because I am unequal to the subject. It is evident that some of these articles are too much for one professor & must therefore be ramified; others may be ascribed in groups to a single professor. This is the difficult part of the work, & requires a head perfectly knowing the extent of each branch, & the limits within which it may be circumscribed, so as to bring the whole within the powers of the fewest professors possible, & consequently within the degree of expence practicable for us. We should propose that the professors follow no other calling, so that their whole time may be given to their academical functions; and we should propose to draw from Europe the first characters in science, by considerable temptations, which would not need to be repeated after the first set should have prepared fit successors & given reputation to the institution. From some splendid characters I have received offers most perfectly reasonable & practicable.

I do not propose to give you all this trouble merely of my own head, that would be arrogance. It has been the subject of consultation among the ablest and highest characters of our State, who only wait for a plan to make a joint & I hope successful effort to get the thing carried into effect. They will receive your ideas with the greatest deference & thankfulness. We shall be here certainly for two months to come; but should you not have leisure to think of it before Congress adjourns, it will come safely to me afterwards by post, the nearest post office being Milton.

Will not the arrival of Dupont tempt you to make a visit to this quarter? I have no doubt the alarmists are already whetting their shafts for him also, but their glass is nearly run out, and the day I believe is approaching when we shall be as free to pursue what is true wisdom as the effects of their follies will permit; for some of them we shall be forced to wade through because we are emerged in them.

Wishing you that pure happiness which your pursuits and circumstances offer, and which I am sure you are too wise to suffer a diminution of by the pigmy assaults made on you, and with every sentiment of affectionate esteem & respect, I am, dear Sir, your most humble, and most obedient servant.

"A SUBLIME LUXURY"

√ *To Dr. Joseph Priestley*

Philadelphia, Jan. 27, 1800

DEAR SIR,—In my letter of the 18th, I omitted to say any thing of the languages as part of our proposed university. It was not that I think, as some do, that they are useless. I am of a very different opinion. I do not think them essential to the obtaining eminent degrees of science; but I think them very useful towards it. I suppose there is a portion of life during which our faculties are ripe enough for this, & for nothing more useful. I think the Greeks & Romans have left us the present models which exist of fine composition, whether we examine them as works of reason, or of style & fancy; and to them we probably owe these characteristics of modern composition. I know of no composition of any other antient people, which merits the least regard as a model for it's matter or style. To all this I add, that to read the Latin & Greek authors in their original, is a sublime luxury; and I deem luxury in science to be at least as justifiable as in architecture, painting, gardening, or the other arts. I enjoy Homer in his own language infinitely beyond Pope's translation of him, & both beyond the dull narrative of the same events by Dares Phrygius; & it is an innocent enjoyment. I thank on my knees, him who directed my early education, for having put into my possession this rich source of delight; and I would not exchange it for anything which I could then have acquired, & have not since acquired. With this regard for those languages, you will acquit me of meaning to omit them.

About 20. years ago, I drew a bill for our legislature, which proposed to lay off every county into hundreds or townships of 5. or 6. miles square, in the centre of each of which was to be a free English school; the whole state was further laid off into 10. districts, in each of which was to be a college for teaching the languages, geography, surveying, and other useful things of that grade; and then a single University for the sciences. It was received with enthusiasm; but as I had proposed that Wm & Mary, under an improved form, should be the University, & that was at that time pretty highly Episcopal, the dissenters after a while began to apprehend some secret design of a preference to that sect and nothing could then be done. About 3. years ago they enacted that part of my bill which related to English schools, except that instead of obliging, they left it optional in the court of every county to carry it into execution or not. I think it probable the part of the plan for the middle grade of education, may also be brought forward in due time. In the meanwhile, we are not without a sufficient number of good country schools, where the languages, geography, & the first elements of Mathematics, are taught. Having omitted this information in my former letter, I thought it necessary now to supply it, that you might know on what base your superstructure was to be reared. I have a letter from M. Dupont, since his arrival at N. York, dated the 20th, in which he says he will be in Philadelphia within about a fortnight from that time; but only on a visit. How much would it delight me if a visit from you at the same time, were to shew us two such illustrious foreigners embracing each other in my country, as the asylum for whatever is great & good. Pardon, I pray you, the temporary delirium which has been excited here, but which is fast passing away. The Gothic idea that we are to look backwards instead of forwards for the improvement of the human mind, and to recur to the annals of our ancestors for what is most perfect in government, in religion & in learning, is worthy of those bigots in religion & government, by whom it has been recommended, & whose purposes it would answer. But it is not an idea which this country will endure; and the moment of their showing it is fast ripening; and the signs of it will be their respect for you,

& growing detestation of those who have dishonored our country by endeavors to disturb our tranquility in it. No one has felt this with more sensibility than, my dear Sir, your respectful & affectionate friend & servant.

THE 18TH BRUMAIRE
To John Breckinridge

Philadelphia, Jan. 29, 1800

DEAR SIR,—Your favor of the 13th has been duly received, as had been that containing the resolutions of your legislature on the subject of the former resolutions. I was glad to see the subject taken up, and done with so much temper, firmness and propriety. From the reason of the thing I cannot but hope that the Western country will be laid off into a separate Judiciary district. From what I recollect of the dispositions on the same subject at the last session, I should expect that the partiality to a general & uniform system would yield to geographical & physical impracticabilities. I was once a great advocate for introducing into chancery vivâ voce testimony, & trial by jury. I am still so as to the latter, but have retired from the former opinion on the information received from both your state & ours, that it worked inconveniently. I introduced it into the Virginia law, but did not return to the bar, so as to see how it answered. But I do not understand how the vivâ voce examination comes to be practiced in the Federal court with you, & not in your own courts; the Federal courts being decided by law to proceed & decide by the laws of the states.

A great revolution has taken place at Paris. The people of that country having never been in the habit of self-government, are not yet in the habit of acknoleging that fundamental law of nature, by which alone self government can be exercised by a society, I mean the *lex majoris partis*. Of the sacredness of this law, our countrymen are impressed from their cradle, so that with them it is almost innate. This single circumstance may possibly decide the fate of the two nations. One party appears to have been prevalent in the Directory &

council of 500. the other in the council of antients. Sieyes & Ducos, the minority in the Directory, not being able to carry their points there seem to have gained over Buonaparte, & associating themselves with the majority of the Council of antients, have expelled* 120. odd members the most obnoxious of the minority of the Elders, & of the majority of the council of 500. so as to give themselves a majority in the latter council also. They have established Buonaparte, Sieyes & Ducos into an executive, or rather Dictatorial consulate, given them a committee of between 20. & 30. from each council, & have adjourned to the 20th of Feb. Thus the Constitution of the 3d year which was getting consistency & firmness from time is demolished in an instant, and nothing is said about a new one. How the nation will bear it is yet unknown. Had the Consuls been put to death in the first tumult & before the nation had time to take sides, the Directory & councils might have reestablished themselves on the spot. But that not being done, perhaps it is now to be wished that Buonaparte may be spared, as, according to his protestations, he is for liberty, equality & representative government, and he is more able to keep the nation together, & to ride out the storm than any other. Perhaps it may end in their establishing a single representative & that in his person. I hope it will not be for life, for fear of the influence of the example on our countrymen. It is very material for the latter to be made sensible that their own character & situation are materially different from the French; & that whatever may be the fate of republicanism there, we are able to preserve it inviolate here: we are sensible of the duty & expediency of submitting our opinions to the will of the majority and can wait with patience till they get right if they happen to be at any time wrong. Our vessel is moored at such a distance, that should theirs blow up, ours is still safe, if we will but think so.

I had recommended the enclosed letter to the care of the postmaster at Louisville; but have been advised it is better to get a friend to forward it by some of the boats. I will ask that

---

*60. were expelled from the 500, so as to change the majority there to the other side. It seems doubtful whether any were expelled from the Antients. The majority there was already with the Consular party.

favor of you. It is the duplicate of one with the same address which I inclosed last week to mr. Innes & should therefore go by a different conveyance. I am with great esteem dear sir your friend & servant.

ILLUMINATISM

To Bishop James Madison

Philadelphia, Jan. 31, 1800

DEAR SIR,—I have received your favor of the 17th, & communicated it to Mr. Smith. I lately forwarded your letter from Dr. Priestley, endorsed ' with a book'; I struck those words through with my pen, because no book had then come. It is now received, & shall be forwarded to Richmond by the first opportunity: but such opportunities are difficult to find; gentlemen going in the stage not liking to take charge of a packet which is to be attended to every time the stage is changed. The best chance will be by some captain of a vessel going round to Richmond. I shall address it to the care of Mr. George Jefferson there.

I have lately by accident got a sight of a single volume (the 3d.) of the Abbe Barruel's 'Antisocial conspiracy,' which gives me the first idea I have ever had of what is meant by the Illuminatism against which 'illuminate Morse' as he is now called, & his ecclesiastical & monarchical associates have been making such a hue and cry. Barruel's own parts of the book are perfectly the ravings of a Bedlamite. But he quotes largely from Wishaupt whom he considers as the founder of what he calls the order. As you may not have had an opportunity of forming a judgment of this cry of 'mad dog' which has been raised against his doctrines, I will give you the idea I have formed from only an hour's reading of Barruel's quotations from him, which you may be sure are not the most favorable. Wishaupt seems to be an enthusiastic Philanthropist. He is among those (as you know the excellent Price and Priestley also are) who believe in the indefinite perfectibility of man. He thinks he may in time be rendered so perfect that he will be able to govern himself in every circumstance so as to injure

none, to do all the good he can, to leave government no occasion to exercise their powers over him, & of course to render political government useless. This you know is Godwin's
doctrine, and this is what Robinson, Barruel & Morse had
called a conspiracy against all government. Wishaupt believes
that to promote this perfection of the human character was
the object of Jesus Christ. That his intention was simply to
reinstate natural religion, & by diffusing the light of his morality, to teach us to govern ourselves. His precepts are the
love of god & love of our neighbor. And by teaching innocence of conduct, he expected to place men in their natural
state of liberty & equality. He says, no one ever laid a surer
foundation for liberty than our grand master, Jesus of Nazareth. He believes the Free masons were originally possessed
of the true principles & objects of Christianity, & have still
preserved some of them by tradition, but much disfigured.
The means he proposes to effect this improvement of human
nature are 'to enlighten men, to correct their morals & inspire
them with benevolence. Secure of our success, sais he, we ab-
stain from violent commotions. To have foreseen the happiness of posterity & to have prepared it by irreproachable
means, suffices for our felicity. The tranquility of our consciences is not troubled by the reproach of aiming at the ruin
or overthrow of states or thrones.' As Wishaupt lived under
the tyranny of a despot & priests, he knew that caution was
necessary even in spreading information, & the principles of
pure morality. He proposed therefore to lead the Free masons
to adopt this object & to make the objects of their institution
the diffusion of science & virtue. He proposed to initiate new
members into his body by gradations proportioned to his
fears of the thunderbolts of tyranny. This has given an air of
mystery to his views, was the foundation of his banishment,
the subversion of the masonic order, & is the colour for the
ravings against him of Robinson, Barruel & Morse, whose
real fears are that the craft would be endangered by the
spreading of information, reason, & natural morality among
men. This subject being new to me, I have imagined that if it
be so to you also, you may receive the same satisfaction in
seeing, which I have had in forming the analysis of it: & I
believe you will think with me that if Wishaupt had written

here, where no secrecy is necessary in our endeavors to render men wise & virtuous, he would not have thought of any secret machinery for that purpose. As Godwin, if he had written in Germany, might probably also have thought secrecy & mysticism prudent. I will say nothing to you on the late revolution of France, which is painfully interesting. Perhaps when we know more of the circumstances which gave rise to it, & the direction it will take, Buonaparte, its chief organ, may stand in a better light than at present. I am with great esteem, dear sir, your affectionate friend.

"A FEW PLAIN DUTIES"
To Gideon Granger

Monticello, Aug. 13, 1800

DEAR SIR,—I received with great pleasure your favor of June 4, and am much comforted by the appearance of a change of opinion in your state; for tho' we may obtain, & I believe shall obtain, a majority in the legislature of the United States, attached to the preservation of the Federal constitution according to it's obvious principles, & those on which it was known to be received; attached equally to the preservation to the states of those rights unquestionably remaining with them; friends to the freedom of religion, freedom of the press, trial by jury & to economical government; opposed to standing armies, paper systems, war, & all connection, other than commerce, with any foreign nation; in short, a majority firm in all those principles which we have espoused and the federalists have opposed uniformly; still, should the whole body of New England continue in opposition to these principles of government, either knowingly or through delusion, our government will be a very uneasy one. It can never be harmonious & solid, while so respectable a portion of it's citizens support principles which go directly to a change of the federal constitution, to sink the state governments, consolidate them into one, and to monarchize that. Our country is too large to have all its affairs directed by a single government. Public servants at such a distance, & from under the eye of their constituents, must, from the circumstance of distance, be unable to administer & overlook all the details necessary for the good government of the citizens, and the same circumstance, by rendering detection impossible to their constituents, will invite the public agents to corruption, plunder & waste. And I do verily believe, that if the principle were to prevail, of a common law being in force in the U S, (which principle possesses the general government at once of all the powers of the state governments, and reduces us to a single consolidated government,) it would become the most corrupt government on the earth. You have seen the practises by which the public servants have been able to cover their conduct, or, where that could not be done, delusions by which they have varnished it for the eye of their constituents. What an augmentation of the field for jobbing, speculating, plundering, office-building & office-hunting would be produced by an assumption of all the state powers into the hands of the general government. The true theory of our constitution is surely the wisest & best, that the states are independent as to everything within themselves, & united as to everything respecting foreign nations. Let the general government be reduced to foreign concerns only, and let our affairs be disentangled from those of all other nations, except as to commerce, which the merchants will manage the better, the more they are left free to manage for themselves, and our general government may be reduced to a very simple organization, & a very unexpensive one; a few plain duties to be performed by a few servants. But I repeat, that this simple & economical mode of government can never be secured, if the New England States continue to support the contrary system. I rejoice, therefore, in every appearance of their returning to those principles which I had always imagined to be almost innate in them. In this State, a few persons were deluded by the X. Y. Z. duperies. You saw the effect of it in our last Congressional representatives, chosen under their influence. This experiment on their credulity is now seen into, and our next representation will be as republican as it has heretofore been. On the whole, we hope, that by a part of the Union having held on to the principles of the constitution, time has been given to the states to recover from the temporary frenzy

into which they had been decoyed, to rally round the constitution, & to rescue it from the destruction with which it had
been threatened even at their own hands. I see copied from
the American Magazine two numbers of a paper signed Don
Quixotte, most excellently adapted to introduce the real truth
to the minds even of the most prejudiced.

I would, with great pleasure, have written the letter you
desired in behalf of your friend, but there are existing circumstances which render a letter from me to that magistrate as
improper as it would be unavailing. I shall be happy, on some
more fortunate occasion, to prove to you my desire of serving
your wishes.

I sometime ago received a letter from a Mr. M'Gregory of
Derby, in your State; it is written with such a degree of good
sense & appearance of candor, as entitles it to an answer. Yet
the writer being entirely unknown to me, and the stratagems
of the times very multifarious, I have thought it best to avail
myself of your friendship, & enclose the answer to you. You
will see it's nature. If you find from the character of the person to whom it is addressed, that no improper use would
probably be made of it, be so good as to seal & send it.
Otherwise suppress it.

How will the vote of your State and R I be as to A. and
P.?

I am, with great and sincere esteem, dear Sir, your friend
and servant.

"I HAVE SWORN UPON THE ALTAR OF GOD . . ."

To Dr. Benjamin Rush

Monticello, Sep. 23, 1800

DEAR SIR,—I have to acknolege the receipt of your favor of
Aug. 22, and to congratulate you on the healthiness of your
city. Still Baltimore, Norfolk & Providence admonish us that
we are not clear of our new scourge. When great evils happen, I am in the habit of looking out for what good may arise
from them as consolations to us, and Providence has in fact
so established the order of things, as that most evils are the

means of producing some good. The yellow fever will discourage the growth of great cities in our nation, & I view great cities as pestilential to the morals, the health and the liberties of man. True, they nourish some of the elegant arts, but the useful ones can thrive elsewhere, and less perfection in the others, with more health, virtue & freedom, would be my choice.

I agree with you entirely, in condemning the mania of giving names to objects of any kind after persons still living. Death alone can seal the title of any man to this honor, by putting it out of his power to forfeit it. There is one other mode of recording merit, which I have often thought might be introduced, so as to gratify the living by praising the dead. In giving, for instance, a commission of chief justice to Bushrod Washington, it should be in consideration of his integrity, and science in the laws, and of the services rendered to our country by his illustrious relation, &c. A commission to a descendant of Dr. Franklin, besides being in consideration of the proper qualifications of the person, should add that of the great services rendered by his illustrious ancestor, Bn Fr, by the advancement of science, by inventions useful to man, &c. I am not sure that we ought to change all our names. And during the regal government, sometimes, indeed, they were given through adulation; but often also as the reward of the merit of the times, sometimes for services rendered the colony. Perhaps, too, a name when given, should be deemed a sacred property.

I promised you a letter on Christianity, which I have not forgotten. On the contrary, it is because I have reflected on it, that I find much more time necessary for it than I can at present dispose of. I have a view of the subject which ought to displease neither the rational Christian nor Deists, and would reconcile many to a character they have too hastily rejected. I do not know that it would reconcile the *genus irritabile vatum* who are all in arms against me. Their hostility is on too interesting ground to be softened. The delusion into which the X. Y. Z. plot shewed it possible to push the people; the successful experiment made under the prevalence of that delusion on the clause of the constitution, which, while it secured the freedom of the press, covered also the freedom of religion, had given to the clergy a very favorite hope of obtaining an establishment of a particular form of Christianity thro' the U. S.; and as every sect believes its own form the true one, every one perhaps hoped for his own, but especially the Episcopalians & Congregationalists. The returning good sense of our country threatens abortion to their hopes, & they believe that any portion of power confided to me, will be exerted in opposition to their schemes. And they believe rightly; for I have sworn upon the altar of god, eternal hostility against every form of tyranny over the mind of man. But this is all they have to fear from me: & enough too in their opinion, & this is the cause of their printing lying pamphlets against me, forging conversations for me with Mazzei, Bishop Madison, &c., which are absolute falsehoods without a circumstance of truth to rest on; falsehoods, too, of which I acquit Mazzei & Bishop Madison, for they are men of truth.

But enough of this: it is more than I have before committed to paper on the subject of all the lies that has been preached and printed against me. I have not seen the work of Sonnoni which you mention, but I have seen another work on Africa, (Parke's,) which I fear will throw cold water on the hopes of the friends of freedom. You will hear an account of an attempt at insurrection in this state. I am looking with anxiety to see what will be it's effect on our state. We are truly to be pitied. I fear we have little chance to see you at the Federal city or in Virginia, and as little at Philadelphia. It would be a great treat to receive you here. But nothing but sickness could effect that; so I do not wish it. For I wish you health and happiness, and think of you with affection. Adieu.

"PHILOSOPHICAL VEDETTE" AT A DISTANCE

To William Dunbar

Washington, Jan. 12, 1801

DEAR SIR,—Your favor of July 14, with the papers accompanying it, came safely to hand about the last of October. That containing remarks on the line of demarcation I perused according to your permission, and with great satisfaction, and then enclosed to a friend in Philadelphia, to be forwarded to it's address. The papers addressed to me, I took the liberty of communicating to the Philosophical society. That on the language by signs is quite new. Soon after receiving your meteorological diary, I received one of Quebec; and was struck with the comparison between -32 & $+19\frac{3}{4}$ the lowest depression of the thermometer at Quebec & the Natchez. I have often wondered that any human being should live in a cold country who can find room in a warm one. I have no doubt but that cold is the source of more sufferance to all animal nature than hunger, thirst, sickness, & all the other pains of life & of death itself put together. I live in a temperate climate, and under circumstances which do not expose me often to cold. Yet when I recollect on one hand all the sufferings I have had from cold, & on the other all my other pains, the former preponderate greatly. What then must be the sum of that evil if we take in the vast proportion of men who are obliged to be out in all weather, by land & by sea, all the families of beasts, birds, reptiles, & even the vegetable kingdom! for that too has life, and where there is life there may be sensation. I remark a rainbow of a great portion of the circle observed by you when on the line of demarcation. I live in a situation which has given me an opportunity of seeing more than the semicircle often. I am on a hill 500 f. perpendicularly high. On the east side it breaks down abruptly to the base, where a river passes through. A rainbow, therefore, about sunset, plunges one of it's legs down to the river, 500 f. below the level of the eye on the top of the hill. I have twice seen bows formed by the moon. They were of the color of the common circle round the moon, and were very near, being within a few paces of me in both instances. I thank you for the little vocabularies of Bedais, Jankawis and Teghas. I have it much at heart to make as extensive a collection as possible of the Indian tongues. I have at present about 30. tolerably full, among which the number radically different, is truly wonderful. It is curious to consider how such handfuls of men came by different languages, & how they have preserved them so distinct. I at first thought of reducing them all to one orthography, but I soon become sensible that this would occasion two sources of error instead of one. I therefore think it best to keep them in the form of orthography in which they were taken, only noting whether that were English, French, German, or what. I have never been a very punctual correspondent, and it is possible that new duties may make me less so. I hope I shall not on that account lose the benefit of your communications. Philosophical vedette at the distance of one thousand miles, and on the verge of the terra incognita of our continent, is precious to us here. I pray you to accept assurances of my high consideration & esteem, and friendly salutations.

THE REVOLUTION OF 1800
To John Dickinson

Washington, Mar. 6, 1801

DEAR SIR,—No pleasure can exceed that which I received from reading your letter of the 21st ult. It was like the joy we expect in the mansions of the blessed, when received with the embraces of our fathers, we shall be welcomed with their blessing as having done our part not unworthily of them. The storm through which we have passed, has been tremendous indeed. The tough sides of our Argosie have been thoroughly tried. Her strength has stood the waves into which she was steered, with a view to sink her. We shall put her on her republican tack, & she will now show by the beauty of her motion the skill of her builders. Figure apart, our fellow citizens have been led hood-winked from their principles, by a most extraordinary combination of circumstances. But the band is removed, and they now see for themselves. I hope to see shortly a perfect consolidation, to effect which, nothing shall be spared on my part, short of the abandonment of the principles of our revolution. A just and solid republican government maintained here, will be a standing monument & example for the aim & imitation of the people of other countries; and I join with you in the hope and belief that they will see, from our example, that a free government is of all others the most energetic; that the inquiry which has been excited among the mass of mankind by our revolution & it's consequences, will ameliorate the condition of man over a great portion of the globe. What a satisfaction have we in the contemplation of the benevolent effects of our efforts, compared with those of the leaders on the other side, who have discountenanced all advances in science as dangerous innovations, have endeavored to render philosophy and republicanism terms of reproach, to persuade us that man cannot be governed but by the rod, &c. I shall have the happiness of living & dying in the contrary hope. Accept assurances of my constant & sincere respect and attachment, and my affectionate salutations.

SOMETHING NEW UNDER THE SUN
To Dr. Joseph Priestley

Washington, Mar. 21, 1801

DEAR SIR,—I learnt some time ago that you were in Philadelphia, but that it was only for a fortnight; & supposed you were gone. It was not till yesterday I received information that you were still there, had been very ill, but were on the recovery. I sincerely rejoice that you are so. Yours is one of the few lives precious to mankind, & for the continuance of which every thinking man is solicitous. Bigots may be an exception. What an effort, my dear Sir, of bigotry in Politics & Religion have we gone through! The barbarians really flattered themselves they should be able to bring back the times of Vandalism, when ignorance put everything into the hands of power & priestcraft. All advances in science were proscribed as innovations. They pretended to praise and encourage education, but it was to be the education of our ancestors. We were to look backwards, not forwards, for improvement; the President himself declaring, in one of his answers to addresses, that we were never to expect to go beyond them in real science. This was the real ground of all the attacks on you. Those who live by mystery & *charlatanerie*, fearing you would render them useless by simplifying the Christian philosophy,—the most sublime & benevolent, but most perverted system that ever shone on man,—endeavored to crush your well-earnt & well-deserved fame. But it was the Lilliputians upon Gulliver. Our countrymen have recovered from the alarm into which art & industry had thrown them; science & honesty are replaced on their high ground; and you, my dear Sir, as their great apostle, are on it's pinnacle. It is with heartfelt satisfaction that, in the first moments of my public action, I can hail you with welcome to our land, tender to you the homage of it's respect & esteem, cover you under the protection of those laws which were made for the wise and good like you, and disdain the legitimacy of that libel on legislation, which under the form of a law, was for some time placed among them.

As the storm is now subsiding, and the horizon becoming serene, it is pleasant to consider the phenomenon with attention. We can no longer say there is nothing new under the sun. For this whole chapter in the history of man is new. The great extent of our Republic is new. Its sparse habitation is new. The mighty wave of public opinion which has rolled over it is new. But the most pleasing novelty is, it's so quickly subsiding over such an extent of surface to it's true level again. The order & good sense displayed in this recovery from delusion, and in the momentous crisis which lately arose, really bespeak a strength of character in our nation which augurs well for the duration of our Republic; & I am much better satisfied now of it's stability than I was before it was tried. I have been, above all things, solaced by the prospect which opened on us, in the event of a non-election of a President; in which case, the federal government would have been in the situation of a clock or watch run down. There was no idea of force, nor of any occasion for it. A convention, invited by the Republican members of Congress, with the virtual President & Vice President, would have been on the ground in 8. weeks, would have repaired the Constitution where it was defective, & wound it up again. This peaceable & legitimate resource, to which we are in the habit of implicit obedience, superseding all appeal to force, and being always within our reach, shows a precious principle of self-preservation in our composition, till a change of circumstances shall take place, which is not within prospect at any definite period.

But I have got into a long disquisition on politics, when I

only meant to express my sympathy in the state of your
health, and to tender you all the affections of public & private
hospitality. I should be very happy indeed to see you here. I
leave this about the 30th inst., to return about the twenty-
fifth of April. If you do not leave Philadelphia before that, a
little excursion hither would help your health. I should be
much gratified with the possession of a guest I so much esteem, and should claim a right to lodge you, should you make
such an excursion.

WISDOM AND PATRIOTISM
To Moses Robinson

Washington, March 23, 1801

DEAR SIR,—I have to acknowledge the receipt of your favor
of the 3rd instant, and to thank you for the friendly expressions it contains. I entertain real hope that the whole body of
your fellow citizens (many of whom had been carried away
by the X. Y. Z. business) will shortly be consolidated in the
same sentiments. When they examine the real principles of
both parties, I think they will find little to differ about. I
know, indeed, that there are some of their leaders who have
so committed themselves, that pride, if no other passion, will
prevent their coalescing. We must be easy with them. The
eastern States will be the last to come over, on account of the
dominion of the clergy, who had got a smell of union between Church and State, and began to indulge reveries which
can never be realised in the present state of science. If, indeed,
they could have prevailed on us to view all advances in science
as dangerous innovations, and to look back to the opinions
and practices of our forefathers, instead of looking forward,
for improvement, a promising groundwork would have been
laid. But I am in hopes their good sense will dictate to them,
that since the mountain will not come to them, they had better go to the mountain: that they will find their interest in
acquiescing in the liberty and science of their country, and
that the Christian religion, when divested of the rags in which
they have enveloped it, and brought to the original purity and

simplicity of its benevolent institutor, is a religion of all others most friendly to liberty, science, and the freest expansion of the human mind.

I sincerely wish with you, we could see our government so secured as to depend less on the character of the person in whose hands it is trusted. Bad men will sometimes get in, and with such an immense patronage, may make great progress in corrupting the public mind and principles. This is a subject with which wisdom and patriotism should be occupied.

I pray you to accept assurances of my high respect and esteem.

RECONCILIATION AND REFORM

To Elbridge Gerry

Washington, Mar. 29, 1801

MY DEAR SIR,—Your two letters of Jan. 15 and Feb. 24, came safely to hand, and I thank you for the history of a transaction which will ever be interesting in our affairs. It has been very precisely as I had imagined. I thought, on your return, that if you had come forward boldly, and appealed to the public by a full statement, it would have had a great effect in your favor personally, & that of the republican cause then oppressed almost unto death. But I judged from a tact of the southern pulse. I suspect that of the north was different and decided your conduct; and perhaps it has been as well. If the revolution of sentiment has been later, it has perhaps been not less sure. At length it is arrived. What with the natural current of opinion which has been setting over to us for 18. months, and the immense impetus which was given it from the 11th to the 17th of Feb., we may now say that the U.S. from N.Y. southwardly, are as unanimous in the principles of '76, as they were in '76. The only difference is, that the leaders who remain behind are more numerous & bolder than the apostles of toryism in '76. The reason is, that we are now justly more tolerant than we could safely have been then, circumstanced as we were. Your part of the Union tho' as absolutely republican as ours, had drunk deeper of the delusion, & is therefore slower in recovering from it. The ægis of government, & the temples of religion & of justice, have all been prostituted there to toll us back to the times when we burnt witches. But your people will rise again. They will awake like Sampson from his sleep, & carry away the gates & posts of the city. You, my friend, are destined to rally them again under their former banner, and when called to the post, exercise it with firmness & with inflexible adherence to your own principles. The people will support you, notwithstanding the howlings of the ravenous crew from whose jaws they are escaping. It will be a great blessing to our country if we can once more restore harmony and social love among its citizens. I confess, as to myself, it is almost the first object of my heart, and one to which I would sacrifice everything but principle. With the people I have hopes of effecting it. But their Coryphæi are incurables. I expect little from them.

I was not deluded by the eulogiums of the public papers in the first moments of change. If they could have continued to get all the loaves & fishes, that is, if I would have gone over to them, they would continue to eulogise. But I well knew that the moment that such removals should take place, as the justice of the preceding administration ought to have exe- cuted, their hue and cry would be set up, and they would take their old stand. I shall disregard that also. Mr. Adams' last appointments, when he knew he was naming counsellors & aids for me & not for himself, I set aside as far as depends on me. Officers who have been guilty of gross abuses of office, such as marshals packing juries, &c., I shall now remove, as my predecessor ought in justice to have done. The instances will be few, and governed by strict rule, & not party passion. The right of opinion shall suffer no invasion from me. Those who have acted well have nothing to fear, however they may have differed from me in opinion: those who have done ill, however, have nothing to hope; nor shall I fail to do justice lest it should be ascribed to that difference of opinion. A co- alition of sentiments is not for the interest of printers. They, like the clergy, live by the zeal they can kindle, and the schisms they can create. It is contest of opinion in politics as well as religion which makes us take great interest in them, and bestow our money liberally on those who furnish aliment to our appetite. The mild and simple principles of the Christian philosophy would produce too much calm, too much regularity of good, to extract from it's disciples a support for a numerous priesthood, were they not to sophisticate it, ramify it, split it into hairs, and twist it's texts till they cover the divine morality of it's author with mysteries, and require a priesthood to explain them. The Quakers seem to have discovered this. They have no priests, therefore no schisms. They judge of the text by the dictates of common sense & common morality. So the printers can never leave us in a state of perfect rest and union of opinion. They would be no longer useful, and would have to go to the plough. In the first moments of quietude which have succeeded the election, they seem to have aroused their lying faculties beyond their ordinary state, to re-agitate the public mind. What appointments to office have they detailed which had never been thought of, merely to found a text for their calumniating commentaries. However, the steady character of our countrymen is a rock to which we may safely moor; and notwithstanding the efforts of the papers to disseminate early discontents, I expect that a just, dispassionate and steady conduct, will at length rally to a proper system the great body of our country. Unequivocal in principle, reasonable in manner, we shall be able I hope to do a great deal of good to the cause of freedom & harmony. I shall be happy to hear from you often, to know your own sentiments & those of others on the course of things, and to concur with you in efforts for the common good. Your letters through the post will now come safely. Present my best respects to Mrs. Gerry, & accept yourself assurances of my constant esteem and high consideration.

"FREE SHIPS MAKE FREE GOODS"
To the U.S. Minister to France
(ROBERT R. LIVINGSTON)

Monticello, Sep. 9, 1801

DEAR SIR,—You will receive, probably by this post, from the Secretary of State, his final instructions for your mission to France. We have not thought it necessary to say anything in them on the great question of the maritime law of nations, which at present agitates Europe; that is to say, whether free ships shall make free goods; because we do not mean to take any side in it during the war. But, as I had before communicated to you some loose thoughts on that subject, and have since considered it with somewhat more attention, I have thought it might not be unuseful that you should possess my ideas in a more matured form than that in which they were before given. Unforeseen circumstances may perhaps oblige you to hazard an opinion, on some occasion or other, on this subject, and it is better that it should not be at variance with ours. I write this, too, myself, that it may not be considered as official, but merely my individual opinion, unadvised by those official counsellors whose opinions I deem my safest guide, & should unquestionably take in form, were circumstances to call for a solemn decision of the question.

When Europe assumed the general form in which it is occupied by the nations now composing it, and turned its attention to maritime commerce, we found among its earliest practices, that of taking the goods of an enemy from the ship of a friend; and that into this practice every maritime State went sooner or later, as it appeared on the theatre of the ocean. If, therefore, we are to consider the practice of nations as the sole & sufficient evidence of the law of nature among nations, we should unquestionably place this principle among those of natural laws. But it's inconveniences, as they affected neutral nations peaceably pursuing their commerce, and it's tendency to embroil them with the powers happening to be at war, and thus to extend the flames of war, induced nations to introduce by special compacts, from time to time, a more convenient rule; that "free ships should make free goods;" and this latter principle has by every maritime nation of Europe been established, to a greater or less degree, in it's treaties with other nations; insomuch, that all of them have, more or less frequently, assented to it, as a rule of action in particular cases. Indeed, it is now urged, and I think with great appearance of reason, that this is genuine principle dictated by national morality; & that the first practice arose from accident, and the particular convenience of the States which first figured on the water, rather than from well-digested reflections on the relations of friend and enemy, on the rights of territorial jurisdiction, & on the dictates of moral law applied to these. Thus it had never been supposed lawful, in the territory of a friend to seize the goods of an enemy. On an element which nature has not subjected to the jurisdiction of any particular nation, but has made common to all for the purposes to which it is fitted, it would seem that the particular portion of it which happens to be occupied by the vessel of any nation, in the course of it's voyage, is for the moment, the exclusive property of that, and nation, with the vessel, is exempt from intrusion by any other, & from it's jurisdiction, as much as if it were lying in the harbor of it's sovereign. In no country, we believe, is the rule otherwise, as to the subjects of property common to all. Thus the place occupied by an individual in a highway, a church, a theatre, or other public assembly, cannot be intruded on, while it's occupant holds it for the purposes of it's institution. The persons on board a vessel traversing the ocean, carry with them the laws of their nation, have among themselves a jurisdiction, a police, not established by their individual will, but by the authority of their nation, of whose territory their vessel still seems to compose a part, so long as it does not enter the exclusive territory of another. No nation ever pretended a right to govern by their laws the ship of another nation navigating the ocean. By what law then can it enter that ship while in peaceable & orderly use of the common element? We recognize no natural precept for submission to such a right; & perceive no distinction between the movable & immovable jurisdiction of a friend, which would authorize the entering the one & not the other, to seize the property of an enemy.

It may be objected that this proves too much, as it proves you cannot enter the ship of a friend to search for contraband of war. But this is not proving too much. We believe the practice of seizing what is called contraband of war, is an abusive practice, not founded in natural right. War between two nations cannot diminish the rights of the rest of the world remaining at peace. The doctrine that the rights of nations remaining quietly under the exercise of moral & social duties, are to give way to the convenience of those who prefer plundering & murdering one another, is a monstrous doctrine;

and ought to yield to the more rational law, that "the wrongs which two nations endeavor to inflict on each other, must not infringe on the rights or conveniences of those remaining at peace." And what is *contraband*, by the law of nature? Either everything which may aid or comfort an enemy, or nothing. Either all commerce which would accommodate him is unlawful, or none is. The difference between articles of one or another description, is a difference in degree only. No line between them can be drawn. Either all intercourse must cease between neutrals & belligerents, or all be permitted. Can the world hesitate to say which shall be the rule? Shall two nations turning tigers, break up in one instant the peaceable relations of the whole world? Reason & nature clearly pronounce that the neutral is to go on in the enjoyment of all it's rights, that it's commerce remains free, not subject to the jurisdiction of another, nor consequently it's vessels to search, or to enquiries whether their contents are the property of an enemy, or are of those which have been called contraband of war.

Nor does this doctrine contravene the right of preventing vessels from entering a blockaded port. This right stands on other ground. When the fleet of any nation actually beleaguers the port of its enemy, no other has a right to enter their line, any more than their line of battle in the open sea, or their lines of circumvallation, or of encampment, or of battle array on land. The space included within their lines in any of those cases, is either the property of their enemy, or it is common property assumed and possessed for the moment, which cannot be intruded on, even by a neutral, without committing the very trespass we are now considering, that of intruding into the lawful possession of a friend.

Although I consider the observance of these principles as of great importance to the interests of peaceable nations, among whom I hope the U S will ever place themselves, yet in the present state of things they are not worth a war. Nor do I believe war the most certain means of enforcing them. Those peaceable coercions which are in the power of every nation, if undertaken in concert & in time of peace, are more likely to produce the desired effect.

The opinions I have here given are those which have generally been sanctioned by our government. In our treaties with France, the United Netherlands, Sweden & Prussia, the principle of free bottom, free goods, was uniformly maintained. In the instructions of 1784, given by Congress to their ministers appointed to treat with the nations of Europe generally, the same principle, and the doing away contraband of war, were enjoined, and were acceded to in the treaty signed with Portugal. In the late treaty with England, indeed, that power perseveringly refused the principle of free bottoms, free goods; and it was avoided in the late treaty with Prussia, at the instance of our then administration, lest it should seem to take side in a question then threatening decision by the sword. At the commencement of the war between France & England, the representative of the French republic then residing in the U S, complaining that the British armed ships captured French property in American bottoms, insisted that the principle of "free bottoms, free goods," was of the acknowledged law of nations; that the violation of that principle by the British was a wrong committed on us, and such an one as we ought to repel by joining in a war against that country. We denied his position, and appealed to the universal practice of Europe, in proof that the principle of "free bottoms, free goods," was not acknowledged as of the natural law of nations, but only of it's conventional law. And I believe we may safely affirm, that not a single instance can be produced where any nation of Europe, acting professedly under the law of nations alone, unrestrained by treaty, has, either by it's executive or judiciary organs, decided on the principle of "free bottoms, free goods." Judging of the law of nations by what has been *practised* among nations, we were authorized to say that the contrary principle was their rule, and this but an exception to it, introduced by special treaties in special cases only; that having no treaty with England substituting this instead of the ordinary rule, we had neither the right nor the disposition to go to war for it's establishment. But though we would not then, nor will we now, engage in war to establish this principle, we are nevertheless sincerely friendly to it. We think that the nations of Europe have originally set out in error; that experience has proved the error oppressive to the rights and interests of the peaceable part of mankind; that every nation but one has acknoleged this, by consenting to the change, & that one has consented in particular cases; that nations have a right to correct an erroneous principle, & to establish that which is right as their rule of action; and if they should adopt measures for effecting this in a peaceable way, we shall wish them success, and not stand in their way to it. But should it become, at any time, expedient for us to co-operate in the establishment of this principle, the opinion of the executive, on the advice of it's constitutional counsellors, must then be given; & that of the legislature, an independent & essential organ in the operation, must also be expressed; in forming which, they will be governed, every man by his own judgment, and may, very possibly, judge differently from the executive. With the same honest views, the most honest men often form different conclusions. As far, however, as we can judge, the principle of "free bottoms, free goods," is that which would carry the wishes of our nation.

Wishing you smooth seas and prosperous gales, with the enjoyment of good health, I tender you the assurances of my constant friendship & high consideration and respect.

INTERCHANGEABLE PARTS
To James Monroe

Washington, Nov. 14, 1801

DEAR SIR,—The bearer hereof is Mr. Whitney at Connecticut a mechanic of the first order of ingenuity, who invented the cotton gin now so much used in the South; he is at the head of a considerable gun manufactory in Connecticut, and furnishes the U.S. with muskets undoubtedly the best they receive. He has invented molds and machines for making all the pieces of his locks so exactly equal, that take 100 locks to pieces and mingle their parts and the hundred locks may be put together as well by taking the first pieces which come to hand. This is of importance in repairing, because out of 10 locks e.g. disabled for the want of different pieces, 9 good locks may be put together without employing a smith. Leblanc in France had invented a similar process in 1788 and had extended it to the barrel, mounting & stock. I endeavored to get the U.S. to bring him over, which he was ready for on moderate terms. I failed and I do not know what became of him. Mr. Whitney has not yet extended his improvements beyond the lock. I think it possible he might be engaged in our manufactory of Richmd. tho' I have not asked him the question. I know nothing of his moral character. He is now on his way to S. Carola. on the subject of his gin. Health & happiness cum caeteris votis.

AFRICAN COLONIZATION
To the Governor of Virginia
(JAMES MONROE)

Washington, Nov. 24, 1801

DEAR SIR,—I had not been unmindful of your letter of June 15, covering a resolution of the House of Representatives of Virginia, and referred to in yours of the 17th inst. The importance of the subject, and the belief that it gave us time for consideration till the next meeting of the Legislature, have induced me to defer the answer to this date. You will perceive that some circumstances connected with the subject, & necessarily presenting themselves to view, would be improper but for yours' & the legislative ear. Their publication might have an ill effect in more than one quarter. In confidence of attention to this, I shall indulge greater freedom in writing.

Common malefactors, I presume, make no part of the object of that resolution. Neither their numbers, nor the nature of their offences, seem to require any provisions beyond those practised heretofore, & found adequate to the repression of ordinary crimes. Conspiracy, insurgency, treason, rebellion, among that description of persons who brought on us the alarm, and on themselves the tragedy, of 1800, were doubtless within the view of every one; but many perhaps contemplated, and one expression of the resolution might comprehend, a much larger scope. Respect to both opinions makes it my duty to understand the resolution in all the extent of which it is susceptible.

The idea seems to be to provide for these people by a purchase of lands; and it is asked whether such a purchase can be made of the U S in their western territory? A very great extent of country, north of the Ohio, has been laid off into townships, and is now at market, according to the provisions of the acts of Congress, with which you are acquainted. There is nothing which would restrain the State of Virginia either in the purchase or the application of these lands; but a purchase, by the acre, might perhaps be a more expensive provision than the H of Representatives contemplated. Questions would also arise whether the establishment of such a colony within our limits, and to become a part of our union, would be desirable to the State of Virginia itself, or to the other States—especially those who would be in its vicinity?

Could we procure lands beyond the limits of the U S to form a receptacle for these people? On our northern boundary, the country not occupied by British subjects, is the property of Indian nations, whose title would be to be extinguished, with the consent of Great Britain; & the new settlers would be British subjects. It is hardly to be believed that either Great Britain or the Indian proprietors have so disinterested a regard for us, as to be willing to relieve us, by receiving such a colony themselves; and as much to be doubted whether that race of men could long exist in so rigorous a climate. On our western & southern frontiers, Spain holds an immense country, the occupancy of which, however, is in the Indian natives, except a few insulated spots possessed by Spanish subjects. It is very questionable, indeed, whether the Indians would sell? whether Spain would be willing to receive these people? and nearly certain that she would not alienate the sovereignty. The same question to ourselves would recur here also, as did in the first case: should we be willing to have such a colony in contact with us? However our present interests may restrain us within our own limits, it is impossible not to look forward to distant times, when our rapid multiplication will expand itself beyond those limits, & cover the whole northern, if not the southern continent, with a people speaking the same language, governed in similar forms, & by similar laws; nor can we contemplate with satisfaction either blot or mixture on that surface. Spain, France, and Portugal hold possessions on the southern continent, as to which I am not well enough informed to say how far they might meet our views. But either there or in the northern continent, should the constituted authorities of Virginia fix their attention, of preference, I will have the dispositions of those powers sounded in the first instance.

The West Indies offer a more probable & practicable retreat for them. Inhabited already by a people of their own race & color; climates congenial with their natural constitution; insulated from the other descriptions of men; nature seems to have formed these islands to become the receptacle of the blacks transplanted into this hemisphere. Whether we could obtain from the European sovereigns of those islands leave to send thither the persons under consideration, I cannot say; but I think it more probable than the former propositions, because of their being already inhabited more or less by the same race. The most promising portion of them is the island of St. Domingo, where the blacks are established into a sovereignty *de facto*, & have organized themselves under regular laws & government. I should conjecture that their present ruler might be willing, on many considerations, to receive even that description which would be exiled for acts deemed criminal by us, but meritorious, perhaps, by him. The possibility that these exiles might stimulate & conduct vindicative or predatory descents on our coasts, & facilitate concert with their brethren remaining here, looks to a state of things between that island & us not probable on a contemplation of our relative strength, and of the disproportion daily growing; and it is overweighed by the humanity of the measures proposed, & the advantages of disembarrassing ourselves of such dangerous characters. Africa would offer a last & undoubted resort, if all others more desirable should fail us. Whenever the Legislature of Virginia shall have brought it's mind to a point, so that I may know exactly what to propose to foreign authorities, I will execute their wishes with fidelity & zeal. I hope, however, they will pardon me for suggesting a single question for their own consideration. When we contemplate the variety of countries & of sovereigns towards which we may direct our views, the vast revolutions & changes of circumstances which are now in a course of progression, the possibilities that arrangements now to be made, with a view to any particular plan, may, at no great distance of time, be totally deranged by a change of sovereignty, of government, or of other circumstances, it will be for the Legislature to consider whether, after they shall have made all those general provisions which may be fixed by legislative authority, it would be reposing too much confidence in their Executive to leave the place of relegation to be decided on by *them*. They could accommodate their arrangements to the actual state of things, in which countries or powers may be found to exist at the day; and may prevent the effect of the law from being defeated by intervening changes. This, however, is for them to decide. Our duty will be to respect their decision.

LIMITS OF THE PRACTICABLE
To P. S. Dupont de Nemours

Washington, Jan. 18, 1802

DEAR SIR,—It is rare I can indulge myself in the luxury of philosophy. Your letters give me a few of those delicious moments. Placed as you are in a great commercial town, with little opportunity of discovering the dispositions of the country portions of our citizens, I do not wonder at your doubts whether they will generally and sincerely concur in the sentiments and measures developed in my message of the 7th Jany. But from 40. years of intimate conversation with the agricultural inhabitants of my country, I can pronounce them as different from those of the cities, as those of any two nations known. The sentiments of the former can in no degree be inferred from those of the latter. You have spoken a profound truth in these words, "Il y a dans les etats unis un bon sens silencieux, un esprit de justice froide, qui lorsqu'il est question d'emettre un *vote* comme les bavardages de ceux qui font les habiles." A plain country farmer has written lately a pamphlet on our public affairs. His testimony of the sense of the country is the best which can be produced of the justness of your observation. His words are "The tongue of man is not his whole body. So, in this case, the noisy part of the community was not all the body politic. During the career of fury and contention (in 1800) the sedate, grave part of the people were still; hearing all, and judging for themselves, what method to take, when the constitutional time of action should come, the exercise of the right of suffrage." The majority of the present legislature are in unison with the agricultural part of our citizens, and you will see that there is nothing in the message, to which they do not accord. Some things may perhaps be left undone from motives of compromise for a time, and not to alarm by too sudden a reformation, but with a view to be resumed at another time. I am perfectly satisfied the effect of the proceedings of this session of congress will be to consolidate the great body of well meaning citizens together, whether federal or republican, heretofore called. I do not mean to include royalists or priests. Their opposition is immovable. But they will be vox et preterea nihil, leaders without followers. I am satisfied that within one year from this time were an election to take place between two candidates merely republican and federal, where no personal opposition existed against either, the federal candidate would not get the vote of a single elector in the U.S. I must here again appeal to the testimony of my farmer, who says "The great body of the people are one in sentiment. If the federal party and the republican party, should each of them choose a convention to frame a constitution of government or a code of laws, there would be no radical difference in the results of the two conventions." This is most true. The body of our people, tho' divided for a short time by an artificial panic, and called by different names, have ever had the same object in view, to wit, the maintenance of a federal, republican government, and have never ceased to be all federalists, all republicans: still excepting the noisy band of royalists inhabiting cities chiefly, and priests both of city and country. When I say that in an election between a republican and federal candidate, free from personal objection, the former would probably get every vote, I must not be understood as placing myself in that view. It was my destiny to come to the government when it had for several years been committed to a particular political sect, to the absolute and entire exclusion of those who were in sentiment with the body of the nation. I found the country entirely in the enemies hands. It was necessary to dislodge some of them. Out of many thousands of officers in the U.S. 9. only have been removed for political principle, and 12. for delinquincies chiefly pecuniary. The whole herd have squealed out, as if all their throats were cut. These acts of justice few as they have been, have raised great personal objections to me, of which a new character would be [*faded*]. When this government was first established, it was possible to have kept it going on true principles, but the contracted, English, half-lettered ideas of Hamilton, destroyed that hope in the bud. We can pay off his debt in 15. years; but we can never get rid of his financial system. It mortifies me to be strengthening principles which I deem radically vicious, but this vice is entailed on us by the first error. In other parts of our government I hope we shall be able by degrees to introduce sound principles and make them habitual. What is practicable must often controul what is pure theory; and the habits of the governed determine in a great degree what is practicable. Hence the same original principles, modified in practice according to the different habits of different nations, present governments of very different aspects. The same principles reduced to forms of practice accommodated to our habits, and put into forms accommodated to the habits of the French nation would present governments very unlike each other. I have no doubt but that a great man, thoroughly knowing the habits of France, might so accommodate to them the principles of free government as to enable them to live free. But in the hands of those who have not this coup d'oeil, many unsuccessful experiments I fear are yet to be tried before they will settle down in freedom and tranquility. I applaud therefore your determination to remain here, tho' for yourself and the adults of your family the dissimilitude of our manners and the difference of tongue will be sources of real unhappiness. Yet less so than the horrors and dangers which France would present to you, and as to those of your family still in infancy, they will be formed to the circumstances of the country, and will, I doubt not, be happier here than they could have been in Europe under any circumstances. Be so good as to make my respectful salutations acceptable to Made. Dupont, and all of your family and to be assured yourself of my constant and affectionate esteem.

"TO BE LOVED BY EVERY BODY"

To Anne Cary, Thomas Jefferson, and Ellen Wayles Randolph

Washington, Mar. 2, 1802

MY DEAR CHILDREN—I am very happy to find that two of you can write. I shall now expect that whenever it is inconvenient for your papa and mama to write, one of you will write on a piece of paper these words 'all is well' and send it for me to the post office. I am happy too that Miss Ellen can now read so readily. If she will make haste and read through all the books I have given her, and will let me know when she is through them, I will go and carry her some more. I shall now see whether she wishes to see me as much as she says. I wish to see you all: and the more I perceive that you are all advancing in your learning and improving in good dispositions the more I shall love you, and the more every body will love you. It is a charming thing to be loved by every body: and the way to obtain it is, never to quarrel or be angry with any body and to tell a story. Do all the kind things you can to your companions, give them every thing rather than to yourself. Pity and help any thing you see in distress and learn your books and improve your minds. This will make every body fond of you, and desirous of doing it to you. Go on then my dear children, and, when we meet at Monticello, let me see who has improved most. I kiss this paper for each of you: it will therefore deliver the kisses to yourselves, and two over, which one of you must deliver to your Mama for me; and present my affectionate attachment to your papa. Yourselves love and Adieux.

THE PROGRESS OF REFORM

To General Thaddeus Kosciusko

Washington, April 2, 1802

DEAR GENERAL,—It is but lately that I have received your letter of the 25th Frimaire (December 15) wishing to know whether some officers of your country could expect to be employed in this country. To prevent a suspense injurious to them, I hasten to inform you, that we are now actually engaged in reducing our military establishment one third, and discharging one third of our officers. We keep in service no more than men enough to garrison the small posts dispersed at great distances on our frontiers, which garrisons will generally consist of a captain's company only, and in no case of more than two or three, in not one, of a sufficient number to require a field officer; and no circumstance whatever can bring these garrisons together, because it would be an abandonment of their forts. Thus circumstanced, you will perceive the entire impossibility of providing for the persons you recommend. I wish it had been in my power to give you a more favorable answer; but next to the fulfilling your wishes, the most grateful thing I can do is to give a faithful answer. The session of the first Congress convened since republicanism has recovered its ascendancy, is now drawing to a close. They will pretty completely fulfil all the desires of the people. They have reduced the army and navy to what is barely necessary. They are disarming executive patronage and preponderance, by putting down one half the offices of the United States, which are no longer necessary. These economies have enabled them to suppress all the internal taxes, and still to make such provision for the payment of their public debt as to discharge that in eighteen years. They have lopped off a parasite limb, planted by their predecessors on their judiciary body for party purposes; they are opening the doors of hospitality to the fugitives from the oppressions of other countries; and we have suppressed all those public forms and ceremonies which tended to familiarise the public eye to the harbingers of another form of government. The people are nearly all united; their quondam leaders, infuriated with the sense of their impotence, will soon be seen or heard only in the newspapers, which serve as chimnies to carry off noxious vapors and smoke, and all is now tranquil, firm and well, as it should be. I add no signature because unnecessary for you. God bless you, and preserve you still for a season of usefulness to your country.

THE AFFAIR OF LOUISIANA
To the U.S. Minister to France
(ROBERT R. LIVINGSTON)

Washington, Apr. 18, 1802

DEAR SIR—A favorable and a confidential opportunity offering by Mr. Dupont de Nemours, who is revisiting his native country gives me an opportunity of sending you a cipher to be used between us, which will give you some trouble to understand, but, once understood, is the easiest to use, the most indecipherable, and varied by a new key with the greatest facility of any one I have ever known. I am in hopes the explanation inclosed will be sufficient. Let our key of letters be [*some figures which are illegible*] and the key of lines be [*figures illegible*] and lest we should happen to lose our key or be absent from it, it is so formed as to be kept in the memory and put upon paper at pleasure; being produced by writing our names and residences at full length, each of which containing 27 letters is divided into two parts of 9. letters each; and each of the 9. letters is then numbered according to the place it would hold if the 9. were arranged alphabetically, thus [*so blotted as to be illegible*]. The numbers over the letters being then arranged as the letters to which they belong stand in our names, we can always construct our key. But why a cipher between us, when official things go naturally to the Secretary of State, and things not political need no cipher. 1. matters of a public nature, and proper to go on our records, should go to the secretary of state. 2. matters of a public nature not proper to be placed on our records may still go to the secretary of state, headed by the word 'private.' But 3. there may be matters merely personal to ourselves, and which require the cover of a cipher more than those of any other character. This last purpose and others which we cannot foresee may render it convenient and advantageous to have at hand a mask for whatever may need it. But writing by Mr. Dupont I need no cipher. I require from him to put this into your own and no other hand, let the delay occasioned by that be what it will.

The cession of Louisiana and the Floridas by Spain to France works most sorely on the U.S. On this subject the

Secretary of State has written to you fully. Yet I cannot forbear recurring to it personally, so deep is the impression it makes in my mind. It compleatly reverses all the political relations of the U.S. and will form a new epoch in our political course. Of all nations of any consideration France is the one which hitherto has offered the fewest points on which we could have any conflict of right, and the most points of a communion of interests. From these causes we have ever looked to her as our *natural friend*, as one with which we never could have an occasion of difference. Her growth therefore we viewed as our own, her misfortunes ours. There is on the globe one single spot, the possessor of which is our natural and habitual enemy. It is New Orleans, through which the produce of three-eighths of our territory must pass to market, and from its fertility it will ere long yield more than half of our whole produce and contain more than half our inhabitants. France placing herself in that door assumes to us the attitude of defiance. Spain might have retained it quietly for years. Her pacific dispositions, her feeble state, would induce her to increase our facilities there, so that her possession of the place would be hardly felt by us, and it would not perhaps be very long before some circumstance might arise which might make the cession of it to us the price of something of more worth to her. Not so can it ever be in the hands of France. The impetuosity of her temper, the energy and restlessness of her character, placed in a point of eternal friction with us, and our character, which though quiet, and loving peace and the pursuit of wealth, is high-minded, despising wealth in competition with insult or injury, enterprising and energetic as any nation on earth, these circumstances render it impossible that France and the U.S. can continue long friends when they meet in so irritable a position. They as well as we must be blind if they do not see this; and we must be very improvident if we do not begin to make arrangements on that hypothesis. The day that France takes possession of N. Orleans fixes the sentence which is to restrain her forever within her low water mark. It seals the union of two nations who in conjunction can maintain exclusive possession of the ocean. From that moment we must marry ourselves to the British fleet and nation. We must turn all our attentions to a maritime force, for which our resources place us on very high grounds: and having formed and cemented together a power which may render reinforcement of her settlements here impossible to France, make the first cannon, which shall be fired in Europe the signal for tearing up any settlement she may have made, and for holding the two continents of America in sequestration for the common purposes of the united British and American nations. This is not a state of things we seek or desire. It is one which this measure, if adopted by France, forces on us, as necessarily as any other cause, by the laws of nature, brings on its necessary effect. It is not from a fear of France that we deprecate this measure proposed by her. For however greater her force is than ours compared in the abstract, it is nothing in comparison of ours when to be exerted on our soil. But it is from a sincere love of peace, and a firm persuasion that bound to France by the interests and the strong sympathies still existing in the minds of our citizens, and holding relative positions which ensure their continuance we are secure of a long course of peace. Whereas the change of friends, which will be rendered necessary if France changes that position, embarks us necessarily as a belligerent power in the first war of Europe. In that case France will have held possession of New Orleans during the interval of a peace, long or short, at the end of which it will be wrested from her. Will this short-lived possession have been an equivalent to her for the transfer of such a weight into the scale of her enemy? Will not the amalgamation of a young, thriving, nation continue to that enemy the health and force which are at present so evidently on the decline? And will a few years possession of N. Orleans add equally to the strength of France? She may say she needs Louisiana for the supply of her West Indies. She does not need it in time of peace. And in war she could not depend on them because they would be so easily intercepted. I should suppose that all these considerations might in some proper form be brought into view of the government of France. Tho' stated by us, it ought not to give offence; because we do not bring them forward as a menace, but as consequences not controulable by us, but inevitable from the course of things. We mention them not as things which we desire by any means, but as things we deprecate; and we beseech a friend to look forward and to prevent them for our common interests.

If France considers Louisiana however as indispensable for her views she might perhaps be willing to look about for arrangements which might reconcile it to our interests. If anything could do this it would be the ceding to us the island of New Orleans and the Floridas. This would certainly in a great degree remove the causes of jarring and irritation between us, and perhaps for such a length of time as might produce other means of making the measure permanently conciliatory to our interests and friendships. It would at any rate relieve us from the necessity of taking immediate measures for countervailing such an operation by arrangements in another quarter. Still we should consider N. Orleans and the Floridas as equivalent for the risk of a quarrel with France produced by her vicinage. I have no doubt you have urged these considerations on every proper occasion with the government where you are. They are such as must have effect if you can find the means of producing thorough reflection on them by that government. The idea here is that the troops sent to St. Domingo, were to proceed to Louisiana after finishing their work in that island. If this were the arrangement, it will give you time to return again and again to the charge, for the conquest of St. Domingo will not be a short work. It will take considerable time to wear down a great number of souldiers. Every eye in the U.S. is now fixed on this affair of Louisiana. Perhaps nothing since the revolutionary war has produced more uneasy sensations through the body of the nation. Notwithstanding temporary bickerings have taken place with France, she has still a strong hold on the affections of our citizens generally. I have thought it not amiss, by way of supplement to the letters of the Secretary of State to write you this private one to impress you with the importance we affix to this transaction. I pray you to cherish Dupont. He has the best dispositions for the continuance of friendship between the two nations, and perhaps you may be able to make a good use of him. Accept assurances of my affectionate esteem and high consideration.

DRY-DOCKING THE NAVY

To Benjamin H. Latrobe

Washington, Nov. 2, 1802

DEAR SIR—The placing of a navy in a state of perfect preservation, so that at the beginning of a subsequent war it shall
be as sound as at the end of the preceding one when laid up,
and the lessening the expence of repairs, perpetually necessary
while they lie in the water, are objects of the first importance
to a nation which to a certain degree must be maritime. The
dry docks of Europe, being below the level of tide water, are
very expensive in their construction and in the manner of
keeping them clear of water, and are only practicable at all
where they have high tides: insomuch that no nation has ever
proposed to lay up their whole navy in dry docks. But if the
dry dock were above the level of tide water, and there be any
means of raising the vessels up into them, and of covering the
dock with a roof, thus withdrawn from the rot and the sun,
they would last as long as the interior timbers, doors and
floors of a house. The vast command of running water at this
place, at different heights from 30 to 200 feet above tide water, enables us to effect this desirable object by forming a
lower bason into which the tide water shall float the vessel
and then have its gates closed, and adjoining to this, but 24
feet higher, an upper bason 275 feet wide, and 800 f. long
(sufficient to contain 12 frigates) into which running water
can be introduced from above, so that filling both basons (as
in a lock) the vessel shall be raised up and floated into the
upper one, and the water being discharged leave her dry.
Over a bason not wider than 175 feet, a roof can be thrown,
in the manner of that of the Halle au blé at Paris, which needing no underworks to support it, will permit the bason to be
entirely open and free for the movement of the vessels. I
mean to propose the construction of one of these to the National legislature, convinced it will be a work of no great cost,
that it will save us great annual expence, and be an encouragement to prepare in peace the vessels we shall need in war,
when we find they can be kept in a state of perfect preservation and without expence.

The first thing to be done is to chuse from which of the

streams we will derive our water for the lock. These are the Eastern branch, Tyber, Rock creek, and the Potomak itself. Then to trace the canal, draw plans of that and of the two basons, and calculate the expence of the whole, that we may lead the legislature to no expence in the execution of which they shall not be apprised in the beginning. For this I ask your aid, which will require your coming here. Some surveys and elevations have been already made by Mr. N. King, a very accurate man in that line, and who will assist in any thing you desire, and execute on the ground any tracings you may direct, unless you prefer doing them yourself. It is very material too that this should be done immediately, as we have little more than 4 weeks to the meeting of the legislature, and there will then be but 2 weeks for them to consider and decide before the day arrives (Jan. 1) at which alone any number of labourers can be hired here. Should that pass either the work must lie over for a year, or be executed by day labourers at double expence. I propose that such a force shall be provided as to compleat the work in one year. If this results, as it will receive all our present ships, the next work will be a second one, to build and lay up additional ships. On the subject of your superintending the execution of the work it would be premature to say any thing till the legislature shall have declared their will. Be so good as to let me hear from you immediately, if you cannot come so soon as you can write. Accept my best wishes and respects.

"A NOISELESS COURSE"
To Thomas Cooper

Washington, Nov. 29, 1802

DEAR SIR,—Your favor of Oct 25 was received in due time, and I thank you for the long extract you took the trouble of making from Mr. Stone's letter. Certainly the information it communicates as to Alexander kindles a great deal of interest in his existence, and strong spasms of the heart in his favor. Tho his means of doing good are great, yet the materials on which he is to work are refractory. Whether he engages in private correspondences abroad, as the King of Prussia did much, his grandmother sometimes, I know not; but certainly such a correspondence would be very interesting to those who are sincerely anxious to see mankind raised from their present abject condition. It delights me to find that there are persons who still think that all is not lost in France: that their retrogradation from a limited to an unlimited despotism, is but to give themselves a new impulse. But I see not how or when. The press, the only tocsin of a nation, is compleatly silenced there, and all means of a general effort taken away. However, I am willing to hope, as long as anybody will hope with me; and I am entirely persuaded that the agitations of the public mind advance its powers, and that at every vibration between the points of liberty and despotism, something will be gained for the former. As men become better informed, their rulers must respect them the more. I think you will be sensible that our citizens are fast returning, from the panic into which they were artfully thrown to the dictates of their own reason; and I believe the delusions they have seen themselves hurried into will be useful as a lesson under similar attempts on them in future. The good effects of our late fiscal arrangements will certainly tend to unite them in opinion, and in a confidence as to the views of their public functionaries, legislative & executive. The path we have to pursue is so quiet that we have nothing scarcely to propose to our Legislature. A noiseless course, not meddling with the affairs of others, unattractive of notice, is a mark that society is going on in happiness. If we can prevent the government from wasting the labors of the people, under the pretence of taking care of them, they must become happy. Their finances are now under such a course of application as nothing could derange but war or federalism. The gripe of the latter has shown itself as deadly as the jaws of the former. Our adversaries say we are indebted to their providence for the means of paying the public debt. We never charged them with the want of foresight in providing money, but with the misapplication of it after they have levied it. We say they raised not only enough, but too much; and that after giving back the surplus we do more with a part than they did with the whole.

Your letter of Nov 18 is also received. The places of mid-shipman are so much sought that (being limited) there is never a vacancy. Your son shall be set down for the 2d, which shall happen; the 1st being anticipated. We are not long generally without vacancies happening. As soon as he can be appointed you shall know it. I pray you to accept assurances of my great attachment and respect.

CRISIS ON THE MISSISSIPPI
To the Special Envoy to France
(JAMES MONROE)

Washington, Jan. 13, 1803

DEAR SIR,—I dropped you a line on the 10th informing you of a nomination I had made of you to the Senate, and yesterday I enclosed you their approbation not then having time to write. The agitation of the public mind on occasion of the late suspension of our right of deposit at N. Orleans is extreme. In the western country it is natural and grounded on honest motives. In the seaports it proceeds from a desire for war which increases the mercantile lottery; in the federalists generally and especially those of Congress the object is to force us into war if possible, in order to derange our finances, or if this cannot be done, to attach the western country to them, as their best friends, and thus get again into power. Remonstrances memorials &c. are now circulating through the whole of the western country and signing by the body of the people. The measures we have been pursuing being invisible, do not satisfy their minds. Something sensible therefore was become necessary; and indeed our object of purchasing N. Orleans and the Floridas is a measure liable to assume so many shapes, that no instructions could be squared to fit them, it was essential then to send a minister extraordinary to be joined with the ordinary one, with discretionary powers, first however well impressed with all our views and therefore qualified to meet and modify to these every form of proposition which could come from the other party. This could be done only in full and frequent oral communications. Having determined on this, there could not be two opinions among the republicans as to the person. You possess the unlimited confidence of the administration and of the western people; and generally of the republicans everywhere; and were you to refuse to go, no other man can be found who does this. The measure has already silenced the Feds. here. Congress will no longer be agitated by them: and the country will become calm as fast as the information extends over it. All eyes, all hopes, are now fixed on you; and were you to decline, the chagrin would be universal, and would shake under your feet the high ground on which you stand with the public. Indeed I know nothing which would produce such a shock, for on the event of this mission depends the future destinies of this republic. If we cannot by a purchase of the country insure to ourselves a course of perpetual peace and friendship with all nations, then as war cannot be distant, it behooves us immediately to be preparing for that course, without, however, hastening it, and it may be necessary (on your failure on the continent) to cross the channel.

We shall get entangled in European politics, and figuring more, be much less happy and prosperous. This can only be prevented by a successful issue to your present mission. I am sensible after the measures you have taken for getting into a different line of business, that it will be a great sacrifice on your part, and presents from the season and other circumstances serious difficulties. But some men are born for the public. Nature by fitting them for the service of the human race on a broad scale, has stamped with the evidences of her destination and their duty.

But I am particularly concerned that in the present case you have more than one sacrifice to make. To reform the prodigalities of our predecessors is understood to be peculiarly our duty, and to bring the government to a simple and economical course. They, in order to increase expense, debt, taxation, and patronage tried always how much they could give. The outfit given to ministers resident to enable them to furnish their house, but given by no nation to a temporary minister, who is never expected to take a house or to entertain, but considered on a footing of a voyageur, they gave to their extraordinary missionaries by wholesale. In the beginning of our administration, among other articles of reformation in expense, it was determined not to give an outfit to missionaries extraordinary, and not to incur the expense with any minister of sending a frigate to carry him or bring him. The Boston happened to be going to the Mediterranean, and was permitted therefore to take up Mr. Livingstone and touch in a port of France. A frigate was denied to Charles Pinckney and has been refused to Mr. King for his return. Mr. Madison's friendship and mine to you being so well known, the public will have eagle eyes to watch if we grant you any indulgencies of the general rule; and on the other hand, the example set in your case will be more cogent on future ones, and produce greater approbation to our conduct. The allowance therefore will be in this and all similar cases, all the expenses of your journey and voiage, taking a ship's cabin to yourself, 9,000 D. a year from your leaving home till the proceedings of your mission are terminated, and then the quarter's salary for the expenses of the return as prescribed by law. As to the time of your going you cannot too much hasten it, as the moment in France is critical. St. Domingo delays their taking possession of Louisiana, and they are in the last distress for money for current purposes. You should arrange your affairs for an absence of a year at least, perhaps for a long one. It will be necessary for you to stay here some days on your way to New York. You will receive here what advance you chuse. Accept assurances of my constant and affectionate attachment.

CIVILIZATION OF THE INDIANS
To Benjamin Hawkins

Washington, Feb. 18, 1803

DEAR SIR,—Mr. Hill's return to you offers so safe a conveyance for a letter, that I feel irresistibly disposed to write one, tho' there is but little to write about. You have been so long absent from this part of the world, and the state of society so changed in that time, that details respecting those who compose it are no longer interesting or intelligible to you. One source of great change in social intercourse arose while you were with us, tho' it's effects were as yet scarcely sensible on society or government. I mean the British treaty, which produced a schism that went on widening and rankling till the years '98, '99, when a final dissolution of all bonds, civil & social, appeared imminent. In that awful crisis, the people awaked from the phrenzy into which they had been thrown, began to return to their sober and ancient principles, & have now become five-sixths of one sentiment, to wit, for peace, economy, and a government bottomed on popular election in its legislative & executive branches. In the public counsels the federal party hold still one-third. This, however, will lessen, but not exactly to the standard of the people; because it will be forever seen that of bodies of men even elected by the people, there will always be a greater proportion aristocratic than among their constituents. The present administration had a task imposed on it which was unavoidable, and could not fail to exert the bitterest hostility in those opposed to it. The preceding administration left 99. out of every hundred in public offices of the federal sect. Republicanism had been the mark on Cain which had rendered those who bore it exiles from all portion in the trusts & authorities of their country. This description of citizens called imperiously & justly for a restoration of right. It was intended, however, to have yielded to this in so moderate a degree as might conciliate those who had obtained exclusive possession; but as soon as they were touched, they endeavored to set fire to the four corners of the public fabric, and obliged us to deprive of the influence of office several who were using it with activity and vigilance to destroy the confidence of the people in their government, and thus to proceed in the drudgery of removal farther than would have been, had not their own hostile enterprises rendered it necessary in self-defence. But I think it will not be long before the whole nation will be consolidated in their ancient principles, excepting a few who have committed themselves beyond recall, and who will retire to obscurity & settled disaffection.

Altho' you will receive, thro' the official channel of the War Office, every communication necessary to develop to you our views respecting the Indians, and to direct your conduct, yet, supposing it will be satisfactory to you, and to those with whom you are placed, to understand my personal dispositions and opinions in this particular, I shall avail myself of this private letter to state them generally. I consider the business of hunting as already become insufficient to furnish clothing and subsistence to the Indians. The promotion of agriculture, therefore, and household manufacture, are essential in their preservation, and I am disposed to aid and encourage it liberally. This will enable them to live on much smaller portions of land, and indeed will render their vast forests useless but for the range of cattle; for which purpose, also, as they become better farmers, they will be found useless, and even disadvantageous. While they are learning to do better on less land, our increasing numbers will be calling for more land, and thus a coincidence of interests will be produced between those who have lands to spare, and want other necessaries, and those who have such necessaries to spare, and want lands. This commerce, then, will be for the good of both, and those who are friends to both ought to encourage it. You are in the station peculiarly charged with this interchange, and who have it peculiarly in your power to promote among the Indians a sense of the superior value of a little land, well cultivated, over a great deal, unimproved, and to encourage them to make this estimate truly. The wisdom of the animal which amputates & abandons to the hunter the parts for which he is pursued should be theirs, with this difference, that the former sacrifices what is useful, the latter what is not. In truth, the ultimate point of rest & happiness for them is to let our settlements and theirs meet and blend together, to intermix, and become one people. Incorporating themselves with us as citizens of the U.S., this is what the natural progress of things will of course bring on, and it will be better to promote than to retard it. Surely it will be better for them to be identified with us, and preserved in the occupation of their lands, than be exposed to the many casualties which may endanger them while a separate people. I have little doubt but that your reflections must have led you to view the various ways in which their history may terminate, and to see that this is the one most for their happiness. And we have already had an application from a settlement of Indians to become citizens of the

U.S. It is possible, perhaps probable, that this idea may be so novel as that it might shock the Indians, were it even hinted to them. Of course, you will keep it for your own reflection; but, convinced of its soundness, I feel it consistent with pure morality to lead them towards it, to familiarize them to the idea that it is for their interest to cede lands at times to the U S, and for us thus to procure gratifications to our citizens, from time to time, by new acquisitions of land. From no quarter is there at present so strong a pressure on this subject as from Georgia for the residue of the fork of Oconee & Ockmulgee; and indeed I believe it will be difficult to resist it. As it has been mentioned that the Creeks had at one time made up their minds to sell this, and were only checked in it by some indiscretions of an individual, I am in hopes you will be able to bring them to it again. I beseech you to use your most earnest endeavors; for it will relieve us here from a great pressure, and yourself from the unreasonable suspicions of the Georgians which you notice, that you are more attached to the interests of the Indians than of the U S, and throw cold water on their willingness to part with lands. It is so easy to excite suspicion, that none are to be wondered at; but I am in hopes it will be in your power to quash them by effecting the object.

Mr. Madison enjoys better health since his removal to this place than he had done in Orange. Mr. Giles is in a state of health feared to be irrecoverable, although he may hold on for some time, and perhaps be re-established. Browze Trist is now in the Mississippi territory, forming an establishment for his family, which is still in Albemarle, and will remove to the Mississippi in the spring. Mrs. Trist, his mother, begins to yield a little to time. I retain myself very perfect health, having not had 20. hours of fever in 42 years past. I have sometimes had a troublesome headache, and some slight rheumatic pains; but now sixty years old nearly, I have had as little to complain of in point of health as most people. I learn you have the gout. I did not expect that Indian cookery or Indian fare would produce that; but it is considered as a security for good health otherwise. That it may be so with you, I sincerely pray, and tender you my friendly and respectful salutations.

MACHIAVELLIAN BENEVOLENCE AND THE INDIANS

To Governor William H. Harrison

Washington, February 27, 1803

DEAR SIR,—While at Monticello in August last I received your favor of August 8th, and meant to have acknowledged it on my return to the seat of government at the close of the ensuing month, but on my return I found that you were expected to be on here in person, and this expectation continued till winter. I have since received your favor of December 30th.

In the former you mentioned the plan of the town which you had done me the honor to name after me, and to lay out according to an idea I had formerly expressed to you. I am thoroughly persuaded that it will be found handsome and pleasant, and I do believe it to be the best means of preserving the cities of America from the scourge of the yellow fever, which being peculiar to our country, must be derived from some peculiarity in it. That peculiarity I take to be our cloudless skies. In Europe, where the sun does not shine more than half the number of days in the year which it does in America, they can build their town in a solid block with impunity; but here a constant sun produces too great an accumulation of heat to admit that. Ventilation is indispensably necessary. Experience has taught us that in the open air of the country the yellow fever is not only not generated, but ceases to be infectious. I cannot decide from the drawing you sent me, whether you have laid off streets round the squares thus: or only the diagonal streets therein marked. The former was my idea, and is, I imagine, most convenient.

You will receive herewith an answer to your letter as President of the Convention; and from the Secretary of War you receive from time to time information and instructions as to our Indian affairs. These communications being for the public records, are restrained always to particular objects and occasions; but this letter being unofficial and private, I may with safety give you a more extensive view of our policy respecting the Indians, that you may the better comprehend the parts dealt out to you in detail through the official channel, and observing the system of which they make a part, conduct yourself in unison with it in cases where you are obliged to act without instruction. Our system is to live in perpetual peace with the Indians, to cultivate an affectionate attachment from them, by everything just and liberal which we can do for them within the bounds of reason, and by giving them effectual protection against wrongs from our own people. The decrease of game rendering their subsistence by hunting insufficient, we wish to draw them to agriculture, to spinning and weaving. The latter branches they take up with great readiness, because they fall to the women, who gain by quitting the labors of the field for those which are exercised within doors. When they withdraw themselves to the culture of a small piece of land, they will perceive how useless to them are their extensive forests, and will be willing to pare them off from time to time in exchange for necessaries for their farms and families. To promote this disposition to exchange lands, which they have to spare and we want, for necessaries, which we have to spare and they want, we shall push our trading uses, and be glad to see the good and influential individuals among them run in debt, because we observe that when these debts get beyond what the individuals can pay, they become willing to lop them off by a cession of lands. At our trading houses, too, we mean to sell so low as merely to repay us cost and charges, so as neither to lessen or enlarge our capital. This is what private traders cannot do, for they must gain; they will consequently retire from the competition, and we shall thus get clear of this pest without giving offence or umbrage to the Indians. In this way our settlements will gradually circumscribe and approach the Indians, and they will in time either incorporate with us as citizens of the United States, or remove beyond the Mississippi. The former is certainly the termination of their history most happy for themselves; but, in the whole course of this, it is essential to cultivate their love. As to their fear, we presume that our strength and their weakness is now so visible that they must see we have only to shut our hand to crush them, and that all our liberalities to them proceed from motives of pure humanity only. Should any tribe be fool-hardy enough to take up the hatchet at any time, the seizing the whole country of that tribe, and driving them across the Mississippi, as the only condition of peace, would be an example to others, and a furtherance of our final consolidation.

Combined with these views, and to be prepared against the occupation of Louisiana by a powerful and enterprising people, it is important that, setting less value on interior extension of purchases from the Indians, we bend our whole views to the purchase and settlement of the country on the Mississippi, from its mouth to its northern regions, that we may be able to present as strong a front on our western as on our eastern border, and plant on the Mississippi itself the means of its own defence. We now own from 31 to the Yazoo, and hope this summer to purchase what belongs to the Choctaws from the Yazoo up to their boundary, supposed to be about opposite the mouth of Acanza. We wish at the same time to begin in your quarter, for which there is at present a favorable opening. The Cahokias extinct, we are entitled to their country by our paramount sovereignty. The Piorias, we understand, have all been driven off from their country, and we might claim it in the same way; but as we understand there is one chief remaining, who would, as the survivor of the tribe, sell the right, it is better to give him such terms as will make him easy for life, and take a conveyance from him. The Kaskaskias being reduced to a few families, I presume we may purchase their whole country for what would place every individual of them at his ease, and be a small price to us,—say by laying off for each family, whenever they would choose it, as much rich land as they could cultivate, adjacent to each other, enclosing the whole in a single fence, and giving them such an annuity in money or goods forever as would place them in happiness; and we might take them also under the protection of the United States. Thus possessed of the rights of these tribes, we should proceed to the settling their boundaries with the Poutewatamies and Kickapoos; claiming all doubtful territory, but paying them a price for the relinquishment of their concurrent claim, and even prevailing on them, if possible, to *cede*, for a price, such of their own unquestioned territory as would give us a convenient northern boundary. Before broaching this, and while we are bargaining with the Kaskaskies, the minds of the Poutewatamies and Kickapoos should be soothed and conciliated by liberalities and sincere assurances of friendship. Perhaps by sending a well-qualified character to stay some time in Decoigne's village, as if on other business, and to sound him and introduce the subject by degrees to his mind and that of the other heads of families, inculcating in the way of conversation, all those considerations which prove the advantages they would receive by a cession on these terms, the object might be more easily and effectually obtained than by abruptly proposing it to them at a formal treaty. Of the means, however, of obtaining what we wish, you will be the best judge; and I have given you this view of the system which we suppose will best promote the interests of the Indians and ourselves, and finally consolidate our whole country to one nation only; that you may be enabled the better to adapt your means to the object, for this purpose we have given you a general commission for treating. The crisis is pressing: whatever can now be obtained must be obtained quickly. The occupation of New Orleans, hourly expected, by the French, is already felt like a light breeze by the Indians. You know the sentiments they entertain of that nation; under the hope of their protection they will immediately stiffen against cessions of lands to us. We had better, therefore, do at once what can now be done.

I must repeat that this letter is to be considered as private and friendly, and is not to control any particular instructions which you may receive through official channel. You will also perceive how sacredly it must be kept within your own breast, and especially how improper to be understood by the Indians. For their interests and their tranquillity it is best they should see only the present age of their history. I pray you to accept assurances of my esteem and high consideration.

JESUS, SOCRATES, AND OTHERS
To Dr. Joseph Priestley

Washington, Apr. 9, 1803

DEAR SIR,—While on a short visit lately to Monticello, I received from you a copy of your comparative view of Socrates

& Jesus, and I avail myself of the first moment of leisure after my return to acknolege the pleasure I had in the perusal of it, and the desire it excited to see you take up the subject on a more extensive scale. In consequence of some conversation with Dr. Rush, in the year 1798–99, I had promised some day to write him a letter giving him my view of the Christian system. I have reflected often on it since, & even sketched the outlines in my own mind. I should first take a general view of the moral doctrines of the most remarkable of the antient philosophers, of whose ethics we have sufficient information to make an estimate, say of Pythagoras, Epicurus, Epictetus, Socrates, Cicero, Seneca, Antoninus. I should do justice to the branches of morality they have treated well; but point out the importance of those in which they are deficient. I should then take a view of the deism and ethics of the Jews, and show in what a degraded state they were, and the necessity they presented of a reformation. I should proceed to a view of the life, character, & doctrines of Jesus, who sensible of incorrectness of their ideas of the Deity, and of morality, endeavored to bring them to the principles of a pure deism, and juster notions of the attributes of God, to reform their moral doctrines to the standard of reason, justice & philanthropy, and to inculcate the belief of a future state. This view would purposely omit the question of his divinity, & even his inspiration. To do him justice, it would be necessary to remark the disadvantages his doctrines have to encounter, not having been committed to writing by himself, but by the most unlettered of men, by memory, long after they had heard them from him; when much was forgotten, much misunderstood, & presented in very paradoxical shapes. Yet such are the fragments remaining as to show a master workman, and that his system of morality was the most benevolent & sublime probably that has been ever taught, and consequently more perfect than those of any of the antient philosophers. His character & doctrines have received still greater injury from those who pretend to be his special disciples, and who have disfigured and sophisticated his actions & precepts, from views of personal interest, so as to induce the unthinking part of mankind to throw off the whole system in disgust, and to pass sentence as an impostor on the most innocent, the most benevolent, the most eloquent and sublime character that ever has been exhibited to man. This is the outline; but I have not the time, & still less the information which the subject needs. It will therefore rest with me in contemplation only. You are the person who of all others would do it best, and most promptly. You have all the materials at hand, and you put together with ease. I wish you could be induced to extend your late work to the whole subject. I have not heard particularly what is the state of your health; but as it has been equal to the journey to Philadelphia, perhaps it might encourage the curiosity you must feel to see for once this place, which nature has formed on a beautiful scale, and circumstances destine for a great one. As yet we are but a cluster of villages; we cannot offer you the learned society of Philadelphia; but you will have that of a few characters whom you esteem, & a bed & hearty welcome with one who will rejoice in every opportunity of testifying to you his high veneration & affectionate attachment.

THE MORALS OF JESUS

To Dr. Benjamin Rush, with a Syllabus

Washington, Apr. 21, 1803

DEAR SIR,—In some of the delightful conversations with you, in the evenings of 1798–99, and which served as an anodyne to the afflictions of the crisis through which our country was then laboring, the Christian religion was sometimes our topic; and I then promised you, that one day or other, I would give you my views of it. They are the result of a life of inquiry & reflection, and very different from that anti-Christian system imputed to me by those who know nothing of my opinions. To the corruptions of Christianity I am indeed opposed; but not to the genuine precepts of Jesus himself. I am a Christian, in the only sense he wished any one to be; sincerely attached to his doctrines, in preference to all others; ascribing to himself every *human* excellence; & believing he never claimed any other. At the short intervals since these conversations, when I could justifiably abstract my mind from public affairs, the subject has been under my contemplation. But the more I considered it, the more it expanded beyond the measure of either my time or information. In the moment of my late departure from Monticello, I received from Doctr Priestley, his little treatise of "Socrates & Jesus compared." This being a section of the general view I had taken of the field, it became a subject of reflection while on the road, and unoccupied otherwise. The result was, to arrange in my mind a syllabus, or outline of such an estimate of the comparative merits of Christianity, as I wished to see executed by some one of more leisure and information for the task, than myself. This I now send you, as the only discharge of my promise I can probably ever execute. And in confiding it to you, I know it will not be exposed to the malignant perversions of those who make every word from me a text for new misrepresentations & calumnies. I am moreover averse to the communication of my religious tenets to the public; because it would countenance the presumption of those who have endeavored to draw them before that tribunal, and to seduce public opinion to erect itself into that inquisition over the rights of conscience, which the laws have so justly proscribed. It behoves every man who values liberty of conscience for himself, to resist invasions of it in the case of others; or their case may, by change of circumstances, become his own. It behoves him, too, in his own case, to give no example of concession, betraying the common right of independent opinion, by answering questions of faith, which the laws have left between God & himself. Accept my affectionate salutations.

SYLLABUS OF AN ESTIMATE OF THE MERIT OF THE DOC-
TRINES OF JESUS, COMPARED WITH THOSE OF OTHERS

April, 1803

In a comparative view of the Ethics of the enlightened nations of antiquity, of the Jews and of Jesus, no notice should be taken of the corruptions of reason among the ancients, to wit, the idolatry & superstition of the vulgar, nor of the corruptions of Christianity by the learned among its professors.

Let a just view be taken of the moral principles inculcated

by the most esteemed of the sects of ancient philosophy, or of their individuals; particularly Pythagoras, Socrates, Epicurus, Cicero, Epictetus, Seneca, Antoninus.

I. PHILOSOPHERS. 1. Their precepts related chiefly to ourselves, and the government of those passions which, unrestrained, would disturb our tranquillity of mind. In this branch of philosophy they were really great.

2. In developing our duties to others, they were short and defective. They embraced, indeed, the circles of kindred & friends, and inculcated patriotism, or the love of our country in the aggregate, as a primary obligation: toward our neighbors & countrymen they taught justice, but scarcely viewed them as within the circle of benevolence. Still less have they inculcated peace, charity & love to our fellow men, or embraced with benevolence the whole family of mankind.

II. JEWS. 1. Their system was Deism; that is, the belief of one only God. But their ideas of him & of his attributes were degrading & injurious.

2. Their Ethics were not only imperfect, but often irreconcilable with the sound dictates of reason & morality, as they respect intercourse with those around us; & repulsive & antisocial, as respecting other nations. They needed reformation, therefore, in an eminent degree.

III. JESUS. In this state of things among the Jews, Jesus appeared. His parentage was obscure; his condition poor; his education null; his natural endowments great; his life correct and innocent: he was meek, benevolent, patient, firm, disinterested, & of the sublimest eloquence.

The disadvantages under which his doctrines appear are remarkable.

1. Like Socrates & Epictetus, he wrote nothing himself.

2. But he had not, like them, a Xenophon or an Arrian to write for him. On the contrary, all the learned of his country, entrenched in its power and riches, were opposed to him, lest his labors should undermine their advantages; and the committing to writing his life & doctrines fell on the most unlettered & ignorant men; who wrote, too, from memory, & not till long after the transactions had passed.

3. According to the ordinary fate of those who attempt to enlighten and reform mankind, he fell an early victim to the

jealousy & combination of the altar and the throne, at about 33. years of age, his reason having not yet attained the *maximum* of its energy, nor the course of his preaching, which was but of 3. years at most, presented occasions for developing a complete system of morals.

4. Hence the doctrines which he really delivered were defective as a whole, and fragments only of what he did deliver have come to us mutilated, misstated, & often unintelligible.

5. They have been still more disfigured by the corruptions of schismatising followers, who have found an interest in sophisticating & perverting the simple doctrines he taught by engrafting on them the mysticisms of a Grecian sophist, frittering them into subtleties, & obscuring them with jargon, until they have caused good men to reject the whole in disgust, & to view Jesus himself as an impostor.

Notwithstanding these disadvantages, a system of morals is presented to us, which, if filled up in the true style and spirit of the rich fragments he left us, would be the most perfect and sublime that has ever been taught by man.

The question of his being a member of the Godhead, or in direct communication with it, claimed for him by some of his followers, and denied by others, is foreign to the present view, which is merely an estimate of the intrinsic merit of his doctrines.

1. He corrected the Deism of the Jews, confirming them in their belief of one only God, and giving them juster notions of his attributes and government.

2. His moral doctrines, relating to kindred & friends, were more pure & perfect than those of the most correct of the philosophers, and greatly more so than those of the Jews; and they went far beyond both in inculcating universal philanthropy, not only to kindred and friends, to neighbors and countrymen, but to all mankind, gathering all into one family, under the bonds of love, charity, peace, common wants and common aids. A development of this head will evince the peculiar superiority of the system of Jesus over all others.

3. The precepts of philosophy, & of the Hebrew code, laid hold of actions only. He pushed his scrutinies into the heart of man; erected his tribunal in the region of his thoughts, and purified the waters at the fountain head.

4. He taught, emphatically, the doctrines of a future state, which was either doubted, or disbelieved by the Jews; and wielded it with efficacy, as an important incentive, supplementary to the other motives to moral conduct.

EXPEDITION TO THE PACIFIC
Instructions to Captain Lewis

June 20, 1803

To Merryweather Lewis, Esq., Captain of the 1st Regiment of Infantry of the United States of America.

Your situation as Secretary of the President of the United States has made you acquainted with the objects of my confidential message of Jan. 18, 1803, to the legislature. You have seen the act they passed, which, tho' expressed in general terms, was meant to sanction those objects, and you are appointed to carry them into execution.

Instruments for ascertaining by celestial observations the geography of the country thro' which you will pass, have been already provided. Light articles for barter, & presents among the Indians, arms for your attendants, say for from 10 to 12 men, boats, tents, & other travelling apparatus, with ammunition, medicine, surgical instruments & provision you will have prepared with such aids as the Secretary at War can yield in his department; & from him also you will receive authority to engage among our troops, by voluntary agreement, the number of attendants above mentioned, over whom you, as their commanding officer are invested with all the powers the laws give in such a case.

As your movements while within the limits of the U.S. will be better directed by occasional communications, adapted to circumstances as they arise, they will not be noticed here. What follows will respect your proceedings after your departure from the U.S.

Your mission has been communicated to the Ministers here from France, Spain, & Great Britain, and through them to their governments: and such assurances given them as to it's objects as we trust will satisfy them. The country of Louisiana having been ceded by Spain to France, the passport you have from the Minister of France, the representative of the present sovereign of the country, will be a protection with all it's subjects: And that from the Minister of England will entitle you to the friendly aid of any traders of that allegiance with whom you may happen to meet.

The object of your mission is to explore the Missouri river, & such principal stream of it, as, by it's course & communication with the water of the Pacific Ocean may offer the most direct & practicable water communication across this continent, for the purposes of commerce.

Beginning at the mouth of the Missouri, you will take observations of latitude and longitude at all remarkable points on the river, & especially at the mouths of rivers, at rapids, at islands & other places & objects distinguished by such natural marks & characters of a durable kind, as that they may with certainty be recognized hereafter. The courses of the river between these points of observation may be supplied by the compass, the log-line & by time, corrected by the observations themselves. The variations of the compass too, in different places should be noticed.

The interesting points of the portage between the heads of the Missouri & the water offering the best communication with the Pacific Ocean should be fixed by observation & the course of that water to the ocean, in the same manner as that of the Missouri.

Your observations are to be taken with great pains & accuracy, to be entered distinctly, & intelligibly for others as well as yourself, to comprehend all the elements necessary, with the aid of the usual tables to fix the latitude & longitude of the places at which they were taken, & are to be rendered to the war office, for the purpose of having the calculations made concurrently by proper persons within the U.S. Several copies of these as well as of your other notes, should be made at leisure times & put into the care of the most trustworthy of your attendants, to guard by multiplying them against the accidental losses to which they will be exposed. A further guard would be that one of these copies be written on the paper of the birch, as less liable to injury from damp than common paper.

The commerce which may be carried on with the people inhabiting the line you will pursue, renders a knolege of these people important. You will therefore endeavor to make yourself acquainted, as far as a diligent pursuit of your journey shall admit.

with the names of the nations & their numbers;

the extent & limits of their possessions;

their relations with other tribes or nations;

their language, traditions, monuments;

their ordinary occupations in agriculture, fishing, hunting, war, arts, & the implements for these;

their food, clothing, & domestic accommodations;

the diseases prevalent among them, & the remedies they use;

moral and physical circumstance which distinguish them from the tribes they know;

peculiarities in their laws, customs & dispositions;

and articles of commerce they may need or furnish & to what extent.

And considering the interest which every nation has in extending & strengthening the authority of reason & justice among the people around them, it will be useful to acquire what knolege you can of the state of morality, religion & information among them, as it may better enable those who endeavor to civilize & instruct them, to adapt their measures to the existing notions & practises of those on whom they are to operate.

Other objects worthy of notice will be

the soil & face of the country, its growth & vegetable productions; especially those not of the U.S.

the animals of the country generally, & especially those not known in the U.S.

The remains & accounts of any which may be deemed rare or extinct;

the mineral productions of every kind; but more particularly metals, limestone, pit coal & saltpetre; salines & mineral waters, noting the temperature of the last & such circumstances as may indicate their character; volcanic appearances;

climate as characterized by the thermometer, by the proportion of rainy, cloudy & clear days, by lightening, hail, snow, ice, by the access & recess of frost, by the winds, prevailing at different seasons, the dates at which particular plants put forth or lose their flowers, or leaf, times of appearance of particular birds, reptiles or insects.

Altho' your route will be along the channel of the Missouri, yet you will endeavor to inform yourself by inquiry, of the character and extent of the country watered by its branches, and especially on it's southern side. The north river or Rio Bravo which runs into the gulph of Mexico, and the north river, or Rio colorado, which runs into the gulph of California, are understood to be the principal streams heading opposite to the waters of the Missouri, & running Southwardly. Whether the dividing grounds between the Missouri & them are mountains or flatlands, what are their distance from the Missouri, the character of the intermediate country, & the people inhabiting it, are worthy of particular enquiry. The northern waters of the Missouri are less to be enquired after, because they have been ascertained to a considerable degree, and are still in a course of ascertainment by English traders & travellers. But if you can learn anything certain of the most northern source of the Mississippi, & of it's position relative to the lake of the woods, it will be interesting to us. Some account too of the path of the Canadian traders from the Mississippi, at the mouth of the Ouisconsin river, to where it strikes the Missouri and of the soil and rivers in it's course, is desirable.

In all your intercourse with the natives treat them in the most friendly & conciliatory manner which their own conduct will admit; allay all jealousies as to the object of your journey, satisfy them of it's innocence, make them acquainted with the position, extent, character, peaceable & commercial dispositions of the U.S., of our wish to be neighborly, friendly & useful to them, & of our dispositions to a commercial intercourse with them; confer with them on the points most convenient as mutual emporiums, & the articles of most desirable interchange for them & us. If a few of their influential chiefs, within practicable distance, wish to visit us, arrange such a visit with them, and furnish them with authority to call on our officers, on their entering the U.S. to have them conveyed to this place at the public expense. If any of them should wish to have some of their young people brought up with us, & taught such arts as may be useful to them, we will receive, instruct & take care of them. Such a mission, whether of influential chiefs, or of young people, would give some security to your own party. Carry with you some matter of the kine-pox, inform those of them with whom you may be of it's efficacy as a preservative from the small-pox; and instruct & encourage them in the use of it. This may be especially done wherever you may winter.

As it is impossible for us to foresee in what manner you will be received by those people, whether with hospitality or hostility, so is it impossible to prescribe the exact degree of perseverance with which you are to pursue your journey. We value too much the lives of citizens to offer them to probably destruction. Your numbers will be sufficient to secure you against the unauthorized opposition of individuals, or of small parties: but if a superior force, authorized or not authorized, by a nation, should be arrayed against your further passage, & inflexibly determined to arrest it, you must decline it's further pursuit, & return. In the loss of yourselves, we should lose also the information you will have acquired. By returning safely with that, you may enable us to renew the essay with better calculated means. To your own discretion therefore must be left the degree of danger you may risk, & the point at which you should decline, only saying we wish you to err on the side of your safety, & to bring back your party safe, even if it be with less information.

As far up the Missouri as the white settlements extend, an intercourse will probably be found to exist between them and the Spanish posts at St. Louis, opposite Cahokia, or Ste. Genevieve opposite Kaskaskia. From still farther up the river, the traders may furnish a conveyance for letters. Beyond that you may perhaps be able to engage Indians to bring letters for the government to Cahokia or Kaskaskia on promising that they shall there receive such special compensation as you shall have stipulated with them. Avail yourself of these means to communicate to us at seasonable intervals a copy of your journal, notes & observations of every kind, putting into cipher whatever might do injury if betrayed.

Should you reach the Pacific Ocean inform yourself of the circumstances which may decide whether the furs of those parts may not be collected as advantageously at the head of the Missouri (convenient as is supposed to the waters of the Colorado & Oregon or Columbia) as at Nootka Sound or any other point of that coast; & that trade be consequently conducted through the Missouri & U.S. more beneficially than by the circumnavigation now practised.

On your arrival on that coast endeavor to learn if there be any port within your reach frequented by the sea-vessels of any nation, and to send two of your trusted people back by sea, in such way as shall appear practicable, with a copy of your notes. And should you be of opinion that the return of your party by the way they went will be eminently dangerous, then ship the whole, & return by sea by way of Cape Horn or the Cape of Good Hope, as you shall be able. As you will be without money, clothes or provisions, you must endeavor to use the credit of the U.S. to obtain them; for which purpose open letters of credit shall be furnished you authorizing you to draw on the Executive of the U.S. or any of its officers in any part of the world, in which drafts can be disposed of, and to apply with our recommendations to the consuls, agents, merchants or citizens of any nation with which we have intercourse, assuring them in our name that any aids they may furnish you, shall be honorably repaid and on demand. Our consuls Thomas Howes at Batavia in Java, William Buchanan of the Isles of France and Bourbon & John Elmslie at the Cape of Good Hope will be able to supply your necessities by drafts on us.

Should you find it safe to return by the way you go, after sending two of your party round by sea, or with your whole party, if no conveyance by sea can be found, do so; making such observations on your return as may serve to supply, correct or confirm those made on your outward journey.

In re-entering the U.S. and reaching a place of safety, discharge any of your attendants who may desire & deserve it: procuring for them immediate paiment of all arrears of pay & cloathing which may have incurred since their departure & assure them that they shall be recommended to the liberality of the Legislature for the grant of a souldier's portion of land each, as proposed in my message to Congress: & repair your-self with your papers to the seat of government.

To provide, on the accident of your death, against anarchy, dispersion & the consequent danger to your party, and total failure of the enterprise, you are hereby authorized by any instrument signed & written in your own hand to name the person among them who shall succeed to the command on your decease, & by like instruments to change the nomination from time to time, as further experience of the characters ac-companying you shall point out superior fitness: and all the powers & authorities given to yourself are, in the event of your death transferred to & vested in the successor so named, with further power to him, & his successors in like manner to name each his successor, who, on the death of his prede-cessor shall be invested with all the powers & authorities given to yourself.

Given under my hand at the city of Washington, this 20th day of June, 1803.

A NATIONAL AGRICULTURAL SOCIETY
To Sir John Sinclair

Washington, June 30, 1803

DEAR SIR,—It is so long since I have had the pleasure of writing to you, that it would be vain to look back to dates to connect the old and the new. Yet I ought not to pass over my acknowledgments to you for various publications received from time to time, and with great satisfaction and thankful-ness. I send you a small one in return, the work of a very unlettered farmer, yet valuable, as it relates plain facts of im-portance to farmers. You will discover that Mr. Binns is an enthusiast for the use of gypsum. But there are two facts which prove he has a right to be so: 1. He began poor, and has made himself tolerably rich by his farming alone. 2. The county of Loudon, in which he lives, had been so exhausted and wasted by bad husbandry, that it began to depopulate, the inhabitants going Southwardly in quest of better lands. Binns' success has stopped that emigration. It is now becoming one of the most productive counties of the State of Virginia, and the price given for the lands is multiplied manifold.

We are still uninformed here whether you are again at war. Bonaparte has produced such a state of things in Europe as it would seem difficult for him to relinquish in any sensible degree, and equally dangerous for Great Britain to suffer to go on, especially if accompanied by maritime preparations on his part. The events which have taken place in France have lessened in the American mind the motives of interest which it felt in that revolution, and its amity towards that country now rests on its love of peace and commerce. We see, at the same time, with great concern, the position in which Great Britain is placed, and should be sincerely afflicted were any disaster to deprive mankind of the benefit of such a bulwark against the torrent which has for some time been bearing down all before it. But her power and powers at sea seem to render everything safe in the end. Peace is our passion, and the wrongs might drive us from it. We prefer trying *ever* other just principles, right and safety, before we would recur to war.

I hope your agricultural institution goes on with success. I consider you as the author of all the good it shall do. A better idea has never been carried into practice. Our agricultural society has at length formed itself. Like our American Philosophical Society, it is voluntary, and unconnected with the public, and is precisely an execution of the plan I formerly sketched to you. Some State societies have been formed heretofore; the others will do the same. Each State society names two of its members of Congress to be their members in the Central society, which is of course together during the sessions of Congress. They are to select matter from the proceedings of the State societies, and to publish it; so that their publications may be called *l'esprit des sociétes d'agriculture*, &c. The Central society was formed the last winter only, so that it will be some time before they get under way. Mr. Madison, the Secretary of State, was elected their President.

Recollecting with great satisfaction our friendly intercourse while I was in Europe, I nourish the hope it still preserves a place in your mind; and with my salutations, I pray you to accept assurances of my constant attachment and high respect.

PEACE FOUNDED ON INTEREST

To the Earl of Buchan

Washington, July 10, 1803

MY LORD,—I received, through the hands of Mr. Lenox, on his return to the United States, the valuable volume you were so good as to send me on the life and writings of Fletcher, of Saltoun. The political principles of that patriot were worthy the purest periods of the British Constitution; they are those which were in vigor at the epoch of the American emigration. Our ancestors brought them here, and they needed little strengthening to make us what we are. But in the weakened condition of English whigism at this day, it requires more firmness to publish and advocate them than it then did to act on them. This merit is peculiarly your Lordship's; and no one honors it more than myself. While I freely admit the right of a nation to change its political principles and constitution at will, and the impropriety of any but its own citizens censuring that change, I expect your Lordship has been disappointed, as I acknowledge I have been, in the issue of the convulsions on the other side the channel. This has certainly lessened the interest which the philanthropist warmly felt in those struggles. Without befriending human liberty, a gigantic force has risen up which seems to threaten the world. But it hangs on the thread of opinion, which may break from one day to another. I feel real anxiety on the conflict to which imperious circumstances seem to call your nation, and bless the Almighty Being, who, in gathering together the waters under the heavens into one place, divided the dry land of your hemisphere from the dry lands of ours, and said, at least be there peace. I hope that peace and amity with all nations will long be the character of our land, and that its prosperity under the Charter will react on the mind of Europe, and profit her by the example. My hope of preserving peace for our country is not founded in the greater principles of non-resistance under every wrong, but in the belief that a just and friendly conduct on our part will procure justice and friendship from others. In the existing contest, each of the combatants will find an interest in our friendship. I cannot say we shall be unconcerned spectators of this combat. We feel for human sufferings, and we wish the good of all. We shall look on, therefore, with the sensations which these dispositions and the events of the war will produce.

I feel a pride in the justice which your Lordship's sentiments render to the character of my illustrious countryman, Washington. The moderation of his desires, and the strength of his judgment, enabled him to calculate correctly, that the road to that glory which never dies is to use power for the support of the laws and liberties of our country, not for their destruction; and his will accordingly survives the wreck of everything now living.

Accept, my lord, the tribute of esteem, from one who renders it with warmth to the disinterested friend of mankind, and assurances of my high consideration and respect.

PHILOSOPHY AND BLASTED HOPES
To Pierre J. G. Cabanis

Washington, July 12, 1803

DEAR SIR,—I lately received your friendly letter of 28 Vendem. an. 11, with the two volumes on the relations between the physical and moral faculties of man. This has ever been a subject of great interest to the inquisitive mind, and it could not have got into better hands for discussion than yours. That thought may be a faculty of our material organization, has been believed in the gross; and though the "modus operandi" of nature, in this, as in most other cases, can never be developed and demonstrated to beings limited as we are, yet I feel confident you will have conducted us as far on the road as we can go, and have lodged us within reconnoitering distance of the citadel itself. While *here*, I have time to read nothing. But our annual recess for the months of August and September is now approaching, during which time I shall be at the Montrials, where I anticipate great satisfaction in the presence of these volumes. It is with great satisfaction, too, I recollect the agreeable hours I have past with yourself and M. de La Roche, at the house of our late excellent friend, Madame Helvetius, and elsewhere; and I am happy to learn you continue your residence there. Antevil always appeared to me a delicious village, and Madame Helvetius's the most delicious spot in it. In those days how sanguine we were! and how soon were the virtuous hopes and confidence of every good man blasted! and how many excellent friends have we lost in your efforts towards self-government, *et cui bono*? But let us draw a veil over the dead, and hope the best for the living. If the hero who has saved you from a combination of enemies, shall also be the means of giving you as great a portion of liberty as the opinions, habits and character of the nation are prepared for, progressive preparation may fit you for progressive portions of that first of blessings, and you may in time attain what we erred in supposing could be hastily seized and maintained, in the present state of political information among your citizens at large. In this way all may end well.

You are again at war, I find. But we, I hope, shall be permitted to run the race of peace. Your government has wisely removed what certainly endangered collision between us. I now see nothing which need ever interrupt the friendship between France and this country. Twenty years of peace, and the prosperity so visibly flowing from it, have but strengthened our attachment to it, and the blessings it brings, and we do not despair of being always a peaceable nation. We think that peaceable means may be devised of keeping nations in the path of justice towards us, by making justice their interest, and injuries to react on themselves. Our distance enables us to pursue a course which the crowded situation of Europe renders perhaps impracticable there.

Be so good as to accept for yourself and M. de La Roche, my friendly salutations, and assurances of great consideration and respect.

THE LOUISIANA PURCHASE
To John C. Breckinridge

Monticello, Aug. 12, 1803

DEAR SIR,—The enclosed letter, tho' directed to you, was intended to me also, and was left open with a request, that when perused, I would forward it to you. It gives me occasion to write a word to you on the subject of Louisiana, which being a new one, an interchange of sentiments may produce correct ideas before we are to act on them.

Our information as to the country is very incompleat; we have taken measures to obtain it in full as to the settled part, which I hope to receive in time for Congress. The boundaries, which I deem not admitting question, are the high lands on the western side of the Missisipi enclosing all it's waters, the Missouri of course, and terminating in the line drawn from the northwestern point of the Lake of the Woods to the nearest source of the Missipi, as lately settled between Gr Britain and the U S. We have some claims, to extend on the sea coast Westwardly to the Rio Norte or Bravo, and better, to go Eastwardly to the Rio Perdido, between Mobile & Pensacola, the antient boundary of Louisiana. These claims will be a subject of negociation with Spain, and if, as soon as she is at war, we push them strongly with one hand, holding out a price in the other, we shall certainly obtain the Floridas, and all in good time. In the meanwhile, without waiting for permission, we shall enter into the exercise of the natural right we have always insisted on with Spain, to wit, that of a nation holding the upper part of streams, having a right of innocent passage thro' them to the ocean. We shall prepare her to see us practise on this, & she will not oppose it by force.

Objections are raising to the Eastward against the vast extent of our boundaries, and propositions are made to exchange Louisiana, or a part of it, for the Floridas. But, as I have said, we shall get the Floridas without, and I would not give one inch of the waters of the Mississippi to any nation, because I see in a light very important to our peace the exclusive right to it's navigation, & the admission of no nation into it, but as into the Potomak or Delaware, with our consent & under our police. These federalists see in this acquisition the formation of a new confederacy, embracing all the waters of the Missipi, on both sides of it, and a separation of it's Eastern waters from us. These combinations depend on so many circumstances which we cannot foresee, that I place little reliance on them. We have seldom seen neighborhood produce affection among nations. The reverse is almost the universal truth. Besides, if it should become the great interest of those nations to separate from this, if their happiness should depend on it so strongly as to induce them to go through that convulsion, why should the Atlantic States dread it? But especially why should we, their present inhabitants, take side in such a question? When I view the Atlantic States, procuring for those on the Eastern waters of the Missipi friendly instead of hostile neighbors on it's Western waters, I do not view it as an Englishman would the procuring future blessings for the French nation, with whom he has no relations of blood or affection. The future inhabitants of the Atlantic & Missipi States will be our sons. We leave them in distinct but bordering establishments. We think we see their happiness in their union, & we wish it. Events may prove it otherwise; and if they see their interest in separation, why should we take side with our Atlantic rather than our Missipi descendants? It is the elder and the younger son differing. God bless them both, & keep them in union, if it be for their good, but separate them, if it be better. The inhabited part of Louisiana, from Point Coupée to the sea, will of course be immediately a territorial government, and soon a State. But above that, the best use we can make of the country for some time, will be to give establishments in it to the Indians on the East side of the Missipi, in exchange for their present country, and open land offices in the last, & thus make this acquisition the means of filling up the Eastern side, instead of drawing off it's population. When we shall be full on this side, we may lay off a range of States on the Western bank from the head to the mouth, & so, range after range, advancing compactly as we multiply.

This treaty must of course be laid before both Houses, because both have important functions to exercise respecting it. They, I presume, will see their duty to their country in ratifying & paying for it, so as to secure a good which would otherwise probably be never again in their power. But I suppose they must then appeal to *the nation* for an additional article to the Constitution, approving & confirming an act which the nation had not previously authorized. The constitution has made no provision for our holding foreign territory, still less for incorporating foreign nations into our Union. The Executive in seizing the fugitive occurrence which so much advances the good of their country, have done an act beyond the Constitution. The Legislature in casting behind them metaphysical subtleties, and risking themselves like faithful servants, must ratify & pay for it, and throw themselves on their country for doing for them unauthorized what we know they would have done for themselves had they been in a situation to do it. It is the case of a guardian, investing the money of his ward in purchasing an important adjacent territory; & saying to him when of age, I did this for your good; I pretend to no right to bind you: you may disavow me, and I must get out of the scrape as I can: I thought it my duty to risk myself for you. But we shall not be disavowed by the nation, and their act of indemnity will confirm & not weaken the Constitution, by more strongly marking out its lines.

We have nothing later from Europe than the public papers give. I hope yourself and all the Western members will make a sacred point of being at the first day of the meeting of Congress; for *vestra res agitur.*

Accept my affectionate salutations & assurances of esteem & respect.

A CONSTITUTIONAL AMENDMENT
To Wilson Cary Nicholas

Monticello, Sep. 7, 1803

DEAR SIR,—Your favor of the 3d was delivered me at court; but we were much disappointed at not seeing you here, Mr. Madison & the Gov. being here at the time. I enclose you a letter from Monroe on the subject of the late treaty. You will observe a hint in it, to do without delay what we are bound to do. There is reason, in the opinion of our ministers, to believe, that if the thing were to do over again, it could not be obtained, & that if we give the least opening, they will declare the treaty void. A warning amounting to that has been given to them, & an unusual kind of letter written by their minister to our Secretary of State, direct. Whatever Congress shall think it necessary to do, should be done with as little debate as possible, & particularly so far as respects the constitutional difficulty. I am aware of the force of the observations you make on the power given by the Constn to Congress, to admit new States into the Union, without restraining the subject to the territory then constituting the U S. But when I consider that the limits of the U S are precisely fixed by the treaty of 1783, that the Constitution expressly declares itself to be made for the U S, I cannot help believing the intention was to permit Congress to admit into the Union new States, which should be formed out of the territory for which, & under whose authority alone, they were then acting. I do not believe it was meant that they might receive England, Ireland, Holland, &c. into it, which would be the case on your construction. When an instrument admits two constructions, the one safe, the other dangerous, the one precise, the other indefinite, I prefer that which is safe & precise. I had rather ask an enlargement of power from the nation, where it is found necessary, than to assume it by a construction which would make our powers boundless. Our peculiar security is in possession of a written Constitution. Let us not make it a blank paper by construction. I say the same as to the opinion of those who consider the grant of the treaty making power as boundless. If it is, then we have no Constitution. If it has bounds, they can be no others than the definitions of the powers which that instrument gives. It specifies & delineates the operations permitted to the federal government, and gives all the powers necessary to carry these into execution. Whatever of these enumerated objects is proper for a law, Congress may make the law; whatever is proper to be executed by way of a treaty, the President & Senate may enter into the treaty; whatever is to be done by a judicial sentence, the judges may pass the sentence. Nothing is more likely than that their enumeration of powers is defective. This is the ordinary case of all human works. Let us go on then perfecting it, by adding, by way of amendment to the Constitution, those powers which time & trial show are still wanting. But it has been taken too much for granted, that by this rigorous construction the treaty power would be reduced to nothing. I had occasion once to examine its effect on the French treaty, made by the old Congress, & found that out of thirty odd articles which that contained, there were one, two, or three only which could not now be stipulated under our present Constitution. I confess, then, I think it important, in the present case, to set an example against broad construction, by appealing for new power to the people. If, however, our friends shall think differently, certainly I shall acquiesce with satisfaction; confiding, that the good sense of our country will correct the evil of construction when it shall produce ill effects.

No apologies for writing or speaking to me freely are necessary. On the contrary, nothing my friends can do is so dear to me, & proves to me their friendship so clearly, as the information they give me of their sentiments & those of others on interesting points where I am to act, and where information & warning is so essential to excite in me that due reflection which ought to precede action. I leave this about the 21st, and shall hope the District Court will give me an opportunity of seeing you.

Accept my affectionate salutations, & assurances of cordial esteem & respect.

JESUS, LOUISIANA, AND MALTHUS
To Dr. Joseph Priestley

Washington, Jan. 29, 1804

DEAR SIR,—Your favor of December 12 came duly to hand, as did the 2.ᵈ letter to Doctor Linn, and the treatise of Phlogiston, for which I pray you to accept my thanks. The copy for Mr. Livingston has been delivered, together with your letter to him, to Mr. Harvie, my secretary, who departs in a day or two for Paris, & will deliver them himself to Mr. Livingston, whose attention to your matter cannot be doubted. I have also to add my thanks to Mr. Priestley, your son, for the copy of your Harmony, which I have gone through with great satisfaction. It is the first I have been able to meet with, which is clear of those long repetitions of the same transaction, as if it were a different one because related with some different circumstances.

I rejoice that you have undertaken the task of comparing

the moral doctrines of Jesus with those of the ancient Philosophers. You are so much in possession of the whole subject,
that you will do it easier & better than any other person living. I think you cannot avoid giving, as preliminary to the
comparison, a digest of his moral doctrines, extracted in his
own words from the Evangelists, and leaving out everything
relative to his personal history and character. It would be
short and precious. With a view to do this for my own satisfaction, I had sent to Philadelphia to get two testaments
Greek of the same edition, & two English, with a design to
cut out the morsels of morality, and paste them on the leaves
of a book, in the manner you describe as having been pursued
in forming your Harmony. But I shall now get the thing
done by better hands.

I very early saw that Louisiana was indeed a speck in our
horizon which was to burst in a tornado; and the public are
unapprized how near this catastrophe was. Nothing but a
frank & friendly development of causes & effects on our part,
and good sense enough in Bonaparte to see that the train was
unavoidable, and would change the face of the world, saved
us from that storm. I did not expect he would yield till a war
took place between France and England, and my hope was to
palliate and endure, if Messrs. Ross, Morris, &c. did not force
a premature rupture, until that event. I believed the event not
very distant, but acknolege it came on sooner than I had expected. Whether, however, the good sense of Bonaparte
might not see the course predicted to be necessary & unavoidable, even before a war should be imminent, was a
chance which we thought it our duty to try; but the immediate prospect of rupture brought the case to immediate decision. The *dénoument* has been happy; and I confess I look
to this duplication of area for the extending a government so
free and economical as ours, as a great achievement to the
mass of happiness which is to ensue. Whether we remain in
one confederacy, or form into Atlantic and Mississippi confederacies, I believe not very important to the happiness of
either part. Those of the western confederacy will be as much
our children & descendants as those of the eastern, and I feel
myself as much identified with that country, in future time,
as with this; and did I now foresee a separation at some fu-

ture day, yet I should feel the duty & the desire to promote the western interests as zealously as the eastern, doing all the good for both portions of our future family which should fall within my power.

Have you seen the new work of Malthus on population? It is one of the ablest I have ever seen. Altho' his main object is to delineate the effects of redundancy of population, and to test the poor laws of England, & other palliations for that evil, several important questions in political economy, allied to his subject incidentally, are treated with a masterly hand. It is a single 4.to volume, and I have been only able to read a borrowed copy, the only one I have yet heard of. Probably our friends in England will think of you, & give you an opportunity of reading it. Accept my affectionate salutations, and assurances of great esteem & respect.

MALTHUS AND THE NEW WORLD
To Jean Baptiste Say

Washington, February 1, 1804

DEAR SIR,—I have to acknowledge the receipt of your obliging letter, and with it, of two very interesting volumes on Political Economy. These found me engaged in giving the leisure moments I rarely find, to the perusal of Malthus' work on population, a work of sound logic, in which some of the opinions of Adam Smith, as well as of the economists, are ably examined. I was pleased, on turning to some chapters where you treat the same questions, to find his opinions corroborated by yours. I shall proceed to the reading of your work with great pleasure. In the meantime, the present conveyance, by a gentleman of my family going to Paris, is too safe to hazard a delay in making my acknowledgments for this mark of attention, and for having afforded to me a satisfaction, which the ordinary course of literary communications could not have given me for a considerable time.

The differences of circumstance between this and the old countries of Europe, furnish differences of fact whereon to reason, in questions of political economy, and will consequently produce sometimes a difference of result. There, for instance, the quantity of food is fixed, or increasing in a slow and only arithmetical ratio, and the proportion is limited by the same ratio. Supernumerary births consequently add only to your mortality. Here the immense extent of uncultivated and fertile lands enables every one who will labor to marry young, and to raise a family of any size. Our food, then, may increase geometrically with our laborers, and our births, however multiplied, become effective. Again, there the best distribution of labor is supposed to be that which places the manufacturing hands alongside the agricultural; so that the one part shall feed both, and the other part furnish both with clothes and other comforts. Would that be best here? Egoism and first appearances say yes. Or would it be better that all our laborers should be employed in agriculture? In this case a double or treble portion of fertile lands would be brought into culture; a double or treble creation of food be produced, and its surplus go to nourish the now perishing births of Europe, who in return would manufacture and send us in exchange our clothes and other comforts. Morality listens to this, and so invariably do the laws of nature create our duties and interests, that when they seem to be at variance, we ought to suspect some fallacy in our reasonings. In solving this question, too, we should allow its just weight to the moral and physical preference of the agricultural, over the manufacturing, man. My occupations permit me only to ask questions. They deny me the time, if I had the information, to answer them. Perhaps, as worthy the attention of the author of the Traité d'Economie Politique, I shall find them answered in that work. If they are not, the reason will have been that you wrote for Europe; while I shall have asked them because I think for America. Accept, Sir, my respectful salutations, and assurances of great consideration.

GRIEF AND GRIEVANCES

To Abigail Adams

Washington, June 13, 1804

DEAR MADAM—The affectionate sentiments which you have had the goodness to express in your letter of May 20. towards my dear departed daughter, have awakened in me sensibilities natural to the occasion, and recalled your kindnesses to her which I shall ever remember with gratitude and friendship. I can assure you with truth they had made an indelible impression on her mind, and that, to the last, on our meetings after long separations, whether I had heard lately of you, and how you did, were among the earliest of her enquiries. In giving you this assurance I perform a sacred duty for her, and at the same time am thankful for the occasion furnished me of expressing my regret that circumstances should have arisen which have seemed to draw a line of separation between us. The friendship with which you honoured me has ever been valued, and fully reciprocated; and altho' events have been passing which might be trying to some minds, I never believed yours to be of that kind, nor felt that my own was. Neither my estimate of your character, nor the esteem founded in that, have ever been lessened for a single moment, although doubts whether it would be acceptable may have forbidden manifestations of it. Mr. Adams's friendship and mine began at an earlier date. It accompanied us thro' long and important scenes. The different conclusions we had drawn from our political reading and reflections were not permitted to lessen mutual esteem, each party being conscious they were the result of an honest conviction in the other. Like differences of opinion existing among our fellow citizens attached them to the one or the other of us, and produced a rivalship in their minds which did not exist in ours. We never stood in one another's way: for if either had been withdrawn at any time, his favorers would not have gone over to the other, but would have sought for some one of homogeneous opinions. This consideration was sufficient to keep down all jealousy between us, and to guard our friendship from any disturbance by sentiments of rivalship: and I can say with truth that one act of Mr. Adams's life, and one only, ever gave me a moment's personal displeasure. I did consider his last appointments to office as personally unkind. They were from among my most ardent political enemies, from whom no faithful cooperation could ever be expected, and laid me under the embarrasment of acting thro' men whose views were to defeat mine; or to encounter the odium of putting others

in their places. It seemed but common justice to leave a successor free to act by instruments of his own choice. If my
respect for him did not permit me to ascribe the whole blame
to the influence of others, it left something for friendship to
forgive, and after brooding over it for some little time, and
not always resisting the expression of it, I forgave it cordially,
and returned to the same state of esteem and respect for him
which had so long subsisted. Having come into life a little
later than Mr. Adams, his career has preceded mine, as mine
is followed by some other, and it will probably be closed at
the same distance after him which time originally placed between us. I maintain for him, and shall carry into private life
an uniform and high measure of respect and good will, and
for yourself a sincere attachment. I have thus, my dear
Madam, opened myself to you without reserve, which I have
long wished an opportunity of doing; and, without knowing
how it will be recieved, I feel relief from being unbosomed.
And I have now only to entreat your forgiveness for this transition from a subject of domestic affliction to one which
seems of a different aspect. But tho connected with political
events, it has been viewed by me most strongly in it's unfortunate bearings on my private friendships. The injury these
have sustained has been a heavy price for what has never
given me equal pleasure. That you may both be favored with
health, tranquility and long life, is the prayer of one who
tenders you the assurances of his highest consideration and
esteem.

FREEDOM OF THE PRESS
To Judge John Tyler

Washington, June 28, 1804

DEAR SIR,—Your favor of the 10th instant has been duly received. Amidst the direct falsehoods, the misrepresentations
of truth, the calumnies and the insults resorted to by a faction
to mislead the public mind, and to overwhelm those entrusted with its interests, our support is to be found in the
approving voice of our conscience and country, in the testi-

mony of our fellow citizens, that their confidence is not shaken by these artifices. When to the plaudits of the honest multitude, the sober approbation of the sage in his closet is added, it becomes a gratification of an higher order. It is the sanction of wisdom superadded to the voice of affection. The terms, therefore, in which you are so good as to express your satisfaction with the course of the present administration cannot but give me great pleasure. I may err in my measures, but never shall deflect from the intention to fortify the public liberty by every possible means, and to put it out of the power of the few to riot on the labors of the many. No experiment can be more interesting than that we are now trying, and which we trust will end in establishing the fact, that man may be governed by reason and truth. Our first object should therefore be, to leave open to him all the avenues to truth. The most effectual hitherto found, is the freedom of the press. It is therefore, the first shut up by those who fear the investigation of their actions. The firmness with which the people have withstood the late abuses of the press, the discernment they have manifested between truth and falsehood, show that they may safely be trusted to hear everything true and false, and to form a correct judgment between them. As little is it necessary to impose on their senses, or dazzle their minds by pomp, splendor, or forms. Instead of this artificial, how much surer is that real respect, which results from the use of their reason, and the habit of bringing everything to the test of common sense.

I hold it, therefore, certain, that to open the doors of truth, and to fortify the habit of testing everything by reason, are the most effectual manacles we can rivet on the hands of our successors to prevent their manacling the people with their own consent. The panic into which they were artfully thrown in 1798, the frenzy which was excited in them by their enemies against their apparent readiness to abandon all the principles established for their own protection, seemed for awhile to countenance the opinions of those who say they cannot be trusted with their own government. But I never doubted their rallying; and they did rally much sooner than I expected. On the whole, that experiment on their credulity has confirmed my confidence in their ultimate good sense and virtue.

I lament to learn that a like misfortune has enabled you to estimate the afflictions of a father on the loss of a beloved child. However terrible the possibility of such another accident, it is still a blessing for you of inestimable value that you would not even then descend childless to the grave. Three sons, and hopeful ones too, are a rich treasure. I rejoice when I hear of young men of virtue and talents, worthy to receive, and likely to preserve the splendid inheritance of self-government, which we have acquired and shaped for them.

The complement of midshipmen for the Tripoline squadron, is full; and I hope the frigates have left the Capes by this time. I have, however, this day, signed warrants of midshipmen for the two young gentlemen you recommended. These will be forwarded by the Secretary of the Navy. He tells me that their first services will be to be performed on board the gun boats.

Accept my friendly salutations, and assurances of great esteem and respect.

"THE OFFICE OF HANGMAN"
To Larkin Smith

Washington, Nov. 26, 1804

SIR,—Your letter of the 10th came to hand yesterday evening. It was written with frankness and independance and will be answered in the same way. You complain that I did not answer your letters applying for office. But if you will reflect a moment you may judge whether this ought to be expected. To the successful applicant for an office the commission is the answer. To the unsuccessful multitude am I to go with every one into the reasons for not appointing him? Besides that this correspondence would literally engross my whole time, into what controversies would it lead me. Sensible of this dilemma, from the moment of coming into office I laid it down as a rule to leave the applicants to collect their answer from the facts. To entitle myself to the benefit of the rule in any case it must be observed in every one: and I never have departed from it in a single case, not even for my bosom friends.

You observe that you are, or probably will be appointed an elector. I have no doubt you will do your duty with a conscientious regard to the public good & to that only. Your decision in favor of another would not excite in my mind the slightest dissatisfaction towards you. On the contrary I should honor the integrity of your choice. In the nominations I have to make, do the same justice to my motives. Had you hundreds to nominate, instead of one, be assured they would not compose for you a bed of roses. You would find yourself in most cases with one loaf and ten wanting bread. Nine must be disappointed, perhaps become secret, if not open enemies. The transaction of the great interests of our country costs us little trouble or difficulty. There the line is plain to men of some experience. But the task of appointment is a heavy one indeed. He on whom it falls may envy the lot of a Sisyphus or Ixion. Their agonies were of the body: this of the mind. Yet, like the office of hangman it must be executed by some one. It has been assigned to me and made my duty. I make up my mind to it therefore, & abandon all regard to consequences. Accept my salutations & assurances of respect.

BLUEPRINT OF THE UNIVERSITY
To Littleton Waller Tazewell

Washington, Jan. 5, 1805

DEAR SIR,—Your favor of December 24 never came to my hands till last night. It's importance induces me to hasten the answer. No one can be more rejoiced at the information that the legislature of Virginia are likely at length to institute an University on a liberal plan. Convinced that the people are the only safe depositories of their own liberty, & that they are not safe unless enlightened to a certain degree, I have looked on our present state of liberty as a short-lived possession unless the mass of the people could be informed to a certain degree. This requires two grades of education. First some institution where science in all it's branches is taught, and in the highest degree to which the human mind has carried it. This would prepare a few subjects in every State, to whom nature has given minds of the first order. Secondly such a degree of learning given to every member of the society as will enable him to read, to judge & to vote understandingly on what is passing. This would be the object of the township schools. I understand from your letter that the first of these only is under present contemplation. Let us receive with contentment what the legislature is now ready to give. The other branch will be incorporated into the system at some more favorable moment.

The first step in this business will be for the legislature to pass an act of establishment equivalent to a charter. This should deal in generals only. It's provisions should go 1. to the object of the institution. 2. it's location. 3. it's endowment. 4. it's Direction. On each of these heads I will hazard a first thought or two. 1. It's object should be defined only generally for teaching the useful branches of science, leaving the particulars to the direction of the day. Science is progressive. What was useful two centuries ago is now become useless, e.g. one half the professorships of Wm & Mary. What is now deemed useful will in some of it's parts become useless in another century. The visitors will be the best qualified to keep their institution up in even pace with the science of the times. Every one knows that Oxford, Cambridge, the Sorbonne, etc. are now a century or two behind the science of the age. 2. The location. The legislature is the proper judges of a general position, within certain limits, as for instance the county in which it shall be. To fix on the spot identically they would not be so competent as persons particularly appointed to examine the grounds. This small degree of liberty in location would place the landholders in the power of the purchasers: to fix the spot would place the purchaser in the power of the landholder. 3. It's endowment. Bank stock, or public stock of any kind should be immediately converted into real estate. In the form of stock it is a dead fund, it's depreciation being equal to it's interest. Every one must see that money put into our funds when first established (in 1791) with all its interest from that day would not buy more now than the principal would then have done. Mr. Pitt states to parliament that the expenses of living in England have, in the last 20 years, increased 50. percent: that is that money has depreciated that much. Even the precious metals depreciate slowly so that in perpetual institutions, as colleges, that ought to be guarded against. But in countries admitting paper, the abusive emissions of that produces two, three or four courses of depreciation & annihilation in a century. Lands will keep *advancing* nominally so as to keep *even* really. Canal shares are as good as lands, perhaps better: but the whole funds should not be risked in any one form. They should be vested in the visitors, without any power given them to lessen their capital, or even to *change* what is real. 4. The Direction. This would of course be in the hands of Visitors. The legislature would name the first set, & lay down the laws of their succession. On death or resignation the legislature or the Chancellor might name three persons of whom the visitors should chuse one. The visitors should be few. If many, those half qualified would by their numbers bring every thing down to the level of their own capacities, by out-voting the few of real science. I doubt if they should exceed five. For this is an office for which good sense alone does not qualify a man. To analyse science into it's different branches, to distribute these into professorships, to superintend the course practiced by each professor, he must know what these sciences are and possess their outlines at least. Can any state in the union furnish more than 5. men so qualified as to the whole field of the sciences. The Visitors should receive no pay. Such qualifications are properly rewarded by honor, not by money.

The charter being granted & the Visitors named, these become then the agents as to every thing else. Their first objects will be 1. the special location. 2. the institution of professorships. 3. the employment of their capital. 4. the necessary buildings. A word on each. 1. Special location needs no explanation. 2. Professorships. They would have to select all the branches of science deemed useful at this day, & in this country: to groupe as many of these together as could be taught by one professor and thus reduce the number of professors to the minimum consistent with the essential object. Having for some years entertained the hope that our country would some day establish an institution on a liberal scale, I have been taking measures to have in readiness such materials as would require time to collect. I have from Dr. Priestley a designation of the branches of science grouped into professorships which he furnished at my request. He was an excellent judge of what may be called the old studies, of those useful and those useless. I have the same thing from Mr. Dupont, a good judge of the new branches. His letter to me is quite a treatise. I have the plan of the institutions of Edinburgh, & those of the National institute of France; and I expect from Mr. Pictet, one of the most celebrated professors of Geneva, their plan, in answer to a letter written some time ago. From these the Visitors could select the branches useful for the country & how to groupe them. A hasty view of the subject on a former occasion led me to believe 10. professorships would be necessary, but not all immediately. Half a dozen of the most urgent would make a good beginning. The salaries of the first professors should be very liberal, that we might draw the first names of Europe to our institution in order to give it a celebrity in the outset, which will draw to it the youth of all the states, and make Virginia their cherished & beloved Alma mater. I have good reasons to believe we can command the services of some of the first men of Europe. 3. The emploiment of their capital. On this subject others are so much better judges than myself that I shall say nothing. 4. Buildings. The greatest danger will be their over-building themselves, by attempting a large house in the beginning, sufficient to contain the whole institution. Large houses are always ugly, inconvenient, exposed to the accident of fire, and bad in cases of infection. A plain small house for the school & lodging of each professor is best. These connected by covered ways out of which the rooms of the students should open would be best. These may then be built only as they shall be wanting. In fact an University should not be an house but a village. This will much lessen their first expenses.

Not having written any three lines of this without interruption it has been impossible to keep my ideas rallied to the subject. I must let these hasty outlines go therefore as they are. Some are premature, some probably immature: but make what use you please of them except letting them get into print. Should this establishment take place on a plan worthy of approbation, I shall have a valuable legacy to leave it, to wit, my library, which certainly has not cost less than 15,000

Dollars. But it's value is more in the selection, a part of which, that which respects America, is the result of my own personal searches in Paris for 6. or 7. years, & of persons employed by me in England, Holland, Germany and Spain to make similar searches. Such a collection on that subject can never again be made. With my sincere wishes for the success of this measure accept my salutations & assurances of great esteem & respect.

THE TWO-TERM PRECEDENT

To John Taylor

Washington, Jan. 6, 1805

DEAR SIR,—Your favor of Dec. 26th has been duly received, and was received as a proof of your friendly partialities to me, of which I have so often had reason to be sensible. My opinion originally was that the President of the U.S. should have been elected for 7. years, & forever ineligible afterwards. I have since become sensible that 7. years is too long to be irremovable, and that there should be a peaceable way of withdrawing a man in midway who is doing wrong. The service for 8. years with a power to remove at the end of the first four, comes nearly to my principle as corrected by experience. And it is in adherence to that that I determined to withdraw at the end of my second term. The danger is that the indulgence & attachments of the people will keep a man in the chair after he becomes a dotard, that reelection through life shall become habitual, & election for life follow that. Genl. Washington set the example of voluntary retirement after 8. years. I shall follow it, and a few more precedents will oppose the obstacle of habit to anyone after a while who shall endeavor to extend his term. Perhaps it may beget a disposition to establish it by an amendment of the constitution. I believe I am doing right, therefore, in pursuing my principle. I had determined to declare my intention, but I have consented to be silent on the opinion of friends, who think it best not to put a continuance out of my power in defiance of all circumstances. There is, however, but one circumstance which could engage my acquiescence in another election, to wit, such a division about a successor as might bring in a Monarchist. But this circumstance is impossible. While, therefore, I shall make no formal declarations to the public of my purpose, I have freely let it be understood in private conversation. In this I am persuaded yourself & my friends generally will approve of my views: and should I at the end of a 2d term carry into retirement all the favor which the 1st has acquired, I shall feel the consolation of having done all the good in my power, and expect with more than composure the termination of a life no longer valuable to others or of importance to myself. Accept my affectionate salutations & assurances of great esteem & respect.

CLIMATE, FEVERS, AND THE POLYGRAPH
To C. F. de C. Volney

Washington, February 8, 1805

DEAR SIR,—Your letter of November the 26th came to hand May the 14th; the books some time after, which were all distributed according to direction. The copy for the East Indies went immediately by a safe conveyance. The letter of April the 28th, and the copy of your work accompanying that, did not come to hand till August. That copy was deposited in the Congressional library. It was not till my return here from my autumnal visit to Monticello, that I had an opportunity of reading your work. I have read it, and with great satisfaction. Of the first part I am less a judge than most people, having never travelled westward of Staunton, so as to know any thing of the face of the country; nor much indulged myself in geological inquiries, from a belief that the skin-deep scratches which we can make or find on the surface of the earth, do not repay our time with as certain and useful deductions, as our pursuits in some other branches. The subject of our winds is more familiar to me. On that, the views you have taken are always great, supported in their outlines by your facts; and though more extensive observations, and longer continued, may produce some anomalies, yet they will probably take their place in this first great canvass which you have sketched. In no case, perhaps, does habit attach our choice or judgment more than in climate. The Canadian glows with delight in his sleigh and snow, the very idea of which gives me the shivers. The comparison of climate between Europe and North America, taking together its corresponding parts, hangs chiefly on three great points. 1. The changes between heat and cold in America, are greater and more frequent, and the extremes comprehend a greater scale on the thermometer in America than in Europe. Habit, however, prevents these from affecting us more than the smaller changes of Europe affect the European. But he is greatly affected by ours. 2. Our sky is always clear; that of Europe always cloudy. Hence a greater accumulation of heat here than there, in the same parallel. 3. The changes between wet and dry are much more frequent and sudden in Europe than in America. Though we have double the rain, it falls in half the time. Taking all these together, I prefer much the climate of the United States to that of Europe. I think it a more cheerful one. It is our cloudless sky which has eradicated from our constitutions all disposition to hang ourselves, which we might otherwise have inherited from our English ancestors. During a residence of between six and seven years in Paris, I never, but once, saw the sun shine through a whole day, without being obscured by a cloud in any part of it: and I never saw the moment, in which, viewing the sky through its whole hemisphere, I could say there was not the smallest speck of a cloud in it. I arrived at Monticello, on my return from France, in January, and during only two months' stay there, I observed to my daughters, who had been with me to France, that twenty odd times within that term, there was not a speck of a cloud in the whole hemisphere. Still I do not wonder that an European should prefer his grey to our azure sky. Habit decides our taste in this, as in most other cases.

The account you give of the yellow fever, is entirely agreeable to what we then knew of it. Further experience has developed more and more its peculiar character. Facts appear to have established that it is originated here by a local atmosphere, which is never generated but in the lower, closer, and dirtier parts of our large cities, in the neighborhood of the water; and that, to catch the disease, you must enter the local atmosphere. Persons having taken the disease in the infected quarter, and going into the country, are nursed and buried by their friends, without an example of communicating it. A vessel going from the infected quarter, and carrying its atmosphere in its hold into another State, has given the disease to every person who there entered her. These have died in the arms of their families without a single communication of the disease. It is certainly, therefore, an epidemic, not a contagious disease; and calls on the chemists for some mode of purifying the vessel by a decomposition of its atmosphere, if ventilation be found insufficient. In the long scale of bilious fevers, graduated by many shades, this is probably the last and most mortal term. It seizes the native of the place equally with strangers. It has not been long known in any part of the United States. The shade next above it, called the stranger's fever, has been coeval with the settlement of the larger cities in the southern parts, to wit, Norfolk, Charleston, New Orleans. Strangers going to these places in the months of July, August or September, find this fever as mortal as the genuine yellow fever. But it rarely attacks those who have resided in them some time. Since we have known that kind of yellow fever which is no respecter of persons, its name has been extended to the stranger's fever, and every species of bilious fever which produces a black vomit, that is to say, a discharge of very dark bile. Hence we hear of yellow fever on the Alleganey mountains, in Kentucky, &c. This is a matter of definition only: but it leads into error those who do not know how loosely and how interestedly some physicians think and speak. So far as we have yet seen, I think we are correct in saying, that the yellow fever which seizes on all indiscriminately, is an ultimate degree of bilious fever never known in the United States till lately, nor farther south, as yet, than Alexandria, and that what they have recently called the yellow fever in New Orleans, Charleston and Norfolk, is what has always been known in those places as confined chiefly to strangers, and nearly as mortal *to them*, as the other is to *all* its subjects. But both grades are local: the stranger's fever less so, as it sometimes extends a little into the neighborhood; but the yellow fever rigorously so, confined within narrow and well defined limits, and not communicable out of those limits. Such a constitution of atmosphere being requisite to originate this disease as is generated only in low, close, and ill-cleansed parts of a town, I have supposed it practicable to prevent its generation by building our cities on a more open plan. Take, for instance, the chequer board for a plan. Let the black squares only be building squares, and the white ones be left open, in turf and trees. Every square of houses will be surrounded by four open squares, and every house will front an open square. The atmosphere of such a town would be like that of the country, insusceptible of the miasmata which produce yellow fever. I have accordingly proposed that the enlargements of the city of New Orleans, which must immediately take place, shall be on this plan. But it is only in case of enlargements to be made, or of cities to be built, that this means of prevention can be employed.

The *genus irritabile vatum* could not let the author of the Ruins publish a new work, without seeking in it the means of discrediting that puzzling composition. Some one of those holy calumniators has selected from your new work every scrap of a sentence, which, detached from its context, could displease an American reader. A cento has been made of these, which has run through a particular description of newspapers, and excited a disapprobation even in friendly minds, which nothing but the reading of the book will cure. But time and truth will at length correct error.

Our countrymen are so much occupied in the busy scenes of life, that they have little time to write or invent. A good invention here, therefore, is such a rarity as it is lawful to offer to the acceptance of a friend. A Mr. Hawkins of Frankford, near Philadelphia, has invented a machine which he calls a polygraph, and which carries two, three, or four pens. That of two pens, with which I am now writing, is best; and is so perfect that I have laid aside the copying-press, for a twelve month past, and write always with the polygraph. I have directed one to be made, of which I ask your acceptance. By what conveyance I shall send it while Havre is blockaded, I do not yet know. I think you will be pleased with it, and will use it habitually as I do; because it requires only that degree of mechanical attention which I know you to possess. I am glad to hear that M. Cabanis is engaged in writing on the reformation of medicine. It needs the hand of a reformer, and cannot be in better hands than his. Will you permit my respects to him and the Abbé de la Roche to find a place here.

A word now on our political state. The two parties which prevailed with so much violence when you were here, are almost wholly melted into one. At the late Presidential election I have received one hundred and sixty-two votes against fourteen only. Connecticut is still federal by a small majority; and Delaware on a poise, as she has been since 1775, and will be till Anglomany with her yields to Americanism. Connecticut will be with us in a short time. Though the people in mass have joined us, their leaders had committed themselves too far to retract. Pride keeps them hostile; they brood over their angry passions, and give them vent in the newspapers which they maintain. They still make as much noise as if they were the whole nation. Unfortunately, these being the mercantile papers, published chiefly in the sea ports, are the only ones which find their way to Europe, and make very false impressions there. I am happy to hear that the late derangement of your health is going off, and that you are re-established. I sincerely pray for the continuance of that blessing, and with my affectionate salutations, tender you assurances of great respect and attachment.

P. S. The sheets which you receive are those of the copying pen of the polygraph, not of the one with which I have written.

NEWS OF CAPTAIN LEWIS
To C. F. de C. Volney

Washington, Feb. 11, 1806

DEAR SIR,—Since mine of Feb. 18 of the last year, I have received yours of July 2. I have been constantly looking out for an opportunity of sending your Polygraph; but the blockade of Havre has cut off that resource, and I have feared to send it to a port from which there would be only land carriage. A safe conveyance now offering to Nantes, & under the particular care of Mr. Skipwith, who is returning to France, he will take care of it from Nantes by land if an easy carriage is found, or if not, then by the canal of Briare. Another year's constant use of a similar one attaches me more and more to it as a most valuable convenience. I send you also a pamphlet published here against the English doctrine which denies to neutrals a trade in war not open to them in peace in which you will find it pulverized by a logic not to be controverted.

Our last news of Captn Lewis was that he had reached the upper part of the Missouri, & had taken horses to cross the Highlands to the Columbia river. He passed the last winter among the Manians 1610 miles above the mouth of the river. So far he had delineated it with as great accuracy as will probably be ever applied to it, as his courses & distances by mensuration were corrected by almost daily observations of latitude and longitude. With his map he sent us specimens or information of the following animals not before known to the northern continent of America. 1. The horns of what is perhaps a species of Ovis Ammon. 2. A new variety of the deer having a black tail. 3. An antelope. 4. The badger, not before known out of Europe. 5. A new species of marmotte. 6. A white weasel. 7. The magpie. 8. The Prairie hen, said to resemble the Guinea hen (peintade). 9. A prickly lizard. To these are added a considerable collection of minerals, not yet analyzed. He wintered in Lat. 47° 20′ and found the maximum of cold 43° below the zero of Fahrenheit. We expect he has reached the Pacific, and is now wintering on the head of the Missouri, and will be here next autumn. Having been disappointed in our view of sending an exploring party up the Red river the last year, they were sent up the Washita, as far as the hot springs, under the direction of Mr. Dunbar. He found the temperature of the springs 150° of Fahrenheit & the water perfectly potable when cooled. We obtain also the geography of that river, so far with perfect accuracy. Our party is just at this time setting out from Natchez to ascend the Red river. These expeditions are so laborious, & hazardous, that men of science, used to the temperature & inactivity of their closet, cannot be induced to undertake them. They are headed therefore by persons qualified expressly to give us the geography of the rivers with perfect accuracy, and of good common knolege and observation in the animal, vegetable &

mineral departments. When the route shall be once open and known, scientific men will undertake, & verify & class it's subjects. Our emigration to the western country from these states the last year is estimated at about 100,000. I conjecture that about one-half the number of our increase will emigrate westwardly annually. A newspaper paragraph tells me, with some details, that the society of agriculture of Paris had thought a mould-board of my construction worthy their notice & Mr. Dupont confirms it in a letter, but not specifying anything particular. I send him a model with an advantageous change in the form, in which however the principle is rigorously the same. I mention this to you lest he should have left France for America, and I notice it no otherwise lest there should have been any error in the information. Present my respectful salutations to Doctr. Cabanis & accept them yourself with assurances of my constant friendship & attachment.

A NATIONAL ACADEMY
To Joel Barlow

Feb. 24, 1806

I return you the draft of the bill for the establishment of a National Academy & University at the city of Washington, with such alterations as we talked over the last night. They are chiefly verbal. I have often wished we could have a Philosophical society or academy so organized as that while the central academy should be at the seat of government, it's members dispersed over the states, should constitute filiated academies in each state, publish their communications, from which the central academy should select unpublished what should be most choice. In this way all the members wheresoever dispersed might be brought into action, and an useful emulation might arise between the filiated societies. Perhaps the great societies now existing might incorporate themselves in this way with the National one. But time does not allow me to pursue this idea, nor perhaps had we time at all to get it into the present bill. I procured an Agricultural society to be established (voluntarily) on this plan, but it has done nothing. Friendly salutations.

COURTING ALEXANDER

To the Emperor Alexander

Washington, April 19, 1806

I owe an acknowledgment to your Imperial Majesty for the great satisfaction I have received from your letter of Aug. 20, 1805, and embrace the opportunity it affords of giving expression to the sincere respect and veneration I entertain for your character. It will be among the latest and most soothing comforts of my life, to have seen advanced to the government of so extensive a portion of the earth, and at so early a period of his life, a sovereign whose ruling passion is the advancement of the happiness and prosperity of his people; and not of his own people only, but who can extend his eye and his good will to a distant and infant nation, unoffending in its course, unambitious in its views.

The events of Europe come to us so late, and so suspiciously, that observations on them would certainly be stale, and possibly wide of their actual state. From their general aspect, however, I collect that your Majesty's interposition in them has been disinterested and generous, and having in view only the general good of the great European family. When you shall proceed to the pacification which is to re-establish peace and commerce, the same dispositions of mind will lead you to think of the general intercourse of nations, and to make that provision for its future maintenance which, in times past, it has so much needed. The northern nations of Europe, at the head of which your Majesty is distinguished, are habitually peaceable. The United States of America, like them, are attached to peace. We have then with them a common interest in the neutral rights. Every nation indeed, on the continent of Europe, belligerent as well as neutral, is interested in maintaining these rights, in liberalizing them progressively with the progress of science and refinement of morality, and in relieving them from restrictions which the extension of the arts has long since rendered unreasonable and vexatious.

Two personages in Europe, of which your Majesty is one, have it in their power, at the approaching pacification, to render eminent service to nations in general, by incorporating into the act of pacification, a correct definition of the rights of neutrals on the high seas. Such a definition, declared by all the powers lately or still belligerent, would give to those rights a precision and notoriety, and cover them with an authority, which would protect them in an important degree against future violation; and should any further sanction be necessary, that of an exclusion of the violating nation from commercial intercourse with all the others, would be preferred to war, as more analogous to the offence, more easy and likely to be executed with good faith. The essential articles of these rights, too, are so few and simple as easily to be defined.

Having taken no part in the past or existing troubles of Europe, we have no part to act in its pacification. But as principles may then be settled in which we have a deep interest, it is a great happiness for us that they are placed under the protection of an umpire, who, looking beyond the narrow bounds of an individual nation, will take under the cover of his equity the rights of the absent and unrepresented. It is only by a happy concurrence of good characters and good occasions, that a step can now and then be taken to advance the well-being of nations. If the present occasion be good, I am sure your Majesty's character will not be wanting to avail the world of it. By monuments of such good offices, may your life become an epoch in the history of the condition of man; and may He who called it into being, for the good of the human family, give it length of days and success, and have it always in His holy keeping.

A TRIBUTE OF GRATITUDE

To Dr. Edward Jenner

Monticello, May 14, 1806

SIR,—I have received a copy of the evidence at large respecting the discovery of the vaccine inoculation which you have been pleased to send me, and for which I return you my thanks. Having been among the early converts, in this part of the globe, to its efficiency, I took an early part in recommending it to my countrymen. I avail myself of this occasion of rendering you a portion of the tribute of gratitude due to you from the whole human family. Medicine has never before produced any single improvement of such utility. Harvey's discovery of the circulation of the blood was a beautiful addition to our knowledge of the animal economy, but on a review of the practice of medicine before and since that epoch, I do not see any great amelioration which has been derived from that discovery. You have erased from the calendar of human afflictions one of its greatest. Yours is the comfortable reflection that mankind can never forget that you have lived. Future nations will know by history only that the loathsome small-pox has existed and by you has been extirpated.

Accept my fervent wishes for your health and happiness and assurances of the greatest respect and consideration.

SCHISM AND THE MAJORITY LEADERSHIP
To Barnabas Bidwell

Washington, July 5, 1806

SIR,—Your favor of June the 21st has been duly received. We have not as yet heard from General Skinner on the subject of his office. Three persons are proposed on the most respectable recommendations, and under circumstances of such equality as renders it difficult to decide between them. But it shall be done impartially. I sincerely congratulate you on the triumph of republicanism in Massachusetts. The Hydra of federalism has now lost all its heads but two. Connecticut I think will soon follow Massachusetts. Delaware will probably remain what it ever has been, a mere county of England, conquered indeed, and held under by force, but always disposed to counter-revolution. I speak of its majority only.

Our information from London continues to give us hopes of an accommodation there on both the points of 'accustomed commerce and impressment.' In this there must probably be some mutual concession, because we cannot expect to obtain every thing and yield nothing. But I hope it will be such an one as may be accepted. The arrival of the Hornet in

France is so recently known, that it will yet be some time before we learn our prospects there. Notwithstanding the efforts made here, and made professedly to assassinate that negotiation in embryo, if the good sense of Buonaparte should prevail over his temper, the present state of things in Europe may induce him to require of Spain that she should do us justice at least. That he should require her to sell us East Florida, we have no right to insist: yet there are not wanting considerations which may induce him to wish a permanent foundation for peace laid between us. In this treaty, whatever it shall be, our old enemies the federalists, and their new friends, will find enough to carp at. This is a thing of course, and I should suspect error where they found no fault. The buzzard feeds on carrion only. Their rallying point is 'war with France and Spain, and alliance with Great Britain:' and every thing is wrong with them which checks their new ardor to be fighting for the liberties of mankind; on the sea always excepted. There one nation is to monopolise all the liberties of the others.

I read, with extreme regret, the expressions of an inclination on your part to retire from Congress. I will not say that this time, more than all others, calls for the service of every man; but I will say, there never was a time when the services of those who possess talents, integrity, firmness and sound judgment, were more wanted in Congress. Some one of that description is particularly wanted to take the lead in the House of Representatives, to consider the business of the nation as his own business, to take it up as if he were singly charged with it, and carry it through. I do not mean that any gentleman, relinquishing his own judgment, should implicitly support all the measures of the administration; but that, where he does not disapprove of them, he should not suffer them to go off in sleep, but bring them to the attention of the House, and give them a fair chance. Where he disapproves, he will of course leave them to be brought forward by those who concur in the sentiment. Shall I explain my idea by an example? The classification of the militia was communicated to General Varnum and yourself merely as a proposition, which, if you approved, it was trusted you would support. I knew, indeed, that General Varnum was opposed to any thing which might break up the present organization of the militia: but when so modified as to avoid this, I thought he might, perhaps, be reconciled to it. As soon as I found it did not coincide with your sentiments, I could not wish you to support it; but using the same freedom of opinion, I procured it to be brought forward elsewhere. It failed there also, and for a time perhaps, may not prevail: but a militia can never be used for distant service on any other plan; and Buonaparte will conquer the world, if they do not learn his secret of composing armies of young men only, whose enthusiasm and health enable them to surmount all obstacles. When a gentleman, through zeal for the public service, undertakes to do the public business, we know that we shall hear the cant of backstairs counsellors. But we never heard this while the declaimer was himself a backstairs man, as he calls it, but in the confidence and views of the administration, as may more properly and respectfully be said. But if the members are to know nothing but what is important enough to be put into a public message, and indifferent enough to be made known to all the world; if the executive is to keep all other information to himself, and the House to plunge on in the dark, it becomes a government of chance and not of design. The imputation was one of those artifices used to despoil an adversary of his most effectual arms; and men of mind will place themselves above a gabble of this order. The last session of Congress was indeed an uneasy one for a time: but as soon as the members penetrated into the views of those who were taking a new course, they rallied in as solid a phalanx as I have ever seen act together. Indeed I have never seen a House of better dispositions. They want only a man of business & in whom they can confide to conduct things in the house; and they are as much disposed to support him as can be wished. It is only speaking a truth to say that all eyes look to you. It was not perhaps expected from a new member, at his first session, & before the forms & style of doing business were familiar. But it would be a subject of deep regret were you to refuse yourself to the conspicuous part in the business of the house which all assign you. Perhaps I am not entitled to speak with so much frankness; but it proceeds from no motive which has not a right to your forgiveness. Opportunities of candid explanation are so seldom afforded me, that I must not lose them when they occur.

The information I receive from your quarter agrees with that from the south; that the late schism has made not the smallest impression on the public, and that the seceders are obliged to give to it other grounds than those which we know to be the true ones. All we have to wish is, that at the ensuing session, every one may take the part openly which he secretly befriends. I recollect nothing new and true, worthy communicating to you. As for what is not true, you will always find abundance in the newspapers. Among other things, are those perpetual alarms as to the Indians, for no one of which has there ever been the slightest ground. They are the suggestions of hostile traders, always wishing to embroil us with the Indians, to perpetuate their own extortionate commerce. I salute you with esteem and respect.

GARDENS FOR MONTICELLO
To William Hamilton

Washington, July, 1806

Your favor of the 7th came duly to hand and the plant you are so good as to propose to send me will be thankfully rec'd. The little Mimosa Julibrisin you were so kind as to send me the last year is flourishing. I obtained from a gardener in this nbh'd [neighborhood] 2 plants of the paper mulberry; but the parent plant being male, we are to expect no fruit from them, unless your [trees] should chance to be of the sex wanted. at a future day, say two years hence I shall ask from you some seeds of the Mimosa Farnesiana or Nilotica, of which you were kind enough before to furnish me some. but the plants have been lost during my absence from home. I remember seeing in your greenhouse a plant of a couple of feet height in a pot the fragrance of which (from it's gummy bud if I recollect rightly) was peculiarly agreeable to me and you were so kind as to remark that it required only a greenhouse, and that you would furnish me one when I should be in a situation to preserve it. but it's name has entirely escaped me & I cannot suppose you can recollect or conjecture in your vast collection what particular plant this might be. I must acquiese therefore in a privation which my own defect of memory has produced, unless indeed I could some of these days make an impromptu visit to Phila. & recognise it myself at the Woodlands.

Having decisively made up my mind for retirement at the end of my present term, my views and attentions are all turned homewards. I have hitherto been engaged in my buildings which will be finished in the course of the present year. The improvement of my grounds has been reserved for my occupation on my return home. For this reason it is that I have put off to the fall of the year after next the collection of such curious trees as will bear our winters in the open air.

The grounds which I destine to improve in the style of the English gardens are in a form very difficult to be managed. They compose the northern quadrant of a mountain for about ⅔ of its height & then spread for the upper third over its whole crown. They contain about three hundred acres, washed at the foot for about a mile, by a river of the size of the Schuylkill. The hill is generally too steep for direct ascent, but we make level walks successively along it's side, which in it's upper part encircle the hill & intersect these again by others of easy ascent in various parts. They are chiefly still in their native woods, which are majestic, and very generally a close undergrowth, which I have not suffered to be touched, knowing how much easier it is to cut away than to fill up. The upper third is chiefly open, but to the South is covered with a dense thicket of Scotch broom (Spartium scoparium Lin.) which being favorably spread before the sun will admit of advantageous arrangement for winter enjoyment. You are sensible that this disposition of the ground takes from me the first beauty in gardening, the variety of hill & dale, & leaves me as an awkward substitute a few hanging hollows & ridges, this subject is so unique and at the same time refractory, that to make a disposition analogous to its character would require much more of the genius of the landscape painter & gardener than I pretend to. I had once hoped to get Parkins to go and give me some outlines, but I was disappointed. Certainly I could never wish your health to be such as to render travelling necessary; but should a journey at any time promise improvement to it, there is no one on which you would be received with more pleasure than at Monticello. Should I be there you will have an opportunity of indulging on a new field some of the taste which has made the Woodlands the only rival which I have known in America to what may be seen in England.

Thither without doubt we are to go for models in this art. Their sunless climate has permitted them to adopt what is certainly a beauty of the very first order in landscape. Their canvas is of open ground, variegated with clumps of trees distributed with taste. They need no more of wood than will serve to embrace a lawn or a glade. But under the beaming, constant and almost vertical sun of Virginia, shade is our Elysium. In the absence of this no beauty of the eye can be enjoyed. This organ must yield it's gratification to that of the other senses; without the hope of any equivalent to the beauty relinquished. The only substitute I have been able to imagine is this. Let your ground be covered with trees of the loftiest stature. Trim up their bodies as high as the constitution & form of the tree will bear, but so as that their tops shall still unite & yeild dense shade. A wood, so open below, will have nearly the appearance of open grounds. Then, when in the open ground you would plant a clump of trees, place a thicket of shrubs presenting a hemisphere the crown of which shall distinctly show itself under the branches of the trees. This may be effected by a due selection & arrangement of the shrubs, & will I think offer a group not much inferior to that of trees. The thickets may be varied too by making some of them of evergreens altogether, our red cedar made to grow in a bush, evergreen privet, pyrocanthus, Kalmia, Scotch broom. Holly would be elegant but it does not grow in my part of the country.

Of prospect I have a rich profusion and offering itself at every point of the compass. Mountains distant & near, smooth & shaggy, single & in ridges, a little river hiding itself among the hills so as to shew in lagoons only, cultivated grounds under the eye and two small villages. To prevent a satiety of this is the principal difficulty. It may be successively offered, & in different portions through vistas, or which will be better, between thickets so disposed as to serve as vistas, with the advantage of shifting the scenes as you advance on your way.

You will be sensible by this time of the truth of my information that my views are turned so steadfastly homeward that the subject runs away with me whenever I get on it. I sat down to thank you for kindnesses received, & to bespeak permission to ask further contributions from your collection & I have written you a treatise on gardening generally, in which art lessons would come with more justice from you to me.

DISCONTENTS IN THE WEST

To John Dickinson

Washington, Jan. 13, 1807

MY DEAR AND ANCIENT FRIEND,—I have duly received your favor of the 1st inst., and am ever thankful for communications which may guide me in the duties which I wish to perform as well as I am able. It is but too true that great discontents exist in the territory of Orleans. Those of the French inhabitants have for their sources, 1, the prohibition of importing slaves. This may be partly removed by Congress permitting them to receive slaves from the other States, which, by dividing that evil, would lessen its danger; 2, the administration of justice in our forms, principles, & language, with all of which they are unacquainted, & are the more abhorrent, because of the enormous expense, greatly exaggerated by the corruption of bankrupt & greedy lawyers, who have gone there from the Ud S. & engrossed the practice; 3, the call on them by the land commissioners to produce the titles of their lands. The object of this is really to record & secure their rights. But as many of them hold on rights so ancient that the title papers are lost, they expect the land is to be taken from them wherever they cannot produce a regular deduction of title in writing. In this they will be undeceived by the final result, which will evince to them a liberal disposition of the government towards them. Among the American inhabitants it is the old division of federalists & republicans.

The former are as hostile there as they are everywhere, & are the most numerous & wealthy. They have been long endeavoring to batter down the Governor, who has always been a firm republican. There were characters superior to him whom I wished to appoint, but they refused the office: I know no better man who would accept of it, and it would not be right to turn him out for one not better. But it is the 2d. cause, above mentioned, which is deep-seated & permanent. The French members of the Legislature, being the majority in both Houses, lately passed an act declaring that the civil, or French laws, should be the laws of their land, and enumerated about 50 folio volumes, in Latin, as the depositories of these laws. The Governor negatived the act. One of the houses thereupon passed a vote for self-dissolution of the Legislature as a useless body, which failed in the other House by a single vote only. They separated, however, & have disseminated all the discontent they could. I propose to the members of Congress in conversation, the enlisting 30,000 volunteers, Americans by birth, to be carried at the public expense, & settled immediately on a bounty of 160 acres of land each, on the west side of the Mississippi, on the condition of giving two years of military service, if that country should be attacked within 7 years. The defence of the country would thus be placed on the spot, and the additional number would entitle the territory to become a State, would make the majority American, & make it an American instead of a French State. This would not sweeten the pill to the French; but in making that acquisition we had some view to our own good as well as theirs, and I believe the greatest good of both will be promoted by whatever will amalgamate us together.

I have tired you, my friend, with a long letter. But your tedium will end in a few lines more. Mine has yet two years to endure. I am tired of an office where I can do no more good than many others, who would be glad to be employed in it. To myself, personally, it brings nothing but unceasing drudgery & daily loss of friends. Every office becoming vacant, every appointment made, me donne un ingrat, et cent ennemis. My only consolation is in the belief that my fellow citizens at large give me credit for good intentions. I will certainly endeavor to merit the continuance of that good-will which follows well-intended actions, and their approbation will be the dearest reward I can carry into retirement.

God bless you, my excellent friend, and give you yet many healthy and happy years.

LAWS OF VIRGINIA

To William Waller Hening

Washington, January 14, 1807

SIR,—Your letter of Dec. 26th, was received in due time. The only object I had in making my collection of the laws of Virginia, was to save all those for the Public which were not then already lost, in the hope that at some future day they might be republished. Whether this be by public or private enterprise, my end will be equally answered. The work divides itself into two very distinct parts; to wit, the printed and the unprinted laws. The former begin in 1682, (Purvis' collection.) My collection of these is in strong volumes, well bound, and therefore may safely be transported anywhere. Any of these volumes which you do not possess, are at your service for the purpose of republication, but the unprinted laws are dispersed through many MS. volumes, several of them so decayed that the leaf can never be opened but once without falling into powder. These can never bear removal further than from their shelf to a table. They are, as well as I recollect, from 1622 downwards. I formerly made such a digest of their order, and the volumes where they are to be found, that, under my own superintendence, they could be copied with once handling. More they would not bear. Hence the impracticability of their being copied but at Monticello. But independent of them, the printed laws, beginning in 1682, with all our former printed collections, will be a most valuable publication, & sufficiently distinct. I shall have no doubt of the exactness of your part of the work, but I hope you will take measures for having the typography & paper worthy of the work. I am lead to this caution by the scandalous volume of our laws printed by Pleasants in 1803, & those by Davis, in 1796 were little better; both unworthy the history of Tom

Thumb. You can have them better & cheaper printed anywhere north of Richmond. Accept my salutations & assurances of respect.

LESSONS OF THE BURR CONSPIRACY
To Governor William C. C. Claiborne

Washington, February 3, 1807

DEAR SIR,—I pray you to read the enclosed letter, to seal and
deliver it. It explains itself so fully, that I need say nothing. I
am sincerely concerned for Mr. Reibelt, who is a man of excellent understanding and extensive science. If you had any
academical berth, he would be much better fitted for that
than for the bustling business of life. I enclose to General
Wilkinson my message of January 22d. I presume, however,
you will have seen it in the papers. It gives the history of
Burr's conspiracy, all but the last chapter, which will, I hope,
be that of his capture before this time, at Natchez. Your situations have been difficult, and we judge of the merit of our
agents there by the magnitude of the danger as it appeared to
them, not as it was known to us. On great occasions every
good officer must be ready to risk himself in going beyond
the strict line of law, when the public preservation requires it;
his motives will be a justification as far as there is any discretion in his ultra-legal proceedings, and no indulgence of private feelings. On the whole, this squall, by showing with
what ease our government suppresses movements which in
other countries requires armies, has greatly increased its
strength by increasing the public confidence in it. It has been
a wholesome lesson too to our citizens, of the necessary obedience to their government. The Feds, and the little band of
Quids, in opposition, will try to make something of the infringement of liberty by the military arrest and deportation of
citizens, but if it does not go beyond such offenders as Swart-
wout, Bollman, Burr, Blennerhasset, Tyler, &c., they will be
supported by the public approbation. Accept my friendly salutations, and assurances of esteem and respect.

THE BURR TRIAL
To William Branch Giles

Monticello, April 20, 1807

DEAR SIR,—Your favor of the 6th, on the subject of Burr's offences, was received only 4 days ago. That there should be anxiety & doubt in the public mind, in the present defective state of the proof, is not wonderful; and this has been sedulously encouraged by the tricks of the judges to force trials before it is possible to collect the evidence, dispersed through a line of 2000 miles from Maine to Orleans. The federalists, too, give all their aid, making Burr's cause their own, mortified only that he did not separate the Union or overturn the government, & proving, that had he had a little dawn of success, they would have joined him to introduce his object, their favorite monarchy, as they would any other enemy, foreign or domestic, who could rid them of this hateful republic for any other government in exchange.

The first ground of complaint was the supine inattention of the administration to a treason stalking through the land in open day. The present one, that they have crushed it before it was ripe for execution, so that no overt acts can be produced. This last may be true; tho' I believe it is not. Our information having been chiefly by way of letter, we do not know of a certainty yet what will be proved. We have set on foot an inquiry through the whole of the country which has been the scene of these transactions, to be able to prove to the courts, if they will give time, or to the public by way of communication to Congress, what the real facts have been. For obtaining this, we are obliged to appeal to the patriotism of particular persons in different places, of whom we have requested to make the inquiry in their neighborhood, and on such information as shall be voluntarily offered. Aided by no process or facilities from the *federal* courts, but frowned on by their new born zeal for the liberty of those whom we would not permit to overthrow the liberties of their country, we can expect no revealments from the accomplices of the chief offender. Of treasonable intentions, the judges have been obliged to confess there is probable appearance. What loophole they will find in it, when it comes to trial, we cannot foresee. Eaton, Stoddart, Wilkinson, and two others whom I must not name, will satisfy the world, if not the judges, on that head. And I do suppose the following overt acts will be proved. 1. The enlistment of men in a regular way. 2. The regular mounting of guard round Blennerhassett's island when they expected Governor Tiffin's men to be on them, *modo guerrino arraiali*. 3. The rendezvous of Burr with his men at the mouth of the Cumberland. 4. His letter to the acting Governor of Mississippi, holding up the prospect of civil war. 5. His capitulation regularly signed with the aids of the Governor, as between two independent & hostile commanders.

But a moment's calculation will shew that this evidence cannot be collected under 4 months, probably 5. from the moment of deciding when & where the trial shall be. I desired Mr. Rodney expressly to inform the Chief Justice of this, inofficially. But Mr. Marshall says, "more than 5 weeks have elapsed since the opinion of the Supreme court has declared the necessity of proving the overt acts, if they exist. Why are they not proved?" In what terms of decency can we speak of this? As if an express could go to Natchez, or the mouth of Cumberland, & return in 5 weeks, to do which has never taken less than twelve. Again, "If, in Nov. or Dec. last, a body of troops had been assembled on the Ohio, it is impossible to suppose the affidavits establishing the fact could not have been obtained by the last of March." But I ask the judge where they should have been lodged? At Frankfort? at Cincinnati? at Nashville? St. Louis? Natchez? New Orleans? These were the probable places of apprehension & examination. It was not known at *Washington* till the 26th of March that Burr would escape from the Western tribunals, be retaken & brought to an Eastern one; and in 5 days after, (neither 5. months nor 5. weeks, as the judge calculated,) he says, it is "impossible to suppose the affidavits could not have been obtained." Where? At Richmond he certainly meant, or meant only to throw dust in the eyes of his audience. But all the principles of law are to be perverted which would bear on the favorite offenders who endeavor to overrun this odious Republic. "I understand," sais the judge, "*probable* cause of guilt to be a case made out by *proof* furnishing good reason to believe," &c. Speaking as a lawyer, he must mean legal proof, i. e., proof on oath, at least. But this is confounding *probability* and *proof.* We had always before understood that where there was reasonable ground to believe guilt, the offender must be put on his trial. That guilty intentions were probable, the judge believed. And as to the overt acts, were not the bundle of letters of information in Mr. Rodney's hands, the letters and facts published in the local newspapers, Burr's flight, & the universal belief or rumor of his guilt, probable ground for presuming the facts of enlistment, military guard, rendezvous, threats of civil war, or capitulation, so as to put him on trial? Is there a candid man in the U S who does not believe some one, if not all, of these overt acts to have taken place?

If there ever had been an instance in this or the preceding administrations, of federal judges so applying principles of law as to condemn a federal or acquit a republican offender, I should have judged them in the present case with more charity. All this, however, will work well. The nation will judge both the offender & judges for themselves. If a member of the Executive or Legislature does wrong, the day is never far distant when the people will remove him. They will see then & amend the error in our Constitution, which makes any branch independent of the nation. They will see that one of the great co-ordinate branches of the government, setting itself in opposition to the other two, and to the common sense of the nation, proclaims impunity to that class of offenders which endeavors to overturn the Constitution, and are themselves protected in it by the Constitution itself; for impeachment is a farce which will not be tried again. If their protection of Burr produces this amendment, it will do more good than his condemnation would have done. Against Burr, personally, I never had one hostile sentiment. I never indeed thought him an honest, frank-dealing man, but considered him as a crooked gun, or other perverted machine, whose aim or stroke you could never be sure of. Still, while he possessed the confidence of the nation, I thought it my duty to respect in him their confidence, & to treat him as if he deserved it; and if this punishment can be commuted now for any useful amendment of the Constitution, I shall rejoice in it. My sheet being full, I perceive it is high time to offer you my friendly salutations, and assure you of my constant and affectionate esteem and respect.

HISTORY, HUME, AND THE PRESS
To John Norvell

Washington, June 14, 1807

SIR,—Your letter of May 9 has been duly received. The subject it proposes would require time & space for even moderate development. My occupations limit me to a very short notice of them. I think there does not exist a good elementary work on the organization of society into civil government: I mean a work which presents in one full & comprehensive view the system of principles on which such an organization should be founded, according to the rights of nature. For want of a single work of that character, I should recommend Locke on Government, Sidney, Priestley's Essay on the first Principles of Government, Chipman's Principles of Government, & the Federalist. Adding, perhaps, Beccaria on crimes & punishments, because of the demonstrative manner in which he has treated that branch of the subject. If your views of political inquiry go further, to the subjects of money & commerce, Smith's Wealth of Nations is the best book to be read, unless Say's Political Economy can be had, which treats the same subject on the same principles, but in a shorter compass & more lucid manner. But I believe this work has not been translated into our language.

History, in general, only informs us what bad government is. But as we have employed some of the best materials of the British constitution in the construction of our own government, a knolege of British history becomes useful to the American politician. There is, however, no general history of that country which can be recommended. The elegant one of

Hume seems intended to disguise & discredit the good principles of the government, and is so plausible & pleasing in it's style & manner, as to instil it's errors & heresies insensibly into the minds of unwary readers. Baxter has performed a good operation on it. He has taken the text of Hume as his ground work, abridging it by the omission of some details of little interest, and wherever he has found him endeavoring to mislead, by either the suppression of a truth or by giving it a false coloring, he has changed the text to what it should be, so that we may properly call it Hume's history republicanised. He has moreover continued the history (but indifferently) from where Hume left it, to the year 1800. The work is not popular in England, because it is republican; and but a few copies have ever reached America. It is a single 4to. volume. Adding to this Ludlow's Memoirs, Mrs. M'Cauley's & Belknap's histories, a sufficient view will be presented of the free principles of the English constitution.

To your request of my opinion of the manner in which a newspaper should be conducted, so as to be most useful, I should answer, 'by restraining it to true facts & sound principles only.' Yet I fear such a paper would find few subscribers. It is a melancholy truth, that a suppression of the press could not more compleatly deprive the nation of it's benefits, than is done by it's abandoned prostitution to falsehood. Nothing can now be believed which is seen in a newspaper. Truth itself becomes suspicious by being put into that polluted vehicle. The real extent of this state of misinformation is known only to those who are in situations to confront facts within their knolege with the lies of the day. I really look with commiseration over the great body of my fellow citizens, who, reading newspapers, live & die in the belief, that they have known something of what has been passing in the world in their time; whereas the accounts they have read in newspapers are just as true a history of any other period of the world as of the present, except that the real names of the day are affixed to their fables. General facts may indeed be collected from them, such as that Europe is now at war, that Bonaparte has been a successful warrior, that he has subjected a great portion of Europe to his will, &c., &c.; but no details can be relied on. I will add, that the man who never looks into a newspaper is better informed than he who reads them; inasmuch as he who knows nothing is nearer to truth than he whose mind is filled with falsehoods & errors. He who reads nothing will still learn the great facts, and the details are all false.

Perhaps an editor might begin a reformation in some such way as this. Divide his paper into 4 chapters, heading the 1st, Truths. 2d, Probabilities. 3d, Possibilities. 4th, Lies. The first chapter would be very short, as it would contain little more than authentic papers, and information from such sources, as the editor would be willing to risk his own reputation for their truth. The 2d would contain what, from a mature consideration of all circumstances, his judgment should conclude to be probably true. This, however, should rather contain too little than too much. The 3d & 4th should be professedly for those readers who would rather have lies for their money than the blank paper they would occupy.

Such an editor too, would have to set his face against the demoralising practice of feeding the public mind habitually on slander, & the depravity of taste which this nauseous aliment induces. Defamation is becoming a necessary of life; insomuch, that a dish of tea in the morning or evening cannot be digested without this stimulant. Even those who do not believe these abominations, still read them with complaisance to their auditors, and instead of the abhorrence & indignation which should fill a virtuous mind, betray a secret pleasure in the possibility that some may believe them, tho they do not themselves. It seems to escape them, that it is not he who prints, but he who pays for printing a slander, who is it's real author.

These thoughts on the subjects of your letter are hazarded at your request. Repeated instances of the publication of what has not been intended for the public eye, and the malignity with which political enemies torture every sentence from me into meanings imagined by their own wickedness only, justify my expressing a solicitude, that this hasty communication may in nowise be permitted to find it's way into the public papers. Not fearing these political bull-dogs, I yet avoid putting myself in the way of being baited by them, and do not wish to volunteer away that portion of tranquillity, which a firm execution of my duties will permit me to enjoy.

I tender you my salutations, and best wishes for your success.

A SUBPŒNA FOR THE PRESIDENT
To George Hay

Washington, June 20, 1807

DEAR SIR,—Mr. Latrobe now comes on as a witness against Burr. His presence here is with great inconvenience dispensed with, as 150 workmen require his constant directions on various public works of pressing importance. I hope you will permit him to come away as soon as possible. How far his testimony will be important as to the prisoner, I know not; but I am desirous that those meetings of Yrujo with Burr and his principal accomplices, should come fully out, and judicially, as they will establish the just complaints we have against his nation.

I did not see till last night the opinion of the Judge on the *subpœna duces tecum* against the President. Considering the question there as *coram non judice*, I did not read his argument with much attention. Yet I saw readily enough, that, as is usual where an opinion is to be supported, right or wrong, he dwells much on smaller objections, and passes over those which are solid. Laying down the position generally, that all persons owe obedience to subpœnas, he admits no exception unless it can be produced in his law books. But if the Constitution enjoins on a particular officer to be always engaged in a particular set of duties imposed on him, does not this supersede the general law, subjecting him to minor duties inconsistent with these? The Constitution enjoins his constant agency in the concerns of 6. millions of people. Is the law paramount to this, which calls on him on behalf of a single one? Let us apply the Judge's own doctrine to the case of himself & his brethren. The sheriff of Henrico summons him from the bench, to quell a riot somewhere in his county. The federal judge is, by the general law, a part of the *posse* of the

State sheriff. Would the Judge abandon major duties to perform lesser ones? Again; the court of Orleans or Maine commands, by subpœnas, the attendance of all the judges of the Supreme Court. Would they abandon their posts as judges, and the interests of millions committed to them, to serve the purposes of a single individual? The leading principle of our Constitution is the independence of the Legislature, executive and judiciary of each other, and none are more jealous of this than the judiciary. But would the executive be independent of the judiciary, if he were subject to the *commands* of the latter, & to imprisonment for disobedience; if the several courts could bandy him from pillar to post, keep him constantly trudging from north to south & east to west, and withdraw him entirely from his constitutional duties? The intention of the Constitution, that each branch should be independent of the others, is further manifested by the means it has furnished to each, to protect itself from enterprises of force attempted on them by the others, and to none has it given more effectual or diversified means than to the executive. Again; because ministers can go into a court in London as witnesses, without interruption to their executive duties, it is inferred that they would go to a court 1000. or 1500. miles off, and that ours are to be dragged from Maine to Orleans by every criminal who will swear that their testimony 'may be of use to him.' The Judge says, '*it is apparent* that the President's duties as chief magistrate do not demand his whole time, & are not unremitting.' If he alludes to our annual retirement from the seat of government, during the sickly season, he should be told that such arrangements are made for carrying on the public business, at and between the several stations we take, that it goes on as unremittingly there, as if we were at the seat of government. I pass more hours in public business at Monticello than I do here, every day; and it is much more laborious, because all must be done in writing. Our stations being known, all communications come to them regularly, as to fixed points. It would be very different were we always on the road, or placed in the noisy & crowded taverns where courts are held. Mr. Rodney is expected here every hour, having been kept away by a sick child.

I salute you with friendship and respect.

"UNLEARNED VIEWS OF MEDICINE"
To Dr. Caspar Wistar

Washington, June 21, 1807

DEAR SIR,—I have a grandson, the son of Mr. Randolph, now about 15 years of age, in whose education I take a lively interest. His time has not hitherto been employed to the greatest advantage, a frequent change of tutors having prevented the steady pursuit of any one plan. Whether he possesses that lively imagination, usually called genius, I have not had opportunities of knowing. But I think he has an observing mind & sound judgment. He is assiduous, orderly, & of the most amiable temper & dispositions. As he will be at ease in point of property, his education is not directed to any particular possession, but will embrace those sciences which give to retired life usefulness, ornament or amusement. I am not a friend to placing growing men in populous cities, because they acquire there habits & partialities which do not contribute to the happiness of their after life. But there are particular branches of science, which are not so advantageously taught anywhere else in the U.S. as in Philadelphia. The garden at the Woodlands for Botany, Mr. Peale's Museum for Natural History, your Medical school for Anatomy, and the able professors in all of them, give advantages not to be found elsewhere. We propose, therefore, to send him to Philadelphia to attend the schools of Botany, Natural History, Anatomy, & perhaps Surgery; but not of Medicine. And why not of Medicine, you will ask? Being led to the subject, I will avail myself of the occasion to express my opinions on that science, and the extent of my medical creed. But, to finish first with respect to my grandson, I will state the favor I ask of you, which is the object of this letter.

Having been born & brought up in a mountainous & healthy country, we should be unwilling he should go to Philadelphia until the autumnal diseases cease. It is important therefore for us to know, at what period after that, the courses of lectures in Natural history, Botany, Chemistry, Anatomy & Surgery begin and end, and what days or hours they occupy? The object of this is that we may be able so to marshal his pursuits as to bring their accomplishment within the shortest space practicable. I shall write to Doctor Barton for information as to the courses of natural history & botany but not having a sufficient acquaintance with professors of chemistry & surgery, if you can add the information respecting their school to that of your own, I shall be much obliged to you. What too are the usual terms of boarding? What the compensations to professors? And can you give me a conjectural estimate of other necessary expenses? In these we do not propose to indulge him beyond what is necessary, decent, & usual, because all beyond that leads to dissipation & idleness, to which, at present, he has no propensities. I think Mr. Peale has not been in the habit of receiving a boarder. His house & family would, of themselves, be a school of virtue & instruction; & hours of leisure there would be as improving as busy ones elsewhere. But I say this only on the possibility of so desirable a location for him, and not with the wish that the thought should become known to Mr. Peale, unless some former precedent should justify it's suggestion to him. I am laying a heavy tax on your busy time, but I think your goodness will pardon it in consideration of it's bearing on my happiness.

This subject dismissed, I may now take up that which it led to, and further tax your patience with unlearned views of medicine; which, as in most cases, are, perhaps, the more confident in proportion as they are less enlightened.

We know, from what we see & feel, that the animal body in it's organs and functions is subject to derangement, inducing pain, & tending to it's destruction. In this disordered state, we observe nature providing for the re-establishment of order, by exciting some salutary evacuation of the morbific matter, or by some other operation which escapes our imperfect senses and researches. She brings on a crisis, by stools, vomiting, sweat, urine, expectoration, bleeding, &c., which, for the most part, ends in the restoration of healthy action. Experience has taught us, also, that there are certain substances, by which, applied to the living body, internally or externally, we can at will produce these same evacuations, and thus do, in a short time, what nature would do but slowly, and do effectually, what perhaps she would not have strength to accomplish. Where, then, we have seen a disease, characterized by specific signs or phenomena, and relieved by a certain natural evacuation or process, whenever that disease recurs under the same appearances, we may reasonably count on producing a solution of it, by the use of such substances as we have found produce the same evacuation or movement. Thus, fulness of the stomach we can relieve by emetics; diseases of the bowels, by purgatives; inflammatory cases, by bleeding; intermittents, by the Peruvian bark; syphilis, by mercury: watchfulness, by opium; &c. So far, I bow to the utility of medicine. It goes to the well-defined forms of disease, & happily, to those the most frequent. But the disorders of the animal body, & the symptoms indicating them, are as various as the elements of which the body is composed. The combinations, too, of these symptoms are so infinitely diversified, that many associations of them appear too rarely to establish a definite disease; and to an unknown disease, there cannot be a known remedy. Here then, the judicious, the moral, the humane physician should stop. Having been so often a witness to the salutary efforts which nature makes to re-establish the disordered functions, he should rather trust to their action, than hazard the interruption of that, and a greater derangement of the system, by conjectural experiments on a machine so complicated & so unknown as the human body, & a subject so sacred as human life. Or, if the appearance of doing something be necessary to keep alive the hope & spirits of the patient, it should be of the most innocent character. One of the most successful physicians I have ever known, has assured me, that he used more bread pills, drops of colored water, & powders of hickory ashes, than of all other medicines put together. It was certainly a pious fraud. But the adventurous physician goes on, & substitutes presumption for knolege. From the scanty field of what is known, he launches into the boundless region of what is unknown. He establishes for his guide some fanciful theory of corpuscular attraction, of chemical agency, of mechanical powers, of stimuli, of irritability accumulated or exhausted, of depletion by the lancet & repletion by mercury, or some other ingenious dream, which lets him into all nature's secrets at short hand. On the principle which he thus assumes, he forms his table of nosology, arrays his diseases into families, and extends his curative treatment, by analogy, to all the cases he has thus arbitrarily marshalled together. I have lived myself to see the disciples of Hoffman, Boerhaave, Stalh, Cullen, Brown, succeed one another like the shifting figures of a magic lantern, & their fancies, like the dresses of the annual doll-babies from Paris, becoming, from their novelty, the vogue of the day, and yielding to the next novelty their ephemeral favor. The patient, treated on the fashionable theory, sometimes gets well in spite of the medicine. The medicine therefore restored him, & the young doctor receives new courage to proceed in his bold experiments on the lives of his fellow creatures. I believe we may safely affirm, that the inexperienced & presumptuous band of medical tyros let loose upon the world, destroys more of human life in one year, than all the Robinhoods, Cartouches, & Macheaths do in a century. It is in this part of medicine that I wish to see a reform, an abandonment of hypothesis for sober facts, the first degree of value set on clinical observation, and the lowest on visionary theories. I would wish the young practitioner, especially, to have deeply impressed on his mind, the real limits of his art, & that when the state of his patient gets beyond these, his office is to be a watchful, but quiet spectator of the operations of nature, giving them fair play by a well-regulated regimen, & by all the aid they can derive from the excitement of good spirits & hope in the patient. I have no doubt, that some diseases not yet understood may in time be transferred to the table of those known. But, were I a physician, I would rather leave the transfer to the slow hand of accident, than hasten it by guilty experiments on those who put their lives into my hands. The only sure foundations of medicine are, an intimate knolege of the human body, and observation on the effects of medicinal substances on that. The anatomical & clinical schools, therefore, are those in which the young physician should be formed. If he enters with innocence that of the theory of medicine, it is scarcely possible he should come out untainted with error. His mind must be strong indeed, if, rising above juvenile credulity, it can maintain a wise infidelity against the authority of his instructors, & the bewitching delusions of their theories. You see that I estimate justly that portion of instruction which our medical students derive from your labors; &, associating with it one of the chairs which my old & able friend, Doctor Rush, so honorably fills, I consider them as the two fundamental pillars of the edifice. Indeed, I have such an opinion of the talents of the professors in the other branches which constitute the school of medicine with you, as to hope & believe, that it is from this side of the Atlantic, that Europe, which has taught us so many other things, will at length be led into sound principles in this branch of science, the most important of all others, being that to which we commit the care of health & life.

I dare say, that by this time, you are sufficiently sensible that old heads as well as young, may sometimes be charged with ignorance and presumption. The natural course of the human mind is certainly from credulity to scepticism; and this is perhaps the most favorable apology I can make for venturing so far out of my depth, & to one too, to whom the strong as well as the weak points of this science are so familiar. But having stumbled on the subject in my way, I wished to give a confession of my faith to a friend; & the rather, as I had perhaps, at time, to him as well as others, expressed my scepticism in medicine, without defining it's extent or foundation. At any rate, it has permitted me, for a moment, to abstract myself from the dry & dreary waste of politics, into which I have been impressed by the times on which I happened, and to indulge in the rich fields of nature, where alone I should have served as a volunteer, if left to my natural inclinations & partialities.

I salute you at all times with affection & respect.

TORPEDOES AND SUBMARINES
To Robert Fulton

Monticello, August 16, 1807

SIR,—Your letter of July 28, came to hand just as I was about leaving Washington, & it has not been sooner in my power to acknolege it. I consider your torpedoes as very valuable means of defence of harbors, & have no doubt that we should adopt them to a considerable degree. Not that I go the whole length (as I believe you do) of considering them as solely to be relied on. Neither a nation nor those entrusted with it's affairs, could be justifiable, however sanguine their expectations, in trusting solely to an engine not yet sufficiently tried, under all the circumstances which may occur, & against which we know not as yet what means of parrying may be devised. If, indeed, the mode of attaching them to the cable of a ship be the only one proposed, modes of prevention cannot be difficult. But I have ever looked to the submarine boat as most to be depended on for attaching them, & tho' I see no mention of it in your letter, or your publications, I am in hopes it is not abandoned as impracticable. I should wish to see a corps of young men trained to this service. It would belong to the engineers if at land, but being nautical, I suppose we must have a corps of naval engineers, to practise & use them. I do not know whether we have authority to put any part of our existing naval establishment in a course of training, but it shall be the subject of a consultation with the Secretary of the Navy. Genl Dearborne has informed you of the urgency of our want of you at N Orleans for the locks there.

I salute you with great respect & esteem.

RELIGIOUS FREEDOM
To Rev. Samuel Miller

Washington, Jan. 23, 1808

SIR,—I have duly received your favor of the 18th and am thankful to you for having written it, because it is more agreeable to prevent than to refuse what I do not think myself authorized to comply with. I consider the government of the U S. as interdicted by the Constitution from intermeddling with religious institutions, their doctrines, discipline, or exercises. This results not only from the provision that no law shall be made respecting the establishment, or free exercise, of religion, but from that also which reserves to the states the powers not delegated to the U.S. Certainly no power to prescribe any religious exercise, or to assume authority in religious discipline, has been delegated to the general government. It must then rest with the states, as far as it can be in any human authority. But it is only proposed that I should *recommend*, not prescribe a day of fasting & prayer. That is, that I should *indirectly* assume to the U.S. an authority over religious exercises which the Constitution has directly precluded them from. It must be meant too that this recommendation is to carry some authority, and to be sanctioned by some penalty on those who disregard it; not indeed of fine and imprisonment, but of some degree of proscription perhaps in public opinion. And does the change in the nature of the penalty make the recommendation the less *a law* of conduct for those to whom it is directed? I do not believe it is for the interest of religion to invite the civil magistrate to direct it's exercises, it's discipline, or it's doctrines; nor of the religious societies that the general government should be invested with the power of effecting any uniformity of time or matter among them. Fasting & prayer are religious exercises. The enjoining them an act of discipline. Every religious society has a right to determine for itself the times for these exercises, & the objects proper for them, according to their own particular tenets; and this right can never be safer than in their own hands, where the constitution has deposited it.

I am aware that the practice of my predecessors may be quoted. But I have ever believed that the example of state executives led to the assumption of that authority by the general government, without due examination, which would have discovered that what might be a right in a state government, was a violation of that right when assumed by another. Be this as it may, every one must act according to the dictates of his own reason, & mine tells me that civil powers alone have been given to the President of the U S. and no authority to direct the religious exercises of his constituents.

I again express my satisfaction that you have been so good as to give me an opportunity of explaining myself in a private letter, in which I could give my reasons more in detail than might have been done in a public answer: and I pray you to accept the assurances of my high esteem & respect.

"SUBJECTS FOR A MAD-HOUSE"

To Dr. Thomas Leib

Washington, June 23, 1808

SIR,—I have duly received your favor covering a copy of the talk to the Tammany society, for which I thank you, and particularly for the favorable sentiments expressed towards myself. Certainly, nothing will so much sweeten the tranquillity and comfort of retirement, as the knoledge that I carry with me the good will & approbation of my republican fellow citizens, and especially of the individuals in unison with whom I have so long acted. With respect to the federalists, I believe we think alike; for when speaking of them, we never mean to include a worthy portion of our fellow citizens, who consider themselves as in duty bound to support the constituted authorities of every branch, and to reserve their opposition to the period of election. These having acquired the appellation of federalists, while a federal administration was in place, have not cared about throwing off their name, but adhering to their principle, are the supporters of the present order of things. The other branch of the federalists, those who are so in principle as well as in name, disapprove of the republican principles & features of our Constitution, and would, I believe, welcome any public calamity (war with England excepted) which might lessen the confidence of our country in those principles & forms. I have generally considered them rather as subjects for a mad-house. But they are now playing a game of the most mischevious tendency, without perhaps being themselves aware of it. They are endeavoring to convince England that we suffer more by the embargo than they do, & that if they will but hold out awhile, we must abandon it. It is true, the time will come when we must abandon it. But if this is before the repeal of the orders of council, we must abandon it only for a state of war. The day is not distant, when that will be preferable to a longer continuance of the embargo. But we can never remove that, & let our vessels go out & be taken under these orders, without making reprisal. Yet this is the very state of things which these federal monarchists are endeavoring to bring about; and in this it is but too possible they may succeed. But the fact is, that if we have war with England, it will be solely produced by their manœuvres. I think that in two or three months we shall know what will be the issue.

I salute you with esteem & respect.

BONES FOR THE NATIONAL INSTITUTE
To Lacépède, with a Catalogue

Washington, July 14, 1808

Sir,—If my recollection does not deceive me, the collection of the remains of the animal incognitum of the Ohio (sometimes called mammoth), possessed by the Cabinet of Natural History at Paris, is not very copious. Under this impression, and presuming that this Cabinet is allied to the National Institute, to which I am desirous of rendering some service, I have lately availed myself of an opportunity of collecting some of those remains. General Clarke (the companion of Governor Lewis in his expedition to the Pacific Ocean) being, on a late journey, to pass by the Big-bone Lick of the Ohio, was kind enough to undertake to employ for me a number of laborers, and to direct their operations in digging for these bones at this important deposit of them. The result of these researches will appear in the enclosed catalogue of specimens which I am now able to place at the disposal of the National Institute. An aviso being to leave this place for some port of France on public service, I deliver the packages to Captain Haley, to be deposited with the Consul of the United States, at whatever port he may land. They are addressed to Mr. Warden of our legation at Paris, for the National Institute, and he will have the honor of delivering them. To these I have added the horns of an animal called by the natives the Mountain Ram, resembling the sheep by his head, but more nearly the deer in his other parts; as also the skin of another animal, resembling the sheep by his fleece but the goat in his other parts. This is called by the natives the Fleecy Goat, or in the style of the natural historian, the Pokotragos. I suspect it to be nearly related to the Pacos, and were we to group the fleecy animals together, it would stand perhaps with the

Vigogne, Pacos, and Sheep. The Mountain Ram was found in abundance by Messrs. Lewis and Clarke on their western tour, and was frequently an article of food for their party, and esteemed more delicate than the deer. The Fleecy Goat they did not see, but procured two skins from the Indians, of which this is one. Their description will be given in the work of Governor Lewis, the journal and geographical part of which may be soon expected from the press; but the parts relating to the plants and animals observed in his tour, will be delayed by the engravings. In the meantime, the plants of which he brought seeds, have been very successfully raised in the botanical garden of Mr. Hamilton of the Woodlands, and by Mr. McMahon, a gardener of Philadelphia; and on the whole, it is with pleasure I can assure you that the addition to our knowledge in every department, resulting from this tour of Messrs. Lewis and Clarke, has entirely fulfilled my expectations in setting it on foot, and that the world will find that those travellers have well earned its favor. I will take care that the Institute as well as yourself shall receive Governor Lewis's work as it appears.

It is with pleasure I embrace this occasion of returning you my thanks for the favor of your very valuable works, *sur les poissons et les cetacées*, which you were so kind as to send me through Mr. Livingston and General Turreau, and which I find entirely worthy of your high reputation in the literary world. That I have not sooner made this acknowledgment has not proceeded from any want of respect and attachment to yourself, or a just value of your estimable present, but from the strong and incessant calls of duty to other objects. The candor of your character gives me confidence of your indulgence on this head, and I assure you with truth that no circumstances are more welcome to me than those which give me the occasion of recalling myself to your recollection, and of renewing to you the assurances of sincere personal attachment, and of great respect and consideration.

Contents of the large square Box.

A Fibia.
A Radius.
Two ribs belonging to the upper part of the thorax.

Two ribs from a lower part of the thorax.

One entire vertebra.

Two spinous processes of the vertebra broken from the bodies.

Dentes molares, which appear to have belonged to the full-grown animal.

A portion of the under-jaw of a young animal with two molar teeth in it.

These teeth appear to have belonged to a first set, as they are small, and the posterior has but three grinding ridges, instead of five, the common number in adult teeth of the lower jaw.

Another portion of the under-jaw, including the symphisis, or chin. In this portion the teeth of one side are every way complete; to wit, the posterior has five transverse ridges, and the anterior three.

A fragment of the upper-jaw with one molar tooth much worn.

Molar teeth which we suppose to be like those of the mammoth or elephant of Siberia. They are essentially different from those of the mammoth or elephant of this country, and although similar in some respects to the teeth of the Asiatic elephant, they agree more completely with the description of the teeth found in Siberia in the arrangement and size of the transverse lamina of enamel. This idea, however, is not derived from actual comparison of the different teeth with each other, for we have no specimens of Siberian teeth in this country; but from inferences deduced from the various accounts and drawings of these teeth to be found in books. A few of these teeth have been found in several places where the bones of the American animal have existed.

An Astragalus.

An Oscalcis.

Os naviculare.

In the large box in which the preceding bones are, is a small one containing a promiscuous mass of small bones, chiefly of the feet.

In the large irregular-shaped box, a tusk of large size. The spiral twist in all the specimens of these tusks which we have seen, was remarked so long ago as the time of Breyneus, in his description of the tusks of the Siberian mammoth in the Philosophical Transactions, if that paper is rightly recollected, for the book is not here to be turned to at present. Many fragments of tusks have been sent from the Ohio, generally resembling portions of such tusks as are brought to us in the course of commerce. But of these spiral tusks, in a tolerable complete state, we have had only four. One was found near the head of the north branch of the Susquehanna. A second possessed by Mr. Peale, was found with the skeleton, near the Hudson. A third is at Monticello, found with the bones of this collection at the Big-bone lick of Ohio, and the fourth is that now sent for the Institute, found at the same place and larger than that at Monticello.

The smallest box contains the horns of the mountain ram, and skin of the fleecy goat.

PLOUGHS
To Monsieur Sylvestre

Washington, July 15, 1808

SIR,—I had received from you on a former occasion the four first volumes of the Memoirs of the Agricultural Society of the Seine, and since that, your letter of September 19th, with the 6th, 7th, 8ths, and 9th volumes, being for the years 1804 '5 '6, with some separate memoirs. These I have read with great avidity and satisfaction, and now return you my thanks for them. But I owe particular acknowledgments for the valuable present of the Theatre de De Serres, which I consider as a prodigy for the age in which it was composed, and shows an advancement in the science of agriculture which I had never suspected to have belonged to that time. Brought down to the present day by the very valuable notes added, it is really such a treasure of agricultural knowledge, as has not before been offered to the world in a single work.

It is not merely for myself, but for my country, that I must do homage to the philanthropy of the Society, which has dictated their destination for me of their newly-improved plough. I shall certainly so use it as to answer their liberal views, by making the opportunities of profiting by it as general as possible.

I have just received information that a plough addressed to me has arrived at New York, *from England*, but unaccompanied by any letter or other explanation. As I have had no intimation of such an article to be forwarded to me from that country, I presume it is the one sent by the Society of the Seine, that it has been carried into England under their orders of council, and permitted to come on from thence. This I shall know within a short time. I shall with great pleasure attend to the construction and transmission to the Society of a plough with my mould board. This is the only part of that useful instrument to which I have paid any particular attention. But knowing how much the perfection of the plough must depend, 1st, on the line of traction; 2d, on the direction of the share; 3d, on the angle of the wing; 4th, on the form of the mould-board; and persuaded that I shall find the three first advantages eminently exemplified in that which the Society sends me, I am anxious to see combined with these a mould-board of my form, in the hope it will still advance the perfection of that machine. But for this I must ask time till I am relieved from the cares which have now a right to all my time, that is to say, till the next Spring. Then giving, in the leisure of retirement, all the time and attention this construction merits and requires, I will certainly render to the Society the result in a plough of the best form I shall be able to have executed. In the meantime, accept for them and yourself the assurances of my high respect and consideration.

EDUCATION OF A GRANDSON
To Thomas Jefferson Randolph

Washington, Nov. 24th, 1808

MY DEAR JEFFERSON—I have just recieved the inclosed letter under cover from Mr. Bankhead which I presume is from Anne and will inform you she is well. Mr. Bankhead has consented to go and pursue his studies at Monticello, and live with us till his pursuits or circumstances may require a separate establishment. Your situation, thrown at such a distance from us and alone, cannot but give us all, great anxieties for you. As much has been secured for you, by your particular position and the acquaintance to which you have been recommended, as could be done towards shielding you from the dangers which surround you. But thrown on a wide world, among entire strangers without a friend or guardian to advise so young too and with so little experience of mankind, your dangers are great, and still your safety must rest on yourself. A determination never to do what is wrong, prudence, and good humor, will go far towards securing to you the estimation of the world. When I recollect that at 14. years of age, the whole care and direction of my self was thrown on my self entirely, without a relation or friend qualified to advise or guide me, and recollect the various sorts of bad company with which I associated from time to time, I am astonished I did not turn off with some of them, and become as worthless to society as they were. I had the good fortune to become acquainted very early with some characters of very high standing, and to feel the incessant wish that I could even become what they were. Under temptations and difficulties, I could ask myself what would Dr. Small, Mr. Wythe, Peyton Randolph do in this situation? What course in it will ensure me their approbation? I am certain that this mode of deciding on my conduct tended more to it's correctness than any reasoning powers I possessed. Knowing the even and dignified line they pursued, I could never doubt for a moment which of two courses would be in character for them. Whereas seeking the same object through a process of moral reasoning, and with the jaundiced eye of youth, I should often have erred. From the circumstances of my position I was often thrown into the society of horseracers, cardplayers, Foxhunters, scientific and professional men, and of dignified men; and many a time have I asked myself, in the enthusiastic moment of the death of a fox, the victory of a favorite horse, the issue of a question eloquently argued at the bar or in the great Council of the nation, well, which of these kinds of reputation should I prefer? That of a horse jockey? A foxhunter? An Orator? Or the honest advocate of my country's rights? Be assured my dear Jefferson, that these little returns into ourselves, this selfcathechising habit, is not trifling, nor useless, but leads to the prudent selection and steady pursuits of what is right? I have mentioned good humor as one of the preservatives of our peace and tranquillity. It is among the most effectual, and it's effect is so well imitated and aided artificially by politeness, that this also becomes an acquisition of first rate value. In truth, politeness is artificial good humor, it covers the natural want of it, and ends by rendering habitual a substitute nearly equivalent to the real virtue. It is the practice of sacrificing to those whom we meet in society all the little conveniences and preferences which will gratify them, and deprive us of nothing worth a moment's consideration; it is the giving a pleasing and flattering turn to our expressions which will conciliate others, and make them pleased with us as well as themselves. How cheap a price for the good will of another! When this is in return for a rude thing said by another, it brings him to his senses, it mortifies and corrects him in the most salutary way, and places him at the feet of your good nature in the eyes of the company. But in stating prudential rules for our government in society I must not omit the important one of never entering into dispute or argument with another. I never yet saw an instance of one of two disputants convincing the other by argument. I have seen many on their getting warm, becoming rude, and shooting one another. Conviction is the effect of our own dispassionate reasoning, either in solitude, or weighing within ourselves dispassionately what we hear from others standing uncommitted in argument ourselves. It was one of the rules which above all others made Doctr. Franklin the most amiable of men in society, 'never to contradict any body.' If he was urged to anounce an opinion, he did it rather by asking questions, as if for information, or by suggesting doubts. When I hear another express an opinion, which is not mine, I say to myself, He has a right to his opinion, as I to mine; why should I question it. His error does me no injury, and shall I become a Don Quixot to bring all men by force of argument, to one opinion? If a fact be misstated, it is probable he is gratified by a belief of it, and I have no right to deprive him of the gratification. If he wants information he will ask it, and then I will give it in measured terms; but if he still believes his own story, and shows a desire to dispute the fact with me, I hear him and say nothing. It is his affair, not mine, if he prefers error. There are two classes of disputants most frequently to be met with among us. The first is of young students just entered the threshold of science, with a first view of it's outlines, not yet filled up with the details and modifications which a further progress would bring to their knoledge. The other consists of the ill-tempered and rude men in society who have taken up a passion for politics. (Good humor and politeness never introduce into mixed society a question on which they foresee there will be a difference of opinion.) From both of these classes of disputants, my dear Jefferson, keep aloof, as you would from the infected subjects of yellow fever or pestilence. Consider yourself, when with them, as among the patients of Bedlam needing medical more than moral counsel. Be a listener only, keep within yourself, and endeavor to establish with yourself the habit of silence, especially in politics. In the fevered state of our country, no good can ever result from any attempt to set one of these fiery zealots to rights either in fact or principle. They are determined as to the facts they will believe, and the opinions on which they will act. Get by them, therefore as you would by an angry bull: it is not for a man of sense to dispute the road with such an animal. You will be more exposed than others to have these animals shaking their horns at you, because of the relation in which you stand with me and to hate me as a chief in the antagonist party your presence will be to them what the vomit-grass is to the sick dog a nostrum for producing an ejaculation. Look upon them exactly with that eye, and pity them as objects to whom you can administer only occasional ease. My character is not within their power. It is in the hands of my fellow citizens at large, and will be consigned to honor or infamy by the verdict of the republican mass of our country, according to what themselves will have seen, not what their enemies and mine shall have said. Never therefore consider these puppies in politics as requiring any notice from you, and always shew that you are not afraid to leave my character to the umpirage of public opinion. Look steadily to the pursuits which have carried you to Philadelphia, be very select in the society you attach yourself to; avoid taverns,

drinkers, smoakers, and idlers and dissipated persons generally; for it is with such that broils and contentions arise, and
you will find your path more easy and tranquil. The limits of
my paper warn me that it is time for me to close with my
affectionate Adieux.

P. S. Present me affectionately to Mr. Ogilvie, and in doing
the same to Mr. Peale tell him I am writing with his polygraph and shall send him mine the first moment I have leisure
enough to pack it.

SOWING THE UPLAND RICE
To Dr. Benjamin Waterhouse

Washington, December 1, 1808

SIR,—In answer to the inquiries of the benevolent Dr. De
Carro on the subject of the upland or mountain rice, Oryza
Mutica, I will state to you what I know of it. I first became
informed of the existence of a rice which would grow in up-
lands without any more water than the common rains, by
reading a book of Mr. De Porpre, who had been Governor
of the Isle of France, who mentions it as growing there and
all along the coast of Africa successfully, and as having been
introduced from Cochin-China. I was at that time (1784–89)
in France, and there happening to be there a Prince of
Cochin-China, on his travels, and then returning home, I obtained his promise to send me some. I never received it however, and mention it only as it may have been sent, and
furnished the ground for the inquiries of Dr. De Carro, respecting my receiving it from China. When at Havre on my
return from France, I found there Captain Nathaniel Cutting,
who was the ensuing spring to go on a voyage along the coast
of Africa. I engaged him to inquire for this; he was there just
after the harvest, procured and sent me a thirty-gallon cask of
it. It arrived in time the ensuing spring to be sown. I divided
it between the Agricultural Society of Charleston and some
private gentlemen of Georgia, recommending it to their care,
in the hope which had induced me to endeavor to obtain it,

that if it answered as well as the swamp rice, it might rid them of that source of their summer diseases. Nothing came of the trials in South Carolina, but being carried into the upper hilly parts of Georgia, it succeeded there perfectly, has spread over the country, and is now commonly cultivated; still, however, for family use chiefly, as they cannot make it for sale in competition with the rice of the swamps. The former part of these details is written from memory, the papers being at Monticello which would enable me to particularize exactly the dates of times and places. The latter part is from the late Mr. Baldwin, one of those whom I engaged in the distribution of the seed in Georgia, and who in his annual attendance on Congress, gave me from time to time the history of its progress. It has got from Georgia into Kentucky, where it is cultivated by many individuals for family use. I cultivated it two or three years at Monticello, and had good crops, as did my neighbors, but not having conveniences for husking it, we declined it. I tried some of it in a pot, while I lived in Philadelphia, and gave seed to Mr. Bartram. It produced luxuriant plants with us both, but no seed; nor do I believe it will ripen in the United States as far north as Philadelphia. Business and an indisposition of some days must apologize for this delay in answering your letter of October 24th, which I did not receive till the 6th of November. And permit me here to add my salutations and assurances of esteem and respect.

"LAST TRIAL FOR PEACE"
To James Monroe

Washington, January 28, 1809

DEAR SIR,—Your favor of the 18th was received in due time, and the answer has been delayed as well by a pressure of business, as by the expectation of your absence from Richmond.

The idea of sending a special mission to France or England is not entertained at all here. After so little attention to us from the former, and so insulting an answer from Canning, such a mark of respect as an extraordinary mission, would be a degradation against which all minds revolt here. The idea was hazarded in the House of Representatives a few days ago, by a member, and an approbation expressed by another, but rejected indignantly by every other person who spoke, and very generally in conversation by all others; and I am satisfied such a proposition would get no vote in the Senate. The course the Legislature means to pursue, may be inferred from the act now passed for a meeting in May, and a proposition before them for repealing the embargo in June, and then resuming and maintaining by force our right of navigation. There will be considerable opposition to this last proposition, not only from the federalists, old and new, who oppose everything, but from sound members of the majority. Yet it is believed it will obtain a good majority, and that it is the only proposition which can be devised that could obtain a majority of any kind. Final propositions will, therefore, be soon despatched to both the belligerents through the resident ministers, so that their answers will be received before the meeting in May, and will decide what is to be done. This last trial for peace is not thought desperate. If, as is expected, Bonaparte should be successful in Spain, however every virtuous and liberal sentiment revolts at it, it may induce both powers to be more accommodating with us. England will see here the only asylum for her commerce and manufactures, worth more to her than her orders of council. And Bonaparte, having Spain at his feet, will look immediately to the Spanish colonies, and think our neutrality cheaply purchased by a repeal of the illegal parts of his decrees, with perhaps the Floridas thrown into the bargain. Should a change in the aspect of affairs in Europe produce this disposition in both powers, our peace and prosperity may be revived and long continue. Otherwise, we must again take the tented field, as we did in 1776 under more inauspicious circumstances.

There never has been a situation of the world before, in which such endeavors as we have made would not have secured our peace. It is probable there never will be such another. If we go to war now, I fear we may renounce forever the hope of seeing an end of our national debt. If we can keep at peace eight years longer, our income, liberated from debt, will be adequate to any war, without new taxes or loans, and our position and increasing strength put us *hors d'insulte* from any nation. I am now so near the moment of retiring, that I take no part in affairs beyond the expression of an opinion. I think it fair that my successor should now originate those measures of which he will be charged with the execution and responsibility, and that it is my duty to clothe them with the forms of authority. Five weeks more will relieve me from a drudgery to which I am no longer equal, and restore me to a scene of tranquillity, amidst my family and friends, more congenial to my age and natural inclinations. In that situation, it will always be a pleasure to me to see you, and to repeat to you the assurances of my constant friendship and respect.

THE REPUBLIC OF SCIENCE

To John Hollins

Washington, February 19, 1809

DEAR SIR,—A little transaction of mine, as innocent an one as I ever entered into, and where an improper construction was never less expected, is making some noise, I observe, in your city. I beg leave to explain it to you, because I mean to ask your agency in it. The last year, the Agricultural Society of Paris, of which I am a member, having had a plough presented to them, which, on trial with a graduated instrument, did equal work with half the force of their best ploughs, they thought it would be a benefit to mankind to communicate it. They accordingly sent one to me, with a view to its being made known here, and they sent one to the Duke of Bedford also, who is one of their members, to be made use of for England, although the two nations were then at war. By the Mentor, now going to France, I have given permission to two individuals in Delaware and New York, to import two parcels of Merino sheep from France, which they have procured there, and to some gentlemen in Boston, to import a very valuable machine which spins cotton, wool and flax equally. The last spring, the Society informed me they were cultivat-

ing the cotton of the Levant and other parts of the Mediterranean, and wished to try also that of our southern States. I
immediately got a friend to have two tierces of seed forwarded to me. They were consigned to Messrs. Falls and
Brown of Baltimore, and notice of it being given me, I immediately wrote to them to re-ship them to New York, to be
sent by the Mentor. Their first object was to make a show of
my letter, as something very criminal, and to carry the subject
into the newspapers. I had, on a like request, some time ago,
(but before the embargo) from the President of the Board of
Agriculture of London, of which I am also a member, to send
them some of the genuine May wheat of Virginia, forwarded
to them two or three barrels of it. General Washington, in his
time, received from the same Society the seed of the perennial
succory, which Arthur Young had carried over from France
to England, and I have since received from a member of it
the seed of the famous turnip of Sweden, now so well known
here. I mention these things, to shew the nature of the correspondence which is carried on between societies instituted
for the benevolent purpose of communicating to all parts of
the world whatever useful is discovered in any one of them.
These societies are always in peace, however their nations may
be at war. Like the republic of letters, they form a great fraternity spreading over the whole earth, and their correspondence is never interrupted by any civilized nation. Vaccination
has been a late and remarkable instance of the liberal diffusion
of a blessing newly discovered. It is really painful, it is mortifying, to be obliged to note these things, which are known
to every one who knows any thing, and felt with approbation
by every one who has any feeling. But we have a faction to
whose hostile passions the torture even of right into wrong is
a delicious gratification. Their malice I have long learned to
disregard, their censure to deem praise. But I observe, that
some republicans are not satisfied (even while we are receiving liberally from others) that this small return should be
made. They will think more justly at another day: but in the
mean time, I wish to avoid offence. My prayer to you, therefore, is, that you will be so good, under the inclosed order,
as to receive these two tierces of seed from Falls and Brown,

and pay them their disbursements for freight, &c. which I will immediately remit you on knowing the amount. Of the seed, when received, be so good as to make manure for your garden. When rotted with a due mixture of stable manure or earth, it is the best in the world. I rely on your friendship to excuse this trouble, it being necessary I should not commit myself again to persons of whose honor, or the want of it, I know nothing.

Accept the assurances of my constant esteem and respect.

THE NEGRO RACE
To Henri Gregoire

Washington, February 25, 1809

SIR,—I have received the favor of your letter of August 17th, and with it the volume you were so kind as to send me on the "Literature of Negroes." Be assured that no person living wishes more sincerely than I do, to see a complete refutation of the doubts I have myself entertained and expressed on the grade of understanding allotted to them by nature, and to find that in this respect they are on a par with ourselves. My doubts were the result of personal observation on the limited sphere of my own State, where the opportunities for the development of their genius were not favorable, and those of exercising it still less so. I expressed them therefore with great hesitation; but whatever be their degree of talent it is no measure of their rights. Because Sir Isaac Newton was superior to others in understanding, he was not therefore lord of the person or property of others. On this subject they are gaining daily in the opinions of nations, and hopeful advances are making towards their re-establishment on an equal footing with the other colors of the human family. I pray you therefore to accept my thanks for the many instances you have enabled me to observe of respectable intelligence in that race of men, which cannot fail to have effect in hastening the day of their relief; and to be assured of the sentiments of high and just esteem and consideration which I tender to yourself with all sincerity.

"A PRISONER, RELEASED FROM HIS CHAINS"
To P. S. Dupont de Nemours

Washington, March 2, 1809

DEAR SIR,—My last to you was of May the 2nd; since which I have received yours of May the 25th, June the 1st, July the 23rd, 24th, and September the 5th, and distributed the two pamphlets according to your desire. They are read with the delight which every thing from your pen gives.

After using every effort which could prevent or delay our being entangled in the war of Europe, that seems now our only resource. The edicts of the two belligerents, forbidding us to be seen on the ocean, we met by an embargo. This gave us time to call home our seamen, ships and property, to levy men and put our sea ports into a certain state of defence. We have now taken off the embargo, except as to France and England and their territories, because fifty millions of exports, annually sacrificed, are the treble of what war would cost us; besides, that by war we should take something, and lose less than at present. But to give you a true description of the state of things here, I must refer you to Mr. Coles, the bearer of this, my secretary, a most worthy, intelligent and well in-formed young man, whom I recommend to your notice, and conversation on our affairs. His discretion and fidelity may be relied on. I expect he will find you with Spain at your feet, but England still afloat, and a barrier to the Spanish colonies. But all these concerns I am now leaving to be settled by my friend Mr. Madison. Within a few days I retire to my family, my books and farms; and having gained the harbor myself, I shall look on my friends still buffeting the storm, with anxiety indeed, but not with envy. Never did a prisoner, released from his chains, feel such relief as I shall on shaking off the shackles of power. Nature intended me for the tranquil pur-suits of science, by rendering them my supreme delight. But the enormities of the times in which I have lived, have forced me to take a part in resisting them, and to commit myself on the boisterous ocean of political passions. I thank God for the opportunity of retiring from them without censure, and car-rying with me the most consoling proofs of public approba-tion. I leave every thing in the hands of men so able to take care of them, that if we are destined to meet misfortunes, it will be because no human wisdom could avert them. Should you return to the United States, perhaps your curiosity may lead you to visit the hermit of Monticello. He will receive you with affection and delight; hailing you in the mean time with his affectionate salutations, and assurances of constant esteem and respect.

P.S. If you return to us, bring a couple of pair of true-bred shepherd's dogs. You will add a valuable possession to a country now beginning to pay great attention to the raising sheep.

A PARTING BLESSING
To Mrs. Samuel H. Smith

Washington, Mar. 6, 1809

Th: Jefferson presents his respectful salutations to mrs. Smith, and sends her the Geranium she expressed a willingness to receive. it is in very bad condition, having been neglected latterly, as not intended to be removed. he cannot give it his parting blessing more effectually than by consigning it to the nourishing hand of mrs. Smith. If plants have sensibility, as the analogy of their organisation with ours seems to indicate, it cannot but be proudly sensible of her fostering attentions. of his regrets at parting with the society of Washington, a very sensible portion attaches to mrs. Smith, whose friendship he has particularly valued. her promise to visit Monticello is some consolation; and he can assure her she will be received with open arms and hearts by the whole family. he prays her to accept the homage of his affectionate attachment and respect.

THE POTATO AND HARPER'S FERRY
To Horatio G. Spafford

Monticello, May 14, 1809

SIR,—I have duly received your favor of April 3d, with the copy of your "General Geography," for which I pray you to accept my thanks. My occupations here have not permitted me to read it through, which alone could justify any judgment expressed on the work. Indeed, as it appears to be an abridgment of several branches of science, the scale of abridgment must enter into that judgment. Different readers require different scales according to the time they can spare, and their views in reading, and no doubt that the view of the sciences which you have brought into the compass of a 12mo volume will be accommodated to the time and object of many who may wish for but a very general view of them

In passing my eye rapidly over parts of the book, I was struck with two passages, on which I will make observations, not doubting your wish, in any future edition, to render the work as correct as you can. In page 186 you say the potatoe is a native of the United States. I presume you speak of the Irish potatoe. I have inquired much into the question, and think I can assure you that plant is not a native of North America. Zimmerman, in his "Geographical Zoology," says it is a native of Guiana; and Clavigero, that the Mexicans got it from South America, *its native country*. The most probable account I have been able to collect is, that a vessel of Sir Walter Raleigh's, returning from Guiana, put into the west of Ireland in distress, having on board some potatoes which they called earth-apples. That the season of the year, and circumstance of their being already sprouted, induced them to give them all out there, and they were no more heard or thought of, till they had been spread considerably into that island, whence they were carried over into England, and therefore called the Irish potatoe. From England they came to the United States, bringing their name with them.

The other passage respects the description of the passage of the Potomac through the Blue Ridge, in the Notes on Virginia. You quote from Volney's account of the United States what his words do not justify. His words are, "on coming from Fredericktown, one does not see the rich perspective mentioned in the Notes of Mr. Jefferson. On observing this to him a few days after, he informed me he had his information from a French engineer who, during the war of Independence, ascended the height of the hills, and I conceive that at that elevation the perspective must be as imposing as a wild

country, whose horizon has no obstacles, may present." That
the scene described in the "Notes" is not visible from any part
of the road from Fredericktown to Harper's ferry is most certain. That road passes along the valley, nor can it be seen
from the tavern after crossing the ferry; and we may fairly
infer that Mr. Volney did not ascend the height back of the
tavern from which alone it can be seen, but that he pursued
his journey from the tavern along the high road. Yet he admits, that at the elevation of that height the perspective may
be as rich as a wild country can present. But you make him
"surprised to find, *by a view of the spot*, that the description
was *amazingly exaggerated*." But it is evident that Mr. Volney
did not ascend the hill to *get a view of the spot*, and that he
supposed that that height may present as imposing a view as
such a country admits. But Mr. Volney was mistaken in saying I told him I had received the description from a French
engineer. By an error of memory he has misapplied to this
scene what I mentioned to him as to the Natural Bridge. I
told him I received a *drawing* of that from a French engineer
sent there by the Marquis de Chastellux, and who has published that drawing in his travels. I could not tell him I had
the description of the passage of the Potomac from a French
engineer, because I never heard any Frenchman say a word
about it, much less did I ever receive a description of it from
any mortal whatever. I visited the place myself in October
1783, wrote the description some time after, and printed the
work in Paris in 1784–5. I wrote the description from my own
view of the spot, stated no fact but what I saw, and can now
affirm that no fact is exaggerated. It is true that the same
scene may excite very different sensations in different spectators, according to their different sensibilities. The sensations
of some may be much stronger than those of others. And
with respect to the Natural Bridge, it was not a description,
but a drawing only, which I received from the French engineer. The description was written before I ever saw him. It is
not from any merit which I suppose in either of these descriptions, that I have gone into these observations, but to correct
the imputation of having given to the world as my own,
ideas, and false ones too, which I had received from another.
Nor do I mention the subject to you with a desire that it

should be any otherwise noticed before the public than by a more correct statement in any future edition of your work.

You mention having enclosed to me some printed letters announcing a design in which you ask my aid. But no such letters came to me. Any facts which I possess, and which may be useful to your views, shall be freely communicated, and I shall be happy to see you at Monticello, should you come this way as you propose. You will find me engaged entirely in rural occupations, looking into the field of science but occasionally and at vacant moments.

I sowed some of the Benni seed the last year, and distributed some among my neighbors; but the whole was killed by the September frost. I got a little again the last winter, but it was sowed before I received your letter. Colonel Fen of New York receives quantities of it from Georgia, from whom you may probably get some through the Mayor of New York. But I little expect it can succeed with you. It is about as hardy as the cotton plant, from which you may judge of the probability of raising it at Hudson.

I salute you with great respect.

CIRCULATING LIBRARIES
To John Wyche

Monticello, May 19, 1809

SIR,—Your favor of March 19th came to hand but a few days ago, and informs me of the establishment of the Westward Mill Library Society, of its general views and progress. I always hear with pleasure of institutions for the promotion of knowledge among my countrymen. The people of every country are the only safe guardians of their own rights, and are the only instruments which can be used for their destruction. And certainly they would never consent to be so used were they not deceived. To avoid this, they should be instructed to a certain degree. I have often thought that nothing would do more extensive good at small expense than the establishment of a small circulating library in every county, to consist of a few well-chosen books, to be lent to the people of the county, under such regulations as would secure their safe return in due time. These should be such as would give them a general view of other history, and particular view of that of their own country, a tolerable knowledge of Geography, the elements of Natural Philosophy, of Agriculture and Mechanics. Should your example lead to this, it will do great good. Having had more favorable opportunities than fall to every man's lot of becoming acquainted with the best books on such subjects as might be selected, I do not know that I can be otherwise useful to your society than by offering them any information respecting these which they might wish. My services in this way are freely at their command, and I beg leave to tender to yourself my salutations and assurances of respect.

"THE SPIRIT OF MANUFACTURE"

To P. S. Dupont de Nemours

Monticello, June 28, 1809

DEAR SIR,—The interruption of our commerce with England, produced by our embargo and non-intercourse law, and the general indignation excited by her barefaced attempts to make us accessories and tributaries to her usurpations on the high seas, have generated in this country an universal spirit for manufacturing for ourselves, and of reducing to a minimum the number of articles for which we are dependent on her. The advantages, too, of lessening the occasions of risking our peace on the ocean, and of planting the consumer in our own soil by the side of the grower of produce, are so palpable, that no temporary suspension of injuries on her part, or agreements founded on that, will now prevent our continuing in what we have begun. The spirit of manufacture has taken deep root among us, and its foundations are laid in too great expense to be abandoned. The bearer of this, Mr. Ronaldson, will be able to inform you of the extent and perfection of the works produced here by the late state of things; and to his information, which is greatest as to what is doing in the cities, I can add my own as to the country, where the principal articles wanted in every family are now fabricated within itself. This mass of *household* manufacture, unseen by the public eye, and so much greater than what is seen, is such at present, that let our intercourse with England be opened when it may, not one half the amount of what we have heretofore taken from her will ever again be demanded. The great call from the country has hitherto been of coarse goods. These are now made in our families, and the advantage is too sensible ever to be relinquished. It is one of those obvious improvements in our condition which needed only to be once forced on our attention, never again to be abandoned.

Among the arts which have made great progress among us is that of printing. Heretofore we imported our books, and with them much political principle from England. We now print a great deal, and shall soon supply ourselves with most of the books of considerable demand. But the foundation of printing, you know, is the type-foundry, and a material essential to that is antimony. Unfortunately that mineral is not among those as yet found in the United States, and the difficulty and dearness of getting it from England, will force us to discontinue our type-founderies, and resort to her again for our books, unless some new source of supply can be found. The bearer, Mr. Ronaldson, is of the concern of Binney & Ronaldson, type-founders of Philadelphia. He goes to France for the purpose of opening some new source of supply, where we learn that this article is abundant; the enhancement of the price in England has taught us the fact, that its exportation thither from France must be interrupted, either by the war or express prohibition. Our relations, however, with France, are too unlike hers with England, to place us under the same interdiction. Regulations for preventing the transportation of the article to England, under the cover of supplies to America, may be thought requisite. The bearer, I am persuaded, will readily give any assurances which may be required for this object, and the wants of his own type-foundry here are a sufficient pledge that what he gets is *bonâ fide* to supply them. I do not know that there will be any obstacle to his bringing from France any quantity of antimony he may have occasion for; but lest there should be, I have taken the liberty of recommending him to your patronage. I know your enlightened and liberal views on subjects of this kind, and the friendly interest you take in whatever concerns our welfare. I place Mr. Ronaldson, therefore, in your hands, and pray you to advise him, and patronize the object which carries him to Europe, and is so interesting to him and to our country. His knowledge of what is passing among us will be a rich source of information for you, and especially as to the state and progress of our manufactures. Your kindness to him will confer an obligation on me, and will be an additional title to the high and affectionate esteem and respect of an ancient and sincere friend.

AN EDITION OF WRITINGS
To John W. Campbell

Monticello, September 3, 1809

Sɪʀ,—Your letter of July 29th came to hand some time since, but I have not sooner been able to acknowledge it. In answer to your proposition for publishing a complete edition of my different writings, I must observe that no writings of mine, other than those merely official, have been published, except the Notes on Virginia and a small pamphlet under the title of a Summary View of the rights of British America. The Notes on Virginia, I have always intended to revise and enlarge, and have, from time to time, laid by materials for that purpose. It will be long yet before other occupations will permit me to digest them, and observations and inquiries are still to be made, which will be more correct in proportion to the length of time they are continued. It is not unlikely that this may be through my life. I could not, therefore, at present, offer anything new for that work.

The Summary View was not written for publication. It was a draught I had prepared for a petition to the king, which I meant to propose in my place as a member of the convention of 1774. Being stopped on the road by sickness, I sent it on to the Speaker, who laid it on the table for the perusal of the members. It was thought too strong for the times, and to become the act of the convention, but was printed by sub-scription of the members, with a short preface written by one of them. If it had any merit, it was that of first taking our true ground, and that which was afterwards assumed and maintained.

I do not mention the Parliamentary Manual, published for the use of the Senate of the United States, because it was a mere compilation, into which nothing entered of my own but the arrangement, and a few observations necessary to explain that and some of the cases.

I do not know whether your view extends to official papers of mine which have been published. Many of these would be like old newspapers, materials for future historians, but no longer interesting to the readers of the day. They would con-sist of reports, correspondences, messages, answers to ad-dresses; a few of my reports while Secretary of State, might perhaps be read by some as essays on abstract subjects. Such as the report on measures, weights and coins, on the mint, on the fisheries, on commerce, on the use of distilled sea-water, &c. The correspondences with the British and French minis-ters, Hammond and Genet, were published by Congress. The messages to Congress, which might have been interesting at the moment, would scarcely be read a second time, and an-swers to addresses are hardly read a first time.

So that on a review of these various materials, I see nothing encouraging a printer to a re-publication of them. They would probably be bought by those only who are in the habit of preserving State papers, and who are not many.

I say nothing of numerous draughts of reports, resolutions, declarations, &c., drawn as a Member of Congress or of the Legislature of Virginia, such as the Declaration of Indepen-dence, Report on the Money Mint of the United States, the act of religious freedom, &c., &c.; these having become the acts of public bodies, there can be no personal claim to them, and they would no more find readers now, than the journals and statute books in which they are deposited.

I have presented this general view of the subjects which might have been within the scope of your contemplation, that they might be correctly estimated before any final decision.

They belong mostly to a class of papers not calculated for popular reading, and not likely to offer profit, or even indemnification to the re-publisher. Submitting it to your consideration, I tender you my salutations and respects.

INDIAN VOCABULARIES

To Dr. Benjamin S. Barton

Monticello, September 21, 1809

DEAR SIR,—I received last night your favor of the 14th, and would with all possible pleasure have communicated to you any part or the whole of the Indian vocabularies which I had collected, but an irreparable misfortune has deprived me of them. I have now been thirty years availing myself of every possible opportunity of procuring Indian vocabularies to the same set of words: my opportunities were probably better than will ever occur again to any person having the same desire. I had collected about fifty, and had digested most of them in collateral columns, and meant to have printed them the last year of my stay in Washington. But not having yet digested Captain Lewis's collection, nor having leisure then to do it, I put it off till I should return home. The whole, as well digest as originals, were packed in a trunk of stationary, and sent round by water with about thirty other packages of my effects, from Washington, and while ascending James river, this package, on account of its weight and presumed precious contents, was singled out and stolen. The thief being disappointed on opening it, threw into the river all its contents, of which he thought he could make no use. Among these were the whole of the vocabularies. Some leaves floated ashore and were found in the mud; but these were very few, and so defaced by the mud and water that no general use can ever be made of them. On the receipt of your letter I turned to them, and was very happy to find, that the only morsel of an original vocabulary among them, was Captain Lewis's of the Pani language, of which you say you have not one word. I therefore inclose it to you, as it is, and a little fragment of some other, which I see is in his hand writing, but no indication remains on it of what language it is. It is a specimen of the condition of the little which was recovered. I am the more concerned at this accident, as of the two hundred and fifty words of my vocabularies, and the one hundred and thirty words of the great Russian vocabularies of the languages of the other quarters of the globe, severty-three were common to both, and would have furnished materials for a comparison from which something might have resulted. Although I believe no general use can ever be made of the wrecks of my loss, yet I will ask the return of the Pani vocabulary when you are done with it. Perhaps I may make another attempt to collect, although I am too old to expect to make much progress in it.

I learn, with pleasure, your acquisition of the pamphlet on the astronomy of the antient Mexicans. If it be antient and genuine, or modern and rational, it will be of real value. It is one of the most interesting countries of our hemisphere, and merits every attention.

I am thankful for your kind offer of sending the original Spanish for my perusal. But I think it a pity to trust it to the accidents of the post, and whenever you publish the translation, I shall be satisfied to read that which shall be given by your translator, who is, I am sure, a greater adept in the language than I am.

Accept the assurances of my great esteem and respect.

AMERICAN QUAKERISM
To Samuel Kercheval

Monticello, January 19, 1810

SIR,—Yours of the 7th instant has been duly received, with the pamphlet inclosed, for which I return you my thanks. Nothing can be more exactly and seriously true than what is there stated; that but a short time elapsed after the death of the great reformer of the Jewish religion, before his principles were departed from by those who professed to be his special servants, and perverted into an engine for enslaving mankind, and aggrandising their oppressors in Church and State; that the purest system of morals ever before preached to man, has been adulterated and sophisticated by artificial constructions, into a mere contrivance to filch wealth and power to themselves; that rational men not being able to swallow their impious heresies, in order to force them down their throats, they raise the hue and cry of infidelity, while themselves are the greatest obstacles to the advancement of the real doctrines of Jesus, and do in fact constitute the real Anti-Christ.

You expect that your book will have some effect on the prejudices which the society of Friends entertain against the present and late administrations. In this I think you will be disappointed. The Friends are men, formed with the same passions, and swayed by the same natural principles and prejudices as others. In cases where the passions are neutral, men will display their respect for the religious *professions* of their sect. But where their passions are enlisted, these *professions* are no obstacle. You observe very truly, that both the late and present administration conducted the government on principles *professed* by the Friends. Our efforts to preserve peace, our measures as to the Indians, as to slavery, as to religious freedom, were all in consonance with their *professions*. Yet I never expected we should get a vote from them, and in this I was neither deceived nor disappointed. There is no riddle in this, to those who do not suffer themselves to be duped by the *professions* of religious sectaries. The theory of American Quakerism is a very obvious one. The mother society is in England. Its members are English by birth and residence, devoted to their own country, as good citizens ought to be. The Quakers of these States are colonies or filiations from the mother society, to whom that society sends its yearly lessons. On these the filiated societies model their opinions, their conduct, their passions and attachments. A Quaker is, essentially, an Englishman, in whatever part of the earth he is born or lives. The outrages of Great Britain on our navigation and commerce, have kept us in perpetual bickerings with her. The Quakers here have taken side against their own government; not on their *profession* of peace, for they saw that peace was our object also; but from devotion to the views of the mother society. In 1797 and 8, when an administration sought war with France, the Quakers were the most clamorous for war.

Their principle of peace, as a secondary one, yielded to the primary one of adherence to the Friends in England, and what was patriotism in the original became treason in the copy. On that occasion, they obliged their good old leader, Mr. Pemberton, to erase his name from a petition to Congress, against war, which had been delivered to a Representative of Pennsylvania, a member of the late and present administration. He accordingly permitted the old gentleman to erase his name. You must not, therefore, expect that your book will have any more effect on the society of Friends here, than on the English merchants settled among us. I apply this to the Friends in general, not universally. I know individuals among them as good patriots as we have.

I thank you for the kind wishes and sentiments towards myself, expressed in your letter, and sincerely wish to yourself the blessings of health and happiness.

NEPOTISM AND THE REPUBLIC
To John Garland Jefferson

Monticello, January 25, 1810

DEAR SIR,—Your favor of December 12th was long coming to hand. I am much concerned to learn that any disagreeable impression was made on your mind, by the circumstances which are the subject of your letter. Permit me first to explain the principles which I had laid down for my own observance. In a government like ours, it is the duty of the Chief Magistrate, in order to enable himself to do all the good which his station requires, to endeavor, by all honorable means, to unite in himself the confidence of the whole people. This alone, in any case where the energy of the nation is required, can produce a union of the powers of the whole, and point them in a single direction, as if all constituted but one body and one mind, and this alone can render a weaker nation unconquerable by a stronger one. Towards acquiring the confidence of the people, the very first measure is to satisfy them of his disinterestedness, and that he is directing their affairs with a single eye to their good, and not to build up fortunes for himself and family, and especially, that the officers appointed to transact their business, are appointed because they are the fittest men, not because they are his relations. So prone are they to suspicion, that where a President appoints a relation of his own, however worthy, they will believe that favor and not merit was the motive. I therefore laid it down as a law of conduct for myself, never to give an appointment to a relation. Had I felt any hesitation in adopting this rule, examples were not wanting to admonish me what to do and what to avoid. Still, the expression of your willingness to act in any office for which you were qualified, could not be imputed to you as blame. It would not readily occur that a person qualified for office ought to be rejected merely because he was related to the President, and the then more recent examples favored the other opinion. In this light I considered the case as presenting itself to your mind, and that the application might be perfectly justifiable on your part, while, for reasons occurring to none perhaps, but the person in my situation, the public interest might render it unadvisable. Of this, however, be assured that I consider the proposition as innocent on your part, and that it never lessened my esteem for you, or the interest I felt in your welfare.

My stay in Amelia was too short, (only twenty-four hours,) to expect the pleasure of seeing you there. It would be a happiness to me any where, but especially here, from whence I am rarely absent. I am leading a life of considerable activity as a farmer, reading little and writing less. Something pursued with ardor is necessary to guard us from the *tedium-vitæ,* and the active pursuits lessen most our sense of the infirmities of age. That to the health of youth you may add an old age of vigor, is the sincere prayer of

Yours, affectionately.

PROSTRATION OF REASON

To Cæsar A. Rodney

Monticello, February 10, 1810

MY DEAR SIR,—I have to thank you for your favor of the 31st ultimo, which is just now received. It has been peculiarly unfortunate for us, personally, that the portion in the history of mankind, at which we were called to take a share in the direction of their affairs, was such an one as history has never before presented. At any other period, the even-handed justice we have observed towards all nations, the efforts we have made to merit their esteem by every act which candor or liberality could exercise, would have preserved our peace, and secured the unqualified confidence of all other nations in our faith and probity. But the hurricane which is now blasting the world, physical and moral, has prostrated all the mounds of reason as well as right. All those calculations which, at any other period, would have been deemed honorable, of the existence of a moral sense in man, individually or associated, of the connection which the laws of nature have established between his duties and his interests, of a regard for honest fame and the esteem of our fellow men, have been a matter of reproach on us, as evidences of imbecility. As if it could be a folly for an honest man to suppose that others could be honest also, when it is their interest to be so. And when is this state of things to end? The death of Bonaparte would, to be sure, remove the first and chiefest apostle of the desolation of men and morals, and might withdraw the scourge of the land. But what is to restore order and safety on the ocean? The death of George III? Not at all. He is only stupid; and his ministers, however weak and profligate in morals, are ephemeral. But his nation is permanent, and it is that which is the tyrant of the ocean. The principle that force is right, is become the principle of the nation itself. They would not permit an honest minister, were accident to bring such an one into power, to relax their system of lawless piracy. These were the difficulties when I was with you. I know they are not lessened, and I pity you.

It is a blessing, however, that our people are reasonable; that they are kept so well informed of the state of things as to judge for themselves, to see the true sources of their difficulties, and to maintain their confidence undiminished in the wisdom and integrity of their functionaries. *Macte virtute* therefore. Continue to go straight forward, pursuing always that which is right, as the only clue which can lead us out of the labyrinth. Let nothing be spared of either reason or passion, to preserve the public confidence entire, as the only rock of our safety. In times of peace the people look most to their representatives; but in war, to the executive solely. It is visible that their confidence is even now veering in that direction; that they are looking to the executive to give the proper direction to their affairs, with a confidence as auspicious as it is well founded.

I avail myself of this, the first occasion of writing to you, to express all the depth of my affection for you; the sense I entertain of your faithful co-operation in my late labors, and the debt I owe for the valuable aid I received from you. Though separated from my fellow laborers in place and pursuit, my affections are with you all, and I offer daily prayers that ye love one another, as I love you. God bless you.

"THE BOOK OF KINGS"

To Governor John Langdon

Monticello, March 5, 1810

Your letter, my dear friend, of the 18th ultimo, comes like the refreshing dews of the evening on a thirsty soil. It recalls antient as well as recent recollections, very dear to my heart. For five and thirty years we have walked together through a land of tribulations. Yet these have passed away, and so, I trust, will those of the present day. The toryism with which we struggled in '77, differed but in name from the federalism of '99, with which we struggled also; and the Anglicism of 1808, against which we are now struggling, is but the same thing still, in another form. It is a longing for a King, and an English King rather than any other. This is the true source of their sorrows and wailings.

The fear that Buonaparte will come over to us and conquer us also, is too chimerical to be genuine. Supposing him to have finished Spain and Portugal, he has yet England and Russia to subdue. The maxim of war was never sounder than in this case, not to leave an enemy in the rear; and especially where an insurrectionary flame is known to be under the embers, merely smothered, and ready to burst at every point.

These two subdued, (and surely the Anglomen will not think the conquest of England alone a short work) antient Greece and Macedonia, the cradle of Alexander, his prototype, and Constantinople, the seat of empire for the world, would glitter more in his eye than our bleak mountains and rugged forests. Egypt, too, and the golden apples of Mauritania, have for more than half a century fixed the longing eyes of France; and with Syria, you know, he has an old affront to wipe out. Then come 'Pontus and Galatia, Cappadocia, Asia and Bithynia,' the fine countries on the Euphrates and Tigris, the Oxus and Indus, and all beyond the Hyphasis, which bounded the glories of his Macedonian rival; with the invitations of his new British subjects on the banks of the Ganges, whom, after receiving under his protection the mother country, he cannot refuse to visit. When all this is done and settled, and nothing of the old world remains unsubdued, he may turn to the new one. But will he attack us first, from whom he will get but hard knocks and no money? Or will he first lay hold of the gold and silver of Mexico and Peru, and the diamonds of Brazil? A *republican* Emperor, from his affection to republics, independent of motives of expediency, must grant to ours the Cyclop's boon of being the last devoured. While all this is doing, we are to suppose the chapter of accidents read out, and that nothing can happen to cut short or to disturb his enterprises.

But the Anglomen, it seems, have found out a much safer dependance, than all these chances of death or disappointment. That is, that we should first let England plunder us, as she has been doing for years, for fear Buonaparte should do it; and then ally ourselves with her, and enter into the war. A conqueror, whose career England could not arrest when aided by Russia, Austria, Prussia, Sweden, Spain and Portugal, she is now to destroy, with all these on his side, by the aid of the United States alone. This, indeed, is making us a mighty people. And what is to be our security, that when embarked for her in the war, she will not make a separate peace, and leave us in the lurch? Her good faith! The faith of a nation of merchants! The *Punica fides* of modern Carthage! Of the friend and protectress of Copenhagen! Of the nation who never admitted a chapter of morality into her political code! And is now boldly avowing, that whatever power can make hers, is hers of right. Money, and not morality, is the principle of commerce and commercial nations. But, in addition to this, the nature of the English government forbids, of itself, reliance on her engagements; and it is well known she has been the least faithful to her alliances of any nation of Europe, since the period of her history wherein she has been distinguished for her commerce and corruption, that is to say, under the houses of Stuart and Brunswick. To Portugal alone she has steadily adhered, because, by her Methuin treaty she had made it a colony, and one of the most valuable to her. It may be asked, what, in the nature of her government, unfits England for the observation of moral duties? In the first place, her King is a cypher; his only function being to name the oligarchy which is to govern her. The parliament is, by corruption, the mere instrument of the will of the administration. The real power and property in the government is in the great aristocratical families of the nation. The nest of office being too small for all of them to cuddle into at once, the contest is eternal, which shall crowd the other out. For this purpose, they are divided into two parties, the Ins and the Outs, so equal in weight that a small matter turns the balance. To keep themselves in, when they are in, every stratagem must be practised, every artifice used which may flatter the pride, the passions or power of the nation. Justice, honor, faith, must yield to the necessity of keeping themselves in place. The question whether a measure is moral, is never asked; but whether it will nourish the avarice of their merchants, or the piratical spirit of their navy, or produce any other effect which may strengthen them in their places. As to engagements, however positive, entered into by the predecessors of the Ins, why, they were their enemies; they did every thing which was wrong; and to reverse every thing they did, must, therefore, be right. This is the true character of the English government in practice, however different its theory; and it presents the singular phenomenon of a nation, the individuals of which are as faithful to their private engagements and duties, as honorable, as worthy, as those of any nation on earth, and whose government is yet the most unprincipled at this day known. In an absolute government there can be no such equiponderant parties. The despot is the government. His power suppressing all opposition, maintains his ministers firm in their places. What he has contracted, therefore, through them, he has the power to observe with good faith; and he identifies his own honor and faith with that of his nation.

When I observed, however, that the King of England was a cypher, I did not mean to confine the observation to the mere individual now on that throne. The practice of Kings marrying only into the families of Kings, has been that of Europe for some centuries. Now, take any race of animals, confine them in idleness and inaction, whether in a stye, a stable, or a state room, pamper them with high diet, gratify all their sexual appetites, immerse them in sensualities, nourish their passions, let every thing bend before them, and banish whatever might lead them to think, and in a few generations they become all body and no mind: and this, too, by a law of nature, by that very law by which we are in the constant practice of changing the characters and propensities of the animals we raise for our own purposes. Such is the regimen in raising Kings, and in this way they have gone on for centuries. While in Europe, I often amused myself with contemplating the characters of the then reigning sovereigns of Europe. Louis the XVI. was a fool, of my own knowledge, and in despite of the answers made for him at his trial. The King of Spain was a fool, and of Naples the same. They passed their lives in hunting, and despatched two couriers a week, one thousand miles, to let each other know what game they had killed the preceding days. The King of Sardinia was a fool. All these were Bourbons. The Queen of Portugal, a Braganza, was an idiot by nature. And so was the King of Denmark. Their sons, as regents, exercised the powers of government. The King of Prussia, successor to the great Frederick, was a mere hog in body as well as in mind. Gustavus of Sweden, and Joseph of Austria, were really crazy, and George of England you know was in a straight waistcoat. There remained, then, none but old Catherine, who had been too lately picked up to have lost her common sense. In this state Buonaparte found Europe; and it was this state of its rulers which lost it with scarce a struggle. These animals had be-

come without mind and powerless; and so will every hereditary monarch be after a few generations. Alexander, the
grandson of Catherine, is as yet an exception. He is able to
hold his own. But he is only of the third generation. His race
is not yet worn out. And so endeth the book of Kings, from
all of whom the Lord deliver us, and have you, my friend,
and all such good men and true, in his holy keeping.

"AN ACADEMICAL VILLAGE"

To Messrs. Hugh L. White and Others

Monticello, May 6, 1810

GENTLEMEN,—I received, some time ago, your letter of February 28th, covering a printed scheme of a lottery for the benefit of the East Tennessee College, and proposing to send
tickets to me to be disposed of. It would be impossible for
them to come to a more inefficient hand. I rarely go from
home, and consequently see but a few neighbors and friends,
who occasionally call on me. And having myself made it a rule
never to engage in a lottery or any other adventure of mere
chance, I can, with the less candor or effect, urge it on others,
however laudable or desirable its object may be. No one more
sincerely wishes the spread of information among mankind
than I do, and none has greater confidence in its effect towards supporting free and good government. I am sincerely
rejoiced, therefore, to find that so excellent a fund has been
provided for this noble purpose in Tennessee. Fifty-thousand
dollars placed in a safe bank, will give four thousand dollars
a year, and even without other aid, must soon accomplish
buildings sufficient for the object in its early stage. I consider
the common plan followed in this country, but not in others,
of making one large and expensive building, as unfortunately
erroneous. It is infinitely better to erect a small and separate
lodge for each separate professorship, with only a hall below
for his class, and two chambers above for himself; joining
these lodges by barracks for a certain portion of the students,
opening into a covered way to give a dry communication between all the schools. The whole of these arranged around an

open square of grass and trees, would make it, what it should be in fact, an academical village, instead of a large and common den of noise, of filth and of fetid air. It would afford that quiet retirement so friendly to study, and lessen the dangers of fire, infection and tumult. Every professor would be the police officer of the students adjacent to his own lodge, which should include those of his own class of preference, and might be at the head of their table, if, as I suppose, it can be reconciled with the necessary economy to dine them in smaller and separate parties, rather than in a large and common mess. These separate buildings, too, might be erected successively and occasionally, as the number of professorships and students should be increased, or the funds become competent.

I pray you to pardon me if I have stepped aside into the province of counsel; but much observation and reflection on these institutions have long convinced me that the large and crowded buildings in which youths are pent up, are equally unfriendly to health, to study, to manners, morals and order; and, believing the plan I suggest to be more promotive of these, and peculiarly adapted to the slender beginnings and progressive growth of our institutions, I hoped you would pardon the presumption, in consideration of the motive which was suggested by the difficulty expressed in your letter, of procuring funds for erecting the building. But, on whatever plan you proceed, I wish it every possible success, and to yourselves the reward of esteem, respect and gratitude due to those who devote their time and efforts to render the youths of every successive age fit governors for the next. To these accept, in addition, the assurances of mine.

A PLAN FOR THE MERINOS

To the President of the United States
(JAMES MADISON)

Monticello, May 13, 1810

DEAR SIR,—I thank you for your promised attention to my portion of the Merinos, and if there be any expenses of trans-

portation, &c., and you will be so good as to advance my
portion of them with yours and notify the amount, it shall be
promptly remitted. What shall we do with them? I have been
so disgusted with the scandalous extortions lately practised in
the sale of these animals, and with the description of patriotism and praise to the sellers, as if the thousands of dollars
apiece they have not been ashamed to receive were not reward
enough, that I am disposed to consider as right, whatever is
the reverse of what they have done. Since fortune has put the
occasion upon us, is it not incumbent upon us so to dispense
this benefit to the farmers of our country, as to put to shame
those who, forgetting their own wealth and the honest simplicity of the farmers, have thought them fit objects of the
shaving art, and to excite, by a better example, the condemnation due to theirs? No sentiment is more acknowledged in
the family of Agriculturists than that the few who can afford
it should incur the risk and expense of all new improvements,
and give the benefit freely to the many of more restricted circumstances. The question then recurs, What are we to do
with them? I shall be willing to concur with you in any plan
you shall approve, and in order that we may have some proposition to begin upon, I will throw out a first idea, to be
modified or postponed to whatever you shall think better.

Give all the full-blooded males we can raise to the different
counties of our State, one to each, as fast as we can furnish
them. And as there must be some rule of priority for the distribution, let us begin with our own counties, which are contiguous and nearly central to the State, and proceed, circle
after circle, till we have given a ram to every county. This will
take about seven years, if we add to the full descendants those
which will have past to the fourth generation from common
ewes, to make the benefit of a single male as general as practicable to the county, we may ask some known character in
each county to have a small society formed which shall receive
the animal and prescribe rules for his care and government.
We should retain ourselves all the full-blooded ewes, that they
may enable us the sooner to furnish a male to every county.
When all shall have been provided with rams, we may, in a
year or two more, be in a condition to give an ewe also to
every county, if it be thought necessary. But I suppose it will

not, as four generations from their full-blooded ram will give them the pure race from common ewes.

In the meantime we shall not be without a profit indemnifying our trouble and expense. For if of our present stock of common ewes, we place with the ram as many as he may be competent to, suppose fifty, we may sell the male lambs of every year for such reasonable price as in addition to the wool, will pay for the maintenance of the flock. The first year they will be half bloods, the second three-quarters, the third seven-eights, and the fourth full-blooded, if we take care in selling annually half the ewes also, to keep those of highest blood, this will be a fund for kindnesses to our friends, as well as for indemnification to ourselves; and our whole State may thus, from this small stock, so dispersed, be filled in a very few years with this valuable race, and more satisfaction result to ourselves than money ever administered to the bosom of a shaver. There will be danger that what is here proposed, though but an act of ordinary duty, may be perverted into one of ostentation, but malice will always find bad motives for good actions. Shall we therefore never do good? It may also be used to commit us with those on whose example it will truly be a reproof. We may guard against this perhaps by a proper reserve, developing our purpose only by its execution.

> Vive, vale, et siquid novisti rectius istis
> Candidus imperti sinon, his ulere mecum.

SCHOOLS AND "LITTLE REPUBLICS"
To John Tyler

Monticello, May 26, 1810

DEAR SIR,—Your friendly letter of the 12th has been duly received. Although I have laid it down as a law to myself, never to embarrass the President with my solicitations, and have not till now broken through it, yet I have made a part of your letter the subject of one to him, and have done it with all my heart, and in the full belief that I serve him and the public in urging that appointment. We have long enough suffered under the base prostitution of law to party passions in one judge, and the imbecility of another. In the hands of one the law is nothing more than an ambiguous text, to be explained by his sophistry into any meaning which may subserve his personal malice. Nor can any milk-and-water associate maintain his own dependance, and by a firm pursuance of what the law really is, extend its protection to the citizens or the public. I believe you will do it, and where you cannot induce your colleague to do what is right, you will be firm enough to hinder him from doing what is wrong, and by opposing sense to sophistry, leave the juries free to follow their own judgment.

I have long lamented with you the depreciation of law science. The opinion seems to be that Blackstone is to us what the Alcoran is to the Mahometans, that everything which is necessary is in him, and what is not in him is not necessary. I still lend my counsel and books to such young students as will fix themselves in the neighborhood. Coke's institutes and reports are their first, and Blackstone their last book, after an intermediate course of two or three years. It is nothing more than an elegant digest of what they will then have acquired from the real fountains of the law. Now men are born scholars, lawyers, doctors; in our day this was confined to poets. You wish to see me again in the legislature, but this is impossible; my mind is now so dissolved in tranquillity, that it can never again encounter a contentious assembly; the habits of thinking and speaking off-hand, after a disuse of five and twenty years, have given place to the slower process of the pen. I have indeed two great measures at heart, without which no republic can maintain itself in strength. 1. That of general education, to enable every man to judge for himself what will secure or endanger his freedom. 2. To divide every county into hundreds, of such size that all the children of each will be within reach of a central school in it. But this division looks to many other fundamental provisions. Every hundred, besides a school, should have a justice of the peace, a constable and a captain of militia. These officers, or some others within the hundred, should be a corporation to manage all its concerns, to take care of its roads, its poor, and its police by patrols, &c., (as the select men of the Eastern townships.)

Every hundred should elect one or two jurors to serve where requisite, and all other elections should be made in the hundreds separately, and the votes of all the hundreds be brought together. Our present Captaincies might be declared hundreds for the present, with a power to the courts to alter them occasionally. These little republics would be the main strength of the great one. We owe to them the vigor given to our revolution in its commencement in the Eastern States, and by them the Eastern States were enabled to repeal the embargo in opposition to the Middle, Southern and Western States, and their large and lubberly division into counties which can never be assembled. General orders are given out from a centre to the foreman of every hundred, as to the sergeants of an army, and the whole nation is thrown into energetic action, in the same direction in one instant and as one man, and becomes absolutely irresistible. Could I once see this I should consider it as the dawn of the salvation of the republic, and say with old Simeon, "nunc dimittas Domine." But our children will be as wise as we are, and will establish in the fulness of time those things not yet ripe for establishment. So be it, and to yourself health, happiness and long life.

HUME AND MONTESQUIEU
To William Duane

Monticello, August 12, 1810

SIR,—Your letter of July 16th has been duly received, with the paper it enclosed, for which accept my thanks, and especially for the kind sentiments expressed towards myself. These testimonies of approbation, and friendly remembrance, are the highest gratifications I can receive from any, and especially from those in whose principles and zeal for the public good I have confidence. Of that confidence in yourself the military appointment to which you allude was sufficient proof, as it was made, not on the recommendations of others, but on our own knowledge of your principles and qualifications. While I cherish with feeling the recollections of my friends, I banish from my mind all political animosities which might disturb its tranquillity, or the happiness I derive from my present pursuits. I have thought it among the most fortunate circumstances of my late administration that, during its eight years continuance, it was conducted with a cordiality and harmony among all the members, which never were ruffled on any, the greatest or smallest occasion. I left my brethren with sentiments of sincere affection and friendship, so rooted in the uniform tenor of a long and intimate intercourse, that the evidence of my own senses alone ought to be permitted to shake them. Anxious, in my retirement, to enjoy undisturbed repose, my knowledge of my successor and late coadjutors, and my entire confidence in their wisdom and integrity, were assurances to me that I might sleep in security with such watchmen at the helm, and that whatever difficulties and dangers should assail our course, they would do what could be done to avoid or surmount them. In this confidence I envelope myself, and hope to slumber on to my last sleep. And should difficulties occur which they cannot avert, if we follow them in phalanx, we shall surmount them without danger.

I have been long intending to write to you as one of the associated company for printing useful works.

Our laws, language, religion, politics and manners are so deeply laid in English foundations, that we shall never cease to consider their history as a part of ours, and to study ours in that as its origin. Every one knows that judicious matter and charms of style have rendered Hume's history the manual of every student. I remember well the enthusiasm with which I devoured it when young, and the length of time, the research and reflection which were necessary to eradicate the poison it had instilled into my mind. It was unfortunate that he first took up the history of the Stuarts, became their apologist, and advocated all their enormities. To support his work, when done, he went back to the Tudors, and so selected and arranged the materials of their history as to present their arbitrary acts only, as the genuine samples of the constitutional power of the crown, and, still writing backwards, he then reverted to the early history, and wrote the Saxon and Norman periods with the same perverted view. Although all this is known, he still continues to be put into the hands of all our young people, and to infect them with the poison of his own principles of government. It is this book which has undermined the free principles of the English government, has persuaded readers of all classes that these were usurpations on the legitimate and salutary rights of the crown, and has spread universal toryism over the land. And the book will still continue to be read here as well as there. Baxter, one of Horne Tooke's associates in persecution, has hit on the only remedy the evil admits. He has taken Hume's work, corrected in the text his misrepresentations, supplied the truths which he suppressed, and yet has given the mass of the work in Hume's own words. And it is wonderful how little interpolation has been necessary to make it a sound history, and to justify what should have been its title, to wit, "Hume's history of England abridged and rendered faithful to fact and principle." I cannot say that his amendments are either in matter or manner in the fine style of Hume. Yet they are often unperceived, and occupy so little of the whole work as not to depreciate it. Unfortunately he has *abridged* Hume, by leaving out all the less important details. It is thus reduced to about one half its original size. He has also continued the history, but very summarily, to 1801. The whole work is of 834 quarto pages, printed close, of which the continuation occupies 283. I have read but little of this part. As far as I can judge from that little, it is a mere chronicle, offering nothing profound. This work is so unpopular, so distasteful to the present Tory palates and principles of England, that I believe it has never reached a second edition. I have often inquired for it in our book shops, but never could find a copy in them, and I think it possible the one I imported may be the only one in America. Can we not have it re-printed here? It would be about four volumes 8vo.

I have another enterprise to propose for some good printer. I have in my possession a MS. work in French, confided to me by a friend, whose name alone would give it celebrity were it permitted to be mentioned. But considerations insuperable forbid that. It is a Commentary and Review of Montesquieu's Spirit of Laws. The history of that work is well known. He had been a great reader, and had commonplaced everything he read. At length he wished to undertake some work into which he could bring his whole commonplace

book in a digested form. He fixed on the subject of his Spirit
of Laws, and wrote the book. He consulted his friend Helvetius about publishing it, who strongly dissuaded it. He
published it, however, and the world did not confirm Helvetius' opinion. Still, every man who reflects as he reads, has
considered it as a book of paradoxes; having, indeed, much
of truth and sound principle, but abounding also with inconsistencies, apochryphal facts and false inferences. It is a correction of these which has been executed in the work I
mention, by way of commentary and review; not by criticis-
ing words or sentences, but by taking a book at a time, considering its general scope, and proceeding to confirm or
confute it. And much of confutation there is, and of substitution of true for false principle, and the true principle is ever
that of republicanism. I will not venture to say that every sentiment in the book will be approved, because, being in manuscript, and the French characters, I have not read the whole,
but so much only as might enable me to estimate the soundness of the author's way of viewing his subject; and, judging
from that which I have read, I infer with confidence that we
shall find the work generally worthy of our high approbation,
and that it everywhere maintains the preëminence of representative government, by showing that its foundations are laid in
reason, in right, and in general good. I had expected this
from my knowledge of the other writings of the author,
which have always a precision rarely to be met with. But to
give you an idea of the manner of its execution, I translate
and enclose his commentary on Montesquieu's eleventh book,
which contains the division of the work. I wish I could have
added his review at the close of the twelve first books, as this
would give a more complete idea of the extraordinary merit
of the work. But it is too long to be copied. I add from it,
however, a few extracts of his reviews of some of the books,
as specimens of his plan and principles. If printed in French,
it would be of about 180 pages 8vo, or 23 sheets. If any one
will undertake to have it translated and printed on their own
account, I will send on the MS. by post, and they can take
the copyright as of an original work, which it ought to be
understood to be. I am anxious it should be ably translated
by some one who possesses style as well as capacity to do

justice to abstruse conceptions. I would even undertake to revise the translation if required. The original sheets must be returned to me, and I should wish the work to be executed with as little delay as possible.

I close this long letter with assurances of my great esteem and respect.

A LAW BEYOND THE CONSTITUTION
To John B. Colvin

Monticello, September 20, 1810

SIR,—Your favor of the 14th has been duly received, and I have to thank you for the many obliging things respecting myself which are said in it. If I have left in the breasts of my fellow citizens a sentiment of satisfaction with my conduct in the transaction of their business, it will soften the pillow of my repose through the residue of life.

The question you propose, whether circumstances do not sometimes occur, which make it a duty in officers of high trust, to assume authorities beyond the law, is easy of solution in principle, but sometimes embarrassing in practice. A strict observance of the written laws is doubtless *one* of the high duties of a good citizen, but it is not *the highest*. The laws of necessity, of self-preservation, of saving our country when in danger, are of higher obligation. To lose our country by a scrupulous adherence to written law, would be to lose the law itself, with life, liberty, property and all those who are enjoying them with us; thus absurdly sacrificing the end to the means. When, in the battle of Germantown, General Washington's army was annoyed from Chew's house, he did not hesitate to plant his cannon against it, although the property of a citizen. When he besieged Yorktown, he leveled the suburbs, feeling that the laws of property must be postponed to the safety of the nation. While the army was before York, the Governor of Virginia took horses, carriages, provisions and even men by force, to enable that army to stay together till it could master the public enemy; and he was justified. A ship at sea in distress for provisions, meets another having abundance, yet refusing a supply; the law of self-preservation authorizes the distressed to take a supply by force. In all these cases, the unwritten laws of necessity, of self-preservation, and of the public safety, control the written laws of *meum* and *tuum*. Further to exemplify the principle, I will state an hypothetical case. Suppose it had been made known to the Executive of the Union in the autumn of 1805, that we might have the Floridas for a reasonable sum, that that sum had not indeed been so appropriated by law, but that Congress were to meet within three weeks, and might appropriate it on the first or second day of their session. Ought he, for so great an advantage to his country, to have risked himself by transcending the law and making the purchase? The public advantage offered, in this supposed case, was indeed immense; but a reverence for law, and the probability that the advantage might still be *legally* accomplished by a delay of only three weeks, were powerful reasons against hazarding the act. But suppose it foreseen that a John Randolph would find means to protract the proceeding on it by Congress, until the ensuing spring, by which time new circumstances would change the mind of the other party. Ought the Executive, in that case, and with that foreknowledge, to have secured the good to his country, and to have trusted to their justice for the transgression of the law? I think he ought, and that the act would have been approved. After the affair of the Chesapeake, we thought war a very possible result. Our magazines were illy provided with some necessary articles, nor had any appropriations been made for their purchase. We ventured, however, to provide them, and to place our country in safety; and stating the case to Congress, they sanctioned the act.

To proceed to the conspiracy of Burr, and particularly to General Wilkinson's situation in New Orleans. In judging this case, we are bound to consider the state of the information, correct and incorrect, which he then possessed. He expected Burr and his band from above, a British fleet from below, and he knew there was a formidable conspiracy within the city. Under these circumstances, was he justifiable, 1st, in seizing notorious conspirators? On this there can be but two opinions; one, of the guilty and their accomplices; the other, that of all honest men. 2d. In sending them to the seat of government, when the written law gave them a right to trial in the territory? The danger of their rescue, of their continuing their machinations, the tardiness and weakness of the law, apathy of the judges, active patronage of the whole tribe of lawyers, unknown disposition of the juries, an hourly expectation of the enemy, salvation of the city, and of the Union itself, which would have been convulsed to its centre, had that conspiracy succeeded; all these constituted a law of necessity and self-preservation, and rendered the *salus populi* supreme over the written law. The officer who is called to act on this superior ground, does indeed risk himself on the justice of the controlling powers of the constitution, and his station makes it his duty to incur that risk. But those controlling powers, and his fellow citizens generally, are bound to judge according to the circumstances under which he acted. They are not to transfer the information of this place or moment to the time and place of his action; but to put themselves into his situation. We knew here that there never was danger of a British fleet from below, and that Burr's band was crushed before it reached the Mississippi. But General Wilkinson's information was very different, and he could act on no other.

From these examples and principles you may see what I think on the question proposed. They do not go to the case of persons charged with petty duties, where consequences are trifling, and time allowed for a legal course, nor to authorize them to take such cases out of the written law. In these, the example of overleaping the law is of greater evil than a strict adherence to its imperfect provisions. It is incumbent on those only who accept of great charges, to risk themselves on great occasions, when the safety of the nation, or some of its very high interests are at stake. An officer is bound to obey orders; yet he would be a bad one who should do it in cases for which they were not intended, and which involved the most important consequences. The line of discrimination between cases may be difficult; but the good officer is bound to draw it at his own peril, and throw himself on the justice of his country and the rectitude of his motives.

I have indulged freer views on this question, on your assurances that they are for your own eye only, and that they will not get into the hands of newswriters. I met their scurrilities without concern, while in pursuit of the great interests with which I was charged. But in my present retirement, no duty forbids my wish for quiet.

Accept the assurances of my esteem and respect.

RELATIONS WITH ADAMS
To Dr. Benjamin Rush

Monticello, January 16, 1811

DEAR SIR,—I had been considering for some days, whether it was not time by a letter, to bring myself to your recollection, when I received your welcome favor of the 2d instant. I had before heard of the heart-rending calamity you mention, and had sincerely sympathized with your afflictions. But I had not made it the subject of a letter, because I knew that condolences were but renewals of grief. Yet I thought, and still think, this is one of the cases wherein we should "not sorrow, even as others who have no hope." I have myself known so many cases of recovery from confirmed insanity, as to reckon it ever among the recoverable diseases. One of them was that of a near relative and namesake of mine, who, after many years of madness of the first degree, became entirely sane, and amused himself to a good old age in keeping school; was an excellent teacher and much valued citizen.

You ask if I have read Hartley? I have not. My present course of life admits less reading than I wish. From breakfast, or noon at latest, to dinner, I am mostly on horseback, attending to my farm or other concerns, which I find healthful to my body, mind and affairs; and the few hours I can pass in my cabinet, are devoured by correspondences; not those with my intimate friends, with whom I delight to interchange sentiments, but with others, who, writing to me on concerns of their own in which I have had an agency, or from motives of mere respect and approbation, are entitled to be answered with respect and a return of good will. My hope is that this obstacle to the delights of retirement, will wear away with the oblivion which follows that, and that I may at length be indulged in those studious pursuits, from which nothing but revolutionary duties would ever have called me.

I shall receive your proposed publication and read it with the pleasure which everything gives me from your pen. Although much of a sceptic in the practice of medicine, I read with pleasure its ingenious theories.

I receive with sensibility your observations on the discontinuance of friendly correspondence between Mr. Adams and myself, and the concern you take in its restoration. This discontinuance has not proceeded from me, nor from the want of sincere desire and of effort on my part, to renew our intercourse. You know the perfect coincidence of principle and of action, in the early part of the Revolution, which produced a high degree of mutual respect and esteem between Mr. Adams and myself. Certainly no man was ever truer than he was, in that day, to those principles of rational republicanism which, after the necessity of throwing off our monarchy, dictated all our efforts in the establishment of a new government. And although he swerved, afterwards, towards the principles of the English constitution, our friendship did not abate on that account. While he was Vice President, and I Secretary of State, I received a letter from President Washington, then at Mount Vernon, desiring me to call together the Heads of departments, and to invite Mr. Adams to join us (which, by-the-bye, was the only instance of that being done) in order to determine on some measure which required despatch; and he desired me to act on it, as decided, without again recurring to him. I invited them to dine with me, and after dinner, sitting at our wine, having settled our question, other conversation came on, in which a collision of opinion arose between Mr. Adams and Colonel Hamilton, on the merits of the British constitution, Mr. Adams giving it as his opinion, that, if some of its defects and abuses were corrected, it would be the most perfect constitution of government ever devised by man. Hamilton, on the contrary, asserted, that with its existing vices, it was the most perfect model of government that could be formed; and that the correction of its vices would render it an impracticable government. And this you may be assured was the real line of difference between the political principles of these two gentlemen. Another incident took place on the same occasion, which will further delineate Mr. Hamilton's political principles. The room being hung around with a collection of the portraits of remarkable men, among them were those of Bacon, Newton and Locke, Hamilton asked me who they were. I told him they were my trinity of the three greatest men the world had ever produced, naming them. He paused for some time: "the greatest man," said he, "that ever lived, was Julius Cæsar." Mr. Adams was honest as a politician, as well as a man; Hamilton honest as a man, but, as a politician, believing in the necessity of either force or corruption to govern men.

You remember the machinery which the federalists played off, about that time, to beat down the friends to the real principles of our constitution, to silence by terror every expression in their favor, to bring us into war with France and alliance with England, and finally to homologize our constitution with that of England. Mr. Adams, you know, was overwhelmed with feverish addresses, dictated by the fear, and often by the pen, of the *bloody buoy*, and was seduced by them into some open indications of his new principles of government, and in fact, was so elated as to mix with his kindness a little superciliousness towards me. Even Mrs. Adams, with all her good sense and prudence, was sensibly flushed. And you recollect the short suspension of our intercourse, and the circumstance which gave rise to it, which you were so good as to bring to an early explanation, and have set to rights, to the cordial satisfaction of us all. The nation at length passed condemnation on the political principles of the federalists, by refusing to continue Mr. Adams in the Presidency. On the day on which we learned in Philadelphia the vote of the city of New York, which it was well known would decide the vote of the State, and that, again, the vote of the Union, I called on Mr. Adams on some official business. He was very sensibly affected, and accosted me with these words: "Well, I understand that you are to beat me in this contest, and I will only say that I will be as faithful a subject as any you will have." "Mr. Adams," said I, "this is no personal contest between you and me. Two systems of principles on the subject of government divide our fellow citizens into two parties. With one of these you concur, and I with the other. As we have been longer on the public stage than most of those now living, our names happen to be more generally known. One of these parties, therefore, has put your name at its head, the other mine. Were we both to die to-day, to-morrow two other names would be in the place of ours, without any change in the motion of the machinery. Its motion is from its principle, not from you or myself." "I believe you are right," said he, "that we are but passive instruments, and should not suffer this matter to affect our personal dispositions." But he did not long retain this just view of the subject. I have always believed that the thousand calumnies which the federalists, in bitterness of heart, and mortification at their ejection, daily invented against me, were carried to him by their busy intriguers, and made some impression. When the election between Burr and myself was kept in suspense by the federalists, and they were mediating to place the President of the Senate at the head of the government, I called on Mr. Adams with a view to have this desperate measure prevented by his negative. He grew warm in an instant, and said with a vehemence he had not used towards me before, "Sir, the event of the election is within your own power. You have only to say you will do justice to the public creditors, maintain the navy, and not disturb those holding offices, and the government will instantly be put into your hands. We know it is the wish of the people it should be so." "Mr. Adams," said I, "I know not what part of my conduct, in either public or private life, can have authorized a doubt of my fidelity to the public engagements. I say, however, I will not come into the government by capitulation. I will not enter on it, but in perfect freedom to follow the dictates of my own judgment." I had before given the same answer to the same intimation from Gouverneur Morris. "Then," said he, "things must take their course." I turned the conversation to something else, and soon took my leave. It was the first time in our lives we had ever parted with anything like dissatisfaction. And then followed those scenes of midnight appointment, which have been condemned by all men. The last day of his political power, the last hours, and even beyond the midnight, were employed in filling all offices, and especially permanent ones, with the bitterest federalists, and providing for me the alternative, either to execute the government by my enemies, whose study it would be to thwart and defeat all my measures, or to incur the odium of such numerous removals from office, as might bear me down. A little time and reflection effaced in my mind this temporary dissatisfaction with Mr. Adams, and restored me to that just estimate of his virtues and passions, which a long acquaintance had enabled me to fix. And my first wish became that of making his retirement easy by any means in my power; for it was understood he was not rich. I suggested to some republican members of the delegation from his State, the giving him, either directly or indirectly, an office, the most lucrative in that State, and then offered to be resigned, if they thought he would not deem it affrontive. They were of opinion he would take great offence at the offer; and more-over, that the body of republicans would consider such a step in the outset as arguing very ill of the course I meant to pursue. I dropped the idea, therefore, but did not cease to wish for some opportunity of renewing our friendly under-standing.

Two or three years after, having had the misfortune to lose a daughter, between whom and Mrs. Adams there had been a considerable attachment, she made it the occasion of writing me a letter, in which, with the tenderest expressions of con-cern at this event, she carefully avoided a single one of friend-ship towards myself, and even concluded it with the wishes "of her who *once* took pleasure in subscribing herself your friend, Abigail Adams." Unpromising as was the complexion of this letter, I determined to make an effort towards remov-ing the cloud from between us. This brought on a correspon-dence which I now enclose for your perusal, after which be so good as to return it to me, as I have never communicated it to any mortal breathing, before. I send it to you, to con-vince you I have not been wanting either in the desire, or the endeavor to remove this misunderstanding. Indeed, I thought it highly disgraceful to us both, as indicating minds not sufficiently elevated to prevent a public competition from affecting our personal friendship. I soon found from the correspondence that conciliation was desperate, and yielding to an intimation in her last letter, I ceased from further explanation. I have the same good opinion of Mr. Adams which I ever had. I know him to be an honest man, an able one with his pen, and he was a powerful advocate on the floor of Congress. He has been alienated from me, by belief in the lying suggestions contrived for electioneering purposes, that I perhaps mixed in the activity and intrigues of the occasion. My most intimate friends can testify that I was perfectly passive. They would sometimes, indeed, tell me what was going on; but no man ever heard me take part in such conversations; and none ever misrepresented Mr. Adams in my presence, without my asserting his just character. With very confidential persons I have doubtless disapproved of the principles and practices of his administration. This was unavoidable. But never with those with whom it could do him any injury. Decency would have required this conduct from me, if disposition had not; and I am satisfied Mr. Adams' conduct was equally honorable towards me. But I think it part of his character to suspect foul play in those of whom he is jealous, and not easily to relinquish his suspicions.

I have gone, my dear friend, into these details, that you might know everything which had passed between us, might be fully possessed of the state of facts and dispositions, and judge for yourself whether they admit a revival of that friendly intercourse for which you are so kindly solicitous. I shall certainly not be wanting in anything on my part which may second your efforts, which will be the easier with me, inasmuch as I do not entertain a sentiment of Mr. Adams, the expression of which could give him reasonable offence. And I submit the whole to yourself, with the assurance, that whatever be the issue, my friendship and respect for yourself will remain unaltered and unalterable.

"THE SEEDS OF CIVILIZATION"

To John Lynch

Monticello, January 21, 1811

SIR,—You have asked my opinion on the proposition of Mrs. Mifflin, to take measures for procuring, on the coast of Africa, an establishment to which the people of color of these

States might, from time to time, be colonized, under the auspices of different governments. Having long ago made up my mind on this subject, I have no hesitation in saying that I have ever thought it the most desirable measure which could be adopted, for gradually drawing off this part of our population, most advantageously for themselves as well as for us. Going from a country possessing all the useful arts, they might be the means of transplanting them among the inhabitants of Africa, and would thus carry back to the country of their origin, the seeds of civilization which might render their sojournment and sufferings here a blessing in the end to that country.

I received, in the first year of my coming into the administration of the General Government, a letter from the Governor of Virginia, (Colonel Monroe,) consulting me, at the request of the Legislature of the State, on the means of procuring some such asylum, to which these people might be occasionally sent. I proposed to him the establishment of Sierra Leone, to which a private company in England had already colonized a number of negroes, and particularly the fugitives from these States during the Revolutionary War; and at the same time suggested, if this could not be obtained, some of the Portuguese possessions in South America, as next most desirable. The subsequent Legislature approving these ideas, I wrote, the ensuing year, 1802, to Mr. King, our Minister in London, to endeavor to negotiate with the Sierra Leone company a reception of such of these people as might be colonized thither. He opened a correspondence with Mr. Wedderburne and Mr. Thornton, secretaries of the company, on the subject, and in 1803 I received through Mr. King the result, which was that the colony was going on, but in a languishing condition; that the funds of the company were likely to fail, as they received no returns of profit to keep them up; that they were therefore in treaty with their government to take the establishment off their hands; but that in no event should they be willing to receive more of these people from the United States, as it was exactly that portion of their settlers which had gone from hence, which, by their idleness and turbulence, had kept the settlement in constant danger of dissolution, which could not have been prevented but for the aid of the Maroon negroes from the West Indies, who were more industrious and orderly than the others, and supported the authority of the government and its laws. I think I learned afterwards that the British Government had taken the colony into its own hands, and I believe it still exists. The effort which I made with Portugal, to obtain an establishment for them within their claims in South America, proved also abortive.

You inquire further, whether I would use my endeavors to procure for such an establishment security against violence from other powers, and particularly from France? Certainly, I shall be willing to do anything I can to give it effect and safety. But I am but a private individual, and could only use endeavors with private individuals; whereas, the National Government can address themselves at once to those of Europe to obtain the desired security, and will unquestionably be ready to exert its influence with those nations for an object so benevolent in itself, and so important to a great portion of its constituents. Indeed, nothing is more to be wished than that the United States would themselves undertake to make such an establishment on the coast of Africa. Exclusive of motives of humanity, the commercial advantages to be derived from it might repay all its expenses. But for this, the national mind is not yet prepared. It may perhaps be doubted whether many of these people would voluntarily consent to such an exchange of situation, and very certain that few of those advanced to a certain age in habits of slavery, would be capable of self-government. This should not, however, discourage the experiment, nor the early trial of it; and the proposition should be made with all the prudent cautions and attentions requisite to reconcile it to the interests, the safety and the prejudices of all parties.

Accept the assurances of my respect and esteem.

THE EXECUTIVE OFFICE
To A. L. C. Destutt de Tracy

Monticello, January 26, 1811

SIR,—The length of time your favor of June the 12th, 1809, was on its way to me, and my absence from home the greater part of the autumn, delayed very much the pleasure which awaited me of reading the packet which accompanied it. I cannot express to you the satisfaction which I received from its perusal. I had, with the world, deemed Montesquieu's work of much merit; but saw in it, with every thinking man, so much of paradox, of false principle and misapplied fact, as to render its value equivocal on the whole. Williams and others had nibbled only at its errors. A radical correction of them, therefore, was a great desideratum. This want is now supplied, and with a depth of thought, precision of idea, of language and of logic, which will force conviction into every mind. I declare to you, Sir, in the spirit of truth and sincerity, that I consider it the most precious gift the present age has received. But what would it have been, had the author, or would the author, take up the whole scheme of Montesquieu's work, and following the correct analysis he has here developed, fill up all its parts according to his sound views of them? Montesquieu's celebrity would be but a small portion of that which would immortalize the author. And with whom? With the rational and high-minded spirits of the present and all future ages. With those whose approbation is both incitement and reward to virtue and ambition. Is then the hope desperate? To what object can the occupation of his future life be devoted so usefully to the world, so splendidly to himself? But I must leave to others who have higher claims on his attention, to press these considerations.

My situation, far in the interior of the country, was not favorable to the object of getting this work translated and printed. Philadelphia is the least distant of the great towns of our States, where there exists any enterprise in this way; and it was not till the spring following the receipt of your letter, that I obtained an arrangement for its execution. The translation is just now completed. The sheets came to me by post, from time to time, for revisal; but not being accompanied by the original, I could not judge of verbal accuracies. I think, however, it is substantially correct, without being an adequate representation of the excellences of the original; as indeed no translation can be. I found it impossible to give it the appearance of an original composition in our language. I therefore think it best to divert inquiries after the author towards a

quarter where he will not be found; and with this view, propose to prefix the prefatory epistle, now enclosed. As soon as
a copy of the work can be had, I will send it to you by duplicate. The secret of the author will be faithfully preserved during his and my joint lives; and those into whose hands my
papers will fall at my death, will be equally worthy of confidence. When the death of the author, or his living consent
shall permit the world to know their benefactor, both his and
my papers will furnish the evidence. In the meantime, the
many important truths the work so solidly establishes, will, I
hope, make it the political rudiment of the young, and manual of our older citizens.

One of its doctrines, indeed, the preference of a plural over
a singular executive, will probably not be assented to here.
When our present government was first established, we had
many doubts on this question, and many leanings towards a
supreme executive council. It happened that at that time the
experiment of such an one was commenced in France, while
the single executive was under trial here. We watched the motions and effects of these two rival plans, with an interest and
anxiety proportioned to the importance of a choice between
them. The experiment in France failed after a short course,
and not from any circumstance peculiar to the times or nation, but from those internal jealousies and dissensions in the
Directory, which will ever arise among men equal in power,
without a principal to decide and control their differences. We
had tried a similar experiment in 1784, by establishing a committee of the States, composed of a member from every State,
then thirteen, to exercise the executive functions during the
recess of Congress. They fell immediately into schisms and
dissensions, which became at length so inveterate as to render
all co-operation among them impracticable: they dissolved
themselves, abandoning the helm of government, and it continued without a head, until Congress met the ensuing winter. This was then imputed to the temper of two or three
individuals; but the wise ascribed it to the nature of man. The
failure of the French Directory, and from the same cause,
seems to have authorized a belief that the form of a plurality,
however promising in theory, is impracticable with men constituted with the ordinary passions. While the tranquil and

steady tenor of our single executive, during a course of twenty-two years of the most tempestuous times the history of the world has ever presented, gives a rational hope that this important problem is at length solved. Aided by the counsels of a cabinet of heads of departments, originally four, but now five, with whom the President consults, either singly or altogether, he has the benefit of their wisdom and information, brings their views to one centre, and produces an unity of action and direction in all the branches of the government. The excellence of this construction of the executive power has already manifested itself here under very opposite circumstances. During the administration of our first President, his cabinet of four members was equally divided by as marked an opposition of principle as monarchism and republicanism could bring into conflict. Had that cabinet been a directory, like positive and negative quantities in algebra, the opposing wills would have balanced each other and produced a state of absolute inaction. But the President heard with calmness the opinions and reasons of each, decided the course to be pursued, and kept the government steadily in it, unaffected by the agitation. The public knew well the dissensions of the cabinet, but never had an uneasy thought on their account, because they knew also they had provided a regulating power which would keep the machine in steady movement. I speak with an intimate knowledge of these scenes, *quorum pars fui*; as I may of others of a character entirely opposite. The third administration, which was of eight years, presented an example of harmony in a cabinet of six person, to which perhaps history has furnished no parallel. There never arose, during the whole time, an instance of an unpleasant thought or word between the members. We sometimes met under differences of opinion, but scarcely ever failed, by conversing and reasoning, so to modify each other's ideas, as to produce an unanimous result. Yet, able and amicable as these members were, I am not certain this would have been the case, had each possessed equal and independent powers. Ill-defined limits of their respective departments, jealousies, trifling at first, but nourished and strengthened by repetition of occasions, intrigues without doors of designing persons to build an importance to themselves on the divisions of others, might,

from small beginnings, have produced persevering opposi-
tions. But the power of decision in the President left no object for internal dissension, and external intrigue was stifled in
embryo by the knowledge which incendiaries possessed, that
no division they could foment would change the course of
the executive power. I am not conscious that my participa-
tions in executive authority have produced any bias in favor
of the single executive; because the parts I have acted have
been in the subordinate, as well as superior stations, and because, if I know myself, what I have felt, and what I have
wished, I know that I have never been so well pleased, as
when I could shift power from my own, on the shoulders of
others; nor have I ever been able to conceive how any rational
being could propose happiness to himself from the exercise of
power over others.

I am still, however, sensible of the solidity of your principle, that, to insure the safety of the public liberty, its depository should be subject to be changed with the greatest ease
possible, and without suspending or disturbing for a moment
the movements of the machine of government. You apprehend that a single executive, with eminence of talent, and
destitution of principle, equal to the object, might, by
usurpation, render his powers hereditary. Yet I think history
furnishes as many examples of a single usurper arising out of
a government by a plurality, as of temporary trusts of power
in a single hand rendered permanent by usurpation. I do not
believe, therefore, that this danger is lessened in the hands of
a plural executive. Perhaps it is greatly increased, by the state
of inefficiency to which they are liable from feuds and divisions among themselves. The conservative body you propose
might be so constituted, as, while it would be an admirable
sedative in a variety of smaller cases, might also be a valuable
sentinel and check on the liberticide views of an ambitious
individual. I am friendly to this idea. But the true barriers of
our liberty in this country are our State governments; and the
wisest conservative power ever contrived by man, is that of
which our Revolution and present government found us possessed. Seventeen distinct States, amalgamated into one as to
their foreign concerns, but single and independent as to their
internal administration, regularly organized with legislature

and governor resting on the choice of the people, and enlightened by a free press, can never be so fascinated by the arts of
one man, as to submit voluntarily to his usurpation. Nor can
they be constrained to it by any force he can possess. While
that may paralyze the single State in which it happens to be
encamped, sixteen others, spread over a country of two thousand miles diameter, rise up on every side, ready organized
for deliberation by a constitutional legislature, and for action
by their governor, constitutionally the commander of the militia of the State, that is to say, of every man in it able to bear
arms; and that militia, too, regularly formed into regiments
and battalions, into infantry, cavalry and artillery, trained under officers general and subordinate, legally appointed, always
in readiness, and to whom they are already in habits of obedience. The republican government of France was lost without a struggle, because the party of *"un et indivisible"* had
prevailed; no provincial organizations existed to which the
people might rally under authority of the laws, the seats of
the directory were virtually vacant, and a small force sufficed
to turn the legislature out of their chamber, and to salute its
leader chief of the nation. But with us, sixteen out of seventeen States rising in mass, under regular organization, and
legal commanders, united in object and action by their Congress, or, if that be in *duresse*, by a special convention, present
such obstacles to an usurper as forever to stifle ambition in
the first conception of that object.

Dangers of another kind might more reasonably be apprehended from this perfect and distinct organization, civil and
military, of the States; to wit, that certain States from local
and occasional discontents, might attempt to secede from the
Union. This is certainly possible; and would be befriended by
this regular organization. But it is not probable that local discontents can spread to such an extent, as to be able to face
the sound parts of so extensive an Union; and if ever they
should reach the majority, they would then become the regular government, acquire the ascendency in Congress, and be
able to redress their own grievances by laws peaceably and
constitutionally passed. And even the States in which local
discontents might engender a commencement of fermentation, would be paralyzed and self-checked by that very divi-

sion into parties into which we have fallen, into which all States must fall wherein men are at liberty to think, speak, and act freely, according to the diversities of their individual conformations, and which are, perhaps, essential to preserve the purity of the government, by the censorship which these parties habitually exercise over each other.

You will read, I am sure, with indulgence, the explanations of the grounds on which I have ventured to form an opinion differing from yours. They prove my respect for your judgment, and diffidence in my own, which have forbidden me to retain, without examination, an opinion questioned by you. Permit me now to render my portion of the general debt of gratitude, by acknowledgements in advance for the singular benefaction which is the subject of this letter, to tender my wishes for the continuance of a life so usefully employed, and to add the assurances of my perfect esteem and respect.

THE LATIN AMERICAN REVOLUTIONS
To Alexander von Humboldt

Monticello, April 14, 1811

MY DEAR BARON,—The interruption of our intercourse with France for some time past, has prevented my writing to you. A conveyance now occurs, by Mr. Barlow or Mr. Warden, both of them going in a public capacity. It is the first safe opportunity offered of acknowledging your favor of September 23d, and the receipt at different times of the IIId part of your valuable work, 2d, 3d, 4th and 5th livraisons, and the IVth part, 2d, 3d, and 4th livraisons, with the *Tableaux de la nature*, and an interesting map of New Spain. For these magnificent and much esteemed favors, accept my sincere thanks. They give us a knowledge of that country more accurate than I believe we possess of Europe, the seat of the science of a thousand years. It comes out, too, at a moment when those countries are beginning to be interesting to the whole world. They are now becoming the scenes of political revolution, to take their stations as integral members of the great family of nations. All are now in insurrection. In several, the Independents are already triumphant, and they will undoubtedly be so in all. What kind of government will they establish? How much liberty can they bear without intoxication? Are their chiefs sufficiently enlightened to form a well-guarded government, and their people to watch their chiefs? Have they mind enough to place their domesticated Indians on a footing with the whites? All these questions you can answer better than any other. I imagine they will copy our outlines of confederation and elective government, abolish distinction of ranks, bow the neck to their priests, and persevere in intolerantism. Their greatest difficulty will be in the construction of their executive. I suspect that, regardless of the experiment of France, and of that of the United States in 1784, they will begin with a directory, and when the unavoidable schisms in that kind of executive shall drive them to something else, their great question will come on whether to substitute an executive elective for years, for life, or an hereditary one. But unless instruction can be spread among them more rapidly than experience promises, despotism may come upon them before they are qualified to save the ground they will have gained. Could Napoleon obtain, at the close of the present war, the independence of all the West India islands, and their establishment in a separate confederacy, our quarter of the globe would exhibit an enrapturing prospect into futurity. You will live to see much of this. I shall follow, however, cheerfully my fellow laborers, contented with having borne a part in beginning this beatific reformation.

I fear, from some expressions in your letter, that your personal interests have not been duly protected, while you were devoting your time, talents and labor for the information of mankind. I should sincerely regret it for the honor of the governing powers, as well as from affectionate attachment to yourself and the sincerest wishes for your felicity, fortunes and fame.

In sending you a copy of my Notes on Virginia, I do but obey the desire you have expressed. They must appear chetif enough to the author of the great work on South America. But from the widow her mite was welcome, and you will add to this indulgence the acceptance of my sincere assurances of constant friendship and respect.

"A YOUNG GARDENER"

To Charles Willson Peale

Poplar Forest, August 20, 1811

It is long, my dear Sir, since we have exchanged a letter. Our former correspondence had always some little matter of business interspersed; but this being at an end, I shall still be anxious to hear from you sometimes, and to know that you are well and happy. I know indeed that your system is that of contentment under any situation. I have heard that you have retired from the city to a farm, and that you give your whole time to that. Does not the museum suffer? And is the farm as interesting? Here, as you know, we are all farmers, but not in a pleasing style. We have so little labor in proportion to our land that, although perhaps we make more profit from the same labor, we cannot give to our grounds that style of beauty which satisfies the eye of the amateur. Our rotations are corn, wheat, and clover, or corn, wheat, clover and clover, or wheat, corn, wheat, clover and clover; preceding the clover by a plastering. But some, instead of clover substitute mere rest, and all are slovenly enough. We are adding the care of Merino sheep. I have often thought that if heaven had given me choice of my position and calling, it should have been on a rich spot of earth, well watered, and near a good market for the productions of the garden. No occupation is so delightful to me as the culture of the earth, and no culture comparable to that of the garden. Such a variety of subjects, some one always coming to perfection, the failure of one thing repaired by the success of another, and instead of one harvest a continued one through the year. Under a total want of demand except for our family table, I am still devoted to the garden. But though an old man, I am but a young gardener.

Your application to whatever you are engaged in I know to be incessant. But Sundays and rainy days are always days of writing for the farmer. Think of me sometimes when you have your pen in hand, and give me information of your health and occupations; and be always assured of my great esteem and respect.

To Dr. Robert Patterson

Monticello, November 10, 1811

DEAR SIR,—Your favor of September 23d came to hand in due time, and I thank you for the nautical almanac it covered for the year 1813. I learn with pleasure that the Philosophical Society has concluded to take into consideration the subject of a fixed standard of measures, weights and coins, and you ask my ideas on it; insulated as my situation is, I am sure I can offer nothing but what will occur to the committee engaged on it, with the advantage on their part of correction by an interchange of sentiments and observations among themselves. I will, however, hazard some general ideas because you desire it, and if a single one be useful, the labor will not be lost.

The subject to be referred to as a standard, whether it be matter or motion, should be fixed by nature, invariable and accessible to all nations, independently of others, and with a convenience not disproportioned to its utility. What subject in nature fulfils best these conditions? What system shall we propose on this, embracing measures, weights and coins? and in what form shall we present it to the world? These are the questions before the committee.

Some other subjects have, at different times, been proposed as standards, but two only have divided the opinions of men: first, a direct admeasurement of a line on the earth's surface, or second, a measure derived from its motion on its axis. To measure directly such a portion of the earth as would furnish an element of measure, which might be found again with certainty in all future times, would be too far beyond the competence of our means to be taken into consideration. I am free, at the same time, to say that if these were within our power in the most ample degree, this element would not meet my preference. The admeasurement would of course be of a portion of some great circle of the earth. If of the equator, the countries over which that passes, their character and remoteness, render the undertaking arduous, and we may say impracticable for most nations. If of some meridian, the varying measures of its degrees from the equator to the pole, require a mean to be sought, of which some aliquot part may furnish what is desired. For this purpose the 45th degree has been recurred to, and such a length of line on both sides of it terminating at each end in the ocean, as may furnish a satisfactory law for a deduction of the unmeasured part of the quadrant. The portion resorted to by the French philosophers, (and there is no other on the globe under circumstances equally satisfactory,) is the meridian passing through their country and a portion of Spain, from Dunkirk to Barcelona. The objections to such an admeasurement as an element of measure, are the labor, the time, the number of highly-qualified agents, and the great expense required. All this, too, is to be repeated whenever any accident shall have destroyed the standard derived from it, or impaired its dimensions. This portion of that particular meridian is accessible of right to no one nation on earth. France, indeed, availing herself of a moment of peculiar relation between Spain and herself, has executed such an admeasurement. But how would it be at this moment, as to either France or Spain? and how is it at all times as to other nations, in point either of right or of practice? Must these go through the same operation, or take their measures from the standard prepared by France? Neither case bears that character of independence which the problem requires, and which neither the equality nor convenience of nations can dispense with. How would it now be, were England the deposit of a standard for the world? At war with all the world, the standard would be inaccessible to all other nations. Against this, too, are the inaccuracies of admeasurements over hills and valleys, mountains and waters, inaccuracies often unobserved by the agent himself, and always unknown to the world. The various results of the different measures heretofore attempted, sufficiently prove the inadequacy of human means to make such an admeasurement with the exactness requisite.

Let us now see under what circumstances the pendulum offers itself as an element of measure. The motion of the earth on its axis from noon to noon of a mean solar day, has been divided from time immemorial, and by very general consent, into 86,400 portions of time called seconds. The length of a pendulum vibrating in one of these portions, is determined by the laws of nature, is invariable under the same parallel, and accessible independently to all men. Like a degree of the meridian, indeed, it varies in its length from the equator to the pole, and like it, too, requires to be reduced to a mean. In seeking a mean in the first case, the 45th degree occurs with unrivalled preferences. It is the mid-way of the celestial ark from the equator to the pole. It is a mean between the two extreme degrees of the terrestrial ark, or between any two equi-distant from it, and it is also a mean value of all its degrees. In like manner, when seeking a mean for the pendulum, the same 45th degree offers itself on the same grounds, its increments being governed by the same laws which determine those of the different degrees of the meridian.

In a pendulum loaded with a Bob, some difficulty occurs in finding the centre of oscillation; and consequently the distance between that and the point of suspension. To lessen this, it has been proposed to substitute for the pendulum, a cylindrical rod of small diameter, in which the displacement of the centre of oscillation would be lessened. It has also been proposed to prolong the suspending wire of the pendulum below the Bob, until their centres of oscillation shall coincide. But these propositions not appearing to have received general approbation, we recur to the pendulum, suspended and charged as has been usual. And the rather as the the laws which determine the centre of oscillation leave no room for error in finding it, other than that minimum in practice to which all operations are subject in their execution. The other sources of inaccuracy in the length of the pendulum need not be mentioned, because easily guarded against. But the great and decisive superiority of the pendulum, as a standard of measure, is in its accessibility to all men, at all times and in all places. To obtain the second pendulum for 45° it is not necessary to go actually to that latitude. Having ascertained its length in our own parallel, both theory and observation give us a law for ascertaining the difference between that and the pendulum of any other. To make a new measure therefore, or verify an old one, nothing is necessary in any place but a well-regulated time-piece, or a good meridian, and such a knowledge of the subject as is common in all civilized nations.

Those indeed who have preferred the other element, do justice to the certainty, as well as superior facilities of the pendulum, by proposing to recur to one of the length of their standard, and to ascertain its number of vibrations in a day. These being once known, if any accident impair their standard it is to be recoved by means of a pendulum which shall make the requisite number of vibrations in a day. And among the several commissions established by the Academy of Sciences for the execution of the several branches of their work on measures and weights, that respecting the pendulum was assigned to Messrs. Borda, Coulomb & Cassini, the result of whose labors, however, I have not learned.

Let our unit of measures then be a pendulum of such length as in the latitude of 45°, in the level of the ocean, and in a given temperature, shall perform its vibrations, in small and equal arcs, in one second of mean time.

What ratio shall we adopt for the parts and multiples of this unit? The decimal without a doubt. Our arithmatic being founded in a decimal numeration, the same numeration in a system of measures, weights and coins, tallies at once with that. On this question, I believe, there has been no difference of opinion.

In measures of length, then, the pendulum is our unit. It is a little more than our yard and less than the ell. Its tenth or dime, will not be quite .4 inches. Its hundredth, or cent, not quite .4 of an inch; its thousandth, or mill, not quite .04 of an inch, and so on. The traveller will count his road by a longer measure. 1,000 units, or a kiliad, will not be quite two-thirds of our present mile, and more nearly a thousand paces than that.

For measures of surface, the square unit, equal to about ten square feet, or one-ninth more than a square yard, will be generally convenient. But for those of lands a larger measure will be wanted. A kiliad would be not quite a rood, or quarter of an acre; a myriad not quite 2½ acres.

For measures of capacity, wet and dry,

The cubic Unit = .1 would be about .35 cubic feet, .28 bushels dry, or ⅞ of a ton liquid.

Dime = .1 would be about 3.5 cubic feet, 2.8 bushels, or about ⅞ of a barrel liquid.

Cent = .o1 about 50 cubic inches, or ⅞ of a
quart.

Mill = .oo1 = .5 of a cubic inch, or ⅔ of a gill.

To incorporate into the same system our weights and coins,
we must recur to some natural substance, to be found everywhere, and of a composition sufficiently uniform. Water has
been considered as the most eligible substance, and rain-water
more nearly uniform than any other kind found in nature.
That circumstance renders it preferable to distilled water, and
its variations in weight may be called insensible.

The cubic unit of this = .1 would weigh about 2,165 lbs. or
a ton between the long and short.

The Dime = .1 a little more than 2. kentals.

Cent = .o1 a little more than 20 lb.

Mill = .oo1 a little more than 2 lb.

Decimmil = .ooo1 about 3½ oz. avoirdupoise.

Centimmil = .oooo1 a little more than 6 dwt.

Millionth = .oooo01 about 15 grains.

Decimmillionth = .ooooo01 about 1½ grains.

Centimmillionth = .oooooo01 about .14 of a grain.

Billionth = .ooooooo01 about .014 of a grain.

With respect to our coins, the pure silver in a dollar being
fixed by law at 347¼ grains, and all debts and contracts being
bottomed on that value, we can only state the pure silver in
the dollar, which would be very nearly 23 millionths.

I have used loose and round numbers (the exact unit being
yet undetermined) merely to give a general idea of the measures and weights proposed, when compared with those we
now use. And in the names of the subdivisions I have followed the metrology of the ordinance of Congress of 1786,
which for their series below unit adopted the Roman numer-
als. For that above unit the Grecian is convenient, and has
been adopted in the new French system.

We come now to our last question, in what form shall we
offer this metrical system to the world? In some one which
shall be altogether unassuming; which shall not have the appearance of taking the lead among our sister institutions in
making a general proposition. So jealous is the spirit of equality in the republic of letters, that the smallest excitement of
that would mar our views, however salutary for all. We are in

habits of correspondence with some of these institutions, and identity of character and of object, authorize our entering into correspondence with all. Let us then mature our system as far as can be done at present, by ascertaining the length of the second pendulum of 45° by forming two tables, one of which shall give the equivalent of every different denomination of measures, weights and coins in these States, in the unit of that pendulum, its decimals and multiples; and the other stating the equivalent of all the decimal parts and multiples of that pendulum, in the several denominations of measures, weights and coins of our existing system. This done, we might communicate to one or more of these institutions in every civilized country a copy of those tables, stating as our motive, the difficulty we had experienced, and often the impossibility of ascertaining the value of the measures, weights and coins of other countries, expressed in any standard which we possess; that desirous of being relieved from this, and of obtaining information which could be relied on for the purposes of science, as well as of business, we had concluded to ask it from the learned societies of other nations, who are especially qualified to give it with the requisite accuracy; that in making this request we had thought it our duty first to do ourselves, and to offer to others, what we meant to ask from them, by stating the value of our own measures, weights and coins, in some unit of measure already possessed, or easily obtainable, by all nations; that the pendulum vibrating seconds of mean time, presents itself as such an unit; its length being determined by the laws of nature, and easily ascertainable at all times and places; that we have thought that of 45° would be the most unexceptionable, as being a mean of all other parallels, and open to actual trial in both hemispheres. In this, therefore, as an unit, and in its parts and multiples in the decimal ratio, we have expressed, in the tables communicated, the value of all the measures, weights and coins used in the United States, and we ask in return from their body a table of the weights, measures and coins in use within their country, expressed in the parts and multiples of the same unit. Having requested the same favor from the learned societies of other nations, our object is, with their assistance, to place within the reach of our fellow citizens at large a perfect knowledge of the measures, weights and coins of the countries with which they have commercial or friendly intercourse; and should the societies of other countries interchange their respective tables, the learned will be in possession of an uniform language in measures, weights and coins, which may with time become useful to other descriptions of their citizens, and even to their governments. This, however, will rest with their pleasure, not presuming, in the present proposition, to extend our views beyond the limits of our own nation. I offer this sketch merely as the outline of the kind of communication which I should hope would excite no jealousy or repugnance.

Peculiar circumstances, however, would require letters of a more special character to the Institute of France, and the Royal Society of England. The magnificent work which France has executed in the admeasurement of so large a portion of the meridian, has a claim to great respect in our reference to it. We should only ask a communication of their metrical system, expressed in equivalent values of the second pendulum of 45° as ascertained by Messrs. Borda, Coulomb and Cassini, adding, perhaps, the request of an actual rod of the length of that pendulum.

With England, our explanations will be much more delicate. They are the older country, the mother country, more advanced in the arts and sciences, possessing more wealth and leisure for their improvement, and animated by a pride more than laudable.* It is their measures, too, which we undertake to ascertain and communicate to themselves. The subject should therefore be opened to them with infinite tenderness and respect, and in some way which might give them due place in its agency. The parallel of 45° being within our latitude and not within theirs, the actual experiments under that would be of course assignable to us. But as a corrective, I

---

*We are all occupied in industrious pursuits. They abound with persons living on the industry of their fathers, or on the earnings of their fellow citizens, given away by their rulers in sinecures and pensions. Some of these, desirous of laudable distinction, devote their time and means to the pursuits of science, and become profitable members of society by an industry of a higher order.

would propose that they should ascertain the length of the pendulum vibrating seconds in the city of London, or at the observatory of Greenwich, while we should do the same in an equi-distant parallel to the south of 45°, suppose in 38° 29'. We might ask of them, too, as they are in possession of the standards of Guildhall, of which we can have but an unauthentic account, to make the actual application of those standards to the pendulum when ascertained. The operation we should undertake under the 45th parallel, (about Passamaquoddy,) would give us a happy occasion, too, of engaging our sister society of Boston in our views, by referring to them the execution of that part of the work. For that of 38° 29' we should be at a loss. It crosses the tide waters of the Potomac, about Dumfries, and I do not know what our resources there would be unless we borrow them from Washington, where there are competent persons.

Although I have not mentioned Philadelphia in these operations, I by no means propose to relinquish the benefit of observations to be made there. Her science and perfection in the arts would be a valuable corrective to the less perfect state of them in the other places of observation. Indeed, it is to be wished that Philadelphia could be made the point of observation south of 45°, and that the Royal Society would undertake the counterpoint on the north, which would be somewhere between the Lizard and Falmouth. The actual pendulums from both of our points of observation, and not merely the measures of them, should be delivered to the Philosophical Society, to be measured under their eye and direction.

As this is really a work of common and equal interest to England and the United States, perhaps it would be still more respectful to make our proposition to her Royal Society in the outset, and to agree with them on a partition of the work. In this case, any commencement of actual experiments on our part should be provisional only, and preparatory to the ultimate results. We might, in the meantime, provisionally also, form a table adapted to the length of the pendulum of 45°, according to the most approved estimates, including those of the French commissioners. This would serve to introduce the subject to the foreign societies, in the way before proposed, reserving to ourselves the charge of communicating to them a more perfect one, when that shall have been completed.

We may even go a step further, and make a general table of the measures, weights and coins of all nations, taking their value hypothetically for the present, from the tables in the commercial dictionary of the encyclopedia methodique, which are very extensive, and have the appearance of being made with great labor and exactness. To these I expect we must in the end recur, as a supplement for the measures which we may fail to obtain from other countries directly. Their reference is to the foot or inch of Paris, as a standard, which we may convert into parts of the second pendulum of 45°.

I have thus, my dear sir, committed to writing my general ideas on this subject, the more freely as they are intended merely as suggestions for consideration. It is not probable they offer anything which would not have occurred to the committee itself. My apology on offering them must be found in your request. My confidence in the committee, of which I take for granted you are one, is too entire to have intruded a single idea but on that ground.

Be assured of my affectionate and high esteem and respect.

RECONCILIATION
To John Adams

Monticello, Jan. 21, 1812

DEAR SIR—I thank you before hand (for they are not yet arrived) for the specimens of homespun you have been so kind as to forward me by post. I doubt not their excellence, knowing how far you are advanced in these things in your quarter. Here we do little in the fine way, but in coarse and midling goods a great deal. Every family in the country is a manufactory within itself, and is very generally able to make within itself all the stouter and midling stuffs for it's own cloathing and household use. We consider a sheep for every person in the family as sufficient to clothe it, in addition to the cottom, hemp and flax which we raise ourselves. For fine stuff we shall depend on your Northern manufactures. Of these, that is to say, of company establishments, we have none. We use little machinery. The Spinning Jenny and loom with the flying shuttle can be managed in a family; but nothing more complicated. The economy and thriftiness resulting from our household manufactures are such that they will never again be laid aside; and nothing more salutary for us has ever happened than the British obstructions to our demands for their manufactures. Restore free intercourse when they will, their commerce with us will have totally changed it's form, and the articles we shall in future want from them will not exceed their own consumption of our produce.

A letter from you calls up recollections very dear to my mind. It carries me back to the times when, beset with difficulties and dangers, we were fellow laborers in the same cause, struggling for what is most valuable to man, his right of self-government. Laboring always at the same oar, with some wave ever ahead threatening to overwhelm us and yet passing harmless under our bark, we knew not how, we rode through the storm with heart and hand, and made a happy port. Still we did not expect to be without rubs and difficulties; and we have had them. First the detention of the Western posts: then the coalition of Pilnitz, outlawing our commerce with France, and the British enforcement of the outlawry. In your day French depredations: in mine English, and the Berlin and Milan decrees: now the English orders of council, and the piracies they authorise: when these shall be over, it will be the impressment of our seamen, or something else: and so we have gone on, and so we shall go on, puzzled and prospering beyond example in the history of man. And I do believe we shall continue to growl, [i.e., grow] to multiply and prosper until we exhibit an association, powerful, wise and happy, beyond what has yet been seen by men. As for France and England, with all their pre-eminence in science, the one is a den of robbers, and the other of pirates. And if science produces no better fruits than tyranny, murder, rapine and destitution of national morality, I would rather wish our country to be ignorant, honest and estimable as our neighboring savages are.

But whither is senile garrulity leading me? Into politics, of which I have taken final leave. I think little of them, and say less. I have given up newspapers in exchange for Tacitus and Thucydides, for Newton and Euclid; and I find myself much the happier. Sometimes indeed I look back to former occurrences, in remembrance of our old friends and fellow laborers, who have fallen before us. Of the signers of the Declaration of Independance I see now living not more than half a dozen on your side of the Potomak, and, on this side, myself alone. You and I have been wonderfully spared, and myself with remarkable health, and a considerable activity of body and mind. I am on horseback 3. or 4. hours of every day; visit 3. or 4. times a year a possession I have 90 miles distance, performing the winter journey on horseback. I walk little however; a single mile being too much for me; and I live in the midst of my grandchildren, one of whom has lately promoted me to be a great grandfather. I have heard with pleasure that you also retain good health, and a greater power of exercise in walking than I do. But I would rather have heard this from yourself, and that, writing a letter, like mine, full of egotisms, and of details of your health, your habits, occupations and enjoyments, I should have the pleasure of knowing that, in the race of life, you do not keep, in it's physical decline, the same distance ahead of me which you have done in political honors and atchievements. No circumstances have lessened the interest I feel in these particulars respecting yourself; none have suspended for one moment my sincere esteem for you; and I now salute you with unchanged affections and respect.

CONCERNING THE INDIANS

To John Adams

Monticello, June 11, 1812

DEAR SIR—By our post preceding that which brought your letter of May 21, I had recieved one from Mr. Malcolm on the same subject with yours, and by the return of the post had stated to the President my recollections of him. But both of your letters were probably too late; as the appointment had been already made, if we may credit the newspapers.

You ask if there is any book that pretends to give any account of the traditions of the Indians, or how one can acquire an idea of them? Some scanty accounts of their traditions, but fuller of their customs and characters are given us by most of the early travellers among them. These you know were chiefly French. Lafitau, among them, and Adair an Englishman, have written on this subject; the former two volumes, the latter one, all in 4to [quarto]. But unluckily Lafitau had in his head a preconcieved theory on the mythology, manners, institutions and government of the antient nations of Europe, Asia, and Africa, and seems to have entered on those of America only to fit them into the same frame, and to draw from them a confirmation of his general theory. He keeps up a perpetual parallel, in all those articles, between the Indians of America, and the antients of the other quarters of the globe. He selects therefore all the facts, and adopts all the falsehoods which favor his theory, and very gravely retails such absurdities as zeal for a theory could alone swallow. He was a man of much classical and scriptural reading, and has rendered his book not unentertaining. He resided five years among the Northern Indians, as a Missionary, but collects his matter much more from the writings of others, than from his own observation.

Adair too had his kink. He believed all the Indians of American to be descended from the Jews: the same laws, usages; rites and ceremonies, the same sacrifices, priests, prophets, fasts and festivals, almost the same religion, and that they all spoke Hebrew. For altho he writes particularly of the Southern Indians only, the Catawbas, Creeks, Cherokees, Chickasaws and Choctaws, with whom alone he was personally acquainted, yet he generalises whatever he found among them, and brings himself to believe that the hundred languages of America, differing fundamentally every one from every other, as much as Greek from Gothic, have yet all one common prototype. He was a trader, a man of learning, a self-taught Hebraist, a strong religionist, and of as sound a mind as Don Quixot in whatever did not touch his religious chivalry. His book contains a great deal of real instruction on it's subject, only requiring the reader to be constantly on his guard against the wonderful obliquities of his theory.

The scope of your enquiry would scarcely, I suppose, take in the three folio volumes of Latin by De Bry. In these fact and fable are mingled together, without regard to any favorite system. They are less suspicious therefore in their complexion, more original and authentic, than those of Lafitau and Adair. This is a work of great curiosity, extremely rare, so as never to be bought in Europe, but on the breaking up, and selling some antient library. On one of these occasions a bookseller procured me a copy, which, unless you have one, is probably the only one in America.

You ask further, if the Indians have any order of priesthood among them, like the Druids, Bards or Minstrels of the Celtic nations? Adair alone, determined to see what he wished to see in every object, metamorphoses their Conjurers into an order of priests, and describes their sorceries as if they were the great religious ceremonies of the nation. Lafitau calls them by their proper names, Jongleurs, Devins, Sortileges; De Bry praestigiatores, Adair himself sometimes Magi, Archimagi, cunning men, Seers, rain makers, and the modern Indian interpreters, call them Conjurers and Witches. They are persons pretending to have communications with the devil and other evil spirits, to foretel future events, bring down rain, find stolen goods, raise the dead, destroy some, and heal others by enchantment, lay spells etc. And Adair, without departing from his parallel of the Jews and Indians, might have found their counterpart, much more aptly, among the Soothsayers, sorcerers and wizards of the Jews, their Jannes and Jambres, their Simon Magus, witch of Endor, and the young damsel whose sorceries disturbed Paul so much; instead of placing them in a line with their High-priest, their Chief priests, and their magnificent hierarchy generally. In the solemn ceremonies of the Indians, the persons who direct or officiate, are their chiefs, elders and warriors, in civil ceremonies or in those of war; it is the Head of the Cabin, in their private or particular feasts or ceremonies; and sometimes the Matrons, as in their Corn feasts. And, even here, Adair might have kept up his parallel, with ennobling his Conjurers. For the antient Patriarchs, the Noahs, the Abrahams, Isaacs and

Jacobs, and, even after the consecration of Aaron, the Samuels and Elijahs, and we may say further every one for himself, offered sacrifices on the altars. The true line of distinction seems to be, that solemn ceremonies, whether public or private, addressed to the Great Spirit, are conducted by the worthies of the nation, Men, or Matrons, while Conjurers are resorted to only for the invocation of evil spirits. The present state of the several Indian tribes, without any public order of priests, is proof sufficient that they never had such an order. Their steady habits permit no innovations, not even those which the progress of science offers to increase the comforts, enlarge the understanding, and improve the morality of mankind. Indeed so little idea have they of a regular order of priests, that they mistake ours for their Conjurers, and call them by that name.

So much in answer to your enquiries concerning Indians, a people with whom, in the very early part of my life, I was very familiar, and acquired impressions of attachment and commiseration for them which have never been obliterated. Before the revolution they were in the habit of coming often, and in great numbers to the seat of our government, where I was very much with them. I knew much the great Outassete [i.e., Outacity], the warrior and orator of the Cherokees. He was always the guest of my father, on his journeys to and from Williamsburg. I was in his camp when he made his great farewell oration to his people, the evening before his departure for England. The moon was in full splendor, and to her he seemed to address himself in his prayers for his own safety on the voyage, and that of his people during his absence. His sounding voice, distinct articulation, animated actions, and the solemn silence of his people at their several fires, filled me with awe and veneration, altho' I did not understand a word he uttered. That nation, consisting now of about 2000. wariors, and the Creeks of about 3000. are far advanced in civilisation. They have good Cabins, inclosed fields, large herds of cattle and hogs, spin and weave their own clothes of cotton, have smiths and other of the most necessary tradesmen, write and read, are on the increase in numbers, and a branch of the Cherokees is now instituting a regular representative government. Some other tribes were advancing in the same line. On those who have made any progress, English seductions will have no effect. But the backward will yeild, and be thrown further back. These will relapse into barbarism and misery, lose numbers by war and want, and we shall be obliged to drive them, with the beasts of the forest into the Stony mountains. They will be conquered however in Canada. The possession of that country secures our women and children for ever from the tomahawk and scalping knife, by removing those who excite them: and for this possession, orders I presume are issued by this time; taking for granted that the doors of Congress will re-open with a Declaration of war. That this may end in indemnity for the past, security for the future, and compleat emancipation from Anglomany, Gallomany, and all the manias of demoralized Europe, and that you may live in health and happiness to see all this, is the sincere prayer of   Yours affectionately.

WAR WITH ENGLAND
To General Thaddeus Kosciusko

Monticello, June 28, 1812

Nous voila donc, mon cher ami, en guerre avec l'Angleterre. This was declared on the 18th instant, thirty years after the signature of our peace in 1782. Within these thirty years what a vast course of growth and prosperity we have had! It is not ten years since Great Britain began a series of insults and injuries which would have been met with war in the threshold by any European power. This course has been unremittingly followed up by increasing wrongs, with glimmerings indeed of peaceable redress, just sufficient to keep us quiet, till she has had the impudence at length to extinguish even these glimmerings by open avowal. This would not have been borne so long, but that France has kept pace with England in iniquity of principle, although not in the power of inflicting wrongs on us. The difficulty of selecting a foe between them has spared us many years of war, and enabled us to enter into it with less debt, more strength and preparation. Our present enemy will have the sea to herself, while we shall be equally predominant at land, and shall strip her of all her possessions on this continent. She may burn New York, indeed, by her ships and congreve rockets, in which case we must burn the city of London by hired incendiaries, of which her starving manufacturers will furnish abundance. A people in such desperation as to demand of their government *aut parcem, aut furcam*, either bread or the gallows, will not reject the same alternative when offered by a foreign hand. Hunger will make them brave every risk for bread. The partisans of England here have endeavored much to goad us into the folly of choosing the ocean instead of the land, for the theatre of war. That would be to meet their strength with our own weakness, instead of their weakness with our strength. I hope we shall confine ourselves to the conquest of their possessions, and defence of our harbors, leaving the war on the ocean to our privateers. These will immediately swarm in every sea, and do more injury to British commerce than the regular fleets of all Europe would do. The government of France may discontinue their license trade. Our privateers will furnish them much more abundantly with colonial produce, and whatever the license trade has given them. Some have apprehended we should be overwhelmed by the new improvements of war, which have not yet reached us. But the British possess them very imperfectly, and what are these improvements? Chiefly in the management of artillery, of which our country admits little use. We have nothing to fear from their armies, and shall put nothing in prize to their fleets. Upon the whole, I have known no war entered into under more favorable auspices.

Our manufacturers are now very nearly on a footing with those of England. She has not a single improvement which we do not possess, and many of them better adapted by ourselves to our ordinary use. We have reduced the large and expensive machinery for most things to the compass of a private family, and every family of any size is now getting machines on a small scale for their household purposes. Quoting myself as an example, and I am much behind many others in this business, my household manufactures are just getting into operation on the scale of a carding machine costing $60 only, which may be worked by a girl of twelve years old, a spinning machine, which may be made for $10, carrying 6 spindles for wool, to be worked by a girl also, another which can be made for $25, carrying 12 spindles for cotton, and a loom, with a flying shuttle, weaving its twenty yards a day. I need 2,000 yards of linen, cotton and woollen yearly, to clothe my family, which this machinery, costing $150 only, and worked by two women and two girls, will more than furnish. For fine goods there are numerous establishments at work in the large cities, and many more daily growing up; and of merinos we have some thousands, and these multiplying fast. We consider a sheep for every person as sufficient for their woollen clothing, and this State and all to the north have fully that, and those to the south and west will soon be up to it. In other articles we are equally advanced, so that nothing is more certain than that, come peace when it will, we shall never again go to England for a shilling where we have gone for a dollar's worth. Instead of applying to her manufacturers there, they must starve or come here to be employed. I give you these details of peaceable operations, because they are within my present sphere. Those of war are in better hands, who know how to keep their own secrets. Because, too, although a soldier yourself, I am sure you contemplate the peaceable employment of man in the improvement of his condition, with more pleasure than his murders, rapine and devastations.

Mr. Barnes, some time ago, forwarded you a bill of exchange for 5,500 francs, of which the enclosed is a duplicate. Apprehending that a war with England would subject the remittances to you to more casualties, I proposed to Mr. Morson, of Bordeaux, to become the intermediate for making remittances to you, which he readily acceded to on liberal ideas arising from his personal esteem for you, and his desire to be useful to you. If you approve of this medium I am in hopes it will shield you from the effect of the accidents to which the increased dangers of the seas may give birth. It would give me great pleasure to hear from you oftener. I feel great interest in your health and happiness. I know your feelings on the present state of the world, and hope they will be cheered by the successful course of our war, and the addition of Canada to our confederacy. The infamous intrigues of

Great Britain to destroy our government (of which Henry's is but one sample), and with the Indians to tomahawk our women and children, prove that the cession of Canada, their fulcrum for these Machiavelian levers, must be a *sine qua non* at a treaty of peace. God bless you, and give you to see all these things, and many and long years of health and happiness.

"A RADICAL DIFFERENCE OF POLITICAL PRINCIPLE"

To John Melish

Monticello, January 13, 1813

DEAR SIR,—I received duly your favor of December the 15th, and with it the copies of your map and travels, for which be pleased to accept my thanks. The book I have read with extreme satisfaction and information. As to the western States, particularly, it has greatly edified me: for of the actual condition of that interesting portion of our country, I had not an adequate idea. I feel myself now as familiar with it as with the condition of the maritime States. I had no conception that manufactures had made such progress there, and particularly of the number of carding and spinning machines dispersed through the whole country. We are but beginning here to have them in our private families. Small spinning jennies of from half a dozen to twenty spindles, will soon, however, make their way into the humblest cottages, as well as the richest houses; and nothing is more certain, than that the coarse and middling clothing for our families, will forever hereafter continue to be made within ourselves. I have hitherto myself depended entirely on foreign manufactures; but I have now thirty-five spindles agoing, a hand carding machine, and looms with the flying shuttle, for the supply of my own farms, which will never be relinquished in my time. The continuance of the war will fix the habit generally, and out of the evils of impressment and of the orders of council, a great blessing for us will grow. I have not formerly been an advocate for great manufactories. I doubted whether our labor, employed in agriculture, and aided by the spontaneous energies of the earth, would not procure us more than we could make ourselves of other necessaries. But other considerations entering into the question, have settled my doubts.

The candor with which you have viewed the manners and condition of our citizens, is so unlike the narrow prejudices of the French and English travellers preceding you, who, considering each the manners and habits of their own people as the only orthodox, have viewed everything differing from that test as boorish and barbarous, that your work will be read here extensively, and operate great good.

Amidst this mass of approbation which is given to every other part of the work, there is a single sentiment which I cannot help wishing to bring to what I think the correct one; and, on a point so interesting, I value your opinion too highly not to ambition its concurrence with my own. Stating in volume one, page sixty-three, the principle of difference between the two great political parties here, you conclude it to be, 'whether the controlling power shall be vested in this or that set of men.' That each party endeavors to get into the administration of the government, and exclude the other from power, is true, and may be stated as a motive of action: but this is only secondary; the primary motive being a real and radical difference of political principle. I sincerely wish our differences were but personally who should govern, and that the principles of our constitution were those of both parties. Unfortunately, it is otherwise; and the question of preference between monarchy and republicanism, which has so long divided mankind elsewhere, threatens a permanent division here.

Among that section of our citizens called federalists, there are three shades of opinion. Distinguishing between the *leaders* and *people* who compose it, the *leaders* consider the English constitution as a model of perfection, some, with a correction of its vices, others, with all its corruptions and abuses. This last was Alexander Hamilton's opinion, which others, as well as myself, have often heard him declare, and that a correction of what are called its vices, would render the English an impracticable government. This government they wished to have established here, and only accepted and held fast, *at first*, to the present constitution, as a stepping-stone to the final establishment of their favorite model. This party therefore always clung to England as their prototype, and great auxiliary in promoting and effecting this change. A weighty MINOR- ITY, however, of these *leaders*, considering the voluntary con- version of our government into a monarchy as too distant, if not desperate, wish to break off from our Union its eastern fragment, as being, in truth, the hot-bed of American mon- archism, with a view to a commencement of their favorite government, from whence the other States may gangrene by degrees, and the whole be thus brought finally to the desired point. For Massachusetts, the prime mover in this enterprise, is the last State in the Union to mean a *final* separation, as being of all the most dependent on the others. Not raising bread for the sustenance of her own inhabitants, not having a stick of timber for the construction of vessels, her principal occupation, nor an article to export in them, where would she be, excluded from the ports of the other States, and thrown into dependence on England, her direct and natural, but now insidious rival? At the head of this MINORITY is what is called the Essex Junto of Massachusetts. But the MAJORITY of these *leaders* do not aim at separation. In this, they adhere to the known principle of General Hamilton, never, under any views, to break the Union. Anglomany, monarchy, and sepa- ration, then, are the principles of the Essex federalists. Anglo- many and monarchy, those of the Hamiltonians, and Anglomany alone, that of the portion among the *people* who call themselves federalists. These last are as good republicans as the brethren whom they oppose, and differ from them only in their devotion to England and hatred of France which they have imbibed from their leaders. The moment that these lead- ers should avowedly propose a separation of the Union, or the establishment of regal government, their popular adher- ents would quit them to a man, and join the republican stan- dard; and the partisans of this change, even in Massachusetts, would thus find themselves an army of officers without a soldier.

The party called republican is steadily for the support of the present constitution. They obtained at its commencement, all the amendments to it they desired. These reconciled them to it perfectly, and if they have any ulterior view, it is only, perhaps, to popularize it further, by shortening the Senatorial term, and devising a process for the responsibility of judges, more practical than that of impeachment. They esteem the people of England and France equally, and equally detest the governing powers of both.

This I verily believe, after an intimacy of forty years with the public councils and characters, is a true statement of the grounds on which they are at present divided, and that it is not merely an ambition for power. An honest man can feel no pleasure in the exercise of power over his fellow citizens. And considering as the only offices of power those conferred by the people directly, that is to say, the executive and legislative functions of the General and State governments, the common refusal of these and multiplied resignations, are proofs sufficient that power is not alluring to pure minds, and is not, with them, the primary principle of contest. This is my belief of it; it is that on which I have acted; and had it been a mere contest who should be permitted to administer the government according to its genuine republican principles, there has never been a moment of my life in which I should have relinquished for it the enjoyments of my family, my farm, my friends and books.

You expected to discover the difference of our party principles in General Washington's valedictory, and my inaugural address. Not at all. General Washington did not harbor one principle of federalism. He was neither an Angloman, a monarchist, nor a separatist. He sincerely wished the people to have as much self-government as they were competent to exercise themselves. The only point on which he and I ever differed in opinion, was, that I had more confidence than he had in the natural integrity and discretion of the people, and in the safety and extent to which they might trust themselves with a control over their government. He has asseverated to me a thousand times his determination that the existing government should have a fair trial, and that in support of it he would spend the last drop of his blood. He did this the more repeatedly, because he knew General Hamilton's political bias, and my apprehensions from it. It is a mere calumny, therefore, in the monarchists, to associate General Washington with their principles. But that may have happened in this case which has been often seen in ordinary cases, that, by oft repeating an untruth, men come to believe it themselves. It is a mere artifice in this party to bolster themselves up on the revered name of that first of our worthies. If I have dwelt longer on this subject than was necessary, it proves the estimation in which I hold your ultimate opinions, and my desire of placing the subject truly before them. In so doing, I am certain I risk no use of the communication which may draw me into contention before the public. Tranquillity is the *summum bonum* of a Septagenaire.

To return to the merits of your work: I consider it as so lively a picture of the real state of our country, that if I can possibly obtain opportunities of conveyance, I propose to send a copy to a friend in France, and another to one in Italy, who, I know, will translate and circulate it as an antidote to the misrepresentations of former travellers. But whatever effect my profession of political faith may have on your general opinion, a part of my object will be obtained, if it satisfies you as to the principles of my own action, and of the high respect and consideration with which I tender you my salutations.

TYRANTS OF LAND AND SEA

To Madame de Staël

United States of America, May 24, 1813

I received with great pleasure, my dear Madam and friend, your letter of November the 10th, from Stockholm, and am sincerely gratified by the occasion it gives me of expressing to you the sentiments of high respect and esteem which I entertain for you. It recalls to my remembrance a happy portion of my life, passed in your native city; then the seat of the most amiable and polished society of the world, and of which yourself and your venerable father were such distinguished members. But of what scenes has it since been the theatre, and with what havoc has it overspread the earth! Robespiere met the fate, and his memory the execration, he so justly merited.

The rich were his victims, and perished by thousands. It is by millions that Buonaparte destroys the poor, and he is eulogised and deified by the sycophants even of science. These merit more than the mere oblivion to which they will be consigned; and the day will come when a just posterity will give to their hero the only pre-eminence he has earned, that of having been the greatest of the destroyers of the human race. What year of his military life has not consigned a million of human beings to death, to poverty and wretchedness! What field in Europe may not raise a monument of the murders, the burnings, the desolations, the famines and miseries it has witnessed from him! And all this to acquire a reputation, which Cartouche attained with less injury to mankind, of being fearless of God or man.

To complete and universalise the desolation of the globe, it has been the will of Providence to raise up, at the same time, a tyrant as unprincipled and as overwhelming, for the ocean. Not in the poor maniac George, but in his government and nation. Buonaparte will die, and his tyrannies with him. But a nation never dies. The English government and its piratical principles and practices, have no fixed term of duration. Europe feels, and is writhing under the scorpion whips of Buonaparte. We are assailed by those of England. The one continent thus placed under the gripe of England, and the other of Buonaparte, each has to grapple with the enemy immediately pressing on itself. We must extinguish the fire kindled in our own house, and leave to our friends beyond the water that which is consuming theirs. It was not till England had taken one thousand of our ships, and impressed into her service more than six thousand of our citizens; till she had declared, by the proclamation of her Prince Regent, that she would not repeal her aggressive orders *as to us*, until Buonaparte should have repealed his *as to all nations*; till her minister, in formal conference with ours, declared, that no proposition for protecting our seamen from being impressed, under color of taking their own, was practicable or admissible; that, the door to justice and to all amicable arrangement being closed, and negotiation become both desperate and dishonorable, we concluded that the war she had been for years waging against us, might as well become a war on both sides.

She takes fewer vessels from us since the declaration of war than before, because they venture more cautiously; and we now make full reprisals where before we made none. England is, in principle, the enemy of all maritime nations, as Buonaparte is of the continental; and I place in the same line of insult to the human understanding, the pretension of conquering the ocean, to establish continental rights, as that of conquering the continent, to restore maritime rights. No, my dear Madam; the object of England is the *permanent dominion of the ocean*, and the *monopoly of the trade of the world*. To secure this, she must keep a larger fleet than her own resources will maintain. The resources of other nations, then, must be impressed to supply the deficiency of her own. This is sufficiently developed and evidenced by her successive strides towards the usurpation of the sea. Mark them, from her first war after William Pitt the little, came into her administration. She first forbade to neutrals all trade with her enemies in time of war, which they had not in time of peace. This deprived them of their trade from port to port of the same nation. Then she forbade them to trade from the port of one nation to that of any other at war with her, although a right fully exercised in time of peace. Next, instead of taking vessels only *entering* a blockaded port, she took them over the whole ocean, if destined to that port, although ignorant of the blockade, and without intention to violate it. Then she took them returning from that port, as if infected by previous infraction of blockade. Then came her paper blockades, by which she might shut up the whole world without sending a ship to sea, except to take all those sailing on it, as they must, of course, be bound to some port. And these were followed by her orders of council, forbidding every nation to go to the port of any other, without coming first to some port of Great Britain, there paying a tribute to her, regulated by the cargo, and taking from her a license to proceed to the port of destination; which operation the vessel was to repeat with the return cargo on its way home. According to these orders, we could not send a vessel from St. Mary's to St. Augustine, distant six hours' sail, on our own coast, without crossing the Atlantic four times, twice with the outward cargo, and twice with the inward. She found this too daring and outrageous for a single step, retracted as to certain articles of commerce, but left it in force as to others which constitute important branches of our exports. And finally, that her views may no longer rest on inference, in a recent debate, her minister declared in open parliament, that the object of the present war is a *monopoly of commerce.*

In some of these atrocities, France kept pace with her fully in speculative wrong, which her impotence only shortened in practical execution. This was called retaliation by both; each charging the other with the initiation of the outrage. As if two combatants might retaliate on an innocent bystander, the blows they received from each other. To make war on both would have been ridiculous. In order, therefore, to single out any enemy, we offered to both, that if either would revoke its hostile decrees, and the other should refuse, we would interdict all intercourse whatever with that other; which would be war of course, as being an avowed departure from neutrality. France accepted the offer, and revoked her decrees as to us. England not only refused, but declared by a solemn proclamation of her Prince Regent, that she would not revoke her orders *even as to us*, until those of France should be annulled *as to the whole world*. We thereon declared war, and with abundant additional cause.

In the mean time, an examination before parliament of the ruinous effects of these orders on her own manufacturers, exposing them to the nation and to the world, their Prince issued a palinodial proclamation, *suspending* the orders on certain conditions, but claiming to renew them at pleasure, as a matter of right. Even this might have prevented the war, if done and known here before its declaration. But the sword being once drawn, the expense of arming incurred, and hostilities in full course, it would have been unwise to discontinue them, until effectual provision should be agreed to by England, for protecting our citizens on the high seas from impressment by her naval commanders, through error, voluntary or involuntary; the fact being notorious, that these officers, entering our ships at sea under pretext of searching for their seamen, (which they have no right to do by the law or usage of nations, which they neither do, nor ever did, as to any other nation but ours, and which no nation ever before pretended to do in any case,) entering our ships, I say, under pretext of searching for and taking out their seamen, they took ours, native as well as naturalised, knowing them to be ours, merely because they wanted them; insomuch, that no American could safely cross the ocean, or venture to pass by sea from one to another of our own ports. It is not long since they impressed at sea two nephews of General Washington, returning from Europe, and put them, as common seamen, under the ordinary discipline of their ships of war. There are certainly other wrongs to be settled between England and us; but of a minor character, and such as a proper spirt of concil-iation on both sides would not permit to continue them at war. The sword, however, can never again be sheathed, until the personal safety of an American on the ocean, among the most important and most vital of the rights we possess, is completely provided for.

As soon as we heard of her partial repeal of her orders of council, we offered instantly to suspend hostilities by an ar-mistice, if she would suspend her impressments, and meet us in arrangements for securing our citizens against them. She refused to do it, because impracticable by any arrangement, as she pretends; but, in truth, because a body of sixty to eighty thousand of the finest seamen in the world, which we possess, is too great a resource for manning her exaggerated navy, to be relinquished, as long as she can keep it open. Peace is in her hand, whenever she will renounce the practice of aggression on the persons of our citizens. If she thinks it worth eternal war, eternal war we must have. She alleges that the sameness of language, of manners, of appearance, renders it impossible to distinguish us from her subjects. But because we speak English, and look like them, are we to be punished? Are free and independent men to be submitted to their bond-age?

England has misrepresented to all Europe this ground of the war. She has called it a new pretension, set up since the repeal of her orders of council. She knows there has never been a moment of suspension of our reclamations against it, from General Washington's time inclusive, to the present day: and that it is distinctly stated in our declaration of war, as one of its principal causes. She has pretended we have entered into the war to establish the principle of 'free bottoms, free goods,' or to protect her seamen against her own right over them. We contend for neither of these. She pretends we are partial to France; that we have observed a fraudulent and un- faithful neutrality between her and her enemy. She knows this to be false, and that if there has been any inequality in our proceedings towards the belligerents, it has been in her favor. Her ministers are in possession of full proofs of this. Our accepting at once, and sincerely, the mediation of the virtuous Alexander, their greatest friend, and the most aggravated en- emy of Buonaparte, sufficiently proves whether we have par- tialities on the side of her enemy. I sincerely pray that this mediation may produce a just peace. It will prove that the immortal character, which has first stopped by war the career of the destroyer of mankind, is the friend of peace, of justice, of human happiness, and the patron of unoffending and in- jured nations. He is too honest and impartial to countenance propositions of peace derogatory to the freedom of the seas.

Shall I apologise to you, my dear Madam, for this long political letter? But yours justifies the subject, and my feelings must plead for the unreserved expression of them; and they have been the less reserved, as being from a private citizen, retired from all connection with the government of his coun- try, and whose ideas, expressed without communication with any one, are neither known, nor imputable to them.

The dangers of the sea are now so great, and the possibili- ties of interception by sea and land such, that I shall subscribe no name to this letter. You will know from whom it comes, by its reference to the date of time and place of yours, as well as by its subject in answer to that. This omission must not lessen in your view the assurances of my great esteem, of my sincere sympathies for the share which you bear in the afflic- tions of your country, and the deprivations to which a lawless will has subjected you. In return, you enjoy the dignified sat- isfaction of having met them, rather than be yoked with the abject, to his car; and that, in withdrawing from oppression, you have followed the virtuous example of a father, whose name will ever be dear to your country and to mankind. With my prayers that you may be restored to it, that you may see it re-established in that temperate portion of liberty which does not infer either anarchy or licentiousness, in that high degree of prosperity which would be the consequence of such a government, in that, in short, which the constitution of 1789 would have insured it, if wisdom could have stayed at that point the fervid but imprudent zeal of men, who did not know the character of their own countrymen, and that you may long live in health and happiness under it, and leave to the world a well educated and virtuous representative and descendant of your honored father, is the ardent prayer of the sincere and respectful friend who writes this letter.

LIGHT AND LIBERTY AND THE PARTIES

To John Adams

Monticello, June 15, 1813

DEAR SIR—I wrote you a letter on the 27th. of May, which probably would reach you about the 3d. inst. and on the 9th. I recieved yours of the 29th. of May. Of Lindsay's Memoirs I had never before heard, and scarcely indeed of himself. It could not therefore but be unexpected that two letters of mine should have any thing to do with his life. The name of his editor was new to me, and certainly presents itself, for the first time, under unfavorable circumstances. Religion, I suppose, is the scope of his book: and that a writer on that subject should usher himself to the world in the very act of the grossest abuse of confidence, by publishing private letters which passed between two friends, with no views to their ever being made public, is an instance of inconsistency, as well as of infidelity of which I would rather be the victim than the author. By your kind quotation of the dates of my two letters I have been enabled to turn to them. They had compleatly evanished from my memory. The last is on the subject of religion, and by it's publication will gratify the priesthood with new occasion of repeating their Comminations against me. They wish it to be believed that he can have no religion who advocates it's freedom. This was not the doctrine of Priestley, and I honored him for the example of liberality he set to his order. The first letter is political. It recalls to our recollection the gloomy transactions of the times, the doctrines they witnessed, and the sensibilities they excited. It was a confidential communication of reflections on these from one friend to another, deposited in his bosom, and never meant to trouble the public mind. Whether the character of the times is justly portrayed or not, posterity will decide. But on one feature of them they can never decide, the sensations excited in free yet firm minds, by the terrorism of the day. None can concieve who did not witness them, and they were felt by one party only. This letter exhibits their side of the medal. The Federalists no doubt have presented the other, in their private correspondences, as well as open action. If these correspondencies should ever be laid open to the public eye, they will probably be found not models of comity towards their adversaries. The readers of my letter should be cautioned not to confine it's view to this country alone. England and it's alarmists were equally under consideration. Still less must they consider it as looking personally towards you. You happen indeed to be quoted because you happened to express, more pithily than had been done by themselves, one of the mottos of the party. This was in your answer to the address of the young men of Philadelphia. [See Selection of patriotic addresses. pa. 198.] One of the questions you know on which our parties took different sides, was on the improvability of the human mind, in science, in ethics, in government etc. Those who advocated reformation of institutions, pari passu, with the progress of science, maintained that no definite limits could be assigned to that progress. The enemies of reform, on the other hand, denied improvement, and advocated steady adherence to the principles, practices and institutions of our fathers, which they represented as the consummation of wisdom, and akmé of excellence, beyond which the human mind could never advance. Altho' in the passage of your answer alluded to, you expressly disclaim the wish to influence the freedom of enquiry, you predict that that will produce nothing more worthy of transmission to posterity, than the principles, institutions, and systems of education recieved from their ancestors. I do not consider this as your deliberate opinion. You possess, yourself, too much science, not to see how much is still ahead of you, unexplained and unexplored.

Your own consciousness must place you as far before our ancestors, as in the rear of our posterity. I consider it as an expression lent to the prejudices of your friends; and altho' I happened to cite it from you, the whole letter shews I had them only in view. In truth, my dear Sir, we were far from considering you as the author of all the measures we blamed. They were placed under the protection of your name, but we were satisfied they wanted much of your approbation. We ascribed them to their real authors, the Pickerings, the Wolcotts, the Tracys, the Sedgwicks, et id genus omne ["and all of their kind"], with whom we supposed you in a state of Duresse. I well remember a conversation with you, in the morning of the day on which you nominated to the Senate a substitute for Pickering, in which you expressed a just impatience under 'the legacy of Secretaries which Gen. Washington had left you' and whom you seemed therefore to consider as under public protection. Many other incidents shewed how differently you would have acted with less impassioned advisers; and subsequent events have proved that your minds were not together. You would do me great injustice therefore by taking to yourself what was intended for men who were then your secret, as they are now your open enemies. Should you write on the subject, as you propose, I am sure we shall see you place yourself farther from them than from us.

As to myself, I shall take no part in any discussions. I leave others to judge of what I have done, and to give me exactly that place which they shall think I have occupied. Marshall has written libels on one side; others, I suppose, will be written on the other side; and the world will sift both, and separate the truth as well as they can. I should see with reluctance the passions of that day rekindled in this, while so many of the actors are living, and all are too near the scene not to participate in sympathies with them. About facts, you and I cannot differ; because truth is our mutual guide. And if any opinions you may express should be different from mine, I shall recieve them with the liberality and indulgence which I ask for my own, and still cherish with warmth the sentiments of affectionate respect of which I can with so much truth tender you the assurance.

DEBT, TAXES, BANKS, AND PAPER

To John Wayles Eppes

Monticello, June 24, 1813

DEAR SIR,—This letter will be on politics only. For although
I do not often permit myself to think on that subject, it sometimes obtrudes itself, and suggests ideas which I am tempted
to pursue. Some of these relating to the business of finance, I
will hazard to you, as being at the head of that committee,
but intended for yourself individually, or such as you trust,
but certainly not for a mixed committee.

It is a wise rule and should be fundamental in a government disposed to cherish its credit, and at the same time to
restrain the use of it within the limits of its faculties, "never
to borrow a dollar without laying a tax in the same instant
for paying the interest annually, and the principal within a
given term; and to consider that tax as pledged to the creditors on the public faith." On such a pledge as this, sacredly
observed, a government may always command, on a *reasonable interest*, all the lendable money of their citizens, while the
necessity of an equivalent tax is a salutary warning to them
and their constituents against oppressions, bankruptcy, and
its inevitable consequence, revolution. But the term of redemption must be moderate, and at any rate within the limits
of their rightful powers. But what limits, it will be asked,
does this prescribe to their powers? What is to hinder them
from creating a perpetual debt? The laws of nature, I answer.
The earth belongs to the living, not to the dead. The will and
the power of man expire with his life, by nature's law. Some
societies give it an artificial continuance, for the encouragement of industry; some refuse it, as our aboriginal neighbors,
whom we call barbarians. The generations of men may be
considered as bodies or corporations. Each generation has the
usufruct of the earth during the period of its continuance.
When it ceases to exist, the usufruct passes on to the succeeding generation, free and unincumbered, and so on, successively, from one generation to another forever. We may
consider each generation as a distinct nation, with a right, by
the will of its majority, to bind themselves, but none to bind
the succeeding generation, more than the inhabitants of an-

other country. Or the case may be likened to the ordinary one of a tenant for life, who may hypothecate the land for his debts, during the continuance of his usufruct; but at his death, the reversioner (who is also for life only) receives it exonerated from all burthen. The period of a generation, or the term of its life, is determined by the laws of mortality, which, varying a little only in different climates, offer a general average, to be found by observation. I turn, for instance, to Buffon's tables, of twenty-three thousand nine hundred and ninety-four deaths, and the ages at which they happened, and I find that of the numbers of all ages living at one moment, half will be dead in twenty-four years and eight months. But (leaving out minors, who have not the power of self-government) of the adults (of twenty-one years of age) living at one moment, a majority of whom act for the society, one half will be dead in eighteen years and eight months. At nineteen years then from the date of a contract, the majority of the contractors are dead, and their contract with them. Let this general theory be applied to a particular case. Suppose the annual births of the State of New York to be twenty-three thousand nine hundred and ninety-four, the whole number of its inhabitants, according to Buffon, will be six hundred and seventeen thousand seven hundred and three, of all ages. Of these there would constantly be two hundred and sixty-nine thousand two hundred and eighty-six minors, and three hundred and forty-eight thousand four hundred and seventeen adults, of which last, one hundred and seventy-four thousand two hundred and nine will be a majority. Suppose that majority, on the first day of the year 1794, had borrowed a sum of money equal to the fee-simple value of the State, and to have consumed it in eating, drinking and making merry in their day; or, if your please, in quarrelling and fighting with their unoffending neighbors. Within eighteen years and eight months, one half of the adult citizens were dead. Till then, being the majority, they might rightfully levy the interest of their debt annually on themselves and their fellow-revellers, or fellow-champions. But at that period, say at this moment, a new majority have come into place, in their own right, and not under the rights, the conditions, or laws of their predecessors. Are they bound to acknowledge the debt, to consider the preceding generation as having had a right to eat up the whole soil of their country, in the course of a life, to alienate it from them, (for it would be an alienation to the creditors,) and would they think themselves either legally or morally bound to give up their country and emigrate to another for subsistence? Every one will say no; that the soil is the gift of God to the living, as much as it had been to the deceased generation; and that the laws of nature impose no obligation on them to pay this debt. And although, like some other natural rights, this has not yet entered into any declaration of rights, it is no less a law, and ought to be acted on by honest governments. It is, at the same time, a salutary curb on the spirit of war and indebtment, which, since the modern theory of the perpetuation of debt, has drenched the earth with blood, and crushed its inhabitants under burthens ever accumulating. Had this principle been declared in the British bill of rights, England would have been placed under the happy disability of waging eternal war, and of contracting her thousand millions of public debt. In seeking, then, for an ultimate term for the redemption of our debts, let us rally to this principle, and provide for their payment within the term of nineteen years at the farthest. Our government has not, as yet, begun to act on the rule of loans and taxation going hand in hand. Had any loan taken place in my time, I should have strongly urged a redeeming tax. For the loan which has been made since the last session of Congress, we should now set the example of appropriating some particular tax, sufficient to pay the interest annually, and the principal within a fixed term, less than nineteen years. And I hope yourself and your committee will render the immortal service of introducing this practice. Not that it is expected that Congress should formally declare such a principle. They wisely enough avoid deciding on abstract questions. But they may be induced to keep themselves within its limits.

I am sorry to see our loans begin at so exorbitant an interest. And yet, even at that you will soon be at the bottom of the loan-bag. We are an agricultural nation. Such an one employs its sparings in the purchase or improvement of land or stocks. The lendable money among them is chiefly that of orphans and wards in the hands of executors and guardians, and that which the farmer lays by till he has enough for the purchase in view. In such a nation there is one and one only resource for loans, sufficient to carry them through the expense of war; and that will always be sufficient, and in the power of an honest government, punctual in the preservation of its faith. The fund I mean, is *the mass of circulating coin*. Every one knows, that although not literally, it is nearly true, that every paper dollar emitted banishes a silver one from the circulation. A nation, therefore, making its purchases and payments with bills fitted for circulation, thrusts an equal sum of coin out of circulation. This is equivalent to borrowing that sum, and yet the vendor receiving payment in a medium as effectual as coin for his purchases or payments, has no claim to interest. And so the nation may continue to issue its bills as far as its wants require, and the limits of the circulation will admit. Those limits are understood to extend with us at present, to two hundred millions of dollars, a greater sum than would be necessary for any war. But this, the only resource which the government could command with certainty, the States have unfortunately fooled away, nay corruptly alienated to swindlers and shavers, under the cover of private banks. Say, too, as an additional evil, that the disposal funds of individuals, to this great amount, have thus been withdrawn from improvement and useful enterprise, and employed in the useless, usurious and demoralizing practices of bank directors and their accomplices. In the war of 1755, our State availed itself of this fund by issuing a paper money, bottomed on a specific tax for its redemption, and, to insure its credit, bearing an interest of five per cent. Within a very short time, not a bill of this emission was to be found in circulation. It was locked up in the chests of executors, guardians, widows, farmers, &c. We then issued bills bottomed on a redeeming tax, but bearing no interest. These were readily received, and never depreciated a single farthing. In the revolutionary war, the old Congress and the States issued bills without interest, and without tax. They occupied the channels of circulation very freely, till those channels were overflowed by an excess beyond all the calls of circulation. But although we have so improvidently suffered the field of circulating medium to be filched from us by private individuals, yet I think we may recover it in part, and even in the whole, if the States will co-operate with us. If treasury bills are emitted on a tax appropriated for their redemption in fifteen years, and (to insure preference in the first moments of competition) bearing an interest of six per cent. there is no one who would not take them in preference to the bank paper now afloat, on a principle of patriotism as well as interest; and they would be withdrawn from circulation into private hoards to a considerable amount. Their credit once established, others might be emitted, bottomed also on a tax, but not bearing interest; and if ever their credit faltered, open public loans, on which these bills alone should be received as specie. These, operating as a sinking fund, would reduce the quantity in circulation, so as to maintain that in an equilibrium with specie. It is not easy to estimate the obstacles which, in the beginning, we should encounter in ousting the banks from their possession of the circulation; but a steady and judicious alternation of emissions and loans, would reduce them in time. But while this is going on, another measure should be pressed, to recover ultimately our right to the circulation. The States should be applied to, to transfer the right of issuing circulating paper to Congress exclusively, *in perpetuum*, if possible, but during the war at least, with a saving of charter rights. I believe that every State west and South of Connecticut river, except Delaware, would immediately do it; and the others would follow in time. Congress would, of course, begin by obliging uncharted banks to wind up their affairs within a short time, and the others as their charters expired, forbidding the subsequent circulation of their paper. This they would supply with their own, bottomed, every emission, on an adequate tax, and bearing or not bearing interest, as the state of the public pulse should indicate. Even in the non-complying States, these bills would make their way, and supplant the unfunded paper of their banks, by their solidity, by the universality of their currency, and by their receivability for customs and taxes. It would be in their power, too, to curtail those banks to the amount of their actual specie, by gathering up their paper, and running it constantly on them. The national paper might thus take place even in the non-complying States. In this way, I am not without a hope, that this great, this sole resource for loans in an agricultural country, might yet be recovered for the use of the nation during war; and, if obtained *in perpetuum*, it would always be sufficient to carry us through any war; provided, that in the interval between war and war, all the outstanding paper should be called in, coin be permitted to flow in again, and to hold the field of circulation until another war should require its yielding place again to the national medium.

But it will be asked, are we to have no banks? Are merchants and others to be deprived of the resource of short accommodations, found so convenient? I answer, let us have banks; but let them be such as are alone to be found in any country on earth, except Great Britain. There is not a bank of discount on the continent of Europe, (at least there was not one when I was there,) which offers anything but cash in exchange for discounted bills. No one has a natural right to the trade of a money lender, but he who has the money to lend. Let those then among us, who have a monied capital, and who prefer employing it in loans rather than otherwise, set up banks, and give cash or national bills for the notes they discount. Perhaps, to encourage them, a larger interest than is legal in the other cases might be allowed them, on the condition of their lending for short periods only. It is from Great Britain we copy the idea of giving paper in exchange for discounted bills; and while we have derived from that country some good principles of government and legislation, we unfortunately run into the most servile imitation of all her practices, ruinous as they prove to her, and with the gulph yawning before us into which these very practices are precipitating her. The unlimited emission of bank paper has banished all her specie, and is now, by a depreciation acknowledged by her own statesmen, carrying her rapidly to bankruptcy, as it did France, as it did us, and will do us again, and every country permitting paper to be circulated, other than that by public authority, rigorously limited to the just measure for circulation. Private fortunes, in the present state of our circulation, are at the mercy of those self-created money lenders, and are prostrated by the floods of nominal money with which their avarice deluges us. He who lent his money to the public or to an individual, before the institution

of the United States Bank, twenty years ago, when wheat was
well sold at a dollar the bushel, and receives now his nominal
sum when it sells at two dollars, is cheated of half his fortune;
and by whom? By the banks, which, since that, have thrown
into circulation ten dollars of their nominal money where was
one at that time.

Reflect, if you please, on these ideas, and use them or not
as they appear to merit. They comfort me in the belief, that
they point out a resource ample enough, without overwhelming war taxes, for the expense of the war, and possibly still
recoverable; and that they hold up to all future time a resource within ourselves, ever at the command of government,
and competent to any wars into which we may be forced. Nor
is it a slight object to equalize taxes through peace and war.

I was in Bedford a fortnight in the month of May, and did
not know that Francis and his cousin Baker were within 10.
miles of me at Lynchburg. I learnt it by letters from themselves after I had returned home. I shall go there early in August and hope their master will permit them to pass their
Saturdays & Sundays with me. Ever affectionately yours.

NO PATENTS ON IDEAS

To Isaac McPherson

Monticello, August 13, 1813

SIR,—Your letter of August 3d asking information on the
subject of Mr. Oliver Evans' exclusive right to the use of what
he calls his Elevators, Conveyers, and Hopper-boys, has been
duly received. My wish to see new inventions encouraged,
and old ones brought again into useful notice, has made me
regret the circumstances which have followed the expiration
of his first patent. I did not expect the retrospection which
has been given to the reviving law. For although the second
proviso seemed not so clear as it ought to have been, yet it
appeared susceptible of a just construction; and the retrospective one being contrary to natural right, it was understood to
be a rule of law that where the words of a statute admit of
two constructions, the one just and the other unjust, the for-

mer is to be given them. The first proviso takes care of those who had lawfully used Evans' improvements under the first patent; the second was meant for those who had lawfully erected and used them after that patent expired, declaring they "should not be liable to damages therefor." These words may indeed be restrained to uses already past, but as there is parity of reason for those to come, there should be parity of law. Every man should be protected in his lawful acts, and be certain that no *ex post facto* law shall punish or endamage him for them. But he is endamaged, if forbidden to use a machine lawfully erected, at considerable expense, unless he will pay a new and unexpected price for it. The proviso says that he who erected and used lawfully should not be liable to pay damages. But if the proviso had been omitted, would not the law, construed by natural equity, have said the same thing. In truth both provisos are useless. And shall useless provisos, inserted *pro majori cautela* only, authorize inferences against justice? The sentiment that *ex post facto* laws are against natural right, is so strong in the United States, that few, if any, of the State constitutions have failed to proscribe them. The federal constitution indeed interdicts them in criminal cases only; but they are equally unjust in civil as in criminal cases, and the omission of a caution which would have been right, does not justify the doing what is wrong. Nor ought it to be presumed that the legislature meant to use a phrase in an unjustifiable sense, if by rules of construction it can be ever strained to what is just. The law books abound with similar instances of the care the judges take of the public integrity. Laws, moreover, abridging the natural right of the citizen, should be restrained by rigorous constructions within their narrowest limits.

Your letter, however, points to a much broader question, whether what have received from Mr. Evans the new and proper name of Elevators, are of his invention. Because, if they are not, his patent gives him no right to obstruct others in the use of what they possessed before. I assume it is a Lemma, that it is the invention of the machine itself, which is to give a patent right, and not the application of it to any particular purpose, of which it is susceptible. If one person invents a knife convenient for pointing our pens, another cannot have a patent right for the same knife to point our pencils. A compass was invented for navigating the sea; another could not have a patent right for using it to survey land. A machine for threshing *wheat* has been invented in Scotland; a second person cannot get a patent right for the same machine to thresh *oats*, a third *rye*, a fourth *peas*, a fifth *clover*, &c. A string of buckets is invented and used for raising water, ore, &c., can a second have a patent right to the same machine for raising wheat, a third oats, a fourth rye, a fifth peas, &c? The question then whether such a string of buckets was invented first by Oliver Evans, is a mere question of fact in mathematical history. Now, turning to such books only as I happen to possess, I find abundant proof that this simple machinery has been in use from time immemorial. Doctor Shaw, who visited Egypt and the Barbary coast in the years 1727–8–9, in the margin of his map of Egypt, gives us the figure of what he calls a Persian wheel, which is a string of round cups or buckets hanging on a pully, over which they revolved, bringing up water from a well and delivering it into a trough above. He found this used at Cairo, in a well 264 feet deep, which the inhabitants believe to have been the work of the patriarch Joseph. Shaw's travels, 341, Oxford edition of 1738 in folio, and the Universal History, I. 416, speaking of the manner of watering the higher lands of Egypt, says, "formerly they made use of Archimedes's screw, thence named the Egyptian pump, but they now generally use wheels (wallowers) which carry a rope or chain of earthen pots holding about seven or eight quarts apiece, and draw the water from the canals. There are besides a vast number of wells in Egypt, from which the water is drawn in the same manner to water the gardens and fruit trees; so that it is no exaggeration to say, that there are in Egypt above 200,000 oxen daily employed in this labor." Shaw's name of Persian wheel has been since given more particularly to a wheel with buckets, either fixed or suspended on pins, at its periphery. Mortimer's husbandry, I. 18, Duhamel III. II., Ferguson's Mechanic's plate, XIII; but his figure, and the verbal description of the Universal History, prove that the string of buckets is meant under that name. His figure differs from Evans' construction in the circumstances of the buckets being round, and strung through their bottom on a chain.

But it is the principle, to wit, a string of buckets, which constitutes the invention, not the form of the buckets, round, square, or hexagon; nor the manner of attaching them, nor the material of the connecting band, whether chain, rope, or leather. Vitruvius, L. x. c. 9, describes this machinery as a windlass, on which is a chain descending to the water, with vessels of copper attached to it; the windlass being turned, the chain moving on it will raise the vessel, which in passing over the windlass will empty the water they have brought up into a reservoir. And Perrault, in his edition of Vitruvius, Paris, 1684, fol. plates 61, 62, gives us three forms of these water elevators, in one of which the buckets are square, as Mr. Evans' are. Bossut, Histoire de Mathematiques, i. 86, says, "the drum wheel, the wheel with buckets and the *Chapelets*, are hydraulic machines which come to us from the ancients. But we are ignorant of the time when they began to be put into use." The *Chapelets* are the revolving bands of the buckets which Shaw calls the Persian wheel, the moderns a chain-pump, and Mr. Evans elevators. The next of my books in which I find these elevators is Wolf's Cours de Mathematiques, i. 370, and plate 1, Paris 1747, 8vo; here are two forms. In one of them the buckets are square, attached to two chains, passing over a cylinder or wallower at top, and under another at bottom, by which they are made to revolve. It is a nearly exact representation of Evans' Elevators. But a more exact one is to be seen in Desagulier's Experimental Philosophy, ii. plate 34; in the Encyclopedie de Diderot et D'Alembert, 8vo edition of Lansanne, 1st volume of plates in the four subscribed Hydraulique. Norie, is one where round eastern pots are tied by their collars between two endless ropes suspended on a revolving lantern or wallower. This is said to have been used for raising ore out of a mine. In a book which I do not possess, L'Architecture Hidraulique de Belidor, the 2d volume of which is said [De la Lande's continuation of Montuclas' Historie de Mathematiques, iii. 711] to contain a detail of all the pumps, ancient and modern, hydraulic machines, fountains, wells, &c, I have no doubt this Persian wheel, chain pump, chapelets, elevators, by whichever name you choose to call it, will be found in various forms. The last book I have to quote for it is Prony's Architecture Hydraulique i., Avertissement vii., and § 648, 649, 650. In the latter of which passages he observes that the first idea which occurs for raising water is to lift it in a bucket by hand. When the water lies too deep to be reached by hand, the bucket is suspended by a chain and let down over a pulley or windlass. If it be desired to raise a continued stream of water, the simplest means which offers itself to the mind is to attach to an endless chain or cord a number of pots or buckets, so disposed that, the chain being suspended on a lanthorn or wallower above, and plunged in water below, the buckets may descend and ascend alternately, filling themselves at bottom and emptying at a certain height above, so as to give a constant stream. Some years before the date of Mr. Evans' patent, a Mr. Martin of Caroline county in this State, constructed a drill-plough, in which he used the band of buckets for elevating the grain from the box into the funnel, which let them down into the furrow. He had bands with different sets of buckets adapted to the size of peas, of turnip seed, &c. I have used this machine for sowing Benni seed also, and propose to have a band of buckets for drilling Indian Corn, and another for wheat. Is it possible that in doing this I shall infringe Mr. Evans' patent? That I can be debarred of any use to which I might have applied my drill, when I bought it, by a patent issued after I bought it?

These verbal descriptions, applying so exactly to Mr. Evans' elevators, and the drawings exhibited to the eye, flash conviction both on reason and the senses that there is nothing new in these elevators but their being strung together on a strap of leather. If this strap of leather be an invention, entitling the inventor to a patent right, it can only extend to the strap, and the use of the string of buckets must remain free to be connected by chains, ropes, a strap of hempen girthing, or any other substance except leather. But, indeed, Mr. Martin had before used the strap of leather.

The screw of Archimedes is as ancient, at least, as the age of that mathematician, who died more than 2,000 years ago. Diodorus Siculus speaks of it, L. i., p. 21, and L. v., p. 217, of Stevens' edition of 1559, folio; and Vitruvius, xii. The cutting of its spiral worm into sections for conveying flour or grain, seems to have been an invention of Mr. Evans, and to be a fair subject of a patent right. But it cannot take away from others the use of Archimedes' screw with its perpetual spiral, for any purposes of which it is susceptible.

The hopper-boy is an useful machine, and so far as I know, original.

It has been pretended by some, (and in England especially,) that inventors have a natural and exclusive right to their inventions, and not merely for their own lives, but inheritable to their heirs. But while it is a moot question whether the origin of any kind of property is derived from nature at all, it would be singular to admit a natural and even an hereditary right to inventors. It is agreed by those who have seriously considered the subject, that no individual has, of natural right, a separate property in an acre of land, for instance. By an universal law, indeed, whatever, whether fixed or movable, belongs to all men equally and in common, is the property for the moment of him who occupies it; but when he relinquishes the occupation, the property goes with it. Stable ownership is the gift of social law, and is given late in the progress of society. It would be curious then, if an idea, the fugitive fermentation of an individual brain, could, of natural right, be claimed in exclusive and stable property. If nature has made any one thing less susceptible than all others of exclusive property, it is the action of the thinking power called an idea, which an individual may exclusively possess as long as he keeps it to himself; but the moment it is divulged, it forces itself into the possession of every one, and the receiver cannot dispossess himself of it. Its peculiar character, too, is that no one possesses the less, because every other possesses the whole of it. He who receives an idea from me, receives instruction himself without lessening mine; as he who lights his taper at mine, receives light without darkening me. That ideas should freely spread from one to another over the globe, for the moral and mutual instruction of man, and improvement of his condition, seems to have been peculiarly and benevolently designed by nature, when she made them, like fire, expansible over all space, without lessening their density in any point, and like the air in which we breathe, move, and have our physical being, incapable of confinement or exclusive appropriation. Inventions then cannot, in nature, be a subject of property. Society may give an exclusive right to the profits arising from them, as an encouragement to men to pursue ideas which may produce utility, but this may or may not be done, according to the will and convenience of the society, without claim or complaint from any body. Accordingly, it is a fact, as far as I am informed, that England was, until we copied her, the only country on earth which ever, by a general law, gave a legal right to the exclusive use of an idea. In some other countries it is sometimes done, in a great case, and by a special and personal act, but, generally speaking, other nations have thought that these monopolies produce more embarrassment than advantage to society; and it may be observed that the nations which refuse monopolies of invention, are as fruitful as England in new and useful devices.

Considering the exclusive right to invention as given not of natural right, but for the benefit of society, I know well the difficulty of drawing a line between the things which are worth to the public the embarrassment of an exclusive patent, and those which are not. As a member of the patent board for several years, while the law authorized a board to grant or refuse patents, I saw with what slow progress a system of general rules could be matured. Some, however, were established by that board. One of these was, that a machine of which we were possessed, might be applied by every man to any use of which it is susceptible, and that this right ought not to be taken from him and given to a monopolist, because the first perhaps had occasion so to apply it. Thus a screw for crushing plaster might be employed for crushing corn-cobs. And a chain-pump for raising water might be used for raising wheat: this being merely a change of application. Another rule was that a change of material should not give title to a patent. As the making a ploughshare of cast rather than of wrought iron; a comb of iron instead of horn or of ivory, or the connecting buckets by a band of leather rather than of hemp or iron. A third was that a mere change of form should give no right to a patent, as a high-quartered shoe instead of a low one; a round hat instead of a three-square; or a square bucket instead of a round one. But for this rule, all the changes of fashion in dress would have been under the tax of patentees. These were among the rules which the uniform decisions of the board had already established, and under each of them Mr. Evans' patent would have been refused. First, because it was a mere change of application of the chain-pump, from raising water to raise wheat. Secondly, because the using a leathern instead of a hempen band, was a mere change of material; and thirdly, square buckets instead of round, are only a change of form, and the ancient forms, too, appear to have been indifferently square or round. But there were still abundance of cases which could not be brought under rule, until they should have presented themselves under all their aspects; and these investigations occupying more time of the members of the board than they could spare from higher duties, the whole was turned over to the judiciary, to be matured into a system, under which every one might know when his actions were safe and lawful. Instead of refusing a patent in the first instance, as the board was authorized to do, the patent now issues of course, subject to be declared void on such principles as should be established by the courts of law. This business, however, is but little analogous to their course of reading, since we might in vain turn over all the lubberly volumes of the law to find a single ray which would lighten the path of the mechanic or the mathematician. It is more within the information of a board of academical professors, and a previous refusal of patent would better guard our citizens against harrassment by law-suits. But England had given it to her judges, and the usual predominancy of her examples carried it to ours.

It happened that I had myself a mill built in the interval between Mr. Evans' first and second patents. I was living in Washington, and left the construction to the mill-wright. I did not even know he had erected elevators, conveyers and hopper-boys, until I learnt it by an application from Mr. Evans' agent for the patent price. Although I had no idea he had a right to it by law, (for no judicial decision had then been given,) yet I did not hesitate to remit to Mr. Evans the old and moderate patent price, which was what he then asked, from a wish to encourage even the useful revival of ancient inventions. But I then expressed my opinion of the law in a letter, either to Mr. Evans or to his agent.

I have thus, Sir, at your request, given you the facts and

ideas which occur to me on this subject. I have done it without reserve, although I have not the pleasure of knowing you personally. In thus frankly committing myself to you, I trust you will feel it as a point of honor and candor, to make no use of my letter which might bring disquietude on myself. And particularly, I should be unwilling to be brought into any difference with Mr. Evans, whom, however, I believe too reasonable to take offence at an honest difference of opinion. I esteem him much, and sincerely wish him wealth and honor. I deem him a valuable citizen, of uncommon ingenuity and usefulness. And had I not esteemed still more the establishment of sound principles, I should now have been silent. If any of the matter I have offered can promote that object, I have no objection to its being so used; if it offers nothing new, it will of course not be used at all. I have gone with some minuteness into the mathematical history of the elevator, because it belongs to a branch of science in which, as I have before observed, it is not incumbent on lawyers to be learned; and it is possible, therefore, that some of the proofs I have quoted may have escaped on their former arguments. On the law of the subject I should not have touched, because more familiar to those who have already discussed it; but I wished to state my own view of it merely in justification of myself, my name and approbation being subscribed to the act. With these explanations, accept the assurance of my respect.

A "DUCTILE AND COPIOUS" LANGUAGE

To John Waldo

Monticello, August 16, 1813

SIR,—Your favor of March 27th came during my absence on a journey of some length. It covered your "Rudiments of English Grammar," for which I pray you to accept my thanks. This acknowledgment of it has been delayed, until I could have time to give the work such a perusal as the avocations to which I am subject would permit. In the rare and short intervals which these have allotted me, I have gone over with pleasure a considerable part, although not yet the whole of it.

But I am entirely unqualified to give that critical opinion of it which you do me the favor to ask. Mine has been a life of business, of that kind which appeals to a man's conscience, as well as his industry, not to let it suffer, and the few moments allowed me from labor have been devoted to more attractive studies, that of grammar having never been a favorite with me. The scanty foundation, laid in at school, has carried me through a life of much hasty writing, more indebted for style to reading and memory, than to rules of grammar. I have been pleased to see that in all cases you appeal to usage, as the arbiter of language; and justly consider that as giving law to grammar, and not grammar to usage. I concur entirely with you in opposition to Purists, who would destroy all strength and beauty of style, by subjecting it to a rigorous compliance with their rules. Fill up all the ellipses and syllepses of Tacitus, Sallust, Livy, &c., and the elegance and force of their sententious brevity are extinguished.

"Auferre, trucidare, rapere, falsis nominibus, imperium appellant." "Deorum injurias, diis curæ." "Allieni appetens, sui profusus; ardens in cupiditatibus; satis loquentiæ, sapientiæ parum." "Annibal peto pacem." "Per diem Sol non *uret* te, neque Luna per noctem." Wire-draw these expressions by filling up the whole syntax and sense, and they become dull paraphrases on rich sentiments. We may say then truly with Quinctilian, "Aliud est Grammaticé, aliud Latiné loqui." I am no friend, therefore, to what is called *Purism*, but a zealous one to the *Neology* which has introduced these two words without the authority of any dictionary. I consider the one as destroying the nerve and beauty of language, while the other improves both, and adds to its copiousness. I have been not a little disappointed, and made suspicious of my own judgment, on seeing the Edinburgh Reviews, the ablest critics of the age, set their faces against the introduction of new words into the English language; they are particularly apprehensive that the writers of the United States will adulterate it. Certainly so great growing a population, spread over such an extent of country, with such a variety of climates, of productions, of arts, must enlarge their language, to make it answer its purpose of expressing all ideas, the new as well as the old. The new circumstances under which we are placed, call for new words, new phrases, and for the transfer of old words to new objects. An American dialect will therefore be formed; so will a West-Indian and Asiatic, as a Scotch and an Irish are already formed. But whether will these adulterate, or enrich the English language? Has the beautiful poetry of Burns, or his Scottish dialect, disfigured it? Did the Athenians consider the Doric, the Ionian, the Æolic, and other dialects, as disfiguring or as beautifying their language? Did they fastidiously disavow Herodotus, Pindar, Theocritus, Sappho, Alcæus, or Grecian writers? On the contrary, they were sensible that the variety of dialects, still infinitely varied by poetical license, constituted the riches of their language, and made the Grecian Homer the first of poets, as he must ever remain, until a language equally ductile and copious shall again be spoken.

Every language has a set of terminations, which make a part of its peculiar idiom. Every root among the Greeks was permitted to vary its termination, so as to express its radical idea in the form of any one of the parts of speech; to wit, as a noun, an adjective, a verb, participle, or adverb; and each of these parts of speech again, by still varying the termination, could vary the shade of idea existing in the mind.

       *   *   *

It was not, then, the number of Grecian roots (for some other languages may have as many) which made it the most copious of the ancient languages; but the infinite diversification which each of these admitted. Let the same license be allowed in English, the roots of which, native and adopted, are perhaps more numerous, and its idiomatic terminations more various than of the Greek, and see what the language would become. Its idiomatic terminations are:—

Subst. Gener-ation—ator; degener-acy; gener-osity—ousness—alship—alissimo; king-dom—ling; joy-ance; enjoy-er—ment; herb-age—alist; sanct-uary—imony—itude; royal-ism; lamb-kin; child-hood; bishop-ric; proceed-ure; horsemanship; worthi-ness.

Adj. Gener-ant—ative—ic—ical—able—ous—al; joy-ful—less—some; herb-y; accous-escent—ulent; child-ish; wheat-en.

Verb. Gener-ate—alize.
Part. Gener-ating—ated.
Adv. Gener-al—ly.

I do not pretend that this is a complete list of all the terminations of the two languages. It is as much so as a hasty recollection suggests, and the omissions are as likely to be to the disadvantage of the one as the other. If it be a full, or equally fair enumeration, the English are the double of the Greek terminations.

But there is still another source of copiousness more abundant than that of termination. It is the composition of the root, and of every member of its family, 1, with prepositions, and 2, with other words. The prepositions used in the composition of Greek words are:—

*   *   *

Now multiply each termination of a family into every preposition, and how prolific does it make each root! But the English language, besides its own prepositions, about twenty in number, which it compounds with English roots, uses those of the Greek for adopted Greek roots, and of the Latin for Latin roots. The English prepositions, with examples of their use, are a, as in a-long, a-board, a-thirst, a-clock; be, as in be-lie; mis, as in mis-hap; these being inseparable. The separable, with examples, are above-cited, after-thought, gain-say, before-hand, fore-thought, behind-hand, by-law, for-give, fro-ward, in-born, on-set, over-go, out-go, thorough-go, under-take, up-lift, with-stand. Now let us see what copiousness this would produce, were it allowed to compound every root and its family with every preposition, where both sense and sound would be in its favor. Try it on an English root, the verb "to place," Anglo Saxon *plæce*,* for instance, and the Greek and Latin roots, of kindred meaning, adopted in English, to wit, θεσις and locatio, with their prepositions.

---

*Johnson derives "place" from the French "place," an open square in a town. But its northern parentage is visible in its syno-nime *platz*, Teutonic, and *plattse*, Belgic, both of which signify locus, and the Anglo-Saxon *plæce, platea, vicus*.

mis-place	amphi-thesis	a-location	inter-location
after-place	ana-thesis	ab-location	intro-location
gain-place	anti-thesis	abs-location	juxta-location
fore-place	apo-thesis	al-location	ob-location
hind-place	dia-thesis	anti-location	per-location
by-place	ek-thesis	circum-location	post-location
for-place	en-thesis	cis-location	pre-location
fro-place	epi-thesis	col-location	preter-location
in-place	cata-thesis	contra-location	pro-location
on-place	para-thesis	de-location	retro-location
over-place	peri-thesis	di-location	re-location
out-place	pro-thesis	dis-location	se-location
thorough-place	pros-thesis	e-location	sub-location
under-place	syn-thesis	ex-location	super-location
up-place	hyper-thesis	extra-location	trans-location
with-place	hypo-thesis	il-location	ultra-location

Some of these compounds would be new; but all present distinct meanings, and the synonisms of the three languages offer a choice of sounds to express the same meaning; add to this, that in some instances, usage has authorized the compounding an English root with a Latin preposition, as in de-place, dis-place, re-place. This example may suffice to show what the language would become, in strength, beauty, variety, and every circumstance which gives perfection to language, were it permitted freely to draw from all its legitimate sources.

The second source of composition is of one family of roots with another. The Greek avails itself of this most abundantly, and beautifully. The English once did it freely, while in its Anglo-Saxon form, *e. g. boc-cræft*, book-craft, learning, *riht-ʒeleaf-full*, right-belief-ful, orthodox. But it has lost by desuetude much of this branch of composition, which it is desirable however to resume.

If we wish to be assured from experiment of the effect of a judicious spirit of Neology, look at the French language. Even before the revolution, it was deemed much more copious than the English; at a time, too, when they had an academy which endeavored to arrest the progress of their language, by fixing it to a Dictionary, out of which no word was ever to be sought, used, or tolerated. The institution of parliamentary assemblies in 1789, for which their language had no opposite terms or phrases, as having never before needed them, first obliged them to adopt the Parliamentary vocabulary of England; and other new circumstances called for corresponding new words; until by the number of these adopted, and by the analogies for adoption which they have legitimated, I think we may say with truth that a Dictionaire Neologique of these would be half as large as the dictionary of the academy; and that at this time it is the language in which every shade of idea, distinctly perceived by the mind, may be more exactly expressed, than in any language at this day spoken by man. Yet I have no hesitation in saying that the English language is founded on a broader base, native and adopted, and capable, with the like freedom of employing its materials, of becoming superior to that in copiousness and euphony. Not indeed by holding fast to Johnson's Dictionary; not by raising a hue and cry against every word he has not licensed; but by encouraging and welcoming new compositions of its elements. Learn from Lye and Benson what the language would now have been if restrained to their vocabularies. Its enlargement must be the consequence, to a certain degree, of its transplantation from the latitude of London into every climate of the globe; and the greater the degree the more precious will it become as the organ of the development of the human mind.

These are my visions on the improvement of the English language by a free use of its faculties. To realize them would require a course of time. The example of good writers, the approbation of men of letters, the judgment of sound critics, and of none more than of the Edinburgh Reviewers, would give it a beginning, and once begun, its progress might be as rapid as it has been in France, where we see what a period of only twenty years has effected. Under the auspices of British science and example it might commence with hope. But the dread of innovation there, and especially of any example set by France, has, I fear, palsied the spirit of improvement. Here, where all is new, no innovation is feared which offers good. But we have no distinct class of literati in our country. Every man is engaged in some industrious pursuit, and science is but a secondary occupation, always subordinate to the main business of his life. Few therefore of those who are qualified, have leisure to write. In time it will be otherwise. In the meanwhile, necessity obliges us to neologize. And should the language of England continue stationary, we shall probably enlarge our employment of it, until its new character may separate it in name as well as in power, from the mother-tongue.

Although the copiousness of a language may not in strictness make a part of its grammar, yet it cannot be deemed foreign to a general course of lectures on its structure and character; and the subject having been presented to my mind by the occasion of your letter, I have indulged myself in its speculation, and hazarded to you what has occurred, with the assurance of my great respect.

THE CODE OF JESUS
To John Adams

Monticello, Oct. 12, 1813

DEAR SIR—Since mine of Aug. 22. I have recieved your favors of Aug. 16. Sep. 2. 14. 15. and—and Mrs. Adams's of Sep. 20. I now send you, according to your request a copy of the Syllabus. To fill up this skeleton with arteries, with veins, with nerves, muscles and flesh, is really beyond my time and information. Whoever could undertake it would find great aid in Enfield's judicious abridgment of Brucker's history of Philosophy, in which he has reduced 5. or 6. quarto vols. of 1000. pages each of Latin closely printed, to two moderate 8 vos. of English, open, type.

To compare the morals of the old, with those of the new testament, would require an attentive study of the former, a search thro' all it's books for it's precepts, and through all it's history for it's practices, and the principles they prove. As commentaries too on these, the philosophy of the Hebrews must be enquired into, their Mishna, their Gemara, Cabbala, Jezirah, Sohar, Cosri, and their Talmud must be examined and understood, in order to do them full justice. Brucker, it should seem, has gone deeply into these Repositories of their ethics, and Enfield, his epitomiser, concludes in these words. 'Ethics were so little studied among the Jews, that, in their whole compilation called the Talmud, there is only one trea-

tise on moral subjects. Their books of Morals chiefly consisted in a minute enumeration of duties. From the law of
Moses were deduced 613. precepts, which were divided into
two classes, affirmative and negative, 248 in the former, and
365 in the latter. It may serve to give the reader some idea of
the low state of moral philosophy among the Jews in the
Middle age, to add, that of the 248. affirmative precepts, only
3. were considered as obligatory upon women; and that, in
order to obtain salvation, it was judged sufficient to fulfill any
one single law in the hour of death; the observance of the rest
being deemed necessary, only to increase the felicity of the
future life. What a wretched depravity of sentiment and manners must have prevailed before such corrupt maxims could
have obtained credit! It is impossible to collect from these
writings a consistent series of moral Doctrine.' Enfield, B. 4.
chap. 3. It was the reformation of this 'wretched depravity'
of morals which Jesus undertook. In extracting the pure principles which he taught, we should have to strip off the artificial vestments in which they have been muffled by priests,
who have travestied them into various forms, as instruments
of riches and power to them. We must dismiss the Platonists
and Plotinists, the Stagyrites and Gamalielites, the Eclectics
the Gnostics and Scholastics, their essences and emanations,
their Logos and Demi-urgos, Aeons and Daemons male and
female, with a long train of Etc. Etc. Etc. or, shall I say at
once, of Nonsense. We must reduce our volume to the simple
evangelists, select, even from them, the very words only of
Jesus, paring off the Amphibologisms into which they have
been led by forgetting often, or not understanding, what had
fallen from him, by giving their own misconceptions as his
dicta, and expressing unintelligibly for others what they had
not understood themselves. There will be found remaining
the most sublime and benevolent code of morals which has
ever been offered to man. I have performed this operation for
my own use, by cutting verse by verse out of the printed
book, and arranging, the matter which is evidently his, and
which is as easily distinguishable as diamonds in a dunghill.
The result is an 8 vo. of 46. pages of pure and unsophisticated
doctrines, such as were professed and acted on by the *unlettered* apostles, the Apostolic fathers, and the Christians of the

1st. century. Their Platonising successors indeed, in after times, in order to legitimate the corruptions which they had incorporated into the doctrines of Jesus, found it necessary to disavow the primitive Christians, who had taken their principles from the mouth of Jesus himself, of his Apostles, and the Fathers cotemporary with them. They excommunicated their followers as heretics, branding them with the opprobrious name of Ebionites or Beggars.

For a comparison of the Graecian philosophy with that of Jesus, materials might be largely drawn from the same source. Enfield gives a history, and detailed account of the opinions and principles of the different sects. These relate to

the gods, their natures, grades, places and powers;

the demi-gods and daemons, and their agency with man;

the Universe, it's structure, extent, production and duration;

the origin of things from the elements of fire, water, air and
     earth;

the human soul, it's essence and derivation;

the summum bonum and finis bonorum; with a thousand idle dreams and fancies on these and other subjects the knolege of which is withheld from man, leaving but a short chapter for his moral duties, and the principal section of that given to what he owes himself, to precepts for rendering him impassible, and unassailable by the evils of life, and for preserving his mind in a state of constant serenity.

Such a canvas is too broad for the age of seventy, and especially of one whose chief occupations have been in the practical business of life. We must leave therefore to others, younger and more learned than we are, to prepare this euthanasia for Platonic Christianity, and it's restoration to the primitive simplicity of it's founder. I think you give a just outline of the theism of the three religions when you say that the principle of the Hebrew was the fear, of the Gentile the honor, and of the Christian the love of God.

An expression in your letter of Sep. 14. that 'the human understanding is a revelation from it's maker' gives the best solution, that I believe can be given, of the question, What did Socrates mean by his Daemon? He was too wise to believe, and too honest to pretend that he had real and familiar converse with a superior and invisible being. He probably considered the suggestions of his conscience, or reason, as revelations, or inspirations from the Supreme mind, bestowed, on important occasions, by a special superintending providence.

I acknolege all the merit of the hymn of Cleanthes to Jupiter, which you ascribe to it. It is as highly sublime as a chaste and correct imagination can permit itself to go. Yet in the contemplation of a being so superlative, the hyperbolic flights of the Psalmist may often be followed with approbation, even with rapture; and I have no hesitation in giving him the palm over all the Hymnists of every language, and of every time. Turn to the 148th. psalm, in Brady and Tate's version. Have such conceptions been ever before expressed? Their version of the 15th. psalm is more to be esteemed for it's pithiness, than it's poetry. Even Sternhold, the leaden Sternhold, kindles, in a single instance, with the sublimity of his original, and expresses the majesty of God descending on the earth, in terms not unworthy of the subject.

'The Lord descended from above
And underneath his feet he cast
On Cherubim and Seraphim
And on the wings of mighty winds
And bowed the heav'ns most high;
The darkness of the sky.
Full royally he rode;
Came flying all abroad.'
Psalm xviii. 9. 10.

The Latin versions of this passage by Buchanan and by Johnston, are but mediocres. But the Greek of Duport is worthy of quotation.

> Ουρανον αγκλινας κατεβη· ὑπο ποσσι δ' ἑοισιν
> Αχλυς αμφι μελαινα χυθη και νυξ ερεβεννη.
> Ριμφα ποτᾶτο Χερουβῳ οχευμενος, ωσπερ εφ' ἱππῳ.
> Ἱπτατο δε πτερυγεσσι πολυπλαγκτου ανεμοιο.

The best collection of these psalms is that of the Octagonian dissenters of Liverpool, in their printed Form of prayer; but they are not always the best versions. Indeed bad is the best of the English versions; not a ray of poetical genius having ever been employed on them. And how much depends on this may be seen by comparing Brady and Tate's XVth. psalm with Blacklock's Justum et tenacem propositi virum ["a man just and steadfast of purpose"] of Horace, quoted in Hume's history, Car. 2. ch. 65. A translation of David in this style, or in that of Pompei's Cleanthes, might give us some idea of the merit of the original. The character too of the poetry of these hymns is singular to us. Written in monostichs, each divided into strophe and antistrophe, the sentiment of the 1st. member responded with amplification or antithesis in the second.

On the subject of the Postscript of yours of Aug. 16. and of Mrs. Adams's letter, I am silent. I know the depth of the affliction it has caused, and can sympathise with it the more sensibly, inasmuch as there is no degree of affliction, produced by the loss of those dear to us, which experience has not taught me to estimate. I have ever found time and silence the only medecine, and these but assuage, they never can suppress, the deep-drawn sigh which recollection for ever brings up, until recollection and life are extinguished together. Ever affectionately yours

P. S. Your's of Sep—just recieved

THE NATURAL ARISTOCRACY
To John Adams

Monticello, Oct. 28, 1813

DEAR SIR—According to the reservation between us, of taking up one of the subjects of our correspondence at a time, I turn to your letters of Aug. 16. and Sep. 2.

The passage you quote from Theognis, I think has an Ethical, rather than a political object. The whole piece is a moral *exhortation,* παραίνεσις, and this passage particularly seems to be a reproof to man, who, while with his domestic animals he is curious to improve the race by employing always the finest male, pays no attention to the improvement of his own race, but intermarries with the vicious, the ugly, or the old, for considerations of wealth or ambition. It is in conformity with the principle adopted afterwards by the Pythagoreans, and expressed by Ocellus in another form. Περι δε τῆς ἐκ τῶν αλληλων ανθρωπων γενεσεως etc.—ουχ ἡδονης ἐνεκα ἡ μιξις. Which, as literally as intelligibility will admit, may be thus translated. 'Concerning the interprocreation of men, how, and of whom it shall be, in a perfect manner, and according to the laws of modesty and sanctity, conjointly, this is what I think right. First to lay it down that we do not commix for the sake of pleasure, but of the procreation of children. For the powers, the organs and desires for coition have not been given by god to man for the sake of pleasure, but for the procreation of the race. For as it were incongruous for a mortal born to partake of divine life, the immortality of the race being taken away, god fulfilled the purpose by making the generations uninterrupted and continuous. This therefore we are especially to lay down as a principle, that coition is not for the sake of pleasure.' But Nature, not trusting to this moral and abstract motive, seems to have provided more securely for the perpetuation of the species by making it the effect of the oestrum implanted in the constitution of both sexes. And not only has the commerce of love been indulged on this unhallowed impulse, but made subservient also to wealth and ambition by marriages without regard to the beauty, the healthiness, the understanding, or virtue of the subject from which we are to breed. The selecting the best male for a Haram of well chosen females also, which Theognis seems to recommend from the example of our sheep and asses, would doubtless improve the human, as it does the brute animal, and produce a race of veritable αριστοι ["aristocrats"]. For experience proves that the moral and physical qualities of man, whether good or evil, are transmissible in a certain degree from father to son. But I suspect that the equal rights of men will rise up against this privileged Solomon, and oblige us to continue acquiescence under the Ἀμαυρωσις γενεος ἀστων ["the degeneration of the race of men"] which Theognis complains of, and to content ourselves with the accidental aristoi produced by the fortuitous concourse of breeders. For I agree with you that there is a natural aristocracy among men. The grounds of this are virtue and talents. Formerly bodily powers gave place among the aristoi. But since the invention of gunpowder has armed the weak as well as the strong with missile death, bodily strength, like beauty, good humor, politeness and other accomplishments, has become but an auxiliary ground of distinction. There is also an artificial aristocracy founded on wealth and birth, without either virtue or talents; for with these it would belong to the first class. The natural aristocracy I consider as the most precious gift of nature for the instruction, the trusts, and government of society. And indeed it would have been inconsistent in creation to have formed man for the social state, and not to have provided virtue and wisdom enough to manage the concerns of the society. May we not even say that that form of government is the best which provides the most effectually for a pure selection of these natural aristoi into the offices of government? The artificial aristocracy is a mischievous ingredient in government, and provision should be made to prevent it's ascendancy. On the question, What is the best provision, you and I differ; but we differ as rational friends, using the free exercise of our own reason, and mutually indulging it's errors. *You* think it best to put the Pseudo-aristoi into a separate chamber of legislation where they may be hindered from doing mischief by their coordinate branches, and where also they may be a protection to wealth against the Agrarian and plundering enterprises of the Majority of the people. I think that to give them power in order to prevent them from doing mischief, is arming them for it, and increasing instead of remedying the evil. For if the coordinate branches can arrest their action, so may they that of the coordinates. Mischief may be done negatively as well as positively. Of this a cabal in the Senate of the U.S. has furnished many proofs. Nor do I believe them necessary to protect the wealthy; because enough of these will find their way into every branch of the legislation to protect themselves. From 15. to 20. legislatures of our own, in action for 30. years past, have proved that no fears of an equalisation of property are to be apprehended from them.

I think the best remedy is exactly that provided by all our constitutions, to leave to the citizens the free election and separation of the aristoi from the pseudo-aristoi, of the wheat from the chaff. In general they will elect the real good and wise. In some instances, wealth may corrupt, and birth blind them; but not in sufficient degree to endanger the society.

It is probable that our difference of opinion may in some

measure be produced by a difference of character in those among whom we live. From what I have seen of Massachusets and Connecticut myself, and still more from what I have heard, and the character given of the former by yourself, [vol. I. pa. III.] who know them so much better, there seems to be in those two states a traditionary reverence for certain families, which has rendered the offices of the government nearly hereditary in those families. I presume that from an early period of your history, members of these families happening to possess virtue and talents, have honestly exercised them for the good of the people, and by their services have endeared their names to them.

In coupling Connecticut with you, I mean it politically only, not morally. For having made the Bible the Common law of their land they seem to have modelled their morality on the story of Jacob and Laban. But altho' this hereditary succession to office with you may in some degree be founded in real family merit, yet in a much higher degree it has proceeded from your strict alliance of church and state. These families are canonised in the eyes of the people on the common principle 'you tickle me, and I will tickle you.' In Virginia we have nothing of this. Our clergy, before the revolution, having been secured against rivalship by fixed salaries, did not give themselves the trouble of acquiring influence over the people. Of wealth, there were great accumulations in particular families, handed down from generation to generation under the English law of entails. But the only object of ambition for the wealthy was a seat in the king's council. All their court then was paid to the crown and it's creatures; and they Philipised in all collisions between the king and people. Hence they were unpopular; and that unpopularity continues attached to their names. A Randolph, a Carter, or a Burwell must have great personal superiority over a common competitor to be elected by the people, even at this day.

At the first session of our legislature after the Declaration of Independence, we passed a law abolishing entails. And this was followed by one abolishing the privilege of Primogeniture, and dividing the lands of intestates equally among all their children, or other representatives. These laws, drawn by myself, laid the axe to the root of Pseudo-aristocracy. And had another which I prepared been adopted by the legislature, our work would have been compleat. It was a Bill for the more general diffusion of learning. This proposed to divide every county into wards of 5. or 6. miles square, like your townships; to establish in each ward a free school for reading, writing and common arithmetic; to provide for the annual selection of the best subjects from these schools who might recieve at the public expence a higher degree of education at a district school; and from these district schools to select a certain number of the most promising subjects to be compleated at an University, where all the useful sciences should be taught. Worth and genius would thus have been sought out from every condition of life, and compleatly prepared by education for defeating the competition of wealth and birth for public trusts.

My proposition had for a further object to impart to these wards those portions of self-government for which they are best qualified, by confiding to them the care of their poor, their roads, police, elections, the nomination of jurors, administration of justice in small cases, elementary exercises of militia, in short, to have made them little republics, with a Warden at the head of each, for all those concerns which, being under their eye, they would better manage than the larger republics of the county or state. A general call of ward-meetings by their Wardens on the same day thro' the state would at any time produce the genuine sense of the people on any required point, and would enable the state to act in mass, as your people have so often done, and with so much effect, by their town meetings. The law for religious freedom, which made a part of this system, having put down the aristocracy of the clergy, and restored to the citizen the freedom of the mind, and those of entails and descents nurturing an equality of condition among them, this on Education would have raised the mass of the people to the high ground of moral respectability necessary to their own safety, and to orderly government; and would have compleated the great object of qualifying them to select the veritable aristoi, for the trusts of government, to the exclusion of the Pseudalists: and the same Theognis who has furnished the epigraphs of your two letters assures us that 'ουδεμιαν πω, Κυρν· ἀγαθοι πολιν ὤλεσαν ἀνδρες, ["Curnis, good men have never harmed any city"]'. Altho' this law has not yet been acted on but in a small and inefficient degree, it is still considered as before the legislature, with other bills of the revised code, not yet taken up, and I have great hope that some patriotic spirit will, at a favorable moment, call it up, and make it the key-stone of the arch of our government.

With respect to Aristocracy, we should further consider that, before the establishment of the American states, nothing was known to History but the Man of the old world, crouded within limits either small or overcharged, and steeped in the vices which that situation generates. A government adapted to such men would be one thing; but a very different one that for the Man of these states. Here every one may have land to labor for himself if he chuses; or, preferring the exercise of any other industry, may exact for it such compensation as not only to afford a comfortable subsistence, but wherewith to provide for a cessation from labor in old age. Every one, by his property, or by his satisfactory situation, is interested in the support of law and order. And such men may safely and advantageously reserve to themselves a wholsome controul over their public affairs, and a degree of freedom, which in the hands of the Canaille of the cities of Europe, would be instantly perverted to the demolition and destruction of every thing public and private. The history of the last 25. years of France, and of the last 40. years in America, nay of it's last 200. years, proves the truth of both parts of this observation.

But even in Europe a change has sensibly taken place in the mind of Man. Science had liberated the ideas of those who read and reflect, and the American example had kindled feelings of right in the people. An insurrection has consequently begun, of science, talents and courage against rank and birth, which have fallen into contempt. It has failed in it's first effort, because the mobs of the cities, the instrument used for it's accomplishment, debased by ignorance, poverty and vice, could not be restrained to rational action. But the world will recover from the panic of this first catastrophe. Science is progressive, and talents and enterprize on the alert. Resort may be had to the people of the country, a more governable power from their principles and subordination; and rank, and birth, and tinsel-aristocracy will finally shrink into insignificance, even there. This however we have no right to meddle with. It suffices for us, if the moral and physical condition of our own citizens qualifies them to select the able and good for the direction of their government, with a recurrence of elections at such short periods as will enable them to displace an unfaithful servant before the mischief he meditates may be irremediable.

I have thus stated my opinion on a point on which we differ, not with a view to controversy, for we are both too old to change opinions which are the result of a long life of inquiry and reflection; but on the suggestion of a former letter of yours, that we ought not to die before we have explained ourselves to each other. We acted in perfect harmony thro' a long and perilous contest for our liberty and independance. A constitution has been acquired which, tho neither of us think perfect, yet both consider as competent to render our fellow-citizens the happiest and the securest on whom the sun has ever shone. If we do not think exactly alike as to it's imperfections, it matters little to our country which, after devoting to it long lives of disinterested labor, we have delivered over to our successors in life, who will be able to take care of it, and of themselves.

Of the pamphlet on aristocracy which has been sent to you, or who may be it's author, I have heard nothing but thro' your letter. If the person you suspect it may be known from the quaint, mystical and hyperbolical ideas, involved in affected, new-fangled and pedantic terms, which stamp his writings. Whatever it be, I hope your quiet is not to be affected at this day by the rudeness of intemperance of scribblers; but that you may continue in tranquility to live and to rejoice in the prosperity of our country until it shall be your own wish to take your seat among the Aristoi who have gone before you. Ever and affectionately yours.

P. S. Can you assist my memory on the enquiries of my letter of Aug. 22.?

To Alexander von Humboldt

December 6, 1813

MY DEAR FRIEND AND BARON,—I have to acknowledge your two letters of December 20 and 26, 1811, by Mr. Correa, and am first to thank you for making me acquainted with that most excellent character. He was so kind as to visit me at Monticello, and I found him one of the most learned and amiable of men. It was a subject of deep regret to separate from so much worth in the moment of its becoming known to us.

The livraison of your astronomical observations, and the 6th and 7th on the subject of New Spain, with the corresponding atlasses, are duly received, as had been the preceding cahiers. For these treasures of a learning so interesting to us, accept my sincere thanks. I think it most fortunate that your travels in those countries were so timed as to make them known to the world in the moment they were about to become actors on its stage. That they will throw off their European dependence I have no doubt; but in what kind of government their revolution will end I am not so certain. History, I believe, furnishes no example of a priest-ridden people maintaining a free civil government. This marks the lowest grade of ignorance, of which their civil as well as religious leaders will always avail themselves for their own purposes. The vicinity of New Spain to the United States, and their consequent intercourse, may furnish schools for the higher, and example for the lower classes of their citizens. And Mexico, where we learn from you that men of science are not wanting, may revolutionize itself under better auspices than the Southern provinces. These last, I fear, must end in military despotisms. The different casts of their inhabitants, their mutual hatreds and jealousies, their profound ignorance and bigotry, will be played off by cunning leaders, and each be made the instrument of enslaving others. But of all this you can best judge, for in truth we have little knowledge of them to be depended on, but through you. But in whatever governments they end they will be *American* governments, no longer to be involved in the never-ceasing broils of Europe. The European nations constitute a separate division of the globe; their localities make them part of a distinct system; they have a set of interests of their own in which it is our business never to engage ourselves. America has a hemisphere to itself. It must have its separate system of interests, which must not be subordinated to those of Europe. The insulated state in which nature has placed the American continent, should so far avail it that no spark of war kindled in the other quarters of the globe should be wafted across the wide oceans which separate us from them. And it will be so. In fifty years more the United States alone will contain fifty millions of inhabitants, and fifty years are soon gone over. The peace of 1763 is within that period. I was then twenty years old, and of course remember well all the transactions of the war preceding it. And you will live to see the epoch now equally ahead of us; and the numbers which will then be spread over the other parts of the American hemisphere, catching long before that the principles of our portion of it, and concurring with us in the maintenance of the same system. You see how readily we run into ages beyond the grave; and even those of us to whom that grave is already opening its quiet bosom. I am anticipating events of which you will be the bearer to me in the Elsyian fields fifty years hence.

You know, my friend, the benevolent plan we were pursuing here for the happiness of the aboriginal inhabitants in our vicinities. We spared nothing to keep them at peace with one another. To teach them agriculture and the rudiments of the most necessary arts, and to encourage industry by establishing among them separate property. In this way they would have been enabled to subsist and multiply on a moderate scale of landed possession. They would have mixed their blood with ours, and been amalgamated and identified with us within no distant period of time. On the commencement of our present war, we pressed on them the observance of peace and neutrality, but the interested and unprincipled policy of England has defeated all our labors for the salvation of these unfortunate people. They have seduced the greater part of the tribes within our neighborhood, to take up the hatchet against us, and the cruel massacres they have committed on the women and children of our frontiers taken by surprise, will oblige us now to pursue them to extermination, or drive them to new seats beyond our reach. Already we have driven their patrons and seducers into Montreal, and the opening season will force them to their last refuge, the walls of Quebec. We have cut off all possibility of intercourse and of mutual aid, and may pursue at our leisure whatever plan we find necessary to secure ourselves against the future effects of their savage and ruthless warfare. The confirmed brutalization, if not the extermination of this race in our America, is therefore to form an additional chapter in the English history of the same colored man in Asia, and of the brethren of their own color in Ireland, and wherever else Anglo-mercantile cupidity can find a two-penny interest in deluging the earth with human blood. But let us turn from the loathsome contemplation of the degrading effects of commercial avarice.

That their Arrowsmith should have stolen your Map of Mexico, was in the piratical spirit of his country. But I should be sincerely sorry if our Pike has made an ungenerous use of your candid communications here; and the more so as he died in the arms of victory gained over the enemies of his country. Whatever he did was on a principle of enlarging knowledge, and not for filthy shillings and pence of which he made none from that work. If what he has borrowed has any effect it will be to excite an appeal in his readers from his defective information to the copious volumes of it with which you have enriched the world. I am sorry he omitted even to acknowledge the source of his information. It has been an oversight, and not at all in the spirit of his generous nature. Let me solicit your forgiveness then of a deceased hero, of an honest and zealous patriot, who lived and died for his country.

You will find it inconceivable that Lewis's journey to the Pacific should not yet have appeared; nor is it in my power to tell you the reason. The measures taken by his surviving companion, Clarke, for the publication, have not answered our wishes in point of despatch. I think, however, from what I have heard, that the mere journal will be out within a few weeks in two volumes 8vo. These I will take care to send you with the tobacco seed you desired, if it be possible for them to escape the thousand ships of our enemies spread over the ocean. The botanical and zoological discoveries of Lewis will probably experience greater delay, and become known to the world through other channels before that volume will be ready. The Atlas, I believe, waits on the leisure of the engraver.

Although I do not know whether you are now at Paris or ranging the regions of Asia to acquire more knowledge for the use of men, I cannot deny myself the gratification of an endeavor to recall myself to your recollection, and of assuring you of my constant attachment, and of renewing to you the just tribute of my affectionate esteem and high respect and consideration.

WAR AND BOTANICAL EXCHANGES
To Madame de Tessé

December 8, 1813

While at war, my dear Madam and friend, with the leviathan of the ocean, there is little hope of a letter escaping his thousand ships; yet I cannot permit myself longer to withhold the acknowledgment of your letter of June 28 of the last year, with which came the memoirs of the Margrave of Bareuth. I am much indebted to you for this singular morsel of history which has given us a certain view of kings, queens and princes, disrobed of their formalities. It is a peep into the state of the Egyptian god Apis. It would not be easy to find grosser manners, coarser vices, or more meanness in the poorest huts of our peasantry. The princess shows herself the legitimate sister of Frederic, cynical, selfish, and without a heart. Notwithstanding your wars with England, I presume you get the publications of that country. The memoirs of Mrs. Clarke and of her *darling* prince, and the book emphatically so called, because it is the Biblia Sacra Deorum et Dearum sub-cœlestium, the Prince Regent, his Princess and the minor deities of his sphere, form a worthy sequel to the memoirs of Bareuth; instead of the vulgarity and penury of the court of Berlin, giving us the vulgarity and profusion of that of London, and the gross stupidity and profligacy of the latter, in lieu of the genius and misanthropism of the former. The whole might be published as a supplement of M. de Buffon, under the title of the "Natural History of Kings and Princes," or as a separate work and called "Medicine for Monarchists." The "Intercepted Letters," a later English publication of great wit and humor, has put them to their proper use by holding them up as butts for the ridicule and contempt of mankind. Yet by such worthless beings is a great nation to be governed and even made to deify their old king because he is only a fool and a maniac, and to forgive and forget his having lost to them a great and flourishing empire, added nine hundred millions sterling to their debt, for which the fee simple of the whole island would not sell, if offered farm by farm at public auction, and increased their annual taxes from eight to seventy millions sterling, more than the whole rent-roll of the island. What must be the dreary prospect from the son when such a father is deplored as a national loss. But let us drop these odious beings and pass to those of an higher order, the plants of the field. I am afraid I have given you a great deal more trouble than I intended by my inquiries for the Maronnier or Castanea Sativa, of which I wished to possess my own country, without knowing how rare its culture was even in yours. The two plants which your researches have placed in your own garden, it will be all but impossible to remove hither. The war renders their safe passage across the Atlantic extremely precarious, and, if landed anywhere but in the Chesapeake, the risk of the additional voyage along the coast to Virginia, is still greater. Under these circumstances it is better they should retain their present station, and compensate to you the trouble they have cost you.

I learn with great pleasure the success of your new gardens at Auenay. No occupation can be more delightful or useful. They will have the merit of inducing you to forget those of Chaville. With the botanical riches which you mention to have been derived to England from New Holland, we are as yet unacquainted. Lewis's journey across our continent to the Pacific has added a number of new plants to our former stock. Some of them are curious, some ornamental, some useful, and some may by culture be made acceptable to our tables. I have growing, which I destine for you, a very handsome little shrub of the size of a currant bush. Its beauty consists in a great produce of berries of the size of currants, and literally as white as snow, which remain on the bush through the winter, after its leaves have fallen, and make it an object as singular as it is beautiful. We call it the snow-berry bush, no botanical name being yet given to it, but I do not know why we might not call it Chionicoccos, or Kallicoccos. All Lewis's plants are growing in the garden of Mr. McMahon, a gardener of Philadelphia, to whom I consigned them, and from whom I shall have great pleasure, when peace is restored, in ordering for you any of these or of our other indigenous plants. The port of Philadelphia has great intercourse with Bordeaux and Nantes, and some little perhaps with Havre. I was mortified not long since by receiving a letter from a merchant in Bordeaux, apologizing for having suffered a box of plants addressed by me to you, to get accidentally covered in his warehouse by other objects, and to remain three years undiscovered, when every thing in it was found to be rotten. I have learned occasionally that others rotted in the warehouses of the English pirates. We are now settling that account with them. We have taken their Upper Canada and shall add the Lower to it when the season will admit; and hope to remove them fully and finally from our continent. And what they will feel more, for they value their colonies only for the bales of cloth they take from them, we have established manufactures, not only sufficient to supersede our demand from them, but to rivalize them in foreign markets. But for the course of our war I will refer you to M. de La Fayette, to whom I state it more particularly.

Our friend Mr. Short is well. He makes Philadelphia his winter quarters, and New York or the country, those of the summer. In his fortune he is perfectly independent and at ease, and does not trouble himself with the party politics of our country. Will you permit me to place here for M. de Tessé the testimony of my high esteem and respect, and accept for yourself an assurance of the warm recollections I retain of your many civilities and courtesies to me, and the homage of my constant and affectionate attachment and respect.

THE CHARACTER OF WASHINGTON

To Dr. Walter Jones

Monticello, January 2, 1814

DEAR SIR,—Your favor of November the 25th reached this place December the 21st, having been near a month on the way. How this could happen I know not, as we have two mails a week both from Fredericksburg and Richmond. It found me just returned from a long journey and absence, during which so much business had accumulated, commanding the first attentions, that another week has been added to the delay.

I deplore, with you, the putrid state into which our newspapers have passed, and the malignity, the vulgarity, and mendacious spirit of those who write for them; and I enclose you a recent sample, the production of a New England judge, as a proof of the abyss of degradation into which we are fallen. These ordures are rapidly depraving the public taste, and lessening its relish for sound food. As vehicles of information, and a curb on our functionaries, they have rendered themselves useless, by forfeiting all title to belief. That this has, in a great degree, been produced by the violence and malignity of party spirit, I agree with you; and I have read with great pleasure the paper you enclosed me on that subject, which I now return. It is at the same time a perfect model of the style of discussion which candor and decency should observe, of the tone which renders difference of opinion even amiable, and a succinct, correct, and dispassionate history of the origin and progress of party among us. It might be incorporated as it stands, and without changing a word, into the history of the present epoch, and would give to posterity a fairer view of the times than they will probably derive from other sources. In reading it with great satisfaction, there was but a single passage where I wished a little more development of a very sound and catholic idea; a single intercalation to rest it solidly on true bottom. It is near the end of the first page, where you make a statement of genuine republican maxims; saying, "that the people ought to possess as much political power as can possibly exist with the order and security of society." Instead of this, I would say, "that the people, being the only safe depository of power, should exercise in person every function which their qualifications enable them to exercise, consistently with the order and security of society; that we now find them equal to the election of those who shall be invested with their executive and legislative powers, and to act themselves in the judiciary, as judges in questions of fact; that the range of their powers ought to be enlarged," &c. This gives both the reason and exemplification of the maxim you express, "that they ought to possess as much political power," &c. I see nothing to correct either in your facts or principles.

You say that in taking General Washington on your shoulders, to bear him harmless through the federal coalition, you encounter a perilous topic. I do not think so. You have given the genuine history of the course of his mind through the trying scenes in which it was engaged, and of the seductions by which it was deceived, but not depraved. I think I knew General Washington intimately and thoroughly; and were I called on to delineate his character, it should be in terms like these.

His mind was great and powerful, without being of the very first order; his penetration strong, though not so acute as that of a Newton, Bacon, or Locke; and as far as he saw, no judgment was ever sounder. It was slow in operation, being little aided by invention or imagination, but sure in conclusion. Hence the common remark of his officers, of the advantage he derived from councils of war, where hearing all suggestions, he selected whatever was best; and certainly no General ever planned his battles more judiciously. But if deranged during the course of the action, if any member of his plan was dislocated by sudden circumstances, he was slow in re-adjustment. The consequence was, that he often failed in the field, and rarely against an enemy in station, as at Boston and York. He was incapable of fear, meeting personal dangers with the calmest unconcern. Perhaps the strongest feature in his character was prudence, never acting until every circumstance, every consideration, was maturely weighed; refraining if he saw a doubt, but, when once decided, going through with his purpose, whatever obstacles opposed. His integrity was most pure, his justice the most inflexible I have ever

known, no motives of interest or consanguinity, of friendship
or hatred, being able to bias his decision. He was, indeed, in
every sense of the words, a wise, a good, and a great man.
His temper was naturally high toned; but reflection and resolution had obtained a firm and habitual ascendency over it.
If ever, however, it broke its bonds, he was most tremendous
in his wrath. In his expenses he was honorable, but exact;
liberal in contributions to whatever promised utility; but
frowning and unyielding on all visionary projects and all unworthy calls on his charity. His heart was not warm in its
affections; but he exactly calculated every man's value, and
gave him a solid esteem proportioned to it. His person, you
know, was fine, his stature exactly what one would wish, his
deportment easy, erect and noble; the best horseman of his
age, and the most graceful figure that could be seen on horseback. Although in the circle of his friends, where he might be
unreserved with safety, he took a free share in conversation,
his colloquial talents were not above mediocrity, possessing
neither copiousness of ideas, nor fluency of words. In public,
when called on for a sudden opinion, he was unready, short
and embarrassed. Yet he wrote readily, rather diffusely, in an
easy and correct style. This he had acquired by conversation
with the world, for his education was merely reading, writing
and common arithmetic, to which he added surveying at a
later day. His time was employed in action chiefly, reading
little, and that only in agriculture and English history. His
correspondence became necessarily extensive, and, with jour-
nalizing his agricultural proceedings, occupied most of his leisure hours within doors. On the whole, his character was, in
its mass, perfect, in nothing bad, in few points indifferent;
and it may truly be said, that never did nature and fortune
combine more perfectly to make a man great, and to place
him in the same constellation with whatever worthies have
merited from man an everlasting remembrance. For his was
the singular destiny and merit, of leading the armies of his
country successfully through an arduous war, for the establishment of its independence; of conducting its councils
through the birth of a government, new in its forms and principles, until it had settled down into a quiet and orderly train;
and of scrupulously obeying the laws through the whole of

his career, civil and military, of which the history of the world furnishes no other example.

How, then, can it be perilous for you to take such a man on your shoulders? I am satisfied the great body of republicans think of him as I do. We were, indeed, dissatisfied with him on his ratification of the British treaty. But this was short lived. We knew his honesty, the wiles with which he was encompassed, and that age had already begun to relax the firmness of his purposes; and I am convinced he is more deeply seated in the love and gratitude of the republicans, than in the Pharisaical homage of the federal monarchists. For he was no monarchist from preference of his judgment. The soundness of that gave him correct views of the rights of man, and his severe justice devoted him to them. He has often declared to me that he considered our new constitution as an experiment on the practicability of republican government, and with what dose of liberty man could be trusted for his own good; that he was determined the experiment should have a fair trial, and would lose the last drop of his blood in support of it. And these declarations he repeated to me the oftener and more pointedly, because he knew my suspicions of Colonel Hamilton's views, and probably had heard from him the same declarations which I had, to wit, "that the British constitution, with its unequal representation, corruption and other existing abuses, was the most perfect government which had ever been established on earth, and that a reformation of those abuses would make it an impracticable government." I do believe that General Washington had not a firm confidence in the durability of our government. He was naturally distrustful of men, and inclined to gloomy apprehensions; and I was ever persuaded that a belief that we must at length end in something like a British constitution, had some weight in his adoption of the ceremonies of levees, birth-days, pompous meetings with Congress, and other forms of the same character, calculated to prepare us gradually for a change which he believed possible, and to let it come on with as little shock as might be to the public mind.

These are my opinions of General Washington, which I would vouch at the judgment seat of God, having been formed on an acquaintance of thirty years. I served with him in the Virginia legislature from 1769 to the Revolutionary war, and again, a short time in Congress, until he left us to take command of the army. During the war and after it we corresponded occasionally, and in the four years of my continuance in the office of Secretary of State, our intercourse was daily, confidential and cordial. After I retired from that office, great and malignant pains were taken by our federal monarchists, and not entirely without effect, to make him view me as a theorist, holding French principles of government, which would lead infallibly to licentiousness and anarchy. And to this he listened the more easily, from my known disapprobation of the British treaty. I never saw him afterwards, or these malignant insinuations should have been dissipated before his just judgment, as mists before the sun. I felt on his death, with my countrymen, that "verily a great man hath fallen this day in Israel."

More time and recollection would enable me to add many other traits of his character; but why add them to you who knew him well? And I cannot justify to myself a longer detention of your paper.

Vale, proprieque tuum, me esse tibi persuadeas.

CHRISTIANITY AND THE COMMON LAW
To Dr. Thomas Cooper

Monticello, February 10, 1814

DEAR SIR,—In my letter of January 16, I promised you a sample from my common-place book, of the pious disposition of the English judges, to connive at the frauds of the clergy, a disposition which has even rendered them faithful allies in practice. When I was a student of the law, now half a century ago, after getting through Coke Littleton, whose matter cannot be abridged, I was in the habit of abridging and common-placing what I read meriting it, and of sometimes mixing my own reflections on the subject. I now enclose you the extract from these entries which I promised. They were written at a time of life when I was bold in the pursuit of knowledge, never fearing to follow truth and reason to whatever results they led, and bearding every authority which stood in their way. This must be the apology, if you find the conclusions bolder than historical facts and principles will warrant. Accept with them the assurances of my great esteem and respect.

Common-place Book.

873. In Quare imp. in C. B. 34, H. 6, fo. 38, the def. Br. of Lincoln pleads that the church of the pl. became void by the death of the incumbent, that the pl. and J. S. each pretending a right, presented two several clerks; that the church being thus rendered litigious, he was not obliged, by the *Ecclesiastical law* to admit either, until an inquisition de jure patronatus, in the ecclesiastical court: that, by the same law, this inquisition was to be at the suit of either claimant, and was not *ex-officio* to be instituted by the bishop, and at his proper costs; that neither party had desired such an inquisition; that six months passed whereon it belonged to him of right to present as on a lapse, which he had done. The pl. demurred. A question was, How far the *Ecclesiastical law* was to be respected in this matter by the common law court? and Prisot C. 3, in the course of his argument uses this expression, "A tiels leis que ils de seint eglise ont en *ancien scripture*, covient a nous a donner credence, car ces common ley sur quel touts manners leis sont fondés: et auxy, sin, nous sumus obligés de conustre nostre ley; et, sin, si poit apperer or á nous que liévesque ad fait comme un ordinary fera en tiel cas, adong nous devons ces adjuger bon autrement nemy," &c. It does not appear that judgment was given. Y. B. ubi supra. S. C. Fitzh. abr. Qu. imp. 89. Bro. abr. Qu. imp. 12. Finch mistakes this in the following manner: "To such laws of the church as have warrant in *Holy Scripture*, our law giveth credence," and cites the above case, and the words of Prisot on the margin. Finch's law. B. 1, ch. 3, published 1613. Here we find "ancien scripture" converted into "Holy Scripture," whereas it can only mean the *ancien written* laws of the church. It cannot mean the Scriptures, 1, because the "ancien scripture" must then be understood to mean the "Old Testament" or Bible, in opposition to the "New Testament," and to the exclusion of that, which would be absurd and contrary to the wish of those

who cite this passage to prove that the Scriptures, or Christianity, is a part of the common law. 2. Because Prisot says,
"Ceo [est] common ley, sur quel touts manners leis sont
fondés." Now, it is true that the ecclesiastical law, so far as
admitted in England, derives its authority from the common
law. But it would not be true that the Scriptures so derive
their authority. 3. The whole case and arguments show that
the question was how far the Ecclesiastical law in general
should be respected in a common law court. And in Bro. abr.
of this case, Littleton says, "Les juges del common ley pren-
dra conusans quid est *lax ecclesiæ*, vel admiralitatis, et trujus
modi." 4. Because the particular part of the Ecclesiastical law
then in question, to wit, the right of the patron to present to
his advowson, was not founded on the law of God, but subject to the modification of the lawgiver, and so could not introduce any such general position as Finch pretends. Yet
Wingate [in 1658] thinks proper to erect this false quotation
into a maxim of the common law, expressing it in the very
words of Finch, but citing Prisot, wing. max. 3. Next comes
Sheppard, [in 1675,] who states it in the same words of Finch,
and quotes the Year-Book, Finch and Wingate. 3. Shepp. abr.
tit. Religion. In the case of the King *v.* Taylor, Sir Matthew
Hale lays it down in these words, "Christianity is parcel of
the laws of England." 1 Ventr. 293, 3 Keb. 607. But he quotes
no authority, resting it on his own, which was good in all
cases in which his mind received no bias from his bigotry, his
superstitions, his visions above sorceries, demons, &c. The
power of these over him is exemplified in his hanging of the
witches. So strong was this doctrine become in 1728, by additions and repetitions from one another, that in the case of
the King *v.* Woolston, the court would not suffer it to be
debated, whether to write against Christianity was punishable
in the temporal courts at common law, saying it had been so
settled in Taylor's case, ante 2, stra. 834; therefore, Wood, in
his Institute, lays it down that all blasphemy and profaneness
are offences by the *common law*, and cites Strange ubi supra.
Wood 409. And Blackstone [about 1763] repeats, in the words
of Sir Matthew Hale, that "Christianity is part of the laws of
England," citing Ventris and Strange ubi supra. 4. Blackst. 59.
Lord Mansfield qualifies it a little by saying that "The essen-

tial principles of revealed religion are part of the common law." In the case of the Chamberlain of London *v.* Evans, 1767. But he cities no authority, and leaves us at our peril to find out what, in the opinion of the judge, and according to the measure of his foot or his faith, are those essential principles of revealed religion obligatory on us as a part of the common law.

Thus we find this string of authorities, when examined to the beginning, all hanging on the same hook, a perverted expression of Prisot's, or on one another, or nobody. Thus Finch quotes Prisot; Wingate also; Sheppard quotes Prisot, Finch and Wingate; Hale cites nobody; the court in Woolston's case cite Hale; Wood cites Woolston's case; Blackstone that and Hale; and Lord Mansfield, like Hale, ventures it on his own authority. In the earlier ages of the law, as in the year-books, for instance, we do not expect much recurrence to authorities by the judges, because in those days there were few or none such made public. But in latter times we take no judge's word for what the law is, further than he is warranted by the authorities he appeals to. His decision may bind the unfortunate individual who happens to be the particular subject of it; but it cannot alter the law. Though the common law may be termed "Lex non Scripta," yet the same Hale tells us " when I call those parts of our laws Leges non Scriptæ, I do not mean as if those laws were only oral, or communicated from the former ages to the latter merely by word. For all those laws have their several monuments in writing, whereby they are transferred from one age to another, and without which they would soon lose all kind of certainty. They are for the most part extant in records of pleas, proceedings, and judgments, in books of reports and judicial decisions, in tractates of learned men's arguments and opinions, preserved from ancient times and still extant in writing." Hale's H. c. d. 22. Authorities for what is common law may therefore be as well cited, as for any part of the Lex Scripta, and there is no better instance of the necessity of holding the judges and writers to a declaration of their authorities than the present; where we detect them endeavoring to make law where they found none, and to submit us at one stroke to a whole system, no particle of which has its foundation in the common law. For we know that the common law is that system of law which was introduced by the Saxons on their settlement in England, and altered from time to time by proper legislative authority from that time to the date of Magna Charta, which terminates the period of the common law, or lex non scripta, and commences that of the statute law, or Lex Scripta. This settlement took place about the middle of the fifth century. But Christianity was not introduced till the seventh century; the conversion of the first christian king of the Heptarchy having taken place about the year 598, and that of the last about 686. Here, then, was a space of two hundred years, during which the common law was in existence, and Christianity no part of it. If it ever was adopted, therefore, into the common law, it must have been between the introduction of Christianity and the date of the Magna Charta. But of the laws of this period we have a tolerable collection by Lambard and Wilkins, probably not perfect, but neither very defective; and if any one chooses to build a doctrine on any law of that period, supposed to have been lost, it is incumbent on him to prove it to have existed, and what were its contents. These were so far alterations of the common law, and became themselves a part of it. But none of these adopt Christianity as a part of the common law. If, therefore, from the settlement of the Saxons to the introduction of Christianity among them, that system of religion could not be a part of the common law, because they were not yet Christians, and if, having their laws from that period to the close of the common law, we are all able to find among them no such act of adoption, we may safely affirm (though contradicted by all the judges and writers on earth) that Christianity neither is, nor ever was a part of the common law. Another cogent proof of this truth is drawn from the silence of certain writers on the common law. Bracton gives us a very complete and scientific treatise of the whole body of the common law. He wrote this about the close of the reign of Henry III., a very few years after the date of the Magna Charta. We consider this book as the more valuable, as it was written about fore gives us the former in its ultimate state. Bracton, too, was an ecclesiastic, and would certainly not have failed to inform us of the adoption of Christianity as a part of the common law, had any such adoption ever taken place. But no word of his, which intimates anything like it, has ever been cited. Fleta and Britton, who wrote in the succeeding reign (of Edward I.), are equally silent. So also is Glanvil, an earlier writer than any of them, (viz.: temp. H. 2,) but his subject perhaps might not have led him to mention it. Justice Fortescue Aland, who possessed more Saxon learning than all the judges and writers before mentioned put together, places this subject on more limited ground. Speaking of the laws of the Saxon kings, he says, "the ten commandments were made part of their laws, and consequently were *once* part of the law of England; so that to break any of the ten commandments was then esteemed a breach of the common law, of England; and why it is not so now, perhaps it may be difficult to give a good reason." Preface to Fortescue Aland's reports, xvii. Had he proposed to state with more minuteness how much of the scriptures had been made a part of the common law, he might have added that in the laws of Alfred, where he found the ten commandments, two or three other chapters of Exodus are copied almost verbatim. But the adoption of a part proves rather a rejection of the rest, as municipal law. We might as well say that the Newtonian system of philosophy is a part of the common law, as that the Christian religion is. The truth is that Christianity and Newtonianism being reason and verity itself, in the opinion of all but infidels and Cartesians, they are protected under the wings of the common law from the dominion of other sects, but not erected into dominion over them. An eminent Spanish physician affirmed that the lancet had slain more men than the sword. Doctor Sangrado, on the contrary, affirmed that with plentiful bleedings, and draughts of warm water, every disease was to be cured. The common law protects both opinions, but enacts neither into law. See post. 879.

879. Howard, in his Contumes Anglo-Normandes, 1.87, notices the falsification of the laws of Alfred, by prefixing to them four chapters of the Jewish law, to wit: the 20th, 21st, 22d and 23d chapters of Exodus, to which he might have added the 15th chapter of the Acts of the Apostles, v. 23, and precepts from other parts of the scripture. These he calls a *hors d'œuvre* of some pious copyist. This awkward monkish fabrication makes the preface to Alfred's genuine laws stand

in the body of the work, and the very words of Alfred himself prove the fraud; for he declares, in that preface, that he has collected these laws from those of Ina, of Offa, Aethelbert and his ancestors, saying nothing of any of them being taken from the Scriptures. It is still more certainly proved by the inconsistencies it occasions. For example, the Jewish legislator Exodus xxi. 12, 13, 14, (copied by the Pseudo Alfred § 13,) makes murder, with the Jews, death. But Alfred himself, Le. xxvi., punishes it by a fine only, called a Weregild, proportioned to the condition of the person killed. It is remarkable that Hume (append. 1 to his History) examining this article of the laws of Alfred, without perceiving the fraud, puzzles himself with accounting for the inconsistency it had introduced. To strike a pregnant woman so that she die is death by Exodus, xxi. 22, 23, and Pseud. Alfr. § 18; but by the laws of Alfred ix., pays a Weregild for both woman and child. To smite out an eye, or a tooth, Exod. xxi. 24–27. Pseud. Alfr. § 19, 20, if of a servant by his master, is freedom to the servant; in every other case retaliation. But by Alfr. Le. xl. a fixed indemnification is paid. Theft of an ox, or a sheep, by the Jewish law, Exod. xxii. 1, was repaid five-fold for the ox and four-fold for the sheep; by the Pseudograph § 24, the ox double, the sheep four-fold; but by Alfred Le. xvi., he who stole a cow and a calf was to repay the worth of the cow and 40l for the calf. Goring by an ox was the death of the ox, and the flesh not to be eaten. Exod. xxi. 28. Pseud. Alfr. § 21 by Alfred Le. xxiv., the wounded person had the ox. The Pseudograph makes municipal laws of the ten commandments, § 1–10, regulates concubinage, § 12, makes it death to strike or to curse father or mother, § 14, 15, gives an eye for an eye, tooth for a tooth, hand for hand, foot for foot, burning for burning, wound for wound, strife for strife, § 19; sells the thief to repay his theft, § 24; obliges the fornicator to marry the woman he has lain with, § 29; forbids interest on money, § 35; makes the laws of bailment, § 28, very different from what Lord Holt delivers in Coggs *v.* Bernard, ante 92, and what Sir William Jones tells us they were; and punishes witchcraft with death, § 30, which Sir Matthew Hale, 1 H. P. C. B. 1, ch. 33, declares was not a felony before the Stat. 1, Jac. 12. It was under that statute, and not this forgery, that he hung

Rose Cullendar and Amy Duny, 16 Car. 2, (1662,) on whose trial he declared "that there were such creatures as witches he made no doubt at all; for first the Scripture had affirmed so much, secondly the wisdom of all nations had provided laws against such persons, and such hath been the judgment of this kingdom, as appears by that act of Parliament which hath provided punishment proportionable to the quality of the offence." And we must certainly allow greater weight to this position that "it was no felony till James' Statute," laid down deliberately in his H. P. C., a work which he wrote to be printed, finished, and transcribed for the press in his life time, than to the hasty scripture that "at *common law* witchcraft was punished with death as heresy, by writ de Heretico Comburendo" in his Methodical Summary of the P. C. p. 6, a work "not intended for the press, not fitted for it, and which he declared himself he had never read over since it was written;" Pref. Unless we understand his meaning in that to be that witchcraft could not be punished at common law as witchcraft, but as heresy. In either sense, however, it is a denial of this pretended law of Alfred. Now, all men of reading know that these pretended laws of homicide, concubinage, theft, retaliation, compulsory marriage, usury, bailment, and others which might have been cited, from the Pseudograph, were never the laws of England, not even in Alfred's time; and of course that it is a forgery. Yet palpable as it must be to every lawyer, the English judges have piously avoided lifting the veil under which it was shrouded. In truth, the alliance between Church and State in England has ever made their judges accomplices in the frauds of the clergy; and even bolder than they are. For instead of being contented with these four surreptitious chapters of Exodus, they have taken the whole leap, and declared at once that the whole Bible and Testament in a lump, make a part of the common law; ante 873: the first judicial declaration of which was by this same Sir Matthew Hale. And thus they incorporate into the English code laws made for the Jews alone, and the precepts of the gospel, intended by their benevolent author as obligatory only in *foro concientiæ*; and they arm the whole with the coercions of municipal law. In doing this, too, they have not even used the Connecticut caution of declaring, as is done in their blue laws, that the laws of God shall be the laws of their land, except where their own contradict them; but they swallow the yea and nay together. Finally, in answer to Fortescue Aland's question why the ten commandments should not now be a part of the common law of England? we may say they are not because they never were made so by legislative authority, the document which has imposed that doubt on him being a manifest forgery.

CLASSIFICATION IN NATURAL HISTORY
To Dr. John Manners

Monticello, February 22, 1814

SIR,—The opinion which, in your letter of January 24, you are pleased to ask of me, on the comparative merits of the different methods of classification adopted by different writers on Natural History, is one which I could not have given satisfactorily, even at the earlier period at which the subject was more familiar; still less, after a life of continued occupation in civil concerns has so much withdrawn me from studies of that kind. I can, therefore, answer but in a very general way. And the text of this answer will be found in an observation in your letter, where, speaking of nosological systems, you say that disease has been found to be an unit. Nature has, in truth, produced units only through all her works. Classes, orders, genera, species, are not of her work. Her creation is of individuals. No two animals are exactly alike; no two plants, nor even two leaves or blades of grass; no two crystallizations. And if we may venture from what is within the cognizance of such organs as ours, to conclude on that beyond their powers, we must believe that no two particles of matter are of exact resemblance. This infinitude of units or individuals being far beyond the capacity of our memory, we are obliged, in aid of that, to distribute them into masses, throwing into each of these all the individuals which have a certain degree of resemblance; to subdivide these again into smaller groups, according to certain points of dissimilitude observable in them, and so on until we have formed what we call a system of classes, orders, genera and species. In doing this, we fix arbitrarily on such characteristic resemblances and differences as seem to us most prominent and invariable in the several subjects, and most likely to take a strong hold in our memories. Thus Ray formed one classification on such lines of division as struck him most favorably; Klein adopted another; Brisson a third, and other naturalists other designations, till Linnæus appeared. Fortunately for science, he conceived in the three kingdoms of nature, modes of classification which obtained the approbation of the learned of all nations. His system was accordingly adopted by all, and united all in a general language. It offered the three great desiderata: First, of aiding the memory to retain a knowledge of the productions of nature. Secondly, of rallying all to the same names for the same objects, so that they could communicate understandingly on them. And Thirdly, of enabling them, when a subject was first presented, to trace it by its character up to the conventional name by which it was agreed to be called. This classification was indeed liable to the imperfection of bringing into the same group individuals which, though resembling in the characteristics adopted by the author for his classification, yet have strong marks of dissimilitude in other respects. But to this objection every mode of classification must be liable, because the plan of creation is inscrutable to our limited faculties. Nature has not arranged her productions on a single and direct line. They branch at every step, and in every direction, and he who attempts to reduce them into departments, is left to do it by the lines of his own fancy. The objection of bringing together what are disparata in nature, lies against the classifications of Blumenbach and of Cuvier, as well as that of Linnæus, and must forever lie against all. Perhaps not in equal degree; on this I do not pronounce. But neither is this so important a consideration as that of uniting all nations under one language in Natural History. This had been happily effected by Linnæus, and can scarcely be hoped for a second time. Nothing indeed is so desperate as to make all mankind agree in giving up a language they possess, for one which they have to learn. The attempt leads directly to the confusion of the tongues of Babel. Disciples of Linnæus, of Blumenbach, and of Cuvier, exclusively possessing their own nomenclatures, can no longer communicate intelligibly with one another. However much, therefore, we are indebted to both these naturalists, and to Cuvier especially, for the valuable additions they have made to the sciences of nature, I cannot say they have rendered her a service in this attempt to innovate in the settled nomenclature of her productions; on the contrary, I think it will be a check on the progress of science, greater or less, in proportion as their schemes shall more or less prevail. They would have rendered greater service by holding fast to the system on which we had once all agreed, and by inserting into that such new genera, orders, or even classes, as new discoveries should call for. Their systems, too, and especially that of Blumenbach, are liable to the objection of giving too much into the province of anatomy. It may be said, indeed, that anatomy is a part of natural history. In the broad sense of the word, it certainly is. In that sense, however, it would comprehend all the natural sciences, every created thing being a subject of natural history in extenso. But in the subdivisions of general science, as has been observed in the particular one of natural history, it has been necessary to draw arbitrary lines, in order to accommodate our limited views. According to these, as soon as the structure of any natural production is destroyed by art, it ceases to be a subject of natural history, and enters into the domain ascribed to chemistry, to pharmacy, to anatomy, &c. Linnæus' method was liable to this objection so far as it required the aid of anatomical dissection, as of the heart, for instance, to ascertain the place of any animal, or of a chemical process for that of a mineral substance. It would certainly be better to adopt as much as possible such exterior and visible characteristics as every traveller is competent to observe, to ascertain and to relate. But with this objection, lying but in a small degree, Linnæus' method was received, understood, and conventionally settled among the learned, and was even getting into common use. To disturb it then was unfortunate. The new system attempted in botany, by Jussieu, in mineralogy, by Haüiy, are subjects of the same regret, and so also the no-system of Buffon, the great advocate of individualism in opposition to classification. He would carry us back to the days and to the confusion of Aristotle and Pliny, give up the im-

provements of twenty centuries, and co-operate with the
neologists in rendering the science of one generation useless
to the next by perpetual changes of its language. In botany,
Wildenow and Persoon have incorporated into Linnæus the
new discovered plants. I do not know whether any one has
rendered us the same service as to his natural history.
It would be a very acceptable one. The materials furnished by
Humboldt, and those from New Holland particularly, require
to be digested into the Catholic system. Among these, the
Ornithorhyncus mentioned by you, is an amusing example of
the anomalies by which nature sports with our schemes of
classification. Although without mammæ, naturalists are
obliged to place it in the class of mammiferæ; and Blumenbach, particularly, arranges it in his order of Palmipeds and
toothless genus, with the walrus and manatie. In Linnæus'
system it might be inserted as a new genus between the
anteater and manis, in the order of Bruta. It seems, in truth,
to have stronger relations with that class than any other in the
construction of the heart, its red and warm blood, hairy in-
teguments, in being quadruped and viviparous, and may we
not say, in its *tout ensemble*, which Buffon makes his sole principle of arrangement? The mandible, as you observe, would
draw it towards the birds, were not this characteristic over-
balanced by the weightier ones before mentioned. That of the
Cloaca is equivocal, because although a character of birds, yet
some mammalia, as the beaver and sloth, have the rectum and
urinary passage terminating at a common opening. Its ribs
also, by their number and structure, are nearer those of the
bird than of the mammalia. It is possible that further opportunities of examination may discover the mammæ. Those of
the Opossum are asserted, by the Chevalier d'Aboville, from
his own observations on that animal, made while here with
the French army, to be not discoverable until pregnancy, and
to disappear as soon as the young are weaned. The Duckbill
has many additional particularities which liken it to other
genera, and some entirely peculiar. Its description and history
needs yet further information.

In what I have said on the method of classing, I have not
at all meant to insinuate that that of Linnæus is intrinsically
preferable to those of Blumenbach and Cuvier. I adhere to

the Linnean because it is sufficient as a ground-work, admits
of supplementary insertions as new productions are discovered, and mainly because it has got into so general use that it
will not be easy to displace it, and still less to find another
which shall have the same singular fortune of obtaining the
general consent. During the attempt we shall become unintelligible to one another, and science will be really retarded by
efforts to advance it made by its most favorite sons. I am not
myself apt to be alarmed at innovations recommended by reason. That dread belongs to those whose interests or prejudices shrink from the advance of truth and science. My
reluctance is to give up an universal language of which we are
in possession, without an assurance of general consent to receive another. And the higher the character of the authors
recommending it, and the more excellent what they offer, the
greater the danger of producing schism.

I should seem to need apology for these long remarks to
you who are so much more recent in these studies, but I find
it in your particular request and my own respect for it, and
with that be pleased to accept the assurance of my esteem and
consideration.

THE CENSORSHIP OF BOOKS
To N. G. Dufief

Monticello, April 19, 1814

DEAR SIR,—Your favor of the 6th instant is just received, and
I shall with equal willingness and truth, state the degree of
agency you had, respecting the copy of M. de Becourt's book,
which came to my hands. That gentleman informed me, by
letter, that he was about to publish a volume in French, "Sur
la Création du Monde, un Systême d'Organisation Primitive,"
which, its title promised to be, either a geological or astronomical work. I subscribed; and, when published, he sent me
a copy; and as you were my correspondent in the book line
in Philadelphia, I took the liberty of desiring him to call on
you for the price, which, he afterwards informed me, you
were so kind as to pay him for me, being, I believe, two dol-

lars. But the sole copy which came to me was from himself directly, and, as far as I know, was never seen by you.

I am really mortified to be told that, *in the United States of America*, a fact like this can become a subject of inquiry, and of criminal inquiry too, as an offence against religion; that a question about the sale of a book can be carried before the civil magistrate. Is this then our freedom of religion? and are we to have a censor whose imprimatur shall say what books may be sold, and what we may buy? And who is thus to dogmatize religious opinions for our citizens? Whose foot is to be the measure to which ours are all to be cut or stretched? Is a priest to be our inquisitor, or shall a layman, simple as ourselves, set up his reason as the rule for what we are to read, and what we must believe? It is an insult to our citizens to question whether they are rational beings or not, and blasphemy against religion to suppose it cannot stand the test of truth and reason. If M. de Becourt's book be false in its facts, disprove them; if false in its reasoning, refute it. But, for God's sake, let us freely hear both sides, if we choose. I know little of its contents, having barely glanced over here and there a passage, and over the table of contents. From this, the Newtonian philosophy seemed the chief object of attack, the issue of which might be trusted to the strength of the two combatants; Newton certainly not needing the auxiliary arm of the government, and still less the holy author of our religion, as to what in it concerns him. I thought the work would be very innocent, and one which might be confided to the reason of any man; not likely to be much read if let alone, but, if persecuted, it will be generally read. Every man in the United States will think it a duty to buy a copy, in vindication of his right to buy, and to read what he pleases. I have been just reading the new constitution of Spain. One of its fundamental basis is expressed in these words: "The *Roman Catholic* religion, the only true one, is, and always shall be, that of the Spanish nation. The government protects it by wise and just laws, and prohibits the exercise of any other whatever." Now I wish this presented to those who question what you may sell, or we may buy, with a request to strike out the words, "Roman Catholic," and to insert the denomination of their own religion. This would ascertain the code of dogmas which each wishes should domineer over the opinions of all others, and be taken, like the Spanish religion, under the "protection of wise and just laws." It would shew to what they wish to reduce the liberty for which one generation has sacrificed life and happiness. It would present our boasted freedom of religion as a thing of theory only, and not of practice, as what would be a poor exchange for the theoretic thraldom, but practical freedom of Europe. But it is impossible that the laws of Pennsylvania, which set us the first example of the wholesome and happy effects of religious freedom, can permit the inquisitorial functions to be proposed to their courts. Under them you are surely safe.

At the date of yours of the 6th, you had not received mine of the 3d inst., asking a copy of an edition of Newton's Principia, which I had seen advertised. When the cost of that shall be known, it shall be added to the balance of $4.93, and incorporated with a larger remittance I have to make to Philadelphia. Accept the assurance of my great esteem and respect.

THE MORAL SENSE

To Thomas Law

Poplar Forest, June 13, 1814

DEAR SIR,—The copy of your Second Thoughts on Instinctive Impulses, with the letter accompanying it, was received just as I was setting out on a journey to this place, two or three days' distant from Monticello. I brought it with me and read it with great satisfaction, and with the more as it contained exactly my own creed on the foundation of morality in man. It is really curious that on a question so fundamental, such a variety of opinions should have prevailed among men, and those, too, of the most exemplary virtue and first order of understanding. It shows how necessary was the care of the Creator in making the moral principle so much a part of our constitution as that no errors of reasoning or of speculation might lead us astray from its observance in practice. Of all the theories on this question, the most whimsical seems to have been that of Wollaston, who considers *truth* as the foundation of morality. The thief who steals your guinea does wrong only inasmuch as he acts a lie in using your guinea as if it were his own. Truth is certainly a branch of morality, and a very important one to society. But presented as its foundation, it is as if a tree taken up by the roots, had its stem reversed in the air, and one of its branches planted in the ground. Some have made the *love of God* the foundation of morality. This, too, is but a branch of our moral duties, which are generally divided into duties to God and duties to man. If we did a good act merely from the love of God and a belief that it is pleasing to Him, whence arises the morality of the Atheist? It is idle to say, as some do, that no such being exists. We have the same evidence of the fact as of most of those we act on, to-wit: their own affirmations, and their reasonings in support of them. I have observed, indeed, generally, that while in protestant countries the defections from the Platonic Christianity of the priests is to Deism, in catholic countries they are to Atheism. Diderot, D'Alembert, D'Holbach, Condorcet, are known to have been among the most virtuous of men. Their virtue, then, must have had some other foundation than the love of God.

The Tò χυλον of others is founded in a different faculty, that of taste, which is not even a branch of morality. We have indeed an innate sense of what we call beautiful, but that is exercised chiefly on subjects addressed to the fancy, whether through the eye in visible forms, as landscape, animal figure, dress, drapery, architecture, the composition of colors, &c., or to the imagination directly, as imagery, style, or measure in prose or poetry, or whatever else constitutes the domain of criticism or taste, a faculty entirely distinct from the moral one. Self-interest, or rather self-love, or *egoism*, has been more plausibly substituted as the basis of morality. But I consider our relations with others as constituting the boundaries of morality. With ourselves we stand on the ground of identity, not of relation, which last, requiring two subjects, excludes self-love confined to a single one. To ourselves, in strict language, we can owe no duties, obligation requiring also two parties. Self-love, therefore, is no part of morality. Indeed it is exactly its counterpart. It is the sole antagonist of virtue, leading us constantly by our propensities to self-gratification in violation of our moral duties to others. Accordingly, it is against this enemy that are erected the batteries of moralists and religionists, as the only obstacle to the practice of morality. Take from man his selfish propensities, and he can have nothing to seduce him from the practice of virtue. Or subdue those propensities by education, instruction or restraint, and virtue remains without a competitor. Egoism, in a broader sense, has been thus presented as the source of moral action. It has been said that we feed the hungry, clothe the naked, bind up the wounds of the man beaten by thieves, pour oil and wine into them, set him on our own beast and bring him to the inn, because we receive ourselves pleasure from these acts. So Helvetius, one of the best men on earth, and the most ingenious advocate of this principle, after defining "interest" to mean not merely that which is pecuniary, but whatever may procure us pleasure or withdraw us from pain, [*de l'esprit* 2, 1,] says, [ib. 2, 2,] "the humane man is he to whom the sight of misfortune is insupportable, and who to rescue himself from this spectacle, is forced to succor the unfortunate object." This indeed is true. But it is one step short of the ultimate question. These good acts give us pleasure, but how happens it that they give us pleasure? Because nature hath implanted in our breasts a love of others, a sense of duty to them, a moral instinct, in short, which prompts us irresistibly to feel and to succor their distresses, and protests against the language of Helvetius, [ib. 2, 5,] " what other motive than self-interest could determine a man to generous actions? It is as impossible for him to love what is good for the sake of good, as to love evil for the sake of evil." The Creator would indeed have been a bungling artist, had he intended man for a social animal, without planting in him social dispositions. It is true they are not planted in every man, because there is no rule without exceptions; but it is false reasoning which converts exceptions into the general rule. Some men are born without the organs of sight, or of hearing, or without hands. Yet it would be wrong to say that man is born without these faculties, and sight, hearing, and hands may with truth enter into the general definition of man. The want or imperfection of the moral sense in some men, like the want or imperfection of the senses of sight and hearing in others, is no proof that it is a general characteristic of the species. When it is wanting, we endeavor to supply the defect by education, by appeals to reason and calculation, by presenting to the being so unhappily conformed, other motives to do good and to eschew evil, such as the love, or the hatred, or rejection of those among whom he lives, and whose society is necessary to his happiness and even existence; demonstrations by sound calculation that honesty promotes interest in the long run; the rewards and penalties established by the laws; and ultimately the prospects of a future state of retribution for the evil as well as the good done while here. These are the correctives which are supplied by education, and which exercise the functions of the moralist, the preacher, and legislator; and they lead into a course of correct action all those whose disparity is not too profound to be eradicated. Some have argued against the existence of a moral sense, by saying that if nature had given us such a sense, impelling us to virtuous actions, and warning us against those which are vicious, then nature would also have designated, by some particular ear-marks, the two sets of actions which are, in themselves, the one virtuous and the other vicious. Whereas, we find, in fact, that the same actions are deemed virtuous in one country and vicious in another. The answer is that nature has constituted *utility* to man the standard and best of virtue. Men living in different countries, under different circumstances, different habits and regimens, may have different utilities; the same act, therefore, may be useful, and consequently virtuous in one country which is injurious and vicious in another differently circumstanced. I sincerely, then, believe with you in the general existence of a moral instinct. I think it the brightest gem with which the human character is studded, and the want of it as more degrading than the most hideous of the bodily deformities. I am happy in reviewing the roll of associates in this principle which you present in your second letter, some of which I had not before met with. To these might be added Lord Kaims, one of the ablest of our advocates, who goes so far as to say, in his Principles of Natural Religion, that a man owes no duty to which he is not urged by some impulsive feeling. This is correct, if referred to the standard of general feeling in the given case, and not to the feeling of a single individual. Perhaps I may misquote him, it being fifty years since I read his book.

The leisure and solitude of my situation here has led me to the indiscretion of taxing you with a long letter on a subject whereon nothing new can be offered you. I will indulge myself no farther than to repeat the assurances of my continued esteem and respect.

BONAPARTE AND PLATO
To John Adams

Monticello, July 5, 1814

DEAR SIR—Since mine of Jan. 24. yours of Mar. 14. was recieved. It was not acknoleged in the short one of May 18. by Mr. Rives, the only object of that having been to enable one of our most promising young men to have the advantage of making his bow to you. I learned with great regret the serious illness mentioned in your letter: and I hope Mr. Rives will be able to tell me you are entirely restored. But our machines have now been running for 70. or 80. years, and we must expect that, worn as they are, here a pivot, there a wheel, now a pinion, next a spring, will be giving way: and however we may tinker them up for awhile, all will at length surcease motion. Our watches, with works of brass and steel, wear out within that period. Shall you and I last to see the course the seven-fold wonders of the times will take? The Attila of the age dethroned, the ruthless destroyer of 10. millions of the human race, whose thirst for blood appeared unquenchable, the great oppressor of the rights and liberties of the world, shut up within the circuit of a little island of the Mediterranean, and dwindled to the condition of an humble and degraded pensioner on the bounty of those he had most injured. How miserably, how meanly, has he closed his inflated career! What a sample of the Bathos will his history present! He should have perished on the swords of his enemies, under the walls of Paris.

'Leon piagato a morte
Sente mancar la vita,
Guarda la sua ferita,
Ne s'avilisce ancor.

Cosi fra l'ire estrema
rugge, minaccia, e freme,
Che fa tremar morendo
Tal volta il cacciator.'

Metast Adriano.

But Bonaparte was a lion in the field only. In civil life a cold-blooded, calculating unprincipled Usurper, without a virtue, no statesman, knowing nothing of commerce, political economy, or civil government, and supplying ignorance by bold presumption. I had supposed him a great man until his entrance into the Assembly des cinq cens, 18. Brumaire (an. 8.) From that date however I set him down as a great scoundrel only. To the wonders of his rise and fall, we may add that of a Czar of Muscovy dictating, *in Paris*, laws and limits to all the successors of the Caesars, and holding even the balance in which the fortunes of this new world are suspended. I own that, while I rejoice, for the good of mankind, to the deliverance of Europe from the havoc which would have never ceased while Bonaparte should have lived in power, I see with anxiety the tyrant of the ocean remaining in vigor, and even participating in the merit of crushing his brother tyrant. While the world is thus turned up side down, on which side of it are we? All the strong reasons indeed place us on the side of peace; the interests of the continent, their friendly dispositions, and even the interests of England. Her passions alone are opposed to it. Peace would seem now to be an easy work, the causes of the war being removed. Her orders of council will no doubt be taken care of by the allied powers, and, war ceasing, her impressment of our seamen ceases of course. But I fear there is foundation for the design intimated in the public papers, of demanding a cession of our right in the fisheries. What will Massachusets say to this? I mean her majority, which must be considered as speaking, thro' the organs it has appointed itself, as the Index of it's will. She chose to sacrifice the liberty of our seafaring citizens, in which we were all interested, and with them her obligations to the Co-states; rather than war with England. Will she now sacrifice the fisheries to the same partialities? This question is interesting to her alone: for to the middle, the Southern and Western States they are of no direct concern; of no

more than the culture of tobacco, rice and cotton to Massachusets. I am really at a loss to conjecture what our refractory
sister will say on this occasion. I know what, as a citizen of
the Union, I would say to her. 'Take this question ad referendum. It concerns you alone. If you would rather give up
the fisheries than war with England, we give them up. If you
had rather fight for them, we will defend your interests to the
last drop of our blood, chusing rather to set a good example
than follow a bad one.' And I hope she will determine to fight
for them. With this however you and I shall have nothing to
do; ours being truly the case wherein 'non tali auxilio, nec
defensoribus istis Tempus eget.' Quitting this subject therefore I will turn over another leaf.

I am just returned from one of my long absences, having
been at my other home for five weeks past. Having more leisure there than here for reading, I amused myself with reading seriously Plato's republic. I am wrong however in calling
it amusement, for it was the heaviest task-work I ever went
through. I had occasionally before taken up some of his other
works, but scarcely ever had patience to go through a whole
dialogue. While wading thro' the whimsies, the puerilities,
and unintelligible jargon of this work, I laid it down often to
ask myself how it could have been that the world should have
so long consented to give reputation to such nonsense as this?
How the soi-disant Christian world indeed should have done
it, is a piece of historical curiosity. But how could the Roman
good sense do it? And particularly how could Cicero bestow
such eulogies on Plato? Altho' Cicero did not wield the dense
logic of Demosthenes, yet he was able, learned, laborious,
practised in the business of the world, and honest. He could
not be the dupe of mere style, of which he was himself the
first master in the world. With the Moderns, I think, it is
rather a matter of fashion and authority. Education is chiefly
in the hands of persons who, from their profession, have an
interest in the reputation and the dreams of Plato. They give
the tone while at school, and few, in their after-years, have
occasion to revise their college opinions. But fashion and authority apart, and bringing Plato to the test of reason, take
from him his sophisms, futilities, and incomprehensibilities,
and what remains? In truth, he is one of the race of genuine

Sophists, who has escaped the oblivion of his brethren, first by the elegance of his diction, but chiefly by the adoption and incorporation of his whimsies into the body of artificial Christianity. His foggy mind, is forever presenting the semblances of objects which, half seen thro' a mist, can be defined neither in form or dimension. Yet this which should have consigned him to early oblivion really procured him immortality of fame and reverence. The Christian priesthood, finding the doctrines of Christ levelled to every understanding, and too plain to need explanation, saw, in the mysticisms of Plato, materials with which they might build up an artificial system which might, from it's indistinctness, admit everlasting controversy, give employment for their order, and introduce it to profit, power and pre-eminence. The doctrines which flowed from the lips of Jesus himself are within the comprehension of a child; but thousands of volumes have not yet explained the Platonisms engrafted on them: and for this obvious reason that nonsense can never be explained. Their purposes however are answered. Plato is canonized; and it is now deemed as impious to question his merits as those of an Apostle of Jesus. He is peculiarly appealed to as an advocate of the immortality of the soul; and yet I will venture to say that were there no better arguments than his in proof of it, not a man in the world would believe it. It is fortunate for us that Platonic republicanism has not obtained the same favor as Platonic Christianity; or we should now have been all living, men, women and children, pell mell together, like beasts of the field or forest. Yet 'Plato is a great Philosopher,' said La Fontaine. But says Fontenelle 'do you find his ideas very clear'? 'Oh no! he is of an obscurity impenetrable.' 'Do you not find him full of contradictions?' 'Certainly,' replied La Fontaine, 'he is but a Sophist.' Yet immediately after, he exclaims again, 'Oh Plato was a great Philosopher.' Socrates had reason indeed to complain of the misrepresentations of Plato; for in truth his dialogues are libels on Socrates.

But why am I dosing you with these Ante-diluvian topics? Because I am glad to have some one to whom they are familiar, and who will not recieve them as if dropped from the moon. Our post-revolutionary youth are born under happier stars than you and I were. They acquire all learning in their mothers' womb, and bring it into the world ready-made. The information of books is no longer necessary; and all knolege which is not innate, is in contempt, or neglect at least. Every folly must run it's round; and so, I suppose, must that of self-learning, and self sufficiency; of rejecting the knolege acquired in past ages, and starting on the new ground of intuition. When sobered by experience I hope our successors will turn their attention to the advantages of education. I mean of education on the broad scale, and not that of the petty *academies*, as they call themselves, which are starting up in every neighborhood, and where one or two men, possessing Latin, and sometimes Greek, a knolege of the globes, and the first six books of Euclid, imagine and communicate this as the sum of science. They commit their pupils to the theatre of the world with just taste enough of learning to be alienated from industrious pursuits, and not enough to do service in the ranks of science. We have some exceptions indeed. I presented one to you lately, and we have some others. But the terms I use are general truths. I hope the necessity will at length be seen of establishing institutions, here as in Europe, where every branch of science, useful at this day, may be taught in it's highest degrees. Have you ever turned your thoughts to the plan of such an institution? I mean to a specification of the particular sciences of real use in human affairs, and how they might be so grouped as to require so many professors only as might bring them within the views of a just but enlightened economy? I should be happy in a communication of your ideas on this problem, either loose or digested. But to avoid my being run away with by another subject, and adding to the length and ennui of the present letter, I will here present to Mrs. Adams and yourself the assurance of my constant and sincere friendship and respect.

EMANCIPATION AND THE YOUNGER GENERATION
To Edward Coles

Monticello, August 25, 1814

DEAR SIR,—Your favour of July 31, was duly received, and was read with peculiar pleasure. The sentiments breathed through the whole do honor to both the head and heart of the writer. Mine on the subject of slavery of negroes have long since been in possession of the public, and time has only served to give them stronger root. The love of justice and the love of country plead equally the cause of these people, and it is a moral reproach to us that they should have pleaded it so long in vain, and should have produced not a single effort, nay I fear not much serious willingness to relieve them & ourselves from our present condition of moral & political reprobation. From those of the former generation who were in the fulness of age when I came into public life, which was while our controversy with England was on paper only, I soon saw that nothing was to be hoped. Nursed and educated in the daily habit of seeing the degraded condition, both bodily and mental, of those unfortunate beings, not reflecting that that degradation was very much the work of themselves & their fathers, few minds have yet doubted but that they were as legitimate subjects of property as their horses and cattle. The quiet and monotonous course of colonial life has been disturbed by no alarm, and little reflection on the value of liberty. And when alarm was taken at an enterprize on their own, it was not easy to carry them to the whole length of the principles which they invoked for themselves. In the first or second session of the Legislature after I became a member, I drew to this subject the attention of Col. Bland, one of the oldest, ablest, & most respected members, and he undertook to move for certain moderate extensions of the protection of the laws to these people. I seconded his motion, and, as a younger member, was more spared in the debate; but he was denounced as an enemy of his country, & was treated with the grossest indecorum. From an early stage of our revolution other & more distant duties were assigned to me, so that from that time till my return from Europe in 1789, and I may say till I returned to reside at home in 1809, I had little opportunity of knowing the progress of public sentiment here on this subject. I had always hoped that the younger generation receiving their early impressions after the flame of liberty had been kindled in every breast, & had become as it were the vital spirit of every American, that the generous temperament of youth, analogous to the motion of their blood, and above the suggestions of avarice, would have sympathized with oppression wherever found, and proved their love of liberty beyond their own share of it. But my intercourse with them, since my return has not been sufficient to ascertain that they had made towards this point the progress I had hoped. Your solitary but welcome voice is the first which has brought this sound to my ear; and I have considered the general silence which prevails on this subject as indicating an apathy unfavorable to every hope. Yet the hour of emancipation is advancing, in the march of time. It will come; and whether brought on by the generous energy of our own minds; or by the bloody process of St Domingo, excited and conducted by the power of our present enemy, if once stationed permanently within our Country, and offering asylum & arms to the oppressed, is a leaf of our history not yet turned over. As to the method by which this difficult work is to be effected, if permitted to be done by ourselves, I have seen no proposition so expedient on the whole, as that as emancipation of those born after a given day, and of their education and expatriation after a given age. This would give time for a gradual extinction of that species of labour & substitution of another, and lessen the severity of the shock which an operation so fundamental cannot fail to produce. For men probably of any color, but of this color we know, brought from their infancy without necessity for thought or forecast, are by their habits rendered as incapable as children of taking care of themselves, and are extinguished promptly wherever industry is necessary for raising young. In the mean time they are pests in society by their idleness, and the depredations to which this leads them. Their amalgamation with the other color produces a degradation to which no lover of his country, no lover of excellence in the human character can innocently consent. I am sensible of the partialities with which you have looked towards me as the person who should undertake this salutary but arduous work. But this, my dear sir, is like bidding old Priam to buckle the armour of Hector "trementibus æquo humeris et inutile ferruncingi." No, I have overlived the generation with which mutual labors & perils begat mutual confidence and influence. This enterprise is for the young; for those who can follow it up, and bear it through to its con-

summation. It shall have all my prayers, & these are the only
weapons of an old man. But in the mean time are you right
in abandoning this property, and your country with it? I
think not. My opinion has ever been that, until more can be
done for them, we should endeavor, with those whom fortune has thrown on our hands, to feed and clothe them well,
protect them from all ill usage, require such reasonable labor
only as is performed voluntarily by freemen, & be led by no
repugnancies to abdicate them, and our duties to them. The
laws do not permit us to turn them loose, if that were for
their good: and to commute them for other property is to
commit them to those whose usage of them we cannot control. I hope then, my dear sir, you will reconcile yourself to
your country and its unfortunate condition; that you will not
lessen its stock of sound disposition by withdrawing your
portion from the mass. That, on the contrary you will come
forward in the public councils, become the missionary of this
doctrine truly christian; insinuate & inculcate it softly but
steadily, through the medium of writing and conversation;
associate others in your labors, and when the phalanx is
formed, bring on and press the proposition perseveringly until its accomplishment. It is an encouraging observation that
no good measure was ever proposed, which, if duly pursued,
failed to prevail in the end. We have proof of this in the history of the endeavors in the English parliament to suppress
that very trade which brought this evil on us. And you will
be supported by the religious precept, "be not weary in well-
doing." That your success may be as speedy & complete, as it
will be of honorable & immortal consolation to yourself, I
shall as fervently and sincerely pray as I assure you of my
great friendship and respect.

A SYSTEM OF EDUCATION

To Peter Carr

Monticello, September 7, 1814

DEAR SIR,—On the subject of the academy or college proposed to be established in our neighborhood, I promised the

trustees that I would prepare for them a plan, adapted, in the first instance, to our slender funds, but susceptible of being enlarged, either by their own growth or by accession from other quarters.

I have long entertained the hope that this, our native State, would take up the subject of education, and make an establishment, either with or without incorporation into that of William and Mary, where every branch of science, deemed useful at this day, should be taught in its highest degree. With this view, I have lost no occasion of making myself acquainted with the organization of the best seminaries in other countries, and with the opinions of the most enlightened individuals, on the subject of the sciences worthy of a place in such an institution. In order to prepare what I have promised our trustees, I have lately revised these several plans with attention; and I am struck with the diversity of arrangement observable in them—no two alike: Yet, I have no doubt that these several arrangements have been the subject of mature reflection, by wise and learned men, who, contemplating local circumstances, have adapted them to the conditions of the section of society for which they have been framed. I am strengthened in this conclusion by an examination of each separately, and a conviction that no one of them, if adopted without change, would be suited to the circumstances and pursuit of our country. The example they set, then, is authority for us to select from their different institutions the materials which are good for us, and, with them, to erect a structure, whose arrangement shall correspond with our own social condition, and shall admit of enlargement in proportion to the encouragement it may merit and receive. As I may not be able to attend the meetings of the trustees, I will make you the depository of my ideas on the subject, which may be corrected, as you proceed, by the better view of others, and adapted, from time to time, to the prospects which open upon us, and which cannot be specifically seen and provided for.

In the first place, we must ascertain with precision the object of our institution, by taking a survey of the general field of science, and marking out the portion we mean to occupy at first, and the ultimate extension of our views beyond that, should we be enabled to render it, in the end, as comprehensive as we would wish.

1. Elementary schools.

It is highly interesting to our country, and it is the duty of its functionaries, to provide that every citizen in it should receive an education proportioned to the condition and pursuits of his life. The mass of our citizens may be divided into two classes—the laboring and the learned. The laboring will need the first grade of education to qualify them for their pursuits and duties; the learned will need it as a foundation for further acquirements. A plan was formerly proposed to the legislature of this State for laying off every county into hundreds or wards of five or six miles square, within each of which should be a school for the education of the children of the ward, wherein they should receive three years' instruction gratis, in reading, writing, arithmetic as far as fractions, the roots and ratios, and geography. The Legislature at one time tried an ineffectual expedient for introducing this plan, which having failed, it is hoped they will some day resume it in a more promising form.

2. General schools.

At the discharging of the pupils from the elementary schools, the two classes separate—those destined for labor will engage in the business of agriculture, or enter into apprenticeships to such handicraft art as may be their choice; their companions, destined to the pursuits of science, will proceed to the college, which will consist, 1st of general schools; and, 2d, of professional schools. The general schools will constitute the second grade of education.

The learned class may still be subdivided into two sections: 1, Those who are destined for learned professions, as means of livelihood; and, 2, The wealthy, who, possessing independent fortunes, may aspire to share in conducting the affairs of the nation, or to live with usefulness and respect in the private ranks of life. Both of these sections will require instruction in all the higher branches of science; the wealthy to qualify them for either public or private life; the professional section will need those branches, especially, which are the basis of their future profession, and a general knowledge of the others, as auxiliary to that, and necessary to their standing and association with the scientific class. All the branches, then, of useful science, ought to be taught in the general schools, to a competent degree, in the first instance. These sciences may be arranged into three departments, not rigorously scientific, indeed, but sufficiently so for our purposes. These are, I. Language; II. Mathematics; III. Philosophy.

I. Language. In the first department, I would arrange a distinct science. 1, Languages and History, ancient and modern; 2, Grammar; 3, Belles Lettres; 4, Rhetoric and Oratory; 5, A school for the deaf, dumb and blind. History is here associated with languages, not as a kindred subject, but on the principle of economy, because both may be attained by the same course of reading, if books are selected with that view.

II. Mathematics. In the department of Mathematics, I should give place distinctly: 1, Mathematics pure; 2, Physico-Mathematics; 3, Physic; 4, Chemistry; 5, Natural History, to wit: Mineralogy; 6, Botany; and 7, Zoology; 8, Anatomy; 9, the Theory of Medicine.

III. Philosophy. In the Philosophical department, I should distinguish: 1, Ideology; 2, Ethics; 3, the Law of Nature and Nations; 4, Government; 5, Political Economy.

But, some of these terms being used by different writers, in different degrees of extension, I shall define exactly what I mean to comprehend in each of them.

I. 3. Within the term of Belles Lettres I include poetry and composition generally, and criticism.

II. 1. I consider pure mathematics as the science of, 1, Numbers, and 2, Measure in the abstract; that of numbers comprehending Arithmetic, Algebra and Fluxions; that of Measure (under the general appellation of Geometry), comprehending Trigonometry, plane and spherical, conic sections, and transcendental curves.

II. 2. Physico-Mathematics treat of physical subjects by the aid of mathematical calculation. These are Mechanics, Statics, Hydrostatics, Hydrodynamics, Navigation, Astronomy, Geography, Optics, Pneumatics, Acoustics.

II. 3. Physics, or Natural Philosophy (not entering the limits of Chemistry) treat of natural substances, their properties, mutual relations and action. They particularly examine the subjects of motion, action, magnetism, electricity, galvanism, light, meteorology, with an etc. not easily enumerated. These definitions and specifications render immaterial the question whether I use the generic terms in the exact degree of comprehension in which others use them; to be understood is all that is necessary to the present object.

3. Professional Schools.

At the close of this course the students separate; the wealthy retiring, with a sufficient stock of knowledge, to improve themselves to any degree to which their views may lead them, and the professional section to the professional schools, constituting the third grade of education, and teaching the particular sciences which the individuals of this section mean to pursue, with more minuteness and detail than was within the scope of the general schools for the second grade of instruction. In these professional schools each science is to be taught in the highest degree it has yet attained. They are to be the

1st Department, the fine arts, to wit: Civil Architecture, Gardening, Painting, Sculpture, and the Theory of Music; the

2nd Department, Architecture, Military and Naval; Projectiles, Rural Economy (comprehending Agriculture, Horticulture and Veterinary), Technical Philosophy, the Practice of Medicine, Materia Medica, Pharmacy and Surgery. In the

3rd Department, Theology and Ecclesiastical History; Law, Municipal and Foreign.

To these professional schools will come those who separated at the close of their first elementary course, to wit:

The lawyer to the law school.

The ecclesiastic to that of theology and ecclesiastical history.

The physican to those of medicine, materia medica, pharmacy and surgery.

The military man to that of military and naval architecture and projectiles.

The agricultor to that of rural economy.

The gentleman, the architect, the pleasure gardener, painter and musician to the school of fine arts.

And to that of technical philosophy will come the mariner, carpenter, shipwright, pumpmaker, clockmaker, machinist, optician, metallurgist, founder, cutler, druggist, brewer, vintner, distiller, dyer, painter, bleacher, soapmaker, tanner, powdermaker, saltmaker, glassmaker, to learn as much as shall be necessary to pursue their art understandingly, of the sciences of geometry, mechanics, statics, hydrostatics, hydraulics, hydrodynamics, navigation, astronomy, geography, optics, pneumatics, physics, chemistry, natural history, botany, mineralogy and pharmacy.

The school of technical philosophy will differ essentially in its functions from the other professional schools. The others are instituted to ramify and dilate the particular sciences taught in the schools of the second grade on a general scale only. The technical school is to abridge those which were taught there too much *in extenso* for the limited wants of the artificer or practical man. These artificers must be grouped together, according to the particular branch of science in which they need elementary and practical instruction; and a special lecture or lectures should be prepared for each group. And these lectures should be given in the evening, so as not to interrupt the labors of the day. The school, particularly, should be maintained wholly at the public expense, on the same principles with that of the ward schools. Through the whole of the collegiate course, at the hours of recreation on certain days, all the students should be taught the manual exercise; military evolutions and manœuvers should be under a standing organization as a military corps, and with proper officers to train and command them,

A tabular statement of this distribution of the sciences will place the system of instruction more particularly in view:

1st or Elementary Grade in the Ward Schools.
Reading, Writing, Arithmetic, Geography.
2d, or General Grade.
1. Language and History, ancient and modern.
2. Mathematics, viz: Mathematics pure, Physico-Mathematics, Physics, Chemistry, Anatomy, Theory of Medicine, Zoology, Botany and Mineralogy.

3. Philosophy, viz: Ideology, and Ethics, Law of Nature and Nations, Government, Political Economy.

3d, or Professional Grades.

Theology and Ecclesiastical History; Law, Municipal and Foreign; Practice of Medicine; Materia Medica and Pharmacy; Surgery; Architecture, Military and Naval, and Projectiles; Technical Philosophy; Rural Economy; Fine Arts.

On this survey of the field of science, I recur to the question, what portion of it we mark out for the occupation of our institution? With the first grade of education we shall have nothing to do. The sciences of the second grade are our first object; and, to adapt them to our slender beginnings, we must separate them into groups, comprehending many sciences each, and greatly more, in the first instance, than ought to be imposed on, or can be competently conducted by a single professor permanently. They must be subdivided from time to time, as our means increase, until each professor shall have no more under his care than he can attend to with advantage to his pupils and ease to himself. For the present, we may group the sciences into professorships, as follows, subject, however, to be changed, according to the qualifications of the persons we may be able to engage.

I. Professorship.
Languages and History, ancient and modern.
Belles-Lettres, Rhetoric and Oratory.
II. Professorship.
Mathematics pure, Physico-Mathematics.
Physics, Anatomy, Medicine, Theory.
III. Professorship.
Chemistry, Zoology, Botany, Mineralogy.
IV. Professorship.
Philosophy.

The organization of the branch of the institution which respects its government, police and economy, depending on principles which have no affinity with those of its institution, may be the subject of separate and subsequent consideration.

With this tribute of duty to the board of trustees, accept assurances of my great esteem and consideration.

A LIBRARY FOR CONGRESS
To Samuel H. Smith

Monticello, September 21, 1814

DEAR SIR,—I learn from the newspapers that the Vandalism of our enemy has triumphed at Washington over science as well as the arts, by the destruction of the public library with the noble edifice in which it was deposited. Of this transaction, as of that of Copenhagen, the world will entertain but one sentiment. They will see a nation suddenly withdrawn from a great war, full armed and full handed, taking advantage of another whom they had recently forced into it, unarmed, and unprepared, to indulge themselves in acts of barbarism which do not belong to a civilized age. When Van Ghent destroyed their shipping at Chatham, and De Ruyter rode triumphantly up the Thames, he might in like manner, by the acknowledgment of their own historians, have forced all their ships up to London bridge, and there have burnt them, the tower, and city, had these examples been then set. London, when thus menaced, was near a thousand years old, Washington is but in its teens.

I presume it will be among the early objects of Congress to re-commence their collection. This will be difficult while the war continues, and intercourse with Europe is attended with so much risk. You know my collection, its condition and extent. I have been fifty years making it, and have spared no pains, opportunity or expense, to make it what it is. While residing in Paris, I devoted every afternoon I was disengaged, for a summer or two, in examining all the principal bookstores, turning over every book with my own hand, and putting by everything which related to America, and indeed whatever was rare and valuable in every science. Besides this, I had standing orders during the whole time I was in Europe, on its principal book-marts, particularly Amsterdam, Frankfort, Madrid and London, for such works relating to America as could not be found in Paris. So that in that department particularly, such a collection was made as probably can never again be effected, because it is hardly probable that the same opportunities, the same time, industry, perseverance and expense, with some knowledge of the bibliography of the subject, would again happen to be in concurrence. During the same period, and after my return to America, I was led to procure, also, whatever related to the duties of those in the high concerns of the nation. So that the collection, which I suppose is of between nine and ten thousand volumes, while it includes what is chiefly valuable in science and literature generally, extends more particularly to whatever belongs to the American statesman. In the diplomatic and parliamentary branches, it is particularly full. It is long since I have been sensible it ought not to continue private property, and had provided that at my death, Congress should have the refusal of it at their own price. But the loss they have now incurred, makes the present the proper moment for their accommodation, without regard to the small remnant of time and the barren use of my enjoying it. I ask of your friendship, therefore, to make for me the tender of it to the library committee of Congress, not knowing myself of whom the committee consists. I enclose you the catalogue, which will enable them to judge of its contents. Nearly the whole are well bound, abundance of them elegantly, and of the choicest editions existing. They may be valued by persons named by themselves, and the payment made convenient to the public. It may be, for instance, in such annual instalments as the law of Congress has left at their disposal, or in stock of any of their late loans, or of any loan they may institute at this session, so as to spare the present calls of our country, and await its days of peace and prosperity. They may enter, nevertheless, into immediate use of it, as eighteen or twenty wagons would place it in Washington in a single trip of a fortnight. I should be willing indeed, to retain a few of the books, to amuse the time I have yet to pass, which might be valued with the rest, but not included in the sum of valuation until they should be restored at my death, which I would carefully provide for, so that the whole library as it stands in the catalogue at this moment should be theirs without any garbling. Those I should like to retain would be chiefly classical and mathematical. Some few in other branches, and particularly one of the five encyclopedias in the catalogue. But this, if not acceptable, would not be urged. I must add, that I have not revised the library since I came home to live, so that it is probable some of the books may be missing, except in the chapters of Law and Divinity, which have been revised and stand exactly as in the catalogue. The return of the catalogue will of course be needed, whether the tender be accepted or not. I do not know that it contains any branch of science which Congress would wish to exclude from their collection; there is, in fact, no subject to which a member of Congress may not have occasion to refer. But such a wish would not correspond with my views of preventing its dismemberment. My desire is either to place it in their hands entire, or to preserve it so here. I am engaged in making an alphabetical index of the author's names, to be annexed to the catalogue, which I will forward to you as soon as completed. Any agreement you shall be so good as to take the trouble of entering into with the committee, I hereby confirm. Accept the assurance of my great esteem and respect.

A JUST BUT SAD WAR

To William Short

Monticello, November 28, 1814

DEAR SIR,—Yours of October 28th came to hand on the 15th instant only. The settlement of your boundary with Colonel Monroe, is protracted by circumstances which seem foreign to it. One would hardly have expected that the hostile expedition to Washington could have had any connection with an operation one hundred miles distant. Yet preventing his attendance, nothing could be done. I am satisfied there is no unwillingness on his part, but on the contrary a desire to have it settled; and therefore, if he should think it indispensable to be present at the investigation, as is possible, the very first time he comes here I will press him to give a day to the decision, without regarding Mr. Carter's absence. Such an occasion must certainly offer soon after the fourth of March, when Congress rises of necessity, and be assured I will not lose one possible moment in effecting it.

Although withdrawn from all anxious attention to political concerns, yet I will state my impressions as to the present war, because your letter leads to the subject. The essential grounds of the war were, 1st, the orders of council; and 2d, the impressment of our citizens; (for I put out of sight from the love of peace the multiplied insults on our government and aggressions on our commerce, with which our pouch, like the Indian's, had long been filled to the mouth.) What immediately produced the declaration was, 1st, the proclamation of the Prince Regent that he would never repeal the orders of council as to us, until Bonaparte should have revoked his decrees as to all other nations as well as ours; and 2d, the declaration of his minister to ours that no arrangement whatever could be devised admissible in lieu of impressment. It was certainly a misfortune that *they* did not know themselves at the date of this silly and insolent proclamation, that within one month they would repeal the orders, and that *we*, at the date of our declaration, could not know of the repeal which was then going on one thousand leagues distant. Their determinations, as declared by themselves, could alone guide us, and they shut the door on all further negotiation, throwing down to us the gauntlet of war or submission as the only alternatives. We cannot blame the government for choosing that of war, because certainly the great majority of the nation thought it ought to be chosen, not that they were to gain by it in dollars and cents; all men know that war is a losing game to both parties. But they know also that if they do not resist encroachment at some point, all will be taken from them, and that more would then be lost even in dollars and cents by submission than resistance. It is the case of giving a part to save the whole, a limb to save life. It is the melancholy law of human societies to be compelled sometimes to choose a great evil in order to ward off a greater; to deter their neighbors from rapine by making it cost them more than honest gains. The enemy are accordingly now disgorging what they had so ravenously swallowed. The orders of council had taken from us near one thousand vessels. Our list of captures from them is now one thousand three hundred, and, just become sensible that it is small and not large ships which gall them most, we shall probably add one thousand prizes a year to their past losses. Again, supposing that, according to the confession of their own minister in parliament, the Americans they had impressed were something short of two thousand, the war against us alone cannot cost them less than twenty millions of dollars a year, so that each American impressed has already cost them ten thousand dollars, and every year will add five thousand dollars more to his price. We, I suppose, expend more; but had we adopted the other alternative of submission, no mortal can tell what the cost would have been. I consider the war then as entirely justifiable on our part, although I am still sensible it is a deplorable misfortune to us. It has arrested the course of the most remarkable tide of prosperity any nation ever experienced, and has closed such prospects of future improvement as were never before in the view of any people. Farewell all hopes of extinguishing public debt! farewell all visions of applying surpluses of revenue to the improvements of peace rather than the ravages of war. Our enemy has indeed the consolation of Satan on removing our first parents from Paradise: from a peaceable and agricultural nation, he makes us a military and manufacturing one. We shall indeed survive the conflict. Breeders enough will remain to carry on population. We shall retain our country, and rapid advances in the art of war will soon enable us to beat our enemy, and probably drive him from the continent. We have men enough, and I am in hopes the present session of Congress will provide the means of commanding their services. But I wish I could see them get into a better train of finance. Their banking projects are like dosing dropsy with more water. If anything could revolt our citizens against the war, it would be the extravagance with which they are about to be taxed. It is strange indeed that at this day, and in a country where English proceedings are so familiar, the principles and advantages of funding should be neglected, and expedients resorted to. Their new bank, if not abortive at its birth, will not last through one campaign; and the taxes proposed cannot be paid. How can a people who cannot get fifty cents a bushel for their wheat, while they pay twelve dollars a bushel for their salt, pay five times the amount of taxes they ever paid before? Yet that will be the case in all the States south of the Potomac. Our resources are competent to the maintenance of the war if duly economized and skillfuly employed in the way of anticipation. However, we must suffer,

LETTERS 1814

I suppose, from our ignorance in funding, as we did from that of fighting, until necessity teaches us both; and, fortunately, our stamina are so vigorous as to rise superior to great mismanagement. This year I think we shall have learnt how to call forth our force, and by the next I hope our funds, and even if the state of Europe should not by that time give the enemy employment enough nearer home, we shall leave him nothing to fight for here. These are my views of the war. They embrace a great deal of sufferance, trying privations, and no benefit but that of teaching our enemy that he is never to gain by wanton injuries on us. To me this state of things brings a sacrifice of all tranquillity and comfort through the residue of life. For although the debility of age disables me from the services and sufferings of the field, yet, by the total annihilation in value of the produce which was to give me subsistence and independence, I shall be like Tantalus, up to the shoulders in water, yet dying with thirst. We can make indeed enough to eat, drink and clothe ourselves; but nothing for our salt, iron, groceries and taxes, which must be paid in money. For what can we raise for the market? Wheat? we can only give it to our horses, as we have been doing ever since harvest. Tobacco? it is not worth the pipe it is smoked in. Some say Whiskey; but all mankind must become drunkards to consume it. But although we feel, we shall not flinch. We must consider now, as in the revolutionary war, that although the evils of resistance are great, those of submission would be greater. We must meet, therefore, the former as the casualties of tempests and earthquakes, and like them necessarily resulting from the constitution of the world. Your situation, my dear friend, is much better. For, although I do not know with certainty the nature of your investments, yet I presume they are not in banks, insurance companies, or any other of those gossamer castles. If in ground-rents, they are solid; if in stock of the United States, they are equally so. I once thought that in the event of a war we should be obliged to suspend paying the interest of the public debt. But a dozen years more of experience and observation on our people and government, have satisfied me it will never be done. The sense of the necessity of public credit is so universal and so deeply rooted, that no other necessity will prevail against it; and I am glad to see that while the former eight millions are steadfastly applied to the sinking of the old debt, the Senate have lately insisted on a sinking fund for the new. This is the dawn of that improvement in the management of our finances which I look to for salvation; and I trust that the light will continue to advance, and point out their way to our legislators. They will soon see that instead of taxes for the whole year's expenses, which the people cannot pay, a tax to the amount of the interest and a reasonable portion of the principal will command the whole sum, and throw a part of the burthens of war on times of peace and prosperity. A sacred payment of interest is the only way to make the most of their resources, and a sense of that renders your income from our funds more certain than mine from lands. Some apprehend danger from the defection of Massachusetts. It is a disagreeable circumstance, but not a dangerous one. If they become neutral, we are sufficient for one enemy without them, and in fact we get no aid from them now. If their administration determines to join the enemy, their force will be annihilated by equality of division among themselves. Their federalists will then call in the English army, the republicans ours, and it will only be a transfer of the scene of war from Canada to Massachusetts; and we can get ten men to go to Massachusetts for one who will go to Canada. Every one, too, must know that we can at any moment make peace with England at the expense of the navigation and fisheries of Massachusetts. But it will not come to this. Their own people will put down these factionists as soon as they see the real object of their opposition; and of this Vermont, New Hampshire, and even Connecticut itself, furnish proofs.

You intimate a possibility of your return to France, now that Bonaparte is put down. I do not wonder at it, France, freed from that monster, must again become the most agreeable country on earth. It would be the second choice of all whose ties of family and fortune gives a preference to some other one, and the first of all not under those ties. Yet I doubt if the tranquillity of France is entirely settled. If her Pretorian bands are not furnished with employment on her external enemies, I fear they will recall the old, or set up some new cause.

God bless you and preserve you in bodily health. Tranquillity of mind depends much on ourselves, and greatly on due
reflection "how much pain have cost us the evils which have
never happened." Affectionately adieu.

WAR, REVOLUTION, AND RESTORATION

To Lafayette

Monticello, February 14, 1815

MY DEAR FRIEND, —Your letter of August the 14th has been
received and read again, and again, with extraordinary pleasure. It is the first glimpse which has been furnished me of
the interior workings of the late unexpected but fortunate revolution of your country. The newspapers told us only that the
great beast was fallen; but what part in this the patriots acted,
and what the egotists, whether the former slept while the latter were awake to their own interests only, the hireling scribblers of the English press said little and knew less. I see now
the mortifying alternative under which the patriot there is
placed, of being either silent, or disgraced by an association
in opposition with the remains of Bonapartism. A full measure of liberty is not now perhaps to be expected by your
nation, nor am I confident they are prepared to preserve it.
More than a generation will be requisite, under the administration of reasonable laws favoring the progress of knowledge
in the general mass of the people, and their habituation to an
independent security of person and property, before they will
be capable of estimating the value of freedom, and the necessity of a sacred adherence to the principles on which it rests
for preservation. Instead of that liberty which takes root and
growth in the progress of reason, if recovered by mere force
or accident, it becomes, with an unprepared people, a tyranny
still, of the many, the few, or the one. Possibly you may remember, at the date of the *jeu de paume*, how earnestly I
urged yourself and the patriots of my acquaintance, to enter
then into a compact with the king, securing freedom of religion, freedom of the press, trial by jury, *habeas corpus*, and a
national legislature, all of which it was known he would then

yield, to go home, and let these work on the amelioration of
the condition of the people, until they should have rendered
them capable of more, when occasions would not fail to arise
for communicating to them more. This was as much as I then
thought them able to bear, soberly and usefully for themselves. You thought otherwise, and that the dose might still
be larger. And I found you were right; for subsequent events
proved they were equal to the constitution of 1791. Unfortunately, some of the most honest and enlightened of our patriotic friends, (but closet politicians merely, unpractised in
the knowledge of man,) thought more could still be obtained
and borne. They did not weigh the hazards of a transition
from one form of government to another, the value of what
they had already rescued from those hazards, and might hold
in security if they pleased, nor the imprudence of giving up
the certainty of such a degree of liberty, under a limited monarch, for the uncertainty of a little more under the form of a
republic. You differed from them. You were for stopping
there, and for securing the constitution which the National
Assembly had obtained. Here, too, you were right; and from
this fatal error of the republicans, from their separation from
yourself and the constitutionalists, in their councils, flowed all
the subsequent sufferings and crimes of the French nation.
The hazards of a second change fell upon them by the way.
The foreigner gained time to anarchise by gold the government he could not overthrow by arms, to crush in their own
councils the genuine republicans, by the fraternal embraces of
exaggerated and hired pretenders, and to turn the machine of
Jacobinism from the change to the destruction of order; and,
in the end, the limited monarchy they had secured was exchanged for the unprincipled and bloody tyranny of Robespierre, and the equally unprincipled and maniac tyranny of
Bonaparte. You are now rid of him, and I sincerely wish you
may continue so. But this may depend on the wisdom and
moderation of the restored dynasty. It is for them now to
read a lesson in the fatal errors of the republicans; to be contented with a certain portion of power, secured by formal
compact with the nation, rather than, grasping at more, hazard all upon uncertainty, and risk meeting the fate of their
predecessor, or a renewal of their own exile. We are just in-

formed, too, of an example which merits, if true, their most profound contemplation. The gazettes say that Ferdinand of Spain is dethroned, and his father re-established on the basis of their new constitution. This order of magistrates must, therefore, see, that although the attempts at reformation have not succeeded in their whole length, and some secession from the ultimate point has taken place, yet that men have by no means fallen back to their former passiveness, but on the contrary, that a sense of their rights, and a restlessness to obtain them, remain deeply impressed on every mind, and, if not quieted by reasonable relaxations of power, will break out like a volcano on the first occasion, and overwhelm everything again in its way. I always thought the present king an honest and moderate man; and having no issue, he is under a motive the less for yielding to personal considerations. I cannot, therefore, but hope, that the patriots in and out of your legislature, acting in phalanx, but temperately and wisely, pressing unremittingly the principles omitted in the late capitulation of the king, and watching the occasions which the course of events will create, may get those principles engrafted into it, and sanctioned by the solemnity of a national act.

With us the affairs of war have taken the most favorable turn which was to be expected. Our thirty years of peace had taken off, or superannuated, all our revolutionary officers of experience and grade; and our first draught in the lottery of untried characters had been most unfortunate. The delivery of the fort and army of Detroit by the traitor Hull; the disgrace at Queenstown, under Van Rensellaer; the massacre at Frenchtown under Winchester; and surrender of Boerstler in an open field to one-third of his own numbers, were the inauspicious beginnings of the first year of our warfare. The second witnessed but the single miscarriage occasioned by the disagreement of Wilkinson and Hampton, mentioned in my letter to you of November the 30th, 1813, while it gave us the capture of York by Dearborne and Pike; the capture of Fort George by Dearborne also; the capture of Proctor's army on the Thames by Harrison, Shelby and Johnson, and that of the whole British fleet on Lake Erie by Perry. The third year has been a continued series of victories, to-wit: of Brown and

Scott at Chippewa, of the same at Niagara; of Gaines over Drummond at Fort Erie; that of Brown over Drummond at the same place; the capture of another fleet on Lake Champlain by M'Donough; the entire defeat of their army under Prevost, on the same day, by M'Comb, and recently their defeats at New Orleans by Jackson, Coffee and Carroll, with the loss of four thousand men out of nine thousand and six hundred, with their two Generals, Packingham and Gibbs killed, and a third, Keane, wounded, mortally, as is said.

This series of successes has been tarnished only by the conflagration at Washington, a *coup de main* differing from that at Richmond, which you remember, in the revolutionary war, in the circumstance only, that we had, in that case, but forty-eight hours' notice that an enemy had arrived within our capes; whereas, at Washington, there was abundant previous notice. The force designated by the President was double of what was necessary; but failed, as is the general opinion, through the insubordination of Armstrong, who would never believe the attack intended until it was actually made, and the sluggishness of Winder before the occasion, and his indecision during it. Still, in the end, the transaction has helped rather than hurt us, by arousing the general indignation of our country, and by marking to the world of Europe the Vandalism and brutal character of the English government. It has merely served to immortalize their infamy. And add further, that through the whole period of the war, we have beaten them single-handed at sea, and so thoroughly established our superiority over them with equal force, that they retire from that kind of contest, and never suffer their frigates to cruize singly. The Endymion would never have engaged the frigate President, but knowing herself backed by three frigates and a razee, who, though somewhat slower sailers, would get up before she could be taken. The disclosure to the world of the fatal secret that they can be beaten at sea with an equal force, the evidence furnished by the military operations of the last year that experience is rearing us officers who, when our means shall be fully under way, will plant our standard on the walls of Quebec and Halifax, their recent and signal disaster at New Orleans, and the evaporation of their hopes from the Hartford convention, will probably raise a clamor in the British nation, which will force their ministry into peace. I say *force* them, because, willingly, they would never be at peace. The British ministers find in a state of war rather than of peace, by riding the various contractors, and receiving *douceurs* on the vast expenditures of the war supplies, that they recruit their broken fortunes, or make new ones, and therefore will not make peace as long as by any delusions they can keep the temper of the nation up to the war point. They found some hopes on the state of our finances. It is true that the excess of our banking institutions, and their present discredit, have shut us out from the best source of credit we could ever command with certainty. But the foundations of credit still remain to us, and need but skill which experience will soon produce, to marshal them into an order which may carry us through any length of war. But they have hoped more in their Hartford convention. Their fears of republican France being now done away, they are directed to republican America, and they are playing the same game for disorganization here, which they played in your country. The Marats, the Dantons and Robespierres of Massachusetts are in the same pay, under the same orders, and making the same efforts to anarchise us, that their prototypes in France did there.

I do not say that all who met at Hartford were under the same motives of money, nor were those of France. Some of them are Outs, and wish to be Inns; some the mere dupes of the agitators, or of their own party passions, while the Maratists alone are in the real secret; but they have very different materials to work on. The yeomanry of the United States are not the *canaille* of Paris. We might safely give them leave to go through the United States recruiting their ranks, and I am satisfied they could not raise one single regiment (gambling merchants and silk-stocking clerks excepted) who would support them in any effort to separate from the Union. The cement of this Union is in the heart-blood of every American. I do not believe there is on earth a government established on so immovable a basis. Let them, in any State, even in Massachusetts itself, raise the standard of separation, and its citizens will rise in mass, and do justice themselves on their own incendiaries. If they could have induced the government to some effort of suppression, or even to enter into discussion with them, it would have given them some importance, have brought them into some notice. But they have not been able to make themselves even a subject of conversation, either of public or private societies. A silent contempt has been the sole notice they excite; consoled, indeed, some of them, by the *palpable* favors of Philip. Have then no fears for us, my friend. The grounds of these exist only in English newspapers, endited or endowed by the Castlereaghs or the Cannings, or some other such models of pure and uncorrupted virtue. Their military heroes, by land and sea, may sink our oyster boats, rob our hen roosts, burn our negro huts, and run off. But a campaign or two more will relieve them from further trouble or expense in defending their American possessions.

You once gave me a copy of the journal of your campaign in Virginia, in 1781, which I must have lent to some one of the undertakers to write the history of the revolutionary war, and forgot to reclaim. I conclude this, because it is no longer among my papers, which I have very diligently searched for it, but in vain. An author of real ability is now writing that part of the history of Virginia. He does it in my neighborhood, and I lay open to him all my papers. But I possess none, nor has he any, which can enable him to do justice to your faithful and able services in that campaign. If you could be so good as to send me another copy, by the very first vessel bound to any port in the United States, it might be here in time; for although he expects to begin to print within a month or two, yet you know the delays of these undertakings. At any rate it might be got in as a supplement. The old Count Rochambeau gave me also his *memoire* of the operations at York, which is gone in the same way, and I have no means of applying to his family for it. Perhaps you could render them as well as us, the service of procuring another copy.

I learn, with real sorrow, the deaths of Monsieur and Madame de Tessé. They made an interesting part in the idle reveries in which I have sometimes indulged myself, of seeing all my friends of Paris once more, for a month or two; a thing impossible, which, however, I never permitted myself to despair of. The regrets, however, of seventy-three at the loss of friends, may be the less, as the time is shorter within which we are to meet again, according to the creed of our education.

This letter will be handed you by Mr. Ticknor, a young gentleman of Boston, of great erudition, indefatigable industry, and preparation for a life of distinction in his own country. He passed a few days with me here, brought high recommendations from Mr. Adams and others, and appeared in every respect to merit them. He is well worthy of those attentions which you so kindly bestow on our countrymen, and for those he may receive I shall join him in acknowledging personal obligations.

I salute you with assurances of my constant and affectionate friendship and respect.

P. S. February 26th. My letter had not yet been sealed, when I received news of our peace. I am glad of it, and especially that we closed our war with the eclat of the action at New Orleans. But I consider it as an armistice only, because no security is provided against the impressment of our seamen. While this is unsettled we are in hostility of mind with England, although actual deeds of arms may be suspended by a truce. If she thinks the exercise of this outrage is worth eternal war, eternal war it must be, or extermination of the one or the other party. The first act of impressment she commits on an American, will be answered by reprisal, or by a declaration of war here; and the interval must be merely a state of preparation for it. In this we have much to do, in further fortifying our seaport towns, providing military stores, classing and disciplining our militia, arranging our financial system, and above all, pushing our domestic manufactures, which have taken such root as never again can be shaken. Once more, God bless you.

LIBRARY CLASSIFICATION

To George Watterston

Monticello, May 7, 1815

SIR,—I have duly received your favor of April 26th, in which you are pleased to ask my opinion on the subject of the arrangement of libraries. I shall communicate with pleasure what occurs to me on it. Two methods offer themselves, the one alphabetical, the other according to the subject of the book. The former is very unsatisfactory, because of the medley it presents to the mind, the difficulty sometimes of recalling an author's name, and the greater difficulty, where the name is not given, of selecting the word in the title, which shall determine its alphabetical place. The arrangement according to subject is far preferable, although sometimes presenting difficulty also, for it is often doubtful to what particular subject a book should be ascribed. This is remarkably the case with books of travels, which often blend together the geography, natural history, civil history, agriculture, manufactures, commerce, arts, occupations, manners, &c., of a country, so as to render it difficult to say to which they chiefly relate. Others again, are polygraphical in their nature, as Encyclopedias, magazines, etc. Yet on the whole I have preferred arrangement according to subject, because of the peculiar satisfaction, when we wish to consider a particular one, of seeing at a glance the books which have been written on it, and selecting those from which we effect most readily the information we seek. On this principle the arrangement of my library was formed, and I took the basis of its distribution from Lord Bacon's table of science, modifying it to the changes in scientific pursuits which have taken place since his time, and to the greater or less extent of reading in the science which I proposed to myself. Thus the law having been my profession, and politics the occupation to which the circumstances of the times in which I have lived called my particular attention, my provision of books in these lines, and in those most nearly connected with them was more copious, and required in particular instances subdivisions into sections and paragraphs, while other subjects of which general views only were contemplated are thrown into masses. A physician or theologist would have modified differently, the chapters, sections, and paragraphs of a library adapted to their particular pursuits.

You will receive my library arranged very perfectly in the

order observed in the catalogue, which I have sent with it. In placing the books on their shelves, I have generally, but not always, collocated distinctly the folios, quarto, octavo, and duodecimo, placing with the last all smaller sizes. On every book is a label, indicating the chapter of the catalogue to which it belongs, and the other it holds among those of the same format. So that, although the numbers seem confused on the catalogue, they are consecutive on the volumes as they stand on their shelves, and indicate at once the place they occupy there. Mr. Milligan in packing them has preserved their arrangement so exactly, in their respective presses, that on setting the presses up on end, he will be able readily to replace them in the order corresponding with the catalogue, and thus save you the immense labor which their rearrangement would otherwise require.

To give to my catalogue the convenience of the alphabetical arrangement I have made at the end an alphabet of authors' names and have noted the chapter or chapters, in which the name will be found; where it occurs several times in the same chapter, it is indicated, by one or more perpendicular scores, thus ||||, according to the number of times it will be found in the chapter. Where a book bears no author's name, I have selected in its title some leading word for denoting it alphabetically. This member of the catalogue would be more perfect if, instead of the score, the number on the book were particularly noted. This could not be done when I made the catalogue, because no label of numbers had then been put on the books. That alteration can now be readily made, and would add greatly to the convenient use of the catalogue. I gave to Mr. Milligan a note of three folio volumes of the laws of Virginia belonging to the library, which being in known hands, will be certainly recovered, and shall be forwarded to you. One is a MS. volume from which a printed copy is now preparing for publication.

This statement meets, I believe, all the enquiries of your letter, and where it is not sufficiently minute, Mr. Milligan, from his necessary acquaintance with the arrangement, will be able to supply the smaller details. Accept the assurances of my respect and consideration.

MANUFACTURES

To Benjamin Austin

Monticello, January 9, 1816

DEAR SIR,—Your favor of December 21st has been received, and I am first to thank you for the pamphlet it covered. The same description of persons which is the subject of that is so much multiplied here too, as to be almost a grievance, and by their numbers in the public councils, have wrested from the public hand the direction of the pruning knife. But with us as a body, they are republican, and mostly moderate in their views; so far, therefore, less objects of jealousy than with you. Your opinions on the events which have taken place in France, are entirely just, so far as these events are yet developed. But they have not reached their ultimate termination. There is still an awful void between the present and what is to be the last chapter of that history; and I fear it is to be filled with abominations as frightful as those which have already disgraced it. That nation is too high-minded, has too much innate force, intelligence and elasticity, to remain under its present compression. Samson will arise in his strength, as of old, and as of old will burst asunder the withes and the cords, and the webs of the Philistines. But what are to be the scenes of havoc and horror, and how widely they may spread between brethren of the same house, our ignorance of the interior feuds and antipathies of the country places beyond our ken. It will end, nevertheless, in a representative government, in a government in which the will of the people will be an effective ingredient. This important element has taken root in the European mind, and will have its growth; their despots, sensible of this, are already offering this modification of their governments, as if on their own accord. Instead of the parricide treason of Bonaparte, in perverting the means confided to him as a republican magistrate, to the subversion of that republic and erection of a military despotism for himself and his family, had he used it honestly for the establishment and support of a free government in his own country, France would now have been in freedom and rest; and her example operating in a contrary direction, every nation in Europe would have had a government over which the will of the people would have had some control. His atrocious egotism has checked the salutary progress of principle, and deluged it with rivers of blood which are not yet run out. To the vast sum of devastation and of human misery, of which he has been the guilty cause, much is still to be added. But the object is fixed in the eye of nations, and they will press on to its accomplishment and to the general amelioration of the condition of man. What a germ have we planted, and how faithfully should we cherish the parent tree at home!

You tell me I am quoted by those who wish to continue our dependence on England for manufactures. There was a time when I might have been so quoted with more candor, but within the thirty years which have since elapsed, how are circumstances changed! We were then in peace. Our independent place among nations was acknowledged. A commerce which offered the raw material in exchange for the same material after receiving the last touch of industry, was worthy of welcome to all nations. It was expected that those especially to whom manufacturing industry was important, would cherish the friendship of such customers by every favor, by every inducement, and particularly cultivate their peace by every act of justice and friendship. Under this prospect the question seemed legitimate, whether, with such an immensity of unimproved land, courting the hand of husbandry, the industry of agriculture, or that of manufactures, would add most to the national wealth? And the doubt was entertained on this consideration chiefly, that to the labor of the husbandman a vast addition is made by the spontaneous energies of the earth on which it is employed: for one grain of wheat committed to the earth, she renders twenty, thirty, and even fifty fold, whereas to the labor of the manufacturer nothing is added. Pounds of flax, in his hands, yield, on the contrary, but pennyweights of lace. This exchange, too, laborious as it might seem, what a field did it promise for the occupations of the ocean; what a nursery for that class of citizens who were to exercise and maintain our equal rights on that element? This was the state of things in 1785, when the "Notes on Virginia" were first printed; when, the ocean being open to all nations, and their common right in it acknowledged and exercised under regulations sanctioned by the assent and usage of all, it was thought that the doubt might claim some consideration. But who in 1785 could foresee the rapid depravity which was to render the close of that century the disgrace of the history of man? Who could have imagined that the two most distinguished in the rank of nations, for science and civilization, would have suddenly descended from that honorable eminence, and setting at defiance all those moral laws established by the Author of nature between nation and nation, as between man and man, would cover earth and sea with robberies and piracies, merely because strong enough to do it with temporal impunity; and that under this disbandment of nations from social order, we should have been despoiled of a thousand ships, and have thousands of our citizens reduced to Algerine slavery. Yet all this has taken place. One of these nations interdicted to our vessels all harbors of the globe without having first proceeded to some one of hers, there paid a tribute proportioned to the cargo, and obtained her license to proceed to the port of destination. The other declared them to be lawful prize if they had touched at the port, or been visited by a ship of the enemy nation. Thus were we completely excluded from the ocean. Compare this state of things with that of '85, and say whether an opinion founded in the circumstances of that day can be fairly applied to those of the present. We have experienced what we did not then believe, that there exists both profligacy and power enough to exclude us from the field of interchange with other nations: that to be independent for the comforts of life we must fabricate them ourselves. We must now place the manufacturer by the side of the agriculturist. The former question is suppressed, or rather assumes a new form. Shall we make our own comforts, or go without them, at the will of a foreign nation? He, therefore, who is now against domestic manufacture, must be for reducing us either to dependence on that foreign nation, or to be clothed in skins, and to live like wild beasts in dens and caverns. I am not one of these; experience has taught me that manufactures are now as necessary to our independence as to our comfort; and if those who quote me as of a different opinion, will keep pace with me in purchasing nothing foreign where an equivalent of domestic fabric can be obtained, without regard to difference of price, it will not be our fault if we do not soon have a supply at home equal to our demand, and wrest that weapon of distress from the hand which has wielded it. If it shall be proposed to go beyond our own supply, the question of '85 will then recur, will our *surplus* labor be then most beneficially employed in the culture of the earth, or in the fabrications of art? We have time yet for consideration, before that question will press upon us; and the maxim to be applied will depend on the circumstances which shall then exist; for in so complicated a science as political economy, no one axiom can be laid down as wise and expedient for all times and circumstances, and for their contraries. Inattention to this is what has called for this explanation, which reflection would have rendered unnecessary with the candid, while nothing will do it with those who use the former opinion only as a stalking horse, to cover their disloyal propensities to keep us in eternal vassalage to a foreign and unfriendly people.

I salute you with assurances of great respect and esteem.

"A REAL CHRISTIAN"
To Charles Thomson

Monticello, January 9, 1816

MY DEAR AND ANCIENT FRIEND,—An acquaintance of fifty-two years, for I think ours dates from 1764, calls for an interchange of notice now and then, that we remain in existence, the monuments of another age, and examples of a friendship unaffected by the jarring elements by which we have been surrounded, of revolutions of government, of party and of opinion. I am reminded of this duty by the receipt, through our friend Dr. Patterson, of your synopsis of the four Evangelists. I had procured it as soon as I saw it advertised, and had become familiar with its use; but this copy is the more valued as it comes from your hand. This work bears the stamp of that accuracy which marks everything from you, and will be useful to those who, not taking things on trust, recur for themselves to the fountain of pure morals. I, too, have made a wee-little book from the same materials, which I call the Philosophy of Jesus; it is a paradigma of his doctrines, made by cutting the texts out of the book, and arranging them on the pages of a blank book, in a certain order of time or subject. A more beautiful or precious morsel of ethics I have never seen; it is a document in proof that *I* am a *real Christian*, that is to say, a disciple of the doctrines of Jesus, very different from the Platonists, who call *me* infidel and *themselves* Christians and preachers of the gospel, while they draw all their characteristic dogmas from what its author never said nor saw. They have compounded from the heathen mysteries a system beyond the comprehension of man, of which the great reformer of the vicious ethics and deism of the Jews, were he to return on earth, would not recognize one feature. If I had time I would add to my little book the Greek, Latin and French texts, in columns side by side. And I wish I could subjoin a translation of Gosindi's Syntagma of the doctrines of Epicurus, which, notwithstanding the calumnies of the Stoics and caricatures of Cicero, is the most rational system remaining of the philosophy of the ancients, as frugal of vicious indulgence, and fruitful of virtue as the hyperbolical extravagances of his rival sects.

I retain good health, am rather feeble to walk much, but ride with ease, passing two or three hours a day on horseback, and every three or four months taking in a carriage a journey of ninety miles to a distant possession, where I pass a good deal of my time. My eyes need the aid of glasses by night, and with small print in the day also; my hearing is not quite so sensible as it used to be; no tooth shaking yet, but shivering and shrinking in body from the cold we now experience, my thermometer having been as low as 12° this morning. My greatest oppression is a correspondence afflictingly laborious, the extent of which I have been long endeavoring to curtail. This keeps me at the drudgery of the writing-table all the prime hours of the day, leaving for the gratification of my appetite for reading, only what I can steal from the hours of sleep. Could I reduce this epistolary corvée within the limits of my friends and affairs, and give the time redeemed from it to reading and reflection, to history, ethics, mathematics, my life would be as happy as the infirmities of age would admit, and I should look on its consummation with the composure of one *"qui summum nec me tuit diem nec optat."*

So much as to myself, and I have given you this string of egotisms in the hope of drawing a similar one from yourself. I have heard from others that you retain your health, a good degree of activity, and all the vivacity and cheerfulness of your mind, but I wish to learn it more minutely from yourself. How has time affected your health and spirits? What are your amusements, literary and social? Tell me everything about yourself, because all will be interesting to me who retains for you ever the same constant and affectionate friendship and respect.

YOUR PROPHECY AND MINE

To John Adams

Monticello, Jan. 11, 1816

DEAR SIR—Of the last five months I have past four at my other domicil, for such it is in a considerable degree. No letters are forwarded to me there, because the cross post to that place is circuitous and uncertain. During my absence therefore they are accumulating here, and awaiting acknolegments. This has been the fate of your favor of Nov. 13.

I agree with you in all it's eulogies on the 18th. century. It certainly witnessed the sciences and arts, manners and morals, advanced to a higher degree than the world had ever before seen. And might we not go back to the aera of the Borgias, by which time the barbarous ages had reduced national morality to it's lowest point of depravity, and observe that the arts and sciences, rising from that point, advanced gradually thro' all the 16th. 17th. and 18th. centuries, softening and correcting the manners and morals of man? I think too we may add, to the great honor of science and the arts, that their natural effect is, by illuminating public opinion, to erect it into a Censor, before which the most exalted tremble for their future, as well as present fame. With some exceptions only, through the 17th. and 18th. centuries morality occupied an honorable chapter in the political code of nations. You must have observed while in Europe, as I thought I did, that those who administered the governments of the greater powers at least, had a respect to faith, and considered the dignity of their government as involved in it's integrity. A wound indeed was inflicted on this character of honor in the 18th. century by the partition of Poland. But this was the atrocity of a barbarous government chiefly, in conjunction with a smaller one still scrambling to become great, while one only of those already great, and having character to lose, descended to the baseness of an accomplice in the crime. France, England, Spain shared in it only inasmuch as they stood aloof and permitted it's perpetration. How then has it happened that these nations, France especially and England, so great, so dignified, so distinguished by science and the arts, plunged at once into all the depths of human enormity, threw off suddenly and openly all the restraints of morality, all sensation to character, and unblushingly avowed and acted on the principle that power was right? Can this sudden apostacy from national rectitude be accounted for? The treaty of Pilnitz seems to have begun it, suggested perhaps by the baneful precedent of Poland. Was it from the terror of monarchs, alarmed at the light returning on them from the West, and kindling a Volcano under their thrones? Was it a combination to extinguish that light, and to bring back, as their best auxiliaries, those enumerated by you, the Sorbonne, the Inquisition, the Index expurgatorius, and the knights of Loyola? Whatever it was, the close of the century saw the moral world thrown back again to the age of the Borgias, to the point from which it had departed 300. years before. France, after crushing and punishing the conspiracy of Pilnitz, went herself deeper and deeper into the crimes she had been chastising. I say France, and not Bonaparte; for altho' he was the head and mouth, the nation furnished the hands which executed his enormities. England, altho' in opposition, kept full pace with France, not indeed by the manly force of her own arms, but by oppressing the weak, and bribing the strong. At length the whole choir joined and divided the weaker nations among them. Your prophecies to Dr. Price proved truer than mine; and yet fell short of the fact, for instead of a million, the destruction of 8. or 10. millions of human beings has probably been the ef-

LETTERS 1816

fect of these convulsions. I did not, in 89. believe they would
have lasted so long, nor have cost so much blood. But altho'
your prophecy has proved true so far, I hope it does not preclude a better final result. That same light from our West
seems to have spread and illuminated the very engines employed to extinguish it. It has given them a glimmering of
their rights and their power. The idea of representative government has taken root and growth among them. Their masters feel it, and are saving themselves by timely offers of this
modification of their own powers. Belguim, Prussia, Poland,
Lombardy etc. are now offered a representative organization:
illusive probably at first, but it will grow into power in the
end. Opinion is power, and that opinion will come. Even
France will yet attain representative government. You observe
it makes the basis of every constitution which has been demanded or offered: of that demanded by their Senate; of that
offered by Bonaparte; and of that granted by Louis XVIII.
The idea then is rooted, and will be established, altho' rivers
of blood may yet flow between them and their object. The
allied armies now couching upon them are first to be destroyed, and destroyed they will surely be. A nation united
can never be conquered. We have seen what the ignorant bigotted and unarmed Spaniards could do against the disciplined
veterans of their invaders. What then may we not expect from
the power and character of the French nation? The oppressors
may cut off heads after heads, but like those of the Hydra,
they multiply at every stroke. The recruits within a nation's
own limits are prompt and without number; while those of
their invaders from a distance are slow, limited, and must
come to an end. I think too we percieve that all these allies
do not see the same interest in the annihilation of the power
of France. There are certainly some symptoms of foresight in
Alexander that France might produce a salutary diversion of
force were Austria and Prussia to become her enemies. France
too is the natural ally of the Turk, as having no interfering
interests, and might be useful in neutralizing and perhaps
turning that power on Austria. That a re-acting jealousy too
exists with Austria and Prussia I think their late strict alliance
indicates; and I should not wonder if Spain should discover a
sympathy with them. Italy is so divided as to be nothing.

JOSEPH C. CABELL 1377

Here then we see new coalitions in embrio which after France shall in turn have suffered a just punishment for her crimes, will not only raise her from the earth on which she is prostrate, but give her an opportunity to establish a government of as much liberty as she can bear, enough to ensure her happiness and prosperity. When insurrection begins, be it where it will, all the partitioned countries will rush to arms, and Europe again become an Arena of gladiators. And what is the definite object they will propose? A restoration certainly of the status quo prius, of the state of possession of 89. I see no other principle on which Europe can ever again settle down in lasting peace. I hope your prophecies will go thus far, as my wishes do, and that they, like the former, will prove to have been the sober dictates of a superior understanding, and a sound calculation of effects from causes well understood. Some future Morgan will then have an opportunity of doing you justice, and of counterbalancing the breach of confidence of which you so justly complain, and in which no one has had more frequent occasion of fellow-feeling than myself. Permit me to place here my affectionate respects to Mrs. Adams, and to add for yourself the assurances of cordial friendship and esteem.

THE WARD SYSTEM
To Joseph C. Cabell

Monticello, February 2, 1816

DEAR SIR,—Your favors of the 23d and 24th ult., were a week coming to us. I instantly enclosed to you the deeds of Capt. Miller, but I understand that the Post Master, having locked his mail before they got to the office, would not unlock it to give them a passage.

Having been prevented from retaining my collection of the acts and journals of our legislature by the lumping manner in which the Committee of Congress chose to take my library, it may be useful to our public bodies to know what acts and journals I had, and where they can now have access to them. I therefore enclose you a copy of my catalogue, which I pray you to deposit in the council office for public use. It is in the eighteenth and twenty-fourth chapters they will find what is interesting to them. The form of the catalogue has been much injured in the publication; for although they have preserved my division into chapters, they have reduced the books in each chapter to alphabetical order, instead of the chronological or analytical arrangements I had given them. You will see sketches of what were my arrangements at the heads of some of the chapters.

The bill on the obstructions in our navigable waters appears to me proper; as do also the amendments proposed. I think the State should reserve a right to the use of the waters for navigation, and that where an individual landholder impedes that use, he shall remove that impediment, and leave the subject in as good a state as nature formed it. This I hold to be the true principle; and to this Colonel Green's amendments go. All I ask in my own case is, that the legislature will not take from me *my own works*. I am ready to cut my dam in any place, and at any moment requisite, so as to remove that impediment, if it be thought one, and to leave those interested to make the most of the natural circumstances of the place. But I hope they will never take from me my canal, made through the body of my own lands, at an expense of twenty thousand dollars, and which is no impediment to the navigation of the river. I have permitted the riparian proprietors above (and they not more than a dozen or twenty) to use it gratis, and shall not withdraw the permission unless they so use it as to obstruct too much the operations of my mills, of which there is some likelihood.

Doctor Smith, you say, asks what is the best elementary book on the principles of government? None in the world equal to the Review of Montesquieu, printed at Philadelphia a few years ago. It has the advantage, too, of being equally sound and corrective of the principles of political economy; and all within the compass of a thin 8vo. Chipman's and Priestley's Principles of Government, and the Federalists, are excellent in many respects, but for fundamental principles not comparable to the Review. I have no objections to the printing my letter to Mr. Carr, if it will promote the interests of science; although it was not written with a view to its publication.

My letter of the 24th ult. conveyed to you the grounds of the two articles objected to the College bill. Your last presents one of them in a new point of view, that of the commencement of the ward schools as likely to render the law unpopular to the country. It must be a very inconsiderate and rough process of execution that would do this. My idea of the mode of carrying it into execution would be this: Declare the county *ipso facto* divided into wards for the present, by the boundaries of the militia captaincies; somebody attend the ordinary muster of each company, having first desired the captain to call together a full one. There explain the object of the law to the people of the company, put to their vote whether they will have a school established, and the most central and convenient place for it; get them to meet and build a log school-house; have a roll taken of the children who would attend it, and of those of them able to pay. These would probably be sufficient to support a common teacher, instructing gratis the few unable to pay. If there should be a deficiency, it would require too trifling a contribution from the county to be complained of; and especially as the whole county would participate, where necessary, in the same resource. Should the company, by its vote, decide that it would have no school, let them remain without one. The advantages of this proceeding would be that it would become the duty of the alderman elected by the county, to take an active part in pressing the introduction of schools, and to look out for tutors. If, however, it is intended that the State government shall take this business into its own hands, and provide schools for every county, then by all means strike out this provision of our bill. I would never wish that it should be placed on a worse footing than the rest of the State. But if it is believed that these elementary schools will be better managed by the governor and council, the commissioners of the literary fund, or any other general authority of the government, than by the parents within each ward, it is a belief against all experience. Try the principle one step further, and amend the bill so as to commit to the governor and council the management of all our farms, our mills, and merchants' stores. No, my friend, the way to have good and safe government, is not to trust it all to one, but to divide it among the many, distributing to every one exactly the functions he is competent to. Let the national government be entrusted with the defence of the nation, and its foreign and federal relations; the State governments with the civil rights, laws, police, and administration of what concerns the State generally; the counties with the local concerns of the counties, and each ward direct the interests within itself. It is by dividing and subdividing these republics from the great national one down through all its subordinations, until it ends in the administration of every man's farm by himself; by placing under every one what his own eye may superintend, that all will be done for the best. What has destroyed liberty and the rights of man in every government which has ever existed under the sun? The generalizing and concentrating all cares and powers into one body, no matter whether of the autocrats of Russia or France, or of the aristocrats of a Venetian senate. And I do believe that if the Almighty has not decreed that man shall never be free, (and it is a blasphemy to believe it,) that the secret will be found to be in the making himself the depository of the powers respecting himself, so far as he is competent to them, and delegating only what is beyond his competence by a synthetical process, to higher and higher orders of functionaries, so as to trust fewer and fewer powers in proportion as the trustees become more and more oligarchical. The elementary republics of the wards, the county republics, the States republics, and the republic of the Union, would form a gradation of authorities, standing each on the basis of law, holding every one its delegated share of powers, and constituting truly a system of fundamental balances and checks for the government. Where every man is a sharer in the direction of his ward-republic, or of some of the higher ones, and feels that he is a participator in the government of affairs, not merely at an election one day in the year, but every day; when there shall not be a man in the State who will not be a member of some one of its councils, great or small, he will let the heart be torn out of his body sooner than his power be wrested from him by a Cæsar or a Bonaparte. How powerfully did we feel the energy of this organization in the case of embargo? I felt the foundations of the government shaken under my feet by the New England townships. There was not an individual in their States whose body was not thrown with all its momentum into action; and although the whole of the other States were known to be in favor of the measure, yet the organization of this little selfish minority enabled it to overrule the Union. What would the unwieldy counties of the middle, the south, and the west do? Call a county meeting, and the drunken loungers at and about the court houses would have collected, the distances being too great for the good people and the industrious generally to attend. The character of those who really met would have been the measure of the weight they would have had in the scale of public opinion. As Cato, then, concluded every speech with the words, *"Carthago delenda est,"* so do I every opinion, with the injunction, "divide the counties into wards." Begin them only for a single purpose; they will soon show for what others they are the best instruments. God bless you, and all our rulers, and give them the wisdom, as I am sure they have the will, to fortify us against the degeneracy of one government, and the concentration of all its powers in the hands of the one, the few, the well-born or the many.

"HOPE IN THE HEAD . . . FEAR ASTERN"

To John Adams

Monticello, Apr. 8, 1816

DEAR SIR—I have to acknolege your two favors of Feb. 16. and Mar. 2. and to join sincerely in the sentiment of Mrs. Adams, and regret that distance separates us so widely. An hour of conversation would be worth a volume of letters. But we must take things as they come.

You ask if I would agree to live my 70. or rather 73. years over again? To which I say Yea. I think with you that it is a good world on the whole, that it has been framed on a principle of benevolence, and more pleasure than pain dealt out to us. There are indeed (who might say Nay) gloomy and hypocondriac minds, inhabitants of diseased bodies, disgusted with the present, and despairing of the future; always count- ing that the worst will happen, because it may happen. To these I say How much pain have cost us the evils which have never happened? My temperament is sanguine. I steer my bark with Hope in the head, leaving Fear astern. My hopes in- deed sometimes fail; but not oftener than the forebodings of the gloomy. There are, I acknolege, even in the happiest life, some terrible convulsions, heavy set-offs against the opposite page of the account. I have often wondered for what good end the sensations of Grief could be intended. All our other pas- sions, within proper bounds, have an useful object. And the perfection of the moral character is, not in a Stoical apathy, so hypocritically vaunted, and so untruly too, because impossible, but in a just equilibrium of all the passions. I wish the patholo- gists then would tell us what is the use of grief in the economy, and of what good it is the cause, proximate or remote.

Did I know Baron Grimm while at Paris? Yes, most inti- mately. He was the pleasantest, and most conversible member of the diplomatic corps while I was there: a man of good fancy, acuteness, irony, cunning, and egoism: no heart, not much of any science, yet enough of every one to speak it's language. His fort was Belles-lettres, painting and sculpture. In these he was the oracle of the society, and as such was the empress Catharine's private correspondent and factor in all things not diplomatic. It was thro' him I got her permission for poor Ledyard to go to Kamschatka, and cross over thence to the Western coast of America, in order to penetrate across our continent in the opposite direction to that afterwards adopted for Lewis and Clarke: which permission she with- drew after he had got within 200. miles of Kamschatska, had him siesed, brought back and set down in Poland. Altho' I never heard Grimm express the opinion, directly, yet I always supposed him to be of the school of Diderot, D'Alembert, D'Holbach, the first of whom committed their system of atheism to writing in 'Le bon sens,' and the last in his 'Sys- teme de la Nature.' It was a numerous school in the Catholic countries, while the infidelity of the Protestant took generally the form of Theism. The former always insisted that it was a mere question of definition between them, the hypostasis of which on both sides was 'Nature' or 'the Universe:' that both agreed in the order of the existing system, but the one supposed it from eternity, the other as having begun in time. And when the atheist descanted on the unceasing motion and circulation of matter thro' the animal vegetable and mineral kingdoms, never resting, never annihilated, always changing form, and under all forms gifted with the power of reproduction; the Theist pointing 'to the heavens above, and to the earth beneath, and to the waters under the earth,' asked if these did not proclaim a first cause, possessing intelligence and power; power in the production, and intelligence in the design and constant preservation of the system; urged the palpable existence of final causes, that the eye was made to see, and the ear to hear, and not that we see because we have eyes, and hear because we have ears; an answer obvious to the senses, as that of walking across the room was to the philosopher demonstrating the nonexistence of motion. It was in D'Holbach's conventicles that Rousseau imagined all the machinations against him were contrived; and he left, in his Confessions the most biting anecdotes of Grimm. These appeared after I left France; but I have heard that poor Grimm was so much afflicted by them, that he kept his bed several weeks. I have never seen these Memoirs of Grimm. Their volume has kept them out of our market.

I have been lately amusing myself with Levi's book in answer to Dr. Priestley. It is a curious and tough work. His style is inelegant and incorrect, harsh and petulent to his adversary, and his reasoning flimsey enough. Some of his doctrines were new to me, particularly that of his two resurrections: the first a particular one of all the dead, in body as well as soul, who are to live over again, the Jews in a state of perfect obedience to god, the other nations in a state of corporeal punishment for the sufferings they have inflicted on the Jews. And he explains this resurrection of bodies to be only of the original stamen of Leibnitz, or the homunculus in semine masculino, considering that as a mathematical point, insusceptible of separation, or division. The second resurrection a general one of souls and bodies, eternally to enjoy divine glory in the presence of the supreme being. He alledges that the Jews alone preserve the doctrine of the unity of god.

Yet their god would be deemed a very indifferent man with us: and it was to correct their Anamorphosis of the deity that Jesus preached, as well as to establish the doctrine of a future state. However Levi insists that that was taught in the old testament, and even by Moses himself and the prophets. He agrees that an anointed prince was prophecied and promised: but denies that the character and history of Jesus has any analogy with that of the person promised. He must be fearfully embarrassing to the Hierophants of fabricated Christianity; because it is their own armour in which he clothes himself for the attack. For example, he takes passages of Scripture from their context (which would give them a very different meaning) strings them together, and makes them point towards what object he pleases; he interprets them figuratively, typically, analogically, hyperbolically; he calls in the aid of emendation, transposition, ellipsis, metonymy, and every other figure of rhetoric; the name of one man is taken for another, one place for another, days and weeks for months and years; and finally avails himself of all his advantage over his adversaries by his superior knolege of the Hebrew, speaking in the very language of the divine communication, while they can only fumble on with conflicting and disputed translations. Such is this war of giants. And how can such pigmies as you and I decide between them? For myself I confess that my head is not formed tantas componere lites. And as you began your Mar. 2. with a declaration that you were about to write me the most frivolous letter I had ever read, so I will close mine by saying I have written you a full match for it, and by adding my affectionate respects to Mrs. Adams, and the assurance of my constant attachment and consideration for yourself.

"CONSTITUTIONALLY AND CONSCIENTIOUSLY DEMOCRATS"

To P. S. Dupont de Nemours

Poplar Forest, April 24, 1816

I received, my dear friend, your letter covering the constitution for your Equinoctial republics, just as I was setting out for this place. I brought it with me, and have read it with great satisfaction. I suppose it well formed for those for whom it was intended, and the excellence of every government is its adaptation to the state of those to be governed by it. For us it would not do. Distinguishing between the structure of the government and the moral principles on which you prescribe its administration, with the latter we concur cordially, with the former we should not. We of the United States, you know, are constitutionally and conscientiously democrats. We consider society as one of the natural wants with which man has been created; that he has been endowed with faculties and qualities to effect its satisfaction by concurrence of others having the same want; that when, by the exercise of these faculties, he has procured a state of society, it is one of his acquisitions which he has a right to regulate and control, jointly indeed with all those who have concurred in the procurement, whom he cannot exclude from its use or direction more than they him. We think experience has proved it safer, for the mass of individuals composing the society, to reserve to themselves personally the exercise of all rightful powers to which they are competent, and to delegate those to which they are not competent to deputies named, and removable for unfaithful conduct, by themselves immediately. Hence, with us, the people (by which is meant the mass of individuals composing the society) being competent to judge of the facts occurring in ordinary life, they have retained the functions of judges of facts, under the name of jurors; but being unqualified for the management of affairs requiring intelligence above the common level, yet competent judges of human character, they chose, for their management, representatives, some by themselves immediately, others by electors chosen by themselves. Thus our President is chosen by ourselves, directly in *practice*, for we vote for A as elector only on the condition he will vote for B, our representatives by ourselves immediately, our Senate and judges of law through electors chosen by ourselves. And we believe that this proximate choice and power of removal is the best security which experience has sanctioned for ensuring an honest conduct in the functionaries of society. Your three or four alembications have indeed a seducing appearance. We should

conceive *primâ facie*, that the last extract would be the pure
alcohol of the substance, three or four times rectified. But in
proportion as they are more and more sublimated, they are
also farther and farther removed from the control of the society; and the human character, we believe, requires in general
constant and immediate control, to prevent its being biased
from right by the seductions of self-love. Your process produces therefore a structure of government from which the
fundamental principle of ours is excluded. You first set down
as zeros all individuals not having lands, which are the greater
number in every society of long standing. Those holding
lands are permitted to manage in person the small affairs of
their commune or corporation, and to elect a deputy for the
canton; in which election, too, every one's vote is to be an
unit, a plurality, or a fraction, in proportion to his landed
possessions. The assemblies of cantons, then, elect for the districts; those of districts for circles; and those of circles for the
national assemblies. Some of these highest councils, too, are
in a considerable degree self-elected, the regency partially, the
judiciary entirely, and some are for life. Whenever, therefore,
an *esprit de corps*, or of party, gets possession of them, which
experience shows to be inevitable, there are no means of
breaking it up, for they will never elect but those of their own
spirit. Juries are allowed in criminal cases only. I acknowledge
myself strong in affection to our own form, yet both of us act
and think from the same motive, we both consider the people as our children, and love them with parental affection.
But you love them as infants whom you are afraid to trust
without nurses; and I as adults whom I freely leave to self-
government. And you are right in the case referred to you;
my criticism being built on a state of society not under your
contemplation. It is, in fact, like a critic on Homer by the
laws of the Drama.

But when we come to the moral principles on which the
government is to be administered, we come to what is proper
for all conditions of society. I meet you there in all the benevolence and rectitude of your native character; and I love myself always most where I concur most with you. Liberty,
truth, probity, honor, are declared to be the four cardinal
principles of your society. I believe with you that morality,

compassion, generosity, are innate elements of the human constitution; that there exists a right independent of force; that a right to property is founded in our natural wants, in the means with which we are endowed to satisfy these wants, and the right to what we acquire by those means without violating the similar rights of other sensible beings; that no one has a right to obstruct another, exercising his faculties innocently for the relief of sensibilities made a part of his nature; that justice is the fundamental law of society; that the majority, oppressing an individual, is guilty of a crime, abuses its strength, and by acting on the law of the strongest breaks up the foundations of society; that action by the citizens in person, in affairs within their reach and competence, and in all others by representatives, chosen immediately, and removable by themselves, constitutes the essence of a republic; that all governments are more or less republican in proportion as this principle enters more or less into their composition; and that a government by representation is capable of extension over a greater surface of country than one of any other form. These, my friend, are the essentials in which you and I agree; however, in our zeal for their maintenance, we may be perplexed and divaricate, as to the structure of society most likely to secure them.

In the constitution of Spain, as proposed by the late Cortes, there was a principle entirely new to me, and not noticed in yours, that no person, born after that day, should ever acquire the rights of citizenship until he could read and write. It is impossible sufficiently to estimate the wisdom of this provision. Of all those which have been thought of for securing fidelity in the administration of the government, constant ralliance to the principles of the constitution, and progressive amendments with the progressive advances of the human mind, or changes in human affairs, it is the most effectual. Enlighten the people generally, and tyranny and oppressions of body and mind will vanish like evil spirits at the dawn of day. Although I do not, with some enthusiasts, believe that the human condition will ever advance to such a state of perfection as that there shall no longer be pain or vice in the world, yet I believe it susceptible of much improvement, and most of all, in matters of government and religion;

and that the diffusion of knowledge among the people is to be the instrument by which it is to be effected. The constitution of the Cortes had defects enough; but when I saw in it this amendatory provision, I was satisfied all would come right in time, under its salutary operation. No people have more need of a similar provision than those for whom you have felt so much interest. No mortal wishes them more success than I do. But if what I have heard of the ignorance and bigotry of the mass be true, I doubt their capacity to understand and to support a free government; and fear that their emancipation from the foreign tyranny of Spain, will result in a military despotism at home. Palacios may be great; others may be great; but it is the multitude which possess force: and wisdom must yield to that. For such a condition of society, the constitution you have devised is probably the best imaginable. It is certainly calculated to elicit the best talents; although perhaps not well guarded against the egoism of its functionaries. But that egoism will be light in comparison with the pressure of a military despot, and his army of Janissaries. Like Solon to the Athenians, you have given to your Columbians, not the best possible government, but the best they can bear. By-the-bye, I wish you had called them the Columbian republics, to distinguish them from our American republics. Theirs would be the most honorable name, and they best entitled to it; for Columbus discovered their continent, but never saw ours.

To them liberty and happiness; to you the meed of wisdom and goodness in teaching them how to attain them, with the affectionate respect and friendship of,

CAPTAIN LEWIS'S PAPERS
To Corrèa da Serra

Poplar Forest, April 26, 1816

DEAR SIR—Your favor of Mar. 29. was recieved just as I was setting out for this place. I brought it with me to be answered hence. Since you are so kind as to interest yourself for Capt. Lewis's papers, I will give you a full statement of them.

1. Ten or twelve such pocket volumes, Morocco bound, as that you describe, in which, in his own hand writing, he had journalised all occurences, day by day, as he travelled. They were small 8vos and opened at the end for more convenient writing. Every one had been put into a separate tin case, cemented to prevent injury from wet. But on his return the cases, I presume, had been taken from them, as he delivered me the books uncased. There were in them the figures of some animals drawn with the pen while on his journey. The gentlemen who published his travels must have had these Ms. volumes, and perhaps now have them, or can give some account of them.

2. Descriptions of animals and plants. I do not recollect whether there was such a book or collection of papers, distinct from his journal; altho' I am inclined to think there was one: because his travels as published, do not contain all the new animals of which he had either descriptions or specimens. Mr. Peale, I think, must know something of this, as he drew figures of some of the animals for engraving, and some were actually engraved. Perhaps Conrad, his bookseller, who was to have published the work, can give an account of these.

3. Vocabularies. I had myself made a collection of about 40. vocabularies of the Indians on this side of the Missisipi, and Capt. Lewis was instructed to take those of every tribe beyond, which he possibly could: the intention was to publish the whole, and leave the world to search for affinities between these and the languages of Europe and Asia. He was furnished with a number of printed vocabularies of the same words and form I had used, with blank spaces for the Indian words. He was very attentive to this instruction, never missing an opportunity of taking a vocabulary. After his return, he asked me if I should have any objection to the printing his separately, as mine were not yet arranged as I intended. I assured him I had not the least; and I am certain he contemplated their publication. But whether he had put the papers out of his own hand or not, I do not know. I imagine he had not: and it is probable that Doctr. Barton, who was particularly curious on this subject, and published on it occasionally, would willingly recieve and take care of these papers after Capt. Lewis's death, and that they are now among his papers.

4. His observations of longitude and latitude. He was instructed to send these to the war-office, that measures might be taken to have the calculations made. Whether he delivered them to the war-office, or to Dr. Patterson, I do not know; but I think he communicated with Dr. Patterson concerning them. These are all-important: because altho', having with him the Nautical almanacs, he could & did calculate some of his latitudes, yet the longitudes were taken merely from estimates by the log-line, time and course. So that it is only as to latitudes that his map may be considered as tolerably correct; not as to its longitudes.

5. His Map. This was drawn on sheets of paper, not put together, but so marked that they could be joined together with the utmost accuracy; not as one great square map, but ramifying with the courses of the rivers. The scale was very large, and the sheets numerous, but in perfect preservation. This was to await publication, until corrected by the calculations of longitude and latitude. I examined these sheets myself minutely, as spread on the floor, and the originals must be in existence, as the Map published with his travels must have been taken from them.

These constitute the whole. They are the property of the government, the fruits of the expedition undertaken at such expense of money and risk of valuable lives. They contain exactly the whole of the information which it was our object to obtain for the benefit of our own country and of the world. But we were willing to give to Lewis and Clarke whatever pecuniary benefits might be derived from the publication, and therefore left the papers in their hands, taking for granted that their interests would produce a speedy publication, which would be better if done under their direction. But the death of Capt. Lewis, the distance and occupations of General Clarke, and the bankruptcy of their bookseller, have retarded the publication, and rendered necessary that the government should attend to the reclamation & security of their papers. Their recovery is now become an imperious duty. Their safest deposit as fast as they can be collected, will be the Philosophical Society, who no doubt will be so kind as to receive and preserve them, subject to the orders of government; and their publication, once effected in any way, the originals will probably be left in the same deposit. As soon as I can learn their present situation, I will lay the matter before the government to take such order as they think proper. As to any claims of individuals to these papers, it is to be observed that, as being the property of the public, we are certain neither Lewis nor Clarke would undertake to convey away the right to them, and that they could not convey them, had they been capable of intending it. Yet no interest of that kind is meant to be disturbed, if the individual can give satisfactory assurance that he will promptly & properly publish them. Otherwise they must be restored to the government, & the claimant left to settle with those on whom he has any claim. My interference will, I trust, be excused, not only from the portion which every citizen has in whatever is public, but from the peculiar part I have had in the design and execution of this expedition.

To you, my friend, apology is due for involving you in the trouble of this inquiry. It must be found in the interest you take in whatever belongs to science, and in your own kind offers to me of aid in this research. Be assured always of my affectionate friendship and respect.

THE TEST OF REPUBLICANISM

To John Taylor

Monticello, May 28, 1816

DEAR SIR,—On my return from a long journey and considerable absence from home, I found here the copy of your "Enquiry into the principles of our government," which you had been so kind as to send me; and for which I pray you to accept my thanks. The difficulties of getting new works in our situation, inland and without a single bookstore, are such as had prevented my obtaining a copy before; and letters which had accumulated during my absence, and were calling for answers, have not yet permitted me to give to the whole a thorough reading; yet certain that you and I could not think differently on the fundamentals of rightful government, I was impatient, and availed myself of the intervals of repose from the writing table, to obtain a cursory idea of the body of the work.

I see in it much matter for profound reflection; much which should confirm our adhesion, in practice, to the good principles of our constitution, and fix our attention on what is yet to be made good. The sixth section on the good moral principles of our government, I found so interesting and replete with sound principles, as to postpone my letter-writing to its thorough perusal and consideration. Besides much other good matter, it settles unanswerably the right of instructing representatives, and their duty to obey. The system of banking we have both equally and ever reprobated. I contemplate it as a blot left in all our constitutions, which, if not covered, will end in their destruction, which is already hit by the gamblers in corruption, and is sweeping away in its progress the fortunes and morals of our citizens. Funding I consider as limited, rightfully, to a redemption of the debt within the lives of a majority of the generation contracting it; every generation coming equally, by the laws of the Creator of the world, to the free possession of the earth he made for their subsistence, unincumbered by their predecessors, who, like them, were but tenants for life. You have successfully and completely pulverized Mr. Adams' system of orders, and his opening the mantle of republicanism to every government of laws, whether consistent or not with natural right. Indeed, it must be acknowledged, that the term *republic* is of very vague application in every language. Witness the self-styled republics of Holland, Switzerland, Genoa, Venice, Poland. Were I to assign to this term a precise and definite idea, I would say, purely and simply, it means a government by its citizens in mass, acting directly and personally, according to rules established by the majority; and that every other government is more or less republican, in proportion as it has in its composition more or less of this ingredient of the direct action of the citizens. Such a government is evidently restrained to very narrow limits of space and population. I doubt if it would be practicable beyond the extent of a New England township. The first shade from this pure element, which, like that of pure vital air, cannot sustain life of itself, would be where the powers of the government, being divided, should be exercised each by representatives chosen either *pro hac vice*, or for such short terms as should render secure the duty of expressing the will of their constituents. This I should consider as the nearest approach to a pure republic, which is practicable on a large scale of country or population. And we have examples of it in some of our States constitutions, which, if not poisoned by priest-craft, would prove its excellence over all mixtures with other elements; and, with only equal doses of poison, would still be the best. Other shades of republicanism may be found in other forms of government, where the executive, judiciary and legislative functions, and the different branches of the latter, are chosen by the people more or less directly, for longer terms of years or for life, or made hereditary; or where there are mixtures of authorities, some dependent on, and others independent of the people. The further the departure from direct and constant control by the citizens, the less has the government of the ingredient of republicanism; evidently none where the authorities are hereditary, as in France, Venice, &c., or self-chosen, as in Holland; and little, where for life, in proportion as the life continues in being after the act of election.

The purest republican feature in the government of our own State, is the House of Representatives. The Senate is equally so the first year, less the second, and so on. The Executive still less, because not chosen by the people directly. The Judiciary seriously anti-republican, because for life; and the national arm wielded, as you observe, by military leaders irresponsible but to themselves. Add to this the vicious constitution of our county courts (to whom the justice, the executive administration, the taxation, police, the military appointments of the county, and nearly all our daily concerns are confided), self-appointed, self-continued, holding their authorities for life, and with an impossibility of breaking in on the perpetual succession of any faction once possessed of the bench. They are in truth, the executive, the judiciary, and the military of their respective counties, and the sum of the counties makes the State. And add, also, that one half of our brethren who fight and pay taxes, are excluded, like Helots, from the rights of representation, as if society were instituted for the soil, and not for the men inhabiting it; or one half of these could dispose of the rights and the will of the other half, without their consent.

> "What constitutes a State?
> Not high-raised battlements, or labor'd mound,
>   Thick wall, or moated gate;
> Not cities proud, with spires and turrets crown'd;
>   No: men, high minded men;
>   Men, who their duties know;
> But know their rights; and knowing, dare maintain.
>   These constitute a State."

In the General Government, the House of Representatives is mainly republican; the Senate scarcely so at all, as not elected by the people directly, and so long secured even against those who do elect them; the Executive more republican than the Senate, from its shorter term, its election by the people, in *practice*, (for they vote for A only on an assurance that he will vote for B,) and because, *in practice also*, a principle of rotation seems to be in a course of establishment; the judiciary independent of the nation, their coercion by impeachment being found nugatory.

If, then, the control of the people over the organs of their government be the measure of its republicanism, and I confess I know no other measure, it must be agreed that our governments have much less of republicanism than ought to have been expected; in other words, that the people have less regular control over their agents, than their rights and their interests require. And this I ascribe, not to any want of republican dispositions in those who formed these constitutions, but to a submission of true principle to European authorities, to speculators on government, whose fears of the people have been inspired by the populace of their own great cities, and were unjustly entertained against the independent, the happy, and therefore orderly citizens of the United States. Much I apprehend that the golden moment is past for reforming these heresies. The functionaries of public power rarely strengthen in their dispositions to abridge it, and an unorganized call for timely amendment is not likely to prevail against an organized opposition to it. We are always told that things are going on well; why change them? *"Chi sta bene, non si muove,"* said the Italian, "let him who stands well, stand still." This is true; and I verily believe they would go on well with us under an absolute monarch, while our present character remains, of order, industry and love of peace, and restrained, as he would be, by the proper spirit of the people. But it is while it remains such, we should provide against the consequences of its deterioration. And let us rest in the hope that it will yet be done, and spare ourselves the pain of evils which may never happen.

On this view of the import of the term *republic*, instead of saying, as has been said, "that it may mean anything or nothing," we may say with truth and meaning, that governments are more or less republican as they have more or less of the element of popular election and control in their composition; and believing, as I do, that the mass of the citizens is the safest depository of their own rights, and especially, that the evils flowing from the duperies of the people, are less injurious than those from the egoism of their agents, I am a friend to that composition of government which has in it the most of this ingredient. And I sincerely believe, with you, that banking establishments are more dangerous than standing armies; and that the principle of spending money to be paid by posterity, under the name of funding, is but swindling futurity on a large scale.

I salute you with constant friendship and respect.

REFORM OF THE VIRGINIA CONSTITUTION
To Samuel Kercheval

Monticello, July 12, 1816

SIR,—I duly received your favor of June the 13th, with the copy of the letters on the calling a convention, on which you are pleased to ask my opinion. I have not been in the habit of mysterious reserve on any subject, nor of buttoning up my opinions within my own doublet. On the contrary, while in public service especially, I thought the public entitled to frankness, and intimately to know whom they employed. But I am now retired: I resign myself, as a passenger, with confidence to those at present at the helm, and ask but for rest, peace and good will. The question you propose, on equal representation, has become a party one, in which I wish to take no public share. Yet, if it be asked for your own satisfaction only, and not to be quoted before the public, I have no motive to withhold it, and the less from you, as it coincides with your own. At the birth of our republic, I committed that opinion to the world, in the draught of a constitution annexed to the "Notes on Virginia," in which a provision was inserted for a representation permanently equal. The infancy of the subject at that moment, and our inexperience of self-government, occasioned gross departures in that draught from genuine republican canons. In truth, the abuses of monarchy had so much filled all the space of political contemplation, that we imagined everything republican which was not monarchy. We had not yet penetrated to the mother principle, that "governments are republican only in proportion as they embody the will of their people, and execute it." Hence, our first constitutions had really no leading principles in them. But experience and reflection have but more and more confirmed me in the particular importance of the equal representation then proposed. On that point, then, I am entirely in sentiment with your letters; and only lament that a copy-right of your pamphlet prevents their appearance in the newspapers, where alone they would be generally read, and produce general effect. The present vacancy too, of other matter, would give them place in every paper, and bring the question home to every man's conscience.

But inequality of representation in both Houses of our legislature, is not the only republican heresy in this first essay of our revolutionary patriots at forming a constitution. For let it be agreed that a government is republican in proportion as every member composing it has his equal voice in the direction of its concerns (not indeed in person, which would be impracticable beyond the limits of a city, or small township, but) by representatives chosen by himself, and responsible to him at short periods, and let us bring to the test of this canon every branch of our constitution.

In the legislature, the House of Representatives is chosen by less than half the people, and not at all in proportion to those who do choose. The Senate are still more disproportionate, and for long terms of irresponsibility. In the Executive, the Governor is entirely independent of the choice of the people, and of their control; his Council equally so, and at best but a fifth wheel to a wagon. In the Judiciary, the judges of the highest courts are dependent on none but themselves. In England, where judges were named and removable at the will of an hereditary executive, from which branch most misrule was feared, and has flowed, it was a great point gained, by fixing them for life, to make them independent of that executive. But in a government founded on the public will, this principle operates in an opposite direction, and against that will. There, too, they were still removable on a concurrence of the executive and legislative branches. But we have made them independent of the nation itself. They are irremovable, but by their own body, for any depravities of conduct, and even by their own body for the imbecilities of dotage. The justices of the inferior courts are self-chosen, are for life, and perpetuate their own body in succession forever, so that a faction once possessing themselves of the bench of a county, can never be broken up, but hold their county in chains, forever indissoluble. Yet these justices are the real executive as well as judiciary, in all our minor and most ordinary concerns. They tax us at will; fill the office of sheriff, the most important of all the executive officers of the county; name nearly all our military leaders, which leaders, once named, are removable but by themselves. The juries, our judges of all fact, and of law when they choose it, are not selected by the people, nor amenable to them. They are chosen by an officer named by the court and executive. Chosen, did I say? Picked up by the sheriff from the loungings of the court yard, after everything respectable has retired from it. Where then is our republicanism to be found? Not in our constitution certainly, but merely in the spirit of our people. That would oblige even a despot to govern us republicanly. Owing to this spirit, and to nothing in the form of our constitution, all things have gone well. But this fact, so triumphantly misquoted by the enemies of reformation, is not the fruit of our constitution, but has prevailed in spite of it. Our functionaries have done well, because generally honest men. If any were not so, they feared to show it.

But it will be said, it is easier to find faults than to amend them. I do not think their amendment so difficult as is pretended. Only lay down true principles, and adhere to them inflexibly. Do not be frightened into their surrender by the alarms of the timid, or the croakings of wealth against the ascendency of the people. If experience be called for, appeal to that of our fifteen or twenty governments for forty years, and show me where the people have done half the mischief in these forty years, that a single despot would have done in a single year; or show half the riots and rebellions, the crimes and the punishments, which have taken place in any single nation, under kingly government, during the same period. The true foundation of republican government is the equal right of every citizen, in his person and property, and in their management. Try by this, as a tally, every provision of our constitution, and see if it hangs directly on the will of the people. Reduce your legislature to a convenient number for full, but orderly discussion. Let every man who fights or pays, exercise his just and equal right in their election. Submit them to approbation or rejection at short intervals. Let the executive be chosen in the same way, and for the same term, by those whose agent he is to be; and leave no screen of a council behind which to skulk from responsibility. It has been thought that the people are not competent electors of judges *learned in the law*. But I do not know that this is true, and, if doubtful, we should follow principle. In this, as in many other elections, they would be guided by reputation, which would not err oftener, perhaps, than the present mode of appointment. In one State of the Union, at least, it has long been tried, and with the most satisfactory success. The judges of Connecticut have been chosen by the people every six months, for nearly two centuries, and I believe there has hardly ever been an instance of change; so powerful is the curb of incessant responsibility. If prejudice, however, derived from a monarchical institution, is still to prevail against the vital elective principle of our own, and if the existing example among ourselves of periodical election of judges by the people be still mistrusted, let us at least not adopt the evil, and reject the good, of the English precedent; let us retain amovability on the concurrence of the executive and legislative branches, and nomination by the executive alone. Nomination to office is an executive function. To give it to the legislature, as we do, is a violation of the principle of the separation of powers. It swerves the members from correctness, by temptations to intrigue for office themselves, and to a corrupt barter of votes; and destroys responsibility by dividing it among a multitude. By leaving nomination in its proper place, among executive functions, the principle of the distribution of power is preserved, and responsibility weighs with its heaviest force on a single head.

The organization of our county administrations may be thought more difficult. But follow principle, and the knot unties itself. Divide the counties into wards of such size as that every citizen can attend, when called on, and act in person. Ascribe to them the government of their wards in all things relating to themselves exclusively. A justice, chosen by themselves, in each, a constable, a military company, a patrol, a school, the care of their own poor, their own portion of the public roads, the choice of one or more jurors to serve in some court, and the delivery, within their own wards, of their own votes for all elective officers of higher sphere, will relieve the county administration of nearly all its business, will have it better done, and by making every citizen an acting member of the government, and in the offices nearest and most interesting to him, will attach him by his strongest feelings to the independence of his country, and its republican constitution. The justices thus chosen by every ward, would constitute the county court, would do its judiciary business, direct roads and bridges, levy county and poor rates, and administer all the matters of common interest to the whole country. These wards, called townships in New England, are the vital principle of their governments, and have proved themselves the wisest invention ever devised by the wit of man for the perfect exercise of self-government, and for its preservation. We should thus marshal our government into, 1, the general federal republic, for all concerns foreign and federal; 2, that of the State, for what relates to our own citizens exclusively; 3, the county republics, for the duties and concerns of the county; and 4, the ward republics, for the small, and yet numerous and interesting concerns of the neighborhood; and in government, as well as in every other business of life, it is by division and subdivision of duties alone, that all matters, great and small, can be managed to perfection. And the whole is cemented by giving to every citizen, personally, a part in the administration of the public affairs.

The sum of these amendments is, 1. General Suffrage. 2. Equal representation in the legislature. 3. An executive chosen by the people. 4. Judges elective or amovable. 5. Justices, jurors, and sheriffs elective. 6. Ward divisions. And 7. Periodical amendments of the constitution.

I have thrown out these as loose heads of amendment, for consideration and correction; and their object is to secure self-government by the republicanism of our constitution, as well as by the spirit of the people; and to nourish and perpetuate that spirit. I am not among those who fear the people. They, and not the rich, are our dependence for continued freedom. And to preserve their independence, we must not let our rulers load us with perpetual debt. We must make our election between *economy and liberty*, or *profusion and servitude*. If we run into such debts, as that we must be taxed in our meat and in our drink, in our necessaries and our comforts, in our labors and our amusements, for our callings and our creeds, as the people of England are, our people, like them, must come to labor sixteen hours in the twenty-four, give the earnings of fifteen of these to the government for their debts and daily expenses; and the sixteenth being insufficient to afford us bread, we must live, as they now do, on oatmeal and potatoes; have no time to think, no means of calling the mismanagers to account; but be glad to obtain subsistence by hiring ourselves to rivet their chains on the necks of our fellow-sufferers. Our landholders, too, like theirs, retaining indeed the title and stewardship of estates called theirs, but held really in trust for the treasury, must wander, like theirs, in foreign countries, and be contented with penury, obscurity, exile, and the glory of the nation. This example reads to us the salutary lesson, that private fortunes are destroyed by public as well as by private extravagance. And this is the tendency of all human governments. A departure from principle in one instance becomes a precedent for a second; that second for a third; and so on, till the bulk of the society is reduced to be mere automatons of misery, and to have no sensibilities left but for sinning and suffering. Then begins, indeed, the *bellum omnium in omnia*, which some philosophers observing to be so general in this world, have mistaken it for the natural, instead of the abusive state of man. And the fore horse of this frightful team is public debt. Taxation follows that, and in its train wretchedness and oppression.

Some men look at constitutions with sanctimonious reverence, and deem them like the arc of the covenant, too sacred to be touched. They ascribe to the men of the preceding age a wisdom more than human, and suppose what they did to be beyond amendment. I knew that age well; I belonged to it, and labored with it. It deserved well of its country. It was very like the present, but without the experience of the present; and forty years of experience in government is worth a century of book-reading; and this they would say themselves, were they to rise from the dead. I am certainly not an advocate for frequent and untried changes in laws and constitutions. I think moderate imperfections had better be borne with; because, when once known, we accommodate ourselves to them, and find practical means of correcting their ill effects. But I know also, that laws and institutions must go hand in hand with the progress of the human mind. As that becomes more developed, more enlightened, as new discoveries are made, new truths disclosed, and manners and opinions change with the change of circumstances, institutions must advance also, and keep pace with the times. We might as well require a man to wear still the coat which fitted him when a boy, as civilized society to remain ever under the regimen of their barbarous ancestors. It is this preposterous idea which has lately deluged Europe in blood. Their monarchs, instead of wisely yielding to the gradual change of circumstances, of favoring progressive accommodation to progressive improvement, have clung to old abuses, entrenched themselves behind steady habits, and obliged their subjects to seek through blood and violence rash and ruinous innovations, which, had they been referred to the peaceful deliberations and collected wisdom of the nation, would have been put into acceptable and salutary forms. Let us follow no such examples, nor weakly believe that one generation is not as capable as another of taking care of itself, and of ordering its own affairs.

Let us, as our sister States have done, avail ourselves of our reason and experience, to correct the crude essays of our first and unexperienced, although wise, virtuous, and well-meaning councils. And lastly, let us provide in our constitution for its revision at stated periods. What these periods should be, nature herself indicates. By the European tables of mortality, of the adults living at any one moment of time, a majority will be dead in about nineteen years. At the end of that period, then, a new majority is come into place; or, in other words, a new generation. Each generation is as independent as the one preceding, as that was of all which had gone before. It has then, like them, a right to choose for itself the form of government it believes most promotive of its own happiness; consequently, to accommodate to the circumstances in which it finds itself, that received from its predecessors; and it is for the peace and good of mankind, that a solemn opportunity of doing this every nineteen or twenty years, should be provided by the constitution; so that it may be handed on, with periodical repairs, from generation to generation, to the end of time, if anything human can so long endure. It is now forty years since the constitution of Virginia was formed. The same tables inform us, that, within that period, two-thirds of the adults then living are now dead. Have then the remaining third, even if they had the wish, the right to hold in obedience to their will, and to laws heretofore made by them, the other two-thirds, who, with themselves, compose the present mass of adults? If they have not, who has? The dead? But the dead have no rights. They are nothing; and nothing cannot own something. Where there is no substance, there can be no accident. This corporeal globe, and everything upon it, belong to its present corporeal inhabitants, during their generation. They alone have a right to direct what is the concern of themselves alone, and to declare the law of that direction; and this declaration can only be made by their majority. That majority, then, has a right to depute representatives to a convention, and to make the constitution what they think will be the best for themselves. But how collect their voice? This is the real difficulty. If invited by private authority, or county or district meetings, these divisions are so large that few will attend; and their voice will be imperfectly, or falsely pronounced. Here, then, would be one of the advantages of the ward divisions I have proposed. The mayor of every ward, on a question like the present, would call his ward together, take the simple yea or nay of its members, convey these to the county court, who would hand on those of all its wards to the proper general authority; and the voice of the whole people would be thus fairly, fully, and peaceably expressed, discussed, and decided by the common reason of the society. If this avenue be shut to the call of sufferance, it will make itself heard through that of force, and we shall go on, as other nations are doing, in the endless circle of oppression, rebellion, reformation; and oppression, rebellion, reformation, again; and so on forever.

These, Sir, are my opinions of the governments we see among men, and of the principles by which alone we may prevent our own from falling into the same dreadful track. I have given them at greater length than your letter called for. But I cannot say things by halves; and I confide them to your honor, so to use them as to preserve me from the gridiron of the public papers. If you shall approve and enforce them, as you have done that of equal representation, they may do some good. If not, keep them to yourself as the effusions of withered age and useless time. I shall, with not the less truth, assure you of my great respect and consideration.

"NEVER AN INFIDEL, IF NEVER A PRIEST"
To Mrs. Samuel H. Smith

Monticello, August 6, 1816

I have received, dear Madam, your very friendly letter of July 21st, and assure you that I feel with deep sensibility its kind expressions towards myself, and the more as from a person than whom no others could be more in sympathy with my own affections. I often call to mind the occasions of knowing your worth, which the societies of Washington furnished; and none more than those derived from your much valued visit to Monticello. I recognize the same motives of goodness in the solicitude you express on the rumor supposed to proceed from a letter of mine to Charles Thomson, on the subject of the Christian religion. It is true that, in writing to the translator of the Bible and Testament, that subject was mentioned; but equally so that no adherence to any particular mode of Christianity was there expressed, nor any change of opinions suggested. A change from what? the priests indeed have heretofore thought proper to ascribe to me religious, or rather anti-religious sentiments, of their own fabric, but such as soothed their resentments against the act of Virginia for establishing religious freedom. They wished him to be thought atheist, deist, or devil, who could advocate freedom from their religious dictations. But I have ever thought religion a concern purely between our God and our consciences, for which we were accountable to him, and not to the priests. I never told my own religion, nor scrutinized that of another. I never attempted to make a convert, nor wished to change another's creed. I have ever judged of the religion of others by their lives, and by this test, my dear Madam, I have been satisfied yours must be an excellent one, to have produced a life of such exemplary virtue and correctness. For it is in our lives, and not from our words, that our religion must be read. By the same test the world must judge me. But this does not satisfy the priesthood. They must have a positive, a declared assent to all their interested absurdities. My opinion is that there would never have been an infidel, if there had never been a priest. The artificial structures they have built on the purest of all moral systems, for the purpose of deriving from it pence and power, revolts those who think for themselves, and who read in that system only what is really there. These, therefore, they brand with such nick-names as their enmity chooses gratuitously to impute. I have left the world, in silence, to judge of causes from their effects; and I am consoled in this course, my dear friend, when I perceive the candor with which I am judged by your justice and discernment; and that, notwithstanding the slanders of the saints, my fellow citizens have thought me worthy of trusts. The imputations of irreligion having spent their force; they think an imputation of change might now be turned to account as a holster for their duperies. I shall leave them, as heretofore, to grope on in the dark.

Our family at Monticello is all in good health; Ellen speaking of you with affection, and Mrs. Randolph always regretting the accident which so far deprived her of the happiness of your former visit. She still cherishes the hope of some future renewal of that kindness; in which we all join her, as in the assurances of affectionate attachment and respect.

HORIZONTAL PLOUGHING

To Tristam Dalton

Monticello, May 2, 1817

DEAR SIR,—I am indebted to you for your favor of Apr. 22, and for the copy of the Agricultural magazine it covered, which is indeed a very useful work. While I was an amateur in Agricultural science (for practical knolege my course of life never permitted me) I was very partial to the drilled husbandry of Tull, and thought still better of it when reformed by Young to 12 rows. But I had not time to try it while young, and now grown old I have not the requisite activity either of body or mind.

With respect to field culture of vegetables for cattle, instead of the carrot and potato recommended by yourself and the magazine, & the best of others, we find the Jerusalem artichoke best for winter, & the Succory for Summer use. This last was brought over from France to England by Arthur Young, as you will see in his travels thro' France, & some of the seed sent by him to Genl. Washington, who spared me a part of it. It is as productive as the Lucerne, without its laborious culture, & indeed without any culture except the keeping it clean the first year. The Jerusalem artichoke far exceeds the potato in produce, and remains in the ground thro' the winter to be dug as wanted. A method of ploughing over hill sides horizontally, introduced into the most hilly part of our country by Colo. T. M. Randolph, my son in law, may be worth mentioning to you. He has practised it a dozen or 15 years, and it's advantages were so immediately observed that it has already become very general, and has entirely changed and renovated the face of our country. Every rain, before that, while it gave a temporary refreshment, did permanent evil by carrying off our soil: and fields were no sooner cleared than wasted. At present we may say that we lose none of our soil, the rain not absorbed in the moment of it's fall being retained in the hollows between the beds until it can be absorbed. Our practice is when we first enter on this process, with a rafter level of 10 f. span, to lay off guide lines conducted horizontally around the hill or valley from one end to the other of the field, and about 30 yards apart. The steps of the level on the ground are marked by a stroke of a hoe, and immediately followed by a plough to preserve the trace. A man or a lad, with the level, and two small boys, the one with sticks, the other with the hoe, will do an acre of this in an hour, and when once done it is forever done. We generally level a field the year it is put into Indian corn laying it into beds of 6 ft. wide, with a large water furrow between the beds, until all the fields have been once leveled. The intermediate furrows are run by the eye of the ploughman governed by these guide lines, & occasion gores which are thrown into short beds. As in ploughing very steep hill sides horizontally the common ploughman can scarcely throw the furrow uphill, Colo. Randolph has contrived a very simple alteration of the share, which throws the furrow down hill both going and coming. It is as if two shares were welded together at their straight side, and at a right angle with each other. This turns on it's bar as on a pivot, so as to lay either share horizontal, when the other becoming verticle acts as a mould board. This is done by the ploughman in an instant by a single motion of the hand, at the end of every furrow. I enclose a bit of paper cut into the form of the double share, which being opened at the fold to a right angle, will give an idea of it's general principle. Horizontal and deep ploughing, with the use of plaister and clover, which are but beginning to be used here will, as we believe, restore this part of our country to it's original fertility, which was exceeded by no upland in the state. Believing that some of these things might be acceptable to you I have hazarded them as testimonials of my great esteem & respect.

ERA OF GOOD FEELINGS
To Lafayette

Monticello, May 14, 1817

Although, dear Sir, much retired from the world, and meddling little in its concerns, yet I think it almost a religious duty to salute at times my old friends, were it only to say and to know that "all's well." Our hobby has been politics; but all here is so quiet, and with you so desperate, that little matter is furnished us for active attention. With you too, it has long been forbidden ground, and therefore imprudent for a foreign friend to tread, in writing to you. But although our speculations might be intrusive, our prayers cannot but be acceptable, and mine are sincerely offered for the well-being of France. What government she can bear, depends not on the state of science, however exalted, in a select band of enlightened men, but on the condition of the general mind. That, I am sure, is advanced and will advance; and the last change of government was fortunate, inasmuch as the new will be less obstructive to the effects of that advancement. For I consider your foreign military oppressions as an ephemeral obstacle only.

Here all is quiet. The British war has left us in debt; but that is a cheap price for the good it has done us. The establishment of the necessary manufactures among ourselves, the proof that our government is solid, can stand the shock of war, and is superior even to civil schism, are precious facts for us; and of these the strongest proofs were furnished, when, with four eastern States tied to us, as dead to living bodies, all doubt was removed as to the achievements of the war, had it continued. But its best effect has been the complete suppression of party. The federalists who were truly American, and their great mass was so, have separated from their brethren who were mere Anglomen, and are received with cordiality into the republican ranks. Even Connecticut, as a State, and the last one expected to yield its steady habits (which were essentially bigoted in politics as well as religion), has chosen a republican governor, and republican legislature. Massachusetts indeed still lags; because most deeply involved in the parricide crimes and treasons of the war. But her gangrene is contracting, the sound flesh advancing on it, and all there will be well. I mentioned Connecticut as the most hopeless of our States. Little Delaware had escaped my attention. That is essentially a Quaker State, the fragment of a religious sect which, there, in the other States, in England, are a homogeneous mass, acting with one mind, and that directed by the mother society in England. Dispersed, as the Jews, they still form, as those do, one nation, foreign to the land they live in. They are Protestant Jesuits, implicitly devoted to the will of their superior, and forgetting all duties to their country in the execution of the policy of their order. When war is proposed with England, they have religious scruples; but when with France, these are laid by, and they become clamorous for it. They are, however, silent, passive, and give no other trouble than of whipping them along. Nor is the election of Monroe an inefficient circumstance in our felicities. Four and twenty years, which he will accomplish, of administration in republican forms and principles, will so consecrate them in the eyes of the people as to secure them against the danger of change. The evanition of party dissensions has harmonized intercourse, and sweetened society beyond imagination. The war then has done us all this good, and the further one of assuring the world, that although attached to peace from a sense of its blessings, we will meet war when it is made necessary.

I wish I could give better hopes of our southern brethren. The achievement of their independence of Spain is no longer a question. But it is a very serious one, what will then become of them? Ignorance and bigotry, like other insanities, are incapable of self-government. They will fall under military despotism, and become the murderous tools of the ambition of their respective Bonapartes; and whether this will be for their greater happiness, the rule of one only has taught you to judge. No one, I hope, can doubt my wish to see them and all mankind exercising self-government, and capable of exercising it. But the question is not what we wish, but what is practicable? As their sincere friend and brother then, I do believe the best thing for them, would be for themselves to come to an accord with Spain, under the guarantee of France,

Russia, Holland, and the United States, allowing to Spain a nominal supremacy, with authority only to keep the peace among them, leaving them otherwise all the powers of self-government, until their experience in them, their emancipation from their priests, and advancement in information, shall prepare them for complete independence. I exclude England from this confederacy, because her selfish principles render her incapable of honorable patronage or disinterested co-operation; unless, indeed, what seems now probable, a revolution should restore to her an honest government, one which will permit the world to live in peace. Portugal, grasping at an extension of her dominion in the south, has lost her great northern province of Pernambuco, and I shall not wonder if Brazil should revolt in mass, and send their royal family back to Portugal. Brazil is more populous, more wealthy, more energetic, and as wise as Portugal. I have been insensibly led, my dear friend, while writing to you, to indulge in that line of sentiment in which we have been always associated, forgetting that these are matters not belonging to my time. Not so with you, who have still many years to be a spectator of these events. That these years may indeed be many and happy, is the sincere prayer of your affectionate friend.

"THE FLATTERIES OF HOPE"
To François de Marbois

Monticello, June 14, 1817

I thank you, dear Sir, for the copy of the interesting narrative of the Complet d'Arnold, which you have been so kind as to send me. It throws light on that incident of history which we did not possess before. An incident which merits to be known as a lesson to mankind, in all its details. This mark of your attention recalls to my mind the earlier period of life at which I had the pleasure of your personal acquaintance, and renews the sentiments of high respect and esteem with which that acquaintance inspired me. I had not failed to accompany your personal sufferings during the civil convulsions of your country, and had sincerely sympathized with them. An awful period, indeed, has passed in Europe since our first acquaintance. When I left France at the close of '89, your revolution was, as I thought, under the direction of able and honest men. But the madness of some of their successors, the vices of others, the malicious intrigues of an envious and corrupting neighbor, the tracasserie of the Directory, the usurpations, the havoc, and devastations of your Attila, and the equal usurpations, depredations and oppressions of your hypocritical deliverers, will form a mournful period in the history of man, a period of which the last chapter will not be seen in your day or mine, and one which I still fear is to be written in characters of blood. Had Bonaparte reflected that such is the moral construction of the world, that no national crime passes unpunished in the long run, he would not now be in the cage of St. Helena; and were your present oppressors to reflect on the same truth, they would spare to their own countries the penalties on their present wrongs which will be inflicted on them on future times. The seeds of hatred and revenge which they are now sowing with a large hand, will not fail to produce their fruits in time. Like their brother robbers on the highway, they suppose the escape of the moment a final escape, and deem infamy and future risk countervailed by present gain. Our lot has been happier. When you witnessed our first struggles in the war of independence, you little calculated, more than we did, on the rapid growth and prosperity of this country; on the practical demonstration it was about to exhibit, of the happy truth that man is capable of self-government, and only rendered otherwise by the moral degradation designedly superinduced on him by the wicked acts of his tyrants.

I have much confidence that we shall proceed successfully for ages to come, and that, contrary to the principle of Montesquieu, it will be seen that the larger the extent of country, the more firm its republican structure, if founded, not on conquest, but in principles of compact and equality. My hope of its duration is built much on the enlargement of the resources of life going hand in hand with the enlargement of territory, and the belief that men are disposed to live honestly, if the means of doing so are open to them. With the consolation of this belief in the future result of our labors, I have that of other prophets who foretell distant events, that I shall not live to see it falsified. My theory has always been, that if we are to dream, the flatteries of hope are as cheap, and pleasanter than the gloom of despair. I wish to yourself a long life of honors, health and happiness.

FEMALE EDUCATION

To Nathaniel Burwell

Monticello, March 14, 1818

DEAR SIR,—Your letter of February 17th found me suffering under an attack of rheumatism, which has but now left me at sufficient ease to attend to the letters I have received. A plan of female education has never been a subject of systematic contemplation with me. It has occupied my attention so far only as the education of my own daughters occasionally required. Considering that they would be placed in a country situation, where little aid could be obtained from abroad, I thought it essential to give them a solid education, which might enable them, when become mothers, to educate their own daughters, and even to direct the course for sons, should their fathers be lost, or incapable, or inattentive. My surviving daughter accordingly, the mother of many daughters as well as sons, has made their education the object of her life, and being a better judge of the practical part than myself, it is with her aid and that of one of her élèves that I shall subjoin a catalogue of the books for such a course of reading as we have practiced.

A great obstacle to good education is the inordinate passion prevalent for novels, and the time lost in that reading which should be instructively employed. When this poison infects the mind, it destroys its tone and revolts it against wholesome reading. Reason and fact, plain and unadorned, are rejected. Nothing can engage attention unless dressed in all the figments of fancy, and nothing so bedecked comes amiss. The result is a bloated imagination, sickly judgment, and disgust towards all the real businesses of life. This mass of trash, however, is not without some distinction; some few modelling their narratives, although fictitious, on the incidents of real life, have been able to make them interesting and useful vehicles of sound morality. Such, I think, are Marmontel's new moral tales, but not his old ones, which are really immoral. Such are the writings of Miss Edgeworth, and some of those of Madame Genlis. For a like reason, too, much poetry should not be indulged. Some is useful for forming style and taste. Pope, Dryden, Thompson, Shakspeare, and of the French, Molière, Racine, the Corneilles, may be read with pleasure and improvement.

The French language, become that of the general intercourse of nations, and from their extraordinary advances, now the depository of all science, is an indispensable part of education for both sexes. In the subjoined catalogue, therefore, I have placed the books of both languages indifferently, according as the one or the other offers what is best.

The ornaments too, and the amusements of life, are entitled to their portion of attention. These, for a female, are dancing, drawing, and music. The first is a healthy exercise, elegant and very attractive for young people. Every affectionate parent would be pleased to see his daughter qualified to participate with her companions, and without awkwardness at least, in the circles of festivity, of which she occasionally becomes a part. It is a necessary accomplishment, therefore, although of short use, for the French rule is wise, that no lady dances after marriage. This is founded in solid physical reasons, gestation and nursing leaving little time to a married lady when this exercise can be either safe or innocent. Drawing is thought less of in this country than in Europe. It is an innocent and engaging amusement, often useful, and a qualification not to be neglected in one who is to become a mother and an instructor. Music is invaluable where a person has an ear. Where they have not, it should not be attempted. It furnishes a delightful recreation for the hours of respite from the cares of the day, and lasts us through life. The taste of this country, too, calls for this accomplishment more strongly than for either of the others.

I need say nothing of household economy, in which the mothers of our country are generally skilled, and generally careful to instruct their daughters. We all know its value, and that diligence and dexterity in all its processes are inestimable treasures. The order and economy of a house are as honorable to the mistress as those of the farm to the master, and if either be neglected, ruin follows, and children destitute of the means of living.

This, Sir, is offered as a summary sketch on a subject on which I have not thought much. It probably contains nothing but what has already occurred to yourself, and claims your acceptance on no other ground than as a testimony of my respect for your wishes, and of my great esteem and respect.

THE CLASSICAL PRESS
To Wells and Lilly

Monticello, April 1, 1818

You must have thought me very tardy in acknoleging the receipt of your letter of Jan. 13. and in returning my thanks, which I now do, for the very handsome copy of Cicero's works from your press, which you have been so kind as to present me. I waited first the receipt of that and the books accompanying it, but I happened at the time of their arrival to be reading the 5th book of Cicero's Tusculans, which I followed by that of his Offices, and concluded to lay aside the variorum edition, and to use yours, after which I might write more understandingly on the subject. having been extremely disgusted with the Philadelphia and New York Delphin editions, some of which I had read, and altho executed with a good type on good paper, yet so full of errors of the press as not to be worth the paper they were printed on, I wished to see the state of the classical press with you. their editions had on an average about one error for every page. I read therefore the portions of your's above mentioned with a pretty sharp eye, and in something upwards of 200. pages I found the errors noted on the paper inclosed, being an average of one for every 13. pages. this is a good advance on the presses of N.Y. and Philada., and gives hopes of rapid improvements. the errors in the Variorum editions however are fewer than these, the Elzevirs still fewer: but the perfection of accuracy is to be found in the folio edition of Homer by the Foulis of Glasgow. I have understood they offered 1000 guineas for the discovery of any error in it, even of an accent, and that the reward was never claimed. I am glad to find you are thinking of printing Livy. there should be no hesitation between that and Quinctilian. this last is little wanting. we have Blair's and Adams's books which give us the rhetoric of our own language and that of a foreign and a dead one will interest few readers. but of Livy there is not, nor ever has been an edition meriting the name of an editio optima. the Delphin edition might have been, but for it's numerous errors of the press, and unmanageable size in 4to. it's notes are valuable, and it has the whole of Freinsheim's supplement with the marginal references to his authorities. Clerk's edition is of a handy size, has the whole of Freinsheim, but without the references, which we often wish to turn to, and it is without notes. the late Paris edition of La Malle has only the supplement of the 2d decad and no notes. I possess these two last mentioned editions, but would gladly become a subscriber to such a one as I describe, that is to say, an 8vo edition with the Delphin notes and all Freinsheim's supplements and references. if correctly executed it would be the editio optima, be called for in Europe and do us honor there. since consigning my library to Congress I have supplied myself from Europe with most of the classics, and of the best editions, in which I have been much aided by mr. Ticknor, your most learned and valuable countryman.

I make you my acknolegement for the sermon on the Unity of God, and am glad to see our countrymen looking that question in the face. it must end in a return to primitive christianity, and the disbandment of the unintelligible Athanasian jargon of 3. being 1. and 1. being 3. this sermon is one of the strongest pieces against it. I observe you are about printing a work of Belsham's on the same subject, for which I wish to be a subscriber, and inclose you a 5 D. bill, there being none of fractional denominations. the surplus therefore may stand as I shall be calling for other things. Accept the assurance of my great respect.

INFLATION AND DEMORALIZATION
To Nathaniel Macon

Monticello, January 12, 1819

DEAR SIR,—The problem you had wished to propose to me was one which I could not have solved; for I knew nothing of the facts. I read no newspaper now but Ritchie's, and in that chiefly the advertisements, for they contain the only truths to be relied on in a newspaper. I feel a much greater interest in knowing what has passed two or three thousand years ago, than in what is now passing. I read nothing, therefore, but of the heroes of Troy, of the wars of Lacedæmon and Athens, of Pompey and Cæsar, and of Augustus too, the Bonaparte and parricide scoundrel of that day. I have had, and still have, such entire confidence in the late and present Presidents, that I willingly put both soul and body into their pockets. While such men as yourself and your worthy colleagues of the legislature, and such characters as compose the executive administration, are watching for us all, I slumber without fear, and review in my dreams the visions of antiquity. There is, indeed, one evil which awakens me at times, because it jostles me at every turn. It is that we have now no measure of value. I am asked eighteen dollars for a yard of broadcloth, which, when we had dollars, I used to get for eighteen shillings; from this I can only understand that a dollar is now worth but two inches of broadcloth, but broadcloth is no standard of measure or value. I do not know, therefore, whereabouts I stand in the scale of property, nor what to ask, or what to give for it. I saw, indeed, the like machinery in action in the years '80 and '81, and without dissatisfaction; because in wearing out, it was working out our salvation. But I see nothing in this renewal of the game of "Robin's alive" but a general demoralization of the nation, a filching from industry its honest earnings, wherewith to build up palaces, and raise gambling stock for swindlers and shavers, who are to close too their career of piracies by fraudulent bankruptcies. My dependence for a remedy, however, is with the wisdom which grows with time and suffering. Whether the succeeding generation is to be more virtuous than their predecessors, I cannot say; but I am sure they will have more worldly wisdom, and enough, I hope, to know that honesty is the first chapter in the book of wisdom. I have made a great exertion to write you thus much; my antipathy to taking up a pen being so intense that I have never given you a stronger proof, than in the effort of writing a letter, how much I value you, and of the superlative respect and friendship with which I salute you.

HABITS OF "A HARD STUDENT"

To Dr. Vine Utley

Monticello, March 21, 1819

SIR,—Your letter of February the 18th came to hand on the 1st instant; and the request of the history of my physical habits would have puzzled me not a little, had it not been for the model with which you accompanied it, of Doctor Rush's answer to a similar inquiry. I live so much like other people, that I might refer to ordinary life as the history of my own. Like my friend the Doctor, I have lived temperately, eating little animal food, and that not as an aliment, so much as a condiment for the vegetables, which constitute my principal diet. I double, however, the Doctor's glass and a half of wine, and even treble it with a friend; but halve its effects by drinking the weak wines only. The ardent wines I cannot drink, nor do I use ardent spirits in any form. Malt liquors and cider are my table drinks, and my breakfast, like that also of my friend, is of tea and coffee. I have been blest with organs of digestion which accept and concoct, without ever murmuring, whatever the palate chooses to consign to them, and I have not yet lost a tooth by age. I was a hard student until I entered on the business of life, the duties of which leave no idle time to those disposed to fulfil them; and now, retired, and at the age of seventy-six, I am again a hard student. Indeed, my fondness for reading and study revolts me from the drudgery of letter writing. And a stiff wrist, the consequence of an early dislocation, makes writing both slow and painful. I am not so regular in my sleep as the Doctor says he was, devoting to it from five to eight hours, according as my company or the book I am reading interests me; and I never go to bed without an hour, or half hour's previous reading of something moral, whereon to ruminate in the intervals of sleep. But whether I retire to bed early or late, I rise with the sun. I use spectacles at night, but not necessarily in the day, unless in reading small print. My hearing is distinct in particular conversation, but confused when several voices cross each other, which unfits me for the society of the table. I have been more fortunate than my friend in the article of health. So free from catarrhs that I have not had one, (in the breast, I mean) on an average of eight or ten years through life. I ascribe this exemption partly to the habit of bathing my feet in cold water every morning, for sixty years past. A fever of more than twenty-four hours I have not had above two or three times in my life. A periodical headache has afflicted me occasionally, once, perhaps, in six or eight years, for two or three weeks at a time, which seems now to have left me; and except on a late occasion of indisposition, I enjoy good health; too feeble, indeed, to walk much, but riding without fatigue six or eight miles a day, and sometimes thirty or forty. I may end these egotisms, therefore, as I began, by saying that my life has been so much like that of other people, that I might say with Horace, to every one *"nomine mutato, narratur fabula de te."* I must not end, however, without due thanks for the kind sentiments of regard you are so good as to express towards myself; and with my acknowledgments for these, be pleased to accept the assurances of my respect and esteem.

SETTING THE RECORD STRAIGHT
To Samuel Adams Wells

Monticello, May 12, 1819

SIR,—An absence of some time at an occasional and distant residence must apologize for the delay in acknowledging the receipt of your favor of April 12th. And candor obliges me to add that it has been somewhat extended by an aversion to writing, as well as to calls on my memory for facts so much obliterated from it by time as to lessen my confidence in the traces which seem to remain. One of the inquiries in your letter, however, may be answered without an appeal to the memory. It is that respecting the question whether committees of correspondence originated in Virginia or Massachusetts? On which you suppose me to have claimed it for Virginia. But certainly I have never made such a claim. The idea, I suppose, has been taken up from what is said in Wirt's history of Mr. Henry, p. 87, and from an inexact attention to its precise term. It is there said "this house [of burgesses of Virginia] had the merit of originating that powerful engine of resistance, corresponding committees *between the legislatures* of the *different colonies*." That the fact as here expressed is true, your letter bears witness when it says that the resolutions of Virginia for this purpose were transmitted to the speakers of the different Assemblies, and by that of Massachusetts was laid at the next session before that body, who appointed a committee for the specified object: adding, "thus in Massachusetts there were two committees of correspondence, one chosen by the people, the other appointed by the House of Assembly; in the former, Massachusetts preceded Virginia; in the latter, Virginia preceded Massachusetts." To the origination of committees for the interior correspondence between the counties and towns of a State, I know of no claim on the part of Virginia; but certainly none was ever made by myself. I perceive, however, one error into which memory had led me. Our committee for national correspondence was appointed in March, '73, and I well remember that going to Williamsburg in the month of June following, Peyton Randolph, our chairman, told me that messengers, bearing despatches between the two States, had crossed each other by the way; that of Virginia carrying our propositions for a committee of national correspondence, and that of Massachusetts bringing, as my memory suggested, a similar proposition. But here I must have misremembered; and the resolutions brought us from Massachusetts were probably those you mention of the town meeting of Boston, on the motion of Mr. Samuel Adams, appointing a committee "to state the rights of the colonists, and of that province in particular, and the infringements of them, to communicate them to the several towns, as the sense of the town of Boston, and to request of each town a free communication of its sentiments on this subject"? I suppose, therefore, that these resolutions were not received, as you think, while the House of Burgesses was in session in March, 1773; but a few days after we rose, and were probably what was sent by the messenger who crossed ours by the way. They may, however, have been still different. I must therefore have been mistaken in supposing and stating to Mr. Wirt, that the proposition of a committee for national correspondence was nearly simultaneous in Virginia and Massachusetts.

A similar misapprehension of another passage in Mr. Wirt's book, for which I am also quoted, has produced a similar reclamation of the part of Massachusetts by some of her most distinguished and estimable citizens. I had been applied to by Mr. Wirt for such facts respecting Mr. Henry, as my intimacy with him, and participation in the transactions of the day, might have placed within my knowledge. I accordingly committed them to paper, and Virginia being the theatre of his action, was the only subject within my contemplation, while speaking of him. Of the resolutions and measures here, in which he had the acknowledged lead, I used the expression that "Mr. Henry certainly gave the first impulse to the ball of revolution." [Wirt, p. 41.] The expression is indeed general, and in all its extension would comprehend all the sister States. But indulgent construction would restrain it, as was really meant, to the subject matter under contemplation, which was Virginia alone; according to the rule of the lawyers, and a fair canon of general criticism, that every expression should be construed *secundum subjectam materiem*. Where the first attack was made, there must have been of course, the first act of resistance, and that was of Massachusetts. Our first overt act of war was Mr. Henry's embodying a force of militia from several counties, regularly armed and organized, marching them in military array, and making reprisal on the King's treasury at the seat of government for the public powder taken away by his Governor. This was on the last days of April, 1775. Your formal battle of Lexington was ten or twelve days before that, which greatly overshadowed in importance, as it preceded in time our little affray, which merely amounted to a levying of arms against the King, and very possibly you had had military affrays before the regular battle of Lexington.

These explanations will, I hope, assure you, Sir, that so far as either facts or opinions have been truly quoted from me they have never been meant to intercept the just fame of Massachusetts, for the promptitude and perseverance of her early resistance. We willingly cede to her the laud of having been (although not exclusively) "the cradle of sound principles," and if some of us believe she has deflected from them in her course, we retain full confidence in her ultimate return to them.

I will now proceed to your quotation from Mr. Galloway's statements of what passed in Congress on their declaration of independence, in which statement there is not one word of truth, and where, bearing some resemblance to truth, it is an entire perversion of it. I do not charge this on Mr. Galloway himself; his desertion having taken place long before these measures, he doubtless received his information from some of the loyal friends whom he left behind him. But as yourself, as well as others, appear embarrassed by inconsistent accounts of the proceedings on that memorable occasion, and as those who have endeavored to restore the truth have themselves committed some errors, I will give you some extracts from a written document on that subject, for the truth of which I pledge myself to heaven and earth; having, while the question of independence was under consideration before Congress, taken written notes, in my seat, of what was passing, and reduced them to form on the final conclusion. I have now before me that paper, from which the following are extracts: *   *   *

Governor McKean, in his letter to McCorkle of July 16th, 1817, has thrown some lights on the transactions of that day, but trusting to his memory chiefly at an age when our memories are not to be trusted, he has confounded two questions, and ascribed proceedings to one which belonged to the other. These two questions were, 1. The Virginia motion of June 7th to declare independence, and 2. The actual declaration, its matter and form. Thus he states the question on the declaration itself as decided on the 1st of July. But it was the Virginia motion which was voted on that day in committee of the whole; South Carolina, as well as Pennsylvania, then voting against it. But the ultimate decision in *the House* on the report of the committee being by request postponed to the next morning, all the States voted for it, except New York, whose vote was delayed for the reason before stated. It was not till the 2d of July that the declaration itself was taken up, nor till the 4th that it was decided; and it was signed by every member present, except Mr. Dickinson.

The subsequent signatures of members who were not then present, and some of them not yet in office, is easily explained, if we observe who they were; to wit, that they were of New York and Pennsylvania. New York did not sign till the 15th, because it was not till the 9th, (five days after the general signature,) that their convention authorized them to do so. The convention of Pennsylvania, learning that it had been signed by a minority only of their delegates, named a new delegation on the 20th, leaving out Mr. Dickinson, who had refused to sign, Willing and Humphreys who had withdrawn, reappointing the three members who had signed, Morris who had not been present, and five new ones, to wit, Rush, Clymer, Smith, Taylor and Ross; and Morris and the five new members were permitted to sign, because it manifested the assent of their full delegation, and the express will of their convention, which might have been doubted on the former signature of a minority only. Why the signature of Thornton of New Hampshire was permitted so late as the 4th of November, I cannot now say; but undoubtedly for some particular reason which we should find to have been good, had it been expressed. These were the only post-signers, and you see, Sir, that there were solid reasons for receiving those of New York and Pennsylvania, and that this circumstance in no wise affects the faith of this declaratory charter of our rights and of the rights of man.

With a view to correct errors of fact before they become inveterate by repetition, I have stated what I find essentially material in my papers; but with that brevity which the labor of writing constrains me to use.

On the fourth particular articles of inquiry in your letter, respecting your grandfather, the venerable Samuel Adams, neither memory nor memorandums enable me to give any information. I can say that he was truly a great man, wise in council, fertile in resources, immovable in his purposes, and had, I think, a greater share than any other member, in advising and directing our measures, in the northern war especially. As a speaker he could not be compared with his living colleague and namesake, whose deep conceptions, nervous style, and undaunted firmness, made him truly our bulwark in debate. But Mr. Samuel Adams, although not of fluent elocution, was so rigorously logical, so clear in his views, abundant in good sense, and master always of his subject, that he commanded the most profound attention whenever he rose in an assembly by which the froth of declamation was heard with the most sovereign contempt. I sincerely rejoice that the record of his worth is to be undertaken by one so much disposed as you will be to hand him down fairly to that posterity for whose liberty and happiness he was so zealous a laborer.

With sentiments of sincere veneration for his memory, accept yourself this tribute to it with the assurances of my great respect.

P. S. August 6th, 1822, since the date of this letter, to wit, this day, August 6th, '22, I received the new publication of the secret Journals of Congress, wherein is stated a resolution, July 19th, 1776, that the declaration passed on the 4th be fairly engrossed on parchment, and when engrossed, be signed by every member; and another of August 2d, that being engrossed and compared at the table, was signed by the members. That is to say the copy engrossed on parchment (for durability) was signed by the members after being compared at the table with the original one, signed on paper as before stated. I add this P.S. to the copy of my letter to Mr. Wells, to prevent confounding the signature of the original with that of the copy engrossed on parchment.

THE VALUE OF CLASSICAL LEARNING

To John Brazier

Poplar Forest, August 24, 1819

SIR,—The acknowledgment of your favor of July 15th, and thanks for the Review which it covered of Mr. Pickering's

Memoir on the Modern Greek, have been delayed by a visit to an occasional but distant residence from Monticello, and to an attack here of rheumatism which is just now moderating. I had been much pleased with the memoir, and was much also with your review of it. I have little hope indeed of the recovery of the ancient pronunciation of that finest of human languages, but still I rejoice at the attention the subject seems to excite with you, because it is an evidence that our country begins to have a taste for something more than merely as much Greek as will pass a candidate for clerical ordination.

You ask my opinion on the extent to which classical learning should be carried in our country. A sickly condition permits me to think, and a rheumatic hand to write too briefly on this litigated question. The utilities we derive from the remains of the Greek and Latin languages are, first, as models of pure taste in writing. To these we are certainly indebted for the national and chaste style of modern composition which so much distinguishes the nations to whom these languages ae familiar. Without these models we should probably have continued the inflated style of our northern ancestors, or the hyperbolical and vague one of the east. Second. Among the values of classical learning, I estimate the luxury of reading the Greek and Roman authors in all the beauties of their originals. And why should not this innocent and elegant luxury take its preeminent stand ahead of all those addressed merely to the senses? I think myself more indebted to my father for this than for all the other luxuries his cares and affections have placed within my reach; and more now than when younger, and more susceptible of delights from other sources. When the decays of age have enfeebled the useful energies of the mind, the classic pages fill up the vacuum of *ennui*, and become sweet composers to that rest of the grave into which we are all sooner or later to descend. Third. A third value is in the stores of real science deposited and transmitted us in these languages, to-wit: in history, ethics, arithmetic, geometry, astronomy, natural history, &c.

But to whom are these things useful? Certainly not to all men. There are conditions of life to which they must be forever estranged, and there are epochs of life too, after which the endeavor to attain them would be a great misemployment of time. Their acquisition should be the occupation of our early years only, when the memory is susceptible of deep and lasting impressions, and reason and judgment not yet strong enough for abstract speculations. To the moralist they are valuable, because they furnish ethical writings highly and justly esteemed: although in my own opinion, the moderns are far advanced beyond them in this line of science, the divine finds in the Greek language a translation of his primary code, of more importance to him than the original because better understood; and, in the same language, the newer code, with the doctrines of the earliest fathers, who lived and wrote before the simple precepts of the founder of this most benign and pure of all systems of morality became frittered into subtleties and mysteries, and hidden under jargons incomprehensible to the human mind. To these original sources he must now, therefore, return, to recover the virgin purity of his religion. The lawyer finds in the Latin language the system of civil law most conformable with the principles of justice of any which has ever yet been established among men, and from which much has been incorporated into our own. The physician as good a code of his art as has been given us to this day. Theories and systems of medicine, indeed, have been in perpetual change from the days of the good Hippocrates to the days of the good Rush, but which of them is the true one? the present, to be sure, as long as it is the present, but to yield its place in turn to the next novelty, which is then to become the true system, and is to mark the vast advance of medicine since the days of Hippocrates. Our situation is certainly benefited by the discovery of some new and very valuable medicines; and substituting those for some of his with the treasure of facts, and of sound observations recorded by him (mixed to be sure with anilities of his day) and we shall have nearly the present sum of the healing art. The statesman will find in these languages history, politics, mathematics, ethics, eloquence, love of country, to which he must add the sciences of his own day, for which of them should be unknown to him? And all the sciences must recur to the classical languages for the etymon, and sound understanding of their fundamental terms. For the merchant I should not say that the languages are a necessary. Ethics, mathematics, geography, political economy, history, seem to constitute the immediate foundations of his calling. The agriculturist needs ethics, mathematics, chemistry and natural philosophy. The mechanic the same. To them the languages are but ornament and comfort. I know it is often said there have been shining examples of men of great abilities in all the businesses of life, without any other science than what they had gathered from conversations and intercourse with the world. But who can say what these men would not have been had they started in the science on the shoulders of a Demosthenes or Cicero, of a Locke or Bacon, or a Newton? To sum the whole, therefore, it may truly be said that the classical languages are a solid basis for most, and an ornament to all the sciences.

I am warned by my aching fingers to close this hasty sketch, and to place here my last and fondest wishes for the advancement of our country in the useful sciences and arts, and my assurances of respect and esteem for the Reviewer of the Memoir on modern Greek.

LIMITS TO JUDICIAL REVIEW
To Judge Spencer Roane

Poplar Forest, September 6, 1819

DEAR SIR,—I had read in the Enquirer, and with great approbation, the pieces signed Hampden, and have read them again with redoubled approbation, in the copies you have been so kind as to send me. I subscribe to every tittle of them. They contain the true principles of the revolution of 1800, for that was as real a revolution in the principles of our government as that of 1776 was in its form; not effected indeed by the sword, as that, but by the rational and peaceable instrument of reform, the suffrage of the people. The nation declared its will by dismissing functionaries of one principle, and electing those of another, in the two branches, executive and legisltaive, submitted to their election. Over the judiciary department, the constitution had deprived them of their control. That, therefore, has continued the reprobated system, and although new matter has been occasionally incorporated into the old, yet the leaven of the old mass seems to assimilate to itself the new, and after twenty years' confirmation of the federal system by the voice of the nation, declared through the medium of elections, we find the judiciary on every occasion, still driving us into consolidation.

In denying the right they usurp of exclusively explaining the constitution, I go further than you do, if I understand rightly your quotation from the Federalist, of an opinion that "the judiciary is the last resort in relation *to the other departments* of the government, but not in relation to the rights of the parties to the compact under which the judiciary is derived." If this opinion be sound, then indeed is our constitution a complete *felo de se*. For intending to establish three departments, co-ordinate and independent, that they might check and balance one another, it has given, according to this opinion, to one of them alone, the right to prescribe rules for the government of the others, and to that one too, which is unelected by, and independent of the nation. For experience has already shown that the impeachment it has provided is not even a scare-crow; that such opinions as the one you combat, sent cautiously out, as you observe also, by detachment, not belonging to the case often, but sought for out of it, as if to rally the public opinion beforehand to their views, and to indicate the line they are to walk in, have been so quietly passed over as never to have excited animadversion, even in a speech of any one of the body entrusted with impeachment. The constitution, on this hypothesis, is a mere thing of wax in the hands of the judiciary, which they may twist and shape into any form they please. It should be remembered, as an axiom of eternal truth in politics, that whatever power in any government is independent, is absolute also; in theory only, at first, while the spirit of the people is up, but in practice, as fast as that relaxes. Independence can be trusted nowhere but with the people in mass. They are inherently independent of all but moral law. My construction of the constitution is very different from that you quote. It is that each department is truly independent of the others, and has an equal right to decide for itself what is the meaning of the constitution in the cases submitted to its action; and es-

pecially, where it is to act ultimately and without appeal. I will explain myself by examples, which, having occurred while I was in office, are better known to me, and the principles which governed them.

A legislature had passed the sedition law. The federal courts had subjected certain individuals to its penalties of fine and imprisonment. On coming into office, I released these individuals by the power of pardon committed to executive discretion, which could never be more properly exercised than where citizens were suffering without the authority of law, or, which was equivalent, under a law unauthorized by the constitution, and therefore null. In the case of Marbury and Madison, the federal judges declared that commissions, signed and sealed by the President, were valid, although not delivered. I deemed delivery essential to complete a deed, which, as long as it remains in the hands of the party, is as yet no deed, it is in *posse* only, but not in *esse*, and I withheld delivery of the commissions. They cannot issue a mandamus to the President or legislature, or to any of their officers.* When the British treaty of ———— arrived, without any provision against the impressment of our seamen, I determined not to ratify it. The Senate thought I should ask their advice. I thought that would be a mockery of them, when I was predetermined against following it, should they advise its ratification. The constitution had made their advice necessary to confirm a treaty, but not to reject it. This has been blamed by some; but I have never doubted its soundness. In the cases of two persons, *antenati*, under exactly similar circumstances, the federal court had determined that one of them (Duane) was not a citizen; the House of Representatives nevertheless determined that the other (Smith, of South Carolina) was a citizen, and admitted him to his seat in their body. Duane was a republican, and Smith a federalist, and these decisions were made during the federal ascendancy.

These are examples of my position, that each of the three departments has equally the right to decide for itself what is its duty under the constitution, without any regard to what the others may have decided for themselves under a similar

*The constitution controlling the common law in this particular.

question. But you intimate a wish that my opinion should be known on this subject. No, dear Sir, I withdraw from all contest of opinion, and resign everything cheerfully to the generation now in place. They are wiser than we were, and their successors will be wiser than they, from the progressive advance of science. Tranquillity is the *summum bonum* of age. I wish, therefore, to offend no man's opinion, nor to draw disquieting animadversions on my own. While duty required it, I met opposition with a firm and fearless step. But loving mankind in my individual relations with them, I pray to be permitted to depart in their peace; and like the superannuated soldier, *"quadragenis stipendiis emeritis,"* to hang my arms on the post. I have unwisely, I fear, embarked in an enterprise of great public concern, but not to be accomplished within my term, without their liberal and prompt support. A severe illness the last year, and another from which I am just emerged, admonish me that repetitions may be expected, against which a declining frame cannot long bear up. I am anxious, therefore, to get our University so far advanced as may encourage the public to persevere to its final accomplishment. That secured, I shall sing my *nunc demittas*. I hope your labors will be long continued in the spirit in which they have always been exercised, in maintenance of those principles on which I verily believe the future happiness of our country essentially depends. I salute you with affectionate and great respect.

GREEK PRONUNCIATION
To Nathaniel F. Moore

Monticello, September 22, 1819

I thank you, Sir for the remarks on the pronunciation of the Greek language which you have been so kind as to send me. I have read them with pleasure, as I had the pamphlet of Mr. Pickering on the same subject. This question has occupied long and learned inquiry, and cannot, as I apprehend, be ever positively decided. Very early in my classical days, I took up the idea that the ancient Greek language having been changed by degrees into the modern, and the present race of that people having received it by tradition, they had of course better pretensions to the ancient pronunciation also, than any foreign nation could have. When at Paris, I became acquainted with some learned Greeks, from whom I took pains to learn the modern pronunciation. But I could not receive it as genuine *in toto*. I could not believe that the ancient Greeks had provided six different notations for the simple sound of ι, iota, and left the five other sounds which we give to *n, v, ι-ι, οι, υι,* without any characters of notation at all. I could not acknowledge the υ, upsillon, as an equivalent to our *v*, as in *Αχιλλευς*, which they pronounce Achillevs, nor the γ, gamma, to our *y*, as in αλγέ, which they pronounce alye. I concluded, therefore, that as experience proves to us that the pronunciation of all languages changes, in their descent through time, that of the Greek must have done so also in some degree; and the more probably, as the body of the words themselves had substantially changed, and I presumed that the instances above mentioned might be classed with the degeneracies of time; a presumption strengthened by their remarkable cacophony. As to all the other letters, I have supposed we might yield to their traditionary claim of a more orthodox pronunciation. Indeed, they sound most of them as we do, and, where they differ, as in the ε, δ, χ, their sounds do not revolt us, nor impair the beauty of the language.

If we adhere to the Erasmian pronunciation, we must go to Italy for it, as we must do for the most probably correct pronunciation of the language of the Romans, because rejecting the modern, we must argue that the ancient pronunciation was probably brought from Greece, with the language itself; and, as Italy was the country to which it was brought, and from which it emanated to other nations, we must presume it better preserved there than with the nations copying from them, who would be apt to affect its pronunciation with some of their own national peculiarities. And in fact, we find that no two nations pronounce it alike, although all pretend to the Erasmian pronunciation. But the whole subject is conjectural, and allows therefore full and lawful scope to the vagaries of the human mind. I am glad, however, to see the question stirred here; because it may excite among our young countrymen a spirit of inquiry and criticism, and lead them to more attention to this most beautiful of all languages. And wishing that the salutary example you have set may have this good effect, I salute you with great respect and consideration.

"I TOO AM AN EPICUREAN"

To William Short, with a Syllabus

Monticello, October 31, 1819

DEAR SIR,—Your favor of the 21st is received. My late illness, in which you are so kind as to feel an interest, was produced by a spasmodic stricture of the ilium, which came upon me on the 7th inst. The crisis was short, passed over favorably on the fourth day, and I should soon have been well but that a dose of calomel and jalap, in which were only eight or nine grains of the former, brought on a salivation. Of this, however, nothing now remains but a little soreness of the mouth. I have been able to get on horseback for three or four days past.

As you say of yourself, I too am an Epicurian. I consider the genuine (not the imputed) doctrines of Epicurus as containing everything rational in moral philosophy which Greece and Rome have left us. Epictetus indeed, has given us what was good of the stoics; all beyond, of their dogmas, being hypocrisy and grimace. Their great crime was in their calumnies of Epicurus and misrepresentations of his doctrines; in which we lament to see the candid character of Cicero engaging as an accomplice. Diffuse, vapid, rhetorical, but enchanting. His prototype Plato, eloquent as himself, dealing out mysticisms incomprehensible to the human mind, has been deified by certain sects usurping the name of Christians; because, in his foggy conceptions, they found a basis of impenetrable darkness whereon to rear fabrications as delirious, of their own invention. These they fathered blasphemously on him whom they claimed as their founder, but who would disclaim them with the indignation which their caricatures of his religion so justly excite. Of Socrates we have nothing genuine but in the Memorabilia of Xenophon; for Plato makes him

one of his Collocutors merely to cover his own whimsies under the mantle of his name; a liberty of which we are told
Socrates himself complained. Seneca is indeed a fine moralist,
disfiguring his work at times with some Stoicisms, and affecting too much of antithesis and point, yet giving us on the
whole a great deal of sound and practical morality. But the
greatest of all the reformers of the depraved religion of his
own country, was Jesus of Nazareth. Abstracting what is
really his from the rubbish in which it is buried, easily distinguished by its lustre from the dross of his biographers, and as
separable from that as the diamond from the dunghill, we
have the outlines of a system of the most sublime morality
which has ever fallen from the lips of man; outlines which it
is lamentable he did not live to fill up. Epictetus and Epicurus
give laws for governing ourselves, Jesus a supplement of the
duties and charities we owe to others. The establishment of
the innocent and genuine character of this benevolent moralist, and the rescuing it from the imputation of imposture,
which has resulted from artificial systems,* invented by ultra-
Christian sects, unauthorized by a single word ever uttered by
him, is a most desirable object, and one to which Priestley
has successfully devoted his labors and learning. It would in
time, it is to be hoped, effect a quiet euthanasia of the heresies
of bigotry and fanaticism which have so long triumphed over
human reason, and so generally and deeply afflicted mankind;
but this work is to be begun by winnowing the grain from
the chaff of the historians of his life. I have sometimes
thought of translating Epictetus (for he has never been tolerable translated into English) by adding the genuine doctrines
of Epicurus from the Syntagma of Gassendi, and an abstract
from the Evangelists of whatever has the stamp of the eloquence and fine imagination of Jesus. The last I attempted too
hastily some twelve or fifteen years ago. It was the work of
two or three nights only, at Washington, after getting
through the evening task of reading the letters and papers of
the day. But with one foot in the grave, these are now idle

*_e. g._ The immaculate conception of Jesus, his deification, the creation of
the world by him, his miraculous powers, his resurrection and visible ascen-
sion, his corporeal presence in the Eucharist, the Trinity; original sin, atonement, regeneration, election, orders of Hierarchy, &c.

projects for me. My business is to beguile the wearisomeness of declining life, as I endeavor to do, by the delights of classical reading and of mathematical truths, and by the consolations of a sound philosophy, equally indifferent to hope and fear.

I take the liberty of observing that you are not a true disciple of our master Epicurus, in indulging the indolence to which you say you are yielding. One of his canons, you know, was that "the indulgence which prevents a greater pleasure, or produces a greater pain, is to be avoided." Your love of repose will lead, in its progress, to a suspension of healthy exercise, a relaxation of mind, an indifference to everything around you, and finally to a debility of body, and hebetude of mind, the farthest of all things from the happiness which the well-regulated indulgences of Epicurus ensure; fortitude, you know, is one of his four cardinal virtues. That teaches us to meet and surmount difficulties; not to fly from them, like cowards; and to fly, too, in vain, for they will meet and arrest us at every turn of our road. Weigh this matter well; brace yourself up; take a seat with Correa, and come and see the finest portion of your country, which, if you have not forgotten, you still do not know, because it is no longer the same as when you knew it. It will add much to the happiness of my recovery to be able to receive Correa and yourself, and prove the estimation in which I hold you both. Come, too, and see our incipient University, which has advanced with great activitiy this year. By the end of the next, we shall have elegant accommodations for seven professors, and the year following the professors themselves. No secondary character will be received among them. Either the ablest which America or Europe can furnish, or none at all. They will give us the selected society of a great city separated from the dissipations and levities of its ephemeral insects.

I am glad the bust of Condorcet has been saved and so well placed. His genius should be before us; while the lamentable, but singular act of ingratitude which tarnished his latter days, may be thrown behind us.

I will place under this a syllabus of the doctrines of Epicurus, somewhat in the lapidary style, which I wrote some twenty years ago, a like one of the philosophy of Jesus, of nearly the same age, is too long to be copied. *Vale, et tibi persuade carissimum te esse mihi.*

Syllabus of the doctrines of Epicurus.

Physical.—The Universe eternal.

Its parts, great and small, interchangeable.

Matter and Void alone.

Motion inherent in matter which is weighty and declining.

Eternal circulation of the elements of bodies.

Gods, an order of beings next superior to man, enjoying in their sphere, their own felicities; but not meddling with the concerns of the scale of beings below them.

Moral.—Happiness the aim of life.

Virtue the foundation of happiness.

Utility the test of virtue.

Pleasure active and In-do-lent.

In-do-lence is the absence of pain, the true felicity.

Active, consists in agreeable motion; it is not happiness, but the means to produce it.

Thus the absence of hunger is an article of felicity; eating the means to obtain it.

The *summum bonum* is to be not pained in body, nor troubled in mind.

i. e. In-do-lence of body, tranquillity of mind.

To procure tranquillity of mind we must avoid desire and fear, the two principal diseases of the mind.

Man is a free agent.

Virtue consists in 1. Prudence. 2. Temperance. 3. Fortitude. 4. Justice.

To which are opposed, 1. Folly. 2. Desire. 3. Fear. 4. Deceit.

"A FIRE BELL IN THE NIGHT"
To John Holmes

Monticello, April 22, 1820

I thank you, dear Sir, for the copy you have been so kind as to send me of the letter to your constituents on the Missouri question. It is a perfect justification to them. I had for

a long time ceased to read newspapers, or pay any attention
to public affairs, confident they were in good hands, and content to be a passenger in our bark to the shore from which I
am not distant. But this momentous question, like a fire bell
in the night, awakened and filled me with terror. I considered
it at once as the knell of the Union. It is hushed, indeed, for
the moment. But this is a reprieve only, not a final sentence.
A geographical line, coinciding with a marked principle,
moral and political, once conceived and held up to the angry
passions of men, will never be obliterated; and every new irritation will mark it deeper and deeper. I can say, with conscious truth, that there is not a man on earth who would
sacrifice more than I would to relieve us from this heavy reproach, in any *practicable* way. The cession of that kind of
property, for so it is misnamed, is a bagatelle which would
not cost me a second thought, if, in that way, a general emancipation and *expatriation* could be effected; and gradually, and
with due sacrifices, I think it might be. But as it is, we have
the wolf by the ears, and we can neither hold him, nor safely
let him go. Justice is in one scale, and self-preservation in the
other. Of one thing I am certain, that as the passage of slaves
from one State to another, would not make a slave of a single
human being who would not be so without it, so their diffusion over a greater surface would make them individually
happier, and proportionally facilitate the accomplishment of
their emancipation, by dividing the burthen on a greater
number of coadjutors. An abstinence too, from this act of
power, would remove the jealousy excited by the undertaking
of Congress to regulate the condition of the different descriptions of men composing a State. This certainly is the exclusive
right of every State, which nothing in the constitution has
taken from them and given to the General Government.
Could Congress, for example, say, that the non-freemen of
Connecticut shall be freemen, or that they shall not emigrate
into any other State?

I regret that I am now to die in the belief, that the useless
sacrifice of themselves by the generation of 1776, to acquire
self-government and happiness to their country, is to be
thrown away by the unwise and unworthy passions of their
sons, and that my only consolation is to be, that I live not to

weep over it. If they would but dispassionately weigh the blessings they will throw away, against an abstract principle more likely to be effected by union than by scission, they would pause before they would perpetrate this act of suicide on themselves, and of treason against the hopes of the world. To yourself, as the faithful advocate of the Union, I tender the offering of my high esteem and respect.

JESUS AND THE JEWS
To William Short

Monticello, August 4, 1820

DEAR SIR,—I owe you a letter for your favor of June the 29th, which was received in due time; and there being no subject of the day, of particular interest, I will make this a supplement to mine of April the 13th. My aim in that was, to justify the character of Jesus against the fictions of his pseudo-followers, which have exposed him to the inference of being an impostor. For if we could believe that he really countenanced the follies, the falsehoods and the charlatanisms which his biographers father on him, and admit the misconstructions, interpolations and theorizations of the fathers of the early, and fanatics of the latter ages, the conclusion would be irresistible by every sound mind, that he was an impostor. I give no credit to their falsifications of his actions and doctrines, and to rescue his character, the postulate in my letter asked only what is granted in reading every other historian. When Livy and Siculus, for example, tell us things which coincide with our experience of the order of nature, we credit them on their word, and place their narrations among the records of credible history. But when they tell us of calves speaking, of statues sweating blood, and other things against the course of nature, we reject these as fables not belonging to history. In like manner, when an historian, speaking of a character well known and established on satisfactory testimony, imputes to it things incompatible with that character, we reject them without hesitation, and assent to that only of which we have better evidence. Had Plutarch informed us that Cæsar and Cicero passed their whole lives in religious exercises, and abstinence from the affairs of the world, we should reject what was so inconsistent with their established characters, still crediting what he relates in conformity with our ideas of them. So again, the superlative wisdom of Socrates is testified by all antiquity, and placed on ground not to be questioned. When, therefore, Plato puts into his mouth such paralogisms, such quibbles on words, and sophisms, as a school boy would be ashamed of, we conclude they were the whimsies of Plato's own foggy brain, and acquit Socrates of puerilities so unlike his character. (Speaking of Plato, I will add, that no writer, antient or modern, has bewildered the world with more *ignes fatui*, than this renowned philosopher, in Ethics, in Politics and Physics. In the latter, to specify a single example, compare his views of the animal economy, in his Timæus, with those of Mrs. Bryan in her Conversations on Chemistry, and weigh the science of the canonised philosopher against the good sense of the unassuming lady. But Plato's visions have furnished a basis for endless systems of mystical theology, and he is therefore all but adopted as a Christian saint. It is surely time for men to think for themselves, and to throw off the authority of names so artificially magnified. But to return from this parenthasis.) I say, that this free exercise of reason is all I ask for the vindication of the character of Jesus. We find in the writings of his biographers matter of two distinct descriptions. First, a groundwork of vulgar ignorance, of things impossible, of superstitions, fanaticisms and fabrications. Intermixed with these, again, are sublime ideas of the Supreme Being, aphorisms and precepts of the purest morality and benevolence, sanctioned by a life of humility, innocence and simplicity of manners, neglect of riches, absence of worldly ambition and honors, with an eloquence and persuasiveness which have not been surpassed. These could not be inventions of the groveling authors who relate them. They are far beyond the powers of their feeble minds. They shew that there was a character, the subject of their history, whose splendid conceptions were above all suspicion of being interpolations from their hands. Can we be at a loss in separating such materials, and ascribing each to its genuine author? The difference is obvious to the eye and to the understanding, and we may read as we run to each his part; and I will venture to affirm, that he who, as I have done, will undertake to winnow this grain from its chaff, will find it not to require a moment's consideration. The parts fall asunder of themselves, as would those of an image of metal and clay.

There are, I acknowledge, passages not free from objection, which we may, with probability, ascribe to Jesus himself; but claiming indulgence from the circumstances under which he acted. His object was the reformation of some articles in the religion of the Jews, as taught by Moses. That sect had presented for the object of their worship, a being of terrific character, cruel, vindictive, capricious and unjust. Jesus, taking for his type the best qualities of the human head and heart, wisdom, justice, goodness, and adding to them power, ascribed all of these, but in infinite perfection, to the Supreme Being, and formed him really worthy of their adoration. Moses had either not believed in a future state of existence, or had not thought it essential to be explicitly taught to his people. Jesus inculcated that doctrine with emphasis and precision. Moses had bound the Jews to many idle ceremonies, mummeries and observances, of no effect towards producing the social utilities which constitute the essence of virtue; Jesus exposed their futility and insignificance. The one instilled into his people the most anti-social spirit towards other nations; the other preached philanthropy and universal charity and benevolence. The office of reformer of the superstitions of a nation, is ever dangerous. Jesus had to walk on the perilous confines of reason and religion: and a step to right or left might place him within the gripe of the priests of the superstition, a blood thirsty race, as cruel and remorseless as the being whom they represented as the family God of Abraham, of Isaac and of Jacob, and the local God of Israel. They were constantly laying snares, too, to entangle him in the web of the law. He was justifiable, therefore, in avoiding these by evasions, by sophisms, by misconstructions and misapplications of scraps of the prophets, and in defending himself with these their own weapons, as sufficient, *ad homines*, at least. That Jesus did not mean to impose himself on mankind as the son of God, physically speaking, I have been convinced by the writings of men more learned than myself in that lore. But that he might conscientiously believe himself inspired from above, is very possible. The whole religion of the Jews, inculcated on him from his infancy, was founded in the belief of divine inspiration. The fumes of the most disordered imaginations were recorded in their religious code, as special communications of the Deity; and as it could not but happen that, in the course of ages, events would now and then turn up to which some of these vague rhapsodies might be accommodated by the aid of allegories, figures, types, and other tricks upon words, they have not only preserved their credit with the Jews of all subsequent times, but are the foundation of much of the religions of those who have schismatised from them. Elevated by the enthusiasm of a warm and pure heart, conscious of the high strains of an eloquence which had not been taught him, he might readily mistake the coruscations of his own fine genius for inspirations of an higher order. This belief carried, therefore, no more personal imputation, than the belief of Socrates, that himself was under the care and admonitions of a guardian Dæmon. And how many of our wisest men still believe in the reality of these inspirations, while perfectly sane on all other subjects. Excusing, therefore, on these considerations, those passages in the gospels which seem to bear marks of weakness in Jesus, ascribing to him what alone is consistent with the great and pure character of which the same writings furnish proofs, and to their proper authors their own trivialities and imbecilities, I think myself authorised to conclude the purity and distinction of his character, in opposition to the impostures which those authors would fix upon him; and that the postulate of my former letter is no more than is granted in all other historical works.

Mr. Correa is here, on his farewell visit to us. He has been much pleased with the plan and progress of our University, and has given some valuable hints to its botanical branch. He goes to do, I hope, much good in his new country; the public instruction there, as I understand, being within the department destined for him. He is not without dissatisfaction, and reasonable dissatisfaction too, with the piracies of Baltimore; but his justice and friendly dispositions will, I am sure, distinguish between the iniquities of a few plunderers, and the

sound principles of our country at large, and of our government especially. From many conversations with him, I hope
he sees, and will promote in his new situation, the advantages
of a cordial fraternization among all the American nations,
and the importance of their coalescing in an American system
of policy, totally independent of, and unconnected with that
of Europe. The day is not distant, when we may formally
require a meridian of partition through the ocean which separates the two hemispheres, on the hither side of which no
European gun shall ever be heard, nor an American on the
other; and when, during the rage of the eternal wars of Europe, the lion and the lamb, within our regions, shall lie
down together in peace. The excess of population in Europe
and want of room, render war, in their opinion, necessary to
keep down that excess of numbers. Here, room is abundant,
population scanty, and peace the necessary means for producing men, to whom the redundant soil is offering the means
of life and happiness. The principles of society there and here,
then, are radically different, and I hope no American patriot
will ever lose sight of the essential policy of interdicting in
the seas and territories of both Americas, the ferocious and
sanguinary contests of Europe. I wish to see this coalition
begun. I am earnest for an agreement with the maritime powers of Europe, assigning them the task of keeping down the
piracies of their seas and the cannibalisms of the African
coasts, and to us, the suppression of the same enormities
within our seas: and for this purpose, I should rejoice to see
the fleets of Brazil and the United States riding together as
brethren of the same family, and pursuing the same object.
And indeed it would be of happy augury to begin at once this
concert of action here, on the invitation of either to the other
government, while the way might be preparing for withdrawing our cruisers from Europe, and preventing naval collisions
there which daily endanger our peace.

Turning to another part of your letter, I do not think the
obstacles insuperable which you state as opposed to your visit
to us. From one of the persons mentioned, I never heard a
sentiment but of esteem for you and I am certain you would
be recieved with kindness and cordiality. But still the call may
be omitted without notice. The mountain lies between his

residence and the main road, and occludes the expectation of transient visits. I am equally ignorant of any dispositions not substantially friendly to you in the other person. But the alibi there gives you ten free months in the year. But if the visit is to be but once in your life, I would suppress my impatience and consent it should be made a year or two hence. Because, by that time our University will be compleate and in full action: and you would recieve the satisfaction, in the final adieu to your native state, of seeing that she would retain her equal standing in the sisterhood of our republics. However, come now, come then, or come when you please, your visit will give me the gratification I feel in every opportunity of proving to you the sincerity of my friendship and respect for you.

THE UNIVERSITY, NEOLOGY, AND MATERIALISM

To John Adams

Monticello, Aug. 15, 1820

I am a great defaulter, my dear Sir, in our correspondence, but prostrate health rarely permits me to write; and, when it does, matters of business imperiously press their claims. I am getting better however, slowly, swelled legs being now the only serious symptom, and these, I believe, proceed from extreme debility. I can walk but little; but I ride 6. or 8. miles a day without fatigue; and within a few days, I shall endeavor to visit my other home, after a twelve month's absence from it. Our University, 4 miles distant, gives me frequent exercise, and the oftener as I direct it's architecture. It's plan is unique, and it is becoming an object of curiosity for the traveller. I have lately had an opportunity of reading a critique on this institution in your North American Review of January last, having been not without anxiety to see what that able work would say of us: and I was relieved on finding in it much coincidence of opinion, and even, where criticisms were indulged, I found they would have been obviated had the developements of our plan been fuller. But these were restrained by the character of the paper reviewed, being merely a report of outlines, not a detailed treatise, and addressed to a legislative body, not to a learned academy. E.g. as an inducement to introduce the Anglo-Saxon into our plan, it was said that it would reward amply the *few weeks* of attention which alone would be requisite for it's attainment; leaving both term and degree under an indefinite expression, because I know that not much time is necessary to attain it to an useful degree, sufficient to give such instruction in the etymologies of our language as may satisfy ordinary students, while more time would be requisite for those who would propose to attain a critical knolege of it. In a letter which I had occasion to write to Mr. Crofts (who sent you, I believe, as well as myself, a copy of his treatise on the English and German languages, as preliminary to an Etymological dictionary he meditated) I went into explanations with him of an easy process for simplifying the study of the Anglo-Saxon, and lessening the terrors, and difficulties presented by it's rude Alphabet, and unformed orthography. But this is a subject beyond the bounds of a letter, as it was beyond the bounds of a Report to the legislature. Mr. Crofts died, I believe, before any progress was made in the work he had projected.

The reviewer expresses doubt, rather than decision, on our placing Military and Naval architecture in the department of Pure Mathematics. Military architecture embraces fortification and field works, which with their bastions, curtains, hornworks, redoubts etc. are based on a technical combination of lines and angles. These are adapted to offence and defence, with and against the effects of bombs, balls, escalades etc. But lines and angles make the sum of elementary geometry, a branch of Pure Mathematics: and the direction of the bombs, balls, and other projectiles, the necessary appendages of military works, altho' no part of their architecture, belong to the conic sections, a branch of transcendental geometry. Diderot and Dalembert therefore, in their Arbor scientiae, have placed military architecture in the department of elementary geometry. Naval architecture teaches the best form and construction of vessels; for which best form it has recourse to the question of the Solid of least resistance, a problem of transcendental geometry. And it's appurtenant projectiles belong to the same

branch, as in the preceding case. It is true that so far as respects the action of the water on the rudder and oars, and of
the wind on the sails, it may be placed in the department of
mechanics, as Diderot and Dalambert have done: but belonging quite as much to geometry, and allied in it's military character, to military architecture, it simplified our plan to place
both under the same head. These views are so obvious that I
am sure they would have required but a second thought to
reconcile the reviewer to their *location* under the head of Pure
Mathematics. For this word *Location*, see Bailey, Johnson,
Sheridan, Walker etc. But if Dictionaries are to be the Arbi-
ters of language, in which of them shall we find *neologism*. No
matter. It is a good word, well sounding, obvious, and expresses an idea which would otherwise require circumlocu-
tion. The Reviewer was justifiable therefore in using it; altho'
he noted at the same time, as unauthoritative, *centrality*,
grade, *sparse*; all which have been long used in common
speech and writing. I am a friend to *neology*. It is the only way
to give to a language copiousness and euphony. Without it
we should still be held to the vocabulary of Alfred or of Ul-
philas; and held to their state of science also: for I am sure
they had no words which could have conveyed the ideas of
Oxigen, cotyledons, zoophytes, magnetism, electricity, hya-
line, and thousands of others expressing ideas not then existing, nor of possible communication in the state of their
language. What a language has the French become since the
date of their revolution, by the free introduction of new
words! The most copious and eloquent in the living world;
and equal to the Greek, had not that been regularly modifia-
ble almost ad infinitum. Their rule was that whenever their
language furnished or adopted a root, all it's branches, in
every part of speech were legitimated by giving them their
appropriate terminations. αδελφος ["brother"], αδελφη
["sister"], αδελφιδιον ["little brother"], αδελφοτης ["brotherly affection"], αδελφιξις ["brotherhood"], αδελφιδους
["nephew"], αδελφικος ["brotherly," adj.], αδελφιζω ["to
adopt as a brother"], αδελφικως ["brotherly," adv.]. And this
should be the law of every language. Thus, having adopted
the adjective *fraternal*, it is a root, which should legitimate
fraternity, fraternation, fraternisation, fraternism, to frater-

nate, fraternise, fraternally. And give the word neologism to our language, as a root, and it should give us it's fellow substantives, neology, neologist, neologisation; it's adjectives neologous, neological, neologistical, it's verb neologise, and adverb neologically. Dictionaries are but the depositories of words already legitimated by usage. Society is the work-shop in which new ones are elaborated. When an individual uses a new word, if illformed it is rejected in society, if wellformed, adopted, and, after due time, laid up in the depository of dictionaries. And if, in this process of sound neologisation, our transatlantic brethren shall not choose to accompany us, we may furnish, after the Ionians, a second example of a colonial dialect improving on it's primitive.

But enough of criticism: let me turn to your puzzling letter of May 12. on matter, spirit, motion etc. It's croud of scepticisms kept me from sleep. I read it, and laid it down: read it, and laid it down, again and again: and to give rest to my mind, I was obliged to recur ultimately to my habitual anodyne, 'I feel: therefore I exist.' I feel bodies which are not myself: there are other existencies then. I call them *matter*. I feel them changing place. This gives me *motion*. Where there is an absence of matter, I call it *void*, or *nothing*, or *immaterial space*. On the basis of sensation, of matter and motion, we may erect the fabric of all the certainties we can have or need. I can concieve *thought* to be an action of a particular organisation of matter, formed for that purpose by it's creator, as well as that *attraction* in an action of matter, or *magnetism* of loadstone. When he who denies to the Creator the power of endowing matter with the mode of action called *thinking* shall shew how he could endow the Sun with the mode of action called *attraction*, which reins the planets in the tract of their orbits, or how an absence of matter can have a will, and, by that will, put matter into motion, then the materialist may be lawfully required to explain the process by which matter exercises the faculty of thinking. When once we quit the basis of sensation, all is in the wind. To talk of *immaterial* existences is to talk of *nothings*. To say that the human soul, angels, god, are immaterial, is to say they are *nothings*, or that there is no god, no angels, no soul. I cannot reason otherwise: but I believe I am supported in my creed of materialism by Locke, Tracy, and Stewart. At what age of the Christian church this heresy of *immaterialism*, this masked atheism, crept in, I do not know. But a heresy it certainly is. Jesus taught nothing of it. He told us indeed that 'God is a spirit,' but he has not defined what a spirit is, nor said that it is not *matter*. And the antient fathers generally, if not universally, held it to be matter: light and thin indeed, an etherial gas; but still matter. Origen says 'Deus reapse corporalis est; sed graviorum tantum corporum ratione, incorporeus.' Tertullian 'quid enim deus nisi corpus?' and again 'quis negabit deum esse corpus? Etsi deus spiritus, spiritus etiam corpus est, sui generis, in sua effigie.' St. Justin Martyr 'το Θειον φαμεν ειναι ασωματον· ουκ οτι ασωματον'—επειδη δε το μη κρατεισθαι υπο τινος, του κρατεισθαι τιμιωτερον εστι, δια τουτο καλουμεν αυτον ασωματον.' And St. Macarius, speaking of angels says 'quamvis enim subtilia sint, tamen in substantiâ, formâ et figurâ, secundum tenuitatem naturae eorum, corpora sunt tenuia.' And St. Austin, St. Basil, Lactantius, Tatian, Athenagoras and others, with whose writings I pretend not a familiarity, are said by those who are, to deliver the same doctrine. Turn to your Ocellus d'Argens 97. 105. and to his Timaeus 17. for these quotations. In England these Immaterialists might have been burnt until the 29. Car. 2. when the writ de haeretico comburendo was abolished: and here until the revolution, that statute not having extended to us. All heresies being now done away with us, these schismatists are merely atheists, differing from the material Atheist only in their belief that 'nothing made something,' and from the material deist who believes that matter alone can operate on matter.

Rejecting all organs of information therefore but my senses, I rid myself of the Pyrrhonisms with which an indulgence in speculations hyperphysical and antiphysical so uselessly occupy and disquiet the mind. A single sense may indeed be sometimes decieved, but rarely: and never all our senses together, with their faculty of reasoning. They evidence realities; and there are enough of these for all the purposes of life, without plunging into the fathomless abyss of dreams and phantasms. I am satisfied, and sufficiently occupied with the things which are, without tormenting or troubling myself about those which may indeed be, but of which I have no evidence. I am sure that I really know many, many, things, and none more surely than that I love you with all my heart, and pray for the continuance of your life until you shall be tired of it yourself.

JUDICIAL SUBVERSION
To Thomas Ritchie

Monticello, December 25, 1820

DEAR SIR,—On my return home after a long absence, I find here your favor of November the 23d, with Colonel Taylor's "Construction Construed," which you have been so kind as to send me, in the name of the author as well as yourself. Permit me, if you please, to use the same channel for conveying to him the thanks I render you also for this mark of attention. I shall read it, I know, with edification, as I did his Inquiry, to which I acknowledge myself indebted for many valuable ideas, and for the correction of some errors of early opinion, never seen in a correct light until presented to me in that work. That the present volume is equally orthodox, I know before reading it, because I know that Colonel Taylor and myself have rarely, if ever, differed in any political principle of importance. Every act of his life, and every word he ever wrote, satisfies me of this. So, also, as to the two Presidents, late and now in office, I know them both to be of principles as truly republican as any men living. If there be anything amiss, therefore, in the present state of our affairs, as the formidable deficit lately unfolded to us indicates, I ascribe it to the inattention of Congress to their duties, to their unwise dissipation and waste of the public contributions. They seemed, some little while ago, to be at a loss for objects whereon to throw away the supposed fathomless funds of the treasury. I had feared the result, because I saw among them some of my old fellow laborers, of tried and known principles, yet often in their minorities. I am aware that in one of their most ruinous vagaries, the people were themselves betrayed into the same phrenzy with their Representatives. The deficit produced, and a heavy tax to supply it, will, I trust, bring both to their sober senses.

But it is not from this branch of government we have most to fear. Taxes and short elections will keep them right. The judiciary of the United States is the subtle corps of sappers and miners constantly working under ground to undermine the foundations of our confederated fabric. They are construing our constitution from a co-ordination of a general and special government to a general and supreme one alone. This will lay all things at their feet, and they are too well versed in English law to forget the maxim, *"boni judicis est ampliare juris-dictionem."* We shall see if they are bold enough to take the daring stride their five lawyers have lately taken. If they do, then, with the editor of our book, in his address to the public, I will say, that "against this every man should raise his voice," and more, should uplift his arm. Who wrote this admirable address? Sound, luminous, strong, not a word too much, nor one which can be changed but for the worse. That pen should go on, lay bare these wounds of our constitution, expose the decisions *seriatim*, and arouse, as it is able, the attention of the nation to these bold speculators on its patience. Having found, from experience, that impeachment is an impracticable thing, a mere scare-crow, they consider themselves secure for life; they sculk from responsibility to public opinion, the only remaining hold on them, under a practice first introduced into England by Lord Mansfield. An opinion is huddled up in conclave, perhaps by a majority of one, delivered as if unanimous, and with the silent acquiescence of lazy or timid associates, by a crafty chief judge, who sophisticates the law to his mind, by the turn of his own reasoning. A judiciary law was once reported by the Attorney General to Congress, requiring each judge to deliver his opinion *seriatim* and openly, and then to give it in writing to the clerk to be entered in the record. A judiciary independent of a king or executive alone, is a good thing; but independence of the will of the nation is a solecism, at least in a republican government.

But to return to your letter; you ask for my opinion of the work you send me, and to let it go out to the public. This I have ever made a point of declining, (one or two instances only excepted.) Complimentary thanks to writers who have sent me their works, have betrayed me sometimes before the public, without my consent having been asked. But I am far from presuming to direct the reading of my fellow citizens, who are good enough judges themselves of what is worthy their reading. I am, also, too desirous of quiet to place myself in the way of contention. Against this I am admonished by bodily decay, which cannot be unaccompanied by corresponding wane of the mind. Of this I am as yet sensible, sufficiently to be unwilling to trust myself before the public, and when I cease to be so, I hope that my friends will be too careful of me to draw me forth and present me, like a Priam in armor, as a spectacle for public compassion. I hope our political bark will ride through all its dangers; but I can in future be but an inert passenger.

I salute you with sentiments of great friendship and respect.

THE MISSOURI QUESTION
To Albert Gallatin

Monticello, Dec. 26, 1820

DEAR SIR,—'It is said to be an ill wind which blows favorably to no one.' My ill health has long suspended the too frequent troubles I have heretofore given you with my European correspondence. To this is added a stiffening wrist, the effect of age on an antient dislocation, which renders writing slow and painful, and disables me nearly from all correspondence, and may very possibly make this the last trouble I shall give you in that way.

Looking from our quarter of the world over the horizon of yours we imagine we see storms gathering which may again desolate the face of that country. So many revolutions going on, in different countries at the same time, such combinations of tyranny, and military preparations and movements to suppress them. England & France unsafe from internal conflict, Germany, on the first favorable occasion, ripe for insurrection, such a state of things, we suppose, must end in war, which needs a kindling spark in one spot only to spread over the whole. Your information can correct these views which are stated only to inform you of impressions here.

At home things are not well. The flood of paper money, as you well know, had produced an exaggeration of nominal prices and at the same time a facility of obtaining money, which not only encouraged speculations on fictitious capital, but seduced those of real capital, even in private life, to contract debts too freely. Had things continued in the same course, these might have been manageable. But the operations of the U.S. bank for the demolition of the state banks, obliged these suddenly to call in more than half of their paper, crushed all fictitious and doubtful capital, and reduced the prices of property and produce suddenly to ⅓ of what they had been. Wheat, for example, at the distance of two or three days from market, fell to and continues at from one third to half a dollar. Should it be stationary at this for a while, a very general revolution of property must take place. Something of the same character has taken place in our fiscal system. A little while back Congress seemed at a loss for objects whereon to squander the supposed fathomless funds of our treasury. This short frenzy has been arrested by a deficit of 5 millions the last year, and of 7. millions this year. A loan was adopted for the former and is proposed for the latter, which threatens to saddle us with a perpetual debt. I hope a tax will be preferred, because it will awaken the attention of the people, and make reformation & economy the principles of the next election. The frequent recurrence of this chastening operation can alone restrain the propensity of governments to enlarge expence beyond income. The steady tenor of the courts of the US. to break down the constitutional barrier between the coordinate powers of the States, and of the Union, and a formal opinion lately given by 5. lawyers of too much eminence to be neglected, give uneasiness. But nothing has ever presented so threatening an aspect as what is called the Missouri question. The Federalists compleatly put down, and despairing of ever rising again under the old division of whig and tory, devised a new one, of slave-holding, & non-slave-holding states, which, while it had a semblance of being Moral, was at the same time Geographical, and calculated to give them ascendancy by debauching their old opponents to a coalition with them. Moral the question certainly is not, because the removal of slaves from one state to another, no more than their removal from one country to another, would never make a slave of one human being who would not be so without it. Indeed if there were any morality in the question it is on the other side; because by spreading them over a larger surface, their happiness would be increased, & the burthen of their future liberation lightened by bringing a greater number of shoulders under it. However it served to throw dust into the eyes of the people and to fanaticise them, while to the knowing ones it gave a geographical and preponderant line of the Patomac and Ohio, throwing 12. States to the North and East, & 10. to the South & West. With these therefore it is merely a question of power: but with this geographical minority it is a question of existence. For if Congress once goes out of the Constitution to arrogate a right of regulating the conditions of the inhabitants of the States, its majority may, and probably will next declare that the condition of all men within the US. shall be that of freedom, in which case all the whites South of the Patomak and Ohio must evacuate their States; and most fortunate those who can do it first. And so far this crisis seems to be advancing. The Missouri constitution is recently rejected by the House of Representatives. What will be their next step is yet to be seen. If accepted on the condition that Missouri shall expunge from it the prohibition of free people of colour from emigration to their state, it will be expunged, and all will be quieted until the advance of some new state shall present the question again. If rejected unconditionally, Missouri assumes independent self-government, and Congress, after pouting awhile, must recieve them on the footing of the original states. Should the Representative propose force, 1. the Senate will not concur. 2. were they to concur, there would be a secession of the members South of the line, & probably of the three North Western states, who, however inclined to the other side, would scarcely separate from those who would hold the Misisipi from it's mouth to it's source. What next? Conjecture itself is at a loss. But whatever it shall be you will hear from others and from the newspapers. And finally the whole will depend on Pensylvania. While she and Virginia hold together, the Atlantic states can never separate. Unfortunately in the present case she has become more fanaticised than any other state. However useful where you are, I wish you were with them. You might turn the scale there, which would turn it for the whole. Should this scission take place, one of it's most deplorable consequences would be it's discouragement of the efforts of the European nations in the regeneration of their oppressive and Cannibal governments.

Amidst this prospect of evil, I am glad to see one good effect. It has brought the necessity of some plan of general emancipation & deportation more home to the minds of our people than it has ever been before. Insomuch, that our Governor has ventured to propose one to the legislature. This will probably not be acted on at this time. Nor would it be effectual; for while it proposes to devote to that object one third of the revenue of the State, it would not reach one tenth of the annual increase. My proposition would be that the holders should give up all born after a certain day, past, present, or to come, that these should be placed under the guardianship of the State, and sent at a proper age to S. Domingo. There they are willing to recieve them, & the shortness of the passage brings the deportation within the possible means of taxation aided by charitable contributions. In this I think Europe, which has forced this evil on us, and the Eastern states who have been it's chief instruments of importation, would be bound to give largely. But the proceeds of the land office, if appropriated, would be quite sufficient. God bless you and preserve you multos años.

BOLINGBROKE AND PAINE
To Francis Eppes

Monticello, January 19, 1821

DEAR FRANCIS,—Your letter of the 1st came safely to hand. I am sorry you have lost Mr. Elliot, however the kindness of Dr. Cooper will be able to keep you in the track of what is worthy of your time.

You ask my opinion of Lord Bolingbroke and Thomas Paine. They were alike in making bitter enemies of the priests and pharisees of their day. Both were honest men; both advocates for human liberty. Paine wrote for a country which permitted him to push his reasoning to whatever length it would go. Lord Bolingbroke in one restrained by a constitution, and by public opinion. He was called indeed a tory; but his writings prove him a stronger advocate for liberty than any of his countrymen, the whigs of the present day. Irritated by his exile, he committed one act unworthy of him, in connecting himself momentarily with a prince rejected by his country. But he redeemed that single act by his establishment of the principles which proved it to be wrong. These two persons differed remarkably in the style of their writing, each leaving a model of what is most perfect in both extremes of the simple and the sublime. No writer has exceeded Paine in ease and familiarity of style, in perspicuity of expression, happiness of elucidation, and in simple and unassuming language. In this he may be compared with Dr. Franklin; and indeed his Common Sense was, for awhile, believed to have been written by Dr. Franklin, and published under the borrowed name of Paine, who had come over with him from England. Lord Bolingbroke's, on the other hand, is a style of the highest order. The lofty, rhythmical, full-flowing eloquence of Cicero. Periods of just measure, their members proportioned, their close full and round. His conceptions, too, are bold and strong, his diction copious, polished and commanding as his subject. His writings are certainly the finest samples in the English language, of the eloquence proper for the Senate. His political tracts are safe reading for the most timid religionist, his philosophical, for those who are not afraid to trust their reason with discussions of right and wrong.

You have asked my opinion of these persons, and, *to you*, I have given it freely. But, remember, that I am old, that I wish not to make new enemies, nor to give offence to those who would consider a difference of opinion as sufficient ground for unfriendly dispositions. God bless you, and make you what I wish you to be.

THE UNIVERSITY AND THE SCHOOLS
To General James Breckinridge

Monticello, February 15, 1821

DEAR SIR,—I learn, with deep affliction, that nothing is likely to be done for our University this year. So near as it is to the shore that one shove more would land it there, I had hoped that would be given; and that we should open with the next year an institution on which the fortunes of our country may depend more than may meet the general eye. The reflections that the boys of this age are to be the men of the next; that they should be prepared to receive the holy charge which we are cherishing to deliver over to them; that in establishing an institution of wisdom for them, we secure it to all our future generations; that in fulfilling this duty, we bring home to our own bosoms the sweet consolation of seeing our sons rising under a luminous tuition, to destinies of high promise; these are considerations which will occur to all; but all, I fear, do not see the speck in our horizon which is to burst on us as a tornado, sooner or later. The line of division lately marked out between different portions of our confederacy, is such as will never, I fear, be obliterated, and we are now trusting to those who are against us in position and principle, to fashion to their own form the minds and affections of our youth. If, as has been estimated, we send three hundred thousand dollars a year to the northern seminaries, for the instruction of our own sons, then we must have there five hundred of our sons, imbibing opinions and principles in discord with those of their own country. This canker is eating on the vitals of our existence, and if not arrested at once, will be beyond remedy. We are now certainly furnishing recruits to their school. If it be asked what are we to do, or said we cannot give the last lift to the University without stopping our primary schools, and these we think most important; I answer, I know their importance. No body can doubt my zeal for the general instruction of the people. Who first started that idea? I may surely say, myself. Turn to the bill in the revised code, which I drew more than forty years ago, and before which the idea of a plan for the education of the people, generally, had never been suggested in this State. There you will see developed the first rudiments of the whole system of general education we are now urging and acting on: and it is well known to those with thom I have acted on this subject, that I never have proposed a sacrifice of the primary to the ultimate grade of instruction. Let us keep our eye steadily on the whole system. If we cannot do every thing at once, let us do one at a time. The primary schools need no preliminary expense; the ultimate grade requires a considerable expenditure in advance. A suspension of proceeding for a year or two on the primary schools, and an application of the whole income, during that time, to the completion of the buildings necessary for the University, would enable us then to start both institutions at the same time. The intermediate branch, of colleges, academies and private classical schools, for the middle grade, may hereafter receive any necessary aids when the funds shall become competent. In the mean time, they are going on sufficiently, as they have ever yet gone on, at the private expense of those who use them, and who in numbers and means are competent to their own exigencies. The experience of three years has, I presume, left no doubt that the present plan of primary schools, of putting money into the hands of twelve hundred persons acting for nothing, and under no responsibility, is entirely inefficient. Some other must be thought of; and during this pause, if it be only for a year, the whole revenue of that year, with that of the last three years which has not been already thrown away, would place our University in readiness to start with a better organization of primary schools, and both may then go on, hand in hand, for ever. No diminution of the capital will in this way have been incurred; a principle which ought to be deemed sacred. A relinquishment of interest on the late loan of sixty thousand dollars, would so far, also, forward the University without lessening the capital.

But what may be best done I leave with entire confidence to yourself and your colleagues in legislation, who know better than I do the conditions of the literary fund and its wisest applications and I shall acquiesce with perfect resignation to their will. I have brooded, perhaps with fondness, over this establishment, as it held up to me the hope of continuing to be useful while I continued to live. I had believed that the course and circumstances of my life had placed within my power some services favorable to the outset of the institution. But this may be egoism; pardonable, perhaps, when I express a consciousness that my colleagues and successors will do as well, whatever the legislature shall enable them to do.

I have thus, my dear Sir, opened my bosom, with all its anxieties, freely to you. I blame nobody for seeing things in a different light. I am sure that all act conscientiously, and that all will be done honestly and wisely which can be done. I yield the concerns of the world with cheerfulness to those who are appointed in the order of nature to succeed to them; and for yourself, for our colleagues, and for all in charge of our country's future fame and fortune, I offer up sincere prayers.

A DANGEROUS EXAMPLE
To Jedidiah Morse

Monticello, March 6, 1822

Sir,—I have duly received your letter of February the 16th, and have now to express my sense of the honorable station proposed to my ex-brethren and myself, in the constitution of the society for the civilization and improvement of the Indian tribes. The object too expressed, as that of the association, is one which I have ever had much at heart, and never omitted an occasion of promoting, while I have been in situations to do it with effect, and nothing, even now, in the calm of age and retirement, would excite in me a more lively interest than an approvable plan of raising that respectable and unfortunate people from the state of physical and moral abjection, to which they have been reduced by circumstances foreign to them. That the plan now proposed is entitled to unmixed approbation, I am not prepared to say, after mature consideration, and with all the partialities which its professed object would rightfully claim from me.

I shall not undertake to draw the line of demarcation between private associations of laudable views and unimposing numbers, and those whose magnitude may rivalise and jeopardise the march of regular government. Yet such a line does exist. I have seen the days, they were those which preceded the Revolution, when even this last and perilous engine became necessary; but they were days which no man would wish to see a second time. That was the case where the regular authorities of the government had combined against the rights of the people, and no means of correction remained to them, but to organise a collateral power, which, with their support, might rescue and secure their violated rights. But such is not the case with our government. We need hazard no collateral power, which, by a change of its original views, and assumption of others we know not how virtuous or how mischievous, would be ready organised and in force sufficient to shake the established foundations of society, and endanger its peace and the principles on which it is based. Is not the machine now proposed of this gigantic stature? It is to consist of the ex-Presidents of the United States, the Vice President, the Heads of all the executive departments, the members of the supreme judiciary, the Governors of the several States and territories, all the members of both Houses of Congress, all the general officers of the army, the commissioners of the navy, all Presidents and Professors of colleges and theological seminaries, all the clergy of the United States, the Presidents and Secretaries of all associations having relation to Indians, all commanding officers within or near Indian territories, all Indian superintendants and agents; all these *ex-officio*; and as many private individuals as will pay a certain price for membership. Observe too, that the clergy will constitute* nineteen twentieths of this association, and, by the law of the majority, may command the twentieth part, which, composed of all the high authorities of the United States, civil and military, may be outvoted and wielded by the nineteen parts with uncontrollable power, both as to purpose and process. Can this formidable array be reviewed without dismay? It will be said, that in this association will be all the confidential officers of the government; the choice of the people themselves. No man on earth has more implicit confidence than myself in

*The clergy of the United States may probably be estimated at eight thousand. The residue of this society at four hundred; but if the former number be halved, the reasoning will be the same.

the integrity and discretion of this chosen band of servants.
But is confidence or discretion, or is *strict limit*, the principle
of our constitution? It will comprehend, indeed, all the functionaries of the government; but seceded from their constitutional stations as guardians of the nation, and acting not by
the laws of their station, but by those of a voluntary society,
having no limit to their purposes but the same will which
constitutes their existence. It will be the authorities of the
people and all influential characters from among them, arrayed on one side, and on the other, the people themselves
deserted by their leaders. It is a fearful array. It will be said,
that these are imaginary fears. I know they are so at present.
I know it is as impossible for these agents of our choice and
unbounded confidence, to harbor machinations against the
adored principles of our constitution, as for gravity to change
its direction, and gravid bodies to mount upwards. The fears
are indeed imaginary: but the example is *real*. Under its authority, as a precedent, future associations will arise with objects at which we should shudder at this time. The society of
Jacobins, in another country, was instituted on principles and
views as virtuous as ever kindled the hearts of patriots. It was
the pure patriotism of their purposes which extended their
association to the limits of the nation, and rendered their
power within it boundless; and it was this power which degenerated their principles and practices to such enormities, as
never before could have been imagined. Yet these were men;
and we and our descendants will be no more. The present is
a case where, if ever, we are to guard against ourselves; not
against ourselves as we are, but as we may be; for who can
now imagine what we may become under circumstances not
now imaginable? The object too of this institution, seems to
require so hazardous an example as little as any which could
be proposed. The government is, at this time, going on with
the process of civilising the Indians, on a plan probably as
promising as any one of us is able to devise, and with resources more competent than we could expect to command
by voluntary taxation. Is it that the new characters called into
association with those of the government, are wiser than
these? Is it that a plan originated by a meeting of private individuals, is better than that prepared by the concentrated

wisdom of the nation, of men not self-chosen, but clothed with the full confidence of the people? Is it that there is no danger that a new authority, marching, independently, along side of the government, in the same line and to the same object, may not produce collision, may not thwart and obstruct the operations of the government, or wrest the object entirely from their hands? Might we not as well appoint a committee for each department of the government, to counsel and direct its head separately, as volunteer ourselves to counsel and direct the whole, in mass? And might we not do it as well for their foreign, their fiscal, and their military, as for their Indian affairs? And how many societies, auxiliary to the government, may we expect to see spring up, in imitation of this, offering to associate themselves in this and that of its functions? In a word, why not take the government out of its constitutional hands, associate them indeed with us, to preserve a semblance that the acts are theirs, but insuring them to be our own by allowing them a minor vote only?

These considerations have impressed my mind with a force so irresistible, that (in duty bound to answer your polite letter, without which I should not have obtruded an opinion,) I have not been able to withhold the expression of them. Not knowing the individuals who have proposed this plan, I cannot be conceived as entertaining personal disrespect for them. On the contrary, I see in the printed list persons for whom I cherish sentiments of sincere friendship; and others, for whose opinions and purity of purpose I have the highest respect. Yet thinking as I do, that this association is unnecessary; that the government is proceeding to the same object under control of the law; that they are competent to it in wisdom, in means, and inclination; that this association, this wheel within a wheel, is more likely to produce collision than aid; and that it is, in its magnitude, of dangerous example; I am bound to say, that, as a dutiful citizen, I cannot in conscience become a member of this society, possessing as it does my entire confidence in the integrity of its views. I feel with awe the weight of opinion to which I may be opposed, and that, for myself, I have need to ask the indulgence of a belief, that the opinion I have given is the best result I can deduce from my own reason and experience, and that it is sincerely conscientious. Repeating therefore, my just acknowledgments for the honor proposed to me; I beg leave to add the assurances to the society and yourself of my highest confidence and consideration.

A UNITARIAN CREED
To Dr. Benjamin Waterhouse

Monticello, June 26, 1822

DEAR SIR,—I have received and read with thankfulness and pleasure your denunciation of the abuses of tobacco and wine. Yet, however sound in its principles, I expect it will be but a sermon to the wind. You will find it as difficult to inculcate these sanative precepts on the sensualities of the present day, as to convince an Athanasian that there is but one God. I wish success to both attempts, and am happy to learn from you that the latter, at least, is making progress, and the more rapidly in proportion as our Platonizing Christians make more stir and noise about it. The doctrines of Jesus are simple, and tend all to the happiness of man.

1. That there is one only God, and he all perfect.

2. That there is a future state of rewards and punishments.

3. That to love God with all thy heart and thy neighbor as thyself, is the sum of religion. These are the great points on which he endeavored to reform the religion of the Jews. But compare with these the demoralizing dogmas of Calvin.

1. That there are three Gods.

2. That good works, or the love of our neighbor, are nothing.

3. That faith is every thing, and the more incomprehensible the proposition, the more merit in its faith.

4. That reason in religion is of unlawful use.

5. That God, from the beginning, elected certain individuals to be saved, and certain others to be damned; and that no crimes of the former can damn them; no virtues of the latter save.

Now, which of these is the true and charitable Christian? He who believes and acts on the simple doctrines of Jesus? Or the impious dogmatists, as Athanasius and Calvin? Verily

I say these are the false shepherds foretold as to enter not by the door into the sheepfold, but to climb up some other way. They are mere usurpers of the Christian name, teaching a counter-religion made up of the *deliria* of crazy imaginations, as foreign from Christianity as is that of Mahomet. Their blasphemies have driven thinking men into infidelity, who have too hastily rejected the supposed author himself, with the horrors so falsely imputed to him. Had the doctrines of Jesus been preached always as pure as they came from his lips, the whole civilized world would now have been Christian. I rejoice that in this blessed country of free inquiry and belief, which has surrendered its creed and conscience to neither kings nor priests, the genuine doctrine of one only God is reviving, and I trust that there is not a *young man* now living in the United States who will not die an Unitarian.

But much I fear, that when this great truth shall be re-established, its votaries will fall into the fatal error of fabricating formulas of creed and confessions of faith, the engines which so soon destroyed the religion of Jesus, and made of Christendom a mere Aceldama; that they will give up morals for mysteries, and Jesus for Plato. How much wiser are the Quakers, who, agreeing in the fundamental doctrines of the gospel, schismatize about no mysteries, and, keeping within the pale of common sense, suffer no speculative differences of opinion, any more than of feature, to impair the love of their brethren. Be this the wisdom of Unitarians, this the holy mantle which shall cover within its charitable circumference all who believe in one God, and who love their neighbor! I conclude my sermon with sincere assurances of my friendly esteem and respect.

SERIATIM OPINIONS AND THE HISTORY OF PARTIES
To Justice William Johnson

Monticello, Oct. 27, 1822

DEAR SIR,—I have deferred my thanks for the copy of your Life of Genl. Greene, until I could have time to read it. This I have done, and with the greatest satisfaction; and can now more understandingly express the gratification it has afforded me. I really rejoice that we have at length a fair history of the Southern war. It proves how much we were left to defend ourselves as we could, while the resources of the Union were so disproportionately devoted to the North. I am glad too to see the Romance of Lee removed from the shelf of History to that of Fable. Some small portion of the transactions he relates were within my own knolege; and of these I can say he has given more falsehood than fact; and I have heard many officers declare the same as to what had passed under their eyes. Yet this book had begun to be quoted as history. Greene was truly a great man, he had not perhaps all the qualities which so peculiarly rendered Genl. Washington the fittest man on earth for directing so great a contest under so great difficulties. Difficulties proceeding not from lukewarmness in our citizens or their functionaries, as our military leaders supposed; but from the pennyless condition of a people, totally shut out from all commerce & intercourse with the world, and therefore without any means for converting their labor into money. But Greene was second to no one in enterprise, in resource, in sound judgment, promptitude of decision, and every other military talent. In addition to the work you have given us, I look forward with anxiety to that you promise in the last paragraph of your book. Lee's military fable you have put down. Let not the invidious libel on the views of the Republican party, and on their regeneration of the government go down to posterity as hypocritically masked. I was myself too laboriously employed, while in office, and too old when I left it, to do justice to those who had labored so faithfully to arrest our course towards monarchy, and to secure the result of our revolutionary sufferings and sacrifices in a government bottomed on the only safe basis, the elective will of the people. You are young enough for the task, and I hope you will undertake it.

There is a subject respecting the practice of the court of which you are a member, which has long weighed on my mind, on which I have long thought I would write to you, and which I will take this opportunity of doing. It is in truth a delicate undertaking, & yet such is my opinion of your candor and devotedness to the Constitution, in it's true spirit, that I am sure I shall meet your approbation in unbosoming myself to you. The subject of my uneasiness is the habitual mode of making up and delivering the opinions of the supreme court of the US.

You know that from the earliest ages of the English law, from the date of the year-books, at least, to the end of the IId George, the judges of England, in all but self-evident cases, delivered their opinions seriatim, with the reasons and authorities which governed their decisions. If they sometimes consulted together, and gave a general opinion, it was so rarely as not to excite either alarm or notice. Besides the light which their separate arguments threw on the subject, and the instruction communicated by their several modes of reasoning, it shewed whether the judges were unanimous or divided, and gave accordingly more or less weight to the judgment as a precedent. It sometimes happened too that when there were three opinions against one, the reasoning of the one was so much the most cogent as to become afterwards the law of the land. When Ld. Mansfield came to the bench he introduced the habit of caucusing opinions. The judges met at their chambers, or elsewhere, secluded from the presence of the public, and made up what was to be delivered as the opinion of the court. On the retirement of Mansfield, Ld. Kenyon put an end to the practice, and the judges returned to that of seriatim opinions, and practice it habitually to this day, I believe. I am not acquainted with the late reporters, do not possess them, and state the fact from the information of others. To come now to ourselves I know nothing of what is done in other states, but in this our great and good Mr. Pendleton was, after the revolution, placed at the head of the court of Appeals. He adored Ld. Mansfield, & considered him as the greatest luminary of law that any age had ever produced, and he introduced into the court over which he presided, Mansfield's practice of making up opinions in secret & delivering them as the Oracles of the court, in mass. Judge Roane, when he came to that bench, broke up the practice, refused to hatch judgments, in Conclave, or to let others deliver opinions for him. At what time the seriatim opinions ceased in the supreme Court of the US., I am not informed. They continued I know to the end of the 3d Dallas in 1800. Later than which I have no Reporter of that court.

About that time the present C. J. came to the bench. Whether he carried the practice of Mr. Pendleton to it, or who, or when I do not know; but I understand from others it is now the habit of the court, & I suppose it true from the cases sometimes reported in the newspapers, and others which I casually see, wherein I observe that the opinions were uniformly prepared in private. Some of these cases too have been of such importance, of such difficulty, and the decisions so grating to a portion of the public as to have merited the fullest explanation from every judge seriatim, of the reasons which had produced such convictions on his mind. It was interesting to the public to know whether these decisions were really unanimous, or might not perhaps be of 4. against 3. and consequently prevailing by the preponderance of one voice only. The Judges holding their offices for life are under two responsibilities only. 1. Impeachment. 2. Individual reputation. But this practice compleatly withdraws them from both. For nobody knows what opinion any individual member gave in any case, nor even that he who delivers the opinion, concurred in it himself. Be the opinion therefore ever so impeachable, having been done in the dark it can be proved on no one. As to the 2d guarantee, personal reputation, it is shielded compleatly. The practice is certainly convenient for the lazy, the modest & the incompetent. It saves them the trouble of developing their opinion methodically and even of making up an opinion at all. That of seriatim argument shews whether every judge has taken the trouble of understanding the case, of investigating it minutely, and of forming an opinion for himself, instead of pinning it on another's sleeve. It would certainly be right to abandon this practice in order to give to our citizens one and all, that confidence in their judges which must be so desirable to the judges themselves, and so important to the cement of the union. During the administration of Genl. Washington, and while E. Randolph was Attorney General, he was required by Congress to digest the judiciary laws into a single one, with such amendments as might be thought proper. He prepared a section requiring the Judges to give their opinions seriatim, in writing, to be recorded in a distinct volume. Other business prevented this bill from being taken up, and it passed off, but such a volume would have been the best possible book of reports, and the better, as unincumbered with the hired sophisms and perversions of Counsel.

What do you think of the state of parties at this time? An opinion prevails that there is no longer any distinction, that the republicans & Federalists are compleatly amalgamated but it is not so. The amalgamation is of name only, not of principle. All indeed call themselves by the name of Republicans, because that of Federalists was extinguished in the battle of New Orleans. But the truth is that finding that monarchy is a desperate wish in this country, they rally to the point which they think next best, a consolidated government. Their aim is now therefore to break down the rights reserved by the constitution to the states as a bulwark against that consolidation, the fear of which produced the whole of the opposition to the constitution at it's birth. Hence new Republicans in Congress, preaching the doctrines of the old Federalists, and the new nick-names of Ultras and Radicals. But I trust they will fail under the new, as the old name, and that the friends of the real constitution and union will prevail against consolidation, as they have done against monarchism. I scarcely know myself which is most to be deprecated, a consolidation, or dissolution of the states. The horrors of both are beyond the reach of human foresight.

I have written you a long letter, and committed to you thoughts which I would do to few others. If I am right, you will approve them; if wrong, commiserate them as the dreams of a Superannuate about things from which he is to derive neither good nor harm. But you will still receive them as a proof of my confidence in the rectitude of your mind and principles, of which I pray you to receive entire assurance with that of my continued and great friendship and respect.

RELIGION AND THE UNIVERSITY
To Dr. Thomas Cooper

Monticello, November 2, 1822

DEAR SIR,—Your favor of October the 18th came to hand yesterday. The atmosphere of our country is unquestionably charged with a threatening cloud of fanaticism, lighter in some parts, denser in others, but too heavy in all. I had no idea, however, that in Pennsylvania, the cradle of toleration and freedom of religion, it could have arisen to the height you describe. This must be owing to the growth of Presbyterianism. The blasphemy and absurdity of the five points of Calvin, and the impossibility of defending them, render their advocates impatient of reasoning, irritable, and prone to denunciation. In Boston, however, and its neighborhood, Unitarianism has advanced to so great strength, as now to humble this haughtiest of all religious sects; insomuch that they condescend to interchange with them and the other sects, the civilities of preaching freely and frequently in each others' meeting-houses. In Rhode Island, on the other hand, no sectarian preacher will permit an Unitarian to pollute his desk. In our Richmond there is much fanaticism, but chiefly among the women. They have their night meetings and praying parties, where, attended by their priests, and sometimes by a hen-pecked husband, they pour forth the effusions of their love to Jesus, in terms as amatory and carnal, as their modesty would permit them to use to a mere earthly lover. In our village of Charlottesville, there is a good degree of religion, with a small spice only of fanaticism. We have four sects, but without either church or meeting-house. The courthouse is the common temple, one Sunday in the month to each. Here, Episcopalian and Presbyterian, Methodist and Baptist, meet together, join in hymning their Maker, listen with attention and devotion to each others' preachers, and all mix in society with perfect harmony. It is not so in the districts where Presbyterianism prevails undividedly. Their ambition and tyranny would tolerate no rival if they had power. Systematical in grasping at an ascendency over all other sects, they aim, like the Jesuits, at engrossing the education of the country, are hostile to every institution which they do not direct, and jealous at seeing others begin to attend at all to that object. The diffusion of instruction, to which there is now so growing an attention, will be the remote remedy to this fever of fanaticism; while the more proximate one will be the progress of Unitarianism. That this will, ere long, be the religion of the majority from north to south, I have no doubt.

In our university you know there is no Professorship of Divinity. A handle has been made of this, to disseminate an idea that this is an institution, not merely of no religion, but against all religion. Occasion was taken at the last meeting of the Visitors, to bring forward an idea that might silence this calumny, which weighed on the minds of some honest friends to the institution. In our annual report to the legislature, after stating the constitutional reasons against a public establishment of any religious instruction, we suggest the expediency of encouraging the different religious sects to establish, each for itself, a professorship of their own tenets, on the confines of the university, so near as that their students may attend the lectures there, and have the free use of our library, and every other accommodation we can give them; preserving, however, their independence of us and of each other. This fills the chasm objected to ours, as a defect in an institution professing to give instruction in *all* useful sciences. I think the invitation will be accepted, by some sects from candid intentions, and by others from jealousy and rivalship. And by bringing the sects together, and mixing them with the mass of other students, we shall soften their asperities, liberalize and neutralize their prejudices, and make the general religion a religion of peace, reason, and morality.

The time of opening our university is still as uncertain as ever. All the pavilions, boarding houses, and dormitories are done. Nothing is now wanting but the central building for a library and other general purposes. For this we have no funds, and the last legislature refused all aid. We have better hopes of the next. But all is uncertain. I have heard with regret of disturbances on the part of the students in your seminary. The article of discipline is the most difficult in American education. Premature ideas of independence, too little repressed by parents, beget a spirit of insubordination, which is the great obstacle to science with us, and a principal cause of its decay since the revolution. I look to it with dismay in our institution, as a breaker ahead, which I am far from being confident we shall be able to weather. The advance of age, and tardy pace of the public patronage, may probably spare me the pain of witnessing consequences.

I salute you with constant friendship and respect.

CALVIN AND COSMOLOGY

To John Adams

Monticello, April 11, 1823

DEAR SIR,—The wishes expressed, in your last favor, that I may continue in life and health until I become a Calvinist, at least in his exclamation of '*mon Dieu!* jusque à quand'! would make me immortal. I can never join Calvin in addressing *his god*. He was indeed an Atheist, which I can never be; or rather his religion was Dæmonism. If ever man worshipped a false god, he did. The being described in his 5. points is not the God whom you and I acknolege and adore, the Creator and benevolent governor of the world; but a dæmon of malignant spirit. It would be more pardonable to believe in no god at all, than to blaspheme him by the atrocious attributes of Calvin. Indeed I think that every Christian sect gives a great handle to Atheism by their general dogma that, without a revelation, there would not be sufficient proof of the being of a god. Now one sixth of mankind only are supposed to be Christians: the other five sixths then, who do not believe in the Jewish and Christian revelation, are without a knolege of the existence of a god! This gives compleatly a gain de cause to the disciples of Ocellus, Timaeus, Spinosa, Diderot and D'Holbach. The argument which they rest on as triumphant and unanswerable is that, in every hypothesis of Cosmogony you must admit an eternal pre-existence of something; and according to the rule of sound philosophy, you are never to employ two principles to solve a difficulty when one will suffice. They say then that it is more simple to believe at once in the eternal pre-existence of the world, as it is now going on, and may for ever go on by the principle of reproduction which we see and witness, than to believe in the eternal pre-existence of an ulterior cause, or Creator of the world, a being whom we see not, and know not, of whose form substance and mode or place of existence, or of action no sense informs us, no power of the mind enables us to delineate or comprehend. On the contrary I hold (without appeal to revelation) that when we take a view of the Universe, in it's parts general or particular, it is impossible for the human mind not to percieve and feel a conviction of design, consummate skill, and indefinite power in every atom of it's composition. The movements of the heavenly bodies, so exactly held in their course by the balance of centrifugal and centripetal forces, the structure of our earth itself, with it's distribution of lands, waters and atmosphere, animal and vegetable bodies, examined in all their minutest particles, insects mere atoms of life, yet as perfectly organised as man or mammoth, the mineral substances, their generation and uses, it is impossible, I say, for the human mind not to believe that there is, in all this, design, cause and effect, up to an ultimate cause, a fabricator of all things from matter and motion, their preserver and regulator while permitted to exist in their present forms, and their regenerator into new and other forms. We see, too, evident proofs of the necessity of a superintending power to maintain the Universe in it's course and order. Stars, well known, have disappeared, new ones have come into view, comets, in their incalculable courses, may run foul of suns and planets and require renovation under other laws; certain races of animals are become extinct; and, were there no restoring power, all existences might extinguish successively, one by one, until all should be reduced to a shapeless chaos. So irresistible are these evidences of an intelligent and powerful Agent that, of the infinite numbers of men who have existed thro' all time, they have believed, in the proportion of a million at least to Unit, in the hypothesis of an eternal pre-existence of a creator, rather than in that of a self-existent Universe. Surely this unanimous sentiment renders this more probable than that of the few in the other hypothesis. Some early Christians indeed have believed in the coeternal pre-existance of both the Creator and the world, without changing their relation of cause and effect. That this was the opinion of St. Thomas, we are informed by Cardinal Toleto, in these words 'Deus ab æterno fuit jam omnipotens, sicut cum produxit mundum. Ab æterno potuit producere mundum.—Si sol ab æterno esset, lumen ab æterno esset; et si pes, similiter vestigium. At lumen et vestigium effectus sunt efficientis solis et pedis; potuit ergo cum causâ æterna effectus coæterna esse. Cujus sententiæ est S. Thomas Theologorum primus' Cardinal Toleta.

Of the nature of this being we know nothing. Jesus tells us

that 'God is a spirit.' 4. John 24. but without defining what a
spirit is 'πνευμα ὁ Θεος. Down to the 3d. century we know
that it was still deemed material; but of a lighter subtler matter than our gross bodies. So says Origen. 'Deus igitur, cui
anima similis est, juxta Originem, reapte corporalis est; sed
graviorum tantum ratione corporum incorporeus.' These are
the words of Huet in his commentary on Origen. Origen
himself says 'appelatio ἀσωμματον apud nostros scriptores est
inusitata et incognita.' So also Tertullian 'quis autem negabit
Deum esse corpus, etsi deus spiritus? Spiritus etiam corporis
sui generis, in suâ effigie.' Tertullian. These two fathers were
of the 3d. century. Calvin's character of this supreme being
seems chiefly copied from that of the Jews. But the reformation of these blasphemous attributes, and substitution of
those more worthy, pure and sublime, seems to have been the
chief object of Jesus in his discources to the Jews: and his
doctrine of the Cosmogony of the world is very clearly laid
down in the 3 first verses of the 1st. chapter of John, in these
words, 'εν αρχη ην ὁ λογος, και ὁ λογος ην προς τον Θεον
και Θεος ην ὁ λογος. 'ᾰτος ην εν αρχη προς τον Θεον.
Παντα δε αυτᾰ εγενετο, και χωρις αυτᾰ εγενετο ᾰδε ἑν, ὁ
γεγονεν. Which truly translated means 'in the beginning God
existed, and reason (or mind) was with God, and that mind
was God. This was in the beginning with God. All things
were created by it, and without it was made not one thing
which was made'. Yet this text, so plainly declaring the doctrine of Jesus that the world was created by the supreme, intelligent being, has been perverted by modern Christians to
build up a second person of their tritheism by a mistranslation of the word λογος. One of it's legitimate meanings indeed is 'a word.' But, in that sense, it makes an unmeaning
jargon: while the other meaning 'reason', equally legitimate,
explains rationally the eternal preexistence of God, and his
creation of the world. Knowing how incomprehensible it was
that 'a word,' the mere action or articulation of the voice and
organs of speech could create a world, they undertake to
make of this articulation a second preexisting being, and ascribe to him, and not to God, the creation of the universe.
The Atheist here plumes himself on the uselessness of such a
God, and the simpler hypothesis of a self-existent universe.

The truth is that the greatest enemies to the doctrines of Jesus are those calling themselves the expositors of them, who have perverted them for the structure of a system of fancy absolutely incomprehensible, and without any foundation in his genuine words. And the day will come when the mystical generation of Jesus, by the supreme being as his father in the womb of a virgin will be classed with the fable of the generation of Minerva in the brain of Jupiter. But we may hope that the dawn of reason and freedom of thought in these United States will do away with all this artificial scaffolding, and restore to us the primitive and genuine doctrines of this the most venerated reformer of human errors.

So much for your quotation of Calvin's 'mon dieu! jusqu'a quand' in which, when addressed to the God of Jesus, and our God, I join you cordially, and await his time and will with more readiness than reluctance. May we meet there again, in Congress, with our antient Colleagues, and recieve with them the seal of approbation 'Well done, good and faithful servants.'

THE SUPREME COURT AND THE CONSTITUTION
To Justice William Johnson

Monticello, June 12, 1823

DEAR SIR,—Our correspondence is of that accommodating character, which admits of suspension at the convenience of either party, without inconvenience to the other. Hence this tardy acknowledgment of your favor of April the 11th. I learn from that with great pleasure, that you have resolved on continuing your history of parties. Our opponents are far ahead of us in preparations for placing their cause favorably before posterity. Yet I hope even from some of them the escape of precious truths, in angry explosions or effusions of vanity, which will betray the genuine monarchism of their principles. They do not themselves believe what they endeavor to inculcate, that we were an opposition party, not on principle, but merely seeking for office. The fact is, that at the formation of our government, many had formed their political opinions on

European writings and practices, believing the experience of old countries, and especially of England, abusive as it was, to be a safer guide than mere theory. The doctrines of Europe were, that men in numerous associations cannot be restrained within the limits of order and justice, but by forces physical and moral, wielded over them by authorities independent of their will. Hence their organization of kings, hereditary nobles, and priests. Still further to constrain the brute force of the people, they deem it necessary to keep them down by hard labor, poverty and ignorance, and to take from them, as from bees, so much of their earnings, as that unremitting labor shall be necessary to obtain a sufficient surplus barely to sustain a scanty and miserable life. And these earnings they apply to maintain their privileged orders in splendor and idleness, to fascinate the eyes of the people, and excite in them an humble adoration and submission, as to an order of superior beings. Although few among us had gone all these lengths of opinion, yet many had advanced, some more, some less, on the way. And in the convention which formed our government, they endeavored to draw the cords of power as tight as they could obtain them, to lessen the dependence of the general functionaries on their constituents, to subject to them those of the States, and to weaken their means of maintaining the steady equilibrium which the majority of the convention had deemed salutary for both branches, general and local. To recover, therefore, in practice the powers which the nation had refused, and to warp to their own wishes those actually given, was the steady object of the federal party. Ours, on the contrary, was to maintain the will of the majority of the convention, and of the people themselves. We believed, with them, that man was a rational animal, endowed by nature with rights, and with an innate sense of justice; and that he could be restrained from wrong and protected in right by moderate powers, confided to persons of his own choice, and held to their duties by dependence on his own will. We believed that the complicated organization of kings, nobles, and priests, was not the wisest nor best to effect the happiness of associated man; that wisdom and virtue were not hereditary, that the trappings of such a machinery, consumed by their expense, those earnings of industry, they were meant to protect, and, by the inequalities they produced, exposed liberty to sufferance. We believed that men, enjoying in ease and security the full fruits of their own industry, enlisted by all their interests on the side of law and order, habituated to think for themselves, and to follow their reason as their guide, would be more easily and safely governed, than with minds nourished in error, and vitiated and debased, as in Europe, by ignorance, indigence and oppression. The cherishment of the people then was our principle, the fear and distrust of them, that of the other party. Composed, as we were, of the landed and laboring interests of the country, we could not be less anxious for a government of law and order than were the inhabitants of the cities, the strongholds of federalism. And whether our efforts to save the principles and form of our constitution have not been salutary, let the present republican freedom, order and prosperity of our country determine. History may distort truth, and will distort it for a time, by the superior efforts at justification of those who are conscious of needing it most. Nor will the opening scenes of our present government be seen in their true aspect, until the letters of the day, now held in private hoards, shall be broken up and laid open to public view. What a treasure will be found in General Washington's cabinet, when it shall pass into the hands of as candid a friend to truth as he was himself! When no longer, like Cæsar's notes and memorandums in the hands of Anthony, it shall be open to the high priests of federalism only, and garbled to say so much, and no more, as suits their views!

With respect to his farewell address, to the authorship of which, it seems, there are conflicting claims, I can state to you some facts. He had determined to decline re-election at the end of his first term, and so far determined, that he had requested Mr. Madison to prepare for him something valedictory, to be addressed to his constituents on his retirement. This was done, but he was finally persuaded to acquiesce in a second election, to which no one more strenuously pressed him than myself, from a conviction of the importance of strengthening, by longer habit, the respect necessary for that office, which the weight of his character only could effect. When, at the end of his second term, his Valedictory came out, Mr. Madison recognized in it several passages of his draught, several others, we were both satisfied, were from the pen of Hamilton, and others from that of the President himself. These he probably put into the hands of Hamilton to form into a whole, and hence it may all appear in Hamilton's hand-writing, as if it were all of his composition.

I have stated above, that the original objects of the federalists were, 1st, to warp our government more to the form and principles of monarchy, and, 2d, to weaken the barriers of the State governments as coördinate powers. In the first they have been so completely foiled by the universal spirit of the nation, that they have abandoned the enterprise, shrunk from the odium of their old appellation, taken to themselves a participation of ours, and under the pseudo-republican mask, are now aiming at their second object, and strengthened by unsuspecting or apostate recruits from our ranks, are advancing fast towards an ascendancy. I have been blamed for saying, that a prevalence of the doctrines of consolidation would one day call for reformation or *revolution*. I answer by asking if a single State of the Union would have agreed to the constitution, had it given all powers to the General Government? If the whole opposition to it did not proceed from the jealousy and fear of every State, of being subjected to the other States in matters merely its own? And if there is any reason to believe the States more disposed now than then, to acquiesce in this general surrender of all their rights and powers to a consolidated government, one and undivided?

You request me confidentially, to examine the question, whether the Supreme Court has advanced beyond its constitutional limits, and trespassed on those of the State authorities? I do not undertake it, my dear Sir, because I am unable. Age and the wane of mind consequent on it, have disqualified me from investigations so severe, and researches so laborious. And it is the less necessary in this case, as having been already done by others with a logic and learning to which I could add nothing. On the decision of the case of Cohens *vs.* The State of Virginia, in the Supreme Court of the United States, in March, 1821, Judge Roane, under the signature of Algernon Sidney, wrote for the Enquirer a series of papers on the law of that case. I considered these papers maturely as they came out, and confess that they appeared to me to pulverize every word which had been delivered by Judge Marshall, of the extra-judicial part of his opinion; and all was extra-judicial, except the decision that the act of Congress had not purported to give to the corporation of Washington the authority claimed by their lottery law, of controlling the laws of the States within the States themselves. But unable to claim that case, he could not let it go entirely, but went on gratuitously to prove, that notwithstanding the eleventh amendment of the constitution, a State *could* be brought as a defendant, to the bar of his court; and again, that Congress might authorize a corporation of its territory to exercise legislation within a State, and paramount to the laws of that State. I cite the sum and result only of his doctrines, according to the impression made on my mind at the time, and still remaining. If not strictly accurate in circumstance, it is so in substance. This doctrine was so completely refuted by Roane, that if he can be answered, I surrender human reason as a vain and useless faculty, given to bewilder, and not to guide us. And I mention this particular case as one only of several, because it gave occasion to that thorough examination of the constitutional limits between the General and State jurisdictions, which you have asked for. There were two other writers in the same paper, under the signatures of Fletcher of Saltoun, and Somers, who, in a few essays, presented some very luminous and striking views of the question. And there was a particular paper which recapitulated all the cases in which it was thought the federal court had usurped on the State jurisdictions. These essays will be found in the Enquirers of 1821, from May the 10th to July the 13th. It is not in my present power to send them to you, but if Ritchie can furnish them, I will procure and forward them. If they had been read in the other States, as they were here, I think they would have left, there as here, no dissentients from their doctrine. The subject was taken up by our legislature of 1821–'22, and two draughts of remonstrances were prepared and discussed. As well as I remember, there was no difference of opinion as to the matter of right; but there was as to the expediency of a remonstrance at that time, the general mind of the States being then under extraordinary excitement by the Missouri question; and it was dropped on that consideration. But this case is not dead, it only sleepeth. The Indian Chief said he did not go to war for every petty injury by itself, but put it into his pouch, and when that was full, he then made war. Thank Heaven, we have provided a more peaceable and rational mode of redress.

This practice of Judge Marshall, of travelling out of his case to prescribe what the law would be in a moot case not before the court, is very irregular and very censurable. I recollect another instance, and the more particularly, perhaps, because it in some measure bore on myself. Among the midnight appointments of Mr. Adams, were commissions to some federal justices of the peace for Alexandria. These were signed and sealed by him, but not delivered. I found them on the table of the department of State, on my entrance into office, and I forbade their delivery. Marbury, named in one of them, applied to the Supreme Court for a mandamus to the Secretary of State, (Mr. Madison) to deliver the commission intended for him. The court determined at once, that being an original process, they had no cognizance of it; and therefore the question before them was ended. But the Chief Justice went on to lay down what the law would be, had they jurisdiction of the case, to wit: that they should command the delivery. The object was clearly to instruct any other court having the jurisdiction, what they should do if Marbury should apply to them. Besides the impropriety of this gratuitous interference, could anything exceed the perversion of law? For if there is any principle of law never yet contradicted, it is that delivery is one of the essentials to the validity of the deed. Although signed and sealed, yet as long as it remains in the hands of the party himself, it is in *fieri* only, it is not a deed, and can be made so only by its delivery. In the hands of a third person it may be made an escrow. But whatever is in the executive offices is certainly deemed to be in the hands of the President; and in this case, was actually in my hands, because, when I countermanded them, there was as yet no Secretary of State. Yet this case of Marbury and Madison is continually cited by bench and bar, as if it were settled law, without any animadversion on its being merely an *obiter* dissertation of the Chief Justice.

It may be impracticable to lay down any general formula of

words which shall decide at once, and with precision, in every case, this limit of jurisdiction. But there are two canons which will guide us safely in most of the cases. 1st. The capital and leading object of the constitution was to leave with the States all authorities which respected their own citizens only, and to transfer to the United States those which respected citizens of foreign or other States: to make us several as to ourselves, but one as to all others. In the latter case, then, constructions should lean to the general jurisdiction, if the words will bear it; and in favor of the States in the former, if possible to be so construed. And indeed, between citizens and citizens of the same State, and under their own laws, I know but a single case in which a jurisdiction is given to the General Government. That is, where anything but gold or silver is made a lawful tender, or the obligation of contracts is any otherwise impaired. The separate legislatures had so often abused that power, that the citizens themselves chose to trust it to the general, rather than to their own special authorities. 2d. On every question of construction, carry ourselves back to the time when the constitution was adopted, recollect the spirit manifested in the debates, and instead of trying what meaning may be squeezed out of the text, or invented against it, conform to the probable one in which it was passed. Let us try Cohen's case by these canons only, referring always, however, for full argument, to the essays before cited.

1. It was between a citizen and his own State, and under a law of his State. It was a domestic case, therefore, and not a foreign one.

2. Can it be believed, that under the jealousies prevailing against the General Government, at the adoption of the constitution, the States meant to surrender the authority of preserving order, of enforcing moral duties and restraining vice, within their own territory? And this is the present case, that of Cohen being under the ancient and general law of gaming. Can any good be effected by taking from the States the moral rule of their citizens, and subordinating it to the general authority, or to one of their corporations, which may justify forcing the meaning of words, hunting after possible constructions, and hanging inference on inference, from heaven to earth, like Jacob's ladder? Such an intention was impossi-

ble, and such a licentiousness of construction and inference, if exercised by both governments, as may be done with equal right, would equally authorize both to claim all power, general and particular, and break up the foundations of the Union. Laws are made for men of ordinary understanding, and should, therefore, be construed by the ordinary rules of common sense. Their meaning is not to be sought for in metaphysical subtleties, which may make anything mean everything or nothing, at pleasure. It should be left to the sophisms of advocates, whose trade it is, to prove that a defendant is a plaintiff, though dragged into court, *torto collo*, like Bonaparte's volunteers, into the field in chains, or that a power has been given, because it ought to have been given, *et alia talia*. The States supposed that by their tenth amendment, they had secured themselves against constructive powers. They were not lessoned yet by Cohen's case, nor aware of the slipperiness of the eels of the law. I ask for no straining of words against the General Government, nor yet against the States. I believe the States can best govern our home concerns, and the General Government our foreign ones. I wish, therefore, to see maintained that wholesome distribution of powers established by the constitution for the limitation of both; and never to see all offices transferred to Washington, where, further withdrawn from the eyes of the people, they may more secretly be bought and sold as at market.

But the Chief Justice says, "there must be an ultimate arbiter somewhere." True, there must; but does that prove it is either party? The ultimate arbiter is the people of the Union, assembled by their deputies in convention, at the call of Congress, or of two-thirds of the States. Let them decide to which they mean to give an authority claimed by two of their organs. And it has been the peculiar wisdom and felicity of our constitution, to have provided this peaceable appeal, where that of other nations is at once to force.

I rejoice in the example you set of *seriatim* opinions. I have heard it often noticed, and always with high approbation. Some of your brethren will be encouraged to follow it occasionally, and in time, it may be felt by all as a duty, and the sound practice of the primitive court be again restored. Why should not every judge be asked his opinion, and give it from the bench, if only by yea or nay? Besides ascertaining the fact of his opinion, which the public have a right to know, in order to judge whether it is impeachable or not, it would show whether the opinions were unanimous or not, and thus settle more exactly the weight of their authority.

The close of my second sheet warns me that it is time now to relieve you from this letter of unmerciful length. Indeed, I wonder how I have accomplished it, with two crippled wrists, the one scarcely able to move my pen, the other to hold my paper. But I am hurried sometimes beyond the sense of pain, when unbosoming myself to friends who harmonize with me in principle. You and I may differ occasionally in details of minor consequence, as no two minds, more than two faces, are the same in every feature. But our general objects are the same, to preserve the republican form and principles of our constitution and cleave to the salutary distribution of powers which that has established. These are the two sheet anchors of our Union. If driven from either, we shall be in danger of foundering. To my prayers for its safety and perpetuity, I add those for the continuation of your health, happiness, and usefulness to your country.

"RIVERS OF BLOOD MUST YET FLOW"

To John Adams

Monticello, Sep. 4, 1823

DEAR SIR,—Your letter of Aug. 15. was recieved in due time, and with the welcome of every thing which comes from you. With it's opinions on the difficulties of revolutions, from despotism to freedom, I very much concur. The generation which commences a revolution can rarely compleat it. Habituated from their infancy to passive submission of body and mind to their kings and priests, they are not qualified, when called on, to think and provide for themselves and their inexperience, their ignorance and bigotry make them instruments often, in the hands of the Bonapartes and Iturbides to defeat their own rights and purposes. This is the present situation of Europe and Spanish America. But it is not desperate. The light which has been shed on mankind by the art of printing has eminently changed the condition of the world. As yet that light has dawned on the midling classes only of the men of Europe. The kings and the rabble of equal ignorance, have not yet recieved it's rays; but it continues to spread. And, while printing is preserved, it can no more recede than the sun return on his course. A first attempt to recover the right of self-government may fail; so may a 2d. a 3d. etc., but as a younger, and more instructed race comes on, the sentiment becomes more and more intuitive, and a 4th. a 5th. or some subsequent one of the ever renewed attempts will ultimately succeed. In France the 1st. effort was defeated by Robespierre, the 2d. by Bonaparte, the 3d. by Louis XVIII. and his holy allies; another is yet to come, and all Europe, Russia excepted, has caught the spirit, and all will attain representative government, more or less perfect. This is now well understood to be a necessary check on kings, whom they will probably think it more prudent to chain and tame, than to exterminate. To attain all this however rivers of blood must yet flow, and years of desolation pass over. Yet the object is worth rivers of blood, and years of desolation for what inheritance so valuable can man leave to his posterity? The spirit of the Spaniard and his deadly and eternal hatred to a Frenchman, gives me much confidence that he will never submit, but finally defeat this atrocious violation of the laws of god and man under which he is suffering; and the wisdom and firmness of the Cortes afford reasonable hope that that nation will settle down in a temperate representative government, with an Executive properly subordinated to that. Portugal, Italy, Prussia, Germany, Greece will follow suit. You and I shall look down from another world on these glorious atchievements to man, which will add to the joys even of heaven.

I observe your toast of Mr. Jay on the 4th. of July, wherein you say that the omission of his signature to the Declaration of Independance was by *accident*. Our impressions as to this fact being different, I shall be glad to have mine corrected, if wrong. Jay, you know, had been in constant opposition to our laboring majority. Our estimate, at the time, was that he, Dickinson and Johnson of Maryland by their ingenuity, perseverance and partiality to our English connection, had constantly kept us a year behind where we ought to have been in our preparations and proceedings. From about the date of the Virginia instructions of May 15. 76. to declare Independance Mr. Jay absented himself from Congress, and never came there again until Dec. 78. Of course he had no part in the discussions or decision of that question. The instructions to their delegates by the Convention of New York, then sitting, to sign the Declaration, were presented to Congress on the 15th. of July only, and on that day the journals shew the absence of Mr. Jay by a letter recieved from him, as they had done as early as the 29th. of May by another letter. And, I think, he had been omitted by the Convention on a new election of Delegates when they changed their instructions. Of this last fact however having no evidence but an antient impression, I shall not affirm it. But whether so or not, no agency of *accident* appears in the case. This error of fact however, whether yours or mine, is of little consequence to the public. But truth being as cheap as error, it is as well to rectify it for our own satisfaction.

I have had a fever of about three weeks during the last and preceding month, from which I am entirely recovered except as to strength. Ever and affectionately yours

"THE BEST LETTER THAT EVER WAS WRITTEN . . ."

To John Adams

Monticello, Oct. 12, 1823

DEAR SIR,—I do not write with the ease which your letter of Sep. 18. supposes. Crippled wrists and fingers make writing slow and laborious. But, while writing to you, I lose the sense of these things, in the recollection of antient times, when youth and health made happiness out of every thing. I forget for a while the hoary winter of age, when we can think of nothing but how to keep ourselves warm, and how to get rid of our heavy hours until the friendly hand of death shall rid us of all at once. Against this tedium vitae however I am fortunately mounted on a Hobby, which indeed I should have better managed some 30. or 40. years ago, but whose easy amble is still sufficient to give exercise and amusement to an Octogenary rider. This is the establishment of an University, on a scale more comprehensive, and in a country more healthy and central than our old William and Mary, which these obstacles have long kept in a state of languor and inefficiency. But the tardiness with which such works proceed may render it doubtful whether I shall live to see it go into action.

Putting aside these things however for the present, I write this letter as due to a friendship co-eval with our government, and now attempted to be poisoned, when too late in life to be replaced by new affections. I had for some time observed, in the public papers, dark hints and mysterious innuendoes of a correspondence of yours with a friend, to whom you had opened your bosom without reserve, and which was to be made public by that friend, or his representative. And now it is said to be actually published. It has not yet reached us, but extracts have been given, and such as seemed most likely to draw a curtain of separation between you and myself. Were there no other motive than that of indignation against the author of this outrage on private confidence, whose shaft seems to have been aimed at yourself more particularly, this would make it the duty of every honorable mind to disappoint that aim, by opposing to it's impression a seven-fold shield of apathy and insensibility. With me however no such armour is needed. The circumstances of the times, in which we have happened to live, and the partiality of our friends, at a particular period, placed us in a state of apparent opposition, which some might suppose to be personal also; and there might not be wanting those who wish'd to make it so, by filling our ears with malignant falsehoods, by dressing up hideous phantoms of their own creation, presenting them to you under my name, to me under your's, and endeavoring to instill into our minds things concerning each other the most destitute of truth. And if there had been, at any time, a moment when we were off our guard, and in a temper to let the whispers of these people make us forget what we had known of each other for so many years, and years of so much trial, yet all men who have attended to the workings of the human mind, who have seen the false colours under which passion sometimes dresses the actions and motives of others, have seen also these passions subsiding with time and reflection, dissipating, like mists before the rising sun, and restoring to us the sight of all things in their true shape and colours. It would be strange indeed if, at our years, we were to go an age back to hunt up imaginary, or forgotten facts, to disturb the repose of affections so sweetening to the evening of our lives. Be assured, my dear Sir, that I am incapable of recieving the slightest impression from the effort now made to plant thorns on the pillow of age, worth, and wisdom, and to sow tares between friends who have been such for near half a century. Beseeching you then not to suffer your mind to be disquieted by this wicked attempt to poison it's peace, and praying you to throw it by, among the things which have never happened, I add sincere assurances of my unabated, and constant attachment, friendship and respect.

THE MONROE DOCTRINE

To the President of the United States
(JAMES MONROE)

Monticello, October 24, 1823

DEAR SIR,—The question presented by the letters you have sent me, is the most momentous which has ever been offered to my contemplation since that of Independence. That made us a nation, this sets our compass and points the course which we are to steer through the ocean of time opening on us. And never could we embark on it under circumstances more auspicious. Our first and fundamental maxim should be, never to entangle ourselves in the broils of Europe. Our second, never to suffer Europe to intermeddle with cis-Atlantic affairs. America, North and South, has a set of interests distinct from those of Europe, and peculiarly her own. She should therefore have a system of her own, separate and apart from that of Europe. While the last is laboring to become the domicil of despotism, our endeavor should surely be, to make our hemisphere that of freedom. One nation, most of all, could disturb us in this pursuit; she now offers to lead, aid, and accompany us in it. By acceding to her proposition, we detach her from the bands, bring her mighty weight into the scale of free government, and emancipate a continent at one stroke, which might otherwise linger long in doubt and difficulty. Great Britain is the nation which can do us the most harm of any one, or all on earth; and with her on our side we need not fear the whole world. With her then, we should most sedulously cherish a cordial friendship; and nothing would tend more to knit our affections than to be fighting once more, side by side, in the same cause. Not that I would purchase even her amity at the price of taking part in her wars. But the war in which the present proposition might engage us, should that be its consequence, is not her war, but ours. Its object is to introduce and establish the American system, of keeping out of our land all foreign powers, of never permitting those of Europe to intermeddle with the affairs of our nations. It is to maintain our own principle, not to depart from it. And if, to facilitate this, we can effect a division in the body of the European powers, and draw over to our side its most powerful member, surely we should do it. But I am clearly of Mr. Canning's opinion, that it will prevent instead of provoking war. With Great Britain withdrawn from their scale and shifted into that of our two continents, all Europe combined would not undertake such a war. For how would they propose to get at either enemy without superior fleets? Nor is the occasion to be slighted which this proposition offers, of declaring our protest against the atrocious violations of the rights of nations, by the interference of any one in the internal affairs of another, so flagitiously begun by Bonaparte, and now continued by the equally lawless Alliance, calling itself Holy.

But we have first to ask ourselves a question. Do we wish to acquire to our own confederacy any one or more of the Spanish provinces? I candidly confess, that I have ever looked on Cuba as the most interesting addition which could ever be made to our system of States. The control which, with Florida Point, this island would give us over the Gulf of Mexico, and the countries and isthmus bordering on it, as well as all those whose waters flow into it, would fill up the measure of our political well-being. Yet, as I am sensible that this can never be obtained, even with her own consent, but by war; and its independence, which is our second interest, (and especially its independence of England,) can be secured without it, I have no hesitation in abandoning my first wish to future chances, and accepting its independence, with peace and the friendship of England, rather than its association, at the expense of war and her enmity.

I could honestly, therefore, join in the declaration proposed, that we aim not at the acquisition of any of those possessions, that we will not stand in the way of any amicable arrangement between them and the mother country; but that we will oppose, with all our means, the forcible interposition of any other power, as auxiliary, stipendiary, or under any other form or pretext, and most especially, their transfer to any power by conquest, cession, or acquisition in any other way. I should think it, therefore, advisable, that the Executive should encourage the British government to a continuance in the dispositions expressed in these letters, by an assurance of his concurrence with them as far as his authority goes; and that as it may lead to war, the declaration of which requires an act of Congress, the case shall be laid before them for consideration at their first meeting, and under the reasonable aspect in which it is seen by himself.

I have been so long weaned from political subjects, and have so long ceased to take any interest in them, that I am sensible I am not qualified to offer opinions on them worthy of any attention. But the question now proposed involves consequences so lasting, and effects so decisive of our future destinies, as to rekindle all the interest I have heretofore felt on such occasions, and to induce me to the hazard of opinions, which will prove only my wish to contribute still my mite towards anything which may be useful to our country. And praying you to accept it at only what it is worth, I add the assurance of my constant and affectionate friendship and respect.

A PLAN OF EMANCIPATION
To Jared Sparks

Monticello, February 4, 1824

DEAR SIR,—I duly received your favor of the 13th, and with it, the last number of the North American Review. This has anticipated the one I should receive in course, but have not yet received, under my subscription to the new series. The article on the African colonization of the people of color, to which you invite my attention, I have read with great consideration. It is, indeed, a fine one, and will do much good. I learn from it more, too, than I had before known, of the degree of success and promise of that colony.

In the disposition of these unfortunate people, there are two rational objects to be distinctly kept in view. First. The establishment of a colony on the coast of Africa, which may introduce among the aborigines the arts of cultivated life, and the blessings of civilization and science. By doing this, we may make to them some retribution for the long course of injuries we have been committing on their population. And considering that these blessings will descend to the *"nati natorum, et qui nascentur ab illis,"* we shall in the long run have rendered them perhaps more good than evil. To fulfil this object, the colony of Sierra Leone promises well, and that of Mesurado adds to our prospect of success. Under this view, the colonization society is to be considered as a missionary society, having in view, however, objects more humane, more justifiable, and less aggressive on the peace of other nations, than the others of that appellation.

The subject object, and the most interesting to us, as coming home to our physical and moral characters, to our happiness and safety, is to provide an asylum to which we can, by degrees, send the whole of that population from among us, and establish them under our patronage and protection, as a separate, free and independent people, in some country and climate friendly to human life and happiness. That any place on the coast of Africa should answer the latter purpose, I have ever deemed entirely impossible. And without repeating the other arguments which have been urged by others, I will appeal to figures only, which admit no controversy. I shall speak in round numbers, not absolutely accurate, yet not so wide from truth as to vary the result materially. There are in the United States a million and a half of people of color in slavery. To send off the whole of these at once, nobody conceives to be practicable for us, or expedient for them. Let us take twenty-five years for its accomplishment, within which time they will be doubled. Their estimated value as property, in the first place, (for actual property has been lawfully vested in that form, and who can lawfully take it from the possessors?) at an average of two hundred dollars each, young and old, would amount to six hundred millions of dollars, which must be paid or lost by somebody. To this, add the cost of their transportation by land and sea to Mesurado, a year's provision of food and clothing, implements of husbandry and of their trades, which will amount to three hundred millions more, making thirty-six millions of dollars a year for twenty-five years, with insurance of peace all that time, and it is impossible to look at the question a second time. I am aware that at the end of about sixteen years, a gradual detraction from this sum will commence, from the gradual diminution of breeders, and go on during the remaining nine years. Calculate this deduction, and it is still impossible to look at the enterprise a second time. I do not say this to induce an inference that the getting rid of them is forever impossible. For that is neither my opinion nor my hope. But only that it cannot be done in this way. There is, I think, a way in which it can be done; that is, by emancipating the after-born, leaving them, on due compensation, with their mothers, until their services are worth their maintenance, and then putting them to industrious occupations, until a proper age for deportation. This was the result of my reflections on the subject five and forty years ago, and I have never yet been able to conceive any other practicable plan. It was sketched in the Notes on Virginia, under the fourteenth query. The estimated value of the new-born infant is so low, (say twelve dollars and fifty cents,) that it would probably be yielded by the owner gratis, and would thus reduce the six hundred millions of dollars, the first head of expense, to thirty-seven millions and a half; leaving only the expense of nourishment while with the mother, and of transportation. And from what fund are these expenses to be furnished? Why not from that of the lands which have been ceded by the very States now needing this relief? And ceded on no consideration, for the most part, but that of the general good of the whole. These cessions already constitute one fourth of the States of the Union. It may be said that these lands have been sold; are now the property of the citizens composing those States; and the money long ago received and expended. But an equivalent of lands in the territories since acquired, may be appropriated to that object, or so much, at least, as may be sufficient; and the object, although more important to the slave States, is highly so to the others also, if they were serious in their arguments on the Missouri question. The slave States, too, if more interested, would also contribute more by their gratuitous liberation, thus taking on themselves alone the first and heaviest item of expense.

In the plan sketched in the Notes on Virginia, no particular place of asylum was specified; because it was thought possible, that in the revolutionary state of America, then commenced, events might open to us some one within practicable distance. This has now happened. St. Domingo has become independent, and with a population of that color only; and if the public papers are to be credited, their Chief offers to pay their passage, to receive them as free citizens, and to provide them employment. This leaves, then, for the general confederacy, no expense but of nurture with the mother a few years, and would call, of course, for a very moderate appropriation of the vacant lands. Suppose the whole annual increase to be of sixty thousand effective births, fifty vessels, of four hundred tons burthen each, constantly employed in that short run, would carry off the increase of every year, and the old stock would die off in the ordinary course of nature, lessening from the commencement until its final disappearance. In this way no violation of private right is proposed. Voluntary surrenders would probably come in as fast as the means to be provided for their care would be competent to it. Looking at my own State only, and I presume not to speak for the others, I verily believe that this surrender of property would not amount to more, annually, than half our present direct taxes, to be continued fully about twenty or twenty-five years, and then gradually diminishing for as many more until their final extinction; and even this half tax would not be paid in cash, but by the delivery of an object which they have never yet known or counted as part of their property; and those not possessing the object will be called on for nothing. I do not go into all the details of the burthens and benefits of this operation. And who could estimate its blessed effects? I leave this to those who will live to see their accomplishment, and to enjoy a beatitude forbidden to my age. But I leave it with this admonition, to rise and be doing. A million and a half are within their control; but six millions, (which a majority of those now living will see them attain,) and one million of these fighting men, will say, "we will not go."

I am aware that this subject involves some constitutional scruples. But a liberal construction, justified by the object, may go far, and an amendment of the constitution, the whole length necessary. The separation of infants from their mothers, too, would produce some scruples of humanity. But this would be straining at a gnat, and swallowing a camel.

I am much pleased to see that you have taken up the subject of the duty on imported books. I hope a crusade will be kept up against it, until those in power shall become sensible of this stain on our legislation, and shall wipe it from their code, and from the remembrance of man, if possible.

I salute you with assurances of high respect and esteem.

PROFESSORS FROM ABROAD
To Dugald Stewart

Monticello in Virginia, Apr. 26, 1824

DEAR SIR,—It is now 35 years since I had the great pleasure of becoming acquainted with you in Paris, and since we saw together Louis XVI. led in triumph by his people thro' the streets of his capital; these years too have been like ages in the events they have engendered without seeming at all to have bettered the condñ of suffering man. Yet his mind has

been opening and advancing, a sentiment of his wrongs has
been spreading, and it will end in the ultimate establishment
of his rights. To effect this nothing is wanting but a general
concurrence of will, and some fortunate accident will produce
that. At a subsequent period you were so kind as to recall me
to your recollection on the publicñ of your invaluable book
on the Philosophy of the Human Mind, a copy of which you
sent me, and I have been happy to see it become the text
book of most of our colleges & academies, and pass thro'
several reimpressions in the U.S. An occurrence of a character
dear to us both leads again to a renewal of our recollections
and associates us in an occasion of still rendering some service
to those we are about to leave. The State of Virgā, of which
I am a native and resident, is establishing an university on a
scale as extensive and liberal as circumstances permit or call
for. We have been 4 or 5 years in preparing our buildings,
which are now ready to recieve their tenants. We proceed,
therefore, to the engaging professors, and anxious to recieve
none but of the highest grade of science in their respective
lines, we find we must have recourse to Europe, where alone
that grade is to be found, and to Gr. Br. of preference, as the
land of our own language, morals, manners, and habits. To
make the selection we send a special agent, Mr Francis W.
Gilmer, who will have the honor of delivering you this letter.
He is well educated himself in most of the branches of science, of correct morals and habits, an enlarged mind, and a
discretion meriting entire confidence. From the universities of
Oxford and Cambridge, where we expect he will find persons
duly qualified in the particular branches in which these seminaries are respectively eminent, he will pass on to Edinburg,
distinguished for it's school of Medicine as well as of other
sciences, but when arrived there he will be a perfect stranger,
and would have to grope his way in darkness and uncertainty;
you can lighten his path, and to beseech you to do so is the
object of this letter. Your knolege of persons and characters
there can guard him against being misled and lead him to the
consummation of our wishes. We do not expect to engage the
high characters there who are at the head of their schools,
established in offices, honors, & emoluments which can be

bettered no where. But we know there is always a junior set of aspirants, treading on their heels, ready to take their places, and as well & sometimes better qualified than they are. These persons, unsettled as yet, surrounded by competitors of equal claims, and perhaps greater credit and interest, may be willing to accept immediately a comfortable certainty here in place of uncertain hopes there, and a lingering delay of even these. From this description of persons we may hope to procure characters of the first order of science. But how to distinguish them? For we are told that were the mission of our agent once known, he would be overwhelmed with applicants, unworthy as well as worthy, yet all supported on recommendñs and certificates equally exaggerated, and by names so respectable as to confound all discrimination. Yet this discrimination is all important to us. An unlucky selection at first would blast all our prospects. Let me beseech you, then, good Sir, to lead Mr. Gilmer by the hand in his researches, to instruct him as to the competent characters, & guard him against those not so. Besides the first degree of eminence in science, a professor with us must be of sober and correct morals & habits, having the talent of communicating his knolege with facility, and of an accomodating and peaceable temper. The latter is all important for the harmony of the institution. For minuter particulars I will refer you to Mr. Gilmer, who possesses a full knolege of everything & our full confidence in everything. He takes with him plans of our establm't, which will shew the comfortable accommodñs provided for the professors, whether with or without families; and by the expensiveness and extent of the scale they will see it is not an ephemeral thing to which they are invited.

A knolege of your character & disposñs to do good dispenses with all apology for the trouble I give you. While the character and success of this institñ, involving the future hopes and happiness of my country, will justify the anxieties I feel in the choice of it's professors, I am sure the object will excite in your breast such sympathies of kind disposñ, as will give us the benefits we ask of your counsels & attentions. And, with my acknolegements for these, accept assurances of constant and sincere attamt, esteem & respect.

SAXONS, CONSTITUTIONS, AND A CASE OF
PIOUS FRAUD

To Major John Cartwright

Monticello, June 5, 1824

DEAR AND VENERABLE SIR,—I am much indebted for your
kind letter of February the 29th, and for your valuable volume
on the English constitution. I have read this with pleasure
and much approbation, and think it has deduced the constitution of the English nation from its rightful root, the Anglo-
Saxon. It is really wonderful, that so many able and learned
men should have failed in their attempts to define it with correctness. No wonder then, that Paine, who thought more
than he read, should have credited the great authorities who
have declared, that the will of parliament is the constitution
of England. So Marbois, before the French revolution, observed to me, that the Almanac Royal was the constitution of
France. Your derivation of it from the Anglo-Saxons, seems
to be made on legitimate principles. Having driven out the
former inhabitants of that part of the island called England,
they became aborigines as to you, and your lineal ancestors.
They doubtless had a constitution; and although they have
not left it in a written formula, to the precise text of which
you may always appeal, yet they have left fragments of their
history and laws, from which it may be inferred with considerable certainty. Whatever their history and laws shew to have
been practised with approbation, we may presume was permitted by their constitution; whatever was not so practised,
was not permitted. And although this constitution was violated and set at naught by Norman force, yet force cannot
change right. A perpetual claim was kept up by the nation,
by their perpetual demand of a restoration of their Saxon
laws; which shews they were never relinquished by the will of
the nation. In the pullings and haulings for these antient
rights, between the nation, and its kings of the races of Plan-
tagenets, Tudors and Stuarts, there was sometimes gain, and
sometimes loss, until the final re-conquest of their rights from
the Stuarts. The destitution and expulsion of this race broke
the thread of pretended inheritance, extinguished all regal
usurpations, and the nation re-entered into all its rights; and

although in their bill of rights they specifically reclaimed some only, yet the omission of the others was no renunciation of the right to assume their exercise also, whenever occasion should occur. The new King received no rights or powers, but those expressly granted to him. It has ever appeared to me, that the difference between the whig and the tory of England is, that the whig deduces his rights from the Anglo-Saxon source, and the tory from the Norman. And Hume, the great apostle of toryism, says, in so many words, note AA to chapter 42, that, in the reign of the Stuarts, 'it was the people who encroached upon the sovereign, not the sovereign who attempted, as is pretended, to usurp upon the people.' This supposes the Norman usurpations to be rights in his successors. And again, C, 159, 'the commons established a principle, which is noble in itself, and seems specious, but is belied by all history and experience, *that the people are the origin of all just power.*' And where else will this degenerate son of science, this traitor to his fellow men, find the origin of just powers, if not in the majority of the society? Will it be in the minority? Or in an individual of that minority?

Our Revolution commenced on more favorable ground. It presented us an album on which we were free to write what we pleased. We had no occasion to search into musty records, to hunt up royal parchments, or to investigate the laws and institutions of a semi-barbarous ancestry. We appealed to those of nature, and found them engraved on our hearts. Yet we did not avail ourselves of all the advantages of our position. We had never been permitted to exercise self-government. When forced to assume it, we were novices in its science. Its principles and forms had entered little into our former education. We established however some, although not all its important principles. The constitutions of most of our States assert, that all power is inherent in the people; that they may exercise it by themselves, in all cases to which they think themselves competent, (as in electing their functionaries executive and legislative, and deciding by a jury of themselves, in all judiciary cases in which any fact is involved,) or they may act by representatives, freely and equally chosen; that it is their right and duty to be at all times armed; that they are entitled to freedom of person, freedom of religion, freedom of property, and freedom of the press. In the structure of our legislatures, we think experience has proved the benefit of subjecting questions to two separate bodies of deliberants; but in constituting these, natural right has been mistaken, some making one of these bodies, and some both, the representatives of property instead of persons; whereas the double deliberation might be as well obtained without any violation of true principle, either by requiring a greater age in one of the bodies, or by electing a proper number of representatives of persons, dividing them by lots into two chambers, and renewing the division at frequent intervals, in order to break up all cabals. Virginia, of which I am myself a native and resident, was not only the first of the States, but, I believe I may say, the first of the nations of the earth, which assembled its wise men peaceably together to form a fundamental constitution, to commit it to writing, and place it among their archives, where every one should be free to appeal to its text. But this act was very imperfect. The other States, as they proceeded successively to the same work, made successive improvements; and several of them, still further corrected by experience, have, by conventions, still further amended their first forms. My own State has gone on so far with its *premiere ebauche*; but it is now proposing to call a convention for amendment. Among other improvements, I hope they will adopt the subdivision of our counties into wards. The former may be estimated at an average of twenty-four miles square; the latter should be about six miles square each, and would answer to the hundreds of your Saxon Alfred. In each of these might be, 1. An elementary school. 2. A company of militia, with its officers. 3. A justice of the peace and constable. 4. Each ward should take care of their own poor. 5. Their own roads. 6. Their own police. 7. Elect within themselves one or more jurors to attend the courts of justice. And 8. Give in at their Folk-house, their votes for all functionaries reserved to their election. Each ward would thus be a small republic within itself, and every man in the State would thus become an acting member of the common government, transacting in person a great portion of its rights and duties, subordinate indeed, yet important, and entirely within his competence.

The wit of man cannot devise a more solid basis for a free, durable and well administered republic.

With respect to our State and federal governments, I do not think their relations correctly understood by foreigners. They generally suppose the former subordinate to the latter. But this is not the case. They are co-ordinate departments of one simple and integral whole. To the State governments are reserved all legislation and administration, in affairs which concern their own citizens only, and to the federal government is given whatever concerns foreigners, or the citizens of other States; these functions alone being made federal. The one is the domestic, the other the foreign branch of the same government; neither having control over the other, but within its own department. There are one or two exceptions only to this partition of power. But, you may ask, if the two departments should claim each the same subject of power, where is the common umpire to decide ultimately between them? In cases of little importance or urgency, the prudence of both parties will keep them aloof from the questionable ground: but if it can neither be avoided nor compromised, a convention of the States must be called, to ascribe the doubtful power to that department which they may think best. You will perceive by these details, that we have not yet so far perfected our constitutions as to venture to make them unchangeable. But still, in their present state, we consider them not otherwise changeable than by the authority of the people, on a special election of representatives for that purpose expressly: they are until then the *lex legum*.

But can they be made unchangeable? Can one generation bind another, and all others, in succession forever? I think not. The Creator has made the earth for the living, not the dead. Rights and powers can only belong to persons, not to things, not to mere matter, unendowed with will. The dead are not even things. The particles of matter which composed their bodies, make part now of the bodies of other animals, vegetables, or minerals, of a thousand forms. To what then are attached the rights and powers they held while in the form of men? A generation may bind itself as long as its majority continues in life; when that has disappeared, another

majority is in place, holds all the rights and powers their predecessors once held, and may change their laws and institutions
to suit themselves. Nothing then is unchangeable but the inherent and unalienable rights of man.

I was glad to find in your book a formal contradition, at
length, of the judiciary usurpation of legislative powers; for
such the judges have usurped in their repeated decisions, that
Christianity is a part of the common law. The proof of the
contrary, which you have adduced, is incontrovertible; to wit,
that the common law existed while the Anglo-Saxons were
yet Pagans, at a time when they had never yet heard the name
of Christ pronounced, or knew that such a character had ever
existed. But it may amuse you, to shew when, and by what
means, they stole this law in upon us. In a case of *quare im-
pedit* in the Year-book 34. H. 6. folio 38. (anno 1458,) a question was made, how far the ecclesiastical law was to be
respected in a common law court? And Prisot, Chief Justice,
gives his opinion in these words, 'A tiel leis qu' ils de seint
eglise ont en *ancien scripture*, covient à nous à donner credence; car ceo common ley sur quels touts manners leis sont
fondés. Et auxy, Sir, nous sumus oblègés de conustre lour ley
de saint eglise: et semblablement ils sont obligés de conustre
nostre ley. Et, Sir, si poit apperer or à nous que l'evesque ad
fait come un ordinary fera en tiel cas, adong nous devons ceo
adjuger bon, ou auterment nemy,' &c. See S. C. Fitzh. Abr.
Qu. imp. 89. Bro. Abr. Qu. imp. 12. Finch in his first book,
c. 3. is the first afterwards who quotes this case, and mistakes
it thus. 'To such laws of the church as have warrant in *holy
scripture*, our law giveth credence.' And cites Prisot; mistrans-
lating *'ancien scripture,'* into *'holy scripture.'* Whereas Prisot
palpably says, 'to such laws as those of holy church have in
antient writing, it is proper for us to give credence;' to wit, to
their *antient written* laws. This was in 1613, a century and a
half after the dictum of Prisot. Wingate, in 1658, erects this
false translation into a maxim of the common law, copying
the words of Finch, but citing Prisot. Wing. Max. 3. And
Sheppard, title, 'Religion,' in 1675, copies the same mistranslation, quoting the Y. B. Finch and Wingate. Hale expresses it
in these words; 'Christianity is parcel of the laws of England.'
1 Ventr. 293. 3 Keb. 607. But he quotes no authority. By these

echoings and re-echoings from one to another, it had become so established in 1728, that in the case of the King *vs.* Woolston, 2 Stra. 834, the court would not suffer it to be debated, whether to write against Christianity was punishable in the temporal court at common law? Wood, therefore, 409, ventures still to vary the phrase, and say, that all blasphemy and profaneness are offences by the common law; and cites 2 Stra. Then Blackstone, in 1763, IV. 59, repeats the words of Hale, that 'Christianity is part of the laws of England,' citing Ventris and Strange. And finally, Lord Mansfield, with a little qualification, in Evans' case, in 1767, says, that 'the essential principles of revealed religion are part of the common law.' Thus ingulphing Bible, Testament and all into the common law, without citing any authority. And thus we find this chain of authorities hanging link by link, one upon another, and all ultimately on one and the same hook, and that a mistranslation of the words *'ancien scripture,'* used by Prisot. Finch quotes Prisot; Wingate does the same. Sheppard quotes Prisot, Finch and Wingate. Hale cites nobody. The court in Woolston's case, cite Hale. Wood cites Woolston's case. Blackstone quotes Woolston's case and Hale. And Lord Mansfield, like Hale, ventures it on his own authority. Here I might defy the best read lawyer to produce another scrip of authority for this judiciary forgery; and I might go on further to shew, how some of the Anglo-Saxon priests interpolated into the text of Alfred's laws, the 20th, 21st, 22nd and 23rd chapters of Exodus, and the 15th of the Acts of the Apostles, from the 23rd to the 29th verses. But this would lead my pen and your patience too far. What a conspiracy this, between Church and State! Sing Tantarara, rogues all, rogues all, Sing Tantarara, rogues all!

I must still add to this long and rambling letter, my acknowledgments for your good wishes to the University we are now establishing in this State. There are some novelties in it. Of that of a professorship of the principles of government, you express your approbation. They will be founded in the rights of man. That of agriculture, I am sure, you will approve: and that also of Anglo-Saxon. As the histories and laws left us in that type and dialect, must be the text books of the reading of the learners, they will imbibe with the language their free principles of government. The volumes you have been so kind as to send, shall be placed in the library of the University. Having at this time in England a person sent for the purpose of selecting some Professors, a Mr. Gilmer of my neighborhood, I cannot but recommend him to your patronage, counsel and guardianship, against imposition, misinformation, and the deceptions of partial and false recommendations, in the selection of characters. He is a gentleman of great worth and correctness, my particular friend, well educated in various branches of science, and worthy of entire confidence.

Your age of eighty-four and mine of eighty-one years, insure us a speedy meeting. We may then commune at leisure, and more fully, on the good and evil, which, in the course of our long lives, we have both witnessed; and in the mean time, I pray you to accept assurances of my high veneration and esteem for your person and character.

THE PROGRESS OF SOCIETY
To William Ludlow

Monticello, September 6, 1824

SIR,—The idea which you present in your letter of July 30th, of the progress of society from its rudest state to that it has now attained, seems conformable to what may be probably conjectured. Indeed, we have under our eyes tolerable proofs of it. Let a philosophic observer commence a journey from the savages of the Rocky Mountains, eastwardly towards our sea-coast. These he would observe in the earliest stage of association living under no law but that of nature, subscribing and covering themselves with the flesh and skins of wild beasts. He would next find those on our frontiers in the pastoral state, raising domestic animals to supply the defects of hunting. Then succeed our own semi-barbarous citizens, the pioneers of the advance of civilization, and so in his progress he would meet the gradual shades of improving man until he would reach his, as yet, most improved state in our seaport towns. This, in fact, is equivalent to a survey, in time, of the progress of man from the infancy of creation to the present day. I am eighty-one years of age, born where I now live, in the first range of mountains in the interior of our country. And I have observed this march of civilization advancing from the sea coast, passing over us like a cloud of light, increasing our knowledge and improving our condition, insomuch as that we are at this time more advanced in civilization here than the seaports were when I was a boy. And where this progress will stop no one can say. Barbarism has, in the meantime, been receding before the steady step of amelioration; and will in time, I trust, disappear from the earth. You seem to think that this advance has brought on too complicated a state of society, and that we should gain in happiness by treading back our steps a little way. I think, myself, that we have more machinery of government than is necessary, too many parasites living on the labor of the industrious. I believe it might be much simplified to the relief of those who maintain it. Your experiment seems to have this in view. A society of seventy families, the number you name, may very possibly be governed as a single family, subsisting on their common industry, and holding all things in common. Some regulators of the family you still must have, and it remains to be seen at what period of your increasing population your simple regulations will cease to be sufficient to preserve order, peace, and justice. The experiment is interesting; I shall not live to see its issue, but I wish it success equal to your hopes, and to yourself and society prosperity and happiness.

RETURN OF THE HERO
To Lafayette

Monticello, October 9, 1824

I have duly received, my dear friend and General, your letter of the 1st from Philadelphia, giving us the welcome assurance that you will visit the neighborhood which, during the march of our enemy near it, was covered by your shield from his robberies and ravages. In passing the line of your former march you will experience pleasing recollections of the good you have done. My neighbors, too, of our academical village, who well remember their obligations to you, have expressed to you, in a letter from a committee appointed for that purpose, their hope that you will accept manifestations of their feelings, simple indeed, but as cordial as any you will have received. It will be an additional honor to the University of the State that you will have been its first guest. Gratify them, then, by this assurance to their committee, if it has not been done. But what recollections, dear friend, will this call up to you and me! What a history have we to run over from the evening that yourself, Meusnier, Bernau, and other patriots settled, in my house in Paris, the outlines of the constitution you wished! And to trace it through all the disastrous chapters of Robespierre, Barras, Bonaparte, and the Bourbons! These things, however, are for our meeting. You mention the return of Miss Wright to America, accompanied by her sister; but do not say what her stay is to be, nor what her course. Should it lead her to a visit of our University, which, in its architecture only, is as yet an object, herself and her companion will nowhere find a welcome more hearty than with Mrs. Randolph, and all the inhabitants of Monticello. This Athenæum of our country, in embryo, is as yet but promise; and not in a state to recall the recollections of Athens. But everything has its beginning, its growth, and end; and who knows with what future delicious morsels of philosophy, and by what future Miss Wright raked from its ruins, the world may, some day, be gratified and instructed? Your son George we shall be very happy indeed to see, and to renew in him the recollections of your very dear family; and the revolutionary merit of M. le Vasseur has that passport to the esteem of every American, and, to me, the additional one of having been your friend and co-operator, and he will, I hope, join you in making head-quarters with us at Monticello. But all these things *à revoir*; in the meantime we are impatient that your ceremonies at York should be over, and give you to the embraces of friendship.

P. S. Will you come by Mr. Madison's, or let him or me know on what day he may meet you here, and join us in our greetings?

COUNSEL TO A NAMESAKE
To Thomas Jefferson Smith

Monticello, February 21, 1825

This letter will, to you, be as one from the dead. The writer
will be in the grave before you can weigh its counsels. Your
affectionate and excellent father has requested that I would
address to you something which might possibly have a favorable influence on the course of life you have to run, and I
too, as a namesake, feel an interest in that course. Few words
will be necessary, with good dispositions on your part. Adore
God. Reverence and cherish your parents. Love your neighbor as yourself, and your country more than yourself. Be just.
Be true. Murmur not at the ways of Providence. So shall the
life into which you have entered, be the portal to one of eternal and ineffable bliss. And if to the dead it is permitted to
care for the things of this world, every action of your life will
be under my regard. Farewell.

The portrait of a good man by the most sublime of poets,
for your imitation.

Lord, who's the happy man that may to thy blest courts re-
   pair;
Not stranger-like to visit them but to inhabit there?
'Tis he whose every thought and deed by rules of virtue
   moves;
Whose generous tongue disdains to speak the thing his heart
   disproves.
Who never did a slander forge, his neighbor's fame to
   wound;
Nor hearken to a false report, by malice whispered round.
Who vice in all its pomp and power, can treat with just
   neglect;
And piety, though clothed in rags, religiously respect.
Who to his plighted vows and trust has ever firmly stood;
And though he promise to his loss, he makes his promise
   good.
Whose soul in usury disdains his treasure to employ;
Whom no rewards can ever bribe the guiltless to destroy.

The man, who, by his steady course, has happiness insur'd.
When earth's foundations shake, shall stand, by Providence
    secur'd.

   A Decalogue of Canons for observation in practical life.
1. Never put off till to-morrow what you can do to-day.
2. Never trouble another for what you can do yourself.
3. Never spend your money before you have it.
4. Never buy what you do not want, because it is cheap; it
   will be dear to you.
5. Pride costs us more than hunger, thirst and cold.
6. We never repent of having eaten too little.
7. Nothing is troublesome that we do willingly.
8. How much pain have cost us the evils which have never
   happened.
9. Take things always by their smooth handle.
10. When angry, count ten, before you speak; if very angry,
    an hundred.

THE OBJECT OF THE DECLARATION OF INDEPENDENCE

To Henry Lee

Monticello, May 8, 1825

DEAR SIR,— Your favor of Apr. 29 has been duly recieved,
and the offer of mineralogical specimens from Mr. Myer
has been communicated to Dr. Emmet our Professor of
Natural history. The last donation of the legislature to the
University was appropriated specifically to a library and apparatus of every kind. But we apply it first to the more important articles of a library, of an astronomical, physical, &
chemical apparatus. And we think it safest to see what
these will cost, before we venture on collections of mineral
& other subjects, the last we must proportion to what sum
we shall have left only. The Professor possesses already
what he thinks will be sufficient for mineralogical and geological explanations to his school. I do not know how far

he might be tempted to enlarge his possession by a catalogue of articles and prices, if both should be satisfactory. If Mr. Myer chuses to send such a catalogue, it shall be returned to you immediately, if the purchase be not approved.

That George Mason was the author of the bill of rights, and the constitution founded on it, the evidence of the day established fully in my mind. Of the paper you mention, purporting to be instructions to the Virginia delegation in Congress, I have no recollection. If it were anything more than a project of some private hand, that is to say, had any such instructions been ever given by the convention, they would appear in the journals, which we possess entire. But with respect to our rights, and the acts of the British government contravening those rights, there was but one opinion on this side of the water. All American whigs thought alike on these subjects. When forced, therefore, to resort to arms for redress, an appeal to the tribunal of the world was deemed proper for our justification. This was the object of the Declaration of Independence. Not to find out new principles, or new arguments, never before thought of, not merely to say things which had never been said before; but to place before mankind the common sense of the subject, in terms so plain and firm as to command their assent, and to justify ourselves in the independent stand we are compelled to take. Neither aiming at originality of principle or sentiment, nor yet copied from any particular and previous writing, it was intended to be an expression of the American mind, and to give to that expression the proper tone and spirit called for by the occasion. All its authority rests then on the harmonizing sentiments of the day, whether expressed in conversation, in letters, printed essays, or in the elementary books of public right, as Aristotle, Cicero, Locke, Sidney, &c. The historical documents which you mention as in your possession, ought all to be found, and I am persuaded you will find, to be corroborative of the facts and principles advanced in that Declaration. Be pleased to accept assurances of my great esteem and respect.

THE ANGLO-SAXON LANGUAGE
To the Honorable J. Evelyn Denison, M.P.

Monticello, November 9, 1825

DEAR SIR,—Your favor of July 30th was duly received, and we have now at hand the books you have been so kind as to send to our University. They are truly acceptable in themselves, for we might have been years not knowing of their existence; but give the greater pleasure as evidence of the interest you have taken in our infant institution. It is going on as successfully as we could have expected; and I have no reason to regret the measure taken of procuring Professors from abroad where science is so much ahead of us. You witnessed some of the puny squibs of which I was the butt on that account. They were probably from disappointed candidates, whose unworthiness had occasioned their applications to be passed over. The measure has been generally approved in the South and West; and by all liberal minds in the North. It has been peculiarly fortunate, too, that the Professors brought from abroad were as happy selections as could have been hoped, as well for their qualifications in science as correctness and amiableness of character. I think the example will be followed, and that it cannot fail to be one of the efficacious means of promoting that cordial good will, which it is so much the interest of both nations to cherish. These teachers can never utter an unfriendly sentiment towards their native country; and those into whom their instructions will be infused, are not of ordinary significance only: they are exactly the persons who are to succeed to the government of our country, and to rule its future enmities, its friendships and fortunes. As it is our interest to receive instruction through this channel, so I think it is yours to furnish it; for these two nations holding cordially together, have nothing to fear from the united world. They will be the models for regenerating the condition of man, the sources from which representative government is to flow over the whole earth.

I learn from you with great pleasure, that a taste is reviving in England for the recovery of the Anglo-Saxon dialect of our language; for a mere dialect it is, as much as those of Piers Plowman, Gower, Douglas, Chaucer, Spenser, Shakspeare, Milton, for even much of Milton is already antiquated. The Anglo-Saxon is only the earliest we possess of the many shades of mutation by which the language has tapered down to its modern form. Vocabularies we need for each of these stages from Somner to Bailey, but not grammars for each or any of them. The grammar has changed so little, in the descent from the earliest, to the present form, that a little observation suffices to understand its variations. We are greatly indebted to the worthies who have preserved the Anglo-Saxon form, from Doctor Hickes down to Mr. Bosworth. Had they not given to the public what we possess through the press, that dialect would by this time have been irrecoverably lost. I think it, however, a misfortune that they have endeavored to give it too much of a learned form, to mount it on all the scaffolding of the Greek and Latin, to load it with their genders, numbers, cases, declensions, conjugations, &c. Strip it of these embarrassments, vest it in the Roman type which we have adopted instead of our English black letter, reform its uncouth orthography, and assimilate its pronunciation, as much as may be, to the present English, just as we do in reading Piers Plowman or Chaucer, and with the cotemporary vocabulary for the few lost words, we understand it as we do them. For example, the Anglo-Saxon text of the Lord's prayer, as given us 6th Matthew, ix., is spelt and written thus, in the equivalent Roman type: "Faeder ure thu the eart in heofenum, si thin nama gehalgod. to becume thin rice. gewurthe thin willa on eorthan. swa swa on heofenum. urne dæghwamlican hlaf syle us to dæg. and forgyf us ure gyltas, swa swa we forgifath urum gyltendum. and ne ge-lædde thu us on costnunge, ac alys us of yfele'. I should spell and pronounce thus: 'Father our, thou tha art in heavenum. si thine name y-hallowed. come thin ric. y-wurth thine will on earthan. so so on heavenum. ourn daywhamlican loaf sell us to day. and forgive us our guilts so so we forgivath ourum guiltendum. and no y-lead thou us on costnunge, ac a-lease us of evil'. And here it is to be observed by-the-bye, that there is but the single word "temptation" in our present version of

this prayer that is not Anglo-Saxon; for the word "tres-
passes" taken from the French, (οφειληματα in the original)
might as well have been translated by the Anglo-Saxon
"guilts."

The learned apparatus in which Dr. Hickes and his successors have muffled our Anglo-Saxon, is what has frightened us
from encountering it. The simplification I propose may, on
the contrary, make it a regular part of our common English
education.

So little reading and writing was there among our Anglo-
Saxon ancestors of that day, that they had no fixed orthography. To produce a given sound, every one jumbled the letters
together, according to his unlettered notion of their power,
and all jumbled them differently, just as would be done at this
day, were a dozen peasants, who have learnt the alphabet, but
have never read, desired to write the Lord's prayer. Hence the
varied modes of spelling by which the Anglo-Saxons meant
to express the same sound. The word *many*, for example, was
spelt in twenty different ways; yet we cannot suppose they
were twenty different words, or that they had twenty different ways of pronouncing the same word. The Anglo-Saxon
orthography, then, is not an exact representation of the
sounds meant to be conveyed. We must drop in pronunciation the superfluous consonants, and give to the remaining
letters their present English sound; because, not knowing the
true one, the present enunciation is as likely to be right as any
other, and indeed more so, and facilitates the acquisition of
the language.

It is much to be wished that the publication of the present
county dialects of England should go on. It will restore to us
our language in all its shades of variation. It will incorporate
into the present one all the riches of our ancient dialects; and
what a store this will be, may be seen by running the eye over
the county glossaries, and observing the words we have lost
by abandonment and disuse, which in sound and sense are
inferior to nothing we have retained. When these local vocabularies are published and digested together into a single one,
it is probable we shall find that there is not a word in Shakspeare which is not now in use in some of the counties in
England, from whence we may obtain its true sense. And

what an exchange will their recovery be for the volumes of idle commentaries and conjectures with which that divine poet has been masked and metamorphosed. We shall find in him new sublimities which we had never tasted before, and find beauties in our ancient poets which are lost to us now. It is not that I am merely an enthusiast for Palæology. I set equal value on the beautiful engraftments we have borrowed from Greece and Rome, and I am equally a friend to the encouragement of a judicious neology; a language cannot be too rich. The more copious, the more susceptible of embellishment it will become. There are several things wanting to promote this improvement. To reprint the Saxon books in modern type; reform their orthography; publish in the same way the treasures still existing in manuscript. And, more than all things, we want a dictionary on the plan of Stephens or Scapula, in which the Saxon root, placed alphabetically, shall be followed by all its cognate modifications of nouns, verbs, &c., whether Anglo-Saxon, or found in the dialects of subsequent ages. We want, too, an elaborate history of the English language. In time our country may be able to co-operate with you in these labors, of common advantage, but as yet it is too much a blank, calling for other and more pressing attentions. We have too much to do in the improvements of which it is susceptible, and which are deemed more immediately useful. Literature is not yet a distinct profession with us. Now and then a strong mind arises, and at its intervals of leisure from business, emits a flash of light. But the first object of young societies is bread and covering; science is but secondary and subsequent.

I owe apology for this long letter. It must be found in the circumstance of its subject having made an interesting part in the tenor of your letter, and in my attachment to it. It is a hobby which too often runs away with me where I meant not to give up the rein. Our youth seem disposed to mount it with me, and to begin their course where mine is ending.

Our family recollects with pleasure the visit with which you favored us; and join me in assuring you of our friendly and respectful recollections, and of the gratification it will ever be to us to hear of your health and welfare.

A GIFT TO A GRANDDAUGHTER

Ellen Randolph Coolidge

Monticello, Nov. 14, 1825

MY DEAR ELLEN—In my letter of Oct. 13. to Mr. Coolidge, I gave an account of the riot we had at the University, and of it's termination. You will both of course be under anxiety till you know how it has gone off? With the best effects in the world. Having let it be understood, from the beginning, that we wished to trust very much to the discretion of the Students themselves for their own government. With about four fifths of them, this did well, but there were about 15. or 20. bad subjects who were disposed to try whether our indulgence was without limit. Hence the licentious transaction of which I gave an account to Mr. Coolidge. But when the whole mass saw the serious way in which that experiment was met, the Faculty of Professors assembled, the Board of Visitors coming forward in support of that authority, a grand jury taking up the subject, four of the most guilty expelled, the rest reprimanded, severer laws enacted, and a rigorous execution of them declared in future, it gave them a shock and struck a terror, the most severe, as it was less expected. It determined the well disposed among them to frown upon every thing of the kind hereafter, and the ill-disposed returned to order from fear if not from better motives. A perfect subordination has succeeded, entire respect towards the Professors, and industry, order, and quiet the most exemplary, has prevailed ever since. Every one is sensible of the strength which the institution has derived from what appeared at first to threaten it's foundation. We have no further fear of any thing of the kind from the present set. But as at the next term their numbers will be more than doubled by the accession of an additional band, as unbroken as these were, we mean to be prepared, and to ask of the legislature a power to call in the civil authority in the first instant of disorder, and to quell it on the spot by imprisonment and the same legal coercions, provided against disorder generally, committed by other citizens, from whom, at their age, they have no right to distinction.

We have heard of the loss of your baggage, with the vessel

carrying it, and sincerely condole with you on it. It is not to be estimated by it's pecuniary value, but by that it held in your affections. The documents of your childhood, your letters, correspondencies, notes, books, &c., &c., all gone! And your life cut in two, as it were, and a new one to begin, without any records of the former. John Hemmings was the first who brought me the news. He had caught it accidentally from those who first read the letter from Col. Peyton announcing it. He was au desespoir! That beautiful writing desk he had taken so much pains to make for you! Everything else seemed as nothing in his eye, and that loss was everything. Virgil could not have been more afflicted had his Aeneid fallen a prey to the flames. I asked him if he could not replace it by making another? No. His eyesight had failed him too much, and his recollection of it was too imperfect. It has occurred to me however, that I can replace it, not, indeed, to you, but to Mr. Coolidge, by a substitute, not claiming the same value from it's decorations, but from the part it has *borne* in our history and the events with which it has been associated. I recieved a letter from a friend in Philadelphia lately, asking information of the house, and room of the house there, in which the Declaration of Independence was written, with a view to future celebrations of the 4th. of July in it, another, enquiring whether a paper given to the Philosophical society there, as a rough draught of that Declaration was genuinely so? A society is formed there lately for an annual celebration of the advent of Penn to that place. It was held in his antient Mansion, and the chair in which he actually sat when at his writing table was presented by a lady owning it, and was occupied by the president of the celebration. Two other chairs were given them, made of the elm, under the shade of which Penn had made his first treaty with the Indians. If then things acquire a superstitious value because of their connection with particular persons, surely a connection with the great Charter of our Independence may give a value to what has been associated with that; and such was the idea of the enquirers after the room in which it was written. Now I happen still to possess the writing-box on which it was written. It was made from a drawing of my own, by Ben. Randall, a cabinet maker in whose house I took my first lodgings on my arrival in Philadelphia in May 1776. And I have used it ever since. It claims no merit of particular beauty. It is plain, neat, convenient, and, taking no more room on the writing table than a moderate 4to. volume, it yet displays it self sufficiently for any writing. Mr. Coolidge must do me the favor of accepting this. Its imaginary value will increase with the years, and if he lives to my age, or another half century, he may see it carried in the procession of our nation's birthday, as the relics of the saints are in those of the church. I will send it thro' Colonel Peyton, and hope with better fortune than that for which it is to be a substitute.

I remark what you say in your letter to your mother, relative to Mr. Willard and our University clock. Judging from that that he is the person whom Mr. Coolidge would recommend, and having recieved from Dr. Waterhouse a very strong recommendation of him, you may assure the old gentleman from me that he shall have the making of it. We have lately made an important purchase of lands amounting to 7000. D. and the government is taking from us, under their old and new Tariff, 2700. D. duty on the marble caps and bases of the Portico of our Rotunda, of 10 columns only. These things try our funds for the moment. At the end of the year we shall see how we stand, and I expect we may be able to give the final order for the clock by February.

I want to engage you, as my agent at Boston, for certain articles not to be had here, and for such only. But it will be on the indispensable condition that you keep as rigorous an account of Dollars and cents as old Yerragan our neighbor would do. This alone can induce friends to ask services freely, which would otherwise be the asking of presents and amount to a prohibition. We should be very glad occasionally to get small supplies of the fine dumb codfish to be had at Boston, and also of the tongues and sounds of the Cod. This selection of the articles I trouble you for is not of such as are better there than here; for on that ground we might ask for every thing from thence, but such only as are not to be had here at all. Perhaps I should trepass on Mr. Coolidge for one other article. We pay here 2. D. a gallon for bad French brandy. I think I have seen in Degrand's Price current Marseilles brandy, from Dodge and Oxnard, advertised good at 1. Dollar; and another kind called Seignettes, which I am told is good Cognac at 1.25. D. I will ask of you then a supply of a kental of good dumb fish, and about 20 or 30 lbs. of tongues and sounds; and of Mr. Coolidge a 30 gallon cask of Dodge and Oxnard's Marseilles brandy, if tolerable good at 1. D. or thereabouts, but double cased to guard against spoliation. Knowing nothing of the prices of the fish, I will at a venture, desire Col. Peyton to remit 60. D. to Mr. Coolidge immediately, and any little difference between this and actual cost either way, may stand over to your next account. We should be the better perhaps of your recipe for dressing both articles.

I promised Mr. Ticknor to inform him at times how our University goes on. I shall be glad if you will read to him that part of this letter which respects it, presuming Mr. Coolidge may have communicated to him the facts of my former letter to him. These facts may be used ad libitum, only keeping my name out of sight. Writing is so irksome to me, especially since I am obliged to do it in a recumbent posture, that I am sure Mr. Ticknor will excuse my economy in this exercise. To you perhaps I should apologize for the want of it on this occasion. The family is well. My own health changes little. I ride two or three miles in a carriage every day. With my affectionate salutations to Mr. Coolidge, be assured yourself of my tender and constant love.

CONSOLIDATION!
To William Branch Giles

Monticello, December 26, 1825

DEAR SIR,—I wrote you a letter yesterday, of which you will be free to make what use you please. This will contain matters not intended for the public eye. I see, as you do, and with the deepest affliction, the rapid strides with which the federal branch of our government is advancing towards the usurpation of all the rights reserved to the States, and the consolidation in itself of all powers, foreign and domestic; and that, too, by constructions which, if legitimate, leave no limits to their power. Take together the decisions of the federal court, the doctrines of the President, and the misconstructions of the constitutional compact acted on by the legislature of the federal branch, and it is but too evident, that the three ruling branches of that department are in combination to strip their colleagues, the State authorities, of the powers reserved by them, and to exercise themselves all functions foreign and domestic. Under the power to regulate commerce, they assume indefinitely that also over agriculture and manufactures, and call it regulation to take the earnings of one of these branches of industry, and that too the most depressed, and put them into the pockets of the other, the most flourishing of all. Under the authority to establish post roads, they claim that of cutting down mountains for the construction of roads, of digging canals, and aided by a little sophistry on the words "general welfare," a right to do, not only the acts to effect that, which are specifically enumerated and permitted, but whatsoever they shall think, or pretend will be for the general welfare. And what is our resource for the preservation of the constitution? Reason and argument? You might as well reason and argue with the marble columns encircling them. The representatives chosen by ourselves? They are joined in the combination, some from incorrect views of government, some from corrupt ones, sufficient voting together to out-number the sound parts; and with majorities only of one, two, or three, bold enough to go forward in defiance. Are we then *to stand to our arms*, with the hot-headed Georgian? No. That must be the last resource, not to be thought of until much longer and greater sufferings. If every infraction of a compact of so many parties is to be resisted at once, as a dissolution of it, none can ever be formed which would last one year. We must have patience and longer endurance then with our brethren while under delusion; give them time for reflection and experience of consequences; keep ourselves in a situation to profit by the chapter of accidents; and separate from our companions only when the sole alternatives left, are the dissolution of our Union with them, or submission to a government without limitation of powers. Between these two evils, when we must make a choice, there can be no hesitation. But in the meanwhile, the States should be watchful to note every material usurpation on their rights; to denounce them as they occur in the most peremptory terms; to protest against them as wrongs to which our present submission shall be considered, not as acknowledgments or precedents of right, but as a temporary yielding to the lesser evil, until their accumulation shall overweigh that of separation. I would go still further, and give to the federal member, by a regular amendment of the constitution, a right to make roads and canals of intercommunication between the States, providing sufficiently against corrupt practices in Congress, (log-rolling, &c.,) by declaring that the federal proportion of each State of the moneys so employed, shall be in works within the State, or elsewhere with its consent, and with a due *salvo* of jurisdiction. This is the course which I think safest and best as yet.

You ask my opinion of the propriety of giving publicity to what is stated in your letter, as having passed between Mr. John Q. Adams and yourself. Of this no one can judge but yourself. It is one of those questions which belong to the forum of feeling. This alone can decide on the degree of confidence implied in the disclosure; whether under no circumstances it was to be communicated to others? It does not seem to be of that character, or at all to wear that aspect. They are historical facts which belong to the present, as well as future times. I doubt whether a single fact, known to the world, will carry as clear conviction to it, of the correctness of our knowledge of the treasonable views of the federal party of that day, as that disclosed by this, the most nefarious and daring attempt to dissever the Union, of which the Hartford convention was a subsequent chapter; and both of these having failed, consolidation becomes the fourth chapter of the next book of their history. But this opens with a vast accession of strength from their younger recruits, who, having nothing in them of the feelings or principles of '76, now look to a single and splendid government of an aristocracy, founded on banking institutions, and moneyed incorporations under the guise and cloak of their favored branches of manufactures, commerce and navigation, riding and ruling over the plundered ploughman and beggared yeomanry. This will be to them a next best blessing to the monarchy of their first aim, and perhaps the surest stepping-stone to it.

I learn with great satisfaction that your school is thriving well, and that you have at its head a truly classical scholar. He is one of three or four whom I can hear of in the State. We were obliged the last year to receive shameful Latinists into the classical school of the University, such as we will certainly refuse as soon as we can get from better schools a sufficiency of those properly instructed to form a class. We must get rid of this Connecticut Latin, of this barbarous confusion of long and short syllables, which renders doubtful whether we are listening to a reader of Cherokee, Shawnee, Iroquois, or what. Our University has been most fortunate in the five professors procured from England. A finer selection could not have been made. Besides their being of a grade of science which has left little superior behind, the correctness of their moral character, their accommodating dispositions, and zeal for the prosperity of the institution, leave us nothing more to wish. I verily believe that as high a degree of education can now be obtained here, as in the country they left. And a finer set of youths I never saw assembled for instruction. They committed some irregularities at first, until they learned the lawful length of their tether; since which it has never been transgressed in the smallest degree. A great proportion of them are severely devoted to study, and I fear not to say that within twelve or fifteen years from this time, a majority of the rulers of our State will have been educated here. They shall carry hence the correct principles of our day, and you may count assuredly that they will exhibit their country in a degree of sound respectability it has never known, either in our days, or those of our forefathers. I cannot live to see it. My joy must only be that of anticipation. But that you may see it in full fruition, is the probable consequence of the twenty years I am ahead of you in time, and is the sincere prayer of your affectionate and constant friend.

"TAKE CARE OF ME WHEN DEAD"
To James Madison

Monticello. February 17, 1826

DEAR SIR,—My circular was answered by Genl. Breckenridge, approving, as we had done, of the immediate appointment of Terril to the chair of Law. But our four Colleagues, who were together in Richmond, concluded not to appoint until our meeting in April. In the meantime the term of the present lamented Incumbent draws near to a close. About 150. students have already entered; many of those who engaged for a 2d. year, are yet to come; and I think we may count that our dormitories will be filled. Whether there will be any overflowing for the accomodations provided in the vicinage, which are quite considerable, is not yet known. None will enter there while a dormitory remains vacant. Were the Law-chair filled it would add 50. at least to our number.

Immediately on seeing the overwhelming vote of the House of Representatives against giving us another dollar, I rode to the University and desired Mr. Brockenbrough to engage in nothing new, to stop everything on hand which could be done without, and to employ all his force and funds in finishing the circular room for the books, and the anatomical theatre. These cannot be done without; and for these and all our debts we have funds enough. But I think it prudent then to clear the decks thoroughly, to see how we shall stand, and what we may accomplish further. In the meantime, there have arrived for us in different ports of the United States, ten boxes of books from Paris, seven from London, and from Germany I know not how many; in all, perhaps, about twenty-five boxes. Not one of these can be opened until the book-room is completely finished, and all the shelves ready to receive their charge directly from the boxes as they shall be opened. This cannot be till May. I hear nothing definite of the three thousand dollars duty of which we are asking the remission from Congress. In the selection of our Law Professor, we must be rigorously attentive to his political principles. You will recollect that before the revolution, Coke Littleton was the universal elementary book of law students, and a sounder whig never wrote, nor of profounder learning in the orthodox doctrines of the British constitution, or in what were called English liberties. You remember also that our lawyers were then all whigs. But when his black-letter text, and uncouth but cunning learning got out of fashion, and the honied Mansfieldism of Blackstone became the student's hornbook, from that moment, that profession (the nursery of our Congress) began to slide into toryism, and nearly all the young brood of lawyers now are of that hue. They suppose themselves, indeed, to be whigs, because they no longer know what whigism or republicanism means. It is in our seminary that that vestal flame is to be kept alive; it is thence it is to spread anew over our own and the sister States. If we are true and vigilant in our trust, within a dozen or twenty years a majority of our own legislature will be from one school, and many disciples will have carried its doctrines home with them to their several States, and will have leavened thus the whole mass. New York has taken strong ground in vindication of the constitution; South Carolina had already done the same. Although I was against our leading, I am equally against omitting to follow in the same line, and backing them firmly; and I hope that yourself or some other will mark out the track to be pursued by us.

You will have seen in the newspapers some proceedings in the legislature, which have cost me much mortification. My own debts had become considerable, but not beyond the effect of some lopping of property, which would have been little felt, when our friend Nicholas gave me the *coup de grace*. Ever since that I have been paying twelve hundred dollars a year interest on his debt, which, with my own, was absorbing so much of my annual income, as that the maintenance of my family was making deep and rapid inroads on my capital, and had already done it. Still, sales at a fair price would leave me competently provided. Had crops and prices for several years been such as to maintain a steady competition of substantial bidders at market, all would have been safe. But the long succession of years of stunted crops, of reduced prices, the general prostration of the farming business, under levies for the support of manufactures, &c., with the calamitous fluctuations of value in our paper medium, have kept agriculture in a state of abject depression, which has peopled the western States by silently breaking up those on the Atlantic, and glutted the land market, while it drew off its bidders. In such a state of things, property has lost its character of being a resource for debts. Highland in Bedford, which, in the days of our plethory, sold readily for from fifty to one hundred dollars the acre, (and such sales were many then,) would not now sell for more than from ten to twenty dollars, or one-quarter or one-fifth of its former price. Reflecting on these things, the practice occurred to me, of selling, on fair valuation, and by way of lottery, often resorted to before the Revolution to effect large sales, and still in constant usage in every State for individual as well as corporation purposes. If it is permitted in my case, my lands here alone, with the mills, &c., will pay every thing, and leave me Monticello and a farm free. If refused, I must sell everything here, perhaps considerably in Bedford, move thither with my family, where I have not even a log hut to put my head into, and whether ground for burial, will depend on the depredations which, under the form of sales, shall have been committed on my property. The question then with me was *ultrum horum*? But why afflict you with these details? Indeed, I cannot tell, unless pains are lessened by communication with a friend. The friendship which has subsisted between us, now half a century, and the harmony of our political principles and pursuits, have been sources of constant happiness to me through that long period. And if I remove beyond the reach of attentions to the University, or beyond the bourne of life itself, as I soon must, it is a comfort to leave that institution under your care, and an assurance that it will not be wanting. It has also been a great solace to me, to believe that you are engaged in vindicating to posterity the course we have pursued for preserving to them, in all their purity, the blessings of self-government, which we had assisted too in acquiring for them. If ever the earth has beheld a system of administration conducted with a single and steadfast eye to the general interest and happiness of those committed to it, one which, protected by truth, can never know reproach, it is that to which our lives have been devoted. To myself you have been a pillar of support through life. Take care of me when dead, and be assured that I shall leave with you my last affections.

NUNC DIMITTIS ON SLAVERY
To James Heaton

Monticello, May 20, 1826

DEAR SIR,—The subject of your letter of April 20, is one on which I do not permit myself to express an opinion, but when time, place, and occasion may give it some favorable effect. A good cause is often injured more by ill-timed efforts of its friends than by the arguments of its enemies. Persuasion, perseverance, and patience are the best advocates on questions depending on the will of others. The revolution in public opinion which this cause requires, is not to be expected in a day, or perhaps in an age; but time, which outlives all things, will outlive this evil also. My sentiments have been forty years before the public. Had I repeated them forty times, they would only have become the more stale and threadbare. Although I shall not live to see them consummated, they will not die with me; but living or dying, they will ever be in my most fervent prayer. This is written for yourself and not for the public, in compliance with your request of two lines of sentiment on the subject. Accept the assurance of my good will and respect.

LAST LETTER: APOTHEOSIS OF LIBERTY
To Roger C. Weightman

Monticello, June 24, 1826

RESPECTED SIR,—The kind invitation I receive from you, on the part of the citizens of the city of Washington, to be present with them at their celebration on the fiftieth anniversary of American Independence, as one of the surviving signers of an instrument pregnant with our own, and the fate of the world, is most flattering to myself, and heightened by the honorable accompaniment proposed for the comfort of such a journey. It adds sensibly to the sufferings of sickness, to be deprived by it of a personal participation in the rejoicings of that day. But acquiescence is a duty, under circumstances not placed among those we are permitted to control. I should, indeed, with peculiar delight, have met and exchanged there congratulations personally with the small band, the remnant of that host of worthies, who joined with us on that day, in the bold and doubtful election we were to make for our country, between submission or the sword; and to have enjoyed with them the consolatory fact, that our fellow citizens, after half a century of experience and prosperity, continue to approve the choice we made. May it be to the world, what I believe it will be, (to some parts sooner, to others later, but finally to all,) the signal of arousing men to burst the chains under which monkish ignorance and superstition had persuaded them to bind themselves, and to assume the blessings and security of self-government. That form which we have substituted, restores the free right to the unbounded exercise of reason and freedom of opinion. All eyes are opened, or opening, to the rights of man. The general spread of the light of science has already laid open to every view the palpable truth, that the mass of mankind has not been born with saddles on their backs, nor a favored few booted and spurred, ready to ride them legitimately, by the grace of God. These are grounds of hope for others. For ourselves, let the annual return of this day forever refresh our recollections of these rights, and an undiminished devotion to them.

I will ask permission here to express the pleasure with which I should have met my ancient neighbors of the city of Washington and its vicinities, with whom I passed so many years of a pleasing social intercourse; an intercourse which so much relieved the anxieties of the public cares, and left impressions so deeply engraved in my affections, as never to be forgotten. With my regret that ill health forbids me the gratification of an acceptance, be pleased to receive for yourself, and those for whom you write, the assurance of my highest respect and friendly attachments.

Chronology

1743   Born April 13 (April 2, Old Style) at Shadwell, Goochland (now Albemarle) County, Virginia, first son (third of ten children) of Peter Jefferson, surveyor, landowner, mapmaker, and magistrate, and Jane Randolph, a member of the most prominent land-owning and office-holding family of colonial Virginia.

1745   Death of William Randolph (Jane Randolph Jefferson's cousin) leaves three orphaned children, among them Thomas Mann Randolph. Peter Jefferson, fulfilling the request made in Randolph's will, becomes their guardian, occupies the family mansion, and manages the plantation at Tuckahoe on the James River above Richmond. Thomas spends six years there, and with his sisters and cousins attends the one-room plantation schoolhouse, where he is tutored privately.

1752   Returns with family to Shadwell, and enters a Latin school conducted by the Reverend William Douglas, of Scotland.

1757   Father dies.

1758–60   Attends school of the Reverend James Maury, "a correct classical scholar," and boards with Maury's family in Fredericksville; rides twelve miles home each weekend.

1760–62   Attends College of William and Mary, at Williamsburg, studying particularly with the professor of mathematics, William Small of Scotland, the only layman on a faculty of Anglican clerics; Small's teaching is rational and scientific, and his influence, Jefferson later wrote, "probably fixed the destinies of my life."

1762–67   Studies law under the direction of George Wythe, a man of considerable learning, later a signer of the Declaration of Independence, first professor of law at William and Mary, and Chancellor of Virginia. Inherits 2,750 acres from his father's estate when he comes of age in 1764, and enters Virginia society; begins successful law practice in Virginia courts following admission to the bar in 1767.

1769   Following his own architectural designs, begins building Monticello, his country seat, on a mountaintop that was part of his father's original landholdings.

1769–76   Member of Virginia House of Burgesses (until it is closed by the Revolution) for Albemarle County; promotes various measures intended to resist British authority, among them the organization of committees of correspondence.

1772   Marries Martha Wayles Skelton, a 23-year-old widow and heiress, on January 1. Brings his bride to the unfinished Monticello, where, on September 27, Martha (called Patsy), their first child, is born.

1773   Comes into possession of 11,000 acres of land and 135 slaves upon death of his father-in-law, John Wayles. Immediately sells over half the lands to meet debts also inherited from Wayles. The purchasers will pay off their notes in depreciated Revolutionary currency, and Jefferson will struggle for the rest of his life to liquidate his own debt to Wayles's creditors.

1774   Writes, in August, proposed instructions for the Virginia delegates to the first Continental Congress. These are later published in Williamsburg under the title *A Summary View of the Rights of British America*, and are reprinted in Philadelphia and in England.

1775–76   Attends Continental Congress in Philadelphia as a Virginia delegate. Mother dies in March 1776. In June 1776, drafts Declaration of Independence, adopted July 4; also drafts a constitution for Virginia, not adopted.

1776–79   Member of Virginia House of Delegates for Albemarle County.

1777   Correspondence with John Adams begins May 16. First and only son dies, unchristened, in June, aged three weeks.

1778   Another daughter, Mary (called Maria or Polly), born August 1. Of his six children, two, Martha and Mary, grow to maturity, and only Martha survives him.

1779   Elected Governor of Virginia on June 1. On June 18, the "Report of the Committee of Revisors," on which he has labored during years as a legislator, is submitted to the Assembly. Never enacted as a unit, and not printed until 1784, this revision of the laws of the Commonwealth nevertheless becomes, in James Madison's words, "a mine of legislative wealth"; includes Bills for Proportioning Crimes and Punishments, for the More General Diffusion of Knowledge, for Establishing Religious Freedom, etc.

1780   Elected a member of the American Philosophical Society January 21. Reelected Governor of Virginia June 2. On December 29, a British army under the command of Benedict Arnold invades Virginia.

1781   Term as governor expires June 2; on June 4, along with several members of the Assembly, who are his guests, is driven from Monticello by General Tarleton's troops. The House of Delegates, meeting in Staunton, across the Blue Ridge, resolves on June 12 to conduct an inquiry into the conduct of Jefferson and his Council, responding to allegations that they had been negligent in preparing to meet Arnold's invasion; on December 15, the Assembly accepts the report of the committee appointed to make the inquiry, and votes a unanimous resolution "to obviate and remove all unmerited Censure" for his conduct as wartime governor. On December 20, sends answers (first form of *Notes on the State of Virginia*) to a series of questions posed by François Marbois, secretary to the French legation, relating to the laws, institutions, geography, climate, flora and fauna of Virginia.

1782–83   Martha Wayles Jefferson, in poor health since the birth of their sixth child in May, dies on September 6, 1782, plunging him into deep grief. Appointed commissioner by Congress to negotiate peace with Great Britain on November 12, but winter ice and a British fleet block passage to France. Word of a provisional treaty reaches Congress in February and mission is suspended.

1783–84   Serves as Virginia delegate in Congress, at Princeton and
           Annapolis.

1784   Submits "Report of a Plan of Government for the Western
           Territory" to Congress on March 1; when revised,
           amended, and adopted on April 23, it projects a federal
           and republican system for the American West. Appointed
           by Congress May 7 as minister plenipotentiary to join
           John Adams and Benjamin Franklin in negotiation of trea-
           ties of amity and commerce in Europe; travels through
           eastern states, gathering information on industry and
           trade in preparation for mission. In Boston on July 5, em-
           barks for England, accompanied by daughter Patsy.

1785   Appointed to succeed Franklin as minister to France in
           March; signs commercial treaty with Prussia in July. Pub-
           lishes, in Paris, a private edition of *Notes on the State of
           Virginia*.

1786   Collaborates anonymously with Jean Nicholas Démeunier
           on article on the United States for the *Encyclopédie Metho-
           dique*, from January to June. Virginia General Assembly
           enacts Statute for Religious Freedom on January 16. In
           March and April, visits London and tours English gardens
           with John Adams (now minister to England). In June,
           sends model of a new capitol, based on Roman temple, to
           Virginia. Meets Maria Cosway, an Englishwoman and
           painter, who becomes his friend and frequent companion
           in Paris.

1787   Journeys to south of France and northern Italy from
           March to June. In July, nine-year-old daughter Polly ar-
           rives in Paris and *Notes on the State of Virginia* is published
           in England (Stockdale edition). Receives a copy of pro-
           posed United States Constitution in November and sup-
           ports its ratification, but urges Madison and others to add
           a bill of rights to the document.

1788   Journeys to Holland and the Rhineland, from March to
           April. In November, signs a consular convention with
           France, and writes and has printed *Observations on the
           Whale-Fishery*. Awarded honorary Doctorate of Laws by
           Harvard University.

1789   Attends opening of Estates General at Versailles May 5;

observes succeeding events of the French Revolution. When deliberations of the Estates General reach an impasse—the clergy and nobles (First and Second Estates) insisting on preservation of the ancient principle of representation and vote by order, and the commons (Third Estate) demanding a single national assembly—Jefferson suggests that the King come forward with a "charter of rights" including rights of habeas corpus and freedom of the press, giving the Estates General exclusive power to legislate and to levy taxes, and abolishing fiscal privileges and inequities. This compromise solution catches the fancy of the Marquis de Lafayette but avails no further. The King rallies to the nobles and resorts to force; the storming of the Bastille ensues, followed by the King's capitulation and a wave of retributive violence. Jefferson is satisfied with the "legitimacy" of the mobs' actions. In August, Lafayette and other Patriot party leaders meet at Jefferson's house to discuss the formation of a constitution. In September, secures leave of absence from diplomatic post to attend to personal affairs in Virginia and take daughters home. Leaves Paris in October, lands November 23 at Norfolk, Virginia. Upon disembarking, learns that Senate on September 26 confirmed his nomination by President Washington as first secretary of state.

1790   Reluctantly accepts appointment as secretary of state February 14. Martha Jefferson marries Thomas Mann Randolph (her second cousin) on February 23. Takes up duties as secretary of state March 21 in New York. Submits Report on Weights and Measures to Congress July 4. Begins to be disturbed by anti-republican sentiments and courtly forms and ceremonies exhibited in the new administration.

1791   Advises the President on February 15 that the Constitution does not empower the federal government to form a national bank; Washington solicits rebuttal from Alexander Hamilton, secretary of the treasury (who advances the doctrine of "implied powers"), and decides the issue in Hamilton's favor. Administrative rivalry with Hamilton grows steadily more intense. Helps persuade Philip Freneau to come to the capital in Philadelphia to edit an opposition newspaper. Extract of private note of Jefferson's, referring to the "political heresies" of John Adams (vice-president), stirs controversy when it is printed (without permission) as preface to Thomas Paine's *Rights of Man*.

1792   Diplomatic memoir to the British minister, dated May 29, seeks removal of British troops from posts below the Great Lakes and settlement of other issues left unresolved by the treaty of peace; Hamilton's connivance forestalls Jefferson's plan to use commercial discrimination to accomplish these ends. On September 9, appeals to President Washington in dispute with Hamilton, who had attacked him anonymously in the press. Political alignments in Congress begin to take on party character, and Jefferson is widely viewed as leader of the opposition to Federalist policies.

1793   Writes "Opinion on the French Treaties," dated April 28, and prevails upon President Washington to receive the new French minister, Edmond Charles Genet, thus tacitly acknowledging the legitimacy of the Republic of France; also convinces Washington not to renounce the treaties of 1778, which allied the fledgling United States with the French monarchy. Acquiesces in Washington's Proclamation of Neutrality. In August, when Genet's activities and statements threaten to involve the United States in the Anglo-French war, Jefferson prepares papers demanding the diplomat's recall. On December 16, submits Report on Commerce to Congress, urging retaliation in kind against discriminatory British trade policies. Resigns as secretary of state at year's end.

1794   Returns to farming at Monticello.

1795   Denounces Jay's Treaty, which represents the pro-British policies of the Federalists, in private letters.

1796   Begins rebuilding Monticello in February to provide expanded accommodations for family and to conform to his developed taste in architectural design. Writes to Philip Mazzei on April 24 that an "Anglican monarchical aristocratical party has sprung up"; when published a year later, the letter is interpreted as reflecting upon Washington and prompts renewed Federalist attacks on Jefferson. December 7, elected vice-president of the United States, having run second in the electoral balloting to John Adams.

1797   Installed as president of the American Philosophical Society on March 3 at Philadelphia, and inaugurated as vice-president of the United States a day later. On March 10, presents scientific paper on megalonyx, based on recent fossil discoveries in Virginia, to American Philosophical Society. In May, assumes leadership of Republican party at special session of Congress. Mary Jefferson marries her cousin John Wayles Eppes in October.

1798   Anti-Jacobin hysteria envelops Philadelphia, aroused by publication of the "XYZ dispatches," which reveal the attempts by agents of the French foreign minister, Talleyrand, to extort money from the American envoys sent to negotiate for reduction of hostilities. Jefferson strives to prevent war, is calumniated in the press as a traitor and a coward, and retires on June 27 to Monticello. In September and October, secretly drafts resolutions declaring the Alien and Sedition laws (aimed against Republican opposition to Federalist war policy) unconstitutional and arranges for these resolutions to be introduced in the Kentucky legislature, which adopts them in November. In December, the Virginia Resolutions, drafted by Madison in tandem with Jefferson's Kentucky Resolutions, are adopted.

1799   Drafts second set of resolutions in August and September and proposes further actions by Virginia and Kentucky legislatures.

1800   Publishes appendix to *Notes on the State of Virginia* in May, authenticating story of the murder of the family of Logan, a Mingo chief (disputed by Luther Martin, attorney general of Maryland, a political enemy of Jefferson's). Runs for President in first national contest between organized political parties; is vilified by Federalists as an infidel, a Jacobin, and a demagogue, but defeats Adams handily in popular vote. On December 3, however, in the meeting of presidential electors in their respective states, a peculiarity of the electoral system results in a tie vote between Jefferson and his running mate, Aaron Burr, and the election is thrown into the House of Representatives.

1801   *A Manual of Parliamentary Practice*, the product of Jefferson's experience presiding over the Senate as vice-president, published in February. The lame-duck Federalist
majority in the House fails in a last-ditch attempt to deny
Jefferson the presidency by swinging to Burr, and on the
36th ballot Jefferson is elected President of the United
States. On March 4 he is inaugurated, and delivers a conciliatory address. Correspondence with Adams ceases and
is not renewed until 1812. Dispatches naval squadron on
May 20 to cruise the Mediterranean to protect American
vessels against the piracy of the Barbary States. On July
12, replies to the New Haven remonstrance, defending removal of the collector of customs in New Haven (a Federalist holdover) and the appointment of a Republican in
his place. On December 8, communicates his First Annual
Message to Congress in writing, eschewing the formality
of a ceremonial address.

1802   Replies to the Danbury Baptist Association on January 1,
affirming his commitment to the separation of church and
state. March 8, succeeds in repealing the Judiciary Act of
1801, passed by the Federalists in their final weeks of
supremacy, which enlarged the federal judiciary and
expanded its jurisdiction. Writes letter to Robert R. Livingston, American minister to France, on April 18, discussing the danger of a rebirth of French empire in the
New World posed by the retrocession of Louisiana from
Spain to France. In July, James T. Callender, disappointed
office-seeker, commences libels of Jefferson, including
allegation that he fathered children by his slave Sally
Hemings.

1803   Nominates James Monroe on January 11 for extraordinary
mission to France to negotiate for purchase of New Orleans and the Floridas. Sends confidential message to Congress on January 18 regarding proposed expedition to the
Pacific, to be led by Meriwether Lewis. On February 24,
Chief Justice John Marshall of the Supreme Court delivers
opinion in the case of Marbury *vs.* Madison. Opinion establishes precedent for judicial review and Marshall issues
gratuitous rebuke of the President for refusing to deliver
commissions to William Marbury and other "midnight
judges" appointed in the final hours of the Adams administration. On April 21, Jefferson sends his "Syllabus . . .

of the Doctrines of Jesus" to Benjamin Rush. Livingston and Monroe conclude treaty of cession of Louisiana in Paris on April 30. In July, believing he had exceeded his constitutional authority in making the purchase, Jefferson drafts an amendment to sanction it retroactively, although for reasons of expedience he does not press it upon Congress. The amendment includes provisions to remove Indian tribes to the far side of the Mississippi and to bar white settlement in the new territory above the 33rd parallel. The policy of removal is abandoned along with the amendment. In September, writes memoir on the boundaries of Louisiana, hoping to make the most of their uncertainty and acquire the Floridas, which had not been part of the bargain. Sends "An Account of Louisiana" to Congress on November 14, and is ridiculed in the press because of the strange, apocryphal tales it includes. Ten days later sends to Senator John Breckinridge an outline of a plan of government for Louisiana, subsequently enacted by Congress.

1804   Younger daughter, Mary Jefferson Eppes, dies April 17; letter of condolence from Abigail Adams leads to brief correspondence with her, which is curtailed when old political animosities surface. Reelected President by a landslide on December 5.

1805   Proposes plan for university in letter to Littleton W. Tazewell on January 5. Supreme Court Justice Samuel Chase, whose partisan attacks on democratic tendencies in the government had led Jefferson to call for his impeachment, is acquitted March 1 in trial in the Senate. Delivers Second Inaugural Address March 4. Peace treaty with Tripoli brings Mediterranean campaign to successful conclusion June 4. Fifth Annual Message to Congress on December 3 offers vigorous defense of American neutrality. Sends confidential message to Congress December 6, hinting at purchase of Floridas from Spain.

1806   With Europe embroiled in war and American neutrality threatened by captures, impressments, and other acts of aggression, Jefferson seeks to exert economic pressure on Britain in particular. He approves the Non-Importation Act, intended to strengthen the hands of James Monroe and William Pinkney, who are nominated joint commissioners to Britain on April 19. In August, lays foundation for Poplar Forest, an octagonal house of his design, on property acquired from father-in-law's estate in Bedford County, Virginia. Lewis and Clark Expedition returns to St. Louis on September 25. Issues proclamation on November 27 warning against Burr Conspiracy, alleged plot of the former vice-president to separate western states from the union and attack Mexico. Sixth Annual Message, on December 2, calls for constitutional amendment to enlarge powers of Congress to undertake internal improvements.

1807   On January 14, offers his collection of Virginia statutes to W. W. Hening for his *Statutes at Large* (1809–23). Sends special message to Congress February 10, calling for the use of gunboats to protect American harbors. On March 3, refuses to submit Monroe–Pinkney treaty to Senate because it contains no guarantee against impressment. Trial of Aaron Burr for treason opens in Richmond May 22; he is acquitted September 1. On June 22, USS *Chesapeake* is fired upon by HMS *Leopard* off Norfolk after American commander's refusal to allow the British to search his ship for deserters. Incident provokes popular clamor for war, but Jefferson retaliates with vigorous commercial measures. The Embargo Act, suspending all foreign commerce, is enacted on Jefferson's recommendation, effective December 22. On December 10, replying to addresses from legislative bodies urging him to continue in office for a third term, he announces his impending retirement from the presidency.

1808   The economy suffers under the embargo, which is regularly violated, especially in the Northeast. On April 19, in response to the smuggling trade carried on across the Canadian frontier, Jefferson issues proclamation declaring the Lake Champlain region to be in a state of insurrection. In July, ships collection of bones of mammoth to National Institute in Paris. Opposition to embargo grows and diplomatic efforts to end the commercial warfare fail. In his Eighth Annual Message, November 8, Jefferson looks to permanent development of domestic manufacturing, which has expanded during suspension of foreign trade. James Madison is elected President December 7.

1809   Signs Non-Intercourse Act March 1, repealing the em-
        bargo (which had failed to achieve its ends) and reopening
        trade with all nations except Great Britain and France. Re-
        tires as President March 4 and returns to Monticello,
        where he spends the remainder of his life entertaining a
        steady stream of visitors, attending to an extensive corre-
        spondence, struggling with mounting debts, planning a
        university, and engaging in philosophical pursuits.

1810   On May 12 Governor John Tyler invites Jefferson to com-
        ment on public education, and on May 26 he responds by
        affirming his continuing support of the cause "of general
        education, to enable every man to judge for himself what
        will secure or endanger his freedom," and by proposing
        the division of each county into "little republics," each to
        have a central school.

1811   Destutt de Tracy's *A Commentary and Review of Montes-
        quieu's Spirit of the Laws* is translated and published in July
        under Jefferson's direction. Suit against Jefferson, brought
        by Edward Livingston concerning the New Orleans Bat-
        ture and resulting from order given during Jefferson's
        presidency that evicted Livingston from a public beach
        formed by Mississippi silt, is dismissed by federal circuit
        court in Richmond for lack of jurisdiction. In March, the
        following year, Jefferson publishes the complex law argu-
        ments prepared for counsel in the case.

1812   Resumes correspondence with John Adams at the latter's
        initiative. War with Great Britain is declared June 18.

1813   August, writes biographical sketch of Meriwether Lewis,
        published the following year.

1814   Proposes comprehensive plan of public education for Vir-
        ginia in letter to Peter Carr September 7. Offers his library
        for sale to the United States on September 21; it becomes
        the foundation of the Library of Congress. Resigns as
        president of the American Philosophical Society Novem-
        ber 23. War ends with Treaty of Ghent December 24. An-
        drew Jackson defeats English at New Orleans January 8 of
        the following year, before word of the treaty arrives.

1815   Contributes to Louis H. Girardin's continuation of John
            Daly Burk's *History of Virginia*, published the following
            year.

1816   Justifies change of opinion on domestic manufactures in
            celebrated letter of January 9 to Benjamin Austin. Calls
            for reform of Virginia constitution in letter of July 12 to
            Samuel Kercheval, widely reprinted. Reads and corrects
            manuscript of William Wirt's *Life of Patrick Henry* in Sep-
            tember.

1817   Virginia Assembly defeats bill that embodies Jefferson's
            general education plan February 20. Develops architec-
            tural plans for an "academical village" in Charlottesville.
            On October 6 the cornerstone is laid for the first building
            of Central College, which will become the University of
            Virginia.

1818   Writes preface to the *Anas* (a collection of partisan anec-
            dotes and memoranda from his years of service in the fed-
            eral government) on February 4, explaining his conflicts
            with Hamilton during Washington's administration; col-
            lection is not published until after his death. August 1–4,
            presides at Rockfish Gap meeting of commissioners
            charged with planning the University of Virginia, and
            writes the Report. In October, Tracy's *A Treatise on Polit-
            ical Economy* is translated and published under Jefferson's
            direction.

1819   General Assembly charters University of Virginia January
            25. Jefferson possibly completes "The Life and Morals of
            Jesus of Nazareth," not published until 1902, but denies in
            private letters that he has converted to any particular de-
            nomination.

1820   Denounces the Missouri Compromise in private letters,
            predicting it will excite sectional prejudices. In this and
            subsequent years, fulminates against the usurpation of
            power by Supreme Court and the tendency toward "con-
            solidation" of authority in federal government.

1821   Writes *Autobiography*, "for my own more ready reference,
            and for the information of my family," from January 6 to
            July 29.

1823   Letter to President Monroe, October 24, contributes to formulation of the Monroe Doctrine, declaring the western hemisphere closed to European expansion.

1824   Makes final preparations in April for Francis Walker Gilmer's mission to Europe to recruit faculty for University of Virginia. Lafayette, on a triumphal tour of the United States, visits Monticello and is feted at the university November 3 to 15.

1825   University of Virginia opens to students March 7. Jefferson drafts "Declaration and Protest" for Virginia legislature, protesting federal usurpations, in December, but suppresses the document.

1826   Writes "Thoughts on Lotteries" in February, asking permission of the legislature to raffle his property to pay his debts, hoping by this means to realize enough money (which could not be done in the depressed market) to save Monticello for his heirs. General Assembly authorizes the lottery, but it is suspended when friends and admirers organize subscription funds in his behalf. Draws his will in March, providing for emancipation of five of his slaves. Dies at Monticello on July 4.

Note on the Texts

Thomas Jefferson published few of his writings during his lifetime. Most of what he wrote served governmental or private purposes: state papers, drafts of legislation, public addresses, autobiographical reminiscences, and letters to a variety of correspondents. The bulk of his writing, therefore, was published only posthumously, and has come down to us mainly through the mediation of several nineteenth-century editors.

Five major editions of Jefferson's writings have been published. The first, *The Memoirs, Correspondence and Private Papers of Thomas Jefferson*, appeared in four volumes in Charlottesville in 1829. Edited by Jefferson's grandson and executor, Thomas Jefferson Randolph, it first published the *Autobiography* and the *Anas* as well as a large selection of personal letters. For previously unpublished material, Randolph worked from manuscript and document sources, but, in accordance with the accepted editorial practice of his time, he made certain changes in spelling, punctuation, and wording.

Henry A. Washington, Librarian of the Department of State, prepared the nine-volume Congress Edition, *The Writings of Thomas Jefferson*, published in Washington, D.C. in 1853–54, following the federal government's purchase of Jefferson's public papers. In addition to these papers, Washington reprinted many items from the Randolph edition, and like Randolph, he routinely made editorial changes.

Paul Leicester Ford's edition, *The Writings of Thomas Jefferson*, 10 vols. (New York, 1892–99), was undoubtedly the best-edited of the nineteenth-century collections. The large majority of the items in this edition were freshly transcribed from Jefferson's manuscripts following conservative editorial principles. Ford indicated the provenance of each manuscript; in the few cases where he reprinted a document from an earlier published source, he indicated that source. For writings not published by Jefferson himself, Ford's edition has been the preferred source of the texts in this volume.

The Writings of Thomas Jefferson, 20 vols. (Washington, D.C., 1903–04), sometimes called the Memorial Edition, prepared by Andrew A. Lipscomb and Albert Ellery Bergh, is the most comprehensive edition and has a highly useful index. Unfortunately, the edition is largely a compendium of reprints. Sources for specific items are not indicated, but comparison with other texts has shown that in most cases Lipscomb and Bergh reprinted documents from Ford, or from Washington, or elsewhere, without reference to manuscripts. Also, Lipscomb and Bergh routinely modernized spelling, punctuation, and orthography. Several documents in their edition, unavailable in any printed source, were newly edited from manuscript: Vol. XVII, comprising the "Miscellaneous Papers," "Thoughts on English Prosody" in Vol. XVIII, and all of Vol. XIX except two letters. The Lipscomb and Bergh edition, therefore, is the only printed source for those items, and has been the source for those texts in this volume that were published for the first time in that edition.

These older editions are destined to be superseded (eventually) by the edition in progress at Princeton University, *The Papers of Thomas Jefferson*, ed. Julian Boyd, Charles Cullen, *et al.*, 20 vols. to date (Princeton, 1950–82). This edition, of which Jefferson's writings form only the core, is still incomplete. Even that edition makes some alterations in spelling and punctuation; its lengthy and detailed historical notes are invaluable.

The first choice of texts for this volume has been those versions which Jefferson himself supervised or which were published during his lifetime, in the three instances where such a text exists: *A Summary View of the Rights of British America*, *Notes on the State of Virginia*, and the *Observations on the Whale-Fishery*. The text of *A Summary View* is taken from the pamphlet edition, published in Williamsburg in 1774.

The text of the *Notes on the State of Virginia* reprinted here is the edition published by John Stockdale in London in 1787. Jefferson had previously arranged for a small private edition of the book, limited to 200 copies, printed without the author's name on the title page. Upon learning that a French publisher had obtained a copy of this edition and was plan-

ning an unauthorized French translation, he agreed to collab-
orate on an authorized translation; but his dissatisfaction with
the product of his collaboration with the Abbé Morellet led
him to commission Stockdale to issue an authorized English
edition for general distribution. The Stockdale edition, which
carried Jefferson's name, and which he closely supervised,
therefore best represents his intentions, and is the text
selected for this volume. Three appendices in that edition (a
commentary by Charles Thomson, a draft constitution of 1783
for Virginia, and the Statute of Religious Freedom) are omitted from the present volume. (Earlier versions of the draft
constitution and the Statute of Religious Freedom are printed
elsewhere in these pages.) The view of Madison's cave is reprinted here courtesy of The New York Public Library. The
map for *Notes on the State of Virginia* was originally prepared
by Peter Jefferson (Thomas's father) and Joshua Fry in 1751 as
"Map of the Inhabited Parts of Virginia." For the Stockdale
edition of the *Notes*, Thomas Jefferson updated his father's
map and commissioned a new engraving in London. The
map is reprinted here in its original size.

Jefferson had the *Observations on the Whale-Fishery* (1778)
printed in Paris by Jacques-Gabriel Clousier. It appeared in
identical format in both English and French. Only a few of
the small number of copies printed are extant. The present
volume reprints the text from the copy in The Library Company of Philadelphia, which may have been the copy Jefferson
kept for his files; several notes in his handwriting which appear at the head and at the end of the printed text are quoted
in the *Notes* to the present volume.

In selecting texts of documents not prepared for publication by Jefferson, the order of preferred sources has been:
contemporary publications (books, newspapers, published
government reports), then the Ford edition, the Randolph
edition, the Washington edition (where no other source has
been found), and the edition of Lipscomb and Bergh (only
for selections they transcribed from manuscript). A slightly
different order of preference has governed the selection of
texts in the last section, the letters. Among the many editions
of selected Jefferson letters, representing all aspects of his
large and varied correspondence, several have been preferred

because of their superior textual reliability. All letters from Jefferson to John and Abigail Adams, for instance, are reprinted from *The Adams-Jefferson Letters*, 2 vols., ed. Lester J. Cappon (1959). Several letters from Jefferson to members of his family have been taken from *The Family Letters of Thomas Jefferson*, ed. Edwin M. Betts and James A. Bear, Jr. (1966). A few letters to various other persons have been chosen from the large number printed in the *Massachusetts Historical Society Collections*, 7th Ser., Vol. I (1900). A small number of letters has been transcribed for the present volume from manuscript, or from microfilm or photostatic copies of manuscript, when no acceptable printed source was available. Sources for other letters are indicated in the list below. After these exceptional cases, the order of preference stated earlier (Ford, then Randolph, Washington, Lipscomb and Bergh) has governed the selection of texts of the letters. In some instances, omissions in previously published versions of letters have been restored from manuscript text or microfilm copy. The following is a list of these restored passages, all from the Jefferson Papers, Library of Congress, cited by page and line number: 743.3–745.31, [enclosure]; 747.8–20, I . . . years.; 748.19–23, This . . . serv.; 748.26–34, I . . . box.; 751.6–12, P. S. . . . purpose.; 823.9–825.33, [enclosure]; 852.32–853.2, One . . . hands.; 884.6–20, You . . . *Congress.*; 905.10–906.14, [enclosure]; 928.40–929.11, Your . . . indulgence.; 930.32–933.8, The campaign . . . line.; 940.19–34, Since . . . good.; 1017.26–39, Let . . . Adieu.; 1076.8–18, I have . . . there.; 1165.30–38, They . . . you.; 1167.4–6, unless . . . Woodlands.; 1286.15–20, I was . . . yours.; 1368.29–39, I gave . . . consideration.; 1439.35–1440.13, Turning . . . you.; 1500.22–1501.5, Your . . . approved.; 1512.36–1535.11, My circular . . . number.

The following is a list of the writings included in this volume, in the order of their appearance, with the source of each text noted. The five main sources, mentioned above, are cited here as *Ford, Randolph, Washington, L&B,* and *Cappon.*

LIST OF SOURCES

I. AUTOBIOGRAPHY

Autobiography, with the Declaration of Independence. *Ford*, I, 3–162.

II. A SUMMARY VIEW OF THE RIGHTS OF BRITISH AMERICA

A Summary View of the Rights of British America. *A Summary View Of The Rights Of British America. Set Forth In Some Resolutions Intended For The Inspection Of The Present Delegates Of The People Of Virginia. Now In Convention. By A Native, And Member Of The House Of Burgesses* (Williamsburg, [1774]).

III. NOTES ON THE STATE OF VIRGINIA

Notes on the State of Virginia. Thomas Jefferson, *Notes on the State of Virginia* (London: John Stockdale, 1787).

IV. PUBLIC PAPERS

Resolutions of Congress on Lord North's Conciliatory Proposal. *Pennsylvania Packet*, August 7, 1775.

Draft Constitution for Virginia. *Ford*, II, 7–30.

Revisal of the Laws: Drafts of Legislation

    A Bill for Establishing Religious Freedom. *Report of the Committee of Revisors Appointed by the General Assembly of Virginia in MDCCLXXVI* (Richmond, 1784), 58–59.

    A Bill for Proportioning Crimes and Punishments. *Ford*, II 203–20.

    A Bill for the More General Diffusion of Knowledge. *Report of the Committee of Revisors . . .*, 53–55.

    A Bill Declaring Who Shall Be Deemed Citizens of This Commonwealth. *Report of the Committee of Revisors . . .*, 41–42.

Report of a Plan of Government for the Western Territory. *Ford*, III, 407–10.

Observations on the Whale-Fishery. *Observations on the Whale-Fishery* (Paris, 1788). Printed here courtesy of The Library Company of Philadelphia.

Plan for Establishing Uniformity in the Coinage, Weights, and Measures of the United States. *Washington*, VII, 472–95.

Opinion on the Constitutionality of a National Bank. *Ford*, V, 284–89.

Report on the Privileges and Restrictions on the Commerce of the United States in Foreign Countries. *Ford*, V, 470–84.

Draft of the Kentucky Resolutions. *L&B*, XVII, 379–91.

Report of the Commissioners for the University of Virginia. *Early History of the University of Virginia as Contained in the Letters of Thomas Jefferson and Joseph C. Cabell*, ed. Nathaniel F. Cabell (Richmond, 1856), 432–47.

Memorial on the Book Duty. *Annals of the Congress of the United States*, 17th Congress, 1st Session (Washington, D.C., 1855), 531–32.

From the Minutes of the Board of Visitors of the Commonwealth of Virginia. *L&B*, XIX, 413–16, 460–61, 468–70.

Draft Declaration and Protest of the Commonwealth of Virginia. *L&B*, XVII, 442–48.

V. ADDRESSES, MESSAGES, AND REPLIES

Response to the Citizens of Albemarle. *The Portable Jefferson*, ed. Merrill Peterson (New York, 1974), 259–60. © 1975 The Viking Press.

First Inaugural Address. *A Compilation of the Messages and Papers of the Presidents*, ed. James D. Richardson, 10 vols. (Washington, D.C., 1907), 309–12.

To Elias Shipman and Others, A Committee of the Merchants of New Haven. *Ford*, VIII, 67–71.

First Annual Message. *Ford*, VIII, 108–25.

To Messrs. Nehemiah Dodge and Others, A Committee of the Danbury Baptist Association, in the State of Connecticut. *Washington*, VIII, 113–14.

Third Annual Message. *Ford*, VIII, 266–74.

Second Inaugural Address, with "Notes of a Draft." *Ford*, VIII, 341–48.

Sixth Annual Message. *Ford*, VIII, 482–96.

Special Message on the Burr Conspiracy. *Ford*, IX, 14–20.

Special Message on Gun-Boats. *Ford*, IX, 23–27.

Eighth Annual Message. *Ford*, IX, 213–25.

To the Inhabitants of Albemarle County, in Virginia. *Ford*, IX, 250.

Indian Addresses

    To Brother John Baptist de Coigne. *Washington*, VIII, 17–76.

    To Brother Handsome Lake. *Washington*, VIII, 187–89.

    To the Brothers of the Choctaw Nation. *L&B*, XIX, 146–49.

    To the Wolf and People of the Mandan Nation. *Washington*, VIII, 200–02.

VI. MISCELLANY

Reply to the Representations of Affairs in America by British Newspapers. MS, Jefferson Papers, Library of Congress.

Answers and Observations for Démeunier's Article on the United States in the *Encyclopédie Methodique*.

    1. *From* Answers to Démeunier's First Queries, January 24, 1786.

        The Confederation. *Ford*, IV, 141–44, 146–47.

    2. *From* Observations on Démeunier's Manuscript, June 22, 1786,

        Indented servants. *Ford*, IV, 158–60.

        Crimes and punishments. *Ford*, IV, 169–70.

        The Society of the Cincinnati. *Ford*, IV, 170–77.

        Populating the continent. *Ford*, IV, 179–81.

    3. To Jean Nicolas Démeunier, June 26, 1786. *Ford*, IV, 183–85.

Thoughts on English Prosody. *L&B*, XVIII, 41–51.

Travel Journals

    1. A Tour to some of the Gardens of England. *Washington*, IX, 367–73.

    2. Memorandums on a Tour from Paris to Amsterdam, Strasburg, and back to Paris. *Washington*, IX, 373–403.

    3. Travelling notes for Mr. Rutledge and Mr. Shippen. *Washington*, 403–05.

The Anas—Selections

> Explanations, February 4, 1818. *Ford*, I, 154–68.
>
> Conversations with the President, 1792–1793. *Ford*, I, 174–78, 198–210, 202–05, 214–16, 256–59.
>
> "Liberty warring on herself," August 20, 1793. *Ford*, I, 259–61.
>
> Conversations with Aaron Burr, 1804–1806. *Ford*, VII, 44–49.

Notes on Professor Ebeling's Letter of July 30, 1795. *Ford*, VII, 44–49.

A Memorandum (Services to My Country). *Ford*, VII, 475–77.

A Memorandum (Rules of Etiquette). *Ford*, VIII, 276–77.

Epitaph. MS, Jefferson Papers, Library of Congress.

VII. LETTERS

John Harvie, January 14, 1760. *Ford*, I, 340.

John Page, December 25, 1762. *Ford*, I, 341.

John Page, May 25, 1766. *New York Public Library Bulletin*, Vol. 2 (1898), 176–77.

Thomas Turpin, February 5, 1769. *Two Letters from Thomas Jefferson to his Relatives the Turpins who Settled in The Little Miami Valley in 1797*, ed. Marie Dickore (Oxford, Ohio, 1941), 8–9.

Robert Skipwith, with a List of Books, August 3, 1771. *Ford*, I, 396.

Charles McPherson, February 25, 1773. *Ford*, I, 413.

William Small, May 7, 1775. *Ford*, I, 453.

John Randolph, August 25, 1775. *Ford*, I, 482.

Edmund Pendleton, August 13, 1776. *Ford*, II, 78–83.

Edmund Pendleton, August 26, 1776. MS, Massachusetts Historical Society.

John Adams, May 16, 1777. *Cappon*, 4–5.

Giovanni Fabbroni, June 8, 1778. *Ford*, II, 156–60.

David Rittenhouse, July 19, 1778. *Ford*, II, 162–64.

Patrick Henry, March 27, 1779. *Ford*, II, 167–80.

J. P. G. Muhlenberg, January 31, 1781. *Ford*, II, 441–43.

Lafayette, March 10, 1781. *Ford*, II, 493–94.

George Washington, May 28, 1781. *Ford*, III, 41–44.

James Monroe, May 20, 1781. *Ford*, III, 56–60.

Chastellux, November 26, 1782. *Ford*, III, 64–66.

Martha Jefferson, November 28, 1783. *The Family Letters of Thomas Jefferson*, ed. Edwin M. Betts and James A. Bear, Jr. (Columbia, Missouri, 1966), 19–20. Used by permission of the University of Missouri Press. © 1966 The Curators of the University of Missouri.

George Rogers Clark, December 4, 1783. *Letters of the Lewis and Clark Expedition*, ed. Donald Jackson (Urbana, Illinois: The University of Illinois Press, 1962), 654–55.

Martha Jefferson, December 11, 1783. *The Family Letters of Thomas Jefferson*, 20–21. © 1966 The Curators of the University of Missouri.

Chastellux, January 16, 1784. MS, Bixby Collection, Missouri Historical Society.

George Washington, March 15, 1784. *Ford*, III, 420–25.

George Washington, April 16, 1784. *Ford*, III, 464–70.

Dr. Philip Turpin, April 28, 1784. *Two Letters from Thomas Jefferson to his Relatives the Turpins who Settled in The Little Miami Valley in 1797*, ed. Marie Dickore (Oxford, Ohio, 1941), 13–16.

Richard Price, February 1, 1785. *Massachusetts Historical Society Proceedings*, 2d Ser., Vol. XVII (1903), 325–26.

Chastellux, June 7, 1785. *Randolph*, I, 228–31.

James Monroe, June 17, 1785. *Ford*, IV, 49–60.

Abigail Adams, June 21, 1785. *Cappon*, 33–36. © 1959 The University of North Carolina Press.

Virginia Delegates in Congress, July 12, 1785. *Ford*, IV, 72–75.

Peter Carr, August 19, 1785. *Randolph*, I, 285–88.

John Jay, August 23, 1785. *Ford*, IV, 87–90.

James Madison, with a List of Books, September 1, 1785. *Randolph*, I, 299–301.

Chastellux, September 2, 1785. *Thomas Jefferson Correspondence, Printed from the Originals in the Collection of William K. Bixby*, ed. Worthington C. Ford (Boston, 1915), 11–13.

James Madison, September 20, 1785. *Randolph*, I, 315–17.

Abigail Adams, September 25, 1785. *Cappon*, 69–71. © 1959 The University of North Carolina Press.

Charles Bellini, September 30, 1785. *Randolph*, I, 326–28.

G. K. van Hogendorp, October 13, 1785. *Ford*, IV, 102–106.

John Banister, Jr., October 15, 1785. *Randolph*, I, 345–47.

James Madison, October 28, 1785. *L&B*, XIX, 15–20.

Archibald Stuart, January 25, 1786. *Ford*, IV, 187–90.

William Buchanan and James Hay, January 26, 1786. *Randolph*, I, 437–39.

James Madison, February 8, 1786. *Ford*, IV, 192–97.

John Page, May 4, 1786. *Ford*, IV, 212–15.

John Adams, July 11, 1786. *Cappon*, 142–44. © 1959 The University of North Carolina Press.

George Wythe, August 13, 1786. *Ford*, IV, 266–70.

Thomas Mann Randolph, Jr., August 27, 1786. *Ford*, IV, 289–95.

Ezra Stiles, September 1, 1786. *Ford*, IV, 297–300.

Maria Cosway, October 12, 1786. *Ford*, IV, 311–13.

St. John de Crèvecoeur, January 15, 1787. *Randolph*, II, 82–83.

Edward Carrington, January 16, 1787. *Ford*, IV, 357–61.

James Madison, January 30, 1787. *Ford*, IV, 361–69.

Anne Willing Bingham, February 7, 1787. *Randolph*, II, 94–96.

Abigail Adams, February 22, 1787. *Cappon*, 172–73. © 1959 The University of North Carolina Press.

Madame de Tessé, March 20, 1787. *Randolph*, II, 101–04.

Lafayette, April 11, 1787. *Randolph*, II, 104–06.

Martha Jefferson, May 21, 1787. *The Family Letters of Thomas Jefferson*, 41–42. © 1966 The Curators of the University of Missouri.

John Adams, July 1, 1787. *Cappon*, 180–82. © 1959 The University of North Carolina Press.

Maria Cosway, July 1, 1787. Helen D. Bullock, *My Head and My Heart: A Little History of Thomas Jefferson and Maria Cosway* (New York, 1945), 68–69.

Peter Carr, with Enclosure, August 10, 1787. *Ford*, IV, 427–34.

John Adams, August 30, 1787. *Cappon*, 194–96. © 1959 The University of North Carolina Press.

Buffon, October 1, 1787. *Ford*, IV, 457–59.

William S. Smith, November 13, 1787. *Ford*, IV, 465–68.

John Adams, November 13, 1787. *Cappon*, 211–12. © 1959 The University of North Carolina Press.

James Madison, December 20, 1787. *Ford*, IV, 473–80.

Alexander Donald, February 7, 1788. *Randolph*, II, 290–92.

Maria Cosway, April 24, 1788. Bullock, *My Head and My Heart*, 90–92.

Anne Willing Bingham, May 11, 1788. *Ford*, V, 8–10.

The Rev. James Madison, July 19, 1788. *Randolph*, II, 335–38.

St. John de Crèvecoeur, August 9, 1788. *Randolph*, II, 350–52.

George Washington, December 4, 1788. *Ford*, V, 56–60.

Richard Price, January 8, 1789. *Washington*, II, 553–57.

John Trumbull, February 15, 1789. MS, Jefferson Papers, Library of Congress.

Francis Hopkinson, March 13, 1789. *Ford*, V, 75–78.

James Madison, March 15, 1789. *Ford*, V, 80–86.

Joseph Willard, March 24, 1789. *Randolph*, II, 451–53.

John Jay, May 9, 1789. *Randolph*, II, 459–62.

Rabout de St. Etienne, with Draft of a Charter of Rights, June 3, 1789. *Ford*, V, 99–102.

Diodati, August 3, 1789. MS, Massachusetts Historical Society.

James Madison, September 6, 1789. *Ford*, V, 115–24.

Madame d'Enville, April 2, 1790. *Ford*, V, 153–54.

John Garland Jefferson, June 11, 1790. *Ford*, V, 179–82.

Mary Jefferson, June 13, 1790. *The Family Letters of Thomas Jefferson*, 58–59. © 1966 The Curators of the University of Missouri.

Samuel Vaughan, Jr., November 27, 1790. MS, Jefferson Papers, Library of Congress.

Martha Jefferson Randolph, December 23, 1790. *The Family Letters of Thomas Jefferson*, 67. © 1966 The Curators of the University of Missouri.

George Mason, February 4, 1791. *Ford*, V, 274–76.

Ebenezer Hazard, February 18, 1791. *Washington*, III, 211.

The Rev. William Smith, February 19, 1791. *Ford*, V, 290–93.

Major L'Enfant, April 10, 1791. *Washington*, III, 236–37.

Charles Carroll, April 15, 1791. *Washington*, III, 246–47.

The President of the U.S. (George Washington), May 23, 1791. *Ford*, V, 328–30.

Thomas Mann Randolph, Jr., June 5, 1791. *Ford*, V, 340–42.

John Adams, July 17, 1791. *Cappon*, 245–47. © 1959 The University of North Carolina Press.

Benjamin Banneker, August 30, 1791. *Ford*, V, 377–78.

Archibald Stuart, December 23, 1791. *Ford*, V, 408–11.

The President of the U.S. (George Washington), May 23, 1792. *Ford*, VI, 1–6.

Lafayette, June 16, 1792. *Ford*, VI, 78–79.

Thomas Paine, June 19, 1792. *Ford*, VI, 87–88.

The President of the U.S. (George Washington), September 9, 1792. *Ford*, VI, 101–109.

The U.S. Minister to France (Gouverneur Morris), December 30, 1792. *Ford*, VI, 149–52.

William Short, January 3, 1793. *Ford*, VI, 153–57.

James Madison, March 24, 1793. *Ford*, VI, 192–93.

James Madison, May 19, 1793. *Ford*, VI, 259–62.

James Madison, June 9, 1793. *Ford*, VI, 290–94.

Mrs. Church, November 27, 1793. *Ford*, VI, 454–56.

Tench Coxe, May 1, 1794. *Ford*, VI, 507–08.

James Madison, December 28, 1794. *Ford*, VI, 516–19.

John Taylor, December 29, 1794. *Massachusetts Historical Society Collections*, 7th Ser., Vol. I (1900), 49–55.

François D'Ivernois, February 6, 1795. *Ford*, VII, 2–6.

James Madison, April 27, 1795. *Ford*, VII, 8–11.

Jean Nicolas Démeunier, April 29, 1795. *Ford*, VII, 12–15.

Mann Page, August 30, 1795. *Ford*, VII, 23–25.

George Wythe, January 16, 1796. *Ford*, VII, 52–55.

John Adams, February 28, 1796. *Cappon*, 259–60. © 1959 The University of North Carolina Press.

Philip Mazzei, April 24, 1796. *Ford*, VII, 72–78.

James Madison, with Enclosure, January 1, 1797. *Ford*, VII, 98–100.

Elbridge Gerry, May 13, 1797. *Ford*, VII, 119–24.

Thomas Pinckney, May 29, 1797. *Ford*, VII, 127–30.

Martha Jefferson Randolph, June 8, 1797. *The Family Letters of Thomas Jefferson*, 145–47. © 1966 The Curators of the University of Missouri.

John Taylor, June 4, 1798. *Massachusetts Historical Society Collections*, 7th Ser., Vol. I (1900), 61–64.

Philip Nolan, June 24, 1798. *Washington*, IV, 252–53.

Samuel Smith, August 22, 1798. *Ford*, VII, 275–80.

Elbridge Gerry, January 26, 1799. *Ford*, VII, 325–36.

Thomas Lomax, March 12, 1799. *Ford*, VII, 373–74.

William Green Munford, June 18, 1799. MS, Milbank Memorial Library, Teachers College, Columbia University.

Edmund Randolph, August 18, 1799. *Ford*, VII, 383–87.

Dr. Joseph Priestley, January 18, 1800. *Ford*, VII, 406–10.

Dr. Joseph Priestley, January 27, 1800. *Ford*, VII, 413–16.

John Breckinridge, January 29, 1800. *Ford*, VII, 416–19.

Bishop James Madison, January 31, 1800. *Ford*, VII, 419–21.

Gideon Granger, August 13, 1800. *Ford*, VII, 450–53.

Dr. Benjamin Rush, September 23, 1800. *Ford*, VII, 458–61.

William Dunbar, January 12, 1801. *Ford*, VII, 481–83.

John Dickinson, March 6, 1801. *Ford*, VIII, 7–8.

Dr. Joseph Priestley, March 21, 1801. *Ford*, VIII, 21–23.

Moses Robinson, March 23, 1801. *Randolph*, III, 463.

Elbridge Gerry, March 29, 1801. *Ford*, VIII, 40–43.

The U.S. Minister to France (Robert R. Livingston), September 9, 1801. *Ford*, VIII, 88–92.

James Monroe, November 14, 1801. *Ford*, VIII, 101–102.

The Governor of Virginia (James Monroe), November 24, 1801. *Ford*, VIII, 103–06.

P. S. Dupont de Nemours, January 18, 1802. *Ford*, VIII, 125–27.

Anne Cary, Thomas Jefferson, and Ellen Wayles Randolph, March 2, 1802. *The Family Letters of Thomas Jefferson*, 218. © 1966 The Curators of the University of Missouri.

General Thaddeus Kosciusko, April 2, 1802. *Randolph*, III, 490–91.

The U.S. Minister to France (Robert R. Livingston), April 18, 1802. *Ford*, VIII, 143–47.

Benjamin H. Latrobe, November 2, 1802. *The Portable Thomas Jefferson*, ed. Merrill Peterson (New York, 1974), 488–90. © 1975 The Viking Press.

Thomas Cooper, November 29, 1802. *Ford*, VIII, 176–78.

The Special Envoy to France (James Monroe), January 13, 1803. *Ford*, VIII, 190–92.

Benjamin Hawkins, February 18, 1803. *Ford*, VIII, 211–16.

Governor William H. Harrison, February 27, 1803. *Washington*, IV, 471–75.

Dr. Joseph Priestley, April 9, 1803. *Ford*, VIII, 224–25.

Dr. Benjamin Rush, with a Syllabus, April 21, 1803. *Ford*, VIII, 223–28.

Instructions to Captain Lewis, June 20, 1803. *Ford*, VIII, 194–99.

Sir John Sinclair, June 30, 1803. *Washington*, IV, 490–92.

Earl of Buchan, July 10, 1803. *Washington*, IV, 493–94.

Pierre J. G. Cabanis, July 12, 1803. *Washington*, IV, 496–97.

John C. Breckinridge, August 12, 1803. *Ford*, VIII, 242–44.

Wilson Cary Nicholas, September 7, 1803. *Ford*, VIII, 247–48.

Dr. Joseph Priestley, January 29, 1804. *Ford*, VIII, 293–96.

Jean Baptiste Say, February 1, 1804. *Washington*, IV, 526–27.

Abigail Adams, June 13, 1804. *Cappon*, 269–71.

Judge John Tyler, June 28, 1804. *Washington*, IV, 548–50.

Larkin Smith, November 26, 1804. *Ford*, VIII, 337–38.

Littleton Waller Tazewell, January 5, 1805. MS, University of Virginia.

John Taylor, January 6, 1805. *Ford*, VIII, 338–40.

C. F. de C. Volney, February 8, 1805. *Randolph*, IV, 30–34.

C. F. de C. Volney, February 11, 1806. *Ford*, VIII, 419–21.

Joel Barlow, February 24, 1806. *Ford*, VIII, 424–25.

The Emperor Alexander, April 19, 1806. *Ford*, VIII, 439–41.

Dr. Edward Jenner, May 14, 1806. *The Portable Thomas Jefferson*, ed. Peterson, 501. © 1975 The Viking Press.

Barnabas Bidwell, July 5, 1806. *Randolph*, IV, 56–58.

William Hamilton, July, 1806. *Thomas Jefferson's Garden Book, 1766–1824*, ed. Edwin M. Betts (Philadelphia, 1944), 322–24.

John Dickinson, January 13, 1807. *Ford*, IX, 8–10.

William Waller Hening, January 14, 1807. *Ford*, IX, 10.

Governor William C. C. Claiborne, February 3, 1807. *Washington*, V, 40–41.

William Branch Giles, April 20, 1807. *Ford*, IX, 42–46.

John Norvell, June 14, 1807. *Ford*, IX, 71–75.

George Hay, June 20, 1807. *Ford*, IX, 59–60.

Dr. Caspar Wistar, June 21, 1807. *Ford*, IX, 78–85.

Robert Fulton, August 16, 1807. *Ford*, IX, 125.

Rev. Samuel Miller, January 23, 1808. *Ford*, IX, 174–76.

Dr. Thomas Leib, June 23, 1808. *Ford*, IX, 196–97.

Lacépède, with a Catalogue, July 14, 1808. *Washington*, V, 309–12.

Monsieur Sylvestre, July 15, 1808. *Washington*, V, 312–14.

Thomas Jefferson Randolph, November 24, 1808. *Ford*, IX, 230–34.

Dr. Benjamin Waterhouse, December 1, 1808. *Washington*, V, 393–95.

James Monroe, January 28, 1809. *Ford*, IX, 242–44.

John Hollins, February 19, 1809. *Randolph*, IV, 124–25.

Henri Gregoire, February 25, 1809. *Ford*, IX, 246–47.

P. S. Dupont de Nemours, March 2, 1809. *Randolph*, IV, 125–26.

Mrs. Samuel H. Smith, March 6, 1809. *Thomas Jefferson Correspondence, Printed from the Originals in the Collection of William K. Bixby*, ed. Worthington C. Ford (Boston 1915), 177.

Horatio G. Spafford, May 14, 1809. *Washington*, V, 445–48.

John Wyche, May 19, 1809. *Washington*, V, 448–49.

P. S. Dupont de Nemours, June 28, 1809. *Washington*, V, 456–58.

John W. Campbell, September 3, 1809. *Ford*, IX, 257–59.

Dr. Benjamin S. Barton, September 21, 1809. *Randolph*, IV, 132–33.

Samuel Kercheval, January 19, 1810. *Randolph*, IV, 138–39.

John Garland Jefferson, January 25, 1810. *Ford*, IX, 270–71.

Cæsar A. Rodney, February 10, 1810. *Ford*, IX, 271–72.

Governor John Langdon, March 5, 1810. *Randolph*, IV, 144–48.

Messrs. Hugh L. White and Others, May 6, 1810. *Washington*, V, 520–22.

The President of the U.S. (James Madison), May 13, 1810. *Washington*, V, 522–24.

John Tyler, May 26, 1810. *Ford*, IX, 276–78.

William Duane, August 12, 1810. *Washington*, V, 532–36.

John B. Colvin, September 20, 1810. *Ford*, IX, 279–82.

Dr. Benjamin Rush, January 16, 1811. *Ford*, IX, 294–99.

John Lynch, January 21, 1811. *Washington*, V, 563–65.

A. L. C. Destutt de Tracy. January 26, 1811. *Ford*, IX, 305–10.

Alexander von Humboldt, April 14, 1811. *Washington*, V, 580–81.

Charles Willson Peale, August 20, 1811. *Washington*, VI, 6.

Dr. Robert Patterson, November 10, 1811. *Washington*, VI, 17–26.

John Adams, January 21, 1812. *Cappon*, 290–92. © 1959 The University of North Carolina Press.

John Adams, June 11, 1812. *Cappon*, 305–308. © 1959 The University of North Carolina Press.

General Thaddeus Kosciusko, June 28, 1812. *Ford*, IX, 361–64.

John Melish, January 13, 1813. *Ford*, IX, 373–77.

Madame de Staël, May 24, 1813. *Randolph*, IV, 186–91.

John Adams, June 15, 1813. *Cappon*, 331–33. © 1959 The University of North Carolina Press.

John Wayles Eppes, June 24, 1813. *Ford*, IX, 388–95.

Isaac McPherson, August 13, 1813. *Washington*, VI, 175–82.

John Waldo, August 16, 1813. *Washington*, VI, 184–89.

John Adams, October 12, 1813. *Cappon*, 383–86. © 1959 The University of North Carolina Press.

John Adams, October 28, 1813. *Cappon*, 387–92. © 1959 The University of North Carolina Press.

Alexander von Humboldt, December 6, 1813. *Ford*, IX, 430–33.

Madame de Tessé, December 8, 1813. *Ford*, IX, 436–40.

Dr. Walter Jones, January 2, 1814. *Ford*, IX, 446–51.

Dr. Thomas Cooper, February 10, 1814. *Washington*, VI, 311–19.

Dr. John Manners, February 22, 1814. *Washington*, VI, 319–24.

N. G. Dufief, April 19, 1814. *Washington*, VI, 339–41.

Thomas Law, June 13, 1814. *Washington*, VI, 348–51.

John Adams, July 5, 1814. *Cappon*, 431–34. © 1959 The University of North Carolina Press.

Edward Coles, August 25, 1814. *Ford*, IX, 477–79.

Peter Carr, September 7, 1814. *L&B*, XIX, 485–88.

Samuel H. Smith, September 21, 1814. *Ford*, IX, 485–88.

William Short, November 28, 1814. *Washington*, VI, 398–402.

Lafayette, February 14, 1815. *Ford*, IX, 504–11.

George Watterston, May 7, 1815. *The Complete Jefferson*, ed. Saul K. Padover (New York, 1943), 1070–72. © 1943 Saul K. Padover, © renewed 1971 by Saul K. Padover.

Benjamin Austin, January 9, 1816. *Ford*, X, 7–11.

Charles Thomson, January 9, 1816. *Ford*, X, 5–7.

John Adams, January 11, 1816. *Cappon*, 458–61. © 1959 The University of North Carolina Press.

Joseph C. Cabell, February 2, 1816. *Washington*, VI, 540–44.

John Adams, April 8, 1816. *Cappon*, 466–69. © 1959 The University of North Carolina Press.

P. S. Dupont de Nemours, April 24, 1816. *Ford*, X, 22–25.

Corrèa da Serra, April 26, 1816. *Letters of the Lewis and Clark Expedition*, ed. Donald Jackson (Urbana, Illinois: The University of Illinois Press, 1962), 611–13.

John Taylor, May 28, 1816. *Ford*, X, 27–31.

Samuel Kercheval, July 12, 1816. *Ford*, X, 37–45.

Mrs. Samuel H. Smith, August 6, 1816. *Washington*, VII, 27–29.

Tristam Dalton, May 2, 1817. *Ford*, X, 79–80.

Lafayette, May 24, 1817. *Ford*, X, 82–86.

François de Marbois, June 14, 1817. *Washington*, VII, 76–77.

Nathaniel Burwell, March 14, 1818. *Ford*, X, 104–106.

Wells and Lilly, April 1, 1818. *Thomas Jefferson Correspondence, Printed from the Originals in the Collection of William K. Bixby*, ed. Worthington C. Ford (Boston, 1915), 238–39.

Nathaniel Macon, January 12, 1819. *Ford*, X, 119–22.

Dr. Vine Utley, March 21, 1819. *Ford*, X, 125–27.

Samuel Adams Wells, May 12, 1819. *Ford*, X, 127–32.

John Brazier, August 24, 1819. *Washington*, VII, 130–33.

Judge Spencer Roane, September 6, 1819. *Ford*, X, 140–43.

Nathaniel F. Moore, September 22, 1819. *Washington*, VII, 137–38.

William Short, with a Syllabus, October 11, 1819. *Ford*, X, 143–46.

John Holmes, April 22, 1820. *Ford*, X, 157–58.

William Short, August 4, 1820. *Randolph*, IV, 328–29.

John Adams, August 15, 1820. *Cappon*, 565–69. © 1959 The University of North Carolina Press.

Thomas Ritchie, December 25, 1820. *Ford*, X, 169–71.

Albert Gallatin, December 26, 1820. MS, Jefferson Papers, Library of Congress.

Francis Eppes, January 19, 1821. *Ford*, X, 182–83.

General James Breckinridge, February 15, 1821. *Randolph*, IV, 341–43.

Jedidiah Morse, March 6, 1822. *Ford*, X, 203–07.

Justice William Johnson, October 27, 1822. *Ford*, X, 222–26.

Dr. Thomas Cooper, November 2, 1822. *Ford*, X, 242–44.

John Adams, April 11, 1823. *Cappon*, 591–94. © 1959 The University of North Carolina Press.

Justice William Johnson, June 12, 1823. *Ford*, X, 226–32.

John Adams, September 4, 1823. *Cappon*, 596–97. © 1959 The University of North Carolina Press.

John Adams, October 12, 1823. *Cappon*, 599–601. © 1959 The University of North Carolina Press.

The President of the U.S. (James Monroe), October 24, 1823. *Ford*, X, 277–79.

Jared Sparks, February 4, 1824. *Ford*, X, 289–93.

Dugald Stewart, April 26, 1824. *Massachusetts Historical Society Collections*, 7th Ser., Vol. I (1900), 333–36.

Major John Cartwright, June 5, 1824. *Randolph*, IV, 393–99.

William Ludlow, September 6, 1824. *Washington*, VII, 377–78.

Lafayette, October 9, 1824. *Ford*, X, 320–21.

Thomas Jefferson Smith, February 21, 1825. *Ford*, X, 340–41.

Henry Lee, May 8, 1825. *Ford*, X, 342–43.

The Honorable J. Evelyn Denison, M.P., November 9, 1825. *Washington*, VII, 415–19.

Ellen Randolph Coolidge, November 14, 1825. *The Family Letters of Thomas Jefferson*, 460–63. © 1966 The Curators of the University of Missouri.

William Branch Giles, December 26, 1825. *Ford*, X, 354–57.

James Madison, February 17, 1826. *Ford*, X, 375–78.

James Heaton, May 20, 1826. Henry S. Randall, *The Life of Thomas Jefferson*, 3 vols. (New York, 1857), III, 539.

Roger C. Weightman, June 24, 1826. *Ford*, X, 390–92.

The standards for American English continue to undergo modification, and in some ways were conspicuously different in earlier periods from what they are today. In eighteenth and nineteenth-century writing, for example, a word might be spelled in more than one way, even in the same work (and sometimes in the same sentence), and these variations might be carried into print. In Jefferson's lifetime the institution of rigid linguistic norms was frequently recommended as a way of halting the process of linguistic change. Jefferson, however, did not spell consistently, nor, apparently, did he care to. Most editors have not been careful to preserve Jefferson's own spellings, which they have characterized as errors; nor have they preserved the punctuation, italics, and capitals that Jefferson used (as was the ordinary practice at the time) to suggest the movements of voice and to give words significances and emphases they might not otherwise have. Most editors have supplied capitals at the beginnings of sentences (a practice that was not Jefferson's), expanded abbreviations, substituted "and" for "&", etc. The texts in the present volume, since they are printed from different editions, represent varying degrees of regularization, according to the policies and habits of their editors. Examples of Jefferson's writing in an unmodernized and unregularized state can be found in the several letters edited from manuscript for the present volume, which present Jefferson's least official prose in its most characteristic and (except for the use of capitals to begin sentences) unmodernized form. The texts of *Notes on the State of Virginia* and *Observations on the Whale-Fishery* are also relatively close to Jefferson's own practice, since they are printed from editions he supervised or annotated, though some of the spelling and punctuation no doubt reflect the habits of the printers of these works.

The presence of brackets at various points in the text calls for brief comment. Some of the previous editions used brackets for different purposes. Ford, for instance, frequently placed his conjectural readings of faded manuscript words or passages inside brackets and in italics. In some cases, however, brackets in the text are Jefferson's own. Usually it is clear from the context whether brackets are Jefferson's or an editor's, and what their function is. Where it is not clear, the information can be sought in the edition from which the text is taken.

The drawings in the text are reproduced from Jefferson's handwritten manuscripts.

This volume is concerned only with representing the *texts* of the various pieces included; it does not attempt to reproduce features of the typographic design of the editions from which the texts are taken—such as the display capitalization and headings of letters, or the exact placement of drawings. The short titles over individual letters have been supplied by the present editor. Typographical errors have been corrected, and a list of these errors follows, cited by page and line numbers: 4.21, communication; 38.35, criminal; 39.16, it was; 40.29, religion" the; 51.29, states; 64.19, revenue; 64.25, laws; 69.31, country; 78.23, Cachet.; 79.38, dedesirous; 81.21, nouishment; 89.26, offer[ed]; 94.38, Commitee; 95.37, coaliton; 107.36, boronet; 140.5, Bïgbeaver; 149.6, remarkble; 175.20, gerality; 176.12, lynx; 177.1, us,; 177.20–21, they are acquainted; 178.26, Virgina; 203.6, far; 204.9, or or; 234.5, to to; 252.31, It is; 272.12, differents; 274.6, to strict; 303.1, QUERY XXII; 305.37, others; 309.16, 1633; 337.32, privileges; 338.24, to shall; 341.17, anually; 356.34, devant."; 356.42, judgment; 366.10, notice or; 367.7, betwen; 368.1, teacherin; 371.12, mumerical; 372.11, enquie; 372.36, interregatories; 377.6–7, America; 380.12, the; 386.4, in; 387.28, it; 409.34, grain,; 410.2, established (8.); 415.5, it thought; 422.29–30, neutrality.; 425.10, Does; 426.11, party.'; 432.27, word?'; 455.32, (not; 461.17, qualties; 461.20, acquisitions; 470.29, Univresity; 493.12, convulious; 564.3, MANDAR; 574.20, Netherl^{ds}.; 581.12, &c.'; 582.7, &c.'; 586.37, wealthest; 595.7, question; 623.3, Memorandems; 631.4, peasants; 631.33, brother; 639.22–23, thus a centry; 639.34, twenty-one; 639.35–36, as present; 659.6, go the; 665.15, Hamiltion; 686.20, energy; 699.40, orriginally; 701.7, Adam's; 779.27, (providing; 779.28, affording; 779.33–34, Chattelux; 781.5, the contrary; 794.11, give,; 794.25, as.; 843.4, and; 848.15, you; 857.31, gentlemen; 918.9, Montesquien;

923.12, Americans; 936.20, rereflection; 950.15, to to get; 952.4, though; 954.3, goverment; 964.10, right convey; 982.13, it is; 988.18, obvious?; 994.14, ackolege; 1088.22, death,; 1092.14, all,; 1096.4, him,; 1097.27, insolated; 1104.38, session; 1122.30, Christianty; 1123.26, no give to; 1143.29, gentlemen; 1156.31–32, indiscrimately; 1157.16, his; 1160.25, goverment; 1178.9, Possibillities; 1181.23, in in; 1192.13, than than; 1195.23, of; 1209.9, relinqished; 1229.6, continne; 1256.35, live ing; 1274.16, intercouse; 1295.8, though; 1300.29, philosphy; 1315.10, dify; 1315.22, Saliva; 1322.19, Eclcesiastical; 1340.7, Ursurper; 1345.27, wherever; 1350.2, eletricity; 1360.32, *jue*; 1398.34, monarchichal; 1404.31, choses; 1442.10, Bailey; 1454.7, anxities.

Notes

In the notes below, the reference numbers denote page and line of the present volume (the line count includes chapter headings). Considerations of space have made it impractical to annotate the vast number of individual names, correspondents, and others mentioned by Jefferson. No note is made for places included in a standard desk-reference book. Notes at the foot of the page in the text are Jefferson's own.

AUTOBIOGRAPHY

3.1   AUTOBIOGRAPHY]   Jefferson wrote his autobiography, as he says, in order to record "memoranda" and "dates and facts" for his own reference and for his family; and since he never revised it for publication, the text retains his abbreviations: "Gr. Br." at 3.11 is "Great Britain"; "pl. or def." at 3.13 is "plaintiff or defendent." The phrase "committee of correspondence," for instance, appears as "commee of correspondce" at 7.1–2 and at many other places. Patrick Henry appears simply as "P. H." in a number of places, and other initials are substituted for names.

7.22   Marshall II. 151]   John Marshall, *The Life of George Washington*, 5 vols (1804–1807).

13.5   government.]   Here Jefferson inserted several sheets of "notes" he had taken " while these things were going on."

24.25–33   Some . . . manner.]   This paragraph was written on a separate slip of paper and inserted by Jefferson. Ford prints it in a footnote but it is added here in its proper place.

39.23   Feb. 6.]   Jefferson had apparently proceeded through the above paragraph on January 6 and resumed writing on February 6. Similar dating occurs at several subsequent points in the text: 42.30, 54.34, 61.30, 62.31, 65.26, 101.17.

48.23–24   Notes and Reply]   Omitted here by Ford and in this edition.

66.31–67.25   "Extrait . . . Majesté."]   Extract from the despatch of the Count de Vergennes to the Marquis de Verac, Ambassador of France at the Hague, dated March 1, 1786. The original translation appeared in the Randolph edition: "The King will give his aid, as far as it may be in his power, towards the success of the affair, and you will, on his part, invite the Patriots to communicate to him their views, their plans, and their discontents. You may assure them, that the King takes a real interest in themselves, as well as their cause, and that they may rely upon his protection. On this they may place the greatest dependence, as we do not conceal, that if the Stadtholder resumes his former influence, the English system will soon prevail, and our alliance become a mere affair of the imagination. The Patriots will readily feel, that this position would be incompatible both with the dignity and consideration of his Majesty. But in case the chief of the Patriots should have to fear a division, they would have time sufficient to reclaim those whom the Anglomaniacs had misled, and to prepare matters in such a manner, that the question when again agitated, might be decided according to their wishes. In such a hypothetical case, the King authorizes you to act in concert with them, to pursue the direction which they may think proper to give you, and to employ every means to augment the number of partisans of the good cause. It remains for me to speak of the personal security of the Patriots. You may assure them, that under every circumstance, the King will take them under his immediate protection, and you will make known wherever you may judge necessary, that his Majesty will regard, as a personal offence, every undertaking against their liberty. It is to be presumed that this language, energetically maintained, may have some effect on the audacity of the Anglomaniacs, and that the Prince de Nassau will feel that he runs some risk in provoking the resentment of his Majesty."

A SUMMARY VIEW OF THE RIGHTS OF BRITISH AMERICA

105.1–2   A SUMMARY . . . AMERICA]   The epigraph and brief "Preface of the Editors" are omitted. Footnotes in Ford's edition indicated the alterations Jefferson made in his personal copy of the pamphlet and, in one instance, in a manuscript copy. These notes are included below.

106.20–21   Not a shilling]   Altered in Jefferson's copy to "No shilling."

106.30   Portugal, and]   Struck out in Jefferson's copy.

107.27   parted]   Altered to "parcelled" in Jefferson's copy.

107.29   were]   Altered to " was" in Jefferson's copy.

107.31–41   1632 . . . representatives.]   In Jefferson's copy this note is struck out and the following substituted: "In 1621 Nova Scotia was granted by James I. to Sir Wm. Alexander. In 1632 Maryland was granted by Charles I. to Lord Baltimore. In 1664 New York was granted by Charles II. to the D. of York: as also New Jersey, which the D. of York conveied again to Ld Berkely & Sr Geo Carteret. So also were the Delaware counties, which the same Duke conveied again to Wm. Penn. In 1665 the country including North & South Carolina, Georgia & the Floridas, was granted by Charles II. to the E. of Clarendon, D. of Albemarle, E. of Craven, Ld Berkely, Ld Ashley, Sr George Carteret, Sr John Coleton, & Sr. Wm Berkely. In 1681 Pennsylvania was granted by Charles II. to Wm. Penn."

111.19   the]   Altered to "his" in Jefferson's copy.

111.27   common]   Struck out in Jefferson's copy.

112.10   hold]   Altered to "withhold" in Jefferson's copy.

112.30   New England]   Altered to "Massachusetts" in Jefferson's copy.

113.13   knighthood]   "Alluding to the knighting of Sir Francis Bernard."—MS note in Jefferson's copy.

116.3   African]   Altered to "British" in Jefferson's copy.

116.30–31   his majesty's]   Struck out, and "the" substituted in Jefferson's copy.

117.15–16   establishment]   Struck out, and "reign of the Second William" substituted in Jefferson's copy.

117.16   of]   Struck out, and "under which" substituted in Jefferson's copy.

117.16–17   at . . . revolution]   Struck out, and "was settled" substituted in Jefferson's copy.

117.23–24   constitution]   "Since this period the king has several times dissolved the parliament a few weeks before its expiration, merely as an assertion of right."—MS note in Jefferson's copy. "On further inquiry I find two instances of dissolutions before the Parliament would, of itself, have been at an end: viz., the Parliament called to meet August 24, 1698, was dissolved by King William, December 19, 1700, and a new one called, to meet November 11, 1701, which was also dissolved November 30, 1701."—Additional note by Jefferson, in MS copy, Department of State Archives.

118.19   proper]   "insert 'and the frame of government thus dissolved, should the people take upon them to lay the throne of your majesty prostrate, or to discontinue their connection with the British empire, none will be so bold as to decide against the right or the efficacy of such avulsion.' "—MS note in Jefferson's copy.

119.21   farmers]   Struck out, and "laborers" substituted in Jefferson's copy.

121.34   and]   Struck out, and "on" substituted in Jefferson's copy.

NOTES ON THE STATE OF VIRGINIA

149.7–13   'Esta . . . hueco.']   "This cave, or channel, is cut out of the live rock with such precision, that the recesses on one side correspond with the projections on the other side, as if the height had parted expressly, with its turns and tortuosities, to give passage to the waters between the two strong walls that form it; they being so much alike that if they were to come together they would fit with each other without leaving a gap."

170.23–29   'en general . . . tous.']   "in general it appears that the colder countries suit our oxen better than the hot countries, and that they are also weightier and larger where the climate is more humid and the pasturage more abundant. The oxen of Denmark, of Podalie, of the Ukraine, and of Tartary which is inhabited by the Calmoques, are the largest of all."

177.33–36   'J'aime . . . verité.']   "I love a person who releases me from an error, as much as the one who teaches me a truth, since in effect an error corrected is a truth."

182.37–183.36   'Quoique . . . animaux.']   "Although the savage of the new world is of approximately the same stature as the man of our world, this does not suffice for him be an exception to the general fact of the shrinking of living nature on all that continent. The savage is feeble and has small generative organs; he has neither hair, nor beard, and no ardor for his female; although more agile than the European because he is more accustomed to running, he is, however, much less strong in body; he is also much less sensitive, and yet more fearful and more craven; he has no vivacity, no activity of soul; that of his body is less an exercise, a voluntary motion, than an involuntary action caused by need; take away from him hunger and thirst, you simultaneously deprive him of the active principle of all his movements; he will remain stupidly in repose on his legs or lying for whole days. There is no reason for seeking further into the cause of the dispersed way of life of the savages and their aversion to society: the most precious spark of the fire of nature has been denied to them; they are wanting in ardor for their females and, in consequence, in love for their fellow men. Not knowing this most ardent of affections, the most tender of them all, their other sentiments of this kind are cold and languid; they love but feebly their fathers and their children; the most intimate society of all, that of one's own family, is to them a weak bond; the society of one family with another does not exist at all: thus no union, no republic, no social state. For them physical love is the moral ethic; their heart is icy, their society cold, and their dominion harsh. They do not regard their wives other than as servants of labor or as beasts of burdon, on whom they load, without regard, the burdon of their hunting, and whom they compel, without pity, without gratitude, to tasks that are often beyond their strength; they have only a few children and take little care of them; all this manifests their original defect; they are indifferent because they are impotent, and this indifference to sex is the fundamental blemish which blights their nature, which hinders its blossoming, and which destroys the seeds of life, at the same time cutting off society at the root. Man is, therefore, not an exceptional case here. Nature, in refusing him the power of love, has treated him worse and has made him less than the animals."

184.20–21   'Sol Rodomonte . . . sicura']   "Rodomont scorns any way / To wend, except what is least secure." Ludovico Ariosto, *The Orlando Furioso*, trans. William Stewart Rose, Vol. 3 (London, 1825), p. 84.

184.24–35   'Los Indios . . . estado.']   "The vanquished Indians are the most cowardly and pusillanimous that can be seen: they play the innocent,

they humble themselves to contempt, apologize for their inconsiderate boldness, and with supplications and prayers give certain proof of their pusillanimity. Either what is said by the histories of the Conquest about their great
actions is meant figuratively, or the character of these peoples is not now
what it was then; but what is beyond doubt is that the nations of the north
subsist in the same liberty they have always had, without ever having been
subjects of any foreign Prince, and they live according to their government
and customs all their lives, without there having been any reason to change
their character; and in them one sees the same as what happened to the
conquered ones of Peru and of all of South America, and those who never
were conquered."

185.26–27   'los obrages . . . trata.']   "the manufactories annihilate them
on account of the inhumanity with which they are treated."

188.14–20   Col. Cresap . . . whites.]   When the accuracy of this account
was questioned, particularly with regard to Cresap's culpability, Jefferson
conducted an investigation into the facts and published the results in *Appendix to the Notes on Virginia Relative to the Murder of Logan's Family* (Philadelphia, 1800). In this he stated the wish that in future editions of *Notes on the
State of Virginia* the passage on Cresap and the murder should read as follows: "Captain Michael Cresap, and a certain Daniel Great-House, leading
on these parties, surprized, at different times, travelling and hunting parties
of the Indians, having their women and children with them, and murdered
many. Among these were unfortunately the family of Logan, a chief celebrated in peace and war, and long distinguished as a friend of the whites."

190.6–9   'On doit . . . science.']   "One must be astonished that America
has not yet produced one good poet, one able mathematician, one man of
genius in a single art, or a single science."

251.34–36   'Omnia . . . fertur.']   "All bad examples come from good ori-
gins; but when power passes to the ignorant or less good, that new example
is transmitted from the worthy and fit to the unworthy and unfit."

268.38   Τὺϛ . . . θεραπαινισιν.]   "He permitted the male slaves to con-
sort with the bondwomen for a fixed price."

PUBLIC PAPERS

331.1–2   *Resolutions . . . Proposal*]   The resolutions adopted by Congress,
printed here, were based on Jefferson's draft submitted July 25.

336.1   *Draft . . . Virginia*]   This is the third and final draft, which was
carried to Williamsburg by George Wythe and shown to the delegates. It was
first printed in the *Richmond Enquirer,* June 20, 1806. The text here is the MS
which Jefferson endorsed with the title "A Bill for new modelling the form
of government, & for establishing the fundamental principles thereof in future." Below this he added, "It is proposed that this bill, after correction by

the Convention, shall be referred by them to the people, to be assembled in their respective counties and that the suffrages of two thirds of the counties shall be requisite to establish it." Bracketed words in roman were so written by Jefferson; those in italic are Ford's interpolations.

346.2   *A Bill . . . Freedom*]   Jefferson said he drafted the bill in 1777; it was first presented and debated in the General Assembly in June, 1779, when it was also first printed as a broadside. It was enacted on January 16, 1786, but only after considerable deletion by amendment. The statute when passed began, "Whereas Almighty God . . ."

349.1–2   *A Bill . . . Punishments*]   Ford's edition includes Jefferson's notes from the MS, now in the Library of Congress, which were omitted in the published version. In the MS, Jefferson quotes in Anglo-Saxon, Latin, Old French, and English; Ford has transliterated the Anglo-Saxon.

376.1   *Report . . . Territory*]   It was not adopted but led to a revised report, also principally of Jefferson's authorship, which was adopted, after elimination of the prohibition of slavery, on April 23, 1784.

379.1   *Observations . . . Whale-Fishery*]   A manuscript note above the title on the first page of Jefferson's copy of this pamphlet reads: "A Memoire on the Arret of Sep. 8. 1788. prohibiting the importation of whale oils of foreign fishery into France, presented to M. de Montmorin Nov. 19. 1788. by Tho? Jefferson M. P. of the US. at Paris."

392.38   us.]   Another manuscript note appears at the end of the pamphlet: "In compliance with the above Memoire whale oils of the US. were exempted from the prohibition by an Arret of Dec. 7. 1788."

395.38   (1)]   Numbers in parentheses refer to Appendix beginning on 410.30.

416.28   XIIth. amendment]   The Tenth Amendment as finally ratified by the states.

449.1   *Draft . . . Resolutions*]   The resolutions in protest against the Alien and Sedition Laws were adopted by the legislature, after minor amendment, on November 16, 1798.

477.1–2   *From . . . Virginia*]   The reports and resolutions adopted by the Board of Visitors were written and signed by Jefferson as Rector.

482.1–4   *Draft . . . them*]   The paper, enclosed in a letter to Madison, December 24, 1825, was withdrawn and never acted upon.

ADDRESSES, MESSAGES, AND REPLIES

491.1   *Response . . . Albemarle*]   The response was delivered to a group of local citizens after his return from France.

492.2   March 4, 1801]   Date inserted.

493.20–21   We are . . . Federalists.]   In the MS draft, and often in print, this appears as "We are all republicans; we are all federalists."

494.6–7   thousandth . . . generation]   "Thousandth and thousandth" is correct. It appears often in other editions as "hundredth and thousandth."

518.1   *Second Inaugural Address*]   In Jefferson's MS is the following outline:

NOTES OF A DRAFT FOR A SECOND INAUGURAL ADDRESS

The former one was an exposition of the principles on which I thought it my duty to administer the government. The second then should naturally be a conte rendu, or a statement of facts, shewing that I have conformed to those principles. The former was *promise*: this is *performance*. Yet the nature of the occasion requires that details should be avoided, that, the most prominent heads only should be selected and these placed in a strong light but in as few words as possible. These heads are Foreign affairs; Domestic do., viz. Taxes, Debts, Louisiana, Religion, Indians, The Press. None of these heads need any commentary but that of the Indians. This is a proper topic not only to promote the work of humanizing our citizens towards these people, but to conciliate to us the good opinion of Europe on the subject of the Indians. This, however, might have been done in half the compass it here occupies. But every respector of science, every friend to political reformation must have observed with indignation the hue & cry raised against philosophy & the rights of man; and it really seems as if they would be overborne & barbarism, bigotry & despotism would recover the ground they have lost by the advance of the public understanding. I have thought the occasion justified some discountenance of these anti-social doctrines, some testimony against them, but not to commit myself in direct warfare on them, I have thought it best to say what is directly applied to the Indians only, but admits by inference a more general extension.

There are also two papers, as follows:

MADISON'S MEMORANDUM.

Insert

"Thro' the transactions of a portion of our citizens whose intelligence & arrangements best shield them agst the abuses, as well as inconveniences incident to the collection."

substitute

"Religion. As religious exercises, could therefore be neither controuled nor prescribed by us. They have accordingly been left as the Constitution found them, under the direction & discipline acknowledged within the several states."

Indians

"No desire" instead of "nothing to desire."

substitute

Who feeling themselves in the present order of things and fearing to become nothing in any other, inculcate a blind attachment to the customs of their fathers in opposition to every light * example which wd conduct them into a more improved state of existence. But the day I hope is not far distant when their prejudices will yield to their true interests & they will take their stand, &c.

Press—strike out from "their own affairs."

Last page—Alter to "views become manifest to them."

This is endorsed "Dept. State recd Feb. 8, 05 Inaugural."

The second paper reads:

MADISON'S MEMORANDUM.

Is the fact certain that the amt of the internal taxes not objectionable in their nature would not have paid the collectors?

What is the amendment alluded to as necessary to a repartition of liberated revenue amg. the states in time of peace?

Page 3—"in any view" may be better than "in any event" that phrase having just preceded.

Instead of "acts of religious exercise suited to it (religion)" "exercises suited to it" or some equivalent variation is suggested.

Dept. State recd Feb. 21. 05 Inaugural.

MISCELLANY

571.1–2   *Reply . . . Newspapers*]   The text is Jefferson's draft. It was translated and published, with some alterations, in the *Gazette de Leyde*, December 7 and 10, 1784.

590.18   13th . . . articles]   Article 13 of the Prussian treaty (signed in September 1785) provided a restrictive definition of contraband; Article 24 offered guarantees for the humane treatment of prisoners of war.

594.1   *Thoughts . . . Prosody*]   It is conjectured that this essay was written in the summer of 1786. The letter to Chastellux was similarly undated, though Lipscomb and Bergh tentatively date it in October of that year.

604.23   following instance]   Quotation from Virgil missing.

623.4   *Whateley*]   Thomas Whately, *Observations on Modern Gardening* (1770).

629.29   axis in peritrochio]   Similar to a windless or capstan.

630.8   moolen book]   Johannis van Zyl, *Theatrum Machinarum Universale; of Groot Algemeen Moolen-Boek* (Amsterdam, 1761).

644.16   annexed bill]   Not included here.

657.10   pumice]   Pomace, the substance of fruit remaining after pressing of cider or wine.

661.27   only . . . period]   John Marshall, *The Life of George Washington*,
5 vols. (1804–1807).

667.14   5/]   Five shillings.

678.10   My lre of——]   May 23, 1792.

694.26   election]   In the House of Representatives.

695.6   4.]   There is a gap in the MS between "4." and "That."

696.16   signature of]   The MS ends with "of" and the note alluded to
has not been found.

697.1   *Notes . . . 1795*]   Christoph Daniel Ebeling consulted Jefferson
while engaged in research for his *Geography and History of North America*, 5
vols. (1796–1816). The MS is undated but was probably written in late 1795.

706.4–5   Ολιγη . . . λυθεντων]   "And small we must lie, / A dust of
loosened bones." Not by Anacreon, but one of the Anacreontea, poems in
the style of Anacreon attributed to him until the 19th century.

LETTERS

735.34   she]   Rebecca Burwell, sister of a college classmate.

740.13–14   plan of study]   This is missing. At about the same time, Jefferson sent such a plan to another student, Bernard Moore, and although the
original of this, too, is missing, Jefferson later revised the plan and enclosed
it in a letter to John Minor, August 30, 1814. This version of the plan follows.

To Bernard Moore

Before you enter on the study of the law a sufficient groundwork must be
laid. For this purpose an acquaintance with the Latin and French languages
is absolutely necessary. The former you have; the latter must now be acquired. Mathematics and Natural philosophy are so useful in the most familiar occurrences of life, and are so peculiarly engaging & delightful as would
induce every person to wish an acquaintance with them. Besides this, the
faculties of the mind, like the members of the body, are strengthened &
improved by exercise. Mathematical reasoning & deductions are therefore a
fine preparation for investigating the abstruse speculations of the law. In
these and the analogous branches of science the following elementary books
are recommended.

Mathematics. Berout, Cours de Mathematiques. The best for a student
    ever published. Montucla or Bossu's histoire des mathematiques.
Astronomy. Ferguson and Le Monnier, or de la Lande.
Geography. Pinkerton.
Nat. Philosophy. Joyce's Scientific dialogues. Martin's Philosophica Britan-
    nica. Mussenbroek's Cours de Physique.
This foundation being laid, you may enter regularly on the study of the

Laws, taking with it such of it's kindred sciences as will contribute to eminence in it's attainment. The principal of these are Physics, Ethics, Religion, Natural law, Belles lettres, Criticism, Rhetoric and Oratory. The carrying on several studies at a time is attended with advantage. Variety relieves the mind, as well as the eye, palled with too long attention to a single object. But with both, transitions from one object to another may be so frequent and transitory as to leave no impression. The mean is therefore to be steered, and a competent space of time allotted to each branch of study. Again, a great inequality is observable in the vigor of the mind at different periods of the day. It's powers at these periods should therefore be attended to in marshalling the business of the day. For these reasons I should recommend the following distribution of your time.

Till VIII o'clock in the morning employ yourself in Physical studies, Ethics, Religion, natural and sectarian, and Natural law, reading the following books.

Agriculture. Dickson's husbandry of the antients. Tull's horse-shoeing husbandry. Ld Kaim's Gentleman farmer. Young's Rural Economy. V. Hale's body of husbandry. De-Serre's Theatre d'Agriculture.

Chemistry. Lavoisier. Conversations in Chemistry.

Anatomy. John and James Bell's Anatomy.

Zoology. Abregé du Systeme de Linnée par Gilbert. Manuel d'histoire Naturel par Blumenbach. Buffon, including Montbeillard & La Cepede. Wilson's American Ornithology.

Botany. Barton's elements of Botany. Turton's Linnaeus. Person Synopsis Plantarum.

Ethics. & Natl Religion. Locke's Essay. Locke's conduct of the mind in the search after truth. Stewart's Philosophy of the human mind. Enfield's history of Philosophy. Condorcet, Progrès de l'esprit Humain. Cicero de officiis. Tusculana. de Senectute. Somnium Scipionis. Senecae Philosophica. Hutchinson's Introduction to Moral Philosophy. Ld Kaim's Natural Religion. Traite elementaire de Morale et Bonheur. La Sagesse de Charron.

Religion. Sectarian Bible. New Testament. Commentaries on them by Middleton in his works, and by Priestley in his Corruptions of Christianity, & Early opinions of Christ. Volney's Ruins. The sermons of Sterne, Masillon & Bourdaloue.

Natural Law. Vattel Droit des Gens. Reyneval. Institutions du droit de la Nature et des Gens.

From VIII. to XII. read law. The general course of this reading may be formed on the following grounds. Ld Coke has given us the first view of the whole body of law worthy now of being studied: for so much of the admirable work of Bracton is now obsolete that the student should turn to it occasionally only, when tracing the history of particular portions of the law. Coke's Institutes are a perfect Digest of the law as it stood in his day. After this, new laws were added by the legislature, and new developments of the old laws by the Judges, until they had become so voluminous as to require a new Digest. This was ably executed by Matthew Bacon, altho' unfortunately under an Alphabetical instead of Analytical arrangement of matter. The same process of new laws & new decisions on the old laws going on, called at length for the same operation again, and produced the inimitable Commentaries of Blackstone.

In the department of the Chancery, a similar progress has taken place. Ld. Kaim has given us the first digest of the principles of that branch of our jurisprudence, more valuable for the arrangement of matter; than for it's exact conformity with the English decisions. The Reporters from the early time of that branch to that of the same Matthew Bacon are well digested, but alphabetically also, in the Abridgment of the Cases in Equity, the 2d volume of which is said to have been done by him. This was followed by a number of able reporters of which Fonblanque has given us a summary digest by commentaries on the text of the earlier work, ascribed to Ballow, entitled 'a Treatise of equity.' The course of reading recommended then in these two branches of Law is the following.

Common Law. Coke's institutes.

Select cases from the subsequent reporters to the time of Matthew Bacon.

Bacon's Abridgement.

Select cases from the subsequent reporters to the present time.

Select tracts on Law, among which those of Baron Gilbert are all of the first merit.

The Virginia laws. Reports on them.

Chancery. Ld Kaim's principles of Equity. 3d edition.

Select cases from the Chancery reporters to the time of Matthew Bacon.

The Abridgment of Cases in Equity.

Select cases from the subsequent reporters to the present day.

Fonblanque's Treatise of equity.

Blackstone's Commentaries (Tucker's edition) as the last perfect digest of both branches of law.

In reading the Reporters, enter in a common-place book every case of value, condensed into the narrowest compass possible which will admit of presenting distinctly the principles of the case. This operation is doubly useful, inasmuch as it obliges the student to seek out the pith of the case, and habituates him to a condensation of thought, and to an acquisition of the most valuable of all talents, that of never using two words where one will do. It fixes the case too more indelibly in the mind.

From XII to I. Read Politics.

Politics, general. Locke on government. Sidney on Government. Priestley's First principles of Government. Review of Montesquieu's Spirit of Laws. Anon.

De Lolme sur la constitution d'Angleterre. De Burgh's Political disquisitions.

Hatsell's Precedents of the H. of Commons. Select Parliam^y debates on England & Ireland.

Chipman's Sketches of the principles of government. The Federalist.
Political Economy. Say's Economie Politique. Malthus on the principles of
    population.
Tracy's work on Political Economy. *Now* about to be printed (1814).
In the AFTERNOON. Read History.
History. Antient the Greek and Latin originals.
    Select histories from the Universal history. Gibbon's Decline of the Ro-
        man Empire.
    Historie Ancienne de Millot.
Modern. Histoire moderne de Millot. Russell's History of Modern Eu-
    rope; Robertson's Charles V.
English. The original historians, to wit. The Hist. of Ed. II. by E. F. Ha-
    bington's E. IV. More's R. III. Ld. Bacon's H. VIII. Ld. Herbert's H.
    VIII. Goodwin's H. VIII. E. VI. Mary. Cambden's Eliz. & James. Lud-
    low. McCaulay. Fox. Belsham. Baxter's Hist. of England. (Hume repub-
    licanised & abridged) Robertson's Hist. of Scotland.
American. Robertson's History of America.
    Gordon's History of the independence of the U.S. Ramsay's Hist. of the
        Amer. Revolution. Burke's Hist of Virginia.
    Continuation of do. by Jones and Girardin nearly ready for the press.
From Dark to Bed-time. Belles lettres, criticism, Rhetoric, Oratory, to
    wit.
Belles lettres. Read the best of the poets, epic, didactic, dramatic, pastoral,
    lyric &c. But among these Shakespeare must be singled out by one who
    wishes to learn the full powers of the English language. Of him we must
    advise as Horace did of the Grecian models, 'vos exemplaria Graeca Noc-
    turna versate manu, diversate diurna.'
Criticism. Ld Kaim's Elements of criticism. Tooke's Diversions of Purley.
    Of Bibliographical criticism the Edinbg Review furnishes the finest
    models extant.
Rhetoric. Blair's lectures on Rhetoric. Sheridan on Elocution. Mason on
    Poetic and Prosaic numbers.
Oratory. This portion of time (borrowing some of the afternoon when the
    days are long and the nights short) is to be applied to acquiring the art
    of writing & speaking correctly by the following exercises. Criticise the
    style of any books whatever, committing your criticisms to writing.
    Translate into the different styles, to wit, the elevated, the middling and
    the familiar. Orators and poets will furnish subjects of the first, histori-
    ans of the second, & epistolary and Comic writers of the third—Under-
    take, at first, short compositions, as themes, letters &c., paying great
    attention to the correctness and elegance of your language. Read the
    Orations of Demosthenes & Cicero. Analyse these orations, and examine
    the correctness of the disposition, language, figures, states of the cases,
    arguments &c. Read good samples of English eloquence, some of these
    may be found in Small's American speaker, and some in Carey's Crimi-
    nal Recorder, in which last the defence of Eugene Aram is distinguish-

able as a model of logic, condensation of matter, & classical purity of style. Exercise yourself afterwards in preparing orations on feigned cases. In this observe rigorously the disposition of Blair into Introduction, Narration &c. Adapt your language & figures to the several parts of the oration, and suit your arguments to the audience before whom it is supposed to be spoken. This is your last and most important exercise. No trouble should therefore be spared. If you have any person in your neighborhood engaged in the same study, take each of you different sides of the same cause, and prepare pleadings, according to the custom of the bar, where the pl. opens, the def. answers and the pl. replies. It would farther be of great service to pronounce your orations (having only before you only short notes to assist the memory) in the presence of some person who may be considered as your judge.

NOTE. Under each of the preceding heads, the books are to be read in the order in which they are named. These by no means constitute the whole of what might be usefully read in each of these branches of science. The mass of excellent works going more into detail is great indeed. But those here noted will enable the student to select for himself such others of detail as may suit his particular views & dispositions. They will give him a respectable, an useful & satisfactory degree of knolege in these branches, and will themselves form a valuable and sufficient library for a lawyer, who is at the same time a lover of science. (*Ford*, IX, 480–85.)

748.30 violin] Randolph, the King's Attorney General in Virginia, was departing for England, which led to the consummation of an old bargain.

751.24 a . . . production] Jefferson's proposed instructions to the Virginia delegates, published as *A Summary View of the Rights of British America.*

757.38 Colō Hans's] Probably Colonel Edward Hand (1744–1802).

760.17 I enclose . . . list] Enclosure omitted.

764.29 Convention troops] Prisoners of war, from the Battle of Saratoga, encamped near Charlottesville.

792.14–15 The fourth . . . states.] See *Report on Government for Western Territory*, p. 376. The clause was subsequently eliminated by Congress.

805.8–32 *I am . . . money.*] Italicized words were written in code.

826.11–12 paper . . . inclosed] Enclosure omitted.

826.17 a lively picture] Chastellux's flattering portrait of Jefferson appeared in *Voyages . . . dans l'Amerique Septentrionale dans les annees 1780, 1781 et 1782* (Paris, 1786).

828.21–22 I enclose] Enclosure omitted.

848.29 the remonstrance] Madison's *Memorial and Remonstrance against Religious Assessments* (1785).

884.7   *formerly . . . Adams.*]   Here and following in this letter, words in italics were written in code.

889.3   letter of Jan. 29.]   Abigail Adams had written as follows:

London Janry. 29th. 1787

MY DEAR SIR

I received by Col. Franks your obliging favour and am very sorry to find your wrist still continues lame; I have known very salutary effects produced by the use of British oil upon a spraind joint. I have sent a servant to see if I can procure some. You may rest assured that if it does no good: it will not do any injury.

With regard to the Tumults in my Native state which you inquire about, I wish I could say that report had exagerated them. It is too true Sir that they have been carried to so allarming a Height as to stop the Courts of justice in several Counties. Ignorant, wrestless desperadoes, without conscience or principals, have led a deluded multitude to follow their standard, under pretence of grievances which have no existance but in their immaginations. Some of them were crying out for a paper currency, some for an equal distribution of property, some were for annihilating all debts, others complaning that the Senate was a useless Branch of Government, that the Court of common pleas was unnecessary, and that the sitting of the General Court in Boston was a grievance. By this list you will see the materials which compose this rebellion, and the necessity there is of the wisest and most vigorus measures to quell and suppress it. Instead of that laudible spirit which you approve, which makes a people watchfull over their Liberties and alert in the defence of them, these mobish insurgents are for sapping the foundation, and distroying the whole fabrick at once.—But as these people make only a small part of the state, when compared to the more sensible and judicious, and altho they create a just allarm and give much trouble and uneasiness, I cannot help flattering myself that they will prove sallutary to the state at large, by leading to an investigation of the causes which have produced these commotions. Luxury and extravagance both in furniture and dress had pervaded all orders of our Countrymen and women, and was hastning fast to sap their independance by involving every class of citizens in distress, and accumulating debts upon them which they were unable to discharge. Vanity was becoming a more powerfull principal than patriotism. The lower order of the community were prest for taxes, and tho possest of landed property they were unable to answer the demand, whilst those who possest money were fearfull of lending, least the mad cry of the mob should force the Legislature upon a measure very different from the touch of Midas.

By the papers I send you, you will see the beneficial effects already produced. An act of the Legislature laying duties of 15 per cent upon many articles of British manufacture and totally prohibiting others—a number of Vollunteers Lawyers physicians and Merchants from Boston made up a party of Light horse commanded by Col. Hitchbourn, Leit. Col. Jackson and Higgenson, and went out in persuit of the insurgents and were fortunate enough to take 3 of their principal Leaders, Shattucks Parker and Page. Shattucks defended himself and was wounded in his knee with a broadsword. He is in Jail in Boston and will no doubt be made an example of.

Your request my dear sir with respect to your Daughter shall be punctually attended to, and you may be assured of every attention in my power towards her.

You will be so kind as to present my Love to Miss Jefferson, compliments to the Marquiss and his Lady. I am really conscience smitten that I have never written to that amiable Lady, whose politeness and attention to me deserved my acknowledgment.

The little balance which you stated in a former Letter in my favour, when an opportunity offers I should like to have in Black Lace at about 8 or 9 Livres pr. Ell. Tho late in the Month, I hope it will not be thought out of season to offer my best wishes for the Health, Long Life and prosperity of yourself and your family, or to assure you of the Sincere Esteem and Friendship with which I am Your's etc. etc.,

                                                              A. ADAMS

(*Cappon*, 168–69; © 1959 The University of North Carolina Press.)

912.8   *To John Adams*]   Adams replied:

                                                        London Decr. 6. 1787
DEAR SIR

The Project of a new Constitution, has Objections against it, to which I find it difficult to reconcile my self, but I am so unfortunate as to differ somewhat from you in the Articles, according to your last kind Letter.

You are afraid of the one—I, of the few. We agree perfectly that the many should have a full fair and perfect Representation.—You are Apprehensive of Monarchy; I, of Aristocracy. I would therefore have given more Power to the President and less to the Senate. The Nomination and Appointment to all offices I would have given to the President, assisted only by a Privy Council of his own Creation, but not a Vote or Voice would I have given to the Senate or any Senator, unless he were of the Privy Council. Faction and Distraction are the sure and certain Consequence of giving to a Senate a vote in the distribution of offices.

You are apprehensive the President when once chosen, will be chosen again and again as long as he lives. So much the better as it appears to me.—You are apprehensive of foreign Interference, Intrigue, Influence. So am I.—But, as often as Elections happen, the danger of foreign Influence recurs. The less frequently they happen the less danger.—And if the Same Man may be chosen again, it is probable he will be, and the danger of foreign Influence will be less. Foreigners, seeing little Prospect will have less Courage for Enterprize.

Elections, my dear sir, Elections to offices which are great objects of Ambition, I look at with terror. Experiments of this kind have been so often tryed, and so universally found productive of Horrors, that there is great Reason to dread them.

Mr. Littlepage who will have the Honour to deliver this will tell you all the News. I am, my dear Sir, with great Regard,

JOHN ADAMS

(*Cappon,* 213–14; © 1959 The University of North Carolina Press.)

935.7   The observations] *Observations on the Whale-Fishery.*

943.6–7   thoughts . . . 17.] Madison had written: "The little pamphlet herewith inclosed will give you a collective view of the alterations which have been proposed for the new Constitution. Various and numerous as they appear they certainly omit many of the true grounds of opposition. The articles relating to Treaties—to paper money, and to contracts, created more enemies than all the errors in the System positive & negative put together. It is true nevertheless that not a few, particularly in Virginia have contended for the proposed alterations from the most honorable & patriotic motives; and that among the advocates for the Constitution, there are some who wish for further guards to public liberty & individual rights. As far as these may consist of a constitutional declaration of the most essential rights, it is probable they will be added; though there are many who think such addition unnecessary, and not a few who think it misplaced in such a Constitution. There is scarce any point on which the party in opposition is so much divided as to its importance and its propriety. My own opinion has always been in favor of a bill of rights; provided it be so framed as not to imply powers not meant to be included in the enumeration. At the same time I have never thought the omission a material defect, nor been anxious to supply it even by *subsequent* amendment, for any other reason than that it is anxiously desired by others. I have favored it because I supposed it might be of use, and if properly executed could not be of disservice. I have not viewed it in an important light 1. because I conceive that in a certain degree, though not in the extent argued by Mr. Wilson, the rights in question are reserved by the manner in which the federal powers are granted. 2 because there is great reason to fear that a positive declaration of some of the most essential rights could not be obtained in the requisite latitude. I am sure that the rights of Conscience in particular, if submitted to public definition would be narrowed much more than they are likely ever to be by an assumed power. One of the objections in New England was that the Constitution by prohibiting religious tests opened a door for Jews Turks & infidels. 3. because the limited powers of the federal Government and the jealousy of the subordinate Governments, afford a security which has not existed in the case of the State Governments, and exists in no other. 4 because experience proves the inefficacy of a bill of rights on those occasions when its controul is most needed. Repeated violations of these parchment barriers have been committed by overbearing majorities in every State. In Virginia I have seen the bill of rights violated in every instance where it has been opposed to a popular current. Notwithstanding the explicit provision contained in that instrument for the rights of Conscience it is well known that a religious establishment wd. have taken place in that State, if the legislative majority had found as they expected, a majority of the people in favor of the measure; and I am persuaded that if a majority of the people were now of one sect, the measure would still take place and on narrower ground than was then proposed, notwithstanding the additional obstacle which the law has since created. Wherever the real power in a Government lies, there is the danger of oppression. In our Governments the real power lies in the majority of the Community, and the invasion of private rights is *cheifly* to be apprehended, not from acts of Government contrary to the sense of its constituents, but from acts in which the Government is the mere instrument of the major number of the constituents. This is a truth of great importance, but not yet sufficiently attended to: and is probably more strongly impressed on my mind by facts, and reflections suggested by them, than on yours which has contemplated abuses of power issuing from a very different quarter. Wherever there is an interest and power to do wrong, wrong will generally be done, and not less readily by a powerful & interested party than by a powerful and interested prince. The difference, so far as it relates to the superiority of republics over monarchies, lies in the less degree of probability that interest may prompt abuses of power in the former than in the latter; and in the security in the former agst. oppression of more than the smaller part of the society, whereas in the former it may be extended in a manner to the whole. The difference so far as it relates to the point in question—the efficacy of a bill of rights in controuling abuses of power—lies in this, that in a monarchy the latent force of the nation is superior to that of the sovereign, and a solemn charter of popular rights must have a great effect, as a standard for trying the validity of public acts, and a signal for rousing & uniting the superior force of the community; whereas in a popular Government, the political and physical power may be considered as vested in the same hands, that is in a majority of the people, and consequently the tyrannical will of the sovereign is not [to] be controuled by the dread of an appeal to any other force within the community. What use then it may be asked can a bill of rights serve in popular Governments? I answer the two following which though less essential than in other Governments, sufficiently recommend the precaution. 1. The political truths declared in that solemn manner acquire by degrees the character of fundamental maxims of free Government, and as they become incorporated within the national sentiment, counteract the impulses of interest and passion. 2. Altho' it be generally true as above stated that the danger of oppression lies in the interested majorities of the people rather than in usurped acts of the Government, yet there may be occasions on which the evil may spring from the latter sources; and on such, a bill of rights will be a good ground for an appeal to the sense of the community. Perhaps too there may be a certain degree of danger, that a succession of artful and ambitious rulers, may by gradual & well-timed advances, finally erect an independent Government on the subversion of liberty. Should this danger exist at all, it is prudent to guard agst. it, especially when the precaution can do no injury. At the same time I must own that I see no tendency in our governments to danger on that side. It has been remarked that there is a tendency in all Governments to an augmentation of power at the expence of liberty. But the remark as usually understood does not appear to me well founded. Power when it has attained a certain degree of energy and independence goes on generally to further degrees. But when below that degree, the direct tendency is to further degrees of relaxation, until the abuses of liberty beget a sudden transition to an undue degree of power. With this explanation the remark may be true; and in the latter sense only is it in my opinion applicable to the Governments in America. It is a melancholy reflection that liberty should be equally exposed to danger whether the Government have too much or too little power, and that the line which divides these extremes should be so inaccurately defined by experience.

Supposing a bill of rights to be proper the articles which ought to compose it, admit of much discussion. I am inclined to think that *absolute* restrictions in cases that are doubtful, or where emergencies may overrule them, ought to be avoided. The restrictions however strongly marked on paper will never be regarded when opposed to the decided sense of the public; and after repeated violations in extraordinary cases, they will lose even their ordinary efficacy. Should a Rebellion or insurrection alarm the people as well as the Government, and a suspension of the Hab. Corp. be dictated by the alarm, no written prohibitions in earth would prevent the measure. Should an army in time of peace be gradually established in our neighborhood by Britn: or Spain, declarations on paper would have as little effect in preventing a standing force for the public safety. The best security agst. these evils is to remove the pretext for them. With regard to monopolies they are justly classed among the greatest nusances in Government. But is it clear that as encouragements to literary works and ingenious discoveries, they are not too valuable to be wholly renounced? Would it not suffice to reserve in all cases a right to the Public to abolish the privilege at a price to be specified in the grant of it? Is there not also infinitely less danger of this abuse in our Governments, than in most others? Monopolies are sacrifices of the many to the few. Where the power is in the few it is natural for them to sacrifice the many to their own partialities and corruptions. Where the power, as with us, is in the many and not in the few, the danger can not be very great that the few will be thus favored. It is much more to be dreaded that the few will be unnecessarily sacrificed to the many." (*The Papers of James Madison,* ed. Robert A. Rutland and Charles F. Hobson [Charlottesville: Univ. of Virginia Press, 1977], Vol. XI, 295–300.)

957.17   faste]   French: pomp and pageantry.

971.9   Bergere or Grizzle]   Shepherd dogs at Monticello.

973.4   two . . . records]   A substantial part of the manuscript of *Hazard's Historical Collections,* 2 vols. (Philadelphia, 1792–94).

981.18   Publicola]   Pseudonym of John Quincy Adams.

1003.29   these]   The remainder of the letter is lost.

1005.2   *reserve . . . States*]   Italicized passages here and throughout this letter were written in code. A postscript in code is omitted.

1006.34   denunciation]   A public announcement.

1008.7   proclamation]   The President's Proclamation of Neutrality, April 22, 1793.

1008.13   P's]   President's.

1031.10   enclosed paper]   Enclosure omitted.

1036.15–16   E. R. . . . M. P.]   Edmund Randolph and Mann Page.

1036.33   The aspect . . . politics]   This part of the letter was published abroad, first in Italian, then in French, after which it was retranslated into English and published in the United States.

1040.1   ENCLOSURE TO JOHN ADAMS]   Madison did not send the letter on to Adams.

1047.5   partner]   John Wayles Eppes.

1048.11   patent]   For a " wheat-thrashing machine."

1058.12   enclosed paper]   Enclosure omitted.

1066.10–11   Your college]   The College of William and Mary.

1078.16   state]   Connecticut.

1086.11–12   libel . . . them.]   Jefferson wrote in the margin of his copy, "Alien law."

1091.39   States]   Jefferson wrote in the margin, "Venice and Genoa."

1096.15   resolution]   Enacted in the wake of the Gabriel Conspiracy, it directed the governor to investigate the possibility of removing dangerous or criminal slaves to some western territory.

1099.23   7th Jany]   The correct date of the First Annual Message is December 8, 1801.

1165.15   declaimer]   John Randolph.

1170.3   Governor]   William C. C. Claiborne.

1226.1–2   one judge . . . another]   Justice Samuel Chase and Judge John Pickering, both impeached, the latter convicted, during Jefferson's administration.

1242.2   packet]   The manuscript, in French, of Destutt de Tracy's *A Commentary and Review of Montesquieu's Spirit of the Laws*, which was translated and published under Jefferson's direction.

1258.25   *To John Adams*]   Adams had reopened the correspondence:

Quincy January 1st. 1812

DEAR SIR

As you are a Friend to American Manufactures under proper restrictions, especially Manufactures of the domestic kind, I take the Liberty of sending you by the Post a Packett containing two Pieces of Homespun lately produced in this quarter by One who was honoured in his youth with some of your Attention and much of your kindness.

All of my Family whom you formerly knew are well. My Daughter Smith is here and has successfully gone through a perilous and painful Operation, which detains her here this Winter, from her Husband and her Family at Chenango: where one of the most gallant and skilful Officers of our Revolution is probably destined to spend the rest of his days, not in the Field of Glory, but in the hard Labours of Husbandry.

I wish you Sir many happy New Years and that you may enter the next and many succeeding Years with as animating Prospects for the Public as those at present before Us. I am Sir with a long and sincere Esteem your Friend and Servant   JOHN ADAMS

(*Cappon*, 290; © 1959 The University of North Carolina Press. The "Pieces of Homespun" proved to be the two volumes of John Quincy Adams's *Lectures on Rhetoric and Oratory*.)

1277.16   Memoirs] Thomas Belsham, *Memoirs of the Late Reverend Theophilus Lindsay* . . . (London, 1812). This work contained Jefferson's letters of March 21, 1801, and April 9, 1803, to Dr. Joseph Priestley (both included in this volume).

1278.22–23   [See . . . 198.]]   Bracketed title is in Jefferson's original.

1296.22 and 1297.14   mind . . . are:—]   Examples in Greek omitted.

1300.17–18   the Syllabus]   "Syllabus of . . . the Doctrines of Jesus."

1304.24   Aug. 16.]   Adams had written to Jefferson as follows:

> κριοὺς μὲν καὶ ὄνους διζήμεθα, Κύρνε, καί ἵππους
> εὐγενέας· καί τις βούλεται ἐξ ἀγαθῶν
> κτήσασθαι. γῆμαι δὲ κακὴν κακοῦ οὐ μελεδαίνει
> ἐσθλός ἀνήρ, ἤν οἱ χρήματα πολλά διδῷ.

Behold my translation

"My friend Curnis, When We want to purchace, Horses, Asses or Rams, We inquire for the Wellborn. And every one wishes to procure, from the good Breeds. A good Man, does not care to marry a Shrew, the Daughter of a Shrew; unless They give him, a great deal of Money with her."

What think you, of my translation? Compare it with that of Grotius, and tell me, which, is nearest to the Original in letter and in Spirit. Grotius renders it

> Nobilitas asinis et equis simul, arietibusque
> Dat pretium: nec de semine degeneri

Admissura placet. sed pravæ e Sanguine pravo,
Si dos sit, præsto est optima conditio.
This flower of Greek Poetry, is extracted, from the
ΘΕΟΓΝΙΔΟΣ ΜΕΓΑΡΕΩΣ ΠΑΡΑΙΝΕΣΕΙΣ

Theognis lived five hundred and forty four Years before Jesus Christ. Has Science or Morals, or Philosophy or Criticism or Christianity, advanced or improved, or enlightened Mankind upon this Subject, and shewn them, that the Idea of the "Well born" is a prejudice, a Phantasm, a Point no point, a Gape Fly away, a dream? I say it is the Ordonance of God Almighty, in the Constitution of human nature, and wrought into the Fabrick of the Universe. Philosophers and Politicians, may nibble and quibble, but they never will get rid of it. Their only resource is, to controul it. Wealth is another Monster to be subdued. Hercules could not subdue both or either. To subdue them by regular approaches by a regular Seige, and strong fortifications, was my Object in writing on Aristocracy, as I proposed to you in Grovenor Square.

If you deny any one of these Positions, I will prove them to demonstration by Examples drawn from your own Virginia, and from every other State in the Union, and from the History of every Nation civilized and savage, from all We know of the time of the Creation of the World.

Whence is the derivation of the Words Generous, Generously, Generosity etc? Johnson says "Generous. a. Generosus Latin, Not of mean Birth; of good extraction. Noble of mind. Magnanimous, Open of Heart Liberal, munificent. Strong, vigorous." And he might have added, Couragious, heroic, patriotic.

Littleton happens to be at hand. Generosus—εὐγενὴς, γενναῖος. Nobilis, ex præclaro genere ortus: qui a genere non deflectit. Born of a noble Race, a Gentleman born. See his Examples.

What is the Origin of the Word Gentleman?

It would be a curious critical Speculation for a learned Idler to pursue this Idea, through all Languages.

We may call this Sentiment a prejudice, because We can give what names We please, to such things as We please; but in my Opinion it is a part of the Natural History of Man: and Politicians and Philosophers may as well project to make The Animal live without Bones or Blood, as Society can pretend to establish, a free Government without Attention to it.

Quincy August 16. 1813. I can proceed no farther, with this Letter, as I intended.

Your Friend, my only Daughter, expired, Yesterday Morning in the Arms of Her Husband her Son, her Daughter, her Father and Mother, her Husbands two Sisters and two of her Nieces, in the 49th. Year of her Age, 46 of which She was the healthiest and firmest of Us all: Since which, She has been a monument to Suffering and to Patience.

JOHN ADAMS

(*Cappon,* 365–66; © 1959 The University of North Carolina Press.)

1307.4–5   [vol. . . . III.]] Jefferson's bracketed reference is to Adams's *Defence of the Constitutions of the United States* (1787).

1340.1–4   'Leon . . . cacciator.'] Translation in *Cappon*:
                              "The lion stricken to death
                              realizes that he is dying,
                              and looks at his wounds from which
                              he grows ever weaker and weaker.
                              Then with his final wrath
                              He roars, threatens, and screams,
                              which makes the hunter
                              tremble at him dying."

1427.20   treaty] The Monroe-Pinkney treaty, which arrived in Washington, from London, on March 3, 1807.

1441.1   paper reviewed] *The Proceedings and Report of the Commissioners for the University of Virginia.*

1479.25   *To John Adams*] In his reply, November 10, Adams wrote: "Your last letter was brought to me from the Post office when at breakfast with my family. I bade one of the misses open the budget; she reported a letter from Mr. Jefferson and two or three newspapers. A letter from Mr. Jefferson, says I, I know what the substance is before I open it. There is no secrets between Mr. Jefferson and me, and I cannot read it; therefore you may open and read it. When it was done, it was followed by an universal exclamation, The best letter that ever was written, and round it went through the whole table— How generous! how noble! how magnanimous!" (*Cappon*, 601–02; © 1959 The University of North Carolina Press.)

Library of Congress Cataloging in Publication Data

Jefferson, Thomas, 1743–1826.
  Writings.

  (The Library of America; 17)
  "Merrill D. Peterson wrote the notes and selected the texts for this volume"—Prelim. p.v.
  Includes bibliographical references and index.
  Contents: Autobiography—A summary view of the rights of British America—Notes on the State of Virginia—Public papers—Addresses, messages, and replies—Miscellany—Letters
  1. United States—Politics and government—Revolution, 1775–1783—Addresses, essays, lectures. 2. United States—Politics and government—1783–1809—Addresses, essays, lectures. 3. Virginia—Addresses, essays, lectures. 4. Jefferson, Thomas, 1743–1826. I. Peterson, Merrill D. II. Title. III. Series.

E302.J442   1984   973.3   83–19917
ISBN 0–940450–16–X

Index

Abortion, Indian use of, 186.

Adams, Abigail, letters to, 809–12, 830–32, 889–90, 1144–46.

Adams, John, 46, 54–58, 75–77, 591, 632, 978; bonds issued by, 77; on character of, 884–85; Declaration committee, 17; and Federalists, 671–72. Letters to: on abiding friendship immune to slander, 1480–82; on age and metaphysics, 1382–84; on aristocracy, natural and pseudo, 1305–10; on Assembly of Notables, 906–08; Barbary states, war on, 855–57; on Bonaparte and Plato, 1339–43; on Calvin and cosmology, 1466–70; on communications, 759; on the Constitution, 912–14; on Europe's past, present, and future, 1374–77; on experiments in government, 1033–35; first letter, 758–60; on Indians, 1260–64; on Jesus and Christianity, 1300–04; on old politics, 1277–79; on preface to Paine's *Rights of Man*, 980–82; reconciliation, 1258–60; on representation, 759; on 1796 election and Hamilton, 1040–41; on south of France and Italy, 897–99; on Univ. of Va., neology, and materialism, 1440–45; on opposition to T.J., 695; to Rush on break with, 1235–39; taxation debate, Articles of Confederation, 25–26; Vice-President, elected as, 75; voting debate, Articles of Confederation, 29–30.

Adams, Samuel, 1419, 1422.

Addison, Joseph, lines from, 617.

Admiralty court, in Virginia, 257.

Africa, 528, 969, 1082; on colonization by American slaves, 1098, 1239–41, 1484–88.

Agriculture, 495, 970, 972; big farm v. small garden, 1249; cattle feed, 1405; depression in, 1515; English practices, 894; European, need to observe, 659; French practices, 894; on gypsum use, 1132; on horizontal plowing, 1405–07; Indian agriculture, 164, 520, 556, 559–62, 1115, 1119; international exchanges in, 1200–02; livestock feed, 1019–21; manuring practices, 894, 895, 1021; on Merino sheep raising, 1223–25; national society of, 1133; olive trees, 703; one-piece wheel used by New Jersey farmers, 877, 878; plows, 650, 651, 1021–22, 1193; Rhineland agricultural prices, 646; rotation of crops, 1016, 1018–22, 1249; seeding, 1027; small farmer, 842, 1029; threshing machine, 1009; upland rice, 703; Virginia crops, 164, 165; virtues of farming, 301, 818, 918, 1029, 1144.

Aix-en-Provence, mineral waters of, 65, 885, 897.

Alabama Indians, 546.

Albermarle, addresses to people of, 491, 550.

Alcoholic beverages, drunkenness in Europe and America, 834; Indian problems with, 555; personal habits of T.J., 1416.

Aldermen, 366, 367.

Alexander I, 1109, 1110, 1222, 1276, 1340; letter to, 1161–62.

Alexander the Great, 93.

Alexandria, 131, 140, 233, 234.

Alfred the Great, 1326–28.

Algiers, 59, 60, 540, 545, 821.

Alien and Sedition Laws, 1060, 1063; Kentucky resolutions on, 449–56; Virginia resolutions on, 479.

Aliens, national bank and laws regarding, 416; rights in Virginia, 281.

Allegheny Mountains, 127, 142–44, 534.

Allegheny River, 138.

Alvensleben, 70.

American Revolution, causes of, 242–43; cruelties of British during, 590–91; disbanding of troops after, 573, 582; France, effect in, 62–63, 936; French aid, 757, 760; Indian support in, request for, 551–54; Lexington and

This book is set in 10 point Linotron Galliard, a face designed for photocomposition by Matthew Carter and based on the sixteenth-century face Granjon. The paper is Olin Nyalite and conforms to guidelines adopted by the Committee on Book Longevity of the Council on Library Resources. The binding material is Brillianta, a 100% rayon cloth made by Van Heek-Scholco Textielfabrieken, Holland. Composition by Haddon Craftsmen, Inc. and The Clarinda Company. Printing and binding by R. R. Donnelley & Sons Company. Designed by Bruce Campbell.

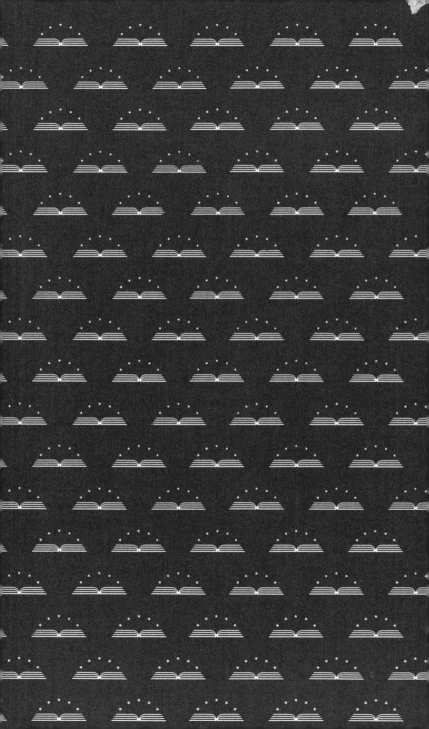